Unproblem JEE

Physical Chemistry I

for JEE Main & Advanced

3000+

Problems with Solutions...

DR. RK GUPTA

ARIHANT PRAKASHAN (Series), MEERUT

Unproblem JEE

ARIHANT PRAKASHAN (Series), MEERUT

All Rights Reserved

© Author

No part of this publication may be re-produced, stored in a retrieval system or by any means, electronic, mechanical, photocopying, recording, scanning, web or otherwise without the written permission of the publisher. Arihant has obtained all the information in this book from the sources believed to be reliable and true. However, Arihant or its editors or authors or illustrators don't take any responsibility for the absolute accuracy of any information published and the damage or loss suffered thereupon.

All disputes subject to Meerut (UP) jurisdiction only.

卐 **Administrative & Production Offices**

Regd. Office

'Ramchhaya' 4577/15, Agarwal Road, Darya Ganj, New Delhi -110002
Tele: 011- 47630600, 43518550

卐 **Head Office**

Kalindi, TP Nagar, Meerut (UP) - 250002
Tel: 0121-7156203, 7156204

卐 **Sales & Support Offices**

Agra, Ahmedabad, Bengaluru, Bareilly, Chennai, Delhi, Guwahati, Hyderabad, Jaipur, Jhansi, Kolkata, Lucknow, Nagpur & Pune.

卐 **ISBN** : 978-93-89204-97-1

卐 **PRICE** : ₹445.00

PO No. : TXT-59-T070597-4-26

Published by Arihant Publications (India) Ltd.

For further information about the books published by Arihant, log on to www.arihantbooks.com or e-mail at info@arihantbooks.com

Follow us on   

Unprblem JEE

Physical Chemistry I

for JEE Main & Advanced

A PRELUDE OF PROBLEMS IN PHYSICAL CHEMISTRY

It is a common phrase among JEE aspirants that Chemistry is the most scoring subject. It is true, no doubt, but partially. It can be realised 100% into dreams if you have the vital tacts of using the basic concepts of theory into applications.

Problems asked in JEE Main & JEE Advanced are not directly related from the theory but based on its applications. Even in many cases, a problem may be a cluster of concepts of two or more units; e.g. a part of ionic equilibrium and a part of electrochemistry may be reinforced to a new complex problem. To tackle such types of problem, an innovative aptitude is the necessity of the time.

Keeping this aspect of chemistry in mind the book **Unproblem JEE Physical Chemistry I** is developed and arranged to provide a logical progression from fundamental to more advanced concepts of the subject. Almost all the problems are designed and presented in the text with an appropriate rigour to satisfy the intellect of the learners and enhance their aptitude. This book will also help to infuse the self-confidence in students to tackle complex JEE Problems.

Innovative features of the book listed below will help you to learn the basic structure of the book;

- Each chapter is divided into separate concept heads.
- Each concept head has quick theory just enough to revise the concepts covering all the important points.
- Different types of Solved Examples under each concept head.
- Each Solved Example followed by 'Immediate Tests' helping in On the Spot practice & assessment.
- Short Exercises under each concept head, 'Knowledge Confirmation Test' give complete practice & assessment of the related concept head.
- After completion of all the concepts, there are separate cumulative exercises for JEE Main & JEE Advanced, 'Acid Test for JEE Main' and 'Acid Test for JEE Advanced' having all types of questions asked in JEE.
- Detailed and explanatory solutions to all the questions just to help you in the case you stuck somewhere while solving a problem.

At the end I can say with great confidence that if you rigorously practice the problems given in this book then surely you will get an edge in chemistry and will increase your chance of getting good JEE Score. A high rank in JEE gives the opportunity to have the engineering branch of your choice in the best IITs.

ACKNOWLEDGEMENT

There are many faculties and students, who helped during the development of this book by their valuable suggestions and unprecedented comments. They know who they are, and I hope that they will accept my sincere thanks for all they did.

It is also a pleasure to acknowledge the many people for their friendly assistance in completing this book, especially Shri YC Jain, Chairman, Arihant Publications India Limited, for encouraging me at each step and for being an exemplary publisher and a good friend too. My special thank also goes to Mr. Keshav Mohan and team who left no stone unturned for completing the book successfully.

I must also thank Almighty God for igniting such a zeal and determination in me without which I would not be able to complete such a comprehensive book.

I would like to appeal all my fellow chemistry teachers to have a look of the book and share their valuable suggestions for its further improvement.

Dr. RK Gupta
Retired Associate Professor,
K (PG) College,
Simbhaoli, Hapur (U.P.)
raghuveshg@gmail.com

CONTENTS

CHAPTER

01

Mole Concept and Stoichiometry

Chapter Topics

- Atomic Number, Mass Number, Isotopes and Isobars
- Mole Concept
- Laws of Chemical Combination
- Concentration Terms
- Stoichiometry (Quantitative Relations in Chemical Reactions)
- Chemical Formula

Atomic Number, Mass Number, Isotopes and Isobars

Atomic number

The **atomic number** (Z) is the number of protons in the nucleus of each atom of an element.

Number of protons = Number of electrons in an atom

- If **cation** is formed, valence electrons are lost but number of protons remains unchanged.
- If **anion** is formed, electrons in valence shell are gained but no effect on the number of protons.

e.g. Na^+ has 10 electrons,

number of protons = 11, so atomic number = 11

O^{2-} has 10 electrons, it means number of protons = 8, so atomic number = 8.

Thus, atomic number = number of protons
= number of electrons in neutral atom

Mass number

The mass number (A) is the total number of neutrons and protons present in the nucleus of each atom of an element. Except for hydrogen (which has only one proton), all atomic nuclei contain both protons and neutrons.

A (mass number) = p (protons) + n (neutrons)
= Z (atomic number) + n (neutrons)

An atom X is represented as

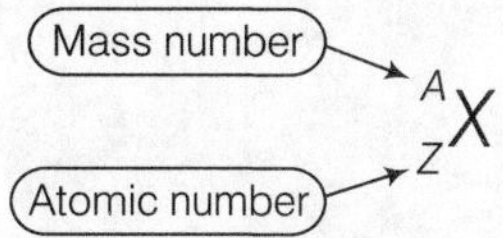

Z, n and A, all must be positive integers.

- Atoms of the same element having same atomic number but different mass number are called **isotopes**.
Examples are

(a)		^1_1H	^2_1H	^3_1H
	Neutrons	0	1	2
(b)		$^{12}_6C$	$^{13}_6C$	$^{14}_6C$
	Neutrons	6	7	8

Different mass number is due to difference in number of neutrons in isotopes.

- **Isotonic** pairs have same number of neutrons.
- Atomic species with same mass number but different atomic number are called **isobars**. Isobars also differ in number of neutrons.

	$^{40}_{18}Ar$	$^{40}_{19}K$	$^{40}_{20}Ca$		
Neutrons	22	21	20	←	Different
Protons	18	19	20	←	Different
Mass number	40	40	40	←	Same

- If A_1, A_2, A_3..... are the atomic masses of the different isotopes with their corresponding percentages or ratios or mole fractions as χ_1, χ_2, χ_3...., then **average atomic mass** or **average atomic weight** or mass number $\overline{A}$ of the element is

$$\overline{A} = \frac{A_1\chi_1 + A_2\chi_2 + A_3\chi_3 + ...}{\chi_1 + \chi_2 + \chi_3 + ...}$$

or $$\overline{A} = \frac{\Sigma A\chi}{\Sigma \chi}$$

- **One atomic mass unit** (amu) is defined as exactly one-twelfth (1/12) the mass of an atom of $^{12}_6C$ and is equal to 1.66056×10^{-24} g.

$$1 \text{ amu} = \frac{1}{12}(\text{mass of one C-atom})$$

$$= \frac{1}{12}\left(\frac{12}{N_0}\right)$$

$$= \frac{1}{N_0} = 1.66056 \times 10^{-24} \text{g}$$

N_0 is called Avogadro's number, it is equal to $6.022 \times 10^{23} \text{ mol}^{-1}$ (Mole is defined in next topic).

$\therefore$ Mass of one H-atom $= \frac{1}{N_0} = 1$ amu

Mass of one O-atom $= \frac{16}{N_0} = 16$ amu

- To convert atomic mass into amu, divide it by N_0. In present notation, 'amu' has been replaced by 'u' (unified mass). amu is also called **Dalton (Da).**
- The **atomic weight** of an element is a number which indicates as to how many times an atom of that element is heavier as compared to 1/12 of the mass of an atom of C-12 ($^{12}_6C$).
- Atomic weight of an element

$$= \frac{\text{weight of an atom}}{\frac{1}{12} \times \text{weight of an atom of } ^{12}C}$$

- The **gram atomic weight** (or the gram-atom) of an element is its atomic weight expressed in grams. Thus, 1 g atom of magnesium stands for 24 g of magnesium.
- The *French Chemists* Dulong and Petit in 1819 found out that the product of the specific heat of an element in the solid state and its atomic weight is constant and is equal to 6.4. It is also called **Dulong and Petit** law.

Specific heat × atomic weight = 6.4 (approx.)

Dalton atomic theory (1808)

Main points of Dalton atomic theory are given below:.

(i) All elements are composed of tiny particles called **atoms,** which do not undergo subdivision during chemical reactions and cannot be created or destroyed by any chemical process **(Taylor).**

(ii) Atoms of the same element are similar to one another in all respects and equal in weights.

(iii) Atoms of different elements have different masses (called atomic masses) and different properties.

(iv) Chemical combination between two or more elements takes place by interaction of their atoms in simple numerical proportions (as 1 : 1 ; 1 : 2; 1 : 3, etc.)

	Ratio of reactants
$H_2 + Cl_2 \longrightarrow 2HCl$	1 : 1
$N_2 + 3H_2 \longrightarrow 2NH_3$	1 : 3
$C + O_2 \longrightarrow CO_2$	1 : 1

(v) Combining masses of the elements represent the combining masses of the atoms.

Solved Examples & Instant Practice

Example 1.1) **A divalent cation M^{2+} is isoelectronic of C_3H_4 and has $(Z + 2)$ neutrons (where Z is the atomic number of the divalent cation). What is the ionic mass of the divalent cation. Also, write the symbol of this cation.**

Atomic mass or mass number is the sum of number of protons and neutrons. In the formation of cation, electrons are lost and in the formation of anion, electrons are gained.
Charge on ion = electrons lost or electron gained. But number of protons and neutrons are not affected. Thus,

Ionic mass = number of (protons + neutrons).

Sol. Electrons in M^{2+} is equal to that in $(C_3H_4) = 3 \times 6 + 4 \times 1 = 22$

In the formation of M^{2+}, two electrons are lost.

Protons in $M^{2+} = 22 + 2 = 24$

Thus, atomic number $= 24 = Z$

Neutrons in $M^{2+} = (Z + 2) = 26$

Ionic mass $= p + n = 24 + 26 = 50$

Symbol $^{50}_{24}M^{2+}$

Immediate Test 1

(i) Ionic mass of X^{2-} is 16. It has 8 neutrons. Determine the number of its (a) protons (b) electrons and (c) atomic number.

(ii) One isotope of a metallic element has mass number 65 and 35 neutrons. The cation derived from the isotope has 28 electrons. Write the symbol for this cation.

Example 1.2) **Carbon occurs in nature as a mixture of atoms of which 98.89% have a mass of 12.0000 u and 1.11% have a mass of 13.00335 u. Calculate the atomic weight of carbon.**

Sol. $\bar{A}$ (Average atomic weight) $= \dfrac{A_1\chi_1 + A_2\chi_2}{\chi_1 + \chi_2}$

$$\bar{A} = \frac{12.0000 \times 98.89 + 13.00335 \times 1.11}{100} = 12.01\,\text{u}$$

Example 1.3) **Naturally occurring boron consists of 80% ^{11}B (atomic weight = 11.01) and 20% of the other isotope. If atomic weight of boron is 10.81. Calculate atomic weight of the other isotope.**

Sol. Average atomic wight $\bar{A} = \dfrac{A_1\chi_1 + A_2\chi_2}{\chi_1 + \chi_2}$

$\bar{A}$, A_1, χ_1 and χ_2 are given, thus A_2 is calculated.

$$10.81 = \frac{11.01 \times 80 + A_2 \times 20}{100}$$

$$\therefore \quad A_2 = 10.01\,\text{u}$$

Immediate Test 2

(i) Calculate the average atomic mass of carbon using the following data of three isotopes with their relative abundance and masses as shown against each of them.

Isotopes of carbon	Relative abundance (%)	Atomic mass (amu)
$^{12}_{6}C$	98.892	12.00000
$^{13}_{6}C$	1.108	13.00335
$^{14}_{6}C$	2×10^{-10}	14.00317

(ii) $^{10}_{5}B$ and $^{11}_{5}B$ are the two isotopes of boron. If the average atomic mass number is 10.2, what is the percentage of each?

KNOWLEDGE CONFIRMATION **Test 1**

1 Consider following species :

I. Atoms of an element having different number of electrons.

II. Atoms of an element having different number of neutrons.

III. $^{40}_{19}K$ and $^{40}_{20}Ca$

IV. $^{90}_{38}Sr$ and $^{88}_{38}Sr$

Which of the above represent isotopes ?

(a) I, IV (b) II, III (c) I, III (d) II, IV

2 Which of the following may contain one proton and one neutron ?

(a) $^{4}_{2}He$ (b) $^{2}_{1}D$ (c) $^{3}_{1}T$ (d) H_2^+

3 An atom has a net charge of –1. It has 18 electrons and 20 neutrons. Its isotopic symbol is

(a) $^{37}_{18}Cl^-$ (b) $^{37}_{17}Cl^-$ (c) $^{37}_{16}Cl^-$ (d) $^{38}_{17}Cl^-$

4 Number of electrons in $^{40}_{19}K^+$ is

(a) 31 (b) 40 (c) 18 (d) 17

5 Select isotonic pairs out of the following (isotonic pair has same number of neutrons)

(a) $^{16}_{8}O$, $^{14}_{6}C$ (b) $^{80}_{35}Br$, $^{79}_{34}Se$ (c) $^{14}_{7}N$, $^{13}_{6}C$ (d) All of these

6 If Avogadro's number would have been $1.0 \times 10^{23}\ \text{mol}^{-1}$, then mass of one atom of nitrogen would be

(a) 14 amu (b) $14 / 1.0 \times 10^{23}$ amu

(c) 14×10^{23} amu (d) 14×6.02 amu

7 Mass of one atom of an element is 6.66×10^{-23} g. It is expressed in amu as

(a) $\frac{1}{N_0}$ (b) $\frac{1}{6.66 \times 10^{-23}}$

(c) $6.66 \times 10^{-23} \times N_0$ (d) $\frac{1}{6.66 \times 10^{-23} \times N_0}$

8 Naturally occurring carbon consists of two isotopes ^{12}C (12) and ^{13}C (13). If atomic weight is taken as 12.01, percentage of ^{13}C is

(a) 1.10 (b) 98.90 (c) 1.00 (d) 99.00

9 Atomic weight of Cl is taken as 35.5. If $^{35}_{17}Cl$ and $^{37}_{17}Cl$ are two isotopes, their ratio of abundance will be **[JEE Main 2020 (II) NTA]**

(a) 3 : 1 (b) 1 : 3 (c) 1 : 4 (d) 4 : 1

10 If we consider that 1/ 6, in place of 1/ 12 mass of carbon atom is taken to be the relative atomic mass unit, the mass of one mole of the substance will **[AIEEE 2005]**

(a) be a function of the molecular mass of the substance
(b) remain unchanged
(c) increases two fold
(d) decreases twice

11 $^{12}_{6}C$ content in the isotopic mixture of $^{12}_{6}C$ and $^{14}_{6}C$ is 98% and rest is $^{14}_{6}C$.

Thus, number of atoms of $^{12}_{6}C$ in 1 kg of mixture is

(a) 6.02×10^{22} (b) 4.90×10^{25} (c) 6.02×10^{23} (d) 1×10^{24}

12 Ions A^-, B^+ and C^{3+} are isoelectronic of peroxide ion (O_2^{2-}) and number of neutrons are Z, $(Z + 1)$ and $(Z + 2)$, respectively where Z is the atomic number of the element B. Thus, number of neutrons in A^-, B^+ and C^{3+} in the increasing order is

(a) $A < B < C$ (b) $B < A < C$ (c) $C < A < B$ (d) $C < B < A$

13 For the following isotopes of Mg, abundance is given.

I.	$^{26}_{12}Mg$	0.15
II.	$^{25}_{12}Mg$	0.05
III.	$^{24}_{12}Mg$	0.80

Which has highest number of neutrons in 24.35 g of mixture of isotopes?

(a) I (b) II (c) III (d) equal

14 In the graph, number of protons are plotted *vs* number of neutrons for the element *A* to *G* and H (hydrogen).

Maximum number of neutrons are present in one formula unit of

(a) DH_4E (b) A_2E (c) GE (d) DE_2

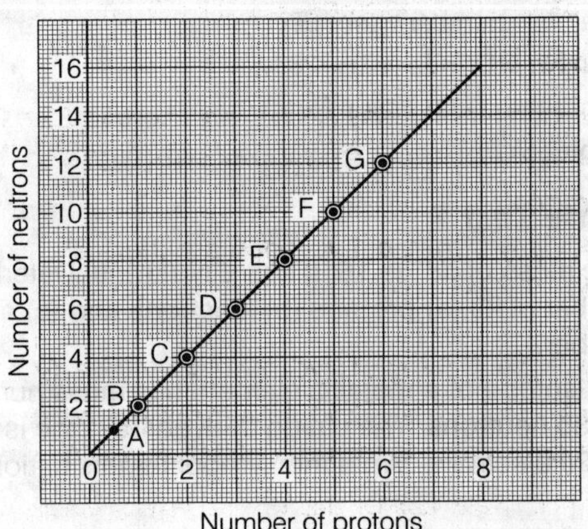

15 Total number of protons, electrons and neutrons are maximum in

(a) $^{16}ND_3$ (b) D_2O^{18}

(c) $^{14}_{6}CD_4$ (d) equal

Mole Concept

The mole (abbreviated as mol) is the base SI unit for a chemical species.

One mole is the amount of a substance that contains as many particles or entities as there are atoms in exactly 12 g of ^{12}C isotope.

- Number of particles in 1 mole of a substance is known as Avogadro's constant or Avogadro's number (N_A or N_0). It is equal to 6.022×10^{23}.

1 mole of H-atom has = 6.022×10^{23} atoms

1 mole of H_2O has = 6.022×10^{23} H_2O molecules

- Number of moles of a substance = $\frac{\text{Mass in grams}}{\text{Molar mass (g mol}^{-1})}$
- Mass of one molecule of any species = $\frac{\text{Molar mass}}{N_0}$
- Mass of one mole of a substance in grams is called its molar mass.

Solved Examples & Instant Practice

Example 1.4) How many molecules of SO_2 are there in 32 g of SO_2 ?

Number of molecules present in one mole of a substance is the Avogadro's number (N_0) 6.02×10^{23}. Number of moles can be derived from the mass divided by its molar mass.

Thus, number of moles $= \dfrac{\text{mass}}{\text{molar mass}}$

and number of molecules = moles $\times N_0$

Sol. Molar mass of $SO_2 = 32 + 2 \times 16 = 64 \text{ g mol}^{-1}$

$\therefore$ Number of moles in 32 g $SO_2 = \dfrac{32}{64} = 0.5$ mol

$\therefore$ Number of molecules in 0.5 mol, i.e. 32 g SO_2

$= 0.5 \times 6.022 \times 10^{23}$ molecules $= 3.011 \times 10^{23}$ molecules

Immediate Test 3

(i) How many molecules of CO_2 are there in 88 g CO_2 ?

(ii) How many moles of $C_2H_4O_2$ contain 6.02×10^{23} atoms of hydrogen?

(iii) How many atoms of hydrogen are there in 36.0 g of H_2O?

Example 1.5) 2.52 g of hydrated salt of Na_2SO_3 has 1.26 g of anhydrous salt. Calculate moles of water and anhydrous salt. What is formula of the hydrated salt ?

Sol. Amount of water can be determined from the weight of hydrated and anhydrous salt.

$$\text{Moles} = \frac{\text{Weight}}{\text{Molar mass}}$$

Mass of hydrated salt = 2.52 g

Mass of anhydrous salt (Na_2SO_3) = 1.26 g

$\therefore$ Mass of water = 2.52 − 1.26 = 1.26 g

Number of moles of anhydrous $Na_2SO_3 = \dfrac{1.26}{126} = 0.01$

Number of moles of water (H_2O) $= \dfrac{1.26}{18} = 0.07$

Ratio of Na_2SO_3 and H_2O = 0.01 : 0.07 = 1 : 7

Thus, formula $= Na_2SO_3 \cdot 7H_2O$

Immediate Test 4

Gypsum is a hydrate calcium sulphate. A 1.0 g sample contains 0.791 g $CaSO_4$. How many moles of $CaSO_4$ and H_2O are there in the sample?

Example 1.6) A metallic spherical ball of radius 7 cm has 0.56% Fe. Calculate number of atoms of iron in it. (Density of metal $= 3.00 \text{ g cm}^{-3}$)

To calculate number of atoms of an element, its number of moles is required. To calculate number of moles, its mass and atomic mass is required.

$$\textit{Number of moles} = \frac{\textit{Mass}}{\textit{Atomic mass}}$$

To calculate mass of spherical ball, volume and density are given.

Mass of the spherical ball $= V \times d$

Volume of spherical ball $= \dfrac{4}{3}\pi r^3$

Sol. Volume of the spherical ball $= \dfrac{4}{3}\pi(7)^3 \text{cm}^3$

Mass of the spherical ball $= \dfrac{4}{3}\pi(7)^3 \times 3$ g

Iron in the ball (0.56%) $= \dfrac{4}{3}\pi(7)^3 \times 3 \times \dfrac{0.56}{100}$

Number of moles of iron in the ball $= \dfrac{4\pi(7)^3 \times 3 \times 0.56}{3 \times 56 \times 100}$

$= 0.431$ mol Fe

$\therefore$ Number of Fe-atoms $= 0.431 \times 6.022 \times 10^{23}$ atoms $= 2.595 \times 10^{23}$

Immediate Test 5

(i) Analysis of chlorophyll shows that it contains 2.88% of magnesium. How many atoms of magnesium does 0.24 g of chlorophyll contain ?

(ii) In a bank there are as many coins as number of molecules in 1.6 μg of CH_4. How many coins are there in the bank ?

Example 1.7) Calculate number of carbon atoms in 3.42 g of $C_{12}H_{22}O_{11}$.

Number of carbon atoms is determined from number of moles which in turn is derived from given mass and molar mass.

Number of moles $= \dfrac{\textit{Mass}}{\textit{Molar mass}}$

Sol. Molar mass of $C_{12}H_{22}O_{11} = 12 \times 12 + 22 \times 1 + 11 \times 16$

$= 342 \text{ g mol}^{-1}$

Number of moles of $C_{12}H_{22}O_{11} = \dfrac{3.42}{3.42} = 0.01$ mol

Number of moles of C-atoms = 12 × 0.01 = 0.12 mol

Number of carbon atoms $= 0.12 \times N_0$

$= 0.12 \times 6.02 \times 10^{23} = 7.224 \times 10^{22}$

Immediate Test 6

(i) What is the mass of 4.00×10^{-3} mole of glucose? How many carbon atoms are there in 4.00×10^{-3} mole of glucose?

(ii) Calculate number of oxygen atoms in 250 g of $CaCO_3$.

KNOWLEDGE CONFIRMATION **Test 2**

1 Which has maximum number of carbon atoms ?
(a) 1.60 g of CH_4 (b) 1.40 g of C_2H_4
(c) 1.35 g of C_4H_6 (d) Equal

2 Number of atoms in 12 g $^{24}_{12}Mg$ is equal to
(a) oxygen atoms in 11 g CO_2
(b) hydrogen atoms in 4 g CH_4
(c) nitrogen atoms in 46 g N_2O_4
(d) sulphur atoms in 79 g $Na_2S_2O_3$

3 The ratio of masses of oxygen and nitrogen in a particular gaseous mixture is 1 : 4. The ratio of number of their molecules is ***[JEE Main 2014]***
(a) 1 : 4 (b) 7 : 32 (c) 1 : 8 (d) 3 : 16

4 Number of atoms in 560 g of Fe (56 g mol^{-1}) is ***[AIEEE 2002]***
(a) twice that of 70 g N (b) half that of 20 g H
(c) Both (a) and (b) (d) None of these

5 A mixture of gases contains H_2 and O_2 gases in the ratio of 1: 4 (*w*/*w*). What is the molar ratio of the two gases in the mixture ?
(a) 1 : 4 (b) 4 : 1 (c) 16 : 1 (d) 2 : 1

6 The number of water molecules is maximum in
(a) 18 molecules of water (b) 1.8 g of water
(c) 18 g of water (d) 18 moles of water

7 3.011×10^{22} atoms of an element weigh 1.15 g. The atomic mass of the element is
(a) 23 (b) 10 (c) 16 (d) 35.5

8 One mole of CH_4 contains
(a) 4 g atoms of H (b) 3.0 g atoms of C
(c) 6.02×10^{23} atoms of H (d) 1.81×10^{23} molecules of CH_4

9 For 14 g of CO, the wrong statement is
(a) it occupies 2.24 L at NTP
(b) it corresponds to 0.5 mole of CO
(c) it corresponds to same mole of CO and N_2 gas
(d) it corresponds to 3.01×10^{23} molecules of CO

10 Number of molecules in 1 L of water is close to
(a) $\frac{18}{22.4} \times 10^{23}$ (b) $55.5 \times 6.02 \times 10^{23}$
(c) $\frac{6.02 \times 10^{23}}{22.4}$ (d) $18 \times 6.02 \times 10^{23}$

11 The total number of electrons in 18 mL of water ($d = 1$ g mL^{-1}) is
(a) 6.023×10^{25} (b) 6.023×10^{24}
(c) $6.023 \times 10^{23} \times 18$ (d) 6.023×10^{23}

12 The total number of electrons in 4.2 g N_3^- ion is (N_0 is Avogadro's number)
(a) 2.4 N_0 (b) 3.2N_0
(c) 2.2N_0 (d) 4.2N_0

13 The weight of a single atom of oxygen is
(a) 1.057×10^{23} g (b) 3.556×10^{23} g
(c) 2.658×10^{-23} g (d) 4.538×10^{-23} g

14 Mass of one atom of *X* is 6.642×10^{-23} g. How many moles would be contained in 20 kg of it ?
(a) 5 mol (b) 50 mol
(c) 500 mol (d) 5×10^3 mol

15 0.1 mole of AB_2 has mass 10 g and 0.1 mole of A_2B has mass 12.5 g. Thus, ratio of atomic weight of *A* to *B* is
(a) 2 : 1 (b) 1: 2
(c) 4 : 5 (d) 5: 4

16 For the two elements *A* and *B* following data are given:

Element	Atomic mass	Amount	Atoms
A	15	*x* g	*y*
B	30	2*x* g	*z*

Thus, *z* is equal to
(a) 2*y* (b) *y*
(c) $\frac{y}{2}$ (d) $\frac{y}{4}$

17 Density of water at 298 K is 1 g cm^{-3}. Radius of water molecule (assuming at to be spherical) is
(a) 192 pm (b) 192 nm
(c) 198 Å (d) 19.2 pm

18 1.806×10^{24} water molecules initially at 277 K and 1 atm are changed to 377 K and 1 atm. Thus, increase in volume is
(a) 11.2 L (b) 27.631 L
(c) 67.2 L (d) 91.816 L

19 100 g of impure sample of $CaCO_3$ contains N_0 atoms of oxygen. Thus, percentage purity of $CaCO_3$ sample is
(a) 50% (b) 33.3%
(c) 66.6% (d) 100%

20 Alum ($K_2SO_4 \cdot Al_2(SO_4)_3 \cdot 24H_2O$) is found to contain 0.8 mole of sulphur in the given sample. Thus, number of moles of oxygen atoms is
(a) 0.8 mol (b) 8 mol
(c) 0.08 mol (d) 80 mol

Laws of Chemical Combination

Law of mass conservation

Mass is neither created nor destroyed in a chemical reaction.

Thus, total mass of the reactants before chemical reaction is equal to the total mass of the products.

$$\underbrace{\underset{84\text{ g}}{MgCO_3(s)}}_{\text{Reactant}} \xrightarrow{\Delta} \underbrace{\underset{40\text{ g}}{MgO(s)} + \underset{44\text{ g}}{CO_2(g)}}_{\text{Products}}$$

Law of definite proportions

Different samples of a pure chemical substance always contain the same proportions of elements by mass.

Thus, every sample of H_2O contains 1 part hydrogen and 8 parts oxygen by mass

$$\begin{array}{c} H_2O \\ \downarrow\downarrow \\ 2 : 16 = 1 : 8 \end{array}$$

Similarly in $CaCO_3$; Ca, C and O are in the ratio of

$\underset{40\ 12\ 48}{CaCO_3} = 10 : 3 : 12$ (by mass).

Law of multiple proportions

If two elements combine in different ways to form different substances, then the masses of one element that combine with a fixed mass of the other element, are in the ratio of small whole number.

$$\underset{2g}{H_2} + \frac{1}{2}\underset{16\text{ g}}{O_2} \longrightarrow H_2O$$

$$\underset{2\text{ g}}{H_2} + \underset{32\text{ g}}{O_2} \longrightarrow H_2O_2$$

H (2 g) — 16 g O_2 → H_2O; H (2 g) — 32 g O_2 → H_2O_2

Ratio of masses of oxygen in H_2O and H_2O_2 that combines with 2 g of hydrogen is 1 : 2.

Law of reciprocal proportions

The masses of two or more different elements which separately combine with a definite mass of another element are either the same or are simple multiple of masses of these different elements when they combine amongst themselves.

In following cases,

I. $C + 2H_2 \longrightarrow CH_4$ II. $O_2 + 2H_2 \longrightarrow 2H_2O$

III. $C + O_2 \longrightarrow CO_2$

4 g of H_2 in I combines with 12 g C.

4 g of H_2 in II combines with 32 g O_2.

Thus, C and O_2 in III combine in the same ratio (as with 4 g H_2), i.e. 12 : 32 or 3 : 8.

Gay-Lussac's law and Avogadro's law

Equal volumes of all gases under the same conditions of temperature and pressure contain equal number of molecules.

$N_2(g)$	+	$3H_2(g)$	$\longrightarrow$	$2NH_3(g)$
1 Vol		3 Vol		2 Vol
1 mole		3 moles		2 moles ($V \propto n$)
6.02×10^{23} molecules		$3 \times 6.02 \times 10^{23}$ molecules		$2 \times 6.02 \times 10^{23}$ molecules

Solved Examples & Instant Practice

Example 1.8) *A* and *B* are two different compounds of P and Cl. Based on the following data, specify the law followed in the formation of *A* and *B*.

Compound	Mass of	
	P	Cl
A	2.0000 g	11.4516 g
B	1.5000 g	8.5887 g

Sol. Based on number of atoms of P and Cl, law of chemical combination can be predicted.

Number of atoms are derived from their masses and atomic masses.

Mass ratio of Cl and P in

$$A = \frac{m_{Cl}}{m_P} = \frac{11.4516}{2.0000} = 5.7258$$

$$B = \frac{m_{Cl}}{m_P} = \frac{8.5887}{1.5000} = 5.7258$$

We find that mass of Cl that combines with 1 g P in *A* and *B* remains constant. Thus, *A* and *B* follow law of definite proportions.

Example 1.9) Two oxides samples of copper were heated in the current of hydrogen and were reduced to the metallic copper. The following data were obtained:

0.795 g of oxide *A* gave 0.635 g copper

1.430 g of oxide *B* gave 1.270 g copper

Show that the data illustrate law of multiple proportion.

Sol. If mass of copper or oxygen are in small whole number ratio w.r.t other element, then law of multiple proportion is followed.

Oxide	Mass of oxide	Mass of copper	Mass of oxygen
A	0.795 g	0.635 g	0.160 g
B	1.430 g	1.270 g	0.160 g

Ratio of mass of Cu and O in $A = \dfrac{0.635}{0.160}$

Ratio of mass of Cu and O in $B = \dfrac{1.270}{0.160}$

Thus, ratio of Cu in A and B (amount of oxygen being same)

$$= \frac{0.635}{1.27} = \frac{1}{2}$$

Ratio being simple multiple of 1 : 2, thus law of multiple proportion is followed.

Example 1.10) Consider following reactions:

I. $S + O_2 \longrightarrow SO_2$ II. $C + O_2 \longrightarrow CO_2$

III. $C + 2S \longrightarrow CS_2$

Which law is followed in the formation of CS_2 in step III ?

Sol. 32 g of O_2 combines with sulphur in I.

32 g of O_2 combines with carbon in II.

Thus, carbon and sulphur in III combine in simple ratio as with 32g O_2.

I. $\underset{32\text{ g}}{S} + \underset{32\text{ g}}{O_2} \longrightarrow SO_2$

II. $\underset{12\text{ g}}{C} + \underset{32\text{ g}}{O_2} \longrightarrow CO_2$

In I and II, 32 g O_2 combines separately with 32 g S or 12 g C. Thus, carbon and sulphur combine in the same ratio or multiple of it.

III. $\underset{12\text{ g}}{C} + \underset{64\text{ g}}{2S} \longrightarrow CS_2$

Thus, C and S in III combine in simple multiple of masses 3:8. Thus, law of multiple proportion is followed.

Immediate Test 7

(i) 10 g of $CaCO_3$ of 50% impurity was heated strongly to form CaO and CO_2. If law of conservation of masses is followed, calculate mass of CaO.

(ii) A metal (*M*) form two oxides *A* and *B*. Following results were obtained:

Oxide	Mass of oxide	O_2 combined
A	1.450 g	0.56 L at STP
B	1.125 g	0.56 L at STP

Assume 1 mol at STP = 22.4L

If the law of multiple proportion is followed, identify the oxides.

(iii) 45.4 L of dinitrogen reacted with 22.7 L of dioxygen and 45.4L of nitrous oxide was formed.

$$2N_2(g) + O_2(g) \longrightarrow 2N_2O(g)$$

What law is being obeyed in the experiment?

[NCERT Exemplar]

(iv) Calculate number of molecules of $SO_3(g)$ formed when N_0 molecules of SO_2 (g) combine with $\frac{N_0}{2}$ molecules of $O_2(g)$ under the identical conditions.

KNOWLEDGE CONFIRMATION Test 3

1 In following reaction, 0.84 g of $MgCO_3(s)$ on heating gave 0.40 g of MgO(*s*). If law of conservation of masses is followed, other compound is

$$MgCO_3(s) \longrightarrow MgO(s) + CO_2(g)$$

(a) 0.44 g CO_2 (b) 0.224 L CO_2 at STP
(c) Both (a) and (b) (d) None of these

2 Consider the following pairs:

I. CH_4, C_2H_6 II. NO, NO_2
III. CO, CO_2 IV. H_2O, H_2O_2

In which cases, law of multiple proportions is followed ?

(a) I and III (b) I, II and III
(c) I, II and IV (d) I, II, III and IV

3 Consider the following experiments:

I. 3 g of the metal when heated with steam gave 5.0 g of metal oxide.

II. 0.9 g of the same metal on heating with oxygen gave 1.5 g of metal oxide.

Above observations verify the

(a) law of multiple proportions
(b) law of reciprocal proportion
(c) law of definite proportion by mass
(d) law of definite proportion by volume

4 A certain element '*X*' forms three different binary compounds with chlorine containing 59.68%, 68.95% and 74.75% chlorine.

These data illustrate the

(a) law of multiple proportions
(b) law of reciprocal proportion
(c) law of definite proportion by mass
(d) law of definite proportion by volume

5 If law of reciprocal proportion holds true,

$$C + 2H_2 \longrightarrow CH_4$$
$$O_2 + 2H_2 \longrightarrow 2H_2O$$

then C and O_2 combine in the mass ratio of

(a) 3 : 8 (b) 3 : 4
(c) 4 : 3 (d) 8 : 3

6 Two oxides of hydrogen follow law of multiple proportion. If percentage of oxygen in one oxide is 88.89, then percentage of oxygen in the other oxide is

(a) 27.16% (b) 53.42%
(c) 91.23% (d) 94.11%

7 Which of the following reactions is not correct according to the law of conservation of masses ? ***[NCERT Exemplar]***

(a) $2Mg(s) + O_2(g) \longrightarrow 2MgO(s)$
(b) $C_3H_8(g) + O_2(g) \longrightarrow CO_2(g) + H_2O(g)$
(c) $P_4(s) + 5O_2(s) \longrightarrow P_4O_{10}(s)$
(d) $CH_4(g) + 2O_2(g) \longrightarrow CO_2(g) + 2H_2O(g)$

8 Which of the following statements indicates that law of multiple proportions is being followed? ***[NCERT Exemplar]***

(a) Sample of carbon dioxide taken from any source will always have carbon and oxygen in the ratio 1 : 2.
(b) Carbon forms two oxides namely CO_2 and CO, where masses of oxygen which combine with fixed mass of carbon are in the simple ratio 2 : 1.
(c) When magnesium burns in oxygen, the amount of magnesium taken for the reaction is equal to the amount of magnesium in magnesium oxide formed.
(d) At constant temperature and pressure 200 mL of hydrogen will combine with 100 mL oxygen to produce 200 mL of water vapour.

9 In three compounds: H_2S : sulphur is 94.12%; H_2O : oxygen is 88.89%, SO_2 : sulphur is 50.00%.

Thus, law of .... is followed.

(a) multiple proportions
(b) reciprocal proportion
(c) definite proportion
(d) Gay-Lussac

10 Which of the following statements about a compound is / are incorrect ? ***[NCERT Exemplar]***

(a) A molecule of a compound has atoms of different elements.
(b) A compound cannot be separated into its constituent elements by physical methods of separation.
(c) A compound retains the physical properties of its constituent elements.
(d) The ratio of atoms of different elements in a compound is fixed.

11 Which of the following statement is correct about the reaction given below? ***[NCERT Exemplar]***

$$4Fe(s) + 3O_2(g) \longrightarrow 2Fe_2O_3(g)$$

(a) Total mass of iron and oxygen in reactants = total mass of iron and oxygen in product therefore it follows the law of conservation of mass
(b) Total mass of reactants = total mass of product; therefore, law of multiple proportions is followed
(c) Amount of Fe_2O_3 can be increased by taking any one of the reactants (iron or oxygen) in excess
(d) Amount of Fe_2O_3 produced will decrease if the amount of any one of the reactants (iron or oxygen) is taken in excess

12 Compounds *X* and *Y* are formed from elements *P* and *Q* in two different experiments.

Compounds	*P*	*Q*
X	0.648 g	0.942 g
Y	0.351 g	1.527 g

Based on the above data, law followed is

(a) law of multiple proportions
(b) law of conservation of mass
(c) law of reciprocal proportion
(d) law of constant definition proportion

13 H_2S contains 97.11% sulphur, SO_2 contains 50% oxygen and H_2O contains 11.11% hydrogen. Thus, one of the following laws of chemical combination can be followed :

(a) Law of multiple proportions
(b) Law of reciprocal proportion
(c) Law of conservation of mass
(d) All of the above

14 0.28 g of nitrogen combines with oxygen when 0.46 g of nitrogen oxides *A* is formed. 0.28 g of nitrogen combines with oxygen when 0.60 g of nitrogen oxide *B* is formed. Thus,

(a) law of multiple proportions is followed
(b) law of conservation of mass is follwed
(c) law of reciprocal proportion is followed
(d) law of definite proportion is followed

15 Consider the following cases :

I. 10 g of $CaCO_3$ of 50% impurity gave 2.24 L CO_2 at STP.
II. 8.7 g of pyrolusite sample (MnO_2 80% pure) on reaction with concentrated HCl displaced 1.792 L Cl_2 at STP.
III. Mixture of 1 mole of Na_2CO_3 and 1 mole of $NaHCO_3$ on heating gave 11.2 L CO_2 at STP.

Select correct cases

(a) I, II (b) I, II, III (c) I, III (d) II, III

Concentration Terms

Solutions are homogeneous mixtures of two or more than two components. By **homogeneous** mixture we mean that its composition and properties are uniform throughout the mixture.

Generally, the component that is present in larger quantity is known as **solvent** (call it 1) and the other component in small quantity called **solute** (call it 2), specifications are as :

Specifications	Solvent	Solute	Solution
Amount	w_1 g	w_2 g	$(w_1 + w_2)$g = Wg
Molar mass	m_1 g mol^{-1}	m_2 g mol^{-1}	$\frac{m_1X_1 + m_2X_2}{X_1 + X_2}$ where, X_1, X_2 are percentages
Moles	$n_1 = \frac{w_1}{m_1}$	$n_2 = \frac{w_2}{m_2}$	$(n_1 + n_2)$
Density	d_1	d_2 (if liquid)	d
Volume	V_1 mL	V_2 mL	$V = (V_1 + V_2)$ mL
	$w_1 = V_1 d_1$	$w_2 = V_2 d_2$	$W = (V_1 + V_2)d$

Concentration of a solution can be expressed through various terms depending on the type of measurements.

Concentration terms Concentration is the amount of solute present in given amount of solvent.

Temperature dependent concentration terms

Name	Symbol	Definition	Formula	Usual SI unit
Volume per cent	C	Amount of solute present in 100 mL of solution.	$C = \frac{100\, w_2}{V}$	
Volume per litre	C	Amount of solute present in 1000 mL of solution.	$C = \frac{1000\, w_2}{V}$	gL^{-1} kg m^{-3}
Molarity	M	Number of moles of solute present in 1 L (1 dm^3, 1000 cm^3) of solution.	$M = \frac{1000 w_2}{m_2 V}$	mol dm^{-3}
Normality	N	Number of gram equivalent of solute present in 1 L (1 dm^3, 1000 cm^3) of solution.	$N = \frac{1000\, w_2}{E_2 V}$ where, E_2 is equivalent mass of solute	g equivalent dm^{-3}

Temperature independent concentration terms

Name	Symbol	Definition	Formula	Usual SI unit
% concentration by mass of solution	%	Amount of solute present in 100 g of solution.	$\% = \frac{100\, w_2}{w_1 + w_2}$	Dimensionless
% concentration by mass of solvent	%	Amount of solute present in 100 g of solvent	$\% = \frac{100\, w_2}{w_1}$	Dimensionless
Molality	m	Number of moles of solute present in 1 kg solvent.	$m = \frac{1000 w_2}{m_2\, w_1}$	mol kg^{-1}
Mole fraction	χ	Fraction of a component out of total moles present in the solution.	$\chi_1 = \frac{n_1}{n_1 + n_2}$, $\chi_2 = \frac{n_2}{n_1 + n_2}$, $\chi_1 + \chi_2 = 1$	Dimensionless

■ Standard notation for molality is m and should not be confused with m_1 (molar mass of solvent) or m_2 (molar mass of solute).

- **Parts per million (ppm) and parts per billion (ppb)**

These are the concentration units which are closely related to weight per cent and particularly useful for dilute solutions.

$$\text{Parts per million (ppm)} = \frac{\text{Mass of solute component}}{\text{Total mass of solution}} \times 10^6$$

$$\text{Parts per billion (ppb)} = \frac{\text{Mass of solute component}}{\text{Total mass of solution}} \times 10^9$$

- Concentration can also be expressed in terms of **ppt (parts per thousand).**

$$\text{Parts per thousand (ppt)} = \frac{\text{Mass of solute component} \times 10^3}{\text{Total mass of solution}}$$

- **Molality (m) related to molarity (M) by relation**

$$m = \frac{1000M}{(1000\, d - Mm_2)}$$

where, d = density of solution in g mL^{-1}

m_2 = molar mass of solute

or
$$M = \frac{1000\, md}{(1000 + mm_2)}$$

- **Molality is also related to mole fraction** of solute (χ_2) by relation

$$m = \frac{1000\chi_2}{(1 - \chi_2)\, m_1}$$

where, m_1 = molar mass of solvent.

- Molarity is also related to mole fraction of solute (χ_2) by relation,

$$M = \frac{1000 d\chi_2}{\chi_2 m_2 + (1 - \chi_2) m_1}$$

- M (molarity) $\times V$(mL) = millimoles of solute

$$\therefore \quad \frac{MV}{1000} = \text{moles of solute.}$$

- **Molarity of solution after dilution** Moles of solute before and after dilution remain constant, so

$$M_1V_1 = M_2V_2$$

where, M_1 and M_2 are the molarities before and after dilution and V_1 and V_2 are initial and final volumes respectively.

- **Molarity of solution after mixing** If V_1 mL of solution of molarity M_1 and V_2 mL of solution of molarity M_2 are mixed, then, the molarity of resultant solution (M_3) may be calculated as

$$M_1V_1 + M_2V_2 = M_3(V_1 + V_2)$$

$$M_3 = \frac{M_1V_1 + M_2V_2}{(V_1 + V_2)}$$

- **Molarity of mixture of acid and base of same basicity and acidity**

Case **I** M_1V_1 (acid) = M_2V_2 (base), then mixture is neutral.

Case **II** M_1V_1 (acid) > M_2V_2 (base), then mixture is acidic.

$$(M) \text{ acid in mixture} = \frac{M_1V_1 - M_2V_2}{(V_1 + V_2)}$$

Case **III** M_1V_1 (acid) < M_2V_2 (base), then mixture is basic.

$$(M) \text{ base in mixture} = \frac{M_2V_2 - M_1V_1}{V_1 + V_2}$$

- **Normality of solution after dilution** Number of gram equivalents before and after dilution remains same, so

$$N_1V_1 = N_2V_2$$

where, N_1 and N_2 are the normalities of solution before and after dilution and V_1 and V_2 are initial and final volumes respectively.

- **Normality of solution after mixing** If V_1 mL of solution of normality N_1 is mixed with V_2 mL of solution, then normality of resultant solution may be calculated as

$$N_1V_1 + N_2V_2 = N_3(V_1 + V_2)$$

$$N_3 = \frac{N_1V_1 + N_2V_2}{V_1 + V_2}$$

- **Normality of mixture of acid and base**

Case **I** If N_1V_1 (acid) = N_2V_2 (base), then mixture is neutral.

Case **II** If N_1V_1 (acid) > N_2V_2 (base), then mixture is acidic

$$(N) \text{ acid in mixture} = \frac{N_1V_1 - N_2V_2}{V_1 + V_2}$$

Case **III** If N_1V_1 (acid) < N_2V_2 (base), then mixture is basic

$$(N) \text{ base in mixture} = \frac{N_2V_2 - N_1V_1}{(V_1 + V_2)}$$

Kjeldahl's method

Percentage of nitrogen in the given compound is determined by Kjeldahl's method:

$$N\% = \frac{1.4\, NV}{w}$$

where, N is the normality of acid and V its volume required to neutralise NH_3 obtained from w g of the compound containing nitrogen.

If percentage of NH_3 is required.

$$NH_3\,(\%) = \frac{1.7\, NV}{w}$$

In this method, compound is digested with NaOH, and NH_3 formed is passed into excess of acid. Unused acid is determined by back titration using alkali solution.

Equivalent mass of an acid or base or salt

- **Equivalent mass** of a substance is the mass which can combine or displace **1 g hydrogen,** or **8 g oxygen** or **35.5 g chlorine** or **80 g bromine** or **127 g iodine** or **12.0 g carbon** or **17 g OH^-**.

Equivalent mass of an element

$$= \frac{\text{Atomic mass of an element}}{\text{Valency of element}}$$

Equivalent mass of a base or an acid or salt can be expressed in terms of *n*-factor.

$$\text{Equivalent mass} = \frac{\text{Molar mass}}{n\text{ - factor}}$$

where ***n*-factor** is the number of ionisable H^+ ions in acid or number of ionisable OH^- ions in base or number of electrons exchanged in a redox reaction.

- $Zn + H_2SO_4 \longrightarrow ZnSO_4 + H_2$

$$H_2 \equiv 2H \equiv H_2SO_4$$

$$\text{Thus, } 1\text{g H} \equiv \frac{H_2SO_4}{2} = 49 \text{ g}$$

1 mol H_2(≡ 2 H) is displaced by 1 mol H_2SO_4.

Thus, 1 g H is displaced by 49 g H_2SO_4.

Thus, equivalent mass of H_2SO_4 = 49 g equiv^{-1}.

- $2H_2 + O_2 \longrightarrow 2H_2O$

$$2H_2O \equiv O_2 \equiv 32 \text{ g } O_2$$

$$32 \text{ g } O_2 \equiv 36 \text{ g } H_2O$$

$$\therefore \quad 8 \text{ g } O_2 \equiv \frac{36}{32} \times 8 = 9 \text{ g } H_2O$$

Alternately 32 g of O_2 is used to form = 36 g H_2O

Thus, 8 g O_2 is used to form = 9 g H_2O.
Thus, equivalent mass of $H_2O = 9$ g equiv^{-1}

- $MnO_2 + 4HCl \longrightarrow MnCl_2 + 2H_2O + Cl_2$

$$MnO_2 \equiv Cl_2 \equiv 2Cl$$

$$\therefore \quad 1\ Cl\ (35.5\ g) \equiv \frac{MnO_2}{2}$$

Thus, equivalent mass of MnO_2 = one-half of its molar mass. ***n*-factor for a base** (i.e. acidity) is the number of replaceable (ionisable) OH^- ions bonded to electropositive metal.

Acidity (or *n*-factor) of Some Common Bases

Base	Type	*n*-factor or number of OH^- ions per unit	Equivalent mass = Molar mass (*m*) / *n* - factor
NaOH	monoacid	1	$= m$
KOH	monoacid	1	$= m$
NH_4OH	monoacid	1	$= m$
CH_3NH_2	monoacid *	1**	$= m$
$C_6H_5NH_2$	monoacid *	1**	$= m$
C_5H_5N	monoacid *	1**	$= m$
$Ca(OH)_2$	diacid	2	$= m/2$
$Ba(OH)_2$	diacid	2	$= m/2$
$Al(OH)_3$	triacid	3	$= m/3$

* Where in aqueous solution, OH^- ion is formed.

$$^{**}RNH_2 + H_2O \longrightarrow RNH_3^{\oplus} + OH^{\ominus}$$

$$\underset{\text{Methyl amine}}{CH_3NH_2} + H^{\oplus} \longrightarrow CH_3NH_3^{\oplus}$$

$$\underset{\text{Aniline}}{C_6H_5NH_2} + H^{\oplus} \longrightarrow C_6H_5NH_3^{\oplus}$$

$$\underset{\text{Pyridine}}{C_5H_5N} + H^{\oplus} \longrightarrow C_5H_5NH^{\oplus}$$

Basicity (or *n*-factor) of Some Common Acids

Acid	Type	*n*-factor or number of H^+ per unit	Equivalent mass = Molar mass (*m*) / *n*-factor
CH_3COOH	monobasic	1	$= m$
HCl	monobasic	1	$= m$
N_3H	monobasic	1	$= m$
HNO_3	monobasic	1	$= m$
HSO_4^-	monobasic	1	$= m$
H_3PO_2	monobasic	1	$= m$
H_2SO_4	dibasic	2	$= m/2$
$H_2C_2O_4$	dibasic	2	$= m/2$
H_3PO_3	dibasic	2	$= m/2$
H_3PO_4	tribasic	3	$= m/3$

- **Note** H_3PO_2, H_3PO_3 and H_3PO_4 all appear tribasic acids but respectively has one, two and three replaceable H^+ ions attached to O-atoms directly (encircled). H attached to P directly exhibit reducing property.

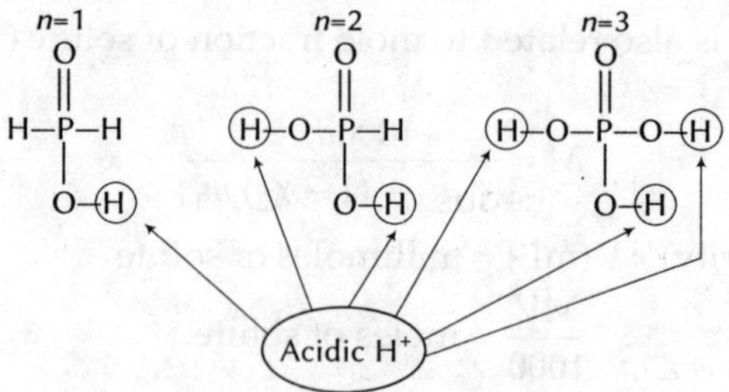

- **For a salt, *n*-factor** is the total positive or negative charge on it.

$$KCl \rightleftharpoons K^+ + Cl^-; n = 1, E = \frac{m}{1}$$

$$K_2SO_4 \rightleftharpoons 2K^+ + SO_4^{2-}; n = 2, E = \frac{m}{2}$$

$$AlPO_4 \rightleftharpoons Al^{3+} + PO_4^{3-}; n = 3, E = \frac{m}{3}$$

$$Fe_2(SO_4)_3 \rightleftharpoons 2Fe^{3+} + 3SO_4^{2-}; n = 6, E = \frac{m}{6}$$

$$K_2SO_4 \cdot Al_2(SO_4)_3 \rightleftharpoons 2K^+ + 2Al^{3+} + 4SO_4^{2-}; n = 8, E = \frac{m}{8}$$

- **For a redox reaction, *n*-factor** is the number of electrons exchanged (gained or lost).

$$Fe^{2+} \longrightarrow Fe^{3+} + e^-; \quad n = 1, E = \frac{\text{ionic mass}}{1}$$

$$MnO_4^- + 5e^- \longrightarrow Mn^{2+}, \quad n = 5, E = \frac{\text{ionic mass}}{5}$$

$$Cr_2O_7^{2-} + 6e^- \longrightarrow 2Cr^{3+}, \quad n = 6, E = \frac{\text{ionic mass}}{6}$$

$$C_2O_4^{2-} \longrightarrow 2CO_2 + 2e^-, \quad n = 2, E = \frac{\text{ionic mass}}{2}$$

$$Sn^{2+} \longrightarrow Sn^{4+} + 2e^-, \quad n = 2, E = \frac{\text{ionic mass}}{2}$$

$$As^{3+} \longrightarrow As^{5+} + 2e^-, \quad n = 2, E = \frac{\text{ionic mass}}{2}$$

e.g. In the following reaction,

$$4Al + 3O_2 \longrightarrow 2Al_2O_3$$

Al has changed into Al^{3+} by loss of three electrons per Al atom and O has changed into O^{2-} by gain of two electrons by O-atom.

Thus, in the formation of one molecule of Al_2O_3, six electrons have been lost by Al and six electrons have been gained by oxygen.

$$\text{Thus, equivalent mass of } Al_2O_3 = \frac{\text{Molar mass of } Al_2O_3}{6}$$

(detailed study in oxidation and reduction)

- **For H_2O_2, strength is measured in terms of volume. For *x* volume H_2O_2**

and $\quad M = \dfrac{x}{11.2} \Rightarrow N = \dfrac{x}{5.6}$

For H_2O_2, molarity = 2 × normality

Solved Examples & Instant Practice

Example 1.11) Aqueous glucose solution is 20% by mass of solution. Calculate the percentage by mass of solvent (H_2O).

Solution is a mixture of solute and solvent. If amount of solute is known in the solution, then amount of solvent can be calculated. Mass per cent of solute by mass of solvent is the amount of solute in 100 g solvent.

Sol. Solvent + Solute (glucose) = 100 g

Since, mass of glucose in 100 g solution is known, mass of solvent (H_2O) is thus also known.

Solute (glucose) = 20 g

$\therefore$ Solvent (H_2O) = 80 g

$$\text{Percentage by mass of solvent} = \frac{\text{Mass of solute} \times 100}{\text{Mass of solvent}}$$

$$\therefore \text{\% by mass of water} = \frac{20}{80} \times 100 = 25\%$$

Example 1.12) A solution is prepared by adding 2 g of a substance A to 18 g water. Calculate mass per cent of solute by mass of solution. ***[NCERT]***

Sol. Mass of solute, $A = 2$ g

Mass of water = 18 g

Mass of solution (solute + water) = 20 g

Mass per cent of solute by mass of solution

$$= \frac{\text{Mass of solute } A \times 100}{\text{Mass of solution}} = \frac{2}{20} \times 100 = 10\%$$

Immediate Test 8

(i) 100 g of aqueous solution contains 1 mole of urea (N_2H_4CO). Calculate percentage concentration by

(a) mass of water (b) mass of solution

(ii) 4.6 g of ethanol (C_2H_5OH) is added to 5.4 g of water (H_2O). Calculate percentage concentration by

(a) mass of water (b) mass of solution

(iii) 100g of an aqueous glucose ($C_6H_{12}O_6$) solution is evaporated when 18 g of residue is recovered. Calculate

(a) mole percentage

(b) mass percentage (by weight of H_2O)

Example 1.13) What is the per cent of free SO_3 in oleum ($H_2S_2O_7$ — a solution of SO_3 in H_2SO_4) that is labelled 109% H_2SO_4?

Sol. Such a designation refers to the total mass of pure H_2SO_4, 109 g of that would be present after dilution of 100 g of the oleum, when all the free SO_3 (in oleum) would combine with water to form H_2SO_4.

$$\text{\% of free } SO_3 \text{ in oleum} = \frac{80}{18} \times \text{\%(strength} - 100)$$

Oleum ($H_2S_2O_7$) = 100 g

Thus, water added = 9 g

Strength = 109%

$$\underset{\substack{1 \text{ mol} \\ 18 \text{ g}}}{H_2O} + \underset{\substack{1 \text{ mol} \\ 80 \text{ g}}}{SO_3 \text{ (in oleum)}} = \underset{\substack{1 \text{ mol} \\ 98 \text{ g}}}{H_2SO_4}$$

18 g H_2O combines with = 80 g SO_3

Thus, 9 g H_2O combines with = 40 g SO_3

Thus, 100 g of the oleum contains 40 g SO_3

$\therefore$ Percentage of free SO_3 in oleum = 40%

Immediate Test 9

Calculate number of moles of water present in oleum that is labelled as 118%.

Example 1.14) 10 g of methanol (CH_3OH) is mixed with water to make total mass 20 g at 298 K. What is volume per cent of methanol (by volume of solution)?

$$d\,(H_2O) = 1.00 \text{ g mL}^{-1}$$
$$d\,(CH_3OH) = 0.75 \text{ g mL}^{-1} \text{ at 298 K}$$

In the solution of two components, mass of each is known. Since, density is also given, hence volume is also known.

$$\textit{Volume} = \frac{\textit{Mass}}{\textit{Density}}$$

From the total volume, per cent of the required components out of total volume.

Sol. $\text{Volume} = \dfrac{\text{Mass}}{\text{Density}}$

$$\text{Volume of methanol} = \frac{10 \text{ g}}{0.75 \text{ g mL}^{-1}} = 13.3 \text{ mL}$$

$$\text{Volume of water} = \frac{10 \text{ g}}{1.00 \text{ g mL}^{-1}} = 10.0 \text{ mL}$$

Total volume of solution = 10 + 13.3 = 23.3 mL

$$\text{Thus, volume per cent of methanol} = \frac{13.3 \times 100}{23.3} = 57.08\%$$

Immediate Test 10

(i) H_2SO_4 solution is 98% by weight of solution with density 1.8 g mL^{-1}. What is per cent H_2SO_4 weight by volume of solution?

(ii) 10 mL each of CH_3CH_2OH and H_2O ($d = 1.00$ g mL^{-1}) has resultant density of 0.90 g mL^{-1}. What is density of CH_3CH_2OH?

Example 1.15) A sample of hard water contains 1 mg $CaSO_4$ per litre of solution. Express this concentration in terms of $CaCO_3$ present in per 10^6 parts of water (ppm of $CaCO_3$).

Sol. Hardness of water is expressed in ppm of $CaCO_3$.

$$CaSO_4 \equiv CaCO_3 \equiv Ca^{2+}$$

Thus, moles of $CaSO_4 \equiv$ moles of $CaCO_3$

Moles of $CaCO_3 \times$ molar mass of $CaCO_3$ = Concentration in g L^{-1}

Thus, (ppm) concentration can be determined.

$$\text{Concentration in ppm} = \frac{\text{Amount of solute} \times 10^6}{\text{Amount of solution}}$$

10^3 mL water has $CaSO_4$ = 1 mg = 0.001 g

$$= \frac{0.001}{136} \text{ mol } CaSO_4 = \frac{0.001}{136} \text{ mol } CaCO_3$$

$$= \frac{0.001}{136} \times (\text{molar mass } CaCO_3)$$

$$= \frac{0.001}{136} \times 100 \text{ g } CaCO_3$$

$$= 7.35 \times 10^{-4} \text{ g } CaCO_3$$

$$\therefore \; CaCO_3 \text{ in } 10^6 \text{ mL } H_2O = \frac{7.35 \times 10^{-4}}{1000} \times 10^6 = 0.735 \text{ ppm}$$

Immediate Test 11

(i) A sample of hard water is 200 ppm of $CaCO_3$. Express this concentration in mg L^{-1} of solution.

(ii) A particular water sample is found to contain 96.0 ppm of SO_4^{2-} and 122.0 ppm of HCO_3^- with Ca^{2+} as the only cation. Express the concentration in ppm of Ca^{2+}.

Example 1.16) **What volume of 95.0% alcohol by weight (density = 0.809 g mL^{-1}) must be used to prepare 150 mL of 30.0 % alcohol by weight (density = 0.957 g mL^{-1})?**

Percentage by weight can be converted to volume. In each of initial and final solution, volume × density × % are compared.

Since, $\frac{\text{Mass}}{\text{Volume}} = \text{Density}$

∴ *Hence, volume of solution is related to mass of solution.*

Sol. Let volume of 95% alcohol required = V mL

Mass of solution with density 0.809 g mL^{-1} = $V \times 0.809$ g

Alcohol in the solution = $V \times 0.809 \times \frac{95}{100}$ g

Similarly, mass of 150 mL in 30% alcohol of density 0.957 g mL^{-1}

$$= 150 \times 0.953 \times \frac{30}{100}$$

∴ Before dilution = after dilution

$$V \times 0.809 \times \frac{95}{100} = 150 \times 0.957 \times \frac{30}{100}$$

$$\therefore \quad V = \frac{150 \times 0.957 \times 30}{0.809 \times 95} = 56.03 \text{ mL}$$

Immediate Test 12

(i) Ammonia gas is passed into water, yielding a solution of density 0.93 g cm^{-3} and containing 18.6% NH_3 by weight. What is the mass of NH_3 per cm^3 of solution?

(ii) Given, 100 mL of pure water at 277 K, what volume of a solution of hydrochloric acid, density 1.175 g mL^{-1} and containing 34.4% HCl by weight, could be prepared?

Example 1.17) **Calculate the mass of $Na_2SO_4 \cdot 10H_2O$ needed to make 50.0 mL of an aqueous solution of concentration 4.6 mg Na^+ per mL.**

Sol. $Na_2SO_4 \rightleftharpoons 2Na^+ + SO_4^{2-}$

Every mole of $Na_2SO_4 \cdot 10H_2O$ or Na_2SO_4 has 2 moles of Na^+ ion. Thus, amount in 50 mL of solution can be determined.

$$4.6 \text{ mg } Na^+ \text{ per mL} = 4.6 \times 10^{-3} \text{ g } \overset{+}{Na} \text{ per mL}$$

$$= \frac{4.6 \times 10^{-3}}{23} \text{ mol } Na^+ \text{ per mL}$$

$$= \frac{4.6 \times 10^{-3}}{23 \times 2} \text{ mol } Na_2SO_4 \cdot 10H_2O$$

$$= \frac{4.6 \times 10^{-3}}{23 \times 2} \times 322 \text{ g } Na_2SO_4 \cdot 10H_2O$$

$$= 0.0322 \text{ g per mL}$$

Thus, $Na_2SO_4 \cdot 10H_2O$ in 50 mL = 0.0322 × 50 = 1.61 g

Immediate Test 13

(i) Calculate the mass of $Al_2(SO_4)_3 \cdot 18H_2O$ (666 g mol^{-1}) needed to make up 50.0 mL of an aqueous solution of concentration 40.0 mg Al^{3+} per mL.

(ii) Describe how you would prepare 50 g of a 12.0% $BaCl_2$ solution, starting with $BaCl_2 \cdot 2H_2O$ and pure water? (Ba = 137)

Example 1.18) **9.2 g of ethanol (C_2H_5OH) is mixed with water to make 20.0 g of solution. What is the mole fraction of each in the solution?**

To calculate mole fraction of any component of a solution, we must know the moles of that component and total moles of solution. Mole fraction of one of the component in the mixture

$$= \frac{\text{Moles of that component}}{\text{Total moles}} = \frac{n_i}{\Sigma n_i}$$

Sol. Ethanol (C_2H_5OH) in mixture = 9.2 g

$$\therefore \quad \text{Number of moles} = \frac{\text{Mass}}{\text{Molar mass}}$$

$$= \frac{9.2}{46} = 0.2 \text{ mol}$$

Water (H_2O) = 20.0 − 9.2 = 10.8 g

$$\text{Number of moles of } H_2O = \frac{10.8}{18} = 0.6 \text{ mol}$$

Total moles = 0.2 + 0.6 = 0.8 mol

$$\therefore \quad \chi_{C_2H_5OH} = \frac{\text{Moles of } C_2H_5OH}{\text{Total moles}}$$

$$= \frac{0.2}{0.8} = 0.25$$

$$\chi_{H_2O} = (1 - 0.25) = \frac{0.6}{0.8} = 0.75$$

Note $\chi_1 + \chi_2 = 1.0$, i.e. Total mole fraction of the components in mixture is always 1.

Example 1.19) Mole fraction of urea (NH_2CONH_2) is an aqueous solution is 0.1. Calculate its per cent concentration by mass of solution.

Sol. $\chi_{\text{solute (urea)}} = 0.1$

$\chi_{\text{solvent (water)}} = 1.0 - 0.1 = 0.9$

$\chi_{H_2O} = n_{H_2O} / n_{\text{Total}}$ and $\chi_{\text{urea}} = n_{\text{urea}} / n_{\text{Total}}$

$$\therefore \quad \frac{\chi_{H_2O}}{\chi_{\text{urea}}} = \frac{9}{1} = \frac{w_1/m_1}{w_2/m_2} \Rightarrow 9 = \frac{w_1 \times 60}{18 \times w_2}$$

$$\therefore \quad \frac{w_1}{w_2} = \frac{162}{60} = \frac{81}{30}$$

Thus, 30 g of solute (urea) is in 81 g of solvent (water)

Total mass of solution is = 30 + 81 = 111 g

$$\therefore \quad \text{Mass per cent of urea} = \frac{\text{Mass of urea} \times 100}{\text{Total mass}} = \frac{30}{111} \times 100$$

$$= 27.03\%$$

Immediate Test 14

(i) Aqueous glucose ($C_6H_{12}O_6$) solution is 18% by mass of solution. Calculate mole fraction of glucose in solution.

(ii) 0.4 g of urea separates when 5 g of 20% aqueous urea (NH_2CONH_2) solution (by mass of solution) is cooled. What is change in mole fraction of urea in solution?

(iii) A solution contains 25 g water, 25 g ethanol and 50 g acetic acid in 100 g solution. Calculate mole fraction of each in the mixture.

(iv) What is mole fraction of H_2 in a gaseous mixture containing 1.0 g H_2, 8.0 g O_2 and 16 g CH_4 ?

Example 1.20) Calculate the molarity of KOH solution prepared by dissolving 0.56 g of it in enough water to make 100 mL of the solution.

Molarity is the number of moles a solute present per litre of solution. If number of moles of solute and volume of solution are known, molarity is calculated.

Sol. $\text{Molarity} = \dfrac{\text{Moles of solute}}{\text{Volume of solution in litre}}$

$$\text{Moles of solute (KOH)} = 0.56\text{ g} = \frac{0.56\text{ g}}{56\text{ g mol}^{-1}} = 0.01\text{ mol}$$

Volume of solution = 100 mL = 0.10 L

$$\therefore \quad \text{Molarity} = \frac{\text{Moles of solute}}{\text{Volume in L (solution)}} = \frac{0.01}{0.10}$$

$$= 0.1\text{ M (mol L}^{-1})$$

Example 1.21) Calculate the volume of 2.50 M sugar solution which contains 0.400 mole sugar.

Sol. $\text{Molarity} = \dfrac{\text{Moles of solute}}{\text{Volume (litres)}}$

$$2.50 = \frac{0.400}{V}$$

$$\therefore \quad V = \frac{0.400\text{ mol}}{2.50\text{ mol L}^{-1}} = 1.160\text{ L}$$

Immediate Test 15

(i) Concentration of glucose ($C_6H_{12}O_6$) in normal blood is 90 mg per 100 mL. What is molarity of glucose solution in blood ?

(ii) The concentration of cholesterol in normal blood is 0.005 M. How many moles of cholesterol are in 750 mL of blood?

(iii) What volume of 1.71 M NaCl solution contains 0.20 mol NaCl ?

Example 1.22) How many mL of water must be added to 200 mL of 0.65 M HCl to dilute the solution to 0.20 M ?

Sol. It is a case of dilution.

Number of moles of solute remains unchanged,

hence $\underset{\text{before dilution}}{M_1V_1} = \underset{\text{after dilution}}{M_2V_2}$

Thus, V_2 (final volume) is known, from where volume of water required can be derived.

200 mL of 0.65 M HCl ≡ V mL of 0.20 M

$$\therefore \quad V = \frac{200 \times 0.65}{0.20} = 650\text{ mL}$$

Thus, water to be added = 650 − 200 = 450 mL

Example 1.23) How much of 1.00 M HCl should be mixed with what volume of 0.250 M HCl in order to prepare 1.00 L of 0.500 M HCl ?

Sol. It is case of mixing of two acid solutions,

So, molarity of resultant solution (say M) can be calculated by using $M_1V_1 + M_2V_2 = M(V_1 + V_2)$

$$M\text{ (resultant)} = \frac{M_1V_1 + M_2V_2}{V_1 + V_2}$$

Total volume is given

$$V_1 + V_2 = 1000\text{ mL}$$

$$\therefore \quad V_2 = (1000 - V_1)$$

$$0.500 = \frac{1 \times V_1 + 0.250\,(1000 - V_1)}{1000}$$

$$\therefore \quad V_1 = 333\text{ mL}$$

$$\therefore \quad V_2 = 667\text{ mL}$$

Thus, 333 mL of 1 M HCl should be mixed with 667 mL of 0.250 M HCl to obtain 1.00 L of 0.500 M HCl.

Immediate Test 16

(i) What volume of 0.30 M Na_2SO_4 solution is required to prepare 2.0 L of a solution 0.40 M in Na^+ ?

(ii) To what extend must a 0.500 M $BaCl_2$ solution is diluted to yield solution of concentration 27.4 mg Ba^{2+} per mL? (Ba = 137)

(iii) Calculate the concentration of diluted HNO_3, if 0.20 mol HNO_3 is added to a beaker containing 2.0 L of 1.1 M HNO_3 and enough pure water is added to give a final volume of 3.0 L.

Example 1.24) H_2SO_4 is 98% by weight of solution. Its density is 1.8 g mL^{-1}. Calculate volume of this solution to prepare 1 L of 0.18 M H_2SO_4.

From mass percentage and density, volume percentage is calculated. Thus, molarity of 98% H_2SO_4 is derived. This solution is diluted to make 1 L of 0.18 M. We use $M_1V_1 = M_2V_2$ as due to dilution, number of moles of solute remains unchanged.

Sol. Mass of H_2SO_4 solution = 100 g

$$\text{Volume of } H_2SO_4 \text{ solution} = \frac{\text{Mass}}{\text{Density}} = \frac{100}{1.8}\text{ mL} = \frac{1}{18}\text{ L}$$

$$H_2SO_4 \text{ present} = 98\text{ g} = \frac{98}{98} = 1\text{ mol}$$

$$\therefore \quad \text{Molarity} = \frac{\text{Mole}}{\text{Litre}} = \frac{1}{1/18} = 18\text{ M}$$

V mL of 18 M H_2SO_4 $H_2SO_4 \equiv$ 1000 mL of 0.18 M H_2SO_4

$\therefore V = 10$ mL

Thus, 10 mL of 98% H_2SO_4 is to be diluted to 1 L to make 0.18 M.

Molarity expressed in terms of density (g mL^{-1}) and %

$$\text{For quick result} = \frac{10d \times \%}{\text{Molar mass}}$$

$$= \frac{10 \times 1.8 \times 98}{98} = 18\text{ M}$$

Immediate Test 17

HNO_3 is 63% by mass of solution. Every 1 mL contains 1.2 g HNO_3. If 1 mL is diluted to 1 L of solution, calculate molarity of dilute HNO_3 solution.

Example 1.25) Calculate molarity of mixture obtained by mixing 100 mL of 0.1 M HCl and 50 mL of 0.25 M NaOH.

Sol. Acid is mixed with a base and depending on the fact of which (MV) factor is larger, resultant molarity is derived.

$$M\text{ (resultant)} = \frac{M_1V_1 - M_2V_2}{(V_1 + V_2)}$$

if $\quad M_1V_1 > M_2V_2$

For acid

100 mL of 0.1 M HCl = 100 × 0.1 = 10 millimoles

For base

50 mL of 0.25 M NaOH = 50 × 0.25 = 12.5 millimoles

Thus, $\quad MV$ (base) > MV (acid)

Hence, mixture is basic.

$$\therefore \quad M(OH^-) = \frac{12.5 - 10.0}{150} = 0.0167\text{ M}$$

Example 1.26) 100 mL of 0.1 M KOH is mixed with 200 mL of 0.1 M $Ca(OH)_2$ and 300 mL of 0.1 M H_2SO_4. What is molarity of resultant solution in terms of H^+ or OH^- ion.

Sol. 100 mL of 0.1 M KOH = 100 mL of 0.1 M $[OH^-]$

200 mL of 0.1 M $Ca(OH)_2$ = 200 mL of 0.2 M $[OH^-]$

300 mL of 0.1 M H_2SO_4 = 300 mL of 0.2 M $[H^+]$

Thus,

$$[OH^-]_{mix} = \frac{100 \times 0.1 + 200 \times 0.2}{300} = 0.167\text{ M}$$

Thus, 300 mL of 0.167 M $[OH^-]$ is mixed with 300 mL of 0.2 M $[H^+]$

Also, 300 × 0.2 M (acid) > 300 × 0.167 M (base)

Mixture is acidic.

$\therefore$ Resultant molarity in terms of $[H^+]$

$$= \frac{300 \times 0.2 - 300 \times 0.167}{600} = 0.0165\text{ M}$$

Immediate Test 18

100 mL of 0.1 M HCl, 200 mL of 0.05 M H_2SO_4 and 100 mL of 0.2 M NaOH are mixed. What is molarity of the resultant solution?

Example 1.27) 1.575 g of oxalic acid ($H_2C_2O_4 \cdot 2H_2O$), a dibasic acid is dissolved in water and solution diluted to 250 mL. Calculate the normality of oxalic acid.

Sol. $$\text{Normality} = \frac{\text{Number of equivalents of acid}}{\text{Volume in L}}$$

$$\text{Also, equivalent mass of acid} = \frac{\text{Molar mass}}{\text{Basicity } (n\text{-factor})}$$

$$\text{Number of equivalents} = \frac{\text{Mass}}{\text{Equivalent mass}}$$

Molar mass of $H_2C_2O_4 \cdot 2H_2O$ = 126 g mol^{-1}

$$\therefore \text{Equivalent mass} = \frac{126}{2} = 63\text{ g equiv}^{-1}$$

$$\therefore \text{Number of equivalents} = \frac{1.575}{63}\text{ equiv}$$

$$\therefore \quad \text{Normality} = \frac{\frac{1.575}{63}}{0.25\text{ L}} = 0.1\text{ N}$$

■ Also, normality (M) = molarity × n-factor

$$M = \frac{1000 \times w_2}{m_2 V}, \quad N = \frac{1000\, w_2}{E_2\, V}$$

where, w_2 = mass of solute, V = volume in mL

E_2 = equivalent mass, m_2 = molar mass of solute

Example 1.28) 8.2 g of a dibasic acid in 100 mL solution forms 0.2 N solution. What is molar mass of dibasic acid?

Sol. If molar mass of the dibasic acid = m_2 g mol^{-1}

$$\text{then its equivalent mass } (E_2) = \frac{m_2}{2}$$

$$\text{Normality} = \frac{\text{Mass of solute (g)}/E_2}{\text{Volume (L)}}$$

$$\Rightarrow \quad 0.2 = \frac{8.2 \times 2}{m_2 \times 0.1}$$

$$\therefore \quad m_2 = 82\text{ g mol}^{-1}$$

■ Direct $N = \frac{1000 \times w_2}{E_2 V}$ and molar mass = E_2 × basicity

Immediate Test 19

(i) 3.267 g of H_3PO_4 in 100 mL solution forms 1 N solution. What is basicity of this acid? (P = 31)

(ii) 2.78 g of $FeSO_4 \cdot xH_2O$ in 100 mL solution forms 0.1 N solution. What is value of x? (Assume n-factor = 1) (Fe = 56)

Example 1.29) Calculate the molarity of the original H_3PO_4 solution, if 20.0 mL of H_3PO_4 solution is required to completely neutralise 40.0 mL of 0.05 M $Ba(OH)_2$ solution.

This is a case in which n-factor of acid (H_3PO_4, $n = 3$) is different from base [$Ba(OH)_2$, $n = 2$]. In such case, convert molarity into normality.

If acids and bases are of different nature in terms of basicity and acidity, then

$$M_1V_1 \neq M_2V_2, \quad \text{but} \quad N_1V_1 = N_2V_2$$

Sol. $2H_3PO_4 + 3Ba(OH)_2 \longrightarrow Ba_3(PO_4)_2 + 6H_2O$

$$H_3PO_4 \rightleftharpoons 3H^+ + PO_4^{3-}$$

Thus, $M_1(H_3PO_4) = 3N_1(H_3PO_4)$

and $M_2(Ba(OH)_2) = 2N_2\ Ba(OH)_2$

For neutralisation reaction,

$$N_1V_1 = N_2V_2$$

$\therefore$ 20 mL of $3N_1\ H_3PO_4 \equiv$ 40 mL of 0.10 $N_2\ Ba(OH)_2$

$M_1 = 0.0667$ M H_3PO_4

Immediate Test 20

(i) 0.4 g of NaOH is dissolved in water and solution diluted to 100 mL. 10 mL of this solution is neutralised by 10 mL of H_2SO_4. Calculate the amount of H_2SO_4 in 100 mL solution.

(ii) 100 mL of 0.01 M H_3PO_4 is completely neutralised by 50 mL of $Ca(OH)_2$ solution. What is molarity and normality of $Ca(OH)_2$ solution.

Example 1.30) 6 g of urea (molar mass 60 g mol^{-1}) is in 54 g of water. What is its molality and mole fraction?

Sol. Molality is the concentration expressed in moles of solute present in 1 kg of solvent.

$$\text{Molality }(m) = \frac{\text{Moles of solute}}{\text{Mass of solvent(kg)}}$$

$$\text{Mole fraction} = \frac{\text{Moles of solute}}{\text{Total moles}}$$

$$\text{Amount of solute (Urea)} = 6\text{ g} = \frac{6}{60} = 0.1\text{ mol}$$

$$\text{Amount of solvent (Water)} = 54\text{ g} = \frac{54}{18}$$

$$= 3.0\text{ mol} = 0.054\text{ kg}$$

Total moles = 0.1 + 3.0 = 3.1 mol

$$\text{Thus, molality} = \frac{0.1\text{ mol}}{0.054\text{ kg}} = 1.852\text{ mol kg}^{-1}$$

$$\text{Mole fraction of urea } \chi_{urea} = \frac{n_{urea}}{n_{total}} = \frac{0.1}{3.1} = 0.0322$$

Immediate Test 21

If 4 g NaOH is dissolved in 36 g H_2O, calculate the mole fraction, molarity and molality of NaOH solution. (Specific gravity of solution is 1g mL^{-1}) ***[NCERT Exemplar]***

Example 1.31) The density of 3M solution of NaCl is 1.25 g mL^{-1}. Calculate the molality of the solution. ***[NCERT Exemplar]***

Sol. Molality is the concentration expressed in moles of solute per kg of solvent while molarity is the number of moles of solute per litre of solution.

Molality (m) is related to molarity (M), density (d) and molar mass

$$m\text{ (molality)} = \frac{1000\,M}{(1000d - Mm_2)}$$ (d is in g mL^{-1}) (m_2) of solute by

$$m_2 = 58.5\text{ g mol}^{-1}$$

$$m = \frac{1000 \times 3}{(1000 \times 1.25 - 3 \times 58.5)} = 2.79\text{ mol kg}^{-1}$$

Immediate Test 22

(i) The density of 3 molal solution of NaOH is 1.11 g mL^{-1}. Calculate the molarity of this solution. ***[NCERT Exemplar]***

(ii) Calculate the (a) molar concentration (b) molality of sulphuric acid solution of density 1.198 g mL^{-1}, containing 27.0% H_2SO_4 by weight.

Example 1.32) Mole fraction of sucrose in aqueous solution is 0.2. Calculate molality of sucrose solution.

Sol. Mole fraction of a component is the fraction of moles out of total moles of all the components.

If, χ_2 = mole fraction of sucrose

and m_1 = molar mass of water (solvent)

$$\text{Then, molality }(m) = \frac{1000\chi_2}{(1-\chi_2)m_1}$$

$$m = \frac{1000 \times 0.2}{0.8 \times 18} = 13.89\text{ molal}$$

Alternately n_1 = moles of water

n_2 = moles of surcrose, then

$$\frac{\chi_2}{\chi_1} = \frac{n_2/n_{Total}}{n_1/n_{Total}} = \frac{n_2}{n_1} = \frac{w_2/m_2}{w_1/m_1} = \frac{w_2m_1}{m_2w_1}$$

$$\frac{0.2}{0.8} = \frac{w_2 \times 18}{w_1 \times 342} \Rightarrow \frac{w_2}{w_1} = \frac{342}{72}$$

Thus, if w_2 (solute) = 342 g = 1 mol

Then w_1 (solvent) = 72 g = 0.072 kg

$$\therefore \quad \text{Molality} = \frac{1}{0.072} = 13.89\text{ molal}$$

Immediate Test 23

(i) Molality of aqueous glucose solution is 1 mol kg^{-1}. What is mole fraction of glucose? Also, calculate percentage of glucose by weight of solution.

(ii) Derive the relation, $M\left[\frac{m_2}{1000} + \frac{1}{m}\right] = d$

where, M = molarity, m = molality

m_2 = molar mass of solute, d = density

KNOWLEDGE CONFIRMATION Test 4

1 NaCl solution is 3.57×10^5 ppm with specific gravity 1.12. Its percentage concentration (w/V) is
(a) 20% (b) 40% (c) 45% (d) 50%

2 Mole fraction of helium in a mixture containing hydrogen (H_2) and helium (He) in 1 : 2 mass ratio, is
(a) 0.5 (b) 0.75 (c) 0.67 (d) 0.33

3 Mole fraction of He in a 2g mixture of H_2 and He is 0.5. Thus, helium present in the mixture is
(a) $\frac{2}{3}$ g (b) $\frac{4}{3}$ g
(c) $\frac{1}{3}$ g (d) $\frac{3}{2}$ g

4 Equal masses of ethanol ($d = 0.75$ g mL^{-1}) and water ($d = 1.00$ g mL^{-1}) are mixed at 298 K. Thus, volume per cent of ethanol in the mixture is
(a) 25.00% (b) 42.86%
(c) 50.00% (d) 57.14%

5 50 mL of concentrated H_2SO_4 ($d = 1.8$ g mL^{-1}) is mixed with 100 mL H_2O ($d = 1.0$ g mL^{-1}) at 298 K. Thus, mass percentage of H_2SO_4 in the mixture is
(a) 33.33% (b) 66.66%
(c) 53.64% (d) 47.36%

6 Concentration of 1 μg mL^{-1} is equal to
(a) 1 ppm (b) 10^3 ppb
(c) 10^{-3} ppt (d) All of these

7 What is molarity of solution which contains 5.85 g NaCl (*s*) per 500 mL solution ? ***[NCERT Exemplar]***
(a) 4 mol L^{-1} (b) 20 mol L^{-1}
(c) 0.2 mol L^{-1} (d) 2 mol L^{-1}

8 If 500 mL of a 5 M solution is diluted to 1500 mL, what will be the molarity of the diluted solution? ***[NCERT Exemplar]***
(a) 1.50 M (b) 1.67 M
(c) 1.59 M (d) 0.017 M

9 6.02×10^{22} molecules of urea (NH_2CONH_2) are present in 500 mL solution. Thus, molar concentration of urea solution is
(a) 0.20 M (b) 0.02 M
(c) 0.10 M (d) 2.0 M

10 60 g of urea is present in 1060 g of aqueous solution. Thus, molality of the solution is
(a) 0.943 (b) 0.893 (c) 1.000 (d) 1.120

11 Ethanol (C_2H_5OH) is 46% by weight in a mixture of water and ethanol. Thus, molality of ethanol solution is
(a) 18.51 molal (b) 0.054 molal
(c) 1.00 molal (d) 2.72 molal

12 On evaporation of 1L of urea solution of density 1.2 g mL^{-1}, 120 g of residue is formed. Thus, molality of solution is
(a) 2.00 molal (b) 1.85 molal
(c) 1.00 molal (d) 1.20 molal

13 100 mL of 1 M HCl is mixed with *x* mL of 2 M HCl giving a solution of 1.67 M HCl. Thus, *x* is
(a) 100 mL (b) 200 mL
(c) 300 mL (d) 400 mL

14 0.530 g of pure Na_2CO_3 required 28.5 mL of aqueous HCl for titration to the neutralisation point. Thus, HCl is
(a) 0.70 M (b) 0.35 M
(c) 0.0875 M (d) 0.175 M

15 0.24 g of a metal combines with oxygen to form 0.40 g of oxide. Thus, equivalent mass of the metal is
(a) 16 (b) 32 (c) 24 (d) 12

16 What volume of 3.0 M NaOH can be prepared with 80.0 g of NaOH?
(a) 0.70 L (b) 0.67 L
(c) 0.50 L (d) 0.80 L

17 2.0 L of 3.0 M sugar solution and 3.0 L of 2.5 M sugar solution are mixed and then diluted to 10 L. Final concentration of sugar is
(a) 1.35 M (b) 3.0 M (c) 2.5 M (d) 1.75 M

18 What volume of 0.50 M $BaCl_2$ will contain 3.0 mol of chloride ion ?
(a) 1.02 L (b) 3.50 L
(c) 3.0 L (d) 4.0 L

19 What volume of 96.0% H_2SO_4 solution (density 1.83 g mL^{-1}) is required to prepare 2.00 L of 3.00 M H_2SO_4 solution.
(a) 335 mL (b) 600 mL
(c) 450 mL (d) 402 mL

20 When 150.0 mL of 2.00 M NaOH was added to 100 mL of H_2SO_4 solution, it required 43.0 mL of 0.5 M HCl to neutralise the excess base. In the original solution, concentration of H_2SO_4 is
(a) 1.502 M (b) 1.392 M
(c) 2.176 M (d) 0.696 M

21 Equal volumes of 0.5 N each of $KMnO_4$ and $K_2Cr_2O_7$ are used to oxidise Fe(II) solution in acidic medium. The amount of Fe(II) oxidised to Fe(III) will be

$$MnO_4^- \xrightarrow{+5e^-} Mn^{2+}$$

$$Cr_2O_7^{2-} \xrightarrow{+6e^-} 2Cr^{3+}$$

(a) more with MnO_4^- (b) more with $Cr_2O_7^{2-}$
(c) MnO_4^- and $Cr_2O_7^{2-}$ (d) can not be predicted

22 10 mL of unknown NH_3 sample was diluted to 100 mL. This solution was treated with 50 mL of 0.1 M HCl (*aq*). Excess of HCl required 10 mL of 0.1 M NaOH solution. Thus, NH_3 in the 10 mL of original solution is

(a) 0.04 M (b) 0.40 M
(c) 0.01 M (d) 0.10 M

23 2.86 g of washing soda $Na_2CO_3 \cdot xH_2O$ was completely neutralised by 200 mL of 0.1 N H_2SO_4.

$$Na_2CO_3 + H_2SO_4 \longrightarrow Na_2SO_4 + H_2O + CO_2$$

Thus, *x* is

(a) 4 (b) 5 (c) 10 (d) 2

24 A sample of H_2SO_4 ($d = 1.8$ g mL^{-1}) with 98% by mass of solution is to be used to prepare 1 L of 0.18 M H_2SO_4. Thus, volume of concentrated H_2SO_4 required is

(a) 10 mL (b) 20 mL
(c) 40 mL (d) 100 mL

25 10 g of NH_4Cl sample is boiled with NaOH to liberated NH_3 which of passed into 60 mL of 0.45 M H_2SO_4. Excess of H_2SO_4 required 10 mL of 0.40 M NaOH. Thus, % of NH_3 in NH_4Cl is

(a) 10.5% (b) 9.5%
(c) 8.5% (d) 7.5%

Stoichiometry (Quantitative Relations in Chemical Reactions)

- **Stoichiometry** deals with the calculation of masses (in terms of moles, molecules and volumes) of the reactants and products involved in a balanced chemical reaction. For combustion of methane (CH_4), balanced chemical equation is

	$CH_4(g)$	$+ 2O_2(g)$	$\rightarrow CO_2(g)$	$+ 2H_2O(g)$
Stoichiometric coefficients ⇒	1	2	1	2
In terms of moles ⇒	1	2	1	2
In terms of molecules ⇒	$1N_0$	$2N_0$	$1N_0$	$2N_0$
In terms of molar volume at STP ⇒	22.4 L	44.8 L	22.4L	44.8 L
In terms of grams ⇒	16g	64 g	44g	36 g
	Reactants		Products	

Thus, moles → molecules → mass → volume → density.

- In a reaction, in which two or more than two reactants (in different quantities) are present, quantity of the product is determined from the reactant present in **limiting quantity.**

  i.e. the reactant which is present in the lesser amount and gets consumed after sometime, limits the amount of products formed, is called the **limiting reactant.** The other reactant is in excess.

- Limiting reactant is a reactant which yields less number of moles of product based on stoichiometry of reaction.

e.g. $\underset{1\text{ mole}}{N_2(g)} + \underset{3\text{ moles}}{3H_2} \longrightarrow \underset{2\text{ moles}}{2NH_3(g)}$

If we take, $\underset{3\text{ moles}}{N_2}$, $\underset{3\text{ moles}}{H_2}$, $\underset{?}{NH_3}$

NH_3 formed 1 mol $N_2 = 2$

NH_3 formed from 3 mol $N_2 = 6$ mol

NH_3 formed from 3 mol $H_2 = 2$ mol

Thus, H_2 is the limiting reactant and N_2 is in excess

N_2 consumed with 3 mol $H_2 = 1$ mol

N_2 left unreacted $= 3 - 1 = 2$ mol

■ Always express quantity in terms of moles.

Yields of chemical reaction

If a reaction goes to completion, then yield of product is 100%. Few reactions behave in such a manner. But due to less purity of reactants or due to some side reactions, yield of the product is always less than theoretical yield (based on stoichiometry).

Per cent yield

$$= \frac{\textbf{Actual yield or observed yield of the product}}{\textbf{Theoretical yield of the product}} \times 100$$

If 2 moles H_2 and 1 mole O_2 form 30 g H_2O, then

$$\underset{2\text{ moles}}{2H_2(g)} + \underset{1\text{ mole}}{O_2(g)} \longrightarrow \underset{2\text{ moles} = 36\text{ g}}{2H_2O(l)}$$

H_2 and O_2 are present in stoichiometry ratio, thus, theoretical yield of $H_2O = 2$ moles (36 g) but experimentally actual yield was formed to be 30 g.

Thus, % yield of $H_2O = \frac{30}{36} \times 100 = 83.33\%$

Solved Examples & Instant Practice

Example 1.33) Calculate the amount of water produced by the combustion of 8 g each of H_2 and O_2.

H_2 and O_2 combine to form water as product. To find out the amount of water, firstly we must have a balanced chemical equation. Determine amount of H_2O formed using both the reactants. Product is taken which is formed in smaller quantity.

Sol. $\underset{\substack{2\text{ moles}\\8\text{ g}\\4\text{ moles}}}{2H_2(g)} + \underset{\substack{1\text{ mole}\\8\text{ g}\\0.25\text{ mole}}}{O_2(g)} \longrightarrow \underset{\substack{2\text{ moles}\\?}}{2H_2O\ (l)}$

2 moles H_2 gives = 2 moles water.

Thus, 4 moles H_2 gives = 4 moles water $= 4 \times 18\text{ g} = 72\text{ g } H_2O$

1 mole O_2 gives = 2 moles water

Thus, 0.25 mole O_2 gives = 0.50 mole water $= 0.50 \times 18\text{ g}$

$= 9\text{ g } H_2O$

Thus, O_2 is the limiting reactant,

H_2 is in excess and quantity of water formed is based on the limiting reactant O_2.

Thus, H_2O formed = 9 g

Immediate Test 24

(i) 1 mole each of N_2 and H_2 react to form NH_3. Calculate moles of NH_3 formed.

(ii) The reaction $2C + O_2 \longrightarrow 2CO$

Is carried out by taking 24 g of carbon and 96 g O_2. Find out

(a) Which reactant is left in excess?

(b) How many moles of CO are formed?

(c) How many grams of other reactant? should be taken extra so that nothing is left (as reactant) at the end of the reaction?

(iii) Calculate the amount of water formed due to combustion of 16 g CH_4. ***[NCERT Exemplar]***

Example 1.34) 0.170 g of $AgNO_3$ is added to 200 mL of 0.5 M HCl. Calculate amount of white precipitate formed. (Ag = 108, Cl = 35.5)

$AgNO_3$ reacts with HCl to form white precipitate of AgCl.

$\underset{1\text{ mole}}{AgNO_3(aq)} + \underset{1\text{ mole}}{HCl\ (aq)} \longrightarrow \underset{1\text{ mole}}{AgCl\ (s)\downarrow} + HNO_3(aq)$

Amount of AgCl formed is decided by the limiting reactant which can be $AgNO_3$ or HCl. One of the reactants ($AgNO_3$) is in grams while other one (HCl) is in millilitres. Both reactants are expressed in number of moles.

$$\text{Number of moles} = \frac{\text{Mass}}{\text{Molar mass}} = \frac{\text{Molarity} \times \text{volume (mL)}}{1000}$$

Sol. 200 mL of 0.5 M HCl = 100 millimoles = 0.1 mol

$$\text{Number of moles of } AgNO_3 = \frac{0.170\text{ g}}{170\text{ g mol}}$$

$= 0.001$ mol

$\underset{1\text{ mole}}{AgNO_3} + \underset{1\text{ mole}}{HCl} \longrightarrow \underset{1\text{ mole}}{AgCl}$

AgCl formed from 0.1 mol HCl = 0.1 mol

AgCl formed from 0.001 mol $AgNO_3$ = 0.001 mol

Thus, $AgNO_3$ is the limiting reactant and AgCl (white precipitate) formed = 0.001 mol

$= 0.001\text{ mol} \times 143.5\text{ g mol}^{-1}$

$= 0.1435$ g

Immediate Test 25

(i) 100 mL of 20.8% $BaCl_2$ solution and 50 mL of 17.4% K_2SO_4 solution are mixed. Calculate mass of $BaSO_4$ formed. (Ba = 137, K = 39, S = 32, O = 16, Cl = 35.5)

(ii) 100 mL of 0.1 M Na_2CO_3 is mixed with 200 mL of 0.1 M $CaCl_2$ solution. Calculate moles of white precipitate of $CaCO_3$ formed.

Example 1.35) In the following reaction,

$$P_4 + 6Cl_2 \longrightarrow 4PCl_3$$

12.4 g of P_4 is treated with excess of Cl_2 when 0.2 mole of PCl_3 is formed. Calculate percentage yield of PCl_3.

From the given data, we have P_4 as the limiting reactant. So, yield depends on it. The given quantity should be coverted to moles.

Sol. $$\%\text{ yield} = \left(\frac{\text{Observed yield}}{\text{Theoretical yield}} \times 100\right)$$

$\underset{1\text{ mole}}{P_4} + 6Cl_2 \longrightarrow \underset{4\text{ moles}}{4PCl_3}$

$$\text{Number of moles of } P_4 = 12.4\text{ g} = \frac{12.4}{124} = 0.1\text{ mol}$$

PCl_3 obtained from 0.1 mol P_4 = 0.4 mol

Thus, theoretical yield = 0.4 mol

and observed yield = 0.2 mol

$$\therefore \quad \text{Percentage yield} = \frac{0.2}{0.4} \times 100 = 50\%$$

Immediate Test 26

Silicon nitride (Si_3N_4) is made by direct combination of silicon and nitrogen at high temperature. How much silicon must react with excess of nitrogen to prepare 140 g of Si_3N_4, if the yield of the product is 75% (Si = 28)

KNOWLEDGE CONFIRMATION **Test 5**

1 In the following reaction,

$$Mg(s) + 2HCl(aq) \longrightarrow MgCl_2(aq) + H_2(g)$$

on reaction of 0.30 mol of Mg with 0.52 mol of HCl, H_2 formed is
(a) 0.30 mol (b) 0.52 mol (c) 0.15 mol (d) 0.26 mol

2 In the following reaction,

$$N_2 + 3H_2 \longrightarrow 2NH_3$$

1 mole each of N_2 and H_2 are allowed to react. NH_3 formed is removed by
(a) 2 mol HCl (b) 1 mol HCl
(c) 0.67 mol HCl (d) 1 mol H_2O

3 1 mol each of CaH_2 and H_2O are allowed to react to form

$$CaH_2 + 2H_2O \longrightarrow Ca(OH)_2 + 2H_2$$

(a) 1.0 mol H_2 (b) 2.0 mol H_2
(c) 0.5 mol H_2 (d) 0.25 mol H_2

4 In the following reactions,

$$Ca(HCO_3)_2 \longrightarrow CaCO_3 + H_2O + CO_2$$
$$CaCO_3 \longrightarrow CO_2 + CaO$$

1 mol of CO_2 is formed from 2 mol $Ca(HCO_3)_2$ of 50% purity. Thus, per cent yield of CO_2 is
(a) 50% (b) 75% (c) 80% (d) 100%

5 A mixture containing 2 mol $NaHCO_3$ and 1 mol Na_2CO_3 forms 22.4 L CO_2 on heating measured at STP. Thus, per cent yield of CO_2 is
(a) 25% (b) 50% (c) 75% (d) 100%

■ Na_2CO_3 is resistant to heat.

6 50 mL of 0.2 M NaOH and 50 mL of 0.4 M HCl react to form NaCl
(a) 0.585 g (b) 5.85 g
(c) 1.17 g (d) 0.117 g

7 In the question (6), above
(a) 25 mL of 0.2 M NaOH is left (b) 25 mL of 0.4 M HCl is left
(c) 15 mL of 0.4 M HCl is left (d) None is left unreacted

8 1 mol SO_2 reacts with 1 mol of H_2S, then S formed is

$$SO_2 + 2H_2S \longrightarrow 2H_2O + 3S$$

(a) 96 g (b) 48 g (c) 24 g (d) 64 g

9 Maximum amount of $Ba_3(PO_4)_2$ that can be obtained in the following reaction on taking 3 mol of each of Na_3PO_4 and $BaCl_2$ is

$$2Na_3PO_4 + 3BaCl_2 \longrightarrow Ba_3(PO_4)_2 + 6NaCl$$

(a) 1 (b) 2 (c) 3 (d) 6

10 Per cent yield of NH_3 in the following reaction is 80%

$$NH_2CONH_2 + 2NaOH \xrightarrow{\Delta} Na_2CO_3 + 2NH_3$$

6 g NH_2CONH_2 reacts with 8 g NaOH to form NH_3. The amount of NH_3 formed is
(a) 3.4 g (b) 2.72 g (c) 4.25 g (d) 11.2 g

11 A sample of dolomite ($CaCO_3 + MgCO_3$) weighing 100 g is ignited to constant weight to yield 22.4 L CO_2 at STP. Thus, percentage of purity of dolomite is
(a) 92.1% (b) 84% (c) 60% (d) 45%

12 NaH_2PO_4 is used to determine P content as $Mg_2P_2O_7$. A solution of NaH_2PO_4 yielded 2.22 g of $Mg_2P_2O_7$. Thus, NaH_2PO_4 is
(a) 2.40 g (b) 1.20 g (c) 3.60 g (d) 4.80 g

13 Alkaline earth metals X, Y, Z on reaction with Cl_2 form chloride. Graph between amount of metal taken (along X-axis) and amount of chloride formed (along Y-axis) is of the type.

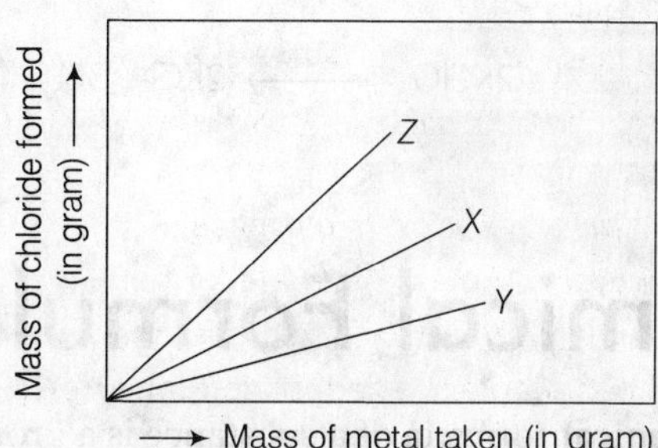

Thus, atomic masses of metals X, Y and Z are in order
(a) $X < Y < Z$ (b) $Y < X < Z$
(c) $Z < X < Y$ (d) $Z < Y < X$

14 A solid mixture weighing 5.00 g of $Pb(NO_3)_2$ and $NaNO_3$ was heated below 600°C until the mass of the residue was constant. If the loss of mass is 28%, number of moles of $Pb(NO_3)_2$ and KNO_3 is (Pb = 207, Na = 23, N = 14, O = 16)

$$2Pb(NO_3)_2 \xrightarrow{\Delta} 2PbO + 4NO_2 + O_2$$
$$2NaNO_3 \xrightarrow{\Delta} 2NaNO_2 + O_2$$

(a) 0.01, 0.01 (b) 0.02, 0.02
(c) 0.02, 0.01 (d) 0.01, 0.02

15 2 g sample containing Na_2CO_3 and $NaHCO_3$ is heated to constant weight when there was a loss of 0.248 g. Thus, $NaHCO_3$ in the sample is
(a) 33.6% (b) 50.0% (c) 66.5% (d) 40.2%

16 10 g each of Li_2CO_3, Na_2CO_3, $CaCO_3$, $MgCO_3$ and K_2CO_3 are heated separately. Centimoles of carbonates are plotted against volume of CO_2 (in L at STP) as shown below. Which of the following is not placed at correct place?
(a) Na_2CO_3 (b) K_2CO_3 (c) Li_2CO_3 (d) $MgCO_3$

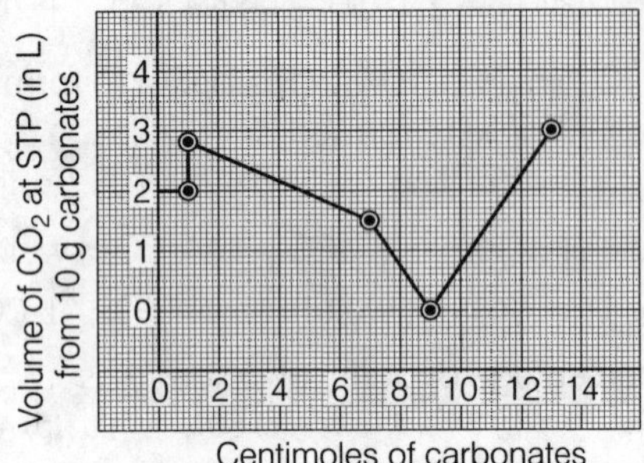

17 In which case percentage yield of O_2 is maximum from 1 mol of the reactant?
(a) $2KClO_3 \longrightarrow 2KCl + 3O_2$ (22.4 L O_2 at STP)
(b) $2Pb(NO_3)_2 \longrightarrow 2PbO + 4NO_2 + O_2$ (10 L at STP)
(c) $2NaNO_3 \longrightarrow 2NaNO_2 + O_2$ (11.2 L at STP)
(d) $2H_2O_2 \longrightarrow 2H_2O + O_2$ (5.6 L at STP).

18 In the following sequence of reactions : percentage yields are shown :

$$2KClO_3 \xrightarrow{50\%} 2KCl + 3O_2$$

$$4Na + O_2 \xrightarrow{40\%} 2Na_2O$$

$$2Na_2O + 2H_2O \xrightarrow{100\%} 4NaOH$$

Starting with 2 moles of $KClO_3$, moles of NaOH in the final stage would be
(a) 2.4 mol (b) 1.2 mol
(c) 0.6 mol (d) 0.3 mol

19 How much metallic chromium can be made in the following reaction, on reaction of 5.0 kg of Al (27) and 20.0 kg of Cr_2O_3 (Cr = 52)?

$$2Al + Cr_2O_3 \longrightarrow Al_2O_3 + 2Cr$$

(a) 13.68 kg (b) 9.63 kg
(c) 5.00 kg (d) 14.20 kg

20 Silver may be removed from a solution of its salt by reaction with metallic zinc

$$Zn + 2Ag^+ \longrightarrow Zn^{2+} + 2Ag$$

A 50 g piece of Zn was treated with a 100 L of Ag^+ containing 3.0 g Ag^+/L. (Ag = 108, Zn = 65.4)
In this case,
(a) Ag^+ is in excess and Zn is completely used
(b) 1.52 mol of Ag^+ is used
(c) 0.76 mol of Zn is used
(d) All of the above are correct

Chemical Formula

- The **Chemical formula** of a substance is a group of symbols representing one molecule of a substance.
- The **Empirical formula** represents the simplest ratio of atoms belonging to different elements in a molecule. If chemical formula of hydrogen peroxide is H_2O_2, then its empirical formula is HO. For the glucose ($C_6H_{12}O_6$), empirical formula is (CH_2O).
- The formula that represents exact number of atoms belonging to different elements in a molecule is called molecular formula. It is related to empirical formula by (empirical formula)$_6$ for glucose.
- In general,
  if empirical formula is $(C_xH_yO_z)$
  and molecular formula is $(C_xH_yO_z)_n$
  Then, $n = \dfrac{\text{Molar mass}}{\text{Empirical formula mass}}$
- Empirical formula (simplest) is derived based on percentage. Given below are the steps to be followed to find empirical formula :
  (i) Calculate the amount of elements and their percentage composition.
  (ii) Divide the percentage of each element by its atomic mass. It gives mole ratio of the elements present in compound.
  (iii) Divide the mole ratio of each element by the minimum value of mole ratio as to get simplest ratio of the atoms of elements present in the compound.
  (iv) If the simplest ratio is fractional, then multiply the values of simplest ratio of each element by a smallest integer to get a simplest whole number for each of the element.
  (v) To get the empirical formula, write symbols of various elements present side by side with their respective whole number ratio as a subscript to the lower right hand corner of the symbol.

Solved Examples & Instant Practice

Example 1.36) A hydrocarbon has 75% carbon. What is its simplest formula?

Sol. *Hydrocarbon is the compound of hydrogen and carbon. Thus, if carbon is 75% then, hydrogen is 25%. Percentage is converted to mole and then mole ratio to derive formula.*

Element	%	Mole mass/atomic mass of C and H	Ratio = $\frac{\text{Mole}}{\text{Least value of mole}}$
C (12)	75	75/12 = 6.25	6.25/6.25 = 1
H (1)	25	24/1 = 25.0	25/6.25 = 4

C and H are in the mol ratio of 1 : 4. Thus, CH_4.

Example 1.37) A compound has 40% calcium, 12% carbon and rest oxygen. Its 0.1 mol has 10 g . Derive empirical and molecular formula.

Sol.

Element	%	Mol = $\frac{\text{Per cent}}{\text{Atomic mass}}$	Ratio = $\frac{\text{Mol}}{\text{Least value of mol}}$
Ca (40)	40	40 / 40 = 1	1
C (12)	12	12 / 12 = 1	1
O (16)	100 – 52 = 48	48 / 16 = 3	3

Ca, C and O atoms are in 1 : 1 : 3 mole ratio, empirical formula = $CaCO_3$

Empirical formula weight = 40 + 12 + 48 = 100

Also, 0.1 mol = 10 g $\quad\therefore$ 1 mol = 100 g mol^{-1}

Thus, molecular formula weight = 100 g mol^{-1}

$$\therefore n = \frac{\text{molecular wt.}}{\text{empirical wt.}} = \frac{100}{100} \qquad \therefore n = 1$$

$\therefore$ Molecular formula = $(CaCO_3)_1$ = $CaCO_3$

Example 1.38) Predict the formula of a compound in which 1 g of Mn reacts with 0.582g of O_2. (Mn = 55).

Sol. Total mass of Mn and oxygen = 1.582

$$\therefore \text{ \% of Mn} = \frac{1}{1.582} \times 100 = 63.21\%, \quad \text{\% of O} = \frac{0.582}{1.582} \times 100 = 36.79\%$$

Element	%	Mole	Ratio
Mn	63.21	$\frac{83.\ 21}{55} = 1.15$	$\frac{1.15}{1.15} = 1$
O	36.79	$\frac{36.79}{16} = 2.30$	$\frac{2.30}{1.15} = 2$

Thus, formula is MnO_2.

Example 1.39) A hydrocarbon on combustion with O_2 gave 0.88 g CO_2 and 0.36 g H_2O. What is the simplest formula of hydrocarbon?

On combustion of hydrocarbon with O_2, each mol of carbon gives 1 mol of CO_2 and each mol of hydrogen gives 0.5 mol of H_2O.

$$C_xH_y + \left(x + \frac{y}{4}\right) O_2 \longrightarrow xCO_2 + \frac{y}{2} H_2O$$

From the mass of CO_2 and H_2O formed, % of carbon and hydrogen, and hence their mole ratio is derived.

Sol. $\underset{12\text{ g}}{C} \longrightarrow \underset{44\text{ g}}{CO_2}$

44 g CO_2 is formed from = 12 g carbon

0.88 g of CO_2 is formed from = $\frac{12}{44} \times 0.88$ g carbon = 024 g

$\underset{1\text{ g}}{H} \longrightarrow \underset{9\text{ g}}{1/2\ H_2O}$

9g H_2O is from = 1 g H

0.36 g H_2O is formed from = $\frac{1}{9} \times 0.36$ = 0.04 g hydrogen

Mass of C and H = 0.24 + 0.04 = 0.28 g

Thus, % carbon = $\frac{0.24}{0.28} \times 100$ = 85.71% and

% hydrogen = $\frac{0.04}{0.28} \times 100$ = 14.29%

Element	%	Mole	Ratio
C	85.71	7.14	1
H	14.29	14.29	2

Simplest formula = CH_2

Since, carbon is tetravalent in nature thus formula is C_2H_4.

Immediate Test 27

(i) A compound on analysis gave the following percentage. ^{39}K = 26.57%, ^{52}Cr = 35.36%. Derive its empirical formula.

(ii) Derive the empirical formula of the compound formed when 7.30 g of iron powder reacts completely with 6.30 g of sulphur.

(iii) A hydrate of iron (III) thiocyanate $Fe(SCN)_3$, was found to contain 19% H_2O. What is the empirical formula of the hydrate? (Fe = 56).

Example 1.40) Glucose or blood sugar has the molecular formula $C_6H_{12}O_6$. Determine % of each element.

Sol. % of a particular element = $\frac{\text{its mass}}{\text{total mass}}$

$C_6H_{12}O_6$ = 72 + 12 + 96 = 180 g mol^{-1}

$\therefore$ % amount of carbon ×100

Total mass = $\frac{72}{180} \times 100$ = 40.0%

% hydrogen = $\frac{12}{180} \times 100$ = 6.67%, % oxygen = $\frac{96}{180} \times 100$ = 53.33%

Oxygen can also be derived by difference.

% oxygen = 100 — (% C + % H)

Immediate Test 28

(i) Determine % of C, H, N and O in CN_2H_4O.

(ii) What is the mass per cent of carbon in carbon dioxide?

KNOWLEDGE CONFIRMATION Test 6

1 What is the empirical formula of a compound which contains 60.0% oxygen and 40% sulphur by mass?
(a) SO_2 (b) SO_3 (c) SO (d) S_2O

2 Hydrocarbon on combustion gave 0.224 L CO_2 at STP and 0.36 g H_2O.

Thus, hydrocarbon is
(a) CH_4 (b) C_2H_4 (c) C_2H_2 (d) C_2H_6

3 An oxide of nitrogen contains 30.4% nitrogen. Its dimer can be written as
(a) N_2O_2 (b) N_2O_4 (c) N_2O (d) NO_2

4 A sample of pure compound contains 2.04 g of sodium, 2.65×10^{22} atoms of carbon and 0.132 mol of oxygen atom. Thus, its empirical formula is
(a) Na_2CO_3 (b) $Na_2C_2O_4$ (c) $Na_2(CO)_2$ (d) None of these

■ Convert each quantity into mol.

5 When $CaCO_3$ is heated to CaO and CO_2, difference in percentage of Ca in product and reactant is
(a) 31.42 % (b) 50.0% (c) 60.00% (d) 68.58%

6 A 15.00 g sample of hydrate salt $Na_2SO_4 \cdot xH_2O$ was found to contain 7.05 g of water. Thus, *x* is
(a) 4 (b) 5 (c) 6 (d) 7

7 A certain element *Z* reacts with oxygen to from Z_2O_5. If 0.375 g of the element forms 0.576 g of the compound, atomic mass of *Z* is
(a) 12.3 g mol^{-1} (b) 74.6 g mol^{-1}
(c) 77.4 g mol^{-1} (d) 153.0 g mol^{-1}

8 The haemoglobin from red cells of blood contain 0.33% iron by weight. If molecular weight of haemoglobin is 68000 g mol^{-1}, number of atoms of iron in each molecule of haemoglobin is
(a) 1 (b) 2 (c) 3 (d) 4

9 When a hydrate of $MgSO_4$ is heated to constant weight (completely anhydrous) it loses 51.2% of its mass. The formula of the hydrate is
(a) $MgSO_4 \cdot 10H_2O$ (b) $MgSO_4 \cdot 7H_2O$
(c) $MgSO_4 \cdot 5H_2O$ (d) $MgSO_4 \cdot H_2O$

10 A compound of nitrogen is found to contain 0.35g of nitrogen per gram of oxygen. Oxide is
(a) NO (b) NO_2 (c) N_2O_3 (d) N_2O_5

11 A crystalline salt on heating becomes anhydrous and loses 45.57% of its weight. It anhydrous hydrate salt contains.

10.50% — Al 15.10 % — K
24.96% — S 49.92% — O

Thus, crystalline salt is
(a) $K_2SO_4 \cdot Al_2(SO_4)_3 \cdot 12H_2O$ (b) $K_2SO_4 \cdot Al_2(SO_4)_3 \cdot 6H_2O$
(c) $KAl(SO_4)_3 \cdot 6H_2O$ (d) $KAl(SO_4)_2 \cdot 12H_2O$

12 A given mass of hydrocarbon on combustion gives 6.72 L CO_2 at STP and 7.20 g H_2O. Thus, hydrocarbon is
(a) C_3H_6 (b) C_3H_4 (c) C_3H_8 (d) C_4H_9

13 A double salt of Fe^{2+} and NH_4^+ loses 27.55% of weight due to moderate heating. It contains 14.26% Fe. NH_3 gas formed from 0.1 mol of salt is neutralised by 200 mL of 1 M HCl. 3.92 g of salt on reaction with excess of $BaCl_2$ gave 4.66 g of white precipitate. Thus, double salt is
(a) $FeSO_4 \cdot (NH_4)_2SO_4 \cdot 6H_2O$
(b) $FeSO_4 \cdot (NH_4)_2SO_4 \cdot 12H_2O$
(c) $FeSO_4 \cdot (NH_4)_2(SO_4)_2 \cdot 12H_2O$
(d) None of the above

14 A sample of pure compound contains 2.04 g of sodium 2.65×10^{22} atoms of carbon and 0.132 mol of oxygen atoms. Thus, its formula is
(a) Na_2CO_3 (b) $Na_2CO)_2$ (c) $NaCO_3$ (d) None of these

15 A certain compound was known to have a formula which could be represented as $[Pd(C_xH_yN_z)](ClO_4)_2$. It contains 30.15% carbon and 5.06% hydrogen. When converted to corresponding thiocyanate $[Pd(C_xH_yN_z)](SCN)_2$, the analysis was 40.46% carbon and 5.94%, hydrogen. Thus, *x*, *y* and *z* are respectively.

	x	*y*	*z*
(a)	14	25	20
(b)	14	28	4
(c)	12	14	16
(d)	14	14	4

ACID TEST
For JEE Main

TYPE I MCQs with Only ONE Correct Alternate

1 If Avogadro's number N_A is changed from $6.022 \times 10^{23}\ mol^{-1}$ to $6.022 \times 10^{20}\ mol^{-1}$, this would change
(a) the definition of amu
(b) the mass of one mole of carbon
(c) the ratio of chemical species to each other in a balanced equation
(d) the ratio of elements to each other in a compound

2 20.0 g magnesium carbonate sample decomposes on heating to give CO_2 (that escapes) and 8.0 g of magnesium oxide. Per cent purity of magnesium carbonate sample is
(a) 75 (b) 96 (c) 60 (d) 84

3 What mass of white precipitate of AgCl is formed when 50 mL of 17% solution of $AgNO_3$ is mixed with 50 mL of 5.85% solution of NaCl ?
(a) 0.05 mol (b) 0.10 mol
(c) 0.15 mol (d) 0.20 mol

4 The mass of $CaCO_3$ required to react completely with 20 mL of 1.0 M HCl in the following reaction is

$$CaCO_3 + 2HCl \longrightarrow CaCl_2 + CO_2 + H_2O$$

(a) 1 g (b) 2 g (c) 10 g (d) 20 g

5 Number of neutrons present in 1.4 mg of ${}^{14}_{6}C$ is
(a) 4.214×10^{20} (b) 3.612×10^{20}
(c) 8.428×10^{20} (d) 4.816×10^{20}

6 Number of electrons present in 6.0 g of CO_3^{2-} is
(a) 1.806×10^{24} (b) 1.9264×10^{24}
(c) 3.7324×10^{24} (d) None of these

7 Mass of calcium that has same number of atoms as in 16g of CH_4 is
(a) 200 g (b) 100 g
(c) 40 g (d) 20 g

8 The volume strength of 1 M H_2O_2 is
(Molar mass of $H_2O_2 = 34\ g\ mol^{-1}$) *[JEE Main 2019 (I) NTA]*
(a) 5.6 (b) 16.8 (c) 22.4 (d) 11.25

9 A 10 mg effervescent tablet containing sodium bicarbonate and oxalic acid releases 0.25 mL CO_2 at 298.15 K and $p = 1$ bar. If molar volume of CO_2 is 25.0 L under such conditions, what is the percentage of sodium bicarbonate in each tablet? (Molar mass of $NaHCO_3 = 84\ g\ mol^{-1}$)
[JEE Main 2019 (I) NTA]
(a) 0.84 (b) 8.4 (c) 16.80 (d) 33.6

10 Largest mass of hydrogen atoms is contained in
(a) 5.0 moles of $C_2H_2O_4$ (b) 1.1 moles of $C_3H_8O_3$
(c) 1.5 moles of $C_6H_8O_6$ (d) 4.0 moles of $C_2H_4O_2$

11 How many moles of Cl^- ions are present in 50.0 mL of 0.20 M $BaCl_2$ solution?
(a) 0.02 mol (b) 10 mol (c) 0.01 mol (d) 20 mol

12 How many moles of Na_2CO_3 are needed to prepare 500 mL of a solution contaning 10.0 mg CO_3^{2-} per mL?
(a) 0.0833 mol (b) 0.0417 mol
(c) 0.167 mol (d) 1.67 mol

13 A solution contains 75 mg NaCl per mL. To what extent must it be diluted to give a solution of 15 mg NaCl per mL?
(a) Five times (b) One-fifth times
(c) Fifty times (d) Two times

14 How many mL of 0.2 M NaOH will completely neutralise 10 mL of 0.25 M H_2SO_4?
(a) 12.5 mL (b) 25.0 mL (c) 50.0 mL (d) 10.0 mL

15 4 g of a mixture of calcium carbonate and sand is treated with an excess of dilute H_2SO_4 and 0.880 g of CO_2 is produced. Thus, per cent of $CaCO_3$ in the original mixture is
(a) 20% (b) 30% (c) 40% (d) 50%

16 A dot mark of a lead pencil has mass of 6 μg of carbon. Thus, number of carbon atoms in one dot mark is
(a) 3.01×10^{17} (b) 6.02×10^{17}
(c) 3.01×10^{20} (d) 6.02×10^{20}

17 Mass of one drop of water molecule is 0.0018 g. Thus, number of water molecules in one drop is
(a) 6.02×10^{23} (b) 3.01×10^{20}
(c) 6.02×10^{20} (d) 6.02×10^{19}

18 For $CuSO_4 \cdot 5H_2O$, which is the correct mole relationship ?
(a) 9 × mole of Cu = mole of O
(b) 5 × mole of Cu = mole of O
(c) 9 × mole of Cu = mole of O_2
(d) Mole of Cu = 9 × mole of O

19 The equivalent mass of a metal is twice that of oxygen. How many times is the equivalent mass of its oxide than the equivalent mass of the metal ?
(a) 4 (b) 3 (c) 2 (d) 1.5

20 0.1596 g of M_2O_3 is reduced to metal M by 0.006 g of hydrogen. The atomic mass of metal M is
(a) 15.58 (b) 5.58 (c) 155.8 (d) 55.8

21 Volume of concentrated $H_2SO_4 (d = 1.84 \text{ g mL}^{-1})$ containing 98.0% H_2SO_4 by weight that would contain 4.0 g H_2SO_4 is
(a) 2.22 mL (b) 1.11 mL (c) 4.44 mL (d) 6.96 mL

22 A mixture of 100 milli. mol of $Ca(OH)_2$ and 2 g of sodium sulphate was dissolved in water and the volume was made upto 100 mL. The mass of $CaSO_4$ formed and the concentration of OH^- in the resulting solution, respectively are: ***[JEE Main 2019 (I) NTA]***
(a) 1.91 g, 0.28 mol L^{-1} (b) 1.9 g, 0.14 mol L^{-1}
(c) 13.6 g, 0.28 mol L^{-1} (d) 13.69, 0.14 mol L^{-1}

23 In the reaction of oxalate with permanganate in acidic medium, the number of electrons involved is producing one mole of CO_2 is ***[JEE Main 2019 (I) NTA]***
(a) 10 (b) 2 (c) 5 (d) 1

24 A 50.0 mL of sample of HCl solution requires 1.0 g of pure $CaCO_3$ for complete neutralisation. Thus, HCl is
(a) 0.2 N (b) 0.1 N (c) 0.04 N (d) 0.4 N

25 The number of lead atoms present in a small piece of lead with a volume of 0.105 cm^3 is (density of lead = 11.34 g / m^3, lead weight = 206).
(a) 3.48×10^{21} (b) 1.56×10^{17}
(c) 5.57×10^{21} (d) 6.50×10^{25}

26 How many moles are there in one atom?
(a) 6.02×10^{23} (b) 1.66×10^{-24}
(c) 1.00 (d) None of these

27 Number of moles in 1 kg electron is
(a) 1.83×10^6 (b) 9.1×10^{-31}
(c) 9.1×10^{-28} (d) 1.1×10^{28}

28 What volume of 0.25 N solution contain 10 milli equivalent of a solute?
(a) 40.0 mL (b) 4.0 mL
(c) 0.40 mL (d) 0.04 mL

29 How many equivalents of a solute are present in 60 mL of 4.0 N solution?
(a) 240 (b) 24.0 (c) 2.4 (d) 0.240

30 Normality of 0.3 M H_3PO_3 solution based on the following reaction is

$$H_3PO_3 + 2OH^- \longrightarrow HPO_3^{2-} + 2H_2O$$

(a) 0.3 N (b) 0.6 N (c) 0.1 M (d) 0.15 N

31 What the ratio of volume of 12.0 N and 3.0 N HCl in a mixture to give 1.00 L of 6.00 N HCl.
(a) 1 : 1 (b) 2 : 1 (c) 1 : 2 (d) 1 : 3

32 90 mL of H_3PO_4 is neutralised by 120 mL of 0.531 N NaOH. Thus, H_3PO_4 is
(a) 0.531 M (b) 1.593 N
(c) Both (a) and (b) (d) None of these

33 The vapour density of a gas is 11.2. The volume occupied by 1 g of the gas at STP is
(a) 1.0 L (b) 11.2 L
(c) 22.4 L (d) None of these

34 What is the atomic weight of an element *X* for a which a sample containing 1.58×10^{22} atoms weigh 1.05 g?
(a) 28 g (b) 20 g (c) 40 g (d) 23 g

35 8 g of a gas at STP occupies 5.6 L, hence number of moles present in 64 g of the gas will be
(a) 1 (b) 2 (c) 3 (d) 8

36 A divalent metal cation has equivalent weight 12. The molecular weight of its oxide is
(a) 16 (b) 32 (c) 40 (d) 52

37 Permanent hardness in hard water is 20 mg Ca^{2+} and 12 mg Mg^{2+} per litre. Thus, volume of 2 N Na_2CO_3 solution to remove hardness is
(a) 1 mL (b) 10 mL (c) 100 mL (d) 2 mL

38 A particular lead-cadmium alloy is 8% cadmium by mass. What mass of this alloy, in grams, must you weight out to obtain a sample containing 6.50×10^{23} Cd -atoms ? (Cd = 112)
(a) 0.121 kg (b) 1.512 kg (c) 0.135 kg (d) 0.0097 kg

39 Volume of 5.00 N H_2SO_4 required to neutralise 2.5 g of NaOH is
(a) 25.0 mL (b) 12.5 mL
(c) 0.25 mL (d) 50.0 mL

40 0.25 g of a sample of an acid was dissolved in water and exactly neutralised by 40.0 mL of 0.125 N base. Thus, equivalent weight of acid is
(a) 25.0 g equiv^{-1} (b) 37.5 g equiv^{-1}
(c) 50.0 g equiv^{-1} (d) 60.5 g equiv^{-1}

41 Volume of concentrated H_2SO_4 ($d = 1.835 \text{ g mL}^{-1}$, 93.2% H_2SO_4 by weight) required to make up 500 mL of 3.00 N H_2SO_4 is
(a) 86.0 mL (b) 21.5 mL
(c) 50.0 mL (d) 43.0 mL

42 Mass of wet NaOH containing 12% water is required to prepare 60 L of 0.50 N solution is
(a) 1.364 kg (b) 0.082 kg
(c) 2.728 kg (d) None of these

43 Equivalents of N, O and Cl in the following reactions formed are in the ratio of

$$N_2 + 3H_2 \longrightarrow 2NH_3$$
$$O_2 + 2H_2 \longrightarrow 2H_2O$$
$$Cl_2 + H_2 \longrightarrow 2HCl$$

(a) 1 : 2 : 3 (b) 3 : 2 : 1
(c) 1 : 1 : 1 (d) 6 : 3 : 2

44 The same amount of metal combines with 0.200 g oxygen and 3.17 g of halogen. Hence, equivalent mass of halogen is
(a) 127 g $equiv^{-1}$ (b) 80 g $equiv^{-1}$
(c) 35.5 g $equiv^{-1}$ (d) 9 g $equiv^{-1}$

45 Daily intake of glucose ($C_6H_{12}O_6$) of a patient is 400 mL of 9% concentration per day. The number of glucose molecules taken by him per hour is
(a) 5.0×10^{21} (b) 1.20×10^{23}
(c) 2.17×10^{25} (d) 5.0×10^{23}

46 Equivalent mass of sulphur in SCl_2 is 16 g $equiv^{-1}$. Thus, equivalent mass of S in S_2Cl_2 is
(a) 32 g $equiv^{-1}$ (b) 16 g $equiv^{-1}$
(c) 8 g $equiv^{-1}$ (d) 64 g $equiv^{-1}$

47 Number of moles of dibasic acid in 0.10 dm^3 of the aqueous solution to give decinormal solution is
(a) 0.10 mol (b) 0.01 mol (c) 0.005 mol (d) 0.50 mol

48 An aqueous solution of glucose is 10% mass by volume. The volume in which 0.1 mole will be dissolved is
(a) 90 mL (b) 900 mL (c) 180 mL (d) 1800 mL

49 Solute and solvent have molar masses in 10 : 1 ratio. If a solution is 10% by mass of solvent, then mole fraction of solute in the solution is
(a) 0.75 (b) 0.50 (c) 1.0×10^{-4} (d) 9.9×10^{-3}

50 50 mL of 0.5 M oxalic acid is needed to neutralise 50 mL of sodium hydroxide solution. The amount of NaOH in 500 mL of the given sodium hydroxide solution is ***[JEE Main 2019 (I) NTA]***
(a) 10 g (b) 40 g (c) 80 g (d) 20 g

51 What is the simplest formula of a compound of elements *X* and *Y* based on following data
X 50% Atomic weight 10
Y 50% Atomic weight 20?
(a) *XY* (b) X_2Y (c) XY_2 (d) X_2Y_3

52 The hardness of water sample (in terms of equivalents of $CaCO_3$) containing 10^{-3} M $CaSO_4$ is (molar mass of $CaSO_4 = 136 \text{ g mol}^{-1}$) ***[JEE Main 2019 (I) NTA]***
(a) 50 ppm (b) 90 ppm (c) 100 ppm (d) 10 ppm

53 8 g of NaOH is dissolved in 18 g H_2O. Mole fraction of NaOH in solution and molality (in mol kg^{-1}) of the solution respectively are ***[JEE Main 2019 (I) NTA]***
(a) 0.2, 11.11 (b) 0.167, 22.20
(c) 0.167, 22.20 (d) 0.107, 11.11

54 If molarity of a solution of solute (50 g mol^{-1}) is 9 mol L^{-1} and molality is 10 mol kg^{-1}, then its density is
(a) 1.0 g mL^{-1} (b) 0.91 g mL^{-1}
(c) 1.05 g mL^{-1} (d) 1.35 g mL^{-1}

55 In rhombic sulphur, S- atoms are joined into S_8 molecules with density 2.07 g / cm^3.

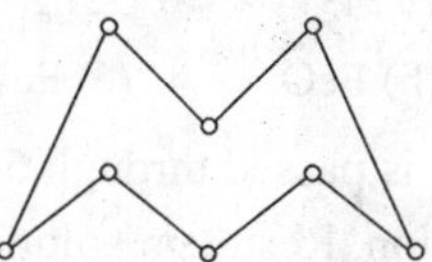

Number of S_8 molecules in a crystal of 0.568 mm^3 is
(a) 1.336×10^{21} (b) 2.212×10^{22}
(c) 2.765×10^{21} (d) 2.765×10^{18}

56 The molarity of a solution obtained by mixing 750 mL of 0.5 M HCl with 250 mL of 2M HCl will be ***[JEE Main 2013]***
(a) 0.875 M (b) 1.00 M
(c) 1.75 M (d) 0.0975 M

57 The density of a solution prepared by dissolving 120 g of urea (molar mass = 60 u) in 1000 g of water is 1.15 g/mL. The molarity of this solution is ***[AIEEE 2012]***
(a) 0.50 M (b) 1.78 M
(c) 1.02 M (d) 2.05 M

58 The molality of a urea solution in which 0.0100 g of urea, $[(NH_2)_2CO]$ is added to 0.3000 dm^3 of water at STP is ***[AIEEE 2011]***
(a) 5.55×10^{-4} M (b) 33.3 M
(c) 3.33×10^{-2} M (d) 0.555 M

59 Number of atoms in 560 g of Fe (atomic mass = 56 g mol^{-1}) is ***[AIEEE 2002]***
(a) twice that 70 g N (b) half that of 20 g H
(c) Both (a) and (b) (d) None of these

60 1 mole each of CaH_2 and H_2O are allowed to react to form
(a) 1 mole H_2 (b) 2 moles H_2
(c) 0.5 mole H_2 (d) 0.25 mole H_2

61 25 mL of the given HCl solution requires 30 mL of 0.1 M Na_2CO_3 solution. What is the volume of this HCl solution required to titrate 30 mL of 0.2 M aqueous NaOH solution? ***[JEE Main 2019 (I) NTA]***
(a) 75 mL (b) 25 mL
(c) 12.5 mL (d) 50 mL

62 Water is evaporated from 135 mL of 0.188 M K_2SO_4 solution until the solution becomes 105 mL. Thus, molarity of the resultant solution is
(a) 0.179 M (b) 0.242 M
(c) 0.146 M (d) None of these

63 A mixture of $CuSO_4$ and $CuSO_4 \cdot 5H_2O$ weight of 1.245g is strongly heated to drive off water, when 0.882 g of residue is formed. Thus, mass percent of anhydrous salt in the mixture is
(a) 19.7 % (b) 70.8% (c) 38.4% (d) 71.6%

64 What is formula of A based on following reaction?

$$\underset{(A)\ 0.5434\ g}{Fe_xO_y} \xrightarrow{H_2} \underset{0.4224\ g}{Fe} + H_2O$$

(a) Fe_2O_3 (b) FeO_2 (c) Fe_3O_4 (d) FeO

65 Excess of CO_2 is passed through 50 mL of 0.5 M $Ca(OH)_2$ solution. Resultant solution was evaporated to dryness and required V mL of 0.1N HCl for complete neutralisation. Thus, V is
(a) 200 mL (b) 500 mL (c) 400 mL (d) 300 mL

66 How many gram of sodium must react with 150 mL H_2O to produce a solution that is 0.175 M NaOH?
(a) 0.312 g (b) 0.543 g (c) 1.085 g (d) 0.604 g

67 A solution of solute X is 40% X by weight of solution. On cooling 800 g of this solution 100 g of solute X is precipitated. Thus, resultant solution is
(a) 31.4% (b) 20.0% (c) 23.0% (d) 24.0%

68 In the following reaction,

$$\underset{0.273\ g}{Mg} \xrightarrow{N_2, \Delta} \underset{0.378\ g}{\text{Product of Mg and N } (A)}$$

empirical formula of A is
(a) MgN (b) Mg_3N_2 (c) MgN_2 (d) Mg_2N

69 Based on the following reaction (unbalanced)

$$\underset{1\ L}{CO_2} + C \longrightarrow \underbrace{CO + CO_2}_{1.5\ L}$$

Thus, moles of CO formed at STP is
(a) 1/11.2 (b) 1/22.4
(c) 14/22.4 (d) 28/22.4

70 $CaCO_3$ sample is 25% pure. 100 g of this sample is heated strongly and CO_2 formed is passed into NaOH solution. Na_2CO_3 formed is
(a) 26.5 g (b) 106.0 g
(c) 13.25 g (d) 53.0 g

71 Per cent yield of NH_3 in the following reaction is 80%.

$$\underset{A}{NH_2\ CONH_2} + \underset{B}{2NaOH} \xrightarrow{\Delta} Na_2CO_3 + 2NH_3$$

If 6 g of (A) reacts with 8 g of (B), then NH_3 formed is
(a) 3.40 g (b) 11.2 g
(c) 4.25 g (d) 2.72 g

72 Aqueous solutions of 1 mole of SO_2Cl_2 is neutralised by
(a) two moles of NaOH (b) three moles of NaOH
(c) two moles of $Ca(OH)_2$ (d) three moles of $Ca(OH)_2$

73 1 mole of BaF_2 is mixed with 2 moles of H_2SO_4. Filtrate required .... moles of NaOH to neutralise acid.
(a) 2 moles of KOH (b) 4 moles of KOH
(c) 3 moles of KOH (d) 1 mole of KOH

74 What mass of $(NH_4)_2CO_3$ contains 6.02×10^{23} hydrogen atoms?
(a) 19.2 g (b) 5.76 g
(c) 12.0 g (d) 6.00 g

75 How many moles of SO_2 contain the same number of atoms as in 1 mole of CH_4O?
(a) 1.0 (b) 2.0 (c) 3.0 (d) 0.5

76 The ratio of masses of oxygen and nitrogen of a particular gaseous mixture is 1 : 4. The ratio of number of their molecules is ***[JEE Main 2014]***
(a) 1 : 4 (b) 7 : 32
(c) 1 : 8 (d) 3 : 16

77 Mixture of x mL of 2 N HCl, 50 mL of 4 N HNO_3 and 62.5 mL of 2M H_2SO_4 is diluted to 1L. 50 mL of this solution required 25 mL of 0.5 M Na_2CO_3 solution for complete reaction. Thus, x is
(a) 25 mL (b) 40 mL (c) 60 mL (d) 100 mL

78 2 g of a mixture containing equal number of moles of Li_2CO_3 (74 g mol^{-1}) and M_2CO_3 required 21.6 mL of 0.5 M H_2SO_4 for complete neutralisation. Thus, atomic mass of M is
(a) 25 (b) 23 (c) 51 (d) 118

79 1 L of hard water required 0.050 g of lime for removing temporary hardness. Thus, temporary hardness in ppm of $CaCO_3$ is
(a) 100 (b) 200 (c) 50 (d) 20

80 Hardness in a sample of hard water containing 1.11 mg $CaCl_2$ and 0.95 mg $MgCl_2$ per litre in terms of ppm of $CaCO_3$ is
(a) 2 ppm (b) 3 ppm
(c) 6 ppm (d) 4 ppm

81 In a sample of hard water with hardness 200 ppm. Select incorrect statement.
(a) Mass ratio of $CaCO_3$ to H_2O is 2×10^{-4}
(b) Mole ratio of $CaCO_3$ to H_2O is 3.0×10^{-5}
(c) $CaCO_3$ is 0.2 g L^{-1}
(d) 1 kg of hard water has 1 milliequivalent

82 A sample of $NaClO_3$ is converted to NaCl and O_2 by heating. There is a loss of 0.16 g O_2. The residue is dissolved in water and precipitated as AgCl. Thus, mass of AgCl obtained is (molar mass of AgCl = 143.5 g mol^{-1} Na = 23, Cl = 35.5) ***[JEE Main 2018]***
(a) 0.41 g (b) 0.35 g
(c) 0.48 g (d) 0.54 g

83 H_2SO_4 is 80% pure (w/V), with density 1.8 g mL^{-1}. Thus, its molality is
(a) 8.16 mol kg^{-1} (b) 1.02 mol kg^{-1}
(c) 4.53 mol kg^{-1} (d) None of these

84 100 mL of 10% NaOH (*w*/*V*) is added to 100 mL of 10% HCl (*w*/*V*), thus resultant mixture is
(a) 0.12 M in terms of H^+ (b) 0.12 M in terms of OH^-
(c) 0.048 M in terms of H^+ (d) 0.192 M in terms of H^+

85 The ammonia (NH_3) released on quantitative reaction of 0.6 g urea (NH_2CONH_2) with sodium hydroxide (NaOH) can be neutralised by ***[JEE Main 2020 (I) NTA]***
(a) 200 mL of 0.2 N HCl (b) 200 mL of 0.4 N HCl
(c) 100 mL of 0.1 N HCl (d) 100 mL of 0.2 N HCl

86 How many millilitres of 0.1 M NaOH must be added to 200 mL of 0.1 M H_2SO_4 to give a solution that is 0.07 M in H_2SO_4?
(a) 100 mL (b) 150 mL
(c) 200 mL (d) 50 mL

87 Public water supply has $CHCl_3$ as impurity to the extent of 0.10 ppb. How many molecules of $CHCl_3$ would be present in 1 mL of this water?
(a) 5.04×10^{11} (b) 5.04×10^{-14}
(c) 1.02×10^{20} (d) 6.02×10^{20}

88 Three types of solutions are supplied to students *A*, *B* and *C*.
A : 5 g of 15 M NaOH ($d = 1$ g mL^{-1})
B : 5 mL of 50% (*w*/*V*) NaOH
C : 5 g of 40% (*w*/*V*) NaOH ($d = 1.25$ g mL^{-1})

Increasing order of mass of NaOH in the above solution is
(a) $A < B < C$ (b) $C < B < A$
(c) $B < C < A$ (d) $B < A < C$

89 The equivalent mass of an element is 4. Its chloride has a vapour density 59.25. Thus, valency of the element is
(a) 1 (b) 2 (c) 3 (d) 4

90 Equivalent mass of a divalent cation is *E*. Thus, molar mass of its oxide and chloride are respectively
(a) $(E + 8)$ $(E + 35.5)$ (b) $(E + 16)$, $(E + 71)$
(c) $2(E + 8)$, $2(E + 35.5)$ (d) $(2E + 8)$, $(2E + 35.5)$

91 Hydrogen has three isotopes (*A*), (*B*) and (*C*). If the number of neutrons in (*A*), (*B*) and (*C*) respectively are (x), (y) and (z), the sum of (x), (y) and (z) is ***[JEE Main 2020 (I) NTA]***
(a) 4 (b) 3 (c) 2 (d) 1

92 The vapour density of a mixture of NO_2 and N_2O_4 is 27.6 at 298 K. Thus mole fraction of N_2O_4 in the mixture is
(a) 0.1 (b) 0.2 (c) 0.5 (d) 0.8

93 One mole of an element *B* is 1.5 times heavier than the element *A*. One mole of an element *A* is half of that of ${}^{16}_{8}O$. Thus, atomic mass of *B* is
(a) 8 (b) 12 (c) 16 (d) 4

94 0.015 mole of an acid HXO_2 has mass 1.695 g. Thus, atomic mass of *X* is
(a) 35.5 (b) 80 (c) 127 (d) 19

95 The sulphate of a metal is isomorphours with $ZnSO_4 \cdot 7H_2O$. It contains 9.87% *M*. Thus, atomic mass of *M* is
(a) 40.3 (b) 36.3
(c) 24.3 (d) 11.3

96 Mass of one proton is 1.675×10^{-24} g. How many moles of proton are present in its 1 kg?
(a) $\frac{1}{1.675 \times 6.023} \times 10^4$ (b) $\frac{10}{1.675 \times 6.023}$
(c) $\frac{1}{6.75} \times 10^{24}$ (d) $\frac{1}{1.675} \times 10^{27}$

97 The strength of 5.6 volume hydrogen peroxide (density 1.0 g mL^{-1}) in terms of mass percentage and molarity respectively are : ***[JEE Main 2020 (II) NTA]***
(a) 0.85 and 0.25 (b) 0.85 and 0.50
(c) 1.70 and 0.50 (d) 1.70 and 0.25

98 The mole fraction of a solvent in aqueous solution of a solute is 0.8. The molality (in mol kg^{-1}) of the aqueous solution is ***[JEE Main 2019 (II) NTA]***
(a) 13.88×10^{-2} (b) 13.88×10^{-1}
(c) 13.88 (d) 13.88×10^{-3}

99 The strength of 11.2 volume solution of H_2O_2 is :
[Given that molar mass of H = 1g mol^{-1} and O = 16 mol^{-1}] ***[JEE Main 2019 (II) NTA]***
(a) 1.7% (b) 34%
(c) 13.6% (d) 3.4%

100 100 mL of a water sample contains 0.81 g of calcium bicarbonate and 0.73 g of magnesium bicarbonate. The hardness of this water sample expressed in terms of equivalents of $CaCO_3$ is (molar mass of calcium bicarbonate is 162 g mol^{-1} and magnesium bicarbonate is 146 g mol^{-1}) ***[JEE Main 2019 (II) NTA]***
(a) 5,000 ppm (b) 1,000 ppm
(c) 100 ppm (d) 20,000 ppm

101 For a reaction,
$N_2(g) + 3H_2(g) \longrightarrow 2NH_3(g)$, identify dihydrogen ($H_2$) as a limiting reagent in the following reaction mixtures. ***[JEE Main 2019 (II) NTA]***
(a) 56 g of N_2 + 10 g of H_2 (b) 35 g of N_2 + 8 g of H_2
(c) 14 g of N_2 + 4 g of H_2 (d) 28 g of N_2 + 6 g of H_2

102 A certain mixture of MnO and MnO_2 contains 66.67 mol % of MnO. What is the approximate weight per cent of Mn in it? (Mn = 55)
(a) 66.67 (b) 33.33
(c) 72 (d) 28

ACID TEST
For JEE Advanced

TYPE I MCQs with Only ONE Correct Alternate

103 10 g of a mixture of BaO and CaO requires 100 mL of 2.50 M HCl to react with it completely. Thus, mole fraction of BaO in the mixture is approximately (Ba = 137, Ca = 40)
(a) 0.25 (b) 0.75 (c) 0.30 (d) 0.70

104 What volume of 6.0 M NaOH would be required to react with SO_2 produced from 10^3 kg of coal containing 0.050% by mass of pyrites impurity (FeS_2)?
(a) 6.0 L (b) 1.4 L
(c) 3.1 L (d) 2.8 L

105 15.0 mL of 2.0 M NaOH was added to 10 mL of a sulphuric acid solution. Resultant mixture required 4.3 mL of 0.5 M HCl to neutralise the excess base. Thus, (H_2SO_4) in the original mixture is
(a) 2.78 M (b) 1.39 M
(c) 0.695 M (d) 0.139 M

106 In the following mixture,
20 mL of 6.0 M HCl + 50 mL of 2.0 M $Ba(OH)_2$ and solution diluted to 100 mL; select correct alternate.

	$[OH^-]$	$[Cl^-]$	$[Ba^{2+}]$
(a)	0.80 M	1.20 M	0.40 M
(b)	0.80 M	0.80 M	0.80 M
(c)	0.80 M	1.20 M	1.00 M
(d)	0.40 M	1.20 M	0.80 M

107 The density of 2.0 M solution of a solute is 1.2 g mL^{-1}. Molar mass of solute is 100 g mol^{-1}. Thus, molality of the solution is
(a) 2.0 m (b) 1.2 m
(c) 1.0 m (d) 0.6 m

108 1.0 g of magnesium is burnt with 0.56 g O_2 in a closed vessel. Which reactant is left in excess and how much?
(a) Mg, 0.16 g (b) O_2, 0.16 g
(c) Mg, 0.44 g (d) O_2, 0.28 g

109 10^{21} molecules are removed from 200 mg of CO_2. Thus, moles of CO_2 left are
(a) 2.88×10^{-3} (b) 2.88×10^{-2}
(c) 2.88×10^{-3} (d) 28.8×10^{3}

110 How many moles of magnesium phosphate will contain 0.25 mole of oxygen atom? *[AIEEE 2005]*
(a) 0.02 (b) 3.125×10^{-2}
(c) 1.25×10^{-2} (d) 2.5×10^{-2}

111 Amount of $FeSO_4 \cdot (NH_4)_2SO_4 \cdot 6H_2O$ (molar mass 392g mol^{-1}) must be dissolved in 250 mL aqueous solution to make Fe^{2+} 1.00 ppm is ($d = 1 \text{g mL}^{-1}$)
(a) 3.50×10^{-3} g (b) 1.75×10^{-3} g
(c) 7.00×10^{-3} g (d) 0.35×10^{-3} g

112 Volume of 98% H_2SO_4 by weight ($d = 1.84 \text{ g mL}^{-1}$) required to prepare 100 mL of 20% H_2SO_4 by weight ($d = 1.14 \text{ g mL}^{-1}$) is
(a) 10.2 mL (b) 12.6 mL (c) 17.7 mL (d) 25.2 mL

113 100 g carbon reacts with 100 g of O_2. Then,
(a) 3.125 mol of CO_2 is formed if CO_2 is the only product
(b) 6.250 mol of CO is formed if CO is the only product
(c) Both of the above are correct
(d) None of the above is correct

114 100 g of oxygen and 60g of carbon are allowed to react. Thus, depending upon the quantity of oxygen available per mole of carbon
(a) 1.25 mol of CO_2 is formed
(b) 3.75 mol of CO is formed
(c) Both of the above are correct
(d) None of the above is correct

115 Number of moles of P_4O_6 and P_4O_{10} formed when 2.0 g each of P_4 and O_2 react such that no P_4 or O_2 is left, is
(a) 0.009, 0.0071 (b) 0.009, 0.009
(c) 0.0071, 0.0071 (d) 0.0071, 0.009

116 How many moles of copper will be replaced from 2.00 L of 1.50 M $CuSO_4$ solution by 40.0 g of aluminium?
(a) 2.22 mol (b) 1.48 mol
(c) 3.00 mol (d) 1.11 mol

117 3.00 L of 1.00 M NaOH solution is prepared from 2.50 M NaOH and 0.40 M NaOH solution. Thus, volume of 2.50 M NaOH solution is
(a) 1.50 L (b) 0.86 L (c) 2.14 L (d) 0.43 L

118 How much $BaCl_2$ would be needed to make 250 mL of a solution having the same concentration of Cl^- as one containing 3.78 g NaCl per 100 mL?
(a) 8.4 g (b) 1.68 g (c) 0.84 g (d) 16.8 g

119 Exactly 4.00 g of solution of H_2SO_4 was diluted with water and excess $BaCl_2$ was added. White precipitate formed weighed 4.08 g. Thus, per cent H_2SO_4 in the original mixture is (Ba = 137)
(a) 86.0 % (b) 67.0 %
(c) 43.0 % (d) 100.0 %

120 On evaporation of 1 L of urea (NH_2CONH_2) solution of density 1.2 g mL^{-1}, 120g of residue is formed. Thus, molality of solution is
(a) 2.000 mol kg (b) 1.852 mol kg
(c) 1.000 mol kg (d) 1.200 mol kg

121 A compound contains 36% carbon by weight. If each molecule contains two carbon atoms, the number of moles of compound in its 10 g is
(a) 66.67 (b) 0.15 (c) 0.30 (d) 0.60

122 What will be percentage concentration of a solution that is obtained by mixing 300g of 25% solution of NaCl with 150g of 40% solution of NaCl? All percentage are mass percentages.
(a) 25% (b) 30%
(c) 35% (d) 40%

123 112.0 mL of NO_2 at 1 atm and 0°C was liquefied, the density of the liquid being 1.15 g mL^{-1}. Calculate the volume and the number of molecules in the liquid NO_2.
(a) 0.10 mL and 3.01×10^{22} (b) 0.20 mL and 3.01×10^{21}
(c) 0.20 mL and 6.02×10^{23} (d) 0.40 mL and 6.02×10^{21}

124 In an experiment, it is found that 2.0769 g of pure *X* produces 3.6769 g of pure X_2O_5. The number of moles of *X* is
(a) 0.04 (b) 0.06 (c) 0.40 (d) 0.02

125 A semiconductor, $YBa_2Cu_3O_7$, is prepared by a reaction involving Y_2O_3, BaO_2 and Cu_2O. The mole ratio in which these compounds should combine, is
(a) 1 : 2 : 4 (b) 1 : 2 : 3
(c) 1 : 4 : 6 (d) 1 : 4 : 3

126 If the mass of neutron is assumed to be half of its original value whereas that of proton is assumed to be the twice of its original value, then the atomic mass of ${}^{14}_{6}C$ will be
(a) same (b) 14.28% less
(c) 14.28% more (d) 28.56% less

127 Volume occupied by 10^6 molecules of water is ($d = 1$ g mL^{-1})
(a) 3.0×10^{-17} mL (b) 6.0×10^{-17} mL
(c) 1.0×10^{-18} mL (d) 6.0×10^{17} mL

128 How many millilitre of 0.715 M NH_4NO_3 solution must be diluted with water to produce 1.00 L of solution of 2.37 mg N per mL ?
(a) 118.4 mL (b) 236.4 mL
(c) 59.2 mL (d) 236.8 mL

129 A solution contains 6.0 micromoles of Na_2SO_4 in 250 mL solution. Assuming no change in volume on dissolution, Na^+ in ppm present in solution is
(a) 0.552 (b) 1.104
(c) 55.2 (d) 552

130 1 mole of N_2 and 4 moles of H_2 are allowed to react in a vessel and after reaction water is added. Aqueous solution required 1 mole of HCl to neutralise the solution. Mole fraction of H_2 in the gaseous mixture (after adding water) is
(a) 1/6 (b) 5/6 (c) 1/3 (d) 5/8

131 To prepare a solution that is 0.50 M KCl using 100 mL 0.40 M KCl (KCl = 74.5 g mol^{-1})
(a) add 0.75 g KCl (b) add 20 mL H_2O
(c) add 0.10 mole KCl (d) evaporate 10 mL H_2O

132 Copper forms two oxides. For the same amount of copper twice as much as oxygen was used to form the first oxide (*A*) than to form second oxide (*B*). Ratio of valencies of copper in the two oxides *A* and *B* is
(a) 1 : 2 (b) 2 : 1 (c) 1 : 1 (d) 1 : 3

133 In the following reaction,

$$M \xrightarrow{H^+} H_2$$

0.7 L of H_2 at STP is formed from *M* (equivalent mass 28 g $equiv.^{-1}$). Thus, *M* taken is
(a) 1.750 g (b) 0.875 g
(c) 3.500 g (d) 7.000 g

134 Given that the abundances of isotopes ${}_{54}Fe$, ${}_{56}Fe$ and ${}_{57}Fe$ are 5%, 90% and 5%, respectively, the atomic mass of Fe is ***[IIT JEE 2009]***
(a) 55.85 (b) 55.95 (c) 55.75 (d) 56.05

135 A mixture of SO_2 and gas *X* (molar mass 80 g mol^{-1}) in the mole ratio *a* : *b* has average molar mass 69.33 g mol^{-1}. If they are mixed in the ratio of b : a, then average molar mass would be
(a) 40.00 (b) 69.33 (c) 32.00 (d) 74.67

136 Consider following solution of HCl.

	A	*B*	*C*	Mixture of *A*, *B* and *C*
Molarity	0.07 M	0.12 M	0.15 M	0.10M
Volume	V_1	V_2	V_3	100 mL

Thus, V_1, V_2 and V_3 respectively (in mL) are given ($V_1 + V_2$) = 75 mL
(a) 50, 25, 25 (b) 15, 60, 25
(c) 45, 30, 25 (d) 55, 20, 25

137 A sample of ammonium phosphate $(NH_4)_3PO_4$ contains 3.18 moles of hydrogen atoms.The number of moles of oxygen atoms in the sample is
(a) 0.265 (b) 0.795 (c) 1.060 (d) 3.180

138 Each molecule of a tear gas Lewisite contains 2 hydrogen atoms, 1.78×10^{-22} g chlorine, 2 carbon atoms and 1.25×10^{-22} g of an unknown metal. Thus, molar mass of the tear gas is
(a) 195.0 (b) 208.0 (c) 280.0 (d) 188.5

139 100 mL of solution of 0.1 M NaOH and 50 mL of 0.2 M HCl react as

$$NaOH(aq) + HCl(aq) \longrightarrow NaCl(aq) + H_2O$$

NaCl formed is
(a) 0.585 g (b) 0.293 g (c) 0.1170 g (d) 0.0365 g

140 NH_3 is formed in the following sequence of reactions.
I. $Ca + 2C \longrightarrow CaC_2$ (50% yield)
II. $CaC_2 + N_2 \longrightarrow CaCN_2 + C$ (100% yield)
III. $CaCN_2 + 3H_2O \longrightarrow 2NH_3 + CaCO_3$ (50% yield)
To form 2 moles of NH_3, calcium should be taken
(a) 1 mole (b) 2 moles (c) 3 moles (d) 4 moles

141 Consider the following reactions :
I. $2KClO_3 \xrightarrow{\Delta} 2KCl + 3O_2$
II. $4Al + 3O_2 \longrightarrow 2Al_2O_3$
2 moles of $KClO_3$ (of 50% impurities) are taken. Based on above reactions, Al_2O_3 formed is
(a) 2 moles (b) 1 mole (c) 3 moles (d) 1.5 moles

142 $\underset{1g}{Zn} \xrightarrow{H_2SO_4} \underset{x\text{ mL}}{H_2}$
$\quad \xrightarrow{NaOH} \underset{y\text{ mL}}{H_2}$
Ratio (*x*/*y*) under identical condition formed from 1 g of Zn (65) is
(a) 1 : 1 (b) 2 : 1 (c) 1 : 2 (d) 9 : 4

143 In the following set of reactions:
I. $CaCO_3 \xrightarrow{\Delta} CaO + CO_2$ (75% yield)
II. $CO_2 + C \xrightarrow{\Delta} 2CO$ (50% yield)
CO formed at STP from 10 g of $CaCO_3$ is
(a) 1.68 L (b) 2.24 L (c) 11.2 L (d) 1.12 L

144 $\underbrace{NaI + NaCl}_{w\,g} \xrightarrow{H_2SO_4} \underbrace{Na_2SO_4}_{w\,g}$ (Na = 23, I = 127)
If above conditions holds true, NaI in the original mixture is
(a) 13.7% (b) 41.7% (c) 28.9% (d) 31.4%

145 Consider the following sequental reactions :
I. $P_4 + 5O_2 \longrightarrow P_4O_{10}$, 85% yield;
II. $P_4O_{10} + 6H_2O \longrightarrow 4H_3PO_4$, 90% yield
Starting with 62 g of P_4, H_3PO_4 formed is
(a) 37.48 g (b) 149.94 g
(c) 125.41 g (d) 564.48 g

146 0.8 mole of a mixture of CO and CO_2 is absorbed by 1 mole of NaOH. On complete oxidation of 0.8 mole of CO and CO_2, it required *x* mole NaOH. Thus, *x* is
(a) 1.2 (b) 1.3 (c) 1.4 (d) 1.6

147 What volume of HCl solution of density 1.2 g mL^{-1} and containing 36.5% by mass HCl must be allowed to react with Mg in order to liberate 2.0 moles of H_2?
(a) 300 mL (b) 333.3 mL
(c) 500 mL (d) 666.6 mL

148 1 L solution of 1 molal aluminium sulphate ($d = 2.684$ g mL^{-1}) is treated with excess of $BaCl_2$. Thus, $BaSO_4$ formed is
(a) 2 moles (b) 3 moles
(c) 6 moles (d) 12 moles

149 Exactly 50.0 mL of Na_2CO_3 solution is equivalent to 50.0 mL of 0.1 N NHCl in an acid -base neutralisation. Amount of $CaCO_3$ that will be precipitated on adding excess of $CaCl_2$ to 100 mL of this Na_2CO_3 solution is
(a) 0.500 g (b) 0.100 g
(c) 1.00 g (d) 0.250 g

150 A 10 g sample of 'gas liquor' is boiled with an excess of NaOH, and the resulting NH_3 is passed into 60 mL of 0.90 N H_2SO_4. If 10 mL of 0.40 N NaOH is required to neutralise the unused H_2SO_4, then percent NH_3 in the gas liquor is
(a) 17.0% (b) 8.5% (c) 2.25% (d) 4.25%

151 54.2 mL of ethanol water mixture has mass of 49.6 g. Density of ethanol 0.80 g mL^{-1} and that of water is 1.00 g mL^{-1}. Thus, percentage of ethanol (by mass) in the solution is
(a) 31.20% (b) 37.10% (c) 33.95% (d) 18.40%

152 A drop of 12.0 M HCl is spread over a sheet of thin aluminium foil. Assume that all the acid reacts with and thus, dissolves through the foil, (20 drops make 1 mL), density of Al foil = 2.7 g/cm^3 and thickness = 0.10 mm. Thus, area of the cylindrical hole (in cm^2) is
(a) 2.0 cm^2 (b) 0.2 cm^2 (c) 4.0 cm^2 (d) 0.1 cm^2

153 In the following graph, number of atoms in 1 g of the solute (along *y* - axis) and solute (along *x* - axis) have been plotted. Which is not placed at correct place?

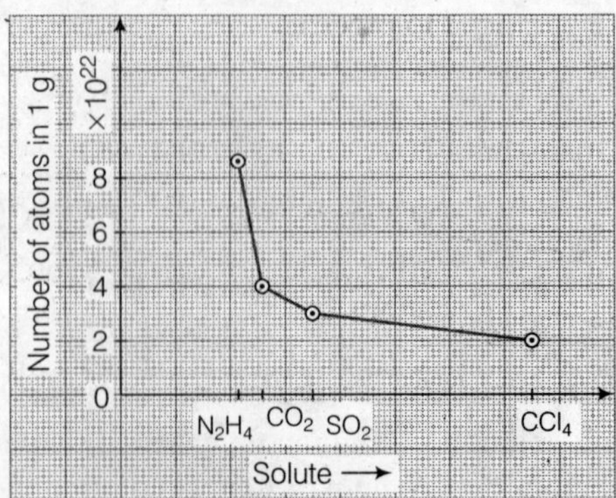

(a) SO_2 (b) N_2H_4 (c) CCl_4
(d) All are placed at correct place

154 For a given element, number of atoms (along *y*- axis) contained in different amount in gram (along *x*- axis) have been plotted. Thus, atomic weight of the element is

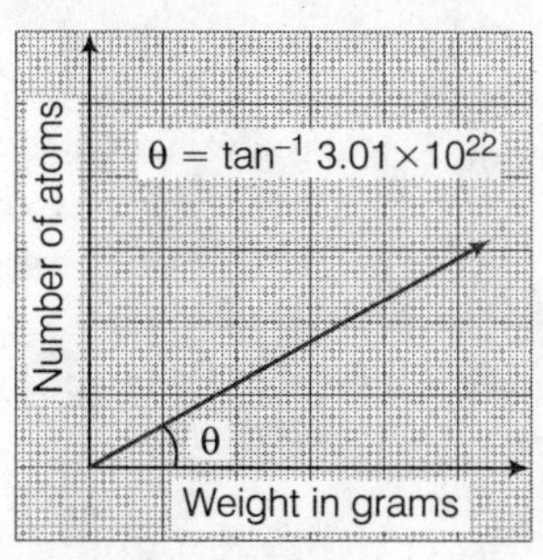

(a) 10 (b) 20 (c) 30 (d) 40

155 A 11.00 g sample of natural gas, consisting of CH_4 and C_2H_4 was burned in excess of oxygen yielding 33 g of CO_2 and some water. Thus, mole fraction of methane in the natural gas is

(a) 0.50 (b) 0.40
(c) 0.30 (d) 0.45

156 About 11.0 g of NaCl is formed when HCl is added to a 15.0 g of mixture of Na_2CO_3 and $NaHCO_3$. Thus, per cent Na_2CO_3 in the mixture is

(a) 91.00% (b) 45.00%
(c) 12.40% (d) 55.00%

157 1.28 g of a mixture of KCl and volatile *M*Cl on reaction with $AgNO_3$ form 2.87 g white precipitate. This mixture is vaporised and passed into $AgNO_3$ when 1.435 g white precipitate is formed.
Thus, ionic mass of M^+ is

(a) 18.0 (b) 39.0 (c) 53.5 (d) 74.5

158 A certain sample of phosphate rock contains 26.26% P_2O_5 . A 0.5428g sample is precipitated as $Mg_2P_2O_7$. Thus, $Mg_2P_2O_7$ obtained is

(a) 0.8486 g (b) 1.1424 g
(c) 0.3648 g (d) 0.2220 g

159 Number of milliliters of a 2.08% $BaCl_2$ solution (*w*/*V*) which is required to precipitate the sulphur as $BaSO_{14}$ in a 0.60 g sample that contains 12% sulphur is (Ba = 137)

(a) 11.40 mL (b) 14.63 mL
(c) 22.50 mL (d) 24.00 mL

160 V_1 mL of 0.2 M NaCl and V_2 mL of 0.1 M $CaCl_2$ solution are mixed resulting in a solution such that molar concentration of cations is 40% more than that of anions.
Assume $(V_1 + V_2) = 1000$ mL then V_1 and V_2 are

	V_1	V_2
(a)	400 mL	600 mL
(b)	600 mL	400 mL
(c)	800 mL	200 mL
(d)	430 mL	570 mL

161 50 g of oleum sample labelled as 118% contains

(a) 18 g of water and 118 g H_2SO_4
(b) 9 g of water and 40 g SO_3
(c) 118 g H_2SO_4
(d) 68 g H_2SO_4

162 12.5 g of fuming H_2SO_4 (labelled as 112%) was diluted by adding 100 L of water. Assume 100% ionisation. Then $[H^+]$ in dilute solution is

(a) 1.67 M (b) 5.72×10^{-3} M
(c) 8.57×10^{-3} M (d) 4.28×10^{-3} M

163 40 mL solution of H_2SO_4 was titrated with 0.1 M $Ca(OH)_2$ solution using phenolphthalein as the indicator. $Ca(OH)_2$ was added drop by drop and pink colour appeared instantly after 30 mL of $Ca(OH)_2$ was added. Colour disappeared on shaking but permanent pink coloured appeared on addition of 35 mL of base.
Thus, H_2SO_4 left after addition of 30 mL of $Ca(OH)_2$ is

(a) 34.3 mL (b) 10.0 mL (c) 5.7 mL (d) 30.0 mL

164 Percentage impurity of lime water $Ca(OH)_2$ can be determined by titrating it against oxalic acid ($H_2C_2O_4$). 1.0 M oxalic acid is added drop by drop to 1L of 1 M $Ca(OH)_2$ solution when following graph is obtained. Thus % purity of $Ca(OH)_2$ solution is

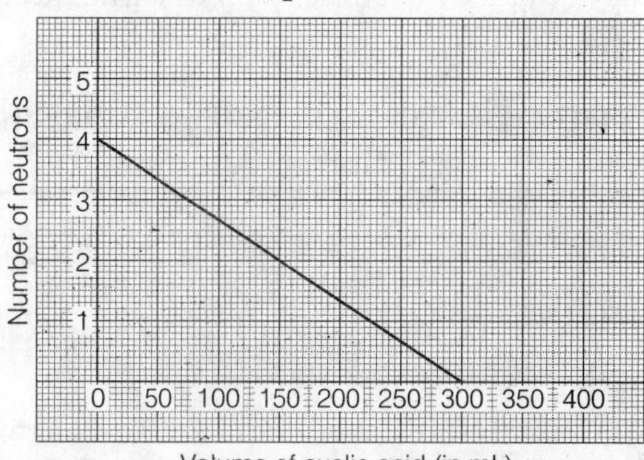

(a) 40.0% (b) 30.0% (c) 60.0% (d) 15.0%

TYPE II Statement Based Questions

Directions Answers of Q. Nos. (165-172) have been based on the following codes.

(a) Statement I is true; Statement II is true; Statement II is the correct explanation of Statement I.
(b) Statement I is true; Statement II is true; Statement II is not the correct explanation of Statement I.
(c) Statement I is true; Statement II is false.
(d) Statement I is false; Statement II is true.

165 Statement I Molarity of pure water is 55.55 M at 298 K.
Statement II Molarity is the concentration in mole $litre^{-1}$.

166 Statement I 0.1 M H_3PO_2 solution is 0.3 N when completely reacted with NaOH.
Statement II NaH_2PO_2 is normal salt.

167 **Statement I** 2 g hydrogen and 16 g oxygen form 18 g H_2O.
Statement II Oxygen is the limiting reactant.

168 **Statement I** SO_2 and SO_3 obey law of multiple proportion.
Statement II Every sample of SO_2 contains 1 part sulphur and 1 part oxygen by mass.

169 **Statement I** In Fe^{2+}, there are 24 electrons and 30 neutrons and thus its ionic mass is 56.
Statement II There are 26 protons in Fe^{2+} and ionic mass is the sum of neutrons and protons.

170 **Statement I** The empirical mass of ethene is half of its molecular mass.
Statement II The empirical formula represents the simplest whole number ratio of atoms present in a compound. ***[NCERT Exemplar]***

171 **Statement I** One atomic mass unit is defined as one-twelfth of the mass of one carbon-12 atom.
Statement II Carbon-12 isotope is the most abundant isotope of carbon and has been chosen as standard. ***[NCERT Exemplar]***

172 **Statement I** 12 g carbon and 16 g oxygen form 1 mole CO.
Statement II CO_2 formed reacts with unreacted carbon to give CO.

TYPE III MCQs with ONE or MORE than ONE Correct Alternate

173 1 g atom of oxygen atom represents
(a) 6.02×10^{23} O_2 molecules
(b) 22.4 L of O_2 gas at 1 atm and 273 K
(c) 11.2 L of O_2 gas at 1 atm and 273 K
(d) 16 g of oxygen

174 Number of electrons in 1 mole of H_2O is equal to number of protons in
(a) 1 mole of CH_4 (b) 1 mole of NH_3
(c) 0.33 mole of C_4H_8 (d) 1 mole of HF

175 In the following reaction,
$$H_3PO_3 + Ca(OH)_2 \longrightarrow CaHPO_3 + 2H_2O$$
(a) equivalent mass of H_3PO_3 is 41
(b) 1 mole of H_3PO_3 is completely neutralised by 1.5 mole of $Ca(OH)_2$
(c) 1 mole of H_3PO_3 is completely neutralised by 1 mole of $Ca(OH)_2$
(d) $CaHPO_3$ is a normal salt

176 In the following reaction,
$$\underset{(A)}{NH_2CONH_2} + NaOH \xrightarrow{\Delta} \underset{(B)}{NH_3}$$
1.2 g of (A) gave (B) which can be neutralised by
(a) 20 mL of 1 M HCl (b) 40 mL of 1 M HCl
(c) 20 mL of 2 M HCl (d) 20 mL of 1 M H_2SO_4

177 Impure sample of $CaCO_3$ weighing 20 g gave 4.4 g of CO_2. Thus, there are
(a) 0.2 N_0 $CaCO_3$ molecules
(b) 0.1 N_0 $CaCO_3$ molecules
(c) N_0 atoms of $CaCO_3$
(d) 0.5 N_0 atoms of $CaCO_3$

178 For the salt $(NH_4)_2CO_3$,
(a) 19.2 g make 0.40 mole of NH_4^+
(b) 12.0 g make 1.0 mole of hydrogen atom
(c) 96.0 g make 1.0 mole of CO_2
(d) 1.92 g is required to prepare 200 mL of 0.2 M NH_4^+ solution.

179 A metal forms two oxides, when 4.29 g of lower oxide is heated 4.77 g of higher oxide is formed. The higher oxide is found to contain 80% metal. Thus,
(a) equivalent mass of metal in lower oxide is 64
(b) equivalent mass of metal in lower oxide is 32
(c) equivalent mass of metal in higher oxide is 64
(d) equivalent mass of metal in higher oxide is 32

180 Select correct statement(s) for 2M $MgCl_2$ aqueous solution ($d = 1.09$ g mL^{-1})
(a) It is 4.44 molal in terms of Cl^-.
(b) Mole fraction of $MgCl_2$ is 0.038.
(c) $MgCl_2$ is 19% (w/V)
(d) $MgCl_2$ is 19×10^4 ppm in given mass of water.

181 In the reaction,
$$4NH_3(g) + 5O_2(g) \longrightarrow 4NO(g) + 6H_2O(l)$$
when 34g of NH_3 and 64g of O_2 are allowed to react
(a) 2.0 moles of NO will be formed
(b) 2.4 moles of H_2O will be formed
(c) all the O_2 will be consumed
(d) all the NH_3 will be consumed

182 F^- is isoelectronic of
(a) O^{2-} (b) N^{3-} (c) Ne (d) Na

183 Select the collection of isoelectronic species.
(a) NH_3, H_2O, CH_4 (b) N_2, C_2^{2-}, CO
(c) NO^+, CO, CH_4 (d) CO_2, N_2O, N_3H

184 In the mixture of 1.6 g CH_4, 1.7 g of NH_3 and 1.8 g of H_2O, which quantity is/are not equal?
(a) Mole (b) Number of atoms
(c) Weight fraction (d) Mole fraction

185 Number of molecules present in 14 g N_2 is equal to that of
(a) 32 g of SO_2 (b) 8 g CH_4
(c) 22 g CO_2 (d) 16 g O_2

186 Which is/are correct about 6.0 g of CH_3COOH?
(a) It contains 0.1 mole of CH_3COOH
(b) It contain 0.1 mole of ionisable H^+ ion
(c) It contains 2.4 g of C atoms
(d) It contains 6.02×10^{22} molecules of CH_3COOH

187 A trivalent metal ion (M^{3+}) has equivalent mass of 9. Then,
(a) equivalent mass of its oxide is 17
(b) molar mass of its oxide is 51
(c) molar mass of its oxide is 102
(d) molar mass of its hydride 10

188 ${}^{12}_{6}C$ and ${}^{13}_{6}C$ differ in
(a) atomic number
(b) number of neutrons
(c) number of electrons
(d) atomic mass

189 Ethanol solution in water is 46% by weight of solution. Then,
(a) mole fraction of ethanol is 0.25
(b) its molality is 18.52 when water is solvent
(c) its molality is 21.74 when ethanol is solvent
(d) mole fraction of ethanol is 0.46

190 4.8 g of magnesium is burnt in a closed vessel which contains 0.224 L O_2 at STP. Thus,
(a) O_2 is the limiting reactant
(b) equivalent of MgO formed is equal to equivalent of oxygen taken
(c) reactants and products are in equal moles
(d) reactants and products are in equal equivalents

191 For the reaction,

$$4Fe + 3O_2 \longrightarrow 2Fe_2O_3$$

4.80 g of O_2 is used to burn 0.150 mole of iron. Thus,
(a) Fe is the limiting reactant and O_2 is in excess
(b) 0.0375 mole of O_2 is left unreacted
(c) 0.075 mole of Fe_2O_3 is formed
(d) Fe and O_2 are in stoichiometric amounts

192 Carbon reacts with oxygen to yield CO or CO_2 or both depending on the quantity of O_2 available per mole of carbon. 100 g of oxygen reacts with 60 g carbon to form
(a) 1.25 moles of CO_2
(b) 3.75 moles of CO
(c) 5.0 moles of CO_2
(d) 5.0 moles of CO

193 RH_2 is an ion exchange resin used to purify water in RO (water purifier). It can replace Ca^{2+} in hard water. If $[H^+] = 0.01\,M$ in water coming out of ion exchange resin, then,
(a) 0.140 g of CaO is required to remove temporary hardness in 1 L H_2O
(b) 1.06 g of Na_2CO_3 is required to remove permanent hardness in 1 L H_2O
(c) hardness of water in ppm of $CaCO_3$ is 200
(d) hardness of water in ppm of Ca^{2+} is 200

194 One takes 0.62 g of P_4 and 4.00 g of O_2 separately for each of the following reactions
I. $P_4 + 5O_2 \longrightarrow P_4O_{10}$
II. $P_4 + 3O_2 \longrightarrow P_4O_6$

Select correct statements about I and II.
(a) P_4 is the limiting reactant in I and O_2 is the limiting reactant in II
(b) P_4 is the limiting reactant in II and O_2 is the limiting reactant in I
(c) 1.42 g of P_4O_{10} in I and 1.10 g of P_4O_6 in II are formed
(d) P_4 is the limiting reactant in both

195 In the synthesis of urea (NH_2CONH_2) as given below

$$2NH_3(g) + CO_2(g) \longrightarrow NH_2CONH_2(aq) + H_2O(l)$$

4.48 L of each gas at STP are allowed to react. In such cases,
(a) NH_3 is the limiting reactant and CO_2 is in excess
(b) CO_2 is the limiting reactant and NH_3 is in excess
(c) 6.0 g of urea is formed
(d) excess reactant can be removed by 0.1 mole of CaO

196 A homogeneous liquid mixture contains 0.1 mole each of CH_3OH and CH_3CH_2OH and 0.2 mole of H_2O. Thus,
(a) molality of CH_3OH is 12.195
(b) molality of component with its maximum amount is 14.706
(c) mass percentage of CH_3CH_2OH is 40.35%
(d) mass percentage of CH_3OH is 59.65%

197 A carbonate of unknown metal (MCO_3) is treated with HCl to produce CO_2. Upon treating 4.2 g of MCO_3 with excess of HCl, 2.2 g of CO_2 is formed. Thus,
(a) weight per cent of the metal is 28.57%
(b) weight per cent of the carbonate is 28.57%
(c) atomic mass of the metal is 24
(d) equivalent mass of the metal carbonate is 42

198 Oleum is labelled 109% H_2SO_4. For such case :
(a) 100 g of oleum has been diluted to 109 g
(b) 9 g of H_2O combines with 40 g SO_3
(c) per cent free SO_3 in oleum is 40%
(d) 0.5 mole of SO_3 is present in the oleum

TYPE IV Numerical Skills

199 The mole fraction of glucose ($C_6H_{12}O_6$) in an aqueous binary solution is 0.1. The mass percentage of water in it, to the nearest integer, is .... ***[JEE Main 2020 (II) NTA]***

200 11 g of A_2O_3 contains 3.0 g of A, then atomic mass of A is .... g

201 6.023×10^{22} molecules are present in 10 g of a substance 'X'. The molarity of a solution containing 5 g of substance 'X' in 2 L solution is .... $\times 10^{-3}$ M. ***[JEE Main 2020 (II) NTA]***

202 A 100 mL solution was made by adding 1.43 g of $Na_2CO_3 \cdot xH_2O$. The normality of the solution is 0.1 N. The value of x is .... ***[JEE Main 2020 (II) NTA]***

203 The volume strength of 8.9 M H_2O_2 solution calculated at 273 K and 1 atm is .... ($R = 0.0821 \text{ L atm K}^{-1} \text{ mol}^{-1}$) (rounded off to the nearest integer) ***[JEE Main 2020 (II) NTA]***

204 An alkene (C_nH_{2n}) occupies 0.8 L g^{-1} at STP. Thus, total number of atoms of carbon and hydrogen in one formula unit of C_nH_{2n} are ....

205 3.36 g of a XBr_2 is completely converted into XCl_2 forming 1.58 g of it (XCl_2).

$$XBr_2 + Cl_2 \longrightarrow XCl_2 + Br_2$$

What is atomic mass of element X ? (Br = 80, Cl = 35.5)

206 Urea solution has density (g mL^{-1}) .... if molarity is 4.0 mol L^{-1} and molality is 2.273 mol kg^{-1} H_2O.

207 Orange coloured solid Sn_xI_y is formed when Sn and I_2 combine. What is value of $(x+y)$ based on following observation?

($Sn = 118.7 \text{ g mol}^{-1}$, $I_2 = 254.0 \text{ g mol}^{-1}$)

Mass of Sn taken = 1 .056 g

Mass of I_2 taken = 1 .947 g

Mass of Sn recovered after reaction = 0.601 g

208 If epsom salt, $MgSO_4 \cdot xH_2O$, is heated to 520 K, all the water of hydration is lost. On heating a 1.687 g sample of the hydrate, 0.824 g of $MgSO_4$ remains. How many molecules of water occur per formula unit of $MgSO_4$?

209 The aluminium sulphate hydrate; $Al_2(SO_4)_3 \cdot xH_2O$ contains 10.71% Al by mass. What is the value of x ? (Al = 27)

210 Ferrous sulphate heptahydrate is used to fortify foods with iron. The amount (in grams) of the salt required to achieve 10 ppm of iron in 100 kg of wheat is .... (Atomic weight : Fe = 55.85, S = 32.00, O = 16.00) ***[JEE Main 2020 (I) NTA]***

211 V mL 90% ethanol (C_2H_5OH) having density 0.8 g mL^{-1} is diluted to prepare 20 mL of 20% ethanol of density 0.9 g mL^{-1}. Thus, value of V is ....

212 50 g of saturated aqueous solution of X on cooling, gives 10 g of X as crystals. What is difference in solubility of X by weight of solvent (H_2O) and by weight of solution ?

213 On heating 2.495 g of $CuSO_4 \cdot xH_2O$, 0.05 mole of H_2O is lost forming anhydrous salt. What is value of x ? (Cu = 63.5)

214 The density of concentrated sulphuric acid is 1.8 g mL^{-1}. What volume of the acid (in mL) would contain 0.1469 mole ?

215 Mole fraction of water in aqueous solution of sucrose is 0.95. Thus, molality of the solution is ....

216 Consider following reaction,

$$\underset{(A)}{[Cr(NH_3)_x Cl_3](aq)} + x\,HCl(aq) \longrightarrow x\,NH_4^+(aq) + Cr^{3+}(aq) + (x+3)\,Cl^-$$

1.585 g of A reacts completely with 24.26 mL of 1.50 M HCl. What is value of x ? (Cr = 52)

217 How many moles of H_2SO_4 in 500 mL of the battery solution are contained if H_2SO_4 used is 30.8% by mass having density 1.303 g mL^{-1}.

218 What is value of x based on the following graph for C_6H_{12}?

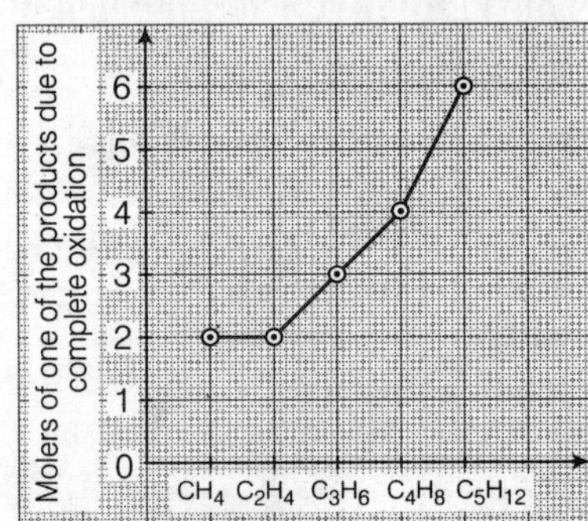

x = mole of one of the products due to complete oxidation of one mole of hydrocarbon. ....

219 Calculate number of moles of water present in oleum that is labelled as 118%

220 The volume (in mL) of 0.1 N NaOH required to neutralise 10 mL of 0.1 N phosphonic acid is .... ***[JEE Main 2020 (II) NTA]***

221 $KClO_4$ may be made by means of the following series of reactions :

$$Cl_2 + 2KOH \longrightarrow KCl + KClO + H_2O$$

$$3KClO \longrightarrow 2KCl + KClO_3$$

$$4KClO_3 \longrightarrow 3KClO_4 + KCl$$

How many moles of Cl_2 are needed to prepare 1 mole $KClO_4$?

222 A sample contains a mixture of $NaHCO_3$ and Na_2CO_3. HCl is added to 15.0 g of the sample, yielding 11.0 g of NaCl. What per cent of the sample is Na_2CO_3 ?

223 H_2SO_4 can be produced by the following sequence of reactions.

$$4FeS_2(s) + 11O_2(g) \longrightarrow 8SO_2(g) + 2Fe_2O_3(s)$$

$$SO_2(g) + \frac{1}{2}O_2(g) \longrightarrow SO_3(g)$$

$$SO_3(g) + H_2O(l) \longrightarrow H_2SO_4(aq)$$

$$H_2SO_4(g) + SO_3(g) \longrightarrow H_2S_2O_7(l)$$

$$H_2S_2O_7(l) + H_2O(l) \longrightarrow 2H_2SO_4$$

What mass of H_2SO_4 could be produced (in kg) in the above sequence of reactions from 5.52 kg of FeS_2?

224 The mass of ammonia in grams produced when 2.8 kg of dinitrogen quantitatively reacts with 1 kg of dihydrogen is .... ***[JEE Main 2020 (II) NTA]***

225 The mole fraction of urea in an aqueour solution containing 900 g of water is 0.05. If the density *d* the solution is 1.2 g cm^{-3}, the molarity of urea solution is ...
(Given data : Molar mass of urea and water are 60 g mol^{-1} and 18 g mol^{-1} respectively). ***[JEE Adv. 2019]***

226 A silver (atomic weight 108 g mol^{-1}) has density of 10.5 g cm^{-3}. The number of silver atoms on a surface area of 10^{-12} m^2 can be expressed in scientific notation as $y \times 10^x$. The value of x is .... ***[IIT JEE 2010]***

227 The volume (in mL) of 0.1 M $AgNO_3$ required for complete precipitation of chloride ions present in 30 mL of 0.01 M solution of $[Cr(H_2O)_5Cl]Cl_2$ as silver chloride is .... ***[IIT JEE 2011]***

228 29.2% (w/w) HCl stock solution has density of 1.25 g mL^{-1}. The molecular weight of HCl is 36.5 g mol^{-1}. The volume (mL) of stock solution required to prepare a 200 mL of 0.4 M HCl solution of is ***[JEE Adv. 2012]***

229 A compound H_2X with molar weight of 80 g is dissolved in a solvent having density of 0.4 g mL^{-1}. Assuming no change in volume upon dissolution, the molality of a 3.2 molar solution is ***[JEE Adv. 2014]***

TYPE V Passage Based MCQ (Comprehension)

Passage 1

Directions (Q. Nos. 230 and 231) Consider following reaction,

$$CO_2 + 2KOH \longrightarrow K_2CO_3 + H_2O$$

0.05 mole of CO_2 is passed into 1.0 L of 0.15 M KOH solution.

230 Resultant molarity of KOH solution is
(a) 0.10 M (b) 0.15 M (c) 0.05 M (d) 0.20 M

231 Molarity of K_2CO_3 solution formed due to above reaction is
(assume no hydrolysis of K_2CO_3)
(a) 0.20 M (b) 0.30 M (c) 0.01 M (d) 0.05 M

Passage 2

Directions (Q. Nos. 232 and 233) 8.075×10^{-2} kg of Glauber's salt is dissolved in water to obtain 1 dm^3 of solution of density 1077.2 kg m^{-3}.

232 Molality of this solution is
(a) 0.24 molal (b) 0.25 molal
(c) 0.28 molal (d) 1.00 molal

233 Difference in molarity and molality is
(a) zero (b) 0.10 (c) 0.25 (d) 0.24

Passage 3

Directions (Q. Nos. 234 and 235) Cupric ammonium sulphate was found to contain 27.03% water of crystallisation. Upon strongly heating, it gave cupric oxide corresponding to 19.89% of starting mass.

234 Water of crystallisation in the complex is
(a) 4 (b) 5 (c) 6 (d) 7

235 Empirical formula is
(a) $CuSO_4 \cdot (NH_4)_2SO_4 \cdot 6H_2O$
(b) $CuSO_4 \cdot (NH_4)_2SO_4 \cdot 4H_2O$
(c) $CuSO_4 \cdot (NH_4)_4 (SO_4)_2 \cdot 6\,H_2O$
(d) $Cu\,NH_4(SO_4)_2 \cdot 4H_2O$

Passage 4

Directions (Q. Nos. 236 and 237) *A* and *B* are two elements which form compounds AB_2 and A_2B_3. 0.2 mole of AB_2 weighs 8 g and 0.1 mole of A_2B_3 weighs 7 g.

236 Ratio of atomic mass of *A* to *B* is :
(a) $\frac{2}{1}$ (b) $\frac{1}{2}$
(c) $\frac{2}{3}$ (d) $\frac{3}{1}$

237 If the above quantities are taken as mixture, then their mole fractions are equal, if
(a) 1 g of A_2B_3 is added (b) 0.1 mole of A_2B_3 is added
(c) 1 g of AB_2 is removed (d) 1 g of AB_2 is added

Passage 5

Directions (Q. Nos. 238 and 239) Brass is a mixture of 90% Cu (63.5) and 10% Zn (65.0). HNO_3 reacts with brass according to the following reactions

$$Cu + 4H^+ + 2NO_3^- \longrightarrow 2NO_2 + Cu^{2+} + 2H_2O$$

$$4Zn + 10H^+ + NO_3^- \longrightarrow NH_4^+ + 4Zn^{2+} + 3H_2O$$

238 What volume of 3.0 M HNO_3 can react with 15.0g of brass?
(a) 303 mL (b) 150 mL
(c) 206 mL (d) 169 mL

239 What volume of NO_2 gas at N.T.P. would be produced ?
(a) 9.52 L (b) 4.76 L
(c) 2.38 L (d) 10.40 L

Passage 6

Directions (Q. Nos. 240 and 241) 100 g of carbon and 100 g oxygen are allowed to react.

240 Select correct statement
(a) 8.33 moles of CO_2 is formed
(b) 3.125 moles of CO_2 is formed
(c) 6.25 moles of CO is formed
(d) None is correct

241 Select correct statement.

(a) Carbon is in excess and CO_2 formed converts excess carbon into CO

(b) Oxygen is in excess and carbon is completely oxidised to CO_2

(c) Carbon and oxygen both are in equal amounts and no reactant is left

(d) 3.125 moles of each of CO and CO_2 are formed at the end of the reaction

Passage 7

Directions (Q. Nos. 242 and 243) A mixture of NaCl and NaBr weighing 3.5084 g was dissolved and treated with excess of $AgNO_3$ to precipitate all of the chlorides and bromides as AgCl and AgBr. The washed precipitate was treated with KCN to dissolve the precipitates

$$AgX + 2KCN \longrightarrow K[Ag(CN)_2] + KX$$

$(X = Cl, Br)$

and the resulting solution was electrolysed.

$$4K[Ag(CN)_2] + 4KOH \longrightarrow 4Ag + 8KCN + O_2 + 2H_2O$$

weight of the metal silver was 5.5028 g.

242 Weight per cent of NaCl is

(a) 65.18% (b) 34.72%
(c) 50.49% (d) 49.51%

243 O_2 formed in this process is

(a) 0.4076 g (b) 0.0127 mol
(c) 285 mL at STP (d) All of the above are correct

Passage 8

Directions (Q. Nos. 244 and 245) A mixture contains CH_3OH, CH_3CH_2OH and H_2O and mole fractions are shown below :

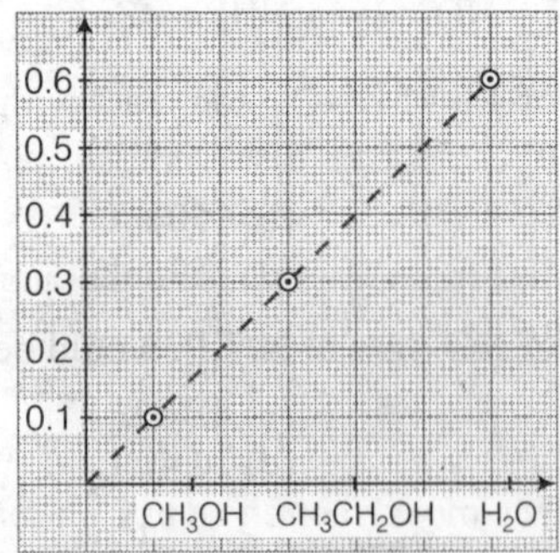

244 Molality of CH_3OH in the above case is

(a) 4.065 (b) 1.312
(c) 4.679 (d) 2.308

245 Mass percentage of CH_3CH_2OH is

(a) 30.00% (b) 49.64%
(c) 98.57% (d) 40.00%

TYPE VI Matrix Matching

Based on One Single Matching Correct

246 Match the given (law of chemical combination) in Column I with the property it holds in Column II. Select the proper answer from the codes given.

Column I	Column II
(i) Law of conservation of mass	(p) CH_4 has carbon and hydrogen in 3 : 1 mass ratio.
(ii) Law of multiple proportion	(q) 10 mL N_2 combines with 30 mL of H_2 to form 20 mL of NH_3.
(iii) Law of definite proportion	(r) S and O_2 combine to form SO_2 and SO_3.
(iv) Law of reciprocal proportion	(s) In H_2S and SO_2 mass ratio of H and O w.r.t. sulphur is 1 : 16, hence, in H_2O mass ratio of H and O is 1 : 8.
(v) Gay Lussac's law	(t) 4.2 g $MgCO_3$ gives 2.0 g residue on heating.

Codes

	(i)	(ii)	(iii)	(iv)	(v)
(a)	(t)	(r)	(p)	(s)	(q)
(b)	(t)	(r)	(p)	(q)	(s)
(c)	(t)	(p)	(r)	(q)	(s)
(d)	(t)	(p)	(r)	(s)	(q)

247 A sugar ($C_{12}H_{22}O_{11}$) syrup (density $= 1.2\, g\, mL^{-1}$) weighing 214.2 g contains 34.2g of sugar. Match the concentration parameters of Column I with their values in Column II. Select the answer from the codes given.

Column I	Column II
(i) Kilomoles of water	(p) 0.555
(ii) Mole fraction of sugar	(q) 9.9×10^{-3}
(iii) Molality of solution	(r) 0.01
(iv) Molarity of solution	(s) 0.56

Codes

	(i)	(ii)	(iii)	(iv)
(a)	(r)	(q)	(p)	(s)
(b)	(p)	(q)	(s)	(p)
(c)	(p)	(r)	(q)	(s)
(d)	(r)	(p)	(s)	(q)

248 Carbon reacts with oxygen to yield CO or CO_2 depending on the quantity of oxygen available per mole of carbon. Initially there is 100 g of O_2.

Quantity of carbon is being given in Column I. Match this quantity of carbon with the quantity of CO or CO_2 formed given in Column II. Select the correct answer from the codes given.

	Column I		Column II
(i)	10 g carbon	(p)	3.125 moles CO_2
(ii)	37.5 g carbon	(q)	0.833 mole CO_2
(iii)	60.0 g carbon	(r)	1.25 moles CO_2
(iv)	100 g carbon	(s)	3.75 moles CO
		(t)	6.25 moles CO

Codes

	(i)	(ii)	(iii)	(iv)
(a)	(q)	(t)	(p)	(s)
(b)	(q)	(t)	(r)	(p)
(c)	(q)	(p)	(r,s)	(t)
(d)	(t)	(s)	(q)	(p)

249 Match the properties of the species in Column I with the calculated number in Column II and select answer the codes given.

Column I		Column II
(i) Number of protons in the element with mass number 81 and having 31.7% more neutrons than protons.	(p)	50
(ii) Ionic mass of M^{2+} which is isoelectronic of CO_2 and has $(Z+2)$ neutrons.	(q)	26
(iii) Ionic mass of X^- with 17 protons and having 11.1% more neutrons than electrons.	(r)	35
(iv) Atomic number of M^{3+} with mass number 56 and having 30.4% more neutrons than electrons.	(s)	37

Codes

	(i)	(ii)	(iii)	(iv)
(a)	(p)	(q)	(r)	(s)
(b)	(s)	(r)	(p)	(q)
(c)	(p)	(q)	(r)	(s)
(d)	(r)	(p)	(s)	(q)

Based on More than One Correct Matching

250 Match the results in Column I with the corresponding compounds in Column II and select the answer from the codes given.

Column I		Column II
(i) Same empirical formula	(p)	CH_3COOH
(ii) Same % of H (6.67)	(q)	NH_2CONH_2
(iii) Same% of C (40)	(r)	HCHO
(iv) Same % of O (53.3)	(s)	$CH_3CH_2CH_2OH$
(v) Equal number of H attached to O-atom	(t)	$HCOOCH_3$

Codes

	(i)	(ii)	(iii)	(iv)	(v)
(a)	(p, t)	(p, t)	(q, s)	(r, s)	(r, t)
(b)	(p, r, t)	(p, q, r)	(q, s)	(r, s)	(q, t)
(c)	(p, t)	(p, q, t)	(q, s)	(r, s)	(q, t)
(d)	(p, r, t)	(p, q, r, t)	(p, r, t)	(p, r, t)	(p, s)

251 Match the item in Column I with the given amount in Column II and select the answer from the codes given.

	Column I		Column II
(i)	N_0 molecules	(p)	8 g oxygen (O)
(ii)	$N_0/2$ molecules	(q)	1 g hydrogen (H)
(iii)	0.5 mole	(r)	35.5 g chlorine (Cl_2)
(iv)	1 equivalent	(s)	66.0 g of H_3PO_2
		(t)	49.0 g of H_2SO_4

Codes

	(i)	(ii)	(iii)	(iv)
(a)	(s)	(r)	(r,t)	(q,r,t)
(b)	(s)	(r,t)	(r,t)	(p,q,r,s,t)
(c)	(q,s)	(p,r,t)	(p,r,t)	(p,q,r,s,t)
(d)	(s)	(r,t)	(r,t)	(q,r,t)

Based on Three Columns

Directions (Q. Nos. 252 to 255) are based on the matching of Columns (1), (2) and (3). Column (1) contains 1g of each gas. Column (2) has mole fraction and Column (3) has total number of atoms of the correspoding gas.

	Column 1		Column (2)		Column (3)
(i)	NH_3	(I)	0.137	(p)	0.235 N_0
(ii)	CO_2	(II)	0.377	(q)	0.068 N_0
(iii)	NO_2	(III)	0.354	(r)	0.3125 N_0
(iv)	CH_4	(IV)	0.131	(s)	0.065 N_0

252 1 g of this gas has mole fraction as in Column (2) and number of atoms as in Column (3).
(a) (i) - (III) - (p) (b) (i) - (III) - (q)
(c) (ii) - (III) - (p) (d) (ii) - (III) - (q)

253 1 g of this gas has mole fraction as in Column (2) and number of atoms as in Column (3).
(a) (ii) - (I) - (p) (b) (ii) - (I) - (q)
(c) (i) - (I) - (r) (d) (iii) - (II) - (q)

254 1 g of this gas has mole fraction as in Column (2) and number of atom as in Column (3).
(a) (ii) - (IV) - (p) (b) (iii) - (IV) - (s)
(c) (iii) - (IV) - (s) (d) (i) - (IV) - (s)

255 1 g of this gas has mole fraction as in Column (2) and number of atoms as in Column (3).
(a) (ii) - (II) - (p) (b) (i) - (II) - (p)
(c) (iii) - (II) - (q) (d) (iv) - (II) - (r)

HINTS & EXPLANATIONS

Immediate Tests

1. (i) Ionic mass of $X^{2-} = 16$

Thus, neutrons + protons = 16

Number of neutrons = 8 (given)

$\therefore$ number of protons = 16 − 8 = 8

Thus, atomic number of $X^{2-} = 8$

number of electrons in $X = 8$

Thus, number of electrons in X^{2-}

= 8 + 2 = 10

$\therefore$ (a) 8 (b) 10 (c) 8

(ii) Isotope can be represented as :

$$\begin{array}{l}\text{Mass number} \longrightarrow A\\ \text{Atomic number} \longrightarrow {}_ZX\end{array}$$

Mass number = 65

Thus, neutron + proton = 65

Since neutron = 35

hence, protons = 65 − 35 = 30

and electrons in X = 30

Cation formed has 28 electrons.

Thus, two electrons are lost in the formation of cation.

$$X \longrightarrow X^{2+} + 2e^-$$

Thus, cation of isotope is ${}^{65}_{30}X^{2+}$.

2. (i) $\bar{A} = \dfrac{A_1\chi_1 + A_2\chi_2 + A_3\chi_3}{\chi_1 + \chi_2 + \chi_3}$

= 12.011 amu

(ii) If ${}^{10}_{5}\text{B} = \chi\%$

then ${}^{11}_{5}\text{B} = (100 - \chi)\%$

$\therefore \quad \bar{A} = \dfrac{10X + 11(100 - \chi)}{100}$

$\therefore \quad 10.2 = \dfrac{10X + 11(100 - \chi)}{100}$

$\chi = 80$

$\therefore \quad {}^{11}_{5}\text{B} = 80\%$

${}^{11}_{5}\text{B} = 20\%$

3. (i) Number of moles = $\dfrac{\text{Mass}}{\text{Molar mass}}$

$= \dfrac{88 \text{ g}}{44 \text{ g mol}^{-1}} = 2 \text{ mol}$

1 mole has molecules = N_0

$\therefore$ 2 moles has molecules = $2N_0$

$= 2 \times 6.02 \times 10^{23}$

$= 12.04 \times 10^{23}$

(ii) 6.02×10^{23} atoms of H = N_0 atoms of H

1 mol of $C_2H_4O_2$ has = 4 mol H-atoms

$= 4N_0$ H-atoms

Thus, N_0 atoms of H are in

$= \dfrac{1}{4}$ mol $C_2H_4O_2$

= 0.25 mol

(iii) 36.0 g $H_2O = \dfrac{36.0}{18} = 2.0$ mol H_2O

= 4.0 mol H-atom

$= 4.0N_0$ H-atom

4. Gypsum = $CaSO_4 \cdot 2H_2O$

If gypsum = 1.0 g and $CaSO_4$ = 0.791 g

then H_2O = 1 − 0.791 = 0.209 g

$\therefore \quad CaSO_4 = \dfrac{0.791}{136} = 0.00582$ mol

$H_2O = \dfrac{0.209}{18} = 0.0116$ mol

5. (i) Chlorophyll = 0.24 g

Mg in chlorophyll (2.88%) = $\dfrac{0.24 \times 2.80}{100}$ g

$= \dfrac{0.24 \times 2.88}{100 \times 24}$ mol

$= 2.88 \times 10^{-4}$ mol

$= 2.88 \times 10^{-4}\ N_0$ atoms

$= 2.88 \times 10^{-4} \times 6.02 \times 10^{23}$ atoms

$= 1.734 \times 10^{20}$ atoms

(ii) 1.6 μg of $CH_4 = 1.6 \times 10^{-6}$ g of CH_4

$= \dfrac{1.6 \times 10^{-6}}{16}$ mol of CH_4

Number of molecules

$= \dfrac{1.6 \times 10^{-6}}{16} \times 6.02 \times 10^{23}$

$= 6.02 \times 10^{16}$

Thus, number of coins = 6.02×10^{16}

6. (i) 1 mol glucose has mass

$(C_6H_{12}O_6) = 6 \times 12 + 12 \times 1 + 6 \times 16$

= 180 g

$\therefore$ 4.00×10^{-3} mol has mass

$= 180 \times 4.00 \times 10^{-3}$ g

= 0.720 g

1 mol of $C_6H_{12}O_6$ has C-atoms = $6N_0$

$\therefore$ 4.0×10^{-3} mol of $C_6H_{12}O_6$ has C-atoms

$= 6N_0 \times 4.0 \times 10^{-3}$

$= 6 \times 6.02 \times 10^{23} \times 4.0 \times 10^{-3}$

$= 1.4448 \times 10^{22}$

(ii) 250 g $CaCO_3 = \dfrac{250}{100}$ mol $CaCO_3$

= 2.5 × 3 mol O-atoms

= 7.50 mol O - atoms

$= 7.50 \times 6.02 \times 10^{23}$ O-atoms

$= 4.515 \times 10^{24}$

7. (i) 10 g impure $CaCO_3 = 10 \times \dfrac{50}{100} = 5.0$ g pure $CaCO_3$

$$\underset{100 \text{ g}}{CaCO_3(s)} \xrightarrow{\Delta} \underset{56 \text{ g}}{CaO(s)} + CO_2(g)$$

100 g gives = 56 g CaO

$\therefore$ 5 g gives = $\dfrac{56}{100} \times 5$

= 2.8 g pure CaO

(ii) In each 0.56 L of O_2 at STP combines with metal A.

22.4 L O_2 at STP = 1 mol = 32 g O_2

$\therefore$ 0.56 g O_2 at STP = 0.8 g of O_2

Oxide	Mass of oxide	Mass of Metal M	Ratio of M
A	1.450	0.650 g	2
B	1.125	0.325 g	1

Thus, $A : M_2O$

$B : MO$

(iii)
$$\begin{array}{ccccc} 2N_2(g) & + & O_2(g) & \longrightarrow & 2N_2O(g)\\ 2 \text{ mol} & & 1 \text{ mol} & & 2 \text{ mol}\\ 45.4 \text{ L} & & 22.7 \text{ L} & & 45.4 \text{ L}\end{array}$$

Equal moles occupy equal volumes. Thus, Gay-Lussac's law of gaseous volume is followed

(iv)
$$\begin{array}{ccccc} SO_2(g) & + & \frac{1}{2}O_2(g) & \longrightarrow & SO_3(g)\\ 1 \text{ mol} & & 0.5 \text{ mol} & & 1 \text{ mol}\\ N_0 \text{ molecules} & & \frac{N_0}{2} \text{ molecules} & & N_0 \text{ molecules}\end{array}$$

8. (i) 1 mol urea (NH_2CONH_2 or N_2H_4CO)

$= 2 \times 14 + 1 \times 4 + 1 \times 12 + 1 \times 16$

= 60 g

Mass of solution = 100 g

$\therefore$ Water + urea = 40 g

(a) % urea by mass of water = $\dfrac{60}{40} \times 100$

= 150%

(b)% urea by mass of solution

$= \dfrac{60}{100} \times 100 = 60\%$

(ii) (a) $\frac{4.6}{5.4} \times 100 = 85.18\%$

(b) $\frac{4.6}{10.0} \times 100 = 46.0\%$

(iii) Solution = 100 g

Residue is glucose.

Glucose = 18 g = $\frac{18}{180} = 0.10$ mol

Water = 100 − 18 = 82 g

(a) Mol % of glucose = $\frac{0.10}{100} \times 100$

= 0.10%

(b) Mass % of glucose (by weight of water)

$= \frac{18}{82} \times 100 = 21.95\%$

9. In 118% oleum, pure H_2SO_4 (in the form of SO_3) = 100 g

water = 18.0 g = $\frac{18}{18} = 1$ mol

10. (i) 100 g of H_2SO_4 solution has

$H_2SO_4 = 98$ g

Since, $\frac{\text{mass}}{\text{volume}} = \text{density}$

$\therefore \frac{100}{1.8}$ mL of H_2SO_4 solution has H_2SO_4

= 98 g

$\therefore$ % H_2SO_4 by volume of solution

$\left(\frac{w}{V}\right) = \frac{98 \times 1.8 \times 100}{100}$

= 176.4%

(ii) $CH_3CH_2OH = 10$ mL

If density = x g mL^{-1}

then mass = $V \times d = 10x$ g

Similarly, 10 mL H_2O = 10 g H_2O

Total mass = $(10x + 10)$ g

$= 10(x + 1)$ g

Density = $\frac{10(x+1)}{20}$ g mL^{-1}

= 0.90 g mL^{-1} (given)

$\therefore \frac{10(x+1)}{20} = 0.90$

$\therefore x = 0.8$ g mL^{-1}

11. (i) 200 ppm, i.e. 200 g in 10^6 mL H_2O.

0.200 g in 10^3 mL (L^{-1}) H_2O.

200 mg in 10^3 mL.

Thus, 200 mg L^{-1}.

■ *x* ppm = *x* mg L^{-1}

(ii) 80 ppm Ca^{2+}

$CaSO_4 \rightleftharpoons Ca^{2+} + SO_4^{2-}$

$Ca(HCO_3)_2 \rightleftharpoons Ca^{2+} + 2HCO_3^-$

Thus, mol of SO_4^{2-} = mol of Ca^{2+}

$= \frac{96}{96} = 1$ mol Ca^{2+}

Thus, $Ca^{2+} = 40$ ppm Ca^{2+}

Mol of $HCO_3^- = 2 \times$ mol of Ca^{2+}

Thus, mol of $Ca^{2+} = \frac{1}{2}$ mol of HCO_3^-

$= \frac{1}{2}\left(\frac{122}{61}\right) = 1$ mol

Thus, $Ca^{2+} = 40$ ppm Ca^{2+}

Total = 80 ppm Ca^{2+}

12. (i) NH_3 in solution = 0.93 g $cm^{-3} \times \frac{18.6}{100}$

= 0.173 g cm^{-3}

(ii) 1.175 g HCl is in = 1 mL

$\therefore$ 34.4 g HCl is in = $\frac{34.4}{1.175}$ mL

= 29.28 mL

Add 29.28 mL HCl into 100 mL solution.

13. (i) 40.0 mg Al^{3+} per mL = 40×10^{-3} g Al^{3+}

Thus, Al^{3+} in 50 mL = $40 \times 10^{-3} \times 50$ g Al^{3+}

$= \frac{40 \times 10^{-3} \times 50}{27}$ mol Al^{3+}

As every mol of $Al_2(SO_4)_3$ has 2 mol Al^{3+}

Al^{3+} in 50 mL = $\left(\frac{40 \times 10^{-3} \times 50}{2 \times 27}\right)$ mol

$Al_2(SO_4)_3 \cdot 18H_2O$

$= \frac{40 \times 10^{-3} \times 50}{54} \times 666$ g

$Al_2(SO_4)_3 \cdot 18H_2O = 24.67$ g

(ii) $BaCl_2$ in 50 g of 12.0% $BaCl_2$ solution

$= \frac{50 \times 12}{100} = 6$ g

Moles of $BaCl_2$ = Moles of $BaCl_2 \cdot 2H_2O$

Moles of $BaCl_2 = \frac{6}{208}$ mol

$\therefore$ Moles of $BaCl_2 \cdot 2H_2O = \frac{6}{208}$ mol

$\therefore$ Mass of $BaCl_2 \cdot 2H_2O$ in 50 g solution

$= \frac{6}{208} \times 244 = 7.04$ g

14. (i) If glucose = 18 g = $\frac{18}{180}$ mol

then water = 100 − 18 = 82 g = $\frac{82}{18}$ mol

$= \frac{820}{180}$ mol (to simplify calculation)

Total moles = $\frac{18 + 820}{180} = \frac{838}{180}$

$\therefore X_{glucose} = \frac{\frac{18}{180}}{\frac{838}{180}} = 0.0215$

(ii) **Before cooling :** Urea in 5 g of 20% aqueous urea solution = $\frac{5 \times 20}{100} = 1$ g

$= \frac{1}{60}$ mol

Water = 5 − 1 = 4 g = $\frac{4}{18}$ mol

$\therefore X_{urea} = \left(\frac{\frac{1}{60}}{\frac{1}{60} + \frac{4}{18}}\right) = 0.67$

After cooling : Urea separates = 0.4 g

Urea in solution = 1 − 0.4 = 0.6 g

$= \frac{0.6}{60}$ mol = 0.01

Water = 4 g = $\frac{4}{18}$ mol

$X'_{urea} = \frac{0.01}{\left(0.01 + \frac{4}{18}\right)} = 0.043$

Change in mole fraction = 0.67 − 0.043

= 0.627

(iii)

	Amount	Moles	Total moles	Mole fraction
Water (H_2O)	5 g	(a) $\frac{25}{18}$	$(a+b+c)$ = 2.349	$\frac{a}{a+b+c}$ = 0.59
Ethanol (C_2H_5OH)	25 g	(b) $\frac{25}{46}$		$\frac{b}{a+b+c}$ = 0.23
Acetic acid (CH_3COOH)	100 g	(c) $\frac{25}{60}$		$\frac{c}{a+b+c}$ 0.18

(iv) $X_{H_2} = \frac{1/2}{\left(\frac{1}{2} + \frac{8}{32} + \frac{16}{16}\right)} = 0.286$

15. (i) Glucose ($C_6H_{12}O_6$), molar mass

$= 6 \times 12 + 12 \times 1 + 6 \times 16 = 180$ g mol^{-1}

90 mg per 100 mL

$= 90 \times 10^{-3}$ g per 100 mL

$= \frac{90 \times 10^{-3} \times 1000}{100}$ gL^{-1}

= 0.90 gL^{-1}

$= \frac{0.90}{180}$ mol L^{-1} = 0.005 M

(ii) Cholesterol in normal blood = 0.005 M

= 0.005 mol L^{-1}

Cholesterol in 750 mL blood

$= \frac{0.005}{1000} \times 750$

$= 3.75 \times 10^{-3}$ mol

(iii) 1.71 M NaCl means 1.71 mol in 1000 mL

$\therefore$ 0.20 mL NaCl is in $= \frac{1000}{1.71} \times 0.20$

$= 117.0$ mL

16. (i) Every Na_2SO_4 gives two Na^+ ions in solution

$0.40 \text{ M } Na^+ \equiv 0.20 \text{ M } Na_2SO_4$

$0.30 \text{ M} \times V = 0.20 \times 2.0$

$\therefore \quad V = 1.33\text{L} = 1330 \text{ mL}$

(ii) 27.4 mg Ba^{2+} $\text{mL}^{-1} = 27.4 \text{ g L}^{-1}$

$= \frac{27.4}{137} = 0.2\text{M}$

Thus, 1 mL of 0.2 M is to be obtained from V mL of 0.5 M

$\therefore \quad V \times 0.5 = 1 \times 0.2$

$V = 0.4$ mL

(iii) $MV(\text{L}) = \text{mol}$

HNO_3 in 2 L of 1.1 M $HNO_3 = (2 \times 1.1)$ mol

Total moles $= 0.20 + 2 \times 1.1$

$= 2.42$ mol in 3.0 L

$\therefore$ Molarity $= \frac{2.42}{3} = 0.81$ M

17. Molarity of 63% $HNO_3 = \frac{10\, d \times \%}{\text{molar mass}}$

$= \frac{10 \times 1.2 \times 63}{63}$

$= 12$ M

$M_1V_1 = M_2V_2$

$1 \times 12 = M_2 \times 1000$

$M_2 = 0.012$ M

18. HCl and H_2SO_4 are of different basicity.

$0.05 \text{ M } H_2SO_4 = 0.10 \text{ N } H_2SO_4$

$N(H^+)$ in mixture

$= \frac{N_1V_1 \text{ (HCl)} + N_2V_2 \text{ } (H_2SO_4)}{V_1 + V_2}$

$= \frac{100 \times 0.1 + 200 \times 0.1}{300} = 0.1$ N

$\therefore \quad (NV)_{H^+} = 300 \times 0.1 = 30$

$(NV)_{OH^-} = 100 \times 0.2 = 20$

$(NV)_{H^+} > (NV)_{OH^-}$

Thus, acidic solution

$N \text{(resultant)} = \frac{(NV)_{H^+} - (NV)_{OH^-}}{V_{\text{Total}}}$

$= \frac{30 - 20}{400} = \frac{10}{400} = 0.025$ M

M in terms of H^+ ion.

19. (i) 3.267 g H_3PO_4 in 100 mL

$= \frac{3.267}{98}$ mol in 0.1 L

$\therefore \quad M\,(H_3PO_4) = \frac{\frac{3.267}{98}}{0.1} = 0.333$ M

$N\,(H_3PO_4) = 1$ N

$M \times \text{Basicity} = \text{Normality}$

$\therefore \; 0.333 \times \text{Basicity} = 1$

$\therefore \quad \text{Basicity} = 3$

■ H—O—P(=O)(—O—H)—O—H

It has the three ionisable H^+ attached to O-atoms

(ii) 2.78 g of $FeSO_4 \cdot xH_2O$ is 100 mL

$\frac{2.78}{(152 + 18x)}$ mol in 100 mL

$\frac{27.8}{(152 + 18x)}$ mol L^{-1}

$\therefore \quad M = N$ (n-factor being 1)

$= \frac{27.8}{(152 + 18x)}$

$\frac{27.8}{(152 + 18x)} = 0.1$

$\therefore \quad x = 7$

20. (i) $N_1 \text{(NaOH)} = \frac{\frac{0.4}{40}}{0.1} = 0.1\, N_1$

$N_2(H_2SO_4) = ?$

$10 \times 0.1 \text{ N} = 10 \times N_2$

$N_2 = 0.1 \text{N } H_2SO_4 = 4.9 \text{ g L}^{-1}$

$= 0.49$ g in 100 mL

(ii) 0.01 M $H_3PO_4 = 0.03 NH_3PO_4$ (being tribasic)

$N_1V_1 = N_2V_2$

$100 \times 0.03 \text{ N} = 50 \times N_2$

$\therefore \; N_2[Ca(OH)_2] = 0.06$ N

$M_2[Ca(OH)_2] = 0.03$ M

■ n-factor of $H_3PO_4 = 3$

n-factor of $Ca(OH)_2 = 2$

21. 4 g NaOH $= \frac{4}{40}$ mol $= 0.1$ mol

36 g $H_2O = \frac{36}{18}$ mol $= 2.0$ mol

Total moles $= 2.1$ mol

$\therefore \quad X_{\text{NaOH}} = \frac{0.1}{2.1} = \frac{1}{21} = 0.048$

Total mass $= 4 + 36 = 40.0 \text{ g} = 40$ mL

$= 0.04 \text{ L } (d = 1 \text{ g mL}^{-1})$

$\therefore$ Molarity (mol L^{-1}) $= \frac{0.1}{0.04} = 2.5$ M

Molality $= \frac{\text{mol (solute)}}{\text{kg } (H_2O)}$

$= \frac{0.1}{0.036} = 2.78$ molal

22. (i) m (molality) $= \frac{100M}{(1000\, d - Mm_2)}$

Molarity $= 2.97$ M (mol L^{-1})

(ii) 1 mL of solution has

$= 1.198 \text{ g } H_2SO_4$ sample

$= 1.198 \times \frac{27}{100}$ g pure H_2SO_4

$= 0.3235 \text{ g} = \frac{0.3235}{98}$

$= 3.30 \times 10^{-3}$ mol

$\therefore$ Molarity $= 3.30$ mol L^{-1}

$\therefore$ Molarity $= 3.30$ M

m (molality) $= \frac{1000M}{(1000\, d - mM_2)}$

$= 3.78$ molal

23. (i) $M(H_2SO_4) = \frac{10d \times \%}{m_2}$

$= \frac{10 \times 1.198 \times 27}{98} = 3.30$ M

Molality $= \frac{1000\, \chi_2}{(1 - \chi_2)\, M_1}$

$1 = \frac{100\, \chi_2}{(1 - \chi_2)\, 18}$

$\frac{1 - \chi_2}{\chi_2} = \frac{1000}{18} = 55.56$

$\chi_2 = 0.0177$

Molality $= 1 \text{ mol kg}^{-1}$

Thus, glucose $= 1$ mol $= 180$ kg

Solvent water $= 1000$ g

$\therefore$ Mass of solution $= 1180$ g

$\therefore$ Percentage by mass of solution

$= \frac{180}{1180} \times 100 = 15.25\%$

(ii) You can use this relation,

$m = \frac{1000\, M}{(1000\, d - Mm_2)}$

to derive the required result.

24. (i) $N_2(g) + 3H_2(g) \longrightarrow 2NH_3(g)$

N_2	H_2	NH_3
1 mol	3 mol	2 mol
1 mol	1 mol	?

H_2 is the limiting reactant.

Thus, NH_3 formed from 1 mol $H_2 = \frac{2}{3}$ mol NH_3

(ii) $2C + O_2 \longrightarrow 2CO$

	2C	O_2	2CO
	2 mol	1 mol	2 mol
	24 g	96 g	?
Given,	2 mol	3 mol	

Thus, carbon is the limiting reactant and O_2 is in excess.

(a) Excess reacant $(O_2) = 3 - 1 = 2$ mol

(b) CO formed = 2 mol

(c) C required by 2 mol excess O_2

= 4 mol

= 4 × 12 = 48 g

(iii) $CH_4 + 2O_2 \longrightarrow CO_2 + 2H_2O$

1 mol 2 mol

16 g = 1 mol 2 mol = 30 g

25. (i) $BaCl_2 + K_2SO_4 \longrightarrow BaSO_4 + 2KCl$

1 mol 1 mol 1 mol

100 mL of 50 mL of

20.8% 17.9%

20.8 g 8.7 g

0.1 mol 0.05 mol (limiting)

$BaSO_4$ formed = 0.05 mol

= 11.65 g $BaSO_4$

(ii) $CaCl_2 + Na_2CO_3 \rightarrow CaCO_3 + 2NaCl$

1 mol 1 mol 1 mol

200 mL 100 mL

of 0.1 M of 0.1 M

= 20 millimol 10 millimol

Na_2CO_3 is the limiting reactant.

Thus, $CaCO_3$ formed

= moles of limiting reactant

= 10 millimol

= 0.01 mol

26. $3Si + 2N_2 \longrightarrow Si_3N_4$

3 mol 2 mol 1 mol

3 × 28 = 84 g 140 g

Si required by 140 g Si_3N_4, if yield is 100%

= 84 g

Si required by 140 g Si_3N_4, if yield is 75%

$$= 84 \times \frac{100}{75} = 112 \text{ g}$$

27. (i)

Elements	%	Mol	Ratio
K (39)	26.57	0.68	1 = 2
Cr (52)	35.36	0.68	1 = 2
O (16)	38.07	2.38	3.5 = 7

Thus, $K_2Cr_2O_7$.

(ii) $x\text{Fe} + y\text{S} \longrightarrow \text{Fe}_x\text{S}_y$

		Mol	Ratio
Fe (56)	7.30 g	0.13	1= 2
S (32)	6.30 g	0.20	1.5 = 3

Thus, Fe_2S_3.

(iii)

		Mole	Ratio
H_2O	19%	$\frac{19}{18} = 1.056$	3
$Fe(SCN)_3$	81%	$\frac{81}{230} = 0.35$	1

∴ Thus, empirical formula is

$Fe(SCN)_3 \cdot 3H_2O$.

28. (i) Molar mass of

$CN_2H_4O = 1 \times 12 + 2 \times 14 + 4 \times 1 + 1 \times 16$

= 60 g mol

$$C = \frac{12}{60} \times 100 = 20.0\%$$

$$N = \frac{28}{60} \times 100 = 46.66\%$$

$$H = \frac{4}{60} \times 100 = 6.667\%$$

$$O = \frac{16}{60} \times 100 = 26.67\%$$

(ii) $\frac{12}{44} \times 100 = 27.27\%$

Knowledge Confirmation Test 1

1. (d) **2.** (b) **3.** (b) **4.** (c) **5.** (d) **6.** (a) **7.** (c) **8.** (c) **9.** (a) **10.** (b)
11. (b) **12.** (a) **13.** (c) **14.** (d) **15.** (d)

Knowledge Confirmation Test 2

1. (d) **2.** (a) **3.** (b) **4.** (c) **5.** (b) **6.** (d) **7.** (a) **8.** (a) **9.** (a) **10.** (b)
11. (b) **12.** (c) **13.** (c) **14.** (c) **15.** (a) **16.** (b) **17.** (a) **18.** (d) **19.** (b) **20.** (b)

Knowledge Confirmation Test 3

1. (c) **2.** (d) **3.** (c) **4.** (a) **5.** (a) **6.** (d) **7.** (b) **8.** (b) **9.** (b) **10.** (c)
11. (a) **12.** (b) **13.** (b) **14.** (a) **15.** (d)

Knowledge Confirmation Test 4

1. (b) **2.** (a) **3.** (b) **4.** (d) **5.** (d) **6.** (d) **7.** (c) **8.** (b) **9.** (a) **10.** (c)
11. (a) **12.** (b) **13.** (b) **14.** (b) **15.** (d) **16.** (b) **17.** (a) **18.** (c) **19.** (a) **20.** (b)
21. (c) **22.** (b) **23.** (c) **24.** (a) **25.** (c)

Knowledge Confirmation Test 5

1. (d) **2.** (c) **3.** (a) **4.** (a) **5.** (d) **6.** (a) **7.** (b) **8.** (b) **9.** (a) **10.** (b)
11. (a) **12.** (a) **13.** (b) **14.** (d) **15.** (a) **16.** (b) **17.** (c) **18.** (a) **19.** (b) **20.** (d)

Knowledge Confirmation Test 6

1. (b) **2.** (a) **3.** (b) **4.** (a) **5.** (a) **6.** (d) **7.** (b) **8.** (d)
9. (b) **10.** (d) **11.** (d) **12.** (c) **13.** (a) **14.** (a) **15.** (b)

Acid Test for JEE Main

Type I. MCQs with Only One Correct Alternate

1. (b) Mass of carbon $= \dfrac{12 \times 6.022 \times 10^{20}}{6.022 \times 10^{23}}$

$= 0.012$ g instead of 12 g

2. (d) $\underset{84\text{ g}}{MgCO_3} \longrightarrow \underset{40\text{ g}}{MgO} + CO_2 \uparrow$

40g of MgO is formed from

$= 84$ g pure MgO

$\therefore$ 8 g of MgO is formed from

$= \dfrac{84}{40} \times 8$ g pure $MgCO_3$

Thus, per cent purity $= \dfrac{84 \times 8 \times 100}{40 \times 20}$

$= 84\%$

3. (a) $AgNO_3 + NaCl \longrightarrow AgCl + HNO_3$

$AgNO_3$	$NaCl$	$AgCl$
1 mol	1 mol	1 mol
170 g	58.5 g	143.5 g
50 mL	50 mL	
(17%)	(5.85%)	
8.5g	2.925 g	?
$\dfrac{8.5}{170}$ mol	$\dfrac{2.925}{58.5}$ mol	
0.05 mol	0.05 mol	

$AgNO_3$ and NaCl are in exact quantity.
Thus, AgCl formed= 0.05 mol.
(Ag = 108, N = 14, Na = 23, Cl = 35.5)

4. (a) $\underset{1\text{ mol}}{CaCO_3} + \underset{2\text{ mol}}{2HCl} \longrightarrow CaCl_2 + CO_2 + H_2O$

we know, $\dfrac{M_{(\text{molarity})}\, V_{(\text{volume})}}{1000} = \text{mol}$

$\therefore$ 20 mL of 1 M HCl $= \dfrac{20 \times 1}{1000} = 0.02$ mol

Thus, $CaCO_3$ required

$= \dfrac{1}{2}$ mol of HCl $= 0.01$ mol

$= 0.01 \times 100 = 1$ g

5. (d) In one atom of ${}^{14}_{6}C$, neutrons

$= 14 - 6 = 8$

1.4 mg ${}^{14}_{6}C = 1.4 \times 10^{-3}$ g ${}^{14}_{6}C$

$= \dfrac{1.4 \times 10^{-3}}{14}$ mol

$= 1 \times 10^{-4}$ mol

Since, each of ${}^{14}_{6}C$ contains N_0 (6.02×10^{23}) atoms, hence

Number of ${}^{14}_{6}C$- atoms

$= 6.02 \times 10^{19}$ atoms

and neutrons $= 6.02 \times 10^{19} \times 8$ neutrons

$= 4.816 \times 10^{20}$ neutrons

6. (b) One CO_3^{2-} ion has electrons

= 6 in C + 8 each in O + 2 due to negative charge = 32

Ionic mass of $CO_3^{2-} = 60$

6 g $CO_3^{2-} = \dfrac{6}{60} = 0.1$ mol CO_3^{2-}

$= 6.02 \times 10^{22}$ CO_3^{2-} ions

$= 6.02 \times 10^{22} \times 32$ electrons

$= 1.9264 \times 10^{24}$ electrons

7. (a) 16 g $CH_4 = \dfrac{16}{16} = 1$ mol CH_4

$= 5\, N_0$ atoms (one C + four H)

= 5 moles of Ca atoms

$= 5 \times 40$ g Ca = 200 g of Ca

8. (d) For x volume H_2O_2

Molarity $= \dfrac{x}{11.2}$

$\therefore \quad 1 = \dfrac{x}{11.2}$

$\therefore \quad x = 11.2$

9. (b) 25 L (= 25000 mL) = 1 mol CO_2

$= 44$ g CO_2

$\therefore$ 0.25 mL $CO_2 = \dfrac{44}{25000} \times 0.25$ g CO_2

$= 4.40 \times 10^{-6}$ g CO_2

$NaHCO_3 + H^+$ (in oxalic acid $= CO_2$

1 mol = 84 g   1 mol = 44 g

44 g CO_2 is from = 84 g $NaHCO_3$

$\therefore 4.4 \times 10^{-6}$ g CO_2 is from

$= \dfrac{84}{44} \times 4.4 \times 10^{-6}$ g

$= 8.40 \times 10^{-4}$ $NaHCO_3$ in

10 mg $= (10 \times 10^{-3}$ g) $NaHCO_3$

$\therefore$ Percentage $= \dfrac{8.4 \times 10^{-4}}{10 \times 10^{-3}} \times 100 = 8.4\%$

10. (d) 5.0 moles of C_2H_5OH = 10.0 moles of H

1.1 moles of $C_3H_8O_3$ = 8.8 moles of H

1.5 moles of $C_6H_8O_6$ = 12.0 moles of H

4.0 moles of $C_4H_4O_2$ = 16.0 moles of H

11. (a) $\dfrac{\text{Molarity} \times \text{volume}}{1000}$

$= \dfrac{50 \times 0.20}{1000}$ mol $BaCl_2$

$= \dfrac{50 \times 0.20 \times 2}{1000}$ mol Cl^- ions

$= 0.02$ mol Cl^- ions

■ Every mol of $BaCl_2$ gives two mol of Cl^- ions.

12. (a) 1 mol of $Na_2CO_3 \equiv 1$ mol of CO_3^{2-}

Ionic mass of $CO_3^{2-} = 60$

10 mg $CO_3^{2-} = \dfrac{10 \times 10^{-3}}{60}$ mol of CO_3^{2-} per mL^{-1}

$= 1.67 \times 10^{-4}$ mol CO_3^{2-} per mL^{-1}

$1.67 \times 10^{-4} \times 500$ mol CO_3^{2-} in 500 mL

$= 0.0833$ mol CO_3^{2-}

or Na_2CO_3 in 500 mL

13. (a) Five times

14. (b)

$2NaOH + H_2SO_4 \longrightarrow Na_2SO_4 + H_2O$

10 mL of 0.25 M H_2SO_4

$\equiv$ 10 mL of 0.50 N H_2SO_4

0.2 M NaOH $\equiv$ 0.2 N NaOH

Apply, $\quad N_1V_1 = N_2V_2$

$0.2 \times V_1 = 0.5 \times 10$

$V_1 = 25$ mL

■ Equivalent of acid $\equiv$ Equivalent of base

V_1 mL of 0.2 M NaOH $= 0.2\, V_1$ millimol

$= 0.2\, V_1$ equivalent

10 mL of 0.25 M H_2SO_4 = 2.5 millimol

= 5.0 equivalent

$0.2\, V_1 = 5.0$

$\therefore \quad V_1 = 25$ mL

Every one mol of H_2SO_4 has two equivalents of H_2SO_4.

15. (d) Only pure $CaCO_3$ reacts.

$\underset{100\text{ g pure}}{CaCO_3} + H_2SO_4 \longrightarrow CaSO_4 + \underset{44\text{ g pure}}{CO_2} + H_2O$

0.88 g pure CO_2 is from $= \dfrac{100}{44} \times 0.88$

= 2 g pure $CaCO_3$ in 4g mixture

Thus, per cent purity = 50%

16. (a) 6 μg $= 6 \times 10^{-6}$ g $= \dfrac{6 \times 10^{-6}}{12}$ mol carbon

$= \dfrac{6 \times 10^{-6}}{12} \times 0.02 \times 10^{23}$ C-atoms

$= 3.01 \times 10^{17}$ C-atoms

(Lead pencil has pure ${}^{12}C$).

17. (d) $\dfrac{0.0018}{18} = 1 \times 10^{-4}$ mol H_2O

$= N_0 \times 10^{-4}$ H_2O molecules

$= 6.02 \times 10^{23} \times 10^{-4}$

$[\because N_0 = 6.02 \times 10^{23}]$

$= 6.02 \times 10^{19}$

■ Number of moles

$= \dfrac{\text{Mass (g)}}{\text{Molar mass (g mol}^{-1})}$

Each mole has N_0 molecules.

18. (d) Each mol of

$CuSO_4 \cdot 5H_2O \equiv 1$ Cu $\equiv 9$(O)

$\equiv 1$(S) $\equiv 10$(H)

Thus, 9 mol (O) $\equiv$ 1 mol of (Cu)

19. (d) Equivalent mass of O = 8

∴ Equivalent mass of metal = 16

∴ Equivalent mass of oxide = 16 + 8 = 24

= 1.5 times that of metal.

20. (d) $3H_2 + M_2O_3 \longrightarrow 2M + 3H_2O$

$(2M + 48)$ g is reduced by = 6 g H_2

0.1596 g of M_2O_3 is reduced by

$$= \frac{6 \times 0.1596}{(2M + 48)} = 0.006 \text{ g (given)}$$

$$\therefore \quad \frac{2M + 48}{0.1596} = \frac{6}{0.006}$$

$$\therefore \quad M = 55.8$$

21. (a) 1 mL H_2SO_4 solution has

= 1.84 g H_2SO_4 (impure)

= 1.84 × 0.98 g pure H_2SO_4

Thus, 4 g pure H_2SO_4 is in

$$= \frac{4}{1.84 \times 0.98} \text{ mL } H_2SO_4 \text{ sample}$$

= 2.22 mL

■ $\frac{\text{Mass}}{\text{Volume}}$ = Density

22. (a) $Ca(OH)_2 + Na_2SO_4 \longrightarrow 2NaOH + CaSO_4$

1 mol	1 mol	2 mol	1 mol
100 millimol	2g = $\frac{2 \text{ mol}}{142}$		
= 0.1 mol	0.014085 mol		

NaOH from 0.1 mol $Ca(OH)_2$ = 0.2 mol

NaOH from 0.014085 mol Na_2SO_4

= 0.028167 mol

Thus, Na_2SO_4 is the limiting reactant

∴ NaOH = 0.028169 mol in 100 mL

= 0.28 mol L^{-1}

$CaSO_4$ = Na_2SO_4 taken

= 0.014085 mol

= 0.014085 × 136 g = 1.91 g

23. (b)

I. $MnO_4^- + 5e^- + 8H^+ \longrightarrow Mn^{2+} + 4H_2O$

II. $C_2O_4^{2-} \longrightarrow CO_2 + 2e^-$

To balance electrons

I × 2 + II × 5

Thus, 5 $CO_2 \equiv 10e^-$

1 $CO_2 \equiv$ 2 electrons

24. (d) $CaCO_3 + 2HCl \rightleftharpoons CaCl_2 + H_2O + CO_2$

$CaCO_3 \equiv 2H^+$

Thus, equivalent mass of $CaCO_3$

$$= \frac{\text{Molar mass}}{2} = 50$$

$$\text{Equivalent of HCl} \left(\frac{NV}{1000}\right) = \frac{50\, N_1}{1000}$$

Equivalent of $CaCO_3$

$$\frac{\text{Mass}}{\text{Equivalent mass}} = \frac{1}{50}$$

Equivalent of $CaCO_3$ = Equivalent of HCl

$$\therefore \quad \frac{50 N_1}{1000} = \frac{1}{50}$$

$$\therefore \quad N_1 = \frac{1000}{2500} = 0.4 \text{ N}$$

25. (a) Mass = Volume × Density

= 0.105 × 11.35 g lead

= 1.191 g lead

$$\therefore \text{Number of moles} = \frac{\text{mass}}{\text{molar mass}}$$

$$\therefore \quad \text{Lead} = \frac{1.191}{206} \text{ mol lead}$$

$$= \frac{1.191\, N_0}{206} \text{ lead atoms}$$

= 3.48×10^{21} lead atoms

■ Every mole of an element has N_0-atoms.

26. (b) $N_0 = 6.02 \times 10^{23}$ atoms mol^{-1}

$$\therefore \text{ 1 atom} = \frac{1}{6.02 \times 10^{23}} \text{ mol}$$

$= 1.66 \times 10^{-24}$ mol

27. (a) Mass of one electron = 9.1×10^{-28} g

∴ Mass of N_0 electrons

$= N_0 \times 9.1 \times 10^{-28}$ g

which is also the molar mass of electron.

$$\therefore \text{ Mol} = \frac{1000 \text{ g}}{N_0 \times 9.1 \times 10^{-28} \text{ g mol}^{-1}}$$

$$= \frac{1000}{6.02 \times 10^{23} \times 9.1 \times 10^{-28}} \text{ mol}$$

$= 1.83 \times 10^6$ mol

28. (a) 10 milli. equiv = 10×10^{-3} equiv

If volume is V mL then number of

$$\text{equivalents} = \frac{0.25 \times V}{1000} = 10^{-2}$$

$$\therefore \quad V = 40 \text{ mL}$$

29. (d) Number of equivalents

$$= \frac{NV}{1000} = \frac{60 \times 4}{1000} = 0.240$$

30. (b) Every mol of H_3PO_3 is neutralises by two mol of OH^-.

Thus, H_3PO_3 has two ionisable H^+

∴ n-factor = 2

∴ Normality of H_3PO_3

= n-factor × molarity

= 2 × 0.3 M = 0.6 N

31. (c) Resultant normality of mixture of acids

$$= \frac{N_1V_1 + N_2V_2}{V_1 + V_2}$$

$$6 = \frac{12\, V + 3\,(1000 - V)}{1000}$$

and V = 333.3 mL of 12N

and V = 666.6 mL of 3 N

Thus, 1 : 2

32. (c) $H_3PO_4 \equiv 3H^+$

Then, n-factor = 3

Molarity × 3 = Normality

$40 \times N_1(H_3PO_4)$

$\equiv 120 \times 0.531\, N_2(NaOH)$

∴ N_1 = 1.593 N

$$\therefore \quad M_1 = \frac{1.593}{3} = 0.531 \text{M}$$

33. (a) Molar mass = vapour density × 2

= 22.4 g mol^{-1}

$$\text{1 g gas at STP} = \frac{1}{22.4} \text{ mol}$$

$$= 22.4 \times \frac{1}{22.4} \text{ L at STP}$$

= 1 L

■ Volume of 1 mole of a gas at STP = 22.4 L

34. (c) 1.58×10^{22} atoms weigh = 1.05 g

∴ 6.02×10^{23} atoms weigh

$$= \frac{1.05 \times 6.02 \times 10^{23}}{1.58 \times 10^{22}} \text{ g}$$

= 40.00 g

∴ Molar mass of the element

= 40.00 g mol^{-1}

35. (b) 5.6 L at STP = 8.0 g,

22.4 L gas at STP = 1 mol = 32 g

$$\text{Thus, number of mol in 64 g} = \frac{64}{32} = 2$$

36. (c) Equivalent weight = 12

∴ Ionic mass of divalent cation

= 12 × valency = 24

∴ Molecular weight of MO

= 24 + 16 = 40

37. (a) $Ca^{2+} + CO_3^{2-} \longrightarrow CaCO_3 \downarrow$

1 mol	1 mol
40 g	1 mol

20 mg Ca^{2+} = 20×10^{-3} g Ca^{2+}

$$= \frac{20 \times 10^{-3}}{40} \text{ mol } Ca^{2+}$$

$= 0.5 \times 10^{-3}$ mol CO_3^{2-}

Similarly, 12 mg Mg^{2+}

$= 5 \times 10^{-4}$ mol CO_3^{2-}

CO_3^{2-} is from Na_2CO_3.

Total Na_2CO_3 = 1×10^{-3} mol

Also, $2\text{ N }Na_2CO_3 = 1\text{ M }Na_2CO_3$
If volume is = V mL

Number of mol in 1 M $Na_2CO_3 = \frac{1 \times V}{1000}$

$\therefore \frac{1 \times V}{1000}$ mol $= 1 \times 10^{-3}$ mol

$\therefore \quad V = 1$ mL

38. (b) Cd in lead-cadmium alloy = 8%

6.02×10^{23} atoms = 1 mol

$= 1 \times 112$

$= 112$ g Cd

6.50×10^{23} atoms $= \frac{112 \times 6.50 \times 10^{23}}{6.02 \times 10^{23}}$ g Cd

$= 120.93$ g Cd of 100% purity

$= \frac{120.93}{0.08}$ g alloy

$= 1511.6$ g $= 1.512$ kg

39. (b) Equivalent of $H_2SO_4 \equiv$ Equivalent of NaOH

2.5 g NaOH $= \frac{2.5}{40}$ equivalent

V mL of 5.0 N $H_2SO_4 = \frac{5V}{1000}$ equivalent

$\therefore \frac{5V}{1000} = \frac{2.5}{40} \Rightarrow V = 12.5$ mL

40. (c) Equivalent of an acid $= \frac{0.25}{E}$

(E = equivalent mass of base)

Equivalent of base $= \frac{40 \times 0.125}{1000}$

Since, equivalent of acid

= equivalent of base

$\therefore \frac{0.25}{E} = \frac{40 \times 0.125}{1000}$

$\therefore \quad E = 50$ of equiv^{-1}

41. (d) H_2SO_4 in 1 mL = 1.835 g impure

$= \frac{1.835 \times 93.2}{100}$ g pure

Normality of concentrated H_2SO_4

$= \frac{\text{mass} \times 1000}{\text{equivalent mass} \times \text{volume}}$

$= \frac{93.2 \times 1.835}{100 \times 49} \times 1000$

$= 34.9$ equiv L^{-1} = 34.9 N

For dilution, if V mL of 34.9 N acid is required then

$N_1V_1 = N_2V_2$

$34.9 \times V = 3 \times 500$

$\therefore \quad V = 43.0$ mL

42. (a) NaOH in 60 L of 0.50 N = 60 × 0.5 mol

= 30 mol = 30 × 40 g NaOH

= 1200 g dry NaOH

$= \frac{1200}{0.88}$ g of wet NaOH = 1.363g

= 1.364 g = 1.364 kg

43. (b) $NH_3 \equiv 3H$, thus equivalent of N in $NH_3 = 3$

$H_2O \equiv 2H$, equivalents of O in $H_2O = 2$

$HCl \equiv 1\,H$, equivalents of Cl in HCl = 1

Thus, 3 : 2 : 1

44. (a) Let mass of metal combined = w g

Equivalent mass of oxygen = 8

Equivalent of oxygen $= \frac{0.200}{8}$

Equivalent of halogen of equivalent mass E

$= \frac{3.17}{E}$

$\therefore \quad \frac{0.200}{8} = \frac{3.17}{E}$

$\therefore \quad E = \frac{3.17 \times 8}{0.200}$

$= 126.8$ g equivalent^{-1}

≈ 127.0 g equivalent^{-1}

45. (a) Glucose intake of 9% glucose solution

$= \frac{400 \times 9}{100}$ g per day

$= \frac{36}{24}$ g per hour

$= \frac{36}{24 \times 180}$ mol per hour

$= \frac{6.02 \times 10^{23}}{120}$ molecules per hour

$= 5.02 \times 10^{21}$

■ Molar mass of glucose ($C_6H_{12}O_6$)

$= 6 \times 12 + 12 \times 1 + 6 \times 16$

$= 180$ g mol^{-1}

1 mol = N_0 molecules

46. (a) $SCl_2 \equiv 2Cl$

$\therefore \quad 2\,Cl \equiv 1\,S$

$1\,Cl \equiv \frac{1S}{2}$ in $SCl_2 = 16$ g equiv^{-1}

In S_2Cl_2, $2Cl \equiv 2S$

$\therefore \quad 1\,Cl \equiv \frac{2S}{2}$

= S = 32 g equiv^{-1}

47. (c) Dibasic acid = 0.1 N (decinormal)

= 0.05 M

$0.05 \times 0.1\text{ dm}^3$ = mol

= 0.005 mol

■ $1\text{ dm}^3 = 1\text{ L}$

Molarity × Basicity = normality

Molarity × Volume in L = mole.

48. (c) 10 g glucose is in = 100 mL

$\frac{10}{180}$ mol glucose is in = 100 mL

$\therefore 0.1$ mol is in $= \frac{100 \times 180 \times 0.1}{10}$

= 180 mL

49. (d) Molar mass of solute = m_2

than molar mass of solvent = $0.1 m_2$

Solute = 10 g $= \frac{10}{m_2}$ mol

Solvent = 100 g $= \frac{100}{0.1\,m_2}$ mol

Total moles $= \frac{10}{m_2} + \frac{1000}{m_2} = \frac{1010}{m_2}$

$\therefore \quad X_{\text{solute}} = \frac{n(\text{solute})}{n(\text{solution})} = \frac{10/m_2}{\frac{1010}{m_2}}$

$= \frac{1}{101} = 9.9 \times 10^{-3}$

50. (d) Oxalic acid is a dibasic acid.

Thus, 0.5 M oxalic acid

= 1.0 N oxalic acid

$N_1V_1 = N_2V_2$

Oxalic acid NaOH

50 mL × 1N ≡ 50 mL × N_2

$\therefore \quad N_2$ (NaOH) = 1 N

NaOH = 1 equiv L^{-1}

= 1 mol L^{-1}

= 40 g L^{-1}

= 20 g in 500 mL

51. (b)

%	Mol	Ratio
X : 50%	5	2
Y : 50%	2.5	1

X and Y are in the molar ratio of 2 : 1.

Thus, X_2Y

52. (c) $CaCO_3 \equiv CaSO_4$

10^{-3} M $CaSO_4 \equiv 10^{-3}$ M $CaCO_3$

$= 10^{-3} \times 100$ g L^{-1}

= 0.1 g L^{-1}

$\therefore$ Hardness in 10^6 mL $= \frac{0.1}{10^3} \times 10^6$

= 100 ppm

53. (d) NaOH = 8 g $= \frac{8}{40} = 0.2$ mol

$H_2O = 18\text{ g} = \frac{18}{18} = 1.0$ mol

Total mol = 1.2 mol

$\therefore \chi_{\text{NaOH}} = \frac{0.2}{1.2} = 0.167$

$$\text{Molality} = \frac{\text{mol (NaOH)}}{\text{kg }(H_2O)} = \frac{0.2}{0.018}$$
$$= 11.11 \text{ mol kg}^{-1}$$

54. (d) $m = \dfrac{100\,M}{(1000\,d - Mm_2)}$

$$d = \frac{1}{1000}\left(\frac{1000M}{m} + Mm_2\right)$$
$$= \frac{1}{1000}\left[\frac{1000 \times 9}{10} + 9 \times 50\right]$$
$$= 1.35 \text{ g mL}^{-1}$$

■ $d = \dfrac{1}{1000}\left[\dfrac{1000M}{m} + Mm_2\right]$

m = molality

M = molarity

d = density (g mL^{-1})

m_2 = molar mass of solute

55. (d) 0.568 mm^3 S_8 crystal $= \dfrac{0.568}{1000}\text{ cm}^3$

Since, $\dfrac{\text{mass}}{\text{volme}} = \text{density}$

$\therefore$ Mass $= 0.568 \times 10^{-3} \times 2.07$ g

$$\text{Moles of } S_8 = \frac{0.568 \times 10^{-3} \times 2.07}{256}\text{mol}$$
$$= 4.59 \times 10^{-6} \text{ mol}$$

Molecules $= 4.59 \times 10^{-6} \times 6.02 \times 10^{23}$ S_8 molecules

$= 2.765 \times 10^{18}$ S_8 molecules

■ One mole of a species has N_0 molecules.

56. (a) $M(\text{resultant}) = \dfrac{M_1V_1 + M_2V_2}{V_1 + V_2}$

$$= \frac{0.5 \times 750 + 2 \times 250}{1000} = 0.875 \text{ M}$$

57. (d) Urea = 120 g $= \dfrac{120}{60} = 2$ mol

Water = 1000 g

$\therefore$ Solution $= 1000 + 120 = 1120$ g

$$= \frac{1120}{1.15}\text{ mL} = 0.9739 \text{ L}$$

$\therefore$ Molarity $= \dfrac{\text{Mole}}{\text{L}} = \dfrac{2}{0.9739}$

$= 2.05$ M

■ Volume $= \dfrac{\text{Mass}}{\text{Density}}$

58. (a) Molality $= \dfrac{\text{Mole}}{\text{kg}} = \dfrac{\frac{0.01}{60}}{0.3}$

$= 5.55 \times 10^{-4}$ M

■ 1 dm^3 = 1L = 1000 mL

= 1000 g = 1 kg

59. (a) 560 g Fe $= \dfrac{560}{50} = 10$ mol atoms Fe

= 10 Fe-atoms

70 g N $= \dfrac{70}{14} = 5$ mol N

= 5 N-atom correct.

20 g H = 20 mol

= 20 H atom incorrect.

(twice that of Fe)

60. (a) $CaH_2 + 2H_2O \longrightarrow Ca(OH)_2 + 2H_2$

1 mol 2 mol 2 mol

1 mol CaH_2 gives = 2 mol H_2

1 mol H_2O gives = 1 mol H_2

Thus, H_2O is limiting reactant and H_2 formed = 1 mol

61. (b) Na_2CO_3 is a diacid base.

0.1 M Na_2CO_3 = 0.2 N Na_2CO_3

25 mL of N_1 HCl ≡ 30 mL of 0.2 N Na_2CO_3

$$\therefore\ N_1\ (\text{HCl}) = \frac{30 \times 0.2}{25} = 0.24 \text{ N}$$

For NaOH, 0.2 M = 0.2 N

V mL of 0.24 N HCl

≡ 30 mL of 0.2 M NaOH

$$\therefore\ V = \frac{30 \times 0.2}{0.24} = 25 \text{ mL}$$

62. (b) K_2SO_4 in 135 mL of

0.188 M solution $= \dfrac{135 \times 0.188}{1000}$

= 0.02538 mol

Water is lost on evaporation but solute remains unaffected.

Thus, volume = 0.105 L

$$\therefore\ \text{Molarity} = \frac{0.02538}{0.105 \text{ L}}\text{ mol} = 0.2417 \text{ M}$$

63. (a) Let $CuSO_4 \cdot 5H_2O = x$ g

Then, $CuSO_4 = (1.245 - x)$ g

Water is lost from x g of hydrated salt.

$CuSO_4 \cdot 5H_2O \longrightarrow CuSO_4$

249.5 g gives 159.5 g $CuSO_4$

x g gives $\left(\dfrac{159.5x}{249.5}\right)$ g $CuSO_4$

$$\text{Then, } (1.245 - x) + \frac{159.5x}{249.5} = 0.882$$

$0.3607x = 0.363$ g

$\therefore$ $x \approx 1$ g

$\therefore$ Anhydrous salt = 1.245 − 1.000

= 0.245 g

$$\text{Per cent} = \frac{0.245}{1.245} \times 100 = 19.7\%$$

64. (d) $Fe_xO_y \longrightarrow x$Fe

$56x + 16y$ $56x$

0.5434 g 0.4224 g

$(56x + 16y)$ g Fe_xO_y gives $= 56x$ g Fe

$$\therefore 0.5434 \text{ g } Fe_xO_y \text{ gives} = \frac{(56x)(0.5434)}{(56x + 16y)}\text{g}$$
$$= 0.4224 \text{ g}$$
$$\frac{56x + 16y}{0.5434} = \frac{56x}{0.4224}$$
$$\frac{56x + 16y}{56x} = \frac{0.5434}{0.4224}$$
$$1 \times \frac{16y}{56x} = 1.2864$$
$$\frac{y}{x} = 1.0$$

Thus, FeO.

65. (b) $Ca(OH)_2 + CO_2 \longrightarrow CaCO_3 + H_2O$

1 mol 1 mol

$CaCO_3$ formed ≡ $Ca(OH)_2$ used.

50 mL of 0.5 M $Ca(OH)_2 = \dfrac{50 \times 0.5}{1000}$ mol

= 0.025 mol $Ca(OH)_2$ or $CaCO_3$

Ca^{2+} is divalent, hence 1 mol Ca^{2+} = 2 equivalents

$\therefore$ 0.025 mol $CaCO_3$

= 0.05 equivalents $CaCO_3$

$CaCO_3$ ≡ HCl

HCl used $= \dfrac{V \times 0.1}{1000}$ equivalent

$$\therefore\ \frac{V \times 0.1}{1000} = 0.05$$

$\therefore$ V = 500 mL

66. (d) $2Na + 2H_2O \longrightarrow 2NaOH$

Na ≡ NaOH

Thus, Na required = 0.02625 mol Na

$$= \frac{150 \times 0.175}{1000} = 0.02625 \text{ mol}$$

= 0.02625 × 23 g

= 0.604 g

67. (a) Solute X in 800 g solution

$$= \frac{800 \times 90}{100} = 320 \text{ g}$$

Solute X precipitated = 100 g

Solute left = 320 − 100 = 220 g

Solution = 800 − 100 = 700 g

$\therefore$ Per cent of X by weight of solution

$$= \frac{220}{700} \times 100 = 31.4\%$$

68. (b) $x\text{Mg} \xrightarrow{N_2} Mg_xN_2$ (Mg is divalent)

$24x$ $(24x + 28)$

0.273 0.378

Moles of Mg = Moles of Mg_3N_2

$$\frac{0.273}{24x} = \frac{0.378}{24x + 28}$$
$$\therefore\ \frac{24x + 28}{24x} = \frac{0.378}{0.273}$$

$\therefore$ $x = 3$

Thus, Mg_3N_2.

69. (b) $CO_2 + C \longrightarrow 2\,CO$

Initial 1 L

After conversion $(1-x)$ $2x$

$\therefore$ Total moles of CO and CO_2

$= (1 - x + 2x) = (1 + x)$

$\therefore$ $(1 + x) = 1.5$ L (given)

$x = 0.5$ L

$\therefore$ CO formed $= 2x = 1.0$ L

At S.T.P, 22.4L = 1 mol

$\therefore$ $1\text{ L} = \dfrac{1}{22.4}$ mol

70. (a) $CaCO_3 \longrightarrow CaO + CO_2$

1mol = 100 g 1 mol

25 g = 0.25 mol 0.25 mol

$2NaOH + CO_2 \longrightarrow Na_2CO_3$

1 mol 1 mol

0.25 mol 0.25 mol

Thus, $Na_2CO_3 = 0.25 \times 106\text{ g} = 26.5\text{ g}$

71. (d) $NH_2CONH_2 + 2\,NaOH \longrightarrow 2NH_3$

60 g 80 g 34 g

6 g 8 g 3.4 g

NH_2CONH_2 and NaOH are in exact quantity

Since, yield is 80%, thus NH_3 formed is

$= 3.4 \times \dfrac{80}{100}$

$= 2.72\text{ g }NH_3$

72. (b) $SO_2Cl_2 + 2H_2O \longrightarrow H_2SO_4 + 2HCl$

1 mol 1 mol 2 mol

$H_2SO_4 \equiv 2H^+,\ HCl \equiv 1H^+$

Thus, H^+ from 1 mol H_2SO_4

$= 2$ and H^+ from 2 mol HCl = 2

Total $H^+ = 3$ mol

Also, $H^+ \equiv OH^-$

Thus, NaOH required = 3 mol

■ Every mol of $Ca(OH)_2$ gives two mol OH^-

73. (b) $BaF_2 + H_2SO_4 \longrightarrow BaSO_4 + 2HF$

1 mol 1 mol 2 mol

H_2SO_4 taken = 2 mol

H_2SO_4 unreacted in mixture

$= 1\text{ mol} = 2H^+$ mol.

Thus, KOH required = 2 mol by 2 mol HF and 2 moles by 1 mol H_2SO_4 = 4 mol

74. (c) $(NH_4)_2CO_3 \equiv 8\text{ mol }H^+$

1 mol

$= 8 \times 6.02 \times 10^{23}$ H atoms

6.02×10^{23} H-atoms are contained in

$= \dfrac{1}{8}\text{ mol }(NH_4)_2CO_3$

$= \dfrac{1}{8} \times 96\text{ g }(NH_4)_2CO_3 = 12\text{ g}$

75. (b) 1 mol $CH_4O = 6\,N_0$ total atoms of C, H and O.

1 mol $SO_2 = 3\,N_0$ total atoms of S and O.

Thus, 2 mol of SO_2 has total $= 6\,N_0$ atom.

76. (b) $O_2 = wg = \dfrac{w}{32}\text{ mol} = \dfrac{wN_0}{32}$ molecules

$N_2 = 4wg = \dfrac{4w}{28}$ mol

$= \dfrac{4wN_0}{28}\text{ molecules} = \dfrac{wN_0}{7}$

Thus, ratio $= \dfrac{1/32}{1/7} = 7 : 32$

77. (a) N_{acid} (resultant)

$= \dfrac{2x + 50 \times 4 + 62.5 \times 4}{1000} = \dfrac{2x + 450}{1000}$

For neutralisation,

$N_1V_1 = N_2V_2$

$50 \times \left(\dfrac{2x + 450}{1000}\right) \equiv 25 \times 0.5\text{ M }Na_2CO_3$

$\equiv 25 \times 1.0\text{ N }Na_2CO_3$

$x = 25$ mL

■ $2M\ H_2SO_4 = 4\ N\ H_2SO_4$

$0.5\ M\ Na_2CO_3 = 1.0\ N\ Na_2CO_3$

78. (d) Let Li_2CO_3 be $= x\text{ g} = \dfrac{x}{74}$ mol

$M_2CO_3 = (2 - x)$ g

$= \dfrac{2 - x}{(2M + 60)}$ mol

Total moles $= \dfrac{x}{74} + \left(\dfrac{2 - x}{2M + 60}\right)$

H_2SO_4 required $= \dfrac{21.6 \times 0.5}{1000}$ mol = 0.0108

Also, moles are equal $\dfrac{x}{74} = \dfrac{2 - x}{2M + 60}$

$\therefore$ $\dfrac{2x}{74} = 0.0108$

$x = 0.40$ g

Thus, $\dfrac{0.40}{74} = \dfrac{1.6}{2M + 60}$

$\therefore$ $M = 118.14\text{ g mol}^{-1}$

79. (b) $CaO + Ca(HCO_3)_2 \rightarrow 2CaCO_3 + H_2O$

56g Temporary hardness 200 g

0.056 g of lime (CaO) required then hardness is $= \dfrac{200}{56} \times 0.056$ g in terms of $CaCO_3$ of = 0.20 g prescott in 1 L hard water

Thus, $CaCO_3$ in ppm $= \dfrac{0.20 \times 10^6}{10^3}$

$= 200$ ppm

■ Temporary hardness is due to $Ca(HCO_3)_2$, which can be removed by CaO.

80. (a) $CaCl_2 \longrightarrow CaCO_3$

1 mol 1 mol

111 g 100 g

1.11 mg 1.0 mg

$MgCl_2 \longrightarrow MgCO_3 \longrightarrow CaCO_3$

95 g 84 g 100 g

0.95 mg 0.84 mg 1.00 mg

Thus, hardness in terms of $CaCO_3$

$= 1.00 + 1.00 = 2.0$ mg

$= 2.0 \times 10^{-3}$ g per litre

Hence, hardness in ppm $= \dfrac{2.0 \times 10^{-3}}{10^3} \times 10^6$

$= 2.0$ ppm

81. (d) 200 ppm $CaCO_3$ means 10^6 g H_2O has $CaCO_3 = 200$ g

(a) Mass ratio of $CaCO_3$ to H_2O

$= \dfrac{200}{10^6} = 2 \times 10^{-4}$

Thus, correct.

(b) Mole ratio of $CaCO_3$ to $H_2O = \dfrac{\dfrac{200}{100}}{\dfrac{10^6}{18}}$

$= 3.6 \times 10^{-5}$

Thus, correct.

(c) $CaCO_3 = 200$ g in 10^6 mL

$= 0.200$ g in 10^3 mL

Thus, correct.

(d) 10^6 g has = 200 g $CaCO_3$

$\dfrac{200}{100} = 2\text{ mol }CaCO_3$

$= 4$ equiv $CaCO_3$

10^3 g has $= 4 \times 10^{-3}$ equiv.

$= 4$ milliequiv.

Thus, incorrect.

■ Ca^{2+} is a divalent cation, thus 1 mol $CaCO_3$ = 2 equivalents $CaCO_3$

82. (c) $NaClO_3 \longrightarrow NaCl + \dfrac{3}{2}O_2$

O_2 lost due to heating = 0.16 g $= \dfrac{0.16}{32}$ mol

$= 5 \times 10^{-3}$ mol

Thus, NaCl formed $= \dfrac{2}{3}$ mol of O_2 lost

$= \dfrac{2}{3} \times 5 \times 10^{-3}$

$= \dfrac{10}{3} \times 10^{-3}$ mol

$NaCl + AgNO_3 \longrightarrow AgCl + NaNO_3$

Thus, AgCl formed $= \dfrac{10}{3} \times 10^{-3}$ mol

$= \dfrac{10}{3} \times 10^{-3} \times 143.5$

$= 0.48$ g

83. (a) 100 mL of H_2SO_4 solution has

$= 80 \text{ g } H_2SO_4$

or (100×1.8) g of H_2SO_4 solution has

$= 80 \text{ g } H_2SO_4$

$\therefore$ Solvent $(H_2O) = 180 - 80 = 100$ g

$= 0.10$ kg

Solute $(H_2SO_4) = 80 \text{ g} = \frac{80}{98}$ mol

$\therefore$ Molality $= \frac{\frac{80}{98}\text{ mol}}{0.1 \text{ kg}} = 8.16 \text{ mol kg}^{-1}$

84. (a) NaOH = 10 g in 100 mL

$= \left(\frac{10}{40}\right)$ mol in 100 mL

$\therefore M(\text{NaOH})\text{ mol/litre} = \frac{10/40}{0.100}$ M

$= 2.5$ M

Similarly $M(\text{HCl}) = \frac{10/36.5}{0.10}\text{M} = 2.74\text{M}$

M_1V_1 (acid) $= 2.74 \times 100$

M_2V_2 (base) $= 2.50 \times 100$

Since, $M_1V_1 > M_2V_2$

Thus, mixture is acidic.

$M(\text{resultant}) = \frac{M_1V_1 - M_2V_2}{V_1 + V_2}$

$= \frac{2.74 - 2.50}{200} \times 100$

$= 0.12$ M in terms of H^+

85. (d) $\underset{\substack{1 \text{ mol urea} \\ 0.6 \text{ g} = 0.01 \text{ mol}}}{NH_2CONH_2} + 2NaOH \longrightarrow \underset{2 \text{ mol}}{2NH_3} + Na_2CO_3$

1 mol urea gives = 2 mol NH_3

Thus, 0.01 mol urea gives = 0.02 mol NH_3

As $\frac{NV}{1000}$ = mol for HCl

$\therefore$ (a) $\frac{200 \times 0.2}{1000} = 0.04$ mol

(b) $\frac{200 \times 0.4}{1000} = 0.08$ mol

(c) $\frac{100 \times 0.1}{1000} = 0.01$ mol

(d) $\frac{100 \times 0.2}{1000} = 0.02$ mol

Thus, (d) is correct.

86. (d) 200 mL of 0.1 M H_2SO_4

= 200 mL of 0.2 N H_2SO_4

Resultant mixture is acidic due to H_2SO_4

0.07 M H_2SO_4 = 0.14 N.

If NaOH added be = V mL

then total volume = $(200 + V)$ mL

$0.14 \text{ N } H_2SO_4 = \frac{200 \times 0.2 - V \times 0.1}{(200 + V)}$

$\therefore$ $V = 50$ mL

87. (a) $CHCl_3$ = 0.10 ppb (parts per billion)

$= 0.10 \text{ g in } 10^9 \text{ mL } H_2O$

$= \frac{0.10}{10^9}$ g in 1 mL H_2O

$= \frac{0.10}{119.5 \times 10^9}$ mol in 1 mL H_2O

$= 8.368 \times 10^{-13} \text{ mol mL}^{-1}$

$= 8.368 \times 10^{-13} \times 6.02 \times 10^{23}$ $CHCl_3$ molecular mL^{-1}

$= 5.04 \times 10^{11}$ molecules mL^{-1}

■ 1 mol = N_0 molecules

88. (b) A : $15 \times 40 \text{ g L}^{-1}$

15×40 g in 1000 g ($d = 1 \text{ g mL}^{-1}$)

$\frac{15 \times 40}{1000} \times 5$ g in 5 g solution = 3 g NaOH

B : mass of 5 mL NaOH solution

$= \frac{50}{100} \times 5 = 2.5$ g

C : 5g of NaOH $= \frac{5}{1.25}$ mL = 4.0 mL

Thus, 40% NaOH is 4.0 mL = 1.6 g

Thus, $C < B < A$

89. (c) Equivalent mass = 4

Vapour density of MCl_x = 59.25

Equivalent mass of its chloride

= 35.5 + 4.0 = 39.5

Molar mass = 59.25 × 2 = 118.50

Thus, valency $= \frac{118.50}{39.50} = 3$

■ Chloride is monovalent.

90. (c) Equivalent mass of divalent cation = E

Its molar mass = $2E$

Molar mass of its oxide = $(2E + 16)$

Molar mass of its chloride = $(2E + 71)$

Thus, $2(E + 8)$ and $2(E + 35.5)$

91. (b)

	Isotope	Atomic mass	Proton	Neutron
A.	${}^1_1H$	1	1	0 (x)
B.	${}^2_1H$	2	1	1 (y)
C.	${}^3_1H$	3	1	2 (z)

Thus, $(x) + (y) + (z) = 3$

92. (b) If mole fraction of $NO_2 = X_1$ then mole fraction of $N_2O_4 = 1 - X_1$

$55.2 = \frac{46 X_1 + 92(1 - X_1)}{1}$

$\therefore$ $X_1 = 0.8$

$\therefore$ Mole fraction of $N_2O_4 = 0.2$

93. (b) One mole of element A is half that of ${}^{16}_8O$.

Thus, atomic mass of $A = \frac{16}{2} = 8.0$

Element B is 1.5 times heavier than A

Thus, atomic mass of $B = 1.5 \times 8.0$

$= 12.0$

94. (b) Molar mass of $HXO_2 = H + X + 2(O)$

$= 1 + x + 32$

$= (33 + x)$

$\therefore$ 1.695 g $HXO_2 = \frac{1.695}{(33 + X)}$ mol

$\therefore$ $\frac{1.695}{(33 + X)} = 0.015$

$\therefore$ $(33 + X) = \frac{1.695}{0.015} = 113$

$\therefore$ $X = 80.0$

95. (c) Salt is $MSO_4 \cdot 7H_2O$

Molar mass = $M + 96 + 126$

Percentage of M

$9.87 = \frac{100\ M}{(M + 96 + 126)}$

$\therefore$ $M = 24.3$

96. (a) Mass of one mol of proton

$= 1.675 \times 10^{-24} \times 6.02 \times 10^{23} \text{ g mol}^{-1}$

Number of mol in 1000 g

$= \frac{1000}{1.675 \times 10^{-24} \times 6.02 \times 10^{23}}$

$= \frac{10^4}{1.675 \times 6.02}$

97. (c) Molarity of x volume H_2O_2

Molarity $= \frac{x}{11.2} = \frac{5.6}{11.2} = 0.5$ M

$\underset{1 \text{ mol}}{H_2O_2} \longrightarrow H_2O + \underset{0.5 \text{ mol } = 11200 \text{ mL at NTP}}{\frac{1}{2}O_2}$

5.6 volume H_2O_2 means that 1 mL of H_2O_2 on decomposition gives 5.6 mL O_2 at NTP.

From stoichiometry :

11200 mL O_2 is formed from = 1 mol H_2O_2

$= 34 \text{ g } H_2O_2$

$\therefore$ 5.6 mL O_2 is formed from

$= \frac{34}{11200} \times 5.6 \text{ g } H_2O_2$

$= 0.017 \text{ g } H_2O_2$

This amount is in 1 mL H_2O_2

or 1 g H_2O_2. ($d = 1 \text{ g mL}^{-1}$)

Thus, mass percentage $= \frac{0.017}{1} \times 100$

$= 1.7\%$

98. (c) $\chi_{solute} + \chi_{solvent} = 1.0$

$\chi_{solvent}(H_2O) = 0.8$

$\chi_{solute} = 0.2$

$\therefore \quad \frac{\chi_{solvent}}{\chi_{solute}} = \frac{n_1}{n_2} = \frac{0.8}{0.2} = \frac{4}{1}$

This if solvent (H_2O) 16 = 4 mol

= 4 × 18 = 72 g = 0.072 kg

then solute = 1 mol.

$\text{Molality} = \frac{\text{moles of solate}}{\text{kg solvent}}$

$= \frac{1 \text{ mol}}{0.072 \text{ kg}} = 13.88 \text{ kg mol}^{-1}$

99. (d) For 'χ' volume H_2O_2

$\text{Molarity} = \frac{\chi}{11.2} \text{mol L}^{-1}$

χ = '11.2' volume

$\therefore$ Molarity = 1 mol L^{-1}

$= 1 \times 34 \text{ g L}^{-1} = 34 \text{ g L}^{-1}$

= 3.4 g in 100 mL

Thus, 3.4%

100. (d) 1 mol $Ca(HCO_3)_2 \equiv 2$ mol $CaCO_3$

0.81 g $Ca(HCO_3)_2$

$= \frac{0.81}{162}$ mol $Ca(HCO_3)_2$

= 0.01 mol $CaCO_3$

0.73 g $Mg(HCO_3)_2$

$= \frac{0.73}{146}$ mol $Mg(HCO_3)_2$

= 0.01 mol $CaCO_3$

Total $CaCO_3$ = 0.02 mol = 0.02 × 100 g

= 2 g $CaCO_3$ in 100 mL

Thus, 100 mL water sample has $CaCO_3$ = 2g Ca

$\therefore 10^6$ mL water has

$CaCO_3 = \frac{2}{100} \times 10^6 = 20{,}000$ ppm

101. (a) $N_2(g) + 3H_2(g) \longrightarrow 2NH_3(g)$

1 mol 3 mol 2 mol

(a) 56 g N_2 = 2 mol N_2 give

= 4 mol NH_3

10 g H_2 = 5 mol H_2

give $= \frac{2}{3} \times 5 = 3.3$ mol NH_3

H_2 is the limiting reagent

(b) 35 g N_2 = 1.25 mol N_2 give

= 2.5 mol NH_3

8 g H_2 = 4 mol $N_2 = \frac{2}{3} \times 4$

= 2.66 mol NH_3

N_2 is the limiting reagent

(c) 14 g N_2 = 0.5 mol N_2 give

= 1.0 mol NH_3

4 g H_2 = 2 mol H_2 give

= 1.33 mol NH_3

N_2 is the limiting reagent

(d) 28 g N_2 = 1 mol N_2 give

= 2.0 mol NH_3

6 g H_2 = 3 mol H_2 give

= 2.0 mol NH_3

Thus, exact

102. (c) MnO = 66.67% mol

MnO_2 = 33.33% mol

Mn in 0.6667 mol of MnO

$= \frac{55}{71} \times 0.6667 = 0.51$ g

Mn in 0.3333 mol MnO_2

$= \frac{55}{87} \times 0.3333 = 0.21$ g

Total = 0.72 g

Thus, % = 72%

Acid Test for JEE Advanced

Type I. MCQs with Only One Correct Alternate

103. (a) Since, $\frac{\text{molarity} \times \text{volume}}{1000} = \text{mol}$

$\text{HCl used} = \frac{100 \times 2.5}{1000} = 0.25 \text{ mol}$

$MO + 2HCl \longrightarrow MCl_2 + H_2O$

(M = Ca, Br)

Thus, metal oxides used

$= \frac{1}{2}$ mol of HCl = 0.125 mol

If amount of BaO = x mol = 153x g

then amount of CaO = (0.125 − x) mol

= 56(0.125 − x) g

$\therefore 153x + 56(0.125 - x) = 10.0$

x = 0.0309 mol BaO

$X_{BaO} = \frac{\text{Mol of BaO}}{\text{Total moles}} = \frac{0.0309}{0.125} = 0.25$

104. (d) $FeS_2 + O_2 \longrightarrow 2SO_2$

120 g 128 g

1 mol 2 mol

FeS_2 in 10^3 kg coal containing 0.050% FeS_2

$= \frac{1000 \times 0.050}{100}$ kg

$= 0.50 \text{ kg} = 500 \text{ g} = \frac{500}{120} = 4.17$ mol

SO_2 from 4.17 mol FeS_2 = 8.34 mol

$2NaOH + SO_2 \longrightarrow Na_2SO_3 + H_2O$

80 g 64 g

2 mol 1 mol

NaOH required by 8.34 mol SO_2

= 16.67 mol

Since, molarity × volume (L) = mol

Thus, M × V (litre) = 16.67

6V = 16.67

V = 2.78 L

105. (b) **Case I** Let excess base be = V mL

Since, $N_1V_1 = N_2V_2$

V mL of 2.0 M NaOH

= 4.3 mL of 0.5 M HCl

$\therefore \quad V = 1.075$ mL

Thus, NaOH used = 15.0 − 1.075

= 13.925 mL

Then 13.925 mL of 2 M NaOH

$\equiv$ 10 mL N of H_2SO_4

$\therefore \quad N(H_2SO_4) = 2.785$ N

Since, for H_2SO_4 molarity × normality

$M(H_2SO_4) = 1.3925$ M

106. (c) Number of moles of HCl $= \frac{M \times V(\text{mL})}{1000}$

$\text{HCl} = \frac{20 \times 6}{1000} \text{mol} = 0.12 \text{ mol}$

= 0.12 equiv. HCl being monobasic

$Ba(OH)_2 = \frac{50 \times 2}{1000} \text{mol} = 0.10 \text{ mol}$

= 0.20 equiv. $Ba(OH)_2$ being diacid base

Solution diluted to 100 mL.

Since, $N_1V_1(Ba(OH)_2) > N_2V_2(HCl)$

Mixture is basic

Equivalent $[OH^-]$ = 0.20 − 0.12 = 0.08

0.08 equivalent is in 100 mL

$\therefore \quad [OH^-] = \frac{0.08 \times 1000}{100} = 0.8$ M

$Ba(OH)_2 + 2HCl \longrightarrow BaCl_2 + 2H_2O$

$BaCl_2$ formed = $Ba(OH)_2$ taken

= 0.10 mol in 100 mL

= 1.0 mol in 1000 mL

$\therefore \quad [Ba^{2+}] = 1.0$ M

$[Cl^-]$ from HCl = 0.12 mol in 100 mL

= 1.2 mol in 1000 mL

$[Cl^-] = 1.2$ M

107. (a) $m = \frac{1000M}{(1000d - Mm_2)} = 2.0$ m

108. (a) $Mg + \frac{1}{2}O_2 \longrightarrow MgO$

1 mol 0.5 mol

24 g 16 g

Taken 1.0g 0.56 g

0.0417 mol 0.0175 mol

O_2 required by 0.0417 mol Mg $= \frac{0.0417}{2}$

= 0.02085 mol

Mg required by 0.0175 mol O_2
= 0.0350 mol

Thus, O_2 is the limiting reactant and Mg is in excess.

Used Mg = Mg taken − Mg required
= 0.0417 − 0.0350 = 0.0067 mol
= 0.0067 × 24 g = 0.1608 g

109. (a) Convert each amount in mol

6.02×10^{23} molecules = 1 mol

$\therefore\ 1.00 \times 10^{21}$ molecules $= \dfrac{1.0 \times 10^{21}}{6.0 \times 10^{23}}$
$= 1.67 \times 10^{-3}$ mol

200 mg $CO_2 = 200 \times 10^{-3}$ g
$= \dfrac{200 \times 10^{-3}}{44}$ mol $= 4.55 \times 10^{-3}$ mol

$\therefore$ CO_2 left $= (4.55 - 1.67) \times 10^{-3}$
$= 2.88 \times 10^{-3}$ mol

110. (b) $\underset{1\text{ mol}}{Mg_3(PO_4)_2} \equiv 8$ mol (O) atoms

8 mol (O) atoms are in 1 mol $Mg_3(PO_4)_2$

$\therefore$ 0.25 mol (O) are in
$= \dfrac{1}{8} \times 0.25 = 3.125 \times 10^{-2}$

111. (b) 10^6 g (or mL) solution has Fe^{2+} = 1 g

$\therefore$ 250 mL solution has Fe^{2+}
$= 250 \times 10^{-6}$ g
$= \dfrac{250 \times 10^{-6}}{56}$ mol
$= 4.464 \times 10^{-6}$ mol

$\therefore$ $FeSO_4(NH_4)_2SO_4 \cdot 6H_2O$
$= 4.464 \times 10^{-6} \times 392$g
$= 1.75 \times 10^{-3}$g

■ Each mol of double salt has one mol Fe^{2+}

112. (b) When one solution of given percentage and density is diluted to lower percentage and density then

$V_1 \times (\%)_1 \times d_1 = V_2 \times (\%)_2 \times d_2$

$V_1 \times (98) \times 1.84 = 100 \times 20 \times 1.14$

$\therefore\quad V_1 = \dfrac{100 \times 20 \times 1.14}{98 \times 1.84}$
= 12.64 mL

■ Molarity in terms of % and density
$= \dfrac{(\%) \times 10d}{\text{molar mass}}$
$= \dfrac{98 \times 10 \times 1.84}{98} = 18.4$ M

For 20% solution,

Molarity $= \dfrac{20 \times 10 \times 1.14}{98} = 2.326$M

$\therefore\quad M_1V_1 = M_2V_2$
$18.4V_1 = 2.326 \times 100$
$V_1 = 12.64$ mL

113. (c)

$$\underset{\substack{1\text{ mol}\\ \frac{100}{12} = 8.33\text{ mol}}}{C} + \underset{\substack{1\text{ mol}\\ \frac{100}{32} = 3.125\text{ mol}}}{O_2} \longrightarrow \underset{\substack{1\text{ mol}\\ ?}}{CO_2}$$

CO_2 formed by 8.33 mol C = 8.33 mol

CO_2 formed by 3.125 mol O_2 = 3.125 mol

Thus, O_2 is the limiting reactant and C is in excess.

Thus, CO_2 formed = 3.125 mol

$$\underset{1\text{ mol}}{C} + \underset{1\text{ mol}}{\frac{1}{2}O_2} \longrightarrow \underset{1\text{ mol}}{CO}$$

If CO is formed, then also O_2 is the limiting reactant and CO formed by 3.125 mol O_2 = 6.250 mol

114. (c) $C + O_2 \longrightarrow CO_2$

$2C + O_2 \longrightarrow 2\,CO$

CO_2 is formed or CO is formed, that will depend on the quantity of O_2 taken.

Carbon $= \dfrac{60}{12} = 5$ mol

Oxygen $= \dfrac{100}{32} = 3.125$ mol

If all the O_2 is consumed.

CO_2 formed = 3.125 mol

Carbon left = 5.0 − 3.125 = 1.875 mol

CO_2 can further react with unreacted carbon to form CO.

$$\underset{1.875\text{ mol}}{C} + \underset{3.125\text{ mol}}{CO_2} \longrightarrow 2\,CO$$

Carbon reacted = 1.875 mol

CO formed (twice of C-reacted) = 2 × 1.875
= 3.75 mol

CO_2 left unreacted = 3.125 − 1.875
= 1.250 mol

115. (a) $P_4 = 2\text{ g} = \dfrac{2}{124}$ mol = 0.0161 mol

$O_2 = 2\text{ g} = \dfrac{2}{32}$ mol = 0.0625 mol

If P_4O_6 is formed

$$\underset{\substack{1\text{ mol}\\0.0161\text{ mol}}}{P_4} + \underset{\substack{3\text{ mol}\\3 \times 0.0161\text{ mol}}}{3O_2} \longrightarrow \underset{\substack{1\text{ mol}\\0.0161\text{ mol}}}{P_4O_6}$$

All the P_4 is consumed.

O_2 consumed = 3 × 0.0161 = 0.0483 mol

O_2 left unreacted = 0.0625 − 0.0483
= 0.0142 mol

P_4O_6 formed = 0.0161 mol

Thus P_4O_6 may combine with unused O_2 to form P_4O_{10}.

$$\underset{1\text{ mol}}{P_4O_6} + \underset{2\text{ mol}}{2O_2} \longrightarrow \underset{1\text{ mol}}{P_4O_{10}}$$

2 mol O_2 combine with = 1 mol P_4O_6

$\therefore$ 0.0142 mol O_2 combines with
= 0.0071 mol P_4O_6

Thus, P_4O_{10} formed = 0.0071 mol

P_4O_6 unreacted = 0.0161 − 0.0071
= 0.009 mol

116. (a) $3CuSO_4 + 2Al \longrightarrow Al_2(SO_4)_3 + 3Cu$

Amount of $CuSO_4$ = 2 × 1.50 = 3.0 mol

Amount of Al $= \dfrac{40}{27} = 1.48$ mol

From reaction,

Al required by 3.0 mol of $CuSO_4$
= 2.0 mol

$CuSO_4$ required by 1.48 mol Al
$= \dfrac{3}{2} \times 1.48 = 2.22$ mol

Thus, Al is the limiting reagent.

$CuSO_4$ reacted = Cu formed
= 2.22 mol

■ Molarity × volume (in L) = mol

117. (b) Let 2.50 M NaOH be = V L

Then, 0.40 M NaOH = $(3 - V)$ L

$[NaOH]_{mix} = \dfrac{2.50V + (3 - V)\,0.4}{3}$

$1 \times 3 = 2.50\,V + (3 - V)\,0.4$

$\therefore\quad V = 0.86$ L

118. (d) 3.78 g NaCl in 100 mL
$= \dfrac{3.78}{58.5}$ mol in 100 mL
= 0.0646 mol in 100 mL

As one mole of NaCl gives one mole of Cl^-, hence

$\therefore\quad (Cl^-) = 0.0646$ mol in 100 mL

Also, every $BaCl_2$ gives $2Cl^-$, hence

$\therefore [BaCl_2] = \dfrac{0.0646}{2}$ mol in 100 mL
$= \dfrac{0.0646}{2} \times \dfrac{250}{100}$ mol in 250 mL
= 0.08077 mol $BaCl_2$ in 250 mL

0.08077 × 208 g = 16.8 g

■ Every $BaCl_2$ furnishes two Cl^- ions.

119. (c)

$$BaCl_2 + \underset{\substack{98\text{ g}\\?}}{H_2SO_4} \longrightarrow \underset{\substack{\text{white ppt.}\\233\text{ g}\\4.08\text{ g}}}{BaSO_4\downarrow} + 2HCl$$

233 g $BaSO_4$ is from = 98 g H_2SO_4

$\therefore$ 4.08 g $BaSO_4$ is from
$= \dfrac{98}{233} \times 4.08$ g H_2SO_4
= 1.716 g H_2SO_4 in 4 g solution

$\therefore$ % $H_2SO_4 = \dfrac{1.716}{4} \times 100 = 42.9\%$

or 43.0%

120. (b) 1 L of urea solution = 1000 mL

$= 1000 \times 1.2 = 1200$ g

Residue (urea) = 120 g = $\frac{120}{60}$ = 2 mol

∴ Water (solvent) = 1200 − 120 = 1080 g = 1.80 kg

∴ Molality $\left(\frac{mol}{kg}\right) = \frac{2}{1.08}$ mol/kg = 1.852 mol kg^{-1}

121. (b) If 36 g carbon, then molar mass = 100

If 24 g carbon, then molar mass

$= \frac{100 \times 24}{36} = 66.67$ g mol^{-1}

Moles in 10 g = $\frac{\text{Mass}}{\text{Molar mass}} = \frac{10}{66.67}$ = 0.15 mol

122. (b) NaCl in 300 g of 25% NaCl solution = 75 g

NaCl in 150 g of 40% solution = 60 g

Total NaCl = 135 g

Total solution = 450 g

∴ % = $\frac{135}{450} \times 100 = 30\%$

123. (b) $n = \frac{pV}{RT} = \frac{1 \times 0.112}{0.0821 \times 273} = 0.005$ mol

$= 3.01 \times 10^{21}$ molecules NO_2

Also, 0.005 mol = 0.005 × 46 g = 0.23 g

$= \frac{0.23}{1.15}$ g/gmL^{-1} = 0.2 mL

■ 1 mol of a gas = N_0 molecules = 6.02×10^{23} molecules

124. (a) $2X \longrightarrow X_2O_5$

$2X$ $(2X + 80)$

2.0769 g 3.6769 g

∴ $\frac{2X}{2.0769} = \frac{2X + 80}{3.6769}$

∴ X (atomic weight of X) = 51.92 g mol^{-1}

∴ 2.0709 g = $\frac{2.0769}{51.92}$ mol X = 0.04 mol X

125. (d) $YBa_2Cu_3O_7$

Thus, $Y_2O_3 = \frac{1}{2} = 0.5 = 1.0$

$BaO_2 = 2 = 2.0 = 4.0$

$Cu_2O = 1.5 = 1.5 = 3.0$

126. (c) $^{14}_{6}C$

	Original	If changed
Neutron	= 8	4
Proton	= 6	12

Total mass = 4 + 12 = 16 units

Excess mass = 16 − 14 = 2 units

∴ % increase = $\frac{2}{14} \times 100 = 14.28\%$

127. (a) 1 mol H_2O

$= 18$ g $H_2O = 18$ g × 1 g mL^{-1} = 18 mL

Also, 1 mol $H_2O = N_0$ molecules = 6.0×10^{23} molecules

Volume of 6.0×10^{23} molecules = 18 mL

∴ Volume of 1.0×10^6 molecules

$= \frac{18 \times 1.0 \times 10^6}{6.0 \times 10^{23}} = 3.0 \times 10^{-17}$ mL

128. (a) 2.37 mg mL^{-1} N = 2.37×10^{-3} g mL^{-1}N

$= 2.37$ g L^{-1} N = $\frac{2.37}{14}$ mol L^{-1} N

$\frac{2.37}{28}$ mol L^{-1} NH_4NO_3

(every NH_4NO_3 has two N-atoms).

Thus, for dilution V mL of 0.715 M NH_4NO_3 = 1000 mL of $\frac{2.37}{28}$ M NH_4NO_3

∴ $V = 118.4$ mL

129. (b) 6 micromol = 6×10^{-6} mol

6.0×10^{-6} mol Na_2SO_4 in 250 mL

12.0×10^{-6} mol Na^+ in 250 mL solution

$12 \times 10^{-6} \times 23$ g Na^+ in 250 mL solution

Thus, Na^+ (ppm) = $\frac{12 \times 10^{-6} \times 10^6 \times 23 \text{ g}}{250}$ = 1.104 ppm

■ 1 ppm ⇒ 1 parts is 10^6 parts

130. (b)

	N_2	+ $3H_2$	$\longrightarrow$ $2NH_3$
Initial	1	4	0
After reaction	$(1-x)$	$(4-3x)$	$2x$

$HCl \equiv NH_3 \equiv 1$ mol

Thus, $2x = 1$ mol, $x = 0.5$

■ H_2O dissolves NH_3 to form NH_4OH.

Thus, only N_2 and H_2 remain

$N_2 = (1 - x) = 0.5$ mol

$H_2 = (4 - 3x) = 2.5$ mol

Total moles = 3.0 mol

∴ $X_{H_2} = \frac{2.5}{3.0} = \frac{5}{6}$

131. (a) 100 mL of 0.50 M KCl

$= \frac{100 \times 0.50}{1000}$ mol KCl = 0.05 mol KCl

100 mL of 0.40 M KCl = $\frac{100 \times 0.4}{1000}$ = 0.04 mol KCl

Extra KCl required = 0.05 − 0.04 = 0.01 mol = 0.745 g

132. (b) $2Cu + O_2 \longrightarrow 2CuO$ (valency = + 2)

$2Cu + \frac{1}{2}O_2 \longrightarrow Cu_2O$ (valency = + 1)

Thus, 2 : 1.

133. (a) $M + H^+ \longrightarrow M^{n+} + H_2$

Equivalent of metal ≡ equivalent of H_2 displaced.

Equivalent volume of H_2 at STP

$= \frac{22.4}{2} = 11.2$ L

11.2 L H_2 is from = 28 g M

0.7 L H_2 is from = 1.750 g

■ 1 equivalents H_2 = 1g H_2 = 0.5 mol H_2

Thus, equivalent volume of 0.5 mol H_2 at STP = 11.2 L

134. (b) $M(\text{Fe}) = \frac{54 \times 5 + 56 \times 90 + 57 \times 5}{100}$ = 55.95

135. (d) M (mixture in ratio $a : b$)

$69.33 = \frac{64a + 80b}{(a + b)}$ (I)

M' (mixture in ratio $b : a$) = $\frac{64b + 80a}{(a + b)}$ (II)

Divide (II) by (I)

∴ $\frac{M'}{69.33} = \frac{64b + 80a}{64a + 80b} = \frac{4b + 5a}{4a + 5b}$ (III)

From (I) $5.33a = 10.67b$

∴ $a = 2b$

Thus, $\frac{M'}{69.33} = \frac{14b}{13b} = \frac{14}{13}$

∴ $M' = 74.67$

136. (d) If $(V_1 + V_2) = 75$ mL

then $V_3 = 25$ mL

If $V_1 = x$ L

then $V_2 = (75 - x)$ mL

∴ $\frac{M_1V_1 + M_2V_2 + M_3V_3}{V_1 + V_2 + V_3} = M$ (Mixture)

$\frac{0.07x + 0.12\,(75 - x) + 0.15 \times 25}{100} = 0.50$

$0.07x + 9 - 0.12x + 3.75 = 10$

$x = 55$ mL

∴ $V_1 = 55$ mL

$V_2 = 20$ mL

$V_3 = 25$ mL

137. (c) 1 mol $(NH_4)_3PO_4 \equiv 12$ mol H ≡ 4 mol O

If 12 mol H then O is = 4 mol

where, 3.18 mol H ≡ $\frac{4}{12} \times 3.18$ = 1.060 mol O-atom

138. (b) Lewisite is a tear gas.

H = 2 atoms and C = 2 atoms

Mass of one Cl atom = $\frac{35.5}{6.02 \times 10^{23}}$ = 5.897×10^{-23} g

Thus, Cl atoms = $\frac{1.78 \times 10^{-22}}{5.897 \times 10^{-23}} = 3$

Mass of 1.25×10^{-22} g of metal
$= 1$ molecule

$\therefore$ Mass of 6.02×10^{23} molecules
$=$ molar mass
$= 1.25 \times 10^{-22} \times 6.02 \times 10^{23}$
$= 75.25 \text{ g mol}^{-1}$

Molar mass $= 2 + 24 + 3 \times 35.5 + 75.25$
≈ 208.0

139. (a) $NaOH = \frac{100 \times 0.1}{1000}$ mol $= 0.01$ mol

$HCl = \frac{50 \times 0.2}{1000}$3 mol $= 0.01$ mol

$NaOH + HCl \longrightarrow NaCl + H_2O$
1 mol   1 mol   1 mol

Both are in exact quantity.

Thus, NaCl formed $= 0.01$ mol
$= 0.01 \times 58.5$ g
$= 0.585$ g

140. (d) From III, $CaCN_2$ required $= 2$ mol if yield is 50%

From II, CaC_2 required $= 2$ mol if yield is 100% for 2 mol of $CaCN_2$

From I, Ca required $= 4$ mol if yield is 50% for 2 mol CaC_2

141. (b) From I, O_2 formed $= 1.5$ mol as $KClO_3$ is 50% pure.

From II, 3 mol O_2 give $= 2$ mol Al_2O_3
Al_2O_3 formed $= 1$ mol from 1.5 mol O_2

142. (a) $Zn + H_2SO_4 \longrightarrow ZnSO_4 + H_2$

$Zn + 2NaOH \longrightarrow Na_2ZnO_2 + H_2$

Thus, H_2 formed in 1 : 1 ratio.

143. (a) I. $CaCO_3 \xrightarrow{\Delta} CaO + CO_2$
1 mol = 100g   1 mol
10 g   0.1 mol for 100% yield
0.075 mol for 75% yield

II. $CO_2 + C \longrightarrow 2CO$
1 mol   2 mol
0.075 mol   0.150 mol

CO formed $= 0.150$ mol for 100% yield
$= 0.075$ mol for 50% yield

Thus, volume of 0.075 mol CO at STP
$= 0.075 \times 22.4 \text{ L} = 1.68$ L

■ 1 mol of an ideal gas at STP occupies 22.4 L.

144. (c) If $NaI = x$ g
$NaCl = (w - x)$ g

$2NaI + H_2SO_4 \longrightarrow Na_2SO_4$
2 mol   1 mol

$\frac{x}{150}$ mol NaI gives $= \frac{x}{300}$ mol Na_2SO_4

$2NaCl + H_2SO_4 \longrightarrow Na_2SO_4$

$\left(\frac{w-x}{58.5}\right)$ mol NaCl gives

$= \left(\frac{w-x}{117}\right)$ mol Na_2SO_4

Total $Na_2SO_4 = \left(\frac{x}{300} + \frac{w-x}{117}\right)$ mol

$= \left(\frac{x}{300} + \frac{w-x}{117}\right) 142$ g Na_2SO_4

Given, $\frac{x}{300} + \frac{w-x}{117} = \frac{w}{142}$

$\therefore \frac{x}{w} = 0.2886$

Thus, % of NaI $= 28.86\%$

145. (b) P atoms are balanced.

Thus, $P_4 \equiv P_4O_{10} = 4H_3PO_4$

P_4 taken $= 62 \text{ g} = \frac{62}{124} = 0.5$ mol

P_4O_{10} formed $= 0.5 \times 0.85$ mol with 85% yield

H_3PO_4 formed with 90% yield
$= 4 \times 0.5 \times 0.85 \times 0.90$
$= 4 \times 0.5 \times 0.85 \times 0.90 \times 98 \text{ g} = 149.94$ g

146. (d) CO_2 is absorbed by NaOH

$2NaOH + CO_2 \longrightarrow Na_2CO_3$
2 mol   1 mol
1 mol   0.5 mol

CO_2 absorbed by 1 mol NaOH $= 0.5$ mol

Thus, CO_2 in the mixture is $= 0.5$ mol
CO in the mixture is $= 0.3$ mol

CO_2 formed by oxidation $= 0.3$ mol of CO

Thus, total $CO_2 = 0.8$ mol

Hence, NaOH required $= 1.6$ mol

147. (b) $Mg + 2HCl \longrightarrow MgCl_2 + H_2$
2 mol HCl   1 mol
4 mol HCl   2 mol H_2

Molarity in terms of density and %
$= \frac{10d \times (\%)}{\text{molar mass}}$

$= \frac{10 \times 1.2 \times 36.5}{36.5} = 12$ M

Let volume of 12 M HCl required V L

$\therefore 12 \times V = 4$ mol

$V = \frac{1}{3} \text{ L} = 333.33$ mL

148. (c)
$Al_2(SO_4)_3 + 3BaCl_2 \longrightarrow 3BaSO_4 + 2AlCl_3$
1 mol = 342 g   3 mol

$Al_2(SO_4)_3$ solution $=$ one litre
$= 1000$ mL
$= 1000 \times 2.684$ g
$= 2684$ g

Total mass of one molal $Al_2(SO_4)_3$ solution
$= (1000 + 342) = 1342$ g

1342 g $Al_2(SO_4)_3$ solution has $Al_2(SO_4)_3 = 342$ g

$Al_2(SO_4)_3$ in 2684 g $Al_2(SO_4)_3$ solution
$= \frac{342}{1342} \times 2684 = 684 \text{ g} = 2$ mol

Thus, $BaSO_4$ formed $= 6$ mol

149. (a) $N_1V_1 = N_2V_2$

$N(Na_2CO_3) = \frac{50 \times 0.1}{50} = 0.1 \text{ N} = 0.05$ M

$CaCl_2 + Na_2CO_3 \longrightarrow CaCO_3$
1 mol   1 mol

Thus, Na_2CO_3 in 100 mL of 0.05 M solution.

$\frac{MV}{1000} = \frac{100 \times 0.05}{1000} = 0.005$ mol

$\therefore$ $CaCO_3$ formed $= 0.005$ mol
$= 0.005 \times 100 = 0.50$ g

150. (b) $2NH_3 + H_2SO_4 \longrightarrow (NH_4)_2SO_4$

Let unused acid be $= V$ mL

V mL of 0.90 N $H_2SO_4 \equiv 10$ mL of 0.4 N NaOH

$\therefore V = \frac{10 \times 0.4}{0.9} = 4.44$ mL

Used $H_2SO_4 = 60 - 4.44 = 55.56$ mL

55.56 mL of 0.90 N H_2SO_4
$= 55.56$ mL of 0.9 N NH_3
$= \frac{55.56 \times 0.9}{1000} = 0.05$ mol NH_3
$= 0.05 \times 17$ g
$= 0.85$ g NH_3 in 10 g sample

$\% NH_3 = \frac{0.85}{10} \times 100 = 8.5\%$

151. (b) Let water be $= x \text{ g} = x$ mL

Then ethanol $= (49.6 - x)$ g
$= \left(\frac{49.6 - x}{0.80}\right)$ mL

$\therefore x + \left(\frac{49.6 - x}{0.80}\right) = 54.2$ (Total volume)

$\therefore x = 31.2$ g

$\therefore$ Ethanol $= (49.6 - 31.2) \text{ g} = 18.4$ g
$= \frac{18.4}{49.6} \times 100 = 37.1\%$

152. (b) $2Al + 6HCl \longrightarrow 2AlCl_3 + 3H_2$
2 mol   6 mol

Volume of 1 drop $= \frac{1}{20} = 0.05$ mL

HCl in 0.05 mL (1 drop)
$= \frac{0.05 \times 12.0}{1000}$ mol
$= 6 \times 10^{-4}$ mol

Al reacted $= \frac{1}{3}$ mol of HCl
$= \frac{6 \times 10^{-4}}{3}$ mol

$= 2\times10^{-4}$ mol

$= 2\times10^{-4}\times 27$ g Al

$= 5.4\times10^{-3}$ g

Density, $d = \dfrac{\text{Mass}}{\text{Volume}}$

Volume $= \dfrac{\text{Mass}}{d} = \dfrac{5.4\times10^{-3}\text{ g}}{2.7\text{ g cm}^{-3}}$

$= 2.0\times10^{-3}$ cm^3

Area × thickness $= 2\times10^{-3}$cm^3

$A\times\dfrac{0.1}{10}$ cm

$\therefore \quad A = 0.2$ cm^2

153. (d) Number of atoms in 1 g $= \dfrac{1\times N_0}{m_2} = \dfrac{N_0}{m_2}$

(m_2 = molar mass of solute)

Thus, larger the molar mass, smaller the number of atoms.

154. (b) Mole $= \dfrac{\text{Mass}}{\text{Atomic weight}}$

∴ One mol has N_0 atoms

Thus, mass ∝ number of atoms

∴ Slope $= \dfrac{N_0}{\text{Atomic weight}}$

Atomic weight $= \dfrac{6.02\times10^{23}}{3.01\times10^{22}}$

$= 20$ g mol^{-1}

155. (a) Let CH_4 be $= x$g $= \dfrac{x}{16}$ mol

Then, $C_2H_4 = (11-x)$g $= \left(\dfrac{11-x}{28}\right)$ mol

CO_2 from $\dfrac{x}{16}$ mol $= \dfrac{x}{16}$ mol CH_4

CO_2 from $\left(\dfrac{11-x}{28}\right)$ mol C_2H_4

$= \dfrac{2(11-x)}{28}$ mol

$\therefore \dfrac{x}{16} + \dfrac{2(11-x)}{28} = \dfrac{33}{44} = \dfrac{3}{4}$ mol

$x = 4$g

Thus, $CH_4 = 4\text{g} = 0.25$ mol

$C_2H_4 = 7\text{g} = 0.25$ mol

Total mol = 0.50 mol

$\therefore \quad \chi_{CH_4} = 0.50$

156. (c) Let Na_2CO_3 be $= x$ g $= \dfrac{x}{106}$ mol

Then $NaHCO_3 = (15-x)$g $= \left(\dfrac{15-x}{84}\right)$ mol

$$\underset{1\text{ mol}}{Na_2CO_3} + 2HCl \longrightarrow \underset{2\text{ mol}}{2NaCl}$$

$\left(\dfrac{x}{106}\right)$ mol $\quad \left(\dfrac{2x}{106}\right)$ mol NaCl

$$\underset{1\text{ mol}}{NaHCO_3} + HCl \longrightarrow \underset{1\text{ mol}}{NaCl} + H_2O + CO_2$$

$\dfrac{(15-x)}{84}$ mol $\quad \left(\dfrac{15-x}{84}\right)$ mol

Total NaCl $= \dfrac{2x}{106} + \left(\dfrac{15-x}{84}\right)$ mol

$= \dfrac{11}{58.5}$ mol (given)

$\therefore \quad x = 1.36$ g

% $Na_2CO_3 = \dfrac{1.36}{11.0}\times100 = 12.36\%$

157. (a) $AgNO_3 + Cl^- \longrightarrow AgCl$

Let KCl $= x$g $= \dfrac{x}{74.5}$ mol

$= \dfrac{x}{74.5}$ mol AgCl

Then, MCl $= (1.28-x)$g $= \dfrac{1.28-x}{M+35.5}$ mol

$= \left(\dfrac{1.28-x}{M+35.5}\right)$ mol AgCl

***Case* I** AgCl formed due to both

$\dfrac{x}{74.5} + \dfrac{1.28-x}{(M+35.5)} = \dfrac{2.87}{143.5}$

***Case* II** AgCl formed due to volatile MCl

$= \dfrac{1.28-x}{(M+35.5)} = \dfrac{1.435}{143.5}$

$\therefore \quad \dfrac{x}{74.5} = \dfrac{1.435}{143.5}$

$\therefore \quad x = 0.745$ g

$\therefore \quad M = 18$

158. (d) P_2O_5 in 0.5428 g sample

$= 0.5428\times0.2626$ g $= 0.1425$g

$= \dfrac{0.1425}{142}$ mol

$$\underset{1\text{ mol (142g)}}{P_2O_5} \longrightarrow \underset{1\text{ mol (222g)}}{Mg_2P_2O_7}$$

$\dfrac{0.1425}{142}$ mol $P_2O_5 \longrightarrow \dfrac{0.1425}{142}$ mol

$Mg_2P_2O_7 = 0.222$ g

159. (c) $\underset{1\text{ mol}}{S} \longrightarrow \underset{1\text{ mol}}{BaSO_4}$

$(0.60\times0.12\text{ g})$

$= 0.072\text{ g} = \dfrac{0.072}{32}$ mol $= 2.25\times10^{-3}$ mol

$BaSO_4$ due to 2.25×10^{-3} mol S

$= 2.25\times10^{-3}$ mol

Thus, $BaCl_2$ required $= 2.25\times10^{-3}$ mol

$= 2.25\times10^{-3}\times208$ g

$= 0.468$ g

2.08 g $BaCl_2$ is in = 100 mL

∴ 0.468 g $BaCl_2$ is in

$= \dfrac{100}{2.08}\times0.468$ mL $= 22.5$ mL

160. (d) $[Na^+]_{mix} = \dfrac{0.2V_1}{1000}$

$[Ca^{2+}]_{mix} = \dfrac{0.1\,V_2}{1000}$

Cation in mixture $= \left(\dfrac{0.2V_1 + 0.1V_2}{1000}\right)$

$[Cl^-]$ in $CaCl_2 = 0.2$ M

$[Cl^-]$ in NaCl = 0.2 M

$\therefore \quad$ [Anion] $= \dfrac{0.2}{1000}(V_1+V_2)$

Cation in mixture is 40% max than that of anion

$\therefore \left(\dfrac{0.2V_1+0.1V_2}{1000}\right)1.40 = \dfrac{0.2}{1000}(V_1+V_2)$

$\therefore \quad V_1 = 430$ mL

$V_2 = 570$ mL

161. (b) Oleum $(H_2S_2O_7) = 100$ g

then water added = 18 g

Thus $H_2S_2O_7$ is 118%.

$$\underset{\substack{1\text{ mol}\\18\text{ g}}}{H_2O} + \underset{\substack{1\text{ mol}\\80\text{ g}}}{SO_3}\text{ (in oleum)} \longrightarrow \underset{\substack{1\text{ mol}\\98\text{ g}}}{H_2SO_4}$$

100 g of oleum contains

$= 18$ g H_2O and 80 g SO_3

∴ 50 g of oleum contains

$= 9$ g H_2O and 40 g SO_3

162. (a) $\underset{18\text{ g}}{H_2O} + \underset{80\text{ g}}{SO_3} \longrightarrow H_2SO_4$

% of free SO_3 in oleum $= \dfrac{80}{18}\times(\%-100)$

$= \dfrac{80}{18}\times(112-100) = 53.33\%$

Thus, SO_3 in 12.5 g oleum

$= \dfrac{53.33\times12.5}{100} = 6.67$ g

$= \dfrac{6.67}{80}$ mol SO_3 or H_2SO_4

$= 0.083$ mol in 100 L

$\therefore \quad [H_2SO_4] = \dfrac{0.083}{100} = 8.33\times10^{-4}$ M

$\therefore \quad [H^+] = 2[H_2SO_4] = 1.67\times10^{-3}$ M

163. (c) $\underset{\text{Dibasic acid}}{H_2SO_4} \equiv \underset{\text{Diacid base}}{Ca(OH)_2}$

$M_1V_1 \equiv M_2V_2$

M_1 (Total H_2SO_4) $\times 40 = 0.1\times35$

$\therefore \quad M_1 = \dfrac{0.1\times35}{40} = 0.0875$ M

H_2SO_4 neutralised after 30 mL of $Ca(OH)_2$ added

$0.0875\times V = 30\times0.1$

$V = \dfrac{30\times0.1}{0.0875} = 34.3$ mL

Thus, H_2SO_4 left unreacted $= 40.0 - 34.3$

$= 5.7$ mL

164. (b) $Ca(OH)_2 + H_2C_2O_4 \longrightarrow CaC_2O_4 + 2H_2O$
1 mol 1 mol

Thus, $M_1V_1 = M_2V_2$

from graph oxalic acid used for reaction $= 300$ mL

$\therefore$ Moles of oxalic acid $= \frac{300 \times 1}{1000} = 0.3$ mol

Moles of $Ca(OH)_2 = 0.3$ mol

Impure $Ca(OH)_2 = \frac{1 \times 1000}{1000} = 1$ mol

% purity $= \frac{0.3}{1.0} \times 100 = 30\%$

Type II. Statement Based Questions

165. (b) **166.** (d) **167.** (c) **168.** (b) **169.** (a) **170.** (b) **171.** (b) **172.** (a)

Type III. MCQs with One or More than One Correct Alternate

173. (c,d) 1 g atom of oxygen atom means

$= 16$ g oxygen atom $= \frac{16}{32}$

$= 0.5$ mol of O_2

$= 11.2$ L O_2 gas at 1 atm and 273 K (at STP)

174. (a, b, d)

	Electron	Proton
H	1	1
O	8	8
N	7	7
C	6	6
F	9	9

1 mol H_2O has electrons $= 10\ N_0$ and protons $= 10\ N_0$

Thus, protons in 1 mol $CH_4 = 10\ N_0$

Protons in 1 mol $NH_3 = 10\ N_0$

Protons in $\frac{1}{3}$ mol $C_4H_8 = \frac{32}{3} N_0$

Protons in 1 mol HF $= 10\ N_0$

175. (a, c, d) $H_3PO_3 \equiv Ca(OH)_2 \equiv 2OH^-$

$\therefore \quad 1\ OH^- \equiv \frac{H_3PO_3}{2} = \frac{82}{2} = 41$

H_3PO_3 is a dibasic acid, thus it is completely neutralised by 1 mol of $Ca(OH)_2$. Since, H_3PO_3 has only two ionisable H^+ shown by dotted circle, hence $CaHPO_3$ is normal salt.

$$H-O-\underset{\underset{H}{|}}{\overset{\overset{O}{||}}{P}}-O-H$$

176. (b,c,d)

$NH_2CONH_2 + 2NaOH \xrightarrow{\Delta} 2NH_3 + Na_2CO_3 + H_2O$
1 mol (*A*) 2 mol (*B*)

$60\ g\ A \longrightarrow 2\ mol\ B$

$1.2\ g\ A = \frac{1.2}{60}\ mol\ A$

$\longrightarrow \frac{2}{60} \times 1.2 = 0.04\ mol\ NH_3$

$1\ mol\ NH_3 \equiv 1\ mol\ HCl \equiv 1\ mol\ H^+$

$\therefore \quad 0.04\ mol\ NH_3 \equiv 0.04\ mol\ H^+$

20 mL of 1 M HCl $\equiv \frac{20 \times 1}{1000} = 0.02$ mol H^+

40 mL of 1 M HCl $= 0.04$ mol H^+

20 mL of 2 M HCl $= 0.04$ mol H^+

20 mL of 1 M H_2SO_4
$\equiv 0.02$ mol $H_2SO_4 \equiv 0.04$ mol H^+

■ $\frac{\text{Molarity} \times \text{volume (mL)}}{1000} = \text{mol}$

177. (b, d) $CaCO_3 \xrightarrow{\Delta} CaO + CO_2$
1 mol 1 mol
100 g 44 g

4.4 g of CO_2 is thus obtained from $= 10$ g $CaCO_3$

Pure $CaCO_3$ in 20 g sample $= 10$ g

$CaCO_3 = \frac{10}{100}$ mol

$= 0.1$ mol $CaCO_3$

$= 0.1\ N_0$ $CaCO_3$ molecules

$= 0.5\ N_0$ atoms in $CaCO_3$

■ Every molecule of $CaCO_3$ has 5 atoms (1 Ca, 1C, 3O).

178. (a,b,c,d) For $(NH_4)_2CO_3$, molar mass $= 96$ g mol^{-1}

(a) $19.2\ g = \frac{19.2}{96} = 0.2\ mol\ (NH_4)_2CO_3$

$= 0.4$ mol NH_4^+

Thus, true.

(b) $12\ g = \frac{12}{96} = 0.125\ mol\ (NH_4)_2CO_3$

$= 0.125 \times 8$ mol H-atoms

$= 1$ mol of H-atoms

Thus, true.

(c) $96\ g = \frac{96}{96} = 1\ mol\ (NH_4)_2CO_3$

$= 1$ mol CO_2

Thus, true.

(d) $1.92\ g = \frac{1.92}{96} = 0.02\ mol\ (NH_4)_2CO_3$

$= 0.04$ mol NH_4^+ in 200 mL

Thus, true.

$\therefore\ NH_4^+ = \frac{0.04}{200} \times 1000 = 0.2$ M

Thus true.

■ Every mol of $(NH_4)_2CO_3$ give two mol of NH_4^+

179. (a, d) Let, lower oxide $= M_2O_x$

Higher oxide $= M_2O_y$

Equivalent mass of metal in lower oxide

$= \frac{\text{atomic mass}}{\text{valency}} = \frac{M}{x}$

Equivalent mass of metal in higher oxide

$= \frac{M}{y}$

$M_2O_x \longrightarrow M_2O_y$
(2M + 16x) (2M + 16y)
4.29 g 4.77 g

$\left(\frac{2M + 16x}{4.29}\right) = \left(\frac{2M + 16y}{4.77}\right)$

$\frac{M + 8x}{4.29} = \frac{M + 8y}{4.77}$

Higher oxide has 80% metal

$\therefore \quad \frac{2M}{2M + 16y} \times 100 = 80$

$\frac{2M + 16y}{2M} = \frac{100}{80} \Rightarrow \frac{M + 8y}{M} = \frac{5}{4}$

$1 + \frac{8y}{M} = \frac{5}{4} \Rightarrow \frac{8y}{M} = \frac{1}{4}$

$\therefore \quad \frac{M}{y} = 32$

$\therefore$ Equivalent mass of higher oxide $= 32$

Similarly, $\frac{M}{x} = 64$

Equivalent mass of lower oxide $= 64$

180. (a, b, c) Molality is related to molarity and density by equation

$m\ (\text{molality}) = \frac{1000\ M\ (\text{molarity})}{(1000d - Mm_2)}$

where, $m_2 =$ molar mass of solute

$m = \frac{1000 \times 2}{(1090 - 95 \times 2)} = 2.22$ molal

$MgCl_2 \rightleftharpoons Mg^{2+} + 2Cl^-$

Thus, Cl^- has molality $= 4.44$ m.

Thus, (a) is correct.

Also mole fraction of solute X_2 related to m_1 (molar mass of solvent) and molality by $m = \frac{1000\ \chi_2}{(1 - \chi_2)m_1}$

$2.22 = \frac{1000\ \chi_2}{(1 - \chi_2)\ 18}$

$\left(\frac{1}{\chi_2} - 1\right) = 25.025$

$\chi_2 = 0.0384$

Thus, (b) is correct.

$2\text{ M }MgCl_2 = 2 \times 95\text{ g L}^{-1} = 190\text{ g L}^{-1}$
$= 19\text{ g in 100 mL}$
$= 19\%\ w/V.$

Thus, (c) is also correct.
Also, 1000 mL solution $= 1000 \times 1.09$ g
$= 1090$ g solution

Solvent $= (1090 - 190)$ g H_2O

Thus, $MgCl_2$ in ppm $= \frac{190}{900} \times 10^6$
$= 21.1 \times 10^4$ ppm

Thus, (d) is incorrect.

■ ppm means 1 part solute in 10^6 g water.

181. (b, c)

$4NH_3(g) + 5O_2(g) \rightarrow 4NO(g) + 6H_2O(l)$
4 mol 5 mol 4 mol 6 mol
34 g = 2 mol 64 g = 2 mol

NO obtained from 2 mol NH_3 = 2 mol
NO obtained from 2 mol O_2 = 1.6 mol
Thus, O_2 is the limiting reactant.
H_2O, obtained from 2 mol O_2 = 2.4 mol
Thus, all the O_2 will be consumed.

182. (a, b, c)

Ion/Element	Z	Electron
F^-	9	10
O^{2-}	8	10
N^{3-}	7	10
Ne	10	10
Na	11	11

183. (a, b, d)

Ion/Element	Z	Electron
N	7	7
H	1	1
C	6	6
O	8	8

Electrons

(a) NH_3 : 7 + 3 = 10
H_2O : 2 + 8 = 10
CH_4 : 6 + 4 = 10
Thus, all are isoelectronic

(b) N_2 : 7 × 2 = 14
C_2^{2-} : 6 × 2 + 2 = 14
CO : 6 + 8 = 14
Thus, all are isoelectronic.

(c) NO^+ : 7 + 8 − 1 = 14
CO : 6 + 8 = 14
CH_4 : 6 + 4 = 10
Thus, they are not isoelectronic.

(d) CO_2 : 6 + 16 = 22
N_2O : 14 + 8 = 22
N_3H : 3 × 7 + 1 = 22
Thus, all are isoelectronic.

184. (b, c)

	Amount	Mole	Atoms	Weight fraction	Mole fraction
CH_4	1.6 g	0.1	$5\ N_0$	0.314	0.33
NH_3	1.7 g	0.1	$4\ N_0$	0.333	0.33
H_2O	1.8 g	0.1	$3\ N_0$	0.353	0.33

■ Weight fraction of the species
$= \frac{\text{weight}}{\text{total weight}}$

185. (a, b, c, d) 14 g N_2 = 0.5 mol
$= 0.5\ N_0$ molecules

(a) 32 g SO_2 = 0.5 mol
$= 0.5\ N_0$ molecules

(b) 8 g CH_4 = 0.5 mol = $0.5 N_0$ molecules

(c) 22 g CO_2 = 0.5 mol
$= 0.5\ N_0$ molecules

(d) 16 g O_2 = 0.5 mol = $0.5\ N_0$ molecules

186. (a, b, c, d)

187. (a, c) Equivalent mass of $M^{3+} = 9$
Equivalent mass of $O^{2-} = 8$
Thus, equivalent mass of its oxide = 17
Oxide is M_2O_3.
Ionic mass of $M^{3+} = 27$
Ionic mass of $O^{2-} = 16$
Thus, molar mass of M_2O_3
$= 2 \times 27 + 3 \times 16 = 102$
Hydride is MH_3.
Molar mass of hydride = 27 + 3 × 1 = 30

188. (b, d)

189. (a, b, c) Ethanol is C_2H_5OH (46 g mol^{-1})

Ethanol = 46 g $= \frac{46}{46} = 1$ mol

Water = 54 g $= \frac{54}{18} = 3$ mol

∴ Mole fraction of ethanol $= \frac{1}{4} = 0.25$

Molality of ethanol, when water is solvent
$= \frac{1\text{ mol}}{0.054\text{ kg }H_2O} = 18.52$ molal

Molality of water, when ethanol is solvent
$= \frac{1\text{ mol}}{0.046\text{ kg ethanol}} = 21.74$ molal

190. (a, b) 22.4 L O_2 at STP = 1 mol
∴ 0.224 L O_2 at STP = 0.01 mol

$Mg + \frac{1}{2}O_2 \longrightarrow MgO$
1 mol 0.5 mol 1 mol
4.8 g
$\frac{4.8}{24}$ mol
0.2 mol 0.01 mol

MgO formed from 0.2 mol Mg = 0.2mol
MgO formed from 0.01 mol O_2 = 0.02 mol
Thus, O_2 is the limiting reactant.
Equivalent MgO formed
= 2 × number of moles = 0.04
Equivalent O_2 taken
= 4 × number of moles of O_2 = 0.04

■ Equivalent in one mole MgO = 2
Equivalent in one mole O_2 = 4

191. (a, b, c) $4Fe + 3O_2 \longrightarrow 2Fe_2O_3$
4 mol 3 mol 2 mol
(4 × 56) g (3 × 32) g (2 × 160)g
(0.15 × 56)g 4.8 g ?
= 8.4 g

Fe_2O_3 formed from 8.4 g Fe
$= \frac{320}{224} \times 8.4 = 12.05$ g

Fe_2O_3 formed from 4.8 g O_2
$= \frac{320}{96} \times 4.8 = 16.0$ g

Thus, Fe is the limiting reactant and O_2 is in excess.

O_2 used by 8.4 g Fe $= \frac{96}{224} \times 8.4 = 3.6$ g

O_2 left unreacted = 4.8 − 3.6
$= 1.2\text{ g} = \frac{1.2}{160}\text{ mol} = 0.0375$ mol

Fe_2O_3 formed $= \frac{12}{160}$ mol = 0.075 mol

192. (a, b) $C + O_2 \longrightarrow CO_2$
1 mol 1 mol 1 mol
$\frac{60}{12} = 5$ mol $\frac{100}{32} = 3.125$ mol ?

$C + \frac{1}{2}O_2 \longrightarrow CO$
1 mol 0.5 mol 1 mol
5 mol 3.125 mol ?

There is excess of O_2 for the formation of CO but insufficient for the formation of CO_2.
CO formed by 5 mol of C = 5 mol
O_2 consumed by 5 mol of C = 2.5 mol
Thus, O_2 left unreacted = 3.125 − 2.50
= 0.625 mol O_2

■ This unreacted O_2 can oxidise CO to CO_2

$CO + \frac{1}{2}O_2 \longrightarrow CO_2$
1 mol 0.5 mol 1 mol
0.625 mol

CO oxidised to CO_2 by 0.625 mol O_2
$= \frac{0.625}{0.5} = 1.25$

Thus, CO_2 formed = 1.25 mol, CO left
= 5.00 − 1.25
= 3.75 mol

193. (a, d) $RH_2 + Ca^{2+} \longrightarrow RCa + 2H^+$

Every Ca^{2+} ion is replaced by two H^+ ions.

$\therefore [Ca^{2+}] = \frac{[H^+]}{2} = \frac{0.01}{2} = 0.005$ M

$= 0.005$ mol L^{-1}

Or$[CaCO_3] = 0.005$ mol L^{-1}

10^3 mL has hardness $= 0.005$ mol Ca^{2+}

$= 0.005 \times 40$ g Ca^{2+}

$= 0.200$ g L^{-1}

$\therefore$ Ca^{2+} in ppm $= 0.200$ g$L^{-1} \times 10^6$

$= 200$ ppm $= 0.200$ g L^{-1}

Hardness in ppm of $CaCO_3$

$= \frac{0.005 \times 100 \times 10^6}{10^3}$

$= 500$ ppm $= 0.500$ g L^{-1}

Temporary hardness is due to HCO_3^- of Ca^{2+} and Mg^{2+}.

$\therefore Ca(HCO_3)_2 + \underset{56\ g}{CaO} \longrightarrow \underset{(2\times100)\ g}{2CaCO_3} + H_2O$

When hardness is 200 g, CaO required $= 56$ g

When hardness is 0.500 g, CaO required is

$= \frac{56 \times 0.500}{200} = 0.14$ g

Permanent hardness is due to dissolved Cl^- and SO_4^{2-} of Ca^{2+} and Mg^{2+}.

$$\underset{\substack{1\ mol\\0.005\ mol}}{Ca^{2+}} + \underset{\substack{1\ mol\\0.005\ mol}}{Na_2CO_3} \longrightarrow CaCO_3 + 2Na^+$$

$\therefore$ Na_2CO_3 required $= 0.005 \times 106$ g $= 0.53$ g

194. (c, d) I : $P_4 + 5O_2 \longrightarrow P_4O_{10}$

	P_4	$5O_2$	P_4O_{10}
	1 mol	5 mol	1 mol
	0.62 g	4g	?
	$\frac{0.62}{124}$ mol,	$\frac{4}{32}$ mol	?

P_4O_{10} formed from $\left(\frac{0.62}{124}\right)$ mol P_4

$= 5 \times 10^{-3}$ mol

P_4O_{10} formed from $\frac{4}{32}$ mol O_2

$= 25 \times 10^{-3}$ mol

Thus, P_4 is the limiting reactant in I.

P_4O_{10} formed $= 5 \times 10^{-3} \times 284 = 1.42$g

II. $\underset{1\ mol}{P_4} + \underset{3\ mol}{3O_2} \longrightarrow \underset{1\ mol}{P_4O_6}$

P_4O_6 formed from $\left(\frac{0.62}{124}\right)$ mol P_4

$= 5 \times 10^{-3}$ mol

P_4O_6 formed from $\left(\frac{4}{32}\right)$ mol O_2

$= 41.7 \times 10^{-3}$ mol

Thus, P_4 is the limiting reactant in II

P_4O_6 formed $= 1.10$ g

195. (a, c, d) 22.4 L of gas at STP = 1 mol

$\therefore$ 4.48 L of gas at STP $= \frac{4.48}{22.4} = 0.2$ mol

	$2NH_3(g)$	$+ CO_2(g)$	$\rightarrow NH_2CONH_2(aq)$	$+ H_2O(l)$
	2 mol	1 mol	1 mol	
Given	0.2 mol	0.2 mol	?	
Reacts	0.2 mol	0.1 mol	0.1 mol (formed)	
Excess	0 mol	0.1 mol		

Thus, NH_3 is the limiting reactant and CO_2 is in excess.

Thus, (a) is correct and (b) is incorrect

0.1 mol NH_2CONH_2 (urea)

$= 0.1 \times 60 = 6.0$ g

Thus, (c) is correct

CaO	+ CO_2	$\longrightarrow$ $CaCO_3$
1 mol	1 mol	
0.1 mol	0.1 mol	

Thus, excess of CO_2(= 0.1 mol) can be removed by 0.1 mol Ca.

Thus, (d) is correct.

196. (a, b, c)

$CH_3OH = 0.1$ mol $= 0.1 \times 32$ g $= 3.2$ g

$CH_3CH_2OH = 0.1$ mol $= 0.1 \times 46$ g $= 4.6$ g

$H_2O = 0.2$ mol $= 0.2 \times 18$ g $= 3.6$ g

Total weight $= 11.4$ g

If CH_3OH is solute and others are solvent then 0.1 mol CH_3OH is in 8.2 g of CH_3OH and H_2O.

$\therefore$ Molarity of $CH_3OH = \frac{0.1\ mol}{0.0082\ kg}$

$= 12.195$ molal

Thus, (a) is correct.

CH_3CH_2OH is in maximum amount.

Thus, its molality

$= \frac{0.1\ mol}{0.0068\ kg} = 14.706$ molal

Thus, (b) is correct.

Mass % of $CH_3CH_2OH = \frac{4.6}{11.4} \times 100$

$= 40.35\%$

Thus, (c) is correct.

Mass % of $CH_3OH = \frac{3.2}{100} \times 100 = 28.07\%$

Thus, (d) is incorrect.

197. (a, c, d)

$MCO_3 + 2HCl \longrightarrow MCl_2 + CO_2$

$(M+60)$g $\qquad$ 44g

4.2g $\qquad$ 2.2g

$\frac{M+60}{4.2} = \frac{44}{2.2}$

$\therefore$ $M = 24$, $MCO_3 = 84$

Thus, atomic mass of M is = 24

M being divalent, equivalent mass of

$MCO_3 = \frac{84}{2} = 42$

Weight % of M in $MCO_3 = \frac{24}{84} \times 100$

$= 28.57\%$

Weight % of $CO_3^{2-} = \frac{60}{84} \times 100 = 71.43\%$

198. (a, b, c, d) 109% H_2SO_4' means that 100 g of oleum has been diluted with 9 g H_2O.

Thus, (a) is true.

$$\underset{\substack{80\ g\\40g}}{SO_3} + \underset{\substack{18\ g\\9\ g}}{H_2O} \longrightarrow H_2SO_4$$

9 g of H_2O combines with 40 g SO_3.

Thus, (b) is true.

% of free $SO_3 = \frac{80}{18} \times (\% - 100)$

$= \frac{80}{18} \times 9 = 40\%$

Thus, (c) is true.

40 g SO_3 = 0.5 mole SO_3.

Thus, (d) is also true.

Type IV. Numerical Skills

199. (47.00)

Let, $n_{glucose} = x$

and $n_{H_2O} = y$

then $x_{glucose} = \frac{x}{x+y} = \frac{0.1}{1}$

Thus, if $x = 0.1$ mol $= 0.1 \times 180 = 18.0$ g

then $\quad y = 0.9$ mol $= 0.9 \times 18 = 16.2$ g

Total mass of solution $= 18.0 + 16.2$

$= 34.2$ g

$\therefore$ Mass % of water $= \frac{16.2}{34.2} \times 100$

$= 47.37\% \approx 47.00\%$

200. Nine (9)

Molar mass of $A_2O_3 = (2A + 48)$

A in 11 g $= \frac{2A \times 11}{(2A + 48)} = 3.0$

$\frac{11A}{A + 24} = 3$

$\therefore \qquad A = 9.0$

201. Twenty Five (25)

6.023×10^{22} molecules of X = 10 g of X

$\therefore$ 6.023×10^{23} molecules of X = 100 g of X

Thus, molar mass of X = 100 g mol^{-1}

$n_X = \frac{5}{100} = 0.05$ mol

Volume = 2 L

$\therefore$ Molarity $= \frac{n_X}{V} = \frac{0.05}{2} = 0.025$
$= 25 \times 10^{-3}$ M

202. Ten (10)
$Na_2CO_3 \cdot xH_2O$ is a diacid base
$\therefore$ Equivalent weight of $Na_2CO_3 \cdot xH_2O$
$= \frac{\text{Molar mass}}{2}$
$= \frac{106 + 18x}{2} = (53 + 9x)$
Equivalent of $Na_2CO_3 \cdot xH_2O = \frac{1.43}{(53 + 9x)}$
Volume = 100 mL = 0.1 L
$\therefore$ Normality $= \frac{\frac{1.43}{(53+9x)}}{0.1} = 0.1$ N (given)
$\therefore$ $53 + 9x = 143$
$9x = 90$
$\therefore$ $x = 10$

203. (100)
Molarity of $H_2O_2 = \frac{\text{Volume strength}}{11.2}$
$8.9 = \frac{\text{Volume strength}}{11.2}$
$\therefore$ Volume strength $= 11.2 \times 8.9 = 99.68$
≈ 100.00

204. Six (6)
Molar mass of alkene
$= \frac{22.4 \text{ L mol}^{-1}}{0.8 \text{ L g}^{-1}} = 28 \text{ g mol}^{-1}$
$C_nH_{2n} = 12n + 2n = 28$
$n = 2$
Thus, alkene is C_2H_4.
Total number of C and H atoms in one formula unit = 6

205. Eight (8)
$$\underset{\substack{(X+160)\\3.36}}{XBr_2} + Cl_2 \longrightarrow \underset{\substack{(X+71)\\1.58}}{XCl_2} + Br_2$$
$\left(\frac{X + 160}{3.36}\right) = \frac{X + 71}{1.58}$
$X = 8$

206. Two (2)
If molality = m mol kg^{-1}
molarity = M mol kg^{-1}
molar mass of solute = m_2 g mol^{-1}
and density = g mL^{-1}
Then, $m = \frac{1000\ M}{(1000\ d - Mm_2)}$
$2.273 = \frac{1000 \times 4}{(1000\ d - 4 \times 60)}$
$d = 2.0$ g mL^{-1}

207. Five (5)
Sn used = 1.056 − 0.601 = 0.455 g
$$\underset{\substack{118.7x\\0.455\text{ g}}}{x\text{Sn}} + \underset{\substack{127y\\1.947\text{ g}}}{\frac{y}{2}I_2} \longrightarrow Sn_xI_y$$
$\frac{118.7x}{127y} = \frac{0.455}{1.947}$ $\therefore$ $\frac{x}{y} = \frac{1}{4}$
$\therefore$ $x + y = 1 + 4 = 5$

208. Seven (7)
$$\underset{\substack{(120+18x)\text{ g}\\1.687}}{MgSO_4 \cdot xH_2O} \longrightarrow \underset{\substack{120\text{ g}\\0.824}}{MgSO_4} + \underset{18x\text{ g}}{H_2O}$$
Thus, $\frac{120 + 18x}{1.687} = \frac{120}{0.824}$
$\Rightarrow$ $x = 7$

209. Nine (9)
$$\underset{2\times27+3\times96+18x}{Al_2(SO_4)_3 \cdot xH_2O} \equiv \underset{54}{2Al}$$
Percentage of Al $= \left(\frac{54}{342 + 18x}\right) \times 100$
$= 10.71$
$\therefore$ $x = 9$

210. (4.97)
Fe in 10^6 g wheat = 10 g
Thus, Fe in 100 kg (= 10^5 g) wheat = 1 g
Every one mole of $FeSO_4 \cdot 7H_2O$ has one mole Fe.
Molar mass of $FeSO_4 \cdot 7H_2O$
$= 55.85 + 96 + 126$
$= 277.85$ g mol^{-1}
Thus, 1 g Fe $= \frac{1}{55.85}$ mole Fe
$= \frac{1}{55.85}$ mole $FeSO_4 \cdot 7H_2O$
$= \frac{1}{55.85} \times 277.85$ g $FeSO_4 \cdot 7H_2O$
$=$ **4.97 g**

211. Five (5)
Amount of ethanol before dilution (volume × density) = $V \times 0.8$
Amount after dilution = 90 × 0.9
Thus, $90 \times V \times 0.8 = 20 \times 20 \times 0.9$
$\therefore$ $V = 5$ mL

212. Five (5)
When 50 g of solution of X % by weight of solution is cooled solute (X) separates = 10 g
Thus, water = 40 g
Solute X = 10 g
Percentage concentration by weight of solvent $H_2O = \frac{10}{40} \times 100 = 25\%$
Percentage concentration by weight of solution $= \frac{10}{(40 + 10)} \times 100 = 20\%$
Difference in two types of concentration
= 25 − 20 = 5%

213. Five (5)
$$\underset{\substack{(159.5+18x)\\2.495\text{ g}}}{CuSO_4 \cdot xH_2O} \longrightarrow \underset{\substack{18x\\0.05\text{ mol}}}{xH_2O}$$
$= 0.05 \times 18$ g
$\therefore$ $\frac{159.5 + 18x}{2.495} = \frac{18x}{0.05 \times 18}$
$\therefore$ $x = 5$

214. Eight (8)
0.1469 mol = 0.1469 × 98 g
Since, $\frac{\text{mass}}{\text{volume}}$ = density
$\therefore V = \frac{\text{mass}}{\text{density}} = \frac{0.1469 \times 98 \text{ g}}{1.8\ g \text{ mL}^{-1}} = 8.0$ mL

215. Three (3)
Relation between molality (m) and mole fraction (χ) of solute is
$m = \frac{1000\chi}{(1 - \chi)m_1}$
where, m_1 is the molar mass of solvent.
$\chi_{\text{solute}} = 1 - 0.95 = 0.05$
Molality (m) $= \frac{1000 \times 0.05}{0.95 \times 18}$
$= 2.92 \approx 3$ mol kg^{-1}

216. Six (6)
$$\underset{(158.5+17x)\text{ g mol}^{-1}}{[Cr(NH_3)_xCl_3]} \equiv xNH_3 \equiv \underset{x\text{ mol}}{xHCl}$$
Moles of HCl used
$= \frac{M \times V(\text{mL})}{1000} = \frac{24.26 \times 1.50}{1000}$
= 0.03639 mol
Thus, $\frac{(158.5 + 17x)}{1.585} = \frac{x}{0.03639}$
$\therefore$ $x = 6$

217. Two (2) H_2SO_4 in 100 g solution = 30.8 g
H_2SO_4 in $\left(\frac{100}{1.303}\right)$ mL solution = 30.8 g
Thus, H_2SO_4 in 500 mL solution
$= \frac{30.8}{100} \times 1.303 \times 500$ g
$= \frac{30.8 \times 1.303 \times 500}{100 \times 98}$ mol = 2.0 mol

218. Six (6)
$$CH_4 \longrightarrow \underset{1\text{ mol}}{CO_2} + \underset{2\text{ mol}}{2H_2O}$$
$$C_2H_4 \longrightarrow \underset{2\text{ mol}}{2CO_2} + \underset{2\text{ mol}}{2H_2O}$$

$$C_3H_6 \longrightarrow \underset{3\text{ mol}}{3CO_2} + \underset{3\text{ mol}}{3H_2O}$$

From the graph, it is clear that y-axis is the number of moles of H_2O formed.

$$C_4H_8 \longrightarrow 4CO_2 + \underset{x=4}{\overset{\uparrow}{4}}H_2O$$

Thus, six H_2O from C_6H_{12}.

219. **One (1)**

$$H_2O + SO_3 \longrightarrow H_2SO_4 \xrightarrow{SO_3} H_2S_2O_7$$

$$H_2S_2O_7 + H_2O \longrightarrow 2H_2SO_4$$

118% means that 100 g of acid has 18 g H_2O.

Thus, moles of $H_2O = \frac{18}{18} = 1$

220. **Ten (10)**

For neutralisation

$$N_1V_1 = N_2V_2$$

NaOH Phosphonic acid

$$0.1 \times V_1 = 0.1 \times 10$$

$\therefore$ $V_1 = 10$ mL

221. **Four (4)**

If stoichiometry amounts (moles) are balanced then

$$12Cl_2 \longrightarrow 12KClO$$

$$12KClO \longrightarrow 4KClO_3$$

$$4KClO_3 \longrightarrow 3KClO_4$$

Thus, $3KClO_4 \equiv 12Cl_2$

$$1\ KClO_4 \equiv 4Cl_2$$

Thus, to prepare 1 mol $KClO_4$, 4 mol of Cl_2 are required.

222. **Nine (9)**

If $NaHCO_3 = x$ g

Then, $Na_2CO_3 = (15 - x)$ g

$$\underset{84\text{ g}}{NaHCO_3} + HCl \longrightarrow \underset{58.5\text{ g}}{NaCl} + H_2O + CO_2$$

$$\underset{106\text{ g}}{Na_2CO_3} + 2HCl \longrightarrow \underset{(2\times 58.5)\text{ g}}{2NaCl} + H_2O + CO_2$$

NaCl formed from x g $NaHCO_3 = \frac{58.5x\text{ g}}{84}$

NaCl formed from $(15 - x)$ g Na_2CO_3

$$= \frac{2 \times 58.5}{106}(15 - x)\text{ g}$$

$$\therefore \frac{58.5x}{84} + \frac{58.5 \times 2\,(15 - x)}{106} = 11$$

$$\frac{x}{84} + \frac{(15 - x)}{53} = \frac{11}{58.5}$$

$$x = 13.64\text{ g}$$

$$Na_2CO_3 = 15 - 13.64 = 1.36\%$$

$$\%\text{ of } Na_2CO_3 = \frac{1.36 \times 100}{15} = 9\%$$

223. **Nine (9)**

Net Reaction

$$FeS_2 \longrightarrow 2H_2SO_4$$

$$120\text{ g} \longrightarrow 2 \times 98\text{ g}$$

$$120\text{ kg} \longrightarrow 2 \times 98\text{ kg}$$

$$\underset{FeS_2}{5.52\text{ kg}} \longrightarrow \frac{2 \times 98}{120} \times 5.52\text{ kg } H_2SO_4$$

$$= 9.0\text{ kg}$$

- Every unit of FeS_2 is a source of two units of H_2SO_4.

224. **(3400)**

$$\underset{\substack{1\text{ mol}\\20\text{ g}}}{N_2} + \underset{\substack{3\text{ mol}\\6\text{ g}}}{3H_2} \longrightarrow \underset{\substack{2\text{ mol}\\34\text{ g}}}{2NH_3}$$

2800 g N_2 give = 3400 g NH_3

1000 g H_2 give $= \frac{34}{6} \times 1000$ g NH_3

$$= 5667\text{ g } NH_3$$

Thus, N_2 is the limiting reactant. NH_3 formed = 3400 g

225. **(2.98)**

Water = 900 g $= \frac{900}{18} = 50$ mol

Let urea be $= x$ mol $= 60x$ g

$$\chi_{urea}\text{ (mole fraction)} = \frac{n_{(urea)}}{n_{(urea)} + n_{(water)}}$$

$$0.05 = \frac{x}{50 + x}$$

$$\therefore \quad x = \frac{50}{19}\text{ mol} = \left(\frac{50}{19} \times 60\right)\text{ g}$$

Total mass of solution

$$= \left(\left(\frac{50}{19} \times 60\right) + 900\right) = \frac{20100}{19}\text{ g}$$

Since density $= \frac{\text{mass}}{\text{volume}}$

$$\therefore \quad \text{Volume} = \frac{20100}{19 \times 1.2}\text{ mL} = \frac{20.1}{19 \times 1.2}\text{ L}$$

$$\text{Molarety} = \frac{\text{mole}}{\text{volume (L)}}$$

$$= \frac{\left(\frac{50}{19}\right)}{\frac{20.1}{19 \times 1.2}} = \frac{50 \times 1.2}{20.1} = 2.985\text{ M}$$

226. **Seven (7)**

Density = 10.5 g cm^{-3}

Thus, 1 cm^3 has Ag = 10.5 g $= \frac{10.5}{108}$ mol

$$= \frac{(10.5 \times 6.02 \times 10^{23})}{108}\text{ atoms} = A$$

1 cm has Ag atoms $= (A)^{1/3}$

10^{-12} m^2 ($= 10^{-8}$ cm^2) has Ag atoms

$$= (A)^{2/3}\ 10^{-8}$$

$$= \left(\frac{10.5 \times 6.02 \times 10^{23}}{108}\right)^{2/3} \times 10^{-8}\text{ Ag atoms}$$

$$= 1.507 \times 10^7 = y \times 10^x$$

Thus, $x = 7$

227. **Six (6)**

$$[Cr(H_2O)_5Cl]Cl_2 \rightleftharpoons [Cr(H_2O)Cl]^{2+} + 2Cl^-$$

Complex has two ionisable Cl^- ions.

Thus, $[Cl^-]$ in 30 mL of 0.01 M solution

$$= \frac{30 \times 0.01 \times 2}{1000} = 6 \times 10^{-4}\text{ mol}$$

Thus, $AgNO_3$ required $= 6 \times 10^{-4}$ mol

$$\therefore \quad 6 \times 10^{-4} = \frac{V \times 0.1}{1000}$$

$$\therefore \quad V = 6\text{ mL}$$

228. **Eight (8)**

100 g of HCl solution has HCl = 29.2 g

or

$\left(\frac{100}{1.25}\right)$ mL of HCl solution has HCl

$$= 29.2\text{ g}$$

$$\therefore M\text{ (stock solution)} = \frac{29.2 / 36.5}{\left(\frac{100}{1.25}\right) / 1000}$$

$$= 10\text{ M}$$

V mL of 10 M HCl = 200 mL of 0.4 M

$\therefore$ $V = 8$ mL

229. **Eight (8)**

There is no change in volume on dissolution.

Thus, 1000 mL solvent = 1000 mL solution

$$= 1000 \times 0.4\text{ g solvent}$$

$$= 400\text{ g solvent} = 0.4\text{ kg}$$

Molarity = 3.2 mol L^{-1} (given)

$$\therefore \text{Molality} = \frac{3.2\text{ mol solute}}{0.4\text{ kg solvent}}$$

$$= 8\text{ mol kg}^{-1}$$

Type V. Passage Based MCQs (Comprehension)

Passage 1

1.0 L of 0.15 KOH = 1 × 0.15 = 0.15 mol

	CO_2 +	$2KOH \longrightarrow$	K_2CO_3 +	H_2O
Initial	0.05	0.15	0	0
After reaction	(0.05–0.05)	(0.15 – 0.10)	0.05 mol	
Resultant	0	0.05 mol	0.05 mol	

Thus, KOH left in 1L solution = 0.05 mol

$$\therefore \text{Molarity of KOH} = \frac{0.05}{1} = 0.05\text{ M}$$

K_2CO_3 formed = 0.05 mol in 1L

$\therefore$ Molarity of K_2CO_3 = 0.05 M

230. (c)

231. (d)

Passage 2

Glauber's salt is $Na_2SO_4 \cdot 10H_2O$

$$= 8.075 \times 10^{-2}\text{ kg}$$

Molar mass = 322 g mol^{-1}

$$\text{Moles} = \frac{8.075\times10^{-2}\times10^3\,\text{g}}{322\text{ g mol}^{-1}}$$
$= 0.25$ mol in 1 dm^3(1L) solution

$\therefore$ Molarity $= \frac{0.25}{1.0} = 0.25$ M

Solution $= 1\ dm^3 = 1000$ mL
$= 1000\times1.0772$ g mL^{-1}
$= 1077.2$ g

■ 1 k $g\,m^{-3} = 0.001\ g\ mL^{-1}$

Solvent $= (1077.20 - 80.75)$ g
$= 996.45\ g = 0.99645$ kg

$\therefore$ Molality $= \frac{\text{moles of solute}}{\text{kg of solvent}}$
$= \frac{0.25}{0.99645} = 0.25$ molal

Thus, difference in molarity and molality = 0

232. (b)

233. (a)

■ $M\text{ (molarity)} = \frac{100\,M}{1000d - Mm_2}$

m_2 = molar mass of solute

Passage 3

Complex $\xrightarrow{\text{Heat}}$ CuO 19.89% of complex 100 g

$\therefore$ CuO formed $= \frac{19.89}{100}\times100 = 19.89$ g
$= \frac{19.89}{79.5}$ mol CuO $= 0.25$ mol

Thus, moles of CuO = moles of $CuSO_4$

$\therefore$ $CuSO_4 = 0.25$ mol
$= 159.5\times0.25\,g = 39.875$ g

Water = 27.03 g

$\therefore$ $(NH_4)_2SO_4 = 100 - (39.875 + 27.03)$
$= 33.095$ g

Empirical formula

	Amount	Mole = mass/molar mass	Ratio
$CuSO_4$ (159.5)	39.875 g	0.25	1
$(NH_4)_2\cdot SO_4$ (132)	33.095 g	0.25	1
H_2O(18)	27.03 g	1.50	6

Thus, empirical formula
$= CuSO_4.(NH_4)_2SO_4\cdot6H_2O$

234. (c)

235. (a)

Passage 4

0.2 mol AB_2 weighs = 8.0 g

Thus, 1 mol of AB_2 weighs = 40.0 g

0.1 mol A_2B_3 weighs = 7.0 g

1 mol A_2B_3 weights = 70 g

$\therefore$ $A + 2B = 40 \Rightarrow 2A + 3B = 70$

$\therefore$ $A = 20 \Rightarrow B = 10$

Thus, $\frac{A}{B} = \frac{2}{1}$

Mole fractions are equal, if moles are equal. Thus, if 0.1 mole of A_2B_3 is added.

Moles of AB_2 = Moles of A_2B_3 = 0.2

236. (a)

237. (b)

Passage 5

Cu in 15 g brass $= 15\times\frac{90}{100} = 13.5$g
$= \frac{13.5}{63.5}$ mol $= 0.2126$ mol

HNO_3 required = 4 times of Cu taken
$= 0.2126\times4$ mol $= 0.8504$ mol

Zn in 15 g brass $= 1.5\ g = \frac{1.5}{65.0}$ mol

HNO_3 required = 2. 5 times of Zn taken
$= \frac{1.5}{65.0}\times2.5 = 0.0577$ mol

Total $HNO_3 = 0.9081$ mol

Since, $\frac{\text{volume (mL)}\times\text{molarity}}{1000} = \text{mol}$

$\therefore$ $V\text{(mL)} = \frac{0.9081\times1000}{3.0} = 303$ mL

NO_2 is due to Cu only.

Thus, NO_2 formed = 2 times of Cu taken
$= 2\times0.2126$ mol

$\therefore$ Volume at STP $= 2\times0.2126\times22.4$ L $= 9.52$ L

238. (a)

239. (a)

Passage 6

100 g carbon $= \frac{\text{mass}}{\text{atomic mass}} = \frac{100}{12} = 8.33$ mol

100 g oxygen $= \frac{100}{32} = 3.125$ mol

$$\begin{array}{ccc} C & + O_2 \longrightarrow & CO_2 \\ 1\text{ mol} & 1\text{ mol} & 1\text{ mol} \\ 8.33\text{ mol} & 3.125\text{ mol} & ? \end{array}$$

O_2 is the limiting reactant.

Thus, initially CO_2 formed = 3.125 mol

Carbon being in excess can reduce CO_2 formed to CO

$$\begin{array}{ccc} C & + CO_2 \longrightarrow & 2CO \\ 3.125\text{ mol} & 3.125\text{ mol} & 2\times3.125\text{ mol} \end{array}$$

Thus, CO formed = 6.25 mol

Carbon left unreacted at the end of complete reaction
$= (8.33 - 2\times3.125)$ mol
$= 2.08$ mol $= 2.08\times12$ g
$= 24.96$ g carbon

240. (c)

241. (a)

Passage 7

Let NaCl $= x\ g = \frac{x}{58.5}$ mol

NaBr $= (3.5084 - x)$ g
$= \left(\frac{3.5084 - x}{103}\right)$ mol

AgBr + AgCl $\xrightarrow[\text{(i) Electrolysis}]{\text{(i) KCN}}$ Ag

Thus, moles of (NaCl + NaBr)
= Moles of (AgCl + AgBr)
= Moles of Ag formed
$= \left(\frac{5.5028}{108}\right)$ mol

$\therefore$ $\frac{x}{58.5} + \frac{3.5084 - x}{103} = \frac{5.5028}{108}$

$x = 2.2870$ g

$\therefore$ NaCl = 2.2870 g

$\% = \frac{2.2870}{3.5084}\times100 = 65.18\%$

Also, moles of $O_2 = \frac{1}{4}$ mole of Ag
$= \frac{5.5028}{4\times108}$ mol $= 0.0127$ mol
$= 0.4076$ g $= 0.0127\times22.4$ L
$= 0.285$ L at STP
$= 285$ mL at STP

242. (a) **243.** (d)

Passage 8

Mole fraction of $CH_3OH = 0.1$

Mole fraction of $CH_2OH = 0.3$

Mole fraction of $H_2O = 0.6$

Sum of mole fraction = 1.0

Thus, moles of $CH_3OH = 1$ (= 32 g)

Moles of $CH_3CH_2OH = 3$ (= 138 g)

Moles of $H_2O = 6$ (= 108 g)

Molality of CH_3OH
$= \frac{\text{Moles of } CH_3OH}{\text{kg of solvent } (H_2O + CH_3CH_2OH)}$
$= \frac{1}{246/1000} = 4.065$ molal

Mass percentage of CH_3CH_2OH
$= \frac{138}{278}\times100 = 49.64\%$

244. (a)

245. (b)

Type VI. Matrix Matching

246. (a)

247. (a) Sugar $(C_{12}H_{22}O_{11}) = 342$ g mol^{-1}

Solution $= 214.2\ g = \frac{214.2}{1.2}$ mL
$= \frac{214.2\text{ L}}{1.2\times1000} = 0.1785$ L

Solute = 34.2 g = $\frac{34.2}{342}$ = 0.1 mol

Water = (214.2 – 34.2) g

= 180 g = 0.180 kg = 10 mol

= 0.01 kilomol

Total moles of solute and water = 10.1

∴ Mole fraction of sugar

$= \frac{0.1}{10.1} = 9.9 \times 10^{-3}$

Molality = $\frac{\text{Moles of solute}}{\text{kg (solvent)}}$

$= \frac{0.1}{0.180} = 0.55$ molal

Molarity = $\frac{\text{Moles of solute}}{\text{Volume of solution in L}}$

$= \frac{0.1 \text{ mol}}{0.1785 \text{ L}} = 0.56$ M

Thus,
(i)-(r)
(ii)-(q)
(iii)-(p)
(iv)-(s)

248. (c) (i) $C + O_2 \longrightarrow CO_2$

12 g 32g 44g
10 g 100 g ?

CO_2 from 10 g C = $\frac{44}{12} \times 10$ = 36.67 g

= 0.833 mol

CO_2 from 100 g O_2 = $\frac{44}{32} \times 100$

= 137.5g = 3.125 mol

Thus, C is the limiting reactant and all the C is oxidised to CO_2.

Thus, (i) - (q)

(ii) $C + O_2 \longrightarrow CO_2$

12 g 32 g 44 g
37.5 g 100 g ?
3.125 mol 3.125 mol 3.125 mol

C and O_2 both are in equal amounts. Thus both are converted to CO_2

∴ (ii)-(p)

(iii) $C + O_2 \longrightarrow CO_2$

12 g 32 g 44 g
60 g 100 g
5 mol 3.125 mol

$C + \frac{1}{2}O_2 \longrightarrow CO$

1 mol 0.5 mol 1 mol
5 mol 2.5 mol 5 mol

■ There is excess of O_2 for the formation of CO but limited for the formation of CO_2.

Initially, all the carbon is converted to CO.

CO formed from 5 mol carbon = 5 mol

O_2 left after CO formed = 3.125 – 2.500

= 0.625 mol

Thus, 0.625 mol O_2 oxidises some CO to CO_2

$CO + \frac{1}{2}O_2 \longrightarrow CO_2$

1 mol 0.5 mol
1.25 mol 0.625 mol 1.25 mol

Thus, CO_2 formed = 1.25 mol

CO left = 5.00 = 1.25 = 3.75 mol

Thus, (iii) -(r, s)

(iv) $C + O_2 \longrightarrow CO_2$

1mol 1 mol ?
8.33 mol 3.125 mol

If CO_2 formed, large amount of C is left unreacted

$2C + O_2 \longrightarrow 2CO$

2 mol 1 mol
8.33 mol 3.125 mol

If CO is formed, all the O_2 is consumed and very small amount of carbon is left.

Thus, CO = 6.25 mol

Thus, (iv)-(t)

249. (d) (i) $n + p = 81$

n = 31.7% more than proton

∴ $n = p + 0.317\,p$

$p + p + 0.317\,p = 81$

$p = 35$

Thus, (1)-(r)

(ii) M^{2+} has electrons = 22

Thus, $p = 24 = Z$

Neutrons (Z + 2) = 26

Thus, ionic mass = 24 + 26 = 50

Thus, (ii)-(p)

(iii) Protons in X^- = 17

Electrons in X^- = 17 + 1 = 18

Neutrons = $18 + \frac{18 \times 11.1}{100} = 20$

Thus, ionic mass of X^-

= 20 + 17 = 37

Thus (iii) -(s)

(iv) $n + p = 56$

Electrons in M^{3+} = (p – 3)

Neutrons in M^{3+}

$= (p-3) + (p-3) \times \frac{30.4}{100} = 56$

$\therefore (p-3)\left[1 + \left(\frac{30.4}{100}\right)\right] + p = 56$

$p = 26$

Thus, (iv)-(q)

250. (d)

(i) p - $C_2H_4O_2$ or $(CH_2O)_2$

r - HCHO or (CH_2O)

t - $HCOOCH_3$ or $(CH_2O)_2$

Thus, (i) - (p, r, t)

(ii) H in CH_3COOH, NH_2CONH_2, HCHO and $HCOOCH_3$

$= \frac{4}{60} \times 100 = 6.666\%$

Thus, (ii) - (p, q, r, t)

(iii) C in CH_3COOH, HCHO, $HCOOCH_3$

$= \frac{24}{60} \times 100 = 40\%$

Thus, (iii) - (p, r, t)

(iv) O in p, r, t = 53.3%

Thus, (iv) - (p, r, t)

(v) H in (p) and (s) attached to O are equal

$CH_3—\overset{\overset{O}{\|}}{C}—O—H$

CH, CH_2—O—H

Thus, (v) - (p, s)

251. (b) $H_3PO_2 \equiv 1H^+$

Thus, molar mass = equivalent mass

$H_2SO_4 \equiv 2H^+$

Thus, 1 mol = 2 equivalents

Solutions for 252 to 255

NH_3 = 1g = $\frac{1}{17}$ mol = $\frac{4N_0}{17}$ atoms

= 0.235 N_0 atoms

CO_2 = 1g = $\frac{1}{44}$ mol = $\frac{3N_0}{44}$ atoms

= 0.068 N_0 atoms

NO_2 = 1g = $\frac{1}{46}$ mol = $\frac{3N_0}{46}$ atoms

= 0.065 N_0 atoms

CH_4 = 1g = $\frac{1}{16}$ mol = $\frac{5N_0}{16}$ atoms

= 0.3125 N_0 atoms

X_{CH_4} = Total moles = 0.1658

$X_{NH_3} = \frac{1/17}{0.1658} = 0.354$

$X_{CO_2} = \frac{1/44}{0.1658} = 0.137$

$X_{NO_2} = \frac{1/46}{0.1658} = 0.131$

$X_{CH_4} = \frac{1/16}{0.1658} = 0.377$

252. (a)

253. (b)

254. (c)

255. (d)

Atomic Structure

Chapter Topics

- Fundamental Aspects
- Bohr's Theory of H-atom
- de-Broglie Equation
- Quantum Numbers

Fundamental Aspects

- All elements are composed of minute particles called **atoms**, which do not undergo sub-division during chemical reactions and cannot be created or destroyed by any chemical process.
- Atoms of same element are similar to one another in all respects and equal in masses.
- Atoms of different elements have different masses (called **atomic masses**) and different properties.
- Fundamental particles of the atom are following **subatomic particles;** electrons, protons and neutrons, which are characterised by their charge and mass.

Properties of the electron, proton and neutron

Properties	Proton, *p*	Neutron, *n*	Electron, *e*
Mass	1.67262×10^{-27} kg	1.67495×10^{-27} kg	9.1091×10^{-31} kg
Absolute charge*	$+1.6022 \times 10^{-19}$ C	0	-1.6022×10^{-19} C
Mass relative to the electron	1836	1839	1
Spin	1/2	1/2	1/2
Charge relative to the proton	+1	0	−1
Discovery	Goldstein	Chadwick	Thomson
Mass (amu)	1.00727	1.00867	0.00054

(1 amu = 1.6605×10^{-27} kg) *determined by M. Faraday

Some sub-nuclear particles

Particle	Mass	Charge	Year of discovery	Spin
Antiproton	Same as that of a proton	Negative	1955 by Serge	$\frac{1}{2}$
μ-meson (muon)	210 times that of an electron	Positive and negative	1937 by Yukawa	$\frac{1}{2}$
π-meson	276 times that of an electron	Positive and negative	1947 by Kemmer	$\frac{1}{2}$
Pion	265 times that of an electron	Zero		
Neutrino	Very much less than that of an electron	Zero	1956 by Fermi	$\frac{1}{2}$
Positron	Same as that of an electron	Positive	1932 by Anderson	$\frac{1}{2}$

Rutherford's atomic model

This is based on gold foil α-particle scattering experiment. In this experiment α-particles were bombarded on gold foil of very small thickness approximately 4×10^{-6} m.

Observation

- The majority of α-particles passed through the foil remain undeflected.
- Some α-particles experienced slight deflections.

- A few (about one in every 20,000) suffered rather serious deflections as they penetrated the foil.
- A small fraction did not pass through the foil at all but "bounced back" in the direction from which they had come.

Conclusion

- Most of the space in an atom is empty as most of the α-particles passed through foil undeflected.
- Only a few positively charged α-particles were deflected due to extreme repulsive force indicating that positive charge of the atom is not spread throughout.
- Positive charge is assumed to be concentrated in very small region that repelled and deflected the positively charged α-particles. This positive centre was called **nucleus.**
- Volume of the nucleus ($r = 10^{-15}$ m) is negligibly small compared to the total volume of the atom ($r = 10^{-10}$ m). Thus, less than 10^{-12} of the volume of the atom is occupied by the material particle.

Moseley's equation

Moseley obtained photographic images of X-ray spectra and assigned frequencies to the spectral line :

$$\nu = a(Z - b)^2$$

or

$$\boxed{\sqrt{\nu} = a(Z - b)}$$

where, ν refers to frequency, Z the nuclear charge (atomic number) and a and b are constants.

Graphically, variation of $\sqrt{\nu}$ with Z is shown below :

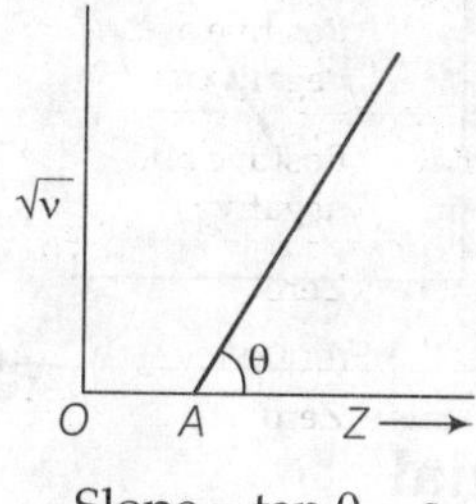

Slope $= \tan\theta = a$

Intercept on y-axis $= -ab$

Nature of light and electromagnetic waves

Wave nature of electromagnetic radiations

- James Maxwell observed that when electrically charged particles move under acceleration, alternating electrical and magnetic fields are produced and transmitted in the form of waves called electromagnetic waves or radiations.
- Wave theory predicts light in the form of wave motion of wavelength (λ) related to frequency (ν) and velocity of light.

$$\boxed{\nu = \frac{c}{\lambda}}$$

$$\nu = c\bar{\nu}$$

when, $\frac{1}{\lambda} = \bar{\nu}$ (wave number)

$\bar{\nu}$ is the number of waves per unit length.

- SI unit of frequency is Hertz (Hz). It is defined as the number of waves that pass a given point in one second. SI unit of wavelength is **m.**

$$1 \text{ pm} = 10^{-12} \text{ m}$$
$$1 \text{ nm} = 10^{-9} \text{ m}$$
$$1 \text{ Å} = 10^{-10} \text{ m} = 10^{-8} \text{ cm}$$

- Various types of electromagnetic radiations having various wavelength (or frequencies) constitute **electromagnetic spectrum.**

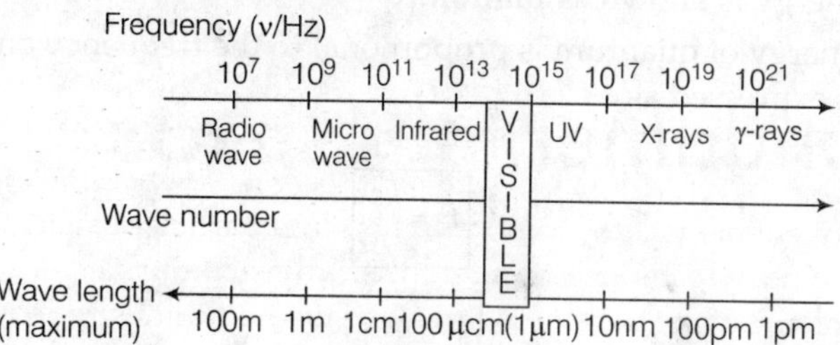

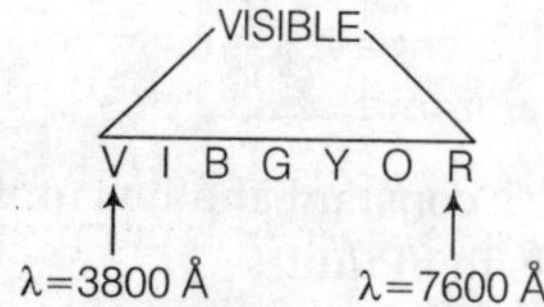

Black body radiations

- The ideal body which emits and absorbs all frequencies of radiations uniformly is called a **black body** and the radiation emitted by this body is called **black body radiation.**
- At a given temperature, the intensity of radiation emitted increases with increase of wavelength, reaches a maximum value and then starts decreasing with further increase of wavelength.
- Shorter wavelengths contribute more to the energy density as the temperature is raised. By **Wien's displacement law**

$$T\lambda_{max} = \text{constant}$$

λ_{max} is the wavelength of the radiation that makes the maximum contribution to the energy density.

As temperature increases, λ_{max} is shifted to lower wavelength.

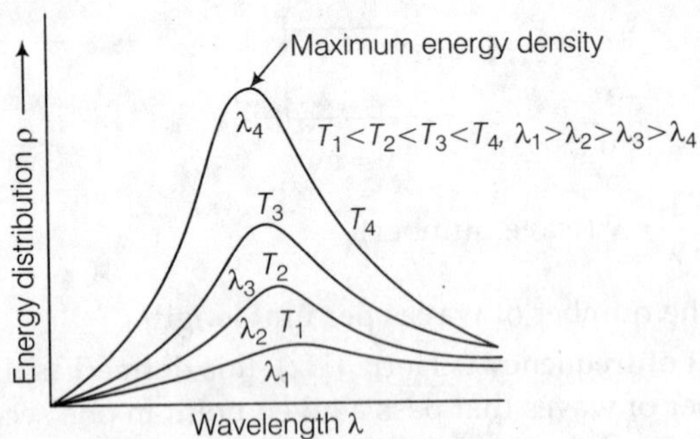

The energy distribution in a black-body cavity at several temperatures; as the temperature is raised, the peak shifts to shorter wavelength.

Planck's quantum theory

- The radiant energy is emitted or absorbed discontinuously in the form of small discrete packets of energy called **quantum.** In case of light, the quantum of energy is known as **photon.**
- Energy of quantum is proportional to the frequency and is expressed as

$$E = h\nu$$

$$\boxed{E = \frac{hc}{\lambda}}$$

$$\boxed{E = hc\bar{\nu}}$$

$$\boxed{\bar{\nu} = \frac{E}{hc}}$$

h is called Planck's constant and has unit of **energy-time.** $h = 6.626 \times 10^{-34}$ Js in SI unit.

$$\frac{E_1}{E_2} = \frac{\nu_1}{\nu_2} = \frac{\lambda_2}{\lambda_1} = \frac{\bar{\nu}_1}{\bar{\nu}_2}$$

Since, energy values are additives

$$E = E_1 + E_2$$

$$h\nu = h\nu_1 + h\nu_2$$

$$\frac{c}{\lambda} = \frac{c}{\lambda_1} + \frac{c}{\lambda_2}$$

$$\therefore \quad \frac{1}{\lambda} = \frac{\lambda_1 + \lambda_2}{\lambda_1\lambda_2}$$

$$\therefore \quad \boxed{\lambda = \frac{\lambda_1\lambda_2}{\lambda_1 + \lambda_2}}$$

- The energy emitted or absorbed by a body is always an integral multiple of $h\nu$.

$$E = nh\nu = \frac{nhc}{\lambda} \qquad (n = 1, 2, 3 \ldots)$$

Photoelectric effect (1889)

H. Hertz performed an experiment in which electrons were ejected when light of certain frequency strikes the surface of a cathode metal (like K, Rb, Cs of low ionisation energy). This phenomenon of ejection of electrons by metals under the given condition is called **photoelectric effect** and electrons emitted are called **photoelectrons.**

Photoelectric equation, $h\nu = h\nu_0 + \text{KE}$

$$= h\nu_0 + \frac{1}{2}mv^2$$

$$h\nu = \phi + \frac{1}{2}mv^2$$

where, ν = frequency of incident light

ν_0 = minimum frequency (threshold frequency) at which electrons are ejected.

$(h\nu_0 = \phi)$ is also called **work function** minimum energy of incident radiation above which electrons are ejected.

Difference of $(h\nu - h\nu_0)$ is used to impart kinetic energy to the ejected electrons. Kinetic energy of the ejected electrons depends upon the frequencies of incident radiations and is independent of its intensity.

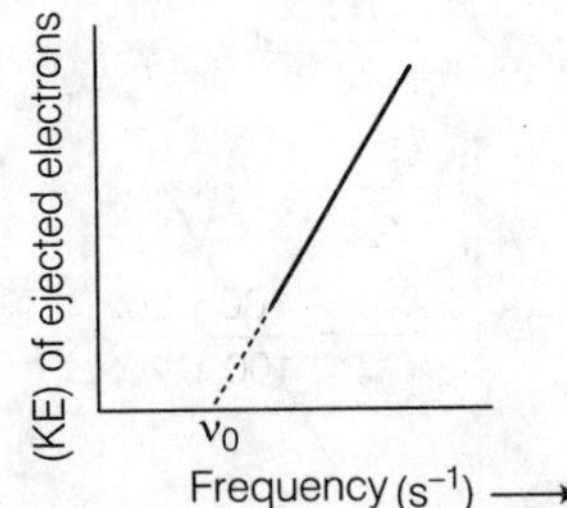

Stopping potential

The stopping potential is the voltage between the metal surface and a cathode, placed closed to the surface in vacuum, which just stops them from producing current. Thus, we can assume that the maximum (KE) of the photo-electrons

$$\text{KE(max)} = eV_s$$

where, V_s the stopping potential

$$\therefore \quad eV_s = \frac{1}{2}mv^2 \qquad (1 \text{ eV} = 1.602 \times 10^{-19} \text{ J})$$

Solved Examples & Instant Practice

Example 2.1) A 100 W bulb emits monochromatic light of 400 nm. Calculate number of photons emitting per second by the bulb. ***[NCERT]***

Sol. Watt (Js^{-1}) is to be related to number of photons by Planck's equation.

$$1\,W = 1\,J\,s^{-1}$$

$$E = nh\nu = \frac{nhc}{\lambda}$$

Thus, $$n = \frac{E\lambda}{hc}$$

$$\text{Number of photons} = \frac{100\,J\,s^{-1} \times 400 \times 10^{-9}\,m}{6.626 \times 10^{-34}\,J\,s \times 3 \times 10^{8}\,m\,s^{-1}}$$

$$= 2.01 \times 10^{20} \text{ photons } s^{-1}$$

For quick calculation, use $hc = 2.0 \times 10^{-25}$ Jm

Immediate Test 1

Calculate the energy of one mole of photons of radiation whose frequency is 5×10^{14} Hz. ***[NCERT]***

Example 2.2) Two waves of 100 nm and 200 nm are ejected when light of certain wavelength falls on the surface of a metal. Calculate the wavelength of the light radiation.

Sol. Energy values are additives, but wavelengths are not additives, thus from this fact relation derived is

$$E = E_1 + E_2$$

$$\therefore \quad \frac{hc}{\lambda} = \frac{hc}{\lambda_1} + \frac{hc}{\lambda_2} \text{ or } \frac{1}{\lambda} = \frac{1}{\lambda_1} + \frac{1}{\lambda_2}$$

or $$\lambda = \frac{\lambda_1 \lambda_2}{\lambda_1 + \lambda_2}$$

$$\lambda = \frac{\lambda_1 \lambda_2}{\lambda_1 + \lambda_2} = \frac{100 \times 200}{100 + 200} = 66.67 \text{ nm}$$

Immediate Test 2

Two photons of wavelength 150 pm and that of unknown wavelength are emitted when a light of 80 pm falls on the surface of a metal. What is wave number of the other photon?

Example 2.3) Moseley's equation can be used to determine atomic number of the element.

$$\sqrt{\nu} = a(Z - b)$$

Graph between frequency (ν) and atomic number Z is of the type

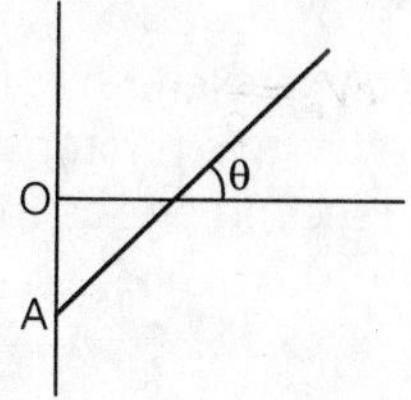

Given, $\theta = 45°$ and $OA = -2$

What is atomic number of the element which gives frequency at 625 Hz?

Sol. $$\sqrt{\nu} = aZ - ab$$

This is linear equation, of the type $y = mx - c$

On comparison of the values, m = Slope = $a = \tan\theta$

Thus, a is known

Intercept on y-axis on the negative side $= -ab$

Thus, b is also known.

$$a = \tan\theta = \tan 45° = 1$$

$$-ab = -2$$

$$\therefore \quad b = 2$$

When, $$\nu = 625\text{ Hz}$$

$$\sqrt{\nu} = 25$$

$$\therefore \quad 25 = aZ - ab = 1 \times Z - 2$$

$$Z = 27$$

Immediate Test 3

What is wavelength of the element of atomic number 25 for the case using Moseley's equation

$$\sqrt{\nu} = a(Z - b)$$

Given, $a = 0.5$ and $b = 2.0$

Example 2.4) The threshold frequency (ν_0) of a metal is $7 \times 10^{14}\ s^{-1}$. Calculate the kinetic energy of an electron emitted when radiation frequency ν of $1 \times 10^{15}\ s^{-1}$ hits the metal. ***[NCERT]***

Emission of electron from a metal when radiation falls on its surface depends on threshold frequency. Difference of energy absorbed and emitted if converted to KE.

Sol. By photoelectric effect,

$$h\nu = h\nu_0 + \frac{1}{2}mv^2$$

$$\frac{1}{2}mv^2 = \text{KE} = h(\nu - \nu_0)$$

$$= 6.626 \times 10^{-34}\,(1 \times 10^{15} - 7 \times 10^{14})\,\text{J}$$

$$= 2 \times 10^{-19} \text{ J per electron}$$

This is also equal to the stopping potential.

Immediate Test 4

Light of wavelength 450 nm strikes on the surface of rubidium (work function = 2.16 eV). Determine the velocity of the ejected electron of (mass of electron = 9.1×10^{-31} kg).

Example 2.5) Voltage required to stop the electron ejection from copper plate is 0.24 V, when the radiation of wavelength 254 nm strikes the plate. Calculate the work function.

Stopping potential is simply the KE which is imparted to electron when light radiations falls on the surface of metal. Thus, work function is calculated.

Sol. Stopping potential = 0.24 V

$\therefore$ KE = 0.24 V $\quad h\nu = \phi + \text{KE}$

$\therefore$ $\phi = (h\nu - \text{KE}) \quad \nu = \dfrac{c}{\lambda}$

$$h\nu = \frac{6.626 \times 10^{-34}\ \text{Js} \times 3 \times 10^{8}\ \text{ms}^{-1}}{254 \times 10^{-9}\ \text{m}} = 7.826 \times 10^{-19}\ \text{J}$$

$$= \frac{7.826 \times 10^{-19}\ \text{J}}{1.6 \times 10^{-19}\ \text{J eV}^{-1}} = 4.89\ \text{eV}$$

$\therefore$ $h\nu = \phi + \text{KE}$

$\therefore$ ϕ (work function) = 4.89 – 0.24 = 4.65 eV

Immediate Test 5

(i) For a photosensitive metal, stopping potential is 0.24 eV, when light radiation of wavelength 100 nm strikes the surface.
What is the stopping potential, if wavelength of the light radiation is made 75 nm?

(ii) In a photoelectric experiment, the collector plate is at 2.25 eV with respect to the emitter plate made of metal with work function at 4.50 eV.
If the metal plate takes a monochromatic light of wavelength 2000 Å, find the minimum and maximum kinetic energy per mol of photoelectrons reacting the collector plate.

KNOWLEDGE CONFIRMATION Test 1

1 For the following dissociation,

$$I_2(g) \longrightarrow 2I(g)$$

one quantum is absorbed per molecule of I_2 gas. If light absorbed has wavelength of 500 nm, energy required (in kJ mol^{-1}) is

(a) 2.39×10^{-4} (b) 4×10^{-22}
(c) 2.39 (d) 239.3

2 What is value of Z in Moseley's equation with $b = 1$ and $\sqrt{\nu} = a$?

(a) 2 (b) 3 (c) 4 (d) $\sqrt{2}$

3 For a photoelectron in Mg, work function is 0.6 eV. What is stopping potential, when wavelength of 200 nm is used for ejection of electron ?

(a) 6.21 eV (b) 0.60 eV (c) 5.61 eV (d) 6.81 eV

4 Energy of one mole of photons having wavelength of 5.42×10^{-6} m is

(a) 2.2078 kJ mol^{-1} (b) 22.078 kJ mol^{-1}
(c) 22.078 J mol^{-1} (d) 2.2078 J mol^{-1}

5 The human eye is most sensitive to visible light having a wavelength of 550 nm. This is equal to

(a) $1.82 \times 10^{6}\ \text{m}^{-1}$ (b) $5.45 \times 10^{14}\ \text{s}^{-1}$
(c) $1.82 \times 10^{4}\ \text{cm}^{-1}$ (d) All of these

6 Maximum wavelength of a photon that can initiate the reaction,

$$Cl_2(g) \longrightarrow 2Cl(g); \quad \Delta H = 247\ \text{kJ mol}^{-1}$$

(a) 484 pm (b) 484 Å
(c) 484 nm (d) None of these

7 The minimum wavelength of light necessary to overcome the work function of Cs-metal, with work function of 2.14 eV is

(a) 193 pm (b) 581 nm (c) 581 pm (d) 193 nm

8 An argon laser operating at a power of 515 mW, emits blue light of wavelength 488 nm. Thus, number of photons emitted in 2s is

(a) 2.53×10^{9} (b) 2.53×10^{18}
(c) 2.53×10^{27} (d) 1.26×10^{18}

9 What is the work function of the metal if the light of wavelength 4000 Å generates photoelectrons of velocity $6 \times 10^{5}\ \text{ms}^{-1}$ from it?

(a) 4.0 eV (b) 3.1 eV
(c) 2.1 eV (d) 0.9 eV

10 Heat treatment of muscular pain involves radiation of wavelength of about 900 nm. Thus, energy associated with it per mol of photon is

(a) 133 kJ mol^{-1} (b) 1.33 kJ mol^{-1}
(c) 13.3 kJ mol^{-1} (d) 133×10^{3} kJ mol^{-1}

11 Which has maximum energy?

(a) A photon with a wavelength 10 nm
(b) A photon with frequency 10 Hz
(c) An electron moving with velocity of light
(d) All have equal energy

12 A near UV photon of wavelength 'x' is absorbed by a gas and then re-emitted as two photons. One photon has wavelength 'y' and second one as 'z'. Thus,

(a) $x = y + z$ (b) $x = (y \times z)$
(c) $x = \dfrac{yz}{y + z}$ (d) $x = \dfrac{y}{z}$

13 Assume that water absorbs light of wavelength 4.20×10^{-6} m with 100% efficiency. How many photons are required to heat 5.75 g of water by 1.00 K. The heat capacity of water is 75.3 J mol^{-1} K^{-1}
(Heat = mol × specific heat × ΔT)
(a) 5.08×10^{20} (b) 5.08×10^{19} (c) 9.15×10^{21} (d) 6.97×10^{21}

14 When an electron falls from a level of energy $\left(\frac{4E}{3}\right)$ to level of energy (E), radiation of wavelength 3λ is observed. If electron falls from a level of energy $2E$ to a level of energy E, wavelength of radiation is
(a) 3λ (b) $\frac{4\lambda}{3}$ (c) $\frac{3\lambda}{4}$ (d) λ

15 When an electromagnetic radiation of wavelength 300 nm falls on the surface of sodium, electrons are emitted with kinetic energy of 1.68×10^5 J mol^{-1}. Thus, minimum energy required for the process is

$$Na(g) \longrightarrow Na^+(g) + e^-$$

(a) 230.88 kJ mol^{-1} (b) −230.88 kJ mol^{-1}
(c) 3.83×10^{-19} kJ mol^{-1} (d) 3.83×10^{10} kJ mol^{-1}

16 $I_2(g) \xrightarrow{4500\ \text{Å}} 2I(g), \Delta H = 240$ kJmol^{-1}. Each molecule of I_2 absorbs one quantum of radiation. Thus, kinetic energy imparted to per iodine atom is
(a) 4.417×10^{-9} J (b) 3.984×10^{-14} J
(c) 2.16×10^{-20} J (d) 4.32×10^{-20} J

17 The minimum energy required of overcome the attractive forces between electron and the surface of Ag metal is 7.52×10^{-19} J. Maximum kinetic energy of electron emitted out from Ag surface which is being radiated with UV-light of wavelength 360 Å is
(a) 5.52×10^{-18} J (b) 4.77×10^{-18} J
(c) 1.03×10^{-17} J (d) None of these

18 Energy required to stop the ejection of electron from a metal surface is 0.25 eV. If radiation of wavelength 200 nm falls on the surface of the metal, then work function is
(a) 6.0 eV (b) 6.50 eV (c) 3.0 eV (d) 7.00 eV

19 Given by

X, **Wien's** contribution, $E_\lambda = \frac{a}{\lambda^5} e^{-b/\lambda T}$

Y, **Rayleigh Jeans,** contribution, $E_\lambda = \frac{8\pi kT}{\lambda^4}$

Z, **Planck's** contribution, $E_\lambda = \frac{a}{\lambda^5 (e^{b/kT} - 1)}$

Thus I, II and III represent.

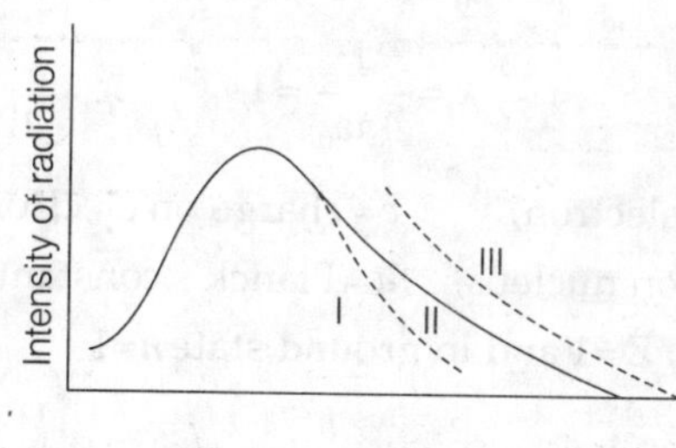

	I	II	III		I	II	III
(a)	X	Y	Z	(b)	X	Z	Y
(c)	Z	X	Y	(d)	Y	X	Z

20 The light of wavelength 400 nm is incident on the sodium surface with work function 2.28 eV. The longest wavelength which can result in the emission of photoelectron from a sodium surface is
(a) 136 nm (b) 272 nm (c) 544 pm (d) 200 nm

Bohr's Theory of H-atom

This theory is applicable for H-atom or species with one electron as He^+, Li^{2+}, Be^{3+} ... Na^{10+}.

Postulates

- The electrons continue revolving in their respective orbits without losing energy. Each orbit is associated with a definite energy, thus **orbit** is also called **energy level.**
- Angular momentum (mvr) of an electron in a given orbit (n) is quantised.

$$mvr_n = \frac{nh}{2\pi}$$

i.e. angular momentum of a moving electron in the nth orbit is an integral multiple of $\frac{h}{2\pi}$.
(m = mass of electron, v = velocity, r_n = radius of the nth orbit, where $n = 1, 2, 3 \ldots$)

- Energy is emitted or absorbed only when an electron moves from one level to another level.

$$\Delta E = (E_2 - E_1) = h\nu = \frac{hc}{\lambda}$$

$$\therefore \quad \frac{1}{\lambda} = \frac{\Delta E}{hc}$$

$$\text{or } \bar{\nu} \text{ (wave number)} = \frac{\Delta E}{hc}$$

Results from Bohr's theory

- Kinetic energy of electron $= \frac{1}{2}mv^2 = \frac{1}{2}\frac{kZe^2}{r_n}$
- Potential energy of electron $= -\frac{kZe^2}{r_n} = -2(\text{KE})$
- Radius of the atom with atomic number (Z) in the nth orbit,

$$r_n = \frac{n^2h^2}{4\pi^2 mkZe^2}$$

where, $k = \frac{1}{4\pi\varepsilon_0}$

ε_0 is called absolute permittivity of the medium (vacuum in this case)

$$\varepsilon_0 = 8.99 \times 10^9 \text{Nm}^2\text{C}^{-2}$$

In CGS unit, $k = \frac{1}{4\pi\varepsilon_0} = 1$

m = mass of electron, e = charge on electron,

Ze = charge on nucleus, h = Planck's constant

For H-atom, Z = 1 and in ground state n = 1

$$\therefore \quad r_1 = \frac{h^2}{4\pi^2 mke^2} = a_0$$

r_n in terms of 'a_0' is

$$r_n = \frac{n^2 a_0}{Z}$$

'a_0' is called Bohr's radius of H-atom in its first orbit (ground state)

$$a_0 = \frac{h^2}{4\pi^2 me^2 k}$$

$$= 0.529\text{Å} = 529 \text{ pm}$$

a_0 defines an atomic unit of length called the Bohr.

For H-atom (Z = 1)	Difference between two successive orbits
$r_1 = a_0$	
	$3a_0$
$r_2 = 4a_0$	
	$5a_0$
$r_3 = 9a_0$	
	$7a_0$
$r_4 = 16a_0$	

Thus, orbits are not equally spaced.

$\therefore \quad \frac{r_1}{r_2} = \frac{n_1^2 Z_2}{n_2^2 Z_1}$ for different orbits in different atoms.

$\frac{r_1}{r_2} = \frac{n_1^2}{n_2^2}$ for different orbits in same atom.

Energy of an electron

- KE in terms of Z, $n = \frac{2\pi ke^2\sqrt{Z}}{nh}$

E_n (energy of the nth orbit) = KE + PE $= \frac{1}{2}\frac{kZe^2}{r_n} - \frac{kZe^2}{r_n}$

$$E_n = -\frac{kZe^2}{2r_n}$$

Thus, total energy of the electron in nth orbit = – KE

$$\boxed{E_n = -\frac{2\pi^2 mZ^2e^4k^2}{n^2h^2}}$$

Here, the negative sign signifies that the energy of the electron in the atom is lower than the energy of a free electron.

Energy of electron in different units

$$E_n = -2.18\times10^{-18}\frac{Z^2}{n^2}\text{ J atom}^{-1}$$

$$E_n = -2.18\times10^{-18}\times6.02\times10^{23}\frac{Z^2}{n^2}\text{ J atom}^{-1}$$

$$E_n = -1.312\times10^{6}\frac{Z^2}{n^2}\text{ J atom}^{-1}$$

Since, $1.6\times10^{-19}\text{ J} = 1 \text{ eV}$

$$\therefore \quad E_n = \frac{-2.18\times10^{-18}\text{ J}}{1.6\times10^{-19}\text{ J / eV}}\left(\frac{Z^2}{n^2}\right) = -13.6\frac{Z^2}{n^2}\text{ eV atom}^{-1}$$

$$= -8.1872\times10^{24}\frac{Z^2}{n^2}\text{ eV mol}^{-1}$$

For H-atom, Z = 1

$$\therefore \quad E_n(\text{H}) = -\frac{13.6}{n^2}\text{ eV atom}^{-1} = -\frac{2.18\times10^{-18}}{n^2}\text{ J atom}^{-1}$$

$$= -\frac{1.312\times10^{6}}{n^2}\text{ J mol}^{-1}$$

Energy	Difference between two successive orbits
$E_1(\text{H}) = -13.6 \text{ eV}$	
	9.2 eV
$E_2(\text{H}) = -4.4 \text{ eV}$	
	2.9 eV
$E_3(\text{H}) = -1.5 \text{ eV}$	
	0.65 eV
$E_4(\text{H}) = -0.85 \text{ eV}$	

Thus, as n increases, the difference in energy decreases. Thus, it is easier to transit an electron from $(n_2 \to n_3)$ than $(n_2$ to $n_1)$.

Ionisation energy

Energy required to remove the electron from the outermost orbit of the atom in gaseous phase is called **ionisation energy (IE)**.

$$\text{H}(g) \longrightarrow \text{H}^+(g) + e^-$$

For H-atom, $(\text{IE})_{\text{H}} = -E_1(\text{H})$

$$= 13.6 \text{ eV atom}^{-1}$$

$$= 2.18 \times 10^{-18} \text{J atom}^{-1}$$

and for an ion (as He^+, Li^{2+}) atom, isoelectronic of H, of atomic number Z

$$\boxed{(\text{IE})_Z = \frac{(\text{IE})_{\text{H}} Z^2}{n^2}}$$

Velocity and time period of the electron

Velocity of the electron in the nth orbit

$$V_n = \frac{2\pi Z e^2 k}{nh} = \frac{(2.182 \times 10^6) Z}{n}$$

$$\frac{V_2}{V_1} = \frac{1}{2}, \quad \frac{V_3}{V_2} = \frac{2}{3}$$

$$\text{Time period } (T) = \frac{2\pi r n}{V_n} = \frac{2\pi^2 n^3 a_0}{(2.1822 \times 10^6) Z^2}$$

$$\therefore \quad T \propto n^3 / Z^2$$

$$\frac{T_2}{T_1} = \left(\frac{n_2}{n_1}\right)^3 \left(\frac{Z_1}{Z_2}\right)^2$$

Hydrogen spectrum

When an electron drops from a higher energy level (or orbit) say n_2 to lower energy level (or orbit) say n_1, the electromagnetic radiations of discrete frequencies are emitted and appear in the form of sharp lines called **spectrum.** The spectrum of white light ranges from violet (at 7.50×10^{14} Hz) to red (4×10^{14} Hz). Such spectrum is called **continuous spectrum.**

Rainbow is a similar type of spectrum. The light of red colour with longest wavelength is deviated the least, while the violet light with shortest wavelength is deviated the most.

Let, E_{n_1} = energy of n_1th level

E_{n_2} = energy of n_2th level $(n_2 > n_1)$

$$\Delta E = (E_{n_2} - E_{n_1})$$

$$= -\frac{2\pi^2 m Z^2 e^4 k^2}{n_2^2 h^2} + \frac{2\pi^2 m Z^2 e^4 k^2}{n_1^2 h^2}$$

$$\boxed{\Delta E = \frac{2\pi^2 m Z^2 e^4 k^2}{h^2}\left[\frac{1}{n_1^2} - \frac{1}{n_2^2}\right]}$$

For H-atom, $Z = 1$

$$\frac{2\pi^2 m e^4 k^2}{h^2} = (\text{IE})_{\text{H}} = 2.18 \times 10^{-18} \text{ J}$$

$$\bar{\nu} = (\text{wave number}) = \frac{1}{\lambda} = \frac{\Delta E}{hc}$$

$$\therefore \quad \bar{\nu} = \frac{2\pi^2 m Z^2 e^4 k^2}{ch^3}\left[\frac{1}{n_1^2} - \frac{1}{n_2^2}\right]$$

$$\boxed{\bar{\nu} = R_{\text{H}} Z^2 \left[\frac{1}{n_1^2} - \frac{1}{n_2^2}\right]}$$

where, $R_{\text{H}} = \dfrac{2\pi^2 m e^4 k^2}{ch^3} = 1.09679 \times 10^7 \text{ m}^{-1}$

R_{H} is called **Rydberg's constant.**

Wave number in terms of (IE) is given by

$$\bar{\nu} = \frac{(\text{IE})_Z}{hc}\left[\frac{1}{n_1^2} - \frac{1}{n_2^2}\right] = \frac{(\text{IE})_{\text{H}} Z^2}{hc}\left(\frac{1}{n_1^2} - \frac{1}{n_2^2}\right)$$

where, $(\text{IE})_Z = (\text{IE})_{\text{H}} \dfrac{Z^2}{n^2}$

Frequency of the emitted radiation

$$\nu = \frac{c}{\lambda} = c\bar{\nu} = \frac{(\text{IE})_{\text{H}} Z^2}{h}\left[\frac{1}{n_1^2} - \frac{1}{n_2^2}\right] = R_{\text{H}} Z^2 c \left[\frac{1}{n_1^2} - \frac{1}{n_2^2}\right]$$

Spectral series

Following series of the H-spectrum is obtained depending on the values of n_1 to which level electron falls from higher level n_2.

Spectral lines of hydrogen atom

Series	n_1	$n_2 > n_1$	$\bar{\nu} = \frac{1}{\lambda} = R_{\text{H}}\left[\frac{1}{n_1^2} - \frac{1}{n_2^2}\right]$	Region of spectrum
Lyman	1	2, 3, ... ∞	$R_{\text{H}}\left[\frac{1}{1^2} - \frac{1}{n_2^2}\right]$	Ultraviolet
Balmer	2	3, 4, ... ∞	$R_{\text{H}}\left[\frac{1}{2^2} - \frac{1}{n_2^2}\right]$	Visible
Paschen	3	4, 5, ... ∞	$R_{\text{H}}\left[\frac{1}{3^2} - \frac{1}{n_2^2}\right]$	Infrared
Brackett	4	5, 6, ... ∞	$R_{\text{H}}\left[\frac{1}{4^2} - \frac{1}{n_2^2}\right]$	Infrared
Pfund	5	6, 7, ... ∞	$R_{\text{H}}\left[\frac{1}{5^2} - \frac{1}{n_2^2}\right]$	Infrared
Humphries	6	7, 8, ... ∞	$R_{\text{H}}\left[\frac{1}{6^2} - \frac{1}{n_2^2}\right]$	Infrared

- When an electron falls from nth, $(n-1)$th, $(n-2)$th ...... level to lower level, then total number of spectral lines $= \dfrac{n(n-1)}{2}$.
- Maximum number of spectral lines in hydrogen like species due to transition of electron from n_2th level to n_1th level $= (n_2 - n_1)(n_2 - n_1 + 1)/2$
- If electron jumps from n_2th level to n_1th level, total number of transitions are $\sum \Delta n = \sum (n_2 - n_1)$

Maximum and minimum wavelength

- Each series of lines converges towards a limit beyond which the spectrum is continuous. This corresponds to the case when $n_2 = \infty$. This also gives spectral line of maximum wave number (minimum wavelength).

Thus, $$\bar{\nu}_{max} = \frac{1}{\lambda_{min}} = \frac{R_H Z^2}{n_1^2}$$

- Minimum wave number is obtained for the case when, $n_2 = (n_1 + 1)$.

Thus, $$\bar{\nu}_{min} = \frac{1}{\lambda_{max}} = R_H Z^2 \left[\frac{1}{n_1^2} - \frac{1}{(n_1+1)^2}\right]$$

This also corresponds to maximum wavelength of the first line called **α-line of the series.**

- First, second, third, ... lines of a series are called α, β, γ, ... lines respectively. Thus, wave number of third line (γ-line) of Balmer series is given by

$$\bar{\nu} = R_H Z^2 \left[\frac{1}{2^2} - \frac{1}{5^2}\right]$$

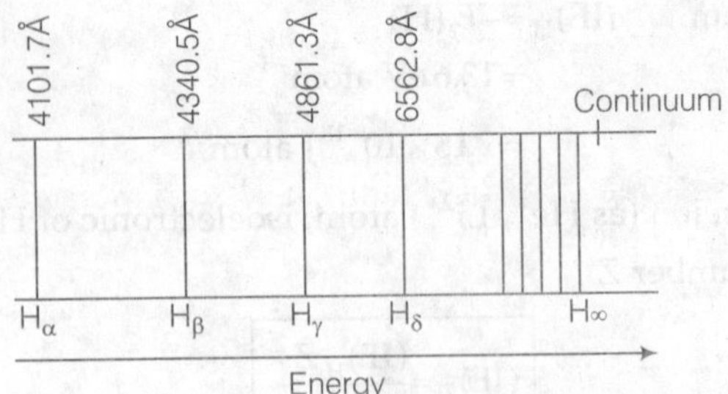

- The energy levels become more closely packed as the height above the lowest level (called the ground state) increases.

They finally converge to a limit whose height above the ground level is the energy necessary to remove the electron completely from the field of the nucleus.

In the observed spectrum, lines become more and more densely packed and finally merge into a continum - a region of continuous absorption or emission of radiation without any line structure.

Solved Examples & Instant Practice

Example 2.6) What is ionic radius of Li^{2+} in second excited state?

Sol. Li^{2+} is isoelectronic of H (one electron), hence ionic radius can be derived from the relation.

$$r_n = \frac{n^2 a_0}{Z}$$

For second excited state, $n = 3$ $a_0 = 52.9$ pm (Bohr's radius)

$Z = 3$

$$\therefore \quad r_3 = \frac{(9)\ (52.9)}{3} = 158.7 \text{ pm}$$

Immediate Test 6

Which is larger out of two

I. a Be^{3+} ion in its second orbit.

II. a He^+ ion in fourth orbit?

Example 2.7) Calculate the velocity of an electron in

(a) second Bohr's orbit of H-atom

(b) second excited state of Li^{2+} ion

Sol. Velocity in the nth orbit can be expressed in terms of atomic number (Z) of any species isoelectronic of H as :

$$v_n = \frac{(2.182 \times 10^6)Z}{n} \text{ ms}^{-1}$$

(a) $Z = 1, n = 2$ $\quad v_2 = \frac{2.182 \times 10^6 \times 1}{2} = 1.091 \times 10^6 \text{ ms}^{-1}$

(b) $n = 3, Z = 3$ $\quad v_3 = 2.182 \times 10^6 \text{ ms}^{-1}$

Immediate Test 7

The circumference of the first orbit of H-atom is 3.322×10^{-10}m. What is the velocity of the electron in this orbit?

Example 2.8) Energy of the electron of the H-atom in ground state is 13.6 eV. What is the energy of the He^+ in first excited state?

Sol. We can relate energy of any species of atomic number Z (but isoelectronic of hydrogen) in the nth orbit to the energy of H-atom.

$$E_n = -\frac{13.6 Z^2}{n^2} \text{eV}$$

For H, $Z = 1$ and $n = 1$

$$\therefore \quad E_1(H) = -13.6 \text{ eV}$$

$$\therefore \quad E_n = E_1(H)\frac{Z^2}{n^2}$$

For first excited state, $n = 2$ and for He^+, $Z = 2$

$$E_2(He^+) = -13.6\left(\frac{2}{2}\right)^2 = -13.6 \text{ eV}$$

Thus, energy of He^+ in first excited state is equal to energy of H-atom in ground state

$$\frac{E_{n_2}}{E_{n_1}} = \left(\frac{n_2}{n_1}\frac{Z_1}{Z_2}\right)^2$$

Immediate Test 8

(i) Calculate kinetic energy, potential energy and total energy of Be^{3+} in its third orbit.

(ii) Calculate the increase in

(a) distance from the nucleus and

(b) energy when an electron in H-atom is excited from the first to the third orbit. Also, calculate the corresponding increase in energy per mole of electrons.

Example 2.9) Calculate the energy of the following process:

$$He^+(g) \longrightarrow He^{2+}(g) + e^-$$

The ionisation energy of H-atom in the ground state is 2.18×10^{-18} J atom^{-1}.

Sol. H and He^+ are isoelectronic thus (IE) can be related by

$$(IE)_Z = (IE)_H \left(\frac{Z^2}{n^2}\right)$$

Given process is the ionisation of $He^+(g)$ (with one electron) to $He^{2+}(g)$.

$$(IE)_{He^+} = 2.18 \times 10^{-18}\left(\frac{2^2}{1^2}\right)$$

$$= 8.72 \times 10^{-18} \text{ J atom}^{-1}$$

$$= 8.72 \times 10^{-18} \times 6.02 \times 10^{23} \text{ J mol}^{-1}$$

$$= 524.944 \times 10^3 \text{ J mol}^{-1}$$

$$= 524.944 \text{ kJ mol}^{-1}$$

Immediate Test 9

Calculate the energy of the following process:

$$He^{2+}(g) + 2e^- \longrightarrow He(g)$$

Given, $He(g) \longrightarrow He^+(g) + e^-$;

$$\Delta H = 3.4 \times 10^{-19} \text{ J atom}^{-1}$$

Example 2.10) Express the Rydberg's constant R_H (= 1.09679×10^5 cm^{-1}) in

(a) J atom^{-1} (b) J mol^{-1}

Sol. R_H has been given in the unit of cm^{-1} (wave number). This value is to be converted into the unit of J (energy).

$$\frac{1}{\lambda} = \bar{\nu} \text{ (in length}^{-1}\text{)}$$

$$\nu = \frac{c}{\lambda}$$

Also, $$E = h\nu = \frac{hc}{\lambda} = hc\bar{\nu}$$

(a) $R_H = 1.09679 \times 10^5 \text{cm}^{-1} = 1.09679 \times 10^7 \text{m}^{-1}$

$$E = hc\bar{\nu}$$

$$= 6.626 \times 10^{-34} \text{ Js} \times 3 \times 10^8 \text{ms}^{-1} \times 1.09679 \times 10^7 \text{m}^{-1}$$

$$= 2.18 \times 10^{-10} \text{ J atom}^{-1}$$

(b) $E = 2.18 \times 10^{-18}$ J atom^{-1}

$$= 2.18 \times 10^{-18} \times 6.02 \times 10^{23} \text{ J mol}^{-1} = 1.3124 \times 10^6 \text{ J mol}^{-1}$$

■ For quick calculation, $hc = 2.0 \times 10^{-25}$ Jm

Immediate Test 10

Frequency of transition from level n_2 to n_1 is given by

$$\nu = 3.2881 \times 10^{15} \text{s}^{-1}\left[\frac{1}{n_1^2} - \frac{1}{n_2^2}\right]$$

Convert this frequency value into

(a) m^{-1} (b) J atom^{-1} (c) J mol^{-1}

Example 2.11) Frequency of a transition in Balmer series of H-atom is given by

$$\nu = 3.2881 \times 10^{15} \text{s}^{-1}\left[\frac{1}{2^2} - \frac{1}{n^2}\right]$$

where, $n = 3, 4 \ldots$

Calculate

(a) wave number and

(b) energy of the transition of β-line in the series.

Sol. Frequency is to be converted into wave number.

For α-line in Balmer series (first line), $n=2+1=3$

and for β-line (second line), $n=2+2=4$

$$\therefore \quad \frac{1}{\lambda} = \frac{\nu}{c}$$

$$\Delta E = h\nu = \frac{hc}{\lambda} = hc\bar{\nu}$$

$$\therefore \quad \bar{\nu} = \frac{\nu}{c}$$

(a) $\nu_\beta = 3.2881 \times 10^{15}\left[\frac{1}{2^2} - \frac{1}{4^2}\right] = 6.1652 \times 10^{14} \text{s}^{-1}$

$$\therefore \bar{\nu} = \frac{6.1652 \times 10^{14} \text{s}^{-1}}{3 \times 10^8 \text{ms}^{-1}} = 2.055 \times 10^6 \text{m}^{-1}$$

(b) $\Delta E = h\nu$

$$= 6.626 \times 10^{-34} \text{ Js} \times 6.1652 \times 10^{14} \text{s}^{-1}$$

$$= 4.085 \times 10^{-19} \text{ J atom}^{-1}$$

$$= 4.085 \times 10^{-19} \times 6.02 \times 10^{23} \text{ J mol}^{-1}$$

$$= 245.92 \times 10^3 \text{ J mol}^{-1} = 245.92 \text{ kJ mol}^{-1}$$

■ 1 mol H = N_0 atoms = 6.02×10^{23} atoms.

Immediate Test 11

(i) What is the frequency, wavelength and wave number of a photon emitted during transition from $n = 5$ to $n = 2$ state in H-atom? ***[NCERT]***

(ii) Calculate the wavelength of the spectral line emitted when an electron in Be^{3+} falls from $n = 5$ to $n = 3$ state.

$(IE)_H = 13.6$ eV

Example 2.12) The Lyman series of the H-spectrum can be represented by the equation,

$$\nu = 3.2881 \times 10^{15} \text{s}^{-1}\left[\frac{1}{1^2} - \frac{1}{n^2}\right]$$

Calculate

(a) maximum and minimum frequency of lines in the given series.

(b) maximum and minimum wavelength

Lyman series corresponds to transition from higher level to a level n = 1.

$$\nu = 3.2881 \times 10^{15} \text{s}^{-1}\left(\frac{1}{1^2} - \frac{1}{n^2}\right)$$

ν is maximum when, $n \rightarrow \infty$

ν is minimum when $\frac{1}{n^2}$ is maximum, i.e. n = 2

$$\nu = \frac{c}{\lambda}$$

If ν is maximum, λ is minimum, and vice-versa.

Sol. (a) $\nu_{max} = 3.2881 \times 10^{15}\left[\frac{1}{1^2} - \frac{1}{\infty}\right]$

$= 3.2881 \times 10^{15} s^{-1}$

$\nu_{min} = 3.2881 \times 10^{15}\left[\frac{1}{1^2} - \frac{1}{2^2}\right]$

$= 2.466 \times 10^{15} s^{-1}$

(b) $\lambda_{min} = \frac{c}{\nu_{max}} = \frac{3.0 \times 10^8 \text{ m s}^{-1}}{3.2881 \times 10^{15} s^{-1}}$

$= 9.12 \times 10^{-8} m$

$= 912 \times 10^{-10}\ m = 912 \text{ Å}$

$\lambda_{max} = \frac{c}{\nu_{min}} = \frac{3.0 \times 10^8 ms^{-1}}{2.466 \times 10^{15} s^{-1}}$

$= 1.21 \times 10^{-7} m$

$= 1210 \times 10^{-10}\ m = 1210 \text{ Å}$

Immediate Test 12

Calculate the maximum and minimum wave number of the Paschen series in He^+ ion.

Example 2.13) What transition in the hydrogen spectrum would have the same wavelength as the Balmer transition $n = 4$ to $n = 2$ of He^+ spectrum?

Sol. $\bar{\nu} = 1.09679 \times 10^7 m^{-1} Z^2\left[\frac{1}{n_1^2} - \frac{1}{n_2^2}\right]$

$\frac{1}{\lambda} = 1.09679 \times 10^7 m^{-1} Z^2\left(\frac{1}{n_1^2} - \frac{1}{n_2^2}\right)$

$\lambda_H = \lambda_{He^+} = 1.09679 \times 10^7 m^{-1}(2)^2\left[\frac{1}{2^2} - \frac{1}{4^2}\right]$

$1.09679 \times 10^7 (1)^2\left[\frac{1}{n_1^2} - \frac{1}{n_2^2}\right] = 4\left[\frac{1}{4} - \frac{1}{16}\right] \Rightarrow \left[\frac{1}{n_1^2} - \frac{1}{n_2^2}\right] = 4 \times \frac{3}{16} = \frac{3}{4}$

If $n_1 = 1$, $n_2 = 2$ then $\frac{1}{1} - \frac{1}{4} = \frac{3}{4}$. Thus, true.

Hence, transition from $n_2 = 2$ to $n_1 = 1$ in H-atom will give spectral line of same wavelength as He^+ for Balmer transition for $n_2 = 4$ to $n_1 = 2$ transition.

Immediate Test 13

(i) Transition between which orbits (less than 5) in He^+ ion would result in the emission of visible light with energy range from 2.84×10^{-19} J to 4.97×10^{-19} J?

(ii) What electronic transition in the He^+ spectrum has the same wave number as the first Lyman transition of H-spectrum?

KNOWLEDGE CONFIRMATION **Test 2**

1 In which case(s), ionic radius of the given ion is equal to Bohr's radius of H-atom?
(a) He^+ in second orbit
(b) Be^{3+} in second orbit
(c) Li^{2+} in second orbit
(d) All of the above

2 In which case, radius of the Column I is larger that of the Column II

	Column I	Column II
(a)	Be^{3+} in second orbit	H in ground state
(b)	He^+ in ground state	H in ground state
(c)	He^+ in second orbit	Be^{3+} in second orbit
(d)	Li^{2+} in second orbit	Be^{3+} in third state

3 Potential energy of the electron is
(a) $\int_{\infty}^{r_n} \frac{kZe^2}{r_n^2} dr$ (b) −2(KE)
(c) $\frac{1}{2}$ (total energy of the electron) (d) All of these

4 Time period of the electron in second orbit of the He^+ ion is t sec then, time period of the electron in third orbit of Li^{2+} is
(a) $\frac{4}{3}t$ (b) $\frac{3}{2}t$ (c) $3t$ (d) $4t$

5 Consider following cases :
I. r_I is the radius of He^+ ion in second orbit
II. r_{II} is the radius of Li^{2+} ion in third orbit
III. r_{III} is the radius of Be^{3+} ion in fourth orbit,
then
(a) $r_I < r_{II} < r_{III}$ (b) $r_I < r_{III} < r_{II}$
(c) $r_{III} < r_{II} < r_I$ (d) $r_I < r_{II} < r_{III}$

6 Ionic radius of M^{n+} (isoelectronic of H) is 2.273 a_0 in 5th orbit. Thus, M^{n+} is
(a) He^+ (b) Li^{2+} (c) Na^{10+} (d) Be^{3+}

7 Maximum wave number of a series is equal to R_H. This corresponds to
(a) Lyman series in H-atom (b) Balmer series in He^+ ion
(c) Paschen series in Li^{2+} ion (d) All of these

8 The Lyman series of the hydrogen spectrum can be represented as :

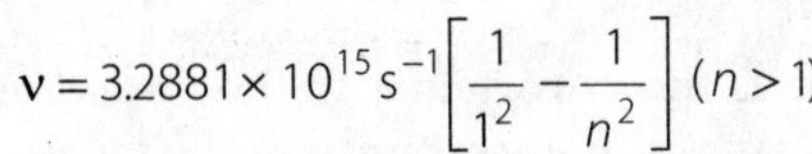

$$\nu = 3.2881 \times 10^{15}\, s^{-1}\left[\frac{1}{1^2} - \frac{1}{n^2}\right] \quad (n > 1)$$

What value of n corresponds to a spectral line at 102.6 nm?
(a) 2 (b) 3 (c) 4 (d) 5

9 Minimum wave number of a series is equal to
(a) 0.75 R_H in Lyman series of H-atom
(b) 3 R_H in Lyman series of He^+ ion
(c) $\frac{7}{9} R_H$ in Paschen series for Be^{3+} ion
(d) All of the above

10 Which has maximum frequency?
(a) α-line in Lyman series in H-atom
(b) β-line in Balmer series in He^+ ion
(c) γ-line in Paschen series in Li^{2+} ion
(d) All have equal frequency

11 For H-like species, wave number is $x\,m^{-1}$ for the first line in Lyman series. Thus, wave number for the first line in Balmer series for the same species
(a) $x\,m^{-1}$ (b) $\frac{5}{27} x\,m^{-1}$ (c) $4x\,m^{-1}$ (d) $\frac{7}{48} x\,m^{-1}$

12 The wave number of the first line of Balmer series of H-atom is 15200 cm^{-1}. Thus, wave number of the first line in the Balmer series of Be^{3+} is :
(a) $2.43 \times 10^5\ cm^{-1}$ (b) $6.08 \times 10^4\ cm^{-1}$
(c) $2.47 \times 10^5\ m^{-1}$ (d) $6.08 \times 10^4\ m^{-1}$

13 Velocity of light is v_1 and that of electron in first Bohr's orbit of H-atom is v_2. Thus, (v_1/v_2) is
(a) $\frac{1}{137}$ (b) $\frac{1}{9}$ (c) 137 (d) 9

14 The energy of an electron in the first Bohr orbit of H-atom is –13.6 eV. Which one of the following is possible excited state for electron on Bohr's orbits of H-atom?
(a) –3.4 eV (b) – 6.8 eV
(c) –1.7 eV (d) +13.6 eV

15 The radii of the any of the first four Bohr's orbits of H-atom are in the 1 : 4 ratio. Thus, energy difference between them is
(a) 10.2 eV or 2.55 eV (b) 13.6 eV or 3.4 eV
(c) 10.2 eV (d) 13.6 eV

16 Which is not the correct variation of velocity of the electron with Z and n?

(a) 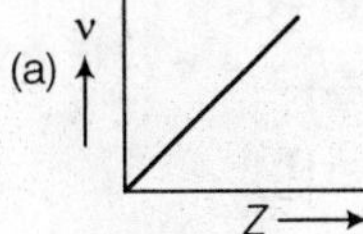

(b) 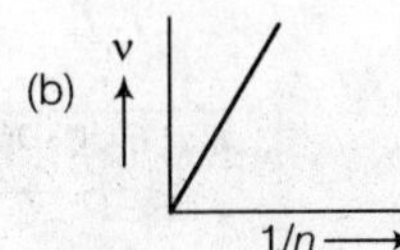

(c) 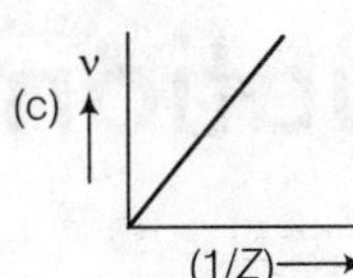

(d) 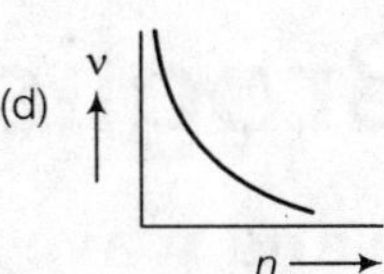

17 An electron in H-atom in its ground state absorbs 1.5 times as much as energy as the minimum required for its escape (13.6 eV) from the atom. Thus, kinetic energy given to the emitted electron is
(a) 13.6 eV (b) 20.4 eV
(c) 34.0 eV (d) 6.8 eV

18 Number of waves made by a Bohr electron in one complete revolution in its fourth orbit is
(a) 2 (b) 3
(c) 4 (d) ∞

19 Rydberg constant (R_H) is $x\,m^{-1}$ for H-atom. For He^+ ion, corresponding value of this constant is
(a) 100 $x\ cm^{-1}$ (b) 4 $x\ cm^{-1}$
(c) 400 $x\ cm^{-1}$ (d) 0.04 $x\ cm^{-1}$

20 Energy of a hydrogen like species in the third excited state is 2.25 times the energy of He^+ in the second excited state. Thus, atomic number of the hydrogen like species is
(a) 4 (b) 3 (c) 2 (d) 1

21 The potential energy of the electron present in the ground state of Be^{3+} ion ($Z = 4$) is
(a) $\frac{-4e^2}{\pi\varepsilon_0 a_0}$ (b) $\frac{-e}{\pi\varepsilon_0 a_0}$ (c) $\frac{-e^2}{\pi\varepsilon_0 a_0^2}$ (d) $\frac{-e^2}{\pi\varepsilon_0 a_0}$

22 The ratio of minimum to maximum wavelengths in Balmer series in any atom/ion is
(a) 5 : 9 (b) 5 : 36
(c) 1 : 4 (d) 3 : 4

23 Which of the following transitions of the electron in H-atom corresponds to the third line from the red end of the spectral lines?
(a) 5→ 2 (b) 2→ 5
(c) 3→ 2 (d) 4 → 1

24 For the following case of transition n_1 to n_2, time periods at n_1th and n_2th states are in the ratio of 8 : 1. Thus,

	n_1	n_2		n_1	n_2
(a)	4	1	(b)	8	2
(c)	4	2	(d)	6	2

25 $\bar{\nu}_1$ and $\bar{\nu}_2$ are the wave numbers of the series limit of Balmer and Paschen series in H-atom, and $\bar{\nu}_3$ is the wave number of the first line of lyman series, then
(a) $\bar{\nu}_3 = 7\bar{\nu}_1 + \frac{4}{9}\bar{\nu}_2$ (b) $\bar{\nu}_3 = \frac{4}{9}\bar{\nu}_1 + 7\bar{\nu}_2$
(c) $\bar{\nu}_3 = \frac{\bar{\nu}_1}{9} + 4\bar{\nu}_2$ (d) None of these

de-Broglie Equation

Particle and wave nature (dual nature) of electron

de-Broglie based on Millikan's oil drop experiment (which showed particle nature) and diffraction study (which showed wave nature) suggested the dual nature of electron, both as a material particle and as a wave. This signifies that electron has both momentum as well as wavelength.

$$E_1 = mc^2 \quad \text{(Particle nature)}$$

$$E_2 = h\nu = \frac{hc}{\lambda} \quad \text{(Wave nature)}$$

If, $E_1 = E_2$, $\lambda = \dfrac{h}{mc}$

$$\lambda = \frac{h}{p\ \text{(momentum)}}$$

or $\lambda = \dfrac{h}{mv}$ or $\lambda = \dfrac{h}{\sqrt{2m(\text{KE})}}$

Also, $\text{KE} = \dfrac{3}{2}\dfrac{RT}{N_0} = \dfrac{3}{2}kT$

$$\lambda = \frac{h}{\sqrt{3mkT}} \Rightarrow \frac{\lambda_1}{\lambda_2} = \sqrt{\frac{m_1T_1}{m_2T_2}}$$

■ Circumference of the *n*th orbit is equal to *n* times the wavelength of the electron

$$2\pi r_n = n\lambda = n\frac{h}{mv}$$

$\therefore$ $mvr_n = n\dfrac{h}{2\pi}$

Thus, angular momentum is an integral multiple of $\dfrac{h}{2\pi}$.

Frequency of the matter wave

$$\nu = \frac{\text{velocity}(v)}{\text{wavelength}} = \frac{v}{h/mv} = \frac{mv^2}{h} = \frac{2\text{KE}}{h}$$

$$\boxed{\text{Frequency} = \frac{2\text{KE}}{h}}$$

If electron is accelerated through a potential difference of V volt, then KE = eV

$\therefore$ $\lambda = h\sqrt{2meV}$

Heisenberg's uncertainty principle

"It is not possible to determine precisely both the position and the momentum (or velocity) of a small moving particle (as electron, proton).

Mathematically, $\Delta x \cdot \Delta p \geq \dfrac{h}{4\pi}\left(\text{or } \dfrac{\hbar}{2}\right)$ $\left(\because \hbar = \dfrac{h}{2\pi}\right)$

$$\Delta x \cdot \Delta v \geq \frac{h}{4\pi m}$$

$$\Delta x \cdot \Delta t \geq \frac{h}{4\pi}$$

where, Δx is the uncertainty in the measurement of **position**, Δp is the uncertainty in the measurement of **momentum** ($\Delta p = m\Delta v$), Δv is the uncertainty in the measurement of velocity and Δt is the uncertainty in the measurement of **time**.

- It is not possible to know exactly the position of an electron moving with a particular velocity as is implied in Bohr's model. Instead, it is possible only to state or predict the probability of locating an electron moving with a particular velocity in a given region of space around the nucleus at a given time.
- This principle rules out existence of definite paths or trajectories of electrons.

Quantum mechanical model of atom (Schrodinger wave equation)

The characteristic wave equation that describes behaviour of a small particle (as electron) for *x*-axis is

$$\psi = A\sin\frac{2\pi x}{\lambda}$$

when ψ is the amplitude of wave called wave function, x is displacement along x-axis and λ the wavelength and A is constant.

$\therefore$ $\dfrac{d^2\psi}{dx^2} = \dfrac{-4\pi^2}{\lambda^2}\psi$

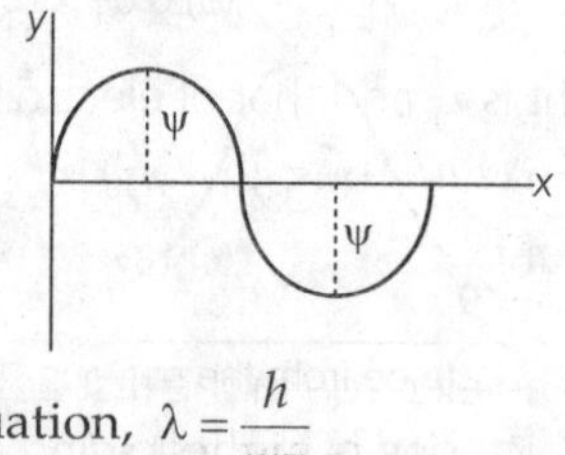

By de-Broglie equation, $\lambda = \dfrac{h}{mv}$

$\therefore$ $\dfrac{1}{\lambda^2} = \dfrac{m^2v^2}{h^2} = \dfrac{m(mv^2)}{h^2}$

But $\text{KE} = \dfrac{1}{2}mv^2$

$\therefore$ $\dfrac{1}{\lambda^2} = \dfrac{2m(\text{KE})}{h^2}$

Total energy, $E = (\text{KE} + \text{PE})$

$\therefore$ $\text{KE} = (E - U)$

$\therefore$ $\dfrac{d^2\psi}{dx^2} = -4\pi^2\psi\dfrac{2m}{h^2}(E-U)$

$\therefore$ $\boxed{\dfrac{d^2\psi}{dx^2} + \dfrac{8\pi^2 m}{h^2}(E-U)\,\psi = 0}$

This equation is called **Schrodinger wave equation.**

For three-dimensional motion of the particle, Schrodinger wave equation is

$$\frac{d^2\psi}{dx^2}+\frac{d^2\psi}{dy^2}+\frac{d^2\psi}{dz^2}+\frac{8\pi^2m}{h^2}(E-U)\psi=0$$

$$\nabla^2\psi+\frac{8\pi^2m}{h^2}(E-U)\psi=0$$

where $\nabla^2=\left(\frac{d^2}{dx^2}+\frac{d^2}{dy^2}+\frac{d^2}{dz^2}\right)$

is called **Laplacian operator.** Potential energy $U=\frac{-Ze^2}{r}$

$$\nabla^2\psi+\frac{8\pi^2m}{h^2}\left(E+\frac{Ze^2}{r}\right)\psi=0$$

Physical significance of ψ and ψ^2

- The energy of a wave at a particular point is proportional to the square of its amplitude.
- For a single particle, the square of the amplitude of wave function (ψ^2) at any point is proportional to the probability of finding the particle at that point.
- The electron density is high in those regions of the orbital where the probability of finding an electron is relatively high and *vice versa.*
- The radial probability density $4\pi r^2\psi^2$ indicates probability of finding the electron within the volume of a very thin spherical shell at a distance r from the nucleus

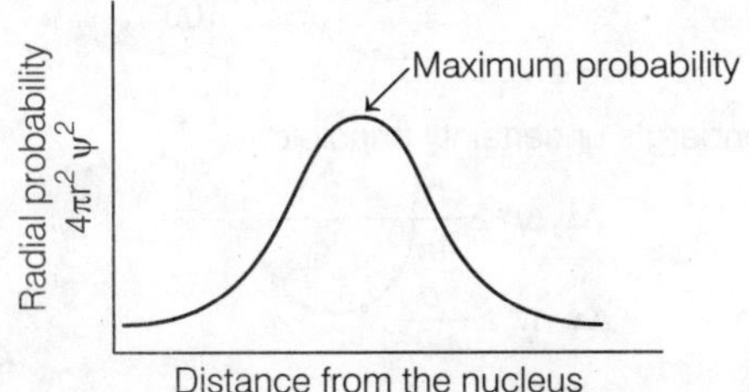

- Electron charge density is highest in the vicinity of the nucleus. It drops to zero at a particular distance from the nucleus (a condition called **spherical node**).
- The probability of finding an electron at the nodal surface is **zero.**
- If there are $(n+1)$ nodes (where, $n=1, 2 \ldots$) in a string of length l, then

$$l=\frac{n\lambda}{2}$$

n	l	$(n+1)$ nodes
1	$\frac{\lambda}{2}$	2
2	λ	3
3	$\frac{3\lambda}{2}$	4
4	2λ	5

- The plots of the radial wave function R (Fig. a), radial probability density R^2 (Fig. b) and radial probability function $4\pi^2r^2R^2$ (Fig. c) for $1s$, $2s$ and $2p$ atomic orbitals as a function of distance r from the nucleus are given (s,p,d...will be discussed in next section)

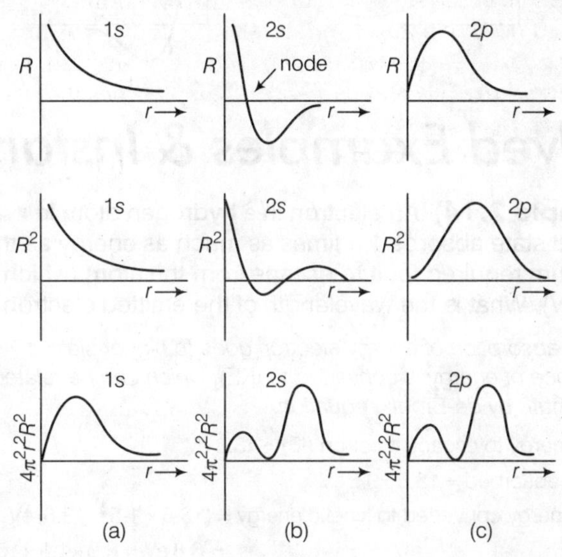

- For $1s$ radial wave function R decays exponentially and approaches zero at $r=\infty$. As is clear from fig. (a), highest electron probability in radial distribution function in $1s$ orbital is at the circumference.
- For $2s$, this radial wave function R is more complicated than for $1s$ orbital. A point at which a wave function is zero is called **node**. In a radial wave function, this node is called **radial node.**
- In case of $2p$ orbital, radial wave function is zero at the nucleus, increases to a maximum value and then decreases towards zero as r increases.

Angular nodes $= l$
Radial nodes $=(n-l-1)$
Total nodes $=(n-1)$

Sub orbit	n	l	Angular nodes	Radial nodes	Total nodes
1s	1	0	0	0	0
2s	2	0	0	1	1
2p	2	1	1	0	1
3s	3	0	0	2	2

- Suborbit is (Refer quantum numbers)
  s if $l=0$, p if $l=1$, d if $l=2$, f if $l=3$,
  based on values of x
  $l=0, 1, 2 \ldots (n-1)$
  Suborbit is designated as nl ← name; ↑ number
  For $n=2, l=0$ it is thus 2s.

- Wave functions ψ, (Fig. a, b) and ψ^2 (Fig. c, d) which also describes probability density of the electron are given

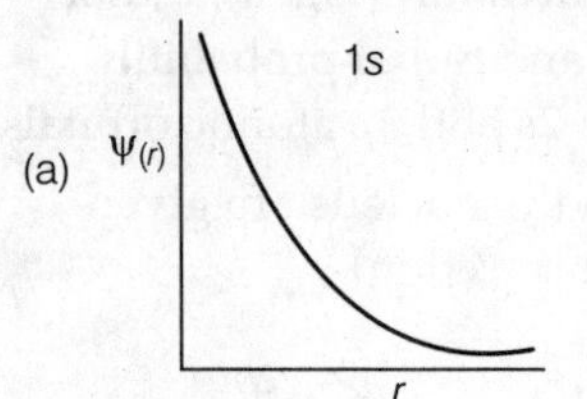

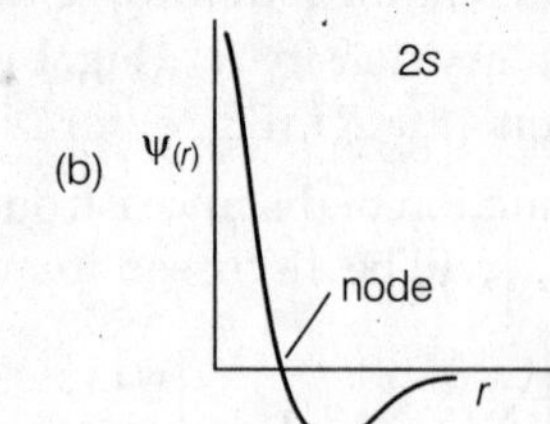

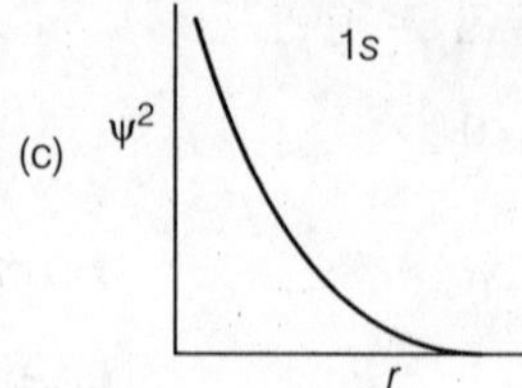

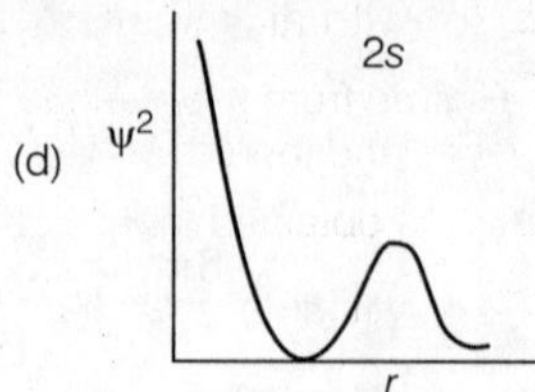

Solved Examples & Instant Practice

Example 2.14) An electron in a hydrogen atom in its ground state absorbs 1.5 times as much as energy as the minimum required for it to escape from the atom (which is 13.6 eV). What is the wavelength of the emitted electron?

By absorption of energy electron goes to higher state. Difference of energy is converted to (KE), which can be related to wavelength by de-Broglie equation.

Sol. Energy to escape electron (IE) = 13.6 eV

Energy absorbed = 13.6 × 1.5 eV

Thus, energy converted to kinetic energy = (13.6 × 1.5 – 13.6) eV

$$= 6.8 \text{ eV} = 6.8 \times 1.6 \times 10^{-19} \text{ J}$$

Thus, velocity is known

$$\therefore \quad \lambda = \frac{h}{mv} = \frac{h}{\sqrt{2mKE}}$$

m (electron) = 9.1×10^{-31} kg

$$\lambda = \frac{6.626 \times 10^{-34} \text{ Js}}{\sqrt{2 \times 9.1 \times 10^{-31} \times 6.8 \times 10^{-19}}} = 4.71 \times 10^{-10} = 471 \text{ pm}$$

Immediate Test 14

(i) The electron wave is associated to kinetic energy of 1.6 eV. Calculate its wavelength.

(ii) de-Broglie wavelength of an electron is 200 pm. Calculate its kinetic energy.

Example 2.15) de-Broglie wavelength of a neutron at 1200 K is 200 pm. Calculate wavelength at 300 K.

Sol. Since KE = $\frac{3}{2}RT$, hence wavelength can also be related to temperature.

$$\lambda = \frac{h}{\sqrt{2m(KE)}} = \frac{h}{\sqrt{2m\left(\frac{3}{2}RT\right)}} = \frac{h}{\sqrt{3mRT}}$$

For the same species, $\frac{\lambda_2}{\lambda_1} = \sqrt{\frac{T_1}{T_2}}$

$T_1 = 1200$ K, $T_2 = 300$ K, $\lambda_1 = 200$ pm, $\lambda_2 = ?$

$$\therefore \quad \lambda_2 = \lambda_1\sqrt{\frac{T_1}{T_2}} = 200\sqrt{\frac{1200}{300}} = 400 \text{ pm}$$

Immediate Test 15

For two atoms X and Y, wavelength ratio and temperature ratio are in 5 : 1 and 1 : 5 respectively. What is the ratio of atomic masses of X and Y?

Example 2.16) The uncertainty for the calculation of ionic radius of Li^{2+} (with one electron) of the third orbit is 0.03%. Calculate uncertainty in the measurement of velocity.

If uncertainty in the measurement of position is known, then uncertainty in the measurement of velocity can be derived using Heisenberg's uncertainty principle. Thus, Δv is calculated.

Sol. By Bohr's theory, radius of the nth orbit is

$$r_n = \frac{n^2 a_0}{Z}$$

$$r_3(Li^{2+}) = \frac{n^2 a_0}{Z} = \frac{(3)^2 \times 0.529}{3} = 3 \times 0.529 \text{ Å}$$

$$= 3 \times 0.529 \times 10^{-10} \text{ m}$$

$\therefore \Delta r$ (uncertainty in measurement of radius)

$$= 3 \times 0.529 \times 10^{-10} \times \frac{0.03 \text{ m}}{100}$$

$$= 4.761 \times 10^{-14} \text{ m}$$

By Heisenberg's uncertainty principle,

$$\Delta x . \Delta p \ge \frac{h}{4\pi}$$

$$\Rightarrow \quad \Delta x . \Delta v \ge \frac{h}{4\pi m}$$

$$\because \quad \Delta v = \frac{h}{4\pi m \Delta r}$$

$$= \frac{6.626 \times 10^{-34} \text{ Js}}{4\pi \times 9.1 \times 10^{-31} \text{ kg} \times 4.761 \times 10^{-14} \text{ m}}$$

$$= 1.217 \times 10^{9} \text{ m s}^{-1}$$

Immediate Test 16

A microscope using suitable photons is employed to locate an electron in an atom within a distance of 0.1 A°. What is the uncertainty in the measurement of velocity? **[NCERT]**

Example 2.17) The normalised wave function of 1s orbital is

$$\psi = \sqrt{N}e^{-Zr/a_0}$$

and the radial distribution function is $4\pi r^2\psi^2$, where N is normalisation constant $= \frac{Z^3}{\pi a_0^3}$.

Calculate the most probable distance at which 1s orbital of H-atom or H-like atom with atomic number Z is to be found.

Sol. As distance of electron from the nucleus increases, radial distribution first increases and then decreases.

Most probable value of r is obtained form.

$$\frac{d}{dr}(4\pi r^2 \psi^2) = 0$$

$$\frac{d}{dr}(4\pi r^2 \psi^2) = 0$$

$$\Rightarrow \quad \frac{d}{dr}(4\pi r^2 N e^{-2Zr/a_0}) = 0$$

$$(4\pi r^2 N e^{-2Zr/a_0})\left(-\frac{2Z}{a_0}\right) + 8\pi r N e^{-2Zr/a_0} = 0$$

$$8\pi N e^{-2Zr/a_0} r\left[\frac{-Zr}{a_0} + 1\right] = 0 \qquad \therefore\ r = \frac{a_0}{Z}$$

Immediate Test 17

Given, $\dfrac{d^2\psi}{dx^2} + \dfrac{8\pi^2 mE}{h^2}\psi = 0$

Show that solution of this equation is $\psi = A \sin\dfrac{2\pi x}{\lambda}$

where, E is the kinetic energy.

KNOWLEDGE CONFIRMATION Test 3

1 If electron and proton move with equal velocity, their de-Broglie's wavelength will be in the ratio of

(a) 1838 (b) $\frac{1}{1838}$ (c) $\frac{1}{3}$ (d) $\frac{3}{1}$

2 Masses of two particles are in the ratio of 3 : 1 and their temperatures are in ratio of 1 : 3, thus their de-Broglie's wavelength will be the ratio of

(a) 1 : 9 (b) 9 : 1 (c) 1 : 3 (d) 1 : 1

3 A baseball of 0.200 kg is moving with a velocity of 30 ms^{-1}. If its position is located with an uncertainty of 500 nm, uncertainty in its momentum is (in kg ms^{-1})

(a) 1.06×10^{-28} (b) 5.27×10^{-28}

(c) 9.43×10^{27} (d) 1.90×10^{27}

4 A N_2 molecule is moving with root mean square velocity $\left(=\sqrt{\frac{3RT}{M}}\right)$ at 300 K. Thus, its de-Broglie's wavelength is

(a) 276 pm (b) 27.6 pm (c) 276 nm (d) 27.6 nm

5 Which is the correct relationship for Heisenberg's uncertainty principle?

(a) $\Delta x \cdot \Delta p \geq \frac{h}{2\pi}$ (b) $\Delta x \cdot \Delta p > \frac{\hbar}{2}$

(c) $\Delta x \cdot \Delta v \geq \frac{h}{2\pi m}$ (d) None of these

6 The de-Broglie's wavelength of the electron in the first excited state of Be^{3+} is

(a) 334 pm (b) 668 pm

(c) 167 pm (d) None of these

7 In some regions of space around the nucleus $\psi^2 = 0$, thus region is called

(a) nucleus (b) spherical nodes

(c) orbital (d) orbit

8 Following are plots of probability density $\psi^2(r)$ as a function of distance r of the electron from the nucleus

(I) 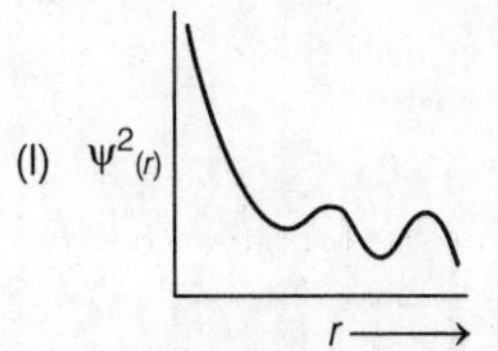

(II) 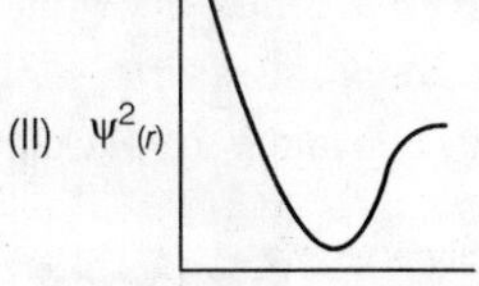

(III) 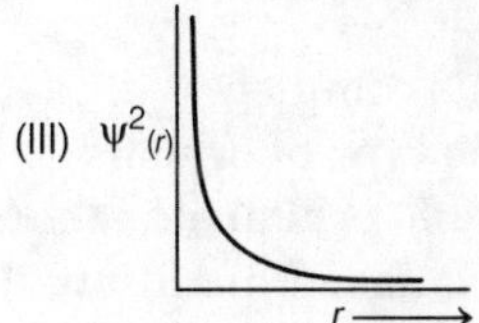

(IV) 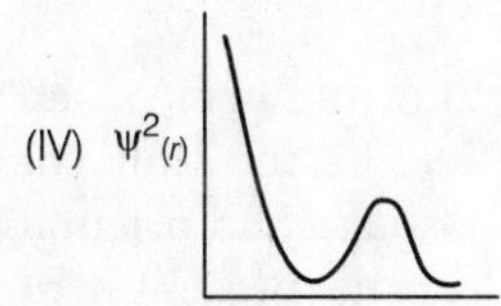

For 1s and 2s orbital, correct plots are

(a) I, II (b) I, III (c) III, IV (d) I, IV

9 The wavelength of the electrons that have been accelerated through a potential difference of 1.00 kV is

(a) 3.88 pm (b) 38.8 pm (c) 388 pm (d) 0.388 pm

10 The speed of a certain projectile of mass 1.0 g is known within 1.0×10^{-16} ms^{-1}. Minimum uncertainty in its position along its line of flight is

(a) 5.3×10^{-26} m (b) 5.3×10^{-16} m

(c) 5.3×10^{-9} m (d) 0.53×10^{-16} m

11 A photon is associated with a wavelength 663 pm. Linear momentum of the photon (in kg ms^{-1}) is

(a) 1×10^{-24} (b) 1×10^{-19}

(c) 1×10^{-22} (d) 1×10^{-26}

12 The de-Broglie wavelength is increased by 1%. Thus, change in kinetic energy is (in joule)

(a) 1% increase (b) 2% increase

(c) 1% decrease (d) 2% decrease

13 How fast would a particle of 1.0 g need to travel to have the same linear momentum as photon of wavelength 300 nm?
(a) 2.21×10^{-12} ms^{-1} (b) 2.21×10^{-16} ms^{-1}
(c) 2.21×10^{-24} ms^{-1} (d) 2.21×10^{-18} ms^{-1}

14 The speed of certain proton ($m_p = 1.67\times10^{-27}$ kg) is half of the velocity of light in vacuum. If uncertainty in its momentum is 0.01%, what uncertainty in its location must be tolerated?
(a) 2.1×10^{-12} m (b) 2.1×10^{-10} m
(c) 2.1×10^{-14} m (d) 2.1×10^{-6} m

15 If uncertainty in its position and momentum of a particle of mass m kg are equal, then uncertainty in its velocity is
(a) $\frac{h}{4\pi m}$ (b) $\frac{1}{2}\sqrt{\frac{h}{\pi m^2}}$
(c) $\sqrt{\frac{h}{4\pi m}}$ (d) $\sqrt{\frac{h}{4\pi}}$

16 $\psi^2 = 0$ represents
(a) node (b) orbital
(c) zero amplitude of wave (d) wave function

17 Number of nodal planes (planes of zero electron density) in the d_{xy} orbital is
(a) 1 (b) 2 (c) 0 (d) 4

18 If radius of first orbit of H-atom is a_0, then de-Broglie wavelength of the electron in the third orbit is
(a) $\frac{a_0}{3}$ (b) $9a_0$ (c) $6\pi a_0$ (d) $2\pi a_0$

19 de-Broglie wavelength of H_2, molecule at 300 K and that of He molecule at 400 K are λ_1 and λ_2, thus λ_1 / λ_2 is equal to
(a) 1.633 (b) 0.612 (c) 1.265 (d) 0.79

20 Which has maximum de-Broglie wavelength?
(a) Electron in first excited state of He^+
(b) Electron in fourth orbit of Be^{3+}
(c) Electron in third orbit of Li^{2+}
(d) Equal in all cases

Quantum Numbers

A set of four numbers which gives us complete information, i.e. location, energy, the type of orbitals occupied, shape and orientation of that orbital etc., about all the electrons present in an atom is called **quantum number.**

Principal quantum number

- This is used to specify the position and energy of the electron in an orbit or shell. This is denoted by n.

$$n = 1, 2, 3, \ldots, \infty \quad \text{(only positive integers)}$$

- Position of the electron from the nucleus in the nth orbit is given by $r_n = \frac{n^2 a_0}{Z}$ and corresponding energy for the species with one electron is

$$E_n = -\frac{13.6\,Z^2}{n^2}.$$

- Smaller the value of n, lower is the energy.
- The size of an orbital also depends on n. The larger the value of n, the larger is the orbital. Orbitals of the same quantum state 'n' are said to belong to the same shell. Shells are also denoted by letters :

Letter	K	L	M	N
n	1	2	3	4

Angular quantum number

- This is also called subsidiary or azimuthal quantum number, denoted by l.

$$l = 0, 1, 2, 3, \ldots (n-1)$$

- This is used to describe subshell $l = 0, 1, 2, 3, 4, 5, \ldots$, subshell $= s, p, d, f, g, \ldots$ where $s, p, d, f, g, \ldots$ are the symbols for sharp, principle, diffused, fundamental, degenerate spectral lines.

Value of l	Subshell (notation)	Number of orbitals $(2l+1)$
0	s (sharp)	1
1	p (principle)	3
2	d (diffused)	5
3	f (fundamental)	7
4	g (degenerate)	9

Any subshell is represented by 'nl' such that we write number for n and name for l.

Thus, $n = 1$, $l = 0$ will indicate (1*s*) subshell; $n = 2$, $l = 1$ will indicate (2*p*) subshell and so on.

Number (1, 2, 3, ...) Name (*s, p, d, f*) nl

Representation of a subshell

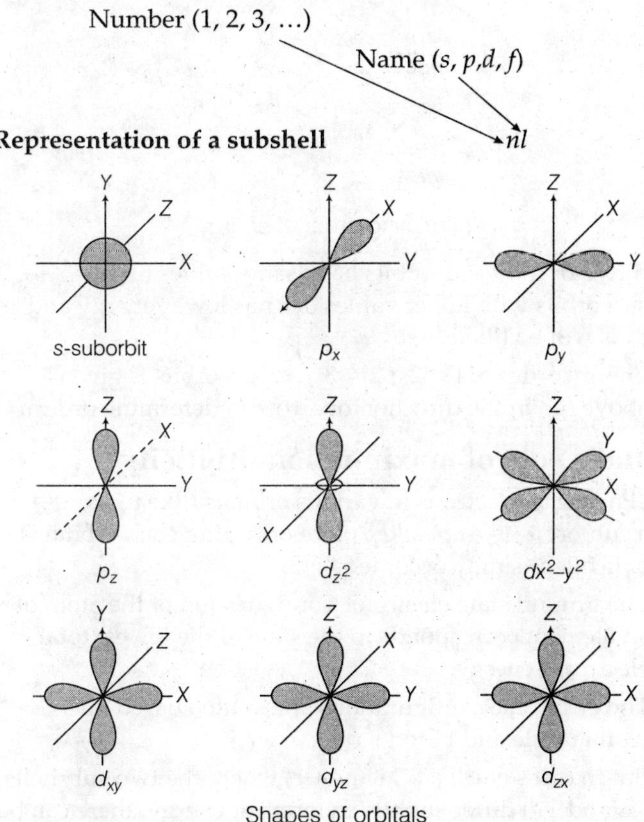

Shapes of orbitals

- Although the energy of an orbital is primarily determined by *n*, the energy also depends on *l* (except for H-atom) for a given *n*, the energy of an orbital increases with *l*.
- A subshell is only possible, if $l < n$.
- *l* also describes the shape of the orbital occupied by the electron, as shown above

$l = 0(s)$ – spherical

$l = 1\ (p)$ – dumb-bell

$l = 2\ (d)$ – double dumb-bell

- In case of 1*s*-orbital, the density of the charge cloud is the greatest at the nucleus and falls off with the distance. The density (at a particular distance) is uniform in all directions.
- In case of 2*s*-orbital, the density is again maximum at the nucleus and become very small at large distance. In between, the density becomes zero; i.e. an electron cannot be found in this region.
- In case of 2*p*-orbital, electron density is concentrated along a particular direction.
- For the $d_{x^2-y^2}$ orbital both nodal planes bisect the *x* and *y* axes.
- For the d_{z^2} orbital there are two nodal cones instead of nodal planes.

- Orbital angular momentum, (*L*) is quantised and is given by

$$L = \sqrt{l(l+1)}\ \frac{h}{2\pi}, \left(\frac{h}{2\pi} = \hbar\right)$$

- The magnitude of magnetic moment (μ_L) is given by

$$\mu_L = \frac{eh}{4\pi mc}\sqrt{l(l+1)}$$

where, $\frac{eh}{4\pi mc} = 9.2732 \times 10^{-14}$ J

Magnetic quantum number

- This quantum number denoted by *m* or m_l determines the preferred orientations of orbitals in space.

$$m \text{ or } m_l = -l, \ldots, 0 \ldots, +l$$

- Total values of $m = (2l + 1)$ = number of orbitals in a subshell (*l*).
- Number of orbitals is equal to the number of ways in which they are oriented. Thus, *s*-subshell ($m = 0$) will have one orbital. *p*-subshell ($m = -1, -0, +1$) has three orbitals (p_x, p_y, p_z). They are identical in energy, (degenerate) shape and size which differ only in their directions in space.
- *d*-subshell ($m = -2, -1, 0, +1, +2$) has five orbitals ($d_{xy}, d_{yz}, d_{zx}, d_{x^2-y^2}$ and d_{z^2}). These are also equal in energy. Degenerate orbitals have the same shape but different orientation in shape.
- Splitting (resolution) of spectral lines occurs when placed in a magnetic field **(Zeeman's effect)** or in an electric field **(Stark's effect)**. Total lines from a single line in the normal spectrum = $(2l + 1)$.

Spin quantum number

- The electron can be regarded as spinning on its axis, like a top, in clockwise or anti-clockwise direction.
- This spin of electron is represented by a number and is called spin quantum number denoted **s of m_s** with value of $\left(\frac{1}{2}\right)$ for all electrons.
- Clockwise or anti-clockwise spins are distinguished by the spin magnetic quantum number m_s.
- If $m_s = +\frac{1}{2}$ or ↑ (spin-up for clockwise) and electron is called **α-electron** if, $m_s = -\frac{1}{2}$ or ↓ (spin-down for anti-clockwise) and electron is called **β-electron**.

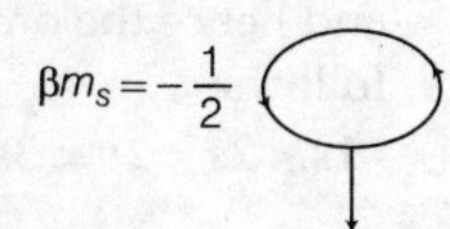

- Spin quantum number refers to magnetic property of electrons called **spin**.
- In an orbital there are maximum of two electrons such that their spins are $+\frac{1}{2}$ and $-\frac{1}{2}$ and sum of spins is zero.

  ⇅ or ⇅

- Spin angular momentum $= \sqrt{s(s+1)}\,\frac{h}{2\pi}$, where, $s = \frac{1}{2}$
- The spin of electrons is responsible for most of the magnetic properties of atoms, molecules or ions. The spin magnetic moment (μ_s) is given by

$$\mu_s = \frac{eh}{2\pi mc}\sqrt{s(s+1)}$$

- There are maximum of 2 electrons in *s*-subshell, 6 in *p*-subshell, 10 in *d* -subshell, 14 in *f*-subshell and 18 in *g*-subshell.
- Total numbers of electrons in a subshell with $(2l+1)$ orbitals $= 2(2l+1)$.

Radial and angular nodes

- For a hydrogen atom wave function of principal quantum number *n*, there are
  (i) $(n-l-1)$ radial nodes
  (ii) l angular nodes
  (iii) $(n-1)$ total nodes
- Thus, $1s(n=1, l=0)$ sub-orbit is without any node.
- $2s(n=2, l=0)$ sub-orbit will have only one radial node. while $2p(n=2, l=1)$ sub-orbit will have only one angular node.
- $3s$ $(n=3, l=0)$ sub-orbit will have two radial nodes, $3p$ $(n=3, l=1)$ sub-orbit will have one radial and one angular node while $3d(n=3, l=2)$ will have two angular nodes.
- **If the node which occurs at $r=\infty$ is being included, then total number of nodes will be n and not $(n-1)$** and number of nodal planes will be *l*.

Rules for filling electrons in orbitals

Aufbau rule

- ('Building up') "Electrons in various sub-orbits of an orbit are filled in the increasing order of their energies". Smaller the value of $(n+l)$, smaller the energy.
- The order in which the energies of the sub-orbits increase and hence the order in which the sub-orbits are filled is as follows:

  $1s < 2s < 2p < 3s < 3p < 4s < 3d < 4p < 5s < 4d < 5p < 4f$

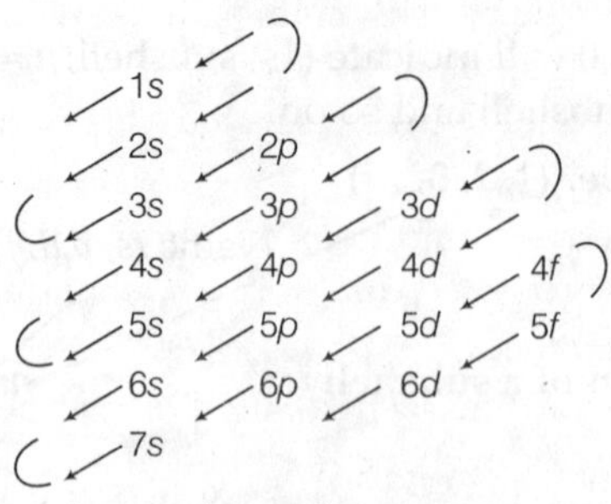

Increasing order of energy

- If two or more sub-orbits have same values of $(n+l)$ sub-orbits with lower values of n has lower energy and thus will be filled first.
- Energy order of $1s$, $2s$, $2p$, $3s$, ... sub-orbits is given above (go in the direction of arrow to determine order).

Hund's rule of maximum multiplicity

- "Pairing of electrons in various orbitals (like p_x, p_y, p_z) of a sub-orbit (like *np*) takes place only after each orbital is half-filled/singly occupied."
- The ground state electronic configuration of the atom of an element corresponds to the state of the lowest total electronic energy.
- The electronic configurations are written based on Aufbau rule and Hund's rule.
- But in cases (such as Cu and Cr) where the two subshells ($4s$ and $3d$) differ slightly in terms of energy, there can be a shift of an electron from a subshell of lower energy ($4s$) to a subshell of higher energy ($3d$) so as to give an electronic configuration of completely filled or half-filled orbitals of a subshell.
- Elements with atomic number 24(Cr), 42(Mo) and 74(W) have $ns^1(n-1)d^5$ configuration and not $ns^2(n-1)d^4$ due to extra stability of these atoms.
- Elements with atomic number 29 (Cu), 47(Ag) and 79(Au) have $ns^1(n-1)d^{10}$ configuration instead of $ns^2(n-1)d^9$ due to extra stability of these atoms.
- There is extra stability associated with these electronic configurations which can be due to :

(i) **Symmetrical distribution of electrons** The completelyf illed or half-filled subshells have symmetrical distribution of electrons in them and therefore more stable.

Electrons in the same subshell (with degenerate orbitals) have equal energy but different spatial distribution.

As a result of it, their shielding of one-another is relatively small and the electrons are more strongly attracted by the nucleus.

(ii) **Exchange energy** This stabilisation effect (of exchange energy) arises whenever two or more electrons with the same spin are present in the degenerate orbitals of a subshell.

These electrons tend to exchange their positions, and the energy released due to this exchange is called exchange energy.

When the subshell is half-filled or completely filled, the number of exchanges can be maximum and thus maximum exchange energy leads to the stabilisation of the atom. Possible exchanges for a d^5-configuration are show below:

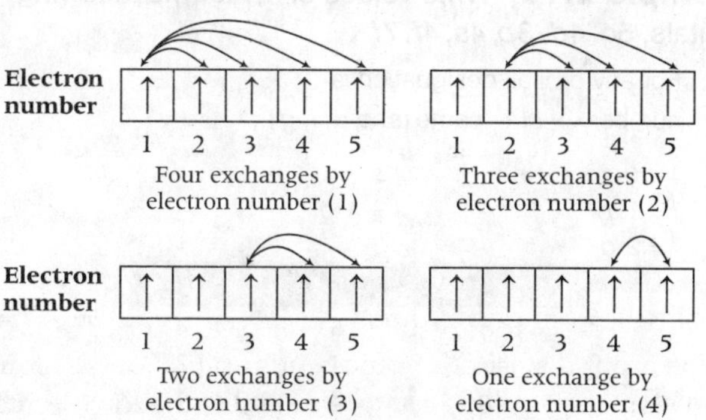

Electrons in various degenerate orbitals of a sub-orbit can be filled by changing spin etc., by following rule

$$\frac{x!}{(x-y)!y!}$$

where, $x = 2 \times$ number of orbitals

$y =$ number of electrons

- Ion/atoms will be paramagnetic if there are unpaired electrons. Magnetic moment is $\mu = \sqrt{N(N+2)}$ BM
- (Bohr Magneton). (1 BM $= 9.27 \times 10^{-24}$ J/T) where, N is the number of unpaired electrons.
- Ion with unpaired electrons in d or f-orbital will be coloured, due to d-d^* or f-f^* transition. Thus, Cu^+ with electronic configuration $[Ar]\,3d^{10}$ is colourless and Cu^{2+} with electronic configuration $[Ar]\,3d^9$ (one unpaired electron in $3d$) is coloured (blue).

Pauli's exclusion principle

- "No two electrons in an atom can have the same set of quantum numbers." This determines the maximum of 2, 6, 10, 14 electrons respectively in s, p, d, f sub-orbits.
- Two electrons in $1s^2$ (helium) have same values of n, l, m but they differ in spin.

Electron	n	l	m	m_s
First electron	1	0	0	$+\frac{1}{2}$
Second electron	1	0	0	$-\frac{1}{2}$

Electronic configuration of certain elements and ions

N (7) [⥮] [⥮] [1 | 1 | 1]
$1s^2$ $2s^2$ $2p^3$

O (8) [⥮] [⥮] [⥮ | 1 | 1] Pairing starts when each orbital is half-filled (Hund's rule).
$1s^2$ $2s^2$ $2p^4$

K (19) $\underbrace{1s^2\,2s^2\,2p^6\,3s^2\,3p^6}_{Ar}\,4s^1$ Energy of $4s < 3d$, thus is filled before $3d$ (Aufbau rule).

Cr (24) $[Ar]_{18}\,4s^1\,3d^5$

[1] [1 | 1 | 1 | 1 | 1]
$4s^1$ $3d^5$

instead of $[Ar]\ 4s^2\,3d^4$ to give maximum stability.

Mn (25) $[Ar]\,4s^2\,3d^5$

[⥮] [1 | 1 | 1 | 1 | 1]
$4s^2$ $3d^5$

Cu (29) (Ar) $4s^1$, $3d^{10}$ [1] [⥮ | ⥮ | ⥮ | ⥮ | ⥮] instead of [Ar]
$4s^1$ $3d^{10}$

$4s^2\,3d^9$ to give maximum stability.

Fe : $[Ar]\,4s^2\,3d^6$

Fe^{2+} ($24e$) $[Ar]\,3d^6 \Rightarrow$ It is different from Cr ($24e$) as when cation is formed, valence electrons ($4s$) are lost.

Thus, when you are asked to write electronic configuration of ion, first write electronic configuration of element and remove (to form cation) or add (to form anion) in valence shell.

Shielding (screening) effect and effective nuclear charge

- A valence electron in a multi-electron atom is attracted by the nucleus and repelled by the core electrons of the inner-shells. The resultant effect of this attractive and repulsive forces acting on the valence electron is, the valence electron experiences less attraction from the nucleus. This is called **shielding** (or screening) **effect.**
- The extent in which the various orbitals penetrate the electron clouds of the other orbitals is:

$$s > p > d > f$$

- Effective nuclear charge (Z^*)

$$Z^* = Z - \sigma$$

when, Z is the atomic number and σ is Slater's screening constant.

Electron in which orbitals ↓ (of shell) →	σ per electrons		
	n	$(n-1)$	$(n-2)(n-3)$
s- or p-orbitals	0.35	0.85	1.00
d- or f-orbitals	0.35	1.00	1.00

e.g. Valence electron ($3s^1$) of Na(Z = 11) experiences repulsive force of
6 electrons in $2p(n-1)$, 2 electrons in $2s(n-1)$
2 electrons in $1s$ $(n-2)$

Thus, σ = 8 electrons in $(n-1) \times 0.85$ + 2 electrons in $(n-2) \times 1.0 = 8.8$

$\therefore \quad Z^* = 11 - 8.8 = 2.2$

Thus, effective nuclear charge of Na is 2.2.

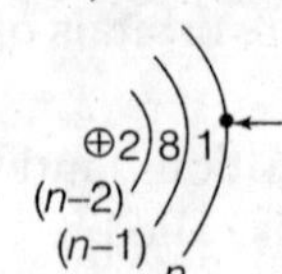

This electron gets repulsive force of 8 electrons in $(n-1)$th orbit and 2 electrons in $(n-2)$th orbit.

Solved Examples & Instant Practice

Example 2.18) Which of the following sets of quantum numbers is (are) not allowed? Why not?

	n	l	m_l
(a)	3	2	–1
(b)	2	3	–1
(c)	3	0	+1
(d)	6	2	–1
(e)	4	4	+4
(f)	4	3	–1

What atomic orbitals do the allowed combinations correspond to?

Sol. For a set of quantum number to be valid

l (azimuthal quantum number) < n (principal quantum number)

m_l (magnetic quantum number) = $-l, \dots 0 \dots + l$

and $\qquad m_s = +\frac{1}{2}$ or $-\frac{1}{2}$

(a) If $n = 3, l = 0, 1, 2$
and $m_l = 0 = -1, 0, +1 = -2, -1, 0, +1, +2$
Thus, allowed (3d)

(b) $n < l$ thus not allowed

(c) $n = 3, l = 0$ is allowed (3s)
but $m_l = +1$ is not allowed;
Thus, not allowed.

(d) $n = 6, l = 2, m_l = -1$ allowed (6d)

(e) not allowed as $n = l$

(f) allowed (4f)

Immediate Test 18

Which of the following sets of quantum numbers are allowed? Also designate allowed atomic orbitals?

	n	l	m_l
(a)	2	2	2
(b)	5	3	–2
(c)	3	–1	1
(d)	2	1	1
(e)	4	0	1

Example 2.19) Write values of n, l for the following orbitals. 5g, 4d, 3p, 4s, 4f, 7f

Sol. For any orbital, designation is

number → nl ← name (s, p, d, f, g)
(1, 2, 3)

$l = 0, s$ $\qquad l = 3, f$
$l = 1, p$ $\qquad l = 4, g$
$l = 2, d$

	n	l
5g	5	4
4d	4	2
3p	3	1
4s	4	0
4f	4	3
7f	7	3

Immediate Test 19

(i) Using s, p, d, f, g notations, describe the orbitals with the following quantum numbers.

	n	l
(a)	3	2
(b)	2	1
(c)	4	0
(d)	5	3
(e)	7	4

(ii) Which of the following sub-orbits are not possible?

(a) 5g (b) 4g
(c) 2d (d) 2f
(e) 1p (f) 3d

Example 2.20)

(a) Write electronic configuration of the atom with atomic number 26.

(b) Its 21st electron has spin +1/2, what will be the spin of 26th electron.

(c) Its divalent cation has 24 electrons. What is to electronic configuration?

(d) Compare magnetic moment of M and M^{2+}.

Electronic configuration is based on
- *Aufbau rule*
- *Hund's rule*
- *Pauli's exclusion principle.*

Magnetic moment of N unpaired electrons = $\sqrt{N(N+2)}$ B.M.
When cation is formed, electrons from the valence shell are removed.

Sol.

(a) $M(Z=26) = 1s^2 2s^2 2p^6 3s^2 3p^6 4s^2 3d^6$

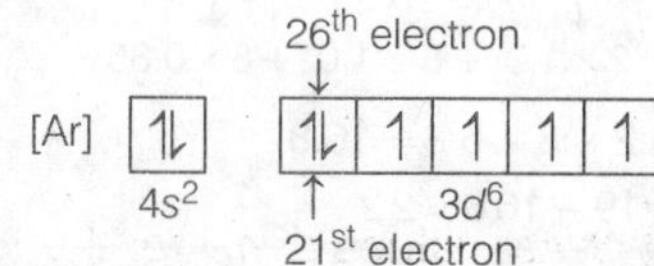

(b) Electrons in 3*d* are filled based on Hund's rule.
Thus, if 21th electron has, $s = +\frac{1}{2}$ then 26th electron has, $s = -\frac{1}{2}$

(c) When M^{2+} is formed, electrons from valence shell (which is 4*s*) are removed.
Thus, M^{2+} : $[Ar]3d^6$

(d) Unpaired electrons in $M = 4$
Unpaired electrons in $M^{2+} = 4$
Thus, both have magnetic moment = $\sqrt{N(N+2)} = \sqrt{24}$ B.M.

- M^{2+} has 24 electrons with electronic configuration $[Ar]3d^6$
  Cr($Z = 24$) has electronic configuration $[Ar]4s^1 3d^5$
  They differ as when M^{2+} is formed valence shell is affected.

Immediate Test 20

I. Cr II. Fe^{2+} III. Mn^+ IV. Co^{3+} are iso-electronic each having 24 electrons.

(a) Compare their magnetic moments.
(b) Select coloured species in the given ions.

Example 2.21) Ion M^{x+} has magnetic moment of $\sqrt{35}$ B.M. There are 26 protons in M^{x+}.

(a) What is charge on M^{x+}?
(b) Write electronic configuration of M^{x+}
(c) Is this coloured ion?

Sol. Number of protons in the given ion have been given. Thus, atomic number (*Z*) is known. From the value of magnetic moment, number of unpaired electrons can be calculated.

Proton = *Z* and magnetic moment of *N* unpaired electron
$= \sqrt{N(N+2)}$ B.M.

From charge of M^{x+} (E.C.) can be written.

$$\sqrt{N(N+2)} = \sqrt{35}$$
$$\therefore \quad N(N+2) = 35$$
$$\therefore \quad N = 5$$

Electronic configuration of $M(Z = 26) = [Ar]\ 4s^2 3d^6$

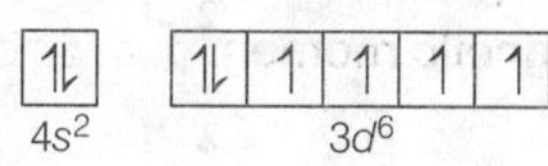

If three electrons are removed from *M*, M^{x+} formed has five unpaired electron

M^{3+} : [Ar] 1 1 1 1 1 ($3d^5$)

(a) Thus, charge on $M^{x+} = +3$
(b) $[Ar]\ 3d^5$
(c) Yes, M^{3+} is coloured ion, as there are unpaired electrons in *d*-orbital

Immediate Test 21

Atomic number of M^{x+} is 28.
Its magnetic moment is $2\sqrt{2}$ B.M.

(a) What is charge on M^{x+}?
(b) Write its electronic configuration.
(c) Is it coloured ion?

Example 2.22) If each orbital can take three electrons instead of two, write (electronic configuration) of the atom with atomic number 19. Assume, all other rules are valid.

Sol. If each orbital can take three electrons then E.C. will be in the form $1s^3 2s^3 2p^6$.........

Electrons in 1*s* = 3
Electrons in 2*s* = 3
Electrons in 2*p* = 9

$Z = (19),\ 1s^3 2s^3 2p^9 3s^3 3p^1$

Immediate Test 22

If *l* can take value 0, 1, 2 ... *n* then write electronic configuration of the element of atomic number 26. Assume all other rules are valid.

Example 2.23) If Aufbau rule is not followed,

(a) write electronic configuration of element of atomic number 25.
(b) calculate its magnetic moment.
(c) make possible coloured ions of the element.

Sol. If Aufbau rule is not followed,

$Z = 25$

(a) $1s^2 2s^2 2p^6 3s^2 3p^6 3d^7$
(4*s* is filled after 3*d*)

(b) [Ar] 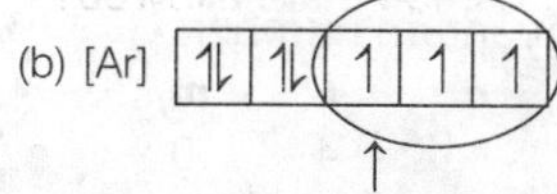

Thus, unpaired electrons=3

$\therefore$ Magnetic moment = $\sqrt{N(N+2)}$ B.M = $\sqrt{15}$ B.M

(c) $M^+\ [Ar]3d^6$ - Coloured
$M^{2+}\ [Ar]3d^5$ - Coloured
$M^{3+}\ [Ar]3d^4$ - Coloured etc.

Example 2.24) Determine effective nuclear charge of the elements of group I (Li, Na, K.)

Sol. Due to repulsive force of inner electrons, force of attraction of nucleus for valence electron is less than the value of Z.

Effective nuclear charge

$$Z^* = (Z - \sigma)$$

where, σ is screening constant.

$\sigma = 0.35$ for electrons in n^{th} orbit.

$\sigma = 0.85$ for electrons in $(n-1)^{\text{th}}$ orbit.

$\sigma = 1.00$ for electrons in $(n-2), (n-3) \ldots$ orbit.

Li $(Z = 3)$ $\quad 1s^2 \; 2s^1$ ($1s^2$: $(n-1)$, $2s^1$: n)

This electron is screened by two electrons in $(n-1)^{\text{th}}$ orbit

$\therefore \; Z^* = 3 - 2 \times 0.85 = 1.3$

Na$(Z = 11)$

$1s^2 \quad 2s^2\,2p^6 \quad 3s^1$

2 electrons in $(n-2)^{\text{th}}$ ($1s^2$); 8 electrons in $(n-1)^{\text{th}}$ ($2s^2 2p^6$); This electron is screened by ($3s^1$)

$\therefore \; Z^* = 11 - (8 \times 0.85 + 2 \times 1.00) = 2.2$

K $(Z = 19)$

$1s^2$ $(n-3)$ $\quad 2s^2\,2p^6$ $(n-2)$ $\quad 3s^2\,3p^6$ $(n-1)$ $\quad 4s^1$ n ← This electron is screened by inner electrons

$\sigma = 2 \times 1.0 + 8 \times 1.0 + 8 \times 0.85$

$= 2 + 8 + 6.8 = 16.8$

$\therefore \quad Z^* = 19 - 16.8 = 2.2$

■ Rb $(Z = 37)$, Cs $(Z = 55)$ have also $Z^* = 2.2$

Thus, increase in size along a group (top to bottom) is predominantly due to n^2 and not due to Z, as effective nuclear charge is almost constant.

KNOWLEDGE CONFIRMATION **Test 4**

1 Valence shell electron of K(19) has quantum numbers as

	n	l	m_l	m_s
(a)	3	2	0	$+\frac{1}{2}$
(b)	4	0	0	$+\frac{1}{2}$
(c)	4	0	1	$-\frac{1}{2}$
(d)	4	1	0	$+\frac{1}{2}$

2 For the four types of sets of quantum numbers

	n	l
I.	3	1
II.	5	3
III.	2	0
IV.	4	2

correct order of their energies is

(a) I < II < III < IV (b) IV < II < IV < I

(c) III < II < IV < I (d) III < I < IV < II

3 Which is not the correct set of quantum numbers?

	n	l	m_l		n	l	m_l
(a)	3	2	−2	(b)	4	4	0
(c)	3	1	0	(d)	5	4	−3

4 Which is not the correct electronic configuration of the ion/atom each having 24 electrons?

(a) Fe^{2+} $(Z = 26)$: [Ar] $3d^5\,4s^1$ (b) Mn^+ $(Z = 25)$: [Ar] $3d^5\,4^1$

(c) Cr $(Z = 24)$: [Ar] $3d^5\,4s^1$ (d) All are correct configurations

5 Magnetic moment of Fe^{3+} in its ground state is

(a) $\sqrt{35}$ B.M (b) $\sqrt{24}$ B.M (c) $\sqrt{15}$ B.M (d) 0

6 Degeneracy occurs in

(a) 3 *s* (b) 4 *s* (c) 4 *g* (d) 5 *g*

7 There are five electrons in $(n-1)d$ or suborbit in

(a) Fe^{2+} (b) Mn^+

(c) Both (a) and (b) (d) None of these

8 *g*-suborbit $(l = 4)$ occurs with minimum value of

(a) 5 (b) 6 (c) 7 (d) 4

9 Suborbit with minimum energy is

(a) $n = 4, l = 2$ (b) $n = 3, l = 2$

(c) $n = 4, l = 0$ (d) $n = 5, l = 1$

10 Consider following statements about Ni^{4+}, Fe^{2+}, Mn^+ and Co^{3+}.

I. They are isoelectronic.

II. All are paramagnetic.

III. All have same electronic configuration except Mn^+.

IV. All form coloured ions.

Select correct statements.

(a) I, II (b) I, II, III (c) II, III, IV (d) I, II, III, IV

11 Electron lost in the oxidation of Cu^+ to Cu^{2+} has set of quantum number as

	n	m	m_l	m_s
(a)	4	0	0	$+\frac{1}{2}$
(b)	3	2	−2	$-\frac{1}{2}$
(c)	3	1	−1	$-\frac{1}{2}$
(d)	3	0	0	$+\frac{1}{2}$

12 A subshell has total number of orbitals equal to
(a) n^2 (b) l (c) $2l$ (d) $(2l+1)$

13 Number of electrons that Cu $(Z=29)$ has in d-orbitals is equal to
(a) number of electrons in p-orbitals in $(Z=16)$
(b) number of electrons in s-orbitals in Ge $(Z=32)$
(c) number of electrons is d-orbitals in Zn $(Z=30)$
(d) All of the above are correct

14 In an atom, 19th and 20th electrons have
$n=4, l=0, m=0, s=+\frac{1}{2}$ and $n=4, l=0, m=0, s=-\frac{1}{2}$
then 21st electron will have
(a) $n=4, l=1, m=0, s=+\frac{1}{2}$ (b) $n=4, l=1, m=-1, s=-\frac{1}{2}$
(c) $n=3, l=2, m=0, s=+\frac{1}{2}$ (d) $n=3, l=1, m=0, s=-\frac{1}{2}$

15 Which of the pair of orbitals have electron density along the axis?
(a) d_{xy}, d_{yz} (b) $d_{x^2-y^2}, d_{z^2}$
(c) d_{xz}, d_{yz} (d) d_{xy}, d_{z^2}

16 In a subshell, there are three radial nodes, This subshell can be
(a) 4s or 5p (b) 4d or 5p
(c) 4s or 4p (d) 3s or 3p

17 Number of nodal planes in 4p-suborbit will be
(a) 3 (b) 2 (c) 1 (d) 0

18 Assume $l=0, 1, 2 \ldots\ldots n$ and $m_s=+\frac{1}{2}, 0, -\frac{1}{2}$
then electronic configuration of Mn (25) will be (assume other rules are not violated.
(a) $1s^3\ 1p^9\ 2s^3\ 2p^9\ 2d^1$ (b) $[Ar]\ 4s^2\ 3d^5$
(c) $1s^3\ 1p^9\ 2s^3\ 2p^6\ 2d^4$ (d) $1s^3\ 1p^9\ 2s^3\ 2p^9\ 3s^1$

19 Magnetic moment of the element with atomic number 29 will be, if concepts of Q. 18 are followed
(a) $\sqrt{8}$ B.M (b) $\sqrt{3}$ B.M
(c) $\sqrt{35}$ B.M (d) zero

20 In which of the following case (s), effective nuclear charge is equal to atomic number?
(a) He^+ $(Z=2)$ (b) Be^{3+} $(Z=4)$
(c) Li^{2+} $(Z=3)$ (d) In all cases

21 While moving along first group top to bottom, atomic radius or ionic radius increases. Which factor is predominant to decide this variation?
(a) Principal quantum number (n)
(b) Effective nuclear charge (Z^*)
(c) Atomic number (Z)
(d) n and Z^*

22 If angular momentum quantum number l can take value of n also (in addition to other possible values), then total number of electrons in the first orbit would have been?
(a) 2 (b) 6 (c) 8 (d) 10

23 A $2p^3$-configuration in N-atom can be written as a many as
(a) three ways (b) nine ways
(c) twelve ways (d) twenty ways

24 In the following electronic configuration some rules have been violated :

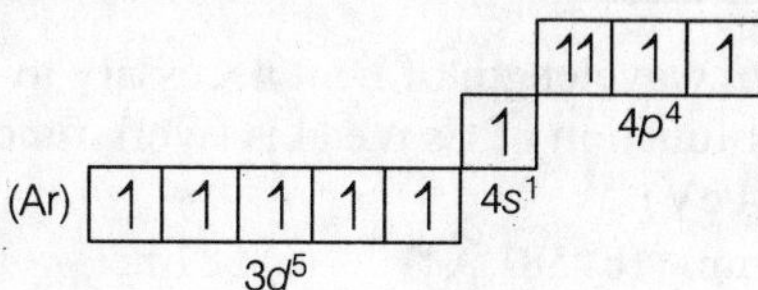

I. Hund's rule
II. Pauli's exclusion rule
III. Aufbau rule
Select the rules which have been violated
(a) I, II (b) I, III
(c) II, III (d) I, II, III

25 In which of the following, do both the ions given in a pair have same magnetic moment?
(a) Cu^{2+} and Ni^{2+} (b) Mn^{4+} and Co^{2+}
(c) Zn^{2+} and Cu^{2+} (d) Mg^{2+} and Sc^+

26 For the electrons of an atom with electronic configuration $1s^2 2s^2 2p^4$, select correct statement(s).
(a) Electrons present in 2s orbital have same spin quantum numbers (m_s) but of opposite sign
(b) Energy of 2p electrons is higher than that of 2s electrons
(c) Shielding of electrons in 1s, 2s and 2p is different
(d) All of the above are correct statements

27 The number of angular nodal planes are same in the orbitals
(a) 3s and 4d (b) 4s and 3p
(c) 4s and 3d (d) 3p and 4p

28 In which of the following cases, $(n+l)$ value is maximum for all the d-electrons?
(a) Fe (b) Cr
(c) Zn (d) equal

29 If 'l' can have value 0, 1, 2 .... n, then (EC) of Cr (24) would be
(a) $1s^2 2s^2 2p^6 3s^2 3p^6 4s^1 3d^5$ (b) $1s^2 1p^6 2s^2 2p^6 2d^8$
(c) $1s^2 1p^6 2s^2 2p^6 2d^5 3s^2 3p^1$ (d) None of the above

30 For the above case, magnetic moment is zero in case of
(a) Zn (30) (b) Mn (25)
(c) Cr (24) (d) Fe (26)

ACID TEST
For JEE Main

TYPE I MCQs with Only ONE Correct Alternate

1 Energy of one mole of photons having a wavelength of 5.0×10^{-6} m is

(a) 23.9 J mol^{-1} (b) 23.9 kJ mol^{-1}
(c) 11.9 kJ mol^{-1} (d) 1.19 kJ mol^{-1}

2 Minimum wavelength of light necessary to overcome the work function of Cs metal is (work function of Cs = 2.14 eV)

(a) 58.1 nm (b) 581 Å (c) 581 nm (d) 581 pm

3 Because of the observation that some α-particles directed at a gold foil are scattered backward at angles larger than 90°, Rutherford was able to conclude that :

(a) All atoms are electrically neutral
(b) The positively charged particles of atoms move with extremely large velocities
(c) The negatively charged electrons are a part of all matter
(d) The positively charged particles of atoms occupy only a small fraction of the volume of atom

4 Which has maximum energy?

(a) A photon with wavelength 10 nm
(b) A photon with frequency 10 Hz
(c) An electron moving with a velocity of light
(d) All have equal energy

5 FM radio in NCR broadcasts at 20 m band. The frequency of this band is

(a) 30 MHz (b) 20 MHz (c) 10 MHz (d) 15 MHz

6 If a photon is associated with energy of 100 kJ mol^{-1}, then its wave number is

(a) $836 \times 10^{3} \text{ m}^{-1}$ (b) $1.2 \times 10^{-6} \text{ m}^{-1}$
(c) $2.51 \times 10^{14} \text{ m}^{-1}$ (d) None of these

7 Electron in He^+ ion in n^{th} level falls successively from nth to n_1th and then n_1th to 1st level, emitting two photons of wavelengths 1000Å and 3000 Å. Thus n corresponds to

(a) 1 (b) 2 (c) 6 (d) 10

8 Consider following statements about black body :

I. The ideal body, which emits and absorbs all frequencies, is called a black body.
II. The exact frequency distribution of the emitted radiation from a black body depends on its temperature.
III. The radiation emitted goes from a lower frequency to a higher frequency as temperature increases.

Select correct statements :

(a) I, II (b) I, III (c) II, III (d) I, II, III

9 Velocity of the electron emitted by Li (ϕ(work function) = 2.90 eV) if light of frequency $4.77 \times 10^{15} \text{ s}^{-1}$ is absorbed, is

(a) $2.435 \times 10^{6} \text{ ms}^{-1}$ (b) $4.870 \times 10^{6} \text{ ms}^{-1}$
(c) $2.435 \times 10^{8} \text{ ms}^{-1}$ (d) $5.927 \times 10^{12} \text{ ms}^{-1}$

10 When an electron falls from a level of energy $\frac{4E}{3}$ to level of energy E, radiation of wavelength 3λ is observed. If electron falls from a level of energy $2E$ to level of energy E, wavelength of radiation is

(a) 3λ (b) $\frac{4\lambda}{3}$
(c) $\frac{3\lambda}{4}$ (d) λ

11 When an electromagnetic radiation of wavelength 300 nm falls on the surface of sodium, electrons are emitted with a kinetic energy of $1.68 \times 10^{5} \text{ J mol}^{-1}$. Minimum energy required to remove an electron from sodium is

(a) 6.63×10^{-19} J (b) 3.99×10^{5} J
(c) 2.31×10^{5} J (d) 3.84×10^{-19} J

12 The energies of the electron in the given orbits are

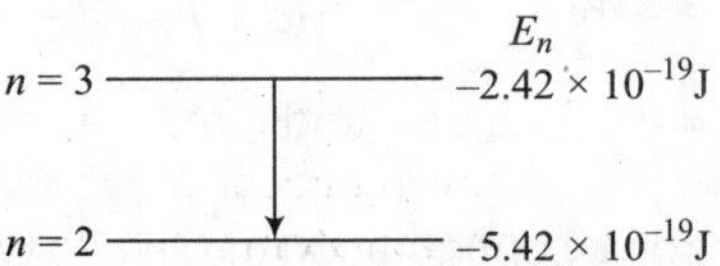

Wavelength of the emitted light when electron drops from third orbit to second orbit is

(a) 440 nm (b) 210 nm
(c) 663 nm (d) None is correct

13 Li^{2+} emits 10 types of lines when it is in the excited state. Ratio of energy of Li^{2+} in this excited state to that of H-atom in the second excited state is

(a) 3.24 (b) 1.44
(c) 0.36 (d) 1.24

14 Electron in H-atom in second orbit and electron in He^+ ion in the fourth orbit are revolving around the nucleus. Thus, ratio of their time periods is

(a) $\frac{1}{2}$ (b) $\frac{1}{3}$ (c) $\frac{1}{6}$ (d) $\frac{1}{8}$

15 He^+, Li^{2+} and Be^{3+} are isoelectronic of H (each having one electron). Which has maximum radius?

(a) H-atom in ground state (b) He^+ ion in second orbit
(c) Li^{2+} ion in third orbit (d) Be^{3+} ion in fourth orbit

16 For H-atom, it is given that

$$\frac{r_{n_2}}{r_{n_1}} = \frac{4}{1}$$

for any two orbits (n_2 or $n_1 \le 4$)
Thus, ΔE for these two orbits is
(a) 10.2 eV or 2.55 eV (b) 13.6 eV or 3.4 eV
(c) 10.2 eV (d) 13.6 eV

17 Increasing order of energy of
I. E_1(H) II. $E_2(He^+)$
III. $E_3(Li^{2+})$ IV. $E_4(Be^{3+})$ is
(a) I < II < III < IV (b) IV < III < II < I
(c) I = II = III = IV (d) I < II = III < IV

18 In a certain electronic transition in the H-atom, from n_2 level to n_1 level, the difference in the radii of two states is 20 times the Bohr's radius. Thus, spectral lines are in ...... series.
(a) Lyman (b) Balmer
(c) Paschen (d) Brackett

19 de-Broglie wavelength is increased by 1%. Thus, change in kinetic energy will be
(a) 0.02 unit (b) 0.20 unit
(c) 0.10 unit (d) 0.01 unit

20 Which have equal number of *d*-electrons out of
I. Fe^{3+} ($Z = 26$) II. Fe^{2+} ($Z = 26$)
III. Cr ($Z = 24$) IV. Mn ($Z = 25$)
(a) I, II (b) I, III, IV
(c) I, III (d) II, III

21 Which one of the following about an electron occupying the 1*s*-orbital in a hydrogen atom is incorrect? (The Bohr radius is represented by a_0) ***[JEE Main 2019 (II) NTA]***
(a) The electron can be found at a distance $2a_0$ from the nucleus
(b) The magnitude of the potential energy is double that of its kinetic energy on an average.
(c) The probability density of finding the electron is maximum at the nucleus.
(d) The total energy of the electron is maximum when it is at a distance a_0 from the nucleus.

22 The orbital angular momentum of an electron in 3*s*-orbital is
(a) $\frac{h}{4\pi}$ (b) zero (c) $\frac{h}{2\pi}$ (d) $\frac{h}{\sqrt{2}\,\pi}$

23 Consider following isoelectronic species (with 24 electrons)
I. Fe^{2+} II. Mn^+ III. Cr IV. Co^{3+}
Their magnetic moments will be in the following order:
(a) I = IV < II = III (b) I < II < III < IV
(c) III < II < I < IV (d) I = II = III = IV

24 de-Broglie's wavelength of an electron in third orbit of H-atom is
(a) $2\pi\, a_0$ (b) $6\pi a_0$ (c) $9\, a_0$ (d) $\frac{a_0}{3}$

25 The ratio of the shortest wavelength of two spectral series of hydrogen spectrum is found to be about (1/9). The spectral series are ***[JEE Main 2019 (II) NTA]***
(a) Lyman and Paschen (b) Brackett and Pfund
(c) Paschen and Pfund (d) Balmer and Brackett

26 Consider the following ions :
I. Mg^+ ($Z = 12$) II. Cu^+ ($Z = 29$)
III. Ni^{2+} ($Z = 28$) IV. Mn^{2+} ($Z = 25$)
V. Zn^{2+} ($Z = 30$)
Select paramagnetic and coloured ions out of
(a) II, III (b) II, III, IV, V (c) II, III, IV (d) III, IV

27 Degeneracy of *s*, *p*, *d*, *f* and *g* suborbits will be respectively

	s	*p*	*d*	*f*	*g*
(a)	1	1	1	1	1
(b)	1	3	5	7	9
(c)	0	1	2	3	4
(d)	1	3	5	7	11

28 The most intense line in the Brackett series of the spectrum of H-atom is given by the transition.
(a) $n_2 = \infty$ to $n_1 = 1$ (b) $n_2 = 8$ to $n_1 = 4$
(c) $n_2 = \infty$ to $n_1 = 4$ (d) $n_2 = 4$ to $n_1 = 3$

29 Einstein unit is defined as the ratio of energy of the given number of photons to the energy of N_0 photons. What is the energy of 7.25×10^{15} photons of 5.37×10^{14} s^{-1} frequency in Einstein unit?
(a) 1.20×10^{-8} (b) 8.33×10^{7} (c) 2.58×10^{-3} (d) 3.56×10^{-19}

30 The number of orbitals associated with quantum numbers $n = 5$, $m_s = +\frac{1}{2}$ is ***[JEE Main 2020 (I) NTA]***
(a) 25 (b) 11 (c) 15 (d) 50

31 Speed of an electron of wavelength 3 cm is
(a) 243 m s^{-1} (b) 24.3 m s^{-1}
(c) 0.243 m s^{-1} (d) 0.0243 m s^{-1}

32 Out of the following electrons with given sets of quantum number, electron with lowest energy is

	n	*l*	m_l	m_s
(a)	3	2	1	$+\frac{1}{2}$
(b)	4	2	−1	$+\frac{1}{2}$
(c)	4	1	0	$-\frac{1}{2}$
(d)	5	0	0	$+\frac{1}{2}$

33 Uncertainty in position of an electron moving with a velocity of 3×10^2 m s^{-1} accurate upto 0.001% will be

(a) 0.0193 m (b) 0.0384 m
(c) 0.0576 m (d) 0.0768 m

34 Longest wavelength of the lines in different series are given. Select the correct value.

	Species	Series	λ_{max}
(a)	H	Balmer	656 nm
(b)	Li^{2+}	Lyman	810 nm
(c)	He^+	Paschen	521 nm

(d) All are correct values

35 Number of orbitals containing electron-pairs in the element with atomic number 38 is

(a) 17 (b) 18
(c) 19 (d) 20

36 There are x, y and z radial nodes in 4s, 3p and 3d orbitals x, y and z are respectively :

	x	y	z
(a)	1	3	2
(b)	3	1	0
(c)	3	1	2
(d)	0	1	2

37 Which H-like species will have same radius as that of Bohr orbit of H-atom?

(a) $n = 2$, Li^{2+} (b) $n = 2$, Be^{2+}
(c) $n = 2$, He^+ (d) $n = 3$, Li^{2+}

38 In the Brackett series of Be^{3+}, successive lines tend towards a limiting value of frequency :

(a) $\frac{\bar{R}_H c}{4}$ (b) $\frac{4R_H}{c}$
(c) $\frac{\bar{R}_H c}{2}$ (d) $\bar{R}_H c$

39 An element of sixth group will have orbitals in the following sequence :

(a) $ns \to np \to (n-1)d \to (n-2)f$
(b) $ns \to (n-2)f \to (n-1)d \to np$
(c) $ns \to (n-1)d \to (n-2)f \to np$
(d) $ns \to (n-2)f \to np \to (n-1)d$

40 If $\bar{\nu} = 0.21\bar{R}_H$ in the emission spectrum of Na^{10+}, then

	n_1	n_2
(a)	10	11
(b)	8	9
(c)	7	8
(d)	16	7

41 de-Broglie wavelength of He atom moving with root mean square velocity at 400 K is

(a) 631 pm (b) 6.31 pm
(c) 0.613 pm (d) 63.1 pm

42 How fast is an electron moving if it has a wavelength equal to the distance it travels in one second ?

(a) $\sqrt{\frac{h}{m}}$ (b) $\sqrt{\frac{m}{h}}$ (c) $\sqrt{\frac{h}{p}}$ (d) $\sqrt{\frac{h}{2(KE)}}$

43 If the de-Broglie wavelength of the electron in the nth Bohr orbit in a hydrogenic atom is equal to 1.5 πa_0 (a_0 is Bohr radius), then the value of n/Z is **[JEE Main 2019 (I) NTA]**

(a) 0.75 (b) 1.0 (c) 0.40 (d) 1.50

44 If the de-Broglie's wavelength of a particle of mass m is 25 times its velocity, then this wavelength is

(a) $\frac{1}{5}\sqrt{\frac{h}{m}}$ (b) $5\sqrt{\frac{h}{m}}$
(c) $\frac{1}{5}\sqrt{\frac{m}{h}}$ (d) $5\sqrt{\frac{m}{h}}$

45 The radius of the second Bohr orbit, in terms of the Bohr radius, a_0 in Li^{2+} is **[JEE Main 2019 (I) NTA]**

(a) $\frac{2a_0}{3}$ (b) $\frac{4a_0}{3}$
(c) $\frac{4a_0}{9}$ (d) $\frac{2a_0}{9}$

46 Electron from Cs surface with threshold frequency ν_0 shows emission of photo-electrons when radiated with frequency ν. Thus, wavelength of the emitted photoelectron is

(a) $\sqrt{\frac{h}{2m\Delta\nu}}$ (b) $\sqrt{\frac{2m\Delta\nu}{h}}$
(c) $\sqrt{\frac{2m}{h\Delta\nu}}$ (d) $\left(\frac{h}{2m\Delta\nu}\right)^2$

47 Highest electron probability in radial distribution function in 1s orbital exists at a point in the vicinity of

(a) spherical nodes (b) circumference
(c) nucleus (d) plane

48 Which of the following combinations of statements is true regarding the interpretation of the atomic orbitals?

I. An electron in an orbital of high angular momentum stays away from the nucleus than an electron in the orbital of lower angular momentum.

II. For a given value of the principal quantum number, the size of the orbit is inversely proportional to the azimuthal quantum number.

III. According to wave mechanics, the ground state angular momentum is equal to $\frac{h}{2\pi}$.

IV. The plot of ψ vs r for various azimuthal quantum numbers, shows peak shifting towards higher r value.

[JEE Main 2019 (I) NTA]

(a) II, III (b) I, IV
(c) I, II (d) I, III

49 What is the maximum number of orbitals that can be identified with the following quantum numbers?

$n = 3, l = 2, m = 0$

(a) 1 (b) 2
(c) 3 (d) 4

50 Which of the graphs shown below does not represent the relationship between incident light and the electron ejected from metal surface? ***[JEE Main 2019 (I) NTA]***

(a) 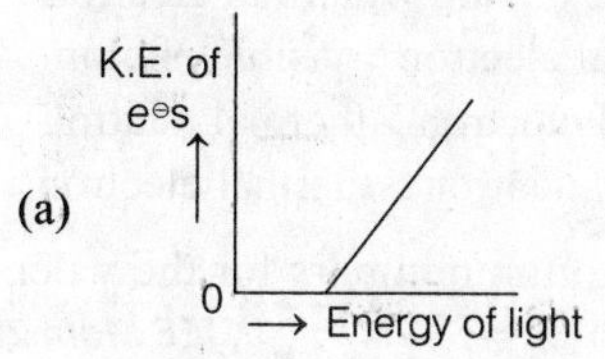

(b) 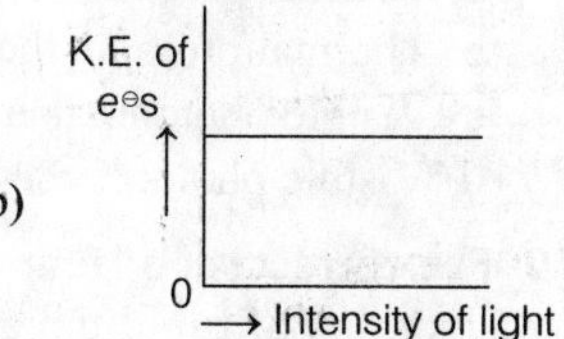

(c) 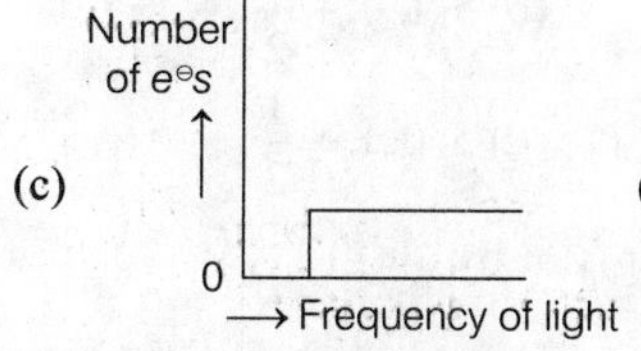

(d) 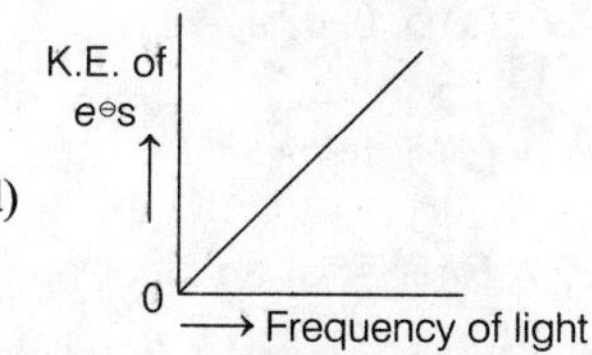

51 Following represents a graph between $\bar{v}$ (wave-number) and $\sqrt{V}$ (V is the potential applied to two sub-atomic particles A and B)

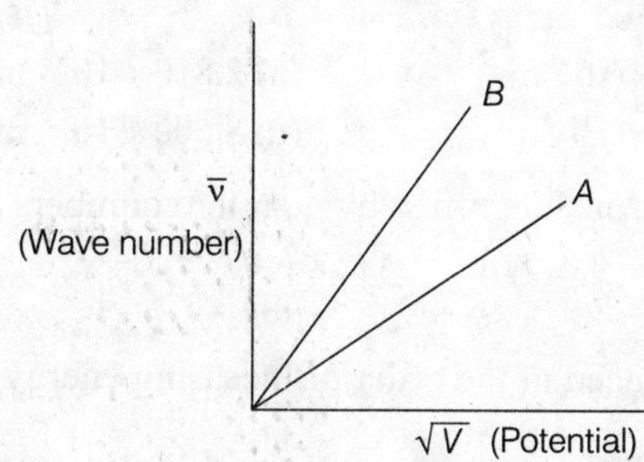

Thus, relative masses of A and B can be

(a) $\frac{m_A}{m_B} = 1$ (b) $\frac{m_A}{m_B} > 1$
(c) $\frac{m_A}{m_B} < 1$ (d) cannot be predicted

52 Helium has two electrons in $1s$ orbital. It is converted to He^+ by losing one electron. Which statement is true about this ion?

(a) Its spectrum resembles the hydrogen spectrum
(b) Ionisation energy of He^+ formed is smaller than that of He
(c) The nuclear charge has decreased by one unit
(d) Ionic mass of He^+ is one

53 For an electron in $1s$ orbital in H-atom, consider following statements.

I. The electron density is independent of angle
II. The electron density is independent of r
III. The electron is at a fixed value of r
IV. The electron has the same angular momentum as in the Bohr atom

Correct statement(s) is/are

(a) I only (b) I, II, III
(c) I, III, IV (d) II, IV

54 The first ionisation potential for s-orbital is lower than that for p-orbital because

(a) Hund's rule is violated
(b) ionisation potential decreases across a representative period
(c) half-filled and filled sets of orbitals are more stable than configuration of one or more fewer electrons.
(d) the statement above is false. The first ionisation potential for s-orbital is higher than that for p-orbital

55 Heat treatment of muscular pain involves radiation of wavelength of about 900 nm. Which spectral line of H-atom is suitable for this purpose? ***[JEE Main 2019 (I) NTA]***

(a) Paschen $5 \rightarrow 3$ (b) Balmer, $\infty \rightarrow 2$
(c) Lyman, $\infty \rightarrow 1$ (d) Paschen, $\infty \rightarrow 3$

56 First line of Lyman series and second line of Balmer series have wavelengths λ_1 and λ_2. Then λ_1 / λ_2 is equal to

(a) $\frac{16}{9}$ (b) $\frac{3}{16}$
(c) $\frac{4}{1}$ (d) $\frac{1}{4}$

57 A particle of m kg and having charge q Coulomb is accelerated from rest by a potential difference of V volts. Thus, its kinetic energy and de-Broglie wavelength are respectively.

(a) $\frac{\text{KE}}{qV}, \frac{\lambda}{h/\sqrt{2mqV}}$ (b) $qV, h/mV$
(c) $h/mV, qV$ (d) $\frac{h}{\sqrt{2mqV}}, qV$

58 The wave number of electromagnetic radiation emitted during transition from n_2 level to n_1 level of Li^{2+} ion such that $n_1 + n_2 = 4$ and $(n_1 - n_2) = 2$, is

(a) $\frac{7}{2}\bar{R}_H$ (b) $4\bar{R}_H$
(c) $8\bar{R}_H$ (d) $\frac{8}{9}\bar{R}_H$

59 Frequency of electron revolving in second Bohr's orbit of H-atom is (in the multiple of 10^{14})

(a) 1.016 (b) 4.496
(c) 0.1626 (d) 8.21

60 In the element with atomic number 20, number of electrons with $(l + m) = 0$, is

(a) 20 (b) 13
(c) 12 (d) 7

61 For the Balmer series in the spectrum of H-atom,
$$\bar{\nu} = R_H\left[\frac{1}{n_1^2} - \frac{1}{n_2^2}\right]$$ **[JEE Main 2020 (I) NTA]**

the correct statements among (I) to (IV) are :

I. As wavelength decreases, the lines in the series converge.

II. The integer n_1 is equal to 2.

III. The lines of longest wavelength corresponds to $n_2 = 3$.

IV. The ionisation energy of hydrogen atom can be calculated from the wave number of these lines.

(a) II, III, IV (b) I, III, IV
(c) I, II, III (d) I, II, IV

62 The de-Broglie's wavelength of electron present in first Bohr orbit of hydrogen atom is **[JEE Main 2018]**

(a) 4×0.529Å (b) $2\pi\times 0.529$Å
(c) $\frac{0.529}{2\pi}$ Å (d) 0.529Å

63 Ejection of the photoelectron from metal in the photoelectric effect experiment can be stopped by applying 0.5V when the radiation of 250 nm is used. The work function of the metal is **[JEE Main 2018]**

(a) 5.5 eV (b) 4.0 eV
(c) 5.0 eV (d) 4.5 eV

64 The radius of the second Bohr orbit for hydrogen atom is (Planck's constant $h = 6.6262\times 10^{-34}$ Js; mass of electron $= 9.1091\times 10^{-31}$ kg; charge of electron $(e) = 1.60210\times 10^{-19}$C; permittivity of vacuum $(\epsilon_0) = 8.854185\times 10^{-12}\ kg^{-1}m^{-3}A^2$) **[JEE Main 2017]**

(a) 1.65 Å (b) 4.76 Å
(c) 0.529 Å (d) 2.12 Å

65 If the shortest wavelength in Lyman series of hydrogen atom is A, then the longest wavelength in Paschen series of He^+ is **[JEE Main 2017, 2020 (II) NTA]**

(a) $\frac{5A}{9}$ (b) $\frac{9A}{5}$
(c) $\frac{36A}{5}$ (d) $\frac{36A}{7}$

66 The electron in the hydrogen atom undergoes transition from higher orbitals to orbital of radius 211.6 pm. This transition is associated with: **[JEE Main 2017]**

(a) Lyman series (b) Balmer series
(c) Paschen series (d) Brackett series

67 A stream of electrons from a heated filament was passed between two charged plates kept at a potential difference of V esu. If e and m are charge and mass of an electron respectively, then the value of h/λ (where, λ is wavelength associated with electron wave) is given by **[JEE Main 2016]**

(a) $2\ meV$ (b) $\sqrt{meV}$
(c) $\sqrt{2\ meV}$ (d) meV

68 Which of the following is the energy of a possible excited state of hydrogen? **[JEE Main 2015]**

(a) 13.6 eV (b) –6.8 eV
(c) – 3.4 eV (d) + 6.8 eV

69 At temperature T, the average kinetic energy of any particle is $\frac{3}{2}kT$. The de-Broglie wavelength follows the order. **[JEE Main 2015]**

(a) Thermal proton > visible photon > thermal electron
(b) Thermal proton > thermal electron > visible photon
(c) Visible photon > thermal electron > thermal neutron
(d) Visible photon > thermal neutron > thermal electron

70 The correct set of four quantum numbers for the valence electrons of rubidium atom $[Z = 37]$ is **[JEE Main 2014]**

(a) $5, 0, 0, +\frac{1}{2}$ (b) $5, 1, 0, +\frac{1}{2}$
(c) $5, 1, 1, +\frac{1}{2}$ (d) $5, 0, 1, +\frac{1}{2}$

71 Energy of an electron is given by $E_n = -2.178\times 10^{-18}\ J\left(\frac{Z^2}{n^2}\right)$. Wavelength of light required to excite an electron in an hydrogen atom from level, $n = 1$ to $n = 2$ will be ($h = 6.62\times 10^{-34}$ Js and $c = 3.0\times 10^8\ ms^{-1}$) **[JEE Main 2013]**

(a) 1.214×10^{-7} m (b) 2.816×10^{-7} m
(c) 6.500×10^{-7} m (d) 8.500×10^{-7} m

72 The electrons identified by quantum numbers n and l.

1. $n = 4, l = 1$ 2. $n = 4, l = 0$
3. $n = 3, l = 2$ 4. $n = 3, l = 1$

can be placed in the order of inceasing energy as **[AIEEE 2012]**

(a) (3) < (4) < (2) < (1) (b) (4) < (2) < (3) < (1)
(c) (2) < (4) < (1) < (3) (d) (1) < (3) < (2) < (4)

73 A gas absorbs photon of 355 nm and emits photons of two wavelengths. If one of the emission is at 680 nm, the other is at **[AIEEE 2011]**

(a) 1035 nm (b) 325 nm
(c) 743 nm (d) 518 nm

74 The frequency of light emitted for the transition $n = 4$ to $n = 2$ of He^+ is equal to the transition in H-atom corresponding to which of the following? **[AIEEE 2011]**

(a) $n = 3$ to $n = 1$ (b) $n = 2$ to $n = 1$
(c) $n = 3$ to $n = 2$ (d) $n = 4$ to $n = 3$

75 The energy required to break one mole of Cl—Cl bonds in Cl_2 is 242 kJ mol^{-1}. The longest wavelength of light capable of breaking a single Cl—Cl bond is **[AIEEE 2010]**

(a) 594 nm (b) 640 nm
(c) 700 nm (d) 494 nm

76 Ionisation energy of He^+ is 19.6×10^{-18} J $atom^{-1}$. The energy of the first stationary state ($n=1$) of Li^{2+} is **[AIEEE 2010]**

(a) 4.41×10^{-16} J $atom^{-1}$ (b) 4.41×10^{-17} J $atom^{-1}$
(c) -2.2×10^{-15} J $atom^{-1}$ (d) 8.82×10^{-17} J $atom^{-1}$

77 In an atom, an electron is moving with a speed of 600 ms^{-1} with an accuracy of 0.05%. Certainity with which the position of the electron can be located is ($h=6.6\times 10^{-34}$ kg $m^2 s^{-1}$, mass of electron, $e_m=9.1\times 10^{-31}$ kg) **[AIEEE 2009]**

(a) 1.52×10^{-4} m (b) 5.10×10^{-3} m
(c) 1.92×10^{-3} m (d) 3.84×10^{-3} m

78 Calculate the wavelength in nanometer associated with a proton moving at 1×10^3 ms^{-1} (mass of proton $=1.67\times 10^{-27}$ kg and $h=6.63\times 10^{-34}$ Js) **[AIEEE 2009]**

(a) 0.032 nm (b) 0.40 nm
(c) 2.5 nm (d) 14 nm

79 The ionisation enthalpy of hydrogen atom is 1.312×10^6 J mol^{-1}. The energy required to excite the electron in the atom from $n=1$ to $n=2$ is **[AIEEE 2008]**

(a) 8.51×10^5 J mol^{-1} (b) 6.56×10^5 J mol^{-1}
(c) 7.56×10^5 J mol^{-1} (d) 9.84×10^5 J mol^{-1}

80 Which of the following sets of quantum numbers represents the highest energy of an atom? **[AIEEE 2007]**

(a) $n=3, l=1, m=1, s=+1/2$
(b) $n=3, l=2, m=1, s=+1/2$
(c) $n=4, l=0, m=0, s=+1/2$
(d) $n=3, l=0, m=0, s=+1/2$

81 Which of the following nuclear reactions will generate an isotope? **[AIEEE 2007]**

(a) Neutron particle emission (b) Positron emission
(c) α-particle emission (d) β-particle emission

82 Uncertainty in the position of an electron (mass $=9.1\times 10^{-31}$ kg) moving with a velocity 300 ms^{-1}, accurate upto 0.001% will be ($h=6.63\times 10^{-34}$ Js) **[AIEEE 2006]**

(a) 19.3×10^{-2}m (b) 5.76×10^{-2}m
(c) 1.93×10^{-2}m (d) 3.84×10^{-2}m

83 According to Bohr's theory, the angular momentum of an electron in 5th orbit is **[AIEEE 2006]**

(a) $25\frac{h}{\pi}$ (b) $1.0\frac{h}{\pi}$
(c) $10\frac{h}{\pi}$ (d) $2.5\frac{h}{\pi}$

84 Which of the following statements in relation to the hydrogen atom is correct? **[AIEEE 2005]**

(a) $3s$, $3p$ and $3d$-orbitals all have the same energy
(b) $3s$ and $3p$-orbitals are of lower energy than $3d$-orbital
(c) $3p$-orbital is lower in energy than $3d$-orbital
(d) $3s$-orbital is lower in energy than $3p$-orbital

85 In a multi-electron atom, which of the following orbitals described by the three quantum numbers will have the same energy in the absence of magnetic and electric field? **[AIEEE 2005]**

A. $n=1, l=0, m=0$
B. $n=2, l=0, m=0$
C. $n=2, l=1, m=1$
D. $n=3, l=2, m=1$
E. $n=3, l=2, m=0$

(a) Both D and E (b) Both C and D
(c) Both B and C (d) Both A and B

86 Pulsed lasers are powerful sources of nearly monochromatic radition. Lasers that emit photons in a pulse of 5.00 ns duration with a total energy in the pulse of 0.175 J at 875 nm are commercially available. Thus, average power energy (s^{-1}) associated with such a pulse and number of photons emitted in such time are

Power energy Js^{-1} (W)	Number of photons emitted
(a) 4.92×10^7	2.166×10^{26}
(b) 3.50×10^7	1.545×10^{26}
(c) 3.50×10^7	7.703×10^{17}
(d) 4.92×10^7	1.083×10^{18}

87 The wavelength of the radiation emitted, when an electron in hydrogen atom falls from infinity to stationary state 1, would be (Rydberg constant $=1.097\times 10^7$ m^{-1}) **[AIEEE 2005]**

(a) 91 nm (b) 192 nm
(c) 406 nm (d) 9.1×10^{-8} nm

88 Which of the following sets of quantum numbers is correct for an electron in $4f$-orbital? **[AIEEE 2004]**

(a) $n=4, l=3, m=+4, s=+1/2$
(b) $n=4, l=4, m=-4, s=+1/2$
(c) $n=4, l=3, m=+1, s=+1/2$
(d) $n=3, l=2, m=-2, s=+1/2$

89 Consider the ground state of Cr-atom ($Z=24$). The numbers of electrons with the azimuthal quantum numbers $l=1$ and 2, respectively are **[AIEEE 2004]**

(a) 12 and 4
(b) 12 and 5
(c) 16 and 4
(d) 16 and 5

90 The figure that is not a direct manifestation of the quantum nature of atoms is ***[JEE Main 2020 (II) NTA]***

(a)

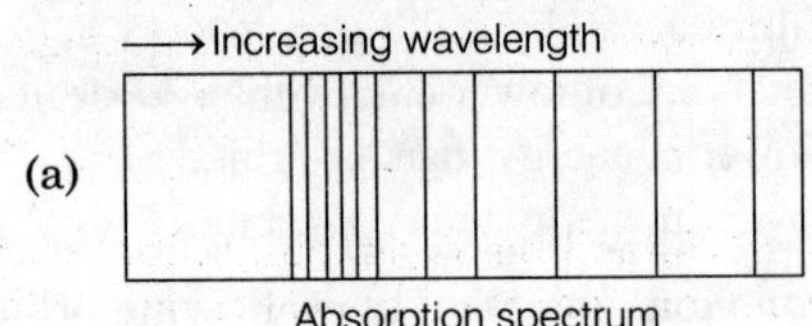

(b)

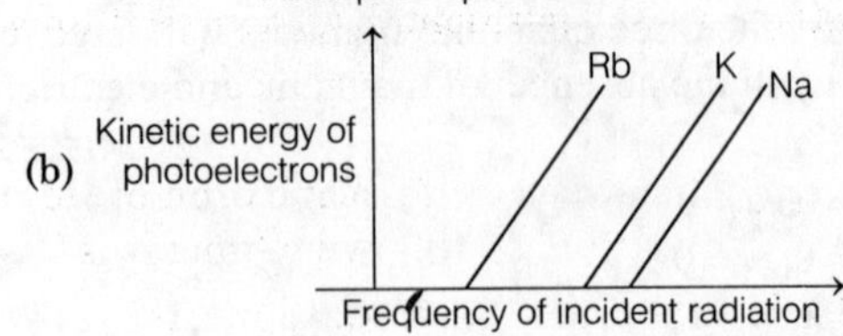

(c)

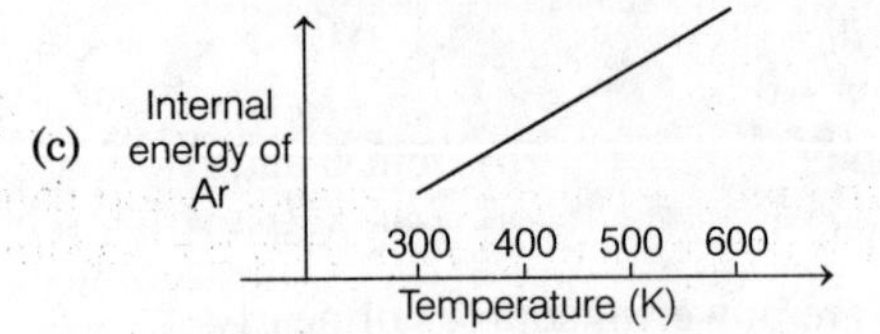

(d)

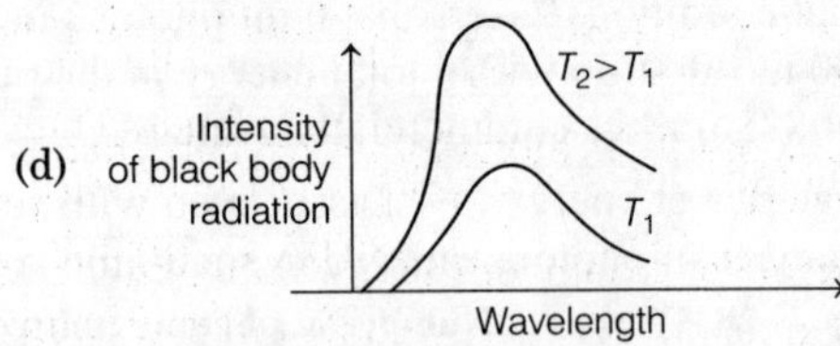

91 The de-Broglie wavelength of a tennis ball of mass 60 g moving with a velocity of 10 ms^{-1} is approximately (Planck's constant, $h = 6.63 \times 10^{-34}$ Js) ***[AIEEE 2003]***

(a) 10^{-33} m (b) 10^{-31} m
(c) 10^{-16} m (d) 10^{25} m

92 In Bohr series of lines of hydrogen spectrum, the third line from the red end corresponds to which one of the following inner - orbit jumps of the electron? ***[AIEEE 2003]***

(a) $3 \rightarrow 2$ (b) $5 \rightarrow 2$
(c) $4 \rightarrow 1$ (d) $2 \rightarrow 5$

93 Consider the hypothetical situation where the azimuthal quantum number, l, takes values 0, 1, 2 ...... $n+1$; where n is the principal quantum number. Then, the element with atomic number ***[JEE Main 2020 (II) NTA]***

(a) 8 is the first noble gas
(b) 13 has a half-filled valence subshell
(c) 9 is the first alkali metal
(d) 6 has a $2p$-valence subshell

94 For any given series of spectral lines of atomic hydrogen, let $\Delta\bar{\nu} = \bar{\nu}_{max} - \bar{\nu}_{min}$ be the difference in maximum and minimum frequencies in cm^{-1}. The ratio $\Delta\bar{\nu}_{Lyman} / \Delta\bar{\nu}_{Balmer}$ is ***[JEE Main (II) 2019 NTA]***

(a) 27 : 5 (b) 5 : 4
(c) 9 : 4 (d) 4 : 1

95 The size of the iso-electronic species Cl^-, Ar and Ca^{2+} is affected by ***[JEE Main 2019 (II) NTA]***

(a) azimuthal quantum number of valence shell
(b) electron-electron interaction in the outer orbitals
(c) principal quantum number of valence shell
(d) nuclear charge

96 If p is the momentum of the fastest electron ejected from a metal surface after the irradiation of light having wavelength λ, then for 1.5 p momentum of the photoelectron, the wavelength of the light should be : (Assume kinetic energy of ejected photoelectron to be very high in comparison to work function) : ***[JEE Main 2019 (II) NTA]***

(a) $\frac{4}{9}\lambda$ (b) $\frac{3}{4}\lambda$
(c) $\frac{2}{3}\lambda$ (d) $\frac{1}{2}\lambda$

97 The number of subshells associated with $n = 4$ and $m = -2$ quantum number is ***[JEE Main 2020 (II) NTA]***

(a) 8 (b) 2
(c) 16 (d) 4

ACID TEST
For JEE Advanced

TYPE I MCQs with Only ONE Correct Alternate

98 Potential energy of an electron present in the *N*-shell of the Be^{3+} ion is
(a) −13.6 eV (b) −27.2 eV
(c) −3.4 eV (d) −6.8 eV

99 Given,
$$Na(g) \longrightarrow Na^{+}(g) + e^{-}, \quad \Delta H = 496 \text{kJ mol}^{-1}$$
Thus, lowest frequency of light that will ionise a sodium atom is
(a) $2.48 \times 10^{15} s^{-1}$ (b) $2.48 \times 10^{14} s^{-1}$
(c) $1.24 \times 10^{14} s^{-1}$ (d) $1.24 \times 10^{15} s^{-1}$

100 The number of possible lines of Paschen series when electron jumps from 7th excited state in hydrogen like species as He^{+} is
(a) 15 (b) 8 (c) 6 (d) 7

101 x number of electrons with magnetic quantum number $m = +1$ and y number of electrons with azimuthal quantum number 0 are present in Cr(24). Thus, x and y are

	x	y
(a)	6	7
(b)	5	7
(c)	7	7
(d)	7	5

102 Iron (II) $(Z = 26)$ has x electrons in $(n-1)d$, y electrons in $(n-1)p$ and z electrons in $(n-2)s$ sub orbits. Thus, x, y and z are respectively :

	x	y	z
(a)	0	6	2
(b)	6	6	2
(c)	6	2	2
(d)	0	6	0

103 In Fe$(Z = 26)$, number of electrons having $(l + m)$ equal to zero is
(a) 7 (b) 12 (c) 13 (d) 20

104 Longest wavelength in the emission of spectrum of H atom is (assume $(n_1 + n_2) = 7$ and $(n_2 - n_1) = 3$)
(a) 8×10^{-6} m (b) 4×10^{-6} m
(c) 1.0×10^{-5} m (d) 1.5×10^{-5} m

105 Kinetic energy of an electron in second orbit of He^{+} is x. Thus, energy required in the following process is
$$Na^{10+}(g) \longrightarrow Na^{11+}(g) + e^{-}$$
assuming the species in ground state
(a) $11x$ (b) $49x$ (c) $121x$ (d) $5x$

106 For the isoelectronic species He^{+} and H, revolving in first and second orbit, ratio of their time periods will be
(a) 1:1 (b) 1:8 (c) 8:1 (d) 1:32

107 Emission spectrum of electron in H-atom falling to ground state consists of maximum of 15 lines. Thus, wavelength of the spectral lines is
(a) 9378Å (b) 950.0Å (c) 480.0Å (d) 468.9Å

108 Magnetic moment of Fe^{2+} is x and that of Co^{3+} is y. Thus, x/y is
(a) $\sqrt{5/7}$ (b) $\sqrt{7/3}$ (c) $7/3$ (d) 1

109 In a sample of H-atom electrons make a transition from fourth excited state to ground state producing all possible types of spectral lines. Number of lines in the (IR) region is
(a) 4 (b) 5 (c) 6 (d) 3

110 Ionisation energy of electron in He^{+} is 19.6×10^{-18} J. Thus, energy of Li^{2+} in second stationary state is
(a) 1.96×10^{-17} J (b) 3.92×10^{-17} J
(c) 1.103×10^{-17} J (d) 1.96×10^{-18} J

111 An orbit in H-atom can be divided into n-waves as shown

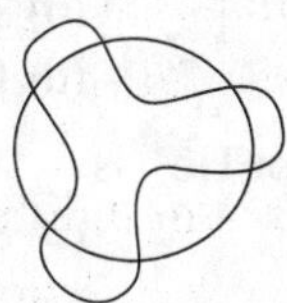

Thus, kinetic energy in the given orbit is
(a) 3.04 eV (b) 1.51 eV
(c) −1.51 eV (d) −3.04 eV

112 A proton accelerated from rest through potential difference of 'V' volts has a wavelength associated with it. What must be accelerated potential for an α-particle (He^{2+}) to have the twice the wavelength of the proton?
(a) $V/4$ (b) $V/8$ (c) $4V$ (d) $2V$

113 The energy required to move a 1.0×10^{-10} C negatively charged body from infinite distance to a point 0.10 cm from a 1.0 C negatively charged body is (constant $k = 9.0\times 10^{11}$ J cm C^{-2})
(a) 9J (b) 900J (c) 0.9J (d) 90J

114 Electrons in H-atom is brought from infinite distance to the point in an orbit of radius r_n, against force of attraction. Work done is
(a) PE, $-\frac{ke^2}{r_n}$ (b) KE, $\frac{ke^2}{r_n}$ (c) PE, $\frac{ke^2}{r_n}$ (d) KE, $-\frac{ke^2}{r_n}$

115 Relationship between the electron volt and the wavelength (in nm) of the energetically equivalent photon is
(a) 1242 nm eV (b) 8.06×10^{-4} nm eV
(c) 1120.3 nm eV (d) None of these

116 Equivalent of energy unit 1.00 cm^{-1} in kJ mol^{-1} of photons is
(a) 2.0×10^{-26} J mol^{-1} (b) 1.20×10^{-2} kJ mol^{-1}
(c) 2.86×10^{-3} kJ mol^{-1} (d) None of these

117 Frequencies of the longest and shortest wavelengths of the visible light are respectively (in multiple of 10^{14})
(a) 7.50, 4.286 (b) 4.286, 7.50
(c) 7.50, 1.50 (d) 1.50, 7.50

118 Consider following dissociation of O_2 molecule

$$O_2 \xrightarrow{h\nu} O + O^*$$

O* is 1.967 eV more energetic than normal O atom. If dissociation energy of O_2 is 498 kJ mol^{-1}, maximum wavelength effective for the photochemical dissociation of O_2 is
(a) 17.4 nm (b) 240nm (c) 24.0nm (d) 174 nm

119 The critical wavelength for producing the photoelectric effect in tungsten is 2600 Å. Thus, wavelength necessary to produce photoelectrons from tungsten having twice the kinetic energy of those produced at 2200 Å is
(a) 950 Å (b) 3900 Å
(c) 1900 Å (d) 1200 Å

120 Rydberg constant for He^+ is
(a) $4.38716\times 10^{7}\ m^{-1}$ (b) 8.271×10^{-18} J
(c) $1.316\times 10^{16}\ s^{-1}$ (d) All of these

121 A photon was absorbed by a H-atom in its ground state, and the electron was promoted to the fifth orbit. When the excited atom returned to its ground state, visible and other quanta were emitted. Thus, wave number of the radiations emitted is
(a) $8.226\times 10^{6}\ m^{-1}$ (b) $1.053\times 10^{7}\ m^{-1}$
(c) $1.028\times 10^{7}\ m^{-1}$ (d) $1.09679\times 10^{7}\ m^{-1}$

122 The wave number of the first line in Balmer series of H-atom is $1.52\times 10^{6}\ m^{-1}$. Thus, wave number of the first line in Balmer series of Be^{3+} is
(a) $6.08\times 10^{6}\ m^{-1}$ (b) $2.432\times 10^{7}\ m^{-1}$
(c) $3.80\times 10^{5}\ m^{-1}$ (d) $9.50\times 10^{4}\ m^{-1}$

123 Ratio of velocity of an electron in the first orbit of H-atom to the velocity of light in vacuum is
(a) 137.5 (b) ∞
(c) 7.273×10^{-3} (d) 1.625×10^{-3}

124 What optical transition in the He^+ spectrum have the same wavelength as the first Lyman transition of hydrogen?
(a) $n=3$ to $n=1$ (b) $n=4$ to $n=3$
(c) $n=3$ to $n=2$ (d) $n=4$ to $n=2$

125 An electron in He^+ ion in its ground state absorbs 1.50 times as much energy as the minimum required for it to escape from the ion. Thus, effective wavelength of the emitted electron is
(a) 2.35 Å (b) 4.70 Å
(c) 9.40 Å (d) 1.175 Å

126 Given,

$$M(g) \longrightarrow M^+(g) + e^-, \qquad \Delta H = 3.44\times 10^{-18}\ J$$

The absorption of photon of wavelength λ ionises the atom $M(g)$ and ejects an electron with a velocity of $1.03\times 10^{6}\ ms^{-1}$. Thus, wavelength λ is
(a) 220.0 Å (b) 110.0 Å
(c) 506.7 Å (d) 902.1 Å

127 In an X-ray photoelectron experiment, a photon of wavelength 150 pm ejects an electron from inner shell of an atom and its emerges with a speed of $2.24\times 10^{7}\ m\ s^{-1}$. Thus, binding energy of the electron is
(a) 1002eV (b) 3425 eV
(c) 510 eV (d) 6856 eV

128 Wavelength of the photon that is emitted when an electron in the second Bohr's orbit returns to the first orbit in the hydrogen atom ($(IE)_H = 2.17\times 10^{-18}$ J $atom^{-1}$) is
(a) 244 nm (b) 122 nm
(c) 122 pm (d) 244 pm

129 Energy of a hydrogen like species in the third excited state is 2.25 times the energy of He^+ in the second excited state. Thus, atomic number of the hydrogen like species is
(a) 4 (b) 5 (c) 6 (d) 3

130 The wavelength of the β-line of the Balmer series in He^+ is 4815Å. Thus, wavelength of the α-line of the Balmer series for the same species is
(a) 4815 Å (b) 2408 Å
(c) 1208 Å (d) 6500 Å

131 Energies of H-atom, He^+ ion, Li^{2+} ion and Be^{3+} are equal in n_1^{th}, n_2^{th}, n_3^{th} and n_4^{th} orbit. Thus, n_1, n_2, n_3 and n_4 are

	n_1	n_2	n_3	n_4
(a)	4	3	2	1
(b)	1	2	3	4
(c)	2	3	1	4
(d)	1	1	1	1

132 The uncertainty in the measurement of position of an electron is equal to its de-Broglie's wavelength. Thus, percentage error in the measurement of velocity is

(a) 7.96% (b) 0.796%
(c) 0.0796% (d) 0.00796%

133 For 1*s* orbital, in terms of normalisation constant *N*, $\psi = \sqrt{N}\, e^{-Zr/a_o}$

radial distribution function is $4\pi r^2 \psi^2$.

Most probable distance at which 1*s* electron of H-atom is to be found is

(a) $1/a_o$ (b) $1/a_o^2$ (c) a_o (d) a_o^2

134 Electron in H-atom is excited to 2*s* level where wave function is given by

$$\psi_{2s} = \frac{1}{4\sqrt{2\pi}}\left(\frac{1}{a_o}\right)^{3/2}\left(2 - \frac{r}{a_o}\right) e^{-r/2a_o}$$

Radius *r* in terms of a_o where radial node in 2*s* occurs is

(a) a_o (b) $1/a_o$ (c) $2a_o$ (d) $\frac{1}{2a_o}$

135 Moseley equation is represented as $\sqrt{v} = a(Z-b)$ where *a* and *b* are constants

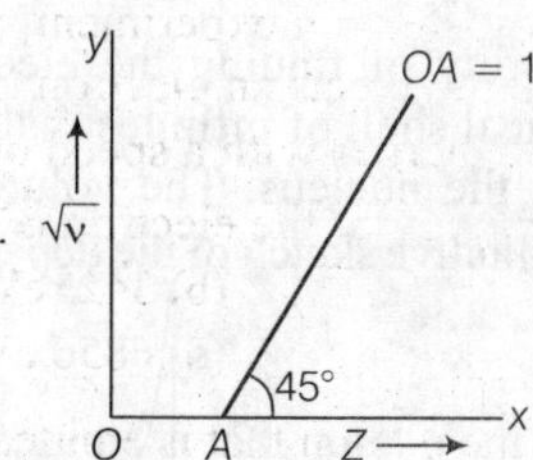

Thus, last filling electron has quantum numbers for the element which has frequency of 400Hz, is

	n	*l*	*m*	*s*
(a)	2	0	0	$+\frac{1}{2}$
(b)	3	2	−2	$+\frac{1}{2}$
(c)	4	0	0	$+\frac{1}{2}$
(d)	3	0	0	$+\frac{1}{2}$

136 Radius of first orbit is a_o. Thus, de-Broglie wavelength of the electron in third orbit of He^+ is nearly,

(a) $2\pi a_o$ (b) $6\pi a_o$ (c) $9a_o$ (d) $3\pi a_o$

137 Shortest wavelength of He^+ ion in Lyman series is *x*, then longest wavelength in Balmer series of Be^{3+} ion is

(a) $\frac{5x}{9}$ (b) $\frac{9x}{5}$ (c) $\frac{x}{4}$ (d) $\frac{36x}{5}$

138 If *n* and *l* are respectively the principal and azimuthal quantum numbers then the expression for calculating the total number of electrons in any energy level is

(a) $\sum_{l=1}^{l=n} 2(2l+1)$ (b) $\sum_{l=1}^{l=(n-1)} 2(2l+1)$

(c) $\sum_{l=0}^{l=(n+1)} 2(2l+1)$ (d) $\sum_{l=0}^{l=(n-1)} 2(2l+1)$

139 If there were the possibilities of electron spin as $\left(+\frac{1}{2}, 0, -\frac{1}{2}\right)$, then K(19) would be placed in

(a) *s*-block (b) *p*-block (c) *d*-block (d) *f*-block

140 If the quantum number *l* could have the value of *n* also, then magnetic moment of Sc(21) would be (other rules followed)

(a) $\sqrt{15}$ B.M (b) $\sqrt{35}$ B.M
(c) $\sqrt{3}$ B.M (d) $\sqrt{8}$ B.M

141 Time taken to produce 1mole of photons emitted by a 100W yellow lamp (wavelength 560 nm) is

(a) 40 min (b) 36 min
(c) 12 min (d) 340 min

142 The position of both, an electron and helium atom is known within 1.0 mm. Further the momentum of the electron is known within 5.0×10^{-26} kg m s^{-1}. The minimum uncertainty in the measurement of the momentum of the helium atom (in kg m s^{-1}) is

(a) 50 (b) 80
(c) 8.0×10^{-26} (d) 3.65×10^{-22}

143 In Schrodinger wave equation given below

$$\nabla^2 \psi + \frac{8\pi m}{h^2}(E - U)\psi = 0$$

∇^2 and *U* are

	∇^2	*U*
(a)	$\frac{d^2}{dx^2} + \frac{d^2}{dy^2} + \frac{d^2}{dz^2}$	Ze/r
(b)	$\frac{d^2}{dx^2} + \frac{d^2}{dy^2} + \frac{d^2}{dz^2}$	$-Ze^2/r$
(c)	$\frac{d}{dx} + \frac{d}{dy} + \frac{d}{dz}$	$-Ze^2/r$
(d)	None of the above	

144 The wavelength of a neutron with translatory kinetic energy equal to *kT* at 300 K is

(a) 178 pm (b) 200 pm (c) 17.8 pm (d) 20.0 pm

145 The shortest wavelength transition in the Paschen series in hydrogen atom occurs at 821 nm; at what wavelength does it occur in Li^{2+} ion?
(a) 91.2 nm (b) 273.6 nm
(c) 821.0 nm (d) 7.4 pm

146 Minimum amount of time required to measure the kinetic energy of an electron with a speed of $100 \pm 1\ \text{m s}^{-1}$ is :
(a) 3.0 μs (b) 0.3 μs
(c) 1.0 μs (d) 1.2 μs

147 A near ultraviolet photon at 300 nm is absorbed by a gas and then remitted as two photons. One photon is red with wavelength 760 nm. Thus, wavelength of second photon is
(a) 460 nm (b) 1060 nm
(c) 230 nm (d) 496 nm

148 Two fast moving particles X and Y are associated with de-Broglie wavelengths of 1 nm and 4 nm respectively. If mass of X is nine times the mass of Y, the ratio of kinetic energies of X and Y would be
(a) 3 : 1 (b) 9 : 1
(c) 5 : 12 (d) 16 : 9

149 The wave function of an electron in the lowest energy state of H-atom is proportional to e^{-r/a_0}, where r is the distance of the electron from the nucleus. Probability is maximum when electron is at
(a) the nucleus (b) a distance a_0 from nucleus
(c) the infinite (d) can't be predicated

150 Assume probability $= 4\pi r^2 \psi^2 \delta r$ and $\psi = \dfrac{e^{-r/a_0}}{(\pi a_0)^{3/2}}$ then probability that an electron will be found between a shell of radius a_0 and a shell of radius 1 pm greater is ($a_0 = 0.529$Å, $e^{-2} = 0.14$)
(a) 0.01 (b) 10 (c) 100 (d) 0.10

151 Photoelectric emission is observed from two surfaces at incident frequencies ν_1 and ν_2 ($\nu_1 > \nu_2$). Maximum kinetic energies of the photoelectrons emitted in the above two cases are in the ratio of 1 : k. If threshold frequency in both cases is ν_0, then this value is
(a) $\dfrac{\nu_2 - \nu_1}{(k-1)}$ (b) $\dfrac{k\nu_1 - \nu_2}{(k-1)}$
(c) $\dfrac{k\nu_2 - \nu_1}{(k-1)}$ (d) $\dfrac{\nu_2 - \nu_1}{k}$

152 Electron in He^+ in excited state returns to the ground state giving spectral line of wavelength λ. In terms of Rydberg constant (R_H) excited state is given by
(a) $\dfrac{4\lambda R_H}{(4\lambda R_H - 1)}$ (b) $\sqrt{\dfrac{\lambda R_H}{(4\lambda R_H - 1)}}$
(c) $\dfrac{2\lambda R_H}{(4\lambda R_H - 1)}$ (d) $2\sqrt{\dfrac{\lambda R_H}{(4\lambda R_H - 1)}}$

153 Consider following cases for Lyman series of Li^{2+} ion. Thus, wavelengths emitted from n_2th and n_3th level are in the ratio of

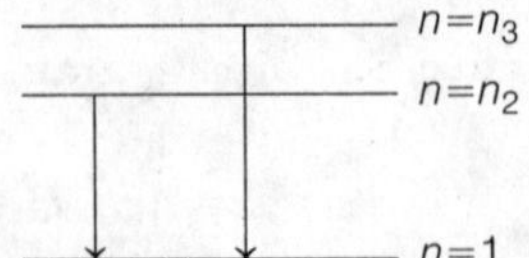

(a) $\left(\dfrac{n_2}{n_3}\right)^2 \left(\dfrac{n_2^2 - 1}{n_3^2 - 1}\right)$ (b) $\left(\dfrac{n_2}{n_3}\right)^2 \left(\dfrac{n_3^2 - 1}{n_2^2 - 1}\right)$
(c) $\left(\dfrac{n_3}{n_2}\right)^2 \left(\dfrac{n_2^2 - 1}{n_3^2 - 1}\right)$ (d) $\dfrac{n_2}{n_3}\left(\dfrac{n_3 - 1}{n_2 - 1}\right)$

154 Balmer series of He^+ ion, wavelength for emission of electron from n^{th} level is given by

$$\lambda = k\frac{n^2}{(n+2)(n-2)}$$

Thus k is equal to
(a) $4R_H$ (b) R_H (c) $\dfrac{1}{R_H}$ (d) $\dfrac{1}{4}R_H$

155 Given energy of H-atom in the ground state is ($-E$), velocity of the photoelectron emitted when a photon of energy E_p strikes a stationary Na^{10+} ion in ground state is given by :
(a) $\sqrt{\dfrac{2(E_p - 121E)}{m}}$ (b) $\sqrt{\dfrac{2(121E - E_p)}{m}}$
(c) $\sqrt{\dfrac{2(E_p + 121E)}{m}}$ (d) $\sqrt{\dfrac{(121E - E_p)}{2m}}$

156 P is the probability of finding the electron of hydrogen atom in a spherical shell of infinitesimal thickness, dr, at a distance r from the nucleus. The volume of this shell is $4\pi r^2 dr$. The qualitative sketch of the dependence of P on r is

(a)
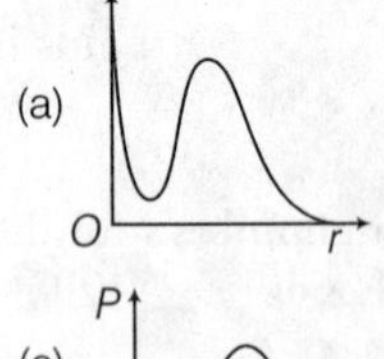

(b)
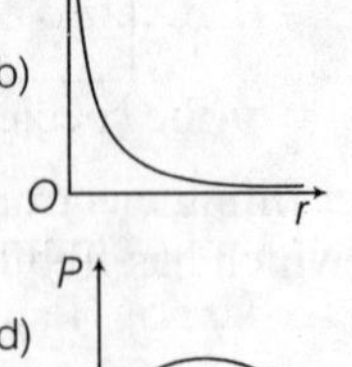

(c) P, O, r
(d) P, O, r

[JEE Adv. 2016]

157 The kinetic energy of an electron in the second Bohr orbit of a hydrogen atom is [a_0 is Bohr radius]. **[JEE Adv. 2012]**
(a) $\dfrac{h^2}{4\pi^2 m a_0^2}$ (b) $\dfrac{h^2}{16\pi^2 m a_0^2}$ (c) $\dfrac{h^2}{32\pi^2 m a_0^2}$ (d) $\dfrac{h^2}{64\pi^2 m a_0^2}$

158 The number of radial nodes in 3s and 2p respectively are **[IIT JEE 2005]**
(a) 2 and 0 (b) 0 and 2 (c) 1 and 2 (d) 2 and 1

TYPE II Statement Based Questions

Directions Answers of Q. Nos. (159-171) have been based on the following codes.

(a) Statement I is true; Statement II is true; Statement II is the correct explanation of Statement I.

(b) Statement I is true; Statement II is true; Statement II is not the correct explanation of Statement I.

(c) Statement I is true; Statement II is false.

(d) Statement I is false; Statement II is true.

159 **Statement I** Cr(24) and Fe^{2+} (26) are isoelectronic but differ is magnetic moment.

Statement II Stability of Cr is increased by $3d^5 4s^1$ configuration and not by $3d^4 4s^2$ configuration.

160 **Statement I** When white light that has passed through sodium vapour is viewed through a spectroscope, the observed spectrum has a dark line at 5890 Å.

Statement II The light of 5890 Å wavelength has precisely the energy absorbed by the sodium atom to promote its outermost electron to a higher level from its ground state level.

161 **Statement I** H, He^+, Li^{2+} and Be^{3+} are iso-electronic, thus they have equal energies.

Statement II Energy of nth orbit of atomic number Z is

$$E_n = \frac{-13.6\, Z^2}{n^2} \text{ eV}$$

162 **Statement I** When work function of an element undergoing photoelectric effect is zero, all the photons absorbed are converted to kinetic energy.

Statement II $h\nu = \text{work function} + \frac{1}{2}mv^2$

163 **Statement I** Li^{2+} and He^+ are iso-electronic and have different values of Bohr's radius.

Statement II In terms of Bohr's radius, ionic radius is $r_n = \frac{n^2 a_0}{Z}$ for the species with one electron only.

164 **Statement I** Wave number of α-line of Be^{3+} is four times the α-line of He^+ of any series.

Statement II $\bar{\nu} = R_H Z^2 \left[\frac{1}{n_1^2} - \frac{1}{n_2^2}\right]$

165 **Statement I** Electronic configuration of N-atom is represented as :

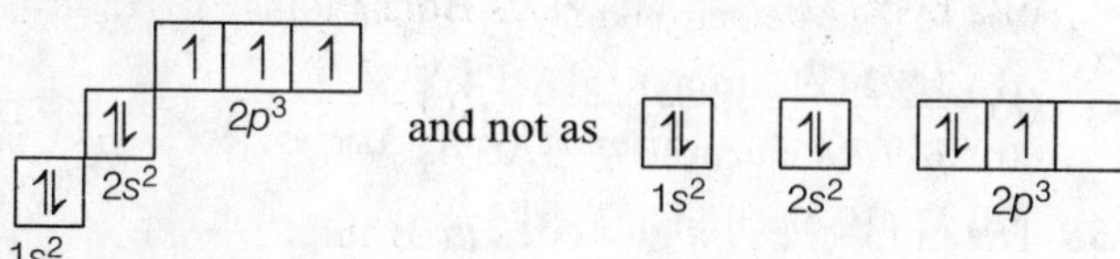

Statement II Aufbau rule has been violated.

166 **Statement I** Electronic configuration of Fe^{2+} is

(Ar) $3d^5 4s^1$ [1 | 1 | 1 | 1 | 1] $3d^5$ [1] $4s^1$

and not as (Ar) $3d^6$ [1⇂ | 1 | 1 | 1 | 1] $3d^6$

Statement II The stable electronic configuration of the ground state of an atom is the one which has the greatest multiplicity.

167 **Statement I** For any axis (say x-axis), Schrodinger wave equation represented as $\frac{d^2\psi}{dx^2} + \frac{4\pi^2}{\lambda^2}\psi = 0$ has the solution $\psi = A \sin\left(\frac{2\pi x}{\lambda}\right)$.

Statement II $\frac{d^2}{dx^2}(Ae^{-2\pi x/\lambda})$ gives $\frac{d^2\psi}{dx^2} + \frac{4\pi^2}{\lambda^2}\psi = 0$

168 **Statement I** Electromagnetic radiations of given frequency consists of a stream of particles called photons.

Statement II The number of photons in the beam are independent of their frequencies.

169 **Statement I** For 2s electron, Schrodinger wave equation for H-atom is $\psi_{2s} = N\left(2 - \frac{r}{a_0}\right)e^{-r/a_0}$, where N is $= \frac{1}{4(2\pi)^{1/2}}\left(\frac{1}{a_0}\right)^{3/2}$.

Statement II If $r_0 = 2a_0$, radial node in 2s orbital is formed.

170 **Statement I** The wavelengths of electron waves in two orbits are in the ratio of 3 : 5 then ratio of their kinetic energies will be in the ratio of 25 : 9.

Statement II $\lambda = \frac{h}{\sqrt{2m\text{KE}}}$

171 **Statement I** It is impossible to determine the exact position and exact momentum of an electron simultaneously.

Statement II The path of an electron in an atom is clearly defined.

TYPE III MCQs with ONE or MORE than ONE Correct Alternate

172 Select the correct statements.

(a) s-orbitals are spherically symmetrical and have non-zero amplitude at the nucleus

(b) Spin with $m_s = +\frac{1}{2}$ is called α-spin and that with $m_s = \frac{-1}{2}$ is called β-spin

(c) A radial distribution function $P(r)$ is the probability density for finding an electron between r and $(r + dr)$ and for s-orbital, $P(r) = 4\pi r^2 \psi^2$

(d) Solution of the Schrodinger wave equation for x-axis $\frac{d^2\psi}{dx^2} + \frac{8\pi^2 mE\psi}{h^2} = 0$ is $\psi = Ae^{-2\pi x/\lambda}$

173 Select correct statements.
(a) $|\psi^2|$ is a measure of electron density at a point in an atom
(b) Radial probability function $(= 4\pi r^2\psi^2)$ gives the probability density of finding the electron at a distance r from the nucleus regardless of direction.
(c) The shape of an orbital is defined as the surface of constant probability density that encloses some large fraction of the probability of finding the electron
(d) For $1s$ orbital $\psi = \sqrt{N} e^{-Zr/a_0}$ and radial distribution function $= 4\pi r^2 \psi^2$. Most probable distance at which $1s$ electron of He^+ ion is to be found is half of Bohr's radius a_0.

174 Based on the equation of the energy of the electron in the nth orbit for the species with one electron and atomic number Z is $E_n = -2.178 \times 10^{-18} J(Z^2/n^2)$
Select correct statement(s)
(a) The negative sign in equation simply means that the energy of electron bound to the nucleus is lower than it would be if the electrons were at the infinite distance from the nucleus.
(b) Larger the value of n, the larger is the orbit radius
(c) It can be used to calculate the energy difference when electron changes its orbit
(d) For $n = 1$, the electron has a more negative value than it does for any value of $n > 1$, which means that the electron is more loosely bound in the smallest allowed orbit.

175 For the electrons of oxygen atom, which of the following statements are incorrect. ***[NCERT Exemplar]***
(a) Effective nuclear charge (Z_{eff}) for an electron in a $2s$-orbital is the same as Z_{eff} for an electron in a $2p$-orbital
(b) An electron in the $2s$-orbital has the same energy as an electron in the $2p$-orbital
(c) Z_{eff} of $1s$ and $2s$ electrons are identical
(d) Electrons present in $2s$-orbital have same spin but opposite sign

176 The ground state energy of hydrogen atom is -13.6 eV. Consider an electronic state ψ of He^+ whose energy, azimuthal quantum number and magnetic quantism number are -3.4 eV, 2 and 0, respectively. Which of the following statement(s) is (are) true for the state ψ ?
(a) It is a $4d$ state ***[JEE Adv. 2019]***
(b) It has 2 angular nodes
(c) It has 3 radial nodes
(d) The nuclear charge experienced by the electron in this state is less than $2e$, where e is the magnitude of the electronic charge.

177 Fe^{2+}, Mn^+, Cr and Co^{3+} are isoelectronic (each having 24 elecrons). Which of these have magnetic moment of 6.93 B.M.?
(a) Fe^{2+} (b) Mn^+
(c) Cr (d) Co^{3+}

178 Energy equivalent to 100 m^{-1} is
(a) 2×10^{-23} J per photon
(b) 1.2×10^{-2} kJ mol^{-1} of photons
(c) 2×10^{-14} erg per photon
(d) 2.9×10^{-3} kcal mol^{-1} of photons

179 Some of the following conclusions could be derived from Rutherford's α-particle scattering experiment. These are ***[NCERT Exemplar]***
(a) most of the space in the atom is empty
(b) the radius of the atom is about 10^{-10} m while that of the nucleus is about 10^{-15} m
(c) electrons move in a circular path of fixed energy called orbits
(d) electrons and the nucleus are held together by electrostatic force of attraction

180 For the helium gas and helium ion,
I. $He(g) \longrightarrow He^{2+}(g) + 2e^-, \Delta H° = 79$ eV
II. $He(g) \longrightarrow He^+(g) + e^-, \Delta H° = x$ eV
III. $He^+(g) \longrightarrow He^{2+}(g) + e^-, \Delta H° = 54.4$ eV
Thus,
(a) first ionisation energy of $He^+(g)$ is 54.4 eV
(b) first ionisation energy of He is 24.6 eV
(c) second ionisation energy of He is 54.4 eV
(d) α-particle gains two electrons by losing 79.0 eV of energy

181 Cathode rays are associated with one or more of the following characteristics ***[NCERT Exemplar]***
(a) they start from the cathode and move towards the anode
(b) they travel in the straight line in the absence of electric or magnetic field
(c) they are independent of the nature of the material of the cathode in the CRT (Cathode Ray Tube)
(d) they are dependent on the nature of the material of the cathode in the CRT

182 If Autbau rule is not followed, incorrect electronic configuration of the given species are
(a) M^{2+} (24 electrons) : [Ar] $4s^1 3d^5$
(b) M (24 electrons) : [Ar] $4s^1 3d^5$
(c) M^+ (24 electrons) : [Ar] $4s^1 3d^5$
(d) M (19 electrons) : [Ar] $3d^1$

183 For 1*s*-orbital of H-atom in the ground state, radial probability density is given by

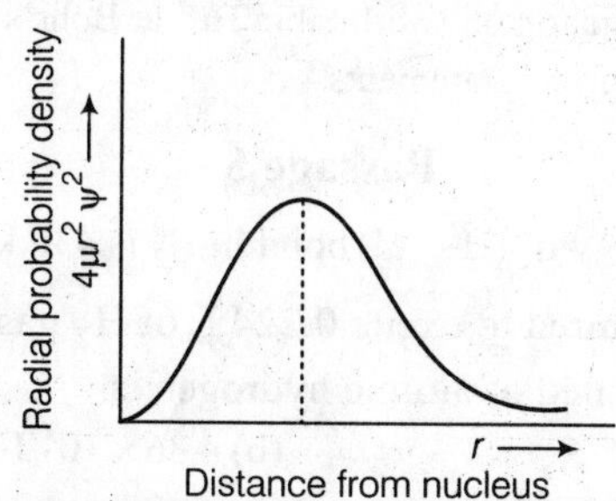

Thus, radial probability density

(a) is maximum when $r = a_0$ (b) is maximum when $r = \frac{1}{a_0}$

(c) falls to zero when $r > 1$ Å (d) is independent of r

184 Energy of $Be^{3+}(g)$ in 4th orbit in equal to that of

(a) H atom in first orbit

(b) $He^+(g)$ in second orbit

(c) $Li^{2+}(g)$ in third orbit

(d) $Na^{10+}(g)$ in eleventh orbit

185 Select correct relationship based on Bohr's theory:

(a) Potential energy = one-half of total energy

(b) Kinetic energy = – total energy

(c) Radius of H-atom or H like species $= \frac{n^2 a_0}{Z}$

(d) Velocity of electron $= \frac{2.18 \times 10^6 Z}{n}$

186 $3d_{xy}$ orbital can be represented as

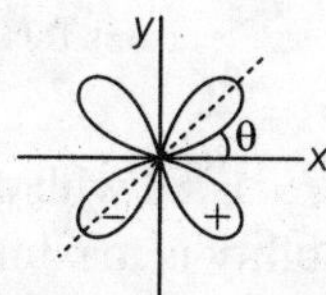

Select correct statements about this $3d_{xy}$ orbital

(a) It is non-axial orbital

(b) Positive and negative signs represent sign of amplitude of electron wave

(c) The orbitals drawn has two nodal planes *xz* and *yz*

(d) The minimum probability point lies along $\theta = 45°$.

187 Given wave number of α-line in Balmer series of He^+ is $x\ m^{-1}$, then

(a) wavelength of α-line in Balmer series of Be^{3+} is $\frac{1}{4x}$ m

(b) wave number of β-line in Balmer series of Be^{3+} is $5.4x\ m^{-1}$

(c) longest wavelength of Balmer series of Li^{2+} is $\left(\frac{4}{9x}\right)$m

(d) shortest wavelength of Paschen series of Be^{3+} is $\left(\frac{5}{16x}\right)$m

188 One electron is revolving around the nucleus of the atom of atomic number Z_1 in n_1^{th} orbit and the second one of the atom of atomic number Z_2 in the n_2^{th} orbit. Thus,

(a) $\frac{(\text{Linear momentum})_1}{(\text{Linear momentum})_2} = \frac{n_1}{n_2}$

(b) $\frac{(\text{Angular momentum})_1}{(\text{Angular momentum})_2} = \frac{Z_1 n_2}{Z_2 n_1}$

(c) $\frac{(\text{KE})_1}{(\text{KE})_2} = \left(\frac{Z_1 n_2}{Z_2 n_1}\right)^2$

(d) $\frac{\nu_1}{\nu_2} = \left(\frac{Z_2}{Z_1}\right)^2 \left(\frac{n_1}{n_2}\right)^3$

189 Select correct statements about photoelectric effect.

(a) Number of electrons ejected is proportional to the intensity or brightness of light but independent of frequency of light

(b) For each metal, there is a characteristic minimum frequency called threshold frequency below which photoelectric effect is not observed

(c) If work function is zero, all the energy falling on the surface of metal is converted to kinetic energy.

(d) If incident frequency is equal to threshold frequency, maximum kinetic energy is obtained

190 The normalised wave function for a 2*s* orbital in H-atom is

$$\psi = \left(\frac{1}{32\pi a_0^3}\right)^{1/2} \left(2 - \frac{r}{a_0}\right) e^{-r/2a_0}$$

Thus, probability of finding an electron that is described by the wave function in a volume of 1 pm^3 is

(a) zero when centred on nucleus

(b) $\left(\frac{1}{32}\pi a_0^3\right)$ when centred at the Bohr's radius

(c) zero when centred at twice the Bohr's radius

(d) $\left(\frac{10^{-12}}{8a_0 e}\right)$ when centred at the Bohr's radius

TYPE IV Passage Based MCQs (Comprehension)

Passage 1

The characteristic X-ray wavelength for the lines of the K_a series in Mg and Cr are 9.87 and 2.29 Å respectively using Moseley's equation

$$\sqrt{\nu} = a(Z - b)$$

a and *b* are independent of the nature of the elements.

191 Constants *a* and *b* are respectively

	a	*b*
(a)	4.90×10^7	0.75
(b)	0.75	4.90×10^7
(c)	0.75	0.75
(d)	4.90×10^7	4.90×10^7

192 Wavelengths associated with Sr($Z=38$) and Cl($Z=17$) are respectively

	λ_{Sr}	λ_{Cl}
(a)	9.01 pm	47.3 pm
(b)	90.1 pm	473 pm
(c)	0.901 pm	47.3 pm
(d)	9.01 pm	47.3 pm

Passage 2

The lowest energy X-rays have $\lambda = 3.05 \times 10^{-8}$ m

193 Minimum difference in energy between two Bohr's orbits such that an electronic transition would correspond to the emission of X-ray is

(a) 6.52×10^{-20} J (b) 6.52×10^{-16} J
(c) 6.52×10^{-18} J (d) None is correct

194 Assume that the electrons in other shells exert no influence, at what Z (minimum) would a transition from the second energy level to the first result in the emission of an X-ray?

(a) 1 (b) 2 (c) 3 (d) 4

Passage 3

Given,	$\Delta H°$
$He(g) \longrightarrow He^+(g) + e^-$,	24.6 eV
$He^+(g) \longrightarrow He^{2+}(g) + e^-$,	54.4 eV

195 Energy required for the following process is:

$$Li^{2+}(g) \longrightarrow Li^{3+}(g) + e^-$$

(a) 13.96 eV (b) 79.00 eV (c) 122.4 eV (d) 54.4 eV

196 What is energy change associated when α-particle changes to He(g) atom?

(a) −13.6 eV (b) −122.4 eV (c) 54.4 eV (d) −79.0 eV

Passage 4

The normalised wave function for a 2s-orbital of H-atom is

$$\psi_{2s} = \left(\frac{1}{32\pi a_0^3}\right)^{1/2}\left(2 - \frac{Zr}{a_0}\right)e^{-Zr/2a_0}$$

197 Probability of finding an electron that is described by this wave function in a volume of 1 pm^3 when electron in H-atom

(a) is centred at the nucleus
(b) is centred at twice the Bohr's radius
(c) is centred both of above sites
(d) probability is never zero

198 Select correct statement(s).

(a) Probability of finding an electron under given condition given in (Q. 197) at Bohr's radius of H atom is $(10^{-12}/8a_0e)$
(b) Wave function of 2s orbital in He^+ in Bohr's orbit is same as that of 2s-orbital in H-atom in twice the Bohr's radius
(c) Wave function of 2s-orbital in He^+ at Bohr's radius is zero
(d) All are correct statements

Passage 5

Dissociation energy of (H—H) bond in H_2 is 436 kJ mol^{-1}

199 Energy required to excite 0.224 L of H_2 gas at S.T.P to the first excited of atomic hydrogen is

(a) 2.40×10^4 J (b) 4.36×10^3 J
(c) 1.965×10^4 J (d) None is correct

200 The minimum wavelength of the radiation required to break (H—H) bond is

(a) 406 nm (b) 137 nm (c) 548 nm (d) 274 nm

Passage 6

Velocity of the electron in the ground state of H-atom is 2.186×10^6 m s^{-1}.

201 What fraction of the velocity of light is this value?

(a) 7.29×10^{-3} (b) 6.00×10^{-3}
(c) 3.00×10^5 (d) 1.37×10^2

202 How many times a second does the electron travel around the nucleus?

(a) 1.522×10^{-16} s^{-1} (b) 7.208×10^{15} s^{-1}
(c) 6.577×10^{15} s^{-1} (d) 9.109×10^{15} s^{-1}

Passage 7

The radial distribution function, $P(r)$ is a probability density and for 1s orbital, it is given by

$$P(r) = \frac{4Z^3}{a_0^3} r^2 e^{-2Zr/a_0}$$

203 For Be^{3+} ion, probability is maximum when

(a) $r = \frac{a_0}{2}$ (b) $r = \frac{a_0}{4}$
(c) $r = 4a_0$ (d) $r = 2a_0$

204 Maximum probability of H-atom under given condition is

(a) $\frac{4}{a_0 e^2}$ (b) $\frac{a_0 e^2}{4}$ (c) $\frac{a_0}{4}$ (d) $\frac{a_0}{2}$

Passage 8

By Planck's contribution

$$E_\lambda = \frac{a}{\lambda^5(e^{b/\lambda T} - 1)}$$

205 At low value of λ, Planck's contribution is reduced to

(a) Wein's contribution
(b) Rayleigh-Jean's contribution
(c) Stefan-Boltzman's contribution
(d) None of the above

206 At high value of λ, planck's contribution is reduced to
(a) Wein's contribution
(b) Rayleigh-Jean's contribution
(c) Stefan-Boltzman's contribution
(d) None of the above

Passage 9

A particle of charge equal to that of an electron and mass 208 times the mass of the electron moves in a circular orbit around a nuclear of charge $+3e$. Assume that the Bohr model is applicable to this system.

207 Radius of the nth Bohr orbit for this case is
(a) $(5.29\times 10^{-11}\ n^2)$ m (b) $(8.50\times 10^{-14}\ n^2)$ m
(c) $(3.66\times 10^{-14}\ n^2)$ m (d) None is correct

208 Value of n for which the radius of the orbit is approximately the same as that of the first Bohr's orbit of H-atom is
(a) $n = 1$ (b) $n = 5$ (c) $n = 25$ (d) $n = 625$

209 The wavelength of the radiation emitted when the revolving particle jumps from the third orbit to the first orbit is
(a) 55.0 pm (b) 5.50 pm (c) 0.550 pm (d) 550 pm

Passage 10

The hydrogen like species Li^{2+} is in a spherically symmetric state S_1 with one radial node. Upon absorbing light the ion undergoes transition to a state S_2. The state S_2 has one radial node and its energy is equal to the ground state energy of the hydrogen atom. ***[IIT JEE 2010]***

210 The state S_1 is
(a) 1s (b) 2s (c) 2p (d) 3s

211 Energy of the state S_1 in the units of ground state energy of the hydrogen atom is
(a) 0.75 (b) 1.50 (c) 2.25 (d) 4.50

212 The orbital angular momentum quantum number of the state S_2 is
(a) 0 (b) 1 (c) 2 (d) 3

TYPE V Numerical Skills

213 Lithium has a work function of 2.96 eV. Light having a wavelength of 1850 Å falls on its surface. Kinetic energy of the ejected electron is $y\times 10^{-19}$ J. Thus, $y = ?$

214 In the nth excited state, ionic radius of Be^{3+} is equal to Bohr's radius of H-atom in the ground state. Thus, n^{th} excited state is ...

215 At what atomic number, a transition from $n = 2$ to $n = 1$ energy level results in the emission of X-rays with wavelength 3.0×10^{-8} m?

216 An electron in H-atom makes a transition from 6th level to 3rd level. Time period of the electron in the initial state is x times that in the final state. Thus, x is ......

217 de-Broglie's wavelength of a proton is x times that of α-particle both moving under same potential difference. Thus, x is ......

218 Ratio of the time required for an electron taking one round of second orbit of H-atom and Li^{2+} ion is ....

219 What electron transition in a hydrogen atom, starting from the orbit $n = 7$, will produce infrared light of wavelength 2170 nm?

220 Most probable distance at which 1s electron of Be^{3+} is to be found is (a_0/y). Given normalised wave function of 1s orbital is $\psi = \sqrt{N}e^{-Zr/a_0}$

$$N = Z^3/\pi a_0^3$$

and radial distribution function is $4\pi r^2\psi^2$. Derive value of y.

221 The normalised wave function for 2s orbital in H-atom is

$$\psi = \left(\frac{1}{32\pi a_0^3}\right)^{1/2}\left(2 - \frac{r}{a_0}\right)e^{-r/2a_0}$$

value of ψ^2 at Bohr's radius is $\left(\frac{1}{2}\right)^n (\pi a_0^3 e)^{-1}$

What is value of n?

222 Balmer series of the species X and Lyman series of H-atom have same value of maximum wave number $\bar{\nu}$. If X and H are isoelectronic, what is atomic number of X?

223 Given :

$$Li^{2+}(g) \longrightarrow Li^{3+}(g) + e^-, \qquad \Delta H° = 122.4 \text{ eV}$$
$$X^{n+}(g) \longrightarrow X^{(n+1)+} + e^-, \qquad \Delta H° = 54.4 \text{ eV}$$

If $Li^{2+}(g)$ and $X^{n+}(g)$ are isoelectronic, what is atomic number of X^{n+}?

224 The work function of sodium metal is 4.41×10^{-19} J. If photons of wavelength 300 nm are incident on the metal, the kinetic energy of the ejected electrons will be $(h = 6.63\times 10^{-34}$ Js, $c = 3\times 10^8$ ms$^{-1})$ .... $\times 10^{-21}$ J ***[JEE Main 2020 (II) NTA]***

225 Energy change associated per mole of atom with an atomic transition giving rise radiations of 1 Hz is $x\times 10^{-10}$ J mol^{-1}. Thus, x is ....

226 How many waves are there made by a Bohr's electron in one complete revolution in its 5th orbit.

227 What is maximum number of emission lines, when the excited electron of H-atom in $n = 4$ drops to the ground state.

228 Consider following cases.

Species	Temperature	de-Broglie's wavelength
He	100 K	750 nm
X	1250 K	150 nm

What is atomic mass of X?

229 An electron is accelerated with a radiation of wavelength 620 pm. Calculate the potential with which electron is accelerated.

230 Energy required to move 1.0×10^{-10} C negatively charged body from infinite distance to a point 1.0 cm from a 1.0 C negatively charged body is $10x$J. If constant is 9.0×10^{11} J cm C^{-2}, what is value of x?

231 When a certain metal was irradiated with light of frequency 3.2×10^{16} Hz, the photoelectrons emitted had twice the kinetic energy as did photoelectrons emitted when the same metal was irradiated with light of frequency 2.0×10^{16} Hz. Threshold frequency is $x \times 10^{15}$ Hz. What is value of x?

232 A 101 watt Na vapour lamp emits yellow light of wavelength 590 nm. Number of photons emitted per second is $y \times 10^{20}$ Thus, y is ... .

233 Assume that an electron can absorb more than one photon in the photoelectric effect. How many photons of wavelength 800.0 nm does an electron in iron need to absorb to escape the iron surface.

(Work function of Fe = 4.67 eV)

234 Electron in He^+ in fourth orbit and electron in H in second orbit are revolving around the nucleus. Thus, their ratio of time periods is ....

235 The orbital degeneracy of the levels in a hydrogen atom that has energy $-\frac{1}{9} hcR_H$ is n^2. Thus, n is ... .

236 For H-atom, the radial distribution function $P(r)$ is given for 1s-orbital.

$$P(r) = \frac{4Z^3}{a_0^3} r^2 e^{-2Zr/a_0}$$

Maximum probability for He^+ is $\frac{n}{a_0 e^2}$

Thus, $n =$ ......

237 Not considering the electronic spin, the degeneracy of the second excited state ($n = 3$) of H-atom is 9.

Thus, the degeneracy of second excited state of H^- is ...... **[JEE Adv. 2015]**

238 In an atom, the total number of electrons having quantum numbers $n = 4$, $|m_l| = 1$ and $m_s = -\frac{1}{2}$ is **[JEE Adv. 2014]**

239 The atomic masses of He and Ne are 4 and 20 amu, respectively.

The value of the de-Broglie wavelength of He gas at −73°C is "M" times that of the de-Broglie wavelength of Ne at 727°C. M is .... **[JEE Adv. 2013]**

240 The maximum number of electrons that can have principal quantum number, $n = 3$ and spin quantum number, $m_s = -1/2$, is **[IIT JEE 2011]**

241 The work function (ϕ) of some metals is listed below. The number of metals which will show photoelectric effect, when light of 300 nm wavelength falls on the metal is ...... **[IIT JEE 2011]**

Metal	ϕ (eV)
Li	2.4
Na	2.3
K	2.2
Mg	3.7
Cu	4.8
Ag	4.3
Fe	4.7
Pt	6.3
W	4.75

TYPE VI Matrix Matching

242 The normalised wave function for a 2s orbital in H-like species is given by

$$\psi_{2s} = \left(\frac{1}{32\pi a_0^3}\right)^{1/2} \left(2 - \frac{Zr}{a_0}\right) e^{-Zr/2a_0}$$

Match the required property given in column I with its value in Column II and select the answer from the codes given :

Column I		Column II
(i) Probability of finding an electron in He^+ that is described by this wave function in a volume of 1 pm^3 centred on the nucleus	(p)	$2a_0$
(ii) Probability at the Bohr's radius in H-atom	(q)	$-\frac{1}{a_0 e^4}$
(iii) Probability at twice the Bohr's radius in He^+	(r)	$\frac{10^{-12}}{8a_0 e}$
(iv) Radius in terms of a_0 if radial node in 2s occurs at a distance equal to a_0 in H-atom	(s)	Zero

Codes

	(i)	(ii)	(iii)	(iv)
(a)	(p)	(q)	(r)	(s)
(b)	(s)	(r)	(p)	(q)
(c)	(s)	(r)	(q)	(p)
(d)	(r)	(p)	(q)	(s)

243 Wavelength of the spectral line of the H-like species (atomic number Z) is given by

$$\frac{1}{\lambda} = \overline{R}_H Z^2 \left[\frac{1}{n_1^2} - \frac{1}{n_2^2} \right]$$

Match the given parameters in column I with their related values in column II and select the answer from the codes given below.

S.No.	Column I		Column II
(i)	Difference in wave number of the α-and β-lines in Balmer series of Be^{3+}	(p)	$\frac{2.89}{\overline{R}_H}$
(ii)	Maximum wave number of spectral line is Brackett series of Li^{2+}.	(q)	$16\overline{R}_H$
(iii)	Difference in the maximum and minimum wavelength of spectral line of Paschen series in He^+	(r)	$\frac{9}{16}\overline{R}_H$
(iv)	Rydberg constant of Be^{3+}	(s)	$\frac{7}{9}\overline{R}_H$

Codes

	(i)	(ii)	(iii)	(iv)
(a)	p	r	q	s
(b)	s	r	q	p
(c)	p	q	r	s
(d)	s	r	p	q

244 For Moseley's equation,

$$\sqrt{v} = a(Z - b)$$

wavelength associated with Sr and Cl are 90.1 pm and 473 pm respectively. Match the parameters given in column I with related their values in column II and select the answer from the codes given.

	Column I		Column II
(i)	Wavelength associated with Mg (in pm)	(p)	377
(ii)	Wavelength associated with K (in pm)	(q)	4.855×10^7
(iii)	Critical wavelength (in pm) for the metal to emit electron if incident wavelength of (ii) is used and kinetic energy of the emitted electron is 3 eV	(r)	402
(iv)	Value of a (in ($s^{-1/2}$))	(s)	983

Codes

	(i)	(ii)	(iii)	(iv)
(a)	(r)	(s)	(p)	(q)
(b)	(p)	(q)	(s)	(r)
(c)	(s)	(p)	(p)	(q)
(d)	(s)	(p)	(q)	(r)

Direction (Q. Nos. 245, 246 and 247) *by appropriately matching the information given in the three columns of the following table.*

The wave function ψ_{n,l,m_l} is a mathematical function whose value depends upon spherical polar coordinates (r, θ, ϕ) of the electron and characterised by the quantum numbers n, l and m_l. Here r is distance from nucleus, θ is colatitude and φ is azimuth. In the mathematical functions given in the table, Z is atomic number a_0 in Bohr radius. ***[JEE Adv. 2017]***

Column-1	Column-2	Column-3
(I) 1s orbital	(i) $\psi_{n,l,m_l} \propto \left(\frac{Z}{a_0}\right)^{3/2} e^{-\left(\frac{Zr}{a_0}\right)}$	(p) [graph: $\psi_{n,l,m_l}(r)$ vs r/a_0, origin 0]
(II) 2s orbital	(ii) One radial node	(q) Probability density at nucleus $\propto \frac{1}{a_0^3}$
(III) $2p_z$ orbital	(iii) $\psi_{n,l,m_l} \propto \left(\frac{Z}{a_0}\right)^{5/2} re^{-\left(\frac{Zr}{2a_0}\right)} \cos\theta$	(r) Probability density is maximum at nucleus.
(IV) $3d_z^2$ orbital	(iv) xy-plane is a nodal plane	(s) Energy needed to excite electron from $n = 2$ state to $n = 4$ state is 27/32 times the energy needed to excite electron from $n = 2$ state to $n = 6$ state.

245 For the given orbital in column 1, the only correct combination for any hydrogen like species is

(a) (IV) (iv) (r) (b) (II) (ii) (p)
(c) (III) (iii) (p) (d) (I) (ii) (s)

246 For He^+ ion, the only incorrect combination is

(a) (II) (ii) (q) (b) (I) (i) (s)
(c) (I) (i) (r) (d) (I) (iii) (r)

247 For hydrogen atom, the only correct combination is

(a) (I) (iv) (r) (b) (I) (i) (p)
(c) (II) (i) (q) (d) (I) (i) (s)

248 Match the entries in Column I with the correctly related quantum number (s) in Column II. ***[IIT JEE 2008]***

	Column I		Column II
(i)	Orbital angular momentum of the electron in a hydrogen-like atomic orbital	(p)	Principal quantum number
(ii)	A hydrogen like one electron wave function obeying Pauli's principle	(q)	Azimuthal quantum number
(iii)	Shape, size and orientation of hydrogen like atomic orbitals	(r)	Magnetic quantum number
(iv)	Probability density of an electron at the nucleus in hydrogen-like atom	(s)	Electron spin quantum number

Codes

	(i)	(ii)	(iii)	(iv)
(a)	(q,p)	(r)	(s)	(p)
(b)	(q)	(s)	(p,q,r)	(p,q,r)
(c)	(p)	(q)	(r, s)	(s)
(d)	(q)	(p)	(p,s)	(r)

249 According to Bohr's theory
E_n = total energy, K_n = kinetic energy
V_n = potential energy r_n = radius of nth orbit *[IIT JEE 2006]*

Column I		Column II
(i) $V_n / K_n = ?$	(p)	0
(ii) If radius of nth orbit $\propto E_n^x$, $x = ?$	(q)	–1
(iii) Angular momentum in lowest orbital	(r)	–2
(iv) $\frac{1}{r^n} \propto Z^y$, $y = ?$	(s)	1

Codes

	(i)	(ii)	(iii)	(iv)
(a)	(r)	(q)	(p)	(s)
(b)	(p)	(q)	(s)	(r)
(c)	(r)	(s)	(p)	(p)
(d)	(q)	(s)	(r)	(p)

250 Consider the Bohr's model of a one-electron atom where the electron moves around the nucleus. In the following, Column-I contains some quantities for the *n*th orbit of the atom and Column-II contains options showing how they depend on *n*. *[JEE Adv. 2019]*

Column I		Column II
(i) Radius of the *n*th orbit	(p)	$\propto n^{-2}$
(ii) Angular momentum of the electron in the *n*th orbit	(q)	$\propto n^{-1}$
(iii) Kinetic energy of the electron in the *n*th orbit	(r)	$\propto n^{0}$
(iv) Potential energy of the electron in the *n*th orbit	(s)	$\propto n^{1}$
	(t)	$\propto n^{2}$
	(u)	$\propto n^{1/2}$

Which of the following option has the correct combination considering Column-I and Column-II?

(a) (i), (t) (b) (ii), (r)
(c) (i), (p) (d) (ii), (q)

HINTS & EXPLANATIONS

Immediate Tests

1. $E = nh\nu$

n = number of photons in one mole $= 6.02 \times 10^{23}\ \text{mol}^{-1}$

$E = 6.02 \times 10^{23} \times 6.626 \times 10^{-34} \times 5 \times 10^{14}$

$= 199.44 \times 10^{3}\ \text{J mol}^{-1}$

$= 199.44\ \text{kJ mol}^{-1}$

2. Energy values are additives

$\therefore \quad E = E_1 + E_2$

$h\nu = h\nu_1 + h\nu_2$

$\frac{hc}{\lambda} = \frac{hc}{\lambda_1} + \frac{hc}{\lambda_2}$

$\frac{1}{\lambda} = \frac{1}{\lambda_1} + \frac{1}{\lambda_2}$

$\frac{1}{\lambda} - \frac{1}{\lambda_1} = \frac{1}{\lambda_2}$

$\therefore \quad \frac{1}{\lambda_2} = \frac{\lambda_1 - \lambda}{\lambda_1 \lambda}$

$\frac{1}{\lambda_2} = \frac{150 - 80}{150 \times 80} = \frac{70}{150 \times 80}\ \text{pm}^{-1}$

Wave number $\bar{\nu}_2 = \frac{1}{\lambda_2}$

$= 5.83 \times 10^{-3}\ \text{pm}^{-1}$

3. $\sqrt{\nu} = a(Z - b)$

$= 0.5(25 - 2) = 11.5$

$\therefore\ \nu = (11.5)^2 = 132.25\ \text{s}^{-1}$

but $\quad \nu = \frac{c}{\lambda}$

$\lambda = \frac{c}{\nu} = \frac{3 \times 10^{8}\ \text{m s}^{-1}}{132.25\ \text{s}^{-1}}$

$= 2.2684 \times 10^{6}\ \text{m}$

4. By photoelectric effect,

$h\nu = \phi + \frac{1}{2}mv^2$

$\therefore \quad \phi = 2.16\ \text{eV}$

$= 2.16 \times 1.6 \times 10^{-19}\ \text{J}$

$h\nu = \frac{hc}{\lambda}$

$= \frac{6.626 \times 10^{-34}\ \text{Js} \times 3 \times 10^{8}\ \text{ms}^{-1}}{450 \times 10^{-9}\ \text{M}}$

$= 4.42 \times 10^{-19}\ \text{J}$

$\therefore\ \frac{1}{2}mv^2 = h\nu - \phi$

$= (4.42 - 2.16 \times 1.6) \times 10^{-19}$

$= 0.96 \times 10^{-19}\ \text{J}$

$\therefore \quad v^2 = \frac{2 \times 0.96 \times 10^{-19}\ \text{J}}{9.1 \times 10^{-31}\ \text{kg}}$

$= 2.11 \times 10^{11}\ \text{m}^2\text{s}^{-2}$

$v = 4.59 \times 10^{5}\ \text{ms}^{-1}$

■ $1\ \text{J} = \text{kg m}^2\text{s}^{-2}$
$1\text{eV} = 1.6 \times 10^{-19}\ \text{J}$

5. (i) By photoelectric effect,

$h\nu = \phi + \frac{1}{2}mu^2$

$h\frac{c}{\lambda} = \phi + \text{stopping potential } (V_s)$

Case I

$\frac{hc}{\lambda_1} = \phi + (V_s)_1$

$\frac{hc}{\lambda_2} = \phi + (V_s)_2$

$\frac{hc}{10^{-9}}\left[\frac{1}{100} - \frac{1}{75}\right] = (V_s)_1 - (V_s)_2$

$-\frac{6.626 \times 10^{-34} \times 3 \times 10^{8}}{1.6 \times 10^{-19} \times 10^{-9}}\left[\frac{25}{7500}\right]$

$= (0.24) - (V_s)_2$

$-4.14 = 0.24 - (V_s)_2$

$(V_s)_2 = 0.24 + 4.14$

$= 4.38\ \text{eV}$

■ $1\ \text{J} = 1.6 \times 10^{-19}\ \text{eV}$

(ii) Potential at the collector plate

$= 2.25\ \text{eV}$

Thus, minimum KE = 2.25 eV

$= 2.25 \times 1.6 \times 10^{-19}$ J per electron

$= 2.25 \times 1.6 \times 10^{-19} \times 6.02 \times 10^{23}\ \text{J mol}^{-1}$

$= 2.1672 \times 10^{5}\ \text{J mol}^{-1}$

$= 216.72\ \text{kJ mol}^{-1}$

Also, energy absorbed = work function + KE

$\frac{hc}{\lambda} = 4.5 \times 1.6 \times 10^{-19} + \text{KE}$

$\frac{hc}{\lambda} = \frac{6.62 \times 10^{-34} \times 3 \times 10^{8}}{2000 \times 10^{-10}}$

$= 9.93 \times 10^{-19}\ \text{J}$

$\therefore$ KE of the emitted electron

$= (9.93 \times 10^{-19} - 7.20 \times 10^{-19})\ \text{J}$

$= 2.73 \times 10^{-19}$ J per electron

$= 2.73 \times 10^{-19} \times 6.02 \times 10^{23}$

$= 164.35 \times 10^{3}\ \text{J mol}^{3}$

$= 164.35\ \text{kJ mol}^{-1}$

Thus, maximum KE = 216.72 + 164.35

$= 381.07$ kJ

6. $r_n = \frac{n^2 a_0}{Z}$

I. $r(\text{Be}^{3+}, Z = 4, n = 2) = \frac{4a_0}{4} = a_0$

II. $r(\text{He}^{+}, Z = 2, n = 4) = \frac{16\,a_0}{2} = 8\,a_0$

Thus, He^{+} is larger than Be^{3+} in ionic radius in their orbits.

7. $mvr_n = \frac{nh}{2\pi}$

$v = \frac{nh}{2\pi r_n m_e}$

$2\pi r_1 = 3.322 \times 10^{-10}\ \text{m}$

$v = \frac{1 \times 6.626 \times 10^{-34}\ \text{Js}}{3.322 \times 10^{-10}\ \text{m} \times 9.1 \times 10^{-31}\ \text{kg}}$

$= 2.192 \times 10^{6}\ \text{m s}^{-1}$

■ $1\ \text{J} = 1\ \text{kg m}^2\text{s}^{-2}$
and $2\pi r$ = circumference of the circular path of radius r.

8. (i) $\text{KE} = -E_n$

$= \frac{13.6Z^2}{n^2}\ \text{eV} = 13.6 \times \frac{(4)^2}{(3)^2} = 24.18\ \text{eV}$

$\text{PE} = -2\text{KE} = -2(24.18) = -48.36\ \text{eV}$

Total energy = PE + KE

$= -48.36 + 24.18$

$= -24.18\ \text{eV}$

or $E_n = -13.6\left(\frac{Z^2}{n^2}\right)$

$E_3 = -13.6\left(\frac{16}{9}\right) = -24.18\ \text{eV}$

(ii) (a) $r_n = \frac{n^2 a_0}{Z}$

$r_1(\text{H}) = (1)^2 \frac{a_0}{1} = a_0$

$r_3(\text{H}) = (3)^2 \frac{a_0}{1} = 9a_0$

Thus, increase $= 9a_0 - a_0 = 8a_0$

$= 8 \times 0.529$ Å

$= 4.232$ Å $= 423.2$ pm

■ 1 Å $= 1 \times 10^{-10}$ m
$= 100 \times 10^{-12}$ pm
$= 100$ pm

(b) $E_n = -13.6\frac{Z^2}{n^2}$ eV

$E_1(\text{H}) = -13.6$ eV

$E_3(\text{H}) = \frac{-13.6}{9}$ eV

Increase $\Delta E = E_3 - E_1$

$= \frac{-13.6}{9} + 13.6$

$= 12.09$ eV atom^{-1}

$= 12.09 \times 1.6 \times 10^{-19}$ J atom^{-1}

$= 12.09 \times 1.6 \times 10^{-19} \times 6.02 \times 10^{23}$ J mol^{-1}

$= 1164.5 \times 10^3$ J mol^{-1}

$= 1164.5$ kJ mol^{-1}

9. $\text{He}(g) \longrightarrow \text{He}^+(g) + e^-$, $(\text{IE})_{\text{He}} = 3.4 \times 10^{-19}$ J atom^{-1}

$\text{He}^+(g) \longrightarrow \text{He}^{2+}(g) + e^-$, $(\text{IE})_{\text{He}^+} = x$

$\text{He}(g) \longrightarrow \text{He}^{2+}(g) + 2e^-$,

$(\text{IE}) = (3.4 \times 10^{-19} + x)$ J

$\text{He}^+(g)$ is isoelectronic of H-atom with one electron each.

Thus,

$(\text{IE})_{\text{He}^+} = 13.6\left(\frac{Z^2}{n^2}\right)$

$= 13.6 \times 2^2 = 54.4$ eV

$= 54.4 \times 1.6 \times 10^{-19}$ J

$= 8.70 \times 10^{-18}$ J

$\therefore (\text{IE})_{\text{He}\longrightarrow\text{He}^{2+}} \longrightarrow (\text{IE})_{\text{He}\longrightarrow\text{He}^+} + (\text{IE})_{\text{He}^+\longrightarrow\text{He}^{2+}}$

$= 3.4 \times 10^{-19} + 8.70 \times 10^{-18}$

$= 9.04 \times 10^{-18}$ J atom^{-1}

Thus, energy of the process :

$\text{He}^{2+}(g) + 2e^- \longrightarrow \text{He}(g)$;

$\Delta H = -9.04 \times 10^{-18}$ J atom^{-1}

10. $\nu = 3.2881 \times 10^{15}\ \text{s}^{-1}\left[\frac{1}{n_1^2} - \frac{1}{n_2^2}\right]$

$= x\left[\frac{1}{n_1^2} - \frac{1}{n_2^2}\right]$

$\nu = \frac{c}{\lambda}$

(a) $\frac{1}{\lambda} = \frac{\nu}{c} = \frac{\text{s}^{-1}}{\text{ms}^{-1}} = \text{m}^{-1}$

$\therefore x = 3.2881 \times 10^{15}\ \text{s}^{-1}$

$= \frac{3.2881 \times 10^{15}\ \text{s}^{-1}}{3 \times 10^8\ \text{m s}^{-1}} = 1.096 \times 10^7\ \text{m}^{-1}$

$\therefore \bar{\nu} = 1.096 \times 10^7\ \text{m}^{-1}\left[\frac{1}{n_1^2} - \frac{1}{n_2^2}\right]$

(b) Also, $\frac{1}{\lambda} = \bar{\nu}\ \text{m}^{-1}$

$= hc\bar{\nu}$ energy atom^{-1}

$x = 6.626 \times 10^{-34} \times 3 \times 10^8 \times 1.096 \times 10^7$ J atom^{-1}

$= 2.18 \times 10^{-18}$ J atom^{-1}

(c) $x = 2.18 \times 10^{-18} \times 6.02 \times 10^{23}$ J mol^{-1}

$= 1.3124 \times 10^6$ J mol^{-1}

$E = 1.3124 \times 10^6\ \text{J mol}^{-1}\left[\frac{1}{n_1^2} - \frac{1}{n_2^2}\right]$

■ $x\text{s}^{-1} = \frac{x}{3 \times 10^8}\ \text{m}^{-1}$

$y\text{m}^{-1} = (1.9878 \times 10^{-25} y)$ J atom^{-1}

$= 0.12y$ J mol^{-1}

11. (i) $\nu = 1.09679 \times 10^7\ \text{m}^{-1} Z^2 c\left[\frac{1}{n_1^2} - \frac{1}{n_2^2}\right]$

$= 1.09679 \times 10^7 (1)^2 \times 3 \times 10^8\left[\frac{1}{2^2} - \frac{1}{5^2}\right]$

$= 6.91 \times 10^{14}\ \text{s}^{-1}$

since, $\nu = \frac{c}{\lambda}$

$\therefore \frac{1}{\lambda} = \frac{\nu}{c} = \frac{6.91 \times 10^{14}\ \text{s}^{-1}}{3.0 \times 10^8\ \text{m s}^{-1}}$

$\bar{\nu} = \frac{1}{\lambda} = 2.303 \times 10^6\ \text{m}^{-1}$

$\therefore \lambda = 4.34 \times 10^{-7}\ \text{m} = 434 \times 10^{-9}$ m

$= 434$ nm

■ 1×10^{-9} m = 1 nm

(ii) In terms of $(\text{IE})_{\text{H}} = 13.6$ eV

$= 13.6 \times 1.6 \times 10^{-19}$ J

$\bar{\nu} = \frac{(\text{IE})_{\text{H}} Z^2}{ch}\left[\frac{1}{n_1^2} - \frac{1}{n_2^2}\right]$

$\frac{1}{\lambda} = \frac{13.6 \times 1.6 \times 10^{-19} \times (4)^2}{3.0 \times 10^8 \times 6.626 \times 10^{-34}}\left[\frac{1}{9} - \frac{1}{25}\right]$

$= 1.245 \times 10^7\ \text{m}^{-1}$

$\therefore \lambda = 8.02 \times 10^{-8}$ m

$= 802 \times 10^{-10}$ m $= 802$ Å

■ $hc = 2.0 \times 10^{-25}$ Jm

12. $\bar{\nu} = R_{\text{H}} Z^2\left[\frac{1}{n_1^2} - \frac{1}{n_2^2}\right]$

For Paschen series, $n_1 = 3$

$R_{\text{H}} = 1.09679 \times 10^7\ \text{m}^{-1}$

$Z(\text{He}^+) = 2$

$\bar{\nu}$ is maximum, when $n_2 \to \infty$

$\therefore \bar{\nu}_{\text{max}} = \frac{R_{\text{H}} Z^2}{n_1^2}$

$= \frac{1.09679 \times 10^7\ \text{m}^{-1} (2)^2}{9}$

$= 4.874 \times 10^6\ \text{m}^{-1}$

$\bar{\nu}$ is minimum, when $n_2 = (n_1 + 1) = 4$

$\bar{\nu}_{\text{min}} = R_{\text{H}} Z^2\left[\frac{1}{3^2} - \frac{1}{4^2}\right]$

$= 1.09679 \times 10^7 (2)^2\left[\frac{7}{144}\right]$

$= 2.132 \times 10^6\ \text{m}^{-1}$

13. (i) Visible region ranges from 2.84×10^{-19} J to 4.97×10^{-19} J

$\therefore \Delta E = (4.97 - 2.84) \times 10^{-19}$ J

$= 2.15 \times 10^{-19}$ J

$\because \Delta E = \frac{2\pi^2 m Z^2 e^4 k^2}{h^2}\left[\frac{1}{n_1^2} - \frac{1}{n_2^2}\right]$

$= 13.6 Z^2\left[\frac{1}{n_1^2} - \frac{1}{n_2^2}\right]$

where, $\frac{2\pi^2 m e^4 k^2}{h^2} = (\text{IE})_{\text{H}} = 13.6$ eV

2.15×10^{-19} J atom^{-1}

$= 13.6 \times 1.6 \times 10^{-19}\ \text{J}\ (2)^2\left[\frac{1}{n_1^2} - \frac{1}{n_2^2}\right]$

$0.0247 = \left[\frac{1}{n_1^2} - \frac{1}{n_2^2}\right]$

If $n_1 = 1$, $n_2 = 2$ then $\frac{1}{1^2} - \frac{1}{2^2} = 0.75$

Thus, false.

If $n_1 = 1$, $n_2 = 3$ then $\frac{1}{1} - \frac{1}{9} = 0.89$

Thus, false.

If $n_1 = 2$, $n_2 = 3$ then $\frac{1}{4} - \frac{1}{9} = 0.14$

Thus, false.

If $n_1 = 4$, $n_2 = 5$ then $\frac{1}{16} - \frac{1}{25} = 0.0225$

Thus, true.

(ii) $\bar{\nu} = R_{\text{H}} Z^2\left[\frac{1}{n_1^2} - \frac{1}{n_2^2}\right]$

$\bar{\nu}_{\text{He}^+} = \bar{\nu}_{\text{H}}$ (Lyman)

$R_{\text{H}}(4)\left[\frac{1}{n_1^2} - \frac{1}{n_2^2}\right] = R_{\text{H}}(1)\left[\frac{1}{1^2} - \frac{1}{2^2}\right] = 0.75$

$\left[\frac{1}{n_1^2} - \frac{1}{n_2^2}\right] = \frac{0.75}{4} = 0.1875$

If $n_1 = 1$, $n_2 = 2$, then $\left(\frac{1}{1} - \frac{1}{9}\right) = 0.75$

$n_1 = 2$, $n_2 = 3$, then $\frac{1}{4} - \frac{1}{9} = \frac{5}{36} = 0.14$

$n_1 = 2$, $n_2 = 4$, then $\frac{1}{4} - \frac{1}{16} = \frac{12}{64} = 0.1875$

Thus, transition is $n_2 = 4$ to $n_1 = 2$

■ This transition is for Balmer β-line.

14. (i) $\lambda = \dfrac{h}{\sqrt{2m\text{KE}}}$

$$\text{KE} = 1.6 \text{ eV} = 1.6 \times 1.6 \times 10^{-19} \text{ J}$$

$$m = 9.1 \times 10^{-31} \text{ kg}$$

$$\therefore \lambda = \frac{6.626 \times 10^{-34} \text{ Js}}{\sqrt{2 \times 9.1 \times 10^{-31} \times 1.6 \times 1.6 \times 0^{-19} \text{ kgJ}}}$$

$$= 9.71 \times 10^{-10} \text{ m}$$

$$= 971 \text{ pm}$$

■ $1 \text{ J} = 1 \text{ kg m}^2\text{s}^{-2}$

(ii) $\lambda = \dfrac{h}{\sqrt{2m(\text{KE})}}$

$$\text{KE} = \frac{h^2}{\lambda^2 \times 2m}$$

$$= \frac{(6.626 \times 10^{-34})^2}{(200 \times 10^{-12})^2 \times 2 \times 9.1 \times 10^{-31}}$$

$$= 6.03 \times 10^{-18} \text{ J}$$

$$= \frac{6.02 \times 10^{-18} \text{ J}}{1.6 \times 10^{-19} \text{ J eV}^{-1}} = 37.69 \text{ eV}$$

15. $\lambda = \dfrac{h}{\sqrt{3mRT}}$

$$\therefore \frac{\lambda_1}{\lambda_2} = \sqrt{\frac{m_2T_2}{m_1T_1}}$$

Given, $\dfrac{\lambda_1}{\lambda_2} = 5, \ \dfrac{T_1}{T_2} = \dfrac{1}{5}$

$$\therefore 5 = \sqrt{\frac{m_2}{m_1} \times 5} \Rightarrow 25 = \frac{m_2}{m_1} \times 5$$

$$\therefore \frac{m_2}{m_1} = 5$$

$$\because \frac{m_1}{m_2} = \frac{1}{5}$$

16. Based on Heisenberg's uncertainty principle,

$$\Delta x \Delta p \geq \frac{h}{4\pi}$$

$$\Delta x m \Delta v \geq \frac{h}{4\pi} \qquad [\because p = mv]$$

$$\therefore \Delta v = \frac{h}{4\pi \Delta x m}$$

$$= \frac{6.626 \times 10^{-34} \text{ Js}}{4\pi \times 0.1 \times 10^{-10} \text{ m} \times 9.1 \times 10^{-31}}$$

$$= 5.794 \times 10^6 \text{ m s}^{-1}$$

■ $1 \text{ J} = 1 \text{ kg m}^2\text{s}^{-2}$

17. $\psi = A \sin\left(\dfrac{2\pi x}{\lambda}\right)$

$$\therefore \frac{d\psi}{dx} = \frac{2\pi}{\lambda} A \cos\left(\frac{2\pi x}{\lambda}\right)$$

$$\therefore \frac{d^2\psi}{dx^2} = -\left(\frac{2\pi}{\lambda}\right)^2 A \sin\left(\frac{2\pi x}{\lambda}\right) = -\frac{4\pi^2}{\lambda^2}\psi$$

$$\therefore \frac{d^2\psi}{dx} + \frac{4\pi^2}{\lambda^2}\psi = 0$$

By de-Broglie equation,

$$\lambda = \frac{h}{mv}$$

$$\therefore \frac{1}{\lambda^2} = \frac{m^2v^2}{h^2}$$

But $\quad \text{E} = \text{KE} = \dfrac{1}{2}mv^2$

$$\therefore 2mE = m^2v^2 (E = \text{KE})$$

$$\frac{1}{\lambda^2} = \frac{2mE}{h^2}$$

$$\therefore \frac{d^2\psi}{dx} + \frac{8\pi^2 mE}{h^2}\psi = 0$$

18. (a) No, (b) Yes, $5f$, (c) No, (d) Yes, $2p$, (e) No

19. (i) (a) $3d$, (b) $2p$, (c) $4s$, (d) $5d$, (e) $7g$

(ii) For a suborbit to exist.

$$l < n$$

Suborbit	n	l	
(a) $5g$	5	4	$l < n$, possible
(b) $4g$	4	4	$l = n$, not possible
(c) $2d$	2	2	$l = n$, not possible
(d) $2f$	2	3	$l > n$, not possible
(e) $1p$	1	1	$l = 1$, not possible
(f) $3d$	3	2	$l < n$, possible

20. I. Cr : [Ar] $4s^1\ 3d^5$

[1] [1 | 1 | 1 | 1 | 1]

II. Fe^{2+} is formed from Fe, and valence shell is affected.

Fe(26) : [Ar] $4s^2$ (valence shell) $3d^6$

Fe^{2+} : [Ar]$3d^6$ [1L | 1 | 1 | 1 | 1]

III. Mn(25) : [Ar]$4s^2 3d^5$

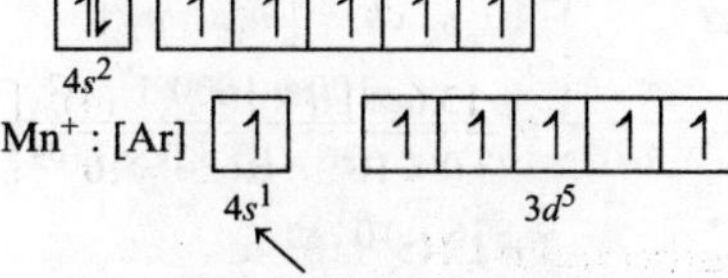

When Mn^+ is formed electron from this valence shell is removed

IV. Co(27):[Ar]$4s^2 3d^7$

[1L] [1L | 1L | 1 | 1 | 1]

Co^{3+} : [Ar]$4s^0 3d^6$

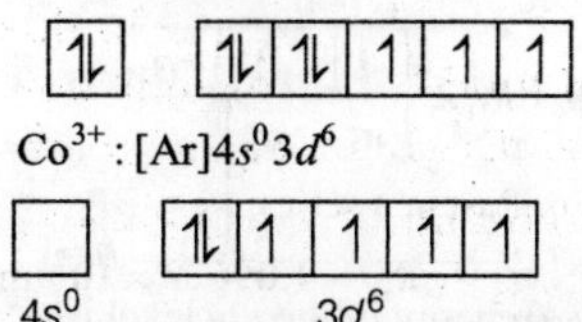

(a)

Species		Unpaired electron	Magnetic moment
(I)	Cr	6	$\sqrt{48}$ BM
(II)	Fe^{2+}	4	$\sqrt{24}$ BM
(III)	Mn^+	6	$\sqrt{48}$ BM
(IV)	Co^{3+}	4	$\sqrt{24}$ BM

The magnetic moment of

$Fe^{2+} = Cr^{3+} < Cr = Mn^+$

(b) Fe^{2+}, Mn^+ and Co^{3+} are coloured ions as they have unpaired electrons in d-orbitals (d—d^* transition)

21. $M(Z = 28)$[Ar]$3d^8, 4s^2$

Magnetic moment of N-unpaired electrons $= \sqrt{N(N+2)}$ BM

$$\sqrt{N(N+2)} = 2\sqrt{2}$$

$$N(N+2) = 8$$

$$N^2 + 2N - 8 = 0$$

$$(N+4)(N-2) = 0$$

$\therefore N = 2$, ($N = -4$, is not possible)

There are two unpaired electrons

$M(Z=28)$ [1L] [1L | 1L | 1L | 1 | 1]
$4s^2$ $3d^8$

If M^{2+} is formed, there will be two unpaired electrons in M^{2+}.

(a) Charge = + 2

(b) M^{2+} : [Ar] $3d^8$, two electrons from valence shell ($4s$) are removed.

(c) It is coloured ion, unpaired electrons being in $3d$-orbital..

22. This is a case in which number of suborbits = (n + 1) as n can take value 0, 1, 2 .... x.

For comparing energies, value of (n + l) is compared.

n	l	m	Spin (for each electron)	Orbital
1	0	0	$\pm\frac{1}{2}$	$1s^2$
	1	−1, + 0, + 1	$\pm\frac{1}{2}$	$1p^6$
2	0	0	$\pm\frac{1}{2}$	$2s^2$
	1	−1, 0, +1	$\pm\frac{1}{2}$	$2p^6$
	2	−2, −1, 0, +1, +2	$\pm\frac{1}{2}$	$2d^{10}$
3	0	0	$\pm\frac{1}{2}$	$3s^2$
	1	−1, 0, +1	$\pm\frac{1}{2}$	$3p^6$
	2	−2, −1, 0, +1, +2	$\pm\frac{1}{2}$	$3d^{10}$
	3	−3, −2, −1, 0, +1, +2, +3	$\pm\frac{1}{2}$	$3f^{14}$

Electronic configuration $1s^2 1p^6 2s^2 2p^6 3s^2 2d^8$

■ $2d$ ($n + l = 4$) is filled after $3s$ ($n + l = 3$)

Knowledge Confirmation Test 1

1. (d) **2.** (a) **3.** (c) **4.** (b) **5.** (d) **6.** (c) **7.** (b) **8.** (b) **9.** (c) **10.** (a)
11. (c) **12.** (c) **13.** (a) **14.** (d) **15.** (a) **16.** (c) **17.** (b) **18.** (a) **19.** (b) **20.** (c)

Knowledge Confirmation Test 2

1. (b) **2.** (c) **3.** (d) **4.** (b) **5.** (d) **6.** (c) **7.** (d) **8.** (b) **9.** (d) **10.** (d)
11. (b) **12.** (a) **13.** (c) **14.** (a) **15.** (a) **16.** (c) **17.** (d) **18.** (c) **19.** (d) **20.** (a)
21. (d) **22.** (a) **23.** (a) **24.** (c) **25.** (b)

Knowledge Confirmation Test 3

1. (a) **2.** (d) **3.** (a) **4.** (b) **5.** (b) **6.** (c) **7.** (b) **8.** (c) **9.** (b) **10.** (b)
11. (a) **12.** (d) **13.** (c) **14.** (a) **15.** (b) **16.** (a) **17.** (b) **18.** (c) **19.** (a) **20.** (d)

Knowledge Confirmation Test 4

1. (b) **2.** (d) **3.** (b) **4.** (a) **5.** (a) **6.** (d) **7.** (b) **8.** (a) **9.** (c) **10.** (d)
11. (b) **12.** (d) **13.** (d) **14.** (c) **15.** (b) **16.** (a) **17.** (c) **18.** (d) **19.** (a) **20.** (d)
21. (a) **22.** (c) **23.** (d) **24.** (d) **25.** (b) **26.** (d) **27.** (d) **28.** (d) **29.** (b) **30.** (d)

Acid Test for JEE Main

Type I. MCQs with Only ONE Correct Alternate

1. (b) Energy of 1 mol of photons = $h\nu$

Since 1 mol = N_0 photon

$$E = N_0 h\bar{\nu} = N_0 \frac{hc}{\lambda}$$

$$= \frac{6.020 \times 10^{23} \times 6.626 \times 10^{-34} \times 3 \times 10^{8}}{5 \times 10^{-6}}$$

$$= 23.9 \times 10^{3}\ \text{J} = 23.9\ \text{kJ}$$

■ All data are in SI units,

2. (c) By photoelectric effect,

$$h\nu = \phi + \frac{1}{2}mu^2$$

For minimum wavelength, electron is simply ejected and KE = 0

as $\quad \nu = \dfrac{c}{\lambda}$

$$\therefore\ h\frac{c}{\lambda} = \phi$$

$$\lambda = \frac{hc}{\phi}$$

$$= \frac{6.626 \times 10^{-34}\ \text{Js} \times 3 \times 10^{8}\ \text{ms}^{-1}}{2.14 \times 1.6 \times 10^{-19}\ \text{J}}$$

$$= 5.805 \times 10^{-7}\ \text{m} = 581 \times 10^{-9}\ \text{m}$$

$$= 581\ \text{nm}$$

$$1\ \text{eV} = 1.6 \times 10^{-19}\ \text{J}$$

■ Time saving factor for exam

$hc = 1.9878 \times 10^{-25}$

$= 2 \times 10^{-25}$ J-m

3. (d)

4. (c) (a) $E = h\bar{\nu} = \dfrac{hc}{\lambda}$

$$= \frac{6.626 \times 10^{-34} \times 3 \times 10^{8}}{10 \times 10^{-9}}\ \text{J}$$

$$= 2 \times 10^{-17}\ \text{J}$$

(b) $E = h\nu = 6.626 \times 10^{-34} \times 10$ J

$$= 6.626 \times 10^{-33}\ \text{J}$$

(c) $E = \dfrac{1}{2}mu^2$

$$= \frac{1}{2} \times 9.1 \times 10^{-31} \times (3 \times 10^{8})^2$$

$$= 4.1 \times 10^{-14}\ \text{J (Maximum)}$$

5. (d) $\nu = \dfrac{c}{\lambda} = \dfrac{3 \times 10^{8}\ \text{m s}^{-1}}{20\,\text{m}} = 15 \times 10^{6}\ \text{s}^{-1}$

$= 15$ MHz

■ 1 MHz = 10^6 Hz (s^{-1})

6. (a) $E = N_0 h\nu = N_0 \dfrac{hc}{\lambda} = N_0 hc\bar{\nu}, \left(\bar{\nu} = \dfrac{1}{\lambda}\right)$

$$\therefore\ \bar{\nu} = \frac{E}{N_0 hc}$$

$$= \frac{100 \times 1000\ \text{J}}{6.02 \times 10^{23} \times 6.626 \times 10^{-3}\ \text{Js} \times 3.0 \times 10^{8}\ \text{ms}^{-1}}$$

$$= 836 \times 10^{3}\ \text{m}^{-1}$$

7. (d) Energy defference of two emissions is given by

$$\Delta E = (E_n - E_{n_1}) + (E_{n_1} - E_1) = (E_n - E_1)$$

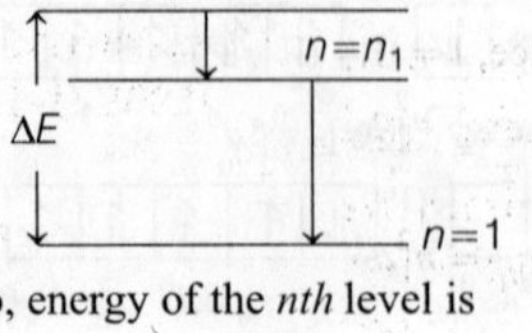

n=n

n=n_1

ΔE

n=1

Also, energy of the *nth* level is

$$E_n = \frac{-2\pi^2 me^4 Z^2}{n^2 h^2}$$

$$= \left(\frac{-2\pi^2 me^4}{h^2}\right)\frac{Z^2}{n^2}$$

$$= \frac{-13.6Z^2}{n^2}\ \text{eV}$$

For He^+, $Z = 2$

$$\therefore\quad \Delta E = \left[\frac{-13.6}{n^2} - \left(\frac{-13.6}{1^2}\right)\right]Z^2$$

$$= 13.6Z^2\left[\frac{1}{1^2} - \frac{1}{n^2}\right]$$

$$= 13.6Z^2\left[\frac{n^2 - 1}{n^2}\right]\text{eV}$$

Also, $\Delta E = \dfrac{hc}{\lambda_1} + \dfrac{hc}{\lambda_2} = hc\dfrac{(\lambda_1 + \lambda_2)}{\lambda_1\lambda_2}$

$$\therefore\ 13.6 \times 4\left(\frac{n^2 - 1}{n^2}\right) \times 1.6 \times 10^{-19}\ \text{J}$$

$$= 6.626 \times 10^{-34} \times 3 \times 10^{8}\left(\frac{1300 \times 10^{-10}}{1000 \times 100 \times 10^{-20}}\right)$$

$$\therefore\quad \frac{n^2 - 1}{n^2} = 0.9896$$

$$n^2 - 1 = n^2(0.9896)$$

$$n^2 = \frac{1}{0.0104} = 96$$

$$n = 9.79 \approx 10$$

8. (d)

9. (a) By photoelectric effect,

$$h\nu = h\nu_0 + \frac{1}{2}mv^2$$

$$h\nu = \phi + \frac{1}{2}mv^2$$

$$v = \sqrt{\frac{2(h\nu - \phi)}{m}}$$

$$= \sqrt{\frac{2(6.626 \times 10^{-34} \times 4.77 \times 10^{15} - 2.90 \times 1.6 \times 10^{-19})}{9.1 \times 10^{-31}}}$$

$$= 2.435 \times 10^{6}\ \text{ms}^{-1}$$

■ 1 eV = 1.6×10^{-19} J

m = mass of electron

10. (d) **Case I**

$$\left(\frac{4E}{3} - E\right) = h\nu = \frac{hc}{3\lambda}$$

$$\frac{E}{3} = \frac{hc}{3\lambda}$$

$$\therefore \quad E = \frac{hc}{\lambda}$$

Case II $(2E - E) = h\nu = \dfrac{hc}{\lambda'}$

$$E = \frac{hc}{\lambda'}$$

$$\therefore \quad \frac{hc}{\lambda} = \frac{hc}{\lambda'}$$

$$\therefore \quad \lambda' = \lambda$$

11. (d) KE $= 1.68 \times 10^5$ J mol^{-1}

$= (1.68 \times 10^5 / N_0)$ J electron^{-1}

By photoelectric effect,

$$h\nu = \phi + \frac{1}{2}mv^2$$

$$\therefore \quad \phi = h\nu - \frac{1}{2}mv^2 = \frac{hc}{\lambda} - \frac{1}{2}mv^2$$

$$= \left(\frac{6.626 \times 10^{-34} \times 3 \times 10^8}{300 \times 10^{-9}}\right) - \left(\frac{1.68 \times 10^5}{6.02 \times 10^{23}}\right)$$

$$= 3.84 \times 10^{-19} \text{ J}$$

■ quick tips for exam, $hc = 2 \times 10^{-25}$

1 nm $= 1 \times 10^{-9}$ m

12. (c) $\Delta E = E_3 - E_2 = 3.0 \times 10^{-19}$ J

$$\therefore \quad \Delta E = h\nu = \frac{hc}{\lambda}$$

$$\therefore \quad \lambda = \frac{hc}{\Delta E}$$

$$= \frac{6.626 \times 10^{-34} \text{ Js} \times 3 \times 10^8 \text{ ms}^{-1}}{3.0 \times 10^{-19} \text{ J}}$$

$$= 6.626 \times 10^{-7} \text{ m} \approx 662.6 \text{ nm}$$

$$\approx 663 \text{ nm}$$

13. (a) Total lines $= \dfrac{n(n-1)}{2} = 10$

$\therefore n = 5$

$$E_n = -\frac{13.6Z^2}{n^2}$$

$$\therefore \quad E_5 = \frac{-13.6 \times (3)^2}{(5)^2} \text{ for Li}^{2+} \text{ ion}$$

E_3 in second excited state ($n = 3$)

$$= \frac{-13.6 \times (1)^2}{(3)^2} \text{ for H-atom}$$

$$\therefore \quad \frac{E_5}{E_3} = \frac{9}{25} \times \frac{9}{1} = \frac{81}{25} = 3.24$$

14. (a) Time period $\propto \dfrac{n^3}{Z^2}$

$$\therefore \quad \frac{T(\text{H})}{T(\text{He}^+)} = \left(\frac{n^3}{Z^2}\right)_{\text{H}} \left(\frac{Z^2}{n^3}\right)_{\text{He}^+}$$

$$= \frac{(2)^3}{(1)^2} \frac{(2)^2}{(4)^3} = \frac{32}{64} = \frac{1}{2}$$

15. (d) Bohr's radius $= a_0$

then $r_n = \dfrac{n^2 a_0}{Z}$

(a) $r_1(\text{H}) = a_0$

(b) $r_2(\text{He}^+) = \dfrac{4a_0}{2} = 2a_0$

(c) $r_3(\text{Li}^{2+}) = \dfrac{9a_0}{3} = 3a_0$

(d) $r_4(\text{Be}^{3+}) = \dfrac{16a_0}{4} = 4a_0$

Hence, Be^{3+} ion has maximum radius.

16. (a) Radius of n th orbit is $r_n = \dfrac{n^2 a_0}{Z}$

$$\frac{r_{n_2}}{r_{n_1}} = \left(\frac{n_2}{n_1}\right)^2 = 4 \Rightarrow \frac{n_2}{n_1} = 2$$

Thus, possible combinations are :

Set I	**Set II**
$n_2 = 2$	$n_2 = 4$
$n_1 = 1$	$n_1 = 2$

Energy of the nth orbit is

$$\therefore \quad E_n = \frac{-13.6Z^2}{n^2}$$

Set I $\Delta E = E_2 - E_1$

$$= 13.6\left(\frac{1}{1^2} - \frac{1}{2^2}\right)$$

$$= 13.6 \times \frac{3}{4}$$

$$= 10.2 \text{ eV}$$

Set II $\Delta E = 13.6\left[\dfrac{1}{2^2} - \dfrac{1}{4^2}\right]$

$$= 13.6 \times \frac{3}{16} = 2.55 \text{ eV}$$

17. (c) Energy of the n th orbit is

$$E_n = \left(\frac{-13.6Z^2}{n^2}\right) \text{eV}$$

$E_1(\text{H}) = -13.6$ eV $(Z = 1)$

$E_2(\text{He}^+) = -13.6$ eV $(Z = 2)$

$E_3(\text{Li}^{2+}) = -13.6$ eV $(Z = 3)$

$E_4(\text{Be}^{3+}) = -13.6$ eV $(Z = 3)$

Hence, I = II = III = IV

18. (d) $r_{n_2} = \dfrac{n_2^2 a_0}{1} = n_2^2 a_0$

$$r_{n_1} = n_1^2 a^0$$

$$\therefore \quad (n_2^2 - n_1^2)a_0 = 20a_0$$

$$\therefore \quad (n_2^2 - n_1^2) = 20$$

$$(n_2 + n_1)(n_2 - n_1) = 20$$

Possible combination is $n_2 = 6$, $n_1 = 4$

Thus, electron falls to fourth level to give lines in **Brackett** series.

19. (a) de-Broglie wavelength is given by

$$\lambda = \frac{h}{\sqrt{2m(\text{KE})}}$$

$$\lambda_1 = \frac{h}{\sqrt{2m(\text{KE})_1}}$$

$$\lambda_2 = 1.01\lambda_1 = \frac{h}{\sqrt{2m(\text{KE})_2}}$$

$$\therefore \quad (\text{KE})_1 = \frac{h^2}{\lambda_1^2 \times 2m}$$

$$(\text{KE})_2 = \frac{h^2}{(1.01)^2 \lambda_1^2 \times 2m}$$

$$\frac{(\text{KE})_2}{(\text{KE})_1} = \frac{1}{(1.01)^2}$$

$$(\text{KE})_2 = 0.98(\text{KE})_1$$

Thus, change in (KE) $= (\text{KE})_2 - (\text{KE})_1$

$= 0.98(\text{KE})_1 - (\text{KE})_1$

$= -0.02(\text{KE})_1$

20. (b)

I. Fe^{3+} ($Z = 26$, 23 electrons) $= [\text{Ar}]3d^5$

II. Fe^{2+} ($Z = 26$, 24 electrons) $= [\text{Ar}]3d^6$

III. Cr ($Z = 24$, 24 electrons) $= [\text{Ar}]3d^5 4s^1$

IV. Mn ($Z = 25$, 25 electrons)

$= [\text{Ar}]3d^5 4s^2$

■ When cation is formed electron is removed from valence shell. Thus electronic configuration of ion is decided by the electronic configuration of the atom.

Fe (26) : $[\text{Ar}]4s^2 3d^6$
Valence shell

Fe^{2+} : $[\text{Ar}]3d^6$

Fe^{2+} is isoelectronic of Cr ($Z = 24$) but electronic configuration of Cr atom is [Ar] $3d^5 4s^1$.

21. (a) (a) For 1*s*-orbital in hydrogen atom, $n = 1$ and is the ground state.

Thus, $r_n = \dfrac{n^2 a_0}{Z}$

$$r_1 = a_0$$

Thus electron is at a distance of a_0 from the nucleus. Thus statement (a) is incorrect.

(b) KE $= \dfrac{Ze^2}{2r}$ and PE $= -\dfrac{Ze^2}{r}$

Thus (PE) is double that of (KE)

Thus (b) is correct.

(c) The probability density of finding the electron is maximum at the nucleus. Thus, (c) is also correct.

(d) Total energy $E_n = (\text{KE} + \text{PE})$

$$= \frac{Ze^2}{2r_n} - \frac{Ze^2}{r_n} = -\frac{Ze^2}{2r_n}$$

When $r_n = a_0$,

$$E_n = -\frac{Ze^2}{2a_0}$$

As r_n increases, E_n decreases, thus maximum. Thus, it is also correct.

22. (b) Orbital angular momentum

$$(L) = \sqrt{l(l+1)}\frac{h}{2\pi}$$

When s-orbital, $l = 0$

$\therefore\ L = 0$

23. (a) Magnetic moment $= \sqrt{N(N+2)}$

where, N is number of unpaired electrons. Thus, larger the value of N larger will be the magnetic moment.

		N
I. Fe^{2+} ($Z = 26$) [Ar]	⇅ ↑ ↑ ↑ ↑ ($3d^6$)	4
II. Mn^+ ($Z = 28$) [Ar]	↑ ↑ ↑ ↑ ↑ ($3d^5$) ↑ ($4s^1$)	6
III. Cr (as in II) [Ar]$3d^5 4s^1$		6
IV. Co^{3+} (as in I) [Ar]$3d^6$		4

Thus, I = IV < II = III

24. (b) de-Broglie's wavelength,

$$\lambda = \frac{h}{mv}$$

Also, angular momentum

$$mvr_n = \frac{nh}{2\pi}$$

$$mv\left(\frac{n^2 a_0}{Z}\right) = \frac{nh}{2\pi}$$

In third orbit,

$$\therefore\quad mv\left(\frac{9a_0}{1}\right) = \frac{3h}{2\pi}$$

$$\therefore\quad mv = \frac{h}{6\pi a_0}$$

$$\therefore\quad \lambda = \frac{h}{h/6\pi a_0} = 6\pi a_0$$

25. (b) For hydrogen spectrum,

$$\bar{\nu} = \frac{1}{\lambda} = \bar{R}_H\left[\frac{1}{n_1^2} - \frac{1}{n_2^2}\right]$$

When $n_2 \to \infty$, $\bar{\nu}$ (wave number) is maximum and λ (wavelength) is shortest. Thus,

$$\bar{\nu}_{max} = \frac{1}{\lambda_{min}} = \frac{\bar{R}_H}{n_1^2}$$

Thus, $\lambda_{min} \propto n_1^2$

$$\therefore\quad \frac{\lambda_{min}\text{ (Lyman)}}{\lambda_{min}\text{ (Paschen)}} = \frac{(1)^2}{(3)^2} = \frac{1}{9}$$

26. (d) Ion is paramagnetic, if it has unpaired electron.

It is also coloured ion if it has unpaired electrons in d-orbitals.

			Paramagnetic	Coloured
I	Mg^+	$[1s^2 2s^2 2p^6 3s^1]$	Yes	No
II	Cu^+	[Ar] $3d^{10}$	No	No
III	Ni^{2+}	[Ar] $3d^8$	Yes	Yes
IV	Mn^{2+}	[Ar] $3d^5$	Yes	Yes
V	Zn^{2+}	[Ar] $3d^{10}$	No	No

In $3d^8$-orbitals, two unpaired electrons make Ni^{2+} paramagnetic and coloured.

27. (b) Total orbitals in a suborbit

$= (2l + 1) =$ degeneracy

$l = 0$ - (s)

Thus, degeneracy = 1

$l = 1$ - (p)

Thus, degeneracy = 3

$l = 2$ - (d)

Thus, degeneracy = 5

$l = 3$ - (f)

Thus, degeneracy = 7

$l = 4$ - (g)

Thus, degeneracy = 9

28. (c) Brackett series is obtained when there is transition to fourth level. For maximum intensity $\bar{\nu}$ (wave number is maximum).

$$\bar{\nu} = \bar{R}_H Z^2\left[\frac{1}{n_1^2} - \frac{1}{n_2^2}\right]$$

$$\Rightarrow\quad \underset{Lt\ n_2 \to \infty}{\bar{\nu}_{max}} = \bar{\nu} = \frac{\bar{R}_H Z^2}{(4)^2} \text{ and } n_1 = 4$$

29. (a) $E = Nh\nu$

E (given number) $= 7.25 \times 10^{15} (h\nu)$

E' (N_0 number) $= 6.02 \times 10^{23} (h\nu)$

$$\therefore\quad \frac{E}{E'} = \frac{7.25 \times 10^{15}}{6.02 \times 10^{23}} = 1.20 \times 10^{-8}$$

30. (a) The number of orbitals associated with quantum number $= n^2$

Thus, when $n = 5$, orbitals = 25

Each orbital can take maximum of two electrons with

$$m_s = +\frac{1}{2} \text{ and } m_s = -\frac{1}{2}$$

Thus, number of orbitals with

$$m_s = +\frac{1}{2} \text{ (in } n = 5) = 25$$

31. (d) de-Broglie's wavelength,

$$\lambda = \frac{h}{mv}$$

$$\therefore\quad v = \frac{h}{m\lambda} = \frac{6.626 \times 10^{-34}\text{ Js}}{9.1 \times 10^{-31}\text{ kg} \times 0.03\text{ m}}$$

$$= 0.0243\text{ m s}^{-1}$$

■ 1 J = 1 kg m^2 s^{-2}

32. (a)

	n	l	Suborbit	(n + l)
(a)	3	2	3d	5
(b)	4	2	4d	6
(c)	4	1	4p	5
(d)	5	0	5s	5

Thus, energy order is : $3d < 4p < 5s < 4d$

Thus, $3d$ electron has lowest energy.

33. (a) By Heisenberg's uncertainty principle, $\Delta x \cdot \Delta p \geq \frac{h}{4\pi}$

$$\Delta x \cdot m\Delta v \geq \frac{h}{4\pi}$$

$$\Delta x \cdot \Delta v \geq \frac{h}{4\pi m}$$

$$\Delta v = 3 \times 10^2 \times \frac{0.001}{100}$$

$$= 3 \times 10^{-3}\text{ m s}^{-1}$$

$$\therefore \Delta x = \frac{6.626 \times 10^{-34}\text{ Js}}{4\pi \times 3 \times 10^{-3}\text{ m s}^{-1} \times 9.1 \times 10^{-31}\text{ kg}}$$

$$= 0.0193\text{ m}$$

■ 1 J = 1kg m^{2}s^{-2}

34. (a) Wave number of a spectral line is given by,

$$\bar{\nu} = \frac{1}{\lambda} = \bar{R}_H Z^2\left[\frac{1}{n_1^2} - \frac{1}{n_2^2}\right]$$

If $\bar{\nu}_{max}$ then $n_2 \to \infty$ and λ is minimum

If $\bar{\nu}_{min}$ then $n_2 = (n_1 + 1)$ and λ is maximum

$$\therefore\quad \frac{1}{\lambda_{max}} = \bar{R}_H Z^2\left[\frac{1}{n_1^2} - \frac{1}{(n_1+1)^2}\right]$$

$$\bar{R}_H = 1.09679 \times 10^7\text{ m}^{-1}$$

(a) For H($Z = 1$) and for Balmer series $n_1 = 2$

$$\therefore\quad \frac{1}{\lambda_{max}} = 1.09679 \times 10^7 (1)^2\left[\frac{1}{2^2} - \frac{1}{3^2}\right]$$

$$= 1.09679 \times 10^7 \times \frac{5}{36}\text{ m}^{-1}$$

$$\lambda_{max} = 6.56 \times 10^{-7}\text{ m}$$

$$= 656 \times 10^{-9}\text{ m} = 656\text{ nm}$$

(b) For Li^{2+} ($Z = 3$) and for Lyman series, $n_1 = 1$

$$\therefore\quad \frac{1}{\lambda_{max}} = 1.09679 \times 10^7 (3)^2\left[\frac{1}{1^2} - \frac{1}{2^2}\right]$$

$$\lambda_{max} = 1.35 \times 10^{-8}\text{ m}$$

$$= 13.5 \times 10^{-9} = 13.5\text{ nm}$$

(c) For He^+ ($Z = 2$) and for Paschen series, $n_1 = 3$

$$\lambda_{max} = 4.68 \times 10^{-7}\text{ m}$$

$$= 468 \times 10^{-9}\text{ nm} = 468\text{ nm}$$

35. (c) $Z(38)$

$1s^2\ 2s^2\ 2p^6\ 3s^2\ 3p^6\ 3d^{10}\ 4s^2\ 4p^6\ 5s^2$

$\downarrow\ \downarrow\ \downarrow\ \downarrow\ \downarrow\ \downarrow\ \downarrow\ \downarrow\ \downarrow$

$1\ \ 1\ \ 3\ \ 1\ \ 3\ \ 5\ \ 1\ \ 3\ \ 1$

All are completely filled.

Thus, electron pairs = 19

36. (b) Angular nodes = l

Radial nodes = $(n - l - 1)$

Orbital	n	l	Radial nodes
4s	4	0	3(x)
3p	3	1	1(y)
3d	3	2	0(z)

37. (b) $r_n = \frac{n^2 a_0}{Z}$

For H, $Z = 1$, $n = 1$ for Bohr's orbit

$r_1 = a_0$

(a) $r_2(\text{Li}^{2+}) = \frac{4a_0}{3}$

(b) $r_2(\text{Be}^{3+}) = \frac{4a_0}{4} = a_0 = r_1$ (H)

(c) $r_2(\text{He}^{+}) = \frac{4a_0}{2} = 2a_0$

(d) $r_3(\text{Li}^{2+}) = \frac{9a_0}{3} = 3a_0$

38. (d) $\bar{\nu} = \frac{1}{\lambda} = \bar{R}_H Z^2\left[\frac{1}{n_1^2} - \frac{1}{n_2^2}\right]$

For Brackett series, $n_1 = 4$

and for limiting values, $n_2 \to \infty$

$$\therefore \quad \bar{\nu} = \frac{1}{\lambda} = \bar{R}_H (4)^2\left[\frac{1}{4^2} - \frac{1}{\infty}\right]$$

$$= \bar{R}_H$$

But, frequency

$$\nu = \frac{c}{\lambda} = c\bar{R}_H$$

39. (b) Sixth period means that electrons are being filled in the orbitals first in 6s and then in subsequent orbitals of higher energy.

	n	l	$n + l$
6s	6	0	6
6p	6	1	7
5d	5	2	7
4f	4	3	7

Thus, ascending order of energy is

$6s < 4f < 5d < 6p$

$ns < (n-2)f < (n-1)d < np$

and sequence of orbitals

$ns \to (n-2)f \to (n-1)d \to np$

40. (a) $\bar{\nu} = \bar{R}_H Z^2\left[\frac{1}{n_1^2} - \frac{1}{n_2^2}\right]$

$$0.21\bar{R}_H = \bar{R}_H (11)^2\left[\frac{1}{n_1^2} - \frac{1}{n_2^2}\right]$$

$$\therefore \quad \left[\frac{1}{n_1^2} - \frac{1}{n_2^2}\right] = \frac{0.21}{(11)^2}$$

$(11)^2$ in the denominator indicates that one of the level is on 11th orbit.

$\therefore n_1 = 10, n_2 = 11$

$$\therefore \quad \left[\frac{1}{(10)^2} - \frac{1}{(11)^2}\right] = \frac{(11)^2 - (10)^2}{(10)^2(11)^2} = \frac{0.21}{(11)^2}$$

Thus, correct.

41. (d) $u_{rms} = \sqrt{\frac{3RT}{M}} = \sqrt{\frac{3 \times 8.3143 \times 400}{4 \times 10^{-3}}}$

$$= 1579.3 \text{ m s}^{-1}$$

■ All data are in S.I. units

$1\text{ J} = 1\text{ kg m}^2\text{s}^{-2}$

$$m \text{ (mass of one H-atom)} = \frac{4 \times 10^{-3}}{N_0} \text{ kg}$$

$$\lambda = \frac{h}{mv} = \frac{6.626 \times 10^{-34} \times 6.02 \times 10^{23}}{4.0 \times 10^{-3} \times 1579.3}$$

$$= 6.31 \times 10^{-11}$$

$$= 63.1 \times 10^{-12} = 63.1 \text{ pm}$$

■ For quick calculation in exam

$N_0 h = 4 \times 10^{-10}$

42. (a) de-Broglie's wavelength, $h = \frac{h}{mv}$

velocity = v m s^{-1}

Then, distance travelled in 1s = vm

$$\therefore \quad \lambda = v = \frac{v}{mv}$$

$$\therefore \quad v^2 = \frac{h}{m}$$

$$\therefore \quad v = \sqrt{\frac{h}{m}}$$

43. (a) By de-Broglie equation,

$$\lambda = \frac{h}{mv} \text{ and } mv = \frac{nh}{2\pi r_n}$$

$$\therefore \quad \lambda = \frac{h}{nh/2\pi r_n}$$

Given, $\lambda = 1.5\pi a_0$

$$\therefore \quad 1.5\pi a_0 = \frac{2\pi r_n}{n}$$

Also, $\quad r_n = \frac{n^2 a_0}{Z}$

$$\therefore \quad 1.5\pi a_0 = \frac{2\pi}{n}\frac{n^2 a_0}{Z}$$

$$\therefore \quad \frac{n}{Z} = 0.75$$

44. (b) $\lambda = \frac{h}{mv}$

Given, $\lambda = 25v$

$$\therefore \quad v = \frac{\lambda}{25}$$

$$\therefore \quad \lambda = \frac{h}{m\left(\frac{\lambda}{25}\right)}$$

$$\therefore \quad \lambda^2 = 25\frac{h}{m}$$

$$\lambda = \sqrt{25\frac{h}{m}} = 5\sqrt{\frac{h}{m}}$$

45. (b) The radius of nth Bohr orbit = $\frac{n^2 a_0}{Z}$

For Li^{2+}, $Z = 3$

and for second orbit $n = 2$,

$$r_2 = \frac{4a_0}{3}$$

46. (a) By photoelectric effect,

$$h\nu = h\nu_0 + \frac{1}{2}mu^2$$

$$\frac{1}{2}mu^2 = h(\nu - \nu_0) = h\Delta\nu$$

$$\therefore \quad u = \sqrt{\frac{2h\Delta\nu}{m}}$$

Also, by de-Broglie's equation,

$$\lambda = \frac{h}{mu} = \frac{h}{m\sqrt{\frac{2h\Delta\nu}{m}}} = \sqrt{\frac{h}{2m\Delta\nu}}$$

47. (b) $\psi \propto e^{-r/a_0}$ for H-atom and radial distribution function is $4\pi r^2\psi^2$

$\therefore$ Probability is maximum, when

$$\frac{d}{dr}(4\pi r^2\psi^2) = 0$$

$$\frac{d}{dr}(4\pi r^2 e^{-2r/a_0}) = 0$$

$$4\pi\left[2re^{-2r/a_0} + r^2\left(\frac{-2}{a_0}\right)e^{-2r/a_0}\right] = 0$$

$$8\pi r e^{-2r/a_0}\left[1 - \frac{r}{a_0}\right] = 0$$

$$\therefore \quad r = a_0$$

Thus, when $r = a_0$ probability is maximum. It is at the circumference of first orbit.

48. (d)

49. (a) If $l = 2$, $m = -2, -1, 0, +1, +2$

Thus, only one orbital with $m = 0$ is allowed.

50. (d)

51. (c) de-Broglie's equation,

$$\lambda = \frac{h}{mv} = \frac{h}{\sqrt{2meV}}$$

$$\therefore \quad \lambda \propto \frac{1}{\sqrt{Vm}}$$

Also, wave number $\bar{\nu} = \dfrac{1}{\lambda}$

$\therefore \qquad \bar{\nu} \propto \sqrt{V_m}$

Thus, greater the mass, greater the slope.

Thus, $\qquad m_B > m_A$ or $\dfrac{m_B}{m_A} > 1$

$$\frac{m_A}{m_B} < 1$$

52. (a) For the change

$$\text{He} \xrightarrow{(\text{IE})_1} \text{He}^+ \xrightarrow{(\text{IE})_2} \text{He}^{2+}$$

(a) He^+ is isoelectronic of H thus Bohr's theory is followed. Hence true.

(b) $(\text{IE})_2 > (\text{IE})_1$ thus given statement is incorrect

(c) Incorrect

(d) Atomic mass does not change as proton and neutrons are not lost.

53. (a)

54. (c)

55. (d) $\dfrac{1}{\lambda} = R_H Z^2 \left[\dfrac{1}{n_1^2} - \dfrac{1}{n_2^2}\right]$

$$\frac{1}{900 \times 10^{-9}\text{ m}} = 1.09679 \times 10^7 \left[\frac{1}{n_1^2} - \frac{1}{n_2^2}\right]$$

$$\therefore \qquad \left[\frac{1}{n_1^2} - \frac{1}{n_2^2}\right] = 0.101$$

(a) $n_1 = 3, n_2 = 5,$

then $\left(\dfrac{1}{3^2} - \dfrac{1}{5^2}\right) = 0.071$, thus false.

(b) $n_1 = 2, \left[\dfrac{1}{2^2} - \dfrac{1}{\infty^2}\right] = 0.25$, thus false.

(c) $n_1 = 1, \left[\dfrac{1}{1^2} - \dfrac{1}{\infty^2}\right] = 1.0$, thus false.

(d) $n_1 = 3, \left[\dfrac{1}{3^2} - \dfrac{1}{\infty^2}\right] = 1$, thus true.

56. (d) $\dfrac{1}{\lambda} = \bar{R}_H Z^2 \left[\dfrac{1}{n_1^2} - \dfrac{1}{n_2^2}\right]$

First line (α-line) of H-atom in Lyman series has $n_1 = 1$, and $n_2 = 2$, $Z = 1$.

$$\therefore \qquad \frac{1}{\lambda_1} = \bar{R}_H \left[\frac{1}{1^2} - \frac{1}{2^2}\right] = \frac{3}{4}\bar{R}_H$$

Second line (β-line) of H-atom in Balmer series has $n_1 = 2$ and $n_2 = 4$.

$$\frac{1}{\lambda_2} = \bar{R}_H \left[\frac{1}{2^2} - \frac{1}{4^2}\right] = \bar{R}_H \left[\frac{1}{4} - \frac{1}{16}\right]$$

$$\frac{1}{\lambda_2} = \frac{3}{16}\bar{R}_H$$

$$\frac{\lambda_1}{\lambda_2} = \frac{3}{16} \times \frac{4}{3} = \frac{1}{4}$$

57. (a) If charge $= q$

and potential difference $= V$

then KE $= qV$

$$\lambda = \frac{h}{mv}$$

Also $\qquad \text{KE} = \dfrac{1}{2}mv^2 = qV$

$$\therefore \qquad m^2v^2 = 2mqV$$

$$\therefore \qquad mv = \sqrt{2mqV}$$

$$\therefore \qquad \lambda = \frac{h}{\sqrt{2mqV}}$$

58. (c) If $n_1 + n_2 = 4$ and $n_2 - n_1 = 2$, then $n_1 = 1$ and $n_2 = 3$

$$\therefore \qquad \bar{\nu} = \bar{R}_H Z^2 \left[\frac{1}{n_1^2} - \frac{1}{n_2^2}\right]$$

$$= \bar{R}_H (3)^2 \left[\frac{1}{1^2} - \frac{1}{3^2}\right]$$

$$= \bar{R}_H (9) \left[\frac{8}{9}\right] = 8\bar{R}_H$$

59. (d) Velocity of the electron in the second

$$\text{orbit} = \frac{(2.182 \times 10^6) Z}{n}$$

$$v = \frac{2.182 \times 10^6}{2}\text{ m s}^{-1}$$

Distance (circumference) $= 2\pi r_n$

$$= 2\pi \left(\frac{n^2 a_0}{Z}\right) = 2\pi(4a_0)$$

$$\therefore \text{ Frequency} = \frac{\text{Velocity}}{\text{Distance}}$$

$$= \frac{2.182 \times 10^6 \text{ms}^{-1}}{2 \times 2\pi(4 \times 0.529 \times 10^{-10})\text{m}}$$

$$= 8.20 \times 10^{14}\text{ s}^{-1}$$

or approx (8.21)

60. (c)

Electronic configuration	l	m	$(l+m)$	Electrons
$1s^2$	0	0	0	2
$2s^2$	0	0	0	2
$2p^6$	1	$\begin{bmatrix}-1\\0\\+1\end{bmatrix}$	0	2
$3s^2$	0	0	0	2
$3p^6$	1	$\begin{bmatrix}-1\\0\\+1\end{bmatrix}$	0	2
$4s^2$	0	0	0	2

In $2p^6$ and $3p^6$ only electrons with $l = 1$ and $m = -1$ were taken.

61. (c) For the Balmer series in the spectrum of H-atom, $n_1 = 2$

$$\bar{\nu} = \frac{1}{\lambda} = \bar{R}_H \left[\frac{1}{n_1^2} - \frac{1}{n_2^2}\right] = \bar{R}_H \left[\frac{1}{2^2} - \frac{1}{n_2^2}\right]$$

When series converge, $n_2 \to \infty$

$$\therefore \qquad \bar{\nu}_{max} = \frac{1}{\lambda_{min}} = \frac{\bar{R}_H}{4}$$

Thus series converge when wavelength is minimum. Thus (I) is correct.

For Balmer series $n_1 = 2$, thus (II) is also correct.

For longest wavelength, or minimum wave number, $n_2 = (n_1 + 1) = 3$. Thus (III) is also correct.

Ionisation energy of H-atom $= -E_1$(H). Thus, (IV) is incorrect.

62. (b) Angular momentum,

$$mvr_n = \frac{nh}{2\pi}$$

For $n = 1$

$$mvr_1 = \frac{h}{2\pi} \Rightarrow 2\pi r_1 = \frac{h}{mv}$$

But $\dfrac{h}{mv} = \lambda$ (de-Broglie's wavelength)

$$\therefore \qquad \lambda = 2\pi r_1 = 2\pi(0.529)\text{ Å}$$

63. (d) By photoelectric effect,

$$h\nu = h\nu_0 + \text{KE}$$

$$\frac{hc}{\lambda} = h\nu_0 + \text{KE} = \phi + \text{KE}$$

$$\phi = \left(\frac{hc}{\lambda} - \text{KE}\right)$$

$$\frac{hc}{\lambda} = \frac{6.62 \times 10^{-34} \times 3 \times 10^8}{250 \times 10^{-9}}\text{ J}$$

$$= 7.944 \times 10^{-19}\text{ J}$$

$$= \frac{7.944 \times 10^{-19}}{1.6 \times 10^{-19}\text{ J/eV}} = 4.97\text{ eV}$$

$$\text{KE} = 0.5\text{ V} = 0.5\text{ eV}$$

$$\therefore \qquad \phi = 4.97 - 0.50 = 4.47\text{ eV}$$

$$\approx 4.50\text{ eV}$$

■ For quick calculation, $hc = 2.0 \times 10^{-25}$

64. (d) Bohr radius,

$$r_n = \frac{n^2 \times 0.53}{Z} = \text{Å}$$

Radius of nth Bohr orbit for H-atom

$$= 0.53\, n^2 \text{Å}\, [Z = 1 \text{ for H-atom}]$$

$\therefore$ Radius 2nd Bohr orbit for H-atom

$$= 0.53 \times (2)^2 = 2.12\text{ Å}$$

■ Do not confuse about constants given. Use direct result.

65. (d) $\bar{\nu} = \dfrac{1}{\lambda} = R_H Z^2 \left[\dfrac{1}{n_1^2} - \dfrac{1}{n_2^2}\right]$

$\bar{\nu}$ is maximum and λ is minimum, if

$$n_2 \longrightarrow \infty$$

For Lyman series, $n_1 = 1$ and for H-atom $Z = 1$

$$\therefore \qquad \frac{1}{A} = R_H$$

For Paschen series, $n_1 = 3$, for He^+, $Z = 2$

λ is maximum, if $n_2 = (n_1 + 1)$

$$\therefore \frac{1}{\lambda_{max}} = R_H Z^2 \left(\frac{1}{n_1^2} - \frac{1}{n_2^2}\right)$$

$$\frac{1}{\lambda_{max}} = \frac{1}{A}(2)^2\left(\frac{1}{9} - \frac{1}{16}\right)$$

$$\frac{1}{\lambda_{max}} = \frac{7}{36A}$$

$$\therefore \lambda_{max} = \frac{36A}{7}$$

66. (b) $r_n = \dfrac{n^2 a_0}{Z}$

$$211.6 \text{ pm} = \frac{n^2 (52.9 \text{ pm})}{1}$$

$$\therefore \quad n = 2$$

Thus, Balmer series.

67. (c) By de-Broglie equation,

$$\lambda = \frac{h}{\sqrt{2meV}} \Rightarrow \frac{h}{\lambda} = \sqrt{2meV}$$

68. (c) Energy of H-atom in the nth state is

$$E_n = -\frac{13.6}{n^2} \text{ eV}$$

$n = 1$, (ground state) $E_1 = -13.6$ eV

$n = 2$, (excited state) $E_2 = -3.4$ eV

69. (d) KE $\propto T$ and $\lambda = \dfrac{h}{\sqrt{2m(\text{KE})}}$

Thus, de-Broglie wavelength will be in order :

Visible photon > thermal neutron > thermal electron.

70. (a) The electronic configuration of rubidium atom ($Z = 37$) is given by:

$$\text{Rb} = [\text{Kr}]\, 5s^1$$

Hence, the quantum numbers for $5s^1$ valence electron is given by

$$n = 5, l = 0, m = 0,$$

$$s = +\frac{1}{2} \quad \text{or} \quad -\frac{1}{2}$$

71. (a) Energy change

$$\Delta E = 2.178 \times 10^{-18}\left(\frac{1}{1^2} - \frac{1}{2^2}\right) = \frac{hc}{\lambda}$$

$$2.178 \times 10^{-18}\left(\frac{1}{1^2} - \frac{1}{2^2}\right)$$

$$= \frac{6.62 \times 10^{-34} \times 3.0 \times 10^8}{\lambda}$$

$$\therefore \quad \lambda \approx 1.214 \times 10^{-7} \text{ m}$$

72. (b)

n	l	nl (suborbit)	$n + l$
(1) 4	1	$4p$	5
(2) 4	0	$4s$	4
(3) 3	2	$3d$	5
(4) 3	1	$3p$	4

Higher the value $(n + l)$, higher is the energy. If $(n + l)$ are same, then suborbit with lower value of n has lower energy. Thus,

$$3p < 4s < 3d < 4p$$
$$(4) < (2) < (3) < (1)$$

73. (c) Energy values are always additive.

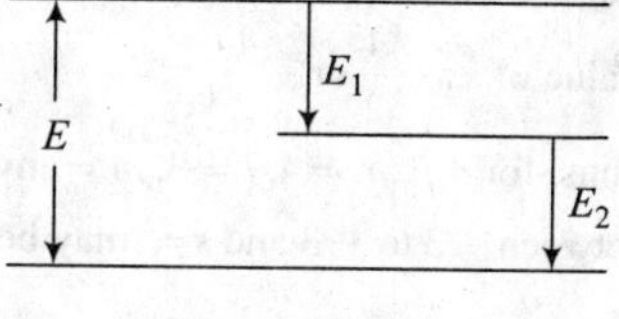

$$E_{total} = E_1 + E_2$$

$$\frac{hc}{\lambda} = \frac{hc}{\lambda_1} + \frac{hc}{\lambda_2}$$

$$\therefore \quad \frac{1}{\lambda} = \frac{1}{\lambda_1} + \frac{1}{\lambda_2}$$

$$\frac{1}{355} = \frac{1}{680} + \frac{1}{\lambda_2}$$

$$\lambda_2 = 742.77 \text{ nm} \approx 743 \text{ nm}$$

74. (b) $\Delta E = h\nu = \dfrac{2\pi^2 m Z^2 e^4 k^2}{h^2}\left[\dfrac{1}{n_1^2} - \dfrac{1}{n_2^2}\right]$

if electron falls from n_2-level to n_1-level.

$\therefore$ In He^+, for $n_2 = 4$ to $n_1 = 2$ transition

$$\nu_{He^+} = \text{constant }(4)\left[\frac{1}{2^2} - \frac{1}{4^2}\right]$$

$$[\because Z_{He^+} = 2]$$

$$= \text{constant} \times 4\left[\frac{3}{16}\right]$$

$$= \frac{3}{4} \times \text{constant}$$

$$\nu(\text{H}) = \text{constant}(1)^2\left[\frac{1}{n_1^2} - \frac{1}{n_2^2}\right]$$

$$= \text{constant}\left[\frac{1}{n_1^2} - \frac{1}{n_2^2}\right]$$

(a) For $n_2 = 3$ and $n_1 = 1$

$$\nu(\text{H}) = \text{constant}\left[\frac{1}{1} - \frac{1}{9}\right]$$

$$= \frac{8}{9} \times \text{constant} \neq \frac{3}{4} \times \text{constant}$$

(b) For $n_2 = 2$ and $n_1 = 1$,

$$\nu\,(\text{H}) = \text{constant} \times \left[\frac{1}{1} - \frac{1}{4}\right]$$

$$= \frac{3}{4} \times \text{constant} = \nu[He^+]$$

(c) For $n = 3$ and $n_1 = 2$

$$\nu(\text{H}) = \text{constant} \times \left[\frac{1}{2^2} - \frac{1}{3^2}\right]$$

$$= \frac{5}{36} \times \text{constant} \neq \nu[He^+]$$

(d) For $n_2 = 4$ and $n_1 = 3$

$$\nu(\text{H}) = \text{constant} \times \left[\frac{1}{3^2} - \frac{1}{4^2}\right]$$

$$= \frac{7}{144} \times \text{constant} \neq \nu[He^+]$$

75. (d) Energy required for breaking bond in one Cl_2 molecule $= \dfrac{242 \times 10^3}{N_A}$ J

$$E = \frac{hc}{\lambda} \quad \text{or} \quad \lambda = \frac{hc}{E}$$

$$= \frac{6.626 \times 10^{-34} \times 3 \times 10^8 \times 6.02 \times 10^{23}}{242 \times 10^3}$$

$$= 494 \times 10^{-9} \text{ m} = 494 \text{ nm}$$

76. (b) Ionisation energy (IE) of H-like species as He^+ is given by,

$$(\text{IE})_Z = (\text{IE})_\text{H}\left(\frac{Z^2}{n^2}\right)$$

For He^+, $Z = 2$, $n = 1$

$$(\text{IE})_{He^+} = 4(\text{IE})_\text{H}$$

and for Li^{2+}, $Z = 3$, $n = 1$

$$(\text{IE})_{Li^{2+}} = 9(\text{IE})_\text{H}$$

$$(\text{IE})_{Li^{2+}} = \frac{9}{4}(\text{IE})_{He^+}$$

$$= \frac{9}{4} \times 19.6 \times 10^{-18} \text{ J atom}^{-1}$$

$$= 4.41 \times 10^{-17} \text{ J atom}^{-1}$$

77. (c) By Heisenberg's uncertainty principle,

$$\Delta x \cdot m\Delta v = \frac{h}{4\pi}$$

Also, $\Delta v = \dfrac{600 \times 0.005}{100} = 0.03 \text{ m s}^{-1}$

$$\Delta x \times 9.1 \times 10^{-31} \times 0.03 = \frac{6.6 \times 10^{-34}}{4 \times 3.14}$$

Hence, $\Delta x = \dfrac{6.6 \times 10^{-34}}{4 \times 3.14 \times 0.03 \times 9.1 \times 10^{-31}}$

$$= 1.92 \times 10^{-3} \text{ m}$$

■ 1 J = 1 kg $m^2 s^{-2}$

78. (b) $\lambda = \dfrac{h}{mv} = \dfrac{6.63 \times 10^{-34}}{1.67 \times 10^{-27} \times 1 \times 10^3}$

$$= 3.97 \times 10^{-10} \text{ m}$$

$$= 0.397 \times 10^{-9} \text{ m}$$

$$\approx 0.40 \text{ nm}$$

79. (d) Ionisation enthalpy of hydrogen atom is 1.312×10^6 J mol^{-1}. It suggests that the energy of electron in the ground state (first orbit) is -1.312×10^6 J mol^{-1}

$$\Delta E = E_2 - E_1$$

$$= -\left(\frac{1.312 \times 10^6}{2^2}\right) - \left(\frac{-1.312 \times 10^6}{1}\right)$$

$$= 9.84 \times 10^5 \text{ J mol}^{-1}$$

80. (b) $n + l = 5$, maximum.

81. (a) $^{A}_{Z}X \longrightarrow {}^{A-1}_{Z}X + {}^{1}_{0}n$

Isotopes are species having same number of protons but different number of neutrons.

82. (c) $\Delta x \cdot \Delta v \geq \frac{h}{4\pi m}$

$\Delta v = 300 \times 0.001 \times 10^{-2}\ \text{m s}^{-1}$

$\Delta x = \frac{6.63 \times 10^{-34}}{4 \times 3.14 \times 9.1 \times 10^{-31} \times 300 \times 0.001 \times 10^{-2}}$

$= 0.01933$

$= 1.93 \times 10^{-2}\ \text{m}$

83. (d) Angular momentum of an electron

$= mvr = \frac{nh}{2\pi}$ [n is orbit number]

In 5th orbit $= \frac{5h}{2\pi} = \frac{2.5h}{\pi}$

84. (a) Hydrogen atom has $1s^1$ configuration and these $3s$, $3p$ and $3d$-orbitals will have same energy *wrt* $1s$-orbital.

85. (a)

(A) $1s$ (B) $2s$

(C) $2p$ (D) $3d$

(E) $3d$

In the absence of any field, $3d$ in (D) and (E) will be of equal energy.

86. (c) $E = 0.175$ J

time = 5 ns = 5×10^{-9} s

$\therefore$ Power $= \frac{0.175\ \text{J}}{5 \times 10^{-9}\ \text{s}}$

$= 5.50 \times 10^{7}\ \text{Js}^{-1}$

$= 3.50 \times 10^{7}$ W

Also, $E = 0.175\ \text{J} = Nh\nu = N\frac{hc}{\lambda}$

$\therefore N = \frac{E\lambda}{hc}$

$= \frac{0.175 \times 875 \times 10^{-9}}{6.626 \times 10^{-34} \times 3 \times 10^{8}}$

$= 7.703 \times 10^{17}$ photons in (5×10^{-9} s)

87. (a) On applying Rydberg formula,

$\frac{1}{\lambda} = \bar{\nu}_H = \bar{R}_H\left[\frac{1}{n_1^2} - \frac{1}{n_2^2}\right]$

$= 1.097 \times 10^{7}\left[\frac{1}{1^2} - \frac{1}{\infty^2}\right]$

$\therefore \lambda = \frac{1}{1.097 \times 10^{7}}$ m

$= 9.11 \times 10^{-8}$ m

$= 91.1 \times 10^{-9}$ m

$= 91.1$ nm [$\because$ 1 nm $= 10^{-9}$ m]

88. (c) Any sub orbit is represented as nl such the n is the principal quantum number (in the form of values) and l is the azimuthal quantum number (its name).

Value of $l < n$

$l = 0\ \ 1\ \ 2\ \ 3\ \ 4$

$s\ \ p\ \ d\ \ f\ \ g$

Value of m : $-l$ to $+l$

Value of s : $+\frac{1}{2}$ or $-\frac{1}{2}$

Thus, for $4f$: $n = 4$, $l = 3$, m = any value between -3 to $+3$ and s = may be $\pm\frac{1}{2}$.

89. (b) Electronic configuration of Cr(Z=24)

	n	l	Electrons
$1s^2$	1	0	2
$2s^2$	2	0	2
$2p^6$	2	1	6
$3s^2$	3	0	2
$3p^6$	3	1	6
$3d^5$	3	2	5
$4s^1$	4	0	2

Thus, electrons with l = 1, are 12 and with l = 2, are 5.

90. (c) Quantum nature of atoms is not associated with its internal energy. Thus, (c) is incorrect.

It is associated with

- absorption spectrum thus (a) is correct.
- black body radiation, thus (d) is correct.
- photo-electric effect, thus (b) is correct.

91. (a) Wavelength associated with the velocity of tennis ball

$\lambda = \frac{h}{mv} = 1.105 \times 10^{-33}$ m

92. (b) The emission is in visible region [V I B G Y O R]. The visible region in H spectrum corresponds to Balmer series [$n_1 = 2$, $n_2 = 3, 4 \ldots \infty$] i.e. either (a) or (b). In (a), there is only one emission. Thus, the third line will be in the jump from $5 \rightarrow 2$.

93. (b) If $n = 1$

Suborbit		Electronic configuration
$l = 0$	$1s$	$1s^2$
$l = 1$	$1p$	$1p^6$
$l = 2$	$1d$	$1d^{10}$

If Z = 8, electronic configuration would be $1s^2 1p^6$

thus, it is not the noble gas.

Thus (a) is incorrect.

If Z = 13, electronic configuration would be $1s^2$, $1p^6$, $1d^5$

Thus d-orbital is half-filled. Thus (b) is correct.

If Z = 9, electronic configuration would be $1s^2$, $1p^6$, $1d^1$

thus it is not she alkali metal. Thus (c) is incorrect.

If Z = 6, electronic configuration would be $1s^2$, $1p^4$, thus it has $1p$ valence shell.

Thus (d) is also incorrect.

94. (c) $\bar{\nu} = \frac{1}{\lambda} = \bar{R}_H Z^2\left[\frac{1}{n_1^2} - \frac{1}{n_2^2}\right]$

$\bar{\nu}_{max}$ when $n_2 \rightarrow \infty$

$\therefore \bar{\nu}_{max} = \frac{\bar{R}_H Z^2}{n_1^2}$

$\bar{\nu}_{min}$ when $n_2 = (n_1 + 1)$

$\therefore \bar{\nu}_{min} = \bar{R}_H Z^2\left[\frac{1}{n_1^2} - \frac{1}{(n_1+1)^2}\right]$

$\therefore (\bar{\nu}_{max} - \bar{\nu}_{min}) = \frac{\bar{R}_H Z^2}{(n_1+1)^2}$

For Lyman series, $n_1 = 1$

$\therefore \Delta\bar{\nu}_{Lyman} = \frac{\bar{R}_H Z^2}{(1+1)^2} = \frac{\bar{R}_H}{4}$

For Balmer series, $n_1 = 2$

$\therefore \Delta\bar{\nu}_{Balmer} = \frac{\bar{R}_H}{(2+1)^2} = \frac{\bar{R}_H}{9}$

$\therefore \frac{\Delta\bar{\nu}_{Lyman}}{\Delta\bar{\nu}_{Balmer}} = \frac{9}{4}$

95. (c) $r_n = \frac{n^2 a_0}{Z}$

For iso-electronic species, n is same

Thus, $r_n \propto \frac{1}{Z}$

96. (c) Momentum $p = mv$

also $\lambda = \frac{h}{mv} = \frac{h}{p}$

$\therefore \frac{\lambda_1}{\lambda_2} = \frac{p_2}{p_1}$

$\frac{\lambda_1}{\lambda_2} = \frac{1.5p}{p}$

$\therefore = \frac{3}{2}$

$\lambda_2 = \frac{2}{3}\lambda_1$

97. (b) $n = 4$

l	*m*
0	0
1	−1
	0
	+1
2	−2 ← subshell
	−1
	0
	+1
	+2
3	−3
	−2 ← subshell
	−1
	0
	+1
	+2
	+3

Thus, two subshells with $m = -2$ are possible.

Acid Test for JEE Advanced

Type I. MCQs with Only ONE Correct Alternate

98. (b) Potential energy $= 2 \times E_n$

$$= 2\left(-\frac{13.6Z^2}{n^2}\right)\text{eV}$$

For Be^{3+}, $Z = 4$

For N-shell, $n = 4$

$$\therefore \quad (\text{PE}) = 2 \times \frac{-13.6 \times (4)^2}{(4)^2}$$

$$= -27.2\,\text{eV}$$

99. (d) $\Delta H = 496\,\text{kJ mol}^{-1}$

$$E = \frac{496 \times 10^3}{6.02 \times 10^{23}}\,\text{J atom}^{-1}$$

$$\therefore \quad E = h\nu$$

$$\nu = \frac{E}{h}$$

$$= \frac{\left(\dfrac{496}{6.02 \times 10^{23}}\right) \times 10^3\,\text{J atom}^{-1}}{6.62 \times 10^{-34}\,\text{Js}}$$

$$= 1.244 \times 10^{15}\,\text{s}^{-1}$$

100. (a) Possible lines due to transition of electron from n_2 level to n_1 level.

$$= \frac{(n_2 - n_1 + 1)(n_2 - n_1)}{2}$$

For Paschen series $n_1 = 3$

$n_2 = 8$ (seventh excited state)

$$\therefore \text{Total lines} = \frac{(8 - 3 + 1)(8 - 3)}{2} = 15$$

101. (b) Cr(24)

$1s^2 2s^2 2p^6 3s^2 3p^6 3d^5 4s^1$

	n	*l*	*m*	Electrons
$1s^2$	1	0	0	2
	1	0	0	
$2s^2$	2	0	0	2
	2	0	0	
$2p^6$	2	0	0	2
		1	−1	2
			0	2
			+1	2
$3s^2$	3	0	0	2
	3	0	0	
$3p^6$	3	1	−1	2
			0	2
			+1	2
$3d^5$	3	2	−2	five
			−1	
			0	
			+1	
			+2	
$4s^1$	4	0	0	1

Thus, electrons with $(m = +1) = 2$ in $2p$, 2 in $3p$ and 1 in $3d = 5$

$$x = 5$$

and electron with $(l = 0) = 2$ each in $1s, 2s, 3s$ and 1 in $4s = 7$

$$\therefore \quad y = 7$$

102. (a) Fe (26) : $1s^2 2s^2 2p^6 3s^2 3p^6 3d^6 4s^2$

Fe (II) (24): $\underbrace{1s^2}_{(n-2)} \; \underbrace{2s^2 2p^6 3s^2 3p^6}_{(n-1)} \; \underbrace{3d^6}_{n}$

Then electrons in $(n-1)d = 0$

electrons in $(n-1)p = 6$

electrons in $(n-2)s = 2$

- If electronic configuration of a cation is required, first write electronic configuration of the atom. In cation formation electrons from valence shell are emitted.

Thus, if

Fe(26) : [Ar]$3d^6 4s^2$

Fe^{2+} : [Ar]$3d^6$

Fe^{3+} : [Ar]$3d^5$

103. (b) Fe (26) : $1s^2 2s^2 2p^6 3s^2 3p^6 4s^2 3d^6$

	l	*m*	$(l+m)$	Electron
$1s^2$	0	0	0	2
$2s^2$	0	0	0	2
$2p^6$	1	−1	0	2
	1	0	1	2
	1	+1	2	2
$3s^2$	0	0	0	2
$3p^6$	1	−1	0	2
	1	0	1	2
	1	+1	1	2
$3d^6$	2	−2	0	2
	2	−1	+1	1
	2	0	2	1
	2	+1	+3	1
	2	+2	+4	1
$4s^2$	0	0	0	2

Thus, two electrons each in $1s, 2s, 2p\,3p$, $3d$ and $4s$ have $(l + m)$ equal to zero.
Thus, total 12 electrons.

104. (b) If $(n_1 + n_2) = 7$ and $(n_2 - n_1) = 3$

Thus, $n_2 = 5$, $n_1 = 2$

$$\therefore \quad \bar{\nu} = \frac{1}{\lambda} = \bar{R}_H Z^2\left[\frac{1}{n_1^2} - \frac{1}{n_2^2}\right]$$

For longest wavelength $n_1 = 4$,

$$n_2 = 5\,[= (n_1 + 1)]$$

(being in boundary lines)

$$\therefore \frac{1}{\lambda} = 1.09679 \times 10^7 \times (1)^2\left[\frac{1}{4^2} - \frac{1}{5^2}\right]$$

$$\therefore \lambda = 4.05 \times 10^{-6}\,\text{m}$$

105. (c) Na^{10+} (*g*) and He^+ (*g*) are isoelectronic.

KE $= -E_n$ (energy of electron in n^{th} orbit)

$$= -\left(-\frac{13.6Z^2}{n^2}\text{eV}\right)$$

$$x = +\frac{13.6Z^2}{n^2} = \frac{+13.6 \times (Z)^2}{(2)^2} = 13.6\text{ eV}$$

Also, $(\text{IE})_{He^+} = -E_n$

$$= 13.6\text{ eV in }2^{\text{nd}}\text{ orbit}$$

$$(\text{IE})_{He^+} = (\text{IE})_H \frac{Z^2}{n^2}$$

$$\therefore \quad (\text{IE})_H = 13.6\,\text{eV} = x$$

$$(\text{IE})_{Na^{10+}} = (\text{IE})_H\left(\frac{Z^2}{n^2}\right) = (x)\frac{(11)^2}{(1)^2}$$

$$= 121x$$

106. (d) Time period $\propto \dfrac{n^3}{Z^2}$

$$\therefore \frac{T(\text{He}^+\text{ in first orbit})}{T(\text{H in second orbit})} = \left(\frac{1^3}{2^2}\right)\left(\frac{1^2}{2^3}\right) = \frac{1}{32}$$

or 1 : 32

107. (a) Total number of lines

$$= \frac{(n_2 - n_1 + 1)(n_2 - 1)}{2}$$

If ground state, $n_1 = 1$

$$\therefore \quad 15 = \frac{n_2(n_2 - 1)}{2}$$

$$30 = n_2(n_2 - 1)$$

Thus, gives $n_2 = 6$

$\therefore \quad \bar{\nu} = \frac{1}{\lambda} = R_H Z^2 \left[\frac{1}{n_1^2} - \frac{1}{n_2^2}\right]$

$= 1.09679 \times 10^7 \, (1)^2 \left[\frac{1}{1^2} - \frac{1}{6^2}\right] \text{m}^{-1}$

$\therefore \quad \lambda = 9.378 \times 10^{-7} \text{m}$

$= 9378 \times 10^{-10} \text{ m} = 9378 \text{ Å}$

108. (d) $Fe^{2+} (Z=26) [Ar] 3d^6$

[Ar] | ⇅ | ↿ | ↿ | ↿ | ↿ |

Four unpaired electron

$\therefore \quad \mu_1 = \sqrt{N(N+2)}, N=4$

$= \sqrt{24} \text{ BM} = x$

$Co^{3+} (Z=27) : [Ar] 3d^6$

It has also four unpaired electrons

Thus, $\quad \mu_2 = \sqrt{24} \text{ BM} = y$

$\therefore \quad x/y = 1$

109. (c) Fourth excited state means, $n=5$

Total lines $= \frac{n(n+1)}{2} = 15$ lines

Lines in visible region = 4

In UV-region = 5

In IR-region = 15 − 9 = 6

110. (c) $\quad (IE)_Z = (IE)_H \frac{Z^2}{n^2}$

$\therefore 19.6 \times 10^{-18} = (IE)_H \left(\frac{2}{1}\right)^2$

$\therefore \quad (IE)_H = \frac{19.6 \times 10^{-18}}{4} J$

$E_1(H) = -(IE)_H$

$= -\frac{19.6 \times 10^{-18}}{4}$

$E_{Li^{2+}} = E_H \left(\frac{Z^2}{n^2}\right)$

$= \frac{-19.6 \times 10^{-18}}{4} \times \frac{9}{4}$

$= 1.1025 \times 10^{-17} J$

111. (b) $KE = -E_n$

$= -\left(\frac{13.6 Z^2}{n^2}\right)$

For H-atom, $Z=1$ and $n=3$ (total waves) = 3 as shown

$\therefore \quad KE = +\frac{13.6 \times (1)^2}{(3)^2} = 1.51 \text{eV}$

112. (a) $\lambda_{proton} = \frac{h}{\sqrt{2m_p (KE)}} = \frac{h}{\sqrt{2 \times 1 \times eV_p}}$

$\lambda_\alpha = \frac{h}{\sqrt{2m_\alpha (KE)}}$

$= \frac{h}{\sqrt{2 \times 4 \times eV_\alpha}}$

Given, $\lambda_\alpha = 2\lambda_p$

$\frac{h}{\sqrt{8eV_\alpha}} = \frac{h}{\sqrt{2eV_p}}$

$\therefore \quad V_\alpha = \frac{V_p}{4}$

113. (b) $E = k\frac{q_1 q_2}{d}$

Where, $k = 9.0 \times 10^{11} \text{ J cm e}^{-2}$

$E = \frac{9.0 \times 10^{11} \times 1.0 \times 10^{-10} \times 1.0}{0.10}$

$= 900 \text{J}$

■ Conversion of cm into m has not been done as these factors are cancelled in final result.

114. (a) Force of attraction between electron and nucleus is, $F = \frac{kZe^2}{r_n^2}$

$\therefore \quad dW = \int_\infty^{r_n} \frac{k Z e^2}{r_n^2}$

$W = -\frac{kZe^2}{r_n}$

This energy is called potential energy.

For H-atom, $Z=1$

$\therefore \quad W = \text{Potential energy} = -\frac{ke^2}{r_n}$

115. (a) Frequency of 1 eV is ($1 \text{ eV} = 1.6 \times 10^{-19} \text{ J}$)

$\nu = \frac{E}{h} = \frac{1.6 \times 10^{-19} \text{ J}}{6.626 \times 10^{-34} \text{Js}}$

$= 2.4147 \times 10^{14} \text{s}^{-1}$

Wavelength, $\lambda = \frac{c}{\nu} = \frac{3.0 \times 10^8 \text{ m s}^{-1}}{2.4147 \times 10^{14} \text{s}^{-1}}$

$= 1.242 \times 10^{-6} \text{m}$

$= 1242 \times 10^{-9} \text{ m}$

$= 1242 \text{ nm}$

$\therefore \quad \lambda_e = 1242 \text{ nm eV}$

116. (b) $E = h\nu = \frac{hc}{\lambda} = hc\bar{\nu}$

$= 6.626 \times 10^{-34} \text{Js} \times 3 \times 10^8 \text{ m s}^{-1} \times 1 \times 100 \text{m}^{-1}$

$= 2.0 \times 10^{-23} \text{J per photon}$

$= 2.0 \times 10^{-23} \times 6.02 \times 10^{23} \text{J mol}^{-1}$

$= 12.04 \text{ J mol}^{-1} = 12.04 \times 10^{-3} \text{ kJ mol}^{-1}$

■ $hc = 2.0 \times 10^{-25}$

117. (b) Longest wavelength of visible light

$= 7000 \text{ Å}$

$= 7000 \times 10^{-10} \text{m}$

$\therefore \quad \nu = \frac{c}{\lambda} = \frac{3 \times 10^8 \text{ m s}^{-1}}{7000 \times 10^{-10} \text{m}}$

$= 4.286 \times 10^{-14} \text{s}^{-1}$

Shortest wavelength of visible light is 4000Å

$\therefore \nu = \frac{3 \times 10^8 \text{ m s}^{-1}}{4 \times 10^{-7} \text{ m}} = 7.50 \times 10^{14} \text{s}^{-1}$

118. (d) Energy required to dissociate O_2 molecule into normal O-atoms

$= \frac{498 \times 10^3}{6.02 \times 10^{23}} \text{ J molecule}^{-1}$

$= 8.2724 \times 10^{-19} \text{ J} \quad (1 \text{ eV} = 1.6 \times 10^{-19} \text{ J})$

∴ Additional energy for excited O* atom

$= 1.6 \times 10^{-19} \times 1.967 \text{ J}$

$= 3.1472 \times 10^{-19} \text{ J}$

Total energy

$= (8.2724 + 3.1472) \times 10^{-19} \text{ J}$

$= 1.142 \times 10^{-18} \text{ J}$

$\therefore \quad \lambda = \frac{hc}{E} = \frac{6.626 \times 10^{-34} \times 3 \times 10^8}{1.142 \times 10^{-18}}$

$= 1.74 \times 10^{-7} \text{ m}$

$= 174 \times 10^{-9} \text{ m} = 174 \text{ nm}$

119. (c) $h\nu = h\nu_0 + (KE)$

Since, $\quad \nu = \frac{c}{\lambda}$

$\therefore \quad (KE) = \frac{hc}{\lambda} - \frac{hc}{\lambda_0}$

$(KE)_{2200} = \frac{hc}{2200} - \frac{hc}{2600}$

$(KE)_{new} = \frac{hc}{\lambda_{new}} - \frac{hc}{2600} = 2(KE)_{2200}$

$2 = \frac{\frac{1}{\lambda_{new}} - \frac{1}{2600}}{\frac{1}{2200} - \frac{1}{2600}}$

$\therefore \quad \lambda = 1900 \text{ Å}$

120. (d) Rydberg constant,

$R_H = 1.09679 \times 10^7 \text{ m}^{-1}$ for H-atom

$\bar{\nu} = R_H Z^2 \left[\frac{1}{n_1^2} - \frac{1}{n_2^2}\right]$

If He^+ is taken, then

$R_{He^+} = 1.09679 \times 10^7 \times 4 \text{m}^{-1}$

$= 4.38716 \times 10^7 \text{ m}^{-1}$

Also, $\quad \bar{\nu} = \frac{1}{\lambda}$

$\therefore \quad E = h\nu = \frac{hc}{\lambda} = hc\bar{\nu} = hc\bar{R}_{He^+}$

$\bar{R}_{He^+} (\text{in J}) = 6.626 \times 10^{-34} \text{Js} \times 3 \times 10^8 \text{ m s}^{-1} \times 4.38716 \times 10^7 \text{ m}^{-1}$

$= 8.721 \times 10^{-18} \text{ J}$

$\nu = \frac{c}{\lambda} = c\bar{\nu} = cR_{He^+} = 1.316 \times 10^{16} \text{s}^{-1}$

121. (a) The emission of visible light implies some transition to the second orbit. After that there must be a transition from second level to first level, so that atom returns to ground state.

$$\therefore \quad \bar{v} = \frac{1}{\lambda} = R_H\left[\frac{1}{n_1^2} - \frac{1}{n_2^2}\right]$$

$$= 1.09679 \times 10^7\ \text{m}^{-1}\left[\frac{1}{1^2} - \frac{1}{2^2}\right]$$

$$= 8.226 \times 10^6\ \text{m}^{-1}$$

122. (b) Species are different but transition is same.

$$\Delta E_{Be^{3+}} = Z^2(\Delta E_H)$$

$$hv_{Be^{3+}} = Z^2(hv_H)$$

$$\frac{hc}{\lambda_{Be^{3+}}} = \left(\frac{hc}{\lambda_H}\right)Z^2$$

$$\therefore \quad \bar{v}_{Be^{3+}} = 4\bar{v}_H$$

$$= 4 \times 1.52 \times 10^6\ \text{m}^{-1}$$

$$= 2.432 \times 10^7\ \text{m}^{-1}$$

123. (c) Velocity of the electron in the nth orbit $= (2.182 \times 10^6)\frac{Z}{n}\ \text{m s}^{-1}$

$$\therefore \quad v_1(H) = 2.182 \times 10^6\ \text{ms}^{-1}$$

$$v_2\ (\text{light}) = 3.0 \times 10^8\ \text{ms}^{-1}$$

$$\therefore \quad \frac{v_1}{v_2} = \frac{2.182 \times 10^6}{3.0 \times 10^8} = 7.273 \times 10^{-3}$$

124. (d) $\frac{1}{\lambda} = R_H Z^2\left[\frac{1}{n_1^2} - \frac{1}{n_2^2}\right]$

For first line of H-atom in Lyman series $n_1 = 1,\ n_2 = 2$

$$\therefore \quad \frac{1}{\lambda_H} = R_H\left[\frac{1}{1^2} - \frac{1}{2^2}\right] = 0.75 R_H$$

For He^+

$$\frac{1}{\lambda_{He^+}} = 4R_H\left[\frac{1}{n_1^2} - \frac{1}{n_2^2}\right]$$

Given, $\lambda_H = \lambda_{He^+}$

$$\therefore \quad 0.75 = 4\left[\frac{1}{n_1^2} - \frac{1}{n_2^2}\right]$$

If $n_1 = 4$ and $n_2 = 2$

then, $0.75 = 4\left[\frac{1}{2^2} - \frac{1}{4^2}\right] = 4\left[\frac{1}{4} - \frac{1}{16}\right]$

$$= 4 \times \frac{12}{64} = 0.75$$

Thus, true.

125. (a) $(\text{IE})_{He^+} = 13.6\left(\frac{Z^2}{n^2}\right) = 13.6 \times 4$

$$= 54.4\ \text{eV}$$

Energy absorbed $= 54.4 \times 1.5 = 81.6\ \text{eV}$

Thus, $\quad \Delta E = 81.6 - 54.4$

$$= 27.2\ \text{eV}$$

$$\therefore \quad \text{KE} = 27.2 \times 1.6 \times 10^{-19}\ \text{J}$$

$$\lambda = \frac{h}{\sqrt{2m\,(\text{KE})}}$$

$$= \frac{6.626 \times 10^{-34}\ \text{Js}}{\sqrt{2 \times 9.1 \times 10^{-31}\ \text{kg} \times 27.2 \times 1.6 \times 10^{-19}}}$$

$$= 2.35 \times 10^{-10}\ \text{m} = 2.35\ \text{Å}$$

126. (c) $hv = \phi + \frac{1}{2}mv^2$

$\phi = 3.44 \times 10^{-18}$ J (work function)

$$\frac{1}{2}mv^2 = \frac{1}{2}(9.1 \times 10^{-31}\ \text{kg})(1.03 \times 10^6\ \text{m s}^{-1})^2$$

$$= 4.83 \times 10^{-19}\ \text{J}$$

■ 1 kg m²s⁻² = 1 J

$$\therefore \quad hv = 3.44 \times 10^{-18} + 4.83 \times 10^{-19}$$

$$= 3.923 \times 10^{-18}\ \text{J}$$

$$\frac{hc}{\lambda} = 3.923 \times 10^{-18}\ \text{J}$$

$$\therefore \quad \lambda = \frac{6.626 \times 10^{-34}\ \text{Js} \times 3 \times 10^8\ \text{m s}^{-1}}{3.923 \times 10^{-18}\ \text{J}}$$

$$= 5.067 \times 10^{-8}\ \text{m}$$

$$= 506.7 \times 10^{-10}\ \text{m} = 506.7\ \text{Å}$$

127. (d) Work function is the binding energy

$$hv = hv_0 + \frac{1}{2}mv^2$$

$$\phi = hv_0 = \frac{hc}{\lambda} - \frac{1}{2}mv^2$$

$$= \frac{6.626 \times 10^{-34} \times 3 \times 10^8}{150 \times 10^{-12}} - \frac{1}{2}[9.1 \times 10^{-31} \times (2.24 \times 10^7)^2]$$

$$= 1.0968 \times 10^{-15}\ \text{J}$$

$$= \frac{1.0968 \times 10^{-15}\ \text{J}}{1.6 \times 10^{-19}\ \text{J eV}^{-1}} = 6856\ \text{eV}$$

■ 1eV = 1.6 × 10⁻¹⁹ J

128. (b) $\Delta E = (E_{n_2} - E_{n_1})$

$$E = -2.17 \times 10^{-18}\left(\frac{Z^2}{n^2}\right)\ \text{J atom}^{-1}$$

$$E_1 = -(\text{IE})_H$$

$$= -2.17 \times 10^{-18}\ \text{J atom}^{-1}$$

$$E_2 = \frac{-2.17 \times 10^{-18}}{4}\ \text{J atom}^{-1}$$

$$\therefore \quad \Delta E = \left(2.17 \times 10^{-18} - \frac{2.17 \times 10^{-18}}{4}\right)$$

$$= 2.17 \times 10^{-18} \times 0.75\ \text{J}$$

$$\therefore \quad \Delta E = hv = \frac{hc}{\lambda}$$

$$\therefore \quad \lambda = \frac{hc}{\Delta E}$$

$$= \frac{6.626 \times 10^{-34} \times 3 \times 10^8\ \text{J m}}{2.17 \times 10^{-18} \times 0.75\ \text{J}}$$

$$= 1.22 \times 10^{-7}\ \text{m}$$

$$= 122 \times 10^{-9}\ \text{m} = 122\ \text{nm}$$

■ For quick calculation, $hc = 2 \times 10^{-25}$ J m

129. (a) $E_n = \frac{-13.6Z^2}{n^2}$

Third excited state, $n = 4$

E_4 (species with atomic number Z)

$$= \frac{13.6Z^2}{4^2}$$

$$E_3(He^+) = \frac{-13.6 \times (2)^2}{3^2}$$

Given, E_4 (H-like species)

$$= 2.25 \times E_3(He^+)$$

$$\frac{-13.6Z^2}{16} = \frac{13.6 \times 4}{9} \times 2.25$$

$$\therefore \quad Z^2 = \frac{64}{9} \times 2.25 = 16$$

$$\therefore \quad Z = 4$$

130. (d) For Balmer series, $n_1 = 2$

For α-line in this series, $n_2 = 3$ and for β-line in this series, $n_2 = 4$

$$\frac{1}{\lambda_\beta} = \bar{R}_H Z^2\left[\frac{1}{n_1^2} - \frac{1}{n_2^2}\right]$$

$$= \bar{R}_H Z^2\left[\frac{1}{2^2} - \frac{1}{4^2}\right] = 4\bar{R}_H\left(\frac{12}{64}\right)$$

$$\frac{1}{\lambda_\alpha} = \bar{R}_H Z^2\left[\frac{1}{2^2} - \frac{1}{3^2}\right] = 4\bar{R}_H\left(\frac{5}{36}\right)$$

$$\frac{\lambda_\alpha}{\lambda_\beta} = \frac{12}{64} \times \frac{36}{5}$$

$$\lambda_\alpha = \lambda_\beta\left(\frac{12}{64} \times \frac{36}{5}\right)$$

$$= 4815\left(\frac{12}{64} \times \frac{36}{5}\right)\text{Å} = 6500\ \text{Å}$$

131. (b) $E_Z = -13.6\frac{Z^2}{n^2}$

$$E_H = \frac{-36.6\ \text{eV}}{n_1^2}$$

$$E_{He^+} = \frac{-13.6(2)^2}{(n^2)} = \frac{-13.6 \times (2)^2}{n_2^2}$$

$$E_{Li^{2+}} = -13.6\left(\frac{3}{n_3}\right)^2$$

$$E_{Be^{3+}} = -13.6\left(\frac{4}{n_4}\right)^2$$

If $E_H = E_{He^+} = E_{Li^{2+}} = E_{Be^{3+}}$

then, $n_1 = 1;\ n_2 = 2$

$n_3 = 3;\ n_4 = 4$

132. (a) de-Broglie equation is

$$\lambda = \frac{h}{p}$$

Also, $\Delta x = \lambda = \frac{h}{p}$

$\Delta x \cdot \Delta p \approx \frac{h}{4\pi}$

$\therefore \frac{h}{p} \Delta p \approx \frac{h}{4\pi}$

$\therefore \frac{\Delta p}{p} = \frac{1}{4\pi} \Rightarrow \frac{m\Delta v}{mv} = \frac{1}{4\pi}$

Thus, % error in the measurement of velocity is

$\therefore \frac{\Delta v}{v} \times 100 = \frac{100}{4\pi} = 7.96\%$

133. (c) Radial distributed function $= 4\pi r^2 \psi^2$

Most probable distance of r is obtained from

$$\frac{d}{dr}[4\pi r^2 \psi^2] = 0$$

$$\therefore \frac{d}{dr}[4\pi r^2 (Ne^{-2Zr/a_0})] = 0$$

$$8\pi N e^{-2Zr/a_0}\left[1 - \frac{Zr}{a_0}\right] = 0$$

$\therefore \quad r = a_0$ (for $Z = 1$)

134. (c) When radial node is formed $\psi^2 = 0$

$$\left[\frac{1}{4\sqrt{2\pi}}\left(\frac{1}{a_0}\right)^{3/2}\left(2 - \frac{r}{a_0}\right)e^{-r/2a_0}\right]^2 = 0$$

or $\left(2 - \frac{r}{a_0}\right) = 0$

$\therefore \quad r = 2a_0$

135. (b) $\sqrt{v} = a(Z - b) = aZ - ab$

It is a straight line, $y = mx - c$

Slope $= a = \tan 45° = 1$

$OA = ab = 1$

$\therefore \; b = 1$

$\therefore \sqrt{400} = Z - 1$

$\therefore \quad Z = 21$ (Sc)

$\therefore$ Electronic configuration is $[Ar]4s^2 3d^1$

For this $n = 3, l = 2, m = -2, s = +\frac{1}{2}$

136. (d) Angular momentum is quantised

$\therefore \; mvr_n = \frac{nh}{2\pi}$

But, $r_n = \frac{n^2 a_0}{Z}$

$\therefore \; mv\left(\frac{n^2 a_0}{Z}\right) = \frac{nh}{2\pi} \Rightarrow mv\left(\frac{na_0}{Z}\right) = \frac{h}{2\pi}$

In third orbit of He^+ ion, $n = 3, Z = 2$

$mv\left(\frac{3a_0}{2}\right) = \frac{h}{2\pi}$

$\therefore \quad mv = \frac{h}{3a_0\pi}$

$\therefore \quad \lambda = \frac{h}{mv} = 3a_0\pi$

137. (b) $\bar{v} = \frac{1}{\lambda} = \bar{R}_H Z^2\left[\frac{1}{n_1^2} - \frac{1}{n_2^2}\right]$

λ is shortest if $n_2 \to \infty$

For Lyman series, $n_1 = 1$

$\therefore \quad \frac{1}{\lambda_{min}} = \frac{4\bar{R}_H}{1^2} = 4\bar{R}_H \quad \therefore \quad \bar{R}_H = \frac{1}{4x}$

λ is longest, if $n_2 = (n_1 + 1)$ and for Balmer series, $n_1 = 2$

$$\therefore \quad \frac{1}{\lambda_{max}} = \bar{R}_H Z^2\left[\frac{1}{n_1^2} - \frac{1}{n_2^2}\right]$$

$$= \frac{1}{4x}(4)^2\left[\frac{1}{2^2} - \frac{1}{3^2}\right] = \frac{4}{x}\left[\frac{1}{4} - \frac{1}{9}\right]$$

$$\frac{1}{\lambda_{max}} = \frac{5}{9x} \quad \therefore \quad \lambda_{max} = \frac{9x}{5}$$

138. (d) If principle quantum number $= n$ then azimuthal quantum number

$l = 0, 1, 2, \ldots (n-1)$

Total orbitals $= (2l + 1)$

Total electrons $= 2(2l + 1)$

For any energy level n

Total electrons $= \sum_{l=0}^{l=(n-1)} 2(2l + 1)$

139. (b) If this condition of three electrons is applicable, K(19) has electronic configuration, each orbital having 3 electrons : $1s^3\, 2s^3\, 2p^9\, 3s^3\, 3p^1$.

Thus, p-block.

140. (a)

n	l	m	s	electron
1	0	0	$\pm\frac{1}{2}$	2 $1s^2$
	1	−1 0 +1	$\pm\frac{1}{2}$ $\pm\frac{1}{2}$ $\pm\frac{1}{2}$ $\pm\frac{1}{2}$	6 $1p^6$
2	0	0	$\pm\frac{1}{2}$	2 $2s^2$
	1	−1 0 +1	$\pm\frac{1}{2}$ $\pm\frac{1}{2}$ $\pm\frac{1}{2}$	6 $2p^6$
	2	−2 −1 0 +1 +2	$\pm\frac{1}{2}$ $\pm\frac{1}{2}$ $\pm\frac{1}{2}$ $\pm\frac{1}{2}$ $\pm\frac{1}{2}$	10 $2d^{10}$

n	l	m	s	electron
3	0	0		2 $3s^2$
	1	−1, 0, +1		6 $3p^6$
	2	−2, −1, 0, +1 , +2		10 $3d^{10}$
	3	−3, −2, −1, 0, +1, +2, +3		14 $3f^{14}$

Energy order is

$1s < 1p < 2s < 2p < 3s < 2d$

Electronic configuration is of Sc(21) is

$1s^2 1p^6 2s^2 2p^6 3s^2 2d^3$

1	1	1		

$2d^3$

Unpaired electrons = 3

$\therefore$ Magnetic moment $= \sqrt{N(N+2)}$ BM

$= \sqrt{15}$ BM

141. (b) $E = N_0 h\nu = N_0 \frac{hc}{\lambda}$

$$= \frac{6.02 \times 10^{23}\, mol^{-1} \times 6.626 \times 10^{-34}\, Js \times 3 \times 10^8\, ms^{-1}}{560 \times 10^{-9}\, m}$$

$= 213688$ J

Lamp power $= 100$ W $= 100\, Js^{-1}$

Thus, time required $= \frac{213688\text{ J}}{100\, Js^{-1}}$

$= 213688$ s $= 36$ min

142. (d) $\Delta x =$ (for electron and helium)

$= 1.0$ mm $= 1.0 \times 10^{-3}$ m

Δp (electron) $= 5.0 \times 10^{-26}$ kg ms^{-1}

$\therefore \quad m_e \Delta v = 5.0 \times 10^{-26}$ kg ms^{-1}

$9.1 \times 10^{-31}\; \Delta v = 5.0 \times 10^{-26}$

$\therefore \quad \Delta v = \frac{5.0 \times 10^{-26}}{9.1 \times 10^{-31}}\, ms^{-1}$

$\therefore \; \Delta p$ (helium) $= m_{He}\, \Delta v$

$= \left(\frac{4 \times 10^{-3}}{6.02 \times 10^{23}}\right)\frac{5.0 \times 10^{-26}}{9.1 \times 10^{-31}}$

$= 3.65 \times 10^{-19}$ kg ms^{-1}

■ Mass of helium atom $= \frac{4}{N_0}$

143. (b) U is potential energy $= \frac{-Ze^2}{r}$

∇^2 is Laplacian operator

144. (a) KE $= kT = \frac{R}{N_0}T$

when k is Boltzmann's constant

$$KE = \frac{8.3143\ \text{Jmol}^{-1}\text{K}^{-1} \times 300\ \text{K}}{6.02 \times 10^{23}\ \text{mol}^{-1}}$$

$$= 4.143 \times 10^{-21}\ \text{J}$$

m (neutron) $= 1.675 \times 10^{-27}$ kg

$$\therefore\ \lambda = \frac{h}{\sqrt{2m\text{KE}}}$$

$$= \frac{6.626 \times 10^{-34}}{\sqrt{2 \times 1.675 \times 10^{-27} \times 4.143 \times 10^{-21}}}$$

$$= 1.778 \times 10^{-10}\ \text{m} = 178 \times 10^{-12}\ \text{m}$$

$$= 178\ \text{pm}$$

■ 1×10^{-12} m = 1 pm

145. (a) $\frac{1}{\lambda} = \overline{R}_H Z^2 \left[\frac{1}{n_1^2} - \frac{1}{n_2^2}\right]$

λ is shortest if $n_2 \to \infty$

$$\frac{1}{\lambda_{\min}} = \overline{R}_H \frac{Z^2}{n_1^2}$$

For Paschen series, $n_1 = 3$

For H-atom

$$\frac{1}{(821 \times 10^{-9})_H} = \frac{\overline{R}_H}{9}$$

For Li^{2+} ion

$$\frac{1}{\lambda_{Li^{2+}}} = \overline{R}_H\left(\frac{9}{9}\right) = \overline{R}_H = \frac{9}{821 \times 10^{-9}}$$

$$\therefore\ \lambda_{Li^{2+}} = \frac{821 \times 10^{-9}}{9}$$

$$= 91.2 \times 10^{-9}\ \text{m} = 91.2\ \text{nm}$$

146. (b) $\Delta E = (E_2 - E_1)$

$$= \frac{1}{2}m(v_2^2 - v_1^2)$$

If $v_1 = 100 - 1 = 99\ \text{ms}^{-1}$ then

$v_2 = 100 + 1 = 101\ \text{ms}^{-1}$

$$\Delta E = \frac{1}{2} \times 9.1 \times 10^{-31}[(101)^2 - (99)^2]$$

$$= 1.82 \times 10^{-28}\ \text{J}$$

By Heisenberg's uncertainty principle

$$\Delta E \cdot \Delta t \geq \frac{h}{4\pi}$$

$$\therefore\ \Delta t = \frac{6.626 \times 10^{-34}}{4\pi \times 1.82 \times 10^{-28}} = 2.89 \times 10^{-7}\ \text{s}$$

$$= 0.289 \times 10^{-6}\ \text{s} = 0.3\ \mu\text{s}$$

■ 1 μs = 1×10^{-6} s

147. (d) Energies are additives

$$E = E_1 + E_2$$

$$\frac{hc}{\lambda} = \frac{hc}{\lambda_1} + \frac{hc}{\lambda_2}$$

$$\therefore\ \frac{1}{\lambda} = \frac{1}{\lambda_1} + \frac{1}{\lambda_2}$$

$$\frac{1}{300} = \frac{1}{760} + \frac{1}{\lambda_2}$$

$$\therefore\ \lambda_2 = 496\ \text{nm}$$

148. (d) $\lambda = \frac{h}{\sqrt{2m\text{KE}}}$

For particle X,

$$\lambda_x = \frac{h}{\sqrt{2m_x(\text{KE})_x}}$$

and for particle Y,

$$\lambda_y = \frac{h}{\sqrt{2m_y(\text{KE})_y}}$$

$$\therefore\ \frac{(\text{KE})_x}{(\text{KE})_y} = \left(\frac{\lambda_y}{\lambda_x}\right)^2\left(\frac{m_y}{m_x}\right) = \left(\frac{4}{1}\right)^2\left(\frac{m_y}{9m_y}\right)$$

$$= \frac{16}{9} \text{ or } 16:9$$

149. (a) $\psi \propto e^{-r/a_0}$

Probability $\propto \psi^2$

$$\psi^2 \propto e^{-2r/a_0}$$

If $r = 0$, (at the nucleus)

$\psi^2 \propto e^0 = 1$ (maximum)

Thus, probability is maximum when electron is at the nucleus.

150. (a) Probability $= 4\pi r^2\psi^2\delta r$

$$= 4\pi r^2\left(\frac{e^{-r/a_0}}{(\pi a_0)^{3/2}}\right)^2 \delta r = 4r^2\left(\frac{e^{-2r/a_0}}{(a_0)^3}\right)\delta r$$

Given, $\delta r = 1.0\ \text{pm} = 1.0 \times 10^{-12}$ m and

$r = a_0$

$$\text{then probability} = 4a_0^2\left(\frac{e^{-2a_0/a_0}}{a_0^3}\right)\delta r$$

$$= \frac{4e^{-2}}{a_0}\delta r$$

$$= \frac{4(0.14) \times 1.0 \times 10^{-12}}{0.529 \times 10^{-10}}$$

$$= 0.01$$

151. (b) By photoelectric effect,

$$hv = hv_0 + (\text{KE})$$

***In case* I**

$$hv_1 = hv_0 + (\text{KE})_1$$

***In case* II**

$$hv_2 = hv_0 + (\text{KE})_2$$

$$(\text{KE})_1 = hv_1 - hv_0 = h(v_1 - v_0)$$

$$(\text{KE})_2 = hv_2 - hv_0 = h(v_2 - v_0)$$

$$\frac{(\text{KE})_1}{(\text{KE})_2} = \frac{1}{k} = \frac{v_1 - v_0}{v_2 - v_0}$$

$$\therefore\ kv_1 - kv_0 = v_2 - v_0$$

$$kv_1 - v_2 = kv_0 - v_0 = (k-1)v_0$$

$$\therefore\ v_0 = \frac{kv_1 - v_2}{(k-1)}$$

152. (d) By Bohr's theory,

$$\overline{v} = \frac{1}{\lambda} = R_H Z^2 \left[\frac{1}{n_1^2} - \frac{1}{n_2^2}\right]$$

For He^+, $Z = 2$

$$\therefore\ \frac{1}{\lambda} = 4R_H\left[\frac{1}{n_1^2} - \frac{1}{n_2^2}\right]$$

For ground state, $n_1 = 1$

$$\therefore\ \frac{1}{\lambda} = 4R_H\left[\frac{1}{1^2} - \frac{1}{n_2^2}\right]$$

$$\frac{1}{4\lambda R_H} = 1 - \frac{1}{n_2^2}$$

$$\frac{1}{n_2^2} = 1 - \frac{1}{4\lambda R_H}$$

$$\frac{1}{n_2^2} = \frac{4\lambda R_H - 1}{4\lambda R_H}$$

$$\therefore\ n_2 = \sqrt{\frac{4\lambda R_H}{4\lambda R_H - 1}} = 2\sqrt{\frac{\lambda R_H}{4\lambda R_H - 1}}$$

153. (b) For spectral line in the H-atom or H-like ion

$$\frac{1}{\lambda} = \overline{R}_H Z^2\left[\frac{1}{n_1^2} - \frac{1}{n_2^2}\right]$$

For Li^{2+} ($Z = 3$) and for lyman series, $n_1 = 1$

$$\therefore\ \frac{1}{\lambda_{n_2}} = 9\overline{R}_H\left(\frac{1}{1^2} - \frac{1}{n_2^2}\right) = 9R_H\left[\frac{n_2^2 - 1}{n_2^2}\right]$$

$$\text{and } \frac{1}{\lambda_{n_3}} = 9\overline{R}_H\left[\frac{1}{1^2} - \frac{1}{n_3^2}\right] = 9R_H\left[\frac{n_3^2 - 1}{n_3^2}\right]$$

$$\therefore\ \frac{\lambda_{n_2}}{\lambda_{n_3}} = \left[\frac{n_3^2 - 1}{n_3^2}\right]\left[\frac{n_2^2}{n_2^2 - 1}\right]$$

$$= \left(\frac{n_2}{n_3}\right)^2\left[\frac{(n_3^2 - 1)}{(n_2^2 - 1)}\right]$$

154. (c) For Balmer series,

$$\frac{1}{\lambda} = \overline{R}_H Z^2\left[\frac{1}{2^2} - \frac{1}{n^2}\right]$$

For He^+, $Z = 2$

$$\therefore\ \frac{1}{\lambda} = 4R_H\left(\frac{1}{2^2} - \frac{1}{n^2}\right)$$

$$= 4R_H\left[\frac{n^2 - 4}{4n^2}\right] = R_H\left[\frac{n^2 - 4}{n^2}\right]$$

$$\therefore\ \lambda = \frac{n^2}{R_H(n^2 - 4)}$$

$$= \frac{1}{R_H}\frac{n^2}{(n+2)(n-2)}$$

$$\lambda = k\frac{n^2}{(n+2)(n-2)}$$

$$\therefore\ k = \frac{1}{R_H}$$

155. (a) By photoelectric effect,

$$h\nu = h\nu_0 + \frac{1}{2}mu^2$$

Energy of electron in H-atom = – E
then its ionisation energy = E

Also, $(IE)_Z = (IE)_H \dfrac{Z^2}{n^2}$

$\therefore$ $(IE)_{Na^{10+}} = (E)\dfrac{(11)^2}{(1)^2} = 121\,E$

$\therefore$ $h\nu = E_p$

and $h\nu_o = 121E$

$\therefore$ $(E_p - 121E) = \frac{1}{2}mu^2$

$\therefore$ $u = \sqrt{\dfrac{2(E_p - 121E)}{m}}$

156. (c) This graph shows the probability (P) of finding the electron within shell at various distances (r) from the nucleus (radial probability). The curve shows maximum, which means that the radial probability is greatest for a given distance from the nucleus. This distance is equal to Bohr's radius = a_0

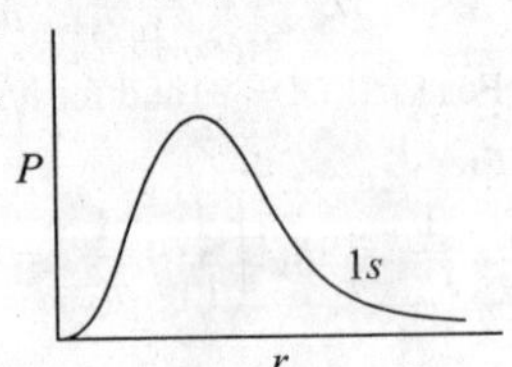

(a) It is for 2s-orbital .
(b) It is radial wave function for 1s orbital
(c) Correct
(d) Probability cannot be zero at a certain distance from nucleus.

157. (c) According to Bohr's model,

$$mvr = \frac{nh}{2\pi} \Rightarrow (mv)^2 = \frac{n^2h^2}{4\pi^2r^2}$$

$$\Rightarrow \quad KE = \frac{1}{2}mv^2 = \frac{n^2h^2}{8\pi^2r^2m} \quad \ldots \text{(i)}$$

Also, Bohr's radius for H-atom is
$r = n^2a_0$

Substituting 'r' in Eq. (i) gives

$$KE = \frac{h^2}{8\pi^2n^2a_0^2m}$$

when n = 2, (given),

$$KE = \frac{h^2}{32\pi^2a_0^2m}$$

158. (a) The number of radial nodes is given by expression $(n - l - 1)$
For 3s, (n = 3, l = 0)
number of nodes = 3 – 0 – 1 = 2
For 2p, (n = 2, l = 1) number of nodes
= 2 – 1 – 1 = 0

Type II. Statement Based Questions

159. (b) **160.** (a) **161.** (d)
162. (a) **163.** (a) **164.** (a)
165. (c) **166.** (c) **167.** (b)
168. (b) **169.** (a) **170.** (a)
171. (c)

Type III. MCQs with ONE or More than One Correct Alternate

172. (a, b, c, d)

173. (a, b, c, d) Most probable distance is when

$$\frac{d}{dr}[4\pi r^2\psi^2] = 0$$

$$N.\frac{d}{dr}[4\pi r^2\, e^{-2Zr/a_o}] = 0$$

This gives $r = \dfrac{a_0}{Z} = \dfrac{a_0}{2}$ for He^+

174. (a, b, c) More negative energy implies that electron is tightly bound. Thus, except (d), all statements are correct.

175. (b, c)

176. (a, b) $E_n = \dfrac{-13.6Z^2}{n^2}$ eV

For He^+, $Z = 2, E_n = -3.4$ eV

$\therefore$ $-3.4 = \dfrac{-13.6 \times (2)^2}{n^2}$

$\therefore$ $n = 4$

Also l = 2 (azimuthal quantum number)
Thus d-orbital
Thus, ψ state is 4d state
Thus (a) is correct
Angular nodes = l = 2
Thus (b) is correct
Radial nodes = $(n - l - 1)$
= (4 – 2 – 1) = 1
Thus (c) is incorrect.

177. (b, c)

Fe^{2+} : (Ar) | ⇅ | 1 | 1 | 1 | 1 |

N (unpaired electrons) = 4

$\therefore$ $\mu = \sqrt{N(N+2)}$ B.M
$= \sqrt{24}$ B.M = 4.90 B.M

Mn^+ : (Ar) | 1 | 1 | 1 | 1 | 1 | | 1 |
$3d^5$ $4s^1$

$N = 6$
$\mu = \sqrt{48}$ = 6.93 B.M

Cr : (Ar) | 1 | 1 | 1 | 1 | 1 | | 1 |

$N = 6$
$\therefore$ μ = 6.93 BM

Co^{3+} : (Ar) | ⇅ | 1 | 1 | 1 | 1 |

$N = 4$
$\therefore$ $\mu = \sqrt{24}$ = 4.90 B.M

178. (a, b, d) $\nu = \dfrac{c}{\lambda} = c\,\bar{\nu}\ s^{-1}$

$E = h\nu = hc\bar{\nu}$
$= 6.626 \times 10^{-34}$ Js $\times 3 \times 10^8$ ms^{-1} $\times 100$ m^{-1}
$= 2.0 \times 10^{-23}$ J per photon (correct)
$= 2.0 \times 10^{-23} \times 6.02 \times 10^{23}$ J per mol of photons
$= 12.04$ J $= 1.2 \times 10^{-2}$ kJ (correct)
$= \dfrac{2.0 \times 10^{-23}}{1.0 \times 10^{-7}} = 2.0 \times 10^{-16}$ ergs per photon (incorrect)
$= \dfrac{1.2 \times 10^{-2} \times 2.0 \times 10^{-3}}{8.314 \times 10^{-3}}$ kcal mol^{-1}
$= 2.9 \times 10^{-3}$ kcal mol^{-1} (correct)

■ 1 J = 1×10^7 ergs

8.314 J = 2.0 cal
Thus, conversion factor joule to cal is
$= \dfrac{2.0}{8.314}$

$hc = 2.0 \times 10^{-25}$ J m

179. (a, b, d)

180. (a, b, c, d)

(a) $He^+(g)$ is ionised to $He^{2+}(g)$ thus, first ionisation energy of $He^+(g)$ is 54.4 eV correct.

(b) (I-III) gives
$He(g) \longrightarrow He^+(g)$, ΔH = 24.6 eV
Thus, correct

(c) $He(g) \longrightarrow He^+(g) + e^-$, first ionisation
$He^+(g) \longrightarrow He^+(g) + e^-$, second ionisation
Thus, second ionisation energy of He(g) is 54.4 eV

(d) $He^{2+}(g) + 2e^- \longrightarrow He(g)$
$\Delta H° = -79$ eV
Thus, correct

181. (a, b, c)

182. (a, b, c) If Aufban rule is not followed, sub-orbits are filled in sequence.
$1s < 2s < 2p < 3s < 3p < 3d < 4s$

(a) M^{2+} (24) : $1s^2\ 2s^2\ 2p^6\ 3s^2\ 3p^6\ 3d^8$ for M
$1s^2\ 2s^2\ 2p^6\ 3s^2\ 3p^6\ 3d^6$ for M^{2+}

(b) M (24) : [Ar] $3d^6$
(c) M^+ (24) : [Ar] $3d^6$
(d) M (19) : [Ar] $3d^1$
Thus, (a), (b) and (c) are incorrect

183. (a, c) $\psi = \sqrt{N}\, e^{-Zr/a_0}$

Radial probability density $= 4\pi r^2\ \psi^2$

$$P = 4\pi r^2\ (N)\ e^{-2Zr/a_0}$$

Density (ρ) is maximum, when

$$\frac{dP}{dr} = 0$$

This gives $r = a_0$, thus (a) is correct when $r > 1$Å, (P) falls to zero as shown by graph.

184. (a, b, c, d) $E_n = \frac{-13.6Z^2}{n^2}$

$$E_4(\text{Be}^{3+}) = -13.6\left(\frac{4}{4}\right)^2 = -13.6 \text{ eV}$$

(a) $E_1(\text{H}) = -13.6$ eV

(b) $E_2(\text{He}^+) = -13.6\left(\frac{2}{2}\right)^2 = -13.6$ eV

(c) $E_3(\text{Li}^{2+}) = -13.6\left(\frac{3}{3}\right)^2 = -13.6$ eV

(d) $E_{11} = (\text{Na}^{10+}) = -13.6\left(\frac{11}{11}\right)^2$

$$= -13.6 \text{ eV}$$

185. (a, b, c, d)

186. (a,b,c)

187. (a, b, c, d) $\bar{\nu} = \frac{1}{\lambda} = \bar{R}_H\ Z^2\left[\frac{1}{n_1^2} - \frac{1}{n_2^2}\right]$

For α-line is Balmer series, $n_1 = 2$, $n_2 = 3$

$$\therefore \quad x\text{m}^{-1} = \bar{R}_H(2)^2\left[\frac{1}{2^2} - \frac{1}{3^2}\right]$$

$$= \bar{R}_H(4)\left(\frac{5}{36}\right)$$

$$\therefore \quad \bar{R}_H = \frac{9}{5}x$$

(a) $\frac{1}{\lambda_\alpha} = (\bar{R}_H)\ (4)^2\left[\frac{1}{2^2} - \frac{1}{3^2}\right]$

$$= \left(\frac{9}{5}x\right)(16)\left(\frac{5}{36}\right) = 4x$$

$$\therefore \lambda_\alpha = \frac{1}{4x}\text{ m}$$

(b) For β-line in Balmer series

$n_1 = 2$, $n_2 = 4$

$$\therefore\ \bar{\nu}_\beta = \bar{R}_H(4)^2\left[\frac{1}{2^2} - \frac{1}{4^2}\right]$$

$$= \left(\frac{9}{5}x\right)(16)\frac{12}{64}$$

$$= \frac{27}{5}x = 5.4x\,\text{m}^{-1}$$

(c) $\frac{1}{\lambda_{max}} = \bar{R}_H\ Z^2\left[\frac{1}{n_1^2} - \frac{1}{n_2^2}\right]$

λ_{max} is when $n_2 = (n_1 + 1)$, $n_1 = 2$ for Balmer series.

$$\frac{1}{\lambda_{max}} = \frac{9}{5}x\ (3)^2\left[\frac{1}{2^2} - \frac{1}{3^2}\right]$$

Thus, it is α-line

$$\frac{1}{\lambda_{max}} = \frac{81\,x}{5}\left(\frac{5}{36}\right)$$

$$\frac{1}{\lambda_{max}} = \frac{9}{4}x$$

$$\therefore \quad \lambda_{max} = \frac{4}{9x}\text{ m}$$

(d) $\frac{1}{\lambda_{min}}$ is when $n_2 \to \infty$

$$\therefore \quad \frac{1}{\lambda_{min}} = \frac{\bar{R}_H\ Z^2}{n_1^2}$$

$$= \frac{9}{5}x\ \frac{(4)^2}{(3)^2} = \frac{16x}{5}$$

$$\therefore \quad \lambda_{min} = \frac{5}{16x}\text{ m}$$

188. (a, b, d)

(a) Linear momentum $p = mv$

$$\text{Velocity} \propto \frac{Z}{n}$$

$$\therefore \quad \frac{p_1}{p_2} = \frac{n_2 Z_1}{n_1 Z_2}$$

Thus, correct

(b) Angular momentum $(L) = mvr_n$

$$\propto m\left(\frac{Z}{n}\right)\left(\frac{n^2 a_0}{Z}\right) \propto n$$

$$\therefore \quad \frac{L_1}{L_2} = \frac{n_1}{n_2}$$

(c) $\text{KE} = \frac{kZe^2}{r_n} = \frac{kZe^2}{n^2 a_0 / Z} = k\frac{Z^2}{n^2}\frac{e^2}{a_0}$

$$\therefore \quad (\text{KE}) \propto \left(\frac{Z}{n}\right)^2$$

$$\frac{(\text{KE})_1}{(\text{KE})_2} = \left(\frac{Z_1 n_2}{Z_2 n_1}\right)^2$$

(d) $\text{Frequency} = \left(\frac{\text{Velocity}}{2\pi r}\right)$

$$\because \text{ Frequency } (\nu) \propto \frac{Z^2}{n^3}$$

Since, velocity $\propto \frac{Z}{n}$ and $r_n \propto \frac{n^2}{Z}$

$$\therefore \quad \frac{\nu_1}{\nu_2} = \left(\frac{Z_1}{Z_2}\right)^2\left(\frac{n_2}{n_1}\right)^3$$

189. (a,b,c) If $\nu = \nu_0$

$$h\nu = h\nu_0 + \frac{1}{2}mv^2$$

then, $\quad \text{KE} = \frac{1}{2}mv^2 = 0$

Thus, statement (d) is incorrect. All the other statements (a), (b) and (c) are correct.

190. (a,c,d) Probability $= 4\pi r^2 \psi^2\ \delta r$

(a) When $r = 0$, $\psi^2 = 0$

(b) When centred at the Bohr's radius

$$r = a_0$$

$$\psi = \left(\frac{1}{32\,\pi a_0^3}\right)^{1/2}\left(2 - \frac{a_0}{a_0}\right)e^{-1/2}$$

$$= \left(\frac{1}{32\pi\, a_0^3\ e}\right)^{1/2}$$

$$\therefore\ \psi^2 = \left(\frac{1}{32\pi a_0^3 e}\right)$$

$$8r^3 = 1\text{ pm}^3 = 1\times10^{-36}\text{ pm}$$

$$8r = 1\times10^{-12}\text{ m}$$

$$\therefore \text{Probability} = 4\pi a_0^2\ \frac{1}{32\pi a_0^3 e}\times1\times10^{-12}$$

$$= \left(\frac{10^{-12}}{8\,a_0 e}\right)$$

Thus, (b) is incorrect but (d) is correct.

(c) When $\quad r = 2a_0$

$$\psi = 0$$

$$\therefore \quad \psi^2 = 0$$

Thus, (c) is correct

Type IV. Passage Based MCQs (Comprehension)

Passage 1

$$\sqrt{\nu} = a(Z - b)$$

For Mg, $\quad \nu = \frac{c}{\lambda} = \frac{3\times10^8\ \text{ms}^{-1}}{9.87\times10^{-10}\ \text{m}}$

$$= 3.04\times10^{17}\ \text{s}^{-1}$$

$$\therefore \quad \sqrt{\nu_{Mg}} = 5.51\times10^8$$

Similarly, for Cr

$$\sqrt{\nu_{Cr}} = 1.14\times10^9$$

$\therefore\ 5.51\times10^8 = a(12 - b)$ for Mg

$1.14\times10^9 = a(24 - b)$ for Cr

$\therefore$ On solving $a = 4.90\times10^7$

and $b = 0.75$

For Sr,

$$\sqrt{\nu_{Sr}} = 4.90\times10^7\,(38 - 0.75)$$

$$\nu_{Sr} = 3.33\times10^{18}\ \text{s}^{-1}$$

$$\lambda = \frac{c}{\nu} = \frac{3\times10^8\ \text{ms}^{-1}}{3.33\times10^{18}\ \text{s}^{-1}}$$

$$= 9.01\times10^{-11}\ \text{m} = 90.1\ \text{pm}$$

and for Cl,

$$\lambda = 4.73\times10^{-10}\text{m}$$

$$= 473\times10^{-12}\ \text{m} = 473\ \text{pm}$$

191. (a) **192.** (b)

Passage 2

$$\Delta E_Z = h\nu = \frac{hc}{\lambda}$$
$$= \frac{6.626 \times 10^{-34}\ \text{Js} \times 3 \times 10^{-8}\ \text{m s}^{-1}}{3.05 \times 10^{-8}\ \text{m}}$$
$$= 6.52 \times 10^{-18}\ \text{J}$$

When transition is from $n = 2$ to $n = 1$ level, for H-atom

$$\Delta E_H = 2.178 \times 10^{-18}\ \text{J}\left[\frac{1}{n_1^2} - \frac{1}{n_2^2}\right]$$
$$= 2.178 \times 10^{-18}\left[\frac{1}{1^2} - \frac{1}{2^2}\right]$$
$$= 0.75 \times 2.178 \times 10^{-18}$$

If atomic number of the element under study is Z, then

$$\Delta E_Z = \Delta E_H\ Z^2$$
$$6.52 \times 10^{-18} = 0.75 \times 2.178 \times 10^{-18}(Z^2)$$
$$Z^2 = 4$$
$$Z = 2$$

193. (c) **194.** (b)

Passage 3

He^+ and Li^{2+} are isoelectronic of H-atom, Li^{2+} (g) is ionised. Thus, energy required is ionisation enthalpy.

Also, $(IE)_Z = Z^2(IE)_H$

$(IE)_{He^+} = 4(IE)_H$

$(IE)_{Li^{2+}} = 9(IE)_H$

$$(IE)_{Li^{2+}} = (IE)_{He^+}\ \frac{9}{4}$$
$$= 54.4 \times \frac{9}{4} = 122.4\ \text{eV}$$

On adding given equations

$$He(g) \longrightarrow He^{2+}(g) + 2e^-,\quad \Delta H° = 79.0\ \text{eV}$$
$$\therefore He^{2+}(g) + 2e^- \longrightarrow He(g)\ \Delta H° = -79.0\ \text{eV}$$

α-particle

195. (c) **196.** (d)

Passage 4

197. (a) When centred at the nucleus

$r = 0$

Probability $= 4\pi r^2 \psi^2\ dr = 0$

Thus, correct

(b) When $r = 2a_0$ for H atom $Z = 1$

$\psi_{2s} = 0$

Thus, probability $= 0$

198. At Bohr's radius $r = a_0$

$$(a) \therefore \psi_{2s} = \left(\frac{1}{32\pi a_0^3}\right)^{1/2} e^{-\frac{1}{2}}$$
$$= \left(\frac{1}{32\ \pi a_0^3\ e}\right)^{1/2}$$
$$dr^3 = 1\ \text{pm}^3 = 1 \times 10^{-36}\ \text{m}^3$$
$$\therefore\ dr = 1 \times 10^{-12}\ \text{m}$$

Pobability $= \psi_{2s}^2\ 4\pi r^2\ dr$

$$= \frac{1}{32\ \pi a_0^3\ e} 4\pi a_0^2\ 10^{-12} = \left(\frac{10^{-12}}{8a_0 e}\right)$$
$$(b)\ \psi_{2s}(He^+) = \left(\frac{1}{32\pi a_0^3}\right)^{1/2}\left(2 - \frac{2a_0}{a_0}\right)$$
$$e^{-1} = 0$$
$$\psi_{2s}(H) = \left(\frac{1}{32\pi a_0^3}\right)^{1/2}\left(2 - \frac{2a_0}{a_0}\right) e^{-1}$$

(c) Is also true as in (b)

197. (c) **198.** (d)

Passage 5

$$pV = nRT$$
$$\therefore\ n = \frac{pV}{RT} = \frac{1 \times 0.224}{0.0821 \times 273}$$
$$= 0.01\ \text{mol}\ H_2\ \text{molecules}$$
$$= 0.02\ \text{mol H atom}$$

■ 0.0821 × 273 = 22.4 L for quick calculation.

Energy required involves two steps :

$$H_2(g) \xrightarrow{(E_1)} 2H(g) \xrightarrow[\text{to } 2^{nd}\ \text{level}]{\text{Excited } (E_2)}$$
$$E_1 = 436\ \text{kJ mol}^{-1} \times 0.01\ \text{mol}$$
$$= 4.36\ \text{kJ} = 4.36 \times 10^3\ \text{J}$$

Energy of H-atom in ground state

$= 13.6\ \text{eV atom}^{-1}$

$= 13.6 \times 1.6 \times 10^{-19}\ \text{J atom}^{-1}$

$= 13.6 \times 1.6 \times 10^{-19} \times 6.02 \times 10^{23}\ \text{J mol}^{-1}$

$= 1.31 \times 10^6\ \text{J mol}^{-1}$

$$\Delta E = 1.31 \times 10^6\left[\frac{1}{1^2} - \frac{1}{2^2}\right]\text{J mol}^{-1}\ \text{H-atom}$$
$$= 0.02 \times 1.31 \times 10^6\left[\frac{3}{4}\right]\text{J}$$

for 0.02 mol H-atom

$= 1.965 \times 10^4\ \text{J}$

$\therefore$ Total energy required

$= 4.36 \times 10^3 + 1.965 \times 10^4\ \text{J}$

$= 2.392 \times 10^4\ \text{J}$

$$\text{BE of one H—H bond} = \frac{4.36 \times 10^3\ \text{J}}{6.02 \times 10^{23}}$$
$$\therefore\ E = h\nu = \frac{hc}{\lambda}$$
$$\therefore\ \lambda = \frac{hc}{E}$$
$$= \frac{6.626 \times 10^{-34} \times 3 \times 10^8 \times 6.02 \times 10^{23}\ \text{m}}{436 \times 10^3}$$
$$= 2.74 \times 10^{-7}\ \text{m} = 274\ \text{nm}$$

■ For quick calculation, $hc = 2 \times 0^{-25}$ J-m

199. (a) **200.** (d)

Passage 6

(a) Velocity of electron in H-atom in ground state $= 2.186 \times 10^6\ \text{m s}^{-1}$

(c) Velocity of light (c) $= 3.0 \times 10^8\ \text{m s}^{-1}$

$$\therefore\ \frac{v}{c} = \frac{2.186 \times 10^6}{3.0 \times 10^8} = 7.29 \times 10^{-3}$$

Distance travelled by an electron in first orbit $= 2\pi r_1$

$= 2\pi \times 0.529 \times 10^{-10}\ \text{m}$

$$\therefore\ \text{Time taken } t = \frac{2\pi \times 0.529 \times 10^{-10}\ \text{m}}{2.186 \times 10^6\text{m s}^{-1}}$$
$$= 1.5205 \times 10^{-16}\ \text{s}$$
$$\therefore\ \text{Number of revolutions per second} = \frac{1}{t}$$
$$= 6.577 \times 10^{15}\ \text{s}$$

201. (a) **202.** (c)

Passage 7

$$P(r) = \frac{4Z^3}{a_0^3} r^2 e^{-2Zr/a_0}$$

For maximum probability $\frac{dP(r)}{dr} = 0$

$$\therefore\ \frac{4Z^3}{a_0^3}\left(2r - \frac{2Zr^2}{a_0}\right) e^{-2Zr/a_0} = 0$$
$$\therefore\ r = \frac{a_0}{Z} = a_0\ \text{(for H-atom)}$$

$\therefore$ Maximum probability for H-atom

$$= \frac{4}{a_0^3}(a_0)^2\ e^{-2} = \frac{4}{a_0 e^2}$$

For Be^{3+}, $Z = 4$

$$\therefore\ r = \frac{a_0}{4}$$

203. (b) **204.** (a)

Passage 8

$$E_\lambda = \frac{a}{\lambda^5\ (e^{b/\lambda T} - 1)}$$

when λ is small

$$e^{b/\lambda T} >> 1$$

Thus, $(e^{b/\lambda T} - 1) \approx 1$

$$E_\lambda = \frac{a}{\lambda^5}\ e^{(-b/\lambda T)}$$

This is identical to Wien's relation.

When λ is high

$$e^{b/\lambda T} \approx 1 + \frac{b}{\lambda T}$$
$$\therefore\ E_\lambda = \frac{a}{\lambda^5}\ \frac{1}{(e^{b/\lambda T} - 1)}$$
$$= \frac{a}{\lambda^5\left(1 + \frac{b}{\lambda T} - 1\right)} = \frac{a\lambda T}{\lambda^5 b}$$
$$= \frac{aT}{\lambda^4 b}\left(= \frac{8\pi kT}{\lambda^4}\right)$$

Thus is identical to Rayleigh-Jeans relation provided $\left(\frac{a}{b}\right) = 8\pi k$

205. (a) **206.** (b)

Passage 9

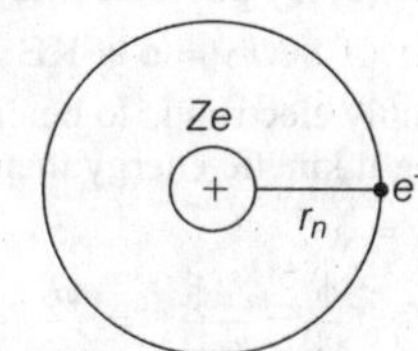

For a general case, when electron of mass m_e revolves round the nucleus of charge Ze,

$$r_n = \frac{n^2h^2}{4\pi^2 m_e kZe^2} = 0.529\times10^{-10}\text{ m}$$

for $Z = 1, n = 1$

When, mass $= 208m_e$

and $Z = +3$ then

$$r_n = \frac{n^2h^2}{4\pi^2 k(208m_e)\times 3e^2}$$

$$= \frac{n^2h^2}{4\pi^2 km_e e^2\times624}$$

$$= \left(\frac{h^2}{4\pi^2 km_e e^2}\right)\frac{n^2}{624}$$

$$= \frac{n^2\times0.529\times10^{-10}}{624}\text{ m}$$

$$= (8.50\times10^{-14}\,n^2)\text{ m}$$

For this radius, $8.50\times10^{-14}\,n^2 = a_0$

$$= 0.529\times10^{-10}$$

$$n^2 = 624$$

$$n \approx 25$$

$$\Delta E = E_2 - E_1$$

$$\frac{1}{\lambda} = \frac{2\pi^2 mZ^2e^4k^2}{ch^3}\left[\frac{1}{n_1^2}-\frac{1}{n_2^2}\right]$$

for H-like species,

In this case, $m = 208m_e$ and $Ze = 3e$

$$\therefore \quad Z^2e^2 = 9e^2$$

$$\therefore \frac{1}{\lambda} = \frac{2\pi^2(208m)(9e^4)k^2}{ch^3}\left[\frac{1}{n_1^2}-\frac{1}{n_2^2}\right]$$

For H-atom, $R_H = \dfrac{2\pi^2me^4k^2}{ch^3}$

$$= 1.09679\times10^7\text{ m}^{-1}$$

$\therefore$ For this present case,

$$R_H' = R_H\times9\times208$$

$$\therefore \frac{1}{\lambda'} = 1.09679\times10^7\times9\times208\text{ m}^{-1}\left[\frac{1}{1^2}-\frac{1}{3^2}\right]$$

$$= 4.87\times10^{-11}\times\frac{8}{9}$$

$$= 5.5\times10^{-11}\text{ m} = 55.0\text{ pm}$$

207. (b) ***208.*** (c)

209. (a)

Passage 10

210. (b) S_1 is spherically symmetrical state, i.e. it corresponds to a *s*-orbital. Also, it has one radial node.

Number of radial nodes $= n - l - 1$

$$n - 0 - 1 = 1$$

$n = 2$, i.e. $S_1 = 2s$ orbital

211. (c) Ground state energy of electron in H-atom (E_H)

$$E_H = \frac{kZ^2}{n^2} = k(Z=1, n=1)$$

For S_1 state of Li^{2+},

$$E = \frac{k(3)^2}{(2^2)} = \frac{9}{4}k = 2.25\,k$$

212. (b) In S_2 state,

$$E(Li^{2+}) = k\text{ (given)}$$

$$k = \frac{9k}{n^2} \Rightarrow n = 3$$

Since, S_2 has one radial node.

$$3 - l - 1 = 1 \Rightarrow l = 1$$

Type V. Numerical Skills

213. **Six (6)** $h\nu = h\nu_0 + \frac{1}{2}mv^2$

$$\therefore \text{KE} = \frac{1}{2}mv^2 = (h\nu - h\nu_0)$$

$$= \left(\frac{hc}{\lambda} - \text{work function}\right)$$

$$= \left(\frac{6.626\times10^{-34}\times3\times10^8}{1850\times10^{-10}}\right) - (2.96\times1.6\times10^{-19})$$

$$= (10.74\times10^{-19} - 4.74\times10^{-19})\text{ J}$$

$$= 6.0\times10^{-19}\text{ J}$$

■ 1 eV = 1.6×10^{-19} J

$hc = 2.0\times10^{-25}$ J - m

214. **One (1)** Bohr's radius of H-atom in ground state $= a_0$

$$\frac{n^2a_0}{Z} = a_0$$

$$n^2 = Z$$

$$n^2 = 4(Be^{3+})$$

$$n = 2$$

But it is ($n = 2$) is n^{th} excited state

Thus, first excited $n = 1$

215. **Two (2)** $\bar{\nu} = \frac{1}{\lambda} = R_H Z^2\left[\frac{1}{n_1^2}-\frac{1}{n_2^2}\right]$

$$\frac{1}{3.0\times10^{-8}} = 1.09679(Z^2)\left[\frac{1}{1^2}-\frac{1}{2^2}\right]$$

$$Z^2 = 4$$

$$\therefore \quad Z = 2$$

216. **Eight (8)** Time period $= \dfrac{\text{Circumference}}{\text{Velocity}}$

$$T = \frac{2\pi r_n}{v}$$

Velocity $\propto \dfrac{Z}{n}$ and $r_n = \dfrac{n^2a_0}{Z}$

$$\therefore \text{ Time period} = \frac{2\pi\left(\dfrac{n^2a_0}{Z}\right)}{Z/n}$$

$$T \propto n^3/Z^2$$

$$\therefore \quad \frac{T_1}{T_3} = \left(\frac{n_1}{n_3}\right)^3 = \left(\frac{6}{3}\right)^3 = 8$$

217. **Two (2)** $\lambda = \dfrac{h}{\sqrt{2m\text{ eV}}}$

$$\therefore \frac{\lambda_{\text{proton}}}{\lambda_{\alpha\text{-particle}}} = \sqrt{\frac{m(\alpha\text{-particle})}{m(\text{proton})}} = \sqrt{\frac{4}{1}} = 2$$

218. **Nine (9)** Ratio of time periods is

$$\frac{T_1}{T_2} = \left(\frac{n_1}{n_2}\right)^3\left(\frac{Z_2}{Z_1}\right)^2$$

$$n_1 = n_2 = 2\text{ given}$$

$$Z_2 = 3\text{ for }Li^{2+}\text{ ion}$$

and $\quad Z_1 = 1$ for H-atom

$$\therefore \quad \frac{T_1\,(\text{H})}{T_2\,(Li^{2+})} = \left(\frac{3}{1}\right)^2 = 9$$

219. **Four (4)** $\bar{\nu} = \frac{1}{\lambda} = (Z^2)R_H\left[\frac{1}{n_1^2}-\frac{1}{n_2^2}\right]$

$$\frac{1}{2170\times10^{-9}} = (1)^2(1.09679\times10^7)\left[\frac{1}{n_1^2}-\frac{1}{7^2}\right]$$

$$\frac{1}{n_1^2} = \left[\frac{1}{49} + \frac{1}{2170\times10^{-9}\times1.09679\times10^7}\right]$$

$$= 0.0204 + 0.042 = 0.0624$$

$$n_1^2 = 16 \Rightarrow n_1 = 4.0$$

220. **Four (4)** Most probable value of r is obtained from

$$\frac{d}{dr}(4\pi r^2\psi^2) = 0$$

$$\frac{d}{dr}[4\pi r^2(\sqrt{N}e^{-Zr/a_0})^2] = 0$$

$$\frac{d}{dr}[4\pi r^2Ne^{-2Zr/a_0}] = 0$$

$$\left[8\pi rNe^{-2Zr/a_0} + 4\pi r^2N\left(-\frac{2Z}{a_0}\right)e^{-2Zr/a_0}\right] = 0$$

$$\therefore \quad 8\pi Nre^{-2Zr/a_0}\left[1-\frac{Zr}{a_0}\right] = 0$$

$$\therefore r(\text{most probable}) = \frac{a_0}{Z} = \frac{a_0}{4} = \frac{a_0}{y}$$

(for Be^{3+})

221. **Five (5)** $\psi = \left(\frac{1}{32\pi a_0^3}\right)^{1/2}\left(2 - \frac{r}{a_0}\right)e^{-r/2a_0}$

If $r = a_0$ (Bohr's radius)

$$\psi = \left(\frac{1}{32\pi a_0^3}\right)^{1/2}\left(2 - \frac{a_0}{a_0}\right)e^{-a_0/2a_0}$$

$$\psi = \left(\frac{1}{32\pi a_0^3}\right)^{1/2} e^{-\frac{1}{2}}$$

$$\psi^2 = \frac{1}{32\pi a_0^3 e} = \left(\frac{1}{2}\right)^5 (\pi a_0^3 e)^{-1}$$

$\therefore \quad n = 5$

222. **Two (2)** $\bar{\nu} = \bar{R}_H Z^2\left[\frac{1}{n_1^2} - \frac{1}{n_2^2}\right]$

For maximum wave number $n_2 \longrightarrow \infty$

$$\therefore \quad \bar{\nu}_{max} = \bar{R}_H Z^2\left(\frac{1}{n_1^2}\right)$$

For Balmer series of species X, $n_1 = 2$ with maximum wave number and for the same case for Lyman series of H-atom, $n_1 = 1$

$$\nu_{max} = \bar{R}_H (Z)^2\left[\frac{1}{2^2}\right] = \bar{R}_H (1)^2\left[\frac{1}{1^2}\right]$$

$$Z^2 = 4$$

$$Z = 2$$

223. **Two (2)** This is the case of ionisation

$$(\text{IE})_Z = 13.6\left(\frac{Z^2}{n^2}\right)$$

For one-electron species, $n = 1$

$$(\text{IE})_{Li^{2+}} = 13.6(9) = 122.4$$

$$(\text{IE})_{X^{n+}} = 13.6\,(Z)^2 = 54.4$$

$$\therefore \quad \frac{Z^2}{9} = \frac{54.4}{122.4}$$

$$Z^2 = 4$$

$$Z = 2$$

224. **(222)** By photoelectric effect

$$h\nu = \phi + \text{KE}$$

$$\therefore \quad \text{KE} = h\nu - \phi$$

$$= \frac{hc}{\lambda} - \text{work function}$$

$$= \frac{6.63\times10^{-34}\times3\times10^8}{300\times10^{-9}} - 4.41\times10^{-19}$$

$$= 6.63\times10^{-19} - 4.41\times10^{19}$$

$$= 2.22\times10^{-19}\ \text{J} = 222\times10^{-21}\ \text{J}$$

225. **Four (4)** $\Delta E = N_0 h\nu$

$$= 6.02\times10^{23}\times6.626\times10^{-34}\times1$$

$$= 4.0\times10^{-10}\ \text{J mol}^{-1}$$

$\therefore \quad x = 4$

226. **Five (5)** If $n = 5$, total waves $= n\lambda$

$2\pi r$ = circumference = total waves

$\therefore n = 5$

227. **Six (6)** Total lines when electron falls from n^{th} level to ground state

$$\frac{n(n-1)}{2} = \frac{4\times3}{2} = 6$$

228. **Eight (8)** $\lambda = \frac{h}{mv} = \frac{h}{\sqrt{2m(\text{KE})}}$

But $\quad \text{KE} = \frac{3}{2}RT$

$$\lambda = \frac{h}{\sqrt{3mRT}}$$

$$\lambda_{He} \text{ at } 100\ \text{K} = \frac{h}{\sqrt{3\times4\times100R}} = 750$$

$$\lambda_X \text{ at } 1250\ \text{K} = \frac{h}{\sqrt{3\times m_x\times1250\ \text{K}}} = 150$$

$$\therefore \quad \frac{750}{150} = \sqrt{\frac{1250m_x}{400}}$$

$$\therefore \quad 25 = \frac{1250m_x}{400}$$

$$\therefore \quad m_x = 8$$

229. **Four (4)** $\lambda = \frac{h}{\sqrt{2m(\text{KE})}}$

$$(\text{KE}) = \frac{h^2}{2\lambda^2 m}$$

$$= \frac{1}{2}\left(\frac{6.626\times10^{-34}}{620\times10^{-12}}\right)^2\frac{1}{9.1\times10^{-31}}$$

$$= 6.3\times10^{-19}\ \text{J}$$

$$\therefore \quad \text{Volt} = \frac{6.3\times10^{-19}\ \text{J}}{1.6\times10^{-19}\ \text{J/eV}} \approx 4.0$$

■ 1 eV = 1.6×10^{-19} J

230. **Nine (9)** $E = K\frac{q_1q_2}{r}$

$$= \frac{9.0\times10^{11}\ \text{J cm C}^{-2}(1.0\times10^{-10}\ \text{C}\times1.0\ \text{C})}{1.0\ \text{cm}}$$

$$= 90\ \text{J} = 10x\ \text{J}$$

$\therefore \quad x = 9$

231. **Eight (8)** $h\nu = h\nu_0 + \text{KE}$

$\therefore$ KE $= h(\nu - \nu_0)$

$(\text{KE})_2 = 2(\text{KE})_1$

$\therefore h(\nu_2 - \nu_0) = 2h(\nu_1 - \nu_0)$

$$\nu_0 = 2\nu_1 - \nu_2$$

$$= 2(2.0\times10^{16}) - 3.2\times10^{16}$$

$$= 0.8\times10^{16} = 8.0\times10^{15}\ \text{Hz}$$

$$= x\times10^{15}\ \text{Hz}$$

Thus, $x = 8$

232. **Three (3)** $E = Nh\nu = N\frac{hc}{\lambda}$

$$\therefore \quad N = \frac{E\lambda}{hc} = \frac{101\times590\times10^{-9}}{6.626\times10^{-34}\times3\times10^8}$$

$$= 3.0\times10^{20} = y\times10^{20}$$

■ $hc = 2.0\times10^{-25}$ J m

233. **Three (3)** By photoelectric effect,

$$Nh\nu = \phi + \text{KE}$$

If simply electron is to be ejected without giving it kinetic energy then

$Nh\nu = \phi$

$$N = \frac{\phi}{h\nu} = \frac{\phi}{hc/\lambda} = \frac{\phi\lambda}{c}$$

$$= \frac{4.67\times1.6\times10^{-19}\ \text{J}\times800\times10^{-9}\ \text{m}}{6.626\times10^{-34}\ \text{Js}\times3\times10^8\ \text{ms}^{-1}}$$

$$= 3.0$$

■ $hc = 2.0\times10^{-25}$ Jm

234. **Two (2)** $T \propto \frac{n^3}{Z^2}$

$$\therefore \quad \frac{T_4\ (\text{He}^+ \text{ in fourth orbit})}{T_2\ (\text{H in second orbit})}$$

$$= \left(\frac{n^3}{Z^2}\right)_{He^+}\left(\frac{Z^2}{n^3}\right)_H = \left(\frac{4^3}{2^2}\right)\left(\frac{1^2}{2^3}\right) = 2$$

235. **Three (3)** Energy $= \frac{-hcR_H}{9}$

degeneracy $= 9 = 3^2$

$n = 3$

236. **Eight (8)** $P(r) = \frac{4Z^3}{a_0^3}r^2e^{-2Zr/a_0}$

For maximum probability, $\frac{dP(r)}{dr} = 0$

$$\therefore \quad \frac{4Z^3}{a_0^3}\left(2r - \frac{2Zr^2}{a_0}\right)e^{-2zr/a_0} = 0$$

$$\therefore \quad r = \frac{a_0}{Z}$$

For He$^+$ ion, $Z = 2$

$$\therefore \quad r = \frac{a_0}{2}$$

$\therefore$ Maximum value of $P(r)$

$$= \frac{4(2)^3}{(a_0)^3}\left(\frac{a_0}{2}\right)^2 e^{\frac{-2(2)a_0}{2a_0}}$$

$$= \frac{8}{a_0}e^{-2}$$

$$= \frac{8}{a_0e^2} = \frac{n}{a_0e^2}$$

237. **Nine (9)** Hydride (H$^-$) has electrons = 2

Thus, (H$^-$) electronic configuration (ground state) = $1s^2$

Ground State [↿⇂] ($1s^2$)

First excited state [1] [1] ($1s^1$ $2s^1$)

Second excited state [1] [ ] [1] [ ] [ ] ($1s^1$ $2s^0$ $2p$)

In second excited state, p_x, p_y and p_z are degenerate. Thus, three-fold degeneracy.

- For a single electron, third orbit is the second excited state which has 3*s*, 3*p* and 3*d*-orbitals.

3s	3p			3d				

Total degeneracy $= n^2 = 9$

238. **Six (6)** $|m_l| = 1$ thus, magnetic quantum number = + 1 and – 1

$$(m_s) = -\frac{1}{2}$$

$n = 4$ can have sub-orbits

	l	m_l	m_s
4s	0	0	$+\frac{1}{2}, -\frac{1}{2}$
4p	1	$\underline{-1}, 0, \underline{+1}$	$+\frac{1}{2}, -\frac{1}{2}$
4d	2	$-2, \underline{-1}, 0, \underline{+1}, +2$	
4f	3	$-3, -2, \underline{-1}, 0, \underline{+1}, +2, +3$	

Thus, underlined electrons with $(m_l = -1, +1)$ and spin $-\left(\frac{1}{2}\right)$ are six.

239. **Five (5)** $\text{KE} = \frac{1}{2}mv^2 = \frac{3}{2}RT$

$\therefore \quad m^2v^2 = 2m\text{KE}$

$\therefore \quad mv = \sqrt{2m\text{KE}}$

$$\lambda(\text{wavelength}) = \frac{h}{mv} = \frac{h}{\sqrt{2m\text{KE}}} \propto \frac{h}{\sqrt{2m(T)}}$$

where, T = Temperature in Kelvin

λ(He at – 73°C = 200 K)

$$= \frac{h}{\sqrt{2 \times 4 \times 200}}$$

λ(Ne at 727°C = 1000 K)

$$= \frac{h}{\sqrt{2 \times 20 \times 1000}}$$

$$\therefore \frac{\lambda(\text{He})}{\lambda(\text{Ne})} = M = \sqrt{\frac{2 \times 20 \times 1000}{2 \times 4 \times 200}} = 5$$

Thus, $M = 5$

240. **Nine (9)** When $n = 3$, $l = 0, 1, 2$, i.e. there are 3*s*, 3*p* and 3*d*-orbitals. If all these orbitals are completely occupied as

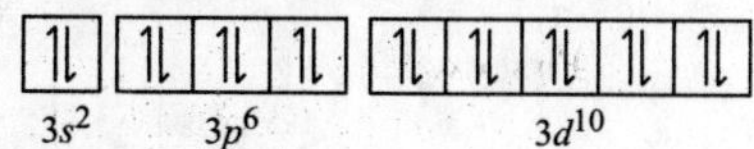

Out of total 18 electrons, 9 electrons with $s = +\frac{1}{2}$ and 9 with $s = -\frac{1}{2}$.

Alternative method in any n^{th} orbit, there can be a maximum of $2n^2$ electrons. Hence, when $n = 3$, number of maximum electrons = 18. Out of these 18 electrons, 9 can have spin $-\frac{1}{2}$ and remaining nine with spin $= +\frac{1}{2}$.

241. **Four (4)** Energy of photon

$$= \frac{hc}{\lambda}\text{ J} = \frac{hc}{e\lambda}\text{ eV}$$

$$= \frac{6.626 \times 10^{-34} \times 3 \times 10^8}{300 \times 10^{-9} \times 1.602 \times 10^{-19}} = 4.14 \text{ eV}$$

For photoelectric effect to occur, energy of incident photons must be greater than work function of metal.

Hence, only Li, Na, K and Mg have work functions less than 4.14 eV.

Type VI. Matrix Matching

242. (c) $\psi_{2s} = \left(\frac{1}{32\pi a_0^3}\right)^{1/2}\left(2 - \frac{Zr}{a_0}\right)e^{-Zr/2a_0}$

Probability $P(r) = 4\pi r^2\psi^2 dr$

$$(dr)^3 = 1\text{pm}^3 = (1 \times 10^{-12})^3\text{m}$$

$$dr = 1 \times 10^{-12}\text{ m}$$

(i) If centred at the nucleas, then $r = 0$

$$P(r) = 0$$

Thus, (i)-(s)

(ii) Electron centered at the Bohr's radius in H-atom

$$r = a_0$$

$$\therefore \quad \psi_{2s} = \left(\frac{1}{32\pi a_0^3}\right)^{\frac{1}{2}} e^{\frac{-1}{2}}$$

$$\therefore \quad \psi_{2s}^2 = \frac{1}{32\pi a_0^3 e}$$

$$P(r) = 4\pi r^2\psi^2 dr$$

$$= 4\pi(a_0)^2\left(\frac{1}{32\pi a_0^3 e}\right)10^{-12}$$

$$= \frac{10^{-12}}{8a_0 e}$$

Thus (ii)-(r)

(iii) $P(r) = 4\pi r^2\psi^2 dr$

$$= 4\pi(2a_0)^2\left(\frac{1}{32\pi a_0^3}\right)\left(2 - \frac{4a_0}{a_0}\right)e^{-2\times 2a_0/a_0}$$

$$= \frac{1}{2a_0}(-2)e^{-4} = -\frac{1}{a_0 e^4}$$

Thus, (iii)-(q)

(iv) When radial node is formed

$$\psi^2 = 0$$

$$\left(\frac{1}{32\pi a_0^3}\right)\left(2 - \frac{r}{a_0}\right)^2 e^{-r/a_0} = 0$$

$$\therefore \quad \left(2 - \frac{r}{a_0}\right) = 0$$

$$\therefore \quad r = 2a_0$$

Thus, (iv)-(p)

243. (d) For α-line in Balmer series, $n_1 = 2$ and $n_2 = 3$

For β-line $n_1 = 2$, $n_2 = 4$

(i) $\therefore \ \bar{\nu} = \frac{1}{\lambda} = \bar{R}_H Z^2\left[\frac{1}{n_1^2} - \frac{1}{n_2^2}\right]$

$$\bar{\nu}_\alpha = \bar{R}_H(4)^2\left[\frac{1}{2^2} - \frac{1}{3^2}\right] = \bar{R}_H(16)\left[\frac{5}{36}\right] = \frac{20\bar{R}_H}{9}$$

$$\bar{\nu}_\beta = \bar{R}_H\,(4)^2\left[\frac{1}{2^2} - \frac{1}{4^2}\right] = \bar{R}_H\,(16)\left[\frac{12}{64}\right] = 3\bar{R}_H$$

$$\text{Difference} = 3\bar{R}_H - \frac{20}{9}\bar{R}_H = \frac{7}{9}\bar{R}_H$$

Thus, (i)-(s)

(ii) For maximum wave number, $n_2 \to \infty$

$$\therefore \quad \bar{\nu}_{\max} = \frac{\bar{R}_H Z^2}{n_1^2}$$

For Brackett series in Li^{2+}, $n_1 = 4$

$$\therefore \quad \bar{\nu}_{\max} = \frac{9}{16}\bar{R}_H$$

Thus, (ii)–(r)

(iii) If $\bar{\nu}$ is maximum, λ is minimum

$$\frac{1}{\lambda_{\min}} = \bar{R}_H Z^2\left[\frac{1}{n_1^2}\right] = \bar{R}_H(2)^2\left[\frac{1}{3^2}\right]$$

$\therefore \ \frac{1}{\lambda_{\min}} = \frac{4}{9}\bar{R}_H$ in Paschen series of He^+

If $\bar{\nu}$ is minimum, λ is maximum and is at $n_2 = (n_1 + 1)$

$$\because \quad \frac{1}{\lambda_{\max}} = 4\bar{R}_H\left[\frac{1}{3^2} - \frac{1}{4^2}\right] = 4\bar{R}_H\left[\frac{7}{144}\right] = \frac{7}{36}\bar{R}_H$$

$$\therefore \quad \lambda_{\max} - \lambda_{\min} = \left[\frac{36}{7} - \frac{9}{4}\right]\frac{1}{\bar{R}_H} = \frac{2.89}{\bar{R}_H}$$

$\therefore$ (iii)–(p)

Rydberg constant of $Be^{3+} = \bar{R}_H(Z^2) = 16\bar{R}_H$

Thus, (iv)–(q)

244. (c) $\sqrt{v} = a(Z - b)$

$$v = \frac{c}{\lambda}$$

$$\therefore \text{ For Sr} = \frac{3 \times 10^8\text{ m s}^{-1}}{90.1 \times 10^{-12}\text{ m}} = 3.293 \times 10^8\text{ s}^{-1}$$

Similarly, for Cl

$$\sqrt{\nu_{Cl}} = 7.964 \times 10^8$$

$$\therefore \quad 1.8147 \times 10^9 = a(38 - b)$$

$$7.964 \times 10^8 = a(17 - b)$$

$$\frac{1.8147 \times 10^9}{7.964 \times 10^8} = \frac{38 - b}{17 - b}$$

$$2.2786 = \frac{38 - b}{17 - b}$$

$b = 0.625$ and $a = 4.855 \times 10^7 \sqrt{s^{-1}}$

Thus, (iv)-(q)

For Mg, $\sqrt{\nu} = 4.855 \times 10^7 (12 - 0.625)$

$$= 552.256 \times 10^6$$

$$\nu = 3.05 \times 10^{17}$$

$$\therefore \quad \lambda = \frac{c}{\nu} = \frac{3 \times 10^8}{3.05 \times 10^{17}}$$

$$= 9.83 \times 10^{-10} = 983 \text{ pm}$$

Thus, (i)-(s)

For (K)

$$\sqrt{\nu} = a(Z - b)$$

$$= 4.855 \times 10^7 (19 - 0.625)$$

$$= 8.92 \times 10^6$$

$$= 7.9585 \times 10^{17} \text{ s}^{-1}$$

$$\therefore \quad \lambda_K = \frac{c}{\nu} = 3.769 \times 10^{-10} \text{ m}$$

$$= 376.9 \text{ pm}$$

Thus, (ii)-(p)

$$h\nu = h\nu_0 + \frac{1}{2}mv^2$$

$$6.626 \times 10^{-34} \times 7.9585 \times 10^{17}$$

$$= h\nu_0 + 3 \times 1.6 \times 10^{-19}$$

$$\therefore \quad \nu_0 = 7.95 \times 10^{17} \text{ s}^{-1}$$

$$\therefore \quad \lambda = \frac{c}{\nu} = \frac{3 \times 10^8 \text{ ms}^{-1}}{7.95 \times 10^{17} \text{ s}^{-1}}$$

$$= 3.77 \times 10^{-10} \text{ m}$$

$$= 377 \text{ pm}$$

Thus, (iii)-(p)

245. (b) (a) (IV) (iv) (r) $\Rightarrow$ incorrect, because, d_{z^2} has no nodal plane.

(b) (II) (ii) (p) $\Rightarrow$ correct, because 2*s*-orbital has 1 radial node.

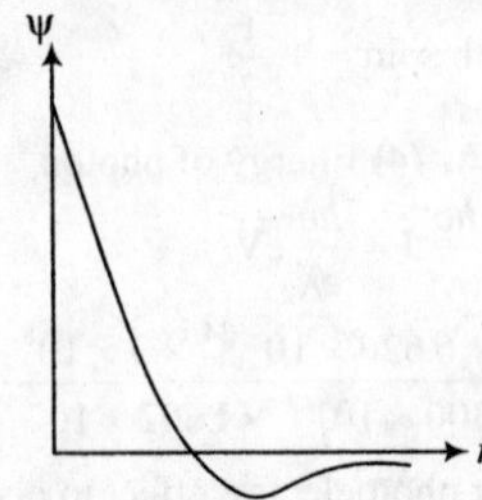

(c) (III) (iii) (P) $\Rightarrow$ incorrect, because probability density for $2p$ at nucleus is zero.

(d) (I) (ii) (S) $\Rightarrow$ incorrect, because 1*s* orbital has no radial node.

246. (d) The option (d) is incorrect because in the wave function of 1*s* orbital, no angular function should be present.

247. (d) We have to select only correct combination hence, the option (d) is correct.

For 1*s* orbital : $\psi_{n,\,l,\,m} \propto \left(\frac{Z}{a_0}\right)^{3/2} e^{\frac{-Zr}{a_0}}$

Energy needed to excite : from $n = 2$ to $n = 4$

$$\Delta E_{2-4} = 13.6\, Z^2 \times \frac{3}{16} \text{ eV}$$

Energy needed to excite from : $n = 2$ to $n = 6$

$$\Delta E_{2-6} = 13.6\, Z^2 \times \frac{8}{36}$$

$$\Delta E_{2-4} = \frac{27}{32} E_{2-6} \text{ (hence, true)}$$

248. (b) (i) Orbital angular momentum (L)

$$= \sqrt{l(l+1)}\, \frac{h}{2\pi}$$

(i)-(q)

i.e. L depends on azimuthal quantum number only.

(ii) To describe a one electron wave function, three quantum numbers n, l and m are needed. Further to abide by exclusion principle, spin quantum number (s) is also needed.

(ii)- (s);'(iii) For shape, size and orientation, only n, l and are needed.

(iii) (p, q, r)

(iv) Probability density (Ψ^2) can be determined if n, l and m are known.

(p, q, r)

249. (a) (i) $V_n = -\frac{1}{4\pi\varepsilon_0}\left(\frac{Ze^2}{r}\right)$

$$K_n = \frac{1}{8\pi\varepsilon_0}\left(\frac{Ze^2}{r}\right)$$

$$\Rightarrow \quad \frac{V_n}{K_n} = -2\,(\Omega)$$

(i)- (r)

(ii) $E_n = -\frac{Ze^2}{8\pi\varepsilon_0 r} \propto r^{-1}$

$$K = -1(q)$$

(ii) - (q)

(iii) Angular momentum

$$= \sqrt{l(l+1)}\, \frac{h}{2\pi} = 0 \text{ in 1s-orbital.}$$

$$l = 0$$

(iii) – (p)

(iv) $r_n = \frac{a_0 n^2}{Z} (p) \Rightarrow \frac{1}{r_n} \propto Z \propto Z^y \quad \therefore$

$$y = 1$$

(iv) - (s)

250. (a) $\text{KE} = \frac{13.6\, Z^2}{n^2}$ eV/atom

$$\text{PE} = -2\text{KE}$$

$$= -\frac{2 \times 13.6 Z^2}{n^2}$$

$$\text{Radius } r_n = \frac{n^2 a_0}{Z} = \frac{0.529 n^2}{Z} \text{ Å}$$

$$\text{Angular momentum} = \frac{nh}{2\pi}$$

States of Matter-I
(Gaseous State)

Chapter Topics
- States of Matter and Intermolecular Forces
- The Gas Laws
- Kinetic Molecular Theory and Molecular Velocities
- Diffusion and Effusion
- Collision Frequency and Mean Free Path
- Real Gas (The van der Waals' Equation)
- Critical Constants

States of Matter and Intermolecular Forces

States of matter

Matter exists in three states; solid, liquid and gas. The states of a matter in the given conditions depend on the net effect of **intermolecular forces** (the forces which act between the molecules of matter) and **thermal energy** (the energy of molecules due to their motion).

In solid state, intermolecular forces are much stronger than thermal energy while in gaseous state the thermal energy is much stronger than intermolecular forces.

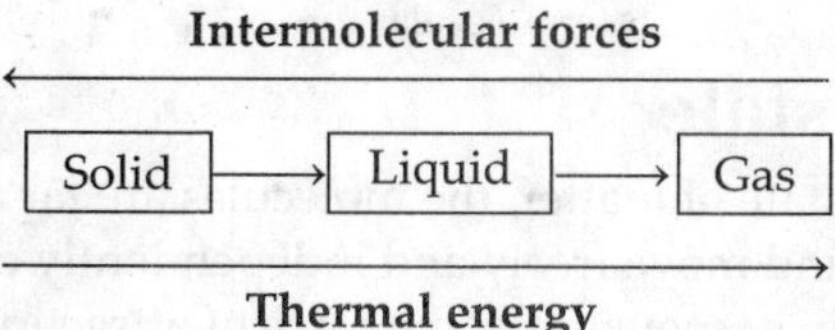

Intermolecular forces

Intermolecular forces are the forces of attraction and repulsion between interacting particles (as atoms and molecules). These are also known as **van der Waals' forces.** Intermolecular forces do not include :

- the electrostatic forces that exist between oppositely charged ions (as Na^+ and Cl^-).
- the forces that hold atoms and molecules together (covalent bonds).

Different types of intermolecular forces are discussed below :

Dispersion forces or London forces

They are weak attractive forces between molecules resulting from the small, instantaneous dipoles that occur because of the varying positions of the electrons during their motion about nuclei.

- Dispersion forces or London forces act mainly in monoatomic or non-polar molecules such as N_2, He, CO_2 etc.
- London forces tend to increase with molecular weight because of more electrons (London forces increase in strength with number of electrons).
- For molecules of about same molecular weight the more compact molecule is less polarisable and thus, London forces are smaller.
- These forces are always attractive in nature and mathematically vary as $\frac{1}{r^6}$, where r is the distance between interactive particles.
- London forces are meaningful only at short distances (~ 500 pm) and are dependent on polarisability of the particle.

Dipole-dipole forces

- These forces act among molecules possessing permanent dipole.
- This dipole-dipole interaction is stronger than the London forces but is weaker than ion-ion interaction as partial charges are involved

$$\overset{\delta+}{\text{H}}-\overset{\delta-}{\text{Cl}}$$

- Dipole-dipole interaction energy between two stationary polar molecules varies as $1/r^3$. Thus, as r increases, dipole-dipole interaction decreases.
- Polar molecules also interact by London forces. Thus, total effect of interaction in polar molecules is due to dipole-dipole interaction and London forces.

Dipole-induced dipole forces

- The forces that act between polar molecules having no dipole moment and molecules having permanent dipole moment are dipole induced dipole forces.
- In neutral molecules, without permanent dipole moment, dipole is induced when it comes in contact with a molecule with permanent dipole moment (by deforming the electron cloud).
- Interaction energy varies as $\frac{1}{r^6}$, due to dipole-induced dipole separated by a distance r.
- Induced dipole moment is dependent on the dipole moment present in the permanent dipole and the polarisability of the electrically neutral molecule.
- Larger the molecule, larger the polarisation and therefore larger the attraction.

Hydrogen bond

- The dipole-dipole interaction between polar hydrogen of one molecule and electronegative atom (N, O, F) of the same molecule (intramolecular) or other molecule (intermolecular) is called **hydrogen bond.**
- This type of interaction gives liquid state to molecules.

$$\cdots\overset{\delta+}{\text{H}}-\overset{\delta-}{\text{F}}\cdots\overset{\delta+}{\text{H}}-\overset{\delta-}{\text{F}}\cdots\overset{\delta+}{\text{H}}-\overset{\delta-}{\text{F}}\cdots \quad \text{(Intermolecular)}$$

(Intramolecular)

- Strength of the H-bonding is determined by the coulombic interaction between the lone pair electrons of electronegative atoms (as N, O, F) of one molecule and the H-atom of the other molecules (or same molecule).
- Larger the electronegativity (F > O > N) and smaller the size (F < O < N), larger the extent of H-bonding.

$$\text{H—F......H} > \text{H—O......H} > \text{H—N......H}$$

Thermal energy

- The energy of constituent particles of matter due to temperature is called thermal energy. It is a measure of average kinetic energy of the particle of the matter and is given by

$$\text{average, KE} = \frac{3}{2}\cdot\frac{RT}{N_0}$$

(R is called gas constant, N_0 the Avogadro's number and $\frac{R}{N_0}$, Boltzmann's constant).

- Thermal energy is responsible for movement of particles.
- When molecular interactions are very weak, molecules do not attract together to give liquid or solid state, unless thermal energy is reduced by lowering the temperature.
- If thermal energy is reduced by lowering the temperature, the gases can be very easily liquefied.
- Extent of thermal energy and intermolecular forces is in order.

$$\text{Solid} \underset{\text{Cool}}{\overset{\Delta}{\rightleftharpoons}} \text{Liquid} \underset{\text{Cool}}{\overset{\Delta}{\rightleftharpoons}} \text{Gas}$$

Thermal energy →

← Intermolecular force

Gaseous state

- In gaseous state of matter, the molecules are far apart from each other and move freely and independently of other molecules. In gaseous state, the force of attraction between the molecules is negligible.

The characteristics properties of gases can be defined in terms of the pressure, temperature, volume, mass and mole.

Several units used for pressure are summarised below :

Name	Symbol	Value
Pascal	Pa	$1\ \text{Pa} = 1\ \text{N m}^{-2} = 1\ \text{kg m}^{-1}\ \text{s}^{-2}$
bar	bar	$1\ \text{bar} = 10^5\ \text{Pa} = 0.987\ \text{atm}$ $1\ \text{atm} = 1.01325\ \text{bar}$
Atmosphere	atm	$1\ \text{atm} = 1.01325 \times 10^5\ \text{Pa}$ $1\ \text{atm} = 1\ \text{g cm}^{-1}\ \text{s}^{-2}$
Torr	Torr	$1\ \text{Torr} = \frac{101325}{760}\ \text{Pa} = 133.322\ \text{Pa}$ $1\ \text{atm} = 760\ \text{Torr}$
Millimetre of mercury	mmHg	$1\ \text{mmHg} = 133.322\ \text{Pa}$

Standard values for reporting data of a gas

Two sets of conditions are widely used as 'standard' values for reporting data.

Condition	T	p	V_m (Molar Volume)
STP/NTP	273.15 K	1 atm	22.414 L
SATP*	298.15 K	1 bar	24.788 L

**Standard Ambient Temperature and Pressure.*

Barometric pressure

Pressure at a height 'h' in the barometer is given by

$$p = h\rho g$$

where 'ρ' is the density of the liquid used in barometer and 'g' is acceleration due to gravity.

If $p°$ is the pressure at sea level, then

$$\log_e \frac{p}{p°} = -\frac{mgh}{RT}$$

or

$$\log_e \frac{p°}{p} = \frac{mgh}{RT}$$

$\left(\frac{mg}{RT}\right)$ being constant, $\log_e \frac{p°}{p}$ increases with height.

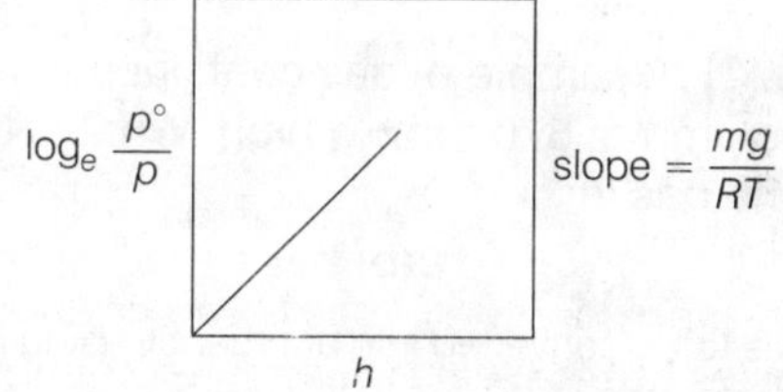

Solved Examples & Instant Practice

Example 3.1) Which would you expect to have the higher force of attraction between molecules? Butane (C_4H_{10}) or acetone (CH_3COCH_3). Also, compare their boiling points.

Force of attraction between the molecules of two compounds can be compared on the basis of their molar mass, in case, molar mass is same then dipole moments need to be compared.

Sol. Both are of equal molar mass (58 g mol^{-1}). Thus, comparison of their dipole moments can give idea about intermolecular forces.

$CH_3CH_2CH_2CH_3$
Butane (non-polar)

$CH_3—C—CH_3$ (C=O) ⟶ $CH_3—C^{\delta+}—CH_3$ (=$O^{\delta-}$)
Acetone (polar)

Thus, intermolecular force of attraction in acetone molecules (due to dipole-dipole interaction) is higher than that in butane. Higher the force of attraction, larger the boiling point. Thus, boiling point of acetone > butane.

Immediate Test 1

Which of the following substances would you expect to have the highest boiling point?

C_3H_8, CO_2, CH_3CN

Example 3.2) Arrange the following substances in the order of increasing intermolecular forces of attraction.

CCl_4, Cl_2, ClNO, N_2

Comparison is based on their molar masses as well as extent of polarity. Larger molar mass implies larger force of attraction.

Sol. Larger the electronegativity difference between bonding atoms, greater the polarity.

CCl_4, Cl_2 and N_2 are non-polar. Thus, strength of dispersion forces should increase with their molar masses.

$$N_2 < Cl_2 < CCl_4$$

Molar mass of Cl_2 (71.0 u) is comparable to that of ClNO (65.5 u), but ClNO is polar. This suggests stronger intermolecular forces in ClNO.

But molar mass of CCl_4 (154.0 u) is much higher than that of ClNO, hence, expected order of intermolecular forces of attraction is

$$N_2 < Cl_2 < ClNO < CCl_4.$$

Immediate Test 2

Arrange the following in increasing order of intermolecular forces of attraction.

Ne, He, Cl_2, $(CH_3)_2CO$, O_2, O_3

Example 3.3) The vapour pressure of water at 298 K is 23.8 Torr. Express this in (a) atm (b) kPa

Sol. We use, 1 atm = 760 Torr = 101.325 kPa

(a) 760 Torr = 1 atm

$$\therefore \ 23.8 \text{ Torr} = \frac{23.8}{760} \text{ atm} = 0.0313 \text{ atm}$$

(b) 760 Torr = 101.325 kPa

$$\therefore \ 23.8 \text{ Torr} = \frac{101.325 \times 23.8}{760} = 3.173 \text{ kPa}$$

Immediate Test 3

(i) A gas in a container had a pressure of 57 kPa. Calculate the pressure in units of atm and mmHg.

(ii) Express the following gas pressures in atm.
(a) 304 cmHg (b) 380 Torr

Example 3.4) A sample of gas contained in a bulb supports a column of 570 mmHg high. What is the pressure of the gas in
(a) Nm^{-2} (b) bar

Sol. One unit is to be converted into another by using conversion factor.

$$1 \text{ Nm}^{-2} = 1 \text{ Pascal}$$

and $$1 \text{ bar} = 1 \times 10^5 \text{ Nm}^{-2}$$

$$1 \text{ atm} = 760 \text{ mmHg} = 101325 \text{ Nm}^{-2} \text{ (Pascal)}$$

$$\text{(a) } 570 \text{ mmHg} = \frac{570}{760} \text{ atm} = \frac{570 \times 101325}{760} \text{Nm}^{-2} \text{ (Pascal)} = 76 \times 10^3 \text{ Pascal (Nm}^{-2})$$

(b) $1 \times 10^5 \text{ Nm}^{-2} = 1 \text{ bar}$

$$\therefore \quad 76 \times 10^3 \text{ Nm}^{-2} = \frac{76 \times 10^3}{1 \times 10^5} = 0.76 \text{ bar}$$

Immediate Test 4

Camphor has been found to undergo a transition at a temperature of 420 K and a pressure of 3.09×10^9 Nm^{-2}. What is transition pressure in
(a) atm (b) bar

Example 3.5) Calculate the difference in pressure between the top and bottom of a vessel 76.00 cm deep when filled at 25° C with
(a) water (b) mercury
Density of mercury at 25° C = 13.6 g cm^{-3} and that of water = 1.0 g cm^{-3}.

Sol. Pressure = $h\rho g$

Take parameters in SI units to get result in Pa.

(a) $p = h \rho g$

$$h = 76 \text{ cm} = \frac{76}{100} = 0.76 \text{ m}, \ \rho = 1.0 \text{ g cm}^{-3} = 1000 \text{ kg m}^{-3},$$

$$g = 9.81 \text{ ms}^{-2}$$

$$p = 0.76 \text{ m} \times 1000 \text{ kg m}^{-3} \times 9.81 \text{ ms}^{-2} = 7.4456 \times 10^3 \text{ kg m}^{-1}\text{s}^{-2} = 7.4456 \times 10^3 \text{ Pa} = 7.4456 \text{ kPa}$$

$$\text{(b) } p = h\rho g = 0.76 \text{ m} \times 13.6 \times 10^3 \text{ kg m}^{-3} \times 9.81 \text{ ms}^{-2} = 101.4 \times 10^3 \text{ kg m}^{-1} \text{ s}^{-2} = 101.4 \text{ kPa}$$

■ $1 \text{ Nm}^{-2} = 1 \text{ kg m}^{-1}\text{s}^{-2} = 1 \text{ Pa}$
$1.0 \text{ g cm}^{-3} = 1000 \text{ kg m}^{-3}$

Example 3.6) What is the gas pressure, if the manometer is filled with mercury ($d = 13.6$ g cm^{-3}), barometric pressure is 748.2 mmHg and the difference in mercury levels is 8.6 mmHg as shown?

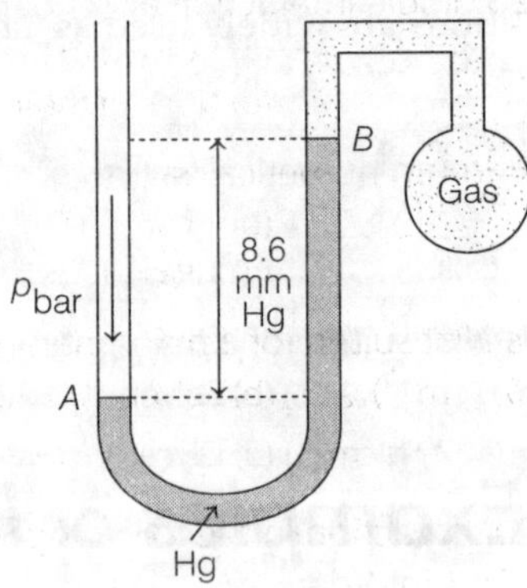

Sol. $p_{gas} = p_{barometric} + \Delta p$

If $A > B$ thus, $\Delta p = (A - B) > 0$
If $A < B$, $\Delta p < 0$

$$p_{gas} = p_{barometric} - \Delta p$$

In this case $A < B$, such that

$$\Delta p < 0 = 8.6 \text{ mmHg}$$

$$\therefore \quad p_{gas} = 748.2 - 8.6 = 739.6 \text{ mmHg}$$

Immediate Test 5

(i) At 298 K, density of mercury is 13.6×10^3 kg m^{-3} and that of water 1.0×10^3 kg m^{-3}. Calculate the height of a column of each liquid that can support a pressure of 1 atm.

(ii) How high a column of air would be necessary to cause the barometer to read 76 cmHg, of the atmosphere of uniform density 1.2 kg m^{-3}? The density of mercury is 13.6×10^3 kg m^{-3}.

(iii) If barometer reads 748.2 mmHg and the gas pressure is 739.6 mmHg, calculate difference in the two levels of liquid, if liquid glycerol is used instead of mercury. d (glycerol) = 1.26 g cm^{-3}.

(iv) A manometer is connected to a bulb containing H_2 gas at 300 K. The open tube reads 400 mm whereas the tube connected to the bulb reads 150 mm.
At the given temperature, barometric pressure is 740 mm. Calculate pressure of the gas in bar.

KNOWLEDGE CONFIRMATION Test 1

1 Arrange the following in the expected order of increasing intermolecular forces of attraction.

I. C_8H_{18} II. $CH_3CH_2CH_2CH_3$
III. C_6H_5CHO IV. SO_3

(a) I < II < III < IV (b) II < IV < I < III
(c) I < II < IV < III (d) I < IV < II < III

2 Highest intermolecular force is in
(a) H_2S (b) H_2O (c) PH_3 (d) CH_4

3 Highest intermolecular force is in
(a) NO (b) O_2 (c) N_2 (d) equal

4 Dipole-induced dipole interaction exists between
(a) HCl and Cl_2 (b) HCl and CH_4
(c) Both of these (d) None of these

5 Which has maximum numerical value?
(a) 1 atm (b) 1 bar
(c) 1 Torr (d) 1 Pascal

6 Which liquid is best suited for a manometer?
(a) H_2O ($d = 1.00$ g cm^{-3}) (b) Solvent ($d = 11.0$ g cm^{-3})
(c) Benzene ($d = 0.879$ g cm^{-3}) (d) Glycerol ($d = 1.25$ g cm^{-3})

7 London force of attraction in the following isomeric pentane (C_5H_{12}) is in order :
I. Pentane II. Isopentane III. Neopentane
(a) I < II < III (b) III < II < I (c) II < III < I (d) I < III < II

8 Dipole-dipole forces act between the molecules possessing permanent dipoles. Ends of dipoles possess partial charges. The partial charge is ***[NCERT Exemplar]***
(a) more than unit electronic charge
(b) equal to unit electronic charge
(c) less than unit electronic charge
(d) double the unit electronic charge

9 Molecules tend to go apart from each other by force *X* and the molecules tend to attract each other by force *Y*. *X* and *Y* are respectively,
(a) intermolecular force and thermal energy
(b) thermal energy and intermolecular forces
(c) both in thermal energy
(d) both in intermolecular forces

10 Select correct order of intermolecular forces (I)/ thermal energy (II) in three phases of matter.
(a) Solid < liquid < gas (II) (b) Solid < liquid < gas (I)
(c) Gas < liquid < solid (II) (d) Liquid < solid < gas (I)

11 Which pair of molecules has the strongest dipole-dipole interactions?
(a) NH_3, CH_4 (b) CH_4, CH_4
(c) CO_2, CO_2 (d) NH_3, NH_3

12 Consider the following compounds :
I. HF II. H_2O
III. (benzene ring with –OH and ortho NO_2) IV. (benzene ring with –OH and COOH)
V. O_2N–(benzene ring)–OH

Intramolecular H-bonding occurs in
(a) I, II, V (b) III, IV, V (c) III, IV (d) III, V

13 Variation of thermal energy with temperature is given by

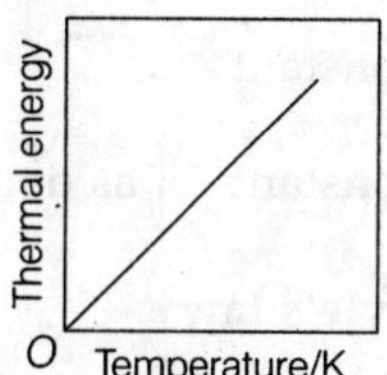

Consider the following facts :
I. Thermal energy is a measure of average kinetic energy given by $= \frac{3}{2}\frac{RT}{N_0}$
II. Thermal energy increases with increase in temperature.
III. Thermal energy is zero at 0°C.
IV. Thermal energy is zero at 0 K.
V. At 0°C, $\left(\frac{\text{Thermal energy}}{273}\right) = \frac{3}{2}\frac{R}{N_0}$

Select correct facts.
(a) All except III (b) All except III and V
(c) All except III, IV and V (d) All except IV and V

14 Dibutylphthalate is commonly used as a liquid in manometers. What pressure is equivalent to a centimetre of this liquid? Density of liquid = 1064.5 kg m^{-3}
(a) 104.43 Nm^{-2} (b) 104.43×10^2 Nm^{-2}
(c) 0.10443 Nm^{-2} (d) None of these

15 Vapour pressure of water is 50 Torr at 313 K. This is equal to
(a) 0.0658 atm (b) 0.0667 bar
(c) 6.667×10^3 Pa (d) All of these

16 If gas pressure is p_1, and barometric pressure p_2, then [Refer Solved Problem (3. 6)]
(a) $p_1 = p_2$, if mercury level in open arm is equal to that attached to closed arm
(b) $p_1 = p_2 + \Delta p$, if mercury level in open arm is higher to that attached to closed arm
(c) $p_1 = p_2 - \Delta p$, if mercury level in open arm is below to that attached to closed arm
(d) All of the above

The Gas Laws

Boyle's law *(Pressure-volume relationship)*

At constant temperature (isothermal condition), the pressure of a fixed amount of a gas (number of moles, n) varies inversely with its volume.

$$(p)_{n,T} \propto \frac{1}{V} \text{ or } (p)_{n,T} = \frac{k}{V}$$

Here, k is constant of proportionality. $(p)_{n,T}$ indicates that fixed amount of gas (in terms of moles n) is taken at constant temperature T

$$pV = \text{constant}$$

- For two or more gases,

$$p_1V_1 = p_2V_2 = \text{constant}$$

Also, $p_1d_2 = p_2d_1 = \text{constant}$ $\left(\text{as density } (d) = \frac{\text{mass}}{\text{volume}}\right)$

Differential form of Boyle's law

$$\therefore \quad \left(\frac{\partial p}{\partial V}\right)_T = -\left(\frac{k}{V^2}\right)_T = -\left(\frac{p}{V}\right)_T$$

Graphical representations of Boyle's law

- **(V-p) Graph** between V and p at constant temperature T is called isotherm.

  Line AB at constant volume can be used to compare pressure of different isotherm $p_3 > p_2 > p_1$ as $T_3 > T_2 > T_1$

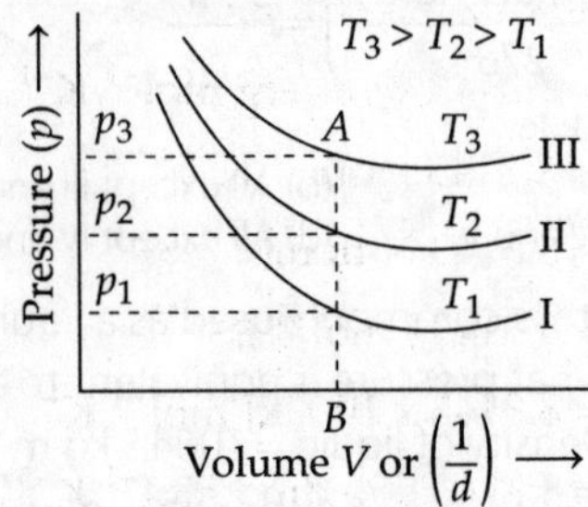

- $\left(\frac{1}{V} - p\right)$ **Graph** is a striaght line, indicates that $\frac{1}{V}$ regularly increases with increase in p.

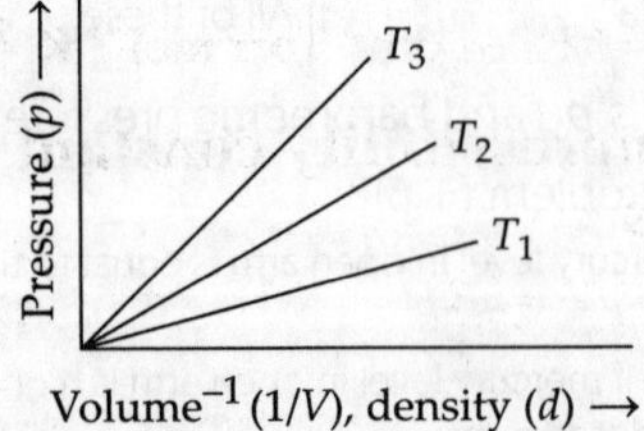

- **(p - pV) Graph** is a straight line parallel to p axis, indicates that value of pV remains constant in spite of regular increase in p at constant temperature.

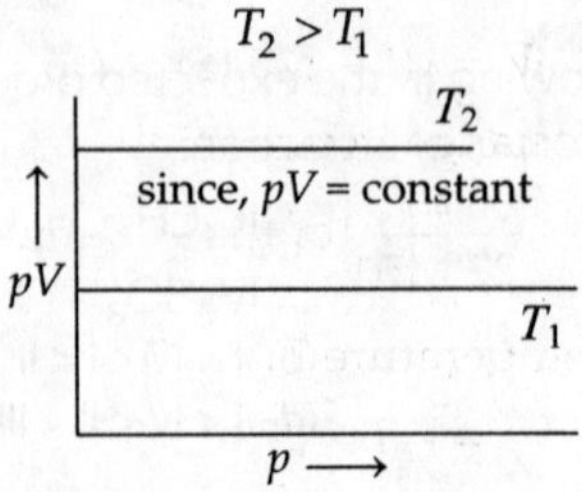

Charles' law

(Temperature-volume relationship)

For a fixed mass of a gas at constant pressure p (under isobaric condition) , volume varies directly with temperature.

$$(V)_{p,n} \propto T$$

$$(V)_{p,n} = kT \qquad (T \text{ is in Kelvin scale})$$

$$\left(\frac{V}{T}\right) = \text{constant}$$

Thus, $V_1T_2 = V_2T_1$

If temperature is taken in °C, then $T = (t + 273.15)$

Differential form of Charle's law

$$\Rightarrow \quad \left(\frac{\partial V}{\partial T}\right)_p = k = \frac{V}{T}$$

Graphical representations of Charle's law

- **(T-V) Graph** is a straight line and a extending it to zero volume, each line intersects the temperature axis at – 273.15°C.

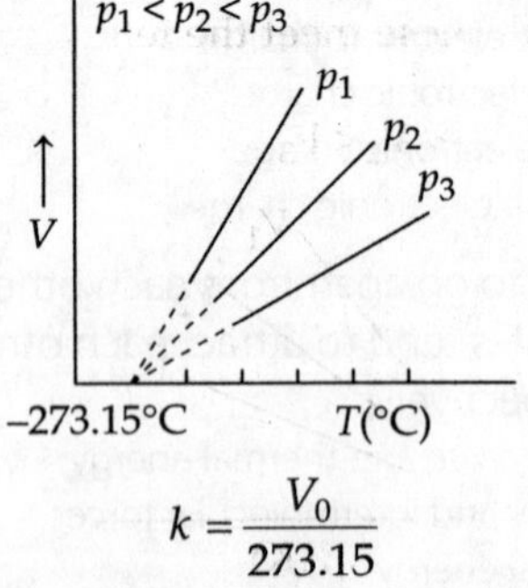

$$k = \frac{V_0}{273.15}$$

- $\left(T - \frac{V}{T}\right)$ **Graph** is a straight line parallel to T-axis indicates that value of $\frac{V}{T}$ remains constant is spite of increase in temperature.

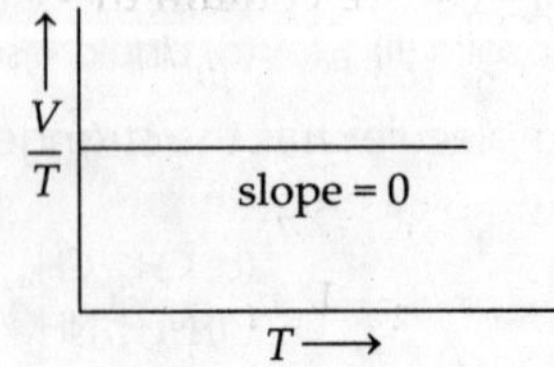

- Also at zero Kelvin, all thermal energy is removed. Thus, no further cooling is possible after all the thermal energy has been removed.

$$V = k(t + 273.15)$$

- Thus, for every 1° change in temperature, the volume of the gas changes by $\left(\frac{1}{273.15}\right)$ of the volume at 0°C.
- Thus, volume at temperature T

$$V_T = V_0 T / 273.15$$

where V_0 is the volume of the gas at 273.15 K.

Gay-Lussac's law

(*Pressure-temperature relationship*)

- At constant volume (For isochoric condition), pressure of the given mass of the gas varies directly with temperature.

$$(p)_{V,n} \propto T$$

$$(p)_{V,n} = kT$$

k = proportionality constant

$$p_1V_1 = p_2V_2 = \text{constant}$$

Also, $$p = p_0\left(1 + \frac{t}{273.15}\right) = p_0(1 + \alpha t)$$

α is called pressure coefficient and p_0 is the pressure of the gas at 273.15 K (0°C).

$$\alpha = \frac{p - p_0}{p_0\, t}$$

Graphical representation of Gay Lussac's law

- p-T graph shows that at different value slopes of graph are different but all these meet the temperature axis on 0 K.

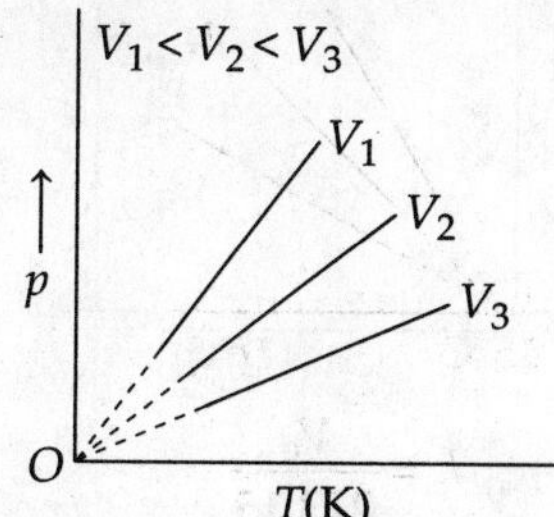

Avogadro's law (*Volume-mole relationship*)

- Equal volumes of any two or more gases at the same temperature and pressure contain the same number of molecules.

$$(V)_{T,p} \propto n \qquad (p \text{ and } T \text{ are constant})$$

$$V = kn$$

$$V_1n_2 = V_2n_1$$

Volume of 1 mole of gas at STP = 22.4 L

$$= 22.4 \times 10^{-3}\ \text{m}^3$$

Differential form of Avogadro's law

$$\left(\frac{\partial V}{\partial n}\right)_{T,p} = k = \frac{V}{n}$$

Ideal gas equation

On the basis of gas laws, the ideal gas equation is

$$\boxed{pV = nRT}$$

where, n = number of moles, R = gas constant.

- R is expressed in the unit of work or energy $\text{mol}^{-1}\ \text{K}^{-1}$.
- In SI unit R has dimension = $\text{Nm K}^{-1}\ \text{mol}^{-1}$ or $(\text{J K}^{-1}\ \text{mol}^{-1})$
- Numerical value of pV by extrapolation at 273.15 K is found to be 22.71 L bar mol^{-1}.

  Thus, $\lim_{p\to} (pV) = 22.71\ \text{L bar mol}^{-1}$

$$\therefore \quad R = \frac{pV}{T} = \frac{22.71\ \text{L bar mol}^{-1}}{273.15\ \text{K}}$$

$$= 0.0831411\ \text{bar mol}^{-1}\ \text{K}^{-1}$$

$$= 0.0831411 \times 0.987\ \text{L atm mol}^{-1}\ \text{K}^{-1}$$

$$= 0.08206\ \text{L atm mol}^{-1}\ \text{K}^{-1}$$

$$= 0.08206 \times 101.325\ \text{J mol}^{-1}\ \text{K}^{-1}$$

$$= 8.314\ \text{J mol}^{-1}\ \text{K}^{-1}$$

Different values of R are summarised below :

$$R = 0.0821\ \text{L atm mol}^{-1}\ \text{K}^{-1}$$

$$= 8.3143 \times 10^7\ \text{erg mol}^{-1}\ \text{K}^{-1}$$

$$= 8.3143\ \text{J mol}^{-1}\ \text{K}^{-1}$$

or $$= 8.3143\ \text{N m mol}^{-1}\ \text{K}^{-1}$$

$$= 8.3143\ \text{J mol}^{-1}\ \text{K}^{-1}$$

$$= 8.3143 \times 10^{-3}\ \text{kJ mol}^{-1}\ \text{K}^{-1}$$

$$= 8.3143\ \text{kPa dm}^3\ \text{mol}^{-1}\ \text{K}^{-1}$$

$$= 1.987\ \text{cal mol}^{-1}\ \text{K}^{-1}$$

$$= 1.987 \times 10^{-3}\ \text{kcal mol}^{-1}\ \text{K}^{-1}$$

$$= 5.189 \times 10^{19}\ \text{eV mol}^{-1}\ \text{K}^{-1}$$

$$= 62.364\ \text{dm}^3\ \text{Torr mol}^{-1}\ \text{K}^{-1}$$

Isothermal compressibility constant for an ideal gas

$$pV = nRT$$

$$\therefore \quad V = \frac{nRT}{p}$$

$$\therefore \quad \left(\frac{\partial V}{\partial p}\right)_{T,n} = -\frac{nRT}{p^2} = -\frac{pV}{p^2} = -\frac{V}{p}$$

$$\therefore \quad -\frac{1}{V}\left(\frac{\partial V}{\partial p}\right)_{T,n} = \frac{1}{p}$$

$-\frac{1}{V}\left(\frac{\partial V}{\partial p}\right)_{T,n}$ is called isothermal compressibility constant for an ideal gas. It is denoted by α.

Similarly, thermal expansion coefficient of an ideal gas is

$$\alpha = \frac{1}{V}\left(\frac{\partial V}{\partial T}\right)_{p,n} = \frac{1}{T}$$

Density and molar mass of gas from ideal gas equation

$$pV = nRT$$

Since, $n = \frac{\text{Mass}}{\text{Molar mass}} = \frac{w}{m}$

$$pV = \frac{w}{m}RT$$

$\therefore$ m (molar mass) $= \frac{wRT}{pV}$

Also, $\frac{w}{V}$ = density $\therefore$ $\boxed{m = \frac{dRT}{p}}$

Dalton's law of partial pressure

When two or more gases, which do not react together chemically, are present in the same container, the total pressure exerted by the mixture is the sum of the partial pressure of each constituent gas.

$$p_{\text{total}} = p_1 + p_2 + p_3 + p_4 + \ldots\ldots \text{ (constant } V, T) = \Sigma p_i$$

where, p_1, p_2, p_3 ...... are the partial pressure of the gases.

Partial pressure of gas $p_i = \chi_i \, p_{\text{total}}$

where, χ_i = mole fraction of gas i.

Gases are generally collected over water and thus moist.

$$\therefore \quad p_{\text{dry air}} = p_{\text{total}} - p_{\text{water vapour}}$$

Pressure of water vapour is called **aqueous tension.**

$$\text{Relative humidity} = \frac{\text{Partial pressure of water in air}}{\text{Vapour pressure of water}}$$

Amagat's law of partial volume

Total volume of a gas mixture is the sum of the partial volumes of the constituents of mixture.

$$V_{\text{total}} = V_1 + V_2 + V_3 + V_4 + \ldots$$

Solved Examples & Instant Practice

Example 3.7) A 38.5 L cylinder of Ar (*g*) is connected to an evacuated 1875 L tank. If the temperature is held constant and the final pressure is 721 mmHg, what must have been the original gas pressure in the cylinder?

Sol. Under isothermal condition, Boyle's law is applicable

Thus, $(p_1V_1)_{T_1} = (p_2V_2)_{T_2}$

$$\therefore \quad p_1 = \frac{p_2V_2}{V_1}$$

If initial $V_1 = 38.5$ L,

final $V_2 = 1875 + 38.5 = 1913.5$ L

$p_1 = ?$ $p_2 = 721$ mmHg

$$p_1 = \frac{721 \times 1913.5}{38.5} \text{ mmHg}$$

$$= 3583.5 \text{ mmHg}$$

$$= \frac{3583.5}{760} = 47.15 \text{ atm}$$

Immediate Test 6

Volume of CO_2 gas equal to 20.0 dm^3 was collected at 300 K and 1.0 bar pressure. What would be the volume of CO_2 collected at 300 K and a pressure reduced by 25%?

Example 3.8) Graphical variation of logarithm form of Boyle's law is represented below such that, $OA = -1.3010$ bar dm^3. What is pressure when volume is 10 dm^3?

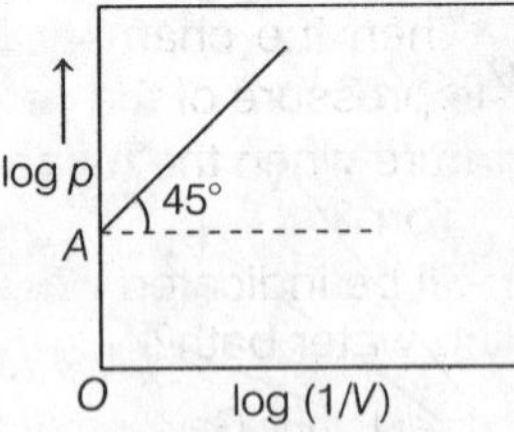

Sol. By Boyle's law, $p = \frac{k}{V}$

This is expressed in logarithm form which is linear.

$$\log p = \log\left(\frac{1}{V}\right) + \log k$$

Compare it with, $y = mx + c$, slope = m, intercept = c = OA

Given, $\log k = -1.3010$ bar dm^3 = OA = $\bar{2}.6990$ bar dm^3

Take antilog, $k = 5 \times 10^{-3}$ bar dm^3

$\therefore$ By Boyle's law, $p = \frac{k}{V} = \frac{5 \times 10^{-3} \text{ bar dm}^3}{10 \text{ dm}^3} = 5 \times 10^{-4}$ bar.

Immediate Test 7

For Boyle's law, isotherm is represented for H_2 gas as given below. What is density of the gas at 0.5 bar?

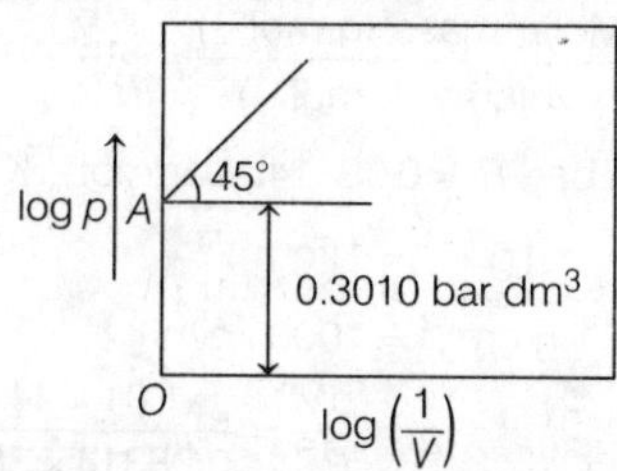

Example 3.9) A given quantity of a gas at 300 K was transferred to new vessel of one-third in volume. What is percentage change in temperature under isobaric condition?

Sol. Under isobaric condition, Charles' law is applicable.

$$V_1T_2 = V_2T_1$$

If $\quad V_1 = V\text{L}$

then, $\quad V_2 = \frac{V}{3}\text{L} \quad$ (One third of initial value)

$$T_1 = 300\text{ K}$$

$\therefore \quad T_2 = \frac{V_2T_1}{V_1} = \frac{V \times 300}{3V} = 100\text{ K}$

Change in temperature (decrease) = 300 − 100 = 200 K

Percentage decrease = $\frac{200}{300} \times 100 = 66.67\%$

Immediate Test 8

On a ship sailing in Pacific Ocean, where temperature is 296.4 K, a balloon is filled with 2 L air. What will be the volume of balloon when the ship reaches Indian Ocean, where the temperature is 299.1K? (assume no change in pressure).

Example 3.10) A quantity of H_2 gas is confined in a chamber of constant volume. When the chamber is immersed in a bath of melting ice, the pressure of the gas is 1000 Torr.

(a) What is temperature when the manometer indicates a pressure of 400 Torr ?

(b) What pressure will be indicated when the chamber is brought in boiling water bath?

Sol. Volume remains constant, thus Gay-Lussac's is applicable

$$p_1T_2 = p_2T_1$$

(a) $p_1T_2 = p_2T_1$

Temperature of melting ice = 0°C = 273 K

$\therefore \quad T_2 = \frac{p_2T_1}{p_1}$

$$T_2 = \frac{400 \times 273}{1000} = 109.2\text{ K}$$

Temperature of boiling water bath = 100° C = 373K

(b) $p_2 = \frac{p_1T_2}{T_1} = \frac{1000 \times 373}{273} = 1366\text{ Torr}$

Immediate Test 9

Based on the following activity, determine temperature T_2 and volume V_{III}

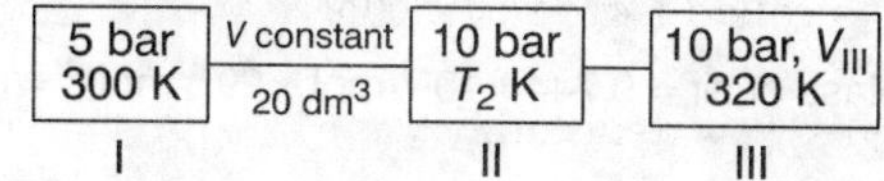

Example 3.11) What volume of N_2 and H_2 will combine to form 3.01×10^{22} molecules of NH_3 at STP ?

Sol. Equation of formation of NH_3

N_2	+	$3H_2$	$\longrightarrow$	$2NH_3$
1 mol		3 mol		2 mol
N_0 molecules		$3\ N_0$ molecules		$2\ N_0$ molecules
1 volume		3 volume		2 volume

At STP, $\quad$ 1 mol = 22.4 L = N_0 molecules

$$6.02 \times 10^{23}\text{ molecules} = 1\text{ mol } NH_3$$

$\therefore \quad 3.01 \times 10^{22}$ molecules = 0.05 mol NH_3

By Avogadro's law, equal volumes of gases contain equal number of molecules or moles.

$$1\text{ mol } NH_3 = 22.4\text{ L at STP}$$

$\therefore \quad 0.05\text{ mol } NH_3 = 1.12\text{ L at STP}$

Thus, $\quad N_2$ required = $\frac{1}{2}$ of NH_3 formed = $\frac{1.12}{2}$ = 0.56 L

H_2 required = $\frac{3}{2}$ of NH_3 formed = $1.12 \times \frac{3}{2}$ = 1.68 L

Immediate Test 10

(i) (a) $Mg_3N_2(s) \longrightarrow 3Mg\,(s) + N_2(g)$

(b) $N_2(g) + 3H_2(g) \longrightarrow 2NH_3(g)$

Calculate moles of Mg_3N_2 that can give enough N_2 that can react with 1 L of H_2 to form NH_3 at STP.

(ii) Based on the following chemical reactions:

(a) $2KClO_3(s) \longrightarrow 2KCl(s) + 3O_2(g)$

(b) $2SO_2(g) + O_2(g) \longrightarrow 2SO_3(g)$

Calculate moles of $KClO_3$ that can give enough O_2 to combine with 2 L SO_2 under standard states.

Example 3.12) What is the mass of air in a 250 mL flask at a laboratory pressure of 715 Torr and a temperature of 21°C. Assume air to be an ideal gas having an average molar mass of 29.0 g mol^{-1}.

Sol. Given data suggests that an ideal gas equation can be used to determine mass of air.

By ideal gas equation, $\quad pV = nRT$

$\therefore \quad n = \frac{pV}{RT}$

Mass of air = $n \times$ molar mass

$$n = \frac{pV}{RT} = \frac{\left(\frac{715}{760}\right) \text{atm} \times (0.250)\,\text{L}}{0.0821\,\text{L atm mol}^{-1}\text{K}^{-1} \times 294\,\text{K}}$$

$$= 9.744 \times 10^{-3}\ \text{mol}$$

$\therefore$ Mass of air $= 9.744 \times 10^{-3}\ \text{mol} \times 29\ \text{g mol}^{-1} = 0.28\ \text{g}$

Example 3.13) What volume of H_2 gas will be produced at 0.963 bar and 27°C from the reaction of 6.5 g of zinc with excess of 6 M HCl? Assume that H_2 is an ideal gas under these conditions (Zn = 65).

Sol.

$$\underset{\substack{1\ \text{mol} \\ 6.5\,\text{g} = 0.1\ \text{mol}}}{Zn} + 2HCl \longrightarrow ZnCl_2 + \underset{\substack{1\ \text{mol} \\ 0.1\ \text{mol}}}{H_2}$$

H_2 formed from 0.1 mol Zn = 0.1 mol

By ideal gas equation,

$$pV = nRT$$

$$\therefore \quad V = \frac{nRT}{p}$$

$$= \frac{0.1\ \text{mol} \times 0.0831\ (\text{L bar mol}^{-1}\text{K}^{-1}) \times 300\ \text{K}}{0.963\ \text{bar}}$$

$$= 2.6\ \text{L}$$

Example 3.14) The relative humidity in a room of volume 48m^3 is 65%. Assuming ideal gas behaviour, what mass of water vapour is in the air at 298 K. The vapour pressure of liquid water is 23.8 Torr at 298 K.

Sol. Relative humidity $= \dfrac{\text{Actual vapour pressure of water in air}}{\text{Equilibrium vapour pressure of water}}$

Actual vapour pressure of water in air

$$p = 0.65 \times 23.8\ \text{Torr}$$

$$= 15.47\ \text{Torr} = \frac{15.47}{760}\ \text{atm} = 0.02036\ \text{atm} \quad (760\ \text{Torr} = 1\ \text{atm})$$

$$V = 48\ \text{m}^3 = 48 \times 10^3\text{L}$$

Thus, moles of water

$$n = \frac{pV}{RT} = \frac{0.02036 \times 48 \times 10^3}{0.0821 \times 298} = 39.93\ \text{mol}$$

$$\text{Amount} = 39.93\ \text{mol} \times 18\ \text{g mol}^{-1} = 719\ \text{g}$$

$$1\ \text{m}^3 = 1 \times 10^3\ \text{dm}^3$$

Immediate Test 11

(i) The vapour pressure of liquid water is 23.8 Torr at 298 K. By what factor does the molar volume of water increase as it vaporises to form an ideal gas under these conditions. The density of liquid water is $0.997\ \text{g cm}^{-3}$ at 298 K.

(ii) An electronic vacuum tube was sealed off during manufacture at a pressure of 1.8×10^{-5} Torr at 300 K. Its volume is 0.1 L. Calculate the number of gas molecules remaining in the tube.

Example 3.15) Assuming ideal gas behaviour, what is the density of carbon dioxide gas at 300 K and pressure 1.01 bar. Express result in kg m^{-3}.

Sol. Density $(\rho) = \dfrac{\text{Molar mass (g mol}^{-1})}{\text{Volume (L mol}^{-1})} = \dfrac{M}{RT/p} = \dfrac{pM}{RT}$

When pressure is in bar, $R = 0.08314\text{L bar mol}^{-1}\ \text{K}^{-1}$ ρ is in g L^{-1}

$$1\ \text{g L}^{-1} = 1\ \text{kg m}^{-3}$$

$$1\ \text{g cm}^{-3} = 1000\ \text{kg m}^{-3}$$

$$\rho = \frac{pM}{RT} = \frac{1.01 \times 44}{0.08314 \times 300}$$

$$= 1.782\ \text{g L}^{-1} = 1.782\ \text{kg m}^{-3}$$

Example 3.16) Density of air at STP is $1.280\ \text{gL}^{-1}$. What is the composition of the air assuming N_2 and O_2 as the main constituents ?

Sol. Molar mass of air $= \dfrac{M_1X_1 + M_2X_2}{(X_1 + X_2)}$

where, M_1 and M_2 are the molar masses of oxygen and nitrogen with their percentages as X_1 and X_2

$$X_1 + X_2 = 100$$

$$\text{Density at STP} = \frac{\text{Molar mass}}{\text{Volume at STP}}$$

Molar mass of air = volume × density

$$= 22.4\ \text{L mol}^{-1} \times 1.286\ \text{g L}^{-1} = 28.806\ \text{g mol}^{-1}$$

$$\therefore \quad 28.806 = \frac{32X_1 + 28\,(100 - X_1)}{100} \quad \therefore X_1 = 20$$

Thus, $\quad O_2 = 20\%,\ N_2 = 80\%$

Immediate Test 12

(i) What is the density of the gaseous mixture of 20% N_2O_4 and 80% NO_2 by masses at 298 K and pressure 1 bar?

(ii) Calculate density of helium at 294 K and 1 bar pressure. Also, calculate lifting force of helium in air.

Example 3.17) A neon ($20\ \text{g mol}^{-1}$) and dioxygen ($32\ \text{g mol}^{-1}$) mixture contains 70.6g dioxygen and 167.5g neon. If pressure of the mixture of gases in the cylinder is 25 bar, what is the partial pressure of dioxygen and neon in the mixture? ***[NCERT]***

Sol. Partial pressure of a gas in a mixture can be calculated using Dalton's law of partial pressure.

$$p_i = \chi_i\, p_{\text{total}} \Rightarrow \chi_i = \frac{n_i}{n_{\text{total}}}$$

where, p_i is the partial pressure of gas (i) with mole fraction (χ_i)

$$\text{mole} = \frac{\text{mass}}{\text{molar mass}}$$

$$n_{\text{neon}} = \frac{167.5}{20} = 8.3750\ \text{mol}$$

$$n_{\text{oxygen}} = \frac{70.6}{32} = 2.2065 \text{ mol}$$

$$n_{\text{Total}} = 10.5815 \text{ mol}$$

$$\chi_{\text{neon}} = \frac{8.3750}{10.5815} = 0.79$$

$$\therefore \quad p_{\text{neon}} = 25 \times 0.79 = 19.75 \text{ bar}$$

$$p_{\text{oxygen}} = 25 - 19.75 = 5.25 \text{ bar}$$

Example 3.18) **A 255 mL sample of Ne at 735 Torr is mixed with a 395 mL sample of Ar at 705 Torr, and the resulting mixture is compressed to a final volume of 315 mL. Assuming, ideal gas behaviour and isothermal conditions, calculate the partial pressure of each gas, the total pressure and the composition of the final mixture.**

Sol. Final volume = 315 mL

For a gas under isothermal condition,

$$p_1V_1 = p_2V_2$$

$$\therefore \quad p_{\text{mix}}(\text{Ne}) = \frac{p_iV_i}{V_f} = \frac{735 \times 255}{315} = 595 \text{ Torr}$$

Similarly, $$p_{\text{mix}}(\text{Ar}) = \frac{705 \times 395}{315} = 884 \text{ Torr}$$

$$p_{\text{total}} \text{ (in mixture)} = 1479 \text{ Torr}$$

$$p_{\text{Ne}} = p_{\text{total}}\, \chi_{\text{Ne}}$$

$$\chi_{\text{Ne}} = \frac{p_{\text{Ne}}}{p_{\text{total}}}$$

$$\chi_{\text{Ne (mix)}} = \frac{595}{1479} = 0.402$$

$$\chi_{\text{Ne (mix)}} = 1 - 0.402 = 0.598$$

Example 3.19) A gaseous mixture at 298 K and 1.0 bar contains 75.0 g He and 75.0 g of Ne. Assuming, ideal behaviour, calculate the partial volume of each gas and the total volume of the gaseous mixture.

Sol. It is based on law of partial volumes (Amagat)

$$n(\text{He}) = \frac{\text{mass}}{\text{molar mass}} = \frac{75}{4} = 18.75 \text{ mol}$$

$$n\,(\text{Ar}) = \frac{75}{20} = 3.75 \text{ mol}$$

$$pV = nRT$$

$$\text{Partial volume of Ne} = \frac{nRT}{p} = \frac{18.75 \times 0.08314 \times 298}{1.0} = 464.50 \text{ L}$$

$$\text{Similarly, partial volume of Ar} = \frac{3.75 \times 0.08314 \times 298}{1.0} = 92.91 \text{ L}$$

$$\text{Total volume} = 557.41 \text{ L}$$

■ Pressure is in bar thus, $R = 0.083 \text{ bar dm}^3 \text{ mol}^{-1} \text{ K}^{-1}$

Immediate Test 13

(i) A 5.0 L flask containing N_2 at 1.00 bar and 298 K is connected to a 4.00 L flask containing O_2 at 2.00 bar and 298 K. What is the composition of the mixture and partial pressure of N_2 in the final mixture?

(ii) A mixture of He and CO_2 has a volume of 63.5 mL at 1.00 bar and 301 K. The system containing the mixture is cooled in liquid N_2 and the remaining gas is evacuated. The system was restored to original conditions, and the volume is 40.5 mL. What was composition of the original mixture?

(iii) Into a 5.00 L container at 291K, are placed 0.2 mol H_2, 20.0 g CO_2 and 1.75 equivalent O_2. Calculate partial pressure of each gas and the total pressure.

KNOWLEDGE CONFIRMATION **Test 2**

1 At 300 K, a gas is compressed to half of its volume. To what temperature, it must now be heated, so that gas occupies its original volume.

(a) 300 K　(b) 600 K　(c) 150 K　(d) 900 K

2 In following two stages volume V is

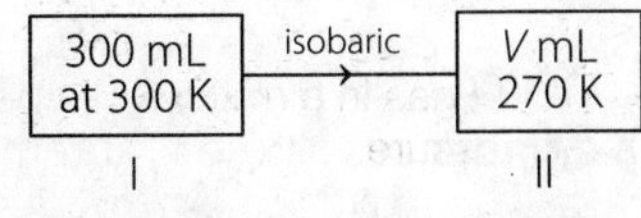

(a) 350 mL　(b) 540 mL　(c) 135 mL　(d) 270 mL

3 Total pressure exerted by the mixture of 14 g N_2, 4 g H_2 and 16.0 g SO_2 gases in the vessel of 12 dm^3 capacity at 300 K is

(a) 2.56 bar　(b) 4.52 bar　(c) 5.72 bar　(d) 10.12 bar

4 Density of methane at 300 K and 1 bar is

(a) 0.71 g dm^{-3}　(b) 0.64 g dm^{-3}
(c) 0.71 g cm^{-3}　(d) 0.64 g cm^{-3}

5 Mass of 5.6 L of a gas at STP is 16g. Thus, gas may be

(a) O_2　(b) SO_2　(c) CO　(d) CO_2

6 An open vessel at 27°C is heated until two- fifth of the air (assumed as an ideal gas) in it has escaped from the vessel. Assuming that the volume of the vessel remains constant, the temperature at which the vessel has been heated is **[JEE Main 2019 (I) NTA]**

(a) 750 K　(b) 500° C　(c) 500 K　(d) 750° C

7 Density of air (N_2 and O_2) is 1.24 g dm^{-3} at 1 bar and 300 K. Thus, partial pressure of N_2 in air is

(a) 0.73 bar　(b) 0.27 bar
(c) 0.80 bar　(d) 0.20 bar

8 Density of gas A is twice that of B and molar mass of gas B is twice that of A under isothermal conditions. Thus, ratio of pressure of gas A to B is

(a) 1 : 6　(b) 1 : 1　(c) 4 : 1　(d) 1 : 4

9 A small bubble of volume 2 cm^3 inside bottom of a water tank at 4°C and 6.0 bar rises to the surface of water where temperature is 27°C and pressure is 1 bar. Thus, volume of the bubble at the surface is

(a) 12.12 cm^3 (b) 6.06 cm^3
(c) 13.00 cm^3 (d) 6.50 cm^3

10 Volume occupied by 32 g CH_4 at 200 K is same as occupied by 4 g of the gas *X* at 400 K under isobaric conditions. Thus, molar mass of gas *X* is

(a) 16 g mol^{-1} (b) 8 g mol^{-1}
(c) 2 g mol^{-1} (d) 4 g mol^{-1}

11 In the following two sets (1) and (2), ratio of pressure *A* to *B* is

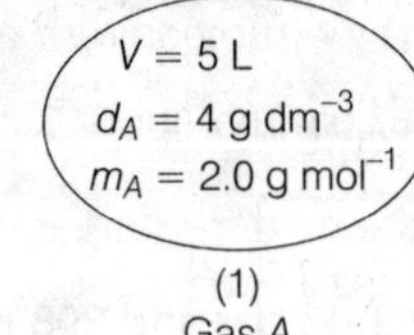

V = 10 L
d_B = 2 g dm^{-3}
m_B = 4.0 g mol^{-1}

(1) Gas *A* (2) Gas *B*

(a) 2 : 1 (b) 1 : 1 (c) 4 : 1 (d) 3 : 1

12 An ideal gas in an open container is heated from 300 K to 400 K. The fraction of the original amount remaining in the gas will be

(a) 0.75 (b) 0.25 (c) 0.50 (d) 0.125

13 If pressure is made one third and volume is made doubled of the original volume without affecting number of moles, then temperature changes by

(a) $\frac{1}{2\times 3}$ (b) $\frac{3}{2}$ (c) 3 × 2 (d) $\frac{2}{3}$

14 A given amount of an ideal gas has volume of 100 dm^3 when collected over water at 288 K and 750 mm pressure. At NTP and in dry state, its volume is 91.9 dm^3. Thus, vapour pressure of water at 288 K is

(a) 20.0 mm (b) 30.0 mm (c) 13.2 mm (d) 42.0 mm

15 A 8.3 L cylinder contains 128.0 g O_2 gas at 300 K. What mass of O_2 gas must be released to reduce the pressure to 6.0 bar?

(a) 64.0 g (b) 32.0 g (c) 16.0 g (d) 8.0 g

16 I, II and III are three isobars respectively at p_1, p_2 and p_3 as shown. Increasing order of pressure is

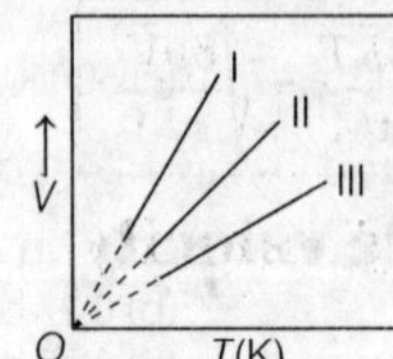

(a) $p_1 < p_3 < p_2$ (b) $p_3 < p_2 < p_1$
(c) $p_1 < p_2 < p_3$ (d) $p_1 = p_2 = p_3$

17 0.50 mole of N_2 at 288 K occupies 10 dm^3. On heating to 323 K, volume changes to 8 dm^3. Thus, change in pressure is

(a) 0.481 bar (b) 0.296 bar
(c) 0.519 bar (d) No change

18 If 150 g of $Al(OH)_3$ is decomposed thermally at 1073 K, $Al_2O_3(s)$ and $H_2O(g)$ are formed. Thus, volume of water vapours formed at 1 atm pressure is

(a) 169.41 dm^3 (b) 254.11 dm^3
(c) 84.71 dm^3 (d) 127.06 dm^3

19 Isothermal compressibility constant of one mole of an ideal gas at 298 K is 0.1 bar^{-1}. Thus, volume occupied is

(a) 24.76 dm^3 (b) 22.40 dm^3
(c) 11.20 dm^3 (d) None of these

20 For an ideal gas at constant pressure $\left(\frac{\partial V}{\partial T}\right)_{p,n}$ is 0.0821 LK^{-1}. Thus, thermal expansion coefficient of an ideal gas is

(a) $3.67\times 10^{-3}\ K^{-1}$ (b) 273 K
(c) $3.00\times 10^{-4}\ K^{-1}$ (d) None of these

21 Which one of the following graphs is not correct for ideal gas?

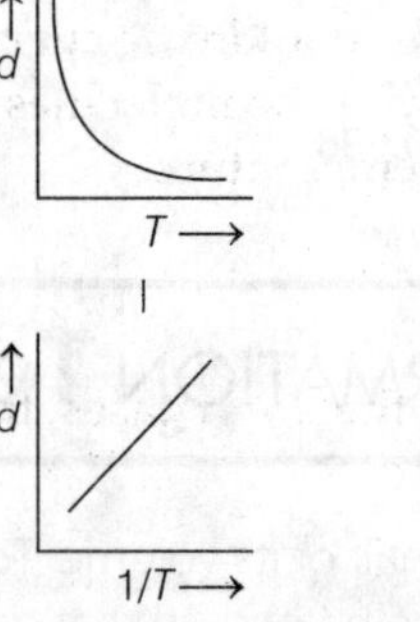

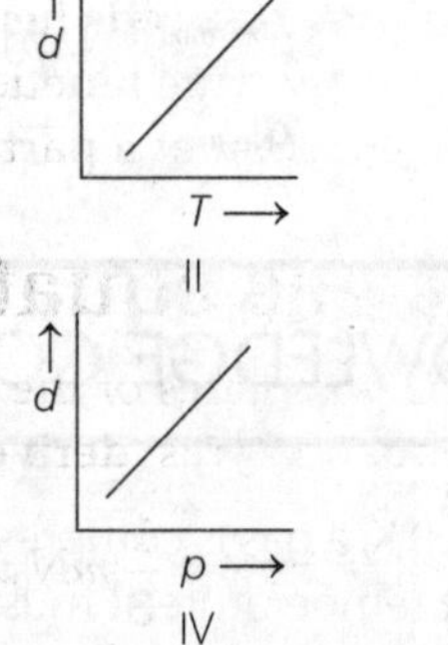

d = density, *p* = pressure, *T* = temperature

[JEE Main 2020 (II) NTA]

(a) III (b) I
(c) IV (d) II

22 A mixture of one mole each of H_2, He and O_2 are enclosed in a cylinder of volume *V*, at temperature *T*. If the partial pressure of H_2 is 2 atm, the total pressure of the gases in the cylinder is ***[JEE Main 2020 (II) NTA]***

(a) 14 atm (b) 38 atm
(c) 22 atm (d) 6 atm

Kinetic Molecular Theory and Molecular Velocities

Kinetic molecular theory of gases

The kinetic molecular theory of gases is based on the following postulates :

(i) A gas consists of large number of tiny particles, either atoms or molecules, moving around randomly.

(ii) The volume of the particles is negligible as compared to total volume of the gas.

(iii) The gas particles act independently of one another. There are no attractive or repulsive forces between particles.

(iv) Collisions of the gas particles, either with other particles or with the walls of the container, are elastic. In other words, the total kinetic energy of the gas particles is constant at constant temperature.

(v) The pressure exerted by a gas is the result of collisions of the particles with the walls of the container or with other molecule.

(vi) The average kinetic energy of the gas particles is proportional to the Kelvin temperature.

(vii) At any particular time, different particles in a gas have different speeds hence, different kinetic energy. However, average kinetic energy of the molecules remain constant at a particular temperature.

Kinetic gas equation

Based on the postulates of the kinetic theory of gases, the following equation was derived

$$\therefore \quad pV = \frac{1}{3} mN_0u^2 = \left[\frac{1}{3} Mu^2\right]$$

This equation is known as kinetic gas equation.

where, $mN_0 = M$ (molar mass),

$N_0 =$ Avogadro's number

$u =$ root mean square velocity (u_{rms})

(u_{rms} is discussed further in this chapter)

- Kinetic energy of n moles is given as :

$$\frac{1}{2} Mu^2 = \frac{3}{2} pV = \frac{3}{2} nRT$$

- If p and T both are given, use equation in terms of temperature. Thus, for root mean square velocity

$$u_{rms} = \sqrt{\frac{3RT}{M}} \text{ and not } \sqrt{\frac{3pV}{M}}$$

$$\left(\frac{du}{dT}\right) = \frac{1}{2}\left(\frac{3RT}{M}\right)^{-\frac{1}{2}}\left(\frac{3R}{M}\right)$$

$$= \frac{1}{2}\left(\frac{3R}{M}\right) \Big/ \sqrt{\frac{3RT}{M}} = \frac{1.5R}{M} / u_{rms}$$

- To have velocity in m s^{-1} (MKS) unit, $R = 8.3143$ J mol^{-1}K^{-1} and M (molar mass) in kg mol^{-1}.
- If density is in kg m^{-3} and pressure in N m^{-2} (kg m^{-1}s^{-2}), then velocity will be in m s^{-1}.
- Average kinetic energy per molecule

$$\boxed{\text{KE} = \frac{3}{2}\frac{RT}{N_0} = \frac{3}{2} kT}$$

where, $k \left(= \frac{R}{N_0}\right)$ is called **Boltzmann's constant.** Its numerical value is 1.38×10^{-23} JK^{-1}.

From kinetic gas equation it is clear that, average kinetic energy is proportional to absolute temperature. If, $T = 0$ K (i.e. $-273.15°$C), then average kinetic energy $= 0$

Thus, absolute zero (0K) is the temperature at which molecular motion ceases.

Molecular velocities

In gaseous state, molecules tend to move in different directions with different speeds. *Based upon the calculations, there are three kinds of molecular velocities :*

Average velocity ($\bar{v}$ or v_{av} or u_{av})

It is the arithmetic mean of the velocities of different molecules of a gas.

Mathematically, $\bar{v} = \frac{v_1 + v_2 + v_3 + \ldots + v_n}{n}$

This is related to temperature T of the gas as

$$\boxed{\bar{v} = \sqrt{\frac{8RT}{\pi M}} = \sqrt{\frac{8pV}{\pi M}}}$$

Root mean square velocity (u or v_{rms} or u_{rms})

It is the square root of the mean of the squares of the velocities of the different molecules of gas.

Mathematically, $u = \sqrt{\frac{v_1^2 + v_2^2 + v_3^2 + \ldots + v_n^2}{n}}$

From kinetic gas equation,

$$u = \sqrt{\frac{3RT}{M}} = \sqrt{\frac{3pV}{M}} = \sqrt{\frac{3p}{d}}$$

where, p = pressure (RT / V) and d = density (M / V)

Most probable velocity (v_{mp} or u_{mp})

It is the velocity, possessed by the largest number of the molecules of gas. Distribution of molecules is maximum at most probable velocity.

From kinetic gas equation, $v = \sqrt{\frac{2RT}{M}} = \sqrt{\frac{2pV}{M}} = \sqrt{\frac{2p}{d}}$

Maxwell-Boltzmann distribution of molecular speeds

Distribution of molecular speeds is given by

$$\frac{1}{N}\left(\frac{dN}{du}\right) = 4\pi u^2 \left(\frac{B}{\pi}\right)^{3/2} e^{-Bu^2}$$

where, dN is the number of molecules distributed out of N molecules between velocities u and $(u + du)$ and $B = \left(\frac{M}{2RT}\right)$

$\frac{1}{u}\left(\frac{dN}{du}\right)$ gives probability of finding molecules having velocity u.

Effect of molar masses on distribution of molecular velocities

Molecules of low molar masses have a broad spectrum of speeds as compared to molecules of higher molar masses.

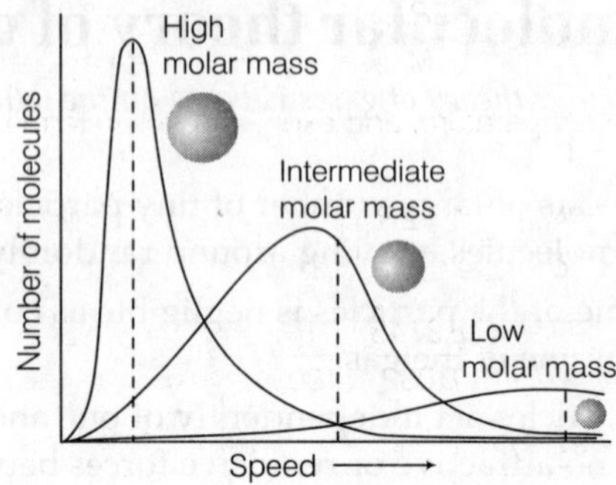

The Maxwell distribution of speed based on molar mass.

- According to this figure, there is only a small number of molecules with very low velocities $(u \to 0)$ or with high velocities $(u \to \infty)$.
- Most molecules have intermediate velocities. The largest number of molecules have a velocity corresponding to the maximum of the curve is called **most probable velocity**.

Solved Examples & Instant Practice

Example 3.20) Calculate most probable velocity of helium gas at 127° C.

Sol. Most probable velocity of a gas of molar mass M is given by

$$u_{mp} = \sqrt{\frac{2RT}{M}}$$

We take R in J mol^{-1}K^{-1} and molar mass in kg mol^{-1} to have result is ms^{-1}.

$$u_{mp} = \sqrt{\frac{2 \times 8.3143 \times 400 \text{ K}}{4 \times 10^{-3}}} = 1289.5 \text{ m s}^{-1}$$

Example 3.21) At what temperature, root mean square velocity of O_2 gas is twice that of most probable velocity of H_2 gas at 27°C ?

Sol.

$$u_{rms} (O_2 \text{ at } T) = 2 \times u_{mp} (H_2 \text{ at } 300 \text{ K})$$

$$\sqrt{\frac{3RT_1}{M_1}} = 2 \times \sqrt{\frac{2RT_2}{M_2}}$$

$$\sqrt{\frac{3 \times T_1}{32 \times 10^{-3}}} = 2\sqrt{\frac{2 \times 300}{2 \times 10^{-3}}}$$

$$\frac{3T_1}{32} = 4 \times 300$$

$$T_1 = 12800 \text{ K}$$

Example 3.22) Root mean square velocity of a gas at 298 K is 411 ms^{-1}. Determine the molar mass of the gas.

Sol.

$$u_{rms} = \sqrt{\frac{3RT}{M}}$$

$$M = \frac{3RT}{u^2_{rms}} = \frac{3 \times 8.314 \times 298}{(411)^2}$$

$$= 0.044 \text{ kg mol}^{-1} = 44 \text{ g mol}^{-1}$$

- When R is J mol^{-1} K^{-1} and velocity in ms^{-1}, molar mass is in kg mol^{-1}.

Immediate Test 14

(i) Calculate root mean square velocity of air assuming it to be a mixture of 80% N_2 and 20% O_2 at 300 K.

(ii) What is the ratio of the average velocity of H_2 to He at 298 K? Is this ratio same for most probable and root mean square velocities?

(iii) Ratio of root mean square velocity of H_2 at 50 K to that of unknown gas at 400 K is 1 : 1. What is the molar mass of the unknown gas?

(iv) Calculate root mean square velocity of H_2 at 298 K. To what temperature, must H_2 be cooled so that it has the same root mean square velocity as He at 298 K?

Example 3.23) Derive the relation showing variation of most probable velocity with temperature. Calculate this value for a gas of molar mass 0.032 kg mol^{-1} having most probable velocity of 100 m s^{-1} at a given temperature.

Sol. $$u_{mp} = \left(\frac{2RT}{M}\right)^{1/2}$$

Differentiate it with temperature, and express result in terms of u_{mp} and molar mass.

$$\frac{du_{mp}}{dT} = \frac{1}{2}\left(\frac{2R}{M}\right)\left(\frac{M}{2RT}\right)^{1/2} = \frac{R}{M}\left(\frac{1}{u_{mp}}\right)$$

$$\frac{du_{mp}}{dT} = \frac{8.3143}{0.032}\left(\frac{1}{100}\right) = 2.6 \text{ ms}^{-1}\text{K}^{-1}$$

Immediate Test 15

What is the increase in root mean square velocity of Ne when temperature is increased from 100 K to 100.1 K? (Molar mass of Ne = 20×10^{-3} kg mol^{-1})

Example 3.24) Calculate root mean square speed of H_2 molecule having density 0.09 g dm^{-3} at 1 atm.

Sol. u_{rms} in terms of pressure and density is

$$u_{same} = \sqrt{\frac{3p}{d}}$$

Take pressure and density in MKS unit.

$p = 1 \text{ atm} = 101325 \text{ Pa}, d = 0.09 \text{ g dm}^{-3} = 0.09 \text{ kg m}^{-3}$

$$\therefore \quad u = \sqrt{\frac{3 \times 101325}{0.09}} = 1838 \text{ ms}^{-1}$$

Immediate Test 16

The root mean square velocity of the molecule of an ideal gas at 298 K and at pressure 2.50 atm is 5.00×10^2 m s^{-1}. What is the density of the gas?

Example 3.25) A gas bulb of 1 dm^3 capacity contains 2×10^{21} molecules of N_2 gas exerting a pressure of 7.57×10^3 Nm^{-2}. Calculate

(a) root mean square velocity.

(b) temperature of the gas molecules.

Sol. By kinetic molecular theory $pV = \frac{1}{3} mNu^2$

where, m = mass of one molecule

N = total number of molecules with rms velocity u

$$u_{rms} = \sqrt{\frac{3pV}{mN}}$$

(a) m (mass of one molecule of N_2) $= \dfrac{28 \times 10^{-3}}{6.02 \times 10^{23}}$ kg

$\therefore$ Mass of 2×10^{21} molecules

$$\therefore \quad mN = \frac{28 \times 10^{-3}}{6.02 \times 10^{23}} \times 2 \times 10^{21} = 9.3 \times 10^{-5} \text{kg}$$

$$V = 1 \text{ dm}^3 = 1 \times 10^{-3} \text{ m}^3$$

$$\therefore \quad u_{rms} = \sqrt{\frac{3 \times 7.57 \times 10^3 \times 1 \times 10^{-3}}{9.3 \times 10^{-5}}}$$

$$= 4.94 \times 10^2 \text{ ms}^{-1}$$

(b) Also, $$u_{rms} = \sqrt{\frac{3RT}{M}}$$

$$4.94 \times 10^2 = \sqrt{\frac{3 \times 8.314\, T}{28 \times 10^{-3}}}$$

$$T = 274 \text{ K}$$

■ M (molar mass of N_2) is in kg mol^{-1}

Immediate Test 17

Calculate the pressure needed to confine 1.0×10^{25} gas molecules each of mass 1.0×10^{-25} kg and u_{rms} of 1.0×10^3 ms^{-1} in a 1.0 m^3 container. Also, calculate the temperature.

Example 3.26) Calculate the average translational kinetic energy for an H_2 molecule and for 1.00 mole of H_2 at 298 K.

Sol.

Average translational kinetic energy for one molecule $= \dfrac{3}{2}\dfrac{RT}{N_0}$

and for n moles (nN_0 molecules) $= \dfrac{3RT}{2N_0} nN_0 = \dfrac{3\, nRT}{2}$

$$\overline{\text{KE}} \text{ (average)} = \frac{3RT}{2\, N_0} = \frac{3 \times 8.3143 \times 298}{2 \times 6.02 \times 10^{23}} = 6.17 \times 10^{-21} \text{ J}$$

Total kinetic energy of one mole of H_2 gas $= \dfrac{3}{2} nRT$

$$= \frac{3}{2} RT = \frac{3 \times 8.3143 \times 298 \text{ J}}{2}$$

$$= 3716 \text{ J} = 3.716 \text{kJ}$$

■ If R is in J mol^{-1} K^{-1}, kinetic energy will be in Joules

Example 3.27) Calculate kinetic energy and average kinetic energy of 1 mole N_2 gas at a temperature at which average speed is 476.3 ms^{-1}.

Sol. $$u_{avg} = \sqrt{\frac{8RT}{\pi M}}$$

$$476.3 = \sqrt{\frac{8 \times 8.3143 \times T}{\pi \times 28 \times 10^{-3}}}$$

$$\therefore \quad T = 300 \text{ K}$$

$$\therefore \quad \text{KE} = \frac{3}{2} nRT = \frac{3}{2} \times x \times 8.3143 \times 300$$

$$= 3741 \text{ J}$$

$$\overline{\text{KE}} = \frac{3}{2}\frac{RT}{N_0} = \frac{3741 \text{J}}{6.02 \times 10^{23}}$$

$$= 6.21 \times 10^{-21} \text{ J molecule}^{-1}$$

Example 3.28) Bond energy of H_2 is 432 kJ mol^{-1}. At what temperature average kinetic energy of gaseous H_2 molecules equals to the energy required to dissociate the molecules into atoms.

Sol. On comparison of bond-energy and average kinetic energy, temperature required T is calculated.

Bond energy of $H_2 = 432 \text{ kJ mol}^{-1} = \dfrac{432 \times 10^3}{N_0}$ J molecule^{-1}

and $$\overline{KE} = \frac{3RT}{2N_0} = \frac{3}{2}\frac{RT}{N_0} = \frac{432 \times 10^3}{N_0}$$

$$\frac{3 \times 8 \cdot 3143T}{2} = 432 \times 10^3 \quad \therefore \; T = 34640 \text{ K}$$

Example 3.29) Temperature of Ne gas is increased from 100 K to 100.1 K. What is increase in average translational kinetic energy?

Sol. Difference of kinetic energy, at two temperature gives increase in kinetic energy.

$$\overline{KE} = \frac{3RT}{2N_0}$$

$$\therefore \quad d\left(\frac{\overline{KE}}{dT}\right) = \frac{3R}{2N_0}$$

$$\therefore \quad d(\overline{KE}) = \frac{3RdT}{2N_0} \Rightarrow dT = 0.1 \text{ K}$$

$$d(\overline{KE}) = \frac{3 \times 8.3143 \times 0.1}{2 \times 6.02 \times 10^{23}} = 2.07 \times 10^{-24} \text{ J}$$

Immediate Test 18

(i) What is the ratio of the average molecular kinetic energy of UF_6 to that of H_2 both at 300 K?

(ii) At what temperature, will hydrogen molecule have the same kinetic energy as nitrogen molecule have at 308K ?

(iii) Average translational kinetic energy of H_2 gas is 6.175×10^{-21}J. Calculate rms velocity at the given temperature.

(iv) The most probable velocity of a gas of mass 6.66×10^{-26} kg molecule^{-1} is 10 ms^{-1}. What is the average kinetic energy?

(v) One mole of H_2 gas is contained in a vessel of volume 1m^3 ? What is the value of $\dfrac{1}{u}\left(\dfrac{dp}{du}\right)$, where u is rms velocity?

(vi) The average velocity of O_2 gas molecules at a certain temperature is 400 ms^{-1}. What would be the average momentum and average kinetic energy of the gas?

(vii) By what ratio translational kinetic energy is increased if temperature of 1 mole of a gas is increased from 300 K to 330 K?

(viii) H_2 and O_2 gases are placed in two separate vessels A and B of same volume, under identical conditions of temperature and pressure. What is the ratio of average momentum of the molecule in A and that of in B?

KNOWLEDGE CONFIRMATION Test 3

1 Temperature at which rms velocity of CO_2 gas is double of most probable velocity of C_3H_8 gas at 300 K is
(a) 300 K (b) 400 K
(c) 500 K (d) 800 K

2 For an ideal gas based on kinetic molecular theory, $\dfrac{1}{u}\left(\dfrac{dp}{du}\right)$ is
(a) $\dfrac{3M}{2u}$ (b) $\dfrac{2M}{3u}$ (c) $\dfrac{3M}{u}$ (d) $\dfrac{M}{2u}$

3 Temperature coefficient showing variation of average translational kinetic energy with temperature is
(a) 1.5 kdT (b) 1.5 RdT
(c) 1.5 R (d) 1.5 k

4 If molecular velocity is given by $u = \sqrt{\dfrac{2RT}{M}}$ then $\left(\dfrac{du}{dT}\right)$ is
(a) $\dfrac{R}{Mu}$ (b) $\dfrac{R}{M}$ (c) $\dfrac{Ru}{M}$ (d) $\dfrac{M}{Ru}$

5 If average translational kinetic energy of a gas molecule at a temperature T is xJ molecule^{-1}, then its rms speed is
(a) $\sqrt{3RT/M}$ (b) $\dfrac{x}{N_0}$ (c) $\sqrt{\dfrac{2xN_0}{M}}$ (d) $\dfrac{N_0T}{x}$

6 If E is the kinetic energy per unit volume, then pressure p can be
(a) $p = \dfrac{2E}{3}$ (b) $p = \dfrac{E}{3}$
(c) $p = \dfrac{3E}{2}$ (d) $p = E$

7 Average molecular kinetic energy of H_2 is E_1 and that of He is E_2 both at temperature 300 K. Thus, E_1/E_2 is
(a) 1.0 (b) 2.0
(c) 4.0 (d) 0.5

8 In the following variation of molecular velocity (u) with probability $\dfrac{1}{N}\left(\dfrac{dN}{du}\right)$, most probable velocity is given by

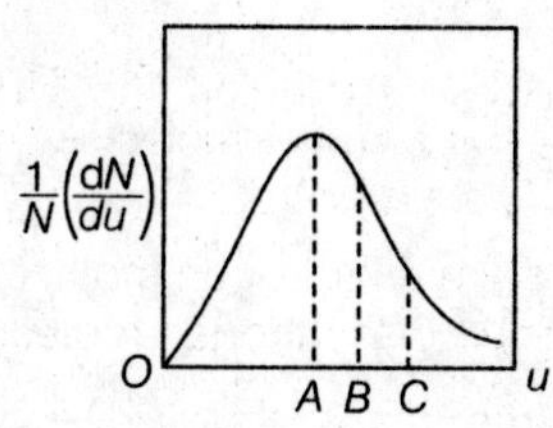

(a) *OA* (b) *OB*
(c) *OC* (d) None of these

9 Arrange u_{rms}, u_{mp} and u_{avg} in increasing order at constant temperature.
(a) $u_{rms} < u_{avg} < u_{mp}$ (b) $u_{mp} < u_{rms} < u_{avg}$
(c) $u_{mp} < u_{avg} < u_{rms}$ (d) $u_{avg} < u_{mp} < u_{rms}$

10 The rms velocity of a monoatomic gas of molar mass '*M*g mol^{-1}' is *u*. Its kinetic energy is per mole (*E*) is related to *u* by equation.
(a) $u = \sqrt{\frac{3E}{M}}$ (b) $u = \sqrt{\frac{2E}{3M}}$
(c) $u = \sqrt{\frac{2E}{M}}$ (d) $u = \sqrt{\frac{E}{3M}}$

11 Two flasks I and II of equal volumes are maintained at temperature 300 K and 600 K respectively. Equal masses of H_2 in I and He in II are placed. Thus, ratio of total translational kinetic energy of gas H_2 in I that of He in II is
(a) 1 : 2 (b) 4 : 1
(c) 2 : 1 (d) 1 : 1

12 Which is correct expression for rms velocity of O_2 gas at 300 K?
(a) $\sqrt{\frac{3 \times 8.314 \times 10^7 \times 300}{32}}$ m s^{-1}
(b) $\sqrt{\frac{3 \times 8.314 \times 10^7 \times 300}{32 \times 10^{-3}}}$ m s^{-1}
(c) $\sqrt{\frac{3 \times 8.314 \times 300}{32 \times 10^{-3}}}$ m s^{-1}
(d) $\sqrt{\frac{3 \times 0.0821 \times 300}{32 \times 10^{-3}}}$ m s^{-1}

13 At 298 K, which of the following gases has the lowest average molecular speed ?
(a) CO_2 at 0.20 atm (b) He at 0.40 atm
(c) CH_4 at 0.80 atm (d) NO at 1.00 atm

14 If molar mass of gas *B* is twice that of *A*, and rms speed of *A* at temperature (*T*) is 200 ms^{-1}, then rms speed of gas *B* at temperature $\left(\frac{T}{2}\right)$ is (*T* is in Kelvin scale)
(a) 200 m s^{-1} (b) 100 m s^{-1} (c) 300 m s^{-1} (d) 400 m s^{-1}

15 *A* and *B* are two ideal gases with the following parameters:

Gas	Molecules	Temperature	Kinetic energy
A	N_A	150 K	E_A
B	N_B	300 K	E_B

If $E_A / E_B = 0.5$, then N_A / N_B is
(a) 1 (b) 0.5 (c) 0.25 (d) 2.0

16 Which of these factors affects the average kinetic energy of the molecules in a gas ?
I : Pressure II : Temperature
(a) I only (b) II only
(c) I and II both (d) Neither of I and II

17 Ratio of number of molecules having speeds in the range of $2u_{mp}$ and $2u_{mp} + du$ to the number of molecules having speeds in the range of (u_{mp}) and ($u_{mp} + du$) is
(a) $\frac{dN_2}{dN_1} = \frac{4}{e^2}$ (b) $\frac{dN_2}{dN_1} = \frac{4}{e^3}$
(c) $\frac{dN_2}{dN_1} = \frac{e^2}{4}$ (d) $\frac{dN_2}{dN_1} = \frac{e^3}{4}$

18 Fraction of N_2 molecules at 101.325 kPa and 300 K whose speeds are in the range of ($u_{mp} \pm 0.005u_{mp}$) is (u_{mp} (N_2) = 422 ms^{-1})
(a) 8.3×10^{-3} (b) 1.6×10^{-3}
(c) 4.1×10^{-2} (d) 8.3×10^{-2}

19 What fraction of molecules in H_2 gas have a KE within (Average KE ± 10) per cent of average KE at 298 K?
(a) 0.001 (b) 0.002
(c) 0.0924 (d) 0.127

20 The escape velocity, defined as the speed at which molecules can escape the earth's gravitational field, is approximately 1.1×10^4 ms^{-1}. At what temperature will the root mean square of H_2 be equal to its escape velocity?
(a) 2.022×10^5 K (b) 1.796×10^4 K
(c) 1.963×10^2 K (d) 1.552×10^5 K

Diffusion and Effusion

Diffusion

Diffusion is the process of intermixing of two or more gases **without any external support**, irrespective of density, gravity etc.

Effusion

It is a special case of diffusion. It is the escape of gas molecules through a tiny hole such as a pinhole in a balloon. Both the rate of diffusion and effusion of a gas are described on the basis of Graham's law.

Graham's law (1848)

It states that "at constant temperature and pressure rate of diffusion (effusion) of gases is inversely proportional to the square root of their densities (or their molar masses)".

$$\text{Rate of diffusion} \propto \frac{1}{\sqrt{d}} \propto \frac{1}{\sqrt{M}}$$

If r_1 and r_2 are rates of diffusion of two gases of molecular weight M_1 and M_2 and their densities are d_1 and d_2 respectively then

$$\frac{\text{Rate of diffusion of gas (1), } r_1}{\text{Rate of diffusion of gas (2), } r_2} = \frac{\sqrt{\text{Density of (2)}}}{\sqrt{\text{Density of (1)}}} = \sqrt{\frac{d_2}{d_1}}$$

$$= \frac{\sqrt{\text{Molar mass of (2)}}}{\sqrt{\text{Molar mass of (1)}}}$$

$$= \sqrt{\frac{M_2}{M_1}}$$

- If V_1 is the volume of gas 1 diffused in time t_1 and V_2 is the volume of gas 2 diffused in time t_2 then

$$r_1 = \frac{V_1}{t_1} \text{ and } r_2 = \frac{V_2}{t_2}$$

$$\Rightarrow \quad \frac{r_1}{r_2} = \sqrt{\frac{M_2}{M_1}} = \frac{V_1 t_2}{V_2 t_1}$$

- If two gases diffuse under different pressures, p_1 and p_2 then,

$$r \propto \frac{p}{\sqrt{M}}$$

or

$$r \propto \frac{p}{\sqrt{d}}$$

$$\therefore \quad \frac{r_1}{r_2} = \frac{p_1}{p_2}\sqrt{\frac{M_2}{M_1}} = \frac{p_1}{p_2}\sqrt{\frac{d_2}{d_1}}$$

Hence, relative rate of diffusion of a gas under different pressures are

$$\frac{r_1}{r_2} = \frac{p_1}{p_2} (M_1 = M_2)$$

Separation factor

- The separation factor is used for enrichment of species present in small concentration.
- The separation factor 'f' of a process of isotopic separation is defined as the ratio of the relative concentration of a given species **after processing** to its relative concentration **before processing.**
- For a single-stage diffusion process, the maximum separation factor is simply the ratio of the rates of diffusion of the isotopic molecules based on Graham's law of diffusion.
- If n_1 and n_2 are the concentration of two isotopic species before processing and n_1' and n_2' after processing then Separation factor,

$$f = \frac{n_1'/n_2'}{n_1/n_2}$$

If enrichment of a mixture of isotopes is carried out in n steps then separation factor,

$$f = \frac{n_1'/n_2'}{n_1/n_2} = \left(\sqrt{\frac{M_2}{M_1}}\right)^n$$

$$n \log \sqrt{\frac{M_2}{M_1}} = \log f$$

$$= \log \frac{n_1'/n_2'}{n_1/n_2}$$

$$\therefore \quad n = \log \frac{n_1'/n_2'}{n_1/n_2} \Big/ \log \sqrt{\frac{M_2}{M_1}}$$

Solved Examples & Instant Practice

Example 3.30) 1.4L of an unknown gas required 57 s to diffuse and the same volume of N_2 gas takes 84 s to diffuse under the same conditions of temperature and pressure. What is molar mass of the unknown gas ?

Sol. Rate of diffusion $\propto \sqrt{\frac{1}{M}} \propto \frac{V}{t}$

Comparison of $\left(\frac{V}{t}\right)$ and $\sqrt{\frac{1}{M}}$ gives molar mass of the unknown gas.

$$\frac{r_X}{r_{N_2}} = \frac{1.4/57}{1.4/84} = \sqrt{\frac{28}{M_X}}$$

$$\therefore \quad \frac{M_X}{28} = \left(\frac{57}{84}\right)^2$$

$$\therefore \quad M_X = 12.9 \text{ g mol}^{-1}$$

Immediate Test 19

CO_2 effuses from an effusion apparatus at rate of 102.0 mL s^{-1}, while unknown gas effuses under identical conditions at the rate of 83.3 mL s^{-1}. What is molar mass of the unknown gas?

Example 3.31) In the experiment as shown, NH_3 and HCl vapours meet at a point where white fumes of NH_4Cl appear. At what fraction of the distance along the tube from the ammonia solution does the white fumes first form ?

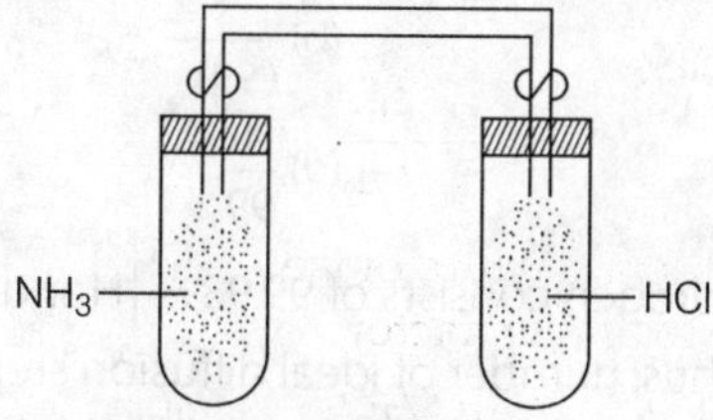

Sol.

$$\frac{r_{HCl}}{r_{NH_3}} = \sqrt{\frac{M_{NH_3}}{M_{HCl}}}$$

NH_3 (lighter gas) moves faster than HCl (heavier gas). Thus, distance travelled by NH_3 is larger than that travelled by HCl in the same time.

$$\frac{r_{HCl}}{r_{NH_3}} = \sqrt{\frac{17.0}{36.5}} = 0.682$$

Thus, if distance travelled by $NH_3 = x$

then distance travelled by HCl = $0.682x$

total length = $x + 0.682x = (1.682)x$

Thus, fraction of distance travelled by

$$NH_3 = \frac{x}{1.682x} = 0.595$$

Immediate Test 20

N_2O makes one laugh and SO_3 makes one tearing. As shown two flasks of uniform size are joined by a tube.

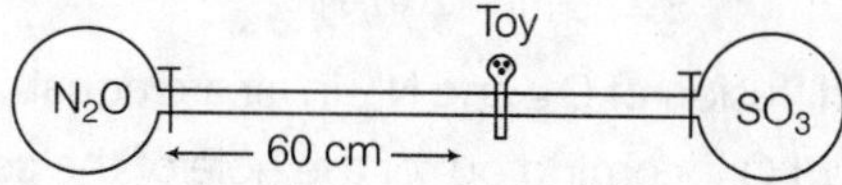

Stopcocks of these flasks are opened and closed at the same time. A toy (hypothetical case) standing at a distance of 60 cm from the side N_2O laughs and has tears at the same moment. Calculate the length of the tube.

Example 3.32) LPG is a mixture of *n*-butane and propane. It effuses from a gas cylinder at the rate of 100 $m^3 h^{-1}$. Oxygen gas effuses from the same type of cylinder at the rate of 132 $m^3 h^{-1}$. What is the composition of the LPG ?

Sol.

$$\frac{r_{LPG}}{r_{O_2}} = \sqrt{\frac{32}{M_{LPG}}} = \frac{100}{132}$$

$$\therefore \quad M_{LPG} = 55.76 \text{ g mol}^{-1}$$

If mole fraction of butane is χ_1 then that of propane is $(1 - \chi_1)$

$$\therefore \quad 55 \cdot 76 = \frac{M_1\chi_1 + M_2(1-\chi_1)}{\chi_1 + \chi_2}$$

$$55.76 = \frac{58\chi_1 + 44(1-\chi_1)}{1}$$

$$\chi_1 = 0.84$$

Thus, *n*-butane = 84 %

Immediate Test 21

(i) Following equilibrium is established at 1500 K and at 1.8 Torr.

$$Cl_2 \rightleftharpoons 2Cl$$

Under these conditions, mixture of Cl_2 and Cl effuses 1.16 times as fast as Kr (84 g mol^{-1}) effuses under the same conditions. Calculate the fraction of chlorine molecules dissociated into atoms.

(ii) What is the composition of the air that comes out of the hole at a pressure *p* atm? Assume, air is a mixture of 80% N_2 and 20% O_2.

(iii) Naturally occurring uranium consists of 99.3% by mass of $^{238}_{92}U$ and 0.7% $^{238}_{92}U$. How many ideal diffusion steps would be required to produce 99.7% pure $^{238}_{92}U$ from UF_6(F = 19).

KNOWLEDGE CONFIRMATION **Test 4**

1 A gas which will diffuse twice as fast as SO_2 is

(a) He (b) CH_4
(c) O_2 (d) HI

2 Rate of diffusion of O_2 and N_2 in air are equal. Thus, mole fraction of O_2 coming out of the hole of the container is

(a) 0.19 (b) 0.81
(c) 0.50 (d) 0.75

3 A given amount of O_2 effused from a container in 32.5 min. It took 23.0 min for the same amount of another gas to effuse from the same container under the same conditions. Thus, molar mass of the second gas is

(a) 64.0 g mol^{-1}
(b) 32.0 g mol^{-1}
(c) 16.0 g mol^{-1}
(d) 4.0 g mol^{-1}

4 N_2 and O_2 combine to form NO under given experimental conditions. NO appears in the form of brown fumes. If N_2 and O_2 are released from the two vessels of equal size at the same moment, then at what fraction of the distance along the tube from O_2 side do the brown fumes appear ?

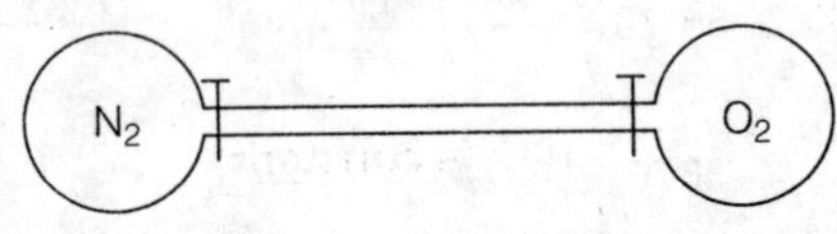

(a) 0.48 (b) 0.52
(c) 2.07 (d) 1.92

5 Compare the rate of diffusion of H_2 gas at pressure p and a temperature T, and He at pressure $2p$ and a temperature T.

(a) 0.705 (b) 1.00
(c) 1.42 (d) 0.295

6 The pressure of the O_2 gas in a vessel dropped from 2000 Torr to 1500 Torr in 55 min as the O_2 leaked through the small hole into vacuum. When the same vessel was filled with another gas same drop in pressure occured in 85 min. Thus, molar mass of the other gas is

(a) 40 g mol^{-1} (b) 85 g mol^{-1}
(c) 80 g mol^{-1} (d) 76 g mol^{-1}

7 A certain hydrocarbon effuses about half as fast as methane. Thus, saturated hydrocarbon is

(a) C_2H_6 (b) C_3H_8
(c) C_5H_4 (d) C_5H_{12}

8 50 mL of H_2 gas diffuse through a small hole from a vessel in 20 min. Time taken by 40mL of O_2 gas to diffuse under similar conditions will be

(a) 12 min (b) 64 min
(c) 8 min (d) 32 min

9 100 mL of O_2 gas diffuse in 10s. 100 mL of gas X diffuse in t s. Gas X and time t respectively can be

(a) H_2, 2.5 s (b) SO_2, 16 s
(c) CO, 10 s (d) He, 4 s

10 At what ratio of N_2 and He (moles) will the rates of effusion of the gases from the toy balloon containing He and N_2 become equal at pressure p

(a) 7 (b) $\sqrt{7}$
(c) 0.378 (d) 0.25

11 1.6 g of methane gas at 2.0 bar takes 40 s to diffusion through a pinhole, whereas 3.2 g gas X at 4.0 bar takes 20 s to diffuse through the same hole. It gas X is SO_n, value of n is

(a) 1 (b) 2
(c) 3 (d) 4

12 Ordinary water H_2O contains about 1% D_2O. Thus, overall separation factor is to get 99.0% D_2O from ordinary water is

(a) $(99)^2$ (b) $\frac{1}{(99)^2}$
(c) (99) (d) $\frac{1}{99}$

13 Natural hydrogen consists of 99.98% ${}_1^1H$ and and 0.02% ${}_1^2H$ by mass. Thus, number of ideal diffusion steps to produce 99% pure (${}^1H^2H$) from ordinary gaseous hydrogen is about

(a) 50 (b) 60
(c) 66 (d) 86

14 Rate of diffusion of helium gas is about 7 times faster than that of PCl_5 which dissociates into PCl_3 and Cl_2. Thus, degree of dissociation of PCl_5 is (P = 31)

(a) 10.1% (b) 6.4%
(c) 5.1% (d) 3.2%

15 A space capsule is filled with neon gas at 1.00 atom at 290 K. The gas effuses through a pinhole into outerspace at such a rate that the pressure drops by 0.30 Torr s^{-1}. The pressure drops if NH_3 is used under identical condition is

(a) 0.30 Torr s^{-1} (b) 0.33 Torr s^{-1}
(c) 0.29 Torr s^{-1} (d) 0.40 Torr s^{-1}

Collision Frequency and Mean Free Path

Collision frequency

During the random motion, the gas molecules collide with other molecules, the number of collisions that a molecule undergoes per second is called collision frequency. It is denoted by Z. It depends on

(i) the distance a molecule moves and

(ii) the number of gas molecules per unit volume (i.e. the pressure).

In a given time period, a molecule will collide with any other molecule whose centre lies within a cylinder with cross-sectional area σ.

$$\sigma = \pi d^2,$$

where, d called collision diameter, is the distance between the centres of two atoms in contact due to collision.

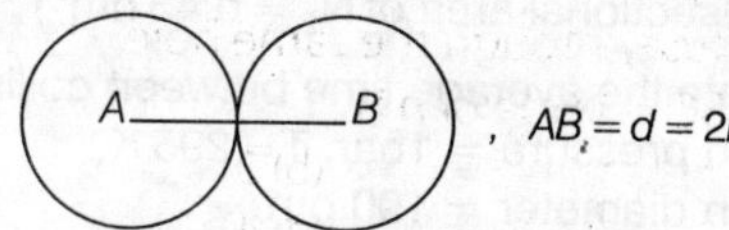

Based on kinetic theory, **collision frequency** is given by

$$Z = \sqrt{2} N_0 (u_{av}) \sigma \left(\frac{p}{RT}\right)$$

where, N_0 = Avogadro's number = $6.02 \times 10^{23}\ mol^{-1}$

u_{av} = Mean speed = $\sqrt{\frac{8RT}{\pi M}}$,

σ = Cross-sectional area,

p = Pressure,

T = Temperature, R = Gas constant.

Mean free path

The average of the distance travelled by a molecule between successive collisions is called mean free path λ.

$$\lambda = \frac{\text{Distance travelled in 1s}}{\text{Number of collisions in 1s}} = \frac{u_{av}}{Z}$$

$$\lambda = \frac{RT}{\sqrt{2} N_0 \sigma p}$$

$$\Rightarrow \quad \lambda = \frac{1}{\sqrt{2} \sigma N^*}$$

where, N^* is the number of molecules per unit volume and $p = N^* kT = N^* \frac{RT}{N_0}$, k is called **Boltzmann's constant.**

- Mean free path (λ) is dependent on temperature $T (\lambda \propto T)$ and cross-sectional area, $\sigma \left(\lambda \propto \frac{1}{\sigma}\right)$.

  Since, $\sigma = \pi (2r)^2 = 4\pi r^2$, hence, smaller molecules have larger mean free path.

- Mean free path is inversely proportional to the pressure $\left(\lambda \propto \frac{1}{p}\right)$, if p increases λ decreases.

$$\lambda \propto \frac{1}{N^*} \quad (N^* = \text{number of molecules per unit volume})$$

As, $$\lambda \propto \frac{T}{p}$$

$$\lambda \propto T \text{ (if } p \text{ is constant)}$$

$$\lambda \propto \frac{1}{p} \text{ (if } T \text{ is constant)}$$

By Gay Lussac's law, $p \propto T$ at constant V, thus λ is constant. Thus, if volume is constant, λ remains constant on changing T of p.

Diffusion coefficient

The diffusion coefficient of an ideal gas is proportional to its mean free path and average speed.

$$\text{Diffusion coefficient} \propto u_{av} \propto \lambda$$

$$\text{Thus, diffusion coefficient} \propto \frac{RT u_{av}}{\sqrt{2} N_0 \sigma p}$$

Solved Examples & Instant Practice

Example 3.33) For N_2 gas, calculate

(a) the collision frequency and

(b) the mean free path at 1 bar and 298 K (standard states)

For N_2, cross-sectional area $\sigma = 0.43\ nm^2$.

Collision frequency is the number of collisions taking place per second.

Collision frequency $(Z) = \sqrt{2} N_0 (u_{av}) \sigma \left(\frac{p}{RT}\right)$

and mean free path $(\lambda) = \frac{\text{Distance travelled sec}^{-1}}{Z}$

where σ *is the cross-sectional area* $= \pi(2r)^2 = 4\pi r^2$

p the pressure, R gas constant, T the temperature and u_{av} *is the average velocity.*

$$u_{av} = \sqrt{\frac{8RT}{\pi M}}$$

Sol.

(a) $u_{av} = \sqrt{\frac{8RT}{\pi M}} = \sqrt{\frac{8 \times 8.3143 \times 298}{\pi \times 28 \times 10^{-3}}} = 474.7\ ms^{-1}$

1 bar $= 1 \times 10^5$ Pa

$\therefore \quad Z = \sqrt{2} \times \frac{(6.02 \times 10^{23}) \times 474.7 \times (0.43 \times 10^{-18})(1 \times 10^5)}{8.3143 \times 298}$

$= 7.01 \times 10^9 s^{-1}$

(b) Distance travelled $s^{-1} = 474.7\ ms^{-1}$

$\therefore$ Mean free path $(\lambda) = \frac{474.7\ ms^{-1}}{7.01 \times 10^9 s^{-1}} = 6.77 \times 10^{-8}$m

Example 3.34) At what pressure, will the mean free path be equal to the collision diameter for He at 298 K? (Collision diameter of He = 0.218 nm).

Sol. Mean free path $(\lambda) = \frac{RT}{\sqrt{2} N_0 \sigma p}$

Given, σ = cross-sectional area $= \pi d^2 = \pi(2r)^2$

$\therefore$ where, $d = 2r$ (d is called collision diameter) $= 0.218 \times 10^{-9}$m

Given, $\lambda = (2r)$

$\therefore \quad 2r = \frac{8.3143 \times 298}{\sqrt{2} \times 6.02 \times 10^{23} \times \pi (2r)^2 \times p}$

put $\quad 2r = 0.218 \times 10^{-9}$m

$\therefore \quad p = \frac{8.3143 \times 298}{\sqrt{2} \times 6.02 \times 10^{23} \times \pi (0.218 \times 10^{-9})^3}$

$= 8.94 \times 10^7$ Pa = 894 bar

Immediate Test 22

(i) Calculate the pressure at which mean free path of N_2 gas is 10 cm at 298 K.
(Cross-sectional area of $N_2 = 0.43\ nm^2$)

(ii) Calculate the average time between collisions in air. Assume pressure = 1bar, T = 295 K, collision diameter = 190 pm.

(iii) Molecular diameter of CO is 3.19×10^{-10}m. Calculate
(a) collision frequency,
(b) number of molecules colliding per second and
(c) mean free path at 300K and 1 bar pressure.

(iv) The mean free path (λ) for N_2 at 273 K and 1 bar pressure is 1×10^{-7}m. Calculate collision diameter for N_2.

KNOWLEDGE CONFIRMATION Test 5

1 Mean free path is maximum for the molecules of
(a) H_2 (b) N_2
(c) O_2 (d) Cl_2

2 If temperature is doubled and pressure is halved, mean free path changes by a factor of
(a) 1 (b) 2 (c) 4 (d) $\frac{1}{4}$

3 Multiple of mean free path and collision frequency is equal to
(a) rms speed (b) average speed
(c) most probable speed (d) translational kinetic energy

4 The diffusion coefficient of an ideal gas is proportional to
(a) mean free path (b) average speed
(c) Both of the above (d) None of these

5 If absolute temperature of an ideal gas is increased 4 times and its pressure is increased 2 times, then diffusion coefficient of the gas increases
(a) 2 times (b) 4 times
(c) 8 times (d) 32 times

6 Xenon has a very large hard sphere of diameter of 4.00 Å. Thus, collision frequency at 1.00 bar and 273 K for one mole of a gas (Xe) is
(a) $1.25 \times 10^8 s^{-1}$ (b) $1.0 \times 10^9 s^{-1}$
(c) $4.2 \times 10^6 s^{-1}$ (d) $2.0 \times 10^6 s^{-1}$

7 The mean free path depends on the ratio T/p. What value of (T/P) is necessary for the mean free path of He ($2r = 65$pm) to equal 130 pm? (In Kelvin/Pascal).
(a) 2.8×10^{-9} (b) 1.77×10^{-10}
(c) 1.77×10^{-7} (d) 2.9×10^{-7}

8 Mean free path of N_2 at 0°C at 1atm is 10^{-7} m. Thus, mean free path at 1 Torr is
(a) 10^{-9} m (b) 10^{-7} m/760
(c) 760×10^{-7} m (d) 76×10^{-7} m

9 Collision diameter, $d(=2r)$ is related to pressure when mean free path λ is equal to d, by
(a) $d = \frac{RT}{\sqrt{2} N_A p\pi}$ (b) $d = \left[\frac{RT}{\sqrt{2} N_A p\pi}\right]^3$
(c) $d = \left[\frac{RT}{\sqrt{2} N_A p\pi}\right]^{1/3}$ (d) None of these

10 Select correct variation of λ
(a) $\frac{d\lambda}{dT} = \frac{R}{\sqrt{2} N_o \sigma p}$ (b) $\frac{d\lambda}{dp} = -\frac{RT}{\sqrt{2} N_o \sigma p^2}$
(c) $\frac{d\lambda}{d\sigma} = -\frac{RT}{\sqrt{2} N_o \sigma^2 p}$ (d) All are correct variation of λ

11 The mean free path of the molecule of a certain gas at 300 K is 2.6×10^{-5} m. The collision diameter of the molecule is 0.26 nm. Thus, number of molecules per unit volume is
(a) 1.281×10^{23} m^{-3} (b) 3.012×10^{23} m^{-3}
(c) 6.912×10^{20} m^{-3} (d) 1.281×10^{17} m^{-3}

12 Two flasks A and B have equal volumes. A is maintained at 300 K and B at 600 K.

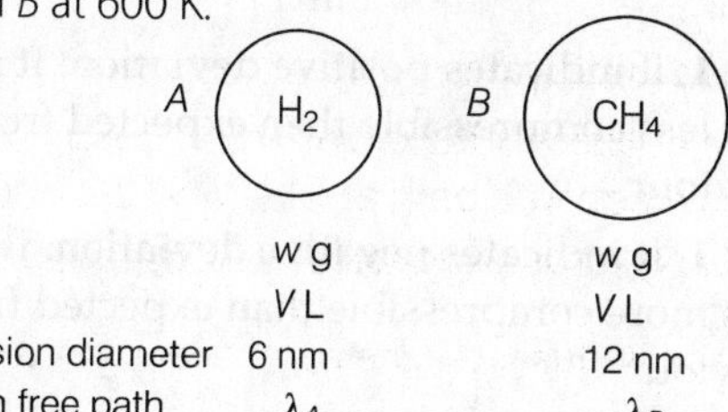

Thus,
(a) $\lambda_A / \lambda_B = 2$ (b) $\lambda_A / \lambda_B = 1/2$
(c) $\lambda_A / \lambda_B = 1$ (d) $\lambda_A / \lambda_B = 4$

13 If 'b' is the van der Waals ' volume correction, then, mean free path can be expressed as
(a) $\frac{RT}{\sqrt{2}(N_0\pi)^{1/3}\, bp}$ (b) $\frac{RT}{\sqrt{2}(N_0\pi)\, bp}$
(c) $\frac{RT\, bp}{\sqrt{2}(N_0\pi)}$ (d) $\frac{RT}{\sqrt{2}(N_0\pi)^{1/3}(1.5b)^{2/3}\, p}$

14 The mean free path of the molecule of a certain gas at 400 K is 2.0×10^{-5} m. The collision diameter of the molecule is 0.20 nm. Thus, pressure of the gas is
(a) 155.4 Pa (b) 15.54 Pa (c) 1554 Pa (d) 0.1554 Pa

Real Gas (The van der Waals' Equation)

Real gases

For an ideal gas, all related gas laws are followed but there is no gas which follows all the gas laws under given conditions of temperature and pressure.

So, particularly ideal gas does not exist. Real gases follow the gas laws only at high temperature and low pressure.

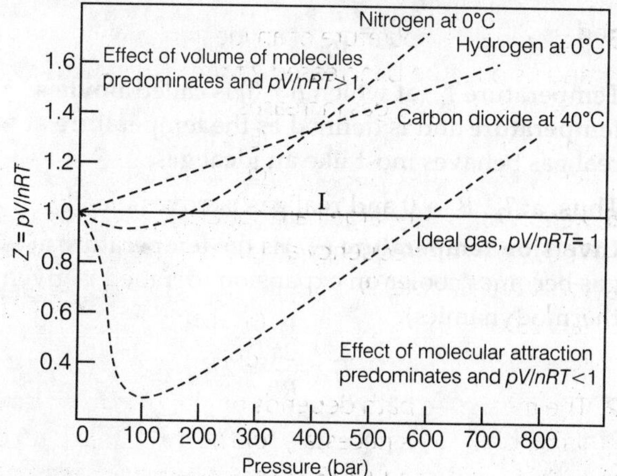

Deviation from ideal gas behaviour, shown by a plot of the compressibility factor, $Z = \frac{pV}{nRT}$ as a function of p for some gases.

Behaviour of real gases

For ideal gas a plot of $\left(\frac{pV}{RT}\right)$ against p at constant temperature is a straight line as shown in figure, and for one mole the value of $\frac{pV}{RT}$ is 1.

But for real gas this value of $\left(\frac{pV}{RT}\right)$ is not equal to 1 and for the real gases the plot of $\frac{pV}{RT}$ against pressure is not a straight line. It means real **gases show deviation from ideal gas behaviour.**

Compressibility factor

The extent to which the measured value of $\left(\frac{pV}{RT}\right)$ called compressibility factor 'Z' deviates from 1, is a measure of non-ideality of a gas.

$$Z = \frac{V_m \text{ (molar volume if gas is real)}}{V_m' \text{(molar volume if gas is ideal)}}$$

$$\frac{pV}{nRT} = Z$$

$Z = 1$ for ideal gas, $Z \neq 1$ for real gas

- In terms of density, $Z = \frac{pm}{dRT}$
- If $Z > 1$, it indicates positive deviation. It implies that the gas is less compressible than expected from ideal behaviour .
- If $Z < 1$, it indicates negative deviation. It implies that the gas is more compressible than expected from ideal behaviour.
- The extent of deviation at any given temperature and pressure depends on the nature of gas.
- Z approaches unity as pressure is lowered, $pV = nRT$ is applicable (at low pressure).

Compressibility factor (Z) for different gases

- $Z = 1$ for ideal gas
- $Z = \left(1 + \frac{pb}{RT}\right)$ for light gases as H_2, He etc. in which force of attraction is negligible.
- $Z = \left(1 - \frac{a}{RTV}\right)$ for gases as CO, CO_2 etc. in low pressure range.
- $Z = \left(1 + \frac{pb}{RT}\right)$ for gases as CO, CO_2 etc. in high pressure range.
- $Z = 1$ for all gases at low pressure and high temperature. Thus, behaviour of real gases approaches ideal behaviour under these conditions.

> ■ For CO, CO_2 etc. there is minimum in isotherms going from low pressure to high pressure.

van der Waals' equation

- For a real gas, van der Waals' equation is followed, it is given by

$$\left[p + \frac{n^2a}{V^2}\right](V - nb) = nRT$$

a and b are called van der Waals' constants.

$\left(\frac{n^2a}{V^2}\right)$ is called **pressure correction,** when force of attraction exists between molecules. Greater the value of 'a', greater the liquefaction. (nb) is called **volume correction** when volume of molecules cannot be neglected as compared to the total volume of the gas. 'b' is also called co-volume or excluded volume.

$$b = 4V$$

where, V = volume of all molecules in one mole of a gas.

- Volume of one molecule $= \frac{4}{3}\pi r^3$. Thus, volume of N_0 molecules in one mole of a gas $= \frac{4}{3}\pi r^3 N_0$

$$\therefore \quad b = 4\left(\frac{4}{3}\pi r^3 N_0\right)$$

Units of van der Waals' constants

Constant	SI Unit	Non SI Unit
$a\,(pV^2\ \text{mol}^{-2})$	Pascal $m^6\,mol^{-2}$	atm $L^2\,mol^{-2}$
$b(V\ \text{mol}^{-1})$	$m^3\,mol^{-1}$	$L\,mol^{-1}$

Kamerlingh Onnes equation of state

$$p = \frac{RT}{V}\left[1 + \frac{B}{V} + \frac{C}{V^2} + \ldots\ldots\right]$$

- This is also called virial equation of state. B and C are called second and third virial coefficients, first virial coefficient = 1, these are temperature dependent. C is meaningless at high volume.
- van der Waals' equation for one mole of a gas in terms of virial equation is

$$p = \frac{RT}{V}\left[1 + \frac{1}{V}\left(b - \frac{a}{RT}\right) + \ldots\ldots\right]$$

On comparison, $B = \left(b - \frac{a}{RT}\right)$

If $B = 0$, $\quad pV = RT$

and $\quad T_b = \frac{a}{Rb}$

- Temperature T_b (at which $B = 0$) is called **Boyle's temperature** and is defined as the temperature at which a real gas behaves most like an ideal gas.

  Thus, at T_b, $B \to 0$ and real gas behaves ideally.
- **Inversion temperature** (T_i) is the temperature at which gas becomes cooler on expansion (detailed is given in thermodynamics).

$$T_i = \frac{2a}{Rb} = 2T_b$$

Solved Examples & Instant Practice

Example 3.35) The density of steam is 0.5974 kgm^{-3} at 373 K and 1.01325 bar. Calculate the compressibility factor Z.

Sol. Compressibility factor Z is to be expressed in terms of density.

$$Z = \frac{pV}{nRT} \text{ for } n \text{ moles} = \frac{pV}{\frac{w}{m}RT} \text{ for } n \text{ moles}$$

Since, $\frac{\text{mass}}{\text{volume}} = \text{density}$

$\therefore$ $d = \frac{w}{V}$

$\therefore$ $Z = \frac{pm}{dRT} = \frac{1.01325 \times 10^5 \times 18 \times 10^{-3}}{0.5974 \times 8.3143 \times 373} = 0.9845$

- All parameters taken in MKS units.
  1 bar = 1.01325 × 10^5 Pa (exact)

Immediate Test 23

(i) 2.2 g CO_2 at 273 K and at a pressure of 1 bar occupies 1.0 dm^3. What is compressibility factor?

(ii) Compressibility factor of a gas behaving non-ideally is 0.90 at 273 K and at a pressure of 1 bar. Calculate molar volume under given conditions.

Example 3.36) Molecular diameter of argon gas (Ar) is 0.2944 nm. What is excluded volume of Ar gas ?

Sol. van der Waals' constant b is called excluded volume. It is four times the volume of molecules present in 1 mole of a gas.

Thus, $b = 4VN_0$

Given, $2r = 0.2944 \times 10^{-9}$ m

$\therefore$ $r = 0.1472 \times 10^{-9}$ m, $V = \frac{4}{3}\pi r^3$

$\therefore$ $b = 4\left(\frac{4}{3}\pi(0.1472 \times 10^{-9})^3\right) \times 6.02 \times 10^{23} = 3.217 \times 10^{-5}\ \text{m}^3\,\text{mol}^{-1}$

Immediate Test 24

Molecular radius of O_2 is 3.81×10^{-10} m. What is value of van der Waals' constant (b)?

Example 3.37) If attractive forces are negligible for a gas under given conditions, what is the pressure exerted by one mole of it at 300 K when it occupies 1000 L. ($b = 3.2 \times 10^{-5}\ \text{m}^3\text{mol}^{-1}$)

Sol. For one mole of a gas, van der Waals' equation is

$$\left(p + \frac{a}{V^2}\right)(V - b) = RT$$

When $\frac{a}{V^2}$ (attractive forces) = 0

$$p = \frac{RT}{(V - b)}$$

Take R in MKS unit.

$1\text{L} = 10^{-3}\ \text{m}^3$

$$p = \frac{8.3143 \times 300}{(1000 \times 10^{-3}\ \text{m}^3 - 3.2 \times 10^{-5})} = 2494.3\ \text{Pa}$$

Immediate Test 25

1 mole of a real gas occupies 22.4 dm^3 at 273 K. What is pressure exerted by it ? (a = 6.865 dm^6 atm mol^{-2}, b = 0.057 dm^{-3} mol^{-1})

Example 3.38) For a different gases, van der Waals' constants are

Gas	a(dm^{2}atm mol^{-2})	b (dm^3 mol^{-1})
H_2	0.244	0.0266
CO_2	3.59	0.0427

Calculate Z.

(a) For one mole H_2 at STP.

(b) For CO_2 at STP when volume occupied is 1000 dm^3 under low pressure at 300 K.

(c) For CO_2 at 1000 atm and 273 K.

Sol. (a) H_2 is a light gas, thus attractive forces are neglected.

$\therefore$ $p(V - b) = RT$

$$Z = \frac{pV}{RT} = \left(1 + \frac{pb}{RT}\right)$$

$$Z = \left(1 + \frac{1 \times 0.0266}{0.0821 \times 273}\right) = 1.0012$$

(b) When volume is very high and pressure is low

$(V - b) \approx V$

$\therefore$ $\left(p + \frac{a}{V^2}\right)V = RT$

$\therefore$ $Z = \left(1 - \frac{a}{RTV}\right)$

$$Z = \left(1 - \frac{3.59}{0.0821 \times 300 \times 1000}\right) = 0.9998$$

(c) Pressure is very high (1000 atm) thus $\left(p + \frac{a}{V^2}\right) \approx p$

$\therefore$ $p(V - b) = RT$

$\therefore$ $Z = \left(1 + \frac{pb}{RT}\right)$

$$= 1 + \frac{1000 \times 0.0427}{(0.0821 \times 273)} = 2.905$$

Immediate Test 26

(i) van der Waals' equation can also be written as

$$p = \frac{RT}{V}\left[1 + \left(b - \frac{a}{RT}\right)\frac{1}{V} + ...\right]$$

If, $Z = 1.000054$ at 273 K and 1 atm, and Boyle's temperature is 107 K, calculate van der Waals' constant a and b.

(ii) A gas obeying the equation $p(V - b) = RT$ has $Z = 1.0018$ at 300 K and 1 atm. Assuming the molecule to be of spherical shape, calculate the diameter.

KNOWLEDGE CONFIRMATION Test 6

1 In the van der Waals' equation, $\left(p+\frac{a}{V^2}\right)(V-b)=RT$ force of attraction between molecules is indicated by

(a) $\frac{a}{V^2}$ (b) b (c) $(V-b)$ (d) $\left(p+\frac{a}{V^2}\right)$

2 van der Waals' constants 'a' of different gases are given in L^2 atm mol^{-2}.

I	II	II	IV
1.70	6.20	5.20	0.70

Which gas is liquefied to maximum extent?

(a) I (b) II (c) III (d) IV

3 A real gas most likely approaches the behaviour of an ideal gas at

(a) high p, low T (b) high p, low T
(c) low p, low T (d) low p, high T

4 Compressibility factor Z is expressed in the unit of

(a) atm-volume (b) atm/volume
(c) atm-volume/ Temperature (d) unitless

5 When second virial coefficient approaches zero ($B\rightarrow 0$), then

(a) $pV=RT$
(b) temperature is called Boyle's temperature
(c) $a=RbT$
(d) All are correct statements

6 Atm L mol^{-1} represents

(a) $\frac{b}{a}$ (b) $\frac{a}{b}$ (c) ab (d) ab^2

7 Compressibility factor Z given below for H_2

$Z=\left(1+\frac{pb}{RT}\right)$ is given by isotherm

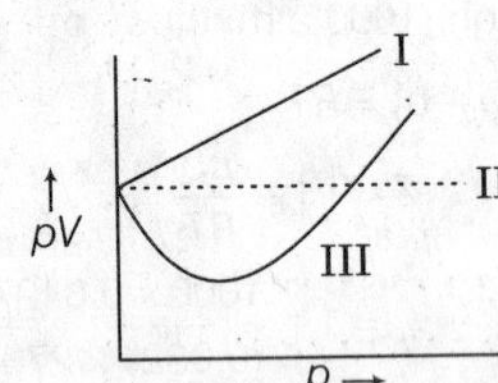

(a) I (b) II (c) II (d) None of these

8 If V is the volume of one molecule, then van der Waals' constant b is

(a) $4V$ (b) V (c) $4V\,N_0$ (d) $\frac{4V}{N_0}$

9 16 g CH_4 at 273 K and 1 bar pressure occupies 21.2 dm^3. Thus, there is

(a) positive deviation from ideal behaviour
(b) negative deviation from ideal behaviour
(c) no deviation from ideal behaviour
(d) no conclusion based on given data

10 In the following isotherms, I (for ideal gas) and II (for real gas), points X and Y on II with respect to I indicate ....deviation

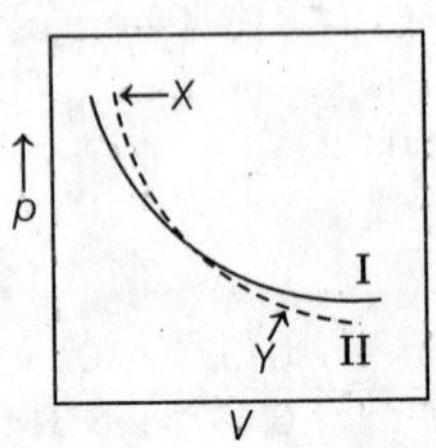

(a) positive, negative (b) positive, positive
(c) negative, negative (d) negative, positive

11 In terms of density, compressibility factor is given by

(a) $\frac{pd}{RTM}$ (b) $\frac{dRT}{pM}$ (c) $\frac{pM}{dRT}$ (d) $\frac{p}{dRT}$

12 Molar density of CO at STP is 1.20. Thus,

(a) $Z>1$ (b) $Z=1$
(c) $Z<1$ (d) $Z>>1$

13 Select correct variation of compressibility factor

(a) $\frac{d(Z)}{dp}=\frac{V}{nRT}$ (b) $\frac{d(Z)}{dV}=\frac{p}{nRT}$
(c) $\frac{d(Z)}{dT}=-\frac{Z}{T}$ (d) All are correct

14 The compressibility factor (Z) of a gas is less than unity at STP. Thus, molar volume (V_m)

(a) $V_m>22.4\,dm^3$ (b) $V_m<22.4\,dm^3$
(c) $V_m=22.4\,dm^3$ (d) $V_m=44.8\,dm^3$

15 For the non-zero volume of the molecules, van der Waals' equation for n moles of the gas will be

(a) $\left(p+\frac{a}{V^2}\right)V=RT$ (b) $pV=nRT+nbp$
(c) $p(V-nb)=nRT$ (d) Both (b) and (c)

16 If V_r = volume of the real gas and V_{id} = volume of the ideal gas under identical conditions of temperature and pressure, then Z (compressibility factor)

(a) $V_{id}V_r$ (b) V_r/V_{id}
(c) V_{id}/V_r (d) V_r^2/V_{id}

17 Which assumption of kinetic molecular theory is not followed when a real gas shows non-ideal behaviour?

(a) Gas molecules move at random with no attractive forces between them
(b) The velocity of gas molecules is dependent on temperature
(c) The amount of space occupied by a gas is much greater than the space occupied by the actual gas molecules
(d) In collisions with the walls of the container or with other molecules, energy is conserved

18 Which of the following gases follows non-ideal behaviour?
(a) N_2 gas having density 1.25 g L^{-1} at STP
(b) 2.8 g CO gas in 0.1 L flask exerting a pressure of 24.63 atm at 300 K
(c) 1.6 g CH_4 in 0.5 L flask at 273 K exerting a pressure of 4 atm
(d) 0.1 g H_2 gas at STP occupies volume of 1.12 L

19 If $b = x$ dm^{3}mol^{-1} of a gas then radius of the molecule will be
(a) $\left(\frac{3x}{16\pi N_0}\right)^{1/3}$ dm (b) $\left(\frac{3x}{16\pi N_0}\right)^{1/2}$ dm
(c) $\left(\frac{3x}{16\pi N_0}\right)$ dm (d) $\left(\frac{3x}{16\pi N_0}\right)^{3}$ dm

20 Assume that the equation, $pV = RT(1 + \alpha p)$ can be used to describe a real gas at low pressure where α is constant. Then $\left(\frac{\partial V}{\partial T}\right)_p$ is
(a) VT (b) V/T (c) $-VT$ (d) $-V/T^2$

21 At STP, compressibility factor of O_2 is 0.927. Thus, amount of O_2 necessary to fill a gas cylinder of 100 dm^3 capacity under the given conditions is
(a) 0.154 kg (b) 1.540 kg (c) 15.4 kg (d) 79.00 kg

22 Based on following observations for given mass of N_2 gas.

T/K	p/MPa	Z	Volume/dm^3
223 K	81.06	1.95	1.0 dm^3
373 K	20.265	1.10	V

volume V is
(a) 1.0 dm^3 (b) 0.1 dm^3 (c) 3.8 dm^3 (d) 7.9 dm^3

23 Select correct statement(s) for two real gases X and Y.
(a) If two gases have same value of 'a' but different value of 'b', then smaller the value of b, larger the compressibility.
(b) If two gases gas have same value of 'b' but different values of 'a' then the gas having a larger value of 'a' will occupy lesser volumes
(c) Both of the above are correct
(d) None of the above is correct

24 For one mole of real gas, isotherm between pV (along y-axis) and p (along X-axis) has intercept OA equal to

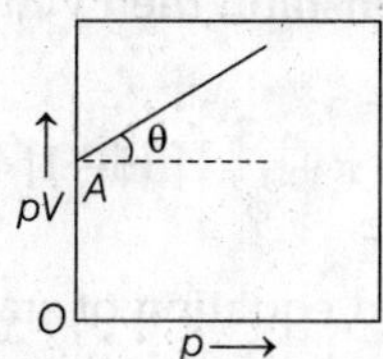

(a) RT (b) pb (c) $\frac{a}{V}$ (d) $\frac{ab}{V^2}$

25 In the above graph, excluded volume is equal to
(a) $\frac{\tan\theta}{RT}$ (b) $\frac{RT}{\tan\theta}$
(c) $\frac{\tan\theta}{p}$ (d) $\frac{p}{\tan\theta}$

26 At 400 K, second virial coefficient of N_2 gas 1.2×10^{-5} m^3 mol^{-1}.
Thus, molar volume of N_2 gas at 400 K and 8.0 bar is
(a) 0.420 m^3 mol^{-1}
(b) 0.042 m^3 mol^{-1}
(c) 1.69 m^3 mol^{-1}
(d) 7.6×10^2 m^3 mol^{-1}

27 Volume occupied by 1 mole of a real gas is $RT/2p$. if b is negligible. Thus,
(a) $RT = 2\sqrt{ap}$ (b) $RT = 2ap$
(c) $\sqrt{ap} = 2RT$ (d) $ap = 2RT$

28 When molecular attraction is negligible, then the slope for an isochore between p and T is

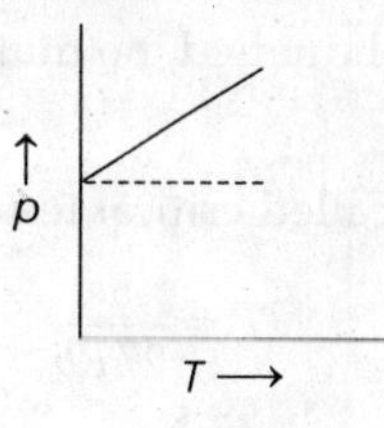

(a) $\frac{R}{V}$ (b) $\frac{R}{p}$
(c) $\frac{R}{V-b}$ (d) zero

29 For values of Z near 1, it is a good approximation to write

$$Z(p) = 1 + \left(\frac{\partial Z}{\partial p}\right)_T p$$

If $Z = 1.0014$ at 298 K and 1 bar and Boyle temperature of the gas is 155 K, then van der Waals' constants a and b are

	a (L^2 bar mol^{-2})	b (L mol^{-1})
(a)	0.692	0.0537
(b)	0.692	0.537
(c)	0.0692	0.0537
(d)	0.0692	0.537

30 For the above data, molar volume of the gas is
(a) 0.248 L mol^{-1} (b) 24.8 L mol^{-1}
(c) 22.4 L mol^{-1} (d) 0.224 L mol^{-1}

Critical Constants

Liquefaction of gases

- Any gas can be liquefied by decreasing its temperature and increasing pressure $\left(\text{as } V \propto \frac{1}{p} \text{ and } V \propto T\right)$.
- Decrease in temperature causes decrease in kinetic energy $\left(\text{KE} = \frac{3}{2}RT\right)$ of the molecules and increase in pressure decreases the average distance between molecules.
- When molecules are close together (with low kinetic energy under given conditions) they do not possess enough energy to overcome the force of attraction between molecules and gas is liquefied.

Critical temperature

For each substance, there exists a temperature above which substance cannot be liquefied, no matter how great the applied pressure.

This temperature is called critical temperature (T_c).

$$T_c = \frac{8a}{27Rb}$$

It is the maximum temperature at which a gas can be liquefied.

Critical pressure

The minimum pressure required to liquefy a gas at its critical temperature is called critical pressure (p_c).

$$p_c = \frac{a}{27b^2}$$

Critical volume

Volume occupied by one mole of a substance at critical temperature and critical pressure is called critical volume (V_c).

$$V_c = 3b$$

As temperature increases, density of gas increases and that of liquid decreases, at $T = T_c$ both (density of liquid and that of gas) are equal.

- **Compressibility factor under critical point**

$$Z = \frac{p_cV_c}{RT_c} = \frac{\left(\frac{a}{27b^2}\right)(3b)}{R\left(\frac{8a}{27Rb}\right)} = \frac{3}{8}$$

$$\therefore \quad \boxed{Z = \frac{p_cV_c}{RT_c} = \frac{3}{8}}$$

- **van der Waals' constants in terms of critical constants**

$$b = \frac{V_c}{3}$$

$$a = 27\,p_c\,b^2 = 27p_c\left(\frac{V_c}{3}\right)^2 = 3p_cV_c^2$$

$$a = \frac{27Rb\,T_c}{8} = \frac{27R}{8}\left(\frac{V_c}{3}\right)T_c = \frac{9\,RV_cT_c}{8}$$

Important points regarding critical constants

- At the critical point, the density of the substance in gaseous and liquid states remains same.
- Gases below their T_c are called **vapours.**
- Fluids above T_c, are called super critical fluids (and is a gas).
- Gaseous substances whose T_c are above room temperature can be liquefied by applying sufficient pressure to the gas.
- Gaseous substances whose T_c are below room temperature can only be liquefied by applying pressure and lowering of temperature (of a value below T_c).
- Vapour can be condensed by applying pressure but to liquefy a gas, we must both apply pressure and lower the temperature.

Reduced constants

If $\frac{p}{p_c} = \pi$, $\frac{V}{V_c} = \phi$ and $\frac{T}{T_c} = \theta$

Here, π is called reduced pressure, ϕ the reduced volume and θ the reduced constant, then van der Waals' equation is reduced to

$$\left[\pi + \frac{3}{\phi^2}\right][3\phi - 1] = 8\theta$$

This is called reduced equation of state and is applicable for gaseous, liquid and solid states.

Solved Examples & Instant Practice

Example 3.39) **Calculate critical volume of one mole of CO_2 at its critical temperature (304 K) and critical pressure (50 bar).**

Sol.

$$p_c V_c = \frac{3n}{8} RT_c$$

$$V_c = \frac{3RT_c}{8p_c} \quad \text{for one mole}$$

$$V_c = \frac{3 \times 0.0831 \times 304}{8 \times 50} = 0.189 \text{ dm}^3$$

Immediate Test 27

Argon has a critical temperature of $-122°C$ and a critical pressure of 48 atm. Calculate its critical density ($Ar = 40 \text{ g mol}^{-1}$)

Example 3.40) **A substance at 300 K (room temperature) can be a gas or vapour. 1 mole of this substance at T_c and p_c of 50 atmosphere occupies volume 0.300 dm^3. What is the nature of substance?**

Sol. Substances above T_c are gaseous fluids.

Substances below T_c are vapour.

Thus, if T_c is known, nature of substance can be decided.

$$T_c = \frac{8}{3}\frac{p_c V_c}{R} = \frac{8}{3}\left(\frac{50 \times 0.300}{0.0821}\right) = 487 \text{ K}$$

Room temperature (300 K) < T_c

Thus, substance is in vapour state.

Example 3.41) **For O_2, van der Waals' constant $b = 0.0319 \text{ L mol}^{-1}$ and Boyle's temperature is 284 K. Calculate T_c, V_c and p_c.**

Sol. $b = 0.0319 \text{ L mol}^{-1}$, $V_c = 3b = 3 \times 0.0319 \text{ L mol}^{-1} = 0.0957 \text{ L mol}^{-1}$

Also, Boyle's temperature $T_b = \dfrac{a}{Rb}$

$$\therefore \quad a = RbT_b = 0.0821 \times 0.0319 \times 284 = 0.744 \text{ L}^2 \text{ atm mol}^{-2}$$

$$p_c = \frac{a}{27b^2} = \frac{0.744}{27\,(0.0319)^2} = 27.08 \text{ atm}$$

$$T_c = \frac{8a}{27Rb} = \frac{8 \times 0.744}{27 \times 0.0821 \times 0.0319} = 84 \text{ K}$$

Immediate Test 28

(i) For CO_2, $T_c = 304$ K and $p_c = 50$ atm. Calculate molecular diameter of CO_2.

(ii) Critical density for CO_2 is 0.44 g dm^{-3}. Calculate van der Waals' constant *b*.

KNOWLEDGE CONFIRMATION Test 7

1 An ideal gas obeying kinetic gas equation can be liquefied if

(a) its temperature is more than critical temperature
(b) its pressure is more than critical pressure
(c) its pressure is more than critical pressure but its temperature is less than critical temperature
(d) it cannot be liquefied at any value of pressure and temperature

2 Critical temperature of CO_2 is 304 K. Thus, CO_2 is

(a) a gas at 308 K and vapour at 298 K
(b) a gas at 308 K as well as at 298 K
(c) vapour at 308 K as well as at 298 K
(d) gas at 308 K and liquid at 298 K

3 Which has maximum numerical value ?

(a) $\dfrac{p_c V_c}{RT_c}$ (b) $\dfrac{T_c}{T_b}$ (c) $\dfrac{27RbT_c}{a}$ (d) $\sqrt{\dfrac{a}{p_c b^2}}$

4 Oxygen can be liquefied more easily than hydrogen because of

(a) $T_c(O_2) > T_c(H_2)$; $T_i(O_2) > T_i(H_2)$
(b) $T_c(O_2) > T_c(H_2)$; $T_i(O_2) < T_i(H_2)$
(c) $T_c(O_2) < T_c(H_2)$; $T_i(O_2) < T_i(H_2)$
(d) $T_c(O_2) < T_c(H_2)$; $T_i(O_2) > T_i(H_2)$

5 For a real gas, T_c, T_b and T_i are arranged as

(a) $T_c < T_b < T_i$ (b) $T_c < T_i < T_b$
(c) $T_i < T_b < T_c$ (d) $T_i < T_c < T_b$

6 The critical temperature of water is higher than that of oxygen because H_2O molecules have

(a) fewer electrons (10) than oxygen (16)
(b) two covalent bonds
(c) V-shaped structure
(d) dipole moment

7 As critical point is approached,

(a) density of CO_2 (*l*) decreases and that CO_2 (*g*) increases and at $T = T_c$ densities are equal
(b) density of CO_2 (*l*) increases and that of CO_2 (*g*) decreases and at $T = T_c$ densities are equal
(c) density of CO_2 (*l*) as well as of CO_2 (*g*) increases
(d) density of CO_2 (*l*) as well as of CO_2 (*g*) decreases

8 Under critical states, variation of compressibility factor $\left(\dfrac{dZ}{dT_c}\right)_{p_c, V_c}$ at the critical temperature of 300 K is

(a) $-\dfrac{3}{8}$ (b) $\dfrac{3}{8}$ (c) $-\dfrac{1}{800}$ (d) -800

9 What is the value of $p_c\left(\dfrac{dZ}{dp_c}\right)_{T_c, V_c}$

(a) $\dfrac{8}{3}$ (b) $\dfrac{3}{8}$ (c) 1 (d) $-\dfrac{3}{8}$

10 In the following variation of $\log V_c$ with $\log T_c$

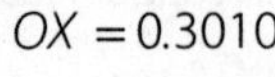

$OX = 0.3010$

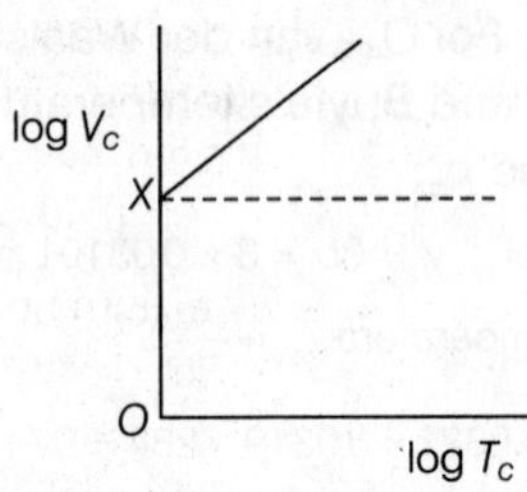

Thus, critical pressure is

(a) $\dfrac{3}{8}R$ (b) $3R$ (c) $\dfrac{3}{16}R$ (d) $\dfrac{16}{3R}$

11 For critical constants, compressibility factor is (3/8) and for reduced constants, its value is (4/3R). Thus, for real gas, its value is

(a) 1 (b) 0.5 (c) 0.75 (d) 0.25

12 Maximum value of Z is for

(a) ideal gas (b) critical constants real
(c) reduced constants (d) equal

13 Volume occupied by 2.0 moles of N_2 at 200 K and 10.1325 M Pa pressure, if compressibility factor

$Z = \dfrac{p_c V_c}{RT_c} = \dfrac{3}{8}$ under critical constant and

$Z = \left(\dfrac{p_r V_r}{RT_r} = \dfrac{2.21}{R}\right)$ under reduced constants is

(a) 0.136 $dm^3\ mol^{-1}$ (b) 0.544 $dm^3\ mol^{-1}$
(c) 0.068 $dm^3\ mol^{-1}$ (d) 0.272 $dm^3\ mol^{-1}$

14 The van der Waals', constants for gases A, B and C are as follow :

Gas	a (dm^6 kPa mol^{-2})	b ($dm^3\ mol^{-1}$)
A	405.3	0.027
B	1215.9	0.030
C	607.95	0.032

Gases having the highest T_C, largest molecular volume and most ideal behaviour around STP are respectively.

	T_C	V	Ideal behaviour
(a)	A	B	C
(b)	B	A	C
(c)	B	C	A
(d)	C	A	B

15 Based on Dieteric's equation, it is found that $V_c = \dfrac{b}{2}$, $a = 2V_c RT_c$ and $p_c = \dfrac{a}{4b^2e^2}$. Thus, $\dfrac{p_c V_c}{RT_c}$ is

(a) 0.375 (b) $\dfrac{2}{e^2}$ (c) $\dfrac{e^2}{2}$ (d) 2.667

ACID TEST
For JEE Main

TYPE I MCQs with Only ONE Correct Alternate

1 Equal masses of He, O_2 and SO_2 are taken in a closed container. The ratio of partial pressure of gases He, O_2 and SO_2 would be
(a) 1:2:8 (b) 8:16:1 (c) 16:8:1 (d) 16:2:1

2 For one mole of an ideal gas under isobaric condition, slope of V *vs* T isobar curve at 2 atm pressure is X (L mol^{-1} K^{-1}). Thus, universal gas constant R is
(a) X L atm $mol^{-1}K^{-1}$ (b) $\frac{X}{2}$ L atm $mol^{-1}K^{-1}$
(c) $2X$ L atm $mol^{-1}K^{-1}$ (d) $2X$ atm L^{-1} $mol^{-1}K^{-1}$

3 Density of CO is maximum at
(a) 2 atm, 600 K (b) 0.5 atm, 273 K
(c) 6 atm, 1092 K (d) 4 atm, 500 K

4 Maximum deviation from ideal behaviour is expected for the gas
(a) H_2 (b) N_2 (c) CH_4 (d) NH_3

5 Equal moles of H_2 and O_2 gases are placed in a container with a pin-hole through which both can escape. What fraction of the oxygen escapes in the time required for one-half of the hydrogen to escape?
(a) 1/8 (b) 1/4 (c) 3/8 (d) 1/2

6 A gas such as CO would be most likely to obey the ideal gas law at
(a) high temperature and low pressure
(b) low temperature and high pressure
(c) high temperature and high pressure
(d) low temperature and low pressure

7 pV values decrease with increase in pressure under isothermal condition when
(a) there is no attractive and repulsive forces between molecules
(b) attractive and repulsive forces between molecules are equal
(c) attractive forces between molecules are predominant
(d) repulsive forces between molecules are predominant

8 How many molecules of gas are in a 0.535 L vacuum system at a pressure of 3.5×10^{-7} Torr and 298K, assuming ideal behaviour?
(a) 1.0×10^{-11} (b) 6.0×10^{12}
(c) 1.0×10^{11} (d) 6.0×10^{-12}

9 Concentration of water vapour in a sample of air at 45°C such that $p_{H_2O}=35$ Torr is
(a) 1.8×10^{-3} M (b) 1.8 M
(c) 1.8×10^{-2} M (d) 0.18 M

10 A mixture of He and CO_2 has a volume of 63.5 mL at 1.00 bar and 291K. The system containing the mixture is cooled in liquid N_2 and the remaining gas is evacuated, and then restored to 1.00 bar and 291K, when volume is 40.5 mL. Thus, mole fraction of He is
(a) 0.638 (b) 0.362 (c) 0.50 (d) 0.75

11 Air contains 18.18 ppm by volume of Ne and 0.934 % by volume of Ar. Thus, ratio of the number of Ar atoms to the number of Ne atoms is
(a) 514 (b) 612 (c) 722 (d) 217

12 The rate of diffusion of two gases A and B is in the ratio of 4:1 and that of B and C in the ratio of 1:3. Thus, rate of diffusion of gases of A and C is
(a) 1:12 (b) 3:4 (c) 4:3 (d) 2:3

13 For two gases A and B, it is found that

$$M_A T_B = M_B T_A$$

where, M_A and M_B are molar masses of the gases A and B respectively. For which of the following property this relation holds good?
(a) Pressure (b) Density
(c) Kinetic energy (d) u_{rms}

14 NH_3 gas at 1 atm was connected to a manometer. After sparking in the flask, NH_3 dissociates as

$$2NH_3(g) \rightleftharpoons N_2(g)+3H_2(g)$$

mercury level in the manometer showed a difference of 10.12 cm. Thus, partial pressure of H_2 gas under given condition is
(a) 0.20 atm (b) 0.40 atm (c) 1.20 atm (d) 0.07 atm

15 CH_4 diffuses four times more faster than a gas X. Thus, number of molecules in 64 g of X gas is
(a) N_0 (b) $2N_0$ (c) $N_0/2$ (d) $N_0/4$

16 Identify the correct lables of A, B and C in the following graph from the options given below :

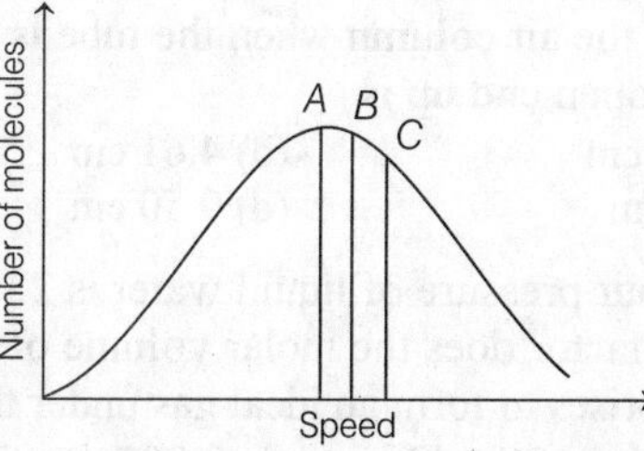

Root mean square speed (v_{rms})
Most probable speed (v_{mp})
Average speed (v_{av})

[JEE Main 2020 (I) NTA]

	A	*B*	*C*
(a)	v_{mp}	v_{av}	v_{rms}
(b)	v_{mp}	v_{rms}	v_{av}
(c)	v_{av}	v_{rms}	v_{mp}
(d)	v_{rms}	v_{mp}	v_{av}

17 As the temperature is raised from 20°C to 40°C. The average kinetic energy of the neon atoms changes by a factor of which of the following? ***[IIT JEE 2004]***
(a) 1/2 (b) $\sqrt{313/293}$
(c) 313/293 (d) 2

18 Which one of the following statements is not true about the effect of an increase in temperature on the distribution of molecular speeds in a gas? ***[IIT JEE 2005]***
(a) The area under the distribution curve remains the same as under the lower temperature
(b) The distribution becomes broader
(c) The fraction of the molecules with the most probable speed increases
(d) The most probable speed increases

19 Compressibility factor for CO_2 at 400 K and 71.0 bar is 0.8697. Molar volume of CO_2 under these conditions is
(a) 22.4 L (b) 2.24 L
(c) 0.41 L (d) 19.5 L

20 1g H_2 gas and x g O_2 gas exert a total pressure of 5 atm. At a given temperature partial pressure of O_2 gas is 4 atm. Thus, O_2 in the mixture is
(a) 1.0 mol (b) 2.0 mol
(c) 3.0 mol (d) 4.0 mol

21 Pressure of 1 g of an ideal gas *A* at 300 K is found to be 2 bar. When 2 g of another ideal gas *B* is introduced in the same flask, at the same temperature, pressure becomes 3 bar. Thus,
(a) $M_A = 4M_B$ (b) $M_B = 4M_A$
(c) $M_A = M_B$ (d) $M_A = 3M_B$

22 A 10.0 cm column of air is trapped by a column of Hg 4.00 cm long in a capillary tube of uniform bore when the tube is held horizontally at 1atm, as shown,

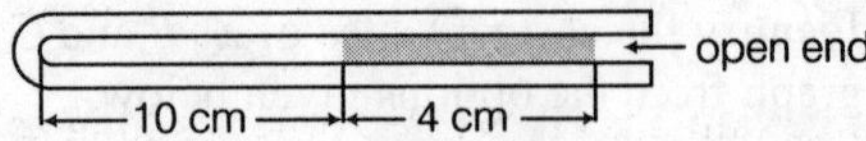

length of the air column when the tube is held vertically with the open end up is
(a) 10.52 cm (b) 4.61 cm
(c) 3.53 cm (d) 9.50 cm

23 The vapour pressure of liquid water is 23.8 Torr at 25°C. By what factor does the molar volume of water increase as it vaporises to form an ideal gas under these conditions? The density of liquid water is 0.997 g cm^{-3} at 298 K.
(a) 4.32×10^4 (b) 2.31×10^{-3}
(c) 2.31×10^{-7} (d) 4.32×10^{-6}

24 *A* and *B* are two ideal gases with following variables.

Gas	Molecules	Temperature	(KE)
A	N_A	−123°C	E_A
B	N_B	27°C	E_B

If $E_A / E_B = 0.5$, then N_B / N_A is equal to
(a) 1 (b) 2 (c) 3 (d) 4

25 Helium atom is two times heavier than H_2 molecule. At 300 K, average kinetic energy of He atom is
(a) two times that of H_2 molecule
(b) same as that of H_2 molecule
(c) four times that of H_2 molecule
(d) half that of H_2 molecule

26 Volume of an ideal gas is to be decreased by 10% by increase of pressure by x% under isothermal condition. Thus, x is
(a) 100/9 (b) 9/100
(c) 10 (d) 1/10

27 Density of an ideal gas at 298 K and 1.0 atm is found to be 1.25 kg m^{-3}. Density of the gas at 1.5 atm and at 298 K is
(a) 1.25 kg m^{-3} (b) 1.875 kg m^{-3}
(c) 1.00 kg m^{-3} (d) 1.20 kg m^{-3}

28 Temperature at which average translational kinetic energy of H_2 molecule is equal to average translational kinetic energy of N_2 molecule at 280 K is
(a) 280 K (b) 40 K (c) 400 K (d) 50 K

29 N_2 gas under the given state I is to be changed to state II. Thus, N_2 escaped from I is

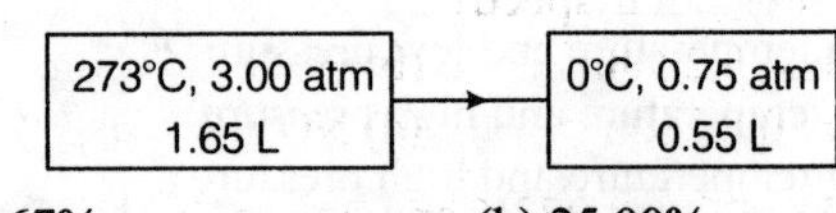

(a) 16.67% (b) 25.00%
(c) 75.00% (d) 83.33%

30 Consider the van der Waals' constants, *a* and *b*, for the following gases.

Gas	Ar	Ne	Kr	Xe
a/(atm dm^6 mol^{-2})	1.3	0.2	5.1	4.1
b/(10^{-2} dm^{-3} mol^{-1})	3.2	1.7	1.0	5.0

Which gas is expected to have the highest critical temperature? ***[JEE Main 2019 (II) NTA]***
(a) Kr (b) Xe (c) Ar (d) Ne

31 A given mass of helium at STP is allowed to expand to 1.4 times its initial volume by changing the temperature and pressure, then its resultant density would be
(a) 0.25 kg m^{-3} (b) 4 kg m^{-3}
(c) 0.13 kg m^{-3} (d) 7.84 kg m^{-3}

32 At a given temperature T, gases Ne, Ar, Xe and Kr are found to deviate from ideal gas behaviour. Their equation of state is given as, $p = \frac{RT}{V-b}$ at T. Here, b is the van der Waals' constant. Which gas will exhibit steepest increase in the plot of Z (compression factor) *vs* p? **[JEE Main 2019 (II) NTA]**

(a) Xe (b) Ar (c) Kr (d) Ne

33 Volume of gaseous PH_3 formed by reaction of 182g of $Ca_3P_2(s)$ with excess of H_2O at STP is (P = 31, Ca = 40)

$$Ca_3P(s) + 6H_2O \longrightarrow 3Ca(OH)_2 + 2PH_3(g)$$

(a) 11.2 L (b) 22.4 L (c) 5.6 L (d) 44.8 L

34 For one mole of an ideal gas $\left(-\frac{\partial V}{\partial p}\right)_{n,T}$ at 1 bar and 273 K is 22.6863 $dm^3\ bar^{-1}$. Thus, isothermal compressibility constant for an ideal gas is

(a) 22.6863 bar^{-1} (b) 0.0441 bar^{-1}

(c) 0.1 bar^{-1} (d) 1 bar^{-1}

35 2 moles each of NO and O_2 in a 20 dm^3 flask react at 300K to form NO_2. Thus, change in pressure due to the reaction $2NO + O_2 \longrightarrow 2NO_2$

(assume that limiting reactant is completely consumed)

(a) 1.247 bar (b) 2.492 bar

(c) 3.738 bar (d) No change

36 The average molecular speed is greatest in which of the following gas samples?

(a) 1 mole of O_2 at 560K (b) 0.50 mole of Ne at 500K

(c) 0.20 mole of CO_2 at 440K (d) 2.0 moles of He at 140K

37 At 298K, which of the following gas has the lowest average molecular speed?

(a) CO_2 and 0.20 atm (b) He at 0.40 atm

(c) CH_4 at 0.80 atm (d) NO at 1 atm

38 One mole of O_2 at 273K and one mole of SO_2 at 546K are taken in two separate containers. Then

(a) KE (O_2) > KE (SO_2) (b) KE (SO_2) > KE (O_2)

(c) KE (SO_2) = KE (O_2) (d) $(KE)_{av}\ SO_2 = (KE)_{av}\ O_2$

39 Points I, II and III in the following plot respectively correspond to (v_{mp} : most probable velocity)

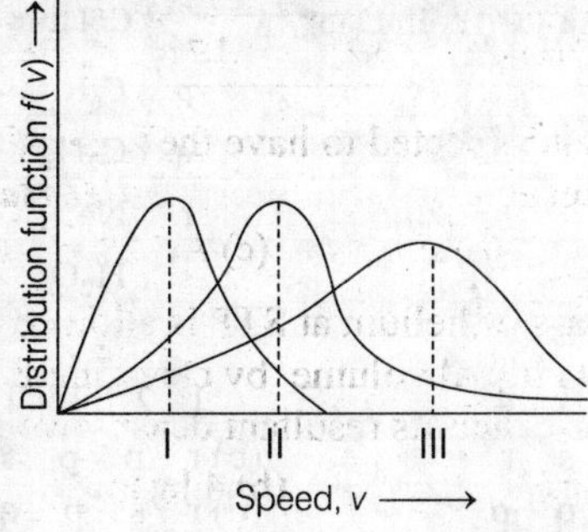

[JEE Main 2019 (II) NTA]

(a) v_{mp} of H_2 (300 K); v_{mp} of N_2 (300 K); v_{mp} of O_2 (400 K)

(b) v_{mp} of O_2 (400 K); v_{mp} of N_2 (300 K); v_{mp} of H_2 (300 K)

(c) v_{mp} of N_2 (300 K); v_{mp} of O_2 (400 K); v_{mp} of H_2 (300 K)

(d) v_{mp} of N_2 (300 K); v_{mp} of H_2 (300 K); v_{mp} of O_2 (400 K)

40 Consider the following table.

Gas	a/(kPa dm^6 mol^{-1})	b/(dm^{-3} mol^{-1})
A	642.32	0.05196
B	155.21	0.04136
C	431.91	0.05196
D	155.21	0.4382

a and b are van der Waals' constants. The correct statement about the gases is **[JEE Main 2019 (II) NTA]**

(a) gas C will occupy lesser volume than gas A; gas B will be lesser compressible than gas D

(b) gas C will occupy more volume than gas A; gas B will be more compressible than gas D

(c) gas C will occupy lesser volume than gas A; gas B will be more compressible than gas D

(d) gas C will occupy more volume than gas A; gas B will be lesser compressible than gas D

41 The compressibility factor (Z) of one mole of a van der Waals' gas of negligible 'a' value is

(a) 1 (b) $\frac{bp}{RT}$ (c) $\left(1+\frac{bp}{RT}\right)$ (d) $\left(1-\frac{bp}{RT}\right)$

42 At a certain temperature, the time required for the complete diffusion of 200 mL of H_2 gas is 30 minute. The time required for the complete diffusion of 50 mL of O_2 gas the same temperature will be

(a) 60 min (b) 30 min (c) 45 min (d) 15 min

43 If 240 mL of a gas x diffuses through a porous membrane in 20 min, whereas the same volume of methane diffuses in 10 min under identical conditions of temperature and pressure, the molar mass of gas x (in g mol^{-1}) is

(a) 8 (b) 64 (c) 32 (d) 123

44 Four gases P, Q, R and S follow van der Waals' equation with same value of 'b' but value of 'a' being in order $P < Q < R < S$ at 300K. Most easily liquefiable gas is

(a) P (b) Q (c) R (d) S

45 A certain gas takes three times as long as to effuse out as helium. Its molar mass will be (g mol^{-1})

(a) 27 (b) 36 (c) 64 (d) 9

46 Thermal expansion coefficient of an ideal gas is maximum at

(a) 273 K (b) 300 K

(c) 400 K (d) 500 K

47 According to Graham's law at a given temperature, the rates of diffusion r_A / r_B of gases A and B is given by (where, p and M are partial pressure and molar masses) **[IIT JEE 1998, 2011]**

(a) $\frac{p_A}{p_B}\left(\frac{M_A}{M_B}\right)^{1/2}$ (b) $\frac{M_A}{M_B}\left(\frac{p_A}{p_B}\right)^{1/2}$

(c) $\left(\frac{p_A}{p_B}\right)\left(\frac{M_B}{M_A}\right)^{1/2}$ (d) $\left(\frac{M_A}{M_B}\right)\left(\frac{p_A}{p_B}\right)^{1/2}$

48 If helium and methane are allowed to diffuse out of the container under the similar conditions of temperature and pressure, then the ratio of rate of diffusion of helium to methane is ***[IIT JEE 2014]***
(a) 2.0 (b) 1.0
(c) 0.5 (d) 4.0

49 Sulphur dioxide and oxygen were allowed to diffuse through a porous partition. 20 dm^3 of SO_2 diffuses through the porous partition in 60 s. The volume of O_2 (in dm^3) which diffuses in 30 s will be (atomic mass of sulphur = 32 u) ***[JEE Main 2014]***
(a) 7.09 (b) 14.1 (c) 10.0 (d) 28.2

50 For CO_2, given that average velocity at T_1 is equal to most probable velocity at T_2. Thus, T_1/T_2 is
(a) 2.26 (b) 0.89
(c) 0.78 (d) 1.13

51 For gaseous state, if most probable speed is denoted by C^*, average speed by $\bar{C}$ and mean square speed of C, then for a large number of molecules, the ratios of these speeds are ***[JEE Main 2013]***

	C^*	:	$\bar{C}$	:	C
(a)	1.225	:	1.128	:	1
(b)	1.128	:	1.225	:	1
(c)	1	:	1.128	:	1.125
(d)	1	:	1.125	:	1.128

52 The compressibility factor for a real gas at high pressure is ***[AIEEE 2012]***
(a) $1+\frac{RT}{pb}$ (b) 1 (c) $1+\frac{pb}{RT}$ (d) $1-\frac{pb}{RT}$

53 a and b are van der Waals' constants for gases. Chlorine is more easily liquefied than ethane because ***[AIEEE 2011]***
(a) a and b for $Cl_2 > a$ and b for C_2H_6
(b) a and b for $Cl_2 < a$ and b for C_2H_6
(c) a for $Cl_2 > a$ for C_2H_6 but b for $Cl_2 > b$ for C_2H_6
(d) a for $Cl_2 > a$ for C_2H_6 but b for $Cl_2 < b$ for C_2H_6

54 At 300K, the density of certain gaseous molecules at 2 bar is double to that of dinitrogen (N_2) at 4 bar. The molar mass of gaseous molecule is ***[JEE Main 2017]***
(a) 28 g mol^{-1} (b) 56 g mol^{-2}
(c) 112 g mol^{-1} (d) 224 g mol^{-1}

55 Two closed bulbs of equal volume (V) containing an ideal gas initially at pressure p_i and temperature (T_i) are connected through a narrow tube of negligible volume shown in the figure below. Temperature of one of the bulbs is raised to T_2. The final pressure p_f is

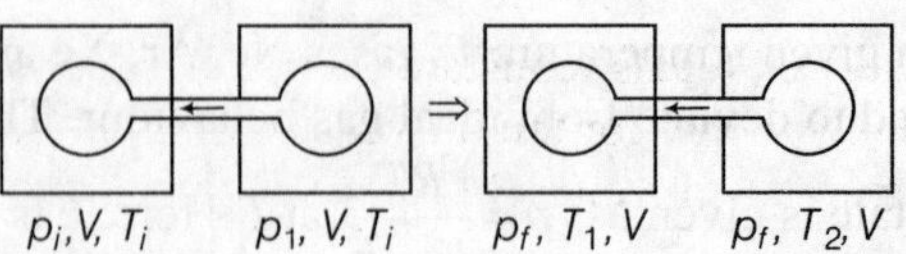

[JEE Main 2016]

(a) $2p_i\left(\frac{T_1}{T_1+T_2}\right)$ (b) $2p_i\left(\frac{T_2}{T_1+T_2}\right)$

(c) $2p_i\left(\frac{T_1T_2}{T_1+T_2}\right)$ (d) $p_i\left(\frac{T_1T_2}{T_1+T_2}\right)$

56 Which of the following is not an assumption of the kinetic theory of gases? ***[JEE Main 2015]***
(a) A gas consists of many identical particles which are in continual motion
(b) Gas particles have negligible volume
(c) At high pressure, gas particles are difficult to compress
(d) Collisions of gas particles are perfectly elastic

57 If Z is a compressibility factor, van der Waals' equation at low pressure can be written as ***[JEE Main 2014]***
(a) $Z=1+\frac{RT}{pb}$ (b) $Z=1-\frac{a}{VRT}$
(c) $Z=1-\frac{pb}{RT}$ (d) $Z=1+\frac{pb}{RT}$

58 Given J-tube has 2.4 mL of air at a pressure of 1 atm. On adding mercury, volume of air is reduced to 1.9 mL as shown. Difference in the level of mercury in two columns is

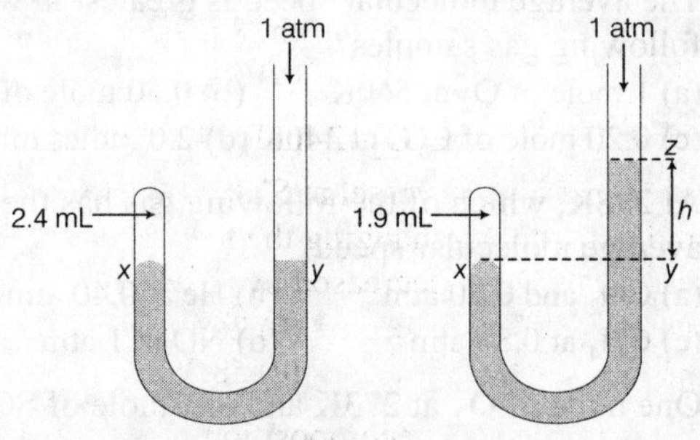

(a) 700 mm (b) 960 mm (c) 900 mm (d) 760 mm

59 The van der Waals' constant 'a' is a correction factor to the ideal gas law for the intermolecular attraction within a substance. Match the following values of 'a' in column I with the gases in column II.

Column I a/(L^2 atm mol^{-2})	Column II (Gases)
1. 0.2107	p. C_6H_6
2. 5.464	q. C_2H_6
3. 18.00	r. Ne
4. 5.51	s. H_2O

Codes

	1	2	3	4		1	2	3	4
(a)	p	q	s	r	(b)	r	p	p	s
(c)	r	s	q	p	(d)	r	s	p	q

60 The van der Waals' constant 'b' is a correction factor to the ideal gas law for the internal volume of the molecule. Match the given values of 'b' in column I with the gases in column II.

Column I ($L\ mol^{-1}$)	Column II (Gases)
1. 0.01709	p. C_6H_6 (benzene)
2. 0.03049	q. $C_6H_5CH_3$ (toluene)
3. 0.1154	r. Ne (neon)
4. 0.1436	s. H_2O (water)

Codes

	1	2	3	4		1	2	3	4
(a)	r	s	q	p	(b)	r	s	p	q
(c)	p	q	r	s	(d)	q	p	r	s

61 If number of molecules of SO_2 effusing through a pin hole at 273K and 1bar pressure is N, the number of He molecules effusing under similar conditions at 546 K and 0.5 bar is

(a) $\frac{N}{2}$ (b) $2N$ (c) $\frac{N}{\sqrt{2}}$ (d) $\sqrt{2}N$

62 Pressure exerted by 10 moles of gaseous mixture of A, B and C is 10 bar. Partial pressure exerted by A and B are 3 bar and 1 bar respectively. Mass of C in the mixture is ($M_C = 2\,g\,mol^{-1}$)

(a) 12 g (b) 8 g
(c) 6 g (d) 3 g

63 1 mole H_2, 3 moles O_2, 2 moles Ne and 4 moles N_2 are placed in a closed vessel at STP. If 2 moles of O_2 are removed without changing the total pressure, partial pressure of O_2 is decreased by

(a) 40% (b) 26%
(c) 13% (d) 58.3%

64 O_2 gas formed by decomposition of $KClO_3$ has volume of 128 mL at 1atm and 297K. If water has vapour pressure of 22.4mmHg, O_2 obtained is

(a) 1.36 g (b) 1.63g
(c) 0.163 g (d) 1.52 g

65 3.06 L of H_2O vapour is taken at a pressure of 1 bar and 373K. On condensation, water vapour (at 298K) volume of liquid formed is (density of water at 298 K = $1\,g\,cm^{-3}$).

(a) 1.78 mL (b) 1.78 L
(c) 3.56 L (d) 0.178 L

66 Two flasks of equal volumes have been joined by a narrow tube of negligible volume. Initially, both flasks are at 300K containing 0.60 mole O_2 gas at 0.5 atm pressure. One of the flasks is placed at 600K. Thus, final pressure exerted by O_2 gases

(a) 0.55 atm (b) 0.67 atm
(c) 0.25 atm (d) None of these

67 Aerated water is CO_2 in water. A 0.2 M CO_2 in 2L aerated water contains same quantity of CO_2 at STP in a volume of

(a) 4.48L (b) 11.2L (c) 2.24L (d) 8.96L

68 Partial pressure of oxygen in air is 22kPa. Thus, O_2 content in per cent volume in air is

(a) 42% (b) 21.7% (c) 11% (d) 5.5%

69 Mole fraction of water vapour in the water saturated air is 0.02. If total pressure is 1.2 atm, partial pressure of dry air is

(a) 1.18 atm (b) 1.22 atm
(c) 1.176 atm (d) 1.222 atm

70 A mixture of C_3H_8 and CH_4 exerts a pressure of 320 mm of Hg at temperature T K in a V L flask. On complete combustion, gaseous mixture contains CO_2 only and exerts a pressure of 448 mm of Hg under identical conditions. Hence, mole fraction of C_3H_8 in the mixture is

(a) 0.2 (b) 0.8 (c) 0.25 (d) 0.75

71 In which case, mean free path is not affected?

(a) H_2 gas at 100K and 1 atm is transferred into a vessel at 50K and 0.5 atm
(b) O_2 gas at 200K and 2 atm is transferred into a vessel at 400K and 1 atm
(c) O_2 gas is replaced by H_2 gas keeping other variables constant
(d) Medium is made more viscous

ACID TEST
For JEE Advanced

TYPE I MCQs with Only ONE Correct Alternate

72 Temperature at which average kinetic energy of a molecule is equal to (kinetic energy) of the electron in first Bohr orbit is (which is 13.6 eV)

(a) 2.02×10^5 K (b) 1.05×10^5 K
(c) 273 K (d) 298 K

73 At what temperature, will the collision frequency in N_2 be equal to that in He at 298 K if both gases are at a pressure of 1.00 bar ?
Collision diameter=0.373 nm for N_2 and=0.218 nm for He.
(Assume equal number of molecules per unit volume)

(a) 40 K (b) 365 K (c) 298 K (d) 400 K

74 The average molar mass of the vapour above solid NH_4Cl is nearly 26.75g mol^{-1}. Thus, vapour consists of (mole fraction)

	NH_4Cl	NH_3	HCl
a.	0.20	0.40	0.40
b.	0.3	0.35	0.35
c.	0.0	0.50	0.50
d.	0.10	0.45	0.45

75 The following arrangement of flasks is set up. Assuming no temperature change, determine the final pressure inside the system after all stopcocks are opened. The connecting tube has zero volume.

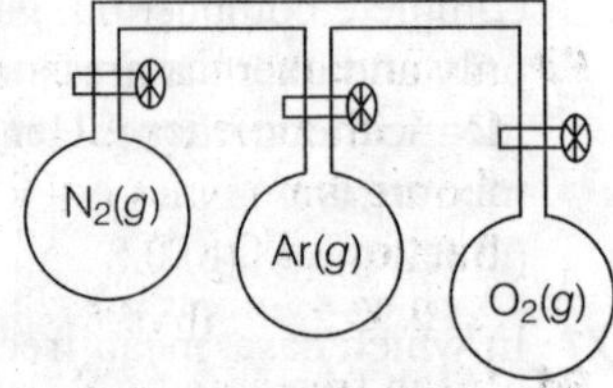

***V* (L)**	4.0,	3.0,	5.0
***p* (atm)**	0.792,	1.23,	2.51

(a) 1.62 atm (b) 4.53 atm (c) 1.51 atm (d) 3.24 atm

76 If the distribution of molecular speeds of a gas is as per the figure shown below, then the ratio of the most probable, the average and the root mean square speeds, respectively, is

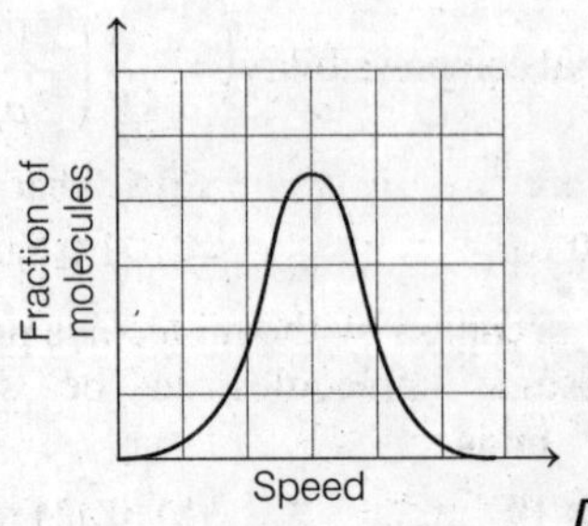

[JEE Adv. 2020]

(a) 1 : 1 : 1 (b) 1 : 1 : 1.224
(c) 1 : 1.128 : 1.224 (d) 1 : 1.128 : 1

77 In an experiment to measure the molar mass of a gas, 250 cm^3 of the gas was confined in a vessel. The pressure was 152 Torr at 298 K, and after correcting for buoyancy effects, the mass of the gas was 33.5mg. Thus, molar mass of the gas is

(a) 164 g mol^{-1} (b) 32.8 g mol^{-1}
(c) 328 g mol^{-1} (d) 16.4g mol^{-1}

78 A 1.0 L sample of dry air at 298 K and 786 mmHg contains 0.925 g N_2 and other gases including O_2, Ar and CO_2.

Thus, partial pressure of N_2 (in mmHg) is

(a) 608 (b) 616 (c) 712 (d) 428

79 Consider the experimental set up shown of equal dimension, under identical conditions:

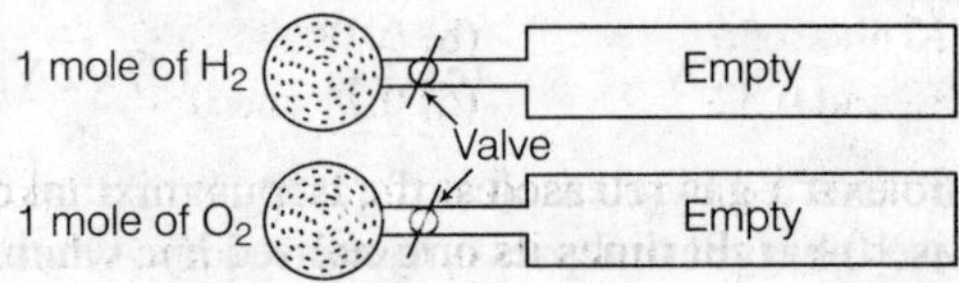

If you wanted the O_2 or H_2 to reach the end of the long tube at the same time as the other gas H_2 or O_2, what experimental condition you could change to make this happen. (no change in experimental apparatus is allowed)?

(a) O_2 is placed at 400 K and H_2 at 25 K
(b) O_2 is placed at 25 K and H_2 at 400 K
(c) H_2 is released before O_2
(d) H_2 is placed at 200 K and O_2 is placed at 50 K

80 Molecular density of N_2 (number of molecules per unit volume) at 1.00 atm and 298 K is

(a) 2.46×10^{12} m^3 (b) 2.46×10^{-25} m^3
(c) 2.46×10^{25} m^{-3} (d) 2.46×10^{25} m^3

81 The density of the vapour of a substance (of molar mass 18 g mol^{-1}) at 1 atm and 500 K is 0.36 kg m^{-3}. Thus, compression factor (*Z*) is

(a) 1.0 (b) 1.220 (c) 0.987 (d) 1.067

82 Average distance between neighbouring molecules at STP for N_2 gas is (assume molecules are spherical)

(a) 41.40 Å (b) 20. 70Å (c) 10.35 Å (d) 3.72 Å

83 5 moles of O_2 in 5 L flask *A* and a mixture of 3 moles of He and 2 moles of N_2 in 5 L flask *B* are allowed to effuse through a small pinhole provided in each flask at constant temperature. Thus, relative rate of effusion of the gases in flask *A* and flask *B* is

(a) 0.652 (b) 0.252 (c) 0.520 (d) 0.480

84 For real gases, van der Waals' equation is

$$\left(p+\frac{n^2a}{V^2}\right)(V-nb)=nRT$$

Two sets of gases are given below:

I. O_2, CO_2, H_2, and He

II. CH_4, O_2, and H_2

Increasing order of 'b' values for set I and that of 'a' values for set II are :

	I	II
(a)	$He < H_2 < CO_2 < O_2$	$CH_4 < H_2 < O_2$
(b)	$O_2 < He < H_2 < CO_2$	$H_2 < O_2 < CH_4$
(c)	$H_2 < He < O_2 < CO_2$	$CH_4 < O_2 < H_2$
(d)	$H_2 < He < O_2 < CO_2$	$H_2 < O_2 < CH_4$

85 What will be the partial pressure of He and O_2 gases respectively (in atm), if 200 mL of He at 0.66 atm and 400 mL of O_2 at 0.52 atm pressure are mixed in 400 mL vessel at 293 K ?

(a) 0.33 and 0.56 (b) 0.33 and 0.52
(c) 0.38 and 0.52 (d) 0.25 and 0.95

86 A bubble of a gas released at the bottom of a lake increases to eight times its original volume when it reaches the surface. Assuming that atmospheric pressure is equivalent to the pressure exerted by a column of water, 10 m height, the depth of the lake is

(a) 80 m (b) 70 m (c) 90 m (d) 10 m

87 The ratio between the root mean square speed of H_2 gas at 50 K and that of O_2 gas at 800 K is ***[IIT JEE 1996]***

(a) 4 (b) 2 (c) 1 (d) 0.25

88 The rms velocity of hydrogen gas is $\sqrt{7}$ times of the rms velocity of nitrogen gas. If T is the temperature of the gas, then ***[IIT JEE 2000]***

(a) $T(H_2)=T(N_2)$ (b) $T(H_2)>T(N_2)$
(c) $T(H_2)<T(N_2)$ (d) $T(H_2)=\sqrt{7}\,T(N_2)$

89 The given graph represents the variations of Z (compressibility factor Z) $=\frac{pV}{nRT}$ *versus p*, for three real gases *A*, *B*, and *C*. ***[IIT JEE 2006]***

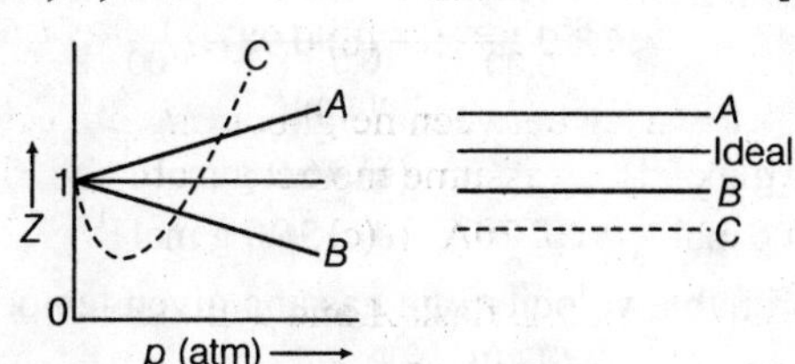

Identify the only incorrect statement.

(a) For the gas *A*, $a=0$ and its dependence on p is linear at all pressure

(b) For the gas *B*, $b=0$ and its dependence on p is linear at all pressure

(c) For the gas *C*, which is typical real gas for which neither a nor $b=0$. By knowing the minima and the point of intersection, with $Z=1$, a and b can be calculated

(d) At high pressure, the slope is positive for all real gases

90 For one mole of a van der Waals' gas when $b=0$ and $T=300$ K, the pV vs $1/V$ plot is shown below. The value of the van der Waals' constant a (atm L^2 mol^{-2}) is

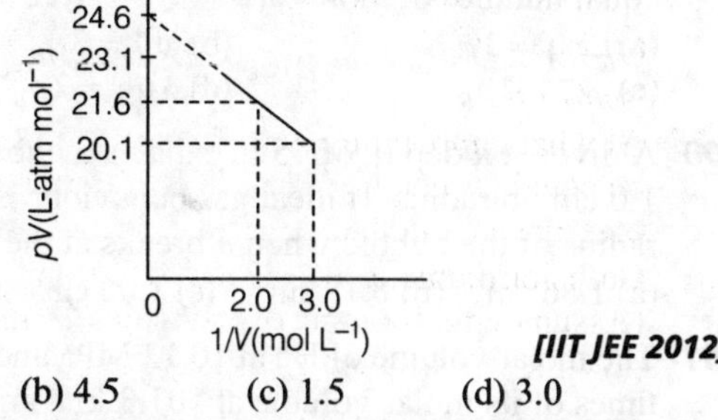

[IIT JEE 2012]

(a) 1.0 (b) 4.5 (c) 1.5 (d) 3.0

91 The term that corrects for the attractive forces present in a real gas in the van der Waals' equation is ***[IIT JEE 2009]***

(a) nb (b) n^2a/V^2
(c) $-(n^2a/V^2)$ (d) $-nb$

92 An equimolar mixture of H_2 and O_2 diffuses through porous disk. What is the composition of the gas that passes through the disk ?

(a) 58.57% H_2 (b) 41.43% H_2
(c) 70.74% H_2 (d) 29.26% H_2

93 Assume that the air in the space vehicle cabin consists of O_2 with mole fraction 0.20. What is the composition of the air that comes out of the hole, in terms of mole fraction of O_2 ?

(a) 0.93 (b) 0.81 (c) 0.48 (d) 0.19

94 Mean free path of N_2 gas is 0.10 m at 298 K. If cross-sectional area is 0.43 nm^2, then pressure maintained is

(a) 2.81×10^5 Pa (b) 2.81×10^3 Pa
(c) 2.81 Pa (d) 0.281 Pa

95 Pressure at which mean free path of helium is equal to its collision diameter at 298 K is (collision diameter of He = 218 pm)

(a) 893 bar (b) 8.93 bar (c) 0.893 bar (d) 89.3 bar

96 Isothermal compressibility $\left(=-\frac{1}{V}\left(\frac{\partial V}{\partial p}\right)_{T,n}\right)$ at 1.00 bar is

(a) 0.10 bar^{-1} (b) 1.0 bar^{-1}
(c) -0.10 bar^{-1} (d) -1.0 bar^{-1}

97 Volume occupied by the molecules present in one mole of gas (assume molecules to be spherical of radius 1×10^{-10} m) is

(a) 22.4×10^{-3} m^3 (b) 0.224 m^3
(c) 1×10^{-30} m^3 (d) 2.52×10^{-6} m^3

98 A quantity of hydrogen gas occupies a volume of 30.0 mL at a certain temperature and pressure. What volume would half of this mass of H_2 occupy at the triple absolute temperature, if the pressure were one-ninth that of the original gas ?
(a) 30.0 mL (b) 60.0 mL (c) 90.0 mL (d) 405.0 mL

99 The volume of gas A is twice than that of gas B. The compressibility factor of gas A is thrice than that of gas B at the same temperature. The pressures of the gases for equal number of moles are *[JEE Main 2019 (I) NTA]*
(a) $2p_A = 3p_B$ (b) $p_A = 3p_B$
(c) $p_A = 2p_B$ (d) $3p_A = 2p_B$

100 A diver at a depth of 45 m exhales a bubble of air that is 1.0 cm in radius. If ideal gas behaviour is applicable, radius of the bubble when it breaks at the surface is
(a) 1.86 cm (b) 0.18 cm (c) 1.06 cm (d) 2.18 cm

101 The molar volume of He at 10.13 MPa and 273 K is 0.011 times of its molar volume at 101.3 kPa and 273 K. If force of attraction between molecules is neglected, the radius of He atom is
(a) 13.1 pm (b) 1.31 pm (c) 1310 pm (d) 131 pm

102 What per cent of a sample of N_2 gas must be allowed to escape if its temperature, pressure and volume are to be changed from 220° C, 3.00 atm and 1.65 L to 110° C, 0.700 atm and 1.00 L respectively
(a) 18.2% (b) 81.8% (c) 40.8% (d) 59.2%

103 Consider two vessels I and II joined by a tube of negligible volume.

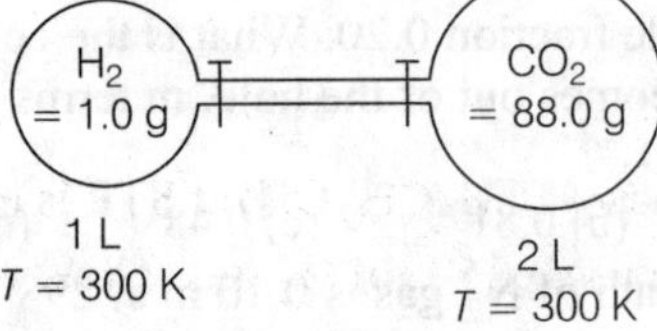

Thus, total pressure of the gaseous mixture if stop cocks are opened will be
(a) 4.1 atm (b) 16.4 atm
(c) 20.5 atm (d) None of these

104 1.0 mole sample of O_2 and 3.0 moles sample of H_2 are mixed isothermally in a 125.3 dm^3 flask at 398 K. Gaseous mixture undergoes reactions to form water vapours. Assume ideal gas behaviour, total pressure before and after $H_2O(g)$ is formed are respectively
(a) 1.056 bar, 0.792 bar (b) 1.056 bar, 1.056 bar
(c) 0.792 bar, 1.056 bar (d) 0.264 bar, 0.528 bar

105 When NO_2 is cooled to room temperature, some of it reacts to form N_2O_4 through the reaction.

$$2NO_2(g) \longrightarrow N_2O_4(g)$$

In a reaction 15.2 g of NO_2 is placed in a 10.0 dm^3 flask at high temperature and the flask is cooled to 25° C. The total pressure is measured to be 0.500 atm. Thus, partial pressure of NO_2 is found to be
(a) 0.19 atm (b) 0.31 atm (c) 0.10 atm (d) 0.40 atm

106 Total pressure of a mixture of H_2 and O_2 is 1.00 bar. The mixture is allowed to react to form water, which is completely removed to leave only pure H_2 at a pressure of 0.35 bar. Assuming ideal gas behaviour and that all pressure measurements were made under the same temperature and volume conditions, the composition of the original mixture is

	X_{H_2}	X_{O_2}		X_{H_2}	X_{O_2}
(a)	0.50	0.50	(b)	0.78	0.22
(c)	0.22	0.78	(d)	0.35	0.65

107 Assume that for every increase in height of 1 m, pressure decreases by 10 mm of Hg. Initially, an experimental air balloon of maximum 200 L capacity has 150 L of air at 1 atm at sea-level. At what height, the balloon is expected to burst?
(a) 15 m above sea-level (b) 19 m above sea-level
(c) 10 m above sea-level (d) 20 m above sea-level

108 Rate of effusion of LPG (a mixture of n-butane and propane) is 1.25 times that of SO_3 gas under identical conditions. Hence, mass fraction of n-butane in LPG is
(a) 0.75 (b) 0.25 (c) 0.51 (d) 0.67

109 Mean free path of krypton atom (radius = 1.85 Å) at 293 K and 1 bar pressure is
(a) 665 Å (b) 26.64 pm (c) 333 nm (d) 472 pm

110 1 mole of a gas at 300 K occupies 5 m^3 under given pressure. Thus, change in pressure per unit change in volume at constant temperature for a given amount of gas is
(a) 100 Pa m^{-3} (b) -100 Pa m^{-3}
(c) 0.01 Pa m^{-3} (d) -0.01 Pa m^{-3}

111 A graph showing variation of $\frac{d}{p}\left(\frac{\text{density}}{\text{pressure}}\right)$ with pressure p is given at 273 K for an unknown gas X. Thus, molar mass of gas X is

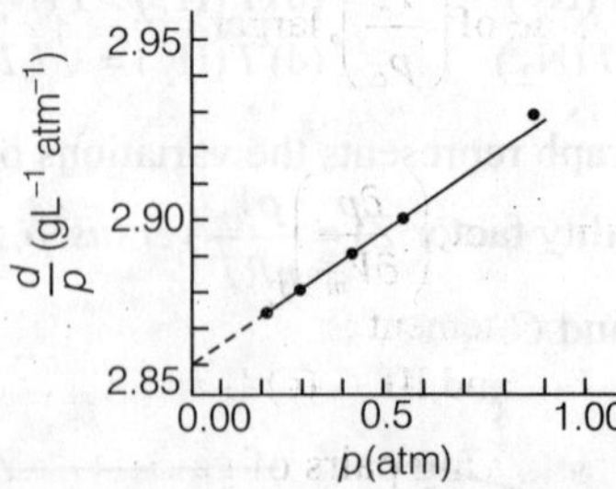

(a) 32.0 g mol^{-1} (b) 46.0 g mol^{-1}
(c) 64.0 g mol^{-1} (d) 156.0 g mol^{-1}

112 Most probable velocity of a gas at a given temperature is 200 ms^{-1}. Thus, $\frac{M}{R}\left(\frac{du_{mp}}{dT}\right)$ for the gas is
(a) 5×10^{-3} s m^{-1} (b) 2.5×10^{-3} s m^{-1}
(c) 200 m s^{-1} (d) 400 m s^{-1}

113 The mean free path of gaseous molecules is 60 cm at a pressure of 1×10^{-4} mm of Hg, what will be its mean free path when the pressure is increased by 100 times at constant temperature ?
(a) 6×10^{-1} cm (b) 6 cm
(c) 6×10^{1} cm (d) 6×10^{2} cm

114 An open ended mercury manometer is used to measure the pressure exerted by a trapped gas as shown in the figure. Atmospheric pressure is 749 mm of Hg . What is the pressure of the trapped gas?

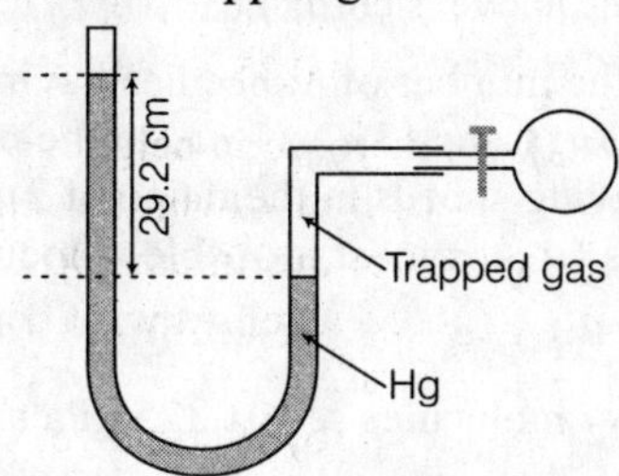

(a) 292 mm of Hg (b) 457 mm of Hg
(c) 749 mm of Hg (d) 1041 mm of Hg

115 **Gas I** N_2O (called laughing gas, molar mass 44 g mol^{-1}) makes one laugh.
Gas II $C_6H_{11}OBr$ (called tear gas, molar mass 179 g mol^{-1}) makes one weep.
In a row of 13 m, having students at equal point, two gases are passed through two gates.

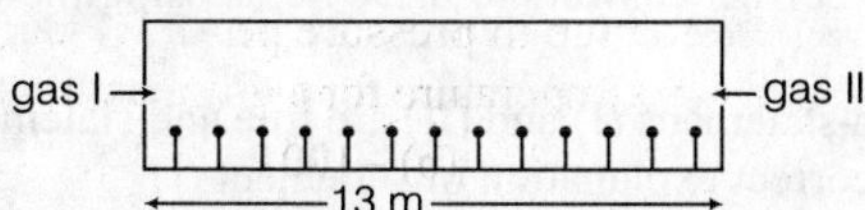

At what point from gas I, a student, will laugh and weep simultaneously ?
(a) 9th (b) 8th (c) 4th (d) 12th

116 Consider following statements on T_c, p_c and u_c:
I. Larger the value of $\left(\frac{T_c}{p_c}\right)$, larger would be the excluded volume
II. $T_c > T_b$
III. At the critical point, $\left(\frac{\partial p}{\partial V_m}\right)_{T_c} = 0$
Select correct statement :
(a) I and II (b) I and III (c) II and III (d) I, II and III

117 Consider the following pairs of gases *A* and *B*.

	A	*B*
I.	CO_2	N_2O
II.	CO	N_2
III.	O_2	O_3
IV.	H_2O	D_2O
V.	$^{235}UF_6$	$^{238}UF_6$

Relative rates of effusion of gases *A* and *B* is in the order
(a) I = II < V < IV < III (b) I = II < III < IV < V
(c) I = II < IV < III < V (d) I < II < III < IV < V

118 A 350 mL sample of ammonia at 1 bar and 300 K is absorbed by 500 mL of solution. Thus, molar concentration of NH_4OH is
(a) 0.014 M (b) 0.028 M
(c) 0.280 M (d) 2.8 M

119 Compressibility factor (*Z*) for N_2 is given as

	T	*p*	*Z*	Volume occupied
I.	330 K	800 atm	1.90	1 dm^3 of given amount
II.	570 K	200 atm	1.10	*V* dm^3 of same amount

What is value of *V*?
(a) 1 L (b) 2 L (c) 3 L (d) 4 L

120 The density of vapour of a substance (*X*) at 1 atm pressure and 500 K is 0.8 kg m^{-3}. The vapour effuses through a small pin hole at a rate $\frac{4}{5}$ times slower than oxygen under same condition. Thus, compressibility factor of vapours of substance (*X*) is
(a) 1.220 (b) 1.520
(c) 0.974 (d) 1.350

121 A mixture contains He, CH_4 and SO_2 in the molar ratio of 1 : 2 : 3. Mixture is allowed to effuse through a pin hole of the container in which mixture is placed. Thus, molar ratio of the gases coming out initially is
(a) 2 : 2 : 3 (b) 4 : 4 : 3
(c) $\sqrt{2} : \sqrt{2} : 3$ (d) 6 : 6 : 1

122 1.75 L of ethanol (CH_3CH_2OH) at STP is exposed to UV radiation using 25 L of O_2 gas. Thus, volume of CO_2 formed is
(a) 16.65 L (b) 3.50 L
(c) 3.821 L (d) None is correct

123 Consider two closed bulbs of equal volume (*V*) having two gases (1) and (2) as shown , are connected through a small tube of negligible volume. Thus, final pressure attained is

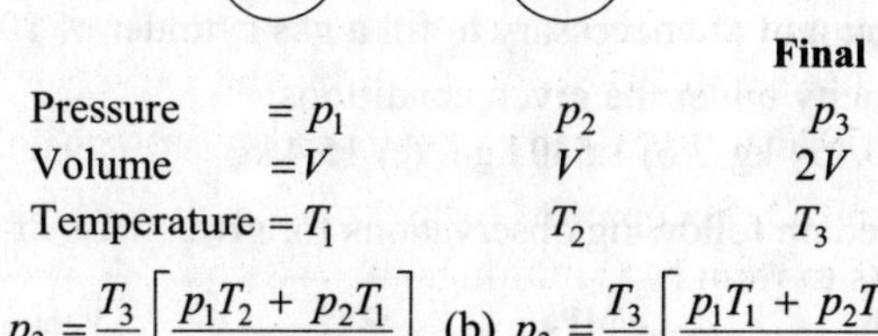

			Final
Pressure	$= p_1$	p_2	p_3
Volume	$= V$	V	$2V$
Temperature	$= T_1$	T_2	T_3

(a) $p_3 = \frac{T_3}{2}\left[\frac{p_1T_2 + p_2T_1}{T_1T_2}\right]$ (b) $p_3 = \frac{T_3}{2}\left[\frac{p_1T_1 + p_2T_2}{T_1T_2}\right]$

(c) $p_3 = \frac{T_3}{2}\left[\frac{p_1 + p_2}{T_1T_2}\right]$ (d) None is correct

124 The pressure exerted by 1.6 g of CH_4 behaving ideally at *T*K in a flask of *V*L is 0.6 bar. On increasing temperature by 10 K under isobaric condition, the pressure increases by 5%. Thus, *V* and *T* are respectively

	$V\,(dm^3)$	T (K)
(a)	1.88	100
(b)	3.00	300
(c)	2.77	200
(d)	6.00	100

125 If u_1 and u_2 are the most probable velocities at STP and $t°$C then in terms of density d_1 (at STP) and pressure p_1 (at STP).

(a) $u_2 = \sqrt{\dfrac{2p_1\,(273+t)}{273 d_1}}$ (b) $u_2 = u_1\sqrt{\dfrac{273+t}{M}}$

(c) $u_2 = u_1\sqrt{\dfrac{2(273+t)\,d_1}{273}}$ (d) None is correct

126 100 mL of gas *X* and gas *Y* (molar mass 100 g mol^{-1}) and having 40% gas *Y* was kept in a closed vessel. Due to fine leakage, mixture effused out as a result of which 40 mL of the mixture was lost and the mixture remained has 55% of gas *Y* by volume. Thus, molar mass of *X* is

(a) 50 g mol^{-1} (b) 2 g mol^{-1}
(c) 10 g mol^{-1} (d) 4 g mol^{-1}

127 The van der Waals' equation for one mole of a gas is

$$\left[p+\frac{a}{V^2}\right][V-b]=RT \quad \ldots(i)$$

and the dielectric's equation is

$$p\,(V-b)=RT\exp\left(-\frac{a}{RTV}\right) \quad \ldots(ii)$$

At low densities, values of *p* using above equation is

(a) $\left(1-\dfrac{a}{RTV}\right)$ by (i) and $\left(\dfrac{RT}{V}-\dfrac{a}{V^2}\right)$ by (ii)

(b) $\left(\dfrac{RT}{V}-\dfrac{a}{V^2}\right)$ by (ii) and $\left(1-\dfrac{a}{RTV}\right)$ by (ii)

(c) $\left(\dfrac{RT}{V}-\dfrac{a}{V^2}\right)$ by both

(d) $\left(1-\dfrac{a}{RTV}\right)$ by both

128 At STP, compressibility factor of O_2 is 0.927. Thus, amount of O_2 necessary to fill a gas cylinder of 100 dm^3 capacity under the given conditions

(a) 0.154 kg (b) 1.540 kg (c) 15.4 kg (d) 79.00 kg

129 Based on following observations for given mass of N_2 gas

T/K	p/MPa	Z	Volume/dm³
223 K	81.06	1.95	1.0 dm³
373 K	20.265	1.10	*V*

volume *V* is

(a) 1.0 dm^3 (b) 0.1 dm^3 (c) 3.8 dm^3 (d) 7.9 dm^3

130 Select correct statement(s) for two real gases *X* and *Y*

(a) If two gases have same value of '*a*' but different values of '*b*', then smaller the value of *b*, larger the compressibility.
(b) If two gases have same value of '*b*' but different values of '*a*', then the gas having a larger value of '*a*' will occupy lesser volume
(c) Both of the above are corret
(d) None of the above is correct

131 The ratio of the number of molecules having speeds in the range of $3u_{mp}$ and $(3u_{mp}+du)$ to the number of molecules having speeds in the range of $2u_{mp}$ and $2u_{mp}+du$) is (u_{mp} is most probable velocity)

(a) $2/e^2$ (b) $4/e^3$ (c) $2.25/e^5$ (d) $1/e^5$

132 Fraction of N_2 molecules at 101.325 kPa and 300 K whose speeds are in the range of ($u_{mp} - 0.005u_{mp}$) to ($u_{mp} + 0.005\,u_{mp}$) is ($e^{-1}=0.3679$)

(a) 8.3×10^{-5} (b) 8.3×10^{-3} (c) 8.3×10^{-6} (d) 8.3×10^{-2}

TYPE II Statement Based Questions

Directions (Q. No. 133-146) The following 4 items consist of two statements. One labelled as the Statement (I) and other as Statement (II). You are to examine these two statements carefully and select the correct answers to these items using the codes given below :

(a) Both statemens (I) and (II) are true and statement (II) is the correct explanation of statement (I).
(b) Both statements (I) and (II) are true, but statement (I) is not the correct explanation of statement (I).
(c) Statement (I) is true, but (II) is false.
(d) Statement (I) is false, but (II) is true.

133 **Statement I** Dipole – dipole interaction between two polar molecules is stronger than the London forces but is weaker than ion-ion interactions.

Statement II Dipole-dipole interaction involves partial charges (δ+ and δ–) between polar molecules.

134 **Statement I** Mean free path decreases as the pressure and molecular size increases.

Statement II Mean free path is dependent on pressure *p* and collision cross-sectional area $\sigma(=4\pi r^2)$ as $\lambda = \dfrac{RT}{(\sqrt{2}\,N_0\sigma p)}$

135 **Statement I** Three states of matter are the result of balance between intermolecular forces and thermal energy of the molecules.

Statements II Intermolecular forces tend to keep the molecules together, but thermal energy of molecules tends to keep them apart.

136 **Statement I** Isotherms showing variation of pV vs p for a real gases are not linear for gases like CO, N_2....

Statement II At high pressure, these gases have $Z > 1$ but at intermediate pressure these gases have $Z < 1$.

137 **Statement I** In van der Waals' equation

$$\left(p + \frac{a}{V^2}\right)(V - b) = RT$$

the term $\left(\frac{a}{V^2}\right)$ is due to force of attraction between molecules.

Statement II Due to force of attraction, volume of molecules cannot be neglected as compared to total volume of the gas.

138 **Statement I** van der Waals' constant 'a' for NH_3 is larger than that for N_2.

Statement II Ammonia has lower molar mass than N_2.

139 **Statement I** Gases do not liquefy above their critical temperature (T_c) even on applying high pressure.

Statement II Above T_c, the molecular speed is high and intermolecular forces of attraction cannot hold the molecules together as they escape with high speed.

140 **Statement I** When second virial coefficient approaches zero, $T = \frac{a}{Rb}$

Statement II $\left(T = \frac{a}{Rb}\right)$ is called Boyle's temperature and real gas shows ideal behaviour.

141 **Statement I** For critical states,

$$T_c\left(\frac{dZ}{dT_c}\right)_{p_c, V_c} = -\frac{3}{8}$$

Statement II $p_c V_c = \frac{3}{8} RT_c$

142 **Statement I** Distribution of molecules with velocity is represented by

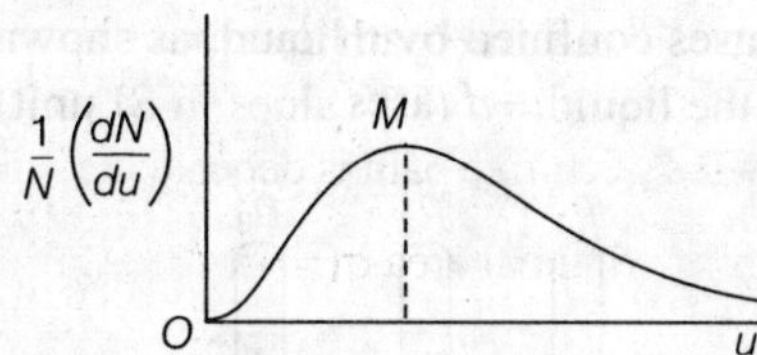

Statement II Probability P (of distribution of molecules) is given by

$$P = \frac{1}{N}\left(\frac{dN}{du}\right) = Au^2 e^{-Bu^2}$$

Increase in P is due to u^2 and decrease in P is due to e^{-Bu^2}.

143 **Statement I** Collision frequency increases with increase of pressure of the gas.

Statement II Under isothermal condition, molecules take lesser time to travel to its neighbour in a denser high pressure before collision.

144 **Statement I** Isobar showing variation of V (in dm^3) and T (in °C) is given by

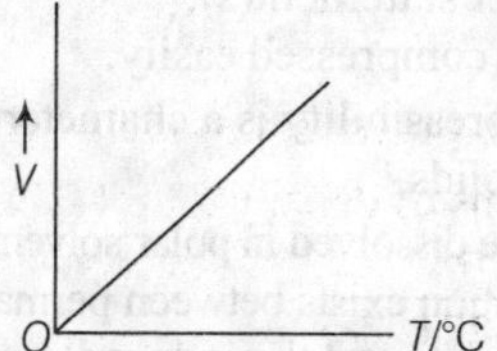

Statement II By Charles' law volume of a given amount of a gas at constant pressure is proportional to temperature (in Kelvin scale).

145 **Statement I** When CO_2 under high pressure is released from the fire extinguisher, particles of solid CO_2 are formed despite the low sublimation temperature (– 77°C) of CO_2 at 1 atm.

Statement II The energy comes from the kinetic energy of the molecules, thus lowering average kinetic energy and thus temperature.

146 **Statement I** Boyle's law cannot be used to calculate the volume of real gas which is changed from its initial state to its final state by an adiabatic expansion.

Statement II The temperature is lowered in an adiabatic expansion.

TYPE III MCQs with ONE or MORE than ONE Correct Alternate

147 Which of the following statements is/are true when comparing 0.5 mole $H_2(g)$ and 1.0 mole He (g) at STP?

The two gases have equal

(a) average molecular kinetic energy
(b) molecular speeds
(c) number of atoms
(d) volumes

148 Which regard to the gaseous state of matter, which of the following statements are correct? ***[NCERT Exemplar]***

(a) Complete order of molecules
(b) Complete disorder of molecules
(c) Random motion of molecules
(d) Fixed position of molecules

149 Consider a mixture of two gases (1 and 2) that have characteristics of ideal behaviour and are non-reactive. If gas (1) with $V_1 = 50$ L at STP is mixed with gas (2) with $V_2 = 10$ L at STP and final volume of the mixture will be 50 L in one case and 10 L in another case. Then partial pressure

(a) of the gas (1) is 1.00 atm and that of the gas (2) is 0.200 atm in one case
(b) of the gas (1) is 5.00 atm and that of gas (2) is 1.00 atm in the other case
(c) of the gas (1) is 5.00 atm and that of gas (2) is 1.00 in one case.
(d) of the gas (1) and gas (2) are respectively 5.00 atm and 1.00 atm in both cases

150 Select the correct statement(s).
(a) Gases can be compressed easily.
(b) Lack of compressibility is a characteristic property of liquids and solids.
(c) Oxygen can be dissolved in polar solvents like water because force of attraction exists between permanent dipole moment (of polar solvent) and the induced dipole of oxygen.
(d) London dispersion forces are the only intermolecular forces that allow non-polar molecules to interact.

151 The interaction energy of London forces is
(a) inversely proportional to sixth power of the distance between two interacting particles
(b) dependent on charge and mass
(c) dependent on polarisability
(d) dependent on strength of permanent dipoles

152 When two gaseous molecules of equal radii 'r' collide
(a) their centres are separated by $2r$ at the point of contact
(b) effective volume occupied by two molecules is eight times of the volume of each molecule
(c) excluded volume is four times of volume of each molecule
(d) greater the excluded volume, greater the deviation from ideal behaviour

153 Select correct variation of gaseous law properties in the following.

(a) 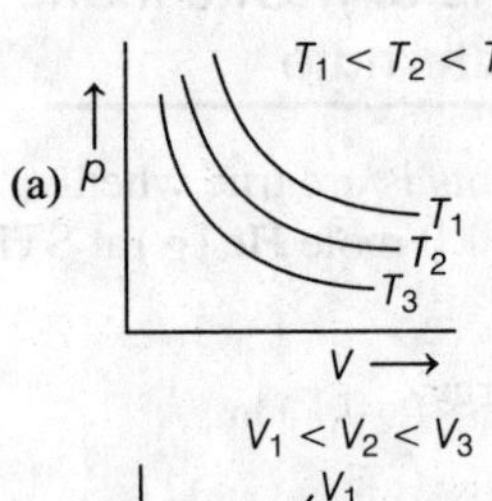

(b) 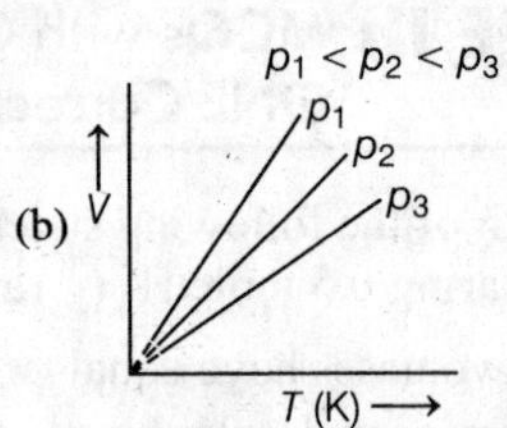

(c) 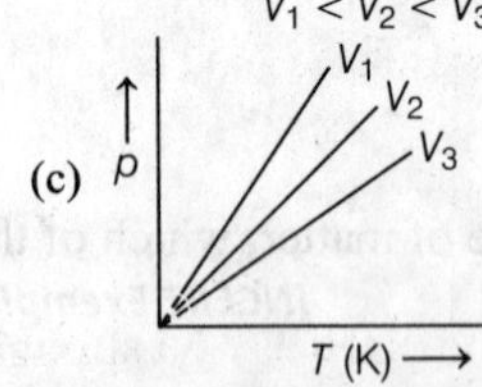

(d) 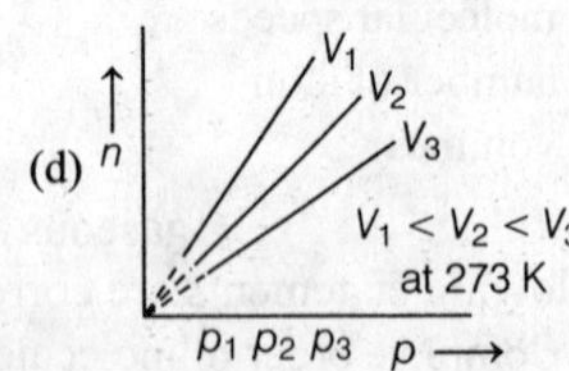

154 Select correct statement(s).
(a) Mass density of O_2 gas at 298 K and 1 atm is 1.31×10^{-3} kg m^{-3}
(b) Number density of O_2 gas at 298 K and 1 atm is 2.46×10^{25} molecules m^{-3}
(c) Mass density differs from gas to gas
(d) Number density at a given temperature and pressure is same for all gases

155 Select correct statement(s).
(a) Kinetic energy of 1 mole of a gas in terms of u_{rms} is $\frac{M}{2}(u_{rms})^2$
(b) Average kinetic energy of 1g H_2 and 8 g O_2 gas at 300 K are equal
(c) Kinetic energy of 1g H_2 at 300 K and that of 8 g O_2 at 600 K are equal
(d) $u_{mp} < u_{av} < u_{rms}$ for different molecular velocities

156 Which of the following statement(s) is/are correct regarding the root mean square speed (u_{rms}) and average translational kinetic energy (ε_{av}) of a molecule in a gas at equilibrium? *[JEE Adv. 2019]*
(a) ε_{av} at a given temperature does not depend on its molecular mass.
(b) u_{rms} is doubled when its temperature is increased four times.
(c) ε_{av} is doubled when its temperature is increased four time.
(d) u_{rms} is inversely proportional to the squqre root of its molecular mass.

157 Select correct statement(s) about Boyle's temperature (T_b).
(a) Above T_b, real gases show positive deviation from ideality and $Z > 1$
(b) Below T_b, real gases show negative deviation from ideality and $Z < 1$, upto certain pressure
(c) Below T_b, Z decreases with increase in p, Z attains minimum value and then increases with increase in p
(d) T_b and T_c are identical

158 Select correct matching of laws with their corresponding relations
(a) $p_1 d_2 = p_2 d_1$ Boyle's law
(b) $\log p = \log V + \log k$ Boyle's law
(c) $\log V = \log T + \log k$ Charles' law
(d) $p_1 T_2 = p_2 T_1$ Gay-Lussac's law

159 Select correct relationship between different units of pressure.
(a) 1 Pa = N m^{-2} = 1 kg m^{-1}s^{-2}
(b) 1 bar = 10^5 Pa = 0.987 atm
(c) 1 atm = 1.01325 bar = 1.01325×10^5 Pa
(d) 1 Torr = 133.322 Pa

160 Consider gases confined by a liquid, as shown in figure. Density of the liquid = d (all values in SI unit)

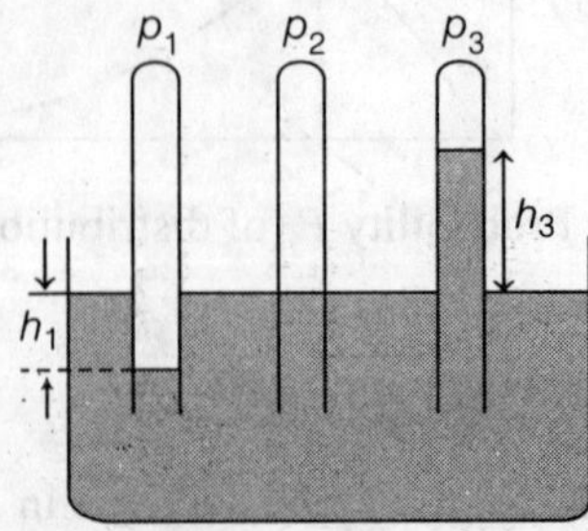

Then
(a) in terms of barometric pressure (p_{atm}), p_1 is $p_{atm} + h_1dg$
(b) barometers pressure is $p_1 + p_2 + p_3$
(c) in terms of barometric pressure (p_{atm}), p_3 is $p_{atm} - h_3dg$
(d) barometric pressure is p_2

161 An ideal gas is at 300 K and 1 atm. Then volume of one mole of gas remains constant if
(a) temperature is doubled and pressure is halved
(b) temperature is halved and pressure is halved
(c) temperature is doubled and pressure is doubled
(d) only temperature is doubled

162 If a gas is expanded at constant temperature
(a) the pressure decreases
(b) the kinetic energy of the molecules remains the same
(c) the kinetic energy of the molecules decreases
(d) the number of molecules of the gas increases

163 According to kinetic theory of gases **[IIT JEE 2011]**
(a) collision are always elastic
(b) heavier molecules transfer more momentum to the walls of the container
(c) only a small number of molecules have very high velocity
(d) between collisions, the molecules move in the straight line with constant velocities

164 Ratio of the rate of diffusion of He to H_2 at 0°C is same
(a) when temperature is changed to 100°C
(b) when O_2 and CH_4 are taken instead of He and H_2
(c) when volume of the flask is doubled
(d) when temperature is changed to 0 K

165 100 mL of H_2 gas diffuse in 10 s. *X* mL of O_2 diffuses in *t* s. Thus, *X* and *t* respectively are
(a) 100 mL, 40 s (b) 25 mL, 10 s
(c) 100 mL, 10 s (d) 5 mL, 2s

166 Based on the following isotherms, select correct statements

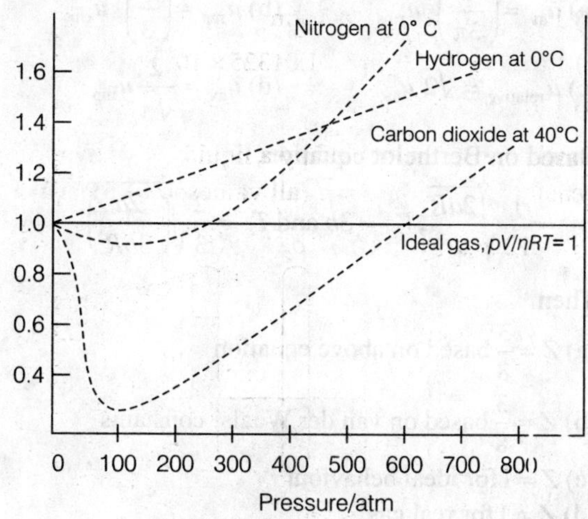

(a) For H_2 at 0°C, molecular attractive forces are weak and size effect dominates its behaviour resulting that ($Z > 1$)
(b) For N_2 at 0°C, attractive forces are large enough to cause negative deviation upto 150 atm thus ($Z < 1$) after which size effect dominates thus ($Z > 1$)
(c) For CO_2, intermolecular attraction is large even at 40°C resulting ($Z < 1$) even at high pressures
(d) For CO_2 and N_2, two effects compensate each other at a particular pressure where, $Z = 1$

167 At Boyle's temperature,
(a) the effects of repulsive and attractive intermolecular forces just off set each other
(b) a non-ideal gas behaves ideally
(c) cooling takes place
(d) heating takes place

168 At 300 K and 100 atm, the second virial coefficient (B) of N_2 and CH_4 are $-4.2\ cm^3\ mol^{-1}$ and $-15\ cm^3\ mol^{-1}$ respectively. Thus,
(a) N_2 gas behaves more ideally than CH_4 gas
(b) CH_4 gas behaves more ideally than that N_2 gas
(c) molar volume of N_2 is larger than that of CH_4
(d) molar volume of CH_4 is larger than that of N_2

169 In the virial equation of state given below :

$$pV_m = RT\left[1 + \frac{B}{V_m} + \frac{C}{V_m^2} + \dots\right]$$

(V_m is molar volume)
Coefficient B
(a) is independent of temperature
(b) is equal to zero at Boyle's temperature $\left(= \frac{a}{Rb}\right)$
(c) has the dimension of molar volume
(d) is equal to $\left(b - \frac{a}{RT}\right)$

170 1 mole of CS_2 was combusted to CO_2 and SO_2 by 4 moles of O_2 at 400 K in a 5 dm^3 flask. Thus,
(a) mole fraction of SO_2 is twice that of CO_2 and O_2
(b) mole fraction of SO_2 is 0.33
(c) mole fraction of CO_2 is 0.25
(d) pressure set up is 26.6 bar

171 Mixture of 3 moles of Na_2CO_3 and $NaHCO_3$ on strongly heating yielded CO_2 exerting a pressure of 8.314 bar at 300 K in 3 dm^3 flask. Thus,
(a) mole fraction of Na_2CO_3 and $NaHCO_3$ in the mixture are equal
(b) mole fraction of Na_2CO_3 is half that of $NaHCO_3$
(c) mole fraction of Na_2CO_3 is twice that of $NaHCO_3$
(d) pressure set up due to CO_2 is 24.942 bar under same conditions if mixture is treated with dil. HCl

172 Select correct statement(s).

(a) For the large temperature change $\Delta u_{\text{rms}} = \left(\frac{3R}{M}\right)^{1/2} (T_2^{1/2} - T_1^{1/2})$

(b) For a very small temperature change $du_{\text{rms}} = \frac{1.5R}{M}\left(\frac{1}{u_{\text{rms}}}\right) dT$

(c) For the large temperature change $\Delta(\text{KE}) = \frac{3}{2}k[T_2 - T_1]$

(d) For a very small temperature change $d(\overline{\text{KE}}) = \frac{(\text{KE})}{T} dT$

173 The van der Waals' equation of state for a non-ideal gas can be rearranged to give $\frac{pV}{RT} = \frac{V}{V-b} - \frac{a}{VRT}$ for 1 mole of gas. The constants a and b are positive numbers. When applied to H_2 at 80 K, the equation gives the curve as shown in the figure. Which one of the following statements is (are) correct?

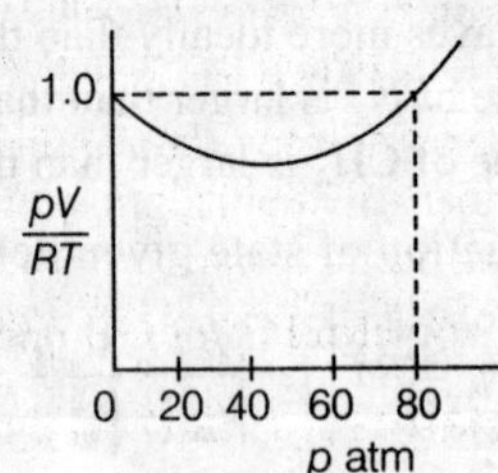

(a) At 40 atm, the two terms $\frac{V}{(V-b)}$ and $\frac{a}{VRT}$ are equal

(b) At 80 atm, the two terms $\frac{V}{(V-b)}$ and $\frac{a}{VRT}$ are equal

(c) At a pressure greater than 80 atm, the term $\frac{V}{(V-b)}$ is greater than $\frac{a}{VRT}$

(d) At 60 atm, term $\frac{V}{(V-b)}$ is smaller than $\left(1+\frac{a}{VRT}\right)$

174 Which of the following statements is/are correct about Boyle temperature T_b

(a) Temperature at which first virial coefficient of van der Waals' equation becomes zero

(b) Temperature at which second virial coefficient of van der Waals' equation becomes zero

(c) According to van der Waals' equation, value of $T_b = \frac{a}{Rb}$

(d) T_b of a gas depends upon the nature of gas

175 Which of the following statements is/are correct?

(a) The difference between rms speed and average speed at any temperature decreases as gases of larger molar masses are involved

(b) Average kinetic energy of the gas molecules at a given temperature is independent of molar mass

(c) Ratio of the rms velocity and average velocity of a given gas is independent of temperature

(d) The square of the average speed is equal to the root mean square speed at a certain temperature

176 Based on the following isotherm

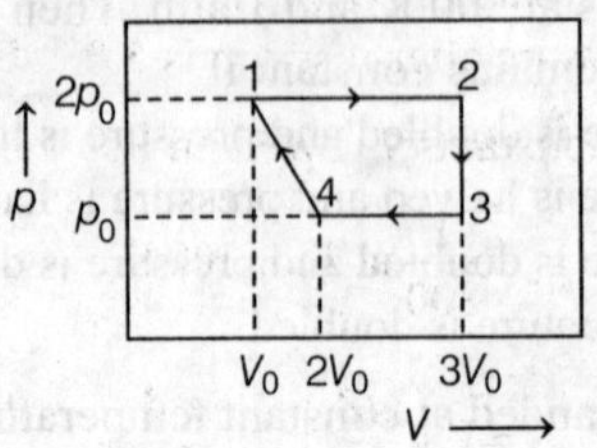

Select correct variation of most probable velocities at different points

(a) u_{mp} at $2 > u_{\text{mp}}$ at 3 (b) u_{mp} at $4 = u_{\text{mp}}$ at 1

(c) u_{mp} at $1 = u_{\text{mp}}$ at 3 (d) u_{mp} at $1 > u_{\text{mp}}$ at 2

177 Which of the following variations of gaseous parameters (p, V, T) given in the form graphs is/are correct?

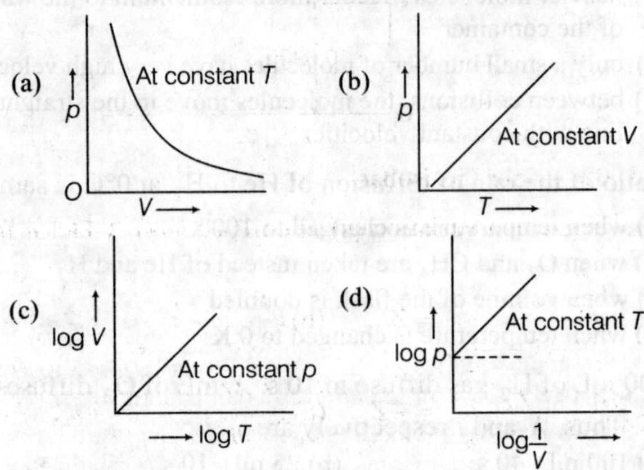

178 Select correct relation for different types of molecular velocities.

(a) $u_{\text{av}} = \left(\frac{8}{3\pi}\right)^{\frac{1}{2}} u_{\text{rms}}$ (b) $u_{\text{mp}} = \left(\frac{2}{3}\right)^{\frac{1}{2}} u_{\text{rms}}$

(c) $u_{\text{relative}} = \sqrt{2}\, u_{\text{av}}$ (d) $u_{\text{av}} = \frac{2}{\sqrt{\pi}} u_{\text{mp}}$

179 Based on Berthelot equation,

$$p_c = \frac{1}{12}\sqrt{\frac{2aR}{3b^3}}, V_c = 3b \text{ and } T_c = \frac{2}{3}\sqrt{\left(\frac{2a}{3bR}\right)}$$

Then

(a) $Z = \frac{3}{8}$ based on above equation

(b) $Z = \frac{3}{8}$ based on van der Waals' constants

(c) $Z = 1$ for ideal behaviour

(d) $Z \neq 1$ for real gas

180 A vessel of volume 22.4 dm^3 contains 2.0 moles H_2 and 1.0 mole N_2 at 273 K.
(a) Total pressure of the mixture before reaction takes place is 3.04 bar
(b) There is no change in pressure after reaction
(c) Partial pressure of NH_3 is maximum
(d) Total pressure after reaction is 5.066 bar

181 For critical constants T_c, p_c and V_c
(a) $\left(\frac{dZ}{dT_c}\right)_{p_c, V_c} = -\frac{1}{800}$ at $T_c = 300$ K
(b) $p_c\left(\frac{dZ}{dp_c}\right)_{T_c V_c} = V_c\left(\frac{dZ}{dV}\right)_{p_c T_c} = \frac{3}{8}$
(c) critical pressure is 6.2×10^{-3} bar for the following isobar

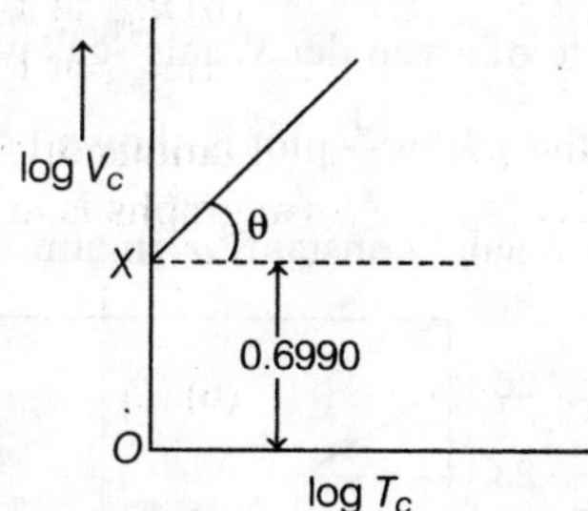

(d) $\theta = 45°$ for this isobar

182 Select correct variation (s) of compressibility factor for an ideal gas.
(a) $p\left(\frac{d(Z)}{dp}\right)_{T, V, n} = Z$ (b) $V\left(\frac{d(Z)}{dV}\right)_{p, T, n} = Z$
(c) $T\left(\frac{d(Z)}{dT}\right)_{V, p, n} = -Z$ (d) $n\left(\frac{dZ}{dn}\right)_{p, V, T} = -n$

183 Select correct statement(s).
(a) Most probable velocity is derived assuming that when maximum distribution of molecules is reached $\frac{dp}{du} = 0$
(b) Boyle's temperature is based on by assuming second virial coefficient to be zero
(c) Compressibility factor $Z = 1$ for all types of real gases
(d) Boyle's temperature is twice of inversion temperature

184 One mole N_2 and four moles H_2 are taken in a 25 L flask at 300 K. Thus,
(a) before they react partial pressure of N_2 is 1 bar
(b) after reaction, partial pressure of NH_3 formed is higher than that of unreacted N_2 and H_2
(c) if 10 L of water is added, pressure set up after reaction is 5 bar
(d) mole fraction of NH_3 gas in the product is 0.67 after H_2O is added

185 Select correct variation of different types of molecular velocities with temperature.
(a) $\frac{du_{mp}}{dT} = \frac{R}{M u_{mp}}$ (b) $\frac{du_{av}}{dT} = \frac{4R}{\pi M u_{av}}$
(c) $\frac{du_{rms}}{dT} = \frac{3R}{2M u_{rms}}$ (d) $\frac{du_{mp}}{dT} = \frac{2R}{M u_{mp}}$

186 For the van der Waals' equation
$$\left(p + \frac{a}{V^2}\right)(V - b) = RT$$
isotherms are given for different gases. Select correct statements.

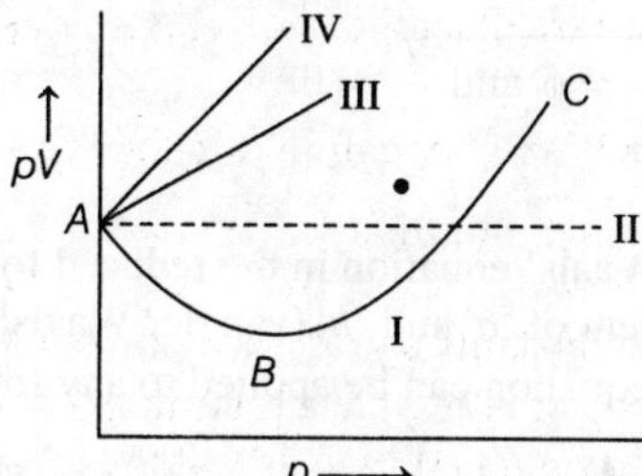

(a) Isotherms III and IV are for H_2 and He and $Z = \left(\frac{pb + RT}{RT}\right)$
(b) Isotherm II is for ideal gas and $Z = 1$
(c) AB part of isotherm I is for CO under low p and $Z = \frac{RTV - a}{RTV}$
(d) BC part of isotherm I is for CO under high p and $Z = \frac{(pb + RT)}{RT}$

187 van der Waals' constants of the two gases X and Y are given below.

Gas	a(dm^3 bar mol^{-2})	b($dm^3 mol^{-1}$)
X	7.1	8.20×10^{-3}
Y	19.98	1.70×10^{-2}

Thus,
(a) $V_c(X) > V_c(Y)$ (b) $p_c(X) < p_c(Y)$
(c) $V_c(X) < V_c(Y)$ (d) $T_b(X) < T_b(Y)$

188 A gas described by van der Waals' equation ***[IIT JEE 2008]***
(a) behaves similar to an ideal gas in the limit of large molar volumes
(b) behaves similar to an ideal gas in the limit of large pressures
(c) is characterised by van der Waals' coefficients that are dependent on the identity of the gas but are independent of the temperature
(d) has the pressure that is lower than the pressure exerted by the same gas behaving ideally

189 He, CH_4 and SO_2 are contained in 10 L flask in the molar ratio of 1 : 2 : 4. If they are allowed to effuse, then
(a) rate of effusion of He and CH_4 is same as rate of He and SO_2
(b) mole fraction of gases coming out of the hole are in 1 : 2 : 4 ratio

(c) mole fraction of gases coming out of the hole are equal

(d) number of moles of gases coming out of the hole are equal

190 On making absolute temperature of an ideal gas 4 times and pressure 2 times, diffusion coefficient becomes 4 times. Thus, diffusion coefficient (DC) is

(a) $DC \propto \frac{\lambda \text{ (mean free path)}}{u_{av} \text{ (average speed)}}$ (b) $(DC) \propto \lambda$

(c) $(DC) \propto u_{av}$ (d) $(DC) \propto \frac{u_{av}}{\lambda}$

191 If $\frac{p}{p_c} = \pi, \frac{V}{V_c} = \phi$ and $\frac{T}{T_c} = \theta$

Then

(a) van der Waals' equation in the reduced form is independent of 'a' and 'b' (van der Waals' constant)

(b) reduced equation can be applied to any form of a matter

(c) equation obtained is $\left(\pi + \frac{3}{\phi^2}\right)(3\phi - 1) = 8\theta$

(d) It is applicable only for gases.

TYPE IV Numerical Skills

192 A spherical balloon of radius 3 cm containing helium gas has a pressure of 48×10^{-3} bar. At the same temperature, the pressure of a spherical balloon of radius 12 cm containing the same amount of gas will be ...... $\times 10^{-6}$ bar **[JEE Main 2020 (II) NTA]**

193 At the top of a mountain, the thermometer reads 273 K and the barometer reads 710 mmHg. At the bottom of the mountain, the temperature is 292 K and the pressure is 760mmHg. Ratio of density of the air at the top to that at the bottom is ....

194 Assuming the same pressure in each case, calculate the mass of H_2 gas required to inflate a balloon to a certain volume V at 373 K, if 5.0 g of He is required to inflate the balloon to half the volume at 298 K.

195 Liquefied natural gas (LNG) is mainly methane. A 10.0 m^3 tank is constructed to store LNG at -164°C and 1.0 atm pressure, under which conditions, the density is 415 kg m^{-3}. Volume of the storage tank capable of holding the same mass of LNG as a gas at 20°C and 1.0 atmospheric pressure is $y \times 10^x$ m^3. What is value of x?

196 Aluminium reacts with sulphuric acid to form aluminium sulphate and hydrogen. What is the volume of hydrogen gas in litres (L) produced at 300 K and 1.0 atm pressure, when 5.4 g of aluminium and 50.0 mL of 5.0 M sulphuric acid are combined for the reaction?

(Use molar mass of aluminium as 27.0 g mol^{-1}, $R = 0.082$ atm L mol^{-1} K^{-1}) **[JEE Adv. 2020]**

197 $x \times 10^3$ g of water vapour is contained in a cubic room of 6.0 m along an edge, if the relative humidity is 50% at 300 K, at which vapour pressure is 19.26 Torr.

198 When 0.75 mol solid "A_4" and 2 mol gaseous O_2 are heated in a sealed vessel, completely using up the reactants, and producing only one compound; it is found that when the temperature is reduced to initial temperature, the contents of the vessel exhibit a pressure equal to half the original pressure. How many total of atoms of A and O are involved in the final product?

199 A closed vessel with rigid walls contains 1 mole of $^{238}_{92}$U and 1 mole of air at 298 K. Considering complete decay of $^{238}_{92}$U to $^{206}_{22}$Pb, the ratio of the final pressure to the initial pressure of the system at 298 K is **[JEE Adv. 2015]**

200 For one mole of a van der Waals' gas when $b = 0$ and $T = 300$ K, the pV vs $\frac{1}{V}$ plot is shown below. The value of the van der Waals' constant 'a' in atm L mol^{-2} is

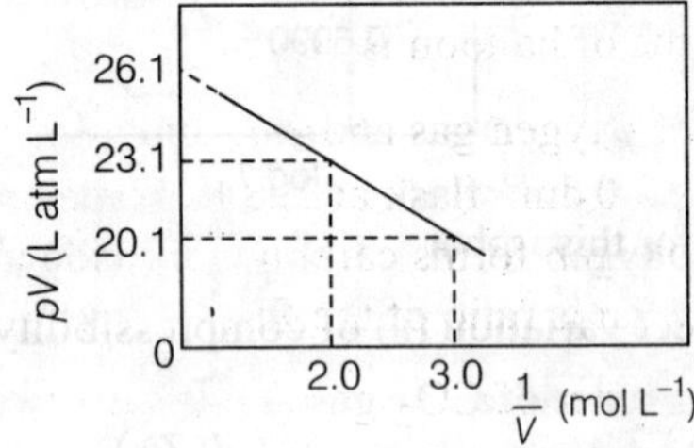

201 At 400 K, the root mean square (rms) speed of a gas X (molecular weight = 40) is equal to the most probable speed of gas Y at 60 K. The molecular weight of the gas Y is **[IIT JEE 2009]**

202 2.00 g of H_2 and 10.00 g of the He are confined to a volume of 10.0 dm^3 at 293 K. Thus, partial pressure of He (in atm) is ....

203 When intermolecular forces of attraction are neglected, graph between V and T at constant p for van der Waals' equation is of the type

Slope = 0.0117 L mol^{-1} K^{-1} and OA = 2.0 L mol^{-1}

Thus, pressure maintained is .... atm.

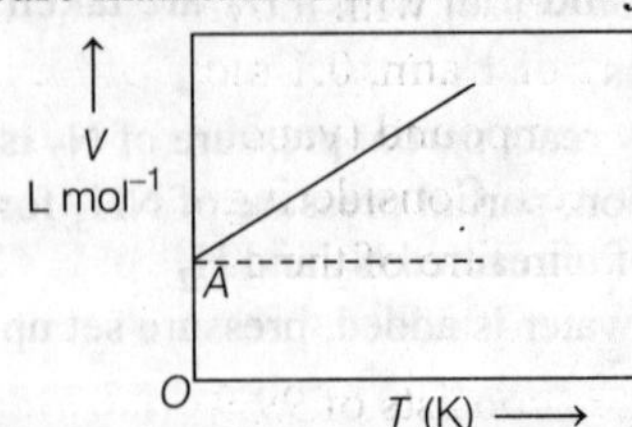

204 Based on Q(203) van der Waals' constant 'b' is ... L mol^{-1}

205 $NaClO_3$ is used, even in spacecrafts to produce O_2. The daily consumption of pure O_2 by a person is 492 L at 1 atm and 300 K. How much amount of $NaClO_3$, in grams, is required to produce O_2 for the daily consumption of a person at 1 atm and 300 K?

$NaClO_3(s) + Fe(s) \longrightarrow O_2(g) + NaCl(s) + FeO(s)$

$R = 0.0821$ L atm mol^{-1} K^{-1} *[JEE Main 2020 (II) NTA]*

206 The density of a steam at 1 bar and at 373 K is 0.6 kg m^{-3}. Thus, compressibility factor (Z) that deviates from the normal value under ideal condition is ..... %.

207 A toy balloon originally held 1 g of He gas and had a radius of 10.0 cm. During overnight, 0.25 g of the gas effused from the balloon. What was the radius of the balloon the next morning? Assume ideal behaviour under isothermal and isobaric conditions (express the result in cm.)

208 Assume air as an ideal gas of molar mass 29.0 g mol^{-1} at 1.00 bar and 298 K. What will be the temperature difference needed in a hot air balloon to lift 1.00 kg of mass? Volume of balloon is 100 m^3.

209 1.23 moles of oxygen gas and 2.73 moles of carbon are placed into a 3.0 dm^3 flask at 298 K. If reaction between carbon and oxygen forms carbon monoxide under given conditions, what is ratio of the final and initial pressure?

210 A 50 dm^3 cylinder of CO_2 gas at 6.00 atm pressure and 304.5 K developed a leak. When the leak was detected, it was found that pressure of CO_2 was 1.5 atm under identical conditions. Thus, number of moles of CO_2 leaked is ....

211 Value of $-\frac{1}{V}\left(\frac{\partial V}{\partial p}\right)_{T,n}$ at 0.2 bar is ...... bar^{-1}.

212 The diffusion coefficient of an ideal gas is proportional to its mean free path and mean speed. The absolute temperature of an ideal gas is increased 4 times and its pressure is increased 2 times. As a result, the diffusion coefficient of the gas increases x times. The value of x is .... *[JEE Adv. 2016]*

213 To an evacuated vessel with movable piston under external pressure of 1 atm, 0.1 mole of He and 1.0 mole of an unknown compound (vapour pressure 0.68 atm at 0°C) are introduced. Considering the ideal gas behaviour, the total volume (in litre of the gases at 0°C is close to) *[IIT JEE 2011]*

214 Natural hydrogen consists of 99.98% ^1_1H and 0.02% ^2_1H by mass. It can be enriched by diffusion to produce 35% $^1_1H^2_1H$ from ordinary gaseous hydrogen in n diffusion steps. What is the value of n?

215 Pressure needed to confine 9×10^{24} gas molecules each of mass 1.0×10^{-25} kg and with root mean square velocity of 1.0×10^3 ms^{-1} in a 1.0 m^3 container is ...... bar.

216 Root mean square velocity of O_2 gas at a given temperature is 129.91 ms^{-1}. What is $\left(\frac{du_{rms}}{dT}\right)$ in ms^{-1}K^{-1}?

217 Observed value of pressure of air (80% N_2 and 20% O_2) at 273 K is 100 atm. What is change from the calculated value of pressure under given condition if air is contained in 0.2175 L flask?

218 For O_2 gas van der Waals' constant (b) at 313 K is 0.034 L mol^{-1}. Its molecular diameter is x Å. What is the value of x? (1 Å $= 1 \times 10^{-10}$ m)

219 A diver at a depth of 45 m exhales a bubble of air that is 1.0 cm in radius, when pressure is 8.09 bar. Assuming ideal gas behaviour, what will be the radius (in cm) of this bubble as it breaks at the surface of the water?

220 What will be the volume of helium (in dm^3) needed to lift 1.00 kg of mass at 298 K and pressure 1 bar? Air (molar mass 29 g mol^{-1}) and helium act ideally.

221 An iron mineral was analysed for its isotopic argon content. The amount of ^{36}Ar was 0.186 mm^3 (STP) per kg of mineral. If each ^{36}Ar atoms had been formed by a single cosmic event, how many such events must there have been per kg of mineral? If this number is $x \times 10^y$, what is the value of $(x + y)$?

TYPE V Passage Based MCQs (Comprehension)

Passage 1

Consider acetaldehyde (CH_3CHO) gas having a volume of 1.75 L at STP which has been mixed with 25 L of O_2 gas at STP. The mixture was exposed to UV-radiation at STP to form CO_2 and H_2O gases (assume H_2O in vapour state at 298 K).

222 Volume of CO_2 gas and H_2O vapour formed at 298 K and 1 atm will be

	CO_2 gas	H_2O vapour
(a)	3.821 L	3.821 L
(b)	3.821 L	1.911 L
(c)	1.911 L	1.911 L
(d)	1.911L	3.821 L

223 Select the correct alternate :

(a) CH_3CHO is the limiting reactant and 0.0781 mol of its are used.

(b) O_2 is the limiting reactant and 1.115 mol of O_2 are used

(c) O_2 is in excess and 0.195 mol of O_2 are used

(d) Alternates (a) and (c) are correct

Passage 2

When intermolecular attractive forces are neglected, isobar formed between V and T at constant p is of the type:

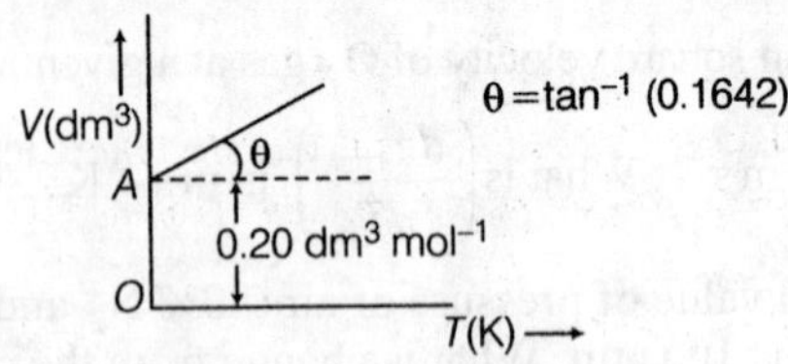

224 Pressure at which isobar is made, is

(a) 2 atm mol^{-1} (b) 0.5 atm mol^{-1}
(c) 1 atm mol^{-1} (d) 4 atm mol^{-1}

225 Volume of molecules present in 1 mole of the gas under given condition is

(a) 0.20 dm^3 mol^{-1} (b) 0.10 dm^3 mol^{-1}
(c) 0.224 dm^3 mol^{-1} (d) 0.05 dm^3 mol^{-1}

Passage 3

Under the condition, when $p \rightarrow 0$, isotherm showing variation of pV with p at 273 K has a slope of $-$ 0.1 dm^3 mol^{-1}.

226 Assume ideal conditions for approximation, van der Waals' constant 'a' (in unit of bar dm^6 mol^{-2}) is

(a) 2.27 (b) 4.54 (c) 0.114 (d) 0.454

227 Intercept on the pV axis in this isotherm is

(a) 2.27 bar dm^3 mol^{-1} (b) 22.7 bar dm^3 mol^{-1}
(c) 0.227 bar dm^3 mol^{-1} (d) None of these

Passage 4

Consider the following arrangements of two vessels (A) and (B) joined by a stopcock of negligible volume. When stopcock is opened, following reaction takes place.

$$2NO(g) + O_2(g) \longrightarrow N_2O_4(s)$$

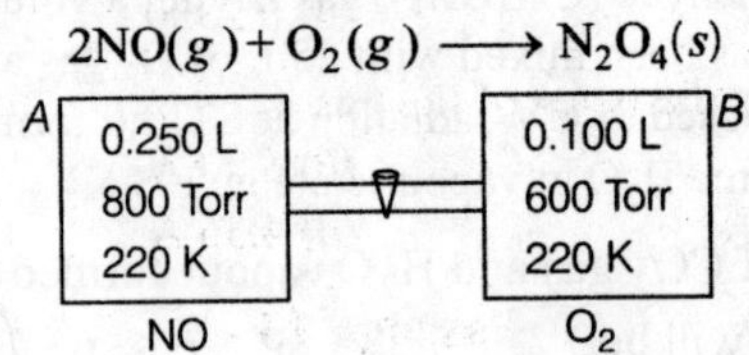

228 Pressure set up at the end of the reaction is

(a) 0.402 atm (b) 0.152 atm
(c) 0.127 atm (d) 0.302 atm

229 $N_2O_4(s)$ formed is

(a) 0.402 g (b) 4.36×10^{-3} g
(c) 0.201 g (d) 0.804 g

Passage 5

Distribution of molecular velocities was studied by Maxwell and is given by

$$\frac{1}{N}\left(\frac{dN}{du}\right) = 4\pi u^2 \left(\frac{M}{2\pi RT}\right)^{3/2} \exp\left(-\frac{Mu^2}{2RT}\right)$$

$\frac{1}{N}\left(\frac{dN}{du}\right)$ is also called probability P. Based on following curves,

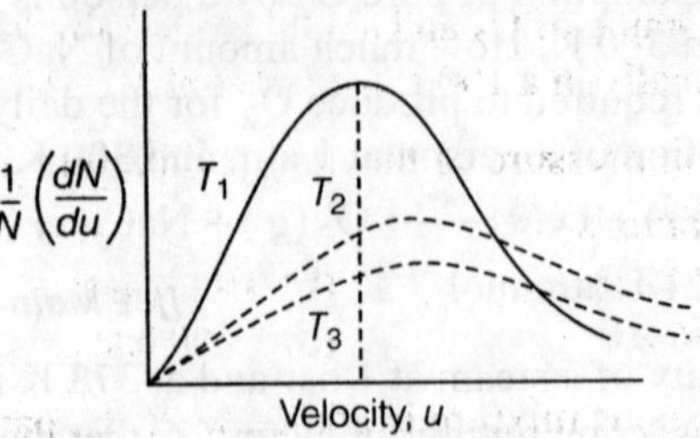

230 Arrange temperatures T_1, T_2 and T_3 in increasing order.

(a) $T_3 < T_2 < T_1$ (b) $T_1 = T_2 = T_3$
(c) $T_1 < T_2 < T_3$ (d) $T_3 < T_2 <<< T_1$

231 As velocity increases, probability also increases. It is maximum at a particular velocity. This is called most probable velocity. At this point, variation of probability P with velocity u is $\left(\frac{dP}{du}\right) = 0$.

Thus, based on this, velocity is

(a) $\sqrt{\frac{3RT}{M}}$ (b) $\sqrt{\frac{2RT}{M}}$ (c) $\sqrt{\frac{8RT}{\pi M}}$ (d) $\sqrt{\frac{2\pi RT}{M}}$

Passage 6

X and Y are two volatile liquids with molar weights of 10 g mol^{-1} and 40 g mol^{-1} respectively. Two cotton plugs, one soaked in X and the other soaked in Y, are simultaneously placed at the ends of the tube of length $l = 24$ cm, as shown in the figure. The tube is filled with an inert gas at 1 atm pressure and temperature of 300 K. Vapours of X and Y react to form a product which is first formed at a distance, a cm from the plug soaked in X. Take X and Y to have equal molecular diameters and assume ideal behaviour for the inert gas and two vapours. **[JEE Adv. 2014]**

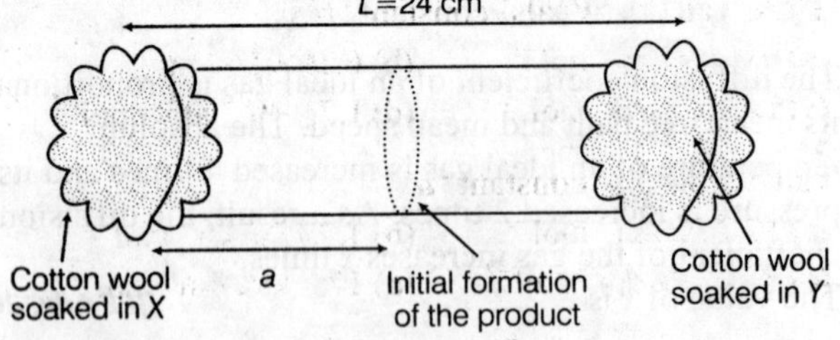

232 The value of 'a' in cm (shown in the figure), as estimated from Graham's law is

(a) 8 (b) 12 (c) 16 (d) 20

233 The experimental value of a is found to be smaller than the estimated value obtained by using Graham's law. This is due to

(a) larger mean free path for X as compared to that of Y
(b) larger mean free path for Y as compared to that of X
(c) increased collision frequency of Y with the inert gas as compared to that of X with the inert gas
(d) increased collision frequency of X with the inert gas as compared to that of Y with the inert gas

Passage 7

A 1.00 mole sample of O_2 and a 3.00 moles sample of H_2 are mixed isothermally in a 100 L container at 127° C.

234 Change in pressure of the gaseous mixture after H_2 and O_2 combine is
(a) 0.3324 bar　(b) 0.9972 bar
(c) 1.3296 bar　(d) 1.000 bar

235 After gaseous mixture is cooled to 25°C, partial pressure of H_2 is
(a) 1.00 bar　(b) 0.2480 bar
(c) 0.3324 bar　(d) 0.2796 bar

Passage 8

A 50 mL sample of a hydrogen-oxygen mixture was placed in a gas buret at 291 K and confined at barometric pressure. A spark was passed through the sample so that the formation of water could go to completion. The resulting pure gas shows a volume of 10 mL at barometric pressure.

236 What is mole fraction of the H_2 in the mixture if the residual gas after sparking was H_2?
(a) 0.482　(b) 0.267　(c) 0.518　(d) 0.733

237 What was the mole fraction of the H_2 in the mixture, if the residual gas after sparking was O_2?
(a) 0.592　(b) 0.408　(c) 0.533　(d) 0.467

Passage 9

Given that, $Z = 1.00054$ at 273 K and 101.325 kPa and Boyle temperature of the gas is 107 K.

Assume, $Z = 1 + \frac{p}{RTZ}\left(b - \frac{a}{RT}\right)$

238 Thus, van der Waals' constant 'b' is
(a) 0.0199 $dm^3\ mol^{-1}$　(b) 0.199 $dm^3\ mol^{-1}$
(c) $1 \times 10^{-4}\ dm^3\ mol^{-1}$　(d) $1.7 \times 10^{-4}\ dm^3\ mol^{-1}$

239 van der Waals' constant 'a'
(a) 17.7 Pa $dm^6\ mol^{-2}$　(b) 1.77 Pa $dm^6\ mol^{-2}$
(c) 1.77 kPa $dm^6\ mol^{-2}$　(d) 17.7 kPa $dm^6\ mol^{-2}$

Passage 10

18.0 g carbon is heated with 5.00 L O_2 at 18°C and 5.00 atm. Gas is passed into 500 mL of 2.0 M NaOH when following reactions occur:

$$NaOH + CO_2 \longrightarrow NaHCO_3$$
$$2NaOH + CO_2 \longrightarrow Na_2CO_3$$

CO formed if any remains unreacted with NaOH.

240 Molar concentrations of $NaHCO_3$ and Na_2CO_3 formed are
(a) 0.80 M, 0.40 M　(b) 0.40 M, 0.80 M
(c) 0.50 M, 0.80 M　(b) 0.60 M, 0.30 M

241 CO formed is
(a) 0.60 mol　(b) 0.40 mol
(c) 0.90 mol　(d) 0.50 mol

Passage 11

When intermolecular forces in a real gas are taken zero, variation of pV with pressure p at a given temperature is shown by following isotherm.

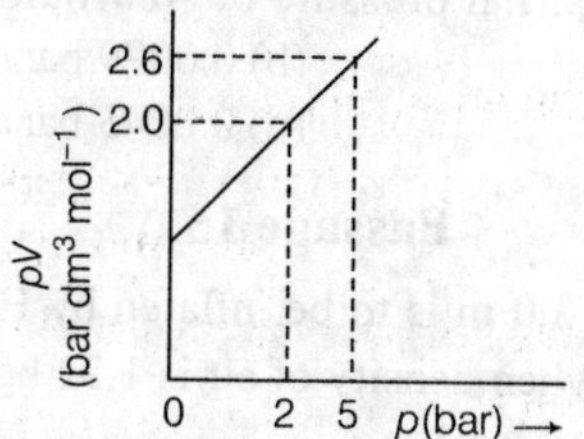

242 Thus, critical volume V_c is
(a) 0.2 $dm^3 mol^{-1}$　(b) 0.6 $dm^3 mol^{-1}$
(c) 1.8 $dm^3 mol^{-1}$　(d) 0.8 $dm^3 mol^{-1}$

243 If, $T_c = 100$ K for this gas then, p_c is
(a) 41.6 bar　(b) 13.8 bar
(c) 124.5 bar　(d) 55.3 bar

Passage 12

Compressibility factor for a van der Waals' gas is 1.008 at 273 K and 1 bar pressure. Its Boyle's temperature is 107 K. Under the given condition, van der Waals' equation followed is

$$pV = RT\left[1 + \left(b - \frac{a}{RT}\right)\frac{1}{V} + \ldots\right]$$

244 van der Waals' constant 'a' is (in bar $dm^6 mol^{-2}$)
(a) 1.1650　(b) 0.2790
(c) 2.67　(d) 0.2330

245 Molecular diameter of the gas is
(a) 2.18 Å　(b) 6.20 Å
(c) 0.545 Å　(d) 4.36 Å

Passage 13

The denisty of air is 3.8×10^{-12} kg m^{-3} at the height of 300 km above sea level. Temperature is 960 K and pressure is 1.6×10^{-8} m bar

246 Assuming ideal gas behaviour, the average molar mass of air at the height and under given conditions is
(a) 19.0 g mol^{-1}　(b) 29.8 g mol^{-1}
(c) 28.2 g mol^{-1}　(d) 32.0 g mol^{-1}

247 Assume air consists of $N_2(g)$ and O-atoms, then mole fraction of $N_2(g)$ is
(a) 0.75　(b) 0.25
(c) 0.66　(d) 0.34

Passage 14

Given that the density of air at 0.987 bar and 300 K is 1.146 kg m^{-3}.

248 Partial pressure of N_2 gas is
(a) 0.494 bar (b) 0.235 bar
(c) 0.617 bar (d) 0.752 bar

249 If air also contains 1 mol per cent Ar (40×10^{-3} kg mol^{-1}) then, partial pressure of Ar would be
(a) 0.772 bar (b) 0.0099 bar
(c) 0.205 bar (d) 0.0045 bar

Passage 15

A balloon of radius 3.0 m is to be inflated by H_2 at a pressure of 1.0 bar and 298 K, when density of air is 1.22 kg m^{-3} at sea level.

250 What amount of H_2 is needed?
(a) 4.565 kmol (b) 9.262 kmol
(c) 2.315 kmol (d) None is correct

251 What mass can the balloon lift at the sea level?
(a) 120.75 kg (b) 124.16 kg (c) 60.12 kg (d) 128.87 kg

Passage 16

A 5.00 L flask containing N_2 at 1.00 bar and 298 K is connected to a 4.00 L flask containing N_2 at 2.00 bar and 273 K. Gases are allowed to mix keeping both flasks at their original temperatures.

252 Amount of N_2 in 5.00 L flask is
(a) 0.296 mol (b) 0.148 mol
(c) 0.444 mol (d) 0.094 mol

253 Final pressure in 5.0 L flask is
(a) 1.00 bar (b) 1.47 bar (c) 2.94 bar (d) 0.74 bar

Passage 17

A Dumas bulb used for determining molar mass of a gas had a mass of 65.2649 g when empty, 65.3324 g when filled with natural gas at 296 K and a pressure 741 Torr, and 170.15 g when filled with water.

254 Density of natural gas is
(a) 6.42×10^{-3} g mL^{-1} (b) 6.42×10^{-6} g mL^{-1}
(c) 0.642 g L^{-1} (d) 6.42×10^{-3} g mL^{-1}

255 Molar mass of the natural gas is
(a) 8.0 g mol^{-1} (b) 16.0 g mol^{-1}
(c) 58.0 g mol^{-1} (d) 32.0 g mol^{-1}

Passage 18

The composition of air inhaled by a person is 21% by volume of O_2 and 0.03% CO_2, and that of exhaled air is 16% by volume of O_2 and 4.4% CO_2 at 37°C and 1.00 bar. Intake of air per day is 7200 L.

256 Mass of O_2 used by a person per day is
(a) 600 g (b) 500 g (c) 450 g (d) 220 g

257 CO_2 generated per day is
(a) 600 g (b) 218 g
(c) 450 g (d) 537 g

Passage 19

For critical states is

$$p_c V_c = \frac{3}{8} R T_c$$

258 If T_c is increased by 10% at a critical atmosphere of 50 bar, Z (compressibility factor) is
(a) decreased by 10% (b) increased by 5%
(c) remains unchanged (d) None is correct

259 In the variation of $\log(p_c V_c)$ with $\log T_c$, at a given pressure gas constant can be determined by
(a) slope of the line (b) intercept
(c) Both of these (d) None of these

TYPE VI Matrix Matching

Based on Two Columns

260 1.00 mole sample of O_2 and 3.00 moles sample of H_2 are mixed isothermally in a 100.0 L container at 400 K. Mixture is cooled to 298 K. Match the partial pressures of different species in Column I with their values in Column II and select answer from codes given below.

	Column I		Column II
(i)	Partial pressure of H_2 before reaction	(p)	0.00 atm
(ii)	Partial pressure of O_2 after reaction	(q)	1.3136 atm
(iii)	Total pressure before reaction	(r)	0.3284 atm
(iv)	Total pressure after reaction	(s)	0.9852 atm
(v)	Total pressure at 298 K	(t)	0.2447 atm

Codes

	(i)	(ii)	(iii)	(iv)	(v)
(a)	p	q	r	s	t
(b)	s	r	q	p	t
(c)	s	p	q	s	t
(d)	s	p	q	s	t

261 Assume that attractive forces are negligible and isobar (using Charles' law) giving variation of V(dm^3) and T(K) constant p(atm) is of the type

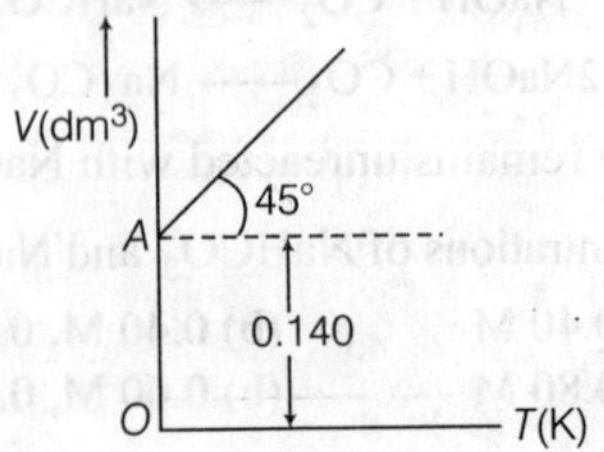

Match the parameters in Column I with their values in Column II and select the answer from the codes given below.

Column I	Column II
(i) Pressure (atm)	(p) 0.043
(ii) van der Waals' constant (b)($dm^3 mol^{-1}$)	(q) 0.140
(iii) Volume at 300 K (dm^3)	(r) 300.14
(iv) van der Waals' constant (a) (dm^6 atm mol^{-2}) if pressure is the critical pressure	(s) 0.0821

Codes

	(i)	(ii)	(iii)	(iv)
(a)	(p)	(q)	(s)	(r)
(b)	(r)	(s)	(p)	(q)
(c)	(s)	(q)	(r)	(p)
(d)	(q)	(r)	(s)	(p)

262 Assume molecules of a real gas of negligible volume isotherm between pV and $\left(\frac{1}{V}\right)$ at 300 K is of the type

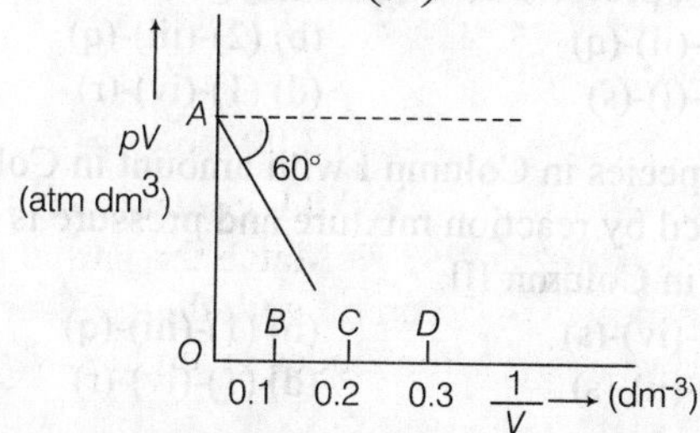

Match the parameters in Column I with their values in Column II and select the answer from the codes given below.

Column I	Column II
(i) Value (OA)	(p) 0.0693
(ii) van der Waals' constant 'a'	(q) 24.11
(iii) (pV) at point (D)	(r) 1.732
(iv) Attractive forces at point (C) in one mole of real gas	(s) 24.63

Codes

	(i)	(ii)	(iii)	(iv)
(a)	(p)	(r)	(s)	(q)
(b)	(s)	(r)	(p)	(q)
(c)	(s)	(p)	(q)	(r)
(d)	(s)	(r)	(q)	(p)

263 An isochore (at 0.1 dm^3) showing Gay-Lussac's law for one mole of a real gas is of the type

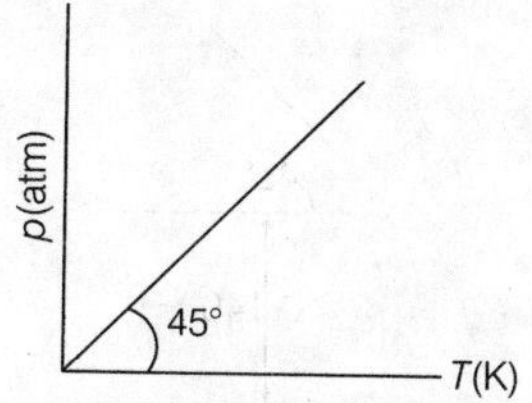

Match the parameters in Column I with their values in Column II and select the answer from codes given below.

Column I	Column II
(i) van der Waals' constant 'b' (dm^3 mol^{-1})	(p) 0.0179
(ii) Temperature (K) at which p is 1 atm	(q) 1.0
(iii) $\left(\frac{\partial p}{\partial T}\right)_V$	(r) 1.21
(iv) Mean free path at the condition of (ii) in Å	(s) 5.24

Codes

	(i)	(ii)	(iii)	(iv)
(a)	(p)	(q)	(r)	(s)
(b)	(p)	(q)	(q)	(s)
(c)	(q)	(r)	(s)	(p)
(d)	(r)	(s)	(p)	(q)

264 Critical constants of a gas are given in $T_c = 27°C$ and $p_c = 24.63$ atm

Match the parameters given in Column I with their values in Column II and select the answer from the codes given below.

Column I	Column II
(i) van der Waals' constant 'b' (dm^3 mol^{-1})	(p) 0.375
(ii) Critical volume (V_c) (dm^3 mol^{-1})	(q) 2.31
(iii) Radius of the molecule (Å)	(r) 462
(iv) Collision diameter (pm)	(s) 0.125

Codes

	(i)	(ii)	(iii)	(iv)
(a)	(s)	(p)	(q)	(r)
(b)	(p)	(s)	(q)	(r)
(c)	(q)	(s)	(p)	(r)
(d)	(p)	(q)	(r)	(s)

265 Match the gaseous mixture in Column I with the composition of lighter gas that comes out of hole of the container in which gaseous mixture is placed and select the answer from the codes given below:

Column I	Column II
(i) Air	(p) 0.64
(ii) He + N_2 (X_{N_2} = 0.60)	(q) 0.94
(iii) CH_4 + O_2(X_{CH_4} = 0.40)	(r) 0.81
(iv) H_2 + O_2 (X_{H_2} = 0.8)	(s) 0.48

Codes

	(i)	(ii)	(iii)	(iv)
(a)	(q)	(r)	(s)	(p)
(b)	(r)	(s)	(q)	(r)
(c)	(r)	(p)	(s)	(q)
(d)	(r)	(p)	(q)	(s)

266 Match the gases under specified conditions listed in Column I with their properties/ laws in column II and select the answer from the codes given below :

Column I		Column II
(i) Hydrogen gas ($p = 200$ atm, $T = 273$ K)	(p)	Compressibility factor $\neq 1$
(ii) Hydrogen gas ($p \sim 0, T = 273$ K)	(q)	Attractive forces are dominant
(iii) $CO_2 (p = 1$ atm, $T = 273$ K)	(r)	$pV = nRT$
(iv) Real gas with very large molar volume	(s)	$p(V - nb) = nRT$

[IIT JEE 2007]

Codes

	(i)	(ii)	(iii)	(iv)
(a)	(p,s)	(r)	(p,q)	(r)
(b)	(s)	(r)	(p)	(q)
(c)	(q)	(p)	(s)	(r)
(d)	(p)	(q)	(r)	(s)

Based on Three Columns

2.645 g mixture of Na_2CO_3, $NaHCO_3$ and KCl on strongly heating gave gas which exerts a pressure of 0.125 bar at 300 K in 1 L flask. This mixture on reaction with dil. HCl gave gases which exert a pressure of 0.375 bar under identical condition.

Questions (267) to (270) are based on matching of Columns I, II and III.

Column I	Column II	Column III
1. HCl	(i) 0.53 g	(p) 0.25 bar
2. KCl	(ii) 0.84 g	(q) 0.125 bar
3. $NaHCO_3$	(iii) 0.745 g	(r) 0.375 bar
4. Na_2CO_3	(iv) 1.095 g	(s) 0.00 bar

267 This species in Column I with amount in Column II exerts a pressure on reaction with HCl given in Column III.

(a) (4)-(i)-(q) (b) (3)-(iv)-(p)
(c) (4)-(iii)-(r) (d) (2)-(iii)-(q)

268 This species in Column I with amount in Column II exerts a pressure on reaction with HCl given in Column III.

(a) (4)-(ii)-(q) (b) (3)-(ii)-(p)
(c) (2)-(ii)-(p) (d) (2)-(iii)-(p)

269 This species in Column I with amount in Column II, exerts a pressure due to heating given in Column III.

(a) (3)-(ii)-(q) (b) (2)-(iii)-(q)
(c) (4)-(i)-(s) (d) (1)-(iv)-(r)

270 This species in Column I with amount in Column II is required by reaction mixture and pressure is set up as given in Column III.

(a) (1)-(iv)-(s) (b) (1)-(iii)-(q)
(c) (1)-(ii)-(s) (d) (1)-(iv)-(r)

HINTS & EXPLANATIONS

Immediate Tests

1. CH_3CN, CO_2, C_3H_8 and CH_3CN are of equal molar masses.

C_3H_8 and CO_2 are non-polar with least force of attraction.

CH_3CN is polar thus, maximum intermolecular force of attraction, hence the maximum boiling point.

2. $He<Ne<O_2<O_3<Cl_2<(CH_3)_2CO$

Based on increasing molar masses.

$(CH_3)_2CO$ molar mass (58) has polarity hence higher intermolecular forces than $Cl_2(71)$.

3. (i) 10^5 Pa = 0.987 atm

100 kpa = 0.987 atm

$$57 \text{ kpa} = \frac{0.987 \times 57}{100} = 0.56 \text{ atm}$$

57 kPa = 0.56 atm = 425.6 mmHg

■ 1 atm = 760 mmHg

(ii) (a) $304 \text{ cmHg} = \frac{304}{76} = 4 \text{ atm}$

(b) $380 \text{ Torr} = \frac{380}{760} = 0.5 \text{ atm}$

4. (a) $1 \text{ Pa} = 1 \text{ Nm}^{-2}$

10^5 Pa = 0.987 atm

$\therefore$ $3.09\times10^9 \text{ Nm}^{-2} = 3.0495\times10^4 \text{ atm}$

(b) $1\times10^5 \text{Nm}^{-2} = 1 \text{ bar}$

$$\therefore\ 3.09\times10^9 \text{ Nm}^{-2} = \frac{3.09\times10^9}{1\times10^5}$$

$$= 3.09\times10^4 \text{ bar}$$

5. (i) h (mercury column) = 0.75 m

h (water column) = 10.2 m

(use $p = h \cdot d \cdot g$, take SI unit)

■ With mercury when used in column, barometer reading is 0.75 m (a reasonable height) but with water it reads 10.2 m (a height of three-storey building) which is not feasible. Hence, mercury is used in instruments (like barometer, manometer) to measure atmospheric pressure. A liquid with still higher density than Hg will give lower barometer reading.

(ii) Pressure of air column

= Pressure of mercury column

$$h_{air}\ l_{air}\ g = h_{(Hg)}\ l_{(Hg)}\ g$$

$$\therefore\ h(\text{air}) = \frac{0.76\times 13.6\times 10^3}{1.2}$$

$$= 8.613\times10^3 \text{m} = 8.613 \text{ km}$$

(iii) Since, liquids are different, hence

$$\Delta p \text{ (Hg column)} = g \cdot h_{Hg}\, d_{Hg}$$

$$\Delta p \text{ (glycerol column)} = g\, h_{glycerol}\, d_{glycerol}$$

$$h_{glycerol} = 8.6\times\frac{13.6}{1.26} = 92.825 \text{ mm}$$

$$= 9.3 \text{ cm}$$

(iv) The height developed due to pressure of the gas

= 400 − 150 = 250 mm = 25 cm

$\therefore$ $p = hdg$

$= 25 \times 13.6 \times 980 \text{ dyne cm}^{-2}$

$$= \frac{25\times 13.6\times 980}{76\times 13.6\times 980} \text{ atm} = 0.33 \text{ atm}$$

$$\therefore\ p_{gas} = p_{atm} + hdg = \frac{740}{760} + 0.33$$

$= 0.97 + 0.33 = 1.3$ atm

As, 0.987 atm = 1 bar

$$\therefore\quad 1.3 \text{ atm} = \frac{1.3}{0.987} \text{ bar} = 1.32 \text{ bar}$$

6. Under isothermal conditions,

$$p_1V_1 = p_2V_2$$

$$V_2 = \frac{p_1V_1}{p_2}$$

Final pressure is 75% of initial value

$\therefore$ $p_2 = (p_1 - 0.25p_1)$

$= p_1\,(1-0.25) = 0.75$ bar

$$\therefore\quad V_2 = \frac{1\times20}{0.75} \text{dm}^3 = 26.67 \text{ dm}^3$$

7. In logarithm form, Boyle's law is

$$\log p = \log\frac{1}{V} + \log k$$

$OA = \log k = 0.3010 \text{ bar dm}^3$

$\therefore$ $k = 2.0 \text{ bar dm}^3$

$$p = \frac{k}{V}$$

$$\therefore\quad \frac{1}{V} = \frac{p}{k} = \frac{0.5 \text{ bar}}{2.0 \text{ bar dm}^3} = 0.25 \text{ dm}^{-3}$$

$$\therefore\quad \text{Density} = \frac{\text{mass}}{\text{volume}}$$

$= 2\times0.25 = 0.50 \text{ g dm}^{-3}$

8. Under isobaric condition,

$$V_2T_1 = V_1T_2$$

$$\therefore\quad V_2 = \frac{V_1T_2}{T_1} = \frac{2\times 299.1}{296.4} = 2.018 \text{ L}$$

9. In going from stage I to stage II, volume is constant, thus Gay-Lussac's law is applicable.

$$\therefore\quad \frac{p_1}{T_1} = \frac{p_2}{T_2}$$

$$\therefore\quad T_2 = \frac{p_2T_1}{p_1} = \frac{10\times300}{5} = 600 \text{ K}$$

In going from stage II to stage III, pressure remains constant, thus Charle's law is applicable.

$$\frac{V}{T_2} = \frac{V_{III}}{T_3}$$

$\therefore$ $V_{III} = 10.67 \text{ dm}^3$

10. (i) (a) $Mg_3N_2(s) \longrightarrow 3Mg(s) + N_2(g)$

(b) $N_2(g) + 3H_2(g) \longrightarrow 2NH_3(g)$

3L H_2 combine with = 1L N_2

$\therefore$ 1L H_2 combines with = $\frac{1}{3}$ L N_2

At STP, 22.4 L N_2 = 1 mol

$$\therefore\quad \frac{1}{3} \text{L } N_2 = \frac{1}{67.2} \text{ mol } N_2$$

1 mol Mg_3N_2 gives = 1 mol N_2

$\therefore$ Mol of Mg_3N_2 to give

$$\frac{1}{67.2} \text{ mol } N_2 = \frac{1}{67.2} \text{ mol} = 0.015 \text{ mol}$$

(ii) $\underset{2L}{2SO_2} + \underset{1L}{O_2} \longrightarrow \underset{2L}{2SO_3}$

O_2 required = 1L = $\frac{1}{22.4}$ mol at STP

$2KClO_3 \longrightarrow 2KCl + 3O_2$

3 mol of O_2 is from = 2 mol $KClO_3$

$$\therefore\ \frac{1}{22.4} \text{ mol } O_2 \text{ is from} = \frac{2}{3}\times\frac{1}{22.4} \text{ mol}$$

$= 0.03$ mol $KClO_3$

11. (i) V_1, Volume of H_2O if it behaves as an ideal gas = RT/p

V_2, Volume of H_2O if it is a liquid

$$= \frac{\text{mass (weight)}}{\text{density}} = \frac{w}{\rho}$$

$$\therefore\quad \frac{V_1}{V_2} = \frac{RT/p}{w/\rho} = \frac{RT\rho}{wp}$$

$$= \frac{0.0821\times298\times0.997\times10^3}{18\times(23.8/760)}$$

$= 4.327\times10^3$

■ $R = 0.0821 \text{L atm mol}^{-1}\text{K}^{-1}$ p is in atm

1 atm = 760 Torr

ρ (density) is in g dm^{-3}

Mass of water is 18g.

(ii) $n = \frac{pV}{RT} = 9.02\times10^{-11}$ mol

1 mol has molecules = N_0

$= 6.023\times10^{23}$

$\therefore$ Molecules $= 9.02 \times 10^{-11} \times 6.02 \times 10^{23}$
$= 5.79 \times 10^{13}$ molecules

12. (i) Molar mass of mixture

$$= \frac{M_1X_1 + M_2X_2}{X_1 + X_2}$$

$$= \frac{92 \times 20 + 46 \times 80}{20 + 80} = 55.20\,\text{g mol}^{-1}$$

$$\text{Density, } \rho = \frac{pM}{RT} = \frac{1 \times 55.20}{0.08314 \times 298}$$

$$= 2.23\,\text{g L}^{-1}$$

■ When pressure is in bar, R is in bar L mol^{-1} K^{-1} (= 0.08314)

$$\text{(ii) } \rho \text{ (density)} = \frac{pM}{RT} = \frac{1 \times 4}{0.08314 \times 294}$$

$$= 0.164\,\text{g L}^{-1}$$

Molar mass of air (80% N_2 and 20% O_2) $= 28.8\,\text{g mol}^{-1}$

Under identical conditions,

$\rho \propto$ molar mass

$$\frac{\rho_2}{\rho_1} = \frac{M_2}{M_1}$$

$$\therefore \rho_2(\text{air}) = 0.164 \times \frac{28.8}{4} = 1.178\,\text{g L}^{-1}$$

■ Mass difference between 1L of air and 1L of He is the lifting force of helium and is equivalent to buoyant.

$\therefore$ Lifting force = (1.178 – 0.164)
= 1.014 g

13. (i) Total volume = 5.0 + 4.0 = 9 L

$$p_{N_2}\text{ (in mixture)} = \frac{1.0 \times 5}{9.0} = 0.556 \text{ bar}$$

$$p_{O_2}\text{ (in mixture)} = \frac{2.0 \times 4}{9.0} = 0.889 \text{ bar}$$

$$p_{mix} = 1.445 \text{ bar}$$

$\therefore$ Also, $X_{N_2} p_{total} = p_{N_2}$

$$\therefore \quad X_{N_2} = \frac{0.556}{1.445} = 0.305$$

(ii) Due to cooling CO_2 is condensed and thus volume of He remained = 40.5 mL

By Amagat's law of partial volume

$$\chi_{He} V_{total} = V_{He}$$

$$\therefore \quad \chi_{He} = \frac{40.5}{63.5} = 0.64$$

$$\chi_{CO_2} = 0.36$$

$$\text{(iii) } n_{total} = 0.2 \text{ mol } H_2 + \frac{2}{44} \text{ mol } CO_2 + \left(\frac{1.75 \times 8}{32}\right) \text{ mol } O_2$$

$= 1.092$ mol

$$p_{total} = n_{total}\frac{RT}{V}$$

$$= \frac{1.092 \times 0.08314 \times 291}{5} = 5.28 \text{ bar}$$

■ Equivalent mass of O_2 = 8 g equiv^{-1}
Thus, 1 equivalent = 8 g

$$\textbf{14. } \text{(i) } u_{rms}(\text{air}) = \sqrt{\frac{3RT}{M}}$$

$$M(\text{air}) = \frac{X_1M_1(N_2) + X_2M_2(O_2)}{X_1 + X_2}$$

$$= \frac{80 \times 28 + 20 \times 32}{100}$$

$= 28.80$ g mol^{-1}
$= 28.8 \times 10^{-3}$ kg mol^{-1}

$$\therefore u_{rms} = \sqrt{\frac{3 \times 8.3143 \times 300}{28.8 \times 10^{-3}}} = 510\,\text{m s}^{-1}$$

$$\text{(ii) } \frac{u_{av}(H_2)}{u_{av}(He)} = \sqrt{\frac{8RT}{\pi M_1(H_2)}} \Bigg/ \sqrt{\frac{8RT}{\pi M_2(He)}}$$

$$= \sqrt{\frac{M_2(He)}{M_1(H_2)}} = \sqrt{\frac{4}{2}} = 1.4142$$

This ratio is same no matter which type of molecular velocity is compared.

(iii) 4 g mol^{-1}

$$\text{(iv) } u_{rms}(H_2) = \sqrt{\frac{3RT}{M}} = \sqrt{\frac{3 \times 8.3143 \times 298}{2 \times 10^{-3}}}$$

$= 1928$ ms^{-1}

$$\text{Also, } \sqrt{\frac{3RT_1(H_2)}{M(H_2)}} = \sqrt{\frac{3RT_2(He)}{M(He)}}$$

$$\therefore \quad \frac{3RT_1}{2 \times 10^{-3}} = \frac{3R \times 298}{4 \times 10^{-3}}$$

$$\therefore \quad T_1 = 149 \text{ K}$$

$$\textbf{15.} \quad u_{rms} = \left(\frac{3RT}{M}\right)^{1/2}$$

$$\therefore \quad \frac{du_{rms}}{dT} = \frac{1}{2}\left(\frac{3R}{M}\right)\left(\frac{M}{3RT}\right)^{1/2}$$

$$= \frac{1}{2}\left(\frac{3R}{M}\right)\left(\frac{1}{u_{rms}}\right)$$

$$u_{rms}(100\text{ K}) = \sqrt{\frac{3 \times 8.3143 \times 100}{20 \times 10^{-3}}}$$

$= 353$ m s^{-1}

$$\therefore \quad \frac{du_{rms}}{dT} = \frac{1}{2}\left(\frac{3 \times 8.3143}{20 \times 10^{-3}}\right)\left(\frac{1}{353.0}\right)$$

$= 1.77$ m s^{-1} K^{-1}

$\therefore \quad du_{rms} = 1.77 \times 0.1$ m s^{-1} ($dT = 0.1$ K)
$= 0.177$ m s^{-1}

$$\textbf{16.} \quad u_{rms} = \sqrt{\frac{3p}{d}}$$

$$5.0 \times 10^2 = \sqrt{\frac{3 \times 2.50 \times 101325}{d}}$$

$$\therefore \quad d = 3.04\,\text{kg m}^{-3}$$

■ 1 atm = 1.01325 × 10^5 Pa

$$\textbf{17. } pV = \frac{1}{3} m N u^2$$

$$\therefore p = \frac{1}{3}\frac{m N u^2}{V}$$

$$= \frac{1}{3} \times \frac{1.0 \times 10^{-25} \times 1.0 \times 10^{25}}{1.0}(1 \times 10^3)^2$$

$= 3.33 \times 10^5$ Pa $= 3.33$ bar

$$\text{Also, } T = \frac{pV}{nR}$$

where, n = number of moles
$= 1.0 \times 10^{25} / 6.02 \times 10^{23} = 16.61$

$$\therefore \quad T = \frac{3.33 \times 10^5}{16.61 \times 8.3143} = 2411 \text{ K}$$

$$\textbf{18. } \text{(i) KE} = \frac{3}{2}\frac{RT}{N_0}$$

Average kinetic energy is independent of molar mass of the substance, thus

$$\overline{(KE)}_{UF_6} / \overline{(KE)}_{H_2} = 1:1$$

$$\text{(ii) } \left(\frac{3}{2}RT\right)_{H_2} = \left(\frac{3}{2}RT\right)_{N_2}$$

Since, (KE) is independent of mass

Thus, $(T)_{H_2} = (T)_{N_2} = 308$ K

$$\text{(iii) (KE)} = \frac{3RT}{2N_0} = 6.175 \times 10^{-21}\text{ J}$$

$$u_{rms} = \sqrt{\frac{3RT}{M}}$$

From (KE),

$3RT = 2 \times 6.02 \times 10^{23} \times 6.175 \times 10^{-21}$
$= 7434.7$

$$\therefore \quad u_{rms} = \sqrt{\frac{7434.7}{2 \times 10^{-3}}} = 1928\,\text{m s}^{-1}$$

(iv) $mN_0 = M$ (molar mass)
$= 6.61 \times 10^{-26} \times 6.02 \times 10^{-23}$ kg mol^{-1}
$= 40 \times 10^{-3}$ kg mol^{-1}

$$u_{mp} = \sqrt{\frac{2RT}{M}}$$

$$10 = \sqrt{\frac{2RT}{40 \times 10^{-3}}}$$

$\therefore RT = 2$

$$\text{(KE)} = \frac{3RT}{2N_0} = \frac{3 \times 2}{2 \times 6.02 \times 10^{23}}$$

$= 5 \times 10^{-24}$ J molecule^{-1}

(v) By kinetic molecular theory,

$$pV = \frac{1}{3} m N_0 u^2$$

$$\therefore \quad p = \frac{1}{3}\frac{mN_0 u^2}{V}$$

$$\therefore \quad \left(\frac{dp}{du}\right)=\frac{2}{3}\frac{mN_0\,u}{V}$$

$$\frac{1}{u}\left(\frac{dp}{du}\right)=\frac{2}{3}\frac{mN_0}{V}=\frac{2}{3}\frac{M}{V}$$

$$=\frac{2}{3}\times\frac{2\times10^{-3}}{1\text{m}^3}\text{kg mol}^{-1}$$

$$=1.33\times10^{-3}\text{kg mol}^{-1}\text{m}^{-3}$$

(vi) Average momentum $= Mu_{av}$

$$=32\times10^{-3}\text{kg mol}^{-1}\times400\,\text{ms}^{-1}$$

$$=12.8\text{ kg ms}^{-1}\text{ mol}^{-1}$$

$$u_{av}=\sqrt{\frac{8RT}{\pi M}}$$

$$400\text{ ms}^{-1}=\sqrt{\frac{8RT}{\pi\times32\times10^{-3}}}$$

$$\therefore \quad RT=2010.6\,\text{J mol}^{-1}$$

$$\therefore \ (\text{KE})_{av}=\frac{3}{2}\frac{RT}{N_0}=\frac{3\times2010.6}{2\times6.02\times10^{23}}$$

$$=5\times10^{-21}\text{J molecule}^{-1}$$

(vii) Since, KE $\propto$ Temperature (K)

$$\frac{(\text{KE})_{T_2}}{(\text{KE})_{T_1}}=\frac{T_2}{T_1}=\frac{330}{300}=1.1$$

(viii) Average momentum $= M\,u_{av}$

$$=M\sqrt{\frac{8RT}{\pi M}}=\sqrt{\frac{8RTM}{\pi}}$$

$$\therefore \quad \frac{(\text{Momentum})_{H_2}}{(\text{Momentum})_{O_2}}=\sqrt{\frac{(M)_{H_2}}{(M)_{O_2}}}=\frac{1}{4}$$

19. $\frac{r_X}{r_{CO_2}}=\sqrt{\frac{M(CO_2)}{M(X)}}=\frac{83.3}{102}$

$$M(X)=66.0\text{ g mol}^{-1}$$

20. $r_{N_2O}=\frac{60}{t}$

$$r_{SO_3}=\frac{x}{t}$$

$$\therefore \quad \frac{r_{N_2O}}{r_{SO_3}}=\frac{60}{x}=\sqrt{\frac{M(SO_3)}{M(N_2O)}}=\sqrt{\frac{80}{44}}$$

$$\therefore \quad x=44.50\text{ cm}$$

Thus, distance travelled by $SO_3 = 44.50$ cm

$\therefore$ Total length of tube $= 60 + 44.50$

$$=104.50\text{ cm}$$

21. (i) $\frac{r_{(Cl+Cl_2)}}{r_{(Kr)}}=1.16=\sqrt{\frac{M_{(Kr)}}{M_{(Mix)}}}$

$$\therefore \ M_{(Mix)}=\frac{(84)}{(1.16)^2}=62.42\,\text{g mol}^{-1}$$

$$\underset{(1-x)}{Cl_2} \rightleftharpoons \underset{2x}{2Cl}$$

Moles of Cl_2 at equilibrium $= (1-x)$

Moles of Cl at equilibrium $= 2x$

Total moles $= (1+x)$

$$\therefore \quad 62.42=\frac{(1-x)71+2x(35.5)}{(1+x)}$$

$$x=0.14$$

Thus, 14% dissociation.

(ii) $\frac{r_{N_2}}{r_{O_2}}=\frac{p_{N_2}}{p_{O_2}}\sqrt{\frac{M_{O_2}}{M_{N_2}}}=\frac{0.80\,p}{0.20\,p}\sqrt{\frac{32}{28}}$

$$=\frac{4.3}{1}$$

If N_2 effuses 4.3 parts O_2 effuses 1 part.

Total = 5.3 parts

Thus, mole fraction of $O_2=\frac{1}{5.3}=0.19$

(iii) **Before processing** $\frac{^{235}U}{^{238}U}=\frac{0.7}{99.3}$

After processing $\frac{^{235}U}{^{238}U}=\frac{99.7}{0.3}$

Thus, overall separation factor

$$f=\frac{\text{Ratio after enrichment}}{\text{Ratio before enrichment}}$$

$$f=\frac{\frac{99.7}{0.3}}{\frac{0.7}{99.3}}=4.7144\times10^4$$

Theoretical separation factor based on Graham's law

$$\frac{r(^{235}U)}{r(^{238}U)}=\sqrt{\frac{M(^{238}UF_6)}{M(^{235}UF_6)}}$$

$$=\sqrt{\frac{352}{349}}=1.0043$$

If enrichment takes place in n-steps, then

$$(1.0043)^n=4.7144\times10^4$$

$$\therefore \ n\log(1.0043)=\log(4.7144\times10^4)$$

$$n=\frac{4.6734}{1.863\times10^{-3}}=2508$$

Thus, enrichment takes place in 2508 diffusion steps.

22. (i) Mean free path,

$$\lambda=\frac{RT}{\sqrt{2}N_0\sigma p}$$

$$\therefore \quad p=\frac{RT}{\sqrt{2}N_0\sigma\lambda}$$

$$=\frac{8.3143\times298}{\sqrt{2}\times6.02\times10^{23}(0.43\times10^{-18})\times10\times10^{-2}}$$

$$=2.82\times10^5\text{Pa}=2.82\text{ bar}$$

■ All parameters in MKS unit.

1×10^5Pa = 1 bar

1 cm = 10^{-2} m

(ii) Average time = (collision frequency)$^{-1}$

$$=\frac{1}{\text{Number of collisions (s}^{-1})}=\frac{1}{Z}$$

$$=\frac{RT}{\sqrt{2}N_0\sqrt{\frac{8RT}{\pi M}}(\pi d^2)p}$$

$$=\frac{1}{4}\sqrt{\frac{RT\,M}{\pi}}\frac{1}{N_0d^2p}$$

$$=5.45\times10^{-10}\text{ s}$$

(iii) (a) Collision frequency

$$Z=\sqrt{2}N_0u_{av}\sigma\left(\frac{p}{RT}\right)$$

$$=\sqrt{2}N_0\left(\sqrt{\frac{8RT}{\pi M}}\right)\pi d^2\left(\frac{p}{RT}\right)$$

$$=4N_0\cdot\sqrt{\frac{\pi}{RTM}}d^2p=5.2\times10^9\text{s}^{-1}$$

(b) Number of collisions per sec

$$=2\times5.2\times10^9$$

(Each molecule has two collisions)

(c) Mean free path

$$=\frac{\text{distance travelled in one second}}{\text{collision frequency}}$$

$$u_{av}=\sqrt{\frac{8RT}{\pi M}}=\sqrt{\frac{8\times8.314\times300}{\pi\times28\times10^{-3}}}$$

$$=476.3\text{ ms}^{-1}$$

$$=\frac{u_{av}\text{ m s}^{-1}}{5.2\times10^9\text{ s}^{-1}}=\frac{476.3}{5.2\times10^9}\text{m}$$

$$=9.16\times10^{-8}\text{ m}$$

$$=916\text{ Å}$$

(iv) Mean free path

$$\lambda=\frac{RT}{\sqrt{2}N_0\sigma p}$$

$$\therefore \quad \sigma=\pi d^2=\frac{RT}{\sqrt{2}N_0\lambda p}$$

$$\pi d^2=\frac{8.3143\times273}{\sqrt{2}\times6.02\times10^{23}\times1\times10^{-7}\times1\times10^5}$$

$$=2.67\times10^{-19}$$

$$\therefore \quad d=2.91\times10^{-10}\text{m}=291\text{ pm}$$

■ 1 bar = 1×10^5 Pa

23. (i) $Z=\frac{pV}{nRT}=\frac{1.0\times1.0}{\left(\frac{2.2}{44}\right)\times0.0831\times273}$

$$=0.88$$

■ R = 0.0831 dm^{3}bar^{-1} K^{-1}

V in dm^3 p in bar

(ii) Molar volume of a gas is the volume of 1 mole of gas

$\therefore \quad pV = nRT$

$\therefore \quad \frac{pV}{nRT} = Z = 0.90$

$V = \frac{0.90\,nRT}{p} = \frac{0.90 \times 1 \times 0.0831 \times 273}{1.0}$

$= 20.4\,dm^3\,mol^{-1}$

24. $b = 4\left(\frac{4}{3}\pi r^3\right)N_0$

$= 4\left(\frac{4}{3}\pi(3.81\times10^{-10})^3\right)6.02\times10^{23}$

$= 5.6\times10^{-4}\,m^3 mol^{-1}$

25. $\left(p + \frac{a}{V^2}\right)(V - b) = RT$

a and b are in (non-SI) units. Thus,

$R = 0.0821\,dm^3 mol^{-1} K^{-1}$

$p = \frac{RT}{V-b} - \frac{a}{V^2}$

$= \frac{0.0821 \times 273}{(22.4 - 0.057)} - \frac{6.865}{(22.4)^2}$

$= 1.003 - 0.0137 = 0.9893$ atm

26. (i) $\frac{pV}{RT} = 1 + \left(b - \frac{a}{RT}\right)\frac{1}{V} + \ldots$

Given, $Z = \frac{pV}{RT} = 1.000054$

T_b (Boyle's temperature) $= \frac{a}{Rb}$

$\therefore \quad a = T_b Rb$

$p = 1$ atm

$\frac{1}{V} = \frac{p}{RT}$

$\therefore \quad \frac{pV}{RT} = 1.000054 = 1 + b\left(1 - \frac{T_b}{T}\right)\frac{p}{RT}$

$= 1 + b\left(1 - \frac{107}{273}\right)\frac{1}{0.0821 \times 273}$

$\therefore \quad b = 1.98\times10^{-3}\,L\,mol^{-1}$

Since, $a = T_b Rb$

$a = 0.0173\,L^2\,atm\,mol^{-2}$

(ii) $p(V - b) = RT \Rightarrow pV - pb = RT$

$\therefore \quad pV = pb + RT$

$\therefore \quad Z = \frac{pV}{RT} = \left(\frac{pb}{RT} + 1\right)$

$1.0018 = \left(\frac{1b}{0.0821 \times 300} + 1\right)$

$b = 0.0443\,L\,mol^{-1}$

$= 0.0443 \times 10^3\,cm^3 mol^{-1}$

Since, $b = 4vN_0$

$b = 4\left(\frac{4}{3}\pi r^3\right)N_0$, thus

$r = 1.64\times10^{-8}$ cm

Diameter $= 2r = 3.28\times10^{-8}$ cm

$= 3.28\times10^{-10}$ m $= 328$ pm

27. Critical density $= \frac{\text{molar mass}}{\text{critical volume}}$

Molar volume $V_C = \frac{3RT_c}{8p_c}$

$= \frac{3}{8}\left(\frac{0.0821\times151}{48}\right)$

$= 0.097\,dm^3 mol^{-1}$

$\therefore$ Critical density $= \frac{40\,g\,mol^{-1}}{0.097\,dm^3\,mol^{-1}}$

$= 412.4\,g\,dm^{-3}$

28. (i) $V_c = \frac{3}{8}\frac{RT_c}{p_c} = \frac{3}{8} \times \frac{0.0821\times304}{50}$

$= 0.187\,dm^3 mol^{-1}$

Also, $V_c = 3b$

$\therefore \quad b = \frac{0.0187}{3}\,dm^3 mol^{-1}$

$= \frac{0.0187\times1000}{3}\,cm^3 mol^{-1}$

Also, $b = 4\left(\frac{4}{3}\pi r^3\right)N_0$

$\therefore \quad \frac{0.0187\times1000}{3} = \frac{16}{3}\pi r^3 \times 6.02\times10^{23}$

$r = 8.51\times10^{-9}$ cm $= 0.851\times10^{-8}$ cm

Diameter $= 2r = 1.702\times10^{-8}$ cm

$= 1.702$ Å

(ii) Critical density $= \frac{\text{mass}}{\text{volume}}$

Critical volume $= \frac{44\,g\,mol^{-1}}{0.44\,g\,dm^{-3}}$

$= 100\,dm^3 mol^{-1}$

$\therefore b = \frac{V_c}{3} = \frac{100}{3} = 33.3\,dm^3 mol^{-1}$

Knowledge Confirmation Test 1

1. (b) **2.** (b) **3.** (a) **4.** (c) **5.** (b) **6.** (b) **7.** (b) **8.** (a) **9.** (b) **10.** (c)
11. (d) **12.** (c) **13.** (a) **14.** (a) **15.** (d) **16.** (d)

Knowledge Confirmation Test 2

1. (b) **2.** (d) **3.** (c) **4.** (b) **5.** (b) **6.** (a) **7.** (b) **8.** (c) **9.** (c) **10.** (d)
11. (c) **12.** (a) **13.** (d) **14.** (c) **15.** (a) **16.** (c) **17.** (a) **18.** (b) **19.** (a) **20.** (a)
21. (d) **22.** (b)

Knowledge Confirmation Test 3

1. (d) **2.** (b) **3.** (d) **4.** (a) **5.** (c) **6.** (a) **7.** (a) **8.** (a) **9.** (c) **10.** (c)
11. (d) **12.** (c) **13.** (a) **14.** (b) **15.** (a) **16.** (c) **17.** (b) **18.** (a) **19.** (c) **20.** (d)

Knowledge Confirmation Test 4

1. (b) **2.** (a) **3.** (c) **4.** (a) **5.** (c) **6.** (d) **7.** (c) **8.** (b) **9.** (a) **10.** (c)
11. (b) **12.** (a) **13.** (c) **14.** (b) **15.** (b)

Knowledge Confirmation Test 5

1. (a) **2.** (c) **3.** (b) **4.** (c) **5.** (b) **6.** (a) **7.** (c) **8.** (c) **9.** (c) **10.** (d)
11. (a) **12.** (b) **13.** (d) **14.** (c)

Knowledge Confirmation Test 6

1. (a) **2.** (b) **3.** (d) **4.** (d) **5.** (d) **6.** (b) **7.** (a) **8.** (c) **9.** (b) **10.** (a)
11. (c) **12.** (a) **13.** (d) **14.** (b) **15.** (c) **16.** (b) **17.** (a) **18.** (c) **19.** (a) **20.** (b)
21. (a) **22.** (c) **23.** (c) **24.** (a) **25.** (c) **26.** (b) **27.** (a) **28.** (c) **29.** (a) **30.** (b)

Knowledge Confirmation Test 7

1. (d) **2.** (a) **3.** (c) **4.** (a) **5.** (a) **6.** (b) **7.** (c) **8.** (c) **9.** (b) **10.** (c)
11. (b) **12.** (a) **13.** (d) **14.** (c) **15.** (b)

Acid Test for JEE Main

Type I. MCQs with Only ONE Correct Alternate

1. (d) Partial pressure of gas $(i) = p_{\text{total}} \chi_i$

$$\propto \frac{n_i}{n_{\text{total}}} \propto n_i$$

But, $$n \propto \frac{1}{\text{molar mass}}$$

Thus, higher the molar mass, smaller the partial pressure.

$$n_{\text{He}} : n_{O_2} : n_{SO_2} :: \frac{1}{4} : \frac{1}{32} : \frac{1}{64}$$

Thus 16 : 2 : 1

2. (c) $V \propto T$

$$V = kT$$

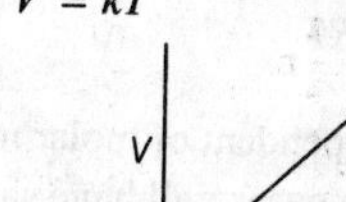

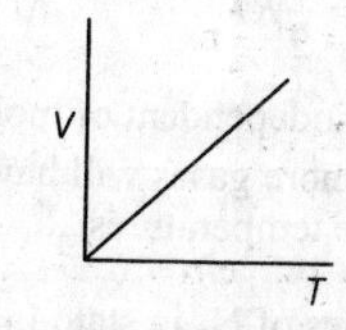

Slope $= k = X$ L mol^{-1}K^{-1} $= \frac{V}{T}$

$$pV = nRT$$

$\therefore \quad R = \frac{pV}{T}$ for one mole

$$= 2X \text{ L atm mol}^{-1}\text{K}^{-1}$$

3. (d) Density d is given by

$$d = \frac{pM}{RT} \Rightarrow d \propto \frac{p}{T}$$

(a) $\frac{p}{T} = \frac{1}{300}$ (b) $\frac{p}{T} = \frac{1}{273 \times 2}$

(c) $\frac{p}{T} = \frac{6}{1092}$ (d) $\frac{p}{T} = \frac{4}{500}$ (maximum)

4. (d) as gas is easily liquefied, due to H-bonding.

5. (a) $n_{H_2} = n_{O_2}$

H_2 escaped $= \frac{V}{2}$

O_2 escaped $= \frac{V}{x}$

$$r_{H_2} = \frac{V/2}{t}$$

$$r_{O_2} = \frac{V/x}{t}$$

$$\therefore \quad \frac{r_{H_2}}{r_{O_2}} = \sqrt{\frac{32}{2}} = \frac{4}{1} \Rightarrow \frac{1/2}{1/x} = 4$$

$$x = 8$$

Thus, fraction of $O_2 = \frac{1}{8}$

6. (a) Real gases show ideal behaviour as temperature is increased and pressure is decreased.

7. (c) By van der Waals' equation,

$$\left(p + \frac{a}{V^2}\right)(V - b) = RT$$

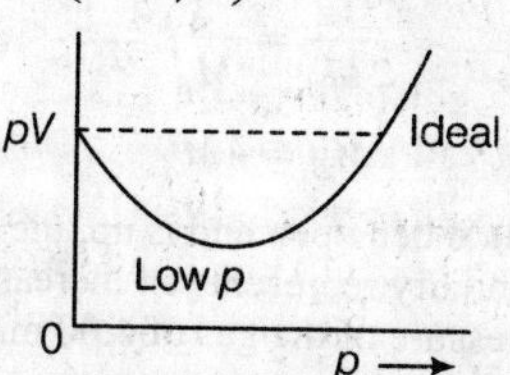

When volume is high, (at low p) $(V - b) \approx V$ and attractive forces are predominant

$$\therefore \quad pV + \frac{a}{V} = RT$$

$$pV = RT - \frac{a}{V} = RT - ap\left(\frac{1}{V} \propto p\right)$$

Thus, pV value decreases as p increases.

8. (b) For ideal gas, $pV = nRT$

$$n = \frac{pV}{RT} = \frac{\left(\frac{3.5 \times 10^{-7}}{760}\right) \times 0.535}{0.0821 \times 298}$$

$$= 1.0 \times 10^{-11} \text{ mol}$$

$\therefore$ Molecules $= xN_0$

$$= 1.0 \times 10^{-11} \times 6.0 \times 10^{23}$$

$$= 6.0 \times 10^{12} \text{ molecules}$$

9. (a) $pV = nRT$

$$\frac{n}{V} = \frac{p}{RT}$$

$$\frac{n}{V} = \frac{\text{mole}}{\text{litre}} = \text{concentration}$$

$$\therefore \frac{n}{V} = \frac{35/760 \text{ atm}}{0.0821 \text{ L atm mol}^{-1} \text{ K}^{-1} \times 318 \text{ K}}$$

$$= 1.8 \times 10^{-3} \text{ mol L}^{-1} \text{ or M}$$

10. (a) Due to cooling in N_2, CO_2 is condensed to liquid CO_2 and thus He remains as gas.

$$\text{He} + CO_2 = 63.5 \text{ mL}$$

$$\text{He} = 40.5 \text{ mL}$$

Thus, by Amagat's law of partial volume,

$$\chi_{\text{He}} = \frac{40.5}{63.5} = 0.638$$

11. (a) $\frac{N_{(\text{Ar})}}{N_{(\text{Ne})}} = \frac{V_{(\text{Ar})}}{V_{(\text{Ne})}} = \frac{9.34 \times 10^{-3}}{18.18 \times 10^{-6}} = 514$

■ $0.934\% = 0.934 \times 10^{-2}$

$18.18 \text{ ppm} = 18.18 \times 10^{-6}$

12. (c) $\frac{r_A}{r_B} = \frac{4}{1}$

$$\frac{r_B}{r_C} = \frac{1}{3}$$

$$\therefore \quad \frac{r_A}{r_C} = \frac{4}{3}$$

13. (d)

(a) If $$p_A = \frac{w_A}{M_A}\frac{RT_A}{V_A}$$

$$\frac{M_A}{T_A} = \frac{w_A R}{p_A V_A}$$

Pressure may differ. Hence,

$$M_A T_B \neq M_B T_A$$

(b) Density $(d) = \frac{pM}{RT}$

If p are different then, density would be different.

(c) Kinetic energy $= \frac{3}{2}nRT = \frac{3}{2}\frac{w_A}{M_A}RT_A$

This would be possible only when w_A and w_B are same.

(d) $u_{\text{rms}} = \sqrt{\frac{3RT}{M}}$

$$u_A = \sqrt{\frac{3RT_A}{M_A}}$$

$$u_B = \sqrt{\frac{3RT_B}{M_B}}$$

Thus if, $u_A = u_B$,

then $M_A T_B = M_B T_A$

14. (a) 1 atm = 76 cm of Hg

	$2NH_3(g)$ ⇌	$N_2(g)$	$+ 3H_2(g)$
Initial pressure	76	0	0
After dissociation	$(76 - 2x)$	x	$3x$

Thus, total pressure $= (76 + 2x)$ cm

Thus, $\quad 2x = 10.12$ cm

$$x = \frac{10.12}{2} \text{ cm}$$

Thus, $\quad p_{H_2} = 3x = \left(\frac{10.12}{2}\right) \times 3$

$$= 15.18 \text{ cm}$$

$$= \frac{15.18}{76} \text{ atm} = 0.20 \text{ atm}$$

15. (d) $\frac{r_X}{r_{CH_4}} = \frac{1}{4} = \sqrt{\frac{M(CH_4)}{M(X)}}$

$$\therefore \quad M(X) = 16 \times 16 = 256 \text{ g mol}^{-1}$$

$$64 \text{ g of } X = \frac{64}{256} = \frac{1}{4} \text{ mol}$$

$$= \frac{N_0}{4} \text{ molecules}$$

16. (c) Different types of molecular speeds are given by

$$V_{\text{mp}} = \sqrt{\frac{2RT}{M}}$$

$$V_{\text{av}} = \sqrt{\frac{8RT}{\pi M}}$$

$$V_{\text{rms}} = \sqrt{\frac{3RT}{M}}$$

Thus, $V_{mp} < V_{av} < V_{rms}$

Thus speeds at $A : V_{mp}$

at $B : V_{av}$

and at $C : V_{rms}$

17. (c) $KE = \frac{3}{2}nRT$

$\therefore \frac{(KE)_{T_2}}{(KE)_{T_1}} = \left(\frac{313}{293}\right)$

18. (c) Fraction of the molecules with most probable velocity decreases with increase in temperature. Thus, statement (c) is incorrect.

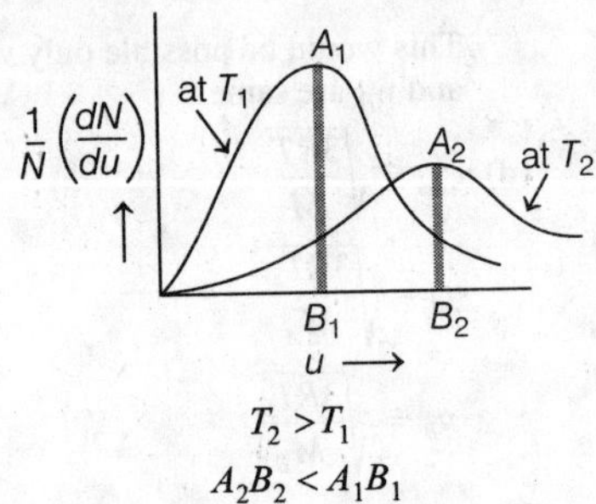

$T_2 > T_1$

$A_2B_2 < A_1B_1$

19. (c) $Z = \frac{pV}{nRT}$

$\therefore V_m$ (Volume of one mole) $= \frac{ZRT}{p}$

$= \frac{0.8697 \times 0.08314 \times 400}{71.0}$

$= 0.41$ L

20. (b) $H_2 = 0.5$ mol, $O_2 = \frac{x}{32}$ mol

$\chi_{O_2} = \frac{\frac{x}{32}}{\left(0.5 + \frac{x}{32}\right)}$

$\therefore p_{O_2} = \frac{5x}{32}\Big/\left(0.5 + \frac{x}{32}\right) = 4$

$x = 64$ g $O_2 = \frac{64}{32}$ mol $= 2$ mol O_2

21. (b) Let molar mass of $A = M_A$

Molar mass of $B = M_B$

$p_A = \frac{n_A RT}{V} = \left(\frac{1}{M_A}\right)\frac{RT}{V}$

$p_B = (n_A + n_B) = \left(\frac{1}{M_A} + \frac{2}{M_B}\right)\frac{RT}{V}$

$\frac{p_B}{p_A} = \frac{\left(\frac{1}{M_A} + \frac{2}{M_B}\right)}{1/M_A}$

$\frac{3}{2} = \frac{\left(\frac{1}{M_A} + \frac{2}{M_B}\right)}{1/M_A}$

$\therefore \frac{3}{2M_A} = \frac{1}{M_A} + \frac{2}{M_B}$

$\frac{1}{2M_A} = \frac{2}{M_B}$

$\therefore M_B = 4M_A$

22. (d) When open end is up, the weight of mercury represents an increase in the pressure of the gas of 4.00 mmHg

= 40 mmHg.

Thus, final pressure = 760 + 40

= 800 mm Hg

Since, volume = area × length

$V_1 = 10 \times a$

$V_2 = l \times a$

$\therefore p_1V_1 = p_2V_2$

$\therefore 760 \times 10 \times a = 800 \times l \times a$

(a = area of cross-section is uniform)

$\therefore l = 9.50$ cm

23. (a) $\frac{\text{Mass}}{\text{Volume}} = \text{Density}$

$\therefore$ Volume of 1 mole H_2O (l)

$= \frac{18 \text{ g mol}^{-1}}{0.997 \text{ g cm}^{-3}}$

$= 18.054 \text{ cm}^3\text{mol}^{-1}$

$V(H_2O \text{ vapours}) = \frac{nRT}{p} = \frac{1 \times 0.0821 \times 298}{23.8/760}$

$= 781.26 \text{ dm}^3$

$= 781.26 \times 10^3 \text{ cm}^3$

Factor by which volume increases

$= \frac{781.26 \times 10^3}{18.054} = 4.327 \times 10^4$

■ 1 dm³ = 1 L = 1000 cm³

24. (a) KE of A, $E_A = \frac{3}{2}N_ART_A$

KE of B, $E_B = \frac{3}{2}N_BRT_B$

$\therefore \frac{E_A}{E_B} = \frac{N_A}{N_B}\frac{T_A}{T_B}$

$0.5 = \frac{N_A}{N_B}\left(\frac{150}{300}\right)$

$\frac{N_B}{N_A} = 1$

25. (b) $\overline{(KE)} = \frac{3}{2}RT$

$\overline{(KE)}$, the average KE is independent of molar mass.

26. (a) $p_2V_2 = p_1V_1$ at constant temperature

If, $V_2 = (V_1 - 0.1\,V_1)$

and $p_2 = (p_1 + 0.01xp_1)$

$\therefore p_1(1 + 0.01\,x)\,V_1(1 - 0.1) = p_1V_1$

$\therefore (1 + 0.01x) = \frac{10}{9}$

$0.01x = \frac{1}{9}$

$x = \frac{100}{9}$

27. (b) $p = \frac{dRT}{M}$

If T and M remain unchanged

$p \propto d$

$\therefore p_2 = p_1\frac{d_2}{d_1}$

$\therefore d_2 = \frac{p_2}{p_1}d_1 = \frac{1.5}{1.0} \times 1.25 = 1.875 \text{ kg m}^{-3}$

28. (a) $\overline{KE} = \frac{3}{2}RT$

$\overline{(KE)}$ is independent of molar mass, thus two or more gases will have same. $\overline{KE}$ at all same temperatures.

29. (d) Moles of N_2 in state I $= \frac{pV}{RT}$

$= \frac{3 \times 1.65}{0.0821 \times 546} = 0.11$

Moles of N_2 in state II

$= \frac{0.75 \times 0.55}{0.0821 \times 273} = 0.0184$

Thus, N_2 escaped = 0.11 − 0.0184

= 0.0916 mol

Percentage of escaped $= \frac{0.0916}{0.11} \times 100$

= 83.3%

30. (a) $T_c = \frac{8a}{27Rb}$

$T_c \propto \left(\frac{a}{b}\right)$

Larger the value of $\left(\frac{a}{b}\right)$ then higher the value of T_c.

Gas		(a/b)
Ar	:	$\left(\frac{1.3}{3.2}\right)$
Ne	:	$\frac{0.2}{1.7}$
Kr	:	$\frac{5.1}{1.0}$ (max.)
Xe	:	$\frac{4.1}{5.0}$

31. (c) Density of He at STP $= \frac{\text{molar mass}}{\text{molar volume}}$

$= \frac{4.0 \times 10^{-3} \text{ kg mol}^{-1}}{22.4 \times 10^{-3} \text{ m}^3 \text{ mol}^{-1}}$

$= 0.1786 \text{ kg m}^{-3}$

Since, $d \propto \frac{1}{V}$

$\therefore \quad \frac{d_2}{d_1} = \frac{V_1}{V_2} = \frac{1}{1.4}$

$\therefore \quad d_2 = \frac{0.1786}{1.4} = 0.13 \text{ kg m}^{-3}$

32. (a) $\left(p + \frac{a}{V^2}\right)(V - b) = RT$

If attractive forces are neglected

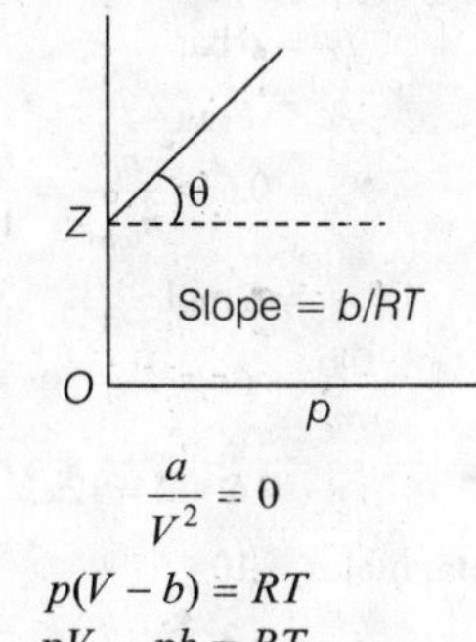

$\frac{a}{V^2} = 0$

$\therefore \quad p(V - b) = RT$

$pV - pb = RT$

$pV = pb + RT$

$\therefore \quad Z = \frac{pV}{RT} = \frac{pb}{RT} + 1$

larger the value of b

larger the angle θ.

Value of 'b' depends on radius.

Size Ne < Ar < Kr < Xe

Thus steepest increase is for Xe.

33. (d) Molar mass of $Ca_3P_2 = 182 g \text{ mol}^{-1}$

Moles of $Ca_3P_2(s) = \frac{182 g}{182 \text{ g mol}^{-1}} = 1 \text{mol}$

PH_3 formed from 1 mol Ca_3P_2 = 2 mol

Volume of PH_3 formed at STP

$= 2 \times 22.4 = 44.8$ L

34. (d) Given,

$-\left(\frac{\partial V}{\partial p}\right)_{n,T} = 22.6863 \text{ dm}^3 \text{ bar}^{-1}$ at STP

Isothermal compressibility constant for an ideal gas is

$\beta = -\frac{1}{V}\left(\frac{\partial V}{\partial p}\right)_{n,T} = \frac{1}{p}$

At 273 K and 1 bar,

$-\left(\frac{\partial V}{\partial p}\right)_{n,T} = 22.6863 \text{ dm}^3$

$\therefore$ Volume of one mole of an ideal gas under given condition

$V = \frac{nRT}{p} = \frac{1.0 \times 0.0831 \times 273}{1}$

$= 22.6863 \text{ dm}^3$

$\beta = -\frac{1}{V}\left(\frac{\partial V}{\partial p}\right)_{n,T} = \frac{22.6863}{22.6863} = 1 \text{ bar}^{-1}$

35. (a) $2NO + O_2 \longrightarrow 2NO_2$

	$2NO$	O_2	$2NO_2$
Before reaction	2	2	0
After reaction	0	1	2

After reaction number of moles of O_2 and $NO_2 = 3$

Before reaction = 4

Thus, change in number of moles = 1

Thus, pressure change due to 1 mole

$= \frac{nRT}{V} = \frac{1 \times 0.0831 \times 300}{20}$

$= 1.247$ bar

36. (d) $u_{av} = \sqrt{\frac{8RT}{\pi M}}$

$\therefore \quad u_{av} \propto \sqrt{\frac{T}{M}}$

$u_{O_2} \propto \sqrt{\frac{560}{32}} = 4.18$

$u_{Ne} \propto \sqrt{\frac{500}{20}} = 5.0$

$u_{CO_2} \propto \sqrt{\frac{440}{44}} = 3.16$

$u_{He} \propto \sqrt{\frac{140}{4}} = 5.92$ (greatest)

■ No effect of number of moles.

37. (a) $u_{av} = \sqrt{\frac{8pV}{M}} \propto \sqrt{\frac{p}{M}}$

As above, compare $\sqrt{\frac{p}{M}}$

(a) $u_{av} \propto \sqrt{\frac{0.20}{44}} = 0.067$

(b) $u_{av} \propto \sqrt{\frac{0.40}{4}} = 0.316$

(c) $u_{av} \propto \sqrt{\frac{0.80}{10}} = 0.224$

(d) $u_{av} \propto \sqrt{\frac{1.0}{30}} = 0.183$

a is lowest.

38. (b) $KE = \frac{3}{2} nRT$

$(\overline{KE})_{av} = \frac{3}{2}\frac{RT}{N_0}$

Thus, $(KE) \propto T$

39. (c) $V_{mp} = \sqrt{\frac{2RT}{M}}$

V_{mp} (H_2 at 300 K) $= \sqrt{\frac{600R}{2}}$

$= \sqrt{300R} = 17.32\ R$

V_{mp} (N_2 at 300 K) $= \sqrt{\frac{600R}{28}} = 4.63\ R$

V_{mp} (O_2 at 400 K) $= \sqrt{\frac{800R}{32}} = 5.0R$

$\therefore V_{mp}$ (N_2 at 300 K) < V_{mp} (O_2 at 400 K) < V_{mp} (H_2 at 300 K)

Thus I : V_{mp} (N_2 at 300 K)

II : V_{mp} (O_2 at 400 K)

III : V_{mp} (H_2 at 300 K)

40. (d) Larger the value of 'a' larger the force of attraction. Thus in gas A molecules are more closely packed than in gas C. Thus gas C will occupy more volume than gas A. Gas B with smaller value of 'b' is less compressible than gas D.

41. (c) When van der Waals' constant 'a' is neglected

$\left(p + \frac{a}{V^2}\right)(V - b) = RT$

reduces to $(pV - pb) = RT$

$pV = RT + pb$

$\therefore \quad \frac{pV}{RT} = Z = \left(1 + \frac{pb}{RT}\right)$

42. (b) $r_{H_2} = \frac{200}{30}$ mL min^{-1}

$r_{O_2} = \frac{50}{t}$ mL min^{-1}

$\therefore \quad \frac{r_{H_2}}{r_{O_2}} = \sqrt{\frac{32}{2}} = \frac{200/30}{50/t} = \frac{4t}{30}$

$\therefore \quad 4 = \frac{4t}{30} \Rightarrow t = 30$ min

43. (c) $r_X = \frac{240}{20} = 12$ mL min^{-1}

$r_{CH_4} = \frac{240}{10} = 24$ mL min^{-1}

Also, $\frac{r_X}{r_{CH_4}} = \sqrt{\frac{16}{M}} = \frac{12}{24} = \frac{1}{2}$

$\therefore \quad M = 32$ g mol^{-1}.

44. (d) Greater the value of 'a', greater the force of attraction hence greater the liquefaction.

45. (b) $\frac{r_X}{r_{He}} = \sqrt{\frac{4}{M}} = \frac{1}{3}$

$\therefore M = 36$ g mol^{-1}

46. (a) Thermal expansion coefficient of an ideal gas is given by

$\alpha = \frac{1}{V}\left(\frac{\partial V}{\partial T}\right)_{p,n} = \frac{1}{T}$

Thus, smaller the temperature of the gas, larger the value of α. Order being

(d) < (c) < (b) < (a).

47. (c) $\frac{r_A}{r_B} = \frac{p_A}{p_B}\sqrt{\frac{M_B}{M_A}}$ in terms of pressure and molar masses.

■ Since, $p \propto n$

$\frac{r_A}{r_B} = \frac{n_A}{n_B}\sqrt{\frac{M_B}{M_A}}$

In cases, when composition of the effusing gases is to be determined.

48. (a) $\frac{r_{He}}{r_{CH_4}} = \sqrt{\frac{M(CH_4)}{M(He)}} = \sqrt{\frac{16}{4}} = 2$

49. (b) $r_{SO_2} = \frac{20}{60} dm^3s^{-1} = \frac{1}{3} dm^3s^{-1}$

$r_{O_2} = \frac{V}{30} dm^3s^{-1}$

$\therefore \frac{r_{SO_2}}{r_{O_2}} = \sqrt{\frac{32}{64}} = \frac{1/3}{V/30} = \frac{10}{V}$

$V = 10\sqrt{2} = 10 \times 1.41 = 14.1 \text{ dm}^3$

50. (c) $u_{av}(T_1) = u_{mp}(T_2)$

$\sqrt{\frac{8RT_1}{\pi M_{(CO_2)}}} = \sqrt{\frac{2RT_2}{M_{(CO_2)}}}$

$\therefore \frac{8RT_1}{\pi M} = \frac{2RT_2}{M}$

$\frac{T_1}{T_2} = \frac{\pi}{4} = 0.78$

51. (c)

C^*	$\bar{C}$	C
(mp)	(av)	(rms)
$\sqrt{2}$	$\sqrt{8/\pi}$	$\sqrt{3}$
1.4142	1.596	1.7320
1	1.128	1.225

52. (c) $\left(p + \frac{a}{V^2}\right)(V - b) = RT$

At high pressure, $\left(p + \frac{a}{V^2}\right) \approx p$

$\therefore \quad p(V - b) = RT$

$pV = RT + pb$

$Z = \frac{pV}{RT} = 1 + \frac{pb}{RT}$

53. (d) Greater the value of 'a', smaller the value of 'b', larger the extent of liquefaction.

'a' is pressure correction, when force of atraction exists. Larger the value of 'a' larger the force of attraction, thus greater the liquefaction.

54. (c) $p = \frac{n}{V}RT$

$= \frac{w}{VM}RT = \frac{dRT}{M} \quad \left(\frac{w}{V} = \text{density}\right)$

$d = \frac{pM}{RT}$

$d \propto pM$ at constant temperature

$\frac{d_1}{d_2} = \frac{p_1M_1}{p_2M_2}$

$d_2(X) = 2d(N_2) = 2d_1$

$\frac{d_1}{2d_1} = \frac{4 \times 28}{2 \times M(X)}$

$M(X) = 112 \text{ g mol}^{-1}$

55. (b) Initially both bulbs are under identical conditions. Hence, number of moles of gases in each contained

$(n_1) = \frac{p_iV}{RT_1}$

Total moles before change of pressure and temperature $(n_2) = \frac{2p_iV}{RT_1}$

When conditions are changed,

moles of gases in LHS $= \frac{p_fV}{RT_1}$

moles of gases in RHS $= \frac{p_fV}{RT_2}$

Total moles $= \left(\frac{p_fV}{RT_1} + \frac{p_fV}{RT_2}\right)$

Total moles are not affected hence,

$\frac{2p_iV}{RT_1} = \frac{p_fV}{R}\left[\frac{1}{T_1} + \frac{1}{T_2}\right]$

$\therefore \quad \frac{2p_i}{T_1} = p_f\left(\frac{T_1 + T_2}{T_1T_2}\right)$

$\therefore \quad p_f = \frac{2p_iT_2}{(T_1 + T_2)}$

56. (c)

57. (b) $\left(p + \frac{a}{V^2}\right)(V - b) = RT$

At low pressure, volume is high.

Thus $\quad V - b = V$

$\therefore \left(p + \frac{a}{V^2}\right)V = RT$

$pV = RT - \frac{a}{V}$

$\therefore \quad Z = \frac{pV}{RT} = \left(1 - \frac{a}{RTV}\right)$

58. (b) Atmospheric pressure = 760 mm of Hg

Since, $p_1V_1 = p_2V_2$, at constant temperature

$\therefore \quad p_2 = \frac{p_1V_1}{V_2} = \frac{760 \times 2.4}{1.9}$

$= 960 \text{ mm of Hg}$

59. (d) Larger the force of attraction, larger the value of a, hence larger the liquefaction. Liquefaction is in order

$Ne < H_2O < C_2H_6 < C_6H_6$

60. (b) $b = uvN_0 = 4\left(\frac{4}{3}\pi r^3\right)N_0$

Larger the size of molecule, larger the value of b.

$r\ (Ne < H_2O < C_6H_6 < C_7H_8)$

61. (d) Rate $\propto \sqrt{\frac{1}{M}}$

$\propto \sqrt{T} \Rightarrow \propto p$

$\therefore \quad \text{Rate} \propto p\sqrt{\frac{T}{M}}$

If p is decreased to (one-fourth) and molar mass is increased to $\sqrt{16} = 4$ times, thus no effect by change of p and molar mass. If temperature is doubled, then number of molecules of He will be $\sqrt{2}$ times of the SO_2.

62. (a) $p_A + p_B + p_C = 10$ bar

$p_A + p_B = 4$ bar

$p_C = 6$ bar

$\therefore \quad p_C = p_{total}\,\chi_C$

$\chi_C = 0.6 = \frac{n_C}{n_{total}} = \frac{n_C}{10}$

$\therefore \quad n_C = 6 \text{ mol}$

$\frac{w_C}{m_C} = 6$

$\therefore \quad w_C = 6 \times 2 = 12\text{g}$

63. (d) Total moles = 10

$\chi_{O_2} = \frac{3}{10}$

If O_2 is not removed

$p_{O_2} = \frac{3}{10}p_{total}$

If O_2 is removed,

$p_{O_2} = \frac{1}{8}p_{total}$

$\therefore$ Decrease $= \left(\frac{3}{10} - \frac{1}{8}\right)p_{total} = \frac{14}{80}p_{total}$

Percentage decrease $= \frac{\frac{14}{80}p_{total}}{\frac{3}{10}p_{total}} \times 100$

$= 58.3\%$

64. (c) $pV = nRT$

$n(O_2) = \frac{pV}{RT}$

$p\ (\text{dry } O_2) = 760 - 22.4$

$= 738.6 \text{ mmHg}$

$= \frac{738.6}{760} \text{ atm}$

$\therefore \quad n(O_2) = \frac{\left(\frac{738.6}{760}\right) \times 0.128}{0.0821 \times 297}$

$= 5.10 \times 10^{-3} \text{ mol}$

$= 5.10 \times 10^{-3} \times 32$

$= 0.163 \text{ g}$

65. (a) $n = \frac{pV}{RT} = \frac{1 \times 3.06}{0.0831 \times 373} = 0.0987 \text{ mol}$

water $= 0.0987 \times 18 = 1.78 \text{ g} = 1.78 \text{ mL}$

■ amount = mol × molar mass

66. (b) Initial, $p_1V_1 = p_2V_2$ at constant temperature

Final, $n_1RT_1 = n_2RT_2$

$$\therefore \quad \frac{n_1}{n_2} = \frac{T_2}{T_1} = \frac{600}{300} = \frac{2}{1} = \frac{4}{2}$$

Total moles $n_1 + n_2 = 0.6$ (given)

$\therefore \quad n_1 = 0.4$ mole at 300 K

and $n_2 = 0.2$ mole at 600 K

Volume of the flask containing 0.3 mole O_2 initially at 300 K $= \dfrac{nRT}{p}$

$$= \frac{0.3 \times 0.0821 \times 300}{0.5}$$

$$\therefore \text{ Final pressure } \frac{n_2RT_2}{V} = \frac{0.2 \times 0.0821 \times 600 \times 0.5}{0.3 \times 0.0821 \times 300}$$

$$= 0.67 \text{ atm}$$

67. (d) 1 L has CO_2 solution = 0.2 mol

$\therefore \quad$ 2 L has CO_2 solution = 0.4 mol

$\because \quad pV = nRT$

$$\therefore \quad V = \frac{nRT}{p} = \frac{0.4 \times 0.0821 \times 273}{1}$$

$$= 8.96 \text{ L}$$

■ At STP, 1 mol = 22.4 L gas

68. (b) $p_{atm} = 1 \text{ atm} = 101.317 \text{ kPa}$

$$p_{O_2} = 22 \text{ kPa}$$

$$\text{Thus } \% = \frac{22}{101.317} \times 100 = 21.7\%$$

69. (c) $\chi_{H_2O} = 0.02$

$\therefore \chi_{\text{dry air}} = 1 - 0.02 = 0.98$ atm

$\therefore p_{\text{dry air}} = 1.2 \times 0.98 = 1.176$ atm

70. (a) $C_3H_8 = n_1$ mol, $CH_4 = n_2$ mol

Total moles $= (n_1 + n_2)$

$\therefore$ Mole fraction of $C_3H_8 = \left(\dfrac{n_1}{n_1 + n_2}\right)$

Before combustion, $p = \dfrac{n}{V}RT$

$$320 = \frac{(n_1 + n_2)}{V}RT$$

$$\underset{n_1}{C_3H_8} \xrightarrow{\text{Air oxidation}} \underset{3n_1}{3CO_2}$$

$$\underset{n_2}{CH_4} \xrightarrow{\text{Air oxidation}} \underset{n_2}{CO_2}$$

After combustion,

$$\therefore \quad 448 = \frac{(3n_1 + n_2)RT}{V}$$

$$\therefore \quad \frac{448}{320} = \frac{3n_1 + n_2}{n_1 + n_2}$$

$$1.4(n_1 + n_2) = 3n_1 + n_2$$

$$n_1 = 0.25n_2$$

$$\therefore \text{ Mole fraction of } C_3H_8 = \frac{0.25n_2}{0.25n_2 + n_2} = 0.2$$

71. (a) Mean free path, $\lambda \propto \dfrac{T}{p}$

(a) $\lambda \propto \dfrac{100}{1}$ or $\dfrac{50}{0.5}$ thus no change.

(b) $\lambda \propto \dfrac{200}{2} \neq \dfrac{400}{1}$

(c) $\sigma(O_2) > \sigma(H_2)$

(d) Movement in more viscous medium is slower than in less viscous medium.

Acid Test for JEE Advanced

Type I. MCQs with Only One Correct Alternate

72. (b) Kinetic energy of the electron in first Bohr's orbit $= 13.6 \text{ eV atom}^{-1}$

$$= 13.6 \times 1.6 \times 10^{-19} \text{ J atom}^{-1}$$

$$\text{Average KE} = \frac{3}{2}\frac{RT}{N_0}$$

$$\text{Thus,} \quad \frac{3RT}{2N_0} = 13.6 \times 1.6 \times 10^{-19}$$

$$T = \frac{13.6 \times 1.6 \times 10^{-19} \times 2 \times 6.02 \times 10^{23}}{3 \times 8.314}$$

$$= 1.0504 \times 10^5 \text{ K}$$

■ $1 \text{ eV} = 1.6 \times 10^{-19}$ J

73. (b) Collision frequency

$$Z = \sqrt{2}N_0(u_{av})\sigma\left(\frac{p}{RT}\right)$$

where, σ = cross-sectional area $= \pi d^2$

d = collision diameter $= 2r$

2r

$$u_{av} = \sqrt{\frac{8RT}{\pi M}}$$

$Z(N_2)$ at $T_1 = Z(\text{He})$ at T_2 (= 298 K)

$$\therefore \quad \sqrt{\frac{8RT_1}{28\pi}}\frac{d_1^2}{T_1} = \sqrt{\frac{8RT_2}{4\pi}}\frac{d_2^2}{T_2}$$

$$\frac{d_1^2}{\sqrt{7T_1}} = \frac{d_2^2}{\sqrt{T_2}} \Rightarrow \sqrt{T_1} = \sqrt{\frac{T_2}{7}} \cdot \left(\frac{d_1}{d_2}\right)^2$$

$$\therefore \quad \sqrt{T_1} = \left(\frac{0.373 \times 10^{-9}}{0.218 \times 10^{-9}}\right)^2 \sqrt{\frac{298}{7}} = 19.1$$

$$T_1 = 365 \text{ K}$$

74. (c) NH_4Cl is in solid state and molar mass of vapour is due to NH_3 and HCl both

$$\therefore \quad \overline{M} = \frac{M_1\chi_1 + M_2\chi_2}{\chi_1 + \chi_2}$$

$$26.75 = \frac{17\chi_1 + 36.5(1 - \chi_1)}{1}$$

$\therefore \chi_1$ = mole fraction of $NH_3 = 0.5$

χ_2 = mole fraction of $HCl = 0.5$

χ_3 = mole fraction of $NH_4Cl = 0.0$

75. (a) $n_{\text{total}} = n_{N_2} + n_{Ar} + n_{O_2}$

Since $n = pV/RT$

$$n_{\text{total}} = \frac{0.792 \times 4 + 1.23 \times 3 + 2.51 \times 5}{RT}$$

$$= \frac{19.408}{RT}, V_{\text{total}} = 12 \text{ L}$$

$$p_{\text{total}} = \frac{nRT}{V} = \frac{19.408}{RT}\frac{RT}{12.0} = 1.62 \text{ atm}$$

76. (b) Fraction of molecules *vs* velocity graph is Maxwell distribution curve. This curve is slightly unsymmetrical as shown below.

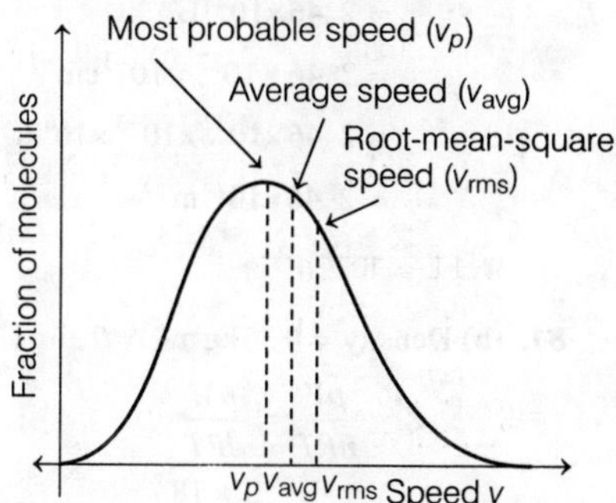

The ratio of most probable, the average and the root mean square speeds for this graph is 1 : 1·128 : 1·224

But the graph in question is completely symmetrical. Therefore, the most probable and the average speed will be same here but root mean square speed will be greater than average speed. So, the correct ratio is 1 : 1 : 1.224.

77. (d) $pV = nRT = \dfrac{w}{m}RT$

$$\therefore \quad m = \frac{wRT}{pV}$$

$$= \frac{(33.5 \times 10^{-3})(0.0821) \times 298}{\left(\frac{152}{760}\right)(0.250)}$$

$$= 16.4 \text{ g mol}^{-1}$$

■ p in atm, V in dm^3, R is in atm dm^3 $mol^{-1}K^{-1}$.

78. (b) $p_{N_2} = \dfrac{n_{N_2}RT}{V} = \left(\dfrac{0.928}{28}\right)\dfrac{0.0821 \times 298}{1}$

$$= 0.811 \text{ atm}$$

$$= 616 \text{ mmHg}$$

79. (a) $\frac{r_{H_2}}{r_{O_2}} = \sqrt{\frac{32}{2}} = 4$

$r_{H_2} = 4r_{O_2}$

H_2 diffuses 4 times faster than O_2,

If temperatures are different,

$$\frac{r_{H_2}}{r_{O_2}} = \sqrt{\frac{T_{H_2} M_{O_2}}{T_{O_2} M_{H_2}}} = \sqrt{\frac{T_{H_2} 16}{T_{O_2}}} = 4\sqrt{\frac{T_{H_2}}{T_{O_2}}}$$

If $\sqrt{\frac{T_{H_2}}{T_{O_2}}} = \sqrt{\frac{25}{400}} = \frac{1}{4}$ then rates are equal.

80. (c) Let number of moles = n

Molecules = nN_0

Molecular density (molecules/ volume)

$$= \frac{nN_0}{V} = \frac{\left(\frac{pV}{RT}\right) N_0}{V} = \frac{pN_0}{RT}$$

$$= \frac{1 \text{ atm} \times 6.02 \times 10^{23} \text{mol}^{-1}}{0.0821 \text{L atm mol}^{-1}\text{K}^{-1} \times 298 \text{K}}$$

$= 2.46 \times 10^{22} \text{L}^{-1}$

$= 2.46 \times 10^{22} \times 10^{-3} \text{cm}^{-3}$

$= 2.46 \times 10^{22} \times 10^{-3} \times 10^{6} \text{m}^{-3}$

$= 2.46 \times 10^{25} \text{m}^{-3}$

■ $1 \text{ L} = 10^{-3} \text{ m}^3$

81. (b) Density = $0.36 \text{kg m}^{-3} = 0.36 \text{g L}^{-1}$

$$Z = \frac{pV}{nRT} = \frac{pM}{dRT}$$

$$= \frac{1 \times 18}{0.36 \times 0.0824 \times 500} = 1.22$$

■ $1 \text{ kg m}^{-3} = 1 \text{ g L}^{-1}$

82. (a) At STP, volume of N_2

$= 22400 \text{cm}^3 \text{mol}^{-1}$

Thus, 6.02×10^{23} molecules have volume

$= 22400 \text{ cm}^3$

and 1 molecule has volume

$$= \frac{22400}{6.02 \times 10^{23}} \text{cm}^3$$

$= 3.72 \times 10^{-20} \text{cm}^3$

Also, $\frac{4}{3}\pi r^3 = 3.72 \times 10^{-20} \text{cm}^3$

$\therefore \quad r = 2.07 \times 10^{-7}$ cm

$= 20.7 \times 10^{-8}$ cm $= 20.7 \times 10^{-10}$ m

$\therefore$ Average distance = $2r$

$= 41.40 \times 10^{-10}$ m

$= 41.40$ Å

83. (c) First we compare the ratio by which N_2 and He (being in different molar ratio effuse from vessel B).

$$\frac{r_{N_2}}{r_{He}} = \frac{n_{N_2}}{n_{He}} \sqrt{\frac{M(\text{He})}{M(N_2)}}$$

$$= \frac{2}{3}\sqrt{\frac{4}{28}} = \frac{2}{3}\sqrt{\frac{1}{7}} = \frac{0.252}{1}$$

Thus, if N_2 effuses 0.252 part, He effuses 1.0 part.

Total part effused = 1.252

$\therefore$ Composition of $N_2 = \frac{0.252}{1.252} = 0.20$

(in mole fraction)

and He = 0.80

$$\therefore \quad M(\text{mixture}) = \frac{M_1\chi_1 + M_2\chi_2}{\chi_1 + \chi_2}$$

$= 0.20 \times 28 + 0.80 \times 4 = 8.8$

$$\therefore \quad \frac{r_{O_2}}{r_{mix}} = \sqrt{\frac{M(\text{mix})}{M(O_2)}}$$

$$= \sqrt{\frac{8.8}{32}} = 0.52$$

84. (d) van der Waals' constant

$$b = 4\left(\frac{4}{3}\pi r^3 N_0\right)$$

Thus, $\quad b \propto r^3$

Larger the molecular size, larger the value of b. Thus, increasing order of value of b is

$H_2 < He < O_2 < CO_2$

Higher the extent of liquefaction, larger the value of a. (which depends on force of attraction)

Thus, $\quad H_2 < O_2 < CH_4$

85. (b) By observation, temperature is constant

$\therefore \quad p_1V_1 = p_2V_2$

$$p_2 \text{ (He in mixture)} = \frac{0.66 \times 200}{400} = 0.33 \text{atm}$$

$$p_2 \text{ (}O_2\text{ in mixture)} = \frac{0.52 \times 400}{400} = 0.52 \text{ atm}$$

86. (b) At bottom = p_1V_1

At surface = $p_2V_2 = (p_1 + p)V_2$

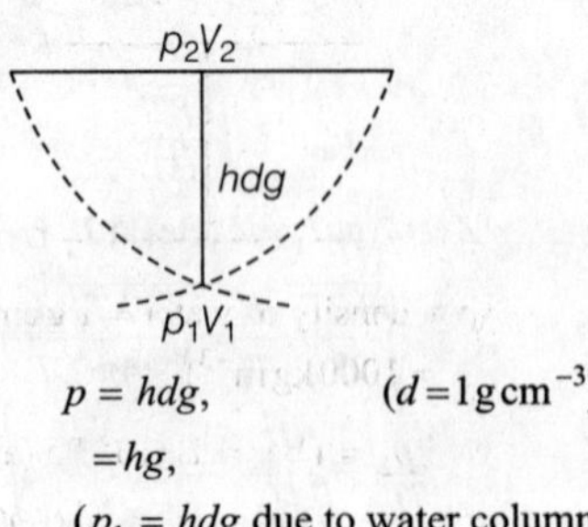

$p = hdg, \qquad (d = 1 \text{g cm}^{-3})$

$= hg,$

($p_1 = hdg$ due to water column)

$= 10$ g

$\therefore \quad p_1V_1 = p_2V_2$

$(h + 10)gV = 10g \times 8$ V

$\therefore \quad h = 70$ m

87. (c) $u_{rms} = \sqrt{\frac{3RT}{M}}$

$$r_{H_2} = \sqrt{\frac{3R \times 50}{2}} = 5\sqrt{3}R$$

$$r_{O_2} = \sqrt{\frac{3R \times 800}{32}} = 5\sqrt{3R}$$

$\therefore \quad \frac{r_{H_2}}{r_{O_2}} = \frac{1}{1}$

88. (c) $u_{rms}(H_2)$

At temperature $T_1 = \sqrt{7}\, u_{rms}(N_2)$

At temperature T_2,

$$\sqrt{\frac{3RT_1}{2}} = \sqrt{7}\sqrt{\frac{3RT_2}{28}}$$

$$\therefore \quad \frac{T_1}{2} = \frac{7T_2}{28} = \frac{T_2}{4} \Rightarrow \frac{T_2}{T_1} = 2$$

Thus, $\quad T_2(N_2) > T_1(H_2)$

89. (d) $\left(p + \frac{a}{V^2}\right)(V - b) = RT$

(a) If $a = 0$, for gas A

$p(V - b) = RT$

$pV = RT + pb$

$$\therefore \quad Z = \frac{pV}{RT} = 1 + \frac{pb}{RT}$$

Thus, Z is dependent on p and is linear as in (A).

(b) If $b = 0$,

$$\left(p + \frac{a}{V^2}\right)V = RT$$

$$pV = \frac{a}{V} = RT$$

$$\therefore \quad Z = \frac{pV}{RT} = 1 - \frac{a}{RTV}$$

$$= 1 - \frac{ap}{RT}\left(\frac{1}{V} \propto p\right)$$

Thus, Z is dependent on p and is linear as shown in (B)

(c) At low p, V is high, $(V - b) \approx V$

and at high p, $\left(p + \frac{a}{V^2}\right) \approx p$

$$\therefore \quad Z = \frac{pV}{RT} = 1 + \frac{pb}{RT}$$

Thus, Z first decreases in low p range and then increases as p increases. At high p, slope changes negative to positive. Thus, incorrect.

90. (c) $\left(p + \frac{a}{V^2}\right)(V - b) = RT$

When $b = 0$

$$pV + \frac{a}{V} = RT$$

$$\therefore \quad pV = RT - \frac{a}{V}$$

when $\frac{1}{V}=2,\ pV=21.6$

when $\frac{1}{V}=3,\ pV=20.1$

$\therefore\quad 21.6=RT-2a$

$20.1=RT-3a$

$\therefore\quad a=1.5\ \text{atm L}^2\ \text{mol}^{-2}$

91. (b) $\frac{n^2a}{V^2}$ is the correction term due to force of attraction.

92. (a) By Graham's law of diffusion,

$$\frac{r_{H_2}}{r_{O_2}}=\sqrt{\frac{4}{2}}=\frac{1.4136}{1}$$

Thus, if H_2 diffuses 1.4136 part, O_2 diffuses 1 part.

$$\therefore\quad X_{H_2}=\frac{1.4136}{1+1.436}=0.5857$$

$\therefore$ percentage = 58.57%

93. (d) $p_{O_2}=0.20\,p$

$p_{N_2}=0.80\,p$

$$\therefore\quad \frac{r_{N_2}}{r_{O_2}}=\frac{p_{N_2}}{p_{O_2}}\sqrt{\frac{M(O_2)}{M(N_2)}}$$

$$=\frac{0.80\,p}{0.20\,p}\sqrt{\frac{32}{28}}=4.276$$

$\therefore$ Thus, if N_2 diffuses 4.276 parts O_2 diffuses 1.0 part.

$$\therefore\quad \chi_{O_2}=\frac{1.0}{5.276}=0.19$$

94. (a) Mean free path, $\lambda=\frac{RT}{\sqrt{2}\,N_0\sigma p}$

$$\therefore\ p=\frac{RT}{\sqrt{2}\,N_0\sigma\lambda}$$

$$p=\frac{8.3143\times 298}{\sqrt{2}\times 6.02\times 10^{23}\times 0.43\times 10^{-18}\times 0.1}$$

$=2.81\times 10^5\,\text{Pa}$

■ 1 nm = 1×10^{-9} m

95. (a) $\lambda=\frac{RT}{\sqrt{2}\,N_A\sigma p}$

Given, $\lambda=2r$ (diameter) $=218\times 10^{-12}\,\text{m}$

and $\sigma=\pi d^2=\pi(2r)^2$

(σ is cross-sectional area)

$$\therefore\quad p=\frac{RT}{\sqrt{2}\,N_A\sigma\lambda}=\frac{RT}{\sqrt{2}\,N_A\pi(2r)^2(2r)}$$

$$=\frac{8.3143\times 298}{\sqrt{2}\times 6.02\times 10^{23}\times\pi(218\times 10^{-12})^3}$$

$=8.93\times 10^7\,\text{Pa}=893$ bar.

■ 1.0×10^5 Pa = 1 bar

96. (b) By Boyle's law,

$pV=RT$

$$\therefore\quad V=\frac{RT}{p}$$

$$\therefore\quad \left(\frac{\partial V}{\partial p}\right)_{T,n}=-\frac{RT}{p^2}=-\frac{V}{p}$$

$$-\frac{1}{V}\left(\frac{\partial V}{\partial p}\right)_{T,n}=\frac{1}{p}=1.0\ \text{bar}^{-1}$$

97. (d) Volume $=\frac{4}{3}\pi r^3 N_0$

$$=\frac{4}{3}\pi(1\times 10^{-10})^3\times 6.02\times 10^{23}$$

$=2.52\times 10^{-6}\,\text{m}^3$

98. (d) $\frac{p_1V_1}{n_1RT_1}=\frac{p_2V_2}{n_2RT_2}$

$p_2=\frac{p_1}{9},\ T_2=3T_1,\ V_1=30\,\text{mL}$

$n_2=\frac{1}{2}n_1,\ V_2=?$

$$\frac{p_1V_1}{n_1RT_1}=\frac{\left(\frac{p_1}{9}\right)(V_2)}{\left(\frac{n_1}{2}\right)R(3T_1)}$$

$$\therefore\quad V_2=\left(\frac{1}{2}\right)(3)\times(9)\times 30=405\ \text{mL}$$

99. (a) Compressibility factor

$$Z=\frac{pV}{nRT}$$

$Z_A=3Z_B$

$$\therefore\quad \frac{p_AV_A}{n_ART_A}=3\frac{p_BV_B}{n_BRT_B}$$

$V_A=2V_B,\ n_A=n_B,\ T_A=T_B$

$\therefore\quad p_A(2V_B)=3p_BV_B$

$\therefore\quad 2p_A=3\,p_B$

100. (a) V_1 (initial) $=\frac{4}{3}\pi r_1^3=\frac{4}{3}\pi(1.0)^3\,\text{cm}^3$

$$V_2(\text{final})=\frac{p_1V_1}{p_2}$$

p_2 (surface), h, p_1 (depth)

(ρ = density of water = $1\,\text{g cm}^{-3}$ = $1000\,\text{kg m}^{-3}$)

$p_2=1\,\text{bar}=1\times 10^5$ Pa (at the surface)

$$p_1=p_2+\rho gh=1+\left(\frac{1000\times 9.81\times 45}{10^5}\right)$$

$=1+4.41=5.41$ bar

$$\therefore\quad V_2=\frac{5.41\times\frac{4}{3}\pi}{1}$$

$$\frac{4}{3}\pi r_2^3=\frac{4}{3}\pi(5.41)$$

$\therefore\quad r_2^3=5.41\,\text{cm}^3$

$\Rightarrow\quad r_2=1.86$ cm

■ 1×10^5 Pascal = 1 bar

$1\,\text{g cm}^{-3}=1000\,\text{kg m}^{-3}$

101. (b) For molar volume, $n=1$, thus

$$\left(p+\frac{a}{V^2}\right)(V-b)=RT$$

If force of attraction is neglected, then $a=0$.

$\therefore\quad p(V-b)=RT$

At 101.3 kPa and 273 K, 101.3 kPa

$(V-b)=8.314\,\text{kPa dm}^3\,\text{K}^{-1}\,\text{mol}^{-1}\times 273$

$\therefore\ (V-b)=22.4\,\text{dm}^3$ ...(i)

At 10.13 MPa (= 10.13×10^3 kPa) and 273 K.

10.13×10^3 kPa $(0.011\,V-b)$

$=8.314\,\text{kPa dm}^3\,\text{K}^{-1}\,\text{mol}^{-1}\times 273$

$\therefore\ (0.011V-b)=0.224\,\text{dm}^3$ ...(ii)

$\therefore$ Multiply (i) by 0.011,

$(0.011V-0.011b)=0.2464\,\text{dm}^3$ ...(iii)

Eq. (ii) – (iii) gives,

$-b(1-0.011)=-0.2464-0.224$

$0.989b=0.0224\,\text{dm}^3$

$\therefore\quad b=0.0226\,\text{dm}^3\,\text{mol}^{-1}$

But, $b=4$ (volume molecules in 1 mole)

$$=4\times\frac{4}{3}\pi r^3 N_0$$

$$\therefore\ r^3=\frac{3b}{16\pi N_0}$$

$$r^3=\frac{3\times 0.0226\,\text{dm}^3}{16\pi\times 6.02\times 10^{23}}$$

$r^3=2.24\times 10^{-27}\,\text{dm}^3$

$\therefore\quad r=1.31\times 10^{-9}$ dm

$=1.31\times 10^{-10}$ m

$=131\times 10^{-12}$ m

$=131$ pm

102. (b) $pV=nRT$

$$\therefore\quad n_1=\frac{3.00\times 1.05}{493\,R}$$

$$n_2=\frac{0.70\times 1.00}{383\,R}$$

$$\therefore\quad \frac{n_2}{n_1}=0.182$$

$\therefore$ Fraction remaining = 0.182

$\therefore$ Fraction escaped = 0.818 (81.8%)

103. (c) $p_{H_2} = \frac{nRT}{V} = \frac{0.5 \times 0.0821 \times 300}{3.0}$

$= 4.1$ atm

$p_{CO_2} = \frac{2 \times 0.0821 \times 300}{3.0} = 16.42$ atm

Total $= 4.10 + 16.42 = 20.52$ atm

■ Total volume = 3 L as two vessels are connected.
H_2 and CO_2 are non-interacting gases.

104. (a) Initially total moles of H_2 and $O_2 = 4$

$\therefore p_{total} = \frac{nRT}{V} = \frac{4 \times 0.0831 \times 398}{125.3}$

$= 1.056$ bar

	$2H_2(g)$	$+ O_2(g) \longrightarrow$	$2H_2O(g)$
Initial	3	1	0
Reacted	2	1	
After reaction	1	0	2

Total moles after reaction = 3

$\therefore p_{total} = \frac{3 \times 0.0831 \times 398}{125.3} = 0.792$ bar

105. (a) NO_2 initially present

$= \frac{15.2\,g}{46\,g\,mol^{-1}} = 0.33$ mol

	$2NO_2(g) \rightleftharpoons$	$N_2O_4(g)$
Initial	0.33	0
At equilibrium	$(0.33 - 2x)$	x

Total moles at equilibrium

$(0.33 - 2x + x) = (0.33 - x)$

$p = \frac{n}{V} RT$

$0.5 = \left(\frac{0.33 - x}{10}\right) \times 0.0821 \times 298$

$\therefore \quad x = 0.126$

$\chi_{NO_2} = \frac{n(NO_2)}{n(\text{Total})}$

$\therefore \quad \chi_{NO_2} = \frac{(0.33 - 2x)}{(0.33 - x)} = \frac{0.33 - 0.252}{(0.33 - 0.126)}$

$= \frac{0.078}{0.204} = 0.38$

$\therefore \quad p_{NO_2} = p_{total}\, \chi_{NO_2} = 0.19$ atm

106. (b) Initially both H_2 and O_2 are present

$n_{H_2} + n_{O_2} = n_{total} = \frac{pV}{RT} = \frac{1 \times V}{RT} = \frac{V}{RT}$

After reaction only unreacted gas is H_2

$p_{H_2} = n_{H_2} \frac{RT}{V}$

Unreacted $(n_{H_2}) = \frac{pV}{RT} = \frac{0.35V}{RT}$

Also,

$\therefore n_{H_2} + n_{O_2} + n_{H_2}$ (unreacted) $= \frac{V}{RT}$

(being under isothermal condition and in a closed vessel)

$n_{H_2} + n_{O_2} = \frac{V}{RT} - \frac{0.35V}{RT} = \frac{0.65V}{RT}$

$2H_2(g) + O_2(g) \longrightarrow 2H_2O(l)$

H_2 and O_2 react in 2:1 molar ratio

$\therefore \quad n_{H_2} = 2n_{O_2}$

$\therefore \quad 3n_{O_2} = \frac{0.65V}{RT}$

$\Rightarrow \quad n_{O_2} = \frac{0.65V}{3RT}$

$\therefore \quad \chi_{O_2} = \frac{n_{O_2}}{n_{total}} = \frac{\frac{0.65V}{3RT}}{\frac{V}{RT}} = 0.22$

$\chi_{H_2} = 0.78$

107. (b) Balloon will burst when volume > 200 L.

At this point $p_2 = \frac{p_1 V_1}{V} = \frac{1 \times 150}{200}$

$= 0.75$ atm $= 570$ mm

pressure decrease = 10 mm per m

Decrease in pressure $= 760 - 570$

$= 190$ mm

Height upto which it can resist bursting

$= \frac{190\text{ mm}}{10\text{ mm/m}} = 19$ m

Thus, at a height above 19 m balloon will burst.

108. (c) $\frac{r_{LPG}}{r_{SO_3}} = \sqrt{\frac{M_{(SO_3)}}{M_{(LPG)}}} = 1.25$

$\therefore M_{(LPG)} = \frac{M_{(SO_3)}}{(1.25)^2} = \frac{80}{(1.25)^2}$

$= 51.2\,g\,mol^{-1}$

Let butane be $= X\,\%$

then propane $= (100 - X)\%$

$51.2 = \frac{M_1 X + M_2(100 - X)}{100}$

$51.2 = \frac{58X + 44(100 - X)}{100}$

$X = 51.43\%$

(mole fraction = 0.51)

109. (a) λ (mean free path) $= \frac{RT}{\sqrt{2}\, N_0 \sigma p}$

where, $\sigma = \pi d^2 = \pi (2r)^2$

(σ is cross-sectional area.)

$\lambda = \frac{8.314 \times 293}{\sqrt{2} \times 6.02 \times 10^{23} \times \pi (3.70 \times 10^{-10})^2 \times 1 \times 10^5}$

$= 6.65 \times 10^{-8}$ m $= 665$ Å

110. (b) $pV = nRT$

$p = \frac{nRT}{V}$

$\left(\frac{\partial p}{\partial V}\right) = -\frac{nRT}{V^2}$

$= -\frac{1\text{ mol} \times 8.3143\,J\,mol^{-1}K^{-1} \times 300\,K}{(5\,m^3)^2}$

$= -100\,J\,m^{-6} = -100\,kg\,m^2 s^{-2} m^{-6}$

$= -100\,kg\,m^{-1}s^{-2}(m^{-3})$

$= -100\,Pa\,m^{-3}$

■ $1\,J = 1\,kg\,m^2 s^{-2}$
$1\,Pa = kg\,m^{-1}s^{-2}$

111. (c) $pV = nRT = \frac{w}{m} RT$

$\therefore \quad p = \frac{w}{Vm} RT = \frac{dRT}{m}$

$\therefore \quad \frac{d}{p} = \frac{m}{RT}$

Extrapolated line cuts $\frac{d}{p}$ axis at

$2.86\,g\,L^{-1} atm^{-1}$

$\therefore \quad \frac{m}{RT} = 2.86\,g\,L^{-1} atm^{-1}$

$\therefore \quad m = 2.86\,g\,L^{-1} atm^{-1} RT$

$= 2.86\,g\,L^{-1} atm^{-1} \times 0.0821\,L\,atm\,mol^{-1}K^{-1} \times 273\,K$

$= 64.10\,g\,mol^{-1}$

112. (a) u_{mp} (most probable velocity)

$= \left(\frac{2RT}{M}\right)^{1/2}$

$\therefore \quad \frac{dU_{mp}}{dT} = \frac{1}{2}\left(\frac{2RT}{M}\right)^{-1/2} \frac{2R}{M}$

$= \frac{R}{M}\left(\frac{M}{2RT}\right)^{1/2} = \frac{R}{M}\left(\frac{1}{U_{mp}}\right)$

$\therefore \quad \frac{M}{R}\left(\frac{dU_{mp}}{dT}\right) = \frac{1}{U_{mp}}$

$= \frac{1}{200\,m\,s^{-1}} = 5 \times 10^{-3}\,s\,m^{-1}$

113. (a) Mean free path $\lambda \propto \frac{T}{p}$

$\therefore \quad \lambda_2 / \lambda_1 = p_1 / p_2$

$\therefore \quad \lambda_2 = \frac{60 \times 1 \times 10^{-4}}{1 \times 10^{-2}} = 0.60$ cm

114. (d) $p_{total} = p_{atm} + p_{gas} = 749 + 29.2 \times 10$

$= 1041$ mmHg

115. (a) $\frac{r_1}{r_2} = \sqrt{\frac{179}{44}} = 2.017$

Thus, N_2O moves 2.017 times faster than $C_6H_{11}OBr$.

Let two gases meet at xth row from gas 1.

Row covered by I $= x$ m

Row covered by II $= (13-x)$ m

$\therefore \quad \frac{x}{13-x} = 2.017 \Rightarrow x = 9$ m

Thus, 9th student from side 1 will weep and laugh at the same time.

116. (b) $\frac{T_c}{p_c} = \frac{8a}{27Rb} \Big/ \frac{a}{27b^2} = 8b$

Thus, larger the value of $\left(\frac{T_c}{p_c}\right)$, larger will be the value of b (excluded volume).

Thus, (I) is correct.

$T_c = \frac{8a}{27\,Rb}, T_b = \frac{a}{Rb} \quad \therefore T_c = \frac{8}{27} T_b$

$\therefore \; T_c < T_b$, thus II is incorrect.

At T_c, $\left(\frac{\partial p}{\partial V}\right)_{T_c} = 0$, thus correct.

117. (a)

Gas	Molar mass (g mol^{-1})
H_2O	18
CO_2	44
N_2O	44
CO	28
N_2	28
O_2	32
O_3	48
D_2O	20

$\therefore \quad \frac{r_A}{r_B} = \sqrt{\frac{M_B}{M_A}}$

Thus, ratio $= \sqrt{\frac{M_B}{M_A}}$

I = 1, II = 1, III $= \sqrt{3/2} = 1.225$

IV $= \sqrt{\frac{20}{18}} = \sqrt{\frac{10}{9}} = 1.054$

V $= \sqrt{\frac{257}{0.254}} = 1.005$

Thus, I = II < V < IV < III

118. (b) $n_{NH_3} = \frac{pV}{RT} = \frac{1 \times 0.350}{0.08314 \times 300}$

$= 0.014$ mol in 500mL

$\therefore$ (NH_4OH) = 0.028 mol in 1000 mL

$\therefore$ Molar concentration = 0.028M

119. (d) $Z = \frac{pV}{nRT}$

$n_I = \frac{pV}{ZRT} = \frac{800 \times 1}{1.9\,R \times 330}$

$n_{II} = n_I = \frac{200\,V}{1.1R \times 570}$

$n_I = n_{II}$ (given)

$\therefore \quad \frac{200\,V}{1.1R \times 570} = \frac{800}{1.9\,R \times 330}$

$V = 4$L

120. (b) $\frac{r_X}{r_{O_2}} = \sqrt{\frac{32}{M_X}} = \frac{4}{5}$

$\therefore \; M_X = 50$ g$mol^{-1} = 0.050$ kgmol^{-1}

$d_X = 0.80$ kgm^{-3}

Since, $\frac{\text{mass}}{\text{volume}} = d$

Molar volume

$(V_m) = \frac{\text{mass}}{\text{density}} = \frac{0.050 \text{ kg mol}^{-1}}{0.80 \text{ kg m}^{-3}}$

$= 0.0625\,m^3 = 62.5$ L

Compressibility factor $(Z) = \frac{pV_m}{RT}$

$\therefore \; Z = \frac{pV_m}{RT} = \frac{1 \times 62.5}{0.0821 \times 500} = 1.52$

■ 1 L = 1 dm^3 = 10^{-3} m^3

121. (b) $\frac{r_1}{r_2} = \frac{p_1}{p_2}\sqrt{\frac{M_2}{M_1}} = \frac{n_1}{n_2}\sqrt{\frac{M_2}{M_1}}$

$\therefore \quad \frac{r_{He}}{r_{CH_4}} = \frac{1}{2}\sqrt{\frac{16}{4}} = 1:1 = 4:4$

$\frac{r_{He}}{r_{SO_2}} = \frac{1}{3}\sqrt{\frac{64}{4}} = 4:3$

Thus, molar ratio of the gases coming out initially = 4:4:3

122. (b) 1.75 L of ethanol at STP is exposed to UV-radiation with 2.5 L of O_2 gas at STP.

$$\underset{1\text{ mol}}{CH_3CH_2OH} + \underset{3\text{ mol}}{3O_2} \longrightarrow \underset{2\text{ mol}}{2CO_2} + \underset{3\text{ mol}}{3H_2O}$$

O_2 required by 1 mol CH_3CH_2OH=3 mol

Since, volume is proportional to number of moles, hence

O_2 required by 1.75 L of CH_3CH_2OH = 3.50 L

O_2 actually taken = 25 L

Thus, O_2 is in excess and CH_3CH_2OH is the limiting reactant.

Thus, CO_2 from 1.75 mol of CH_3CH_2OH

= 2 × mol of CH_3CH_2OH

= 3.50 mol

123. (a) n_1 = number of moles of gas (1) $= \frac{pV}{RT}$

$= \frac{p_1V}{RT_1}$

n_2 = number of moles of gas (2) $= \frac{p_2V}{RT_2}$

Total moles $= (n_1 + n_2)$

$\therefore \quad p_3 = \frac{nRT}{V} = \frac{(n_1+n_2)\,RT_3}{2\,V}$

$= \frac{1}{2\,V}\left(\frac{p_1V}{RT_1} + \frac{p_2V}{RT_2}\right)RT_3$

$= \frac{1}{2}\left[\frac{p_1}{T_1} + \frac{p_2}{T_2}\right]$

$p_3 = \frac{T_3}{2}\left[\frac{p_1T_2 + p_2T_1}{T_1T_2}\right]$

124. (c) Number of moles of CH_4

$= \frac{1.6\text{ g}}{1.6\text{ g mol}^{-1}} = 0.1$ mol

Initial pressure, $p_1 = 0.6$ bar

% increase = 5%

$\therefore$ Final pressure,

$p_2 = \left(p_1 + \frac{5}{100}p_1\right)$

$= 0.6 + 0.05 \times 0.6$

$= 0.63$ bar

Initial temperature, $T_1 = T$ K

$\therefore$ Final temperature, $T_2 = (T + 10)$ K

$\therefore \quad p_1V_1 = RT_1$

$0.6V = nR \times T$

and $\quad p_2V_2 = RT_2$

$\therefore \quad 0.63\,V = nR\,(T+10)$

$\therefore \quad \frac{0.63}{0.60} = \left(\frac{T+10}{T}\right)$

$1.05 = 1 + \frac{10}{T}$

$0.05 = \frac{10}{T}$

$\therefore \quad T = \frac{10}{0.05} = 200$ K

$\therefore \quad 0.6 \times V = 0.1 \times 0.0831 \times 200$

$\therefore \quad V = \frac{0.1 \times 0.0831 \times 200}{0.6}$

$= 2.77\,dm^3$

125. (a) Most propable velocity at STP is

$U_1 = \sqrt{\frac{2R \times 273}{M}} = \sqrt{\frac{2p_1}{d_1}}$

and at t°C, $(273 + t)$ K

$U_2 = \sqrt{\frac{2R\,(273+t)}{M}}$

$\frac{U_2}{U_1} = \sqrt{\frac{273+t}{273}}$

$U_2 = U_1\sqrt{\frac{(273+t)}{273}}$

But, $\quad U_1 = \sqrt{\frac{2p_1}{d_1}}$

$$\therefore \quad U_2 = \sqrt{\frac{2p_1}{d_1}}\sqrt{\frac{(273+t)}{273}}$$

$$U_2 = \sqrt{\frac{2p_1(273+t)}{273d_1}}$$

126. (b) Total volume of gas X and Y = 100 mL

Y in the mixture = 40 mL

and gas X in the mixture = 60 mL

Due to effusion, mixture left

$$= 100 - 40 = 60 \text{ mL}$$

Gas Y in the residual gas mixture

$$= 60 \times \frac{55}{100} = 33 \text{ mL}$$

and gas X in the residual gas mixture

$$= 60 - 33 = 27 \text{ mL}$$

Thus, gas X effused in given time

$$= 60 - 27 = 33 \text{ mL}$$

and gas Y effused in given time

$$= 40 - 33 = 7 \text{ mL}$$

Also, initially $\frac{p_X}{p_Y} = \frac{V_Y}{V_X} = \frac{40}{60}$

$$\therefore \quad \frac{r_X}{r_Y} = \frac{p_X}{p_Y}\sqrt{\frac{M_Y}{M_X}} \Rightarrow \frac{33}{7} = \frac{40}{60}\sqrt{\frac{100}{M_X}}$$

$\therefore M_X = 2 \text{ g mol}^{-1}$

127. (a) $\left(p + \frac{a}{V^2}\right)(V - b) = RT$

If density is low, volume is high, thus

$$(V - b) \approx V$$

$$\therefore \quad \left(p + \frac{a}{V^2}\right)(V) = RT$$

$$\left(p + \frac{a}{V^2}\right) = \frac{RT}{V}$$

$$\therefore \quad p = \left(\frac{RT}{V} - \frac{a}{V^2}\right)$$

By dielectric's equaiton,

$$p(V - b) = RT \exp\left(\frac{-a}{RTV}\right)$$

$$\approx RT\left[1 - \frac{a}{RTV}\right],$$

At low density, $(V - b) \approx V$

$$\therefore \quad p = \frac{RT}{V}\left[1 - \frac{a}{RTV}\right] = \left(\frac{RT}{V} - \frac{a}{V^2}\right)$$

Thus, both equations give same value of pressure at low density.

128. (a) Given at STP,

$$T = 273 \text{ K}$$

$$p = 1 \text{ atm}$$

and Z (compressibility factor) = 0.927

$$Z = \frac{pV}{RT}$$

$$\therefore \quad \text{Molar volume } (V) = \frac{ZRT}{p}$$

$$= \frac{0.927 \times 0.0821 \times 273}{1}$$

$$= 20.78 \text{ dm}^3 \text{ mol}^{-1}$$

$\therefore 20.78 \text{ dm}^3\ O_2 = 32 \text{ g}$

$$\therefore \quad 100 \text{ dm}^3\ O_2 = \frac{32 \times 100}{20.78}$$

$$= 154 \text{ g} = 0.154 \text{ kg}$$

■ R is in $\text{dm}^3 \text{ atm mol}^{-1} \text{K}^{-1}$

129. (c) Let number of moles of N_2 be = n

$$1 \text{ MPa} = 1 \times 10^6 \text{ Pa}$$

At 223 K $\quad n = \frac{pV}{ZRT} = \frac{81.06 \times 1.0}{1.95 \times R \times 223}$

At 373 K $\quad n = \frac{pV}{ZRT}$

$$\therefore V = \frac{nZRT}{p}$$

$$= \frac{81.06 \times 1.0 \times 1.10 \times R \times 373}{1.95 \times R \times 223 \times 20.265}$$

$$= 3.77 \text{ dm}^3$$

■ In both cases, pressure is in MPa, hence conversion into other units have not been taken. R is common, thus cancelled out.

130. (c) If two gases have the same value of 'a' but different values of 'b', then smaller the value of b, larger will be the compressibility because the gas with the smaller value of 'b' will occupy lesser volume and hence will be more compressible.

If the two gases have the same value of 'b' but different values of 'a' then the gas having a larger value of 'a' will occupy lesser volume. This is because the gas with a larger value of 'a' will have larger force of attraction, hence lesser distance between the molecules.

131. (c) By Maxwell's distribution of molecular velocities.

$$\frac{dN}{N} = 4\pi\left(\frac{M}{2\pi RT}\right)^{3/2} u_{mp}^2 \exp\left(-\frac{Mu_{mp}^2}{2RT}\right) du$$

$\therefore$ **Case I** Molecular speeds in the range of $3u_{mp}$ to $(3u_{mp} + du)$

$$\frac{1}{N}\left(\frac{dN_1}{du}\right) = 4\pi\left(\frac{M}{2\pi RT}\right)^{3/2}(9u_{mp}^2)$$

$$\exp\left(-\frac{9Mu_{mp}^2}{2RT}\right)$$

Case II Molecular speeds in the range of $2u_{mp}$ to $(2u_{mp} + du)$

$$\frac{1}{N}\left(\frac{dN_2}{du}\right)$$

$$= 4\pi\left(\frac{M}{2\pi RT}\right)^{3/2}(4u_{mp}^2)\exp\left(-\frac{4Mu_{mp}^2}{2RT}\right)$$

$$\therefore \quad \frac{dN_1}{dN_2} = \frac{9}{4}\exp\left[-\frac{5Mu_{mp}^2}{2RT}\right]$$

As, $\quad u_{mp}^2 = \frac{2RT}{M}$

$$\frac{dN_1}{dN_2} = \frac{9}{4}\exp - \left(\frac{5M}{2RT}\cdot\frac{2RT}{M}\right)$$

$$= \frac{9}{4}\exp(-5) = \frac{9}{4e^5} = \frac{2.25}{e^5}$$

132. (b) Most probable velocity of N_2 gas at 300 K is (in SI Unit)

$$u_{mp} = \sqrt{\frac{2RT}{M}}$$

$$= \sqrt{\frac{2 \times 8.314 \times 300}{28 \times 10^{-3}}} = 422.09 \text{ m s}^{-1}$$

$$du = (u_{mp} + 0.005u_{mp}) - (u_{mp} - 0.005u_{mp})$$

$$= 4.22 \text{ m s}^{-1}$$

By Maxwell distribution law,

$$\frac{dN}{N} = 4\pi\left(\frac{M}{2\pi RT}\right)^{3/2} u^2 e^{-Mu^2/2RT} du$$

$$\left(\frac{M}{2\pi RT}\right)^{3/2} = \left(\frac{28 \times 10^{-3}}{2\pi \times 8.314 \times 300}\right)^{3/2}$$

$$= 2.39 \times 10^{-9} \text{ m}^{-3} \text{ s}^3$$

$$\exp\left(-\frac{Mu^2}{2RT}\right)$$

$$= \exp\left(-\frac{28 \times 10^{-3} \times (422.09)^2}{2 \times 8.314 \times 300}\right)$$

$$= e^{-1} = 0.3679$$

$$\therefore \quad \frac{dN}{N} = 4\pi \times 2.39 \times 10^{-9} \times (422.09)^2 \times 0.3679 \times 4.22$$

$$= 8.303 \times 10^{-3}$$

Type II. Statement Based Questions

133. (a)	**134.** (a)	**135.** (a)
136. (b)	**137.** (c)	**138.** (b)
139. (a)	**140.** (b)	**141.** (a)
142. (a)	**143.** (a)	**144.** (d)
145. (a)	**146.** (a)	

Type III. MCQs with One or More than one Correct Alternate

147. (a, c) 0.5 mole H_2, 1.0 mole He at STP

(a) $\overline{KE} = \frac{3}{2}\frac{R}{N_0}$, same for H_2 and He as number of moles are not involved.

(b) $u \propto \sqrt{\frac{1}{M}}$, thus different molecular speeds.

(c) 0.5 mole $H_2 = 0.5\ N_0$ molecules $= N_0$ H-atoms.

1.0 mole He $= N_0$ He-atoms. Thus, equal.

(d) Volume of 0.5 mole $H_2 = 11.2$ L at STP.

Volume of 1.0 mole He = 22.4 L at STP

Thus, different.

148. (b, c)

149. (a, b) Given, $V_1 = 50$ L, $T = 273$ K, $p = 1$ atm at STP

$V_2 = 10$ L, $T_2 = 273$ K, $p = 1$ atm at STP

$V_1 + V_2 = 50$ L in case (1) as given

$V_1 + V_2 = 10$ L in case (2) as given

Partial pressure of the gases (1) and (2) are required in both cases.

$$n_1 = \frac{pV}{RT} = \frac{1 \times 50}{0.0821 \times 273} = 2.231 \text{ mol}$$

$$n_2 = \frac{pV}{RT} = \frac{1 \times 10}{0.0821 \times 273} = 0.446 \text{ mol}$$

Case I Volume of the mixture = 50 L

$T = 273$ K

$n_1 = 2.31$ mol

$n_2 = 0.446$ mol

$$\therefore \quad p = \frac{nRT}{V}$$

$$\therefore \quad p\text{ (gas)}1 = \frac{2.231 \times 0.0821 \times 273}{50} = 1.00 \text{ atm}$$

$$p\text{ (gas 2)} = \frac{0.446 \times 0.0821 \times 273}{50} = 0.200 \text{ atm}$$

Case II Volume of the mixture = 10 L

$T = 273$ K

$n_1 = 2.31$ mol

$n_2 = 0.446$ mol

$$\therefore \quad p = \text{(gas 1)} = \frac{2.231 \times 0.0821 \times 273}{10} = 5.00 \text{ atm}$$

$$p\text{ (gas 2)} = \frac{0.446 \times 0.0821 \times 273}{10} = 1.00 \text{ atm}$$

150. (a, b, c, d) **151.** (a, c)

152. (a, b, c, d)

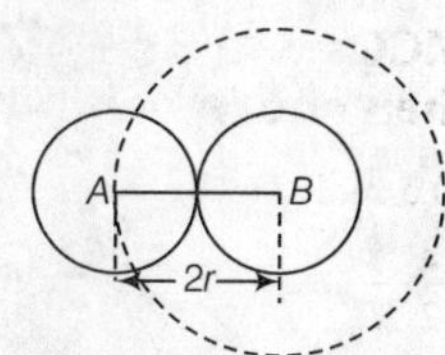

$AB = 2r$ at the point of contact.

Thus, (a) is correct.

Volume of the molecules with radius r

$$= \frac{4}{3}\pi r^3 = V$$

Volume of the molecules with radius $2r$

$$= \frac{4}{3}\pi (2r)^3 = 8\ V$$

Thus, (b) is correct.

b = also excluded volume $= 4N_0\ V$

Thus, (c) is correct.

$V_i = (V - b)$, greater the value of b greater the deviation, thus (d) is correct.

153. (b, c)

(a)

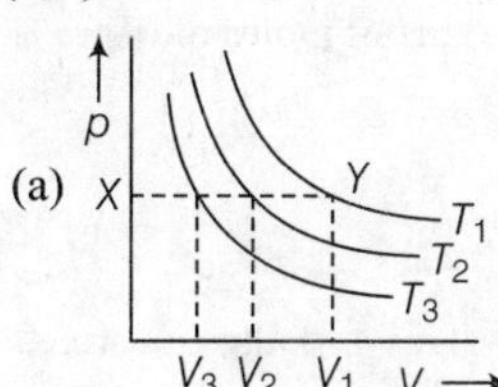

This is Boyle's law. A line (XY) at constant p, gives volume V_1, V_2 and V_3 at these temperature.

$$V_1 > V_2 > V_3$$

Thus, $\quad T_1 > T_2 > T_3$

Thus, (a) is incorrect.

(b)

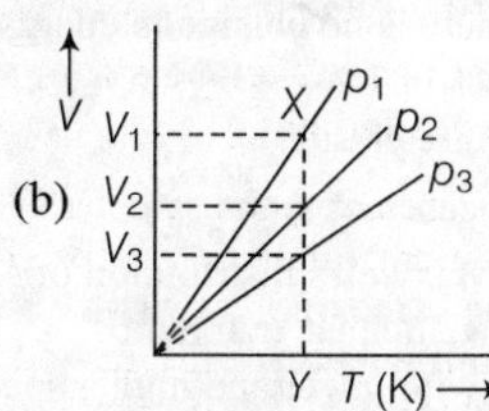

This is Charle's law. Any line XY at constant T, gives volume V_1, V_2 and V_3. Since, $V_1 > V_2 > V_3$, hence $p_1 < p_2 < p_3$. Thus, (b) is correct.

(c)

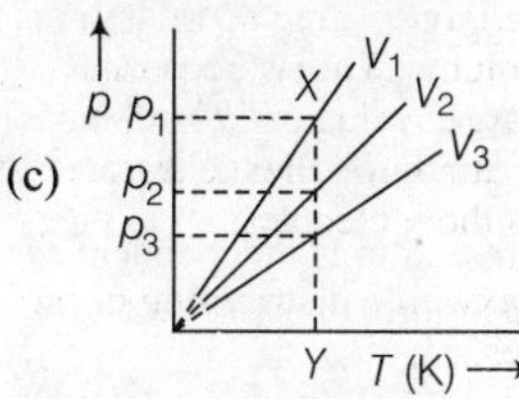

This is Gay-Lussac's law. Any line at constant temperature gives pressures p_1, p_2 and p_3.

Since, $\quad p_1 > p_2 > p_3$

hence, $\quad V_1 < V_2 < V_3$

Thus, (c) is correct.

(d)

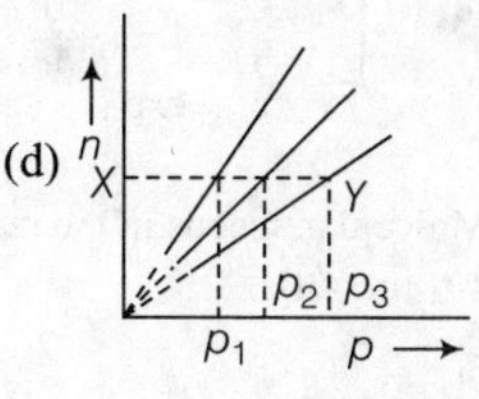

$$pV = nRT$$

At constant temperature,

$$n \propto V, p \Rightarrow p \propto \frac{n}{V}$$

Any line (XY) at constant n, gives p_1, p_2 and p_3.

As, $\quad p_1 < p_2 < p_3$,

hence $\quad V_1 > V_2 > V_3$

Thus, (d) is incorrect.

154. (b, c, d)

(a) Mass density $= \dfrac{pM}{RT}$

$$= \frac{1 \text{ atm} \times 32 \times 10^{-3} \text{kg mol}^{-1}}{0.0821 \text{ dm}^3 \text{atm mol}^{-1}\text{K}^{-1} \times 298 \text{ K}}$$

$$= 1.31 \times 10^{-3} \text{kg dm}^{-3} = 1.31 \text{kg m}^{-3}$$

Thus, (a) is incorrect.

(b) Number density $= \dfrac{pN_0}{RT}$

$$= \frac{1 \text{ atm} \times 6.02 \times 10^{23} \text{ molecules mol}^{-1}}{0.0821 \text{ dm}^3 \text{atm mol}^{-1}\text{K}^{-1} \times 298 \text{ K}}$$

$$= 2.46 \times 10^{22} \text{ molecules dm}^{-3}$$

$$= 2.46 \times 10^{25} \text{ molecules m}^{-3}$$

Thus, (b) is correct.

(c) Mass density $d = \dfrac{\text{mass}}{\text{volume}}$

Since, molar mass differs, hence density differs.

(d) Number density is independent of mass, hence same for all gases.

■ Number density is the number of molecular per unit volume.

155. (a, b, c, d)

$$\text{(a)} \quad (\text{KE}) = \frac{3}{2}RT = \frac{M}{2}\left(\frac{3RT}{M}\right) \quad \text{...(i)}$$

Since, $\quad u_{\text{rms}} = \sqrt{\dfrac{3RT}{M}}$

$$\therefore \quad u_{\text{rms}}^2 = \frac{3RT}{M} \quad \text{......(ii)}$$

$$\therefore \quad \text{KE} = \frac{M}{2}(u_{\text{rms}})^2$$

Thus, (a) is correct.

(b) $\overline{(\text{KE})} = \dfrac{3}{2}kT$

$\overline{\text{KE}}$ (average kinetic energy) is independent of mass, thus correct.

(c) $\text{KE} = \dfrac{3}{2}nRT$

$$(\text{KE})_{H_2} \text{ at 300 K} = \frac{3}{2} \times \frac{1}{2} R \times 300 = \frac{900}{4}R$$

$$(\text{KE})_{O_2} \text{ at 600 K} = \frac{3}{2} \times \frac{1}{4} R \times 600 = \frac{900}{4}R$$

Thus, correct.

(d) $\sqrt{\frac{2RT}{M}} < \sqrt{\frac{8RT}{\pi M}} < \sqrt{\frac{3RT}{M}}$

Thus, correct.

156. (a, b, d)

(a) $\varepsilon_{av} = \frac{3RT}{2N_0}$

Thus independent of molar mass.
Thus correct.

(b) $U_{rms} = \sqrt{\frac{3RT}{M}}$

$\frac{U_2}{U_1} = \sqrt{\frac{T_2}{T_1}} = \sqrt{\frac{4T_1}{T_1}} = 2$

Thus, when temperature is increased four times, U_{rms} is doubled.

Thus, correct.

(c) $\frac{(\varepsilon_{av})_2}{(\varepsilon_{av})_1} = \frac{T_2}{T_1} = \frac{4T_1}{T_1} = 4$

ε_{av} is increased four times, when temperature is increased four times.

Thus, incorrect.

(d) $U_{rms} \propto \sqrt{\frac{1}{M}}$

Thus correct.

157. (a, b, c) $T_b = \frac{a}{Rb}$, $T_c = \frac{8a}{27Rb}$

Thus, diffferent.

158. (a, c, d)

(a) $p \propto \frac{1}{V}$

But, $d = \frac{M}{V}$

$\therefore \quad p \propto d$

$\therefore \quad \frac{p_1}{d_1} = \frac{p_2}{d_2}$ or $p_1 d_2 = p_2 d_1$

Thus, (a) is correct.

(b) $p = \frac{k}{V}$

$\therefore \log p = \log k - \log V$,

Thus, incorrect.

(c) $V = kT$

$\therefore \log V = \log T + \log k$,

Thus, correct.

(d) $p \propto T$, thus $p_1 T_2 = p_2 T_1$

Thus, correct.

159. (a, b, c, d)

160. (a, c, d) This device is called eudiometer, used to compare the pressure of several gases.

Pressure p_1 of the confined gas = barometric pressure + pressure needed to depress of column of liquid = $p_{atm} + h_1 dg$

Thus, (a) is correct.

Similarly, $p_2 = p_{atm} + 0$

= barometric pressure.

Thus, (b) is incorrect and (d) is correct.

Pressure p_3 = barometric pressure – pressure to support the column of liquid = $(p_{atm} - h_3 dg)$

Thus, (c) is correct.

161. (b, c) $p_1 V_1 = n_1 R T_1$

$p_2 V_2 = n_2 R T_2$

If, $V_1 = V_2$, $n_1 = n_2 = 1$ mol

$\frac{p_1}{p_2} = \frac{T_1}{T_2}$

(a) $\frac{p_1}{p_1/2} = \frac{T_1}{2T_1}$

Thus, gives 4 = 1, thus incorrect.

(b) This is correct.

(c) This is correct.

(d) This is incorrect.

162. (a, b) Due to expansion, volumeincreases and pressure decreases, thus (a) is correct.

KE $\propto T$, thus (b) is correct.

163. (a, c, d) There is no change in energy due to collisions.

Thus, they are elastic.

Thus, (a) is correct.

Based on Maxwell's distribution of molecular velocities, number of molecules with lower and higher speeds is small. Thus, (c) is correct.

After collisions, molecules move in a straight line.

Thus, (d) is correct.

164. (a, b, c)

$\frac{r_{H_2}}{r_{He}} = \sqrt{\frac{M_2}{M_1}} = \sqrt{\frac{4}{2}} = \sqrt{2}$

(a) Relative ratio is independent of temperature, thus (a) is correct.

(b) $\frac{r_{CH_4}}{r_{O_2}} = \sqrt{\frac{32}{16}} = \sqrt{2}$

Thus, correct.

(c) is correct.

(d) Motion ceases at 0 K, thus incorrect.

165. (a, b, d)

$\frac{r_{H_2}}{r_{O_2}} = \left(\frac{100/10}{X/t}\right) = \sqrt{\frac{32}{2}} = 4 \Rightarrow \frac{10t}{X} = 4$

$\therefore \quad \frac{X}{t} = 2.5$

(a) $\frac{100}{40} = 2.5$ correct

(b) $\frac{25}{10} = 2.5$ correct

(c) $\frac{100}{10} = 10$ incorrect

(d) $\frac{5}{2} = 2.5$ correct

166. (a, b, c, d)

(a) For H_2, $Z > 1$
Thus, correct.

(b) upto 150 atm for N_2, $Z < 1$
Thus, correct.

(c) For CO_2, $Z < 1$ even at high p.
Thus, correct.

(d) $Z = 1$, when curves intersect at a particular pressure. Thus, correct.

167. (a, b) van der Waals' equation can be written as

$$pV = RT\left[1 + \frac{1}{V}\left(b - \frac{a}{RT}\right) + \dots\right]$$

At $T = T_b = \frac{a}{Rb}$

$$\therefore \; pV = RT\left[1 + \frac{1}{V}\left(b - \frac{a}{R(a/Rb)}\right)\right] \dots +$$

$pV = RT$, thus ideal gas.

Thus, at $T = T_b$ attractive forces just balance the repulsive forces and gas behaves ideally.

168. (a, c) Virial equation of state is

$$pV = RT\left[1 + \frac{B}{V} + \dots\right]$$

$$\therefore \quad Z = \frac{pV}{RT} = \left[1 + \frac{B}{V} + \dots\right] = 1 + \frac{Bp}{RT}$$

$$Z(N_2) = 1 + \frac{-4.2 \times 10^{-3}\,\text{L} \times 100\ \text{atm}}{0.0821\ \text{L atm mol}^{-1}\text{K}^{-1} \times 300\ \text{K}}$$

$= 0.9829$

Similarly, $Z(CH_4) = 0.94$

Thus, N_2 gas approaches ideal behaviour.

Thus, (a) is correct and (b) is incorrect.

Molar volume $\bar{V}(N_2) = \frac{ZRT}{p}$

$= \frac{0.9829 \times 0.0821 \times 300}{100}$

$= 0.242$ L

Similarly, $\bar{V}(CH_4) = 0.2315$ L

Thus, (c) is correct and (d) is incorrect.

169. (b, c, d) $pV_m = RT\left(1 + \frac{B}{V_m} + \frac{C}{V_m^2} + \dots\right)$

van der Waals' equation in terms of virial equation is

$$pV_m = RT\left[1 + \frac{1}{V_m}\left(b - \frac{a}{RT}\right) + \dots\right]$$

Thus, $B = \left(b - \frac{a}{RT}\right)$

Thus, B depends on temperature, thus (a) is incorrect and (d) is correct.

At $T = T_b = \frac{a}{Rb}$, $B = 0$ thus (b) is correct.

B represents molar volume (as it has unit of volume), thus (c) is correct.

170. (a, c, d)

$$\underset{1\text{ mol}}{CS_2} + \underset{3\text{ mol}}{3O_2} \longrightarrow \underset{2\text{ mol}}{2SO_2} + \underset{1\text{ mol}}{CO_2}$$

O_2 taken = 4 mol

O_2 used by 1 mol CS_2 = 3 mol

Thus, unreacted O_2 = 1 mol

Total moles of gaseous (O_2, SO_2 and CO_2) products = 4

$\therefore$ $X_{O_2} = 0.25$

$X_{CO_2} = 0.25$

$X_{SO_2} = 0.50 = 2X_{CO_2}$ or $2X_{O_2}$

Thus, (a) is correct,

(b) is incorrect

(c) is correct.

$$(d)\, p = \frac{n}{V}RT = \frac{4 \times 0.08314 \times 400}{5}$$

$$= 26.6 \text{ bar}$$

Thus, (d) is correct.

171. (b, d)

$$2NaHCO_3 \xrightarrow{\Delta} Na_2CO_3 + H_2O + CO_2$$

$$Na_2CO_3 \xrightarrow{\Delta} \text{no effect}$$

Thus, CO_2 is due to $NaHCO_3$.

$$n_{CO_2} = \frac{pV}{RT} = \frac{8.314 \times 3}{0.08314 \times 300} = 1 \text{ mol}$$

Thus, $NaHCO_3$ used = 2 mol

Na_2CO_3 in mixture = 1 mol

$X_{NaHCO_3} = 2/3$

$Na_2CO_3 = 1/3$

Thus, (a) and (c) are incorrect and (b) is correct.

$$\underset{1\text{ mol}}{NaHCO_3} + \underset{2\text{ mol}}{HCl} \longrightarrow NaCl + CO_2 + H_2O$$

$$\underset{1\text{ mol}}{Na_2CO_3} + 2HCl \longrightarrow 2NaCl + H_2O + \underset{1\text{ mol}}{CO_2}$$

Thus, pressure due to 3 mole CO_2.

$$p = \frac{3 \times 0.08314 \times 300}{3} = 24.942 \text{ bar}$$

Thus, (d) is correct.

172. (a, b, c, d)

$$u_{rms} = \sqrt{\frac{3RT}{M}}$$

$$\therefore \quad \Delta u_{rms} = \left(\frac{3R}{M}\right)^{1/2} [T_2^{1/2} - T_1^{1/2}]$$

Thus, (a) is correct.

$$\frac{du_{rms}}{dT} = \frac{3}{2}\frac{R}{M}\sqrt{\frac{M}{3RT}} = \left(\frac{1.5R}{Mu_{rms}}\right)$$

Thus, (b) is correct.

$$(\overline{KE}) = \frac{3}{2}kT$$

$$\therefore \quad \Delta(\overline{KE}) = \frac{3}{2}k[T_2 - T_1]$$

Thus, (c) is correct.

$$\frac{d(\text{KE})}{dT} = \frac{3}{2}k = \frac{3}{2}\frac{kT}{T} = \frac{(\overline{KE})}{T}$$

Thus, (d) is correct.

173. (c, d) Equation can be straight line

$$y = c - mx$$

where $c = \frac{V}{V - b}$ and m (slope) $= \frac{a}{VR}$

(a) At 40 atm, $\frac{pV}{RT} < 1$, but > 0

$$\left(\frac{V}{V - b}\right) \neq \frac{a}{VRT}$$

Thus, (a) is incorrect.

(b) At 80 atm, $\frac{pV}{RT} = 1$

$$\text{Thus, } \left(\frac{V}{V - b}\right) - \frac{a}{VRT} = 1$$

Thus, (b) is incorrect.

(c) At $p > 80$ atm, $\frac{pV}{RT} > 1$

$$\text{Thus, } \frac{V}{(V - b)} > \frac{a}{VRT}$$

Thus, (c) is correct.

(d) At 60 atm,

$$\frac{pV}{RT} < 1. \text{ but } > 0$$

$$\text{Thus, } \left(\frac{V}{V - b}\right) \text{ is smaller than } \left(1 + \frac{a}{VRT}\right)$$

Thus, (d) is correct.

174. (b, c, d) Second virial coefficient

$$B = \left(b - \frac{a}{RT}\right)$$

when $B = 0$, $T_b = \frac{a}{Rb}$

Thus, (b) and (c) are correct.

T_b depends on 'a' and 'b' and thus nature of the gas thus (d) is correct.

175. (a, b, c) $u_{av} = \sqrt{\frac{8RT}{\pi M}}$, $u_{rms} = \sqrt{\frac{3RT}{M}}$

For H_2 at 300 K,

$(u_{rms} - u_{av}) = 1934 - 1782 = 152 \text{ m s}^{-1}$

For a gas of molar mass 80,

$(u_{rms} - u_{av}) = 306 - 281 = 25 \text{ m s}^{-1}$

Thus, difference decreases.

Thus, (a) is correct.

$$(\text{KE})_{av} = \frac{3}{2}\frac{RT}{N_0}$$

It is independent molar mass.

Thus, (b) is correct

$$\frac{u_{rms}}{u_{av}} = \sqrt{\frac{3RT/M}{8RT/\pi M}} = \sqrt{\frac{3\pi}{8}}$$

independent of temperature.

Thus, (c) is correct.

$$\left(\sqrt{\frac{8RT}{\pi M}}\right)^2 \neq \sqrt{\frac{3RT}{M}}$$

Thus, (d) is incorrect.

176. (a, b) Most probable velocity

$$u_{mp} = \sqrt{\frac{2pV}{M}}$$

At point (2),

$$pV = 6p_0V_0,\ u_{mp} = \sqrt{\frac{12p_0V_0}{M}}$$

At point (3),

$$pV = 3p_0V_0,\ u_{mp} = \sqrt{\frac{6p_0V_0}{M}}$$

Thus, (a) is correct.

At point (4),

$$pV = 2p_0V_0,\ u_{mp} = \sqrt{\frac{4p_0V_0}{M}}$$

At point (1),

$$pV = 2p_0V_0,\ u_{mp} = \sqrt{\frac{4p_0V_0}{M}}$$

Thus, (b) is correct.

u_{mp} at 1 $\neq$ u_{mp} at 3, thus (c) is incorrect.

u_{mp} at 1 < u_{mp} at 2, thus (d) is incorrect.

177. (a, b, d)

178. (a, b, c, d) The mean relative speed is the speed with which one molecule approaches another of the same kind.

$$u_{relative} = 4\sqrt{\frac{RT}{\pi M}} = \sqrt{\frac{16RT}{\pi M}}$$

$$= \sqrt{2 \times \frac{8RT}{\pi M}} = \sqrt{2}\, u_{av}$$

Thus, (a), (b), (c) and (d) are correct.

179. (a, b, c, d) $Z = \frac{p_cV_c}{RT_c}$

(a) $Z = \frac{3}{8}$ correct

(b) $Z = \frac{3}{8}$ correct

(c) is correct

(d) is correct

180. (a, c)

(a) Total moles = 3

$\therefore p_{\text{total}}(\text{before}) = \dfrac{nRT}{V}$

$= \dfrac{3 \times 0.08314 \times 273}{22.4}$

$= 3.04$ bar

Thus, (a) is correct.

$$\begin{array}{lccc} & N_2 & + 3H_2 \longrightarrow & 2NH_3 \\ & 1\text{ mol} & 3\text{ mol} & 2\text{ mol} \\ & 1\text{ mol} & 2\text{ mol} & \\ & \left(1-\frac{2}{3}\right)\text{ mol} & 0\text{ mol} & \frac{4}{3}\text{ mol} \end{array}$$

Thus, N_2 unreacted $= \dfrac{1}{3}$ mol

NH_3 formed $= \dfrac{4}{3}$ mol

Total moles $= \dfrac{1}{3} + \dfrac{4}{3} = \dfrac{5}{3}$

Number of moles decreases thus total pressure changes.

$p\,(\text{after reaction}) = \dfrac{nRT}{V}$

$= \dfrac{5/3 \times 0.0831 \times 273}{22.4} = 1.69$ atm

Thus, (b) is incorrect and (d) is also incorrect.

$\therefore \quad X_{NH_3} = \dfrac{4}{5}$

Thus, partial pressure of NH_3 is also maximum.

Thus, (c) is correct.

181. (a, b, c, d) In terms of critical constants,

$$Z = \frac{p_c V_c}{RT_c} = \frac{3}{8}$$

$$\therefore \left(\frac{dZ}{dT_c}\right)_{p_c, V_c} = -\frac{p_c V_c}{RT_c^2} = -\left(\frac{p_c V_c}{RT_c}\right)\frac{1}{T_c}$$

$$= -\frac{3}{8} \times \frac{1}{300} = -\frac{1}{800}$$

Thus, (a) is correct.

$$\left(\frac{dZ}{dp_c}\right) = \frac{V_c}{RT_c} \Rightarrow \left(\frac{dZ}{dV_c}\right) = \frac{p_c}{RT_c}$$

$$\therefore p_c\left(\frac{dZ}{dp_c}\right)_{T_c, V_c} = V_c\left(\frac{dZ}{dV_c}\right)_{p_c, T_c} = \frac{3}{8}$$

Thus, (b) is correct.

$$\frac{p_c V_c}{RT_c} = \frac{3}{8}$$

$$\therefore \quad V_c = \frac{3}{8}\frac{RT_c}{p_c}$$

$$\therefore \log V_c = \log T_c + \log \frac{3}{8}\left(\frac{R}{p_c}\right)$$

compared to $y = mx + c$

$$\therefore \quad OX = \log\left(\frac{3}{8}\frac{R}{p_c}\right) = 0.6990$$

$$\therefore \quad \frac{3}{8}\left(\frac{R}{p_c}\right) = 5.0$$

$$p_c = \frac{3R}{40} = \frac{3 \times 0.0831}{40}$$

$$= 6.2 \times 10^{-3} \text{ bar}$$

Thus, (c) incorrect.

Slope = 1 = tan θ = tan 45°

Thus, (d) is correct.

182. (a, b, c, d)

$$Z = \frac{pV}{nRT}$$

$$\therefore \quad \left(\frac{dZ}{dp}\right)_{T,V,n} = \frac{V}{nRT}$$

$$\therefore \quad p\left(\frac{dZ}{dp}\right)_{T,V,n} = \frac{pV}{nRT} = Z$$

Thus, (a) is correct.

Similarly,

$$V\left(\frac{dZ}{dV}\right)_{p,T,n} = Z$$

Thus, (b) is correct.

$$\left(\frac{dZ}{dT}\right)_{p,\,V,\,n} = -\frac{pV}{nRT^2} = -\frac{pV}{nRT}\left(\frac{1}{T}\right)$$

$$\therefore \quad T\left(\frac{dZ}{dT}\right)_{p,V,n} = -Z$$

Thus, (c) is correct.

Similarly,

$$n\left(\frac{dZ}{dn}\right)_{p,V,T} = -Z$$

Thus, (d) is correct.

183. (a, b) Distribution of molecular velocities is given by

$$P = \frac{1}{N}\left(\frac{dN}{du}\right) = 4\pi u^2\left(\frac{B}{\pi}\right)^{3/2} e^{-Bu^2}$$

where $B = \left(\dfrac{M}{2RT}\right)$, P = Probability

when $\dfrac{dP}{du} = 0$, $u = \sqrt{\dfrac{2RT}{M}}$

u is called most probable velocity.

In terms of virial coefficient, van der Waals' equation is

$$p = \frac{RT}{V}\left[1 + \frac{1}{V}\left(b - \frac{a}{RT}\right) + \ldots.\right]$$

Virial equation is

$$p = \frac{RT}{V}\left[1 + \frac{B}{V} + \frac{C}{V^2} + \ldots.\right]$$

On comparison, $B = \left(b - \dfrac{a}{RT}\right)$

when $B = 0$,

$$b = \frac{a}{RT}$$

T_b is called Boyle's temperature $T_b = \dfrac{a}{Rb}$

$$\therefore \quad T_b = \frac{a}{Rb}$$

For real gases, $Z \neq 1$, thus, (c) is incorrect.

$T_i = 2T_b$ thus, (d) is incorrect.

184. (a, b)

$$\begin{array}{lccc} & N_2 & + 3H_2 \longrightarrow & 2NH_3 \\ & 1\text{ mol} & 3\text{ mol} & 2\text{ mol} \\ \text{Given,} & 1\text{ mol} & 4\text{ mol} & \\ \text{After reaction} & 0 & 1\text{ mol} & 2\text{ mol} \end{array}$$

Total moles before reaction = 5

Total pressure $= \dfrac{nRT}{V}$

$= \dfrac{5 \times 0.08314 \times 300}{25}$

$= 5.0$ bar

$X_{N_2} = \dfrac{1}{5}$

$\therefore \quad p_{N_2} = X_{N_2}, p_T = 1$ bar.

Thus, (a) is correct.

After reaction

Unreacted $N_2 = 0$ mol,

Unreacted $H_2 = 1$ mol,

NH_3 formed = 2 mol

Thus, $\quad p_{NH_3} > p_{H_2}$

Thus, (b) is correct.

After H_2O is added, all the NH_3 dissolved in H_2O, but H_2 remains insoluble.

Also, volume of empty flask = 15 L

(Due to addition of 10 L H_2O)

$\therefore \quad p = \dfrac{nRT}{V} = \dfrac{1 \times 0.0831 \times 300}{15}$

$= 1.67$ bar

Thus, (c) is incorrect

Since, there is no NH_3, hence

$X_{NH_3} = 0$

Thus, (d) is incorrect.

185. (a, b, c)

$$u_{\text{mp}} = \sqrt{\frac{2RT}{M}}$$

$$\frac{du_{\text{mp}}}{dT} = \frac{1}{2}\left(\frac{2R}{M}\right)\left(\frac{2RT}{M}\right)^{-1/2}$$

$$= \left(\frac{R}{M\,u_{\text{mp}}}\right)$$

Thus, (a) is correct.

$$u_{\text{av}} = \sqrt{\frac{8RT}{\pi M}}$$

$$\therefore \quad \frac{du_{av}}{dT} = \frac{1}{2}\left(\frac{8RT}{\pi M}\right)^{-\frac{1}{2}} \frac{8R}{\pi M} = \frac{4R}{\pi M\, u_{av}}$$

Thus, (b) is correct.

$$u_{rms} = \sqrt{\frac{3RT}{M}}$$

$$\therefore \quad \frac{du_{rms}}{dT} = \frac{1}{2}\left(\frac{3RT}{M}\right)^{-\frac{1}{2}}\left(\frac{3R}{M}\right) = \frac{3R}{2\,Mu_{rms}}$$

Thus, (c) is correct and (d) is incorrect.

186. (a, b, c, d)

H_2 and He are light gases with no force of attraction.

Thus, $\frac{a}{V^2}=0$

$\therefore$ $p(V-b)=RT$

$pV - bp = RT$

$pV = pb + RT$

$\therefore$ $Z=\frac{pV}{RT}=\left(\frac{pb+RT}{RT}\right)$

Thus, (a) is correct.

(b) For ideal gas, $\frac{pV}{RT}=1=Z.$

Thus, (b) is correct.

(c) In lower pressure range, along AB, of isotherm I, volume is high.

Hence, $(V-b)\approx V$

$\therefore$ $V\left(p+\frac{a}{V^2}\right)=RT$

$pV = RT - \frac{a}{V}$

$\therefore$ $Z=\frac{pV}{RT}=\frac{RTV-a}{RTV}$

Thus, (c) is correct.

(d) Under high pressure, V is low

$\therefore$ $\left(p+\frac{a}{V^2}\right)\approx p$

$\therefore$ $p(V-b)=RT$

$\therefore$ $Z=\frac{pV}{RT}=\frac{pb+RT}{RT}$

Thus, (d) is correct.

187. (c, d)

$V_c=3b$

Since, b of $X<b$ of Y, thus (a) is incorrect.

Thus, (c) is correct.

$$p_c=\frac{a}{27b^2}$$

$$p_c(X)=\frac{7.1}{27(8.20^{-3})^2}=3911 \text{ bar mol}^{-1}$$

$$p_c(Y)=\frac{19.91}{27[(1.7\times10^{-2})^2]}=2560 \text{ bar mol}^{-1}$$

Thus, $p_c(X)>p_c(Y)$

Thus, (b) is incorrect.

$T_b(\text{Boyle's})=\frac{a}{Rb}$, $T_b(X)<T_b(Y)$

Thus, (d) is correct.

188. (a, c)

189. (a, c, d) $\frac{r_1}{r_2}=\frac{p_1}{p_2}\sqrt{\frac{m_2}{m_1}}=\frac{n_1}{n_2}\sqrt{\frac{m_2}{m_1}}$

$$\therefore \quad \frac{r_{He}}{r_{CH_4}}=\frac{1}{2}\sqrt{\frac{16}{4}}=\frac{1}{1}$$

$$\frac{r_{He}}{r_{SO_2}}=\frac{1}{4}\sqrt{\frac{64}{4}}=\frac{1}{1}$$

Thus, (a) is correct.

Also number of moles coming out of hole are in 1:1:1 molar ratio.

Also, total moles coming out of hole =3

$$\therefore \quad X_{He}=X_{SO_2}=X_{CH_4}=\frac{1}{3}$$

Thus (b) is incorrect.

Thus, (c) and (d) are correct.

190. (b, c) $(DC)\propto\lambda$ (mean free path)

$\propto u_{av}$

Thus, $(DC)\propto\frac{RTu_{av}}{\sqrt{2}N_0\sigma p}$

But $u_{av}\propto\sqrt{T}$

$\therefore$ $(DC)\propto\frac{T^{3/2}}{p}$

If T is made 4 times and pressure is doubled, then (DC) becomes 4 times

$$(DC)\propto\frac{(8)^{3/2}}{2}=4$$

191. (a, b, c) If $\frac{p}{p_c}=\pi$, $\frac{V}{V_c}=\phi$ and $\frac{T}{T_c}=\theta$

then, $\left(p+\frac{a}{V^2}\right)(V-b)=RT$

is $\left(p_c\pi+\frac{a}{V_c^2\phi^2}\right)(V_c\phi-b)=RT_c\theta$

As, $p_c=\frac{a}{27b^2}$, $V_c=3b$ and $T_c=\frac{8a}{27Rb}$

$$\therefore \left(\frac{a}{27b^2}\pi+\frac{a}{9b^2\phi^2}\right)(3b\phi-b)=\frac{8a}{27Rb}\cdot R\theta$$

$$\left(\pi+\frac{3}{\phi^2}\right)(3\phi-1)=8\theta$$

This is independent of 'a', 'b'. Thus, (a) is correct. It can be applied to any state of matter as it has no T, p and V variables.

Thus, (b) is correct.

Equation (c) is correct.

Type IV. Numerical Skills

192. **(750)** Temperature and number of moles are constant, thus Boyle's law is applicable.

$\therefore$ $p_2V_2=p_1V_1$

$$\therefore \quad p_2=\frac{p_1V_1}{V_2}=\frac{48\times10^{-3}\times\frac{4}{3}\pi r_1^2}{\frac{4}{3}\pi r_2^2}$$

$$=\frac{48\times10^{-3}\times(3)^3}{(12)^3}$$

$$p_2=750\times10^{-6}\text{ bar}$$

193. **One (1)** Since, $p=\frac{dRT}{m}$

$$\frac{d_{top}}{d_{bottom}}=\frac{T_bP_t}{T_tP_b}=\frac{292\times710}{273\times760}=1.0$$

194. **Four (4)** We use, $pV=nRT$

$(pV)_{H_2}=n_{H_2}RT_{H_2}$

$=n_{H_2}R(373)$

$\left(\frac{pV}{2}\right)_{He}=n_{He}R(298)=\left(\frac{5}{4}\right)R(298)$

Also, $p_{H_2}=p_{He}$

$$\therefore \quad \frac{373\times n_{H_2}\times4}{298\times5.00}=2$$

$$n_{H_2}=2.0\text{ mol}=4\text{ g }H_2$$

195. **Three (3)**

Mass (methane) = volume (flask) × density

$=10\text{ m}^3\times415\text{ kg m}^{-3}$

$=4150$ kg

$=\frac{4150\times10^3}{16}$ mol

$V(\text{new})=\frac{nRT}{p}$

$$=\frac{4150\times10^3\text{ mol}\times0.0821\text{ L atm mol}^{-1}\text{ K}^{-1}\times293\text{ K}}{16\times1\text{ atm}}$$

$=6.24\times10^6\text{ L}=6.24\times10^6\times10^3\text{ cm}^3$

$=6.24\times10^3\text{ m}^3=y\times10^x\text{ m}^3$

$\therefore$ $x=3$

■ 1 L = 1 dm^3 = 1× 10^{-3} m^3

196. **(6.15)**

Aluminium reacts with sulphuric acid to form aluminium sulphate and hydrogen.

$$\underset{\left(\frac{5.7}{27}=0.2\text{ mol}\right)}{2Al}+\underset{\left(\frac{50\times5}{1000}=0.25\text{ mol}\right)}{3H_2SO_4}\longrightarrow Al_2(SO_4)_3+3H_2$$

H_2SO_4 is limiting reagent and moles of $H_2(g)$ produced = 0.25 mol

Using ideal gas equation :

$$pV=nRT$$

$$V=\frac{0.25\times0.082\times300}{1\text{ atm}}\Rightarrow 6.15\text{ L}$$

197. **Two (2)** $V_{(room)} = 6 \times 6 \times 6 = 216\ m^3$

$= 216 \times 10^3$ L

$p = 19.26 \times \frac{50}{100} = 9.63$ Torr

$= \frac{9.63}{760}$ atm

$\therefore\ n = \frac{pV}{RT}$

$= \frac{\frac{9.63}{760} \text{ atm} \times 216 \times 10^3 \text{ L}}{0.0821 \text{ L atm mol}^{-1} \text{ K}^{-1} \times 300 \text{ K}}$

$= 111.12$

$= 111.12 \times 18$ g mole water vapour

$= 2000$ g $= 2 \times 10^3$ kg $= x \times 10^3$ kg

Thus, $x = 2$

198. **Seven (7)** 0.75 mol of 'A_4' means 3 atoms of A.

2 mol of O_2 means 4 atoms of O. Product formed exerts considerable pressure indicating that product is a gas. Pressure exerted by product $= \frac{1}{2}$ of O_2.

$\underset{0.75 \text{ mol}}{A_4(s)} + \underset{2 \text{ mol}}{O_2(g)} \longrightarrow$ Product

Since, pressure α is proportional to number of moles hence product formed is one mol (half of O_2 taken due to half of the pressure exerted by product). Hence, product is A_3O_4.

Total numbers of atoms of A and O = 7

199. **Nine (9)** Initial pressure is due to air only

$p_1 = \frac{nRT}{V} = \frac{RT}{V}$

After radioactive decay

${}^{238}_{92}U \longrightarrow {}^{206}_{82}Pb + 8\alpha + 6\beta$

α-particles are $\left({}^4_2He\right)^{2+}$ nuclei

and pressure is exerted due to helium.

Thus, α-particles from 1 mole U = 8 mol

Total moles of air and He = 9 mol

$\therefore\ p_2 = \frac{nRT}{V} = 9RT/V$

Thus, ratio $= \frac{9RT/V}{RT/V} = 9$

200. **Three (3)** van der Waals' equation for one mole of gas is

$\left(p + \frac{a}{V^2}\right)(V - b) = RT$

At 300 K, $b = 0$

$\therefore\ pV + \frac{a}{V} = RT$

$pV = \left(RT - \frac{a}{V}\right)$

At $\frac{1}{V} = 2.0$, $pV = 23.1$

and at $\frac{1}{V} = 3.0$, $pV = 20.1$

$\therefore$ $20.1 = RT - 3a$

$23.1 = RT - 2a$

$\therefore$ $a = 3.0$

201. **Four (4)** $(RMS)_X$ at 400 K = $(MPS)_Y$ at 60 K

$\sqrt{\frac{3RT_1}{M_1}} = \sqrt{\frac{2RT_2}{M_2}}$

$\sqrt{\frac{3R \times 400}{40}} = \sqrt{\frac{2R \times 60}{M_2}}$

$\therefore\ M_2 = \frac{2 \times 60 \times 40}{3 \times 400} = 4$ g mol^{-1}

202. **Six (6)** $n(H_2) = \frac{2.0}{2.0} = 1.0$

$n(He) = \frac{10.0}{4.0} = 2.5$

Total moles = 3.5

$X_{He} = \frac{2.5}{3.5} = \frac{5}{7}$

$p_{total} = \frac{nRT}{V} = \frac{3.5 \times 0.0821 \times 293}{10.0}$

$= 8.42$ atm

$\therefore\ p_{He} = X_{He} \cdot p_{total} = \frac{5}{7} \times 8.42$

$= 6.0$ atm

203. **Seven (7)** When force of attraction are neglected in real gas, van der Waals' equation,

$\frac{a}{V^2} = 0$

$\therefore\ \left(p + \frac{a}{V^2}\right)(V - b) = RT$

reduces to

$p(V - b) = RT$

$pV = RT + pb$

$V = \frac{RT}{p} + b$

Graph between V and T at constant pressure is a straight line.

Slope $\frac{R}{p} = 0.0117$ L mol^{-1} K^{-1}

$p = \frac{0.0821 \text{ L atm mol}^{-1} \text{ K}^{-1}}{0.0117 \text{ L mol}^{-1} \text{ K}^{-1}} = 7$atm

204. **Two (2)** Based on above Q. No. (203)

Intercept $OA = b = 2.0$ L mol^{-1}

Thus, $b = 2$

205. **(2127)** By gas equation

$pV = nRT$

$\therefore\ n = \frac{pV}{RT}$

Thus, number of moles of $O_2(g)$ that occupy 492 L at 1 atm and 300 K is

$n(O_2) = \frac{1 \times 492}{0.0821 \times 300}$

$= 19.976$ mol

By chemical reaction

1 mol $O_2 \equiv$ 1 mol $NaClO_3$

Thus, 19.976 mol O_2 = 19.976 mol $NaClO_3$

Molar mass of $NaClO_3 = 23 + 35.5 + 48$
$= 106.5$ g mol^{-1}

Thus, $NaClO_3$ required

$= 19.976 \times 106.5$ g $= 2127$ g

206. **Three (3)** For n moles of an ideal

$Z = \frac{pV}{nRT}$

$Z = \frac{pV}{\frac{w}{M}RT} = \frac{pM}{dRT} \cdot \left(\frac{w}{V} = d\right)$

At 1 bar (= 1×10^5 Pa),

boiling point = 373 K

$\therefore\ Z = \frac{1 \times 10^5 \times 18 \times 10^{-3}}{0.6 \times 8.314 \times 373} = 0.97$

Normal value under ideal condition = 1.00

Deviation = 0.03

Thus, % deviation = 3%

■ All units are in MKS

M (molar mass of H_2O) = 18×10^{-3} kg mol^{-1}

$R = 8.314$ J mol^{-1} K^{-1}

1 Pa = 1 kg m^{-1} s^{-2}

1 J = 1 kg m^2 s^{-2}

207. **Nine (9)**

$pV = nRT \Rightarrow \frac{V}{n} = \frac{RT}{p}$

Since, T and p remain unchanged

hence $\left(\frac{V}{n}\right)_{initial} = \left(\frac{V}{n}\right)_{final}$

$\frac{\frac{4}{3}\pi r_1^3}{\left(\frac{1}{4}\right)} = \frac{\frac{4}{3}\pi r_2^3}{\left(\frac{0.75}{4}\right)}$

$0.75\,(10)^3 = (r_2)^3$

$\therefore\ r_2^3 = 750$

$r = 9.08$ cm ≈ 9.0 cm

208. **(2.6)**

Lift capacity = mass of cold air − mass of hot air

$pV = nRT$

$$pV = \frac{w}{M}RT$$

$$\therefore \quad w = \frac{pVM}{RT}$$

$$\Delta w = \frac{pV}{R}\left(\frac{1}{T_{cold}} - \frac{1}{T_{hot}}\right)\cdot M$$

$$1000\ g = \frac{1 \times 10^5\ Pa \times 100\ m^3}{8.314\ Pa\ m^3\ mol^{-1}\ K^{-1}}$$

$$\left[\frac{1}{298} - \frac{1}{T_{hot}}\right]\cdot 29 g\ mol^{-1}$$

$$T_{hot} = 300.6 \approx 301\ K$$

$\therefore$ Difference in temperature

$$= 300.6 - 298\ K = 2.6\ K$$

209. Two (2)

p_1 (due to O_2 only as carbon is solid)

$$= \frac{1.23\ RT}{V}$$

	2C	+	$O_2 \longrightarrow$	2CO
Initial	2.73 mol		1.23 mol	
After	(2.73 – 2.46) mol		0 mol	2.46 mol

CO formed = 2.46 mol.

All O_2 is consumed. Thus, final pressure is due to CO only.

$$\therefore \quad p_2 = 2.46\frac{RT}{V}$$

$$\therefore \quad \frac{p_2}{p_1} = 2.0$$

210. Nine (9)

$$pV = nRT$$

$$n = \frac{pV}{RT}$$

$$n_1\ (\text{initial}) = \frac{p_1V}{RT}$$

$$n_2\ (\text{final}) = \frac{p_2V}{RT}$$

Thus, CO_2 escaped.

$$(n_1 - n_2) = (p_1 - p_2)\frac{V}{RT}$$

$$= (6.0 - 1.5)\frac{50}{0.0821 \times 304.5}$$

$$= 9.0\ mol$$

211. Five (5) At constant temperature for a fixed amount

$$V \propto \frac{1}{p}$$

$$V = \frac{k}{p}$$

$$\therefore \quad \left(\frac{\partial V}{\partial p}\right)_{T,n} = -\frac{k}{p^2} = -\frac{pV}{p^2} = -\frac{V}{p}$$

$$\therefore \quad -\frac{1}{V}\left(\frac{\partial V}{\partial p}\right)_{T,n} = \frac{1}{p}$$

At 0.2 bar

$$-\frac{1}{V}\left(\frac{\partial V}{\partial p}\right)_{T,n} = \frac{1}{0.2} = 5\ bar^{-1}$$

212. Four (4) Diffusion coefficient (DC)

$\propto \lambda$ (mean free path)

$\propto U$ (mean speed)

$\therefore$ DC $\propto \lambda U$

But $\lambda = \frac{RT}{\sqrt{2}\, N_0 \sigma P}$ (N_0, σ constant)

$$\therefore \quad \lambda \propto \frac{T}{p}$$

$$U_{mean} = \sqrt{\frac{8RT}{\pi M}}$$

$$U_{mean} \propto \sqrt{T}$$

$$\therefore \quad DC \propto \frac{T}{p}\sqrt{T} \propto \frac{(T)^{3/2}}{p}$$

$$\frac{(DC)_2}{(DC)_1} = \frac{(4T)^{3/2}}{2p}\cdot\frac{p}{(T)^{3/2}} = 4$$

$$\therefore \quad x = 4$$

213. Seven (7)

Pressure of the gas = 1 atm

(as external pressure is 1 atm)

$$p_{He} + p_{unknown} = 1\ atm$$

$$p_{He} + 0.68 = 1\ atm$$

$$p_{He} = 0.32\ atm$$

$$pV = nRT$$

$$\therefore \quad V = \frac{nRT}{p} = \frac{0.1 \times 0.0821 \times 273}{0.32} = 7\ L$$

■ $0.0821 \times 273 = 22.4$

214. (40)

Separation factor required is

$$= \frac{\text{Relative ratio of concentration after enrichment}}{\text{Relative ratio of concentration before enrichment}}$$

$$= \frac{35\% \left({}^1_1H\,{}^2_1H\right)}{65\% \left({}^1_1H\right)} \bigg/ \frac{0.02\%\ {}^2_1H}{99.98\%\ {}^1_1H}$$

$$= \frac{35 \times 99.98}{65 \times 0.02} = 2692$$

Based on rate of diffusion, single step separation factor is

$$\frac{r_{(H_2)}}{r_{\left({}^1_1H\,{}^2_1H\right)}} = \sqrt{\frac{3}{2}} = 1.2247$$

If enrichment requires n-steps

then, $(1.2247)^n = 2692$

$$n \log 1.2247 = \log 2692$$

$$n \times 0.088 = 3.43 \Rightarrow n = 40$$

215. Three (3)

By kinetic molecular theory

$$pV = \frac{1}{3}mNu^2$$

$$\therefore \quad p = \frac{1}{3}\frac{mNu^2}{V}$$

$$= \frac{1 \times 1 \times 10^{-25} \times 9 \times 10^{24} \times (1 \times 10^3)^2}{3 \times 1}$$

$$= 3 \times 10^5\ pa = 3.0\ bar$$

■ All values are in MKS, thus pressure is in kg m^{-1} s^{-2} (Pascal) 1×10^5 Pa = 1 bar

216. Three (3) $u_{rms} = \sqrt{\frac{3RT}{M}} = \left(\frac{3RT}{M}\right)^{1/2}$

$$\therefore \quad \frac{du_{rms}}{dT} = \frac{1}{2}\left(\frac{3R}{M}\right)\left(\frac{M}{3RT}\right)^{1/2}$$

$$= \frac{1}{2}\left(\frac{3R}{M}\right)\left(\frac{1}{u_{rms}}\right)$$

$$= \frac{1}{2}\left(\frac{3 \times 8.314}{32 \times 10^{-3}}\right)\left(\frac{1}{129.91}\right)$$

$$= 3.0\ m\,s^{-1}\ K^{-1}$$

■ Molar mass of O_2 is taken in (kg) and R in J mol^{-1} K^{-1}, both in MKS unit.

217. Three (3) p_{N_2} contained in 1.0 mole air

$$= \frac{nRT}{V} = \frac{0.8 \times 0.0821 \times 273}{0.2175}$$

$$= 82.44\ atm$$

Similarly $p_{O_2} = 20.61$ atm

Total = 82.44 + 20.61 = 103.05 atm

$$p_{observed} = 100\ atm$$

Thus, change = 3 atm

218. Three (3) $b = 0.034\ L\ mol^{-1}$

$$= 0.034 \times 10^{-3}\ m^3 mol^{-1}$$

Also, $b = 4\,N_0V$

where, V = volume of one molecule.

$$\therefore \quad V = \frac{b}{4N_0}$$

$$= \frac{0.034 \times 10^{-3}\ m^3\ mol^{-1}}{4 \times 6.02 \times 10^{23}\ mol^{-1}}$$

$$= 1.412 \times 10^{-29}\ m^3$$

Also, $V = \frac{4}{3}\pi r^3$

$$\therefore \quad \frac{4}{3}\pi r^3 = 1.412 \times 10^{-29}\ m^3$$

$$\therefore \quad r = 1.5 \times 10^{-10}\ m$$

Molecular diameter = $2r$

$$= 3.0 \times 10^{-10}\ m = 3Å$$

219. Two (2) We use

$$p_1V_1 = p_2V_2$$

$$p_1 = 8.09\ bar$$

p_2 = 1.00 bar (at the surface where pressure is atmospheric pressure.)

$$V_1 = \frac{4}{3}\pi r_1^3 = \frac{4}{3}\pi(1.0)^3 = 4.189\ \text{cm}^3$$

$$V_2 = \frac{p_1V_1}{p_2} = \frac{8.09 \times 4.189}{1.0}$$

$$= 33.89\ \text{cm}^3$$

$$\therefore \quad \frac{4}{3}\pi r_2^3 = 33.89\ \text{cm}^3$$

$$r_2^3 = 8.091\ \text{cm}^3 \quad \therefore\ r \approx 2.00\ \text{cm}$$

220. **(991)**

Lifting capacity of a balloon.

$$\Delta m = m(\text{air}) - m(\text{He})$$

$$= n(\text{air})\, m(\text{air}) - n(\text{He}) m(\text{He})$$

Moles being equal

$$\therefore \quad \Delta m = n(29 - 4) = 25\, n\,\text{g}$$

$$= 25 \times \frac{pV}{RT}$$

$$\therefore \quad 1000 = \frac{25 \times 1 \times V}{0.08314 \times 298}$$

$$\therefore \quad V = 991\ \text{dm}^3$$

221. **(20)**

$$n = \frac{pV}{RT}$$

Number of ^{36}Ar atoms = number of events

$$= n\, N_0$$

$$1\ \text{mm}^3 = 0.001\ \text{cm}^3 = 1 \times 10^{-6}\ \text{L}$$

$$n = \frac{pV}{RT}$$

$$\therefore \quad n = \frac{1\ \text{atm} \times 0.186 \times 10^{-6}\text{L}}{0.0821\text{L atm mol}^{-1}\text{K}^{-1} \times 273\text{K}}$$

$$= 8.3 \times 10^{-9}\ \text{moles of}\ ^{36}\text{Ar}$$

∴ Atoms = events

$$= 8.3 \times 10^{-9} \times 6.02 \times 10^{23}$$

$$= 5 \times 10^{15} = x \times 10^{y}$$

$$\therefore \quad x + y = 20$$

Type V. Passage Based MCQs (Comprehension)

Passage 1

At STP

$T = 273$ K, $p = 1$ atm

$V_{CH_3CHO} = 1.75$ L, $V_{O_2} = 25$ L

$$\therefore \quad n_{CH_3CHO} = \frac{pV}{RT} = \frac{1 \times 1.75}{0.0821 \times 273} = 0.0781\text{mol}$$

$$n_{O_2} = \frac{1 \times 25}{0.0821 \times 273} = 1.115\ \text{mol}$$

■ At STP, 1 mol of an ideal gas = 22.4 L

$$\therefore \quad 0.0821 \times 273 = 22.4\ \text{L mol}^{-1}$$

On exposing to UV-radiation, CH_3CHO is oxidised to CO_2 and H_2O.

$$CH_3CHO(g) + 2.5\, O_2(g) \longrightarrow 2CO_2(g) + 2H_2O(l)$$

Stoichiometric : 1 mol 1.5 mol 1 mol 2 mol

O_2 required by 0.0781 mol CH_3CHO

$$= 0.0781 \times 2.5 = 0.195\ \text{mol}$$

Thus, CH_3CHO is the limiting reactant and all its content (0.0781 mol) is used.

O_2 is in excees and 0.195 mol of its is used out of total 1.115 mol.

$CO_2(g)$ formed from 0.0781 mol $CH_3CHO(g) = 0.0781 \times 2 = 0.1562$ mol

$H_2O(g)$ formed from 0.0781 mol $CH_3CHO(g) = 0.1562$ mol

∴ Volume of 0.1562 mol $CO_2(g)$ at 298 K and at 1 atm

$$V_{CO_2} = \frac{nRT}{p} = \frac{0.1562 \times 0.0821 \times 298}{1}$$

$$= 3.821\ \text{L}$$

Since, $n_{H_2O} = n_{CO_2}$ and H_2O is assumed to be is vapour state at 298 K,

$$V_{H_2O} = V_{CO_2} = 3.821\ \text{L}$$

222. (a) ***223.*** (d)

Passage 2

$$\left(p + \frac{a}{V^2}\right)(V - b) = RT$$

When $\frac{a}{V^2} = 0$

(neglected due to force of atraction)

$$p(V - b) = RT$$

$$pV = RT + pb$$

$$V = \left(\frac{RT}{p} + b\right)$$

This is a straight line showing variation of V with T at constant p.

$$\text{Slope} = \frac{R}{p} = \tan\theta = 0.1642\ \text{dm}^3\text{K}^{-1}$$

$$p = \frac{R}{0.1642} = \frac{0.0821\ \text{dm}^3\ \text{atm mol}^{-1}\text{K}^{-1}}{0.1642\ \text{dm}^3\ \text{K}^{-1}}$$

$$= 0.5\ \text{atm mol}^{-1}$$

Also, $b = 0.20\ \text{dm}^3\ \text{mol}^{-1} = OA$ (intercept)

∴ $b = 4V$ (volume of molecules in one mole)

$$V = \frac{b}{4} = \frac{0.20}{4} = 0.05\ \text{dm}^3\text{mol}^{-1}$$

224. (b) ***225.*** (d)

Passage 3

When $p \to 0$, volume is high,

$$(V - b) \approx V$$

$$\text{thus,}\ \left(p + \frac{a}{V^2}\right)V = RT$$

$$pV = RT - \frac{a}{V}$$

Gas behaves ideally (by approximation)

$$\therefore \quad pV = RT \Rightarrow \frac{1}{V} = \frac{p}{RT}$$

$$\therefore \quad pV = RT - \frac{ap}{RT} = \left(-\frac{ap}{RT} + RT\right)$$

This represents a straight line

$$(y = -mx + C)$$

$$\text{Slope} = -\frac{a}{RT} = -0.1\ \text{dm}^3\text{mol}^{-1}$$

$$\therefore\ a = 0.1\ \text{dm}^3 \times 0.08314\ \text{bar dm}^3\ \text{mol}^{-1}\text{K}^{-1} \times 273\ \text{K}$$

$$= 2.27\ \text{bar dm}^6\ \text{mol}^{-2}$$

$$\text{Intercept} = RT$$

$$= 0.08314\ \text{bar dm}^3\ \text{mol}^{-1}\text{K}^{-1} \times 273\ \text{K}$$

$$= 22.7\ \text{bar dm}^3\text{mol}^{-1}$$

226. (a) ***227.*** (b)

Passage 4

$$n = \frac{pV}{RT}$$

$$n_{NO} = \frac{\left(\frac{800}{760}\right)(0.250)}{0.0821 \times 220} = 0.0146\ \text{mol}$$

$n_{O_2} = 0.00437$ moi (limiting reactant)

$$2NO + O_2 \longrightarrow N_2O_4(s)$$

	2 mol	1 mol
Initial	0.0146	0.00437
Reacted	0.00874	0.00437
After reaction	0.00586	0

$N_2O_4(s)$ being in solid state does not exert pressure. Pressure is due to unreacted NO present in 0.350 L (total volume).

$$\therefore \quad p = \frac{nRT}{V} = \frac{0.00586 \times 0.0821 \times 220}{0.350}$$

$$= 0.302\ \text{atm}$$

$N_2O_4(s)$ formed = O_2 reacted

$$= 0.00437\ \text{mol}$$

$$= (0.00437 \times 92)$$

$$= 0.402\ \text{g}$$

228. (d) **229.** (a)

Passage 5

$$\frac{1}{N}\left(\frac{dN}{du}\right) \propto \left(\frac{1}{T}\right)^{3/2} \exp\left(\frac{-Mu^2}{T}\right)$$

As u increases, distribution increases due to u^2 reaches maximum value and then decreases due to $\exp\left(\frac{-Mu^2}{T}\right)$ at a given temperature.

Due to increase in temperature, maximum point is shifted to higher velocity.

Thus, $u \propto \sqrt{T}$

$\therefore \quad T_1 < T_2 < T_3$

Probability

$$P = 4\pi u^2 \left(\frac{M}{2\pi RT}\right)^{3/2} \exp\left(\frac{-Mu^2}{2RT}\right)$$

$$P = 4\pi u^2 B \exp(-Au^2)$$

where, $B = \left(\frac{M}{2\pi RT}\right)$

and $A = \frac{M}{2RT}$

A and B are velocity independent. For maximum distribution,

$$\frac{dP}{du} = 0 \text{ when } u^2 = \frac{1}{A}$$

$$\therefore \quad u = \sqrt{\frac{1}{A}} = \sqrt{\frac{2RT}{M}}$$

This velocity is called most probable velocity.

230. (c) **231.** (b)

Passage 6

$$\frac{r_X}{r_Y} = \sqrt{\frac{40}{10}} = 2$$

Rate of diffusion of X is twice that of Y.

Thus, distance travelled by $X = a$

and distance travelled by $Y = (24 - a)$

$$\therefore \quad r_X = \frac{a}{t} \text{ and } r_Y = \left(\frac{24-a}{t}\right)$$

$$\therefore \quad \frac{r_X}{r_Y} = 2 = \frac{a}{(24-a)} \Rightarrow a = 16 \text{ cm}$$

Collision frequency

$$= \sqrt{2} N_0 (u_{av}) \sigma \left(\frac{p}{RT}\right)$$

where, σ is cross-sectional area

$$= \pi(d)^2 = 4\pi r^2$$

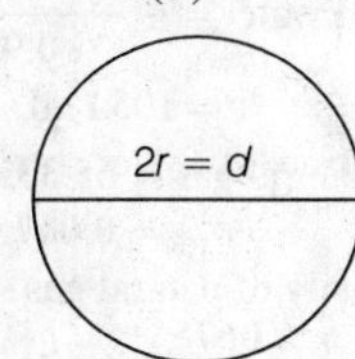

d = diameter = $2r$, r = radius,

N_0 = Avogadro's number

u_{av} = average velocity, p = pressure

If collision frequency is increased, u_{av} is also increased. Thus,

$\frac{r_X}{r_Y} < 2$ and distance $a < 16$ cm.

232. (c) **233.** (c)

Passage 7

For ideal behaviour

$$p_{O_2} = \frac{nRT}{V} = \frac{1 \times 0.0831 \times 400}{100} = 0.3324 \text{ bar}$$

$$p_{H_2} = \frac{3 \times 0.0831 \times 400}{100} = 0.9972 \text{ bar}$$

$$p_{total} = 1.3296 \text{ bar}$$

After reaction at 400 K

	$2H_2(g)$	$+ O_2(g) \longrightarrow$	$2H_2O(g)$
	2 mol	1 mol	2 mol
Moles taken	3 mol	1 mol	
Thus, after reaction	1 mol	0 mol	2 mol

O_2 is the limiting reactant

Thus, total moles of H_2 and H_2O = 3 mol

$$\therefore \quad p = \frac{nRT}{V} = \frac{3 \times 0.0831 \times 400}{100} = 0.9972 \text{ bar}$$

$\therefore$ Change in pressure = 1.3296 − 0.9972 = 0.3324 bar

After cooling to 298 K, $H_2O\ (g)$ is condensed, only H_2 remains. Thus, pressure at 298 K

$$\therefore \quad p_{H_2} = \frac{nRT}{V} = \frac{1 \times 0.08314 \times 298}{100} = 0.248 \text{ bar}$$

234. (a) **235.** (b)

Passage 8

Residual gas = 10 mL

H_2 and O_2 used = 50 − 10 = 40 mL

$$2H_2 + O_2 \longrightarrow 2H_2O$$

If H_2 is residual gas

H_2 used out of 40 mL = $40 \times \frac{2}{3}$ = 26.67 mL

O_2 used out of 40 mL = $40 \times \frac{1}{3}$ = 13.33 mL

Total H_2 = 26.67 + 10 = 36.67 mL

$$\therefore \quad X_{H_2} = \frac{36.67}{50.0} = 0.733$$

If O_2 is residual gas,

H_2 in mixture = 26.67 mL

O_2 in mixture = 23.33 mL

$$\therefore \quad X_{H_2} = \frac{26.07}{50.0} = 0.533$$

236. (d) **237.** (c)

Passage 9

Given, $Z = 1.00054$, $T = 273$ K

$p = 101.325$ kPa

T_B (Boyle temperature) = 107 K = $\frac{a}{Rb}$

Given, $Z = 1 + \frac{p}{RTZ}\left(b - \frac{a}{RT}\right)$

$$\therefore \quad b = (Z-1)\frac{RTZ}{p} + \frac{a}{RT}$$

$$= (Z-1)\frac{RTZ}{p} + \left(\frac{a}{Rb}\right)\frac{b}{T}$$

$$= (Z-1)\frac{RTZ}{p} + \frac{T_B b}{T}$$

$$\therefore \quad \left(b - \frac{T_B b}{T}\right) = (Z-1)\frac{RTZ}{p}$$

$$b\left(\frac{T - T_B}{T}\right) = (Z-1)\frac{RTZ}{p}$$

$$b = \frac{T}{(T - T_B)}(Z-1)\frac{RTZ}{p}$$

Putting, $T = 273$ K, $T_B = 107$ K

$Z = 1.00054$, $R = 8.314$ kPa dm^3 K^{-1} mol^{-1}

and $p = 101.325$ kPa

$b = 0.0199$ dm^3 mol^{-1}

Also, $T_B = \frac{a}{Rb}$

$\therefore \quad a = RT_B b = 17.7$ kPa dm^6 mol^{-2}

238. (a) **239.** (d)

Passage 10

$$n_{O_2} = \frac{pV}{RT} = \frac{5 \times 5}{0.0821 \times 291} = 1.05 \text{ mol}$$

$$n_{Carbon} = \frac{18.0}{12} = 1.50 \text{ mol}$$

$$\underset{1\text{ mol}}{C} + \underset{0.5\text{ mol}}{\frac{1}{2}O_2} \longrightarrow \underset{1\text{ mol}}{CO}$$

$$\underset{1\text{ mol}}{C} + \underset{1\text{ mol}}{O_2} \longrightarrow \underset{1\text{ mol}}{CO_2}$$

Let CO formed = carbon used = x mol

CO_2 formed = carbon used = y mol

O_2 used in the formation of x mol CO = $0.5\,x$ mol

O_2 used in the formation of y mol of $CO_2 = y$

$$\therefore \quad (x + y) = 1.50$$

$$0.5\,x + y = 1.05$$

$\therefore \quad 0.5\,x = 0.45$

$x = 0.90$ mol,

$y = 0.60$ mol

Thus, CO formed = 0..90 mol

$NaOH + CO_2 \longrightarrow NaHCO_3$

$2NaOH + CO_2 \longrightarrow Na_2CO_3 + H_2O$

$$\text{NaOH taken} = \frac{500 \times 2}{1000} = 1 \text{ mol}$$

If CO_2 used by NaOH in the formation of $NaHCO_3 = x_1$ mol

and CO_2 used by NaOH in the formation of $Na_2CO_3 = x_2$ mol

then $(x_1 + x_2) = 0.60$ mol

NaOH used in the formation of $NaHCO_3$ by x_1 mol $CO_2 = x_1$

NaOH used in the formation of Na_2CO_3 by x_2 mol $CO_2 = 2x_2$

$\therefore \quad x_1 + 2x_2 = 1.0$

$x_1 + x_2 = 0.60$

$\therefore \quad x_1 = 0.20$ mol

$x_2 = 0.40$ mol

$\therefore$ 0.40 mole of Na_2CO_3 are in 0.5 L and 0.20 mole of $NaHCO_3$ are in 0.5 L.

$$\therefore \quad Na_2CO_3 = \frac{0.40}{0.5} = 0.80 \text{ M}$$

$$NaHCO_3 = \frac{0.20}{0.5} = 0.40 \text{ M}$$

240. (b) **241.** (c)

Passage 11

$\frac{a}{V^2}$ (intermolecular forces) = 0

$\therefore \quad p(V - b) = RT$

$pV = RT + pb$

$(pV)_2 = RT + p_2 b$

$(pV)_1 = RT + p_1 b$

$$b = \frac{(pV)_2 - (pV)_1}{(p_2 - p_1)} = \frac{2.6 - 2.0}{5 - 2}$$

$= 0.2 \text{ dm}^3\text{mol}^{-1}$

$V_c = 3b = 0.6 \text{ dm}^3\text{mol}^{-1}$

$p_c V_c = 3RT_c$

$$p_c = \frac{3RT_c}{V_c} = 41.6 \text{ bar}$$

242. (b) **243.** (a)

Passage 12

$$pV = RT\left[1 + \frac{1}{V}\left(b - \frac{a}{RT}\right)\right]$$

Z (compressibility factor)

$$= \frac{pV}{RT} = \left[1 + \frac{1}{V}\left(b - \frac{a}{RT}\right)\right]$$

$$1.008 = \left[1 + \frac{b}{V}\left[1 - \frac{a}{bRT}\right]\right]$$

Given, Boyle's temperature

$$T_b = \frac{a}{Rb} = 107 \text{ K}, \text{ and } \frac{1}{V} = \frac{p}{RT}$$

$$= \frac{1}{0.0831 \times 273} = 0.044$$

$$\therefore \quad 1.008 = 1 + 0.044b\left[1 - \frac{107}{273}\right]$$

$$\therefore \quad b = \frac{0.008 \times 273}{166 \times 0.044}$$

$= 0.030 \text{ dm}^3\text{mol}^{-1}$

$\therefore \quad a = T_b Rb$

$= 107 \text{ K} \times 0.08314 \text{ dm}^3 \text{ bar mol}^{-1} \text{ K}^{-1} \times 0.30 \text{ dm}^3\text{mol}^{-1}$

$= 2.67 \text{ bar dm}^6\text{mol}^{-2}$

$$\text{Also, } b = 4\left(\frac{4}{3}\pi r^3\right)N_0$$

$$0.30 \times 10^{-3} \text{ m}^3 = \frac{16}{3}\pi r^3 \times 6.02 \times 10^{23}$$

$r = 3.10 \times 10^{-10}$ m

$\therefore$ Molecular diameter $(2r)$

$= 6.20 \times 10^{-10}$ m = 6.20 Å

244. (c) **245.** (b)

Passage 13

$$pV = nRT = \frac{w}{m}RT$$

$$\therefore \quad m = \frac{w}{p \cdot V}RT = \frac{dRT}{p}$$

$\therefore$ Average molar mass

$$= \frac{3.8 \times 10^{-12} \times 8.314 \times 960}{(1.6 \times 10^{-8} \times 10^{-3}) \times 10^5}$$

$= 0.019 \text{ kg mol}^{-1} = 19 \text{ g mol}^{-1}$

If air is a mixture of N_2 gas and O atoms than

$19 = 28X_{N_2} + 16(1 - X_{N_2})$

$\therefore \quad X_{N_2} = 0.25$

■ 1 m bar = 10^{-3} bar

1 bar = 1×10^5 pascal

246. (a) **247.** (b)

Passage 14

$$p = \frac{n}{V}RT = \frac{w}{VM}RT = \frac{dRT}{M}$$

$$\therefore \quad M = \frac{dRT}{p} = \frac{1.146 \times 0.08314 \times 300}{0.987}$$

$= 28.96 \text{ g mol}^{-1}$

$$\therefore \quad M = \frac{M_1X_1 + M_2X_2}{X_1 + X_2}$$

$$= \frac{28X_1 + 32(1 - X_1)}{1}$$

$28.96 = 28X_1 + 32(1 - X_1)$

$X_1 = 0.76$

Thus, N_2 = 76%, O_2 = 24%

$p_{N_2} = 0.76 \times 0.987 = 0.75$ bar

If Ar is 1.0 mole per cent, that N_2 and O_2 are 99%.

$\therefore \quad p_{Ar} = 0.01 \times 0.987 = 0.00987$ bar

248. (d) **249.** (b)

Passage 15

$$n = \frac{pV}{RT}$$

$$= \frac{1 \text{ bar} \times (4/3)\pi(3)^3 \text{ m}^3}{0.0831 \times 10^{-3} \text{ bar m}^3 \text{ mol}^{-1}\text{K}^{-1} \times 298\text{K}}$$

$= 4.565 \times 10^3$ mol = 4.565 kmol

$= 4.565 \times 2$ kg = 9.130 kg

Density = 1.22 kg m^{-3}

Mass = volume × density

$$= \frac{4}{3}\pi(27) \times 1.22 = 138.00 \text{ kg}$$

Mass that the balloon can lift (pay load)

= mass of air − mass of H_2

= 138.00 kg − 9.130 = 128.87 kg

250. (a) **251.** (d)

Passage 16

$$\text{Before mixing } n_{(N_2 \text{ and } 298)} = \frac{pV}{RT}$$

$$= \frac{1 \times 5}{0.08314 \times 298} = 0.202 \text{ mol}$$

$$n_{(N_2 \text{ at } 273)} = \frac{pV}{RT} = \frac{1 \times 4}{0.08314 \times 273}$$

$= 0.352$ mol

$n_{298} + n_{273}$ = total moles = 0.554 mol

$n_{273} = (0.554 - n_{298})$

After mixing, $p_{\text{hot}} = p_{\text{cold}}$

$$\frac{n_{298}(\text{in mix.}) \times 298}{V_{298}} = \frac{n_{273}(\text{in mix.}) \times 273}{V_{273}}$$

$$\frac{n_{298} \times 298}{5} = \frac{(0.554 - n_{298})273}{4}$$

$n_{298} = (0.554 - n_{298})\,1.145$

$n_{298} = 0.296$ mol

Thus, N_2 after mixing in 5 L flask

= 0.296 mol

$$\therefore \quad p \text{ at } 298 \text{ K} = \frac{0.296 \times 0.08314 \times 298}{5}$$

= 1.47 bar

252. (a) **253.** (b)

Passage 17

$$\text{Volume of water} = \frac{170.15 - 65.2649}{0.998}$$

= 105.1 mL

Mass of natural gas = 65.3324 − 65.2649

= 0.0675 g

Thus, density of natural gas

$$= \frac{\text{mass}}{\text{volume}} = \frac{0.0675}{105.1} = 6.42 \times 10^{-4} \text{g mL}^{-1}$$

$= 6.42 \times 10^{-4} \times 10^3$ g L^{-1} = 0.642 g L^{-1}

$$pV = nRT = \frac{w}{M} RT$$

$$\therefore \quad p = \frac{w}{VM} RT = \frac{dRT}{M}$$

$$\therefore \quad M = \frac{dRT}{p}$$

$$= \frac{0.642 \text{ g L}^{-1} \times 0.0821 \text{ L atm mol}^{-1}\text{K}^{-1} \times 296 \text{ K}}{\left(\frac{741}{760}\right) \text{atm}}$$

$= 16.00$ g mol^{-1}

254. (c) **255.** (b)

Passage 18

The amount of gases inhaled O_2,

$$n(O_2, \text{in}) = \frac{pV}{RT} = \frac{1 \times 7200 \times 0.21}{0.08314 \times 310} = 58.66 \text{ mol}$$

$$\text{Exhaled } O_2, n(O_2, \text{ex}) = \frac{1 \times 7200 \times 0.16}{0.08314 \times 310}$$

$= 44.70$ mol

Thus, O_2 used per day = 58.66 − 44.70

= 13.96mol= 13.96×32 g

= 446.8 ≈ 450 g

$$\text{Similarly, inhaled } CO_2 = \frac{1 \times 7200 \times 0.0003}{0.08314 \times 310}$$

= 0.0838 mol

$$\text{and exhaled } CO_2 = \frac{1 \times 7200 \times 0.044}{0.08314 \times 310}$$

= 12 .29 mol

Thus, CO_2 generated = 12.29 − 0.0838

= 12.207 mol

= 12.207 × 44 = 537 g

256. (c) **257.** (d)

Passage 19

$$p_c V_c = \frac{3}{8} R T_c$$

If T_c increased, at constant p_c, V_c increases and compressibility factor $\left(Z = \frac{p_c V_c}{RT_c} = \frac{3}{8}\right)$ remains unchanged

$$\log(p_c V_c) = \log\left(\frac{3}{8} R\right) + \log T_c$$

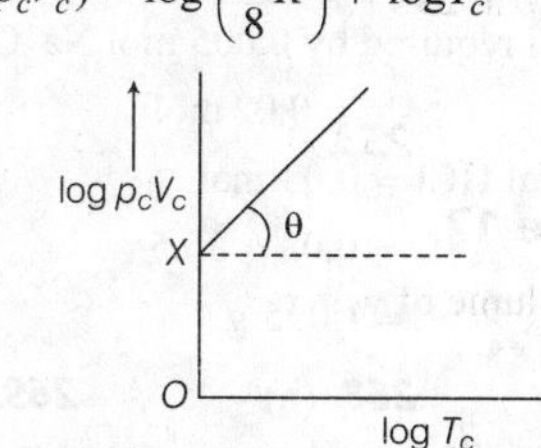

Slope = 1 and intercept = $OX = \log\left(\frac{3}{8} R\right)$

Thus, (R) is determined from intercept.

258. (c) **259.** (b)

Type VI. Matrix Matching

260. (c) $2H_2(g) + O_2(g) \longrightarrow 2H_2O(g)$

	$2H_2(g)$	$O_2(g)$	$2H_2O(g)$
Initial	3 mol	1 mol	0
After reaction	(3 − 2) mol	(1 − 1) mol	2 mol

Before reaction

$$p_{H_2} = \frac{nRT}{V} = \frac{3 \times 0.0821 \times 4.00}{100}$$

= 0.9852 atm

Thus, (i) → (s)

After reaction, O_2 = 0 mol

p_{O_2} = 0.00 atm

Thus, (ii) → (p)

Total pressure before reaction (due to 4 moles) = 1.3136 atm

Thus, (iii) − (q)

Total pressure after reaction (due to 3 moles) = 0.9852 atm

Thus, (iv) → (s)

After cooling to 298 K, H_2O (g) is condensed to liquid, and pressure is due to unreacted H_2.

n_{H_2} (after reaction) = 1 mol

$$p_{H_2} \text{ (at 298 K)} = \frac{nRT}{V}$$

$$= \frac{1 \times 0.0821 \times 298}{100} = 0.2447 \text{ atm}$$

Thus, (v) → (t)

261. (c) When attractive forces are negligible

$$\frac{a}{V^2} = 0$$

Thus, for one mole $p(V - b) = RT$

$$pV - pb = RT$$

$$\Rightarrow \quad V = \left(\frac{RT}{p} + b\right)$$

Isobar at constant p, (between V and T) is of the type as given.

Thus , $OA = b$ = van der Waals' constant

$b = 0.140$ dm^3 mol^{-1}

Thus, (ii)-(q)

Slope of the line = $\frac{R}{p}$ = tan 45°

= 1 dm^3 K^{-1}

∴ $p = R = 0.0821$ atm

Thus , (i)-(s)

$$\text{At 300 K, } V = \frac{0.0821 \times 300}{0.0821} + 0.14$$

$= 300.14$ dm^3

Thus, (iii)-(r)

When $p = p_c = \frac{a}{27b^2}$

∴ $a = 27b^2 p_c$

= 0.0821 atm × 27 × (0.140)^2 dm^6 mol^{-2}

= 0.043 atm dm^6 mol^{-2}

Thus, (iv)-(p)

262. (d) When volume of molecules is negligible $b = 0$

$$\left(p + \frac{a}{V^2}\right)(V - b) = RT$$

$$\therefore \quad \left(p + \frac{a}{V^2}\right) V = RT$$

$$pV = \left(RT - \frac{a}{V}\right)$$

When $\frac{1}{V} = 0$, $pV = RT = OA$ = intercept

At 300 K, $RT = OA = 0.0821 \times 300$

= 24.63 atm dm^{3}mol^{-1}

Thus, (i) → (s)

slope = − a atm dm^6 mol^{-2}

∴ a = slope = tan 60° = $\sqrt{3}$

= 1.732 atm dm^6 mol^{-2}

Thus, (ii)-(r)

At point (D), $= \frac{1}{V} = 0.3$

$$pV = \left(RT - \frac{a}{V}\right) = 24.63 - \sqrt{3} \times 0.3$$

= 24.63 − 0.52 = 24.11 atm dm^3 mol^{-1}

Thus, (iii)-(q)

Attractive forces at $\left(\frac{1}{V} = 0.2\right) = \frac{a}{V^2}$

At point (C) = 1.732×(0.2)^2 = 0.0693 atm

Thus, (iv)-(p)

263. (b) $\left(p + \frac{a}{V^2}\right)(V - b) = RT$

Graph shows that attractive forces are negligible. Thus, $\frac{a}{V^2} = 0$

$$\therefore \quad p = \frac{RT}{(V - b)}$$

Then, $p \propto T$

Isochore is formed between p and T at constant volume.

Thus, slope = $\left(\frac{R}{V - b}\right)$ = tan 45° = 1

∴ $R = (V - b)$

∴ $b = V - R = (0.1 - 0.0821)$

= 0.0179 dm^3 mol^{-1}

Thus, (i) - (p)

$$p = \frac{RT}{(V - b)} = (1)\, T$$

When p = 1 atm, T = 1K. Thus, (ii) - (q)

Also, $\left(\frac{\partial p}{\partial T}\right)_V = \frac{R}{V - b} = 1$

Thus, (iii) - (q)

$$\lambda(\text{Mean free path}) = \frac{RT}{\sqrt{2} N_0 \sigma p}$$

where, σ = cross-sectional area

$= \pi d^2 = \pi(2r)^2$

r = radius of the molecule

Under given conditions (ii), $\frac{T}{p} = 1$

$$b = 0.0179 \text{ dm}^2 \text{ mol}^{-1}$$

Also, $b = 4V = 4N_0\left(\frac{4}{3}\pi r^3\right)$

where, V = volume of molecules in one mole of the gas

$$\therefore r^3 = \frac{3}{16\pi N_0}(b)$$

$$= \frac{3 \times (0.0179) \text{ dm}^3 \text{ mol}^{-1}}{16\pi \times 6.02 \times 10^{23} \text{ mol}^{-1}}$$

$$r^3 = 1.775 \times 10^{-27} \text{ dm}^3$$

$$r = 1.21 \times 10^{-9} \text{ dm}$$

$$\Rightarrow \sigma = \pi d^2 = 4\pi r^2$$

$$= 4\pi(1.21 \times 10^{-9})^2 \text{ dm}^2$$

$$= 1.84 \times 10^{-17} \text{ dm}^2$$

$$\therefore \lambda = \frac{RT}{\sqrt{2}\, N_0\, \sigma\, p}$$

$$= \frac{0.0821 \text{dm}^3 \text{ atm mol}^{-1}\text{K}^{-1} \times 1\text{K}}{\sqrt{2} \times 6.02 \times 10^{23} \text{mol}^{-1} \times 1.84 \times 10^{-17} \text{dm}^2 \times 1 \text{atm}}$$

$$= 5.24 \times 10^{-9} \text{ dm}$$

$$= 5.24 \times 10^{-10} \text{m} = 5.24 \text{ Å}$$

Thus, (iv) - (s)

264. (b) $p_cV_c = \frac{3}{8}RT_c$

$$\therefore \quad V_c = \frac{3\,RT}{8p_c} = \frac{3}{8} \times \frac{0.0821 \times 300}{24.03}$$

$$= \frac{3}{8} \text{ dm}^3 = 0.375 \text{ dm}^3$$

Thus, (i) $\rightarrow$ (p)

$$V_c = 3b$$

$$b = \frac{V_c}{3} = 0.375 = 0.125 \text{ dm}^3 \text{ mol}^{-1}$$

Thus, (ii) $\rightarrow$ (s)

$$b = 4\left(\frac{4}{3}\pi r^3 N_0\right)$$

$$r^3 = \frac{3b}{16\pi N_0} = \frac{3 \times 0.125 \times 10^3 \text{ cm}^3}{16\pi \times 6.02 \times 10^{23}}$$

$$r^3 = 1.24 \times 10^{-23} \text{ cm}^3$$

$$r = 2.31 \times 10^{-8} \text{ cm}$$

$$= 2.31 \times 10^{-10} \text{ m} = 2.31 \text{ Å}$$

$$r = 231 \times 10^{-12} \text{ m} = 231 \text{ pm}$$

Collision diameter $= 2r = 2 \times 2.31$ Å

$$= 4.62 \text{ Å} = 462 \text{ pm}$$

Thus, (iii)-(q) (iv)-(r)

■ $V_c = 3b$

265. (c) Air is a mixture of 80% N_2 and 20% O_2.

$$X_{N_2} = 0.80$$

$$X_{O_2} = 0.20$$

Since, pressure $N_2 \propto X_{N_2}$

$$(\text{pressure})_{O_2} \propto X_{O_2}$$

$$\frac{r_{N_2}}{r_{O_2}} = \frac{p_{N_2}}{p_{O_2}}\sqrt{\frac{M(O_2)}{M(N_2)}} = \frac{0.80}{0.20}\sqrt{\frac{32}{28}}$$

$$\frac{r_{N_2}}{r_{O_2}} = \frac{4.3}{1}$$

Thus, X_{N_2} that comes out of the hole from air $= \frac{4.3}{5.3} = 0.81$ (lighter gas is N_2)

Thus, (i)-(r)

Similarly, $\frac{r_{He}}{r_{N_2}} = \frac{0.40}{0.60}\sqrt{\frac{28}{4}} = \frac{1.764}{1}$

$$\therefore \quad X_{He} = \frac{1.764}{2.764} = 0.64$$

Thus, (ii)-(p)

$$\frac{r_{CH_4}}{r_{O_2}} = \frac{0.40}{0.60}\sqrt{\frac{32}{16}} = \frac{0.943}{1}$$

$$\therefore \quad X_{CH_4} = \frac{0.943}{1.943} = 0.48$$

Thus, (iii)-(s)

$$\frac{r_{H_2}}{r_{O_2}} = \frac{0.8}{0.2}\sqrt{\frac{32}{2}} = 16/1$$

$$n_{H_2} = \frac{16}{17} = 0.94$$

Thus, iv $\rightarrow$ (q)

266. (a) At p = 200 atm (very high)

$$Z > 1$$

Also at high pressure $\frac{n^2a}{V^2} << p$

$$\therefore \quad \left(p + \frac{n^2a}{V^2}\right) \approx p$$

$$\therefore \quad p(V - nb) = nRT$$

Thus, (i)– (p, s)

At $p \approx 0$, gas behave as an ideal gas

$\therefore pV = nRT$

$\therefore$ (ii) — (r)

For CO_2 at 273 K and p = 1 atm

$Z < 1$

$\therefore$ (iii) — (p, q)

At very large volume, $V >> b$

$$\therefore \quad (V - b) \approx V$$

Also when V is large, $\frac{1}{V^2} \approx 0$

(say $V = 1000 \text{ dm}^3$)

Then $\frac{1}{V^2} = \frac{1}{10^6} = 10^{-6} \approx 0)$

Hence, gas behaves ideally.

Thus, (iv) — (r)

Solutions for 267 to 270

$$Na_2CO_3 \xrightarrow{\Delta} \text{no effect}$$

$$KCl \xrightarrow{\Delta} \text{no effect}$$

$$\underset{2 \text{ mol}}{2NaHCO_3} \xrightarrow{\Delta} Na_2CO_3 + H_2O + \underset{1 \text{ mol}}{CO_2}$$

At 300 K, pressure set up is due to CO_2 only (as H_2O is liquid at 300 K) which is from $NaHCO_3$

$n(CO_2)$ due to $NaHCO_3 = pV/RT$

$$= \frac{0.125 \times 1}{0.08314 \times 300}$$

$$= 0.005 \text{ mol}$$

Thus, $NaHCO_3$ in the mixture

$$= 0.01 \text{ mol} = 0.84 \text{ g}$$

(Na_2CO_3 + KCl) in mixture

$$= 2.645 - 0.840 = 1.805 \text{ g}$$

HCl reacts with $NaHCO_3$ and Na_2CO_3 both.

$$\underset{1 \text{ mol}}{NaHCO_3} + HCl \longrightarrow NaCl + H_2O + \underset{1 \text{ mol}}{CO_2}$$

$$\underset{1 \text{ mol}}{Na_2CO_3} + 2HCl \longrightarrow 2NaCl + H_2O + \underset{1 \text{ mol}}{CO_2}$$

CO_2 due to 0.01 mol $NaHCO_3$ = 0.01 mol

Thus, p_{CO_2} (due to $NaHCO_3$) $= \frac{nRT}{V}$

$$= \frac{0.01 \times 0.08314 \times 300}{0.125 \text{ bar}} = 0.25 \text{ bar}$$

Thus, pressure due to CO_2 from Na_2CO_3

$$= 0.375 - 0.250$$

$$= 0.125 \text{ bar}$$

$$\therefore n_{(Na_2CO_3)} = \frac{pV}{RT} = \frac{0.125 \times 1}{0.0831 \times 300}$$

$$= 0.005 \text{ mol}$$

$$= 0.005 \times 106 = 0.53 \text{ g}$$

HCl required by 0.01 mol $NaHCO_3$

$$= 0.01 \text{ mol}$$

HCl required by 0.005 mol Na_2CO_3

$$= 0.02 \text{ mol}$$

Total HCl = 0.03 mol

$$= 0.03 \times 36.5$$

$$= 1.095 \text{ g}$$

267. (a) **268.** (b) **269.** (a) **270.** (d)

States of Matter-II

(The Liquid State)

Chapter Topics

- Vapour Pressure
- Surface Tension and Viscosity

Characteristics of liquids

Liquid is the intermediate state between solid and gas. In case of liquids, magnitude of intermolecular forces is such that they have,

- definite volume
- indefinite shape
- higher density than gases
- less compressibility than gases
- slower diffusion than gases

Vapour pressure, surface tension and viscosity are some of the typical properties of liquids that arise because of two competing forces – the molecular interaction and thermal energy.

Phase transition

	Type	Equilibrium	Enthalpy change (ΔH)
(i)	Fusion	Solid $\rightleftharpoons$ Liquid	Heat is absorbed (endothermic) $\Delta H > 0$
(ii)	Vaporisation	Liquid $\rightleftharpoons$ Vapour	As in (i)
(iii)	Sublimation	Solid $\rightleftharpoons$ Gas (without change into liquid)	As in (i)
(iv)	Freezing	Liquid $\rightleftharpoons$ Solid (reverse of fusion)	Heat is lost (exothermic) $\Delta H < 0$
(v)	Condensation	Vapour $\rightleftharpoons$ Liquid (reverse of vaporisation)	As in (iv)
(vi)	Deposition	Gas $\rightleftharpoons$ Solid (reverse of sublimation)	As in (iv)

Vapour Pressure

- Pressure of vapours in equilibrium with liquid at a given temperature is called its **vapour pressure.**

  Liquid $\rightleftharpoons$ Gas; (vapour) $\Delta H > 0$
- This pressure is sometimes called **saturated vapour pressure** because at this stage, the vapour phase is saturated with vapour.
- Evaporation is endothermic , increase in temperature will shift the above equilibrium towards the side of the formation of vapours, thus vapour pressure increases.

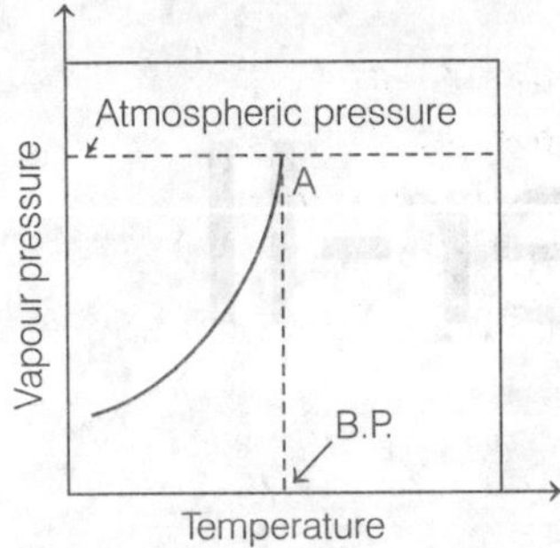

- A liquid boils when the vapour pressure of the vapours escaping from liquid is equal to atmospheric pressure (or external pressure). The temperature at this point (as point *A*) is called **boiling temperature.**
- The temperature of the liquid at which vapour pressure is equal to **1 atm**, is called **normal boiling point.**
- The temperature of liquid at which vapour pressure is equal to **1 bar**, is called **standard boiling point.**

For water

Normal boiling point is 100°C (373.15 K) at 1 atm.

Standard boiling point is 99.6°C (372.75 K) at 1 bar.

Enthalpy of vaporisation (heat required to change 1 mole of liquid into its vapour) is related to boiling point of liquid.

By Trouton's rule,

$$\Delta H_{vap} = 88 \text{ J mol}^{-1} \text{ K}^{-1} \times T_b$$

(boiling point in Kelvin)

Boiling and evaporation

- Boiling takes place only at constant temperature called boiling point while, evaporation takes place spontaneously at all temperatures.
- Evaporation takes place at the surface of the liquid whereas, boiling involves the formation of the bubbles of vapour below the surface of the liquid.
- Evaporation is a surface phenomenon, thus increase in surface area increases rate of evaporation.
- Being endothermic, evaporation causes cooling (when you place some alcohol an your palm, you may feel cooling due to evaporation of alcohol).
- Greater the intermolecular forces between molecules, smaller the extent of evaporation.

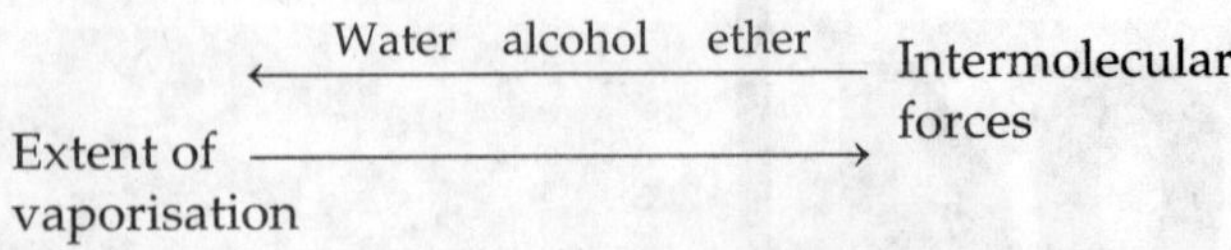

Factors affecting vapour pressure

- **Temperature** By Clausius - Clapeyron equation,

$$\frac{dp}{dt} = \frac{\Delta H_{vap} p}{RT^2}$$

$$\frac{dp}{p} = \frac{\Delta H_{vap}}{R}\left(\frac{dT}{T^2}\right)$$

On integration, $\log_e p = -\dfrac{\Delta H_{vap}}{RT} + \text{constant}$

or $\log_{10} p = -\dfrac{\Delta H_{vap}}{2.303RT} + \text{constant}$

A graph between $\log_{10} p$ and $\dfrac{1}{T}$ is linear as shown :

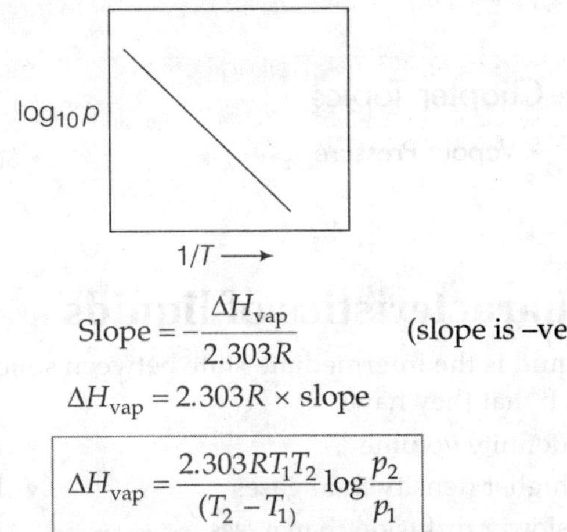

$$\text{Slope} = -\frac{\Delta H_{vap}}{2.303R} \quad \text{(slope is –ve)}$$

$$\therefore \quad \Delta H_{vap} = 2.303R \times \text{slope}$$

$$\boxed{\Delta H_{vap} = \frac{2.303RT_1T_2}{(T_2 - T_1)} \log \frac{p_2}{p_1}}$$

where p_1 is the vapour pressure at temperature T_1 and p_2 at temperature T_2.

As $\left(\dfrac{1}{T}\right)$ increases, or T decreases, log p decreases.

Thus, **vapour pressure increases with increase in temperature.**

- **Nature of liquid** Liquids having **strong** intermolecular attraction have less tendency of evaporation and thus they have low vapour pressure (as in water). Liquids having **weak** intermolecular attraction have more tendency to escape from surface and thus have high vapour pressure.
- Vapour pressure of solution is less than that of solvent as addition of solute lowers the temperature (as in case of sucrose, glucose, etc.).

Vapour pressure of mixture of volatile liquids

$$p_{total} = p_1^\circ \chi_1 + p_2^\circ \chi_2 = p_1 + p_2$$

where, χ_1 = mole fraction of volatile liquid (1)

$\chi_2 = (1 - \chi_1)$, mole fraction of volatile liquid (2)

p_1° = vapour pressure of liquid (1) in pure state

p_2° = vapour pressure of liquid (2) in pure state.

p_1 = vapour pressure of liquid (1) in mixture $= p_1^\circ \chi_1$

p_2 = vapour pressure of liquid (2) in mixture $= p_2^\circ \chi_2$

$$\therefore \quad p_{total} = p_1^\circ \chi_1 + p_2^\circ (1 - \chi_1) = p_2^\circ + \chi_1 (p_1^\circ - p_2^\circ)$$

Effect of pressure on boiling point

$$H_2O(l) \rightleftharpoons H_2O(g)$$

When vapours are formed, vapour pressure increases. On increasing pressure, condensation takes place, thus boiling point increases.

For the case of water,

Pressure	(B.P.)
$p = 1$ atm	100°C
$p > 1$ atm	>100°C (cooking time decreases)
$p < 1$ atm	<100°C (cooking time increases)

The vapour pressure of a liquid in droplet form (p_s) compared to equilibrium pressure (p) is given by Kelvin equation,

$$\ln \left(\frac{p_s}{p} \right) = \frac{2\gamma M}{rdRT}$$

where, γ = surface tension,
M = molar mass,
r = radius of liquid drop,
d = density of the liquid,
T = temperature (K), R = gas constant

Solved Examples & Instant Practice

Example 4.1) The boiling point of n- heptane is 36°C. Estimate its molar heat of vaporisation (ΔH_v), assuming it obeys Trouton's rule.

Sol. By Trouton's rule,

$$\Delta H_v = 88 \text{ J mol}^{-1} \text{ K}^{-1} \times \text{B.P.(K)}$$

$$36°\text{C} = 273 + 36 = 309 \text{ K}$$

$$\Delta H_v = 88 \text{ J mol}^{-1} \text{ K}^{-1} \times 309 \text{ K}$$

$$= 27192 \text{ J mol}^{-1} = 27.192 \text{ kJ mol}^{-1}$$

■ $\dfrac{\text{Quantity mol}^{-1}}{\text{Molar mass}} = \text{Quantity g}^{-1}$

$\therefore \dfrac{27.192 \text{ kJ mol}^{-1}}{\text{Heptane } (100 \text{ g mol}^{-1})} = 0.27192 \text{ kJ g}^{-1}$

Immediate Test 1

(i) The heat of vaporisation of water at 100°C is 2.56 kJ g^{-1} and at 37°C it is 2.41 kJ g^{-1},

(a) Convert these values to molar heat of vaporisation.

(b) Why is the heat of vaporisation greater at 37°C than at 100°C?

(ii) Boiling point of following liquids are given

(a) ethanol 351 K

(b) dimethyl ether 308 K

Determine molar heat of vaporisation in each case.

Example 4.2) Heat of vaporisation of ether (C_2H_6O) is 27.104 kJ mol^{-1}. How much heat is required to vaporise 0.92 kg of ether completely into vapours ?

Sol. Heat required = Heat of vaporisation × moles of liquid

$$\text{Moles} = \frac{\text{Amount in grams}}{\text{Molar mass}}$$

$$\text{Ether} = 0.92 \text{ kg}$$

Molar mass of ether (C_2H_6O)

$$= 2\text{C} + 6\text{H} + \text{O}$$

$$= 24 + 6 + 16$$

$$= 46 \text{ g mol}^{-1}$$

$$= \frac{0.92 \times 1000 \text{ g}}{46 \text{ g mol}^{-1}} = 20 \text{ mol}$$

$$\therefore \text{ Heat required} = 27.104 \text{ kJ mol}^{-1} \times 20 \text{ mol}$$

$$= 542.08 \text{ kJ mol}^{-1}$$

Immediate Test 2

Given, $\Delta H_{vap}(NH_3) = 23.4 \text{ kJmol}^{-1}$

and $\Delta H_{fusion}(\text{ice}) = 6.00 \text{ kJ mol}^{-1}$

(a) How much heat is required to vaporise 1.7 kg of NH_3 liquid?

(b) How many grams of water at 0°C could be converted to ice at 0°C by evaporation of this amount of heat required in evaporation of NH_3?

Example 4.3) Vapour pressure of a volatile liquid is 100 Torr at 27°C and 150 Torr at 57°C. What is enthalpy of vaporisation?

Sol. By Clausius-Clapeyron equation,

$$\Delta H_{vap} = \frac{2.303RT_1T_2}{(T_2 - T_1)} \log \frac{p_2}{p_1}$$

If vapour pressures p_1 and p_2 at the temperatures T_1 and T_2 are known, ΔH_{vap} can be calculated.

$$T(K) = T(°C) + 273$$

■ **Note** Unit of R decides unit of ΔH_{vap}.

Vapour pressure p_1 at 300 K = 100 Torr
Vapour pressure p_2 at 330 K = 150 Torr

$$\Delta H_{vap} = \frac{2.303 \times 8.3143 \text{ J mol}^{-1} \text{ K}^{-1} \times 300 \text{ K} \times 330 \text{ K}}{30 \text{ K}} \log \frac{150}{100}$$

$$= 11127 \text{ J mol}^{-1} = 11.127 \text{ kJ mol}^{-1}$$

Example 4.4) The vapour pressure of benzene is 100.0 mmHg at 300 K and 400 mmHg at 330 K. What is the boiling point of benzene at 760.0 mmHg?

Sol.

Step I. ΔH_{vap} (between T_1 and T_2) $= \frac{2.303RT_1T_2}{(T_2 - T_1)} \log \frac{p_2}{p_1}$

Step II. ΔH_{vap} (between T_1 and T_3) $= \frac{2.303R\,T_1T_3}{(T_3 - T_1)} \log \frac{p_3}{p_1}$

Since, ΔH_{vap} remains constant within given temperature range hence,

$$\frac{2.303\,RT_1T_2}{(T_2 - T_1)} \log \frac{p_2}{p_1} = \frac{2.303\,RT_1T_3}{(T_3 - T_1)} \log \frac{p_3}{p_1}$$

T_1, T_2 and p_1, p_2 and p_3 are given, hence boiling point of benzene T_3 can be calculated.

$$\frac{T_2}{(T_2 - T_1)} \log \frac{p_2}{p_1} = \frac{T_3}{(T_3 - T_1)} \log \frac{p_3}{p_1}$$

$$\frac{330}{30} \log \frac{400}{100} = \frac{T_3}{(T_3 - 300)} \log \frac{760}{100}$$

$$\therefore \quad T_3 = 346 \text{ K}$$

Immediate Test 3

(i) Estimate the vapour pressure of water at 80° C, assume water boils at 1 bar pressure. Heat of vaporisation of water is 40.7 kJ mol^{-1}.

(ii) Freon (CCl_2F_2), one of the ozone layer destroyers, has vapour pressure = 40.0 mmHg at −81.6° C and vapour pressure = 400 mmHg at − 43.9° C. What is the normal boiling point of freon?

Example 4.5) Variation of vapour pressure with temperature is given by

$$\log_{10} p(\text{mm}) = -\frac{4000 \text{ K}}{T(\text{K})} + 10$$

Calculate

(i) ΔH_{vap} (ii) Vapour pressure at 227°C

Sol. Variation of vapour pressure with temperature is studied by Clausius-Clapeyron equation,

$$\log_{10} p = -\frac{\Delta H_{vap}}{2.303RT} + \text{constant}$$

This is **linear equation** of the type ($y = mx + c$) and a graph between ($\log_{10} p$) and $\left(\frac{1}{T}\right)$ is a straight line.

On comparison, ΔH_{vap} can be evaluated.

(i) On comparison, $\frac{\Delta H_{vap}}{2.303R} = 4000$

$$\therefore \quad \Delta H = 2.303 \times 4000 \text{ K} \times R$$
$$= 2.303 \times 4000 \text{ K} \times 8.314 \text{ J mol}^{-1} \text{ K}^{-1}$$
$$= 76591 \text{ J mol}^{-1} = 76.591 \text{ kJ mol}^{-1}$$

(ii) Vapour pressure at 227°C (500 K)

$$\log_{10} p(\text{mm}) = \frac{-4000 \text{ K}}{500 \text{ K}} + 10 = -8 + 10 = 2.0$$

Take (antilog)

$$\therefore \quad p = 100 \text{ mm}$$

Immediate Test 4

The vapour pressure of benzene in the temperature 283 K and 303 K can be expressed as

$$\log_{10} p \text{ (Torr)} = 7.960 - \frac{1780\text{K}}{T(\text{K})}$$

Calculate

(a) the enthalpy of vaporisation

(b) the normal boiling point of benzene

(c) pre-exponential factor of the equation,

$$p = Ae^{-\Delta H/RT}$$

Example 4.6) Vapour pressure of a mixture of volatile liquids A and B can be expressed as (in Torr).

$$p_{total} = 60 + 20\chi_B$$

(i) What are vapour pressures of volatile liquids A and B?

(ii) What is composition of the mixture when total vapour pressure is 68 Torr?

Sol. For volatile liquids A and B.

If vapour pressure of liquid $A = p_A^\circ$ and that of $B = p_B^\circ$ in solution, χ_A is the mole fraction of liquid A and χ_B that of liquid B then

$$p_{total} = \chi_A p_A^\circ + \chi_B p_B^\circ = (1 - \chi_B)p_A^\circ + \chi_B p_B^\circ$$
$$= p_A^\circ + (p_B^\circ - p_A^\circ)\chi_B$$
$$p_{total} = 60 + 20\chi_B$$

Thus, on comparison, p_A° and p_B° and also composition χ_A and χ_B can be determined.

(i) If $\chi_B = 1$, it means pure B, thus $p_B^\circ = 60 + 20 = 80$ Torr

If $\chi_B = 0$, it means pure A, thus $p_A^\circ = 60$ Torr.

(ii) $p_{total} = 68$ Torr

$\therefore \; 68 = 60 + 20\chi_B$

$\therefore \; \chi_B = 0.4 \Rightarrow \chi_A = 0.6$ $\quad (\because \chi_A + \chi_B = 1)$

Immediate Test 5

(i) Calculate total vapour pressure of mixture of 1 mole benzene (vapour pressure = 40 Torr) and 3 moles toluene (vapour pressure = 36 Torr) at 300K.

(ii) A volume of 10.5 dm^3 of N_2 measured at 300 K and 102.66 kPa pressure is bubbled through bromobenzene (C_6H_5Br) at 313 K. The mass of bromobenzene is reduced by 0.856 g. Calculate vapour pressure of bromobenzene at 313 K.

Example 4.7) What is the ratio of the vapour pressure of water in a droplet with $r = 1.0\,\mu m$ compared to that of bulk water at 298 K. For H_2O at 298 K

$$\gamma = 71.97\times10^{-3}\ Nm^{-1},\ d = 0.997\ g\ cm^{-3}$$

Sol. By Kelvin equation,

$$\ln\frac{p_s}{p} = \frac{2\gamma M}{rdRT}$$

Take all data in **SI units**

$$\ln\frac{p_s}{p} = \frac{2\times71.97\times10^{-3}\ Nm^{-1}\times18\times10^{-3}\ kg\ mol^{-1}}{1\times10^{-6} m\times0.999\times10^{3}\ kg\ m^{-3}\times8.314\ JK^{-1}\ mol^{-1}\times298\ K}$$

$$= 1.05\times10^{-5}$$

$$\therefore\quad \frac{p_s}{p} = 1.001$$

Immediate Test 6

What must be the radius of a water droplet if the vapour pressure is 2.7 times greater than that of bulk liquid at 298 K. ($\gamma = 71.97\times10^{-3}$ Nm^{-1}, $d = 0.999$ $g\ cm^{-3}$)

KNOWLEDGE CONFIRMATION **Test 1**

1 Following phase-changes respectively are called

I. Solid $\rightleftharpoons$ Gas II. Gas $\rightleftharpoons$ Liquid

III. Liquid $\rightleftharpoons$ Gas

	I	II	III
(a)	Sublimation	Liquefaction	Vaporisation
(b)	Deposition	Liquefaction	Vaporisation
(c)	Sublimation	Vaporisation	Liquefaction
(d)	Sublimation	Vaporisation	Deposition

2 $\Delta H > 0$ for the processes (in Q. 1 above) will be that of

(a) I, III (b) I, II (c) II, III (d) I, II, III

3 When a phase-change takes place

(a) $\Delta H_{sublimation} = -\Delta H_{deposition}$

(b) $\Delta H_{sublimation} = \Delta H_{fusion} + \Delta H_{vaporisation}$

(c) $-\Delta H_{sublimation} = \Delta H_{condensation} + \Delta H_{freezing}$

(d) All of the above

4 Select correct statement (s) about evaporation:

(a) It is accompanied by cooling

(b) It takes place at all temperature, compared to boiling which takes place only at boiling point

(c) It is a surface phenomenon

(d) All of the above

5 Clausius - Clapeyron equation is

(a) $\dfrac{d\log_{10}p}{dT} = \dfrac{\Delta H}{2.303RT}$ (b) $\dfrac{d\log_{10}p}{dT} = \dfrac{\Delta H}{2.303RT^2}$

(c) $\dfrac{d\log_{10}p}{dT} = -\dfrac{\Delta H}{2.303RT^2}$ (d) $\dfrac{d\log_{10}p}{dT} = -\dfrac{\Delta H}{2.303RT}$

6 If Clausius-Clapeyron equation is written in the form

$$p = Ae^{-\Delta H_{vap}/RT}$$

Then, vapour pressure varies with temperature as

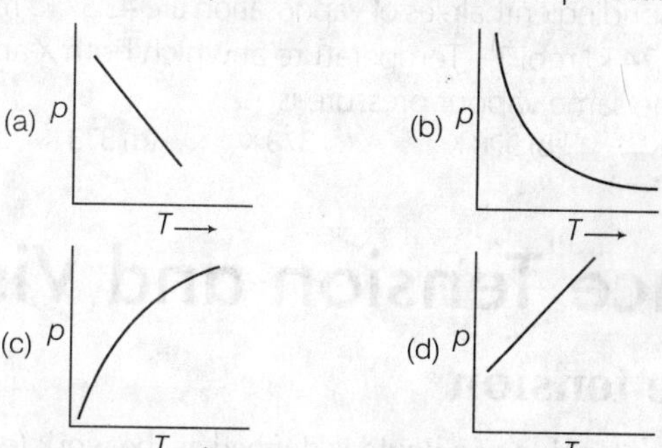

7 Variation of vapour pressure with temperature is given by following graph.

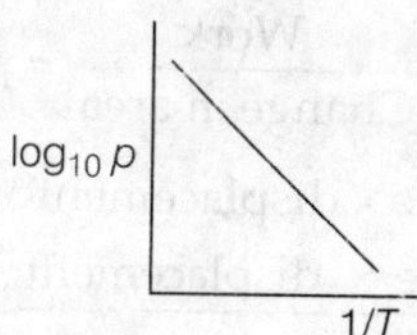

If slope $= \left(\dfrac{-1}{0.02303}\right)$K, then enthalpy of vaporisation is

(a) 8.314 J (b) 0.08314 J

(c) 831.4 J (d) None of these

8 At one place, boiling point of water is found to be 110°C. At this place,

(a) external pressure is less than 1atm

(b) external pressure is greater than 1 atm

(c) external pressure is equal to 1atm

(d) cooking takes longer time

9 If Clausius - Clapeyron equation $p = Ae^{-\Delta H/RT}$ can be written as $\log_{10} p(\text{mm Hg}) = 5 - \frac{400}{T}$ is follow, then ΔH and A are respectively

ΔH(kcal mol^{-1})	A (mmHg)
(a) 400	5
(b) 1.84	10^5
(c) 0.400	10^3
(d) 1.84	5

10 Vapour pressure of a mixture of 0.46g CH_3CH_2OH ($p°$=40 mmHg) and 0.36 g H_2O ($p°$=20 mmHg) at 298 K is
(a) 40 mmHg (b) 50 mmHg
(c) 60 mmHg (d) 27 mmHg

11 The enthalpy of vaporisation of cyclohexane (C_6H_{12}) at its boiling point (353.9 K) is 385.15 Jg^{-1}. Pressure to be reduced to boil it at 298.15 K is
(a) 112.30 mmHg (b) 11.23 mmHg
(c) 76.00 mmHg (d) 56.65 mmHg

12 At 298 K, liquids X and Y have vapour pressures of 13.332 kPa and 26.665 kPa respectively and the corresponding enthalpies of vaporisation are 43.57 kJ mol^{-1} and 16.74 kJ mol^{-1}. Temperature at which both X and Y have the same vapour pressure is
(a) 298 K (b) 328 K (c) 378 K (d) 373 K

13 Number of water molecules in the droplet being formed is so that pure water vapour must be compressed such that $\left(\frac{p_s}{p}\right) = 2.7$ is ($r = 1.1 \times 10^{-9}$ m, $d = 0.999$ g cm^{-3})
(a) 190 (b) 186 (c) 200 (d) 216

14 Ratio $\left(\frac{p_s}{p}\right)$ for a drop of water at 298 K that has $r = 0.1$ cm ($\gamma = 71.97 \times 10^{-3}$ Nm^{-1} and $d = 1 \times 10^3$ kg m^{-3}) is
(a) 1.0 (b) 1.9
(c) 0.1 (d) 2.7

15 What is the minimum size of water droplets such that the vapour pressure does not differ by more than 1% from the bulk value for water 298 K?
(a) 1.05×10^{-9} m (b) 1.05×10^{-6} m
(c) 1.05×10^{-7} m (d) None of these

16 An open beaker of water in equilibrium with water vapour is in a sealed container. When few grams of glucose are added to beaker of water, the rate at which water molecules ***[JEE Main 2020 (II) NTA]***
(a) leaves the solution decreases
(b) leaves the solution increases
(c) leaves the vapour increases
(d) leaves the vapour decreases

Surface Tension and Viscosity

Surface tension

- The surface tension of a liquid is defined as the work (energy) required to expand the surface of a liquid by unit area.

Surface tension = Work to increase surface by unit area

$$= \frac{\text{Work}}{\text{Change in area}} = \gamma$$

Also, work = Force × displacement

$$\therefore \quad \gamma = \frac{\text{Force} \times \text{displacement}}{\text{Change in area}} = \frac{\text{Force} \times \text{length}}{(\text{length})^2}$$

$$\gamma = \text{Force/Length}$$

Thus, surface tension can be assumed as work (energy) per unit area or force per unit length.

- Work necessary to create or extend one unit area of a surface is called the **surface energy.**

Surface energy = Surface tension × area

The difference in pressure between the inside and outside of a liquid drop $= \frac{2\gamma}{r}$.

Units of surface tension are Nm^{-1}, **kg s^{-2}.**

Units of Surface energy are J or Nm

$$1 \text{ dyne cm}^{-1} = 1 \text{ dyne . cm cm}^{-1} \text{ cm}^{-1}$$
$$= 1 \text{ erg cm}^{-2} \text{ (1 dyne.cm} = 1 \text{ erg)}$$
$$= 10^{-3} \text{ Nm}^{-1}$$

Effects of surface tension

- Magnitude of surface tension is a measure of the strength of intermolecular attractive forces.
- Capillary action (rise or fall of liquid in a capillary) is due to surface tension. Capillary action arises due to difference between cohesive forces (I) (forces within liquid) and adhesive forces (II) (forces within liquids and wall of the container).
  If I < II, the liquid rises in the capillary.
  If I > II, the liquid falls in the capillary and solid (glass surface) is not wetted.
- Soaps and detergents lower the surface tension of water to a marked degree and thus, improve the spreading property of these subsances.
- When a drop of mass m ans radius r is formed, surface tension balances the gravitational force.

$$2\pi r\gamma = mg$$

Also, difference in pressure across the curve surface is balanced by weight of the column in the gravitational field.

$$\therefore \quad \frac{2\gamma}{r} = hdg$$

If angle of contact θ is given, then. $h = \frac{2\gamma}{rdg\cos\theta}$

If $\theta = 0$, $\cos\theta = 1$, hence $h = \frac{2\gamma}{rdg}$

Variation of surface tension with temperature

- Surface tension decreases with increase in temperature. At critical temperature, there is no distinction between liquid and vapour phases, thus surface disappears at T_c.

Thus, $\lim_{T \to T_c} \gamma = 0$

- By **Eotvos equation,** $\gamma\left(\frac{M}{d}\right)^{2/3} = a - kt$

where M is the molar mass, d is the density, t is the temperature (in°C), a and k are constants.

At $t = T_c, \gamma = 0 \;\therefore\; a = kT_c$

$$\therefore \quad \gamma\left(\frac{M}{d}\right)^{2/3} = a - kt = k(T_c - t)$$

Thus, as t increases, $(T_c - t)$ decreases. Hence, γ decreases.

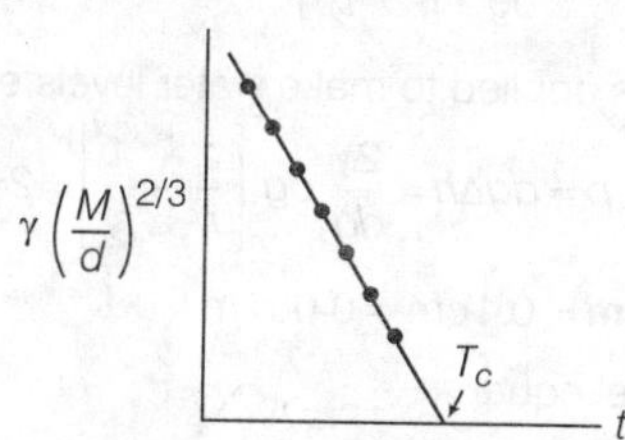

k (Eotvos coefficient) is the slope of the line

$$k = \frac{\gamma_1\left(\frac{M}{d_1}\right)^{2/3} - \gamma_2\left(\frac{M}{d_2}\right)^{2/3}}{(t_2 - t_1)}$$

Viscosity

- Viscosity is the force of friction (F) between two layers of a liquid moving past one another with different velocities.

$$F \propto A\left(\frac{du}{dx}\right) \Rightarrow \frac{F}{A} = -\eta\left(\frac{du}{dx}\right)$$

- η is called coefficient of viscosity. (du) is the difference in velocities of two layers at a distance (dx) apart. $\left(\frac{du}{dx}\right)$ is also called velocity gradient.

If $\left(\frac{du}{dx}\right) = 1\,s^{-1}$, then $\frac{F}{A} = -\eta$.

- Thus, viscosity is the tangential force per unit area required to maintain a unit velocity gradient.

Units : CGS Dyne $cm^{-2}s = g\ cm\ s^{-2}cm^{-2}s$

$= g\ cm^{-1}\ s^{-1}$ (called poise)

1 centipoise = 0.01 poise
1 millipoise = 0.001 poise

MKS $Nm^{-2}s$ (Pascals) $= kg\ m\ s^{-2}m^{-2}s = kg\ m^{-1}s^{-1}$

$1\ \text{poise} = 1\ g\ cm^{-1}\ s^{-1} = 10^{-1} kg\ m^{-1}\ s^{-1}$

■ $1\ N = 1\ kg\ ms^{-2}$

Fluidity (ϕ)

- Reciprocal of viscosity is called fluidity.

$$\phi = \frac{1}{\eta}$$

- Greater the viscosity, smaller the fluidity, the more slowly the liquid flows. Hydrogen bonding and van der Waals' forces are strong enough to cause the liquid to be more viscous.

Effect of temperature on viscosity

- The viscosity of a liquid generally decreases with rise in temperature, as given by 'hole theory'.

$$\eta = Ae^{E_a/RT}$$

where, A is the pre-exponential factor, E_a, is the activation energy required to move into a hole.
In terms of logarithm,

$$\log_e \eta = \log_e A + \log_e e^{E_a/RT} = \log_e A + \frac{E_a}{RT}$$

or $$\log_{10}\eta = \log_{10} A + \frac{E_a}{2.303RT}$$

Graphically, $y = c + mx$

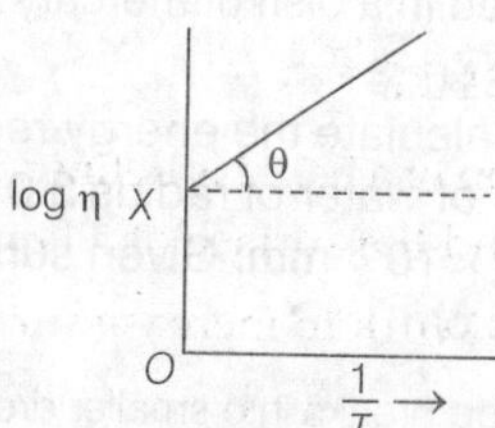

- Thus, as $\left(\frac{1}{T}\right)$ increases (or T decreases) log η increases.

Thus, **viscosity decreases with increase in temperature.**

$$c = \text{intercept} = OX = \log_{10} A$$

$$m = \text{slope} = \tan\theta = \frac{E_a}{2.303R}$$

Also, $$\log_{10}\frac{\eta_2}{\eta_1} = \frac{E_a}{2.303R}\left[\frac{1}{T_1} - \frac{1}{T_2}\right]$$

Effect of pressure

- By Poiseuille's equation, $\eta = \frac{\pi r^4 tp}{8Vl}$

where V is the volume of liquid flowing through a capillary of length l, radius (r) in time t at pressure (p).

$\Rightarrow \quad \eta \propto p$

Thus, **viscosity increases with increase in pressure.**

Solved Examples & Instant Practice

Example 4.8) A liquid of density 800 $kg\,m^{-3}$ and having surface tension of 0.056 Nm^{-1} will rise how far in a glass capillary of inside diameter 1.20 mm ?

Sol. If liquid rises to a height (h) due to surface tension, then

$$2\pi r\gamma = mg$$

Mass can be related to density and volume of the capillary of height h by equation :

$$\frac{m}{V} = \text{density } (d),\ V = \pi r^2 h$$

$$\therefore \quad mg = Vd = \pi r^2 hdg$$

$$\therefore \quad 2\pi r\gamma = \pi r^2 hdg$$

$$\therefore \quad h = \frac{2\gamma}{rdg} \Rightarrow r = \frac{\text{diameter}}{2}$$

$$h = \frac{2 \times 0.056\ Nm^{-1}(kg\ s^{-2})}{(0.60 \times 10^{-3} m) \times 800\ kg\ m^{-3} \times 9.8\ ms^{-2}}$$

$$= 0.0238\ m = 23.8\ mm$$

■ $1\,Nm^{-1} = 1 kg\ ms^{-2} m^{-1} = 1 kg\ s^{-2} \Rightarrow 1\,mm = 1 \times 10^{-3} m$

Immediate Test 7

(i) Calculate the height to which water will rise in a glass capillary of radius 0.02 cm. Surface tension of water is 72.8 dynes cm^{-1}, density $d = 1.0\ g\,cm^{-3}$.

(ii) The surface tension of liquid mercury is 0.490 Nm^{-1}, and its density is $13.6 \times 10^3 kgm^{-3}$. How far will the mercury level be depressed, when a glass capillary with 0.40 mm radius is placed in a dish of mercury?

Example 4.9) Calculate the energy required to disperse one spherical drop of water of radius 3.0 mm into spherical drops of radius 3.0×10^{-3} mm. Given surface tension of water is 72.8 dynes cm^{-1}.

Sol. When a large drop breaks into smaller drops, energy required is the surface energy.

Energy required = γ × change in surface area due to formation of N drops

$$\text{Number of drops} = \frac{\text{Volume of large drop of radius } R}{\text{Volume of small drops of radius } r}$$

$$\text{Surface area} = 4\pi(\text{radius})^2$$

$$N\ (\text{number of drops}) = \frac{\frac{4}{3}\pi(3.0)^3}{\frac{4}{3}\pi(3 \times 10^{-3})^3} = 10^9 \text{ drops}$$

Surface area of one large drop = $4\pi(3)^2 = 36\pi\,mm^2$

$$= 36\,\pi \times 10^{-2}\ cm^2$$

Surface area of 10^9 small drops = $4\pi(3 \times 10^{-3})^2 mm^2 \times 10^9$

$$= 36\pi \times 10^{-8} cm^2 \times 10^9 = 360\pi\,cm^2$$

Increase in surface area = $(360\pi - 0.36\pi)cm^2 = 359.64\pi$

Energy required = γ × increase in surface area

$$= 72.8 \text{ dynes } cm^{-1} \times 359.64\pi$$

$$= 8.2252 \times 10^4 \text{ erg}$$

$$= 8.2252 \times 10^{-3}\ J$$

■ (10^7 erg = 1J)

Immediate Test 8

How much work is required to break up a mole of water at 20°C into spherical droplets of radius 1 cm.

γ for $H_2O = 72.75 \times 10^{-3} Nm^{-1}$ and density = 1000 $kg\,m^{-3}$

Example 4.10) A sample of water at 70°C was placed in a U-tube consisting of one arm with radius of 0.10 mm and the other with a radius of 0.15 mm. What pressure must be applied to the water in the smaller arm to make the water levels equal. ($\gamma = 72.75 \times 10^{-3}\ Nm^{-1}$ for water)

Sol.

$$h = \frac{2\gamma}{drg}$$

Thus,

$$\Delta h = \frac{2\gamma}{dg}\left[\frac{1}{r_1} - \frac{1}{r_2}\right]$$

When pressure p is applied to make water levels equal

$$p = dg\Delta h = \frac{2\gamma}{dg} dg \left[\frac{1}{r_1} - \frac{1}{r_2}\right] = 2\gamma\left[\frac{1}{r_1} - \frac{1}{r_2}\right]$$

$$1\,mm = 0.1\,cm = 0.001\,m$$

To make water level equal

$$p = 2\gamma\left[\frac{1}{r_1} - \frac{1}{r_2}\right]$$

$$= 2 \times 72.75 \times 10^{-3}\left[\frac{1}{0.10 \times 10^{-3}} - \frac{1}{0.15 \times 10^{-3}}\right]$$

$$= 485\ Pa$$

Example 4.11) Coefficient of viscosity of a liquid is 2.76×10^{-4} Pa s at –40° C. If energy of activation for moving a hole is 5.984 kJ mol^{-1}, calculate viscosity at – 50° C.

Sol.

$$\log\frac{\eta_2}{\eta_1} = \frac{E_a}{2.303R}\left[\frac{1}{T_2} - \frac{1}{T_1}\right]$$

$$\log\frac{\eta_2}{(2.76 \times 10^{-4})} = \frac{5.984}{2.303 \times 8.314 \times 10^{-3}}\left[\frac{1}{223} - \frac{1}{233}\right]$$

$$\eta_2 = 3.17 \times 10^{-4}\ \text{Pa s}$$

Immediate Test 9

When temperature is increased from 27°C to 37°C viscosity of a liquid is reduced by 10%. What is energy of activation?

KNOWLEDGE CONFIRMATION Test 2

1 If $\eta = 2.10 \times 10^{-5}$ Pa s, then it is equal to

(a) 2.10×10^{-5} N m^{-2}s
(b) 2.10×10^{-5} kg m^{-1}s^{-1}
(c) 2.10×10^{-4} Poise
(d) All of these

2 Surface tension of water is 73 dynes cm^{-1}. Difference of pressure between the inside and outside of a spherical drop of water of radius 1 mm is

(a) 146 dyne cm^{-2}
(b) 1460 dyne cm^{-2}
(c) 14.6 dyne cm^{-2}
(d) None of these

3 One of the following properties increases with rise in temperature

(a) viscosity
(b) surface tension
(c) vapour pressure
(d) density

4 Consider following properties of liquids :

I. Viscosity II. Surface tension
III. Thermal conductance IV. Diffusion

Select transport properties out of I to IV

(a) all except II
(b) all except II and IV
(c) all except I and II
(d) All of these

5 Effect of temperature on viscosity is given by

(a) adsorption theory
(b) collision theory
(c) hole theory
(d) Arrhenius theory

6 1 poise is equal to

(a) 1 kg m^{-1}s^{-1}
(b) 0.1 kg m^{-1}s^{-1}
(c) 0.01 kg m^{-1}s^{-1}
(d) 10 kg m^{-1}s^{-1}

7 Select the correct statement.

(a) Viscosity of gas increases and that of liquid decreases with rise in temperature
(b) Viscosity of liquid increases and that of gas decreases with rise in temperature
(c) Viscosity of liquid as well as that of gas increases with rise in temperature
(d) Viscosity of liquid as well as that of gas decreases with rise in temperature

8 Select the correct statement(s).

(a) Meniscus of water has convex shape while that of mercury has concave shape
(b) Meniscus of water has concave shape while that of mercury has convex shape
(c) Both have concave shape
(d) Both have convex shape

9 Select the correct statement(s).

(a) Forces holding liquid molecules together are called cohesive forces
(b) Force of attraction between liquid and another surface is called adhesive force
(c) Both of the above
(d) None of the above

10 Surface tension of a liquid is not decreased by

(a) addition of detergent
(b) decrease in temperature
(c) increase in temperature
(d) All of these

11 Consider two bubbles of a liquid of different size connected by a hollow tube

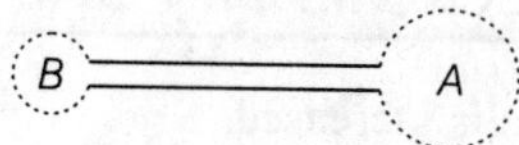

then

(a) B gets smaller and A gets larger
(b) B gets larger and A gets smaller
(c) both gets smaller
(d) both gets larger and ultimately burst

12 Downward force due to gravity when liquid of density 'd' is in a column of radius 'r' set up at a height 'h' is balanced by upward thurst due to surface tension γ. Thus,

(a) $2\pi r\gamma = r^2hdg$
(b) $2\gamma r = hdg$
(c) $2\gamma r = \pi hdg$
(d) $2r = rhdg$

13 A tube was placed in a sample of water at 293 K. As a result of capillary action, the water rose inside the tube to a height of 11.40 cm. Thus, diameter of the tube is [$\gamma = 72.15 \times 10^{-3}$ Nm^{-1}, d (density) $= 0.998$ g cm^{-3} for water]

(a) 0.3012 mm
(b) 0.2176 mm
(c) 0.1304 mm
(d) 0.2608 mm

14 A 0.20 mm capillary tube and a 0.10 mm capillary tube was placed into a sample of liquid H_2O_2. The difference between the heights of the liquid in the tubes is 5.50 cm. If density of H_2O_2 is 1.41 g cm^{-3} at given temperature, its surface tension is

(a) 7.61×10^{-2} N m^{-1}
(b) 7.61×10^{-3} N m^{-1}
(c) 6.93×10^{-2} N m^{-1}
(d) 6.93×10^{-3} N m^{-1}

15 Benzene has a density of 0.879 g, cm^{-3} and has a surface tension of 0.02888 Nm^{-1}. Thus, difference of its height in two capillaries of diameters 0.10 mm and 0.15 mm is

(a) 0.223 cm
(b) 2.23 cm
(c) 2.23 m
(d) 2.33 dm

16 For diethyl ether, viscosity is 2.84 millipoise at 273 K and 2.33 millipoise at 293 K. Thus, activation energy of diethyl ether is

(a) 6.58 kJ mol^{-1}
(b) 4.90 kJ mol^{-1}
(c) 1.58 kJ mol^{-1}
(d) 3.60 kJ mol^{-1}

ACID TEST
For JEE Main

TYPE I MCQs with Only ONE Correct Alternate

1 If surface area is increased,
(a) evaporation increases
(b) boiling point increases
(c) melting point increases
(d) surface tension increases

2 In the following equilibrium,

$$\text{liquid} \rightleftharpoons \text{gas}$$

the pressure of vapours above the liquid is constant at
(a) low temperature
(b) high temperature
(c) constant temperature
(d) None of the above

3 The temperature at which densities of a substance in gaseous as well as in liquid states are same, is called
(a) ideal temperature
(b) isotonic temperature
(c) isoelectric temperature
(d) critical temperature

4 Types of forces that can be present in HF giving it in liquid state is/are
(a) dipole-dipole interaction
(b) London-forces
(c) hydrogen bonding
(d) All of the above

5 Out of the following,most volatile substance is

(a) OH NO_2 (b) OH NO_2

(c) 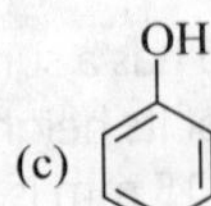

(d) H_2O

6 A person living in Shimla observed that cooking food without using pressure cooker takes more time. The reason for this observation is that at high altitude **[NCERT Exemplar]**
(a) pressure increases (b) temperature decreases
(c) pressure decreases (d) temperature increases

7 If saturated vapours are compressed slowly at constant temperature to half the initial volume, the vapour pressure
(a) becomes double
(b) becomes four times
(c) becomes half
(d) remains unchanged

8 Atmospheric pressure recorded in different cities are as follows:

Cities	Shimla	Bangalore	Delhi	Mumbai
p is N m^{-2}	1.01×10^5	1.2×10^5	1.02×10^5	1.21×10^5

Consider the above data and mark the place at which liquid will boil first. **[NCERT Exemplar]**
(a) Shimla (b) Bangalore
(c) Delhi (d) Mumbai

9 Surface tension of water is 73 dyne cm^{-1} at 293 K. If surface area is increased by 0.08 m^2, work done is
(a) 5.84 erg (b) 584 erg
(c) 5.84×10^{-3} J (d) 5.84×10^{-3} erg

10 If $\log_{10} p(\text{mm}) = -\dfrac{4000\text{K}}{T(\text{K})} + 10$, a logarithm form of Clausius-Clapeyron equation, then
(a) enthalpy of vaporisation is 18.424 kcal
(b) vapour pressure is 20 mm at 459.8 K
(c) Both are correct
(d) None of the above are correct

11 Surface tension of water is 7.29×10^{-2} J m^{-2}. This value is equal to
(a) 7.29×10^{-2} N m^{-1} (b) 72.9 erg cm^{-2}
(c) 72.9 dyne cm^{-1} (d) All of these

12 If change in pressure across the surface of a droplet of water of radius r is

$$\Delta p = \gamma \left(\frac{dA}{dV}\right)$$

where, dA is the change in surface area and dV is the change in volume, then
(a) $\Delta p = \dfrac{4\gamma}{r}$ (b) $\Delta p = \dfrac{2\gamma}{r}$
(c) $\Delta p = \dfrac{\gamma}{r}$ (d) $\Delta p = -\dfrac{4\gamma}{r}$

13 Surface tension at 293 K for several alcohols are given

$\gamma(CH_3OH) = 22.61\,\text{dyne cm}^{-1}$

$\gamma(C_2H_5OH) = 2.275 \times 10^{-2}\ \text{Nm}^{-1}$

$\gamma(C_3H_7OH) = 23.78\,\text{mJ m}^{-2}$

Which has the greatest surface tension out of the above alcohols?

(a) CH_3OH (b) C_2H_5OH
(c) C_3H_7OH (d) Can't be said

14 If pressure is increased for the following equilibrium

$H_2O(l) \xrightleftharpoons{1\,\text{atm}} H_2O(g), \Delta H = 10\,\text{kcal mol}^{-1}$

(a) $H_2O(g)$ is liquefied
(b) boiling point is increased
(c) Both of these
(d) None of the above

15 The heat is removed from a liquid which tends to supercool, its temperature drops below the freezing point and then rises suddenly. What is the source of heat which causes the temperature rise ?

(a) The enthalpy of fusion
(b) The enthalpy of vaporisation
(c) The enthalpy of sublimation
(d) The enthalpy of deposition

16 If soap water has a surface tension of 24.3 dyne cm^{-1}, what is the pressure difference between the inside and outside of a bubble whose radius is 1.75 cm ?

(a) 22.7 bar (b) 55.54 bar
(c) 55.54×10^{-3} bar (d) 5.554×10^{-5} bar

17 Choose the correct statement with respect to the vapour pressure of a liquid among the following.

(a) Increases linearly with increasing temperature
(b) Increases non-linearly with increasing temperature
(c) Decreases linearly with incrasing temperature
(d) Decreases non-linearly with increasing temperature

18 Which of following properties of water can be used to explain the spherical shapes of rain droplets?

(a) Viscosity (b) Surface tension
(c) Critical phenomenon (d) Vapour pressure

19 When temperature of a liquid is increased from 300 K to 400 K, vapour pressure increases 20%. Thus, enthalpy of vaporisation is ($\log 1.2 = 0.0792$)

(a) 438 cal (b) 438 kcal
(c) 3.866 kcal (d) 38.66 cal

20 A liquid of density 850 kg m^{-3} having a surface tension of 0.055 N m^{-1} will rise how far in a glass capillary of 1.40 mm inside diameter?

(a) 1.9 mm (b) 19 mm (c) 0.19 m (d) 0.19 mm

ACID TEST
For JEE Advanced

TYPE I MCQs with Only ONE Correct Alternate

21 Refer to the heating curve for 20.0 g of a compound of molar mass 95.0 g mol^{-1}. Melting point of the compound is

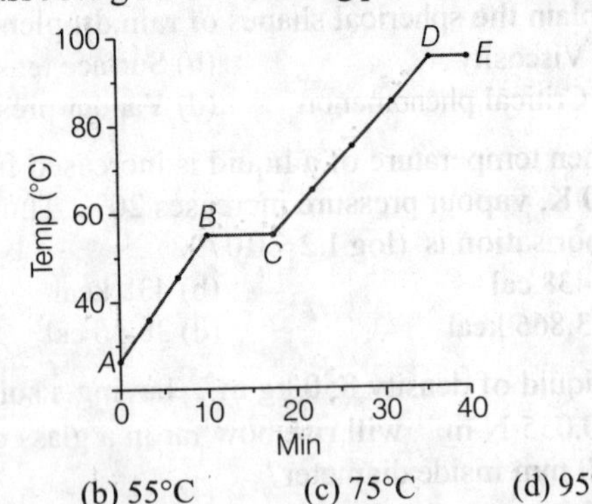

(a) 25°C (b) 55°C (c) 75°C (d) 95°C

22 The vapour pressure of most substances increases with temperature as depicted by the given curve.

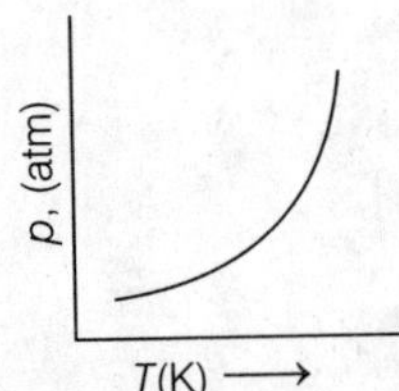

Which way of plotting these data is expected to give a straight line?

(a) $\frac{1}{p}$ vs T (b) p vs $\frac{1}{T}$ (c) $\ln p$ vs T (d) $\ln p$ vs $\frac{1}{T}$

23 10 mL of liquid water are introduced into a 1.0 L flask at 298 K. How many moles of water are in the vapour phase when equilibrium is established ?
Vapour pressure of H_2O at 298 K is 23.8 mm Hg.

(a) 1.28×10^{-3} (b) 5.56×10^{-3}
(c) 1.53×10^{-2} (d) 4.46×10^{-2}

24 If vapour pressure varies with temperature as given by equation.

$$\frac{d \log p}{dT} = + \frac{\Delta H}{RT^2}$$

then

(a) $p = Ae^{-\Delta H / RT}$ (b) $\log p = -\frac{\Delta H}{RT} + \text{constant}$

(c) $\Delta H = \frac{2.303 RT_1 T_2}{(T_2 - T_1)} \log \frac{p_2}{p_1}$ (d) All of these

25 If soap water has a surface tension of 25 dyne cm^{-1}, what is the pressure difference between the inside and outside of a bubble whose diameter is 3.50 cm ?

(a) 28.57 bar (b) 57.14 bar
(c) 5.714×10^{-3} bar (d) 5.714×10^{-5} bar

26 A sample of viscous liquid has its surface decreased from 70.0 cm^2 to 26.2 cm^2. Surface energy associated with this change is ($\gamma = 63.4$ dyne cm^{-1})

(a) 2.8×10^{-4} J (b) 1.45×10^{-4} J
(c) 1.45×10^{-7} J (d) 0.691×10^{-7} J

27 1 mole of water is placed in 1 dm^3 flask at standard boiling point of water. Thus, its vapour pressure is

(a) 30.99 bar (b) 31.01 bar (c) 1.0 bar (d) 1.0 atm

28 In the given variation of vapour pressure with temperature,

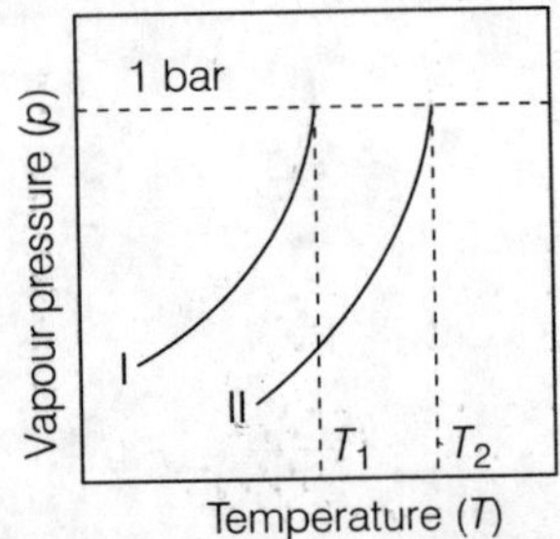

(a) Graph I is for pure solvent and graph II is for a solution containing non-volatile solute
(b) Graph II is for pure solvent and graph I is for a solution containing non-volatile solute
(c) T_2 is the boiling point of solvent, T_1 is the boiling point of solution
(d) $T_1 = T_2$

29 $NH_3(l) \rightleftharpoons NH_3(g)$, $\Delta H = 23.4$ kJ mol^{-1}
$H_2O(l) \rightleftharpoons H_2O(s)$, $\Delta H = -6.01$ kJ mol^{-1}
How many grams of water at 0°C could be converted to ice at 0°C by the heat used in the evaporation of 0.85 kg of ammonia?

(a) 3310 g (b) 2012 g (c) 1735 g (d) 3504 g

30 Two different gases 'A' and 'B' are filled in separate containers of equal capacity under the same conditions of temperature and pressure. On increasing the pressure slightly gas 'A' liquefies, but gas 'B' does not liquefy

even on applying high pressure until it is cooled. This is due to the fact that
(a) gas A is at T_c or below T_c
(b) gas B is at a temperature above T_c
(c) Both are correct
(d) None of the above is correct

31 A liquid film is in a rectangular wire loop in which one side could be moved. A force of 5.0×10^{-3} N is just sufficient to move the loop of 8.0×10^{-2} m wide, then surface tension is
(a) 3.125×10^{-2} N m^{-1} (b) 6.25×10^{-2} N m^{-1}
(c) 0.25 N m^{-1} (d) None is correct

32 Select the correct name(s) of the processes given against them.
(a) Crystals of β-dichlorobenzene used as both repellent, gradually become vapour without passing through liquid phase : **Vaporisation**
(b) As you enter a warm room from the outdoors on a cold winter day, your eye-glasses become fogged with a film of moisture : **Condensation**
(c) On a windly winter day, a pan of water is left outdoors. Some of it turns into vapours, the rest to ice, i.e. (vapour $\rightleftharpoons$ solid) equilibrium is followed : **Sublimation**
(d) All of the above are correct

33 Density of water at 4°C and 1 atm is 1 g mL^{-1}. Thus, density of water vapour under these conditions is
(a) 1.20×10^{-4} g mL^{-1} (b) 7.915×10^{-4} g mL^{-1}
(c) 9.10×10^{-3} g mL^{-1} (d) None of these

34 Water rises through 7.36 cm in a capillary of radius 0.020 cm at 298 K, at which density is 997.1 kg m^{-3}. Thus, surface tension of water is
(a) 0.072 N m^{-1} (b) 0.072 dyne m^{-1}
(c) 7.2 N m^{-1} (d) 72.0 dyne m^{-1}

35 The density of a fluid in the capillary of the plant is 1.3 g cm^{-3}, and its surface tension is 65 dyne cm^{-1}. How high will this fluid rise in the capillary of radius 5×10^{-3} mm?
(a) 4.08 m (b) 1.02 m
(c) 1.26 m (d) 2.04 m

36 In the following graph,

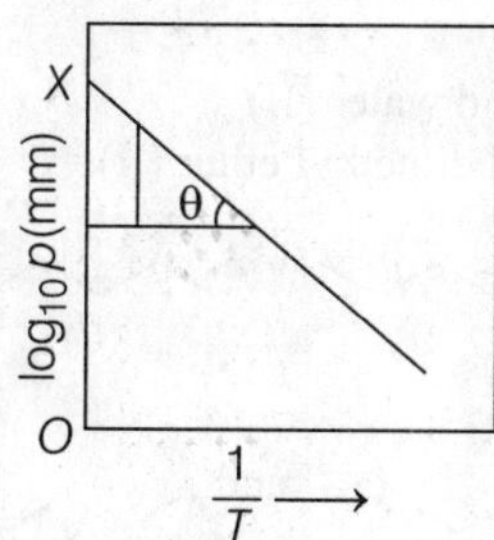

slope = tan θ = – 1.961 and OX = 2.0 mm

Thus, ΔH_{vap} is
(a) 6.73 cal mol^{-1} (b) 6.73 J mol^{-1}
(c) 0.673 cal mol^{-1} (d) 15.60 cal mol^{-1}

37 In the equation,
$\eta = Ae^{E_a/RT}$, $E_a = 5.984$ kJ mol^{-1}. If η is 2.76×10^{-4} Pa s at 233 K, then η at 223 K is
(a) 2.40×10^{-2} Pa s (b) 2.76×10^{-4} Pa s
(c) 2.40×10^{-4} Pa s (d) 6.34×10^{-4} Pa s

38 The vapour pressure of a liquid in the temperature range 25°C and 40°C can be expressed in the equation

$$\log_{10} p(\text{mm}) = 8.0 - \frac{1780\,\text{K}}{T(\text{K})}$$

Thus,
(a) enthalpy of vaporisation is 8.2 kcal mol^{-1}
(b) pre-exponential factor is 10^8 mm
(c) normal boiling point of liquid is 348 K
(d) All of the above are correct

39 $\underset{(A)}{C_6H_{12}(l)} \rightleftharpoons C_6H_{12}(g)$, $\Delta H = 390$ J g^{-1}

Time taken by 1 mole of (A) to convert it into vapours at its boiling point (353.7 K) by heat supplied at the rate of 10.0 J s^{-1} is
(a) 69.0 min (b) 61.2 min (c) 20.0 min (d) 54.6 min

40 Vapour pressure of water at 298 K is 23.8 Torr. A stream of N_2 gas is bubbled through water at 298 K. The water is open to air where the barometric pressure is 759 Torr. Composition of N_2 gas bubbles when they reach the surface of water (in terms of water) is
(a) $\chi_{H_2O} = 0.032$ (b) $\chi_{H_2O} = 0.968$
(c) $\chi_{H_2O} = 0.80$ (d) $\chi_{H_2O} = 0.20$

41 The qualitative sketches I, II and III given below show the variation of surface tension with molar concentration of three different aqueous solutions of KCl, CH_3OH and $CH_3(CH_2)_{11}OSO_3^-Na^+$ at room temperature. The correct assignment of the sketches is **[JEE Adv. 2016]**

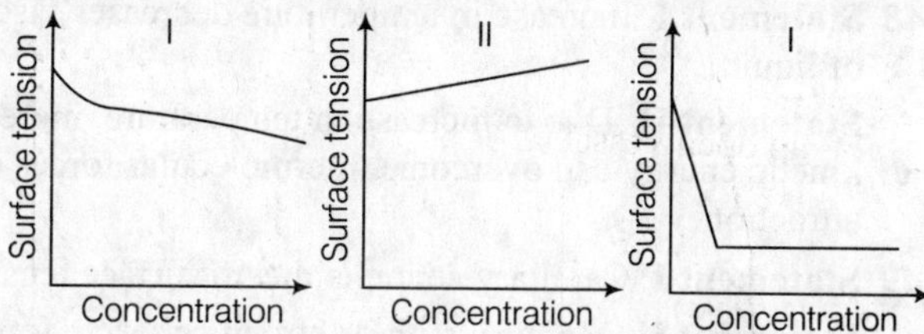

(a) I : KCl, II : CH_3OH, III : $CH_3(CH_2)_{11}OSO_3^-Na^+$
(b) I : $CH_3(CH_2)_{11}OSO_3^-Na^+$, II : CH_3OH, III : KCl
(c) I : KCl, II : $CH_3(CH_2)_{11}OSO_3^-Na^+$, III : CH_3OH
(d) I : CH_3OH, II : KCl, III : $CH_3(CH_2)_{11}OSO_3^-Na^+$

42 When the temperature is increased, surface tension of water **[IIT JEE 2002]**
(a) increases (b) decreases
(c) remains constant (d) shows irregular behaviour

43 At 100°C and 1 atm if the density of the liquid water is 1.0 g cm^{-3} and that of water vapour is 0.0006 g cm^{-3}, then the volume occupied by water molecules in 1 L of steam at this temperature is **[IIT JEE 2000]**
(a) 6 cm^3 (b) 60 cm^3 (c) 0.6 cm^3 (d) 0.06 cm^3

TYPE II Statement Based Questions

Directions (Q. No. 44-56) The following 4 items consist of two statements. One labelled as the 'Statement' (I) and other as 'Statement' (II). You are to examine these two statements carefully and select the correct answers to these items using the codes given below:
(a) Both statemens (I) and (II) are true and statement (II) is the correct explanation of statement (I).
(b) Both statements (I) and (II) are true, but statement (II) is not the correct explanation of statement (I).
(c) Statement (I) is true, but (II) is false.
(d) Statement (I) is false, but (II) is true.

44 **Statement I** Liquids are less compressible than gases.
Statement II Very small free space is available between molecules in gases.

45 **Statement I** Increase in surface area increases the rate of evaporation.
Statement II Evaporation causes cooling.

46 **Statement I** Ethanol (CH_3CH_2OH) has lower vapour pressure than dimethyl ether (CH_3OCH_3).
Statement II Both are functional isomers and have equal London forces of attraction.

47 **Statement I** Standard boiling point of the liquid is less than the normal boiling point.
Statement II Standard state corresponds to 1 bar pressure and temperature 25°C.

48 **Statement I** Increase in temperature decreases viscosity of liquid.
Statement II Due to increase in temperature, increase in kinetic energy can overcome intermolecular forces of attraction.

49 **Statement I** Capillary action is due to surface tension.
Statement II Mercury with its strong cohesive forces and weaker adhesive forces does not show capillary rise.

50 **Statement I** When one end of the tube (open at both ends) is immersed in water, water rises and completely fills a fine capillary.
Statement II The surface tension pulls the water into the capillary.

51 **Statement I** When critical temperature (T_c) is attained, surface tension is reduced to zero.
Statement II At T_c, there is no distinction between liquid and vapour state.

52 **Statement I** The order of viscosities of hexane, water and glycerol is in order

hexane < water < glycerol

Statement II Hexane has the weakest and glycerol the strongest intermolecular forces.

53 **Statement I** Liquids tend to have maximum number of molecules at their surfaces.
Statement II Small liquid drops have spherical shape.

54 **Statement I** A certain amount of minimum energy called activation energy (E_a) is required to move into a hole.
Statement II When state higher than E_a is attained, liquid can flow more easily and viscosity decreases.

55 **Statement I** Water contained in an open container at 100°C is cooled faster than water contained in closed vessel at 100°C.
Statement II In an open vessel, evaporation takes place easily and thus cooling takes place.

56 **Statement I** The temperature at which vapour pressure of liquid is equal to the external pressure is called boiling point.
Statement II At high altitude, atmospheric pressure is high.

TYPE III MCQs with ONE or MORE than ONE Correct Alternate

57 Select correct statements out of the following:
(a) Water drop in vacuum is perfectly spherical
(b) The shape of water drop is distorted due to action of gravity
(c) Soaps and detergents drastically decrease the surface tension of water
(d) As temperature increases, surface tension also increases and becomes maximum at T_c

58 In which of the following pairs, viscosity of I is higher than that of II
(a) ethanol (I) and water (II)
(b) water (I) and dimethyl ether (II)
(c) (I) and (II)
(d) HO, OH, OH (I) and OH, O (II)

59 Variation of η with temperature is given by

$$\eta = A\, e^{Ea/RT}$$

Based on this, select correct statement(s).

(a) A and E_a are temperature dependent

(b) $\dfrac{d\eta}{dT} = \dfrac{E_a}{RT^2}$

(c) $\dfrac{d\log_e \eta}{dT} = -\dfrac{E_a}{RT^2}$

(d) A is expressed in the unit of Pascals

60 Surface tension γ

(a) decreases with increase in temperature
(b) decreases with increase in molar volume
(c) is zero at boiling point
(d) is zero at critical temperature

61 In the following graph, $OX = 5$, $\tan\theta = -2.0$

Thus,

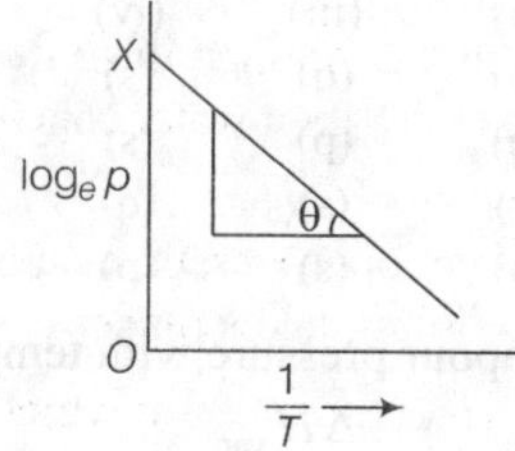

(a) $\log_e p = 5 - \dfrac{2}{T}$ (b) $p = 5e^{2/T}$

(c) $p = 10^5\, e^{-2/T}$ (d) $p = 5\, e^{-2/T}$

62 Select the correct statement(s).

(a) Cohesive forces are the intermolecular forces between like molecules and adhesive forces are between unlike molecules
(b) A drop maintains its shape if cohesive forces are stronger than adhesive forces
(c) If cohesive forces are weak compared to adhesive forces, drop collapses and spreads into film
(d) Cohesive forces in mercury, consist of metallic bonds between atoms, are strong; thus it does not wet glass

63 The temperature dependence of the surface tension of a liquid is given by the Sugden equation,

$\gamma = \gamma_0 \left(1 - \dfrac{T}{T_c}\right)^n$. Select correct statements(s).

(a) Surface tension approaches zero as critical temperature is attained, i.e. at $T = T_c$

(b) Plot of $\log\gamma$ against $\log\left(1 - \dfrac{T}{T_c}\right)$ is linear with a slope equal to n and an intercept equal to $\log\gamma_0$

(c) At reduced temperature $\left(= \dfrac{T}{T_c}\right)$ equal to 1, surface disappears and $\gamma = 0$

(d) $\log\gamma$ decreases on increasing $\log\left(1 - \dfrac{T}{T_c}\right)$

64 Which of the following changes decrease the vapour pressure of water kept in a sealed vessel? ***[NCERT Exemplar]***

(a) Decreasing the quantity of water
(b) Adding salt to water
(c) Decreasing the volume of the vessel to one-half
(d) Decreasing the temperature of water

65 When vaporisation takes place

(a) the molecules moving away from the surface and towards the vapour phase will escape if their kinetic energy is greater than the minimum value of potential energy.
(b) mercury column in the barometer moves downward
(c) mercury column in the barometer moves upward
(d) as the number of molecules in the vapour phase increases, more and more gaseous molecules collide with the liquid water surface exerting pressure

66 Variation of two temperature dependent variables with temperature is given by two lines AB and CD

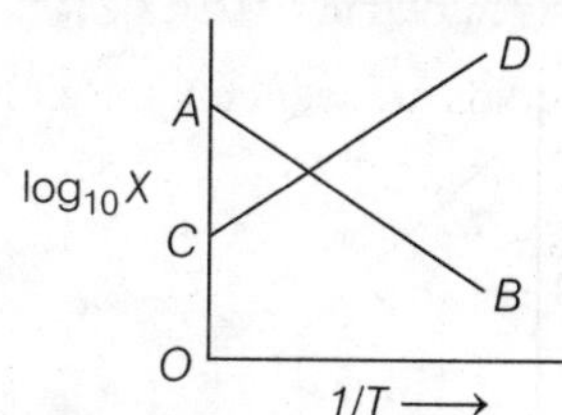

Select correct statement(s).

(a) Line AB is formed when (X) is vapour pressure
(b) Line CD is formed when (X) is viscosity
(c) Line CD is formed when (X) is surface tension
(d) Line AB is formed when (X) is viscosity

TYPE IV Numerical Skills

67 Vapour pressure of benzene is 80 mm and that of toluene is 72 mm. How many moles of toluene should be added to 1 mole benzene so that vapour pressure of benzene is decreased by 6 mm?

68 20% surface sites have adsorbed N_2. On heating N_2 gas evolved from sites and were collected at 0.001 atm and 298 K in a container of volume 2.46 cm^3. Density of surface sites is $6.023 \times 10^{14}/cm^2$ and surface area is 1000 cm^2, find out the number of surface sites occupied per molecule of N_2. ***[IIT JEE 2005]***

69 A liquid of density 850 kg m^{-3} having a surface tension of 0.058 Nm^{-1} rises to $x \times 10^{-2}$ m in a glass capillary of 1.4 mm inside a diameter. What is the value of x?

70 The vapour pressure of benzene, C_6H_6, at 298 K is 95 Torr. 10.0 g of benzene is injected into 10 L bulb at 298 K. Thus, number of grams of benzene remain as liquid is ....

71 For the following equilibrium,

$$CH_3COCH_2CH_3(l) \rightleftharpoons CH_3COCH_2CH_3(g)$$

vapour pressure changes from 304 to 760 Torr on increasing temperature from 329 K to 350 K. What is enthalpy of vaporisation in kcal mol^{-1}? (log 2.5 = 0.40)

72 Surface tension of mercury is 0.490 N m^{-1} at 298 K. When surface area of mercury is increased from 3.0×10^{-4} m^2 to $x \times 10^{-4} m^2$, 2.45×10^{-4} J of energy is used. What is value of x?

73 A tube of $x \times 10^{-4}$ m diameter was placed in a sample of water at 293 K. The water level inside the tube was 10.00 cm due to capillary action.

$\gamma (H_2O) = 73 \times 10^{-3}$ N m^{-1},

$d (H_2O) = 1.0$ g cm^{-3}

What is value of x?

74 In the following variation of $\log_e p$ with $\frac{1}{T}$

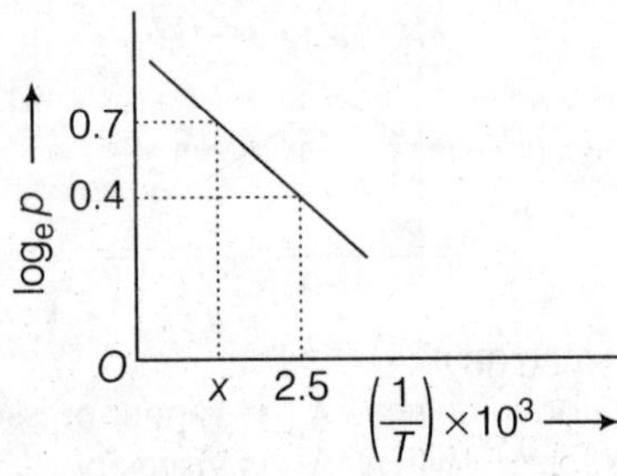

$\Delta H = 400$ cal mol^{-1}.

What is value of x?

75 Surface tension of a liquid is 0.08 Nm^{-1}. Thus, change in pressure across the surface of bubble of diameter 0.04 m is .... N m^{-2}

TYPE V Matrix Matching

76 Match the properties given in Column I with equations in Column II giving their variations with temperature and select the answer from the codes.

Column I	Column II
(i) Mean free path	(p) $Ae^{-\Delta H/RT}$
(ii) Vapour pressure	(q) $Ae^{Ea/RT}$
(iii) Viscosity	(r) $\frac{k(T_c - T)}{(m/d)^{2/3}}$
(iv) Surface tension	(s) $\frac{kT}{p}$

Codes

	(i)	(ii)	(iii)	(iv)
(a)	(p)	(q)	(r)	(s)
(b)	(s)	(p)	(r)	(q)
(c)	(p)	(s)	(r)	(q)
(d)	(s)	(p)	(q)	(r)

77 Match the physical properties in Column I with the corresponding MKS units given in Column II and select the correct answer from the codes given.

Column I	Column II
(i) Latent heat	(p) N m^{-1}
(ii) Viscosity	(q) kg m^{-1} s^{-1}
(iii) Surface tension	(r) J mol^{-1}
(iv) Surface energy	(s) N-m

Codes

	(i)	(ii)	(iii)	(iv)
(a)	(r)	(p)	(q)	(s)
(b)	(r)	(q)	(p)	(s)
(c)	(p)	(r)	(s)	(q)
(d)	(r)	(q)	(s)	(p)

78 Variation of vapour pressure with temperature is given by

$$\log_{10} p = \log_{10} A - \frac{\Delta H_{vap}}{2.303 RT}$$

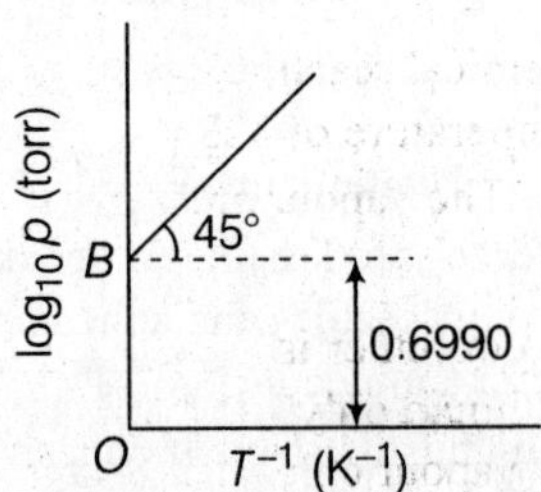

Match the parameters in Column I with their values in Column II and select the answer from the codes given.

Column I	Column II
(i) Constant A	(p) 4.61
(ii) ΔH_{vap} in cal	(q) ∞
(iii) Vapour pressure at 300 K (in Torr)	(r) 5.00
(iv) Vapour pressure when $T \to \infty$	(s) 4.96

Codes

	(i)	(ii)	(iii)	(iv)
(a)	(p)	(r)	(q)	(s)
(b)	(p)	(r)	(s)	(q)
(c)	(r)	(p)	(s)	(r)
(d)	(s)	(r)	(p)	(q)

TYPE VI Passage Based MCQs (Comprehension)

Passage 1

Variation of viscosity (η) with temperature T is given by (viscosity is in poise unit)

$$\log_{10}\eta = C + \frac{B(\text{K})}{T(\text{K})}$$

and graphically

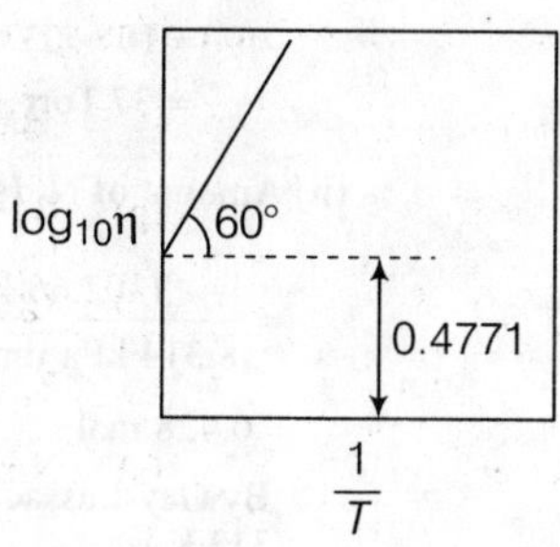

$\tan 60° = \sqrt{3}$

79 Energy of activation required to move into hole is

(a) 14.400 J mol^{-1}　(b) – 14.40 J mol^{-1}
(c) – 33.164 J mol^{-1}　(d) 33.164 J mol^{-1}

80 Viscosity at 150 K is

(a) 1.08 poise　(b) 6.16 poise
(c) 3.08 poise　(d) 1.34 poise

Passage 2

As a result of a chemical reaction, 0.132 g H_2O is produced and maintained at a temperature of 323 K in a closed container of 0.525 dm^3 volume. The vapour pressure of water at 323 K is 92.5 mm Hg.

81 Water in the container is

(a) present as liquid only
(b) present as vapour only
(c) present as liquid $\rightleftharpoons$ vapour equilibrium
(d) can't be present

82 Mass of water present in the container as liquid is

(a) 0.0886 g　(b) 0.0434 g
(c) 0.132 g　(d) 0.066 g

Passage 3

The temperature dependence of the surface tension of a liquid is given by

$$\gamma = \gamma_0\left[1 - \frac{T}{T_c}\right]^n$$

where γ_0 an n are constant for a liquid, T the experimental study temperature, and T_c the critical temperature. Graphically,

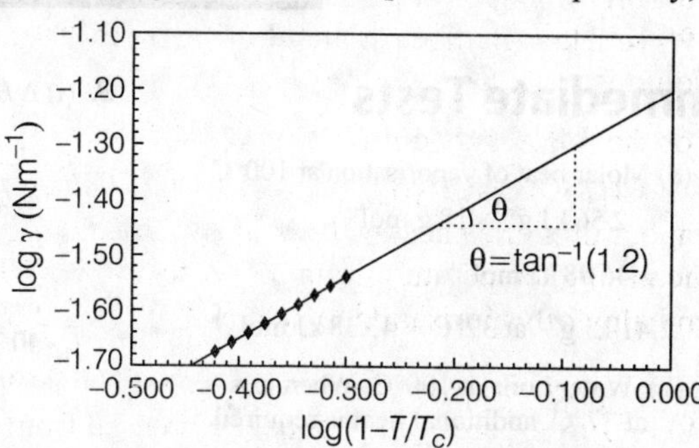

83 Constant γ_0 is

(a) 70.8×10^{-3} N m^{-1}
(b) 70.8×10^{-2} N m^{-1}
(c) 7.08×10^{-3} N m^{-1}
(d) None of the above

84 Constant n is

(a) – 115　(b) – 0.50　(c) 1.2　(d) – 1.2

Passage 4

Based on Clausius-Clapeyron equation

$$p = Ae^{-\Delta H/RT}$$

variation of ($\log_{10} p$) with $\left(\frac{1}{T}\right)$ is given

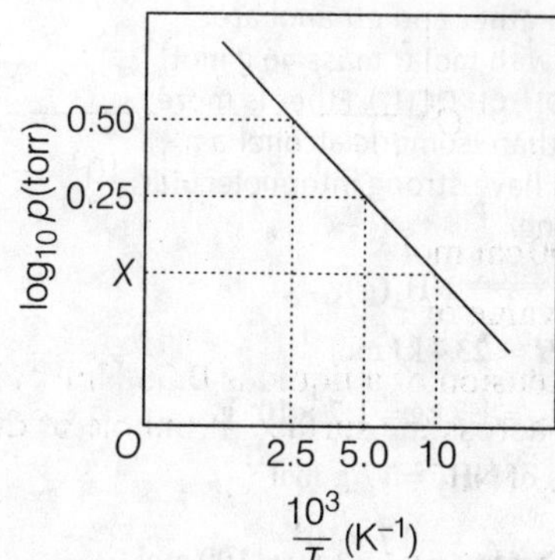

85 Enthalpy of vaporisation based on above data is

(a) 1.915 kJ mol^{-1}　(b) 2.007 kJ mol^{-1}
(c) 1.915 kJ mol^{-1}　(d) 3.217 kJ mol^{-1}

86 $\log_{10} p$ at point (X) is

(a) 0.25　(b) – 0.25
(c) 1.25　(d) – 1.25

HINTS & EXPLANATIONS

Immediate Tests

1. (i) (a) Molar heat of vaporisation at 100°C
$= 2.56\ \text{kJ g}^{-1} \times 18\ \text{g mol}^{-1}$
$= 46.08\ \text{kJ mol}^{-1}$

$2.41\ \text{kJ g}^{-1}$ at $37°\text{C} = 43.38\ \text{kJ mol}^{-1}$

(b) Water boils at 100°C. When it is at 37°C, additional heat is required to convert it into liquid water at 100°C.

(ii) By Trouton's law,
$\Delta H_v = 88\ \text{J mol}^{-1}\ \text{K}^{-1} \times \text{Boiling point (K)}$

(a) ΔH_v (ethanol) $= 88 \times 351$
$= 30888\ \text{J mol}^{-1}$
$= 30.888\ \text{kJ mol}^{-1}$
$= \dfrac{30.888}{46}$
$= 0.6715\ \text{kJ g}^{-1}$

(b) ΔH_v (dimethyl ether) $= 88 \times 308$
$= 27104\ \text{J mol}^{-1}$
$= 27.104\ \text{kJ mol}^{-1}$
$= 0.589\ \text{kJ g}^{-1}$

- Dimethyl ether and ethanol are isomers with molar mass 46 g mol^{-1} (CH_3CH_2OH, CH_3OCH_3). Ether is more volatile than isomeric alcohol as alcohols have strong intermolecular H-bonding.

2. (a) $NH_3(l) \rightleftharpoons NH_3(g)$,
$\Delta H = 23.4\ \text{kJ mol}^{-1}$
$NH_3 = 1.7\ \text{kg} = 1.7 \times 10^3\ \text{g}$

Molar mass of $NH_3 = 17\ \text{g mol}^{-1}$

Number of moles $= \dfrac{1.7 \times 10^3}{17} = 100\ \text{mol}$

Heat required to vaporise 100 mol $NH_3(l)$
$= 23.4\ \text{kJ mol}^{-1} \times 100 = 2340\ \text{kJ}$

(b) $\underset{\text{at } 0°\text{C}}{H_2O(l)} \rightleftharpoons \underset{\text{at } 0°\text{C}}{H_2O(s)}$,
$\Delta H = -\ 6.00\ \text{kJ mol}^{-1}$

$\therefore$ Water converted into ice by the heat required to evaporate NH_3
$= \dfrac{2340\ \text{kJ}}{6.00\ \text{kJ mol}^{-1}} = 390\ \text{mol}$
$= \dfrac{390 \times 18}{1000}\ \text{g} = 7.02\ \text{kg}$

3. (i) $\Delta H_{\text{vap}} = \dfrac{2.303\ RT_1T_2}{(T_2 - T_1)} \log \dfrac{p_2}{p_1}$

T_2 boiling point of water at 1 bar called standard boiling point
$= 99.6°\text{C} = 372.75\ \text{K}$
$T_1 = 353.15\ \text{K}$

$40.7\ \text{kJ mol}^{-1} = 2.303 \times 8.3143 \times 10^{-3}$
$\dfrac{\times\ 353.15 \times 372.75\ \text{K}}{19.60} \log p_1$
$p_1 = 0.4825\ \text{bar}$

(ii) Normal boiling point is taken at 1 atm = 760 mmHg
$\therefore\ \Delta H = \dfrac{2.303\ RT_1T_2}{(T_2 - T_1)} \log \dfrac{p_2}{p_1}$
$= \dfrac{2.303\ RT_1T_3}{(T_3 - T_1)} \log \dfrac{p_3}{p_1}$

On comparison and putting values
$T_3 = -\ 242.4\ \text{K} = -\ 38.6°\text{C}$

4. Clausius-Clapeyron equation can also be written as :
$$p = Ae^{-\Delta H/RT}$$
$\therefore\quad \log_e p = \log_e A - \dfrac{\Delta H}{RT}$
$\log_{10} p = \log_{10} A - \dfrac{\Delta H}{2.303RT}$

Given, $\log_{10} p = 7.960 - \dfrac{1780}{T(\text{K})}$

$\therefore$ (a) $\dfrac{\Delta H}{2.303R} = 1780$
$\Delta H = 1780 \times 2.303R$
$= 1780 \times 2.303 \times 8.3143\ \text{J}$
$= 34083\ \text{J} = 34.083\ \text{kJ}$

(b) Normal boiling point is when
$p = 760\ \text{Torr}\ (= 1\ \text{atm})$
$\log_{10} 760 = 7.960 - \dfrac{1780}{T}$
$2.8808 = 7.960 - \dfrac{1780}{T}$
$\therefore\quad T = 350.45\ \text{K}$

(c) Pre-exponential factor is A
$\log_{10} A = 7.960$
$A = 9.12 \times 10^6$

5. (i) $p_{\text{total}} = \chi_B p_B^\circ + \chi_T p_T^\circ$
$p_B^\circ = 40\ \text{Torr}$
$p_T^\circ = 36\ \text{Torr}$
$n_B + n_T = 4$

$\therefore\quad \chi_B = \dfrac{1}{4}$
$\chi_T = \dfrac{3}{4}$
$\therefore\ p_{\text{total}} = \dfrac{1}{4} \times 40 + \dfrac{3}{4} \times 36$
$= 10 + 27$
$= 37\ \text{Torr}$

(ii) Amount of N_2 (solute), $n_2 = \dfrac{pV}{RT}$
$= \dfrac{(102.66\ \text{kPa}) \times (10.5\ \text{dm}^3)}{8.314\ \text{kPa dm}^3\ \text{mol}^{-1}\ \text{K}^{-1} \times 303\ \text{K}}$
$= 0.428\ \text{mol}$

By Gay-Lussac's law, pressure at 313 K is
$\dfrac{p_2}{p_1} = \dfrac{T_2}{T_1}$
$p_2 = \dfrac{p_1T_2}{T_1} = 102.66 \times \dfrac{313}{303}$
$= 106.05\ \text{kPa}$

Bromobenzene lost (solvent),
$n_1 = \dfrac{0.856\ \text{g}}{157\ \text{g mol}^{-1}}$
$= 0.00555\ \text{mol}$

Thus, total moles of solute and solvent
$= 0.428 + 0.0055$
$= 0.4335\ \text{mol}$

$\therefore\ \chi_{C_6H_5Br} = \dfrac{0.0055}{0.4335} = 0.0127$

$\therefore$ Vapour pressure of bromobenzene at 313 K
$= \chi_{C_6H_5Br} \times p$
$= 0.0127 \times 106.05$
$= 1.347\ \text{kPa}$

6. By Kelvin equation,
$\ln \dfrac{p_s}{p} = \dfrac{2\gamma M}{rdRT}$
$\ln 2.7 = \dfrac{2 \times 71.97 \times 10^{-3} \times 18 \times 10^{-3}}{r \times 0.999 \times 10^3 \times 8.314 \times 298}$
$\therefore\quad r = 1.2 \times 10^{-9}\ \text{m} = 1.2\ \text{nm}$

7. (i) $h = \dfrac{2\gamma}{rdg}$
$= \dfrac{2 \times 72.8\ \text{dynes cm}^{-1}\ (1\ \text{g s}^{-2})}{0.02\ \text{cm} \times 1.0\ \text{g cm}^{-3} \times 980\ \text{cm s}^{-2}}$
$= 7.43\ \text{cm}$

- ($1\ \text{dyne} = 1\ \text{g cm s}^{-2}$)

(ii) $h = \frac{2\gamma}{rdg}$

$= \frac{2 \times 0.49\ N\ m^{-1}\ (kg\ s^{-2})}{0.40 \times 10^{-3}\ m \times 13.6 \times 10^{-3}\ kg\ m^{-3} \times 9.8\ m\ s^{-2}}$

$= 0.0184\ m = 18.4\ mm$

8. 1 mol water = 18 g water

$= 18 \times 10^{-3}$ kg water

Since, $\frac{mass}{volume}$ = density

$\therefore$ volume $= \frac{mass}{volume}$

$= \frac{18 \times 10^{-3}}{1000}$ density/kg m^{-3}

$= 18 \times 10^{-6}\ m^3$

If this is in the form of a drop of radius r

$\frac{4}{3}\pi r^3 = 18 \times 10^{-6}\ m^3$

$\therefore$ r (larger drop) = 0.01626 m

Surface area $= 4\pi r^2 = 4\pi\ (0.01026)^2$

$= 1.0576 \times 10^{-3}\ \pi\ m^2$

volume of each small drop $= \frac{4}{3}\pi(1)^3$

$= \frac{4}{3}\pi\ cm^3 = 1.333 \times 10^{-6}\ \pi\ m^3$

If number of drops = N

then, $N \times 1.333 \times 10^{-6}\ \pi = 18 \times 10^{-6}$

$\therefore$ $N = \frac{18}{1.333\pi} = 4.29 \approx 4.0$ drops

Surface area of four small drops

$= 4\pi(1 \times 10^{-2}) \times 4$

$= 16\pi(1 \times 10^{-4})\ m^2$

Increase in surface area

$= 16\pi\ (1 \times 10^{-4}) - 1.0576 \times 10^{-3}\ \pi$

$= 1.704 \times 10^{-3}\ m^2$

$\therefore$ Work done = γ × increase in surface area

$= 72.75 \times 10^{-3} \times 1.704 \times 10^{-3}$

$= 1.24 \times 10^{-4}$ N m

$= 1.24 \times 10^{-4}$ J

9. $\log_{10}\frac{\eta_2}{\eta_1} = \frac{E_a}{2.303R}\left[\frac{1}{T_2} - \frac{1}{T_1}\right]$

$T_1 = 300\ K, T_2 = 310\ K$

$\eta_1 = \eta$

$\eta_2 = \left(\eta - \frac{10}{100}\eta\right) = 0.9\ \eta$

$\log\frac{0.9\eta}{\eta} = \frac{E_a}{2.303 \times 8.314}\left[\frac{1}{310} - \frac{1}{300}\right]$

$E_a = 8148\ J\ mol^{-1}$

$= 8.148\ kJ\ mol^{-1}$

Knowledge Confirmation Test 1

1. (a)	**2.** (a)	**3.** (d)	**4.** (d)	**5.** (c)	**6.** (c)	**7.** (c)	**8.** (b)	**9.** (b)	**10.** (d)
11. (a)	**12.** (b)	**13.** (b)	**14.** (a)	**15.** (c)	**16.** (d)				

Knowledge Confirmation Test 2

1. (d)	**2.** (b)	**3.** (c)	**4.** (a)	**5.** (c)	**6.** (b)	**7.** (a)	**8.** (b)	**9.** (c)	**10.** (b)
11. (b)	**12.** (d)	**13.** (d)	**14.** (a)	**15.** (b)	**16.** (a)				

Acid Test for JEE Main

Type I. MCQs with Only ONE Correct Alternate

1. (a) Larger the surface area means larger the evaporation.

2. (c) Vapour pressure ∝ temperature. At constant temperature, equilibrium is setup and vapour pressure remains constant. This temperature is called **boiling point**.

3. (d) At T_c distinction between liquid and vapour phase disappears.

4. (d) Due to difference in electronegativity of H and F, there is positive charge on H and negative charge on F, i.e. $\overset{\delta+}{H}—\overset{\delta-}{F}$. This causes intermolecular H-bonding.

5. (b) There is intramolecular H-bonding in this compound, thus force of attraction is least. In (a), (c), and (d) intermolecular H-bonding causes them less volatile.

6. (c) Boiling point is decreased as we go up in mountain.

7. (d) No change as p is constant.

8. (a) Where atmospheric pressure is least, order of boiling

(First) Shimla > Delhi > Bangalore > Mumbai (Last)

9. (c) Work done (energy) = surface tension × increase in area

$= 73\ dyne\,cm^{-1} \times 0.08 \times 10^4 cm^2$

$= 58400\ erg = 5.84 \times 10^{-3} J$

■ $1m^2 = 10^4 cm^2 \Rightarrow 1 \times 10^7 erg = 1\ J$

10. (c) By Clausius-Clapeyron equation,

$\log_{10} p = \log_{10} A - \frac{\Delta H}{2.303RT}$

Given $\log_{10} p = 10 - \frac{4000K}{T(K)}$

$y = c - mx$

Thus, $\frac{\Delta H}{2.303R} = 4000$ (slope)

$\therefore$ $\Delta H = 4000 \times 2.303 \times 2$ cal

$= 18424\ cal = 18.424\ kcal$

$\log_{10} p(mm) = \frac{-4000}{459.8} + 10$

$= -8.699 + 10 = 1.3010$

$\therefore$ $p = 20.00\ mm$

11. (d) $7.29 \times 10^{-2} J\ m^{-2}$

$= 7.29 \times 10^{-2} N\text{-}m\ m^{-2}$

$= 7.29 \times 10^{-2} Nm^{-1}$

Thus, (a) is correct.

Also $1J = 10^7$ erg, $1m^{-2} = 10^{-4} cm^{-2}$

$\therefore$ $7.29 \times 10^{-2} \times 10^7\ erg\ m^{-2}$

$= 7.29 \times 10^{-2} \times 10^7 \times 10^{-4} erg\ cm^{-2}$

$= 7.29 \times 10 = 72.9\ erg\ cm^{-2}$

Thus, (b) is correct.

Also 1 erg = 1 dyne × 1 cm

$72.9\ erg\ cm^{-2} = 72.9 \times dyne \times cm \times cm^{-2}$

$= 72.9\ dyne\,cm^{-1}$

Thus, (c) is also correct.

12. (b) Surface area of a drop, $A = 4\pi r^2$

and volume $V = \frac{4}{3}\pi r^3$

$\therefore$ $\frac{dA}{dr} = 8\pi r \Rightarrow \frac{dV}{dr} = 4\pi r^2$

$\therefore$ $\frac{dA}{dV} = \frac{\frac{dA}{dr}}{\frac{dV}{dr}} = \frac{8\pi r}{4\pi r^2} = \frac{2}{r}$

$\therefore$ $\Delta p = r\left(\frac{dA}{dV}\right) = \frac{2\gamma}{r}$

■ If the system under consideration is a bubble (i.e. a film with an inner and an outer surface) instead of a droplet, then both the surface would contribute surface energy (surface tension)

Thus, $\Delta p = 2\left(\frac{2\gamma}{r}\right) = \frac{4\gamma}{r}$

13. (c) Convert all data in one type of unit and then compare.

$2.275 \times 10^{-2}\ Nm^{-1}$

$= 2.275 \times 10^{-2} kg\ ms^{-2}\ m^{-1}$

$= 2.275 \times 10^{-2} \times 10^3 gs^{-2} = 22.75\ g\ s^{-2}$

$= \frac{22.75\ g\ cm\ s^{-2}}{cm} = 22.75\ dyne\ cm^{-1}$

■ $1\ N\ m^{-1} = 1000\ dyne\ cm^{-1}$
$1\ g\ cm\ s^{-2} = 1\ dyne$

$23.78\ m\ Jm^{-2} = 23.78 \times 10^{-3} J\ m^{-2}$

$= 23.78 \times 10^{-3} kg\ m^2 s^{-2}\ m^{-2}$

$= 23.78 \times 10^{-3} kg\ s^{-2}$

$= 23.78 \times 10^{-3} \times 10^3 gs^{-2}$

$= 23.78\ g\ cm\ s^{-2}\ cm^{-1}$

$= 23.78\ dyne\ cm^{-1}$

■ $1\ g\ cm\ s^{-2} = 1\ dyne$

14. (c) Increase in pressure shifts equilibrium towards the formation of $H_2O(l)$, where p is less (Le-Chatelier). Thus, b.p. is increased.

15. (a)

16. (d) $\Delta p = \frac{\Delta A}{\Delta V} = \frac{4\gamma}{r} = \frac{4 \times 24.3}{1.75}$

$= 55.54\ dyne\ cm^{-2}$

$= 55.54 \times 10^{-1} kg\ m^{-1}\ s^{-2}$

$= 55.54 \times 10^{-1} \times 10^{-5}$ bar

$= 5.554 \times 10^{-5}$ bar

■ $1\ bar = 10^5\ kg\ m^{-1}\ s^{-2}$
$1\ dyne = 1\ g\ cm\ s^{-2}$
$1\ dyne\ cm^{-2} = 1\ g\ cm^{-1}s^{-2}$
$= 0.1\ kg\ m^{-1}\ s^{-2}$

Refer Q. 12.

17. (b)

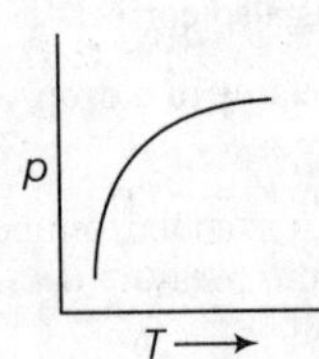

18. (b)

19. (a) $\Delta H = \frac{2.303\, RT_1T_2}{(T_2 - T_1)} \log \frac{p_2}{p_1}$

$= \frac{2.303 \times 2 \times 10^{-3} \times 300 \times 400}{100} \log \frac{120}{100}$

$= 0.438$ kcal $= 438$ cal

20. (b) $h = \frac{2\gamma}{rdg}$

$= \frac{2 \times 0.055\, kg\ s^{-2}}{(0.70 \times 10^{-3} m)(850\, kg\, m^{-3})(9.80\, m\ s^{-2})}$

$= 0.019\, m = 19\, mm$

■ $1\ Nm^{-1} = 1\ kg\ m\ s^{-2}\ m^{-1} = 1\ kg\ s^{-2}$

Acid Test for JEE Advanced

Type I. MCQs with Only ONE Correct Alternate

21. (b) Solid ⟶ liquid ⟶ vapour

At melting point (along BC), temperature line BC remains constant.

22. (d) $\ln p =$ constant $- \frac{\Delta H}{RT}$ then $y = c - mx$

Graph between $\ln p$ and $\left(\frac{1}{T}\right)$ is linear.

23. (a) $n = \frac{pV}{RT}$

$= \frac{\left(\frac{23.8}{760}\right) atm \times 1.0\ L}{0.0821\ L\ atm\ mol^{-1}K^{-1} \times 298\, K}$

$= 1.28 \times 10^{-3}$ mol

24. (d) $\frac{d \log p}{dT} = + \frac{\Delta H}{RT^2}$

$\therefore\ d \log p = + \frac{\Delta H}{RT^2} dT$

$\therefore\ \int d \log p = + \frac{\Delta H}{R} \int \frac{dT}{T^2}$

$\therefore\ \log p = \frac{-\Delta H}{RT} + \log A$ (A = constant)

$\therefore\ p = Ae^{-\Delta H/RT}$

If vapour pressure $= p_1$ at T_1
and vapour pressure $= p_2$ at T_2
then $\Delta H = \frac{2.303\, RT_1T_2}{(T_2 - T_1)} \log \frac{p_2}{p_1}$

Thus, (a), (b) and (c) are correct.

25. (d) Pressure difference between the inside and outside a bubble whose radius is r

$= \frac{4\gamma}{r} = \frac{4 \times 25\ dyne\ cm^{-1}}{1.75\, cm}$

$= 57.14\, dyne\ cm^{-2} = 57.14\, g\, cm\ s^{-2} cm^{-2}$

$= 57.14\ g\ cm^{-1}\ s^{-2}$

$= 57.14 \times 10^{-3} \times 100\ kg\, m^{-1} s^{-2}$

$= 57.14 \times 10^{-1}\ kg\ m^{-1}\ s^{-2}$

$= \frac{57.14 \times 10^{-1} kg\, m^{-1} s^{-2}}{10^5} = 5.714 \times 10^{-5}$ bar

■ $1\ dyne = 1\ g\ cm\ s^{-2}$
$1\ dyne\ cm^{-2} = 1 g\ cm^{-1}s^{-2}$
$= 0.1\ kg\ m^{-1}s^{-2}$
$10^5 kg\ m^{-1}s^{-2} = 1\ bar$

26. (a) Energy $= \gamma \times \Delta A$

$= 63.4\, dyne\ cm^{-1}(70.0 - 26.2)\, cm^2$

$= 63.4\, dyne\ cm^{-1} \times 43.8\, cm^2$

$= 2776.92$ dyne cm

$= 2776.92$ erg $= 2.8 \times 10^{-4}$ J

■ 1 dyne-cm = 1 erg
$10^7 erg = 1\ J$

27. (a) $p = \frac{nRT}{V}$

Standard boiling point of water is 99.6°C at 1 bar (372.75 K).

$p = \frac{1 \times 0.08314 \times 372.75}{1} = 30.99$ bar

28. (a) When a non-volatile solute is added to a pure solvent, temperature falls (due to absorption of heat), hence vapour pressure also falls. T_1 is the boiling point of solvent and T_2 that of the solution.

29. (d) 0.85 kg of NH_3 = 850 g $= \frac{850}{17}$

= 50 mol

Heat required to vaporise 50 mol NH_3

$= 23.4 \times 50 = 1170$ kJ

ΔH (freezing) for water $= -6.01 kJ\ mol^{-1}$

∴ Number of moles of water to be converted into ice by 1170 kJ of heat

$= \frac{1170\ kJ}{6.01 kJ\ mol^{-1}}$

$= 194.6755$ mol $= 3504$ g H_2O

30. (c) A gas is liquefied when it is at or below T_c.

31. (a) Force F is required to displace the side of the liquid film of surface tension γ by distance l, then

$F = 2\gamma l$

$\therefore\ \gamma = \frac{F}{2l} = \frac{5.0 \times 10^{-3} N}{2 \times 8.0 \times 10^{-2} m}$

$= 3.125 \times 10^{-2} N\ m^{-1}$

32. (b) (a) Sublimation (c) Deposition

33. (b) $p = \frac{n}{V} RT = \frac{w}{mV} RT = \frac{dRT}{m}$

$\therefore\ d = \frac{pm}{RT} = \frac{1 atm \times 18\ g mol^{-1} \times 277}{0.0821\ L atm\ mol^{-1} K^{-1}}$

$= 0.7914\ g\ L^{-1}$

$= 0.7914 \times 10^{-3} g\ mL^{-1}$

$= 7.915 \times 10^{-4} g mL^{-1}$

34. (a) $\gamma = \frac{rhdg}{2}$

$= \frac{0.020\ cm \times 7.36\ cm \times 0.9971 g\ cm^{-3} \times 980\, cm\ s^{-2}}{2}$

$= 71.92\ g\ s^{-2} = 71.92$ g-cm $cm^{-1}\ s^{-2}$

$= 71.92$ dyne cm^{-1}

$= \frac{71.92}{10^3} Nm^{-1} = 0.072\, N\ m^{-1}$

■ $d = 1 kg\ m^{-3} = 1 \times 10^3 g\ cm^{-3}$
$1N\ m^{-1} = 10^3 dyne\ cm^{-1}$
$1\ g\ cm\ s^{-2} = 1\ dyne$

35. (d) $\gamma = \frac{rhdg}{2}$

$h = \frac{2\gamma}{rdg} = \frac{2 \times 65}{(5 \times 10^{-4}) \times 1.3 \times 981}$

$= 203.87 \text{ cm} = 2.04 \text{ m}$

36. (a) $\log_{10} p = \log k - \frac{\Delta H}{2.303RT}$

$y = c - mx$

$\tan\theta = \text{Slope} = -m = -1.461$

$\therefore \frac{\Delta H}{2.303R} = 1.461$

$\therefore \Delta H = 2.303 \times 1.461 \times 2 \text{ cal}$

$= 6.73 \text{ cal mol}^{-1}$

37. (c) In the logarithm form,

$\log \eta = \log A - \frac{E_a}{RT}$

$\log \eta_1 = \log A - \frac{E_a}{RT_1}$

$\log \eta_2 = \log A - \frac{E_a}{RT_2}$

$\therefore \log \frac{\eta_1}{\eta_2} = \frac{E_a}{R}\left[\frac{1}{T_2} - \frac{1}{T_1}\right]$

$\therefore \log \frac{\eta_1}{2.76 \times 10^{-4}}$

$= \frac{5.984}{8.314 \times 10^{-3}}\left[\frac{1}{233} - \frac{1}{223}\right]$

$\eta_1 = 2.40 \times 10^{-4} \text{Pa s}$

38. (d) $p = Ae^{-\Delta H/RT}$

$\log_{10} p = 8.0 - \frac{1780\text{K}}{T(\text{K})}$

$\log_{10} p = \log_{10} A - \frac{\Delta H}{2.303RT}$

On comparison, $\log_{10} A = 8$

$A = 10^8$ mm

(pre-exponential factor).

Thus, (b) is correct.

$\frac{\Delta H}{2.303R} = 1780$

$\therefore \Delta H = 1780 \times 2.303 \times 2 \times 10^{-3} \text{kcal mol}^{-1}$

$= 8.2$ kcal

Thus, (a) is correct.

At normal boiling point, $p = 760$ mm

$\therefore \log_{10} 760 = 8 - \frac{1780}{T}$

$\therefore T = 347.7\text{K} \approx 348\text{K}$

Thus, (c) is correct.

39. (d) $\Delta H = 390 \text{ Jg}^{-1} = 390 \times 84 \text{J mol}^{-1}$

Thus, time taken for one mol

$= \frac{390 \times 84 \text{ J}}{10 \text{ J s}^{-1}} = 39 \times 84 \text{ s}$

$= 3276 \text{ s} = 54.6 \text{ min}$

40. (a) Total pressure at the surface

= barometric pressure

$H_2O(l) \rightleftharpoons H_2O(g)$

$p_{\text{total}} = p_{N_2} + p_{H_2O}$

$759 = p_{N_2} + 23.8$

$\therefore p_{N_2} = 759 - 23.8 = 735.2$ Torr

Since, $\chi_{N_2} \cdot p_{N_2} = p_{\text{total}}$

$\therefore \chi_{N_2} = \frac{735.2}{759.0} = 0.968$

$\therefore \chi_{H_2O} = 0.032$

41. (a)

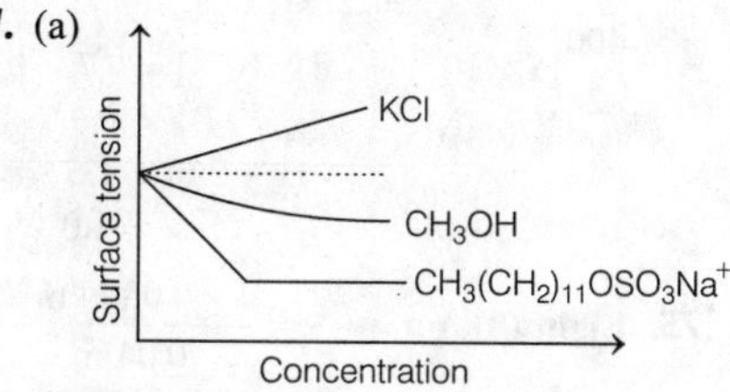

For KCl : Increase in surface tension for inorganic salt.

For CH_3CH_2OH : Decrease of surface tension progressively.

For $CH_3(CH_2)_{11}OSO_2Na$: Decrease of surface tension for CMC (Critical Micelle Concentration) and then almost unchanged.

42. (b)

43. (c) Mass of 1 L of vapour

= volume×density = 1000×0.0006 = 0.6 g

Density of liquid water = 1 g cm^{-3}

$\therefore$ Volume of liquid water $= \frac{0.6 \text{ g}}{1 \text{g cm}^{-3}}$

$= 0.6 \text{ cm}^3$

Type II. Statement Based Questions

44. (d) **45.** (b) **46.** (b) **47.** (b)
48. (a) **49.** (b) **50.** (a) **51.** (a)
52. (a) **53.** (b) **54.** (a) **55.** (a)
56. (c)

Type III. MCQs with One or More than ONE Correct Alternate

57. (a,b,c) **58.** (b,c,d)

59. (c,d,a) $\eta = A e^{E_a/RT}$

$\log_e \eta = \log_e A + \frac{E_a}{RT}$

$\frac{d \log_e \eta}{dT} = 0 - \frac{E_a}{RT^2}$

Thus, (c) is correct. A and E_a are temp. independent. Thus, (a) is incorrect.

A is expressed in unit of viscosity (Pascal). Thus, (d) is correct.

60. (a,b,d) $\gamma\left(\frac{m}{d}\right)^{2/3} = k(t_c - t)$

As t increases, $(t_c - t)$ decreases, hence γ decreases. Thus, (a) is correct.

$\left(\frac{m}{d}\right)$ is molar volume.

Thus, $\gamma \propto \frac{1}{(\text{Molar volume})^{2/3}}$

Thus, γ decreases with increase in molar volume. Thus, (b) is correct.

When $t = t_c, \gamma = 0$.

Thus, (d) is correct.

61. (a,c) This shows variation of $\log p$ with $\frac{1}{T}$.

Thus, it is Clausius-Clapeyron equation,

$\log_e p = \log_e A - \frac{\Delta H}{RT}$

$y = c - mx$

$\log_e A = OX = c = 5.0$ (intercept)

Thus, $A = 10^5$

$-m = \tan\theta = -2.0$

$\therefore \frac{\Delta H}{R} = 2$

$\therefore \log_e p = 5.0 - \frac{2}{T}$

Thus, (a) is correct.

$\therefore p = 10^5 e^{-2/T}$

Thus, (c) is correct.

62. (a,b,c,d)

63. (a,b,c) $\gamma = \gamma_0\left[1 - \frac{T}{T_c}\right]^n$

(a) At $T = T_c, \gamma = \gamma_0$. Thus (b) is correct.

(b) $\log \gamma = \log\gamma_0 + n\log\left[1 - \frac{T}{T_c}\right]$

Thus, straight line, slope $= n$

and intercept $= \log\gamma_0$

Thus, (b) is correct.

(c) T/T_c is called reduced temperature.

When $\frac{T}{T_c} = 1, \gamma = 0$, Thus, (c) is correct.

(d) Incorrect.

64. (b,d) If salt is added, temperature falls, hence vapour pressure decreases.

65. (a,b,c,d)

66. (a,b) $\log_{10} p = \log A - \frac{\Delta H}{2.303RT}$

$\log_{10} \eta = \log_{10} A + \frac{E_a}{2.303RT}$

Line AB is in the form, $y = c + mx$

Thus, (X) is vapour pressure.

Line CD is in the form, $y = c + mx$

Thus, (X) is viscosity.

- Surface tension also decreases with increase in temperature but $\log \gamma$ *vs* $\frac{1}{T}$ is not linear.

Type IV Numerical Skill

67. **Three (3)** If benzene = 1 mol

and toluene = n mol

then $\chi_B = \frac{1}{(1+n)}$ and $\chi_T = \frac{n}{(1+n)}$

$\therefore \quad p_{total} = 74\text{ mm} = p_B^\circ \chi_B + p_T^\circ \chi_T$

$74(1+n) = 80 + 72n$

$74 + 74n = 80 + 72n \Rightarrow n = 3$

68. **Two (2)** Total surface area = 1000 cm^2

Density of surface sites

$= 6.023 \times 10^{14}$ sites/cm^2

Thus, total sites $= 6.023 \times 10^{14} \times 1000$

$= 6.023 \times 10^{17}$ sites

Sites occupied by N_2 molecule (20%)

$= 6.023 \times 10^{17} \times 0.2$

220% N_2 taken $= \frac{pV}{RT} = \frac{0.001 \times 2.46 \times 10^{-3}}{0.0821 \times 298}$

$= 1.00 \times 10^{-7}$ mol

$= 1.00 \times 10^{-7} \times 6.023 \times 10^{23}$ molecules

Thus, sites occupied by each N_2 molecule

$= \frac{\text{Total sites}}{\text{Total molecule}}$

$= \frac{6.023 \times 10^{17} \times 0.2}{6.023 \times 10^{16}} = 2$

69. **Two (2)** Density (d) = 850 kg m^{-3}

(γ) = 0.058 N m^{-1}

radius $r = \frac{\text{diameter}}{2} = 0.7$ mm

$= 0.7 \times 10^{-3}$ m

$h = \frac{2\gamma}{rdg}$

$= \frac{2 \times 0.058}{(0.7 \times 10^{-3})(850)(9.8)}$

$= 2 \times 10^{-2}$ m

70. **Six (6)** Moles of C_6H_6 in vapour state $= \frac{pV}{RT}$

$= \frac{\left(\frac{95}{760}\right)(10)}{0.0821 \times 298} = 0.051\text{ mol} = 4.0\text{ g}$

Thus, benzene as liquid = 10 − 4 = 6.0 g

71. **Eight (8)** $\Delta H = \frac{2.303\, RT_1T_2}{(T_2 - T_1)} \log \frac{p_2}{p_1}$

$= \frac{2.303 \times 0.002 \times 324 \times 350}{26} \log \frac{760}{304}$

$= 20.089 \log 2.5 = 8$ kcal mol^{-1}

72. **Eight (8)** Energy = Surface tension × increase in surface area

$2.45 \times 10^{-4}\text{ J} = 0.490 \times (x-3) \times 10^{-4}$

$\therefore \quad (x-3) = 5$

$\therefore \quad x = 8$

73. **Three (3)** $h = \frac{2\gamma}{rdg}$

$\therefore r = \frac{2\gamma}{hdg} = \frac{2 \times 73 \times 10^{-3}}{(10 \times 10^{-2})(1000)(9.8)}$ m

$= 1.5 \times 10^{-4}$ m

$\therefore$ Diameter $= 3.0 \times 10^{-4}$ m

74. **Four (4)**

$\frac{\Delta H}{R}\left[\frac{1}{T_1} - \frac{1}{T_2}\right] = \log_e p_2 - \log_e p_1$

$\frac{400}{2}[x \times 10^{-3} - 2.5 \times 10^{-3}] = 0.7 - 0.4$

$= 0.3$

$\therefore \quad (x - 2.5) = 1.5$

$x = 4.0$

75. **Eight (8)** $\Delta p = \frac{4\gamma}{r} = \frac{4 \times 0.08\text{ N m}^{-1}}{0.04\text{ m}}$

$= 8$ N m^{-2}

Type V. Matrix Matching

76. (d) **77.** (b)

78. (c) Clausius-Clapeyron equation is

$$\log_{10} p = \log_{10} A - \frac{\Delta H_{vap}}{2.303\, RT}$$

$\uparrow y \qquad \uparrow c \qquad \uparrow m$

On comparison,

$\log_{10} A = c = 0.6990 \Rightarrow A = 5.0$

$\frac{\Delta H_{vap}}{2.303R} = \tan 45° = 1 = m$

$\therefore \quad \Delta H_{vap} = 2.303R = 2.303 \times 2$

$= 4.606$ cal

At 300 K,

$\log_{10} p = 0.6990 - \frac{1}{300} = 0.6957$

$p = 4.96$ Torr

When $T \to \infty$, $\log_{10} p = \log_{10} A$

$\therefore \quad p = A = 5.00$

Thus, (i) - (r) (ii) - (p)

(iii) - (s) (iv) - (r)

Type VI. Passage Based MCQs (Comprehension)

Passage 1

By hole theory,

$\log_{10} \eta = \log_{10} A + \frac{E_a}{2.303\, RT}$

$\log_{10} \eta = C + \frac{B}{T}$

Thus, $\log_{10} A = C = 0.4771$

$B = \frac{E_a}{2.303\, R}$

$= \tan 60° = 1.7320$

$\therefore E_a$ (Energy of activation)

$= 2.303\, R \times 1.7320$

η at 150 K = 33.164 J

$\log_{10} \eta = 0.4771 + \frac{33.164}{2.303 \times 8.314 \times 150}$

$= 0.4886$

$\therefore \quad \eta = 3.08$ poise

79. (d) **80.** (c)

Passage 2

Water given = 0.132 g

Density of water = 1.0 g cm^{-3}

$\therefore$ Volume = 0.132 cm^3

But, volume = 0.525 dm^3 (525 cm^3)

Thus, amount of liquid and vapour differs

Thus, equilibrium,

$H_2O(l) \rightleftharpoons H_2O(g)$

is maintained at 323 K.

Moles of water in vapour state

$n = \frac{pV}{RT} = \frac{\left(\frac{92.5}{760}\right)(0.525)}{0.0821 \times 323}$

$= 2.41 \times 10^{-3}$ mol

Amount in vapour state

$= 2.41 \times 10^{-3} \times 18 = 0.0434$ g

Amount in liquid state

$= 0.132 - 0.0434 = 0.0886$ g

81. (c) **82.** (a)

Passage 3

$\gamma = \gamma_0\left[1 - \frac{T}{T_c}\right]^n$

$y = c + mx$

Slope $= n = \tan\theta = 1.2$

Intercept on ($\log\gamma$) axis $= -1.15 = \log\gamma_0$

$\therefore \quad \gamma_0 = 70.79 \times 10^{-2}$ N m^{-1}

83. (b) **84.** (c)

Passage 4

$\frac{\Delta H}{2.303\, R}\left[\frac{1}{T_1} - \frac{1}{T_2}\right] = \log \frac{p_2}{p_1}$

$= \log p_2 - \log p_1$

$\frac{\Delta H}{2.303 \times 8.314 \times 10^{-3}}[(5.0 - 2.5)10^{-3}]$

$= (0.50 - 0.25)$

$\Delta H = 1.915$ kJ mol^{-1}

Put value of ΔH to calculate ($\log p$) at point X.

$\log p$ (at point X) = − 0.25

85. (c) **86.** (b)

Thermodynamics

Chapter Topics
- Basic Concepts
- Zeroth and First Laws of Thermodynamics
- Carnot's Cycle
- Free Energy

Basic Concepts

System and surroundings

A portion of the universe which is under investigation is called **system,** and everything else in the universe except system is called **surroundings**. The region or interface separating the system from surroundings is called the **boundary**.

System + surroundings = The universe

- System can be **open**, if it can exchange heat and matter with the surroundings.
- System can be **closed**, if it can exchange heat but not the matter with the surroundings.
- System can be **isolated**, if it can neither exchange heat nor the matter with the surroundings.

If, ΔE = change in energy,

Δm = change in mass of matter, then

System	ΔE	Δm
Open	$\neq 0$	$\neq 0$
Closed	$\neq 0$	$= 0$
Isolated	$= 0$	$= 0$

- A system uniform throughout is **homogeneous** and reversely, if it is not uniform then **heterogeneous.**

I. $2NH_3(g) \rightleftharpoons N_2(g) + 3H_2(g)$

II. $NH_4HS(s) \rightleftharpoons NH_3(g) + H_2S(g)$

I is homogeneous system as all species are in gaseous state (uniform).

II is heterogeneous system as species are in different phases.

State functions

In thermodynamics, a state function or function of state is a function defined for a system relating several state variables or state quantities that depend only on the current equilibrium state of system.

- State functions do not depend on the path by which the system arrived at present state.
- A state function describes the equilibrium state of a system and thus also describes the type of system.
- Internal energy, enthalpy and entropy are state functions.

- Mechanical work and heat are not state functions, they are process quantities or path functions.
- A change in a state function describes a difference between two states.
- Change in state functions is independent of path, H(enthalpy) is a state function, if ΔH is independent of path.

Thus, $\Delta H_1 = \Delta H_2 = (H_B - H_A)$

ΔH_1 = change in enthalpy along path I.

ΔH_2 = change in enthalpy along path II.

where, H_A = enthalpy of state A

H_B = enthalpy of state B

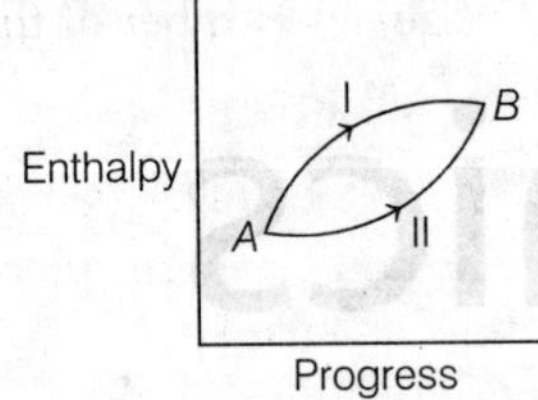

- The thermodynamic state of a system is defined by a set of conditions that completely specify all the properties of system.

State variables

When there is any change in the macroscopic properties, state of the system also changes, hence macroscopic properties are also called state variables.

- For an ideal gas, $pV = nRT$.

  R is gas constant, p, V, and T are called state variables for given amount of gas. If two variables (say p and V) are known, then T can be calculated. Thus, two known variables are independent variables and third one is the dependent variables.
- Common thermodynamic variables are pressure, volume, mole, temperature, work and heat.
- A system in a state of thermodynamic equilibrium is one in which the macroscopic properties do not change with time.

Thermodynamic properties

- **Macroscopic properties** The properties of the system which arise due to bulk behaviour of matter; as pressure, volume, mass, temperature, moles, density, are macroscopic properties.

$$pV = nRT = \frac{w}{m}RT$$

$$p = \frac{w}{Vm}RT = \frac{dRT}{m} \qquad \left(\frac{w}{V} = d\right)$$

- **Intensive properties** The properties of the system that remain unchanged on division as T, p, C (molarity, normality), density, surface tension, viscosity, pH etc. are intensive properties.
- **Extensive properties** The properties of the system that change on division as volume, energy, heat capacity, enthalpy, entropy , free energy, length and mass are extensive properties.

Thermodynamic scale of temperature

The basic SI unit of temperature is Kelvin (K). One Kelvin is $\frac{1}{273.16}$ of the triple point temperature of water (273.16 K at critical pressure 4.58 Torr), is the temperature at which following equilibrium is established.

$$H_2O(s) \rightleftharpoons H_2O(l) \rightleftharpoons H_2O(g)$$

This scale is called thermodynamic temperature scale.

Thermodynamic processes

Process	Description	Condition
• Isothermal	taking place at constant temperature	$T_1 = T_2$ $\Delta T = 0$
• Isobaric	taking place at constant pressure	$p_1 = p_2$ $\Delta p = 0$
• Isochoric	taking place at constant volume	$V_1 = V_2$ $\Delta V = 0$
• Adiabatic	taking place without exchange of heat. Thus, • in expansion , heat is absorbed, temperature falls. • in compression , heat is evolved, hence temperature increases.	Internal energy is decreased, $\Delta E < 0$ Internal energy is increased, $\Delta E > 0$
• Cyclic	• the process in which the system after a number of different changes, or processes returns to initial state.	A B D C

Reversible process

The processes in which system and surroundings are restored to their initial states are called reversible processes.

When the process occurs in such a way that the properties of the system at every instant remain uniform, then it is called reversible (quasi-static).

$$H_2O(l) \rightleftharpoons H_2O(g)$$

$$Zn + Cu^{2+} \rightleftharpoons Cu + Zn^{2+}$$

Irreversible process

The processes in which system and surroundings are not restored to their initial state are called irreversible processes.

All natural processes are irreversible and, thus are spontaneous.

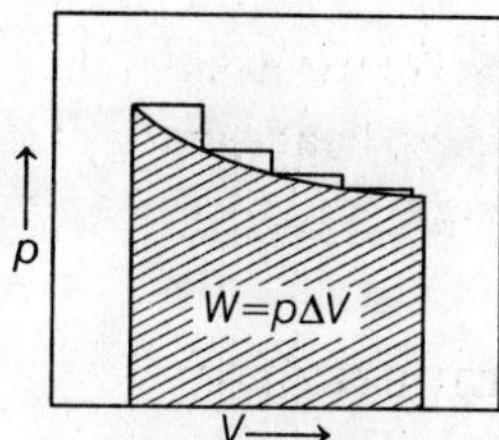

Reversible change
(area under the curve gives work done)

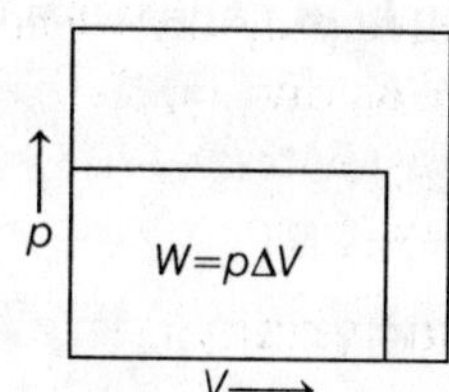

Irreversible
(area under the curve gives work done)

Endothermic process The process which takes place with absorption of heat.

$$A + q \longrightarrow B$$

Let H_A = enthalpy of A

H_B = enthalpy of B

Then $H_A + q = H_B$

Thus, $\Delta H = H_B - H_A = q,\ \Delta H > 0$

Exothermic process The process which takes place with evolution of heat.

$$A - q \longrightarrow B$$

$$\Delta H = H_B - H_A = -q$$

$\therefore\ \Delta H < 0$

Heat and work

SI convention of heat

***Case* I.** Heat involved = x kJ
Then heat absorbed by system = + x kJ
Heat released by system = − x kJ

***Case* II.** Heat involved = − x kJ
Then heat absorbed by the system = − x kJ
Heat released by the system = + x kJ

SI convention of work

Mechanical work = $-p\Delta V$

$$= -p_{ext}\int_{V_1}^{V_2} dV = -\frac{nRT}{V}\int_{V_1}^{V_2} dV$$

(Since, $pV = nRT$)

***Case* I.** Work involved = W kJ
Then work done by the system = − W kJ
and work done on the system = + W kJ

***Case* II.** Work involved = −W kJ
Then work done by the system = +W kJ
and work done on the system = −W kJ

$$W = -p_{ext}(V_f - V_i)$$

$$W = -p_{ext}\Delta V$$

- **During expansion** Work is done by the system on the surroundings

$$W = -p_{ext}(\Delta V)$$

(a negative value) (a positive value)

- **During contraction** Work is done by the surroundings on the system.

$$W = -p_{ext}(\Delta V)$$

(a negative value) (a positive value)

If the pressure is not constant at every stage of compression, but changes in number of finite steps, then work done on the gas is

$$W = -\sum p(\Delta V)$$

- **Free expansion** If the expansion takes place in vacuum ($p_{ex} = 0$), it is called free expansion

$$W = -p_{ex}\,\Delta V = 0$$

> ■ Values of R in different units can be used for energy conversion factor.
>
> $R = 0.0821$ L atm mol^{-1} K^{-1} = 0.0831 bar dm^3 mol^{-1}K^{-1}
> = 1.987 cal mol^{-1} K^{-1} = 8.3143 J mol^{-1} K^{-1}
> = 8.3143×10^{-3} kJ mol^{-1} K^{-1}
>
> 1 L atm = 101.27 J
> 1 cal = 4.184 J
> 1 eV = 1.6×10^{-19} J

Internal or intrinsic energy (E or U)

- Internal energy of the system is simply the total of all the possible kinds of energy associated with the matter in the system.
- Internal energy of the system cannot be measured but its change can be determined.
- Internal energy is a state function, thus ΔE depends on the initial and final values and independent of path.

$$\Delta E_1 \text{ (path I)} = \Delta E_2 \text{ (path II)} = (E_2 - E_1)$$

$$H_2(g) \xrightarrow{436\ \text{kJ}} 2H(g)$$

Internal energy E_R $(E_R + 436)$

$\therefore$ $\Delta E = 436$ kJ

- When work is done on the system, internal energy of the system increases.
- When work is done by the system, internal energy of the system decreases as work is done at the cost of internal energy.

Molar heat capacity

Heat required to raise the temperature of one mole of gas by 1° is called molar heat capacity. If p remains constant, molar heat capacity is C_p and at constant V, molar heat capacity is C_V.

$$C_p = \left(\frac{\Delta H}{\Delta T}\right)_p = \left(\frac{dH}{dT}\right)_p$$

$$C_V = \left(\frac{\Delta E}{\Delta T}\right)_V = \left(\frac{dE}{dT}\right)_V$$

Specific heat capacities for gases

Gas	C_p	C_V	$(C_p - C_V)$	$\gamma = \frac{C_p}{C_V}$
Monoatomic	$\frac{5}{2}R$	$\frac{3}{2}R$	R	1.66
Diatomic	$\frac{7}{2}R$	$\frac{5}{2}R$	R	1.40
Polyatomic	$4R$	$3R$	R	1.33

γ is molar heat capacity ratio.

Solved Examples & Instant Practice

Example 5.1) A sample of an ideal gas undergoes an expansion against a constant external pressure of 1 bar from 1.0 m^3, 10 bar and 273 K to 10.0 m^3, 1.0 bar and 273 K. What is work done by the system on the surroundings?

It is the case of expansion, hence work is done by the system. Thus, it is negative.
Also, 1 bar = 10^5 Pa and 1 m^3 × 1 Pa = 1 J
External pressure is constant. Since, $p \propto 1/V$ hence pressure decrease is associated with expansion.

Sol. Given: $p_{ext} = 1$ bar, $V_1 = 1\,m^3$, $V_2 = 10.0\,m^3$

$$W = -p_{ext}\int_{V_1}^{V_2} dV = -p_{ext}(V_2 - V_1)$$
$$= -1 \times 10^5 \text{ Pa } (10-1)\,m^3$$
$$= -9 \times 10^5 \text{ Pa m}^3 = -9 \times 10^5 \text{ J}$$

Immediate Test 1

Calculate the work done (in kJ) during a process in which the volume expands from 10 L to 20 L against an external pressure of 5.0 bar.

Example 5.2) Calculate the work done when 0.5 mole of aluminium carbide (Al_4C_3) reacts with H_2O in
(a) a closed vessel of fixed volume
(b) an open vessel at 27°C.

(a) In fixed volume, $\Delta V = 0$
(b) $W = -p_{ext}\,\Delta V = -p_{ext}(V_2 - V_1)$
$V_1 \approx 0$, Al_4C_3 being in solid state.

Sol.
(a) $Al_4C_3(s) + H_2O\,(l) \longrightarrow 4Al(OH)_3 + 3\,CH_4(g)$
1 mol ... 3 mol
0.5 mol ... 1.5 mol

In a closed vessel, $\Delta V = 0$ $\quad\therefore W = -p_{ext}\,(\Delta V) = 0$

(b) When $Al_4C_3(s)$ reacts with H_2O, CH_4 gas drives back the atmosphere,

$$W = -p_{ext}(V_2 - V_1) = -p_{ext}(V_2 - 0) = -p_{ext}\left(\frac{nRT}{p_{ext}}\right)$$

$$W = -nRT = -1.5 \times 8.314 \times 300 = -3741.3\text{ J} = -3.7413\text{ kJ}$$

Immediate Test 2

Calculate the work done when 56 g of iron reacts with hydrochloric acid in
(a) a closed vessel (b) an open vessel at 298 K

Example 5.3) For each of the following chemical reactions carried at constant temperature and constant pressure, specify the sign of W (work). Also, mention whether the work is done on the system or by the system (consider the reaction mixture to be the system).
(a) $2NH_4NO_3(s) \longrightarrow 2N_2(g) + 4H_2O(g) + O_2(g)$
(b) $H_2(g) + Cl_2(g) \longrightarrow 2HCl(g)$
(c) $2SO_2(g) + O_2(g) \longrightarrow 2SO_3(g)$
(d) $CaC_2(s) + 2H_2O(l) \longrightarrow Ca(OH)_2(aq) + C_2H_2(g)$
(e) $NH_4HS(s) \longrightarrow NH_3(g) + H_2S(g)$

Sol. Nature of work is decided by the sign of Δn_g.
Δn_g = (moles of gaseous products – moles of gaseous reactants)
- $\Delta n_g = 0$, no change
- Δn_g = –ve, contraction
- Δn_g = +ve, expansion

Chemical change	Δn_g	$W = -p\Delta V$	Nature
a.	+ve	– ve	work is done by the system
b.	0	0	no work
c.	–1	+ ve	work is done on the system
d.	+1	– ve	as in (a)
e.	+2	– ve	as in (a)

Immediate Test 3

Assign the sign of work (based on SI convention) in the following chemical changes taking place against external atmospheric pressure.
(a) $N_2(g) + 2H_2(g) \longrightarrow 2NH_3(g)$
(b) $CH_4(g) + 2O_2(g) \longrightarrow CO_2(g) + 2H_2O(g)$
(c) $CaCO_3(s) \longrightarrow CaO(s) + CO_2(g)$
(d) $C(s) + CO_2(g) \longrightarrow 2CO(g)$
(e) $C_6H_6(l) + 7.5O_2(g) \longrightarrow 6CO_2(g) + 3H_2O(g)$

KNOWLEDGE CONFIRMATION Test 1

1 An ideal gas expands from 2.0 L and 8.0 atm to a final volume of 5.5 L against constant external pressure of 1.75 atm at 298 K. Thus,

	Work done	Final pressure
(a)	−6.125 L atm	2.91 atm
(b)	−620.26 J	2.91 atm

(c) Both (a) and (b) are correct

(d) None of the above is correct

■ 1 L atm = 101.267 J

2 Temperature of one mole of a gas is increased by 1° at constant pressure. Thus, work done by the system is

(a) R (b) $-R$

(c) $\frac{3}{2}R$ (d) $\frac{-3}{2}R$

3 8 g of O_2 gas at STP is expanded, so that volume is doubled. Thus, work done is

(a) −2.268 kJ (b) −1.134 kJ

(c) +567.1 J (d) −567.1 J

4 Out of the following intensive properties are

A. boiling point B. entropy

C. pH D. emf

(a) A, B, C and D (b) Both A and B

(c) A, B and C (d) A, C and D

5 Out of

I. internal energy II. temperature

III. pressure IV. volume

V. work VI. enthalpy,

state functions are

(a) I, II, III and IV (b) I, II, III, V and VI

(c) I, V, VI (d) I, III, V

6 Consider the following chemical changes :

I. $CaC_2(s) + 2H_2O(l) \longrightarrow Ca(OH)_2(s) + C_2H_2(g)$

II. $2SO_2(g) + O_2(g) \longrightarrow 2SO_3(g)$

III. $2Fe(s) + 3H_2O(g) \longrightarrow Fe_2O_3(s) + 3H_2(g)$

Work is done by the system in the case(s) of

(a) I and II (b) II and III

(c) only I (d) None of these

7 Numerical value of the work done is maximum in case of

(a) $C(s) + O_2(g) \longrightarrow CO_2(g)$

(b) $NH_4HS(s) \longrightarrow NH_3(g) + H_2S(g)$

(c) $3Fe(s) + 4H_2O(g) \longrightarrow Fe_3O_4(s) + 4H_2(g)$

(d) $C_3H_8(g) + 5O_2(g) \longrightarrow 3CO_2(g) + 4H_2O(l)$

8 Temperature of one mole of helium gas is increased by 1°, hence increase in internal energy is

(a) 7 cal (b) 5 cal (c) 3.5 cal (d) 3 cal

9 Select the correct statement(s).

(a) When work is done on the system, internal energy of the system increases

(b) When work is done by the system, internal energy of the system decreases

(c) Both are correct

(d) None of the above is correct

10 If $W = -20$ kJ, the negative sign indicates that the

(a) expanding system gains work energy and does work on the surroundings

(b) expanding system loses work energy and does work on the surroundings

(c) expanding system gains work energy and does work on the system

(d) expanding system loses work energy and does work by the surroundings

11 Which of the following represents a closed system ?

(a) Exchange of heat and matter with the surroundings

(b) Exchange of heat but not the matter with the surroundings

(c) Neither exchange of heat nor the matter with the surroundings

(d) None of the above

12 Number of phases present in the following thermodynamic systems are :

I. $NH_4HS(s) \rightleftharpoons NH_3(g) + H_2S(g)$

II. $CaCO_3(s) \rightleftharpoons CaO(s) + CO_2(g)$

III. $N_2(g) + 3H_2(g) \rightleftharpoons 2NH_3(g)$

IV. $CuSO_4 \cdot 5H_2O(s) \rightleftharpoons CuSO_4(s) + 5H_2O(l)$

	I	II	III	IV
(a)	3	2	3	3
(b)	2	3	3	3
(c)	2	3	1	3
(d)	2	1	2	3

13 The following diagram represents the (p-V) changes of an ideal gas. Thus, total work done is

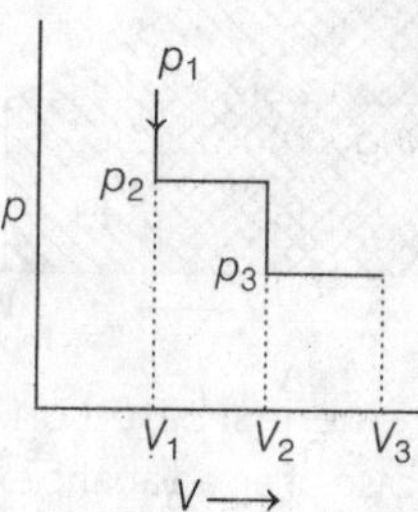

(a) $p_2(V_2 - V_1) + p_3(V_3 - V_2)$

(b) $p_1(V_2 - V_1) + p_3(V_3 - V_2)$

(c) $p_2(V_3 - V_1) + p_3(V_2 - V_1)$

(d) $p_2(V_3 - V_2) + p_3(V_2 - V_1)$

14 A thermodynamic state function is a quantity
(a) used to determine heat changes
(b) whose value is independent of path
(c) used to determine $(p-V)$ work
(d) whose value depends on temperature only

15 For the process to occur under adiabatic conditions, the correct conditions are
(a) $\Delta T = 0, q = 0$ (b) $\Delta p = 0, W = 0$
(c) $q = 0, \Delta T \neq 0$ (d) $\Delta T = 0, W = 0$

16 Following graph shows variation of p with V for adiabatic and isothermal expansion when final volumes are same:

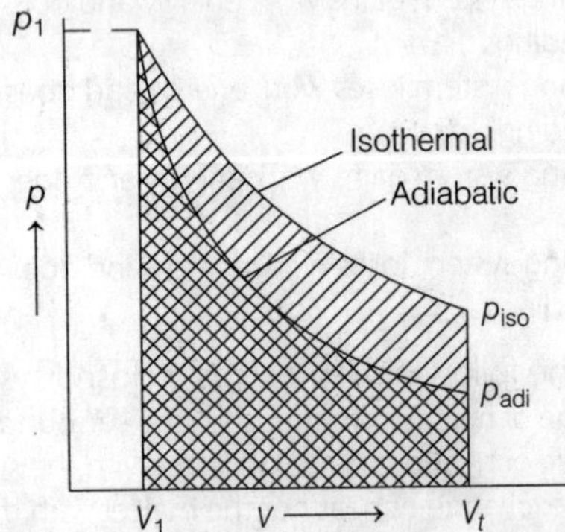

Select correct statement(s) about this graph.
(a) Magnitude of the work involved in the isothermal expansion is greater than that involved in the adiabatic expansion.
(b) In adiabatic expansion, temperature falls whereas in the isothermal expansion, temperature remains the same.
(c) Both of the above are correct
(d) None of the above is correct.

17 Following graph shows variation of p with V for adiabatic and isothermal expansion when final pressures are same:

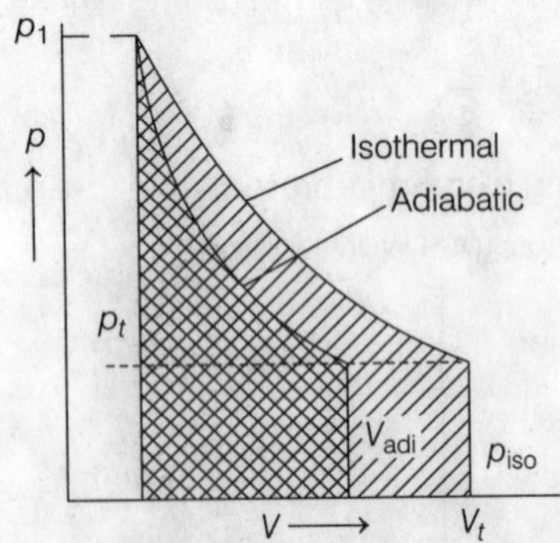

Select correct statement(s) based on this variation.
(a) Final volume in case of an adiabatic expansion is less than the corresponding volume in an isothermal expansion
(b) The magnitude of work involved in an isothermal expansion is greater than that involved in an adiabatic expansion
(c) Both of the above are correct
(d) None of the above is correct

18 Select correct statement (s).
(a) If volume of a fixed amount of an ideal gas is a state function, then

$$\left(\frac{\partial^2 V}{\partial T \partial p}\right) = \left(\frac{\partial^2 V}{\partial p \partial T}\right) = \frac{-nR}{p^2}$$

(b) If pressure is a state function, then

$$\frac{\partial^2 p}{\partial T \partial V} = \frac{\partial^2 p}{\partial V \partial T} = -\frac{R}{V^2}$$

(c) If U is a function of any two variables p, V and T, then

$$\left(\frac{\partial U}{\partial p}\right)_T = \left(\frac{\partial U}{\partial V}\right)_T \left(\frac{\partial V}{\partial p}\right)_T$$

(d) All of the above are correct

19 An ideal gas undergoes a single stage expansion against a constant opposing pressure from p_1, V_1, T to p_2, V_2, T. Thus, the largest mass m which can be lifted through a height h in this expansion is
(a) $m = \frac{nRT}{gh}\left(1 - \frac{p_2}{p_1}\right)$ (b) $m = \frac{nRT}{gh}\left(\frac{p_2}{p_1} - 1\right)$
(c) $m = \frac{nRT}{gh}(p_1 - p_2)^2 / p_1 p_2$ (d) None is correct.

20 The system in Q (19) is restored to its initial state by a single stage compression. Thus, the smallest mass which must fall through the height h to restore the system is
(a) $m = \frac{nRT}{gh}\left(1 - \frac{p_2}{p_1}\right)$ (b) $m = \frac{nRT}{gh}\left(\frac{p_1}{p_2} - 1\right)$
(c) $m = \frac{nRT}{gh}(p_1 - p_2)^2 / p_1 p_2$ (d) $m = \frac{nRT}{gh}(p_2 - p_1)^2 / p_1 p_2$

21 For one mole of an ideal gas, which of these statements must be true? ***[JEE Main 2020 (II) NTA]***
I. U and H each depends only on temperature.
II. Compressibility factor Z is not equal to 1.
III. $C_{p,m} - C_{V,m} = R$ IV. $dU = C_V dT$
(a) II, III and IV (b) I and III
(c) I, III and IV (d) III and IV

22 Five moles of an ideal gas at 1 bar and 298 K is expanded into vacuum to double the volume. The work done is ***[JEE Main 2020 (II) NTA]***
(a) $-RT \ln\left(\frac{V_2}{V_1}\right)$ (b) $-RT(V_2 - V_1)$
(c) $C_V(T_2 - T_1)$ (d) zero

Zeroth and First Laws of Thermodynamics

Zeroth law of thermodynamics

- "Two objects in thermal equilibrium with the third one, are also in thermal equilibrium with each other".
- "If no mechanical work is done by one part of the system on another part of the system, then system is said to be in **mechanical equilibrium.** This is only possible, if process is isobaric, i.e. taking place at constant pressure."
- A chemical equilibrium is set up if composition of the various phases in the system remains the same throughout.

First law of thermodynamics

(Law of conservation of energy)

- "Energy can neither be created nor destroyed, although it can be transformed from one form to another" i.e.
- Total energy of the universe remains constant or the energy of a system that is isolated from its surroundings is constant.

Mathematically, ($\Delta E = q + W$)

where, $\Delta E =$ change in internal energy

$q =$ heat supplied to the system

and $W =$ work done on the system $= -p\Delta V$

$$\therefore \quad \boxed{\Delta E = q - p\Delta V}$$

- In SI convention, W is positive. In non SI convention, W is negative.

$$\therefore \quad \Delta E = q - W = q - (-p\Delta V) = q + p\Delta V$$

- When W or $q > 0$, it means energy has been supplied to the system as heat or work. Then, $\Delta E > 0$.
- When W or $q < 0$, it means energy has been lost by the system as work or as heat. Then, $\Delta E < 0$.
- $\Delta E = -q$ means no work is done on the system but q amount of heat is taken from the system and given to the surroundings.
- $\Delta E = q - W$ means W amount of work is done by the system and q amount of heat is supplied to the system.

Special cases of first law of thermodynamics

(i) If change is **cyclic**, i.e. original state is restored, then $\Delta E = 0$, hence from $\Delta E = q + W$

$$\therefore \quad q = -W = -(-p\Delta V)$$

$= + p\Delta V$ for finite change

$= pdV$ for very small change

Since, $q = -W$, hence system is 100% efficient. Work is thus maximum.

$$q = -W_{\max} = p\int_{V_1}^{V_2} dV$$

$$-W_{\max} = nRT \int_{V_1}^{V_2} \frac{dV}{V} = nRT \log_e \frac{V_2}{V_1}$$

$$\boxed{-W_{\max} = 2.303\, nRT \log_{10} \frac{V_2}{V_1}}$$

or
$$\boxed{-W_{\max} = 2.303 nRT \log_{10} \frac{p_1}{p_2}}$$

as
$$p \propto \frac{1}{V}$$

(ii) The change is **isochoric**, i.e. volume is constant, hence

$$\Delta V = 0$$

$$\because \quad W = p\Delta V = 0$$

$$\therefore \quad \Delta E = q$$

Thus, **heat supplied causes change in internal energy only**.

(iii) If change is **adiabatic** i.e., no exchange of heat then, $q = 0$

$$W = \Delta E = -p\Delta V \quad \text{or} \quad p\Delta V = -\Delta E$$

Thus, work is done at the cost of internal energy. ΔE is negative it means ($E_2 < E_1$), thus, temperature falls in adiabatic expansion of the gas.

Since, $\left(\frac{\Delta E}{\Delta T}\right) = C_V \quad \therefore \quad W = -C_V\, \Delta T = -C_V(T_2 - T_1)$

For adiabatic expansion,

$$\frac{T_2}{T_1} = \left(\frac{V_1}{V_2}\right)^{\gamma - 1} \quad \therefore \quad W = -C_V \left[T_1\left(\frac{V_1}{V_2}\right)^{\gamma - 1} - T_1\right]$$

$$\boxed{W = T_1 C_V \left[1 - \left(\frac{V_1}{V_2}\right)^{\gamma - 1}\right] = T_1 C_V \left(1 - \left(\frac{V_1}{V_2}\right)^{R/C_V}\right)}$$

Also, $\boxed{W = -\frac{(p_1V_1 - p_2V_2)}{(\gamma - 1)}}$ (by mathematical expansion)

$$= \frac{-nR}{\gamma - 1}(T_2 - T_1)$$

where, $\gamma = \frac{C_p}{C_V}$

- For adiabatic change,

$$p_1V_1^{\gamma} = p_2V_2^{\gamma}$$

$$\left(\frac{T_2}{T_1}\right) = \left(\frac{V_1}{V_2}\right)^{\gamma - 1} = \left(\frac{V_1}{V_2}\right)^{\frac{(C_p - C_V)}{C_V}} = \left(\frac{V_1}{V_2}\right)^{R/C_V}$$

$$\left(\frac{T_2}{T_1}\right) = \left(\frac{p_2}{p_1}\right)^{R/C_p} \Rightarrow T_2 = T_1\left[\frac{C_V + p_{\text{ext}}\, R/p_1}{C_V + p_{\text{ext}}\, R/p_2}\right]$$

Also, $\frac{T_2}{T_1} = \frac{C_V + (p_2/p_1)R}{C_p}$

Enthalpy

Enthalpy H is related to internal energy E (or U) by

$$H = E + pV$$

Thus, $\Delta H = \Delta E + p\Delta V$

H is also a state function, then $\Delta H_1 = \Delta H_2 = (H_B - H_A)$

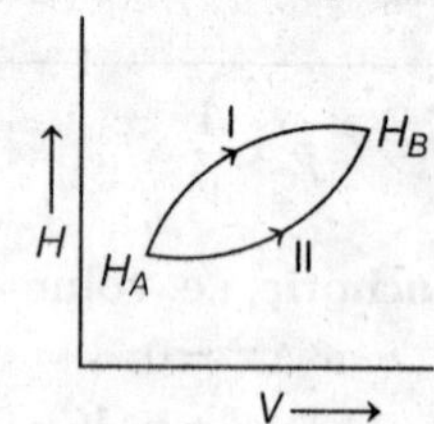

Also, $\Delta H = \Delta E - (-p\Delta V)$

$$\boxed{\Delta H = \Delta E - W} \quad \because \Delta E = \Delta H + W$$

where, $W = -p\Delta V = -p(V_2 - V_1) \Rightarrow \Delta H = \Delta E + \Delta n_g RT$

Under standard states (at 298 K and 1 bar)

$$\Delta H^\circ_{298} = \Delta E^\circ_{298} + \Delta n_g R(298\text{ K})$$

where, Δn_g = moles of gaseous products – moles of gaseous reactants.

Coefficient of Thermal expansion

The rate of change of volume with temperature at constant pressure relative to a volume V is called coefficient of thermal expansion (α),

$$\alpha = \frac{1}{V}\left(\frac{\partial V}{\partial T}\right)_p$$

Joule-Thomson effect

- The phenomenon of change of temperature produced when a gas is made to expand adiabatically from a region of high pressure (low volume) to region of extremely low pressure (high volume) is called Joule-Thomson effect.
- μ_{JT} (Joule-Thomson coefficient)

$$= \left(\frac{dT}{dp}\right)_H = -\left(\frac{\partial H}{\partial p}\right)_T \Big/ C_p = \frac{1}{C_p}\left[\frac{2a}{RT} - b\right]$$

when a and b are van der Waals' constant.

- $\mu_{JT} = 0$, for an ideal gas when it expands in vacuum. No cooling takes place as force of attraction between molecules is zero.

$$W = -p_{ext}\Delta V = 0$$

Thus, by first law, $\Delta E = q + W = q = 0$

Thus, when an ideal gas expands in vacuum, no change takes place in its internal energy.

$$\left(\frac{\partial E}{\partial V}\right)_T = 0$$

For an ideal gas

$$pV = \text{constant} \Rightarrow \left(\frac{\partial E}{\partial V}\right)_T = 0$$

- The temperature below which a gas becomes cooler on expansion is known as the **inversion temperature.**

$$\mu_{JT} = 0 \Rightarrow T_i = \frac{2a}{Rb}$$

Solved Examples & Instant Practice

Example 5.4)

(a) Two litres of an ideal gas at a pressure of 10 atm expands isothermally into a vacuum until its total volume is 10 litres. How much heat is absorbed and how much work is done in the expansion?

(b) If this expansion takes place against a constant external pressure of 1 atm, what is work done?

(c) Calculate the work done, if it takes place reversibly. *[NCERT]*

(a) Expansion under vacuum, $p = 0$

(b) Expansion under external pressure, $W = -p_{ext}\,\Delta V$

(c) Expansion taking place reversibly

$$-W = q = 2.303\, nRT \log\frac{V_2}{V_1}$$

Sol. (a) Under vacuum, $p = 0$

$\therefore \quad W = q = p_{ext}\,(10 - 2) = 0$

(b) $-W = q = p.\Delta V = 1(10 - 2) = 8$ L atm

(c) $-W = q = 2.303 nRT \log\frac{V_2}{V_1}$

Since, $pV = nRT$ (V = total volume)

$\therefore \quad nRT = pV = 1 \times 10$ L atm

$$-W = 2.303 \times 10 \log\frac{10}{2} = 16.097 \text{ L atm}$$

Immediate Test 4

(i) A sample of 4.8 g methane occupies 12.7 L at 310 K.

(a) Calculate the work done when the gas expands isothermally against a constant external pressure of 380 Torr, until the volume doubles.

(b) Calculate the work done if above expansion takes place isothermally and reversibly.

(ii) Calculate the minimum work which must be done to compress 16 g of O_2 gas at 300 K from a pressure of 1 Nm^{-2} to a pressure of 100 Nm^{-2}.

(iii) About 3 dm^3 gastric juice are produced per day in the human body fluids such as blood whose pH is 7.4 at 37°C. Calculate the minimum work required to produce 3 dm^3 gastric juice at body temperature 37°C. The pH of the gastric juice may be taken as unity. log 4 = 0.6,

(iv) Two moles of glucose were dissolved in water to prepare 1 dm^3 solution at 298 K. The solution was further diluted isothermally and gradually until the concentration was 0.2 M. Calculate the work performed.

(v) Five moles of an ideal gas at 300 K are allowed to expand isothermally from an initial pressure of 10.0 atm to a final pressure of 4.0 atm against a constant external pressure of 1.0 atm. Calculate q, W, ΔE and ΔH.

Example 5.5) One mole of CO_2 gas at 300 K is expanded under adiabatic condition such that its volume becomes 64 times.

(a) What is the final temperature ?

(b) What is the work done ?

Sol. For adiabatic expansion, work is done at the cost of internal energy hence, cooling takes place.

$$T_2 = T_1\left(\frac{V_1}{V_2}\right)^{\gamma-1} \Rightarrow \gamma = \frac{C_p}{C_V} = 1.33 \text{ for polyatomic gas}$$

$$T_1 = 300\text{ K}, V_1 = V\text{ L}, V_2 = 64\,V\text{ L}$$

$$\therefore \quad T_2 = 300\left(\frac{1}{64}\right)^{1.33-1} = 300\left(\frac{1}{64}\right)^{1/3} = \frac{300}{4} = 75\text{ K}$$

■ Temperature falls in adiabatic expansion

(b) $q = 0$

For adiabatic change,

$$\therefore W = -\Delta E = -nC_V\Delta T = -nC_V(T_2 - T_1) \qquad [\Delta T = T_2 - T_1]$$

$$W = -1 \times 3R(T_2 - T_1)$$

$$= -1 \times 3 \times 8.314\,(75 - 300) = 5611.95\text{ J} = 5.612\text{ kJ}$$

■ Work is done at the cost of internal energy.

Immediate Test 5

(i) One mole of an inert gas at 339 K is subjected to adiabatic expansion such that pressure changes from 2.44 bar to 0.338 bar.

(a) What is the final temperature?

(b) What is the work done?

(ii) 0.14 kg of CO (assume to be ideal) gas at 298 K is held by a piston under 3×10^4 Nm^{-2} pressure. The pressure is suddenly reduced to one-third of the initial value and the gas expands adiabatically. For CO, $C_V = 20.8$ JK^{-1} mol^{-1}, Calculate

(a) final temperature (b) q, (c) W (d) ΔE and (e) ΔH

Example 5.6) A "0.25 hp" electric motor uses 187 W of electrical energy while, supplying 35 J of work each second. How much energy must be dissipated in the form of heat ?

Sol. Horse power (hp) is the energy supplied per second. It is called Watt

$$1\text{ W} = 1\text{ J s}^{-1} \Rightarrow \Delta E = q + W$$

$$\therefore \quad q = \Delta E - W \Rightarrow \Delta E = 187\text{ W} = 187\text{ J s}^{-1}$$

Thus, in one second

$$\Delta E = 187\text{ J}, W = 35\text{ J} \Rightarrow q = 187 - 35 = 152\text{ J}$$

Immediate Test 6

(i) The work is done when a gas is compressed in a cylinder is 462 J. During this process, there is a heat transfer of 128 J from the gas to the surroundings. Calculate the change in internal energy of the process.

(ii) One mole of benzene is converted reversibly into vapour at its boiling point 80.2°C by supplying heat. The vapour expands against the pressure of 1 atm. The heat of vaporisation of benzene is 395 Jg^{-1}. Calculate q, ΔE, W and ΔH.

Example 5.7) For CO_2, 300 K and 1 atm

$$\left(\frac{\Delta H}{\Delta p}\right)_T = -10.2\text{ cal mol}^{-1}\text{ atm}^{-1}$$

and $\qquad C_p = 8.919\text{ cal mol}^{-1}\text{ K}^{-1}$

Calculate, Joule-Thomson coefficient at the given condition.

Sol. Due to adiabatic expansion cooling takes place and

$$\mu_{JT} = -\frac{1}{C_p}\left(\frac{\Delta H}{\Delta p}\right)_T$$

Given, $\qquad C_p = 8.919\text{ cal mol}^{-1}\text{ K}^{-1}$

and $\qquad \left(\frac{\Delta H}{\Delta p}\right)_T = -10.2\text{ cal mol}^{-1}\text{ atm}^{-1}$

$$\therefore \quad \mu_{JT} = -\frac{1}{8.919} \times (10.2)$$

$$= -1.1436\text{ K atm}^{-1}$$

Example 5.8) At 300 K and 0.60 atm, $\mu_{JT}(N_2) = 0.0142 - 2.60 \times 10^{-4}\,p$. Assume the equation to be independent of temperature near 300 K, what is change in temperature which may be expected due to expansion from 60 atm to 20 atm.?

Sol. $\mu_{JT} = (0.0142 - 2.60 \times 10^{-4}\,p)$

Also, $\mu_{JT} = \left(\frac{dT}{dp}\right)$

$$\therefore \quad \frac{dT}{dp} = (0.0142 - 2.60 \times 10^{-4}\,p)$$

$$\therefore \quad dT = (0.0142 - 2.60 \times 10^{-4}\,p)\,dp$$

$$\therefore \quad \Delta T = \int_{T_1}^{T_2} dT = \int_{p_1}^{p_2} 0.0142\,dp - 2.64 \times 10^{-4}\int_{p_1}^{p_2} p\,dp$$

$$\Delta T = 0.0142(p_2 - p_1) - 2.64 \times 10^{-4}\left(\frac{p_2^2 - p_1^2}{2}\right)$$

$$= (p_2 - p_1)\left[0.0142 - 2.64 \times 10^{-4}\,\frac{(p_2 + p_1)}{2}\right]$$

$$= (20 - 60)\left[0.0142 - 2.64 \times 10^{-4}\left(\frac{20 + 60}{2}\right)\right]$$

$$= -0.152\text{ K}$$

KNOWLEDGE CONFIRMATION **Test 2**

1 0.001 mole of an ideal gas in a piston chamber kept in a constant temperature bath at 298 K expands from 25.0 mL to 75.0 mL very-very slowly. Thus, work done by the system is

(a) –2.72 J (b) +2.72 J (c) – 1.18 J (d) +1.18 J

2 A sample of gas changes in volume from 4.0 L to 6.0 L against an external pressure of 1.50 atm and absorbs 1000 J of heat. Thus, change in internal energy is

(a) 1303.8 J (b) –1303.8 J (c) –696.2 J (d) 696.2 J

3 Of the three forms of water

I. $H_2O(s)$ II. $H_2O(l)$ and III. $H_2O(g)$

highest and lowest enthalpies are for

	Highest	Lowest
(a)	I	II
(b)	I	III
(c)	III	I
(d)	II	III

4 A gas is cooled and loses 50 J of heat. The gas contracts as it cools and work done on the system equal to 20 J is exchanged with the surroundings.

Thus, ΔE is

(a) 70 J (b) –30 J (c) 30 J (d) –70 J

5 For one mole of an ideal gas,

(a) pV = constant under isothermal condition

(b) $\left(\frac{\partial E}{\partial V}\right)_T = 0$

(c) $\frac{\partial(pV)}{\partial T} = R$

(d) All of the above are correct

6 1 g H_2 gas at STP expands under atmospheric pressure such that volume is doubled. Work done is

(a) –11.2 L atm (b) +11.2 L atm

(c) –22.4 L atm (d) +22.4 L atm

7 When 1 mole of $NH_3(g)$ ($\gamma = 1.33$) occupying volume 10 L at 27°C is expanded under adiabatic condition, temperature falls to 150 K. Hence, final volume is

(a) 20 L (b) 5 L (c) 80 L (d) 40 L

8 For the reaction, $O_2(g) \longrightarrow 2O(g)$, $\Delta H = x$ kJ, hence enthalpy of $O_2(g)$ and $O(g)$ are respectively (in kJ)

(a) 0, x (b) 0, $\frac{x}{2}$ (c) x, $\frac{x}{2}$ (d) $\frac{x}{2}$, x

9 A system absorbs 1000 kJ of heat and does 650 kJ of work on the surroundings. Thus, change in internal energy is (in kJ)

(a) 350 (b) –350 (c) 1650 (d) –1650

10 Select the correct statement(s).

(a) Joule-Thomson coefficient $\mu_{JT} = \frac{1}{C_p}\left[\frac{2a}{RT} - b\right]$ for a real gas

(b) $\mu_{JT} = 0$ for an ideal gas

(c) Both are correct

(d) None of the above is correct

11 Consider following change under isothermal and reversible conditions.

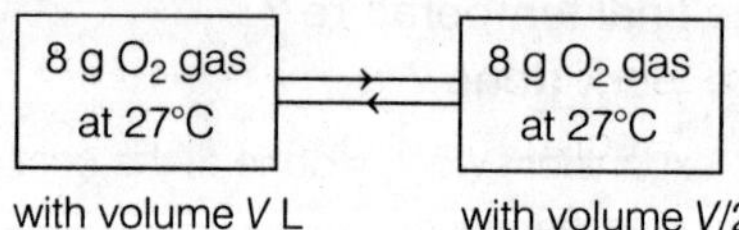

Thus, work done (in cal) on the system is

(a) $W = 0$ (b) $2.303 \times 150 \log 2$

(c) $W = -2.303 \times 150 \log 2$ (d) $-2.303 \times 300 \times 8 \times 2 \log 2$

12 "0.50 hp" electric engine uses 250 W of electrical energy and delivers 48 J of work each second. Thus, energy dissipiated in the form of friction heat is

(a) 298 J (b) –298 J (c) 202 J (d) –202 J

13 When a system releases 10 kJ of energy into the surroundings by doing work, the internal energy of the system decreases by 10 kJ. Thus, W and ΔE in kJ are.

	W	ΔE
(a)	10	10
(b)	–10	–10
(c)	–10	10
(d)	10	–10

14 A 150 W heater was placed in 1.00 kg of methanol and turned on for exactly 1 min. The temperature increased by 3.54° C. Assuming that, all the heat is absorbed by the methanol, molar heat capacity at constant pressure is

(a) 42.375 J K^{-1} mol^{-1} (b) 8.14 J K^{-1} mol^{-1}

(c) 4.237 J K^{-1} mol^{-1} (d) 81.4 J K^{-1} mol^{-1}

15 Given, $\left(\frac{\partial C_p}{\partial p}\right)_T = T\left(\frac{\partial^2 V}{\partial T^2}\right)_p$

Thus,

(a) $\left(\frac{\partial C_p}{\partial P}\right)_T = 0$ (b) $T\left(\frac{\partial^2 V}{\partial T^2}\right)_p = 0$

(c) Both are correct (d) None of these

16 For van der Waals' gas, $(C_p - C_V)$ is equal to

(a) $R\left(1 - \frac{2a(V-b)}{V(pV^2 + a)}\right)^{-1}$ (b) $R\left(1 - \frac{2a(V-b)}{V(pV^2 + a)}\right)$

(c) $R\left(1 + \frac{2a(V-b)}{V(pV^2 + a)}\right)$ (d) R

17 One mole of He gas behaving ideally is subjected to a cyclic process as shown.

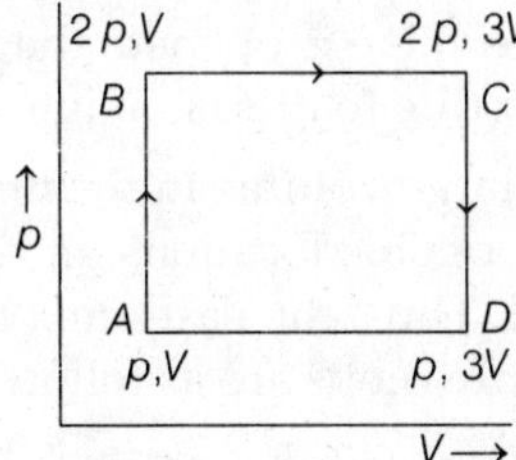

Thus, work done during this cyclic process is

(a) $-pV$ (b) $-2pV$ (c) $-3pV$ (d) zero

18 A gas undergoes adiabatic expansion satisfying the equation $TV^{0.4}$ = constant. Thus, atomicity of the gas is

(a) 1 (b) 2
(c) 3 (d) cannot be predicted

19 A diatomic gas is expanded adiabatically to 8 times of the initial value. Thus, pressure will change to

(a) 0.054 times (b) 0.108 times
(c) $\frac{1}{8}$ times (d) 8 times

20 Consider following (p-V) curve in compression and expansion:

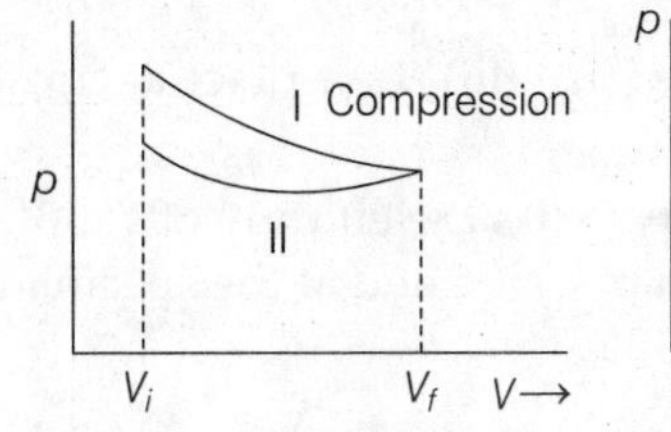

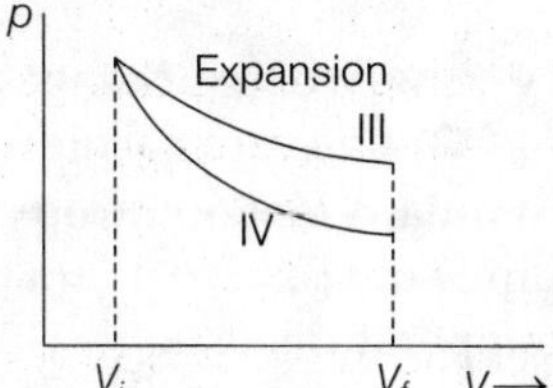

Adiabatic processes are

(a) I, III (b) II, III
(c) I, IV (d) II, IV

Carnot's Cycle

Carnot's cycle is a reversible engine having so many isothermal and adiabatic changes, such that after these processes, engine returns to its original state.

Let heat gained from the source of heat placed at temperature $T_2 = q_2$.

Heat lost to the sink at temperature $T_1 = -q_1, (T_2 > T_1)$, then work done $= (q_2 - q_1)$

$$\text{Efficiency, } \eta = \left(\frac{q_2 - q_1}{q_2}\right) = \left(\frac{T_2 - T_1}{T_2}\right) = \frac{W}{q_2}$$

$$\eta = \left(1 - \frac{T_1}{T_2}\right)$$

If $\quad T_1 = 0\text{ K} (-273°\text{C}), \eta = 1$

Thus, Carnot cycle is 100% efficient, if sink is placed at −273°C. It is practically impossible, thus $\eta \neq 1$.

Since, $T_2 > T_1$, hence $\eta < 1$.

- It is impossible to convert heat into equivalent amount of work.
- Greater the difference between T_2 and T_1, greater the value of η. Thus, superheated steam is used in engine to increase its efficiency. (Steam at elevated pressure is called superheated steam).
- Temperature of the sink at which system is 100% efficient is called absolute zero of the Kelvin scale.

Entropy (S)

- The thermodynamic property that measures the amount of molecular disorder is called **entropy** (S).
- Entropy is a state function, so that change in entropy ΔS is independent of the path used in going from the initial state to the final state.

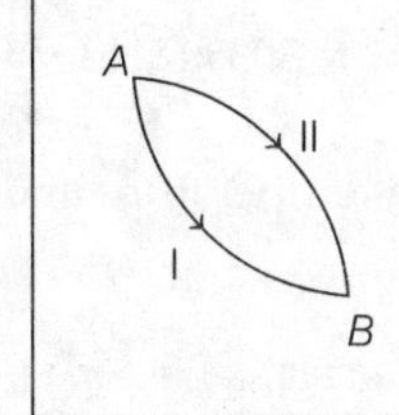

$$\Delta S_1 = \Delta S_2 = (S_B - S_A)$$

Entropy change in an isothermal process,

$$\Delta S = \frac{q_{rev}}{T}$$

As $\quad q_{rev} = -W_{rev} = 2.303\, nRT \log \frac{V_2}{V_1}$

$$\therefore \quad (\Delta S)_{rev} = 2.303\, nR \log \frac{V_2}{V_1} = 2.303\, nR \log \frac{p_1}{p_2}$$

(i) Entropy change of vaporisation

$$\Delta S^\circ_{vap} = \frac{\Delta H^\circ_{vap}}{T(\text{b.p})}$$

(ii) Entropy change of fusion

$$\Delta S^\circ_{\text{fusion}} = \frac{\Delta H^\circ_{\text{fusion}}}{T(\text{f.p})}$$

(iii) Entropy change of transition

$$\Delta S^\circ_{\text{transition}} = \frac{\Delta H^\circ_{\text{trans}}}{T(\text{transition temperature})}$$

All of the above processes [(i) – (iii)] take place at constant temperature.

- **Standard molar entropy** ($S°$) is the entropy of 1 mole of pure substance at 1 atm pressure and at the specified temperature, usually 298 K.

$$\Delta S^\circ = (S^\circ_{\text{product}} - S^\circ_{\text{reactant}})$$

- Standard molar entropy is also called **absolute entropy** because it is measured with reference to the entropy of the perfectly ordered crystalline substance at 0 K.

$$S^\circ = 0 \text{ J K}^{-1} \text{ at } T = 0 \text{ K}$$

- As solid changes to liquid and then to vapour, randomness increases, hence entropy increases. Thus, entropy of vapour > liquid > solid.
- **Entropy change**, due to change in temperature at constant pressure.

$$(\Delta S)_p = 2.303 nC_p \log_{10} \frac{T_2}{T_1}$$

and at constant volume

$$(\Delta S)_V = 2.303\, nC_V \log \frac{T_2}{T_1}$$

- **Entropy change** when temperature and pressure both change

$$\Delta S = 2.303\, n\left[R \log \frac{p_1}{p_2} + C_p \log \frac{T_2}{T_1}\right]$$

and when temperature and volume both change

$$\Delta S = 2.303\, n\left[R \log \frac{V_2}{V_1} + C_V \log \frac{T_2}{T_1}\right]$$

- If, $T_1 = T_2$ (isothermal)

$$(\Delta S)_T = 2.303\, nR \log \frac{p_1}{p_2} = 2.303\, nR \log \frac{V_2}{V_1}$$

If $p_1 = p_2$ (isobaric)

$$(\Delta S)_p = 2.303\, nC_p \log \frac{T_2}{T_1}$$

If $V_1 = V_2$ (isochoric)

$$(\Delta S)_V = 2.303\, nC_V \log \frac{T_2}{T_1}$$

Entropy change of mixing of two gases

Consider a spontaneous process of intermixing of two inert gases. When the valve is opened, the intermixing of two inert gases occur due to diffusion into one another. Each gas occupies a large volume in the final state and thereby, number of possible locations for the molecules of each gas is increased. Thus, the gases mix to achieve more randomness. The expressions are as follow :

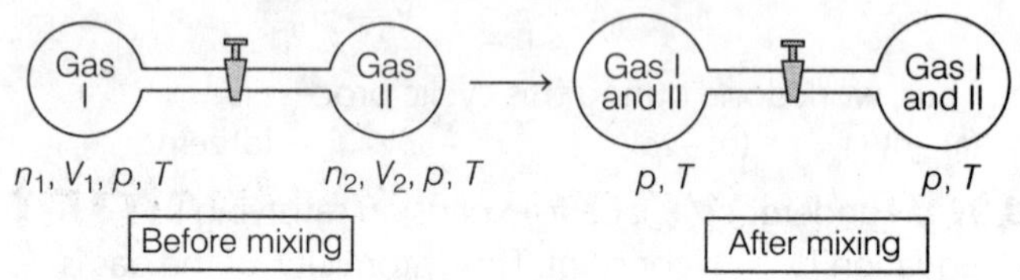

Final volume = $(V_1 + V_2)$

Entropy change for gas I

$$\Delta S_1 = n_1 R \ln \frac{(V_1 + V_2)}{V_1}$$

and for gas II

$$\Delta S_2 = n_2 R \ln\left(\frac{V_1 + V_2}{V_2}\right)$$

$$\chi_1 \text{ (mole fraction) of gas I} = \frac{n_1}{n_1 + n_2} = \frac{V_1}{V_1 + V_2}$$

$$\chi_2 \text{ (mole fraction) of gas II} = \frac{n_2}{n_1 + n_2} = \left(\frac{V_2}{V_1 + V_2}\right)$$

$$\therefore \quad \Delta S_{\text{total}} = \Delta S_1 + \Delta S_2$$

$$= n_1 R \ln \frac{1}{\chi_1} + n_2 R \ln \frac{1}{\chi_2}$$

$$= -[n_1 R \ln \chi_1 + n_2 R \ln \chi_2]$$

$$= -R \sum n_i \ln \chi_i$$

Also,

$$\Delta S_{\text{total}} = -R\left[\frac{n_1}{n_1 + n_2}(n_1 + n_2) \ln \chi_1 + \frac{n_2}{n_1 + n_2}(n_1 + n_2) \ln \chi_2\right]$$

$$\boldsymbol{\Delta S_{\text{Total}} = -R\,(n_1 + n_2)\,[\chi_1 \ln \chi_1 + \chi_2 \ln \chi_2]}$$

Entropy and second law of thermodynamics

In terms of entropy, second law of thermodynamics is defined as "entropy of the system and surrounding remains constant in a reversible equilibrium process while, it increases in an irreversible process".

$$\Delta S_{\text{total}} = \Delta S_{\text{system}} + \Delta S_{\text{surrounding}}$$

- In nature, all the processes are irreversible (spontaneous) going to completion, hence entropy of the universe increases and tends to be maximum.

$$\Delta S_{system} + \Delta S_{surrounding} > 0$$

$\Delta S_{total} > 0 \Rightarrow$ Spontaneous

$\Delta S_{total} < 0 \Rightarrow$ Non-spontaneous

$\Delta S_{total} = 0 \Rightarrow$ Equilibrium

Entropy and third law of thermodynamics

"At the absolute zero of temperature, the entropy of every substance may become zero and does become zero in case of perfectly crystalline structure".

$$\lim_{T \to 0} S = 0$$

In case of CO and NO molecules in solid state, there is randomness even at 0K due to their dipole moment. Hence, entropy in such cases is not zero, even at 0 K.

Solved Examples & Instant Practice

Example 5.9) A Carnot engine operates between two thermal reservoirs at 373 K (source) and 273 K (sink). What amount of work can it produce for each 1000 J of heat absorbed from the source ?

Sol. Efficiency (η) of a Carnot engine is

$$\eta = \frac{T_2 - T_1}{T_2} = \frac{W}{Q} \Rightarrow W = \eta Q = \left(\frac{T_2 - T_1}{T_2}\right)Q$$

Thus, output (work) can be calculated.

Efficiency of the Carnot engine

$$\eta = \frac{T_2 - T_1}{T_2} = \frac{373 - 273}{373} = \frac{100}{373}$$

$$\therefore \quad W = \frac{100}{373} \times 1000\ \text{J} = 268.1\ \text{J}$$

Immediate Test 7

During the operation of the engine operating between 373 K and 273 K. 25% of the work produced is dissipiated by friction. How much heat must the warm reservoir supply in order for the engine to produce 1000 J of useful work ?

Example 5.10) Consider the following thermochemical reactions : **$\Delta H°$ (kJ mol^{-1})**

I. $H_2(g) + \frac{1}{2}O_2(g) \longrightarrow H_2O(l)$, -285.6

II. $H_2(g) + \frac{1}{2}O_2(g) \longrightarrow H_2O(g)$, -243.6

What is entropy change when 1.8 kg of water is vaporised at 1 atm pressure?

Sol. *Liquid water changes to vapour state.*

Thus, $$\Delta S° = \frac{\Delta H°_{vap}}{T}$$

At 1 atm pressure, boiling point of water at which vaporisation takes place is 373 K.

$$H_2O(l) \longrightarrow H_2O(g)$$

Sol. From (i) and (ii) by (ii)–(i)

$$H_2O(l) \longrightarrow H_2O(g), \quad \Delta H°_{vap} = 42.0\ \text{kJ mol}^{-1}$$

$$1.8\ \text{kg}\ H_2O = 1800\ \text{g}\ H_2O = \frac{1800}{18} = 100\ \text{mol water}$$

$\therefore$ Enthalpy change for 100 mol,

$H_2O(l)$ to convert into $H_2O(g) = 42 \times 100 = 4200$ kJ

$$\therefore \quad \Delta S° = \Delta H / T = \frac{4200\ \text{kJ}}{373} = 11.26\ \text{kJ K}^{-1}$$

Immediate Test 8

(i) Exactly 100 J of heat was transferred reversibly to a block of gold at 298 K from a thermal reservoir at 298.01 K and then exactly 100 J of heat was absorbed reversibly from a block of gold by a thermal reservoir at 297.99 K. What is $(\Delta S)_{system}$ for this process?

(ii) Calcuale the entropy change at 373 K for the transformation,

$$H_2O\ (l, 1.01325\ \text{bar}) \longrightarrow H_2O\ (g, 0.101325\ \text{bar})$$

Given, $\Delta H_{vap} = 40.668\ \text{kJ mol}^{-1}$

Example 5.11) Calculate $(\Delta S)_{system}$ for reversibly cooling one mole of an ideal monoatomic gas from 298 K to 273 K under constant volume condition.

Sol. When a process takes place by change in temperature at constant volume, then,

$$\Delta S = nC_V \ln\frac{T_2}{T_1} = 2.303\, nC_V \log_{10}\frac{T_2}{T_1}$$

For monoatomic gas, $C_V = \frac{3}{2}R$

$$\therefore \quad \Delta S = 2.303 \times \frac{3}{2} R \log\frac{T_2}{T_1}$$

$$(\Delta S)_{system} = 2.303 \times 1.5 \times 8.314 \log\frac{273}{298} = -1.09\ \text{J mol}^{-1}\ \text{K}^{-1}$$

Immediate Test 9

Calculate $(\Delta S)_{system}$ for reversibly cooling one mole of an ideal diatomic gas from 300 K to 250 K under constant pressure.

Example 5.12) Consider a reversible expansion of 2.0 moles of O_2 gas ($C_p = 3.5\,R$) from 298 K and 25 L to 596 K and 50 L. Assuming ideal gas behaviour, calculate $(\Delta S)_{\text{system}}$ for the process.

Sol. When temperature and volume both changes,

$$(\Delta S)_{\text{system}} = 2.303\, nC_V \log\frac{T_2}{T_1} + 2.303\, nR \log\frac{V_2}{V_1}$$

$$C_p - C_V = R$$

$$\therefore \quad C_V = (C_p - R) = 3.5R - R = 2.5R$$

$$\therefore \quad \Delta S = 2.303 \times 2 \times 2.5 \times 8.314 \log\frac{596}{298}$$

$$+ 2.303 \times 2 \times 8.314 \log\frac{50}{25}$$

$$= 2.303 \times 2 \times 8.314 \log 2 \times [2.5 + 1] = 40.35\ \text{J K}^{-1}$$

Example 5.13) Consider a mixture of 1 mole of N_2 gas and 3 moles of O_2 gas at 298 K and 1 bar pressure. Calculate the entropy change relative to unmixed gases.

Sol. When two types of gases are mixed,

$$\Delta S_{\text{mix}} = -2.303 nR\, [\chi_1 \log \chi_1 + \chi_2 \log \chi_2]$$

N_2 gas = 1 mol

O_2 gas = 3 mol

Total n = 4 mol

$$\therefore \quad \chi_{N_2} = 0.25 \text{ mol} \Rightarrow \chi_{O_2} = 0.75 \text{ mol}$$

$$\Delta S_{\text{mix}} = -2.303 \times 4 \times 8.314\, [0.25 \log 0.25 + 0.75 \log 0.75]$$

$$= -2.303 \times 4 \times 8.314\, [-0.1505 - 0.0937] = 18.703\ \text{JK}^{-1}$$

Example 5.14) 2 dm^3 of methane gas under 4 bar and 4 dm^3 of oxygen gas under 20 bar and 298 K are forced into a 3 dm^3 evacuated reaction vessel, the temperature being maintained at 298 K. Calculate the change in entropy assuming ideal behaviour of the gases.

Sol. Given : Pressure for CH_4 (p) = 4 bar or 400 kPa

Volume of CH_4 = 2 dm^3

Pressure for O_2(p) = 20 bar

Volume of O_2 = 4 dm^3

$$\text{Moles of } CH_4 = \frac{pV}{RT} = \frac{(400\ \text{kPa})(2\ \text{dm}^3)}{(8.314\ \text{kPa dm}^3\ \text{K}^{-1}\ \text{mol}^{-1})(298\ \text{K})}$$

$$= 0.323 \text{ mol}$$

$$\text{Moles of } O_2 = \frac{pV}{RT} = \frac{200 \times 4}{8.314 \times 298} = 3.23 \text{ mol}$$

$$\Delta S_{\text{mix}} = 2.303\, n_A R \log\frac{V_{\text{final}}}{V_A} + 2.303\, n_B R \log\frac{V_{\text{final}}}{V_B}$$

$$= 2.303 \times 8.314 \left[0.323 \log\frac{3}{2} + 3.23 \log\frac{3}{4}\right] = -6.346\ \text{JK}^{-1}$$

Example 5.15) A 50 g mass of copper at a temperature of 393 K is placed in contact with a 100 g mass of copper at a temperature of 303 K in a thermally insulated container. Calculate entropy change for the reversible process.
Specific heat of copper = 0.4184 JK^{-1} g^{-1}
Atomic mass of Cu = 63.5 g mol^{-1}

System gains heat at the lower temperature and loses heat at the higher temperature. Thus, Heat gained = Heat lost
This gives the thermal equilibrium temperature.

$$\Delta S = nC_p \log\frac{T}{T_i}$$

Thus, ΔS of the hot side and that of cold side are calculated.

$$\Delta S = \Delta S_{\text{cold}} + \Delta S_{\text{hot}}$$

Sol. Let thermal equilibrium temperature be = T

Heat gained by Cu at low temperature = $mC_p\ (T - 303)$
$= 100C_p\ (T - 303)$

Heat lost by Cu at higher temperature = $50C_p\ (393 - T)$

Since, heat gained = heat lost

$$\therefore \quad 100C_p(T - 303) = 50C_p(393 - T)$$

$$\therefore \quad T = 333\ \text{K}$$

$$\text{Thus,} \quad \Delta S_{\text{cold}} = 2.303 nC_p \log\frac{T}{T_c}$$

$$= 2.303 \times \frac{100 \times 0.4184}{63.5} \times 63.5 \log\frac{333}{303}$$

$$= 3.951\ \text{JK}^{-1}$$

$$\text{and} \quad \Delta S_{\text{hot}} = 2.303 \times \frac{50}{63.5} \times 0.4184 \times 63.5 \log\frac{333}{393}$$

$$= -3.466\ \text{JK}^{-1}$$

$$\therefore \quad \Delta S_{\text{Total}} = 3.951 - 3.466$$

$$= 0.485\ \text{JK}^{-1}$$

Immediate Test 10

(i) Calculate ΔS for 2 moles of a diatomic gas, which is heated and compressed from 300 K and 1 bar to 400 K and 5 bar ($C_p = 3.5R$).

(ii) Repeat the above process to calculate $(\Delta S)_{\text{system}}$, if pressure is made one-fourth of the initial value and temperature is doubled.

(iii) A 5.0 g of ice at 273 K is added to 30 g of water at 323 K in a thermally insulated container.
   (a) What is the final temperature?
   (b) What is the total entropy change?
   ΔH_{fusion} (ice) = 334.725 Jg^{-1})
   $C_p(H_2O, l)$ = 4.184 JK^{-1}g^{-1}

KNOWLEDGE CONFIRMATION Test 3

1 When 1.2 g of C(diamond) is combusted 9.1 kcal of heat is supplied to the surrounding. When 2.4 g of C (graphite) is combusted, 18.8 kcal of heat is supplied to the surrounding. Thus, ΔS of transition of 1 mole of C (diamond) to C (graphite) at 300 K (in kcal $mol^{-1} K^{-1}$) is

(Given, $C + O_2 \longrightarrow CO_2$)

(a) 0.01 (b) −0.01
(c) 0.03 (d) −0.03

2 Entropy change of vaporisation of $H_2O(l)$ at 1 atm pressure is 26.81 cal $mol^{-1} K^{-1}$. Thus, latent heat of vaporisation of $H_2O(l)$ is

(a) 26.81 cal mol^{-1} (b) 10.0 kcal mol^{-1}
(c) 10.00 cal mol^{-1} (d) 100.0 kcal mol^{-1}

3 $H_2O(s) \longrightarrow H_2O(l)$, $\Delta H = x_1$ cal mol^{-1} at T(K)

$H_2O(s) \longrightarrow H_2O(g)$, $\Delta H = x_2$ cal mol^{-1} T(K)

Entropy change for $H_2O(l) \longrightarrow H_2O(g)$ is in cal $mol^{-1} K^{-1}$

(a) $\left(\frac{x_1 + x_2}{T}\right)$ (b) $\left(\frac{x_1 - x_2}{T}\right)$
(c) $\left(\frac{x_2 - x_1}{T}\right)$ (d) $-\left(\frac{x_1 + x_2}{T}\right)$

4 1 mole of an ideal gas at 298 K is expanded isothermally and reversibly from 10 L to 100 L. Thus, entropy change is (in JK^{-1})

(a) 2.303×8.314 (b) -2.303×8.314
(c) 8.314 (d) −8.314

5 If for C (diamond) $\longrightarrow$ C (graphite)

$\Delta H° = 12.54$ kJ mol^{-1} at 300 K then $\frac{d}{dT}(\Delta S')$ is J $mol^{-1} K^{-2}$

(a) 0.14 (b) −0.14 (c) −0.042 (d) 0.042

6 Temperature of one mole of an ideal gas changes from T_1 to T_2 and simultaneously volume changes from V_1 to V_2. Thus,

(a) $\Delta S = R \log \frac{V_2}{V_1} + C_p \log \frac{T_2}{T_1}$ (b) $\Delta S = R \log \frac{V_2}{V_1} + (C_V + R) \log \frac{T_2}{T_1}$

(c) $\Delta S = R \log \frac{V_2 T_2}{V_1 T_1} + C_V \log \frac{T_2}{T_1}$ (d) All of these are correct

7 When the following processes are carried out as given for diatomic ideal gas,

I. temperature is made four times and simultaneously,
II. pressure is made one-fourth, then $(\Delta S)_{system}$ is

(a) $9R\ln 2$ (b) $-9R\ln 2$ (c) $4R\ln 2$ (d) $8R\ln 2$

8 Select the correct statement (s).

(a) Entropy of the system and surrounding remains constant in a reversible change.
(b) Entropy of the system and surrounding increases in the irreversible change
(c) Entropy of the nature tends to be maximum
(d) All of the above are correct statements.

9 Which is incorrect relation?

(a) $\Delta S_{(System)} + (\Delta S)_{Surrounding} > 0$ for spontaneous process.
(b) $\Delta S_{(System)} + (\Delta S)_{Surrounding} > 0$ for non-spontaneous process.
(c) $\Delta S_{(System)} + (\Delta S)_{Surrounding} = 0$ for reversible change.
(d) $\Delta S_{(System)} + (\Delta S)_{Surrounding} < 0$ for non-spontaneous change.

10 Entropy change when 2.0 moles of $H_2O(l)$ is heated from 300 K to 350 K is (C_p of $H_2O = 4.2$ J $g^{-1} K^{-1}$, ($\log_{10} 1.17 = 0.068$)

(a) −23.68 J K^{-1} (b) 23.68 J K^{-1}
(c) 10.28 J K^{-1} (d) 151.2 J K^{-1}

11 Entropy change when 36 g of liquid water is completely converted to vapour at 1atm ($\Delta H°_{vap}$ (H_2O) = 40.85 kJ mol^{-1}).

(a) 219.0 J K^{-1} (b) −219.0 J K^{-1}
(c) 6.08 J K^{-1} (d) 109.5 J K^{-1}

12 Consider following statements :

I. Molar entropy of a substance follows the order.

$(S)_{solid} < (S)_{liquid} < (S)_{gas}$

II. Entropy increases when $O_2(g)$ changes to O (g) atoms

$O_2(g) \longrightarrow 2O(g)$

III. Molar entropy of a substance is zero at absolute zero.

Select the correct statement (s).

(a) I, II (b) I, III (c) II, III (d) I, II, III

13 For isoentropic compression at temperature T,

(a) $\Delta S > 0$ (b) $\Delta S < 0$
(c) $\Delta S = 0$ (d) cannot be predicted

14 A Carnot engine absorbs 1000 J of heat and 25% of the heat is lost to the sink. If temperature of the heat reservoir is 400 K, temperature of the sink is ....

(a) 300 K (b) 250 K
(c) 200 K (d) 100 K

15 Which engine has maximum efficiency ?

(a) Engine working in the temperature range 77°C and 27°C
(b) Engine releasing 50% of heat to the surrounding
(c) Engine performing 200 kJ of work by absorbing 500 kJ of heat
(d) Engine working in the temperature range 400 K and 300 K

16 What percentage T_1 is of T_2 for a 10 per cent efficiency of a heat engine?

(a) 10% (b) 20% (c) 90% (d) 80%

17 A Carnot engine uses non-ideal gas and operates between T_2 (source) and T_1 (sink) temperature.
Thus, for non-ideal gas efficiency compared to that of ideal gas is

(a) $\eta_{(non-ideal)} > \eta_{(ideal)}$ (b) $\eta_{(non-ideal)} < \eta_{(ideal)}$
(c) $\eta_{(non-ideal)} = \eta_{(ideal)}$ (d) cannot be predicted

18 Change in entropy when 3 moles of diatomic ideal gas are heated and compressed from 298 K and 1 bar to 398 K and 5 bar ($C_p = 3.5\ R$).

(a) 4.9 JK^{-1} (b) + 14.9 JK^{-1}
(c) −4.9 JK^{-1} (d) − 14.9 JK^{-1}

19 3 moles of a diatomic ideal gas is subjected to a change in temperature from 300 K to 600 K, when entropy change is ΔS_1 at constant pressure and ΔS_2 at constant volume
Thus, $(\Delta S_1 - \Delta S_2)$ is:

(a) 17.29 JK^{-1} (b) −17.29 JK^{-1}
(c) 43.22 JK^{-1} (d) 25.93 JK^{-1}

20 The entropy change at 373 K for the transformation of $H_2O(l)$ at 1.10132 bar to $H_2O(g)$ at 0.101325 bar.
($\Delta H_{vap} = 40.668$ kJ mol^{-1})

(a) 109.03 JK^{-1} mol^{-1} (b) 19.147 JK^{-1} mol^{-1}
(c) 128.1775 JK^{-1} mol^{-1} (d) 89.883 JK^{-1} mol^{-1}

21 Given,

Species	S (JK^{-1} mol^{-1})
Fe_2O_3	87.4
Fe	27.3
O_2	205

and $\Delta S_{surrounding} = 5510\ JK^{-1}\ mol^{-1}$

Thus, $\Delta S_{universe}$ for iron oxidation at 298 K is

$$4\,Fe(s) + 3O_2(g) \longrightarrow 2\,Fe_2O_3(s)$$

(a) −549.4 JK^{-1} mol^{-1} of Fe (b) 4960.6 JK^{-1} mol^{-1} of Fe
(c) 1240.15 JK^{-1} mol^{-1} of Fe (d) None of these

22 Given,

	$CH_4(g)$	$CO_2(g)$	$O_2(g)$	$H_4O(l)$
S (JK^{-1} mol^{-1})	186	214	205	70

and $CH_4(g) + 2O_2(g) \longrightarrow CO_2(g) + 2H_2O(l)$;
$\Delta H = -802.34$ J mol^{-1}

Thus, (in J mol^{-1} K^{-1})

	$\Delta S_{(system)}$	$\Delta S_{(surrounding)}$	$\Delta S_{(universe)}$
(a)	−242.00	2.69	−239.30
(b)	+ 242.00	2.69	+ 239.30
(c)	−242.00	2.69	−239.30
(d)	−239.30	2.69	−242.00

Free Energy

Gibbs free energy (G)

The function G given by equation,

$$G = (H - TS)$$

is called Gibbs free energy (or simply Gibbs energy or Gibbs function). It is a state function because it is composed of functions of the state and, therefore its differential is exact.

As $H = U + pV$

hence, $G = U + pV - TS$

Complete differentiation gives,

$\therefore$ $dG = dU + pdV + Vdp - TdS - SdT$

By first law $dU = q - W = q - pdV$ and $dS = \dfrac{q}{T}$

$$dG = TdS - pdV + pdV + Vdp - TdS - SdT$$
$$dG = Vdp - SdT$$

Also $\Delta G = \Delta H - T\Delta S$

and in standard states

$$\Delta G^\circ = \Delta H^\circ - T\Delta S^\circ$$

ΔG° and ΔS° have opposite sign.

Sign of ΔS can be used to predict the feasibility of a reaction at constant temperature and pressure.

(i) $\Delta S > 0, \Delta G < 0$, then spontaneous
(ii) $\Delta S < 0, \Delta G > 0$, then non-spontaneous
(iii) $\Delta S = 0, \Delta G = 0$, then equilibrium

Relation between ΔG and ΔG°

ΔG and ΔG° are related to reaction quotient Q by equation

$\Delta G = \Delta G^\circ + 2.303RT\ \log Q$

$$A + B \rightleftharpoons C + D,\quad Q = \frac{[C][D]}{[A][B]}$$

if system is in equilibrium, then

$$\Delta G = 0, \text{ and } Q = K_C$$

$\therefore$ $\Delta G^\circ = -2.303\ RT \log K_C$

If $K_C = 1, \Delta G^\circ = 0$
$K_C > 1, \Delta G^\circ < 0$ (spontaneous in forward side)
$K_C < 1, \Delta G^\circ > 0$ (non- spontaneous in forward side)

- Decrease in G (i.e. $-\Delta G$) is equal to net work done

As $dG = Vdp - SdT$

$\therefore$ at constant T, $dT = 0$

$$\therefore \quad dG = Vdp = nRT\frac{dp}{p}$$

$$\therefore \quad \int_{G_1}^{G_2} dG = nRT \int_{p_1}^{p_2} \frac{dp}{p}$$

$$-\Delta G = 2.303\, nRT \log\frac{p_1}{p_2}$$

$$-\Delta G = W_{net} = 2.303 nRT \log\frac{V_2}{V_1}$$

In the mixture of two gases

$$\Delta_{mix} G = nRT\, [\chi_1 \ln \chi_1 + \chi_2 \ln \chi_2]$$

where, n is the total moles of gases (1) and (2) and χ_1 and χ_2 are their mole fractions.

- Net work implies = Total work – mechanical work. It is also called excluded work.

Helmholtz free energy (A)

The function A given by equation,

$$A = U - TS$$

contains only state functions U, T and S, thus, A is also a state function.

Its change is independent of path. A is called the work function or the work content or the Helmholtz free energy. The name of free energy was given to this function by Helmholtz because the decrease in A, $(-\Delta A)$, represents the maximum amount of energy i.e. free or available for being converted into work.

$$A = U - TS \Rightarrow \Delta A = \Delta U - T\Delta S$$

and in standard state

$$\Delta A° = \Delta U° - T\Delta S°$$

where, $\Delta U°$ or ΔU is the change in internal energy.

Decrease in A (i.e. $-\Delta A$) is equal to total work.

$$-\Delta A = nR \ln\frac{V_2}{V_1} = nR \ln\frac{p_1}{p_2}$$

Gibbs Helmholtz equation is

$$\Delta G = \Delta H + T\left(\frac{d\Delta G}{dT}\right)_p$$

Since, $\quad \Delta G = \Delta H - T\Delta S$

$$\therefore \quad \Delta S = -\left[\frac{d(\Delta G)}{dT}\right]_p = -\frac{d(-nFE_{cell})}{dT} = +nF\left(\frac{dE_{cell}}{dT}\right)$$

$\left(\frac{dE_{cell}}{dT}\right)$ is called temperature coefficient of EMF of a cell.

- **van't Hoff equation**

$$\Delta G° = \Delta H° - T\Delta S°$$

Also, $\quad \Delta G° = -2.303RT \log K$

$$2.303RT \log K = -\Delta H° + T\Delta S°$$

$$\therefore \quad \log K = \frac{-\Delta H°}{2.303RT} + \frac{\Delta S°}{2.303R}$$

It is called van't Hoff equation.

Graphically, variation of log K with temperature is linear.

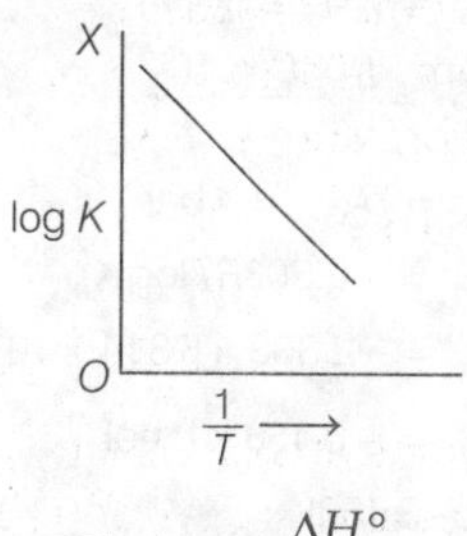

$$\text{Slope} = -\frac{\Delta H°}{2.303\, R}$$

$$OX = \frac{\Delta S°}{2.303\, R}$$

Thus, ΔS is calculated.

Also, $\quad \Delta H = \frac{2.303\, RT_1T_2}{(T_2 - T_1)} \log\frac{K_2}{K_1}$

- **Clapeyron-Clausius equation** (variation of vapour pressure with T).

$$p = Ae^{-\Delta H_v / RT}$$

$$\log_e p = \log_e A - \frac{\Delta H_v}{RT}$$

$$\text{d}\log_{10} p = \log_{10} A - \frac{\Delta H_v}{2.303RT}$$

Graphically, variation of log$p$ with $\left(\frac{1}{T}\right)$ is linear with slope

$$= -\frac{\Delta H_v}{2.303R}$$

$$\log\frac{p_2}{p_1} = \frac{\Delta H_v}{2.303\, R}\left[\frac{1}{T_1} - \frac{1}{T_2}\right]$$

ΔH_v is the latent heat of vaporisation, p_1 and p_2 are vapour pressure at temperature T_1 and T_2.

Solved Examples & Instant Practice

Example 5.16) For the equilibrium at 300 K,

$$CaCO_3(s) \rightleftharpoons CaO(s) + CO_2(g)$$

pressure set up is 4 bar.

$$\Delta H^\circ = 100 \text{ kJ mol}^{-1}$$

Calculate (a) ΔG° and (b) ΔS°

Sol. System is in equilibrium. Activity of solid is taken as unity, hence,

$$K_p = p_{CO_2}$$

Also, $\Delta G^\circ = -2.303\, RT \log K_p$.

Thus, ΔG° is known. Since ΔH° is also given, hence

$$\Delta G^\circ = \Delta H^\circ - T\Delta S^\circ$$

$$\therefore \quad \Delta S^\circ = \left(\frac{\Delta H^\circ - \Delta G^\circ}{T}\right)$$

(a) $K_p = p_{CO_2} = 4 \text{ bar}$

$$\therefore \quad \Delta G^\circ = -2.303 RT \log K_p$$

$$= -2.303 \times 8.314 \times 10^{-3} \times 300 \log 4$$

$$= -3.458 \text{ kJ mol}^{-1}$$

(b) $\Delta S^\circ = \dfrac{100-(-3.458)}{300} = 0.345 \text{ kJ mol}^{-1} \text{ K}^{-1} = 345 \text{ J mol}^{-1} \text{ K}^{-1}$

Immediate Test 11

For the equilibrium at 300 K,

$$COCl_2(g) \rightleftharpoons CO(g) + Cl_2(g)$$

$$\Delta H^\circ = 12 \text{ kJ mol}^{-1}$$

$$\Delta S^\circ = 60 \text{ JK}^{-1} \text{ mol}^{-1}$$

Calculate : (a) ΔG° and (b) equilibrium constant

Example 5.17) For the reaction,

$$CaO(s) + SO_3(g) \longrightarrow CaSO_4(s),$$

$p_{SO_3} = 0.15$ atm, and $\Delta G^\circ_{298} = -245.0 \text{ kJ mol}^{-1}$

Calculate, ΔG_{298}.

Sol. ΔG° in the standard state is given.

ΔG in the given state is calculated.

$$\Delta G_{298} = \Delta G^\circ_{298} + 2.303\, RT \log K$$

$$K = \frac{1}{p_{SO_3}} \text{ (active mass of other species in solid state = 1)}$$

Since, ΔG° is known hence, (ΔG°) is calculated.

Given : $p_{SO_3} = 0.15$ atm

$$K = \frac{1}{p_{SO_3}} = \left(\frac{1}{0.15}\right) \text{atm}^{-1}$$

$$\therefore \quad \Delta G = -245 + 2.303 \times 8.314 \times 10^{-3} \times 298 \times \log\left(\frac{100}{15}\right)$$

$$= -240.3 \text{ kJ mol}^{-1}$$

Immediate Test 12

For the following equilibrium at 298 K

$$NH_4HS(s) \rightleftharpoons NH_3(g) + H_2S(g)$$

total pressure is 12 bar. If ΔG°_{298} is 15 kJ mol^{-1}, calculate ΔG.

Example 5.18) For the following reaction,

$$H_2O(l) \rightleftharpoons H_2O(g)$$

$$\Delta H = 0.5328 \text{ kcal g}^{-1}$$

$$\Delta S = 26 \text{ cal K}^{-1} \text{ mol}^{-1}$$

Specify the condition to make the above reaction spontaneous.

Sol. A reaction is spontaneous, if disorder increases and free energy decreases. ($\Delta H - T\Delta S$) is the driving force for deciding spontaneity,

$$\Delta G = \Delta H - T\Delta S$$

To make the reaction spontaneous,

$$\Delta G < 0$$

Thus, $\quad T\Delta S > \Delta H \Rightarrow T > \dfrac{\Delta H}{\Delta S}$

$$\Delta H = 0.5328 \text{ kcal g}^{-1} = 0.5328 \times 18 \text{ kcal mol}^{-1}$$

$$\Delta S = 26 \times 10^{-3} \text{ kcal K}^{-1} \text{ mol}^{-1}$$

$$\therefore \quad T > \frac{0.5328 \times 18}{26 \times 10^{-3}} \Rightarrow T > 368.86 \text{ K}$$

Thus, reaction is spontaneous above 368.86 K,

Immediate Test 13

For the reaction at 298 K

$$A(g) + B(g) \longrightarrow C(g)$$

$$\Delta E = -3.0 \text{ kcal mol}^{-1}$$

$$\Delta S = -10.0 \text{ cal K}^{-1}$$

Calculate ΔG. Is this reaction spontaneous ?

Example 5.19)

For the reaction, thermodynamic data are in kJ mol^{-1} at 298 K

	$PCl_3(g)$ +	$Cl_2(g)$ $\longrightarrow$	$PCl_5(g)$
$\Delta_f H^\circ$	−287.0		−374.9
$\Delta_f G^\circ$	−267.8		−305.0
S° (kJ K^{-1} mol^{-1})	0.3117,	0.223	?

S° represents absolute entropy.

What is absolute entropy of $PCl_5(g)$?

Sol. $\Delta_f G^\circ = \Delta_f H^\circ - T\Delta_f S^\circ$

$\Delta_f G^\circ = \Delta_f G^\circ$ (product) $- \Delta_f G^\circ$ (reactant)

$\Delta_f H^\circ = \Delta_f H^\circ$ (product) $- \Delta_f H^\circ$ (reactant)

$\Delta G^\circ = \Delta H^\circ - T\Delta S^\circ$

$\Delta S^\circ = S^\circ$ (product) $- S^\circ$ (reactant)

Thus, ΔS° is calculated.

$S^\circ(PCl_5)$, is calculated.

$\Delta_f H^\circ(Cl_2) = 0$, $\Delta_f G^\circ(Cl_2) = 0$ being element

$$\Delta S^\circ = S^\circ[(PCl_5) - (S^\circ(PCl_3) + S^\circ(Cl_2)]$$

and hence, $\Delta_f H^\circ(\text{reaction}) = -374.9 - (-287.0) = -87.9 \text{ kJ mol}^{-1}$

$$\Delta_f G^\circ(\text{reaction}) = -305 - (-267.8) = -37.2 \text{ kJ mol}^{-1}$$

$$\Delta S^\circ = \frac{\Delta H^\circ - \Delta G^\circ}{T} = \frac{-87.9-(-37.2)}{298}$$

$$= -0.170 \text{ kJ mol}^{-1} \text{ K}^{-1}$$

$\therefore \quad \Delta S° = S°(PCl_5) - [S°(PCl_3) + S°(Cl_2)]$

$-0.17 - 0.17° = S°(PCl_5) - [0.3117 + 0.223]$

$\therefore \quad S°(PCl_5) = 0.3646\ \text{kJ mol}^{-1}\ \text{K}^{-1} = 364.6\ \text{J mol}^{-1}\ \text{K}^{-1}$

Immediate Test 14

For $PCl_5(g)$, $\Delta_f H° = -374.9\ \text{kJ mol}^{-1}$ and $\Delta_f G° = -305\ \text{kJ mol}^{-1}$
Calculate $\Delta_f S°$ of PCl_5 (g) at 298 K

Example 5.20) For H_2O, $\Delta H_{vap} = 9.59\ \text{kcal mol}^{-1}$.
Calculate vapour pressure of water at 27°C, if vapour pressure at boiling point is 760 Torr.

Sol. By Clapeyron – Clausius equation is used to study variation of vapour pressure with temperature

$$\log \frac{p_2}{p_1} = \frac{\Delta H_V}{2.303\,R}\left[\frac{T_2 - T_1}{T_1 T_2}\right]$$

$$\log \frac{760}{p_1} = \frac{9.59}{2.303 \times 0.002}\left[\frac{373 - 300}{373 \times 300}\right]$$

$$\log\left(\frac{760}{p_1}\right) = 1.3583$$

$$\therefore \quad \frac{760}{p_1} = 22.82$$

$$\therefore \quad p_1 = \frac{760}{22.82} = 33.30\ \text{Torr}$$

Immediate Test 15

For a given volatile liquid, vapour pressure at different temperatures are given.

	Vapour pressure
I. 300 K	20.0 Torr
II. 350 K	40.0 Torr
III. 400 K	?

Calculate vapour pressure at 400 K.

Example 5.21) For the following cell reaction :

$$Zn + Cu^{2+} \rightleftharpoons Cu + Zn^{2+}$$

EMF of the cell is 1.10 V at 298 K and 1.13 V at 300 K. What is entropy change of the cell reaction?

Sol. EMF of the cell is temperature dependent. Entropy change is related to temperature-coefficient of the EMF of the cell by

$$\Delta S = nF\left(\frac{dE_{cell}}{dT}\right)$$

where, n = number of electrons exchanged

F = Faraday's of electricity

1 F = 96500 C

$\left(\frac{dE_{cell}}{dT}\right) = \left(\frac{E_2 - E_1}{T_2 - T_1}\right)$ called temperature coefficient.

$T_1 = 298\ \text{K}, T_2 = 300\ \text{K}$

$\therefore \quad T_2 - T_1 = 2\ \text{K}$

E_1 (at T_1) = 1.10 V

E_2 (at T_2) = 1.13 V

$\therefore \quad (E_2 - E_1) = 0.03\ \text{V}$

$\therefore \quad \left(\frac{dE_{cell}}{dT}\right) = \frac{0.03}{0.20} = 0.15\ \text{VK}^{-1}$

$n = 2$

$\therefore \quad \Delta S = 2 \times 96500\,(0.15) = 28950\ \text{JK}^{-1} = 28.950\ \text{kJ K}^{-1}$

■ Coulombs volt K^{-1} = Joule K^{-1}

Immediate Test 16

Entropy change of a cell-reaction in a galvanic cell is $0.200\ \text{JK}^{-1}$. What is temperature coefficient of the cell with reaction

$$Al_2O_3 \longrightarrow 2Al^{3+}$$

Example 5.22) Calculate ΔG for the conversion of 3 moles of liquid benzene at 80°C (normal boiling point) to vapour at the same temperature and a pressure of 0.66 bar. Consider the vapour as an ideal gas.

Sol. Above change can be brought about by following steps :

***Step* I :** Benzene (l) (3 mol) $\longrightarrow$ benzene (vapour) (3 mol)

Taking place reversibly at 80°C and at 1 bar.

$\therefore \quad \Delta G = 0$

***Step* II.** Benzene vapour (At 1 bar, 3 mol) $\xrightarrow{\text{At } 80°C}$ Benzene vapour (At 0.66 bar, 3 mol)

$$\therefore \quad \Delta G = 2.303\,nRT \log \frac{p_2}{p_1}$$

$$= 2.303 \times 3 \times 8.314 \times 353 \log \frac{0.66}{1.00}$$

$$= -3659\ \text{J} = -3.66\ \text{kJ}$$

Immediate Test 17

Calculate the free energy change in the freezing of 18 g of water at 263 K, given that the vapour pressure of water and ice at 263 K are 0.287 Pa and 0.200 Pa, respectively.

Example 5.23) Calculate ΔG_{mix} for mixing the constitution of air (80 mol% N_2 and 20 mol % O_2) at 298 K so as to get 1 mol of air.

Sol. When two components are mixed, there is change in free energy given by $\Delta G_{mix} = 2.303\,nRT\,[\chi_1 \log \chi_1 + \chi_2 \log \chi_2]$

where, χ_1 and χ_2 are the mole fraction of the components mixed.

If $\quad n_{O_2} = 0.20\ \text{mol}$ then $n_{N_2} = 0.80\ \text{mol}$

$\therefore \quad \chi_{O_2} = 0.20 \Rightarrow \chi_{N_2} = 0.80 \Rightarrow n = 1$

$\Delta G_{mix} = 2.303 \times 1 \times 8.314 \times 298\,[0.8 \log 0.8 + 0.2 \log 0.2]$

$= -1224.8\ \text{J} = -1.225\ \text{kJ}$

Immediate Test 18

(i) Consider a mixture of 10 moles of gas A and 10 moles of gas B at 298 K. Calculate
(a) ΔG_{mix} (b) ΔS_{mix} (c) ΔH_{mix}

(ii) What is the value of the mole fraction of a mixture of three gases such that free energy of mixing has a minimum value?

KNOWLEDGE CONFIRMATION Test 4

1 For the reactionat 298 K,

$$2A + B \longrightarrow C$$

$$\Delta H = 100 \text{ kcal and}$$

$$\Delta S = 0.050 \text{ kcal K}^{-1}$$

Thus, the temperature above which reaction will be just spontaneous is

(a) 1990 K (b) 200 K
(c) 2010 K (d) 300 K

2 For the reaction

$$2\text{Cl}(g) \longrightarrow \text{Cl}_2(g)$$

Sign of ΔH and ΔS are respectively

	ΔH	ΔS
(a)	+	+
(b)	–	–
(c)	–	+
(d)	+	–

3 A reaction has a value of $\Delta H = -40$ kcal at 400 K. Above, 400 K the reaction is non-spontaneous, below that temperature, it is spontaneous.
Thus, ΔG and ΔS at 400 K are

	ΔG (kcal mol^{-1})	ΔS (kcal mol^{-1} K^{-1})
(a)	0	0
(b)	–100	0
(c)	0	–100
(d)	+100	–100

4 For the reaction,

$$2A(g) + B(g) \longrightarrow 2C(g)$$

$$\Delta E^\circ_{298} = -2.50 \text{ kcal}, \ \Delta S^\circ_{298} = -10.5 \text{ cal K}^{-1}$$

$(R = 0.002 \text{ kcal mol}^{-1} \text{ K}^{-1})$

Thus, ΔG° of the reaction is

(a) 0.04 kcal mol^{-1} (b) –0.04 kcal mol^{-1}
(c) 0.033 kcal mol^{-1} (d) –0.033 kcal mol^{-1}

5 For the following reactions :

$$\text{Ag}_2\text{O}(s) \longrightarrow 2\text{Ag}(s) + \frac{1}{2}\text{O}_2(g)$$

$$\Delta G^\circ = -\Delta G^\circ_f = +11.21 \text{ kJ mol}^{-1}$$

Under what pressure of $O_2(g)$ decomposition of $Ag_2O(s)$ into Ag(s) and $O_2(g)$ will be spontaneous at 25°C ?

(a) 0.10 atm (b) 1.0 atm
(c) 0.01 atm (d) 0.000117 atm

6 $\text{H}_2\text{O}(g) \rightleftharpoons \text{H}_2\text{O}(l), \Delta H = -10 \text{ kcal mol}^{-1}$. Variation of vapour pressure (as log p) with $\left(\frac{1}{T}\right)$ is given as

(a) 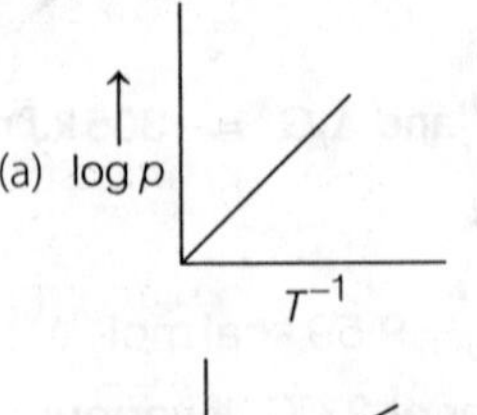

(b) 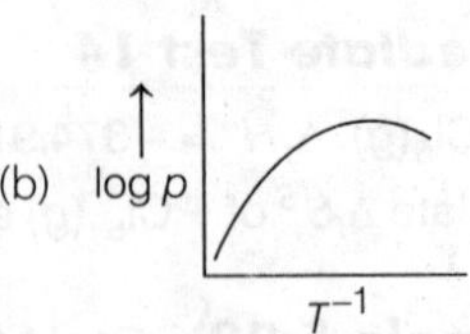

(c) 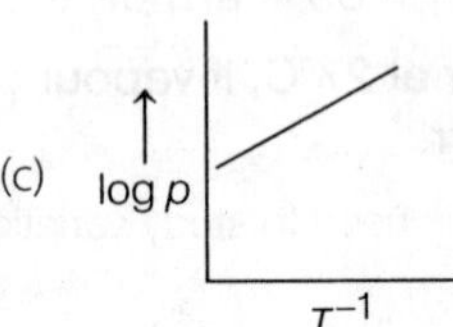

(d) 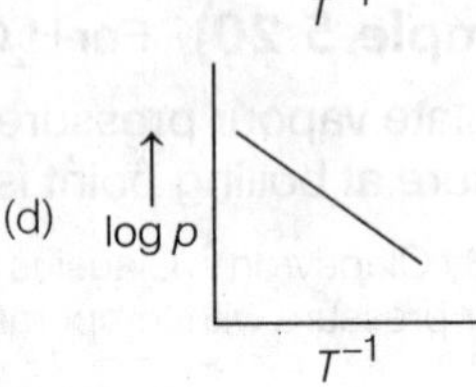

7 Which is not true about G ?

(a) G is a state function
(b) Decrease in G, $(-\Delta G)$ is equal to net work done.
(c) If ΔG is positive, reaction is spontaneous
(d) $\Delta G = \Delta G^\circ$, if K = 1

8 An endothermic reaction is spontaneous, if

(a) $\Delta H > T\Delta S$ (b) $\Delta H < T\Delta S$ (c) $\Delta H = T\Delta S$ (d) $T\Delta S = 0$

9 Formation of ice is favoured based on

$$\text{H}_2\text{O}(s) \rightleftharpoons \text{H}_2\text{O}(l), \Delta H^\circ = +6.01 \text{kJ mol}^{-1}$$

$$\Delta S^\circ = 22.00 \text{ JK}^{-1} \text{ mol}^{-1}$$

(a) above 0°C (b) below 0°C (c) at 0°C (d) above 10°C

10 For the reaction at 298 K

$$X_2\text{O}_4(l) \longrightarrow 2X\text{O}_2(g),$$

$$\Delta H^\circ = 2.1 \text{ kcal mol}^{-1}, \ \Delta S^\circ = 20 \text{ cal mol}^{-1} \text{ K}^{-1}$$

Thus, this reaction is

(a) spontaneous (b) non-spontaneous
(c) in equilibrium (d) unpredictable

11 The molar entropy of $O_2(g)$ at 300 K and 1 atm is 250 J mol^{-1} K^{-1}. ΔG when 1 mole of O_2 is expanded isothermally and reversibly to double the volume is

(a) 1.728 kJ mol^{-1} K^{-1} (b) 0
(c) –1.728 kJ mol^{-1} K^{-1} (d) 0.75 kJ mol^{-1} K^{-1}

12 For the reaction in equilibrium.

	Equilibrium constant (K)	Free energy ΔG°
$A \rightleftharpoons B$	K_1	ΔG°_1
$B \rightleftharpoons C$	K_2	ΔG°_2
$A \rightleftharpoons C$	K_3	ΔG°_3

Thus,

(a) $K_1K_2 = K_3$ (b) $\Delta G_1^\circ + \Delta G^\circ_2 = \Delta G^\circ_3$
(c) Both (a) and (b) (d) None of these

13 For the electrochemical cell reaction,

$$2Cu^+(aq) \longrightarrow Cu(s) + Cu^{2+}(aq)$$

$$E° = 0.368 \text{ V at } 298 \text{ K}$$

Electron exchanged = 1

Thus, maximum useful work that can be obtained from this reaction is

(a) 35.51 kJ (b) −35.51 kJ (c) 71.02 kJ (d) −71.02 kJ

14 For the following reaction,

$$Zn(s) + Cu^{2+}(aq) \rightleftharpoons Cu(s) + Zn^{2+}(aq)$$

$$E°_{cell} = 1.10 \text{ V},$$

$$\Delta H° = -3.0 \text{ kJ at } 300 \text{ K}$$

Thus, temperature coefficient of the emf of the cell is (in $V K^{-1}$)

(a) -5.18×10^{-5} (b) 3.61×10^{-3}

(c) -2.59×10^{-5} (d) $+2.59 \times 10^{-5}$

15 Based on the following graph,

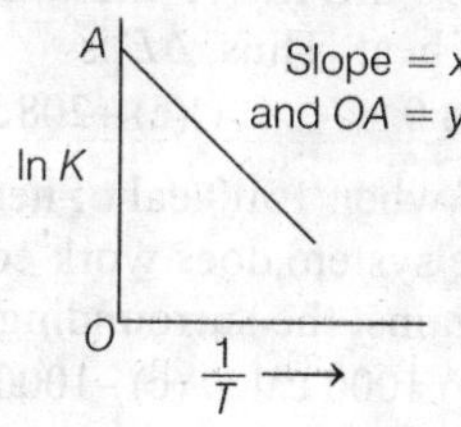

$\Delta G°$ is

(a) $R(x-y)$ (b) $R(x-yT)$ (c) $R(x+y)$ (d) $R(x+yT)$

16 A fixed mass of an ideal gas in 10 dm^3 sealed flask is heated from −73°C to 27°C at constant pressure. If $S(JK^{-1}) = (2 + 10^{-2}T)$, then change in Gibb's free energy is

(a) 450 JK^{-1} (b) −450 JK^{-1} (c) −200 JK^{-1} (d) +200 JK^{-1}

17 Free energy of mixing of *n* gases has a minimum value with respect to each gas only when mole fraction of each of these gases is

(a) $1/n$ (b) n (c) $(n-1)$ (d) $\frac{1}{(n-1)}$

18 Urea $[CO(NH_2)_2]$ can be synthesised using

$$C(\text{graphite} + 2H_2(g) + N_2(g) + \frac{1}{2}O_2(g) \longrightarrow CO(NH_2)_2$$

Given, $CO_2(g) + 2NH_3(g) \longrightarrow H_2O(g) + CO(NH_2)_2$,

$$\Delta G_1 = 1908 \text{ J mol}^{-1}$$

$$H_2O(g) \longrightarrow H_2(g) + \frac{1}{2}O_2(g),$$

$$\Delta G_2 = 227 \text{ kJ mol}^{-1}$$

$$C(g)\text{ (graphite)} + O_2(g) \longrightarrow CO_2(g),$$

$$\Delta G_3 = -394 \text{ kJ mol}^{-1}$$

$$N_2(g) + 3H_2(g) \longrightarrow 2NH_3(g) \quad \Delta G_4 = -33.40 \text{ kJ mol}^{-1}$$

Thus, ΔG of the given reaction is

(a) −198.5 kJ^{-1} mol^{-1} (b) +198.5 kJ^{-1} mol^{-1}

(c) 1707.6 kJ^{-1} mol^{-1} (d) −1707.6 kJ^{-1} mol^{-1}

19 Consider following thermodynamic Maxwell relations

I. $\left(\frac{\partial G}{\partial p}\right)_T = V$, II. $\left(\frac{\partial G}{\partial T}\right)_p = -S$ III. $\left(\frac{\partial S}{\partial p}\right)_T = -\left(\frac{\partial V}{\partial T}\right)_p$

Select correct relations.

(a) I, II (b) II, III (c) I, III (d) I, II, III

20 Consider following graphs :

I. Variation of *G* with *p* II. Variation of *G* with *T*.

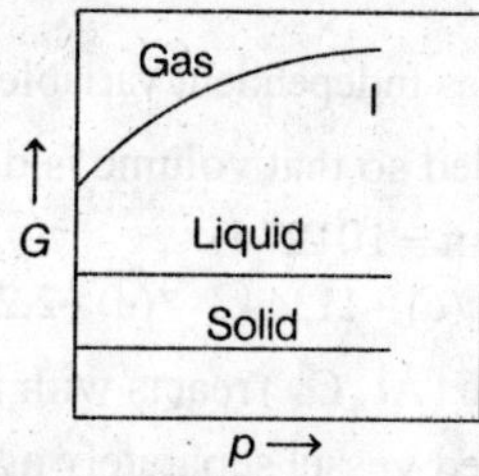

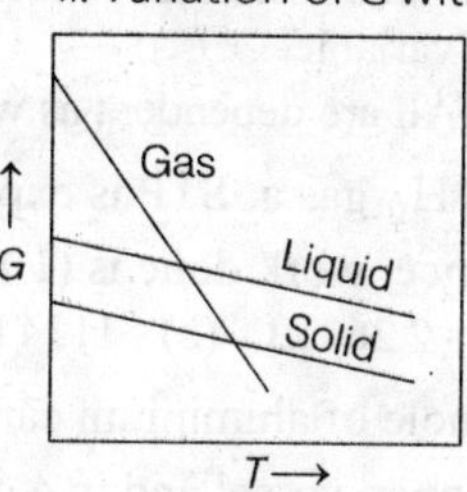

Select correct statements.

(a) In I, variation of *G* with *p* is more rapid for gases as $\left(\frac{\partial G}{\partial p}\right)_T = V$

(b) In II, the negative sign indicates that the function free energy decreases with increase of temperature at constant pressure and decrease is rapid for gases with higher entropies as : $\left(\frac{\partial G}{\partial T}\right)_p = -S$

(c) Both of the above are correct

(d) None of the above is correct

21 A mixture of two gases *A* and *B* contains 10 mol of each at 298 K and 1 bar pressure. Thus, (I) $\Delta_{mix} G°$, (II), $\Delta_{mix} S°$ and (III) $\Delta H°$ are :

	I	II	III
(a)	− 34.35 kJ	115.3 JK^{-1}	0 kJ
(b)	+ 34.35 kJ	− 115.30 JK^{-1}	90.95 kJ
(c)	− 34.35 kJ	− 115.3 JK^{-1}	− 90.95
(d)	None is correct		

22 One dm^3 bulb containing N_2 at 1 bar pressure and 298 K is connected by a tube with a stop-cock to a 3 dm^3 bulb containing CO_2 at 2 bar pressure and 298 K. The stop-cock is opened and the gases are allowed to mix until equilibrium is reached. Assuming ideal behaviour $\Delta_{mix} S$ is

(a) 1.045 JK^{-1} (b) −1.045 JK^{-1}

(c) 0.00 JK^{-1} (d) None of these

[**Hint** $\Delta_{mix} S = n_{N_2} R \ln \frac{V_{final}}{V_{N_2}} + n_{CO_2} R \ln \frac{V_{final}}{V_{CO_2}}$

$n = \frac{pV}{RT}$]

ACID TEST
For JEE Main

TYPE I MCQs with Only ONE Correct Alternate

1 Out of p, V and T
(a) p and V are independent variables and T is dependent variable
(b) p and T are independent variables and V is dependent variable
(c) V and T are independent variables and p is dependent variable
(d) All are dependent as well as independent variables

2 1 g H_2 gas at STP is expanded so that volume is doubled. Hence, work done is (1 L atm = 101.27 J)
(a) −2.268 kJ (b) −1.134 kJ (c) +1.134 kJ (d) −2.268 kJ

3 1 mole of aluminium carbide (Al_4C_3) reacts with H_2O in an open vessel and in a closed vessel separately against atmospheric pressure. Work done in the above case can be (in kJ) at 300 K.

	Open	Closed
(a)	+7.4826	+7.4826
(b)	+7.4826	0
(c)	−7.4826	0
(d)	+7.4826	−7.4826

4 Which has maximum internal energy?
(a) Helium gas (b) Oxygen gas
(c) Ozone gas (d) Equal

5 1 mole each of CaC_2, Al_4C_3 and Mg_2C_3 reacts with H_2O in separate open flasks. Numerical value of the work done by the system is in order :
(a) $CaC_2 < Al_4C_3 < Mg_2C_3$ (b) $CaC_2 < Al_4C_3 = Mg_2C_3$
(c) $CaC_2 = Mg_2C_3 < Al_4C_3$ (d) $CaC_2 = Mg_2C_3 = Al_4C_3$

6 One mole of an ideal gas expands from 2.0 L and 8.0 bar to a final volume 5.0 L against a constant external pressure of 2.0 bar at 298 K. Thus,

	Work done	Final pressure
(a)	−6 L bar	3.2 bar
(b)	+6 L bar	3.2 bar
(c)	−24 L bar	4.0 bar
(d)	+24 L bar	4.0 bar

7. The standard Gibbs energy for the given cell reaction in kJ mol^{-1} at 298 K is
$Zn(s) + Cu^{2+}(aq) \longrightarrow Zn^{2+}(aq) + Cu(s)$,
$E° = 2.0$ V at 298 K **[JEE Main 2019 (II) NTA]**
(a) 384 (b) 192 (c) − 384 (d) − 192

8 An ideal gas undergoes isothermal compression from 5 m^3 to 1 m^3 against a constant external pressure of 4 Nm^{-2}. Heat released in this process is used to increase the temperature of 1 mole of Al. If molar heat capacity of Al is 24 J $mol^{-1}K^{-1}$, the temperature of Al increases by **[JEE Main 2019 (I) NTA]**
(a) $\frac{3}{2}$ K (b) 1 K (c) 2 K (d) $\frac{2}{3}$ K

9 A sample of an ideal gas changes in volume from 4.0 dm^3 to 6.0 dm^3 against an external pressure of 1.50 atm and simultaneously absorbs 1000 J of heat. Thus, change in internal energy is (in Joule)
(a) 1303.8 (b) − 696.2 (c) −1303.8 (d) 696.2

10 A piston filled with 0.04 mole of an ideal gas expands reversibly from 50 mL to 375 mL at 310 K. It also absorbs 208 J of heat. Thus, ΔE is
(a) −208 J (b) 0 (c) +208 J (d) 416 J

11 The value of ΔE when 1500 cal of heat is added to the system while the system does work equivalent to 2500 cal by expanding against the surrounding atmosphere is
(a) 4000 cal (b) 1000 cal (c) −1000 cal (d) − 4000 cal

12 Consider the following physical changes taking place at temperatures (in Kelvin) T_1 and T_2.

I. $H_2O(l) \xrightleftharpoons{T_1} H_2O(g)$, $\Delta H_1^\circ = x$

II. $H_2O(l) \xrightleftharpoons{T_2} H_2O(s)$, $\Delta H_2^\circ = -y$

Thus, $\Delta U°$ (change in internal energy) of the above processes are :

	I. (ΔU_1°)	II. (ΔU_2°)
(a)	$x + RT_1$	$-y + RT_2$
(b)	$-x - RT_1$	$-y - RT_2$
(c)	$x - RT_1$	$-y$
(d)	x	$-y$

13 The standard reaction Gibbs energy for a chemical reaction at an absolute temperature T is given by,
$$\Delta_r G° = A - BT$$
where, A and B are non-zero constants.
Which of the following is true about this reaction? **[JEE Main 2019 (I) NTA]**
(a) Endothermic if, $A < 0$ and $B > 0$
(b) Exothermic if, $B < 0$
(c) Exothermic if, $A > 0$ and $B < 0$
(d) Endothermic if, $A > 0$

14 1.0 mole of a monoatomic gas is expanded from state I to state II at 300 K as shown.

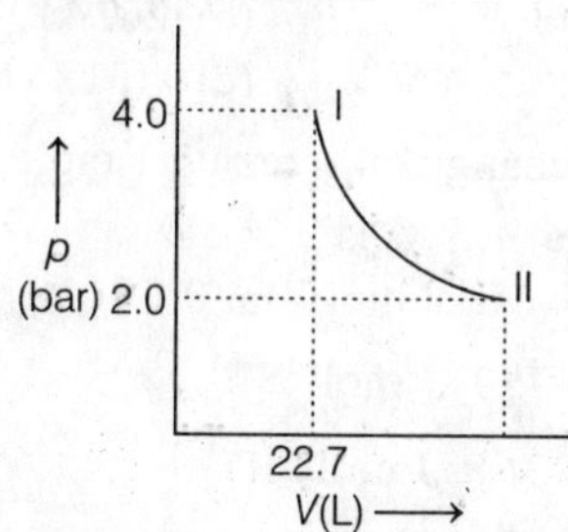

Thus, work done is
(a) −1729 J (b) +1729 J (c) −75.8 J (d) 17.07 J

15 Following graph is between $\left(\frac{-W}{nRT}\right)$ and $\left(\frac{V_2}{V_1}\right)$
(V_1 = initial volume, V_2 = final volume) at different temperatures.

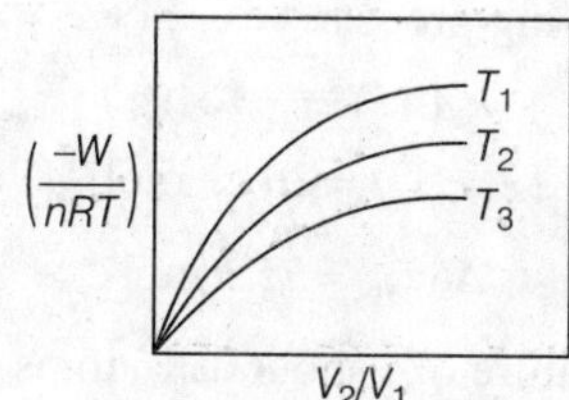

T_1, T_2 and T_3 are arranged in the following order.
(a) $T_1 = T_2 = T_3$ (b) $T_1 < T_2 < T_3$
(c) $T_3 < T_2 < T_1$ (d) Can't be predicted

16 5.85 g of NaCl on melting absorbed 3.05 kJ of heat and its entropy is increased by 28.8 J K^{-1} mol^{-1}. Thus, melting point of sodium chloride is :
(a) 1059 K (b) 729 K (c) 670 K (d) 1208 K

17 A 1.00 g sample of $H_2O(g)$ condenses reversibly at 100°C releasing 2260J of heat into the surroundings. Thus, ΔS (universe) is
(a) 6.06 J K^{-1} (b) −6.06 J K^{-1}
(c) 0 J K^{-1} (d) 12.12 J K^{-1}

18 For the chemical reaction, $X \rightleftharpoons Y$, the standard reaction Gibbs energy depends on temperature T (in K) as

$$\Delta_r G° \text{ (in kJ mol}^{-1}) = 120 - \frac{3}{8}T$$

The major component of the reaction mixture at T is *[JEE Main 2019 (I) NTA]*
(a) Y if $T = 280$ K (b) X if $T = 350$ K
(c) X if $T = 315$ K (d) Y if $T = 300$ K ?

19 For the ionisation of CH_3COOH at 273 K.

$$CH_3COOH + H_2O \rightleftharpoons CH_3COO^- + H_3O^+,$$
$$(K = 1.7 \times 10^{-5})$$

Thus, $\Delta G°$ for the ionisation is
(a) 2.730 ln 1.7 kcal (b) −2.730 ln 1.7 kcal
(c) 2.730 ln 1.7 cal (d) None of these

20 For the following reaction,

$$CaCO_3(s) \longrightarrow CaO(s) + CO_2(g)$$

pressure set up is 10 atm and $\Delta G°_{298} = -200.0$ kJ
Thus, ΔG for the reaction is
(a) −205.7 kJ (b) −194.3 kJ
(c) 0 kJ (d) +194.3 kJ

21 Two blocks of the same metal having same mass and at temperature T_1 and T_2 respectively, are brought in contact with each other and allowed to attain thermal equilibrium at constant pressure. The change in entropy, ΔS, for this process is *[JEE Main 2019 (I) NTA]*

(a) $C_p \ln\left[\frac{(T_1+T_2)^{\frac{1}{2}}}{T_1T_2}\right]$ (b) $C_p \ln\left[\frac{T_1+T_2}{4T_1T_2}\right]$

(c) $C_p \ln\left[\frac{(T_1+T_2)^2}{4T_1T_2}\right]$ (d) $C_p \ln\left[\frac{T_1+T_2}{2T_1T_2}\right]$

22 What is C_p of the gas undergoing reversible adiabatic expansion with following result?

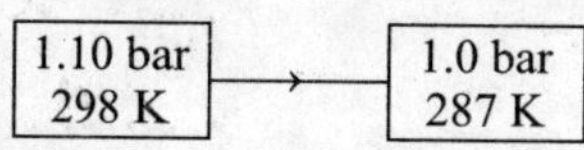

(a) 5.07 cal mol^{-1} (b) 7.0 cal mol^{-1}
(c) 8.0 cal mol^{-1} (d) 3.0 cal mol^{-1}

23 Ratio of slopes $\left(\frac{\partial p}{\partial V}\right)_{\text{isothermal}}$ and $\left(\frac{\partial p}{\partial V}\right)_{\text{adiabatic}}$ for (p-V) plot of an ideal gas is
(a) γ (b) $\frac{1}{\gamma}$ (c) γ^2 (d) $-\gamma$

24 The entropy change associated with the conversion of 1 kg of ice at 273 K to water vapours at 383 K is :
(Specific heat of water liquid and water vapour are 4.2 kJ $K^{-1}kg^{-1}$ and 2.0 kJ K^{-1} kg^{-1}; heat of liquid fusion and vapourisation of water are 334 kJ kg^{-1} and 2491 kJ kg^{-1} respectively).(log 273 = 2.436, log 373 = 2.572, log 383 = 2.583) *[JEE Main 2019 (I) NTA]*
(a) 9.26 kJ kg^{-1} K^{-1} (b) 8.49 kJ $kg^{-1}K^{-1}$
(c) 7.90 kJ $kg^{-1}K^{-1}$ (d) 2.64 kJ $kg^{-1}K^{-1}$

25 $N_2O_4(g)$ is 50% dissociated at 333 K and at 1 atm.

$$N_2O_4(g) \rightleftharpoons 2NO_2(g)$$

Thus, $\Delta G°$ at 333 K is
(a) −1.60 kJ (b) −3.69 kJ (c) − 0.79 kJ (d) + 0.79 kJ

26 Work done when 20 g of neon (20 g mol^{-1}) occupying a volume of 15 dm^3 at 3.5 atm expands adiabatically to 30 dm^3 is (in kJ mol^{-1})
(a) −2.957 (b) +2.957 (c) −1.620 (d) −3.697

27 In general ΔH for any process can be calculated using,

$$\Delta H = \int_{T_1}^{T_2} nC_p dT + \int_{p_1}^{p_2} \left(\frac{\Delta H}{\partial p}\right)_T dp$$

if 1 mole of helium gas (assume ideal behaviour) is expanded from 25.0°C, 5.0 L, 5.0 bar to 125.0° C, 10.0 L and 2.5 bar, ΔH will be

(a) $+350R$ (b) $-250R$ (c) $+300R$ (d) $250R$

28 During a reversible isothermal compression of 1.00 mole of an ideal gas originally at 0° C and 0.525 bar, 975 J of heat was removed. Thus, final pressure is

(a) 1.000 bar (b) 0.807 bar
(c) 1.614 bar (d) 1.721 bar

29 The pressure dependence of C_p is given by

$$\left(\frac{\partial C_p}{\partial p}\right)_T = T\left(\frac{\partial^2 V}{\partial T^2}\right)_p$$

thus, $\left(\frac{\partial C_p}{\partial p}\right)_T$ is

(a) zero (b) $\frac{1}{p}$
(c) $-\frac{1}{p^2}$ (d) p

30 If 1 mole of a diatomic gas contained in a piston absorbs 50 J of heat and does 100 J of work then,

(a) gas will cool by 2.41°C
(b) gas will heat by 2.41°C
(c) gas will cool by 1.2°C
(d) there is no change in temperature

31 A system absorbs 154 J of heat and internal energy of the system decreases by 225 J, then,

(a) work is done by the system equal to -379 J
(b) work is done by the system equal to -71 J
(c) work is done on the system equal to -379 J
(d) work is done on the system equal to $+71$ J

32 Consider following changes

$A \xrightarrow[q = 5\text{ J}]{} B$

work done by the gas = 8 J

$B \xrightarrow[q = -3\text{ J}]{} A$

Thus, going B to A

(a) 10 J of the work will be done by the gas
(b) 6 J of the work will be done by the gas
(c) 10 J of the work will be done by the surrounding on the gas
(d) 6 J of the work will be done by the surrounding on the gas

33 For the given reaction,

$$H_2(g) + Cl_2(g) \longrightarrow 2H^+(aq) + 2Cl^-(aq) \qquad \Delta G° = -262.4 \text{ kJ}$$

Thus, $\Delta G_f^°$ for $Cl^-(aq)$ is (in kJ mol^{-1})

(a) 262.4 kJ mol^{-1} (b) -262.4 kJ mol^{-1}
(c) -131.2 kJ mol^{-1} (d) $+131.2$ kJ mol^{-1}

34 The enthalpy change on freezing 1 mole $H_2O(l)$ at 5° C to $H_2O(s)$, (ice) at -5° C is

given, $\Delta_{fus}H = 6.0$ kJ mol^{-1} at 0°C

$C_p\,(H_2O, l) = 75.3$ J mol^{-1}K^{-1}

$C_p(H_2O, s) = 36.8$ J mol^{-1}K^{-1}

(a) 5.44 kJ mol^{-1} (b) 5.81 kJ mol^{-1}
(c) 6.56 kJ mol^{-1} (d) 6.00 kJ mol^{-1}

35 0.75 mole of an ideal gas expands at STP to 33.6 dm^3 to give maximum work equal to

(a) 142.0 cal (b) -142.0 cal
(c) -166.0 cal (d) $+166.0$ cal

36 For the following process

$$A(l) \rightleftharpoons A(g)$$

$$\Delta H_{vap} = 30 \text{ kJ mol}^{-1}$$

$$\Delta S_{vap} = 75 \text{ J mol}^{-1}$$

Thus, temperature of vapour at 1 atm is

(a) 400 K (b) 350 K
(c) 298 K (d) 250 K

37 For the following change of one mole of a gas from state I to state II

State I		State II
$p_1 = 2.0$ atm $V_1 = 3.0$ L $T_1 = 95$ K	$\longrightarrow$	$p_2 = 4.0$ atm $V_2 = 5.0$ L $T_2 = 245$ K

$$\Delta U = 30.0 \text{ L atm}$$

Thus, ΔH of the process in L atm is

(a) 40.0
(b) 42.3
(c) 44.0
(d) not defined as p is not constant

38 For the different reactions in equilibrium.

		Equilibrium constant K	ΔG (in kJ mol^{-1})
I.	$A \rightleftharpoons B$	$K_I = 10$	-20
II.	$B \rightleftharpoons C$	$K_{II} = 5$	-70

Thus, for the equilibrium

$C \rightleftharpoons A$, K and ΔG are

	K	ΔG (kJ mol^{-1})
(a)	0.02	90
(b)	0.02	-90
(c)	50	50
(d)	50	-50

39 Consider two flasks as shown at 298 K

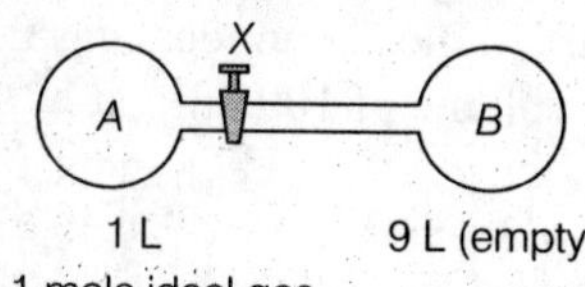

if stopcock X is opened, what is change in entropy?

(a) 4.61 J K^{-1} (b) -19.15 J K^{-1}

(c) -4.61 J K^{-1} (d) 19.15 J K^{-1}

40 An ideal gas is allowed to expand both reversibly and irreversibly in an isolated system. Given, T_i = initial temperature, T_f = final temperature, then,

(a) $(T_f)_{\text{irrev}} > (T_f)_{\text{rev}}$

(b) $T_f > T_i$ for reversible process and $T_f = T_i$ for irreversible process

(c) $(T_f)_{\text{irrev}} < (T_f)_{\text{rev}}$

(d) $T_f = T_f$ for both processes

41 An ideal gas is subjected to free expansion under adiabatic condition . Then

(a) $q = 0, \Delta T < 0, W \neq 0$ (b) $q = 0, \Delta T \neq 0, W = 0$

(c) $q \neq 0, \Delta T = 0, W = 0$ (d) $q = 0, \Delta T = 0, W = 0$

42 Consider three processes I, II and III involved in a cyclic process :

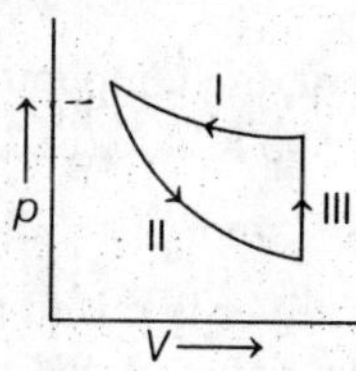

I. Isothermal

II. Adiabatic

III. Constant volume

Sum of the work in this cyclic processes is

(a) zero (b) pV (c) R (d) $-pV$

43 An ideal gas is allowed to expand from 1 L to 10 L against a constant external pressure of 1 bar. The work done in kJ is **[JEE Main 2019 (II) NTA]**

(a) – 9.0 (b) + 10.0

(c) – 0.9 (d) – 2.0

44 Consider following change of 1 mole $H_2O(l)$ at 273 K to 1 mole $H_2O(s)$ at 263 K. Entropy change is the sum of all the steps except.

(a) $\Delta S_1 = C_V \ln \frac{273}{263}$, ($C_V$ = heat capacity of water)

(b) $\Delta S_2 = \frac{\Delta H_{\text{fusion}}}{273}$, ($\Delta H_f$ = enthalpy of fusion of ice)

(c) $\Delta S_3 = -\frac{\Delta H_{\text{fusion}}}{273}$

(d) $\Delta S_4 = C'_V \ln \frac{263}{273}$, ($C'_V$ = heat capacity of 1 ice)

45 8.8 g of CO_2 behaving ideally is heated free 273 to 373 K at constant pressure of 1 bar. Thus, entropy change is

(a) 91.4 JK^{-1} (b) -2.08 JK^{-1} (c) 9.14 JK^{-1} (d) 2.08 JK^{-1}

46 For the following dissolution of $NH_4Cl(s)$ temperature of 1 mole solute changes from 298 K to 295 K. Thus,

(a) $\Delta H < 0, \Delta S < 0, \Delta G < 0$ (b) $\Delta H < 0, \Delta S > 0, \Delta G = 0$

(c) $\Delta H > 0, \Delta S > 0, \Delta G < 0$ (d) $\Delta H = \Delta S = \Delta G = 0$

47 1.0 L of liquid water ($d = 1000 \text{ g L}^{-1}$) freezes under a constant pressure and forms ice with density 909.09 g L^{-1}. Thus, work done is

(a) –0.1 L atm (b) –10.13 J

(c) Both are correct (d) None of these

48 For the following decomposition reaction,

$$NiO(s) \rightleftharpoons Ni(s) + \frac{1}{2}O_2(g)$$

$\Delta G° = 1729 \text{ J mol}^{-1}$ at 300 K (log 2 = 0.3010)

Thus, pressure set up is

(a) 0.3010 atm (b) 0.6990 atm

(c) 0.500 atm (d) 0.25 atm

49 For the following reactions:

	ΔG(kJ)
I. $S_2(s) + 2O_2(g) \longrightarrow 2SO_2(g)$,	–544
II. $2Zn(s) + S_2(s) \longrightarrow 2ZnS(s)$,	–293
III. $2Zn(s) + O_2(g) \longrightarrow 2ZnO(s)$,	–480

Thus, ΔG for the reaction

$2\,ZnS(s) + O_2(g) \longrightarrow 2\,ZnO(s) + 2SO_2(g)$ will be

(a) –357 kJ (b) –731 kJ (c) –773 kJ (d) –229 kJ

50 When one mole of an ideal gas is compressed to half its initial volume and simultaneously heated to twice its initial temperature, the change in entropy is

(a) $C_V \log_e 2$ (b) $C_p \log_e 2$

(c) $R \log_e 2$ (d) $(C_p - R)\log_e 2$

51 An ideal gas undergoes a cyclic process as shown in fig.

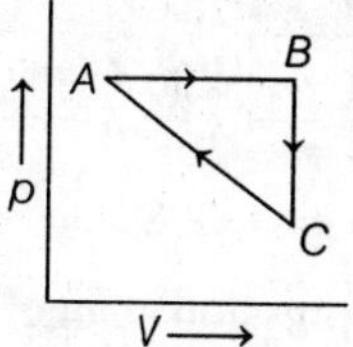

$$\Delta U_{BC} = -5 \text{ kJ mol}^{-1}$$
$$q_{AB} = 2 \text{ kJ mol}^{-1}$$
$$W_{AB} = -5 \text{ kJ mol}^{-1}$$
$$W_{CA} = 3 \text{ kJ mol}^{-1}$$

Heat absorbed by the system during process CA is **[JEE Main 2018]**

(a) 18 kJ mol^{-1} (b) -18 kJ mol^{-1}

(c) -5 kJ mol^{-1} (d) $+5 \text{ kJ mol}^{-1}$

52 Given,

I. $2Fe_2O_3(s) \longrightarrow 4Fe(s) + 3\,O_2(g)$, $\Delta G° = +1487.0$ kJ

II. $2CO(g) + O_2(g) \longrightarrow 2CO_2(g)$, $\Delta G° = -514.4$ kJ^{-1}

III. $2Fe_2O_3 + 6\,CO(g) \longrightarrow 4Fe(s) + 6\,CO_2(g)$, $\Delta G° = ?$

$\Delta G°$ for (III) is **[JEE Main 2018]**

(a) -112.4 kJ mol^{-1} (b) -56.2 kJ mol^{-1}
(c) -208.0 kJ mol^{-1} (d) -168.2 kJ mol^{-1}

53 For which of the following processes, ΔS is negative ? **[JEE Main 2018]**

(a) $N_2(g, 273\text{ K}) \longrightarrow N_2(g, 300\text{ K})$
(b) $N_2(g, 1\text{ atm}) \longrightarrow N_2(g, 5\text{ atm})$
(c) C (diamond) $\longrightarrow$ C (graphite)
(d) $H_2(g) \longrightarrow 2H(g)$

54 ΔU is equal to **[JEE Main 2017]**

(a) isochoric work (b) isobaric work
(c) adiabatic work (d) isothermal work

55 The following reaction is performed at 298 K,

$$2NO(g) + O_2(g) \rightleftharpoons 2NO_2(g)$$

The standard free energy of formation of NO(g) is 86.6 kJ/mol at 298 K. What is the standard free energy of formation of $NO_2(g)$ at 298 K ? ($K_p = 16 \times 10^{12}$) **[JEE Main 2015]**

(a) $R(298)\ln(16 \times 10^{12}) - 86600$
(b) $86600 + R(298)\ln(16 \times 10^{12})$
(c) $86600 - \dfrac{\ln(16 \times 10^{12})}{R(298)}$
(d) $0.5[2 \times 86600 - R(298)\ln(16 \times 10^{12})]$

56 A piston filled with 0.04 mole of an ideal gas expands reversibly from 50.0 mL to 375 mL at a constant temperature of 37.0°C. As it does so, it absorbs 208 J of heat. The values of q and W for the process will be ($R = 8.314$ J/ mol K, ln 7.5 = 2.01) **[JEE Main 2013]**

(a) $Q = +208$ J, $W = -208$ J
(b) $Q = -208$ J, $W = -208$ J
(c) $Q = -208$ J, $W = +208$ J
(d) $Q = +208$ J, $W = +208$ J

57 The incorrect expression among following is **[AIEEE 2012]**

(a) $\dfrac{\Delta G_{\text{system}}}{\Delta S_{\text{total}}} = -T$

(b) in isothermal process, $W_{\text{reversible}} = -nRT \ln \dfrac{V_f}{V_i}$

(c) $\ln K = \dfrac{\Delta H° - T\Delta S°}{RT}$

(d) $K = e^{-\Delta G°/RT}$

58 The entropy change involved in the isothermal reversible expansion of 2 moles of an ideal gas from a volume of 10 dm^3 to a volume of 100 dm^3 at 27° C is **[AIEEE 2011]**

(a) 38.3 J mol^{-1} K^{-1} (b) 35.8 J mol^{-1} K^{-1}
(c) 32.3 J mol^{-1} K^{-1} (d) 42.3 J mol^{-1} K^{-1}

59 In view of the signs of $\Delta_r G°$ for the following reactions,

$$PbO_2 + Pb \longrightarrow 2PbO,\ \Delta_r G° < 0$$
$$SnO_2 + Sn \longrightarrow 2SnO,\ \Delta_r G° > 0$$

which oxidation states are more characteristic for lead and tin ? **[AIEEE 2011]**

(a) For lead + 4, for tin + 2 (b) For lead +2, for tin + 2
(c) For lead + 4, for tin + 4 (d) For lead + 2, for tin + 4

60 For a particular reversible reaction, at temperature T, ΔH and ΔS were found to be both + ve. If T_e is the temperature at equilibrium , the reaction would be spontaneous when **[AIEEE 2010]**

(a) $T_e > T$ (b) $T > T_e$
(c) T_e is 5 times T (d) $T = T_e$

61 Standard entropy of X_2, Y_2 and XY_3 are 60, 40 and 50 JK^{-1} mol^{-1} respectively. For the reaction,

$$\frac{1}{2}X_2 + \frac{3}{2}Y_2 \longrightarrow XY_3;\ \Delta H = -30\text{ kJ}$$

to be at equilibrium, the temperature will be **[AIEEE 2008]**

(a) 1250 K (b) 500 K (c) 750 K (d) 1000 K

62 For silver, C_p(JK^{-1} mol^{-1}) = 23 + 0.01 T. If temperature (T) of 3 moles of silver is raised from 300 K to 1000 K at 1 atm pressure, the value of ΔH will be close to **[JEE Main 2019 (II) NTA]**

(a) 62 kJ (b) 16 kJ (c) 21 kJ (d) 13 kJ

63 5 moles of an ideal gas at 100 K are allowed to undergo reversible compression till its temperature becomes 200 K. If $C_V = 28$ JK^{-1} mol^{-1}, calculate ΔU and $\Delta(pV)$ for this process ($R = 8$ JK^{-1} mol^{-1}) **[JEE Main 2019 (II) NTA]**

(a) $\Delta U = 2.8$ kJ, $\Delta(pV) = 0.8$ kJ
(b) $\Delta U = 14$ J, $\Delta(pV) = 0.8$ kJ
(c) $\Delta U = 14$ kJ, $\Delta(pV) = 4$ kJ
(d) $\Delta U = 14$ kJ, $\Delta(pV) = 18$ kJ

64 In conversion of limestone to lime,

$$CaCO_3(s) \longrightarrow CaO(s) + CO_2(g)$$

the values of $\Delta H°$ and $\Delta S°$ are +179.1 kJ mol^{-1} and 160.2 J/K, respectively at 298 K and 1 bar. Assuming that $\Delta H°$ and $\Delta S°$ do not change with temperature, temperature above which conversion of limestone to lime will be spontaneous is **[AIEEE 2007]**

(a) 1008 K (b) 1200 K
(c) 845 K (d) 1118 K

65 A fixed mass of an ideal gas in a 25 dm^3 sealed rigid flask at 1.2 bar is heated from 27°C to 127°C. Thus, change in Gibb's free energy, if entropy is a function of temperature as

$$S = 3 + 10^{-2} T$$

$$(1 \text{ bar dm}^3 = 100 \text{ J})$$

(a) 700 J (b) 1000 J (c) – 350 J (d) 350 J

66 Free energy of mixing of three gases has a minimum value with respect to each gas only when mole fractions of these gases (χ_1, χ_2 and χ_3) are

(a) $\frac{1}{3}, \frac{1}{3}, \frac{1}{3}$ (b) $\frac{1}{2}, \frac{1}{2}, \frac{1}{2}$

(c) $\frac{1}{4}, \frac{1}{4}, \frac{1}{4}$ (d) $\frac{1}{5}, \frac{1}{5}, \frac{1}{5}$

67 $H_2O(l)$ at 373 K and 1.01325 bar pressure is converted to $H_2O(g)$ at 373 K when pressure is reduced to one-tenth of the initial value. Thus, total entropy change is ($\Delta H_{vap} = 40.67 \text{ kJ mol}^{-1}$)

(a) 109.00 JK^{-1} mol^{-1} (b) 19.15 JK^{-1} mol^{-1}

(c) 128.15 JK^{-1} mol^{-1} (d) 89.85 JK^{-1} mol^{-1}

68 Consider the entropy change of the

(i) system containing 3 moles of an ideal gas at 300 K which is being expanded from a pressure of 2 bar to pressure of 1 bar

(ii) surrounding containing 3 moles of the same gas at 300 K and 1 bar pressure being expanded against constant external pressure of the surrounding.

Thus,

(a) ΔS_{gas} is 17.29 JK^{-1}

(b) ΔS_{surr} is –12.47 JK^{-1}

(c) ΔS_{total} is 4.82 JK^{-1} and process is irreversible.

(d) All of the above statements are correct

69 For a van der Waals' gas, the Joule-Thomson coefficient is given by

$$\mu_{JT} = \frac{1}{C_p}\left[\frac{2a}{RT} - b - \frac{3ab}{R^2T^2}\right]$$

Thus, inversion temperature as a function of temperature is given by

(a) $T_i = \dfrac{a \pm \sqrt{a^2 - 3ab^2 p}}{bR}$

(b) $T_i = \dfrac{a \pm 2\sqrt{a^2 - 3ab^2 p}}{2bR}$

(c) $T_i = \dfrac{2a \pm \sqrt{a^2 - 3ab^2 p}}{2bR}$

(d) None of the correct

70 An ideal monoatomic gas ($C_V = 1.5R$), initially at 298 K and 1.013×10^6 Pa pressure expands adiabatically and irreversibly until it is equilibrium with a constant external pressure of 1.013×10^5 Pa. Thus, final temperature is approximately

(a) 149 K (b) 191 K

(c) 200 K (d) 100 K

ACID TEST

For JEE Advanced

TYPE I MCQs with Only ONE Correct Alternate

71 0.5 mole of a perfect gas is allowed to expand at 300 K from a volume 1 L to a volume of 10 L against a constant pressure of 1 atm. Thus, heat absorbed and entropy change are

	Heat absorbed (J)	Entropy change ($J K^{-1}$)
(a)	−911.4	−9.57
(b)	−911.4	9.57
(c)	+911.4	9.57
(d)	+911.4	−9.57

72 An ideal monoatomic gas undergoes a reversible process by which its volume and absolute temperature, both are doubled. Thus, ΔS is

(a) 7.21 $J mol^{-1} K^{-1}$ (b) 0
(c) −14.41 $J mol^{-1} K^{-1}$ (d) 14.41 $J mol^{-1} K^{-1}$

73 During an isothermal isobaric expansion of 1.0 mole of an ideal gas originally at 273 K and 0.525 atm occupying 43.2 L, 975 J of heat was needed . If external pressure is 2.0 atm, final pressure of the gas is

(a) 2.472 atm (b) 0.472 atm
(c) 1.528 atm (d) 2.971 atm

74 Entropy change on mixing 10.0 L of N_2 with 3.50 L of N_2O at 300 K and 0.550 atm (assuming volumes are additives) is

(a) 2.86 $J K^{-1}$ (b) −1.43 $J K^{-1}$
(c) −2.86 $J K^{-1}$ (d) 1.43 $J K^{-1}$

75 What is entropy change on mixing two gases by opening the stop-cock as shown both at 298 K? Assume ideal behaviour

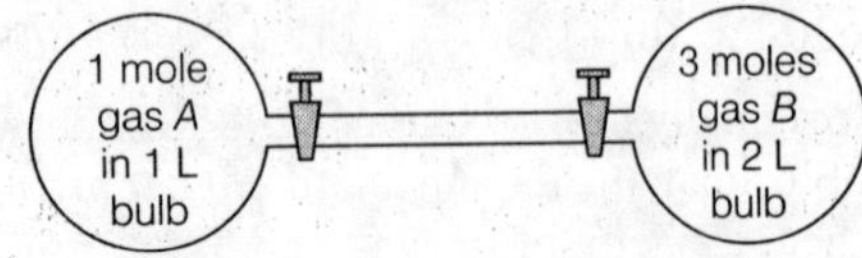

(a) $R[\ln 81 - \ln 8]$ (b) $R[\ln 3 - \ln 2]$
(c) $R[\ln 2 - \ln 3]$ (d) $4R \ln 3$

76 For the chemical reaction,

$$C(s) + CO_2(g) \longrightarrow 2CO(g), \Delta H = 172.0 \text{ kJ}$$

at 1 bar and 300 K. Density of C(*s*) (in graphite form) is 2.25 $g\ cm^{-3}$. Thus, change in internal energy is

(a) 169.5 kJ (b) −2.5 kJ
(c) + 2.5 kJ (d) 174.5 kJ

77 Consider a system consisting of 1 mole of a diatomic gas contained in a piston. If heat absorbed is 50.0 J and workdone by the system is 100.0 J, then change in temperature is

(a) −3.61° (b) 3.61° (c) −2.41° (d) 5.00°

78 In general, ΔU for any process can be calculated using

$$\Delta U = \int_{T_1}^{T_2} nC_V dT + \int_{V_1}^{V_2} \left(\frac{\partial U}{\partial V}\right) dV$$

1 mole of O_2 gas (assume ideal behaviour) is expanded by heating from 25°C, 5.00 L, 4.93 bar to 125.0° C , 6.75 L and 4.90 bar ($C_p = 7/2R$)

Thus, ΔU is

(a) 2.078 kJ (b) −2.078 kJ (c) zero (d) 7.169 kJ

79 A 2-mole sample of an ideal diatomic gas undergoes a reversible isothermal expansion at 298 K from 1.00 bar and 49.6 L to 0.66 bar and 75.0 L. Thus, work done by the system is

(a) zero (b) −491 J (c) −2042 J (d) + 2042 J

80 A sample of $N_2(g)$ underwent a Joule-Thomson expansion from 2.00 bar and 25.0°C to 1.00 bar and 24.95°C. Thus, Joule-Thomson coefficient for $N_2(g)$ is

(a) 20 bar K^{-1} (b) 0.05 K bar^{-1}
(c) 0.05 bar K^{-1} (d) 1.00 K bar^{-1}

81 An ideal refrigerator operates between 273 K and 298 K. This is to be used to produce 1.0 g of ice each second at 273 K from water at 273 K. Thus, work done is (Molar heat of fusion of water = 6.0 kJ mol^{-1}.

(a) 10.0 J (b) 15.6 J
(c) 31.7 J (d) 29.1 J

82 Entropy change for reversibly cooling an ideal monoatomic gas from 298 K to 273 K under constant volume condition is

(a) 1.09 $J K^{-1} mol^{-1}$ (b) −1.09 $J K^{-1} mol^{-1}$
(c) −2.4 $J K^{-1} mol^{-1}$ (d) −1.82 $J K^{-1} mol^{-1}$

83 One mole of an ideal diatomic gas is subjected to reversibly cooling from 300 K to 100 under.

I. isochoric and

II. isobaric conditions

Thus, $d(\Delta S)$ of these two processes I and II would be

(a) 0.693 R (b) $-0.693\, R$

(c) 1.386 R (d) $-1.386\, R$

84 Difference $d(\Delta S)$ of an ideal gas reversibly cooling under isochoric and isobaric conditions is maximum for

(a) monoatomic gas (b) diatomic gas

(c) triatomic gas (d) equal

85 Two flasks A and B each containing 1 mole N_2 gas at 298 K were connected by a tube with stop-cocks as shown

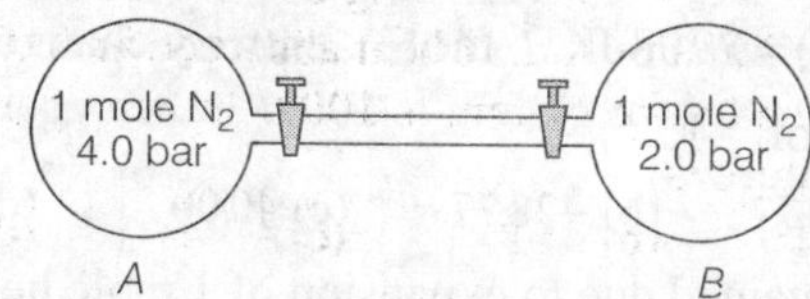

If these two flasks are connected, entropy change will be

(a) $-0.96\ J\ K^{-1}$ (b) $0.96\ J\ K^{-1}$

(c) $6.60\ J\ K^{-1}$ (d) $-6.60\ J\ K^{-1}$

86 Two blocks each made of 1 mole of aluminium, one at 373 K and the other at 273 K, were brought into thermal contact. If C_p (Al) $= 24.35\ J\ K^{-1}\ mol^{-1}$ overall entropy change of the aluminium blocks is

($\log 323 = 2.51$, $\log (273 \times 373) = 5.011$)

(a) $1.12\ J\ K^{-1}$ (b) $0.00\ J\ K^{-1}$

(c) $0.56\ J\ K^{-1}$ (d) $-0.56\ J\ K^{-1}$

87 The composition of a binary mixture of gases (1) and (2) for which $\Delta_{mix} S$(system) is maximum, is

(a) $\chi_1 = 0.5$ (b) $\chi_1 = 0.75$

(c) $\chi_1 = 0.25$ (d) $\chi_1 = 0.90$

88 Entropy change for the system for producing one mole of sample of artificial air consisting of 79% N_2 and 21% O_2, is

($\ln 0.79 = -0.236$, $\ln 0.21 = -1.56$)

(a) $-4.27\ J\ K^{-1}$ (b) $4.27\ J\ K^{-1}$

(c) $0.79\ J\ K^{-1}$ (d) $0.21\ J\ K^{-1}$

89 For the reaction at 1000 K,

$$A \rightleftharpoons B, \qquad \Delta S^\circ = 100\ J\ K^{-1}$$

$$\Delta H^\circ = +102.303\ kJ\ mol^{-1}$$

Thus, equilibrium constant $\log K$ is

(a) 8.314×10^{-3} (b) 8.314

(c) 8.314×10^{3} (d) $\frac{1}{8.314}$

90 With what minimum pressure must a given volume of nitrogen (N_2) originally at 373 K and 1.013×10^5 Pa pressure, be adiabatically compressed in order to raise its temperature by 300 K.

(a) 2.026×10^5 Pa (b) 1.796×10^5 Pa

(c) 3.865×10^5 Pa (d) 3.039×10^5 Pa

91 For the vaporisation of H_2O_2 at 298 K,

$$H_2O_2\,(g.\ p\ \text{bar}) \rightleftharpoons H_2O_2\,(g, 1\ \text{bar})$$

$$\Delta G^\circ = +14.78\ kJ\ mol^{-1}$$

Thus, vapour pressure of H_2O_2 at 298 K is

(a) 2.57×10^{-3} bar (b) 1.00 bar

(c) 1.62×10^{-3} bar (d) 1.97×10^{-3} bar

92. For a reaction,

$$\Delta G^\circ_{300} = -66.9\ kJ\ mol^{-1}$$

and $$\Delta H^\circ_{300} = -41.8\ kJ\ mol^{-1}$$

Thus, ΔG°_{330} for the same reaction is

(a) $-25.1\ kJ\ mol^{-1}$ (b) $+25.1\ kJ\ mol^{-1}$

(c) $18.7\ kJ\ mol^{-1}$ (d) $-69.4\ kJ\ mol^{-1}$

93 5 moles of an ideal gas at 300 K are allowed to expand isothermally from an initial pressure of 10.0 atm to a final pressure of 4.0 atm against external pressure of 1.0 atm. Thus, work done will be

(a) -1870.6 J (b) $+1870.6$ J (c) -18.47 J (d) $+18.47$ J

94 The density of ice at 273 K is $0.915\ g\ cm^{-3}$ and that of liquid water is $1.0\ g\ cm^{-3}$. Work done when 1 mole of ice at 1.00 bar and 273 K is melted is

(a) 0.1675 J (b) -0.1675 J (c) 0.00 J (d) -1.675 J

95 When 1 mole of ice melts at 273 K and at constant pressure of 1 atm, 1440 cal of heat are absorbed by the system. Molar volume V_m of ice = 0.0196 L, and that of water = 0.0180 L

Thus, change in internal energy is

(a) -1439.96 cal (b) -1440.04 cal

(c) $+1439.96$ cal (d) $+1440.04$ cal

96 Two litres of an ideal gas at a pressure of 10 atm expands isothermally and reversibly to a final volume of 10 litres. Thus, work done is (in J)

(a) -1630.4 (b) $+1630.4$ (c) -3260.9 (d) $+3260.9$

97 A gas originally at 1.10 bar and 298 K underwent a reversible adiabatic expansion to 1.0 bar at 287 K. Thus, molar heat capacity of the gas (C_p) is

(a) 21.07 (b) 42.14 (c) 10.58 (d) 5.16

98 A gas is cooled and loses 50 J of heat. The gas contracts and work done on the system equal to 20 J is exchanged with the surroundings. Hence, ΔE is

(a) 70 J (b) -30 J (c) 30 J (d) -70 J

99 Two moles of glucose were dissolved in water to prepare 1 dm^3 solution at 298 K. The solution was further diluted isothermally and gradually until the concentration was 0.2 M. Thus, work done is

(a) −11.41 kJ (b) + 11.41 kJ (c) −38.04 kJ (d) + 38.04 kJ

100 1 mole of a diatomic gas is contained in a piston. It gains 50.0 J of heat and work is done on the surrounding by the system is −100 J. Thus,

(a) the gas will cool by 2.41° (b) the gas will heat by 2.41°
(c) the gas will cool by 3.61° (d) the gas will heat by 3.61°

101 The standard state Gibbs free energies of formation of C(graphite) and C(diamond) at $T = 298$ K are

$$\Delta_f G°[\text{C(graphite)}] = 0 \text{ kJ mol}^{-1}$$
$$\Delta_f G°[\text{C(diamond)}] = 2.9 \text{ kJ mol}^{-1}$$

The standard state means that the pressure should be 1 bar, and substance should be pure at a given temperature. The conversion of graphite [C(graphite)] to diamond [C(diamond)] reduces its volume by 2×10^{-6} m^3 mol^{-1}. If C (graphite) is converted to C(diamond) isothermally at $T = 298$ K, the pressure at which C(graphite) is in equilibrium with C(diamond), is

[Useful information: 1 J = kg $m^2 s^{-2}$; 1 Pa = 1 kg m^{-1} s^{-2}; 1 bar = 10^5 Pa] ***[JEE Adv. 2017]***

(a) 58001 bar (b) 1450 bar
(c) 14501 bar (d) 29001 bar

102 Consider the following equilibrium,

$$CCl_4(l) \rightleftharpoons CCl_4(g), \ \Delta H°_{vap} = 39.4 \text{ kJ mol}^{-1}$$

Entropy of liquid CCl_4 at 298 K is 216 JK^{-1} mol^{-1}. Thus, entropy of 1 mole of the vapour in equilibrium with the liquid at 298 K is (in JK^{-1} mol^{-1})

(a) −348.2 (b) 348.2 (c) 83.8 (d) −83.8

103 Based on the given data, $\Delta G°$ of the given reaction at 298 K is

$$2H_2(g) + O_2(g) \longrightarrow 2H_2O(l)$$

	$2H_2(g)$	$O_2(g)$	$2H_2O(l)$
$\Delta H_f°$(kJ mol^{-1})	0	0	−285.83
$S°$(J mol^{-1} K^{-1})	130.68	205.14	69.91

(a) −474.3 kJ (b) +474.3 kJ
(c) 206.6 kJ (d) −206.6 kJ

104 A system is subjected to the following reversible cycle ($P \rightarrow Q \rightarrow R \rightarrow P$) as shown in graph of entropy (S) *vs* temperature (T). Thus, efficiency of the reversible cycle is

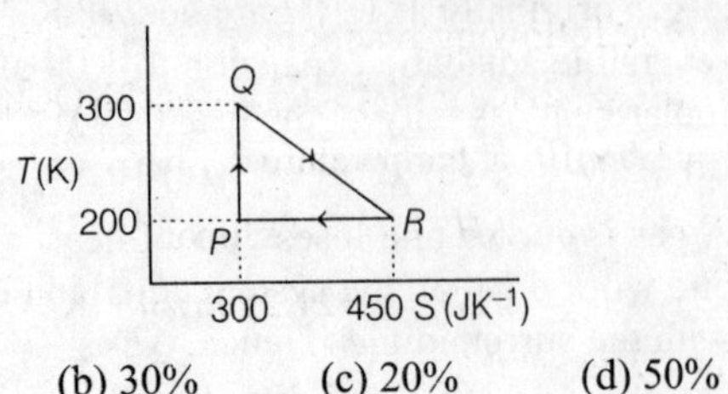

(a) 40% (b) 30% (c) 20% (d) 50%

105 When limestone ($CaCO_3$) decomposes, pressure due to CO_2 is 0.02 atm at 298 K in a closed vessel.

$$CaCO_3(s) \rightleftharpoons CaO(s) + CO_2(g)$$

If, $\Delta H°_{298} = 177.9$ kJ mol^{-1}

and $\Delta S°_{298} = 161.0$ JK^{-1} mol^{-1}

Then, ΔG is

(a) 120.3 kJ mol^{-1} (b) 130.0 kJ mol^{-1}
(c) −120.3 kJ mol^{-1} (d) −130.0 kJ mol^{-1}

106 In the following process from state I to state II

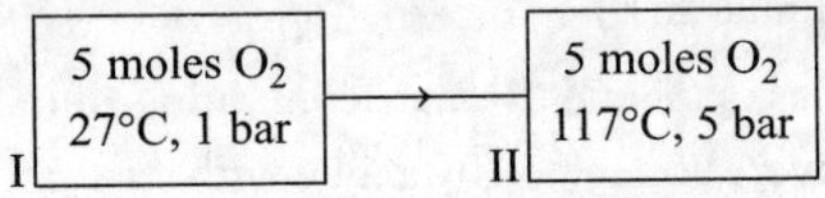

$C_p(O_2) = 29.08$ JK^{-1} mol^{-1}, entropy change is (in J mol^{-1} K^{-1})

(a) + 28.77 (b) −28.77 (c) 40.00 (d) 27.60

107 Heat obtained due to expansion of 1 mole helium gas at 1000 K from 10 dm^3 to 100 dm^3 under isothermal reversible condition is absorbed by an engine having a sink at 300 K Thus, useful work obtained is

(a) 273.53 kJ (b) −13.403 kJ
(c) zero kJ (d) 13.403 kJ

108 For the reaction at 298 K

$$NH_4HS(s) \rightleftharpoons NH_3(g) + H_2S(g);$$
$$\Delta H° = +100 \text{ kJ mol}^{-1}$$
$$\Delta S° = +160 \text{ J mol}^{-1} \text{ K}^{-1}$$

Thus,

(a) reaction is spontaneous at 298 K
(b) as temperature is lowered, reaction becomes more spontaneous in forward side.
(c) reaction is spontaneous in forward side at a temperature just above 625 K
(d) reaction is spontaneous in forward side at a temperature just below 625 K.

109 A piston exerting a pressure of 1.0 atm rests on the surface of water at 373 K. The pressure is reduced to a smaller extent and as a result 10 g of water evaporates and absorbs 22.2 kJ of heat. Thus, change in internal energy is

(a) 20.48 kJ (b) −20.48 kJ
(c) 1.74 kJ (d) −1.74 kJ

110 Consider following transition of $CaCO_3$

$$\text{Calcite} \rightleftharpoons \text{Aragonite}, \ \Delta E = +0.21 \text{ kJ mol}^{-1}$$

density (g cm^{-3}) 2.71 2.93

Thus, enthalpy change at 1 bar is

(a) −0.21 kJ (b) 0.0003 kJ
(c) −0.0003 kJ (d) +0.21 kJ

111 One mole of an ideal diatomic gas undergoes a reversible adiabatic compression from 1 atm, 298 K and 25 L to 1.0 L.

Given, $(5)^{2.8} = 90.6$ and $(5)^{0.8} = 3.624$

Thus, final pressure and final temperature are

	p_f (atm)	T_f (K)
(a)	90.6	1080 K
(b)	10.2	1080 K
(c)	10.2	1200 K
(d)	10.2	1100 K

112 One mole of an ideal diatomic gas underwent an adiabatic expansion from 298 K, 15 bar and 5.25 dm^3 to 2.50 bar against a constant external pressure of 1.0 bar. Thus, cooling takes place by

(a) 10.0° (b) 24.3° (c) 15.0° (d) 17.7°

113 A 0.150 mole sample of an ideal gas is allowed to expand at 294 K from 10.0 atm to 1.00 atm as shown is figure. If external pressure is kept constant at 1.00 atm, work done is

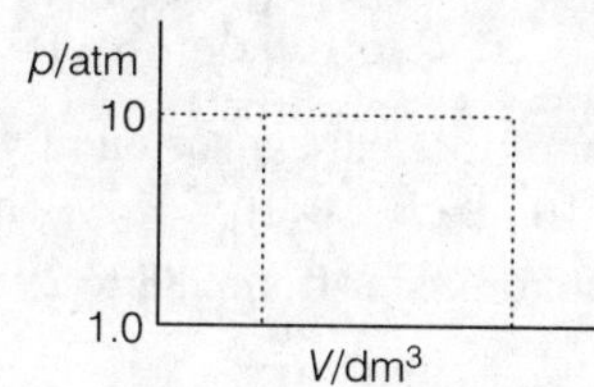

(a) −330 J (b) $-3.26\ dm^3$ atm
(c) Both are correct (d) None of these is correct

114 In the above case (Q. 113), if external pressure is held at 5.00 atm until the expansion stops and then further reduced to 1.00 atm, then work done is

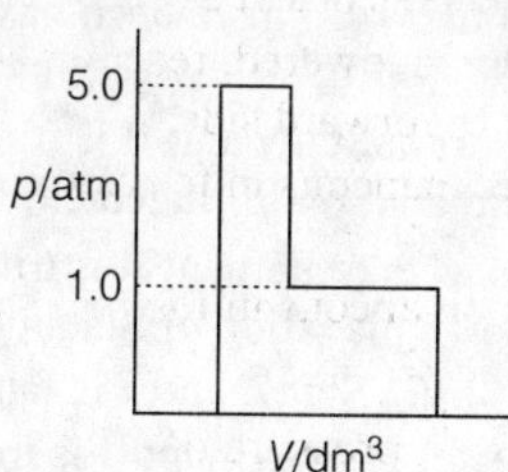

(a) − 6.476 J (b) −4.70 J (c) −476 kJ (d) −1.76 kJ

115 One mole of an ideal gas at 27°C and 10 atm pressure is

I. allowed to expand to 1 atm isothermally and reversibly.
II. allowed to expand against a constant pressure of 1 atm isothermally.
III. allowed of free expansion.

Work obtained in these processes are (in kJ)

	I	II	III
(a)	−5.744	−2.24	0
(b)	+5.744	−2.24	0
(c)	0	−0.0574	−2.24
(d)	−5.744	+ 2.24	0

116 In the following expansion of gas, piston *AB* moves to *A′ B′*. Initially, it occupies 0.500 dm^3 at 298 K and 2 atm. Change in entropy going from *AB* to *A′ B′* is :

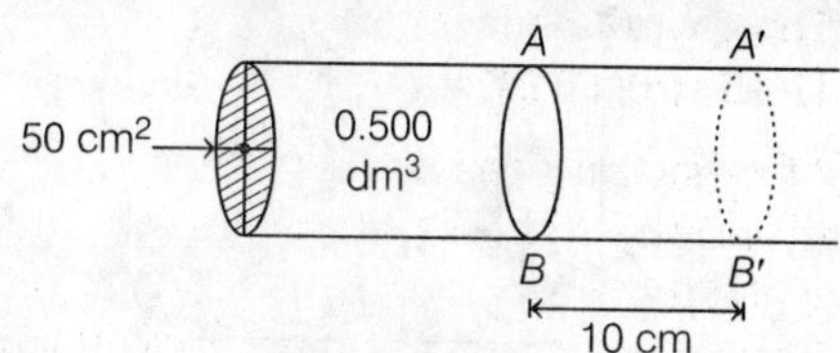

(a) 0.24 JK^{-1} (b) 4.2 JK^{-1} (c) zero (d) −0.24 JK^{-1}

117 One mole of an ideal gas at STP expands isothermally and irreversibly to 44.8 L.

Thus, $\left(\frac{\Delta G}{\Delta S}\right)$ is

(a) 1.4 (b) 273 (c) −273 (d) $\frac{-273}{2.303}$

118 An engine takes up 100 kJ of heat to complete the cycle as shown. Thus, efficiency is

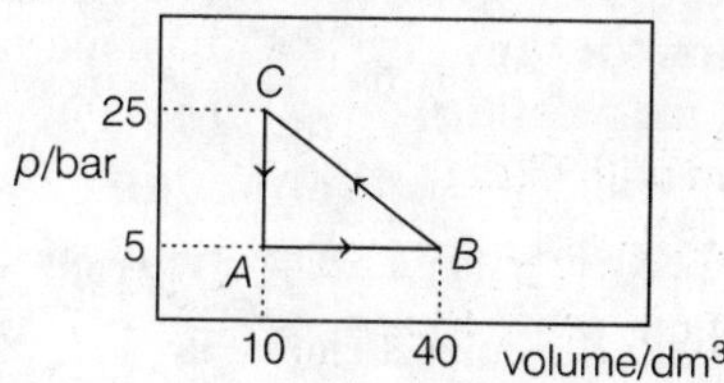

(a) 70.0% (b) 15.0% (c) 75.0% (d) 30.0%

119 Which reaction with the following values of ΔH and ΔS at 400 K is spontaneous and endothermic ?

	ΔH (kJ mol^{-1})	ΔS (kJ mol^{-1})
(a)	−48	+ 0.135
(b)	+ 48	+ 0.135
(c)	−48	− 0.135
(d)	+48	−0.135

120 In the following case :

1 mole CO_2 gas [400 K, 10 dm^3] —— $q = 0$ —— [T K, 80 dm^3]

	Work done	Final temperature
(a)	0.5 kJ	150 K
(b)	1.0 kJ	300 K
(c)	−5 kJ	200 K
(d)	5 kJ	200 K

121 For the following reaction,

$$2NO(g) + Cl_2(g) \longrightarrow 2NOCl(g)$$

$K = 1.0 \times 10^3$ at temperature *T*.

$$\Delta H° = -77.1\ kJ\ mol^{-1}$$

$$\Delta S° = -121.2\ kJ\ mol^{-1}\ K^{-1}$$

Thus, *T* is

(a) 432 K (b) 298 K (c) 412 K (d) 398 K

122 One mole of an ideal gas is put through a series of changes as shown in the figure in which stages I, II and III have been marked . Pressures at the three stages are (in bar)

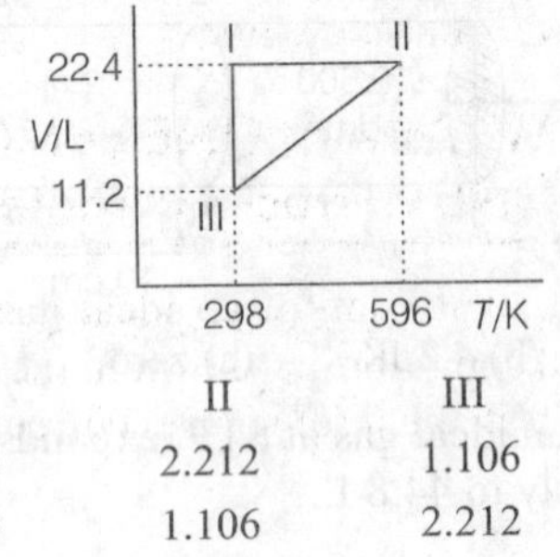

	I	II	III
(a)	1.106	2.212	1.106
(b)	1.106	1.106	2.212
(c)	2.212	1.106	2.212
(d)	1.106	2.212	2.212

123 One mole of an ideal gas at 300 K in thermal contact with surroundings expands isothermally from 1.0 L to 2.0 L against a constant pressure of 3.0 atm. In this process, the change in entropy of surroundings ($\Delta S_{surrounding}$) in $J\ K^{-1}$ is (1 L atm = 101.3 J) ***[JEE Adv. 2016]***

(a) 5.763 (b) 1.013
(c) −1.013 (d) −5.763

124 For the process, $H_2O(l) \longrightarrow H_2O(g)$ at $T = 100°$ C and 1 atm pressure, the correct choice is ***[JEE Adv. 2014]***

(a) $\Delta S_{system} > 0$ and $\Delta S_{surrounding} > 0$
(b) $\Delta S_{system} > 0$ and $\Delta S_{surrounding} < 0$
(c) $\Delta S_{system} < 0$ and $\Delta S_{surrounding} > 0$
(d) $\Delta S_{system} < 0$ and $\Delta S_{surrounding} < 0$

125 For the process, $H_2O(l)$ (1 bar, 373 K) $\longrightarrow H_2O(g)$ (1 bar, 373 K), the correct set of thermodynamic parameters is ***[JEE Adv. 2007]***

(a) $\Delta G = 0, \Delta S = +ve$ (b) $\Delta G = 0, \Delta S = -ve$
(c) $\Delta G = +ve, \Delta S = 0$ (d) $\Delta G = -ve, \Delta S = +ve$

126 The value of $\log_{10} K$ for a reaction ,

$A \rightleftharpoons B$ is (given, $\Delta_r H^\circ_{298\ K} = -54.07\ kJ\ mol^{-1}$,

$\Delta_r S^\circ_{298\ K} = 10\ J\ K^{-1}\ mol^{-1}$ and $R = 8.314\ JK^{-1}\ mol^{-1}$;

$2.303 \times 8.314 \times 298 = 5705$) ***[JEE Adv. 2007]***

(a) 5 (b) 10
(c) 95 (d) 100

127 The direct conversion of A to B is difficult, hence, it is carried out by the following shown path

$$\begin{array}{ccc} C & \longrightarrow & D \\ \uparrow & & \downarrow \\ A & & B \end{array}$$

Given that, $\Delta S_{(A \to C)} = 50$ eu, $\Delta S_{(C \to D)} = 30$ eu

$\Delta S_{(B \to D)} = 20$ eu

where, eu is entropy unit. Then, $\Delta S_{(A \to B)} = 30$ is ***[JEE Adv. 2006]***

(a) + 100 eu (b) + 60 eu (c) −100 eu (d) − 60 eu

128 A monoatomic ideal gas undergoes a process in which the ratio of p to V at any instant is constant and equals to 1. What is the molar heat capacity of the gas? ***[JEE Adv. 2006]***

(a) $\frac{4R}{2}$ (b) $\frac{3R}{2}$ (c) $\frac{5R}{2}$ (d) 0

129 One mole of monoatomic ideal gas expands adiabatically at initial temperature T against a constant external pressure of 1 atm from 1 L to 2 L. Find out the final temperature ($R = 0.0821\ L\ atm\ K^{-1}\ mol^{-1}$) ***[JEE Adv. 2005]***

(a) T (b) $\frac{T}{(2)^{5/3-1}}$

(c) $T - \frac{2}{3 \times 0.082}$ (d) $T + \frac{2}{3 \times 0.082}$

130 Work which could be obtained from an isothermal reversible expansion of 1 mol of chlorine gas from 1 dm^3 to 50 dm^3 at 300 K using van der Waals' behaviour when attractive forces are negligible is ($a = 0-655\ dm^6\ MPa\ mol^{-2}$, $b = 0.055\ dm^3\ mol^{-1}$)

(a) + 8.366 kJ (b) −8.366 kJ
(c) +9.9 kJ (d) −9.9 kJ

131 The coefficient of thermal expansion of water at 293 K and 1.01325×10^5 Pa is $2.1 \times 10^{-4}\ K^{-1}$. Thus, work done in heating 1 mol of water from 288 to 298 K at the given pressure is

(a) $-83.14\ J\ mol^{-1}$ (b) $-3.83 \times 10^{-3}\ J\ mol^{-1}$
(c) $+83.14\ J\ mol^{-1}$ (d) $+3.83 \times 10^{-3}\ J\ mol^{-1}$

TYPE II Statement Based Questions

Directions Q. Nos. (132-143) have been based on the following codes.

(a) Statement I is true; Statement II is true; Statement II is the correct explanation of Statement I.
(b) Statement I is true; Statement II is true; Statement II is not the correct explanation of Statement I.
(c) Statement I is true; Statement II is false.
(d) Statement I is false; Statement II is true.

132 Statement I For two solid-solid transition of iron

Iron	ΔH°
$Fe(\alpha) \longrightarrow Fe(\gamma)$	900 J at 1184 K
$Fe(\gamma) \longrightarrow Fe(\delta)$	837 J at 1665 K

Statement II There is very small increase in randomness due to these transitions.

133 Statement I Entropy change for reversibly cooling an ideal monoatomic gas from 298K to 273K is $-1.09\ J\ K^{-1}\ mol^{-1}$

Statement II Randomness decreases due to reversible cooling.

134 **Statement I** For $CS_2(l) \rightleftharpoons CS_2(g)$ at 298K

$$\Delta H^\circ_{vap} = 27.66 \text{kJ mol}^{-1}$$

$$\Delta S^\circ_{vap} = 86.50 \text{JK}^{-1}\text{mol}^{-1}$$

Statement II Liquid state is more stable at 25°C.

135 **Statement I** Entropy of a crystalline solid increases when temperature is increased from 0 K to 115 K.

Statement II Randomness increases on increasing temperature.

136 **Statement I** For oxidation of iron at 298K

$$4Fe(s) + 3O_2(g) \longrightarrow 2Fe_2O_3(s)$$

$$\Delta S^\circ = -549.4 \text{ JK}^{-1} \text{mol}^{-1}$$

$$\Delta H^\circ = -1648.0 \text{ kJ mol}^{-1}$$

Entropy change is negative, yet reaction is spontaneous.

Statement II Every exothermic reaction is spontaneous.

137 **Statement I** Spontaneous process is an irreversible process and may be reversed by some external agency.

Statement II Decrease in enthalpy is a contributary factor for spontaneity. ***[NCERT Exemplar]***

138 **Statement I** If a liquid crystallises into a solid, it is accompanied by decrease in entropy.

Statement II In crystals, molecules organise in an ordered manner. ***[NCERT Exemplar]***

139 **Statement I** Correct thermodynamic conditions for spontaneous reaction at all temperature is

$$\Delta H < 0 \text{ and } \Delta S > 0$$

Statement II $\Delta G = \Delta H - T\Delta S$

140 **Statement I** For a binary mixture, entropy of the mixture ΔS_{mix} is maximum if mole fraction of each species is 0.5

Statement II $\Delta S_{mix} = -R\ [\chi_1 \ln \chi_1 + (1-\chi_1)\ln(1-\chi_1)]$

and for maximum ΔS_{mix}

$$\left(\frac{\partial \Delta S_{mix}}{\partial \chi}\right) = 0$$

141 **Statement I**

$$\Delta G^\circ = \Delta H^\circ + T\left(d\frac{(\Delta G^\circ)}{dT}\right)_p$$

and $\qquad \Delta G^\circ = -nFE^\circ_{cell}$

Statement II Temperature coefficient of emf of a cell is

$$\left(\frac{dE}{dT}\right) = \frac{\Delta S}{nF}$$

142 **Statement I** For every chemical reaction at equilibrium, standard Gibbs' energy of reaction is zero.

Statement II At constant temperature and pressure, chemical reactions are spontaneous in the direction of decreasing Gibbs' energy. ***[JEE Adv. 2008]***

143 **Statement I** There is a natural asymmetry between converting work to heat and converting heat to work.

Statement II No process is possible in which the sole result is the absorption of heat from a reservoir and its complete conversion into work ***[JEE Adv. 2008]***

TYPE III MCQs with ONE or MORE than ONE Correct Alternate

144 The reversible expansion of an ideal gas under adiabatic and isothermal conditions is shown in the figure. Which of the following statement (s) is (are) correct? ***[JEE Adv. 2012]***

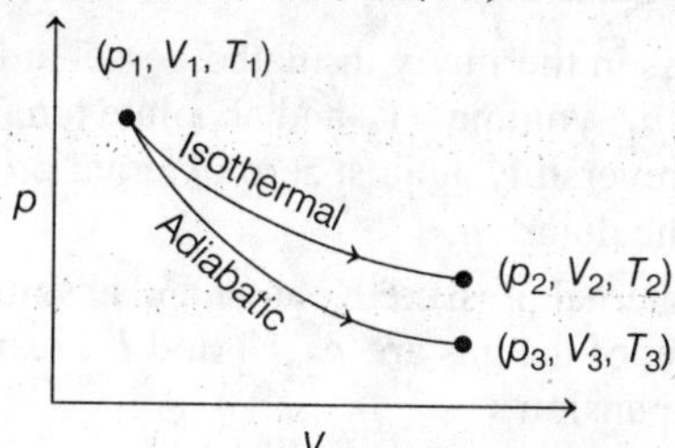

(a) $T_1 = T_2$ (b) $T_3 > T_1$
(c) $W_{isothermal} > W_{adiabatic}$ (d) $\Delta U_{isothermal} > \Delta U_{adiabatic}$

145 For an ideal gas, consider only p-V work in going from initial state X to the final state Z. The final state Z can be reached by either of the two paths shown in the figure.

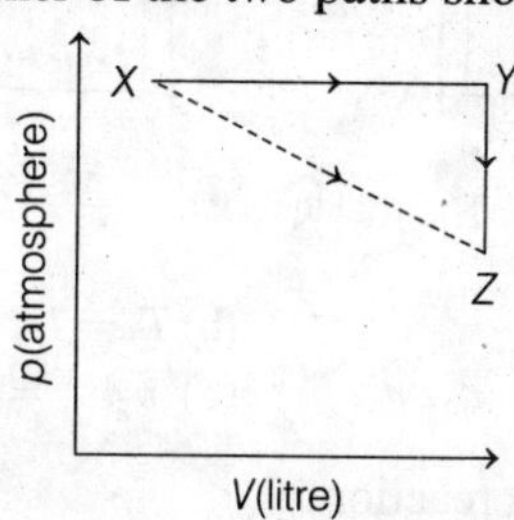

[Takes ΔS as change in entropy and W as work done]
Which of the following choice(s) is (are) correct? ***[JEE Adv. 2012]***

(a) $\Delta S_{X \to Z} = \Delta S_{X \to Y} + \Delta S_{Y \to Z}$
(b) $W_{X \to Z} = W_{X \to Y} + W_{Y \to Z}$
(c) $W_{X \to Y \to Z} = \Delta S_{X \to Y}$
(d) $\Delta S_{X \to Y \to Z} = \Delta S_{X \to Y}$

146 For the two isotherms I and II, between p and V

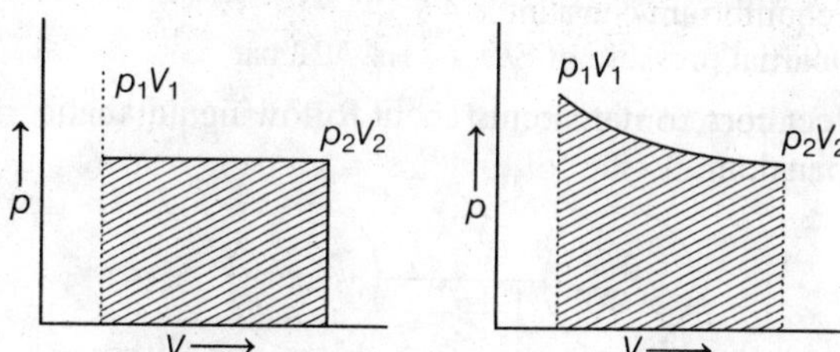

(a) I is a reversible process while II is irreversible process
(b) I is irreversible while II is reversible
(c) $W = -p(V_2 - V_1)$ for the case I
(d) $W = -\int_{V_1}^{V_2} p\,dV$ for the case II

147 In thermodynamics, the p-V work done is given by

$$w = -\int dV\, p_{ext}$$

For a system undergoing a particular process, the work done is

$$w = -\int dV\left(\frac{RT}{V-b} - \frac{a}{V^2}\right)$$

This equation is applicable to a **[JEE Adv. 2020]**

(a) system that satisfies the van der Waals' equation of state
(b) process that is reversible and isothermal
(c) process that is reversible and adiabatic
(d) process that is irreversible and at constant pressure

148 An ideal gas in thermally insulated vessel at internal pressure = p_1, volume = V_1 and absolute temperature = T_1 expands irreversibly against zero external pressure, as shown in the diagram.

The final internal pressure, volume and absolute temperature, of the gas are p_2, V_2 and T_2, respectively. For this expansion

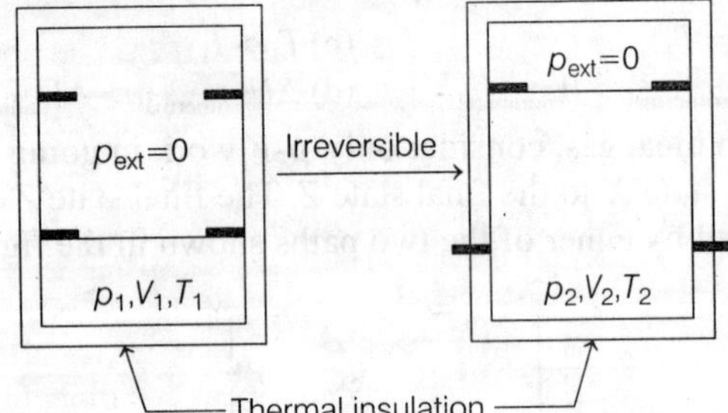

[JEE Adv. 2014]

(a) $q = 0$ (b) $T_2 = T_1$
(c) $p_2V_2 = p_1V_1$ (d) $p_2V_2^{\gamma} = p_1V_1^{\gamma}$

149 In the following reaction,

$$CaSO_3(s) \rightleftharpoons CaO(s) + SO_2(g),$$
$$\Delta H^\circ_{298} = 10\, kJmol^{-1}$$
$$\Delta S^\circ_{298} = 50\, Jmol^{-1}K^{-1}$$

Thus,

(a) the reaction is spontaneous under given condition
(b) minimum temperature upto which decomposition is spontaneous is 200K
(c) equilibrium constant is 4.9
(d) partial pressure of $SO_2(g)$ is 7.22 bar

150 Select correct statements about following adiabatic expansion.

$$(0.5)^{1/3} = 0.7937$$

(a) Work done is 2.02 kJ (b) Work done $= -\Delta U$
(c) $T' = 249K$ (d) $W > \Delta U$

151 10L of N_2 gas and 5L of the gas are mixed at 1atm at 300K

$$\Delta H_{mix} = -10J$$

Thus,

(a) $\Delta S_{mix} = +3.22 JK^{-1}$ (b) $\Delta G_{mix} = -976J$
(c) $\Delta S_{mix} = -3.22 JK^{-1}$ (d) $\Delta G_{mix} = +976J$

152 Consider two isothermal reversible expansion of an ideal gas

	Volume	Temperature	ΔE	Work
Case I	10 L to 100 L	$T = 300$ K	ΔE_1	W_1
Case II	10 L to 100 L	$T = 600$ K	ΔE_2	W_2

Select correct statement(s).

(a) $\Delta E_1 = \Delta E_2 = 0$
(b) $W_1 = 10W_2$
(c) $W_2 = 10W_1$
(d) $W_2 = 2W_1$

153 HCl (g) vapours react immediately with $NH_3(g)$ forming white fumes of NH_4Cl which solidifies as $NH_4Cl(s)$.

For this,

(a) $\Delta G^\circ < 0$, $(\Delta S^\circ)_{universe} > 0$
(b) $\Delta S^\circ_{system} < 0$, $\Delta S^\circ_{surrounding} > 0$
(c) $\Delta H^\circ > 0$, $\Delta G^\circ > 0$
(d) $\Delta S^\circ_{universe} = 0$, $\Delta S^\circ_{system} = -\Delta S^\circ_{surrounding}$

154 Conversion of X to Y can be carried out as shown.

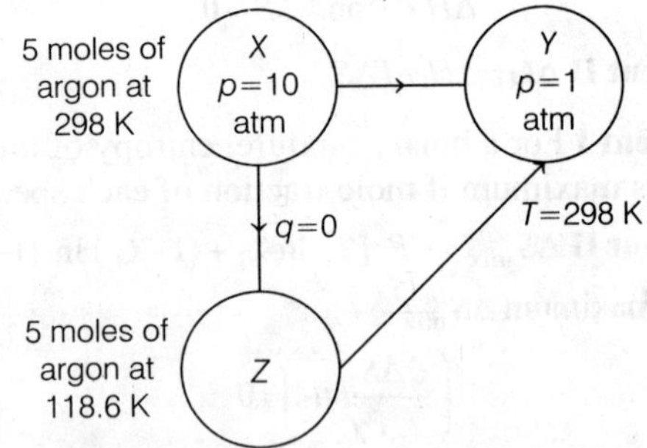

Select correct choices.

(a) $\Delta S_{X\to Y} = 95.7 JK^{-1}$
(b) $\Delta S_{X\to Z} = 0$
(c) $\Delta S_{X\to Y} = \Delta S_{X\to Z} + \Delta S_{Z\to Y} = 95.75 JK^{-1}$
(d) $\Delta S_{X\to Z\to Y} = 0$

155 For an ideal gas which undergoes only adiabatic reversible processes

(a) $\dfrac{dp}{dV} = -\gamma\dfrac{p}{V}$ (b) $\dfrac{1}{C_p}\ln\dfrac{p_2}{p_1} = \dfrac{1}{C_V}\ln\dfrac{V_1}{V_2}$

(c) $\dfrac{dT}{dV} = \left(\dfrac{\gamma-1}{TV}\right)$ (d) $\dfrac{dp}{dV} = -\gamma$

156 In which of the following cases, entropy of I is smaller than that of II.

	I	II
(a)	$NO_2(g)$	$N_2O_4(g)$
(b)	Dry ice (solid CO_2)	$CO_2(g)$
(c)	pure alumina	Ruby
(d)	$N_2(g)$ at 1 bar	$N_2(g)$ at 5 bar

157 A reversible cyclic process for an ideal gas is shown below. Here, p, V and T are pressure, volume and temperature, respectively. The thermodynamic parameters q, W, H and U are heat, work, enthalpy and internal energy, respectively.

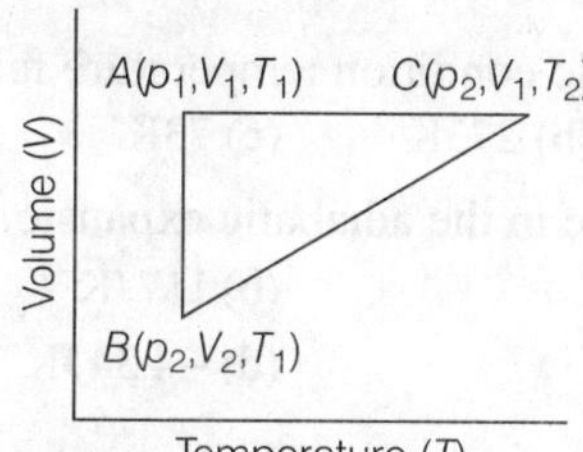

The correct option(s) are **[JEE Adv. 2018]**

(a) $q_{AC} = \Delta U_{BC}$ and $W_{AB} = p_2(V_2 - V_1)$
(b) $W_{BC} = p_2(V_2 - V_1)$ and $q_{BC} = \Delta H_{BC}$
(c) $\Delta H_{CA} < \Delta U_{CA}$ and $q_{AC} = \Delta U_{BC}$
(d) $q_{BC} = \Delta H_{AC}$ and $\Delta H_{CA} > \Delta U_{CA}$

158 For a reaction, $A \rightleftharpoons P$, the plots of $[A]$ and $[P]$ with time at temperatures T_1 and T_2 are given below.

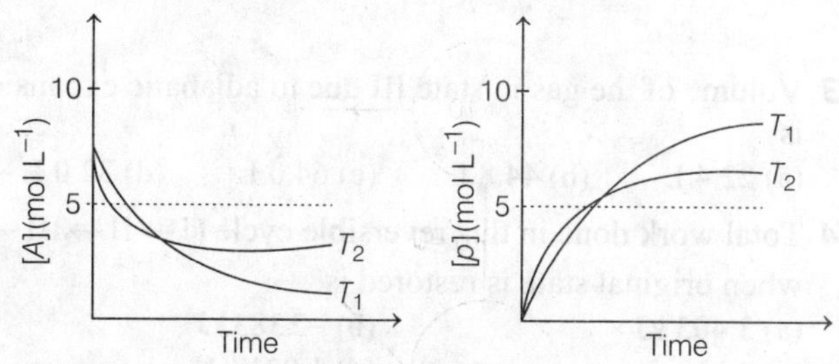

If $T_2 > T_1$, the correct statement(s) is/are

(Assume $\Delta H^\ominus$ and $\Delta S^\ominus$ are independent of temperature and ratio of $\ln K$ at T_1 to $\ln K$ at T_2 is greater than T_2/T_1. Here, H, S, G and K are enthalpy, entropy, Gibbs' energy and equilibrium constant, respectively.) **[JEE Adv. 2018]**

(a) $\Delta H^\ominus < 0, \Delta S^\ominus < 0$
(b) $\Delta G^\ominus < 0, \Delta H^\ominus > 0$
(c) $\Delta G^\ominus < 0, \Delta S^\ominus < 0$
(d) $\Delta G^\ominus < 0, \Delta S^\ominus > 0$

159 An ideal gas is expanded from (p_1, V_1, T_1) to (p_2, V_2, T_2) under different conditions. The correct statement(s) among the following is(are) **[JEE Adv. 2017]**

(a) The work done on the gas is maximum when it is compressed irreversibly from (p_2, V_2) to (p_1, V_1) against constant pressure p_1.
(b) The work done on the gas is less when it is expanded reversibly from V_1 to V_2 under adiabatic conditions as compared to that when expanded reversibly from V_1 to V_2 under isothermal conditions.
(c) The change in internal energy of the gas (i) zero, if it is expanded reversibly with $T_1 = T_2$, and (ii) positive, if it is expanded reversibly under adiabatic conditions with $T_1 \neq T_2$
(d) If the expansion is carried out freely, it is simultaneously both isothermal as well as adiabatic.

160 For a reaction taking place in a container in equilibrium with its surroundings, the effect of temperature on its equilibrium constant K in terms of change in entropy is described by **[JEE Adv. 2017]**

(a) With increase in temperature, the value K for exothermic reaction decreases because the entropy change of the system is positive.
(b) With increase in temperature, the value of K for endothermic reaction increases because unfavourable change in entropy of the surrounding decreases.
(c) With increase in temperature, the value of K for exothermic reaction decreases because favourable change in entropy of the surroundings decreases.
(d) With increase in temperature, the value of K for endothermic reaction increases because the entropy change of the system negative.

TYPE IV Passage Based MCQs (Comprehension)

Passage 1

A 3.18-mole sample of an ideal gas underwent an adiabatic expansion from 298K, 15.0 bar and 5.25 L to 2.50 bar against a constant external pressure of 1 bar.

$$C_V = \frac{5R}{2} \text{ for the given gas}$$

161 Final temperature attained due to expansion is

(a) 290 K (b) 300 K
(c) 264 K (d) 270 K

162 Final volume due to adiabatic expansion is

(a) 22.50 L (b) 27.75 L
(c) 10.25 L (d) 11.50 L

Passage 2

A 1.00 g sample of $H_2O(g)$ at 373K with a pressure of 1.00 atm has a volume of 1.70L. It is isothermally compressed by an external pressure of 2.00 atm until it reaches a volume of 0.850 L.

163 Entropy change of the surrounding is

(a) $0.14\,JK^{-1}$ (b) $-0.32\,JK^{-1}$
(c) $+0.32\,JK^{-1}$ (d) $0.46\,JK^{-1}$

164 Which has maximum numerical value?

(a) ΔS (system)
(b) ΔS (surrounding)
(c) ΔS (universe)
(d) equal

Passage 3

One mole of an ideal gas($C_V = 1.5R$) occupies 1L volume at 100K (initial state) and 2L volume at 200K (final state).
The change from the initial state to the final state is brought about along the two paths ABC and ADC.

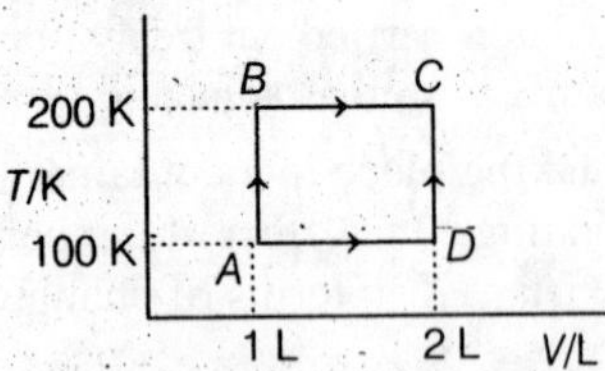

165 For the ADC, thermodynamics, parameters as indicated are

W (J mol^{-1})	q (J mol^{-1})	ΔE (J mol^{-1})
(a) 0	0	576.3
(b) 576.3	1823.4	1247.1
(c) 0	1823.4	1247.1
(d) −576.3	1823.4	576.3

166 Select correct statement(s)
(a) ΔE is path independent but q and W are path dependent
(b) q is path independent but ΔE and W are path dependent
(c) W is path independent but q and ΔE are path dependent
(d) ΔE, W and q all are path independent

Passage 4

Water is brought to boil under a pressure of 1.0 atm. When an electric current of 0.50A from a 12 V is passed for 300s through a resistance in a thermal contact with it, it is found that 0.044 mol of water is vaporised.

167 Thus, molar enthalpy change at 1 atm is
(a) 40.9kJ mol^{-1} (b) 37.5kJ mol^{-1}
(c) -40.9kJ mol^{-1} (d) 1.8kJ mol^{-1}

168 Internal energy change for the above process due to vaporisation of water is
(a) -37.8kJ mol^{-1} (b) 37.8kJ mol^{-1}
(c) 90.9kJ mol^{-1} (d) 1.8kJ mol^{-1}

Passage 5

n moles of an ideal gas change from state (1) to state (2) as shown.

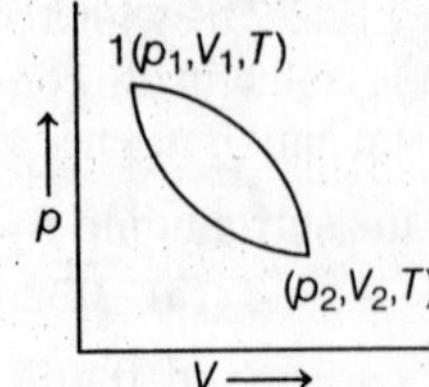

169 Work done under isothermal irreversible condition is
(a) $nRT\left(1-\frac{V_2}{V_1}\right)$ (b) $nRT\left(1-\frac{p_2}{p_1}\right)$
(c) $nRT\ln\frac{V_2}{V_1}$ (d) $nRT\ln\frac{p_2}{p_1}$

170 Difference of work done under reversible and irreversible condition is
(a) $\frac{nRT}{p_1 p_2}(p_1 - p_2)^2$ (b) $\frac{nRT}{p_1 p_2}(V_1 - V_2)^2$
(c) $nRT\left(\frac{V_1 - V_2}{V_1}\right)$ (d) $nRT\ln\frac{V_2}{V_1}$

Passage 6

One mole of O_2 gas expands adiabatically against a constant pressure of 1 atm until the pressure balances. Given, initial temperature = 473K
and initial volume = 20L

171 Due to adiabatic condition temperature falls by
(a) 65.5K (b) 273K (c) 73K (d) 134.5K

172 Entropy change in the adiabatic expansion is
(a) -1.17JK^{-1} (b) 1.17JK^{-1}
(c) 5.51JK^{-1} (d) -4.34JK^{-1}

Passage7

One mole of an ideal gas ($C_V = 1.5R$) initially at STP is put through the following reversible cycle.

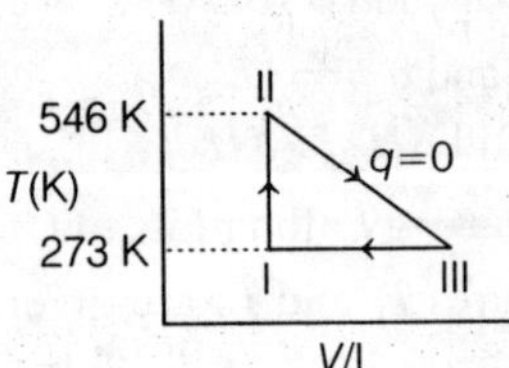

173 Volume of the gas in state III due to adiabatic expansion is
(a) 22.4 L (b) 44.8 L (c) 64.0 L (d) 32.0 L

174 Total work done in this reversible cycle (I→II→III→I) when original state is restored is
(a) 3.405 kJ (b) −2.383 kJ
(c) 0 kJ (d) 1.021 kJ

Passage 8

One mole of an ideal gas is kept in a cylinder fitted with a movable piston with zero friction and negligible mass. It is subjected to expansion in two stages at constant temperature T as shown

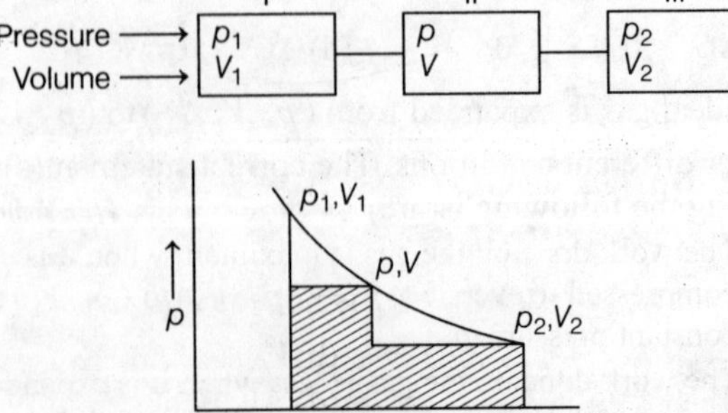

175 Work done in this two-stage expansion is

(a) $p(V_1 - V_2) - 2pV$ (b) $p(V - V_1) + p_2(V_2 - V)$

(c) $RT\left[2 - \frac{(p^2 + p_1 p_2)}{pp_1}\right]$ (d) (b) and (c) are correct

176 If the work obtained is maximum then

(a) $W_{max} = 2RT[1 - \sqrt{p_2/p_1}$

(b) $p = \sqrt{p_1 p_2}$

(c) Both of the above

(d) None of the above

Passage 9

An ideal gas undergoes a cyclic process as shown

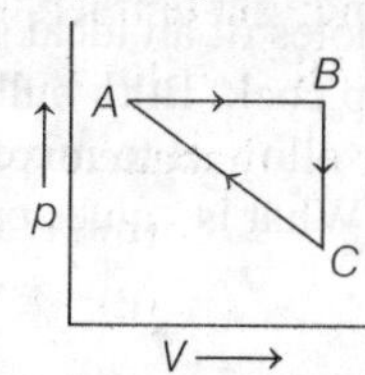

Given, $\Delta U_{BC} = -5\text{kJmol}^{-1}$

$W_{AB} = -5\text{kJmol}^{-1}$

$W_{CA} = 3\text{kJmol}^{-1}$

and $q_{AB} = 2\text{kJmol}^{-1}$

177 ΔU_{CA} (internal energy along CA) is

(a) -8kJmol^{-1} (b) $+8\text{kJmol}^{-1}$

(c) zero (d) -2kJmol^{-1}

178 In going C to A

(a) 5 kJ of heat is absorbed

(b) 5 kJ of heat is evoved

(c) process is adiabatic hence $q=0$

(d) 2 kJ of heat is absorbed

Passage 10

Consider a series of adiabats and isotherms as shown :

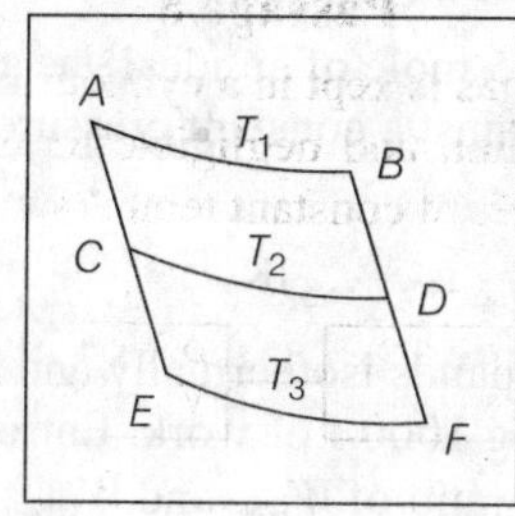

Isotherms AB, CD, EF

Adiabats AC, CE, BD, DF

179 For the above case V_B / V_A is not equal to

(a) V_D / V_C (b) V_F / V_E

(c) V_C / V_D (d) All of these

180 $\Delta S_{(\text{system})}$ $A \rightarrow B$ is equal to

(a) $\Delta S_{(\text{system})}$ $A \rightarrow B \rightarrow D \rightarrow E$

(b) $\Delta S_{(\text{system})}$ $A \rightarrow C \rightarrow E \rightarrow F$

(c) $\Delta S_{(\text{system})}$ $A \rightarrow C \rightarrow D \rightarrow F$

(d) All of the above

Passage 11

For oxidation of iron at 298 K

$$4\text{Fe}(s) + 3\text{O}_2(g) \longrightarrow 2\text{Fe}_2\text{O}_3(s),$$

$$\Delta S^\circ = -549.4 \text{ JK}^{-1}$$

$$\Delta H^\circ = -1648.0 \text{ kJ mol}^{-1}$$

181 Select correct alternate(s)

(a) This reaction is spontaneous

(b) $\Delta S^\circ_{(\text{surrouding})} > 0$

(c) $\Delta S^\circ_{(\text{total})} > 0$

(d) All of the above are correct

182 Free energy change for the reaction is

(a) $-3132.2 \text{ kJ mol}^{-1}$ (b) $+3132.2 \text{ kJ mol}^{-1}$

(c) $-1484.28 \text{ kJ mol}^{-1}$ (d) $+1484.28 \text{ kJ mol}^{-1}$

Passage 12

A system consisting of 1 mole of water vapour $H_2O(g)$ at 100°C and 1 atm with a volume of 3012 L condenses at a constant pressure of 1 atm to liquid water, $H_2O(l)$ at 100°C and 1 atm with a volume of 18.8 cm^3

$$H_2O(g) \longrightarrow H_2O(l), \quad \Delta H = -40.7 \text{ kJ}$$

183 Work done (in kJ) in this transformation is

(a) −3.05 kJ (b) +3.05 kJ

(c) 30.1 kJ (d) −30.1 kJ

184 ΔE (in kJ) of the process is

(a) −37.65 (b) +37.65 kJ

(c) −40.70 (d) +40.70 kJ

Passage 13

A fixed mass m of a gas is subjected to transformation of states from K to L to M to N and back to K as shown in the figure. ***[JEE Adv. 2012]***

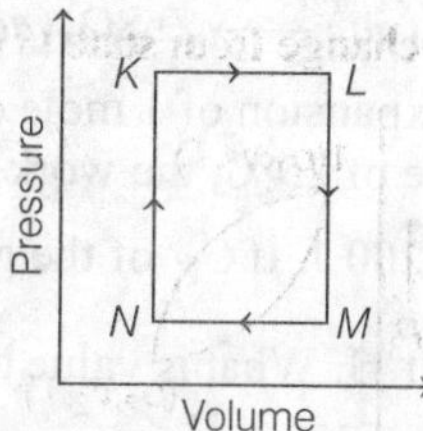

185 The succeeding operations that enable this transformation of states are

(a) heating, cooling, heating, cooling

(b) cooling, heating, cooling, heating

(c) heating, cooling, cooling, heating

(d) cooling, heating, heating cooling

186 The pair of isochoric processes among the transformation of states is

(a) K to L and L to M (b) L to M and N to K
(c) L to M and M to N (d) M to N and N to K

TYPE V Numerical Skills

187 For the reaction,

$A(l) \longrightarrow 2B(g)$

$\Delta U = 2.1$ kcal, $\Delta S = 20$ cal K^{-1} at 300 K

Hence, ΔG in kcal is .... *[JEE Main 2020 (I) NTA]*

188 The magnitude of work done by a gas that undergoes a reversible expansion along the path ABC shown in the figure is ...... *[JEE Main 2020 (I) NTA]*

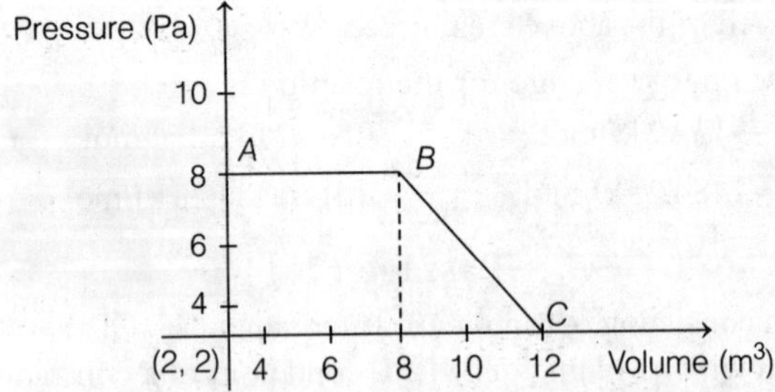

189 At constant volume, 4 mol of an ideal gas when heated from 300 K to 500 K, changes its internal energy by 5000 J. The molar heat capacity at constant volume is ...... *[JEE Main 2020 (I) NTA]*

190 In how many of the following, work is done by the system?

I. $CaC_2(s) + 2H_2O(l) \longrightarrow Ca(OH)_2(s) + C_2H_2(g)$
II. $2SO_2(g) + O_2(g) \longrightarrow 2SO_3(g)$
III. $N_2(g) + 3H_2(g) \longrightarrow 2NH_3(g)$
IV. $PCl_5(g) \longrightarrow PCl_3(g) + Cl_2(g)$
V. $C(s) + O_2(g) \longrightarrow CO_2(g)$
VI. $C(s) + CO_2(g) \longrightarrow 2CO(g)$
VII. $2Fe(s) + 3H_2O(g) \longrightarrow Fe_2O_3(s) + 3H_2(g)$
VIII. $Zn(s) + H_2SO_4(aq) \longrightarrow ZnSO_4(aq) + H_2(g)$

191 In the adiabatic expansion of 1 mole of an ideal gas from initial temperature of 25°C, the work done on the surroundings is 1200 J. If C_V of the gas is $\frac{3}{2}R$, ΔH is found to be $n \times 10^3$ J. What is value of n?

192 The internal energy change (in J) when 90 g of water undergoes complete evaporation at 100°C is ......

(Give, ΔH_{vap} for water at 373 K = 41 kJ mol^{-1}, $R = 8.314$ JK^{-1}mol^{-1}) *[JEE Main 2020 (II) NTA]*

193 Tin is obtained from cassiterite by reduction with coke. Use the data give to determine the minimum temperature (in K) at which the reduction of cassiterite by coke would take place.

At 298 K: $\Delta_f H°[SnO_2(s)] = -581.0$ kJ mol^{-1},
$\Delta_f H°[(CO_2)(g)] = -394.0$ kJ mol^{-1}
$S°[SnO_2(s)] = 56.0$ J K^{-1}mol^{-1},
$S°[Sn(s)] = 52.0$ JK^{-1} mol^{-1},
$S°[C(s)] = 6.0$ J K^{-1} mol^{-1},
$S°[CO_2(g)] = 210.0$ JK^{-1} mol^{-1}.

Assume that the enthalpies and the entropies are temperature independent. *[JEE Adv. 2020]*

194 A 1L bulb containing 1 mole of an ideal gas A and a 2L bulb containing 3 moles of an ideal gas B are connected by a tube with a stop cock. Both bulbs are at 298 K. When two gases are allowed to mixed, entropy of mixing is [n ln 3 – 4.16] cal What is values of n?

($\log_{10} 2 = 0.3010$)

195 The standard Gibbs' free energy ($\Delta G°$) (in cal mol^{-1}), for a certain reaction is given by

$\Delta G° = 300 + 2T \log_{10} T - 15T$.

What is the value of $\Delta S°$ at 100 K?

196 Joule Thomson coefficient of CO_2 is 0.6375 K atm^{-1}. CO_2 at 20.12 atm and 373 K is subjected to a final pressure of 6.0 atm in the expansion. Thus, temperature decrease is ...... K.

197 Following cycle is completed when an engine takes 5×10^4 J of heat.

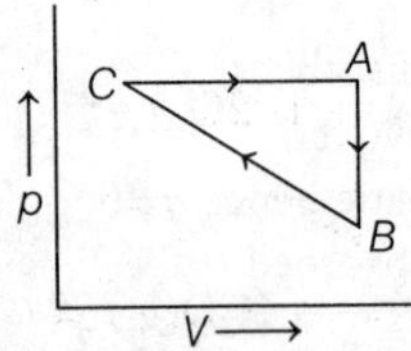

If $AB = 10$ atm and $AC = 20$L then efficiency is $10x$; derive value of $10x$.

198 A quantity of 0.5 mole of an ideal gas at 300 K expands isothermally against a constant pressure of 2.0 atm from 1.0 L to 5.0 L.

Thus, $(\Delta S)_{universe}$ is ...... JK^{-1}.

199 An ideal gas expands isothermally and irreversibly at 298 K producing 1000 J of work. Entropy change is 10 JK^{-1}. Thus, ratio of W_{rev} and W_{irrev} is

200 For a dimerisation reaction,

$$2A(g) \longrightarrow A_2(g)$$

at 298 K, $\Delta U° = -20$ kJ^{-1} mol^{-1}

$\Delta S° = -30$ JK^{-1} mol^{-1}, then $\Delta G°$ will be ......J. *[JEE Main 2020 (II) NTA]*

201 Assume that the human body is a heat engine. For a food intake equivalent to 1.0×10^7 J day^{-1}, a human can work for 6 h per day at a rate equivalent to 0.0374 HP. (1 HP = 746 W). Thus, the efficiency of the human body is ...... %.

202 About 1 dm^3 gastric juice is produced per day in the human body from other body fluids such as blood, whose pH is 7.6021 at 326 K. Calculate the minimum work (in kJ) required to produce 1 dm^3 gastric juice whose pH may be taken as unity? (pH $= -\log[H^+]$ and antilog of $(-0.6021) = 0.25$

203 Consider a reversible isoentropic expansion of 1 mole of an ideal monoatomic gas from 25°C to 75°C. If initial pressure is 1.36 bar, what is the final pressure? $\left(C_p = \frac{5}{2}R\right)$

204 The surface of copper gets tarnished by the formation of copper oxide. N_2 gas was passed to prevent the oxide formation during heating of copper at 1250 K. However, the N_2 gas contains 1 mol% of water vapour as impurity. The water vapour oxidises copper as per the reaction given below

$$2Cu(g) + H_2O(g) \longrightarrow Cu_2O(s) + H_2(g)$$

p_{H_2} is the minimum partial pressure of H_2 (in bar) needed to prevent the oxidation at 1250 K. The value of $\ln(p_{H_2})$ is ....

Given : Total Pressure = 1 bar, R (universal gas constant) = 8 JK^{-1}, ln (10) = 2.30. Cu(s) and $Cu_2O(s)$ are mutually immiscible.

At 1250 K : $2Cu(s) + 1/2O_2(g) \longrightarrow Cu_2O(s)$;

$$\Delta G^{\ominus} = -78{,}000 \text{ J mol}^{-1}$$

$$H_2(g) + \frac{1}{2}O_2(g) \longrightarrow H_2O(g);\ \Delta G^{\ominus} = -1{,}78{,}000 \text{ J mol}^{-1};$$

G is the Gibbs energy. **[JEE Adv. 2018]**

205 Consider the following reversible reaction,

$$A(g) + B(g) \rightleftharpoons AB(g)$$

The activation energy of the backward reaction exceeds that of the forwards reaction by $2RT$ (in J mol^{-1}). If the pre-exponential factor of the forward reaction is 4 times that of the reverse reaction, the absolute value of ΔG^{θ} (in J mol^{-1}) for the reaction at 300 K is ....

(Given ; ln(2) = 0.7, RT = 2500 J mol^{-1} at 300 K and G is the Gibbs energy) **[JEE Adv. 2018]**

206 One mol of an ideal gas is taken from a to b along two paths denoted by the solid and the dashed lines as shown in the graph below. If the work done along the solid line path is W_s and the along the dotted line path is W_d, then the integer closest to the ratio W_d/W_s is **[JEE Adv. 2010]**

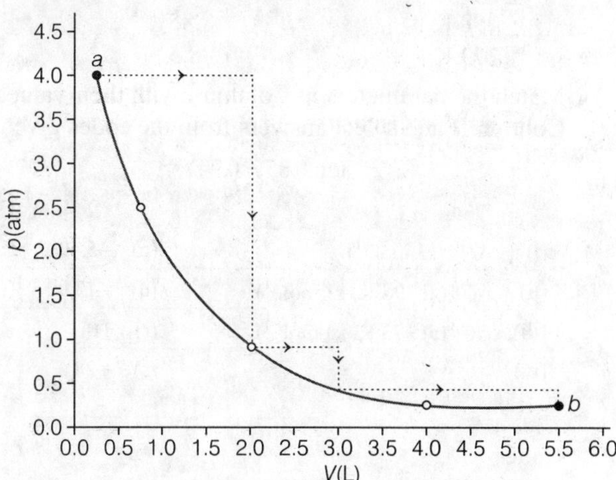

TYPE VI Matrix Matching

207 A 2.00 mol sample of an ideal gas is heated from 1.03 bar, 41.2 L and 255 K to 1.25 bar, 42.2 L and 317 K against a constant external pressure of 1 bar, passing through the stages as shown. $\left(C_p = \frac{7}{2}R\right)$

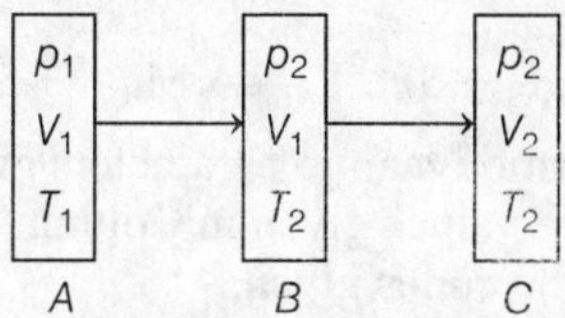

Match the thermodynamic parameters given in Column I with their values given in Column II and select the answer from the codes given,

Column I	Column II
(i) ΔU	(p) 3608 J
(ii) ΔH	(q) 100 J
(iii) q	(r) 2577 J
(iv) W	(s) 2677 J

Codes

	(i)	(ii)	(iii)	(iv)
(a)	(r)	(p)	(q)	(s)
(b)	(r)	(p)	(s)	(q)
(c)	(p)	(r)	(s)	(q)
(d)	(p)	(r)	(q)	(s)

208 Variation of equilibrium constant with temperature is given by

$$\frac{d\log K}{dT} = \frac{\Delta H^{\circ}}{2.303\,RT^2}$$

Given,

Temperature	K_{eq}
298 K	8.85
373 K	88.5

Match the parameters in Column I with their values in Column II and select answers from the codes given

log 8.85 = 0.947

Column I	Column II
(i) $\Delta H°$(kJ mol^{-1})	(p) −5.40
(ii) $\Delta G°$(at 298 K, kJ mol^{-1})	(q) −13.9
(iii) $\Delta G°$(at 373 K, kJ mol^{-1})	(r) 1.0
(iv) $\log \frac{K_2}{K_1}$	(s) +28.4

Codes

	(i)	(ii)	(iii)	(iv)
(a)	(s)	(p)	(q)	(r)
(b)	(s)	(q)	(p)	(r)
(c)	(p)	(q)	(r)	(s)
(d)	(s)	(q)	(p)	(r)

209 Thermodynamic equilibrium constant K is related to temperature T(K) by equation

$$\log_{10} K = -\frac{2303(\text{K})}{T} + 4.06$$

for, $MnO_4^- + 8H^+ + 5Fe^{2+} \longrightarrow Mn^{2+} + 5Fe^{3+} + 4H_2O$

Match the thermodynamic parameters given in Column I with respective values given in Column II and select the answer from the codes given,

Column I	Column II
(i) $\Delta S°$(in kJ mol^{-1} K^{-1})	(p) 20.7
(ii) $\Delta H°$(in kJ mol^{-1})	(q) 0.078
(iii) $\Delta G°$(in kJ mol^{-1}at 300 K)	(r) 44.1
(iv) Temperature coefficient of the emf of a cell (JK^{-1})	(s) 1.62×10^{-4}

Codes

	(i)	(ii)	(iii)	(iv)
(a)	(p)	(r)	(q)	(s)
(b)	(r)	(s)	(q)	(p)
(c)	(q)	(r)	(p)	(s)
(d)	(p)	(q)	(s)	(r)

210 (i) A sample of an ideal gas underwent an expansion against a constant external pressure of 1.0 bar from 1.0 m^3, 10.0 bar and 273 K to 10.0 m^3, 1.0 bar and 273 K. Work done by the surroundings under isothermal condition is W_1 (in J mol^{-1}).

(ii) The external pressure was increased to 10.0 bar and the gas sample was isothermally compressed from 10.0 m^3 and 1.0 bar to 1.0 m^3 and 10.0 bar. Work done on the system by surroundings is W_2 (in J mol^{-1})

(iii) Total work done is W_3 (in J mol^{-1})

(iv) Least amount of work needed to restore the system to the original p-V conditions is W_4 (in J mol^{-1})

Match W_1, W_2, W_3 and W_4 in Column I with the corresponding values in Column II.

Column I	Column II
(i) W_1	(p) 8.1×10^6
(ii) W_2	(q) 9.0×10^6
(iii) W_3	(r) 2.3×10^6
(iv) W_4	(s) -9.0×10^5

Codes

	(i)	(ii)	(iii)	(iv)
(a)	(s)	(q)	(p)	(r)
(b)	(s)	(q)	(r)	(p)
(c)	(q)	(s)	(p)	(r)
(d)	(s)	(p)	(r)	(q)

211 100 g supercooled liquid water at −10.0° C freezes to form ice at −10.0° C.

$$\Delta H_{\text{fusion}} \text{ (at 273 K)} = 6.0 \text{ kJ K}^{-1}\text{mol}^{-1}$$
$$C_p = 75.3 \text{ JK}^{-1} \text{ mol}^{-1} \text{ for liquid water}$$
$$= 38.0 \text{ JK}^{-1} \text{ mol}^{-1} \text{ for ice.}$$

Match the steps in Column I with their entropy change in Column II and select the answer from the codes given.

Column I	Column II
(i) Entropy change for reversibly heating the liquid −10.0°C to 0.0°C.	(p) 15.61 JK^{-1}
(ii) Entropy change for reversibly freezing the liquid at 0.0°C	(q) −114.27 JK^{-1}
(iii) Entropy change for reversibly cooling the ice from 0.0°C to −10.0°C.	(r) −7.88 JK^{-1}
(iv) Entropy change of the total process	(s) −122.0 JK^{-1}

Codes

	(i)	(ii)	(iii)	(iv)
(a)	(r)	(s)	(p)	(q)
(b)	(s)	(r)	(p)	(q)
(c)	(p)	(r)	(s)	(q)
(d)	(p)	(s)	(r)	(q)

212 Match the transformation in Column I with appropriate options in Column II. ***[JEE Adv. 2011]***

Column I	Column II
(i) $CO_2(s) \longrightarrow CO_2(g)$	(p) Phase transition
(ii) $CaCO_3(s) \longrightarrow CaO(s) + CO_2(g)$	(q) Allotropic change
(iii) $2H(g) \longrightarrow H_2(g)$	(r) ΔH is positive
(iv) $P_{(\text{white, solid})} \longrightarrow P_{(\text{red, solid})}$	(s) ΔS is positive
	(t) ΔS is negative

Codes

	(i)	(ii)	(iii)	(iv)
(a)	(p, s)	(r)	(p, q)	(r)
(b)	(p, r, s)	(r, s)	(t)	(p, q, t)
(c)	(q)	(p)	(s)	(r, t)
(d)	(p, t)	(q)	(r)	(r)

213 One mole of a certain gas obeys the equation of state $p(V-b)=RT$ and has a constant molar heat capacity C_V which is independent of temperature. The parameter b is constant. Match the values of ΔH in column II with the given processes in column I and select the answer from the codes given

Column I	Column II
(i) Isothermal reversible process	(p) $C_p(T_2-T_1)+b(p_2-p_1)$
(ii) Isobaric reversible process	(q) $\frac{C_p}{R}(p_2-p_1)(V-b)+b(p_2-p_1)$
(iii) Isochoric reversible process	(r) $b(p_2-p_1)$
(iv) Adiabatic irreversible process	(s) $p(V_2-V_1)\left[\frac{C_V+R}{R}\right]$

Codes

	(i)	(ii)	(iii)	(iv)
(a)	(p)	(q)	(r)	(s)
(b)	(r)	(s)	(q)	(p)
(c)	(p)	(r)	(q)	(s)
(d)	(s)	(p)	(r)	(q)

214 28g of N_2 at 300 K is compressed reversily and adiabatically from 20 dm^3 to 10 dm^3.

Match the thermodynamic parameters given in Column I with their values in Column II and select the answer from the codes given.

Column I	Column II
(i) Final temperature in (K)	(p) Zero
(ii) q (in J)	(q) 1995
(iii) w (in J)	(r) 2794
(iv) ΔU (in J)	(s) 396
(v) ΔH (in J)	(t) 708

Codes

	(i)	(ii)	(iii)	(iv)	(v)
(a)	(p)	(q)	(s)	(r)	(t)
(b)	(t)	(s)	(p)	(q)	(r)
(c)	(s)	(p)	(q)	(q)	(r)
(d)	(p)	(r)	(q)	(s)	(t)

215 One mole of an ideal monoatomic gas ($C_V = 1.5R$) is subjected to the following sequence of steps.

(a) The gas is heated reversibly at constant pressure of 101.325×10^3 Pa from 298 K to 373 K.

(b) Next, the gas is expanded reversibly and isothermally to double its volume.

(c) Finally, the gas is cooled reversibly and adiabatically to 308 K.

Match the given thermodynamic parameters given in Column I with their corresponding values given in Column II and select the answer from the codes given.

Column I	Column II
(i) q	(p) 0.125 kJ mol^{-1}
(ii) W	(q) 3.71 kJ mol^{-1}
(iii) ΔU	(r) 0.208 kJ mol^{-1}
(iv) ΔH	(f) −3.58 kJ mol^{-1}

Codes

	(i)	(ii)	(iii)	(iv)
(a)	(p)	(q)	(s)	(r)
(b)	(q)	(s)	(r)	(p)
(c)	(q)	(s)	(p)	(r)
(d)	(r)	(s)	(p)	(q)

HINTS & EXPLANATIONS

Immediate Tests

1. $W = -p_{ext}\,(V_2 - V_1)$

$= -5.0\text{ bar }(20 - 10)\text{ L}$

$= -5 \times 10\text{ bar L}$

As $1\text{ bar} = 10^5\text{ Pa}$ and $1\text{ L} = 10^3\text{ cm}^3$

$= 10^3 \times 10^{-6}\text{ m}^3 = 10^{-3}\text{ m}^3$

$\therefore -50\text{ bar L} = -50 \times 10^5\text{ Pa} \times 10^{-3}\text{ m}^3$

$= -5000\text{ J} = -5\text{ kJ}$

■ $1\text{ L} = 10^{-3}\text{ m}^3$

2. $\underset{\substack{56\text{ g}\\=1\text{ mol}}}{Fe(s)} + 2HCl(aq) \longrightarrow FeCl_2(aq) + \underset{1\text{ mol}}{H_2(g)}$

(a) $W = -p_{ext}\,(\Delta V)$

In a closed vessel, $\Delta V = 0$

$\therefore W\ 0$

(b) $W = -p_{ext}\,(V_2 - V_1)$

$= -p_{ext}\left(\dfrac{nRT}{p_{ext}} - 0\right) = -nRT$

$= -1 \times 8.314 \times 298 = -2478\text{ J}$

3.

Reaction	Δn_g	$W = -p_{ext}(\Delta V)$	Nature
(a)	-2	$W = +$ ve	on the system
(b)	0	$W = 0$	
(c)	$+1$	$W = -$ ve	by the system
(d)	$+1$	$W = -$ ve	as in (c)
(e)	$+1.5$	$W = -$ ve	as in (c)

4. (i) (a) 4.8 g methane $= \dfrac{4.8}{16} = 0.3$ mol

$V_1 = 12.7\text{ L}$

$V_2 = 25.4\text{ L}$

$W = -p_{ext}\,(V_2 - V_1)$

$= -\dfrac{380}{760}\,(25.4 - 12.7)$

$= -6.35\text{ L atm}$

$= -6.35 \times 101.267\text{ J}$

$= -643.04\text{ J}$

■ $1\text{ L atm} = \dfrac{8.314\text{ J}}{0.0821\text{ L atm}} \times 1\text{ L atm}$

$= 101.267\text{ J}$

(b) $-W = nRT\log_e \dfrac{V_2}{V_1}$

$= 2.303\,nRT\log\dfrac{V_2}{V_1}$

$= 2.303 \times 0.3 \times 8.314 \times 310\log 2$

$= 536.04\text{ J}$

(ii) As minimum work is required, the change is reversible.

$\therefore w = -2.303\,nRT\log\dfrac{p_1}{p_2}$

$= -2.303\left(\dfrac{16}{32}\right) \times 8.314 \times 300\log\dfrac{1}{100}$

$= 5744\text{ J}$

(iii) $[H^+] = 10^{-pH}$

The production of gastric juice from body fluids is a slow process hence change may be considered as reversible process.

$\therefore W = -2.303\,nRT\log\dfrac{C_1}{C_2}$

$C_1 = 10^{-pH} = 10^{-7.4} = 10^{0.6}\,10^{-8}$

$= 4 \times 10^{-8}\text{ M}$

$C_2 = 10^{-1} = 0.1\text{ M}$

n = number of moles of H^+ present in 3 dm^3 of 0.1 M solution.

$= 3 \times 0.1 = 0.3$ mol

$W = -2.303 \times 0.3 \times 8.314 \times 310\log\dfrac{4 \times 10^{-8}}{0.1}$

$= 11393\text{ J} = 11.393\text{ kJ}$

(iv) For isothermal and reversible dilution

$W = -2.303\,nRT\log\dfrac{V_2}{V_1}$

$= -2.303\,nRT\log\dfrac{C_1}{C_2}$

$\left(\text{as } C = \dfrac{\text{mol}}{\text{Litre}},\ C \propto \dfrac{1}{V}\right)$

$C_1 = \dfrac{2\text{ mol}}{1\text{ dm}^3} = 2\text{ M},\ C_2 = 0.2\text{ M}$

$\therefore W = -2.303 \times 2 \times 8.314 \times 298\log\dfrac{2}{0.2}$

$= -11411.7\text{ J} = -11.4117\text{ kJ}$

(v) The gas is allowed to expand against a constant external pressure. Thus

$W = -p_{ext}\,(V_2 - V_1)$

$= -p_{ext}\left(\dfrac{nRT}{p_2} - \dfrac{nRT}{p_1}\right)$

$= -nRT\,p_{ext}\left(\dfrac{1}{p_2} - \dfrac{1}{p_1}\right)$

$= -5 \times 8.314 \times 300 \times 1\left[\dfrac{1}{4} - \dfrac{1}{10}\right]$

$= -1870.65\text{ J}$

$\Delta H = \Delta E = 0$ for isothermal expansion of an ideal gas

$-W = q = 1870.65\text{ J}$

5. (i) (a) For monoatomic gas,

$\gamma = \dfrac{C_p}{C_V} = \dfrac{5/2\pi}{3/2\,\pi} = \dfrac{5}{3}$

$p_1V_1^\gamma = p_2V_2^\gamma$

$\therefore \dfrac{V_1}{V_2} = \left(\dfrac{p_2}{p_1}\right)^{1/\gamma}$

Also, $\dfrac{T_2}{T_1} = \left(\dfrac{V_1}{V_2}\right)^{\gamma - 1} = \left(\dfrac{p_2}{p_1}\right)^{\gamma - 1/\gamma}$

$= \left(\dfrac{p_2}{p_1}\right)^{\left(\frac{5}{3} - 1\right)/\frac{5}{3}} = \left(\dfrac{p_2}{p_1}\right)^{\frac{2}{5}}$

$\therefore T_2 = 339\left(\dfrac{0.338}{2.44}\right)^{2/5} = 154\text{ K}$

(b) $W = -nC_V(T_2 - T_1)$

$= -1 \times \dfrac{3}{2} \times 8.314\,(154 - 339)$

$= +2307\text{ J} = 2.307\text{ kJ}$

(ii) Number of moles of CO $= \dfrac{0.14 \times 1000\text{ g}}{28\text{ g mol}^{-1}}$

$= 5.0$ mol

If, $p_1 = 3 \times 10^4\text{ Nm}^{-2}$

then, $p_2 = \dfrac{p_1}{3} = 1 \times 10^4\text{ Nm}^{-2}$

Change is adiabatic and irreversible (suddenly),

$C_V = 20.8\text{ JK}^{-1}\text{ mol}^{-1}$

$\therefore C_p = C_V + R$

$= (20.8 + 8.314)\text{ JK}^{-1}\text{ mol}^{-1}$

$\therefore T_2 = T_1\left[\dfrac{C_V + (p_2/p_1)\,R}{C_p}\right]$

$= 298\dfrac{\left[20.8 + \dfrac{1}{3} \times 8.314\right]}{[20.8 + 8.314]}$

$= 241.27\text{ K}$

Also, $\Delta E = -nC_V\,[T_2 - T_1]$

$= -5.0 \times 20.8\,[298 - 241.27]$

$= -5900\text{ J} = -5.9\text{ kJ}$

Also, $\Delta E = q + W$

and for adiabatic change, $q = 0$

$\therefore W = \Delta E = -5.9\text{ kJ}$

$\Delta H = -nC_p\,(T_2 - T_1)$

$= -5.0 \times 29.114\,(298 - 241.27)$

$= -82582\text{ J} = -8.2582\text{ kJ}$

6. (i) Gas is compressed, hence W = positive work is done on the system.
As heat is lost to the surrounding
Q = negative
$\Delta E = q + W = -128 + 462 = +334$ J

(ii) $C_6H_6(l) \rightleftharpoons C_6H_6(g)$

$n = 1$ mol $= 78$ g

q (heat supplied) $= \Delta H_V \times$ amount $= 395\ \text{Jg}^{-1} \times 78$ g $= 30810$ J $= 30.81$ kJ

$$-W = p\Delta V = p[V(\text{gas}) - V(\text{liquid})] \approx pV(\text{gas}) \text{ as } V(\text{gas}) >> V(\text{liquid}) = RT = 8.314\,(273 + 80.2) = 2936.5 \text{ J} = 2.9365 \text{ kJ}$$

$$\Delta E = q + W = (30.81 - 2.9365) \text{ kJ} = 27.8735 \text{ kJ}$$

$$\Delta H = \Delta E + p\Delta V = 27.8735 + 2.3965 = 30.27 \text{ kJ}$$

7. $W_{\text{total}} = W_{\text{useful}} + W_{\text{friction}} = 1000 \text{ J} + 0.25\, W_{\text{total}}$

$\therefore\ 0.75\, W_{\text{total}} = 1000$ J

$$\therefore \quad W_{\text{total}} = \frac{1000}{0.75} = 1333 \text{ J}$$

Also, $$\eta = \frac{W_{\text{total}}}{q_{2(\text{absorbed})}} = \frac{T_2 - T_1}{T_1}$$

$$q_2 = \frac{W_{\text{total}}}{\eta} = \frac{1333 \text{ J}}{\left(\frac{373 - 273}{373}\right)} = 4972 \text{ J}$$

8. (i) $(\Delta S)_{\text{system}}$ in case I

when heat is absorbed $= \frac{100}{298}\ \text{JK}^{-1}$

$(\Delta S)_{\text{system}}$ in case II

when heat is released $= \frac{-100}{298}\ \text{JK}^{-1}$

$\therefore \quad (\Delta S)_{\text{total}} = 0$

Entropy is a state function, because the state of the system is unchanged for the process.

$\therefore \quad \Delta S = 0$

(ii) ΔS can be calculated in two steps :

Step I. $H_2O(l, 1.01325 \text{ bar}) \longrightarrow H_2O(g, 1.01325 \text{ bar})$

$$\therefore \quad \Delta S_1 = \frac{40.668 \text{ kJ mol}^{-1}}{373 \text{ K}} = 0.109 \text{ kJ mol}^{-1}\text{ K}^{-1}$$

Step II. $H_2O(g, 1.01325 \text{ bar}) \longrightarrow H_2O(g, 0.101325 \text{ bar})$

$$\therefore \quad \Delta S_2 = 2.303\, R \log \frac{p_1}{p_2} = 2.303 \times 8.314 \log 10 = 19.147 \text{ J mol}^{-1}\text{ K}^{-1} = 0.01915 \text{ kJ mol}^{-1}\text{ K}^{-1}$$

$$\therefore\ \Delta S_{\text{Total}} = \Delta S_1 + \Delta S_2 = 0.109 + 0.01915 = 0.128 \text{ kJ mol}^{-1}\text{ K}^{-1}$$

9. When a process takes place reversibly at constant pressure

$$(\Delta S)_p = 2.303\, n\, C_p \log \frac{T_2}{T_1}$$

For diatomic gas $C_p = \frac{7}{2}R$

$$\therefore\ (\Delta S) = 2.303 \times n \times \frac{7}{2} R \log \frac{T_2}{T_1} = 2.303 \times 1 \times \frac{7}{2} \times 8.314 \log \frac{250}{300} = -5.306 \text{ JK}^{-1}$$

10. (i) $$\Delta S = n\left[C_p \ln \frac{T_2}{T_1} + R \ln \frac{p_1}{p_2}\right] = 2.303\, n\left[C_p \log_{10} \frac{T_2}{T_1} + R \log_{10} \frac{p_1}{p_2}\right]$$

$$= 2.303 \times 2\left[3.5 \times 8.314 \log \frac{400}{300} + 8.314 \log \frac{1}{5}\right] = -10.02 \text{ JK}^{-1}$$

(ii) When temperature and pressure both change,

$C_p = 3.5R$

$$\Delta S_{(\text{system})} = 2.303\, n\left[R \log \frac{p_1}{p_2} + C_p \log \frac{T_2}{T_1}\right]$$

$$= 2.303 \times 2\,[8.314 \log 4 + 3.5 \times 8.314 \log 2] = 2.303 \times 2 \times 8.314[\log 2^2 + 3.5 \log 2] = 63.4 \text{ JK}^{-1}$$

(iii) $H_2O(s, 273 \text{ K}) \longrightarrow H_2O(l, 273 \text{ K})$

$\Delta H = (5 \text{ g}) \times (334.72 \text{ Jg}^{-1}) = 1673.6$ J

If final temperature is T, then

Heat gained by ice = Heat lost by hot water

$$5 \times 334.72 + 5 \times 4.184\,(T - 273) = 30 \times 4.184\,(323 - T)$$

$T = 304.43$ K

$$\Delta S_{\text{ice}} = \frac{\Delta H_{\text{fusion}}}{T} + nC_p \text{ (molar)} \ln \frac{T_2}{T_1} = \frac{1673.6}{273} + \left(\frac{5}{18}\right)\left((4.184 \times 18) \ln \frac{304.43}{273}\right) = 8.410 \text{ JK}^{-1}$$

$$\Delta S_{\text{water}} = nC_p \text{ (molar)} \ln \frac{T_2}{T_1} = \frac{30}{18} \times 4.184 \times 18 \ln \frac{304.43}{323} = -7.434 \text{ JK}^{-1}$$

$$\Delta S_{\text{total}} = \Delta S_{\text{ice}} + \Delta S_{\text{water}} = 8.410 - 7.434 = 0.976 \text{ JK}^{-1}$$

11. (a) $$\Delta G^\circ = \Delta H^\circ - T\,\Delta S^\circ = 12 - 300 \times \frac{60}{1000} = -6 \text{ kJ mol}^{-1}$$

(b) Also $\Delta G^\circ = -2.303\, RT \log K$

$$\therefore\ -6 = -2.303 \times 8.314 \times 10^{-3} \times 300 \log K$$

$\therefore \quad \log K = 1.0445$

$\therefore \quad K = 11.08$

12. $NH_4HS(s) \rightleftharpoons NH_3(g) + H_2S(g)$

$p_{\text{total}} = p_{NH_3} + p_{H_2S} = 12$ bar

Thus, $p_{NH_3} = 6$ bar

$p_{H_2S} = 6$ bar

$\therefore\ K_{\text{eq}} = p_{NH_3} \cdot p_{H_2S} = 36\ \text{bar}^2$

$$\therefore\ \Delta G = \Delta G^\circ + 2.303\, RT \log K = 15 + 2.303 \times 8.314 \times 10^{-3} \times 298 \log 36 = 23.88 \text{ kJ mol}^{-1}$$

13. $A\,(g) + B\,(g) \longrightarrow C(g)$

$\Delta n_g = 1 - 2 = -1$

$$\Delta H = \Delta E + \Delta n_g RT = -3 + (-1) \times 0.002 \times 298 = -3.596 \text{ kcal}$$

$$\Delta G = \Delta H - T\Delta S = -3.596 - 298 \times (-10) \times 10^{-3} = -0.616 \text{ kcal mol}^{-1}$$

As $\Delta G < 0$, hence reaction is spontaneous.

14. $\Delta G^\circ = \Delta H^\circ - T\Delta S^\circ$

$-305 = -374.9 - 298\,\Delta S^\circ$

$$\therefore\ \Delta S^\circ = \frac{-374.9 + 305}{298} = -0.234 \text{ kJ mol}^{-1}\text{K}^{-1} = -234 \text{ J mol}^{-1}\text{K}^{-1}$$

15. $$\Delta H_{\text{vap}} = \frac{2.303\, RT_1T_2}{(T_2 - T_1)} \log \frac{p_2}{p_1}$$ (in temperature range, T_1 and T_2)

$$= \frac{2.303\, RT_1T_3}{(T_3 - T_1)} \log \frac{p_3}{p_1}$$ (in temperature range T_1 and T_3)

$$\therefore \quad \frac{T_2}{(T_2 - T_1)} \log \frac{p_2}{p_1} = \frac{T_3}{(T_3 - T_1)} \log \frac{p_3}{p_1}$$

$$\frac{350}{50} \log \frac{40}{20} = \frac{400}{100} \log \frac{p_3}{20}$$

$$\frac{7 \times 0.3010}{4} = \log \frac{p_3}{20}$$

$\therefore \quad p_3 = 67.3$ Torr.

16. $\Delta S = nF\left(\frac{dE_{cell}}{dt}\right)$

$\Delta S = 0.200\ JK^{-1}$

$Al_2O_3 \longrightarrow 2Al^{3+}$

$\therefore \quad n = 6$

$F = 96500$ C

$\therefore \quad 0.200 = 6 \times 96500\left(\frac{dE_{cell}}{dt}\right)$

$\therefore \quad \left(\frac{dE_{cell}}{dt}\right) = \frac{0.200}{6 \times 96500}$

$= 3.45 \times 10^{-7}\ VK^{-1}$

■ 1 J = (Coulomb × volt)

17. Following change involves three steps :

$H_2O\ (l, 263\ K) \longrightarrow H_2O\ (s, 263\ K)$

I. $H_2O(l, 263\ K, 0.287\ Pa) \longrightarrow H_2O\ (g, 263\ K, 0.287\ Pa)$

It is reversible, thus

$\Delta G_I = 0$

II. $H_2O\ (g, 263\ K, 0.287\ Pa) \longrightarrow H_2O\ (g, 263\ K, 0.260\ Pa)$

Pressure changes, thus

$$\Delta G_{II} = 2.303\ nRT \log \frac{p_2}{p_1}$$

$n = 18$ g water $= 1$ mol

$\therefore \quad \Delta G_{II} = 2.303 \times 1 \times 8.314 \times 263 \log\left(\frac{0.260}{0.287}\right)$

$= -216.07$ J

III. $H_2O(g, 263\ K, 0.260\ Pa) \longrightarrow H_2O\ (s, 263\ K, 0.260\ Pa)$

It is also reversible.

Thus, $\Delta G_{III} = 0$

$\therefore \quad \Delta G_{Total} = \Delta G_I + \Delta G_{II} + \Delta G_{III}$

$= -216.07$ J

18. (i) $n_{Total} = 20, X_A = 0.5, X_B = 0.5$

(a) $\Delta G_{mix} = 2.303\ nRT\ [X_A \log X_A + X_B \log X_B]$

$= 2.303 \times 20 \times 8.314 \times 298[0.5 \log 0.5 + 0.5 \log 0.5]$

$= -34352.6$ J

$= -34.353$ kJ

(b) $\Delta S_{mix} = -\frac{\Delta G_{mix}}{T} = \frac{34352.65\ J}{298\ K}$

$= -115.3\ JK^{-1}$

(c) $\Delta H_{mix} = 0$

(ii) For a mixture of three gases

$\chi_1 + \chi_2 + \chi_3 = 1$

$\therefore \quad \Delta G_{mix} = 2.303\ nRT\ [\chi_1 \log \chi_1 + \chi_2 \log \chi_2 + \chi_3 \log \chi_3]$

$= 2.303\ nRT\ [\chi_1 \log \chi_1 + \chi_2 \log \chi_2 + (1 - \chi_1 - \chi_2) \log (1 - \chi_1 - \chi_2)]$

For minimum value,

$$\frac{d\ (\Delta G)}{dX} = 0$$

If $\left[\frac{d(\Delta G)}{dX_1}\right]_{X_2} = 0$, then,

$$0 = 2.303\ nRT\left[\frac{\chi_1}{\chi_1} + \ln \chi_1 + 0 - 1 - \ln (1 - \chi_1 - \chi_2)\right]$$

$= \ln \chi_1 - \ln (1 - \chi_1 - \chi_2)$

$= \ln \chi_1 - \ln \chi_3$

$\therefore \quad \chi_1 = \chi_3$

Similarly, $\chi_1 = \chi_2$

Thus, $\chi_1 = \chi_2 = \chi_3$

Since, $\chi_1 + \chi_1 + \chi_1 = 1$

$\therefore \quad \chi_1 = \chi_2 = \chi_3 = \frac{1}{3}$

Knowledge Confirmation Test 1

1. (c) **2.** (b) **3.** (d) **4.** (d) **5.** (a) **6.** (c) **7.** (d) **8.** (d) **9.** (c) **10.** (b)
11. (b) **12.** (c) **13.** (a) **14.** (b) **15.** (c) **16.** (c) **17.** (c) **18.** (d) **19.** (a) **20.** (b)
21. (c) **22.** (d)

Knowledge Confirmation Test 2

1. (a) **2.** (d) **3.** (c) **4.** (b) **5.** (d) **6.** (a) **7.** (c) **8.** (b) **9.** (a) **10.** (c)
11. (c) **12.** (c) **13.** (b) **14.** (d) **15.** (c) **16.** (a) **17.** (b) **18.** (b) **19.** (a) **20.** (d)

Knowledge Confirmation Test 3

1. (a) **2.** (b) **3.** (c) **4.** (a) **5.** (b) **6.** (d) **7.** (a) **8.** (d) **9.** (b) **10.** (b)
11. (a) **12.** (a) **13.** (c) **14.** (d) **15.** (b) **16.** (c) **17.** (c) **18.** (d) **19.** (a) **20.** (c)
21. (c) **22.** (a)

Knowledge Confirmation Test 4

1. (b) **2.** (b) **3.** (c) **4.** (c) **5.** (d) **6.** (d) **7.** (c) **8.** (b) **9.** (b) **10.** (a)
11. (c) **12.** (c) **13.** (b) **14.** (a) **15.** (b) **16.** (b) **17.** (a) **18.** (a) **19.** (d) **20.** (c)
21. (a) **22.** (a)

Acid Test for JEE Main

Type I. MCQs with Only ONE Correct Alternate

1. (b) $\left(p \propto \frac{1}{V}, V \propto T\right)$

2. (b) $1 \text{ g } H_2 = \frac{1}{2} = 0.5 \text{ mol } H_2$

Volume of 1 mol at STP = 22.4 L

$\therefore \quad V_i = 11.2 \text{ L at STP}$

$V_f = 22.4 \text{ L at STP}$

$W = -p_{ext}(V_f - V_i)$

$= -1 \times 11.2 = -11.2 \text{ L atm}$

$= -11.2 \times 101.27 \text{ J} = -1.134 \text{ kJ}$

3. (c)

$$\underset{1 \text{ mol}}{Al_4C_3(s)} + 12H_2O(l) \longrightarrow 4Al(OH)_3(s) + \underset{3 \text{ mol}}{3CH_4(g)}$$

Initial volume of solid = 0

$W = -p_{ext}(V_2 - V_1)$

$W = -p_{ext}\left(\frac{nRT}{p_{ext}} - 0\right) = -nRT$

$= -3 \times 8.314 \times 10^{-3} \times 300 = -7.4826 \text{ kJ}$

In a closed vessel, volume remains constant hence, $W = -p\Delta V = 0$.

4. (c) With maximum degrees of freedom.

5. (c) Work is done by the gas formed.

$$\underset{1 \text{ mol}}{CaC_2} + 2H_2O \longrightarrow Ca(OH)_2 + \underset{1 \text{ mol}}{C_2H_2(g)}$$

$$\underset{1 \text{ mol}}{Al_4C_3} + 12H_2O \longrightarrow 4Al(OH)_3 + \underset{3 \text{ mol}}{3CH_4(g)}$$

$$\underset{1 \text{ mol}}{Mg_2C_3} + 4H_2O \longrightarrow 2Mg(OH)_2 + \underset{\substack{1 \text{ mol} \\ \text{(propyne)}}}{C_3H_4(g)}$$

C_2H_2, CH_4 and C_3H_4 are formed in 1 : 3 : 1 molar ratio from 1 mol each of CaC_2, Al_4C_3 and Mg_2C_3.

Thus, work done is in order

$CaC_2 = Mg_2C_3 < Al_4C_3$

6. (a) $W = -p_{ext}\Delta V = -p_{ext}(V_2 - V_1)$

$= -2(5-2) = -6 \text{ L bar}$

Also, $p_1V_1 = p_2V_2$ at 298 K by Boyle's law

$8 \times 2 = p_2 \times 5$

$\therefore \quad p_2 = 3.2 \text{ bar}$

7. (c) $\Delta G° = -nFE°$

$= -2 \times 96000 \times 2 \text{ J} = -384000 \text{ J}$

$= -384 \times 10^3 \text{ J} = -384 \text{ kJ}$

8. (d) It is an irreversible isothermal compression of an ideal gas.

(i) $dE = dq + p(V_f - V_i)$

where, dE = internal energy change

dq = amount of heat released

$0 = dq + p(V_f - V_i)$

[$\because dE = 0$ for an isothermal process]

$\Rightarrow dq = -4(1-5) = 16 \text{ J}$

(ii) $dq = n \times C \times \Delta T$ (for Al)

$16 \text{ J} = 1 \text{ mol} \times 24 \text{ J mol}^{-1} \text{K}^{-1} \times \Delta T$

$\Delta T = \frac{16}{24} \text{ K} = \frac{2}{3} \text{ K}$

9. (d) In the expansion, work is done by the system thus, work is negative.

$W = -p_{ext}(V_2 - V_1)$

$= -1.50(6-4) = -3.0 \text{ atm dm}^3$

$= -3.0 \times 101.27 \text{ J} = -303.81 \text{ J}$

$(1 \text{ dm}^3 \text{ atm} = 101.27 \text{ J})$

Heat absorbed = + 1000 J

$\therefore \Delta E = q + W = 1000 - 303.81$

$= +696.2 \text{ J}$

10. (b) For reversible isothermal expansion.

$W = -2.303\, nRT \log\frac{V_2}{V_1}$

$= -2.303 \times 0.04 \times 8.314 \times 310 \log\left(\frac{375}{50}\right)$

$= -208 \text{ J}$

$Q = +208 \text{ J}$

$\therefore \Delta E = q + W = 0$

11. (a) Heat is absorbed. Hence $q = +1500$ cal, work is done by expanding against surrounding

Hence, $W = +2500$ cal

$\therefore \quad \Delta E = q + W = 4000 \text{ cal}$

12. (c) $\Delta H° = \Delta U° + \Delta n_g RT$

I. $\Delta n_g = +1$

$\therefore \quad x = \Delta U° + RT_1$

$\therefore \Delta U° = x - RT_1$

II. $\Delta n_g = 0$ (solid and liquid being of negligible volume)

$\therefore \quad -y = \Delta U° + 0 \Rightarrow \Delta U° = -y$

13. (d) $\Delta_r G° = A - BT$

Also $\Delta_r G° = \Delta_r H° - T\Delta_r S°$

Thus, $A = \Delta_r H°$ (enthalpy change)

The reaction is endothermic when $\Delta_r H° > 0$

Thus, $A > 0$.

14. (a) Change is reversible and isothermal

$W = -2.303 nRT \log\frac{V_2}{V_1}$

$= -2.303 nRT \log\frac{p_1}{p_2}$

$= -2.303 \times 1 \times 8.314 \times 300 \log\frac{4}{2}$

$= -1729 \text{ J}$

■ In expansion work is done by the system, thus negative.

15. (c) As temperature increases, area under the curve increases. Greater the temperature, greater the work.

Thus, $\quad T_3 < T_2 < T_1$.

16. (a) $\Delta H°_{\text{fusion}}$ of

$NaCl = \frac{3.05 \text{ kJ}}{(5.85/58.5)} = 30.5 \text{ kJ mol}^{-1}$

$\Delta S° = \frac{\Delta H°_{\text{fusion}}}{\text{melting point}}$

$\therefore$ Melting point $= \frac{\Delta H°_{\text{fusion}}}{\Delta S°}$

$= \frac{30.5 \times 1000 \text{ J mol}^{-1}}{28.8 \text{ J mol}^{-1} \text{ K}^{-1}}$

$= 1059 \text{ K}$

17. (c) ΔS_{system} (releasing heat)

$= -\frac{2260}{273} \text{ JK}^{-1}\text{g}^{-1}$

$\Delta S_{\text{surrounding}}$ (gaining heat)

$= \frac{+2260}{273} \text{ JK}^{-1} \text{S}^{-1}$

$\therefore \Delta S_{\text{universe}} = \Delta S_{\text{system}} + \Delta S_{\text{surrounding}}$

$= 0$

18. (c) For a given value of T,

(i) If $\Delta_r G°$ becomes < 0, the forward direction will be spontaneous and then the major and minor components will be Y and X respectively.

(ii) If $\Delta_r G°$ becomes > 0, the forward direction will be non-spontaneous and then the major and minor components will be X and Y respectively.

(a) $\Delta_r G° = 120 - \frac{3}{8} \times 280 = 15$

i.e. $\Delta_r G° > O$ 0, major component $= X$;

(b) $\Delta_r G° = 120 - \frac{3}{8} \times 350 = -11.25$

i.e. $\Delta_r G° < 0$, major component $= Y$

(c) $\Delta_r G° = 120 - \frac{3}{8} \times 315 = 1.875$

i.e. $\Delta_r G° > 0$, major component $= X$

(d) $\Delta_r G° = 120 - \frac{3}{8} \times 300 = 7.5$

i.e. $\Delta_r G° > 0$, major component $= X$

19. (d) $\Delta G° = -RT \ln K$

$= -2 \times 273 \text{ cal} \ln 1.7 \times 10^{-5}$

$= -546 [\ln 1.7 + \ln 10^{-5}] \text{ cal}$

$= [-546 \ln 1.7 + 6286] \text{ cal}$

20. (b) $CaCO_3(s) \rightleftharpoons CaO(s) + CO_2(g)$

$p_{CO_2} = Q = 10 \text{ atm}$

$\therefore \quad \Delta G = \Delta G° + 2.303\, RT \log Q$

where, Q is reaction quotient

$$2.303RT \log Q = 2.303 \times 8.314 \times 10^{-3} \times 298 \log 10$$

$$\Delta G = -200 + 2.303 \times 8.314 \times 10^{-3} \times 298$$

$$= -200 + 5.7 = -194.3 \text{ kJ}$$

21 (c) At the thermal equilibrium,

final temperature, $T_f = \frac{T_1 + T_2}{2}$

for the 1st block, $\Delta S_I = C_p \ln \frac{T_f}{T_1}$

for the 2nd block, $\Delta S_{II} = C_p \ln \frac{T_f}{T_2}$

When brought in contact with each other,

$$\Delta S = \Delta S_I + \Delta S_{II}$$

$$= C_p \ln \frac{T_f}{T_1} + C_p \ln \frac{T_f}{T_2}$$

$$= C_p \ln \left(\frac{T_f}{T_1} \times \frac{T_f}{T_2} \right) = C_p \ln \left[\frac{T_f^2}{T_1 T_2} \right]$$

$$= C_p \ln \left[\frac{(T_1 + T_2/2)^2}{T_1 T_2} \right] = C_p \ln \left[\frac{(T_1 + T_2)^2}{4T_1 T_2} \right]$$

22. (a) For adiabatic expansion,

$$\left(\frac{T_2}{T_1} \right)^{C_p/R} = \left(\frac{p_2}{p_1} \right)$$

$$\left(\frac{287}{298} \right)^{C_p/R} = \left(\frac{1.0}{1.1} \right)$$

$$\frac{C_p}{R} \log \left(\frac{287}{298} \right) = \log \left(\frac{1.0}{1.1} \right)$$

$$C_p = 5.07 \text{ cal mol}^{-1}$$

23. (b) For isothermal condition,

$$pV = \text{constant} = K$$

$$p = \frac{K}{V}$$

$$\left(\frac{\partial p}{\partial V} \right)_{\text{isothermal}} = \left(\frac{\partial p}{\partial V} \right)_T$$

$$= -\frac{K}{V^2} = -\frac{pV}{V^2} = -\frac{p}{V}$$

For adiabatic condition,

$$pV^\gamma = \text{constant}$$

$$p = \frac{K}{V^\gamma} = KV^{-\gamma}$$

$$\left(\frac{\partial p}{\partial V} \right)_{\text{adiabatic}} = \left(\frac{\partial p}{\partial V} \right)_q = -\gamma KV^{-\gamma - 1}$$

$$= -\gamma \frac{K}{V^{\gamma + 1}}$$

$$= -\gamma \frac{pV^\gamma}{V^{\gamma + 1}} = -\frac{\gamma p}{V}$$

$$\frac{\left(\frac{\partial p}{\partial V} \right)_{\text{isothermal}}}{\left(\frac{\partial p}{\partial V} \right)_{\text{adiabatic}}} = \frac{1}{\gamma}$$

24. (a) The conversion of 1 kg of ice at 273 K into water vapours at 383 K takes place as follows:

$$\underset{273\text{K}}{H_2O(s)} \xrightarrow{\Delta S_1} \underset{273\text{K}}{H_2O(l)} \xrightarrow{\Delta S_2} \underset{373\text{K}}{H_2O(l)} \xrightarrow{\Delta S_3} \underset{373\text{K}}{H_2O(g)} \xrightarrow{\Delta S_4} \underset{383\text{K}}{H_2O(g)}$$

$$\Delta S_1 = \frac{\Delta H_{\text{Fusion}}}{\Delta T_{\text{Fusion}}} = \frac{334 \text{ kJ kg}^{-1}}{273 \text{ K}}$$

$$= 1.22 \text{ kJ kg}^{-1}\text{K}^{-1}$$

$$\Delta S_2 = C \ln \frac{T_2}{T_1} = 4.2 \text{ kJ K}^{-1}\text{kg}^{-1} \ln \left(\frac{373 \text{ K}}{273 \text{ K}} \right)$$

$$= 4.2 \times 2.303 (\log 373 - \log 273) \text{ kJ K}^{-1}\text{kg}^{-1}$$

$$= 4.2 \times 2.303 (2.572 - 2.436)$$

$$= 1.31 \text{ kJ K}^{-1}\text{kg}^{-1}$$

$$\Delta S_3 = \frac{\Delta H_{\text{vap.}}}{\Delta T_{\text{vap.}}} = \frac{2491 \text{ kJ kg}^{-1}}{373 \text{ K}}$$

$$= 6.67 \text{ kJ kg}^{-1}\text{K}^{-1}$$

$$\Delta S_4 = C \ln \frac{T_2}{T_1}$$

$$= 2 \text{ kJ K}^{-1}\text{kg}^{-1} \ln \left(\frac{383 \text{ K}}{373 \text{ K}} \right)$$

$$= 2 \times 2.303 (\log 383 - \log 373) \text{ kJ K}^{-1}\text{kg}^{-1}$$

$$= 2 \times 2.303 (2.583 - 2.572) \text{ kJ K}^{-1}\text{kg}^{-1}$$

$$= 0.05 \text{ kJ K}^{-1}\text{kg}^{-1}$$

$$\Delta S_{\text{Total}} = \Delta S_1 + \Delta S_2 + \Delta S_3 + \Delta S_4$$

$$= 1.22 + 1.31 + 6.67 + 0.05$$

$$= 9.26 \text{ kJ kg}^{-1}\text{K}^{-1}$$

25. (c)

	$N_2O_4(g)$ $\rightleftharpoons$	$2NO_2(g)$
Initial mol.	1	0
At equilibrium	$(1 - x)$	$2x$ [total moles $= (1 + x)$ at equilibrium]
Mole fraction	$\left(\frac{1-x}{1+x} \right)$	$\left(\frac{2x}{1+x} \right)$
Partial pressure	$\left(\frac{1-x}{1+x} \right) p$	$\left(\frac{2x}{1+x} \right) p$ [p = 1 atm]

$$K_p = \frac{p_{NO_2}^2}{p_{N_2O_4}} = \frac{4x^2 p}{(1 - x^2)}$$

$$x = 0.5 \text{ (given)}$$

$$\therefore \quad K_p = \frac{4(0.5)^2(1)}{[1 - (0.5)^2]} = 1.33$$

$$\therefore \quad \Delta G^\circ = -2.303RT \log K$$

$$= -2.303 \times 8.314 \times 10^{-3} \times 333 \log 1.33$$

$$= -0.79 \text{ kJ}$$

26. (a) Work done under adiabatic condition,

$$W = -\left(\frac{p_1V_1 - p_2V_2}{\gamma - 1} \right) \text{ for one mole of a gas}$$

$$\text{Neon} = 20 \text{ g} = \frac{20}{20} = 1 \text{ mol}$$

$$\gamma = \frac{C_p}{C_V} = 1.66 \text{ for monoatomic gas}$$

$$p_2 = p_1 \left(\frac{V_1}{V_2} \right)^\gamma = 3.5 \left(\frac{1}{2} \right)^{1.66} = 1.107 \text{ atm}$$

$$\therefore \quad W = -\left[\frac{3.5 \times 15 - 1.107 \times 30}{(1.66 - 1)} \right]$$

$$= -29.2 \text{ atm dm}^3$$

$$(1 \text{ dm}^3 \text{ atm} = 101.27 \text{ J})$$

$$= -29.2 \times 101.27 \text{ J}$$

$$= -2957 \text{ J} = -2.957 \text{ kJ}$$

27. (d) For an ideal gas $\left(\frac{\partial H}{\partial p} \right) = 0$

$$\therefore \quad \Delta H = \int_T^{T_2} nC_p dT = nC_p \Delta T$$

$$= 1 \times 2.5R \times 100 = 250 R$$

28. (b) $q = -975$ J

$$\Delta U = q + W$$

$$\Delta U = 0 \text{ in cyclic process}$$

$$0 = -975 + W$$

$$\therefore \quad W = 975 \text{ J}$$

$$W = -2.303 \, nRT \log \frac{p_1}{p_2}$$

$$975 = -2.303 \times 1 \times 8.314 \times 273 \log \frac{0.525}{p_2}$$

$$\log \frac{p_2}{0.525} = 0.1865$$

$$\frac{p_2}{0.525} = 1.536$$

$$\therefore \quad p_2 = 0.807 \text{ bar}$$

29. (a) $T\left(\frac{\partial^2 V}{\partial T^2} \right)_p = T\left[\frac{\partial}{\partial T} \left(\frac{\partial (RT/p)}{\partial T} \right)_p \right]$

$$= T\frac{\partial}{\partial T} \left(\frac{R}{p} \right)_p = 0$$

At constant temperature,

$$\therefore \quad \left(\frac{\partial C_p}{\partial p} \right)_T = 0$$

30. (a) $q = 50$ J

$$W = -100 \text{ J (by the system)}$$

$$\Delta E = q + W = 50 - 100 = -50 \text{ J}$$

$$\text{But, } C_V = \left(\frac{\Delta E}{\Delta T} \right)_V$$

$$\therefore \quad \Delta T = \left(\frac{\Delta E}{C_V} \right)$$

$$= \frac{-50 \text{ J}}{5/2R} = \frac{-50}{5/2 \times 8.314} = -2.410 \text{ °C}$$

■ For diatomic gas, $C_V = \frac{5}{2}R$

31. (a) $\Delta E = q + W$

$-225 = 154 + W$

$\therefore\ W = -225 - 154 = -379$ J

Thus, work is done by the system.

32. (d) $(\Delta E)_{A-B} = q + W$ (by the gas)

$= 5 - 8 = -3$ J

$\therefore\ (\Delta E)_{B-A} = 3$ J

$\therefore\ 3 = q + W = -3 + W$

$W = +6$ J

Thus, 6J of the work is done by the surroundings on the gas.

33. (c) $\Delta G_f^\circ (H_2) = 0$ (being element)

$\Delta G_f^\circ (Cl_2) = 0$ (being element)

$\Delta G_f^\circ (H^+) = 0$ (by convention)

Thus, $\Delta G^\circ = -262.4 = 2\Delta G_f^\circ (Cl^-)$

$\therefore\ \Delta G_f^\circ(Cl^-) = -131.2$ kJ mol^{-1}

34. (c) It involves (all processes are exothermic)

I. $H_2O(l)$ at 5°C to $H_2O(l)$ at 0°C

II. $H_2O(l)$ at 0°C to $H_2O(s)$ at 0°C

III. $H_2O(s)$ at 0°C to $H_2O(s)$ at –5°C

$\Delta H_I = -nC_p\Delta T = -1 \times 75.3 \times 5$

$= -376.5\ J = -0.3765$ kJ

$\Delta H_{II} = -n\Delta H_{fus} = -1 \times 6.0$

$= -6.0$ kJ

$\Delta H_{III} = -nC_p\Delta T = -1 \times 36.8 \times (+5)$

$= -184\ J = -0.184$ J

$\Delta H_{total} = -0.3765 - 6.0 - 0.184$

$= -6.56$ kJ

35. (b) At STP volume occupied by 0.75 mol of an ideal gas

$= 22.4 \times 0.75$ L

$V_1 = 16.8$ L

$V_2 = 33.6$ L

When work is maximum, expansion is isothermal and reversible and is negative.

$\therefore\ W = -2.303nRT \log\frac{V_2}{V_1}$

$= -2.303 \times 0.75 \times 2 \times 273 \log 2$

$= -142.0$ cal

36. (a) $\Delta G = \Delta H - T\Delta S$

At equilibrium $\Delta G = 0$

$\therefore\ T = \frac{\Delta H}{\Delta S} = \frac{30 \times 1000 \text{ J mol}^{-1}}{75 \text{ J mol}^{-1} \text{ K}^{-1}} = 400$ K

37. (b) $\Delta H = \Delta U + \Delta n\, R(T_2 - T_1)$

$= 30.0 + 1 \times 0.0821 \times (245 - 95)$

$= 42.315$ L atm

■ Since $\frac{p_1V_1}{T_1} \neq \frac{p_2V_2}{T_2}$, gas is not ideal.

38. (a) III. $C \rightleftharpoons A$, – (I + II)

$\therefore\ K_{III} = \frac{1}{K_1K_2} = \frac{1}{50} = 0.02$

$\Delta G = -(-20 - 70)$

$= +90.0$ kJ mol^{-1}

On adding, equilibrium constants are multiplied and free energies are added to get net result.

39. (d) $\Delta S = 2.303nR \log\frac{V_2}{V_1}$

$V_1 = 1$ L

$V_2 = 9$ L

$\therefore\ \Delta S = 2.303 \times 1 \times 8.314 \log\frac{10}{1}$

$= 19.15$ J K^{-1}

40. (a)

41. (a) For adiabatic process, $q = 0$

when expansion takes place, cooling takes place, thus $T_2 < T_1$

i.e. $\Delta T < 0$

$\Delta E = q + W$

$W = \Delta E$

Since temperature falls, $\Delta E < 0$

$W = -C_V\Delta T$

$= -C_V(T_2 - T_1)$

$W \neq 0$

42. (a) Being cyclic, sum of the work = 0

43. (c) $W = -p_{ext}\,\Delta V$

$= -1\,(10 - 1) = -9$ L bar

As 1 L bar $= \frac{8.314 \text{ J}}{0.0831}$

$\therefore\ W = -9 \times \frac{8.314 \text{ J}}{0.0831}$

$= -900\ J = -0.9$ kJ

44. (b) Since, process involved is

$H_2O(l) \rightleftharpoons H_2O(s), \Delta H < 0$

45. (d) C_p (CO_2, polyatomic) $= 4R$

$n = \frac{8.8}{44} = 0.2$

At constant pressure,

$(\Delta S)_p = 2.303\, nC_p \log\frac{T_2}{T_1}$

$= 2.303 \times 0.2 \times 4 \times 8.314 \log\frac{373}{273}$

$= 2.08$ J K^{-1}

46. (c) Temperature falls, hence, endothermic.

Disorder in solid state < in aqueous solution

Thus, entropy increases.

$\therefore\ \Delta S > 0$

Dissolution is spontaneous, $\Delta G < 0$

47. (c) $H_2O(l) \rightleftharpoons H_2O(s)$

$V = 1\text{ L} \Rightarrow V = \frac{\text{Mass}}{\text{Density}} = \frac{1000\text{g}}{909.09\text{gL}^{-1}}$

Mass = 1000 g = 1.1 L

$\therefore\ \Delta V = (1.1 - 1.0) = 0.1$ L

$W = -p\Delta V = -1(0.1) = -0.1$ L atm

Since 1 L atm = 101.27 J

$\therefore$ 0.1 L atm $= -0.1 \times 101.27$ J

$W = -10.127\ J = -10.13$ J

■ Due to ice formation volume increases due to air gap as a result of H-bonding

48. (d) $K_p = (p_{O_2})^{1/2}$

$\therefore\ \Delta G^\circ = -2.303RT \log K_p$

$1729 = -2.303 \times 8.314 \times 300 \log K_p$

$\log K_p = -0.3010 \quad \therefore\ K_p = 0.500$

$(p_{O_2})^{1/2} = 0.5 \quad \therefore\ p_{O_2} = 0.25$ atm

49. (b) From I $\Delta G\ (SO_2) = -\frac{544}{2}$ kJ mol^{-1}

From II. ΔG (ZnS) $= -\frac{293}{2}$ kJ mol^{-1}

From III. ΔG (ZnO) $= -\frac{480}{2}$ kJ mol^{-1}

■ ΔG (elements) = 0

$\therefore\ \Delta G = 2\Delta G(\text{ZnO}) + 2\Delta G(SO_2) - 2G(\text{ZnS})$

$= -480 - 544 - (-293)$

$= -731$ kJ

50. (d) Temperature is doubled

$\therefore\ \frac{T_2}{T_1} = 2$

Volume is halved at constant pressure,

$\therefore\ \frac{V_2}{V_1} = \frac{1}{2}$

Entropy change when temperature and volume both change, is

$\therefore\ \Delta S = nC_p \log_e\frac{T_2}{T_1} + nR\log_e\frac{V_2}{V_1}$

$= C_p \log_e 2 + R\log_e\frac{1}{2}$

$= C_p \log_e 2 - R\log 2$

$= (C_p - R)\log_e 2$

51. (d) $\Delta U_{AB} = q_{AB} + W_{AB}$

$= 2 - 5 = -3$ kJ mol^{-1}

$\Delta U_{BC} = -5$ kJ mol^{-1} (given)

For cyclic process, $\Delta U = 0$

$\therefore\ \Delta U_{AB} + \Delta U_{BC} + \Delta U_{CA} = 0$

$\Delta U_{CA} = -(\Delta U_{AB} + \Delta U_{BC})$

$= -(-3 - 5) = 8$ kJ mol^{-1}

$\Delta U_{CA} = q_{CA} + W_{CA}$

$8 = q_{CA} + 3$

$\therefore\ q_{CA} = 5$ kJ mol^{-1}

52. (b) I + 3(II) = III

$\therefore \quad \Delta G^\circ = 1487.0 + 3(-514.4)$

$= -56.2 \text{ kJ mol}^{-1}$

53. (b) (a) $\Delta S > 0$, as T increases, kinetic energy increases and randomness increases.

(b) $\Delta S > 0$, due to increases in pressure, volume decreases. Molecules come closer, disorder decreases.

(c) Randomness in graphite > diamond

$\therefore \quad \Delta S > 0$

(d) Number of atoms increases

$\therefore \quad \Delta S > 0$

54. (c) According to first law of thermodynamics,

$\Delta U = q + W = q - p\Delta V$

In isochoric process ($\Delta V = 0$), $\Delta U = q$

In isobaric process ($\Delta p = 0$), $\Delta U = q$

In adiabatic process ($q = 0$), $\Delta U = W$

In isothermal process ($\Delta T = 0$) and $\Delta U = 0$

$\therefore$ ΔU is equal to adiabatic work.

55. (d) ΔG° (reaction) $= -RT \ln K$

$= -R \times 298 \ln 1.6 \times 10^{12}$

Also, ΔG° (reaction)

$= 2\Delta G^\circ(NO_2) - [2\Delta G^\circ(NO) + \Delta G^\circ O_2]$

$-R \times 298 \ln 1.6 \times 10^{12} = 2\Delta G^\circ(NO_2) - [2 \times 86600\text{J} + 0]$

$\therefore \Delta G^\circ(NO_2)$

$$= \frac{2 \times 86600}{2} - \frac{R(298) \ln 1.6 \times 10^{12}}{2}$$

$= 86600 - 0.5R(298) \ln 1.6 \times 10^{12}$

$= 0.5\,[2 \times 86600 - R(298) \ln 1.6 \times 10^{12}]$

56. (a) As the process is carrying out at constant temperature therefore this type of expansion is called isothermal reversible expansion, for which, $\Delta U = 0$. Hence, $q = -W$, i.e. heat absorbed by the system is equal to the work done by the system.

Also, $W = -2.303nRT \log \frac{V_2}{V_1}$

$$= -2.303 \times 0.04 \times 8.314 \times 310 \log \frac{375}{50}$$

$= -208$ J

Thus, $q = +208$ J

$W = -208$ J

57. (c)

(a) According to Gibbs-Helmholtz equation,

$\Delta G = \Delta H - T\Delta S$

For a system, total entropy change

$= \Delta S_{\text{total}}$

$\Delta H_{\text{total}} = 0$

$\therefore \quad \Delta G_{\text{system}} = -T\Delta S_{\text{total}}$

$$\therefore \quad \frac{\Delta G_{\text{system}}}{\Delta S_{\text{total}}} = -T$$

Thus, (a) is correct

(b) For isothermal reversible process,

$\Delta E = 0$

By first law of thermodynamics,

$\Delta E = q + W$

$\therefore \quad W_{\text{reversible}} = -q = -\int_{V_i}^{V_f} p dV$

$$W_{\text{reversible}} = -nRT \ln \frac{V_f}{V_i}$$

Thus, (b) is correct

(c) $\Delta G^\circ = \Delta H^\circ - T\Delta S^\circ$,

Also, $\Delta G^\circ = -RT \ln K$

$$\ln K = -\frac{-\Delta G^\circ}{RT}$$

$$\Rightarrow \ln K = -\frac{(\Delta H^\circ - T\Delta S^\circ)}{RT} \quad \text{[From Eq (i)]}$$

Thus, (c) is incorrect

(d) The standard free energy (ΔG°) is related to equilibrium constant K as :

$\Delta G^\circ = -RT \ln K$

$$\ln K = -\frac{\Delta G^\circ}{RT}$$

$K = e^{-\Delta G^\circ / RT}$

58. (a) Entropy change for n moles of isothermal reversible expansion of an ideal gas from volume V_1 to volume V_2 is

$$\Delta S = 2.303nR \log \frac{V_2}{V_1}$$

Here, $n = 2$, $V_2 = 100 \text{ dm}^3$, $V_1 = 10 \text{ dm}^3$

$$= 2.303 \times 2 \times 8.3143 \log \frac{100}{10}$$

$= 38.296 \text{ J mol}^{-1} \text{ K}^{-1}$

59. (d) $PbO_2 + Pb \longrightarrow 2PbO$

Oxidation state +4 0 +2

Since $\Delta_r G^\circ < 0$, i.e it is negative. Therefore, the reaction is spontaneous in the forward direction. This suggests that Pb^{2+} is more stable than Pb^{4+}.

$SnO_2 + Sn \longrightarrow 2SnO$

Oxidation state +4 0 +2

Since, $\Delta_r G^\circ > 0$, i.e., it is positive, therefore the reaction is non-spontaneous in the forward direction. But it will be spontaneous in the backward direction. This suggests that Sn^{4+} will be more stable than Sn^{2+}. These facts are also supported by the inert pair effect which increases down the group.

60. (b) $\Delta G = \Delta H - T\Delta S$

Here, ΔG = Gibbs's free energy change,

ΔH = enthalpy change

ΔS = entropy change, T = temperature

At equilibrium, $\Delta G = 0$. Thus, $T\Delta S = \Delta H$ as ΔH and ΔS are + ve, for a reaction to be feasible (spontaneous) ΔG should be –ve. This can be possible only, when

$T\Delta S > \Delta H$ i.e. $T\Delta S > T_e\Delta S$

or $T > T_e$ [T_e = temperature at equilibrium and $\Delta S = \frac{\Delta H}{T_e}$]

61. (c) $\frac{1}{2}X_2 + \frac{3}{2}Y_2 \longrightarrow XY_3$

$\Delta S_{\text{reaction}} = S_{\text{products}} - S_{\text{reactants}}$

$$\Delta S_{\text{reaction}} = 50 - \left(\frac{3}{2} \times 40 + \frac{1}{2} \times 60\right)$$

$= -40 \text{ J mol}^{-1}$

$\Delta G = \Delta H - T\Delta S$

At equilibrium as $\Delta G = 0$

$\therefore \quad \Delta H = T\Delta S$

$$\Rightarrow \quad T = \frac{\Delta H}{\Delta S} = \frac{30 \times 10^3}{40} = 750 \text{ K}$$

62. (a) $\Delta H = n \int_{T_1}^{T_2} C_p \, dT$

$= n \int (23 + 0.01\,T)\, dT$

$$= n\left[23(T_2 - T_1) + \frac{0.01}{2}(T_2^2 - T_1^2)\right]$$

$= n(T_2 - T_1)[23 + 0.005(T_1 + T_2)]$

$= 3(700)[23 + 0.005 \times 1300]$

$= 61950 \text{ J} = 61.95 \text{ kJ} \approx 62 \text{ kJ}$

63. (c) $C_V = \left(\frac{\Delta U}{\Delta T}\right)$

$\therefore \quad \Delta U = C_V \, \Delta T$ for one mol

$= nC_V \, \Delta T$ for n mol

$= 5 \times 28 \times 100$ J

$= 14000 \text{ J} = 14 \text{ kJ}$

$\Delta(pV) = nR(\Delta T)$

$= 5 \times 8 \times 100$ J

$= 4000 \text{ J} = 4 \text{ kJ}$

64. (d) The entropy change can be given as

$$\Delta S = \frac{\Delta H}{T} \Rightarrow \Delta S = 160.2 \text{ J / K}$$

$\Rightarrow \Delta H = 179.1 \times 10^3 \text{ J / mol}^{-1}$

$$\Rightarrow \quad T = \frac{179.1 \times 10^3 \text{ J / mol}}{160.2 \text{ J / K}}$$

$= 1117.97 \text{ K} \approx 1118 \text{K}$

65. (d) We know,

$G = H - TS$

Also, $H = (U + pV)$

$\therefore \quad G = U + pV - TS$

Complete differentiation gives ,

$dG = dU + pdV + Vdp - TdS - SdT$

Also, by first law

$dU = q - W$

$= q - pdV$

$= TdS - pdV \quad \left[\because dS = \frac{q}{T}\right]$

$\therefore\ dG = TdS - pdV + pdV + Vdp - TdS - SdT$

$= Vdp - SdT$

Also by Gay-Lussac's law,

$p_2 = p_1\frac{T_2}{T_1} = 1.2 \times \frac{400}{300} = 1.6$ bar

$\therefore \int dG = V\int_{p_1}^{p_2} dp - \int_{T_1}^{T_2} S\,dT$

$= V(p_2 - p_1) - \int_{T_1}^{T_2}[3 + 10^{-2}T]dT$

$= V(p_2 - p_1) - [3\int_{T_1}^{T_2} dT + 10^{-2}\int_{T_1}^{T_2} TdT]$

$= V(p_2 - p_1) - \left[3(T_2 - T_1) + 10^{-2}\frac{(T_2^2 - T_1^2)}{2}\right]$

$= V(p_2 - p_1) - \left[3(T_2 - T_1) + 10^{-2}\frac{(T_2 + T_1)(T_2 - T_1)}{2}\right]$

$= 25[1.6 - 1.2] \times 100$ J $- \left[3(400 - 300) + \frac{10^{-2} \times 700 \times 100}{2}\right]$ J

$= 1000 - [300 + 350] = 350$ J

66. (a) $\Delta G_{mix} = nRT[X_1 \ln X_1 + X_2 \ln X_2 + X_3 \ln X_3]$

In terms of mole fractions

$X_1 + X_2 + X_3 = 1$

$\Delta G_{mix} = nRT[X_1 \ln X_i + X_2 \ln X_2 + (1 - X_1 - X_2) \ln (1 - X_1 - X_2)]$

For minimum value of ΔG_{mix},

$\left(\frac{\Delta G}{dX_1}\right)_{X_2} = 0$ and $\left(\frac{\Delta G}{dX_2}\right)_{X_1} = 0$

$\left(\frac{\Delta G_{mix}}{dX_1}\right)_{X_2} = \ln X_1 + \frac{X_1}{X_1} + 0 - \left(\frac{1 - X_1 - X_2}{1 - X_1 - X_2}\right) - \ln(1 - X_1 - X_2)$

$= \ln X_1 + 1 - 1 - \ln X_3 = 0$

$\therefore \ln X_1 = \ln X_3$

$\therefore\ X_1 = X_3$

Similarly, $X_1 = X_2$

Thus, $X_1 = X_2 = X_3 = \frac{1}{3}$

67. (c) **Step I** $H_2O(l) \longrightarrow H_2O(g)$

$p =$ 1.01325 bar   1.01325 bar

$T =$ 373 K   373 K

$\Delta H_{vap} = 40.67 \text{kJ mol}^{-1}$

$\therefore\ \Delta S_1 = \frac{\Delta H_{vap}}{T}$

$= \frac{40.67 \times 1000 \text{J mol}^{-1}}{373 \text{K}}$

$= 109.00 \text{J mol}^{-1} \text{K}^{-1}$

Step II $H_2O(g) \longrightarrow H_2O(l)$

$p =$ 1.013251 bar $\frac{1.01325}{10}$ bar

$T =$ 373 K   373 K

$\therefore\ \Delta S = 2.303 R \log \frac{p_1}{p_2}$

$= 2.303 \times 8.314 \times \log 10$

$= 19.15 \text{J mol}^{-1}\text{K}^{-1}$

$\therefore \Delta S_{Total} = \Delta S_1 + \Delta S_2$

$= 109.00 + 19.15$

$= 128.15 \text{J K}^{-1}\text{mol}^{-1}$

68. 3 mol of an ideal gas $\longrightarrow$ 3 mol of an ideal gas

$T = 300$ K   300 K

$p = 2$ bar   1 bar

$\therefore\ \Delta S_{gas} = 2.303\, nR \log \frac{p_1}{p_2}$

$= 2.303 \times 3 \times 8.314 \log 2 = 17.29 \text{JK}^{-1}$

Thus, (a) is correct.

For surrounding, T = constant

$\Delta T = 0, \Delta U = 0, p_2 = p_{ext}$

$\Delta U = q + W$

$\therefore q = -W = p\Delta V = p_{ext}(V_2 - V_1)$

$= p_2\left(\frac{nRT}{p_2} - \frac{nRT}{p_1}\right)$

$= nRT\left(1 - \frac{p_2}{p_1}\right)$

$= 3 \times 8.314 \times 300\left(1 - \frac{1}{2}\right)$

$= 3741.3$ J

$\Delta S_{surr} = \frac{-q}{T}$

$= \frac{-3741.3}{300}$

$= -12.47 \text{J K}^{-1}$

Thus, (b) is correct

$\therefore\quad \Delta S_{Total} = +4.82 \text{J K}^{-1}$

Since, $\Delta S_{Total} > 0$, the process is **irreversible.** Thus, (c) is also correct.

69. (a) At inversion temperature,

$\mu_{J.T.} = 0$

$\therefore\quad \frac{1}{C_p}\left[\frac{2a}{RT} - b - \frac{3abp}{R^2T^2}\right] = 0$

$\therefore\quad 2aRT - bR^2T^2 - 3abp = 0$

$\therefore\quad bR^2T^2 - 2aRT + 3abp = 0$

Solving this quadratic equation in T,

$T = \frac{2aR \pm \sqrt{4a^2R^2 - 12ab^2p}}{2bR^2}$

$= \frac{2aR \pm 2R\sqrt{a^2 - 3ab^2p}}{2bR^2}$

$= \frac{a \pm \sqrt{a^2 - 3ab^2p}}{bR}$

70. (b) For an adiabatic irreversible process,

$dU = -p_{ext}dV$

But, $\left(\frac{dU}{dT}\right) = nC_V$

$\therefore\quad dU = nC_VdT = nC_V[T_2 - T_1]$

$\therefore\quad nC_V[T_2 - T_1] = -p_{ext}[V_2 - V_1]$

$= -p_{ext}\left[\frac{nRT_2}{p_2} - \frac{nRT_1}{p_1}\right]$

$\therefore 1.5[T_2 - 298]$

$= -1.013 \times 10^5\left[\frac{T_2}{1.013 \times 10^5} - \frac{298}{1.013 \times 10^6}\right]$

$1.5[T_2 - 298] = -\left(T_2 - \frac{298}{10}\right)$

$T_2 = 190.7 \approx 191$ K

Acid Test for JEE Advanced

Type I. MCQs with Only One Correct Alternate

71. (c) When T is constant $\Delta E = 0$

By first law of thermodynamics

$\Delta E = q + W$

$\therefore q = -W$

$= -p\Delta V = -p(V_2 - V_1)$

$= -1$ atm $(10 - 1)$ L $= -9$ L atom

$= -9 \times 101.27$ J (1 L atm = 101.27J)

$= -911.4$ J

Thus, heat absorbed = 911.4 J

$\Delta S = 2.303\, nR \log \frac{V_2}{V_1}$

$= 2.303 \times 0.5 \times 8.314 \log \frac{10}{1}$

$= 9.57$ J

72. (d) $\Delta S = 2.303\, n\left[V \log \frac{T_2}{T_1} + R \log \frac{V_2}{V_1}\right]$

$= 2.303 \times 1[1.5R \log 2 + R \log 2]$

$= 2.303 \times 2.5R \log 2$

$= 2.303 \times 2.5 \times 8.314 \log 2$

$= 14.41 \text{ J mol}^{-1}\text{K}^{-1}$

73. (b) Work = heat absorbed

$= p(V_2 - V_1) = 2(V_2 - 43.2)$ L atm

$975 \text{ J} = 2(V_2 - 43.2) \times 101.27$ J

$\therefore\quad V_2 = 48.0142$ L

Since, $p_1V_1 = p_2V_2$

$\therefore\quad p_2 = \frac{p_1V_1}{V_2} = \frac{0.525 \times 43.2}{48.0142}$ atm

$= 0.472$ atm

■ 1L atm = 101.27J

74. (d) Entropy change of mixing n_1 moles of gas (1) with n_2 moles of gas (2) is

$$\Delta S = -2.303R\,[n_1 \log \chi_1 + n_2 \log \chi_2]$$

χ_1 = mole fraction of gas (1)

χ_2 = mole fraction of gas (2)

Since, $pV = nRT$

$\therefore$ $V \propto n$

$\therefore$ Also, $n = \dfrac{pV}{RT}$

$$n_1(N_2) = \frac{pV}{RT} = \frac{0.550 \times 10}{0.0821 \times 300} = 0.223 \text{ mol}$$

$$n_2(N_2O) = \frac{0.550 \times 3.50}{0.0821 \times 300} = 0.0782 \text{ mol}$$

$n(\text{total}) = 0.3012$ mol

$$\chi_1(N_2) = \frac{0.223}{0.3012} = 0.74$$

$$\chi_2(N_2O) = 1 - \chi_1 = 0.26$$

$$\therefore \Delta S_{mix} = -2.303 \times 8.314\,[0.223 \log 0.74 + 0.0782 \log 0.26] = 1.43 \text{JK}^{-1}$$

75. (a) $p_A = \dfrac{nRT}{V} = RT$

$$p_B = \frac{nRT}{V} = \frac{3RT}{2}$$

Total volume = 3 L,

pressure due to mixing of ideal gas

$$p_A V_A = p'_A V_{total}$$

$$\therefore \frac{p_A}{p'_A} = \frac{V_{total}}{V_A} = \frac{3}{1}$$

Similarly, $\dfrac{p_B}{p'_B} = \dfrac{3}{2}$

$$\Delta S = n_A R \ln \frac{p_A}{p'_A} + n_B R \ln \frac{p_B}{p'_B}$$

$$= R \ln 3 + 3R \ln 1.5$$

$$\Delta S = R \ln 3 + 3R \ln 3 - 3R \ln 2$$

$$= 4R \ln 3 - 3R \ln 2$$

$$= R \ln 3^4 - R \ln 2^3$$

$$= R\,[\ln 81 - \ln 8]$$

76. (a) $\Delta H = \Delta U + p\Delta V$

$\therefore \Delta U = \Delta H - p\Delta V$

$\Delta V = V(CO) - [V(C) + V(CO_2)]$

Since, $pV = nRT$ for ideal gas

$\therefore$ $V = \dfrac{nRT}{p}$

For species is solid state :

$$\frac{\text{Mass}}{\text{Volume}} = \text{Density}$$

$$\therefore \text{Volume} = \frac{\text{Mass}}{\text{Density}}$$

$$\therefore \Delta V = \frac{2RT}{p} - \left[\frac{12 \text{ g mol}^{-1}}{2.25 \text{ g cm}^{-3}} + \frac{RT}{p}\right]$$

$$= \frac{RT}{p} - \frac{12}{2.25} \text{cm}^3 \text{mol}^{-1}$$

$$= \left(\frac{0.0831 \times 300}{1} - \frac{12}{2.25} \times 10^{-3}\right) \text{L mol}^{-1}$$

$$= (24.93 - 5.33 \times 10^{-3} \text{L}) = 24.925 \text{ L}$$

$$\therefore p\Delta V = 24.925 \times 1 \text{ bar L}$$

$$= 24.925 \times 100.0 \text{ J}$$

$$= 249.25 \text{ J} \approx 2.5 \text{ kJ}$$

$$\therefore \Delta U = \Delta H - p\Delta V$$

$$= (172 - 2.5) = 169.5 \text{ kJ}$$

■ 1 L bar = 100.0 J

77. (c) $\Delta E = q + W$

Work is done by the system hence, negative

$\therefore \Delta E = 50 - 100 = -50$ J

Heat capacity $\left(\dfrac{\Delta E}{\Delta T}\right)_V = C_V$

$$= \frac{5}{2}R \text{ for diatomic gas}$$

$$\therefore \Delta T = \frac{\Delta E}{C_V} = \frac{-50 \text{ J mol}^{-1}}{\frac{5}{2}(8.314 \text{ J mol}^{-1} \text{ K}^{-1})}$$

$$= -2.41^\circ$$

Temperature decreases by 2.41°.

78. (a) For an ideal gas $\left(\dfrac{\partial U}{\partial V}\right) = 0$

$$\therefore \Delta U = n\int_{T_1}^{T_2} C_V\, dT$$

$$= n\,C_V(T_2 - T_1) = 1 \times \frac{5}{2}R\,(T_2 - T_1)$$

$$= 2.5 \times 8.314 \times 10^{-3}\,(100)$$

$$= 2.078 \text{ kJ}$$

79. (c) For a reversible isothermal expanstion of an ideal gas

$$\left(\frac{\partial U}{\partial V}\right)_T = \left(\frac{\partial H}{\partial p}\right)_T = 0$$

$$\Delta V = \Delta H = 0$$

$$\frac{p_1}{p_2} = \frac{V_2}{V_1} = 1.51$$

By first law,

$$\Delta U = q + W$$

$$\therefore q = -W$$

$$W = -2.303\, nRT \log \frac{V_2}{V_1}$$

$$= -2.303\, nRT \log \frac{p_1}{p_2}$$

$$= -2.303 \times 2 \times 8.314 \times 298 \log 1.51$$

$$= -2042 \text{ J}$$

80. (b) $\mu_{JT} = \left(\dfrac{\partial T}{\partial p}\right)_n = \dfrac{24.95 - 25.00}{1.00 - 2.00}$

$$= \frac{0.05}{1} = 0.05 \text{ K bar}^{-1}$$

81. (c) $H_2O(l) \rightleftharpoons H_2O(s)$ (reverse of fusion)

273 K   273 K

$$\Delta H^\circ = -6.0 \text{ kJ mol}^{-1}$$

Heat to be removed each second from 1 g water $\left(\dfrac{1}{18} \text{mol}\right)$

$$= \frac{6}{18} \times 1000 \text{ J} = 333 \text{ Js}^{-1}$$

Efficiency of the refrigerator

$$\left(\frac{T_2 - T_1}{T_2}\right) = \frac{298 - 273}{273} = 0.0952$$

Thus, $\dfrac{W}{\text{Heat absorbed}} = 0.0952$

$$W = 333 \times 0.0952 = 31.7 \text{ J}$$

82. (b)

$$\Delta S = 2.303 nR \log \frac{V_2}{V_1} + 2.303\, nC_V \log \frac{T_2}{T_1}$$

$[V_1 = V_2$ (constant V)]

$$C_V = \frac{3}{2}R \text{ for monoatomic gas}$$

$$\because (\Delta S)_V = 2.303\, nC_V \log \frac{T_2}{T_1}$$

$$= 2.303 \times 1 \times 1.5 \times 8.314 \log \frac{273}{298}$$

$$= -1.09 \text{JK}^{-1} \text{mol}^{-1}$$

83. (a) ΔS_I (under isochoric condition)

$C_V = 5/2R$ for diatomic gas

$$\Delta S_1 = 2.303 nC_V \log \frac{T_2}{T_1}$$

$$= 2.303 \times C_V \log \frac{150}{300}$$

ΔS_{II} (under isobaric condition)

$$= 2.303\, nC_p \log \frac{T_2}{T_1}$$

$$= 2.303 \times C_p \log \frac{150}{300}$$

$$\therefore d(\Delta S) = (\Delta S_I - \Delta S_{II})$$

$$= 2.303(C_V - C_p) \log \frac{1}{2}$$

$$= 2.303(C_p - C_V) \log 2$$

$$= 2.303 \times R \log 2 = 0.693R$$

84. (d) $d(\Delta S) = 2.303n(C_p - C_V)\log \dfrac{T_2}{T_1}$ as calculated above

$(C_p - C_V) = R$ for each type of gas.

Thus, $d(\Delta S)$ equal.

85. (b) Volume of the flask A

$$(V_A) = \frac{nRT}{p_A} = \frac{0.0831 \times 298}{4} \text{L}$$

that of the flask $B = \dfrac{0.0831 \times 298}{2}$ L

Total volume = $0.0831 \times 298 \times 0.75$ L

On mixing final pressure $= \frac{nRT}{V}$

$= \frac{2 \times 0.0831 \times 298}{0.0831 \times 298 \times 0.75} = 2.67$ bar

$\therefore$ For flask A,

$(\Delta S)_A = 2.303 nR \log \frac{p_1}{p_2}$

$= 2.303 \times 1 \times 8.314 \log \frac{4.0}{2.67}$

Similarly, for flask B,

$(\Delta S)_B = 2.303 \times 1 \times 8.314 \log \frac{2.0}{2.67}$

$(\Delta S)_{total} = 2.303 \times 8.314 [\log 4 - \log 2.67 + \log 2 - \log 2.67]$

$= 2.303 \times 8.314 [3 \log 2 - 2 \log 2.67]$

$= 0.96 \text{ JK}^{-1}$

86. (c) The final temperature in this case will be

$= \frac{373 + 273}{2}$

$T_{final} = 323$ K

$(\Delta S)_{hot} = 2.303\, n\, C_p \log \frac{T_{final}}{T_{hot}}$

$= 2.303 \times 1 \times C_p \log \frac{323}{373}$

and $(\Delta S)_{cold} = 2.303\, C_p \log \frac{323}{273}$

$(\Delta S)_{total} = 2.303\, C_p \left[\log \frac{323}{373} + \log \frac{323}{273} \right]$

$= 2.303\, C_p\, [\log (323)^2 - \log (373 \times 273)]$

$= 2.303 \times 24.35\, [5.02 - 5.01] = 0.56 \text{ JK}^{-1}$

87. (a) $\chi_1 = \left(\frac{n_1}{n_1 + n_2} \right), \chi_2 = \left(\frac{n_2}{n_1 + n_2} \right)$

$\Delta S_{mix} = -R\, [n_1 \ln \chi_1 + n_2 \ln \chi_2]$

Multiply and divide by $(n_1 + n_2)$

$\therefore \Delta S_{mix} = -R(n_1 + n_2)$

$\left[\frac{n_1}{n_1 + n_2} \ln \chi_1 + \frac{n_2}{n_1 + n_2} \ln \chi_2 \right]$

$-R(n_1 + n_2)[\chi_1 \ln \chi_1 + x_2 \ln \chi_2]$

$= -R(n_1 + n_2)\, [\chi_1 \ln \chi_1 + (1 - \chi_1) \ln(1 - \chi_1)]$

$\therefore$ For maximum value of ΔS_{mix}

$\frac{d(\Delta S_{mix})}{d\chi} = 0$

$\therefore \quad \frac{d\Delta S_{mix}}{dX_1} = -R\, (n_1 + n_2)$

$\left[\frac{\chi_1}{\chi_1} + \ln \chi_1 - \left(\frac{1 - \chi_1}{1 - \chi_1} \right) - \ln\, (1 - \chi_1) \right]$

$0 = -R\, (n_1 + n_2)[1 + \ln \chi_1 - 1 - \ln\, (1 - \chi_1)]$

$\therefore \quad \chi_1 = 0.5$

88. (b)

$\Delta S_{mix} = -R(n_1 + n_2)\, [\chi_1 \ln \chi_1 + \chi_2 \ln X_2]$

$(n_1 + n_2) = 1$

$\chi_1(N_2) = 0.79$

$\chi_2(O_2) = 0.21$

$\therefore \quad \Delta S_{mix} = -8.314\, [0.79 \ln 0.79 + 0.21 \ln 0.21]\ \text{JK}^{-1}$

$= -8.314\, [-0.186 - 0.328]$

$= 4.27 \text{ JK}^{-1}$

89. (d) $\Delta G° = \Delta H° - T\Delta S°$

$= \left(+102.303 - 1000 \times \frac{100}{1000} \right)$ kJ

$= 2.303$ kJ $= 2303$ J

Also, $\Delta G° = -2.303\, RT \log K$

$\therefore \quad 2303 = -2.303 \times 8.314 \times 1000 \log K$

$\log K = \frac{1}{8.314}$

90. (c) For an adiabatic irreversible compression,

$dU = -p_{ext} dV = -p_{ext}\, (V_2 - V_1)$

Also, $\frac{dU}{dT} = C_V \left(C_V = \frac{5}{2} R \text{ for } N_2 \right)$

$\therefore \quad dU = C_V dT = C_V\, (T_2 - T_1)$

and $V = nRT / p$

$\therefore C_V\, (T_2 - T_1) = -p_{ext} \left(\frac{RT_2}{p_2} - \frac{RT_1}{p_1} \right)$

In the given case, $p_2 = p_{ext}$

$\therefore C_V(T_2 - T_1) = -p_2 \left(\frac{RT_2}{p_2} - \frac{RT_1}{p_1} \right)$

$= -RT_2 + \frac{RT_1 p_2}{p_1}$

$\frac{5}{2} R\, (673 - 373) = -R \times 673 + \frac{R \times 373 p_2}{1.013 \times 10^5}$

$\frac{(750 + 673) \times 1.013 \times 10^5}{373} = p_2$

$\therefore \quad p_2 = 3.865 \times 10^5$ pa

91. (a) $H_2O_2(g, p) \rightleftharpoons H_2O_2(g, 1\text{bar})$

$\Delta G° = -2.303 RT \log \frac{V_2}{V_1}$

$= 2.303 RT \log \frac{p_1}{p_2}$

$14.78 = -2.303 \times 8.314 \times 10^{-3} + 298 \log p$

$\log p = -2.59$

$p = 2.57 \times 10^{-3}$ bar

92. (d) $\Delta H°$ and $\Delta S°$ are temperature independent in the given temperature range.

$\Delta G° = \Delta H° - T\Delta S°$

$\therefore (\Delta S°)_{300} = \frac{\Delta H° - \Delta G°}{T} = \frac{-41.8 + 66.9}{300}$

$= \frac{25.1}{300} \text{ kJ K}^{-1}\text{mol}^{-1}$

$\therefore \quad \Delta G°_{330} = -41.8 - 330 \frac{(25.1)}{300}$

$= -69.41 \text{ kJ mol}^{-1}\text{K}^{-1}$

93. (a) Gas is being expanded against external pressure

Thus, work is done by the system and is negative

$W = p_{ext}\, (V_2 - V_1)$

$= -p_{ext} \left(\frac{nRT}{p_2} - \frac{nRT}{p_1} \right)$

$= -nRT\, p_{ext} \left(\frac{1}{p_2} - \frac{1}{p_1} \right)$

$= -5 \times 0.0821 \times 300 \times 1 \left(\frac{1}{4} - \frac{1}{10} \right)$

$= -18.4725$ L atm

$= -18.4725 \times 101.267$ J

$= -1870.6$ J

■ 1 L atm = 101.267 J

94. (a) $W = -p_{ext}\, (V_2 - V_1)$

Since, $\frac{\text{mass}}{\text{volume}} = \text{density } (d)$

$\therefore \quad V = \frac{\text{mass}}{\text{density}} = \frac{\text{g}}{\text{g cm}^{-3}} = \text{cm}^3$

Mass = 1 mol = 18 g

$\therefore W = -1.0 \text{ bar} \left[\frac{18}{1} - \frac{18}{0.915} \right] \text{cm}^3$

$= +1.672 \text{ bar cm}^3$

$= 1.672 \times 10^{-3} \text{ bar dm}^3$

$W = 1.672 \times 10^{-3} \times 100 \text{ J} = 0.167\text{J}$

■ 1 L bar ≈ 100 J

95. (d) Heat absorbed = 1440 cal

$\therefore \Delta H = +1440$ cal

$\Delta V = (0.0180 - 0.0196) = -0.0016$ L

$\therefore p\Delta V = +1 \text{ atm } (-0.0016 \text{ L})$

$= -0.0016$ L atm

$= -0.0016 \times \frac{1.987}{0.0821}$

$= -0.04$ cal

$\therefore \quad \Delta H = \Delta E + p\Delta V$

$\Delta E = \Delta H - p\Delta V$

$= 1440 - (-0.04) = 1440.04$ cal

■ 1 L atm = 24.20 cal

96. (c) $W = -2.303\, nRT \log \frac{V_2}{V_1}$

Initially, $nRT = pV = 10 \times 2 = 20$ L atm

$W = -2.303 \times 20 \log \frac{10}{2}$

$= -32.2 \text{ L atm} = -32.2 \times 101.27\text{J}$

$= -3260.9$ J

■ 1 L atm = 101.27 J

97. (a) For adiabatic change,

$\frac{T_2}{T_1} = \left(\frac{p_2}{p_1} \right)^{R/C_p}$

$\therefore \quad \log\frac{T_2}{T_1} = \frac{R}{C_p}\log\left(\frac{p_2}{p_1}\right)$

$\log\left(\frac{287}{298}\right) = \frac{8.314}{C_p}\log\frac{1.0}{1.1}$

$\therefore \quad C_p = 21.07 \text{ J mol}^{-1}\text{K}^{-1}$

98. (b) $q = -50$ J

$W = +20$ (as done on the system)

$\Delta E = q + W$

$= -50 + 20 = -30$ J

99. (a) Dilution is done gradually, hence reversible.

$W = -2.303nRT\log\frac{V_2}{V_1}$,

concentration $= \frac{\text{mol}}{\text{litre}}$

$\therefore \quad V \propto \frac{1}{C}$

$C_1 = \frac{2 \text{ mol}}{1 \text{ dm}^3} = 2\text{M}$

$\therefore \quad \frac{V_2}{V_1} = \frac{C_1}{C_2} = \frac{2}{0.2} = 10$

$W = -2.303 \times 2 \times 8.314 \times 10^{-3} \times 298 \log 10$

$W = -11.41$ kJ

100. (a) $q = 50$ J (heat is gained)

$W = -100$ J

(work is done by the system)

$\therefore \quad \Delta E = q + W$

$= 50 - 100 = -50 \text{ Jmol}^{-1}$

$\left(\frac{\Delta E}{\Delta T}\right)_V = C_V$

$\therefore (\Delta T) = \left(\frac{\Delta E}{C_V}\right) = \frac{-50}{\frac{5}{2}R} = -\frac{20}{R}$

$= \frac{-20}{8.314} = -2.41°$

Thus, cooling takes place by 2.41°

■ For diatomic gas, $C_V = \frac{5}{2}R$

101. (c) $G = H - TS$

$G = (E + pV) - TS$

Complete differentiation gives,

$dG = dE + pdV + Vdp - TdS - SdT$

By first law.

$dE = q + W = q - pdV$

and $\frac{q}{T} = dS$

$\therefore \quad dE = TdS - pdV$

$\therefore \quad dG = TdS - pdV + pdV + Vdp - TdS - SdT$

$dG = Vdp - SdT$

$(dG)_T = Vdp$ at T = constant

$\Delta G = V\Delta p$

For graphite $G_{gr} - G^\circ_{gr} = V_{gr}\Delta p$

For diamand, $G_d - G^\circ_d = V_d\Delta p$

$(V_d - V_{gr})\Delta p = (G^\circ_{gr} - G^\circ_d) + (G_d - G_r)$

At equilibrium, $G_d = G_{gr}$

$\therefore (V_{gr} - V_d)\Delta p = (G^\circ_d - G^\circ_{gr}) = 2.9 \times 10^3$ J

$\Delta p = \frac{2.9 \times 10^3}{2 \times 10^{-6}}$ Pa

$= 1.45 \times 10^9$ Pa

$= 1.45 \times 10^4$ bar

$\therefore \quad p = p_0 + 14500 \text{ bar} = 14501$ bar

102. (b) $\Delta S^\circ_{\text{vap}} = \frac{\Delta H^\circ_{\text{vap}}}{T} = \frac{39.4 \times 10^3}{298}$

$= 132.2 \text{JK}^{-1} \text{ mol}^{-1}$

$\therefore \Delta S^\circ_{\text{equilibrium}} = \Delta S^\circ_{\text{vap}} + \Delta S^\circ_{\text{equlibrium}}$

$= 132.2 + 216.0$

$= 348.2 \text{ JK}^{-1}\text{mol}^{-1}$

103. (a) $\Delta S^\circ = 2S^\circ[H_2O] - [2S^\circ(H_2) + S^\circ(O_2)]$

$= 2 \times 69.91 - [2 \times 130.68 + 205.14]$

$= -326.68 \text{ J K}^{-1}$

$= -0.327 \text{ kJ K}^{-1}$

$\Delta H^\circ = -285.83 \times 2 = -571.66$ kJ

$\therefore \quad \Delta G^\circ = \Delta H^\circ - T\Delta S^\circ$

$= -571.66 - 298 \times (-0.327)$

$= -474.3$ kJ

104. (c) Efficiency

$= \frac{\text{area of the closed cycle}}{\text{total area under the curve}} \times 100$

Area of the closed cycle $= \frac{1}{2}(PR) \times (PQ)$

$= \frac{1}{2}(450 - 300)(300 - 200)$

$= 7500 \text{ JK}^{-1}\text{K} = 7500$ J

Area under the curve

= Area of the closed cycle

+ area of the rectangle

$= 7500 \text{ J} + 200 \times 150$ J

$= 7500 + 30000 \text{ J} = 37500$ J

$\therefore \quad \eta = \frac{7500}{37500} \times 100 = 20.0\%$

105. (a) $\Delta G = \Delta G^\circ + 2.303\, RT \log Q$

where, Q is reaction quotient

$Q = p_{CO_2} = 0.02$ atm

$\therefore \quad \Delta G^\circ = \Delta H^\circ - T\Delta S^\circ$

$= 177.9 - 298 \times 161 \times 10^{-3}$kJ

$= 130.0$ kJ

$\therefore \quad \Delta G = 130.0 + 2.303 \times 8.314 \times 10^{-3} \times 298 \log 0.02$

$= 130.0 - 9.7 = 120.3 \text{ kJ mol}^{-1}$

106. (b) There is change in pressure and temperature both, thus

$\Delta S = 2.303\, nR\log\frac{p_1}{p_2} + 2.303\, n\, C_p \log\frac{T_2}{T_1}$

$= 2.303 \times 5 \times 8.314 \log\frac{1}{5}$

$+ 2.303 \times 5 \times 29.08 \log\frac{390}{300}$

$= -66.92 + 38.15$

$= -28.77 \text{ J mol}^{-1}\text{ K}^{-1}$

107. (d) Heat absorbed = work

$= 2.303\, nRT\log\frac{V_2}{V_1}$

$= 2.303 \times 1 \times 8.314 \times 1000 \log 10$

$= 19147 \text{ J} = 19.147$ kJ

Efficiency $(\eta) = \frac{T_2 - T_1}{T_2} = \frac{1000 - 300}{1000} = 0.7$

Also, $\eta = \frac{\text{work}}{\text{heat absorbed}}$

$\therefore$ work $= \eta \times$ heat absorbed

$= 0.7 \times 191.47 \text{ kJ} = 13.403$ kJ

108. (c) $\Delta G^\circ = \Delta H^\circ - T\Delta S^\circ$

$\Delta G^\circ = 100 - 298 \times \frac{160}{1000}$

$= 100 - 47.68 = 52.32 \text{ kJ mol}^{-1}$

$\Delta G^\circ > 0$

Thus, non-spontaneous at 298 K.

Thus, (a) is incorrect.

If T is decreased, ΔG° becomes more positive, hence, backward reaction is favoured.

Thus, (b) is incorrect.

The reaction is spontaneous, if $\Delta G^\circ < 0$

i.e. $\quad T\Delta S^\circ > \Delta H^\circ$

$T > \frac{\Delta H^\circ}{\Delta S}$

$T > \frac{100 \times 1000}{160}$

$T > 625$ K

Thus, reaction is spontaneous at a temperature above 625 K.

109. (a) $\Delta H = \Delta E + p\Delta V$

$\Delta H = \Delta E - W$

$\therefore \quad \Delta E = \Delta H + W$

Water vaporesed $= 10\text{g} = \frac{10}{18}$ mol

$W = -nRT$

$= -\left(\frac{10}{18}\right) \times 8.314 \times 10^{-3} \times 373$

$= -1.72$ kJ

$\Delta H = 22.2$ kJ

$\therefore \quad \Delta E = 22.20 - 1.72 = 20.48$ kJ

110. (d) $\Delta H = \Delta E + p\Delta V$

1 mole = 100 g $CaCO_3$

ΔV = volume of aragonite − volume of calcite

$$= \left(\frac{\text{mass}}{\text{density}}\right)_{\text{calcite}} - \left(\frac{\text{mass}}{\text{density}}\right)_{\text{aragonite}}$$

$$= 100\left[\frac{1}{2.93} - \frac{1}{2.71}\right]$$

$$= -2.77 \text{ cm}^3$$

$$= -2.77 \times 10^{-3} \text{ L mol}^{-1}$$

$$\therefore p\Delta V = 1 \times (-2.77 \times 10^{-3}) \text{ bar L}$$

$$= -2.77 \times 10^{-3} \times 100 \text{ J}$$

$$= -0.277 \text{ J} = -0.0003 \text{ kJ}$$

$$\Delta H = \Delta E + p\Delta V$$

$$= 0.21 - 0.0003 \text{ kJ} \approx 0.21 \text{ kJ}$$

■ 1 L bar = 100 J

111. (a) For diatomic gas, $\gamma = \frac{C_p}{C_V} = 1.4$

$$p_1V_1^\gamma = p_2V_2^\gamma$$

$$\therefore \quad p_2 = p_1\left(\frac{V_1}{V_2}\right)^\gamma = 1 \text{ atm}$$

$$\left(\frac{25}{1}\right)^{1.4} = 1(5)^{2.8}$$

$$p_2 = 90.6 \text{ atm}$$

Also, $\frac{T_2}{T_1} = \left(\frac{V_1}{V_2}\right)^{\gamma-1} = \left(\frac{25}{1}\right)^{1.4-1} = (25)^{0.4}$

$$T_2 - T_1(5)^{0.8} = 298 \times 3.624 = 1080.0 \text{ K}$$

112. (b) This is an isobaric adiabatic expansion against constant external pressure, but overall pressure decreases (volume increases, gas expands). For diatomic gas, $C_V = \frac{5}{2}R$

$$T_2 = T_1\left[\frac{C_V + p_{\text{ext}}\frac{R}{p_1}}{C_V + p_{\text{ext}}\frac{R}{p_2}}\right]$$

$$= 298\left[\frac{\frac{5}{2}R + \frac{R}{15}}{\frac{5}{2}R + \frac{R}{2.5}}\right] = 263.7 \text{ K}$$

$$\therefore \quad T_2 - T_1 = 24.3°$$

113. (c) $W = -p\Delta V = -p(V_2 - V_1)$

$$V_2 = \frac{nRT}{p_2}$$

$$V_1 = \frac{nRT}{p_1}$$

$$\therefore \quad \Delta V = nRT\left[\frac{1}{p_2} - \frac{1}{p_1}\right]$$

$$W = -1 \times 0.15 \times 0.0821 \times 294\left(\frac{1}{1} - \frac{1}{10}\right)$$

$$= -3.26 \text{ dm}^3 \text{ atm}$$

$$= -3.26 \times 101.27 = -330.14 \text{ J}$$

■ 1 dm^3 atm = 101.27 J

114. (d) $V_{\text{initial}} = \frac{nRT}{p}$

$$= \frac{0.150 \times 0.0821 \times 294}{5} \text{ dm}^3$$

$$V_{\text{final}} = \frac{nRT}{p}$$

$$= \frac{0.150 \times 0.0821 \times 294}{1} \text{ dm}^3$$

$$\Delta V = 0.150 \times 0.0821 \times 294\left[\frac{1}{1} - \frac{1}{5}\right] \text{ dm}^3$$

$$= 2.90 \text{ dm}^3$$

Work done, when external pressure is held at 5 atm = − 5 × 2.90

$$= -14.50 \text{ dm}^3 \text{ atm}$$

$$= -14.50 \times 101.27 \text{ J}$$

$$= -1468.41 \text{ J}$$

Work done, when external pressure is held at 1 atm = − 1 × 2.90

$$= -2.90 \text{ dm}^3 \text{ atm}$$

$$= -2.90 \times 101.27 \text{ J}$$

$$= -293.68 \text{ J}$$

$\therefore$ Total work = − (1468.41 + 293.68) J

$$= -1762.1 \text{ J} = -1.762 \text{kJ}$$

115. (a) I : $W_{\text{rev}} = -2.303\, nRT \log\frac{V_2}{V_1}$

$$= -2.303\, nRT \log\frac{p_1}{p_2}$$

$$= -2.303 \times 1 \times 8.314 \times 10^{-3} \times 300 \log 10$$

$$= -5.744 \text{ kJ}$$

II : $W = -p_{\text{ext}}(V_2 - V_1)$

$$= -p_{\text{ext}}\left(\frac{nRT}{p_2} - \frac{nRT}{p_1}\right)$$

$$= -nRT\, p_{\text{ext}}\left[\frac{1}{p_2} - \frac{1}{p_1}\right]$$

$$= -1 \times 0.0821 \times 1 \times 300\left[\frac{1}{1} - \frac{1}{10}\right] \text{ L-atm}$$

$$= -22.167 \text{ L atm}$$

$$= -22.167 \times 101.27 \text{ J} = -2.24 \text{ kJ}$$

III. $W = 0$ in free expansion, when $p = 0$.

116. (a) V_1 (initial volume) = 0.500 dm^3

Volume swept by piston when moved to $A'B'$ = 50 cm^2 × 10 cm

$$= 500 \text{ cm}^3 = 0.500 \text{ dm}^3$$

Thus, final volume = 0.500 + 0.500

$$= 1.000 \text{ dm}^3$$

$$\text{Moles } (n) = \frac{pV}{RT}$$

$$nRT = pV$$

$$= 2 \times 0.50 = 1.0 \text{ L atm}$$

$$nR = \frac{1.0}{298}$$

$$\therefore \quad \Delta S = 2.303\, nR \log\frac{V_2}{V_1}$$

$$= \frac{2.303 \times 1}{298} \log\frac{1}{0.5}$$

$$= 2.326 \times 10^{-3} \text{ L atm K}^{-1}$$

$$= 2.326 \times 10^{-3} \times 101.27 \text{ JK}^{-1}$$

$$= 0.236 \text{ JK}^{-1}$$

117. (c) $\Delta G = -nRT \log_e \frac{V_2}{V_1}$

$$\Delta S = nR \log\frac{V_2}{V_1}$$

$$\therefore \quad \frac{\Delta G}{\Delta S} = -T = -273 \text{ K}$$

118. (d) Heat absorbed = 100 kJ

Work done = area enclosed in ABC

$$= \frac{1}{2}(AB)(AC)$$

$$W = \frac{1}{2}(\Delta V)(\Delta p)$$

$$= \frac{1}{2}(30)(20)$$

$$= 300 \text{ bar dm}^3$$

$$= 300 \times 100 \text{ J} = 3 \times 10^4 \text{ J}$$

$$= 30 \text{ kJ}$$

$$\therefore \text{Efficiency} = \frac{\text{Work}}{\text{Heat absorbed}} \times 100$$

$$= \frac{30}{100} \times 100 = 30\%$$

■ 1 bar dm^3 = 100 J

119. (b) $\Delta G = \Delta H - T\Delta S$

If $\Delta G < 0$, spontaneous

$\Delta H > 0$ endothermic (b and c)

For (b),

$$\Delta G = 48 - 400 \times 0.135 = -6 \text{ kJ}$$

Thus, spontaneous.

For (d),

$$\Delta G = 48 - 400(-0.13 \text{ J})$$

$$= +102 \text{ kJ}$$

Thus, non-spontaneous.

120. (d) Since $q = 0$, hence adiabatic expansion

$$\frac{T_2}{T_1} = \left(\frac{V_1}{V_2}\right)^{\gamma-1}$$

(For CO_2, $\gamma = 1.33$ $C_V = 3R$)

$$T_2 = 400\left(\frac{1}{8}\right)^{0.33} = 200\text{ K}$$

$$W = -nC_V(T_2 - T_1)$$
$$= -1 \times 3 \times 8.3143\,(200 - 400)$$
$$= 5000\text{ J} = 5.0\text{ kJ}$$

121. (a) $\Delta G° = -2.303\,RT\log K$
$$= -2.303 \times 8.314 \times 10^{-3}\,T\log 1 \times 10^3$$
$$= -0.0574\,T$$
$$\Delta G° = \Delta H° - T\Delta S° - 0.0574\,T$$
$$= -77.1 - T \times (-121.2 \times 10^{-3})$$
$$= -77.1 + 0.1212\,T$$
$$T = 432\text{ K}$$

122. (d) **At stage I** :
$$p_{\text{I}} = \frac{nRT}{V} = \frac{1 \times 0.0831 \times 298}{22.4}$$
$$= 1.106\text{ bar}$$
In stage II, temperature is doubled
$\therefore$ $p_{\text{II}} = 2.212$ bar
In state III, volume is halved
$\therefore$ $p_{\text{III}} = 2.212$ bar

123. (c) By first law, $\Delta E = q + W$
For isothermal expansion, $\Delta E = 0$
$\therefore$ $q = -W$
$$-q_{\text{irrev}} = W = p\Delta V$$
$$= 3(2 - 1) = 3\text{ L atm}$$
Also, $\Delta S_{\text{surr}} = \dfrac{q_{\text{irrev}}}{T}$
$$= \frac{(-3 \times 101.3)\text{ J}}{300\text{ K}} = \frac{303.9}{300}$$
$$= -1.013\text{ JK}^{-1}$$

124. (b) $H_2O(l) \longrightarrow H_2O(g)$
It (system) takes heat from the surrounding.
Thus, $\Delta H_{\text{vap}} > 0$
$\therefore$ $(\Delta S)_{\text{system}} = \dfrac{q_{\text{rev}}}{T} > 0$
Surrounding loses heat, thus
$$(\Delta S)_{\text{surrounding}} = -\frac{q_{\text{rev}}}{T} > 0$$
$$(\Delta S)_{\text{universe}} = (\Delta S)_{\text{system}} + (\Delta S)_{\text{surrounding}}$$
$$= 0$$

125. (a) $H_2O(l) \longrightarrow H_2O(g)$
System at equilibrium hence, $\Delta G = 0$.
Due to formation of vapour, randomness increases, hence $\Delta S > 0$.

126. (b) $\Delta G° = -2.303RT\log_{10} K$
$\Rightarrow \Delta G° = \Delta H° - T\Delta S°$
$\therefore$ $-2.303RT\log_{10} K = \Delta H° - T\Delta S°$
$$\log_{10} K = \frac{T\Delta S° - \Delta H°}{2.303\,RT}$$
$$\log K = \frac{298 \times 10 + 54.07 \times 10^3}{2.303 \times 8.314 \times 298}$$
$$= \frac{298 \times 10 + 54070}{5705} = 10$$

127. (b) Entropy is a state function and thus change is independent of path
The
$$\Delta S_{A \to B} = \Delta S_{A \to C} + \Delta S_{C \to D} + \Delta S_{D \to B}$$
$$= \Delta S_{A \to C} + \Delta S_{C \to D} - \Delta S_{B \to D}$$
$$= 50 + 30 - 20 = 60\text{ eu}$$

128. (a) By first law, $dE = dq + dW$
Put, $\dfrac{dE}{dT} = C_V \quad \therefore\ dE = C_V dT$
Also, $dW = -pdV$
$\therefore$ Also, $dq = dE + pdV$
$$dq = C_V dT + pdV$$
$pV = RT$ for one mole
$\Rightarrow$ $pdV + Vdp = RdT$
Also, $p = V \;\Rightarrow\; Vdp = pdV$
$\therefore$ $2pdV = RdT$
$\therefore$ $dq = C_V dT + \dfrac{RdT}{2}$
$$C_p = \frac{dq}{dT} = C_V + \frac{R}{2}$$
$$= \frac{3}{2}R + \frac{R}{2} = 2R$$
(For monoatomic gas, $C_V = \dfrac{3}{2}R$)

129. (c) For an adiabatic expansion $q = 0$ and
$$C_V = \left(\frac{\Delta E}{\Delta T}\right)$$
Also, for irreversible process,
$$W = \Delta E = -p(V_2 - V_1)$$
$$= -1(2 - 1) = -1\text{ L atm}$$
$$\therefore\ C_V = \left(\frac{-1}{\Delta T}\right)$$
$$\Rightarrow \Delta T = \frac{-1}{C_V} = -\frac{1}{3/2R} = \frac{-2}{3R}$$
$$T_2 - T_1 = -\frac{2}{3}R$$
$$\Rightarrow\quad T_2 = T - \frac{2}{3R} = \left(T - \frac{2}{3 \times 0.0821}\right)$$

130. (d) For van der Waals' equation of one mol gas
$$\left(p + \frac{a}{V^2}\right)(V - b) = RT$$
When attractive forces are neglected, $a = 0$
$$\therefore\quad p = \left(\frac{RT}{V - b}\right)$$
For reversible expansion,
$$W = -\int pdV = -RT\int\frac{dV}{(V - b)}$$
When volume changes from V_1 to V_2
$$W = -RT\int_{V_1}^{V_2}\frac{dV}{V - b}$$
$$= -RT\ln\left(\frac{V_2 - b}{V_1 - b}\right)$$
$$\therefore\quad W = -8.3143 \times 300 \times 2.303\log\left(\frac{50 - 0.055}{1 - 0.055}\right)$$
$$= -9897.5\text{ J} = -9.8975\text{ kJ}$$

131. (b) Coefficient of thermal expansion is given by
$$\alpha = \frac{1}{V}\left(\frac{\delta V}{\delta T}\right)$$
$$\therefore\quad dV = \alpha VdT$$
$$dW = -pdV = -p(\alpha VdT)$$
Given, $p = 1.01325 \times 10^5$ pa
$\alpha = 2.1 \times 10^{-4}\text{ K}^{-1}$
V = volume occupied by 1 mol of water $= 18\text{ cm}^3 = 18 \times 10^{-3}\text{ dm}^3$
$$\Delta T = (298 - 288) = 10\text{ K}$$
$$\therefore\quad W = -1.01325 \times 10^5 \times 2.1 \times 10^{-4} \times 18 \times 10^{-3} \times 10\text{ K}$$
$$= -3.83 \times 10^{-3}\text{ J mol}^{-1}$$

Type II. Statement Based Questions

132. (b) $\Delta S° = \dfrac{\Delta H°}{T}$
$(\Delta S°)$ is very small.

133. (b) **134.** (b) **135.** (a) **136.** (c)
137. (c) **138.** (d) **139.** (b) **140.** (a)
141. (b) **142.** (d) **143.** (b)

Type III. MCQs with More than ONE Correct Alternate

144. (a, c, d)
(a) Change of state p_1, V_1, T_1 to p_2, V_2, T_2 is isothermal, thus $T_1 = T_2$
(c) Work done in isothermal condition > in adiabatic condition
(d) $\Delta U_{\text{(isothermal)}} > \Delta V_{\text{(adiabatic)}}$ in isothermal condition temperature remains constant while in adiabatic expansion cooling takes place.

145. (a, c)
(a) Entropy is a state function, change in entropy in a cyclic process is zero.
$$\Delta S_{x \to y} + \Delta S_{y \to z} + \Delta S_{z \to x} = 0$$
$$\Delta S_{z \to x} = -(\Delta S_{x \to y} + \Delta S_{y \to z})$$
$$\Delta S_{x \to z} = \Delta S_{x \to y} + \Delta S_{y \to z}$$
Thus, (a) is correct.
Work is a non-state function.
$$W_{x \to y \to z} = W_{x \to y}$$

146. (b, c, d) Refer text

147. (a, b, c) $w = -\int dV\, p_{ext.}$

For 1 mole van der Waals' gas

$$p = \left(\frac{RT}{V-b} - \frac{a}{V^2}\right)$$

For reversible process $p_{ext} = p_{gas}$

$$w = -\int\left(\frac{RT}{V-b} - \frac{a}{V^2}\right) dV$$

But it is not applicable for irreversible process which are carried out very fast. So, work done is calculated assuming final pressure remains constant throughout the process.

Thus, statement (a), (b) and (c) correct while statement (d) is incorrect.

148. (a, b, c)

Process is adiabatic, thus $q = 0$,

Hence, (a) is correct.

Also, $p_{ext} = 0$

$$W = p_{ext}\,\Delta V = 0$$

By first law,

$$\Delta E = q + W = 0 + 0 = 0$$

Thus, change in internal energy is zero

This indicates process is isothermal ($E \propto T$)

$$\therefore \quad \Delta T = 0$$

$T_1 = T_2$, Thus, (b) is correct.

Under isothermal condition,

$$p_1V_1 = p_2V_2$$

Thus, (c) is correct

but $\quad p_1V_1^\gamma = p_2V_2^\gamma$

is not correct under isothermal reversible condition.

Thus, (d) is incorrect.

149. (a, b, d) $\Delta G° = \Delta H° - T\Delta S°$

$$= 10 - 298 \times \frac{50}{1000} = -4.9 \text{ kJ}$$

Since, $\Delta G° < 0$, thus reaction is spontaneous at this temperature.

Thus, (a) is correct.

To be spontaneous $\Delta G° < 0$

$$\therefore \quad T\Delta S° > \Delta H°$$

$$T > \frac{\Delta H°}{\Delta S°} > \frac{10000}{50} > 200 \text{ K}$$

Thus, (b) is correct.

Also, $\Delta G° = -2.303\, RT \log K$

$$-4.9 = -2.303 \times 8.314 \times 10^{-3} \times 298 \log K$$

$$\therefore \quad K = 7.22$$

Thus, (c) is incorrect.

$$K_p = p_{SO_2} = 7.22 \text{ bar}$$

Thus, (d) is correct.

150. (a, b) 16 g CH_4 = 1 mol CH_4 = 22.4 L at STP.

Then $\quad V_1 = 22.4$ L

$\quad V_2 = 44.8$ L

$\therefore$ For adiabatic expansion,

$$\frac{T_2}{T_1} = \left(\frac{V_1}{V_2}\right)^{\gamma - 1}$$

For CH_4, $\gamma = 1.33$, $C_V = 3R$

$$\therefore \quad T_2 = 273\left(\frac{1}{2}\right)^{0.33}$$

$$= 273 \times 0.7937 = 217 \text{ K}$$

Thus, final temperature $T' = 217$ K

Then (c) is incorrect.

By first law of thermodynamics

$$\Delta U = q - W$$

For adiabatic expansion,

$$q = 0$$

$$\Delta E = -W$$

$$W = -\Delta U$$

$$= -C_V(T_2 - T_1)$$

$$= -3R\,(217 - 298)$$

$$= -3 \times 8.314 \times (-81)$$

$$= +2020 \text{ J} = 2.202 \text{ kJ}$$

151. (a, b)

Gas	Volume	Temperature	Pressure	Mole
N_2	10 L	300 K	1 atm	$\frac{pV}{RT}$ = 0.406
He	5 L	300 K	1 atm	= 0.203

$$\chi_{N_2} = \frac{2}{3} \Rightarrow \chi_{He} = \frac{1}{3}$$

$$\Delta S_{mix} = -R[n_{N_2} \ln \chi_{N_2} + n_{He} \ln \chi_{He}]$$

$$= -2.303\, R\,[n_{N_2} \log_{10} \chi_{N_2} + n_{He} \log_{10} \chi_{He}]$$

$$= -2.303 \times 8.314 \left[0.406 \log_{10}\left(\frac{2}{3}\right) + 0.203 \log_{10}\left(\frac{1}{3}\right)\right]$$

$$= -2.303 \times 8.314\,[-0.0715 - 0.0969]$$

$$= 3.22 \text{ J K}^{-1}$$

Thus, (a) is correct.

$$\Delta G = \Delta H - T\Delta S$$

$$\therefore \quad = -10 - 3.22 \times 300$$

$$= -976 \text{ J mol}^{-1}$$

Thus, (b) is correct.

152. (a, d) In isothermal reversible change,

$$\Delta E = 0$$

$$W_1 = -2.303\, nRT \log\frac{V_2}{V_1}$$

$$= -2.303 \times 300\, R \log 10$$

$$W_2 = -2.303 \times 600R \log 10 = 2W_1$$

153. (a, b) Formation of white fumes is spontaneous

$$NH_3(g) + HCl(g) \rightleftharpoons NH_4Cl(g)$$

Thus, $\Delta S°$(universe) > 0 and $\Delta G° < 0$

Also formation of $NH_4Cl(s)$ is exothermic.

$$\therefore \quad (\Delta S)°_{system} = \frac{\Delta H°}{T} = -\text{ve}$$

$$(\Delta S)_{universe} = (\Delta S)_{system} + (\Delta S)_{surrounding}$$

Since, $\quad (\Delta S)°_{system} < 0$

Hence, $(\Delta S)_{surrounding} > 0$

154. (a, b, c) X to Y takes place at constant temperature

$$\therefore \quad \Delta S_{X-Y} = 2.303 nR \log\frac{P_1}{P_2}$$

$$= 2.303 \times 5 \times 8.314 \log 10$$

$$= 95.7 \text{ J K}^{-1}$$

Thus, (a) is correct.

$$X \longrightarrow Z,\ q = 0$$

$$\therefore \quad \Delta S_{X \longrightarrow Z} = \frac{0}{T} = 0$$

Thus, (b) is correct.

In $Z \longrightarrow Z$, temperature changes,

$$C_p = \frac{5}{2}R \text{ for inert gas}$$

$$\therefore \quad (\Delta S)_{Z \to Y} = 2.303\, nC_p \log\frac{T_2}{T_1}$$

$$= 2.303 \times 5 \times \frac{5}{2} \times 8.314 \log\frac{298}{118.6}$$

$$= 95.7 \text{ J K}^{-1}$$

Thus, $\Delta S_{X \to Y} = \Delta S_{X \to Z} + \Delta S_{Z \longrightarrow Y}$

$$= 0 + 95.7 = 95.7 \text{ JK}^{-1}$$

Thus, (c) is correct.

155. (a, b, c) For adiabatic reversible expansion,

$$pV^\gamma = \text{constant } (C)$$

$$\therefore \quad p = \frac{K}{V^\gamma} \Rightarrow \frac{dp}{dV} = -\gamma\frac{p}{V}$$

Thus, (a) is correct.

Also, for adiabatic reversible expansion.

$$\frac{1}{C_p} \ln\frac{p_2}{p_1} = \frac{1}{C_V} \ln\frac{V_1}{V_2}$$

Thus, (b) is correct.

Also $T_1V_1^{\gamma-1} = T_2V_2^{\gamma-1}$

$$\therefore \quad T = \frac{K}{V^{\gamma-1}} = KV^{(1-\gamma)}$$

$$\therefore \quad \frac{dT}{dV} = (1-\gamma)\,KV^{1-\gamma-1}$$

$$= (1-\gamma)\frac{K}{V^\gamma} = (1-\gamma)\frac{K}{V^{\gamma-1}V}$$

$$= \frac{(1-\gamma)}{(TV)} \quad \left(\because T = \frac{K}{V^{\gamma-1}}\right)$$

Thus, (c) is correct.

156. (a, b, c) Both NO_2 and N_2O_4 are gases.
NO_2 being smaller in size is expected to have smaller entropy.
In $CO_2(s)$, randomness is smaller than in $CO_2(g)$. Thus, entropy is smaller. When Cr^{3+} replaces Al^{3+} in Al_2O_3, ruby is formed.
Since, $Cr^{3+} > Al^{3+}$ (size), thus disorder decreases.
Thus, entropy of alumina < ruby.
Since, $p \propto \frac{1}{V}$, thus when p increases, volume decreases. Hence, disorder decreases thus, entropy decreases.

157. (b, c) In the given curve AC represents isochoric process as volume at both the points is same i.e., V_1.
Similarly, AB represents isothermal process (as both the points are at T_1 temperature) and BC represents isobaric process as both the points are at p_2 pressure.
Now (i) for option (a)

$$q_{AC} = \Delta U_{BC} = nC_V(T_2 - T_1)$$

where, n = number of moles
C_V = specific heat capacity at constant volume
However, $W_{AB} \neq p_2(V_2 - V_1)$ instead

$$W_{AB} = nRT_1 \ln\left(\frac{V_2}{V_1}\right)$$

So, this option is incorrect.
(ii) For option (b)

$$q_{BC} = \Delta H_{AC} = nC_p(T_2 - T_1)$$

where, C_p = specific heat capacity at constant pressure likewise,

$$W_{BC} = -p_2(V_1 - V_2)$$

Hence, this option is correct.
(iii) For option (c)
as $nC_p(T_2 - T_1) < nC_V(T_2 - T_1)$
so, $\Delta H_{CA} < \Delta U_{CA}$ and $q_{AC} = \Delta U_{BC}$
Thus, correct.
(d) As $q_{BC} = \Delta H_{AC}$
but $\Delta H_{CA} \not> U_{CA}$
Thus, incorrect.

158. (a, c) For the reaction,

$$A \rightleftharpoons P$$

Given, $T_1 < T_2$

$$\frac{\ln K_1}{\ln K_2} > \frac{T_2}{T_1} \quad \ldots(i)$$

It shows,
On increasing the temperature, K decreases so reaction is exothermic i.e.,

$$\Delta H° < 0$$

Besides, graph shows $K > 1$
So $\Delta G° < 0$

Now, from Eq. (i)

$$T_1 \ln K_1 > T_2 \ln K_2$$
$$-\Delta G_1° > -\Delta G_2°$$

Likewise

$$(-\Delta H° + T_1\Delta S°) > (-\Delta H° + T_2\Delta S°)$$

or simply

$$T_1\Delta S° > T_2\Delta S°$$

So, $(T_2 - T_1)\Delta S° < 0$

$$\Delta S° < 0$$

In other words, increase of ΔG with increase in temperature is possible only when $\Delta S° < 0$.
Hence, option (a) and (c) are correct.

159. (a, b, d)

(a)

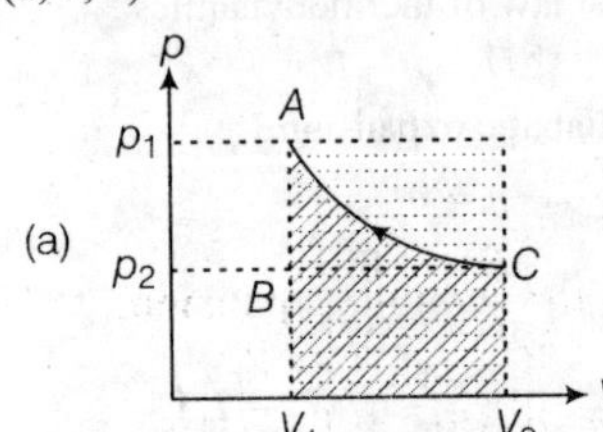

Rev. work (area under the curve)
Irrev. work
$W_{irr} > W_{rev}$

(b)

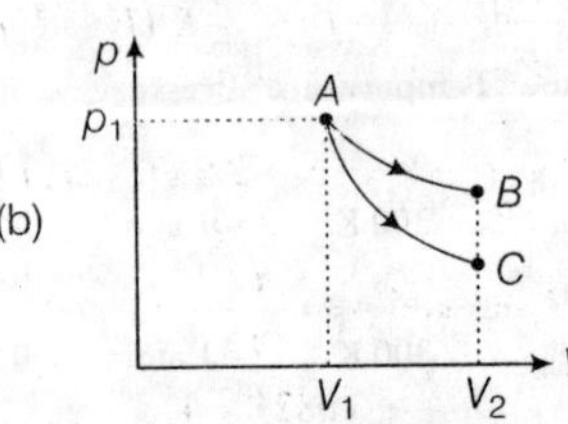

AB : Rev. isothermal
AC : Rev. adiabatic
$|W_{AB}| > |W_{AC}|$

(c) (i) $\Delta U = nC_V\Delta T = 0$ (isothermal hence $\Delta T = 0$)
(ii) $\Delta U = q + W = -$ ve
$(q = 0, W < 0)$
$\Delta U = nC_V \Rightarrow \Delta T < 0$
(d) $q = 0$ (adiabatic), $W = 0$ (free expansion)
$\Delta U = 0 \Rightarrow \Delta T = 0$ (isothermal)

160. (b, c) $\Delta S_{surr} = \frac{-q_{process}}{T_{surr}}$

If $\Delta H > 0$ on $T\uparrow K_{eq}\uparrow$, $\Delta S_{surr} < 0$
(Surrounding in unfavourable)
If $\Delta H < 0$ on $T\uparrow K_{eq}\downarrow$, $\Delta S_{surr} > 0$
(Surrounding is favourable)

Due to increase in pressure, volume decreases, hence molecules are packed in order.
Thus, entropy decreases, greater the volume, greater the randomness

Type IV. Passage Based MCQs (Comprehension)

Passage 1

Due to adiabatic expansion,

$$T_2 = T_1 \frac{C_V + p_{ext}R/p_1}{C_V + p_{ext}R/p_2}$$

$$= 298\,\frac{2.5\,R + R/15}{2.5 + R/2.5} = 264\text{ K}$$

Also, $T_2 = T_1 - \frac{p_{ext}\,\Delta V}{nC_V}$

$$264 = 298 - \frac{\Delta V}{3.18 \times 2.5\,R}$$

$$\Delta V = 34 \times 3.18 \times 2.5 \times 0.0831 = 22.5\text{ L}$$

$\therefore$ Final volume $= V_1 + \Delta V = 5.25 + 22.50 = 27.75$ L

161. (c)

162. (b)

Passage 2

$$\Delta U = q + W$$

For isothermal, $\Delta U = 0$

$\therefore$ $q = -W = -p_{ext}\,\Delta V$
$W = -2$ atm $(0.850 - 1.70)$ L
$= +1.70$ L atm
$= 1.70 \times 101.27$ J
$= 172.16$ J

1 L atm = 101.27 J

$\therefore$ $\Delta S_{surrounding}\, q/T = \frac{172.16}{373} = 0.46\text{ J K}^{-1}$

For reversible process,

$$W = -q_{rev} = -2.303\,nRT\log\frac{V_2}{V_1}$$

$$= -2.303 \times \frac{1}{18} \times 8.314 \times 373 \log\frac{1}{2}$$

$$= 119.44\text{ J}$$

$\therefore$ $q_{rev} = -119.44$ J

$\therefore$ $(\Delta S)_{system} = -\frac{119.44}{373} = -0.32\text{ J K}^{-1}$

$(\Delta S)_{universe} = (\Delta S)_{surrounding} + (\Delta S)_{system}$
$= 0.46 - 0.32 = 0.14\text{ JK}^{-1}$

Thus, (ΔS) of surrounding is maximum.

163. (d)

164. (b)

Passage 3

W (along ADC)
$W_{ADC} = W_{AD}$ (isothermal) $+ W_{DC}$ (adiabatic)
(along DC, volume is constant)

$$= 2.303\,nRT\log\frac{V_2}{V_1} + 2.303\,nRT\log\frac{V_2}{V_2}$$

$$= 2.303 \times 1 \times 8.314\log 2 \times 100$$

$= 576.33 \text{ J mol}^{-1} + 0$

$q = 2.303\, nRT \log \frac{V_2}{V_1} + C_V \Delta T$

$= 576.33 + 1.5 \times 8.314 \times 100$

$= 1823.4 \text{ J mol}^{-1}$

$\Delta E = q - W$

$= 1823.4 - 576.3 = 1247.1 \text{ J mol}^{-1}$

W (along ABC)

$W_{ABC} = W_{AB} + W_{BC}$

$= 0$ (volume constant)

$+ 2.303\, nRT \log \frac{V_2}{V_1}$

$= 2.303 \times 1 \times 8.314 \times 200 \log 2$

$= 1152.6 \text{ Jmol}^{-1}$

$q = 1152.6 + 1247.1$

$= 2399.7 \text{ J mol}^{-1}$

$\Delta E = q - W$

$= 2399.7 - 1152.6$

$= 1247.1 \text{ J mol}^{-1}$

Thus,

$\Delta E_{ABC} = \Delta E_{ADC}$

Thus, ΔE is independent of path

$W_{ABC} \neq W_{ADC}$

and $q_{ABC} \neq q_{ADC}$

Thus, both are path dependent

Thus,

165. (b)

166. (a)

Passage 4

$$H_2O(l) \rightleftharpoons H_2O(g)$$

ΔH = work = i (ampere) × V(volt) × t (second)

$= 0.50 \text{ A} \times 12 \text{ V} \times 300 \text{ s}$

$= 1800 \text{ J} = 1.8 \text{ kJ}$

$\therefore \Delta H_V(\text{molar}) = \frac{1.8 \text{ kJ}}{0.044 \text{ mol}} = 40.9 \text{ kJ mol}^{-1}$

$\Delta H = \Delta E + \Delta n_g RT$

$\Delta n_g = +1$

$\Delta E = \Delta H - \Delta n_g RT$

$= 40.9 - 1 \times 8.314 \times 10^{-3} \times 373$

$= 40.9 - 3.1$

$= 37.8 \text{ kJ mol}^{-1}$

167. (a)

168. (b)

Passage 5

$W_{\text{irrev}} = + p_{\text{ext}}(V_2 - V_1)$

$= p_2\left(\frac{nRT}{p_2} - \frac{nRT}{p_1}\right)$

$= nRT\left(1 - \frac{p_2}{p_1}\right)$

$W_{\text{rev}} = nRT \ln \frac{V_2}{V_1} = nRT \ln \frac{p_1}{p_2}$

$= nRT \ln\left[1 + \frac{p_1 - p_2}{p_2}\right]$

$= nRT\left(\frac{p_1 - p_2}{p_2}\right)$ by expansion

$\therefore W_{\text{rev}} - W_{\text{irrev}} = nRT \frac{(p_1 - p_2)^2}{p_1 p_2}$

■ if $\frac{p_1 - p_2}{p_2} \to 0$, then $\ln\left(1 + \frac{p_1 - p_2}{p_2}\right)$

$= \left(\frac{p_1 - p_2}{p_2}\right)$

169. (b)

170. (a)

Passage 6

In adiabatic irreversible expansion,

$W = p_{\text{ext}}(V_2 - V_1)$

Since, $\Delta E = q - W$ and $q = 0$

$W = -\Delta E$

$= -C_V(T_2 - T_1)$

$p_{\text{ext}}(V_2 - V_1) = -C_V(T_2 - T_1)$

$1 \text{ atm}\left(\frac{RT_2}{p_2} - \frac{RT_1}{p_1}\right) = -\frac{5}{2}R(T_2 - T_1)$

$\left(\frac{T_2}{p_2} - \frac{T_1}{p_2}\right) = -2.5(T_2 - T_1)$

$p_2 = 1 \text{ atm}$ and $p_1 = \frac{RT_1}{V_1}$

$= \frac{0.0821 \times 473}{20} = 1.94 \text{ atm}$

$\therefore \left(T_2 - \frac{T_1}{1.94}\right) = 2.5(T_1 - T_2)$

Given $T_1 = 473 \text{ K}$

$\therefore T_2 = 407.5 \text{ K}$

$\therefore (T_2 - T_1) = 407.5 - 473.0 = 65.5 \text{ K}$

Temperature and pressure both change

$\therefore \Delta S = 2.303\left[C_p \log \frac{T_2}{T_1} + R \log \frac{p_1}{p_2}\right]$

$= 2.303 \times 3.5 \times 8.314 \log \frac{407.5}{473}$

$+ 2.303 \times 8.314 \log \frac{1.94}{1.0}$

$= -4.34 + 5.51 = 1.17 \text{ J K}^{-1}$

171. (a)

172. (b)

Passage 7

$V_1 = 22.4$ L at STP, $T_1 = 273$ K

$V_2 = 22.4$ L $T_2 = 546$K

$V_3 = ?$ $T_3 = 273$K

Process (II → III) is adiabatic.

Since, $q = 0$

$\left(\frac{T_2}{T_3}\right) = \left(\frac{V_3}{V_2}\right)^{\gamma - 1}$

$(2) = \left(\frac{V_3}{22.4}\right)^{0.66}$

$\log(2) = 0.66 \log\left(\frac{V_3}{22.4}\right)$

$\therefore V_3 = 64.0 \text{ L}$

$W_{\text{I — II}} = 0$, since $\Delta V = 0$

$W_{\text{II — III}} = -nC_V(T_3 - T_2)$

$= -1 \times 1.5 \times 8.314(273 - 546)$

$= +3404.5 \text{ J}$

$= 3.405 \text{ kJ}$

$W_{\text{III — I}}$ (isothermal compression)

$= 2.303\, nRT \log \frac{V_1}{V_3}$

$= 2.303 \times 1 \times 8.314 \times 273 \log \frac{22.4}{64.0}$

$= -2383 \text{ J}$

$= -2.383 \text{ kJ}$

$\therefore$ Total work $= 0 + 3.405 - 2.383$

$= 1.021 \text{ kJ}$

173. (d)

174. (d)

Passage 8

Stage I — Stage II $W = p(V - V_1)$

Stage II — Stage III $W_2 = p_2(V_2 - V)$

$\therefore$ Total work $- p(V - V_1) + p_2(V_2 - V)$

$= p\left(\frac{RT}{p} - \frac{RT}{p_1}\right) + p_2\left(\frac{RT}{p_2} - \frac{RT}{p}\right)$

$= RT - \frac{RTp}{p_1} + RT - \frac{RTp_2}{p}$

$= 2RT - RT\left[\frac{p}{p_1} + \frac{p_2}{p}\right]$

$= 2RT - RT\left[\frac{p^2 + p_1 p_2}{pp_1}\right]$

$= RT\left[2 - \frac{(p^2 + p_1 p_2)}{pp_1}\right]$

If work is maximum,

$\frac{dW}{dp} = 0$

$\frac{dW}{dp} = \frac{d}{dp}\left[2RT - RT\left[\frac{p}{p_1} + \frac{p_2}{p}\right]\right]$

$= 0 - RT\left[\frac{1}{p_1} - \frac{p_2}{p^2}\right]$

$\therefore p^2 = p_1 p_2$

$\therefore p = \sqrt{p_1 p_2}$

Put value of p in work

$$W_{max} = RT\left[2 - \frac{p_1p_2 + p_1p_2}{pp_1}\right]$$
$$= RT[2 - 2p_1p_2/pp_1]$$
$$= 2RT\left[1 - \frac{p_2}{p}\right]$$
$$= 2RT\left[1 - \frac{p_2}{\sqrt{p_1p_2}}\right]$$
$$= 2RT\left[1 - \sqrt{\frac{p_2}{p_1}}\right]$$

175. (d)

176. (c)

■ $W = -p_{ext}(V_2 - V_1)$ in expansion, but it has been taken positive in non-SI unit.

Passage 9

$$\Delta U_{AB} = q_{AB} + W_{AB}$$
$$= 2 - 5 = -3 \text{ kJ mol}^{-1}$$

For cyclic process

$$\Delta U_{AB} + \Delta U_{BC} + \Delta U_{CA} = 0$$
$$-3 - 5 + \Delta U_{CA} = 0$$
$$\therefore \quad \Delta U_{CA} = 8 \text{ kJmol}^{-1}$$

Also $\Delta U_{CA} = W_{CA} + q_{CA}$

$$8 = 3 + q_{CA}$$
$$q_{CA} = 5 \text{ kJmol}^{-1}$$

Thus, 5 kJ of heat is absorbed.

177. (b)

178. (a)

Passage 10

Along the adiabats (AC, CE, BD and DF)

$$q = 0$$

Thus, $\Delta S_{(system)} = \frac{q}{T} = 0$

For the isothermal change, ($A \to B$),

$$\Delta S_{system\ (A\to B)} = 2.303\, nR \log\frac{V_B}{V_A}$$

and for isothermal change ($C \to D$),

$$\Delta S_{system\ (C\to D)} = 2.303\, nR \log\frac{V_D}{V_C}$$

For isothermal change ($E \to F$),

$$\Delta S_{system\ (E\to F)} = 2.303\, nR \log\frac{V_F}{V_E}$$

Also for adiabats

$$(AC) \quad \frac{T_2}{T_1} = \left(\frac{V_A}{V_C}\right)^{\gamma-1}$$
$$(CE) \quad \frac{T_3}{T_2} = \left(\frac{V_C}{V_E}\right)^{\gamma-1}$$
$$(BD) \quad \frac{T_2}{T_1} = \left(\frac{V_B}{V_D}\right)^{\gamma-1}$$
$$(DF) \quad \frac{T_3}{T_2} = \left(\frac{V_D}{V_F}\right)^{\gamma-1}$$
$$\therefore \quad \frac{V_A}{V_C} = \frac{V_B}{V_D}$$
$$\therefore \quad \frac{V_B}{V_A} = \frac{V_D}{V_C}$$

and $\frac{V_C}{V_E} = \frac{V_D}{V_F}$

$$\therefore \quad \frac{V_D}{V_C} = \frac{V_F}{V_E} = \frac{V_B}{V_A}$$

Thus, $\frac{V_B}{V_A} = \frac{V_D}{V_C}$ is correct.

$= \frac{V_F}{V_E}$ is correct.

$= \frac{V_C}{V_D}$ is incorrect.

Along $A \to C, C \to E, B \to D$ and $D \to F$ heat absorbed $q = 0$

$$\therefore \quad (\Delta S) = 0$$

(a) $\therefore \Delta S_{system}\ A \to B \to D \to F$

$$= \Delta S_{system}\ (A \to B) + 0 + 0$$
$$= nR \ln\frac{V_B}{V_A}$$

(b) $\Delta S_{system} A \to C \to E \to F$

$$= 0 + 0 + (\Delta S)_{system}\,(E \to F)$$
$$= nR \ln\frac{V_F}{V_E} = nR\ln\frac{V_B}{V_A}$$

(c) Similarly,

$$(\Delta S)_{system}\ (A \to C \to D \to F)$$
$$= nR \ln\frac{V_B}{V_A}$$

179. (c)

180. (d)

Passage 11

$$\Delta S°_{total} = \Delta S°_{surrounding} + \Delta S°_{system}$$
$$\Delta H° = -1648.0 \text{ kJmol}^{-1}$$

(Heat escaped to surrounding)

$$\therefore \Delta S°_{surrounding} = -\frac{\Delta H°}{T}$$
$$= \frac{1648.0 \times 10^3}{298} \text{ Jmol}^{-1}\text{K}^{-1}$$
$$= 5530.2 \text{ Jmol}^{-1}\text{K}^{-1}$$
$$\Delta S°_{system} = -549.4 \text{ Jmol}^{-1}\text{K}^{-1}$$
$$\therefore \Delta S°_{total} = 5530.2 - 549.4$$
$$= 4980.80 \text{ Jmol}^{-1}\text{K}^{-1}$$

$\Delta S° > 0$ Thus, spontaneous

Also, $\Delta G° = \Delta H° - T\Delta S°$

$$= -1484.28 \text{ kJ mol}^{-1}$$

181. (d)

182. (c)

Passage 12

$$H_2O(g) \longrightarrow H_2O(l)$$
$$\Delta V = V_{(liquid)} - V_{(vapour)}$$
$$= 18.8 \times 10^{-3}\text{L} - 30.12\text{ L}$$
$$= -30.1012 \text{ L}$$
$$W = -p\Delta V$$
$$= -1(-30.1012) \text{ L-atm}$$
$$= 30.1012 \times 101.27 \text{ J}$$
$$= 3048 \text{ J}$$
$$= 3.048 \text{ kJ}$$
$$q = -40.7 \text{ kJ}$$
$$\therefore \quad \Delta E = q + W$$
$$= -40.7 + 3.048$$
$$= -37.65 \text{ kJ}$$

183. (b)

184. (a)

Passage 13

185. (c) $K \to L$ (expansion under isobaric condition) thus, heating takes place as $V \propto T$.

$L \to M$ (volume is constant but pressure is decreasing, since $p \propto T$ thus cooling takes place).

$M \to N$ (volume is decreasing under isobaric condition, thus, cooling takes place as $V \propto T$.

$N \to K$ (pressure is increasing at constant volume, since $p \propto T$ thus, temperature increases, heating takes place.

186. (b) Isochoric processes are at constant volume; thus, L to M and N to K are isochoric.

Type V. Numerical Skills

187. (– 2.7) ΔG is related to ΔH and ΔS by equation,

$$\Delta G = \Delta H - T\Delta S$$

and ΔH is related to ΔU by equation

$$\Delta H = \Delta U + \Delta n_g RT$$

Given, $\Delta U = 2.1$ kcal

Δn_g = moles of gaseous product – moles of gaseous reactant

$$= 2 - 0 = 2$$
$$R = 0.002 \text{ kcal mol}^{-1}\text{ K}^{-1}$$
$$T = 300 \text{ K}$$
$$\Delta S = 20 \text{ cal K}^{-1}\text{ mol}^{-1}$$
$$= 0.02 \text{ kcal mol}^{-1}\text{ K}^{-1}$$
$$\therefore \Delta H = 2.1 + 2 \times 0.002 \times 300$$
$$= 3.3 \text{ kcal}$$
$$\therefore \Delta G = 3.3 - 300 \times 0.02$$
$$= -2.7 \text{ kcal}$$

188. (48) Work done is the area under the line ABC.

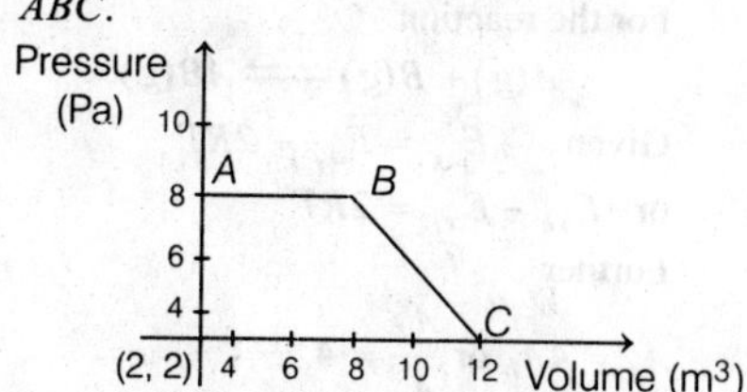

$$\text{Work} = \text{Area} = AB \times BD + \frac{1}{2} BD \times DC$$

$$= (8-2) \times (8-2) + \frac{1}{2} \times (8-2)\,(12-8)$$

$$= 36 + \frac{1}{2} \times 6 \times 4$$

$$= 36 + 12 = 48$$

189. (6.25) $n = 4$

$$nC_V = \left(\frac{\Delta E}{\Delta T}\right)_V = \frac{5000 \text{ J}}{200 \text{ K}}$$

$$\therefore C_V = \frac{50}{8} = 6.25 \text{ J mol}^{-1} \text{ K}^{-1}$$

190. Four (4)

$$W = -nRT$$

If, $\Delta n_g = +\text{ ve}$

$W = -\text{ ve}$

Thus work is done by the system.

	Δn_g
I.	+1
II.	−1
III.	−2
IV.	+1
V.	0
VI.	+1
VII.	0
VIII.	+1

191. Two (2) For adiabatic change

$$q = 0$$

$$\therefore \Delta E = q + W$$

$$\therefore W = \Delta E$$

$$= 1200 \text{ J}$$

$$\therefore \text{Also, } \left(\frac{\Delta E}{\Delta T}\right)_V = C_V$$

$$\therefore \Delta T = \frac{\Delta E}{C_V} = \frac{1200}{1.5\,R}$$

$$\therefore \Delta H = C_p \Delta T$$

$$= \frac{5}{2} R \frac{1200}{1.5\,R}$$

$$= 2000 \text{ J}$$

$$= 2 \times 10^3 \text{ J}$$

$$= n \times 10^3 \text{J}$$

Thus, $n = 2$

192. (189494)

$$H_2O = 90 \text{ g} = \frac{90}{18} = 5 \text{ mol}$$

$$\Delta H_{vap} = 41 \text{ kJ mol}^{-1}$$

$$H_2O(l) \rightleftharpoons H_2O(g)$$

$$\Delta H = \Delta E + \Delta n_g RT$$

$$\therefore \Delta E = \Delta H - \Delta n_g RT$$

$$\Delta n_g = 1 - 0 = 1$$

$$\Delta E = 41 - 1 \times 8.314 \times 10^{-3} \times 373$$

$$= 37.9 \text{ kJ mol}^{-1}$$

$$= 37.9 \times 1000 \text{ J mol}^{-1}$$

$$= 37.9 \times 1000 \times 5 \text{ J for 5 mol } H_2O(l)$$

$$= 189494 \text{ J}$$

193. (935) Tin is obtained from cassiterite by reduction with coke and the balanced chemical reaction is

$$SnO_2(s) + C(s) \longrightarrow Sn(s) + CO_2(g)$$

Standard enthalpy of reaction

$$\Delta H^\circ_{R^n} = (\Delta H^\circ_f\, CO_2(g)) - (\Delta H^\circ_f\, SnO_2(s))$$

$$\Delta H^\circ_{R^n} = -394 - (-581) = 187 \text{ kJ}$$

Standard entropy of reaction

$$\Delta S^\circ_{R^n} = \Delta S^\circ_{\text{Products}} - \Delta S^\circ_{\text{Reactants}}$$

$$\Delta S^\circ_{R^n} = [S^\circ(Sn(s)) + S^\circ(CO_2(g))] - [S^\circ(SnO_2(s)) + S^\circ(C(s))]$$

$$\Delta S^\circ_{R^n} = [52 + 210] - [56 + 6]$$

$$= 200 \text{ JK}^{-1} \text{ mol}^{-1}$$

$$\Delta G^\circ = \Delta H^\circ - T\Delta S^\circ$$

For spontaneous reaction, $\Delta G^\circ < 0$

$$\therefore T\Delta S^\circ > \Delta H^\circ$$

$$\therefore T > \frac{\Delta H^\circ}{\Delta S^\circ} = \frac{187 \times 1000}{200} = 935 \text{ K}$$

For the reaction to be spontaneous, the temperature should be greater than 935 K.

194. Eight (8)

$$\text{Pressure gas } A,\ p_A = \frac{nRT}{V} = \frac{RT}{1} = RT$$

$$\text{gas } B,\ p_B = \frac{3RT}{2} = 1.5\,RT$$

Total volume = 3 L

$\therefore$ In mixture under isothermal condition

$$p_A V_A = p'_A V_{\text{total}}$$

$$\therefore \frac{p_A}{p'_A} = V_{\text{total}} / V_A = 3$$

$$\text{and } \frac{p_B}{p'_B} = \frac{V_{\text{total}}}{V_B} = \frac{3}{2}$$

$$\Delta S_{\text{mix}} = R\left[n_A \ln \frac{p_A}{p'_A} + n_B \ln \frac{p_B}{p'_B}\right]$$

$$= R\left[1 \ \ln 3 + 3 \ln \frac{3}{2}\right]$$

$$= R\,[\ln 3 + 3 \ln 3 - 3 \ln 2]$$

$$= R\,[4 \ln 3 - 3 \ln 2]$$

$$= 4R \ln 3 - 3R \ \ln 2$$

$$= 8 \ln 3 - 3 \times 2 \times 0.3010 \times 2.303 \text{ Cal}$$

$$= (8 \ln 3 - 4.16) \text{ cal}$$

Thus, $n = 8$

195. Nine (9)

By Gibbs's Helmholtz equation

$$\Delta G^\circ = \Delta H^\circ + T\left[\frac{d\Delta G^\circ}{dT}\right]_p$$

Also, $\Delta G^\circ = \Delta H^\circ - T\Delta S^\circ$

$$\therefore \Delta S^\circ = -d\left[\frac{\Delta G^\circ}{dT}\right]_p$$

$$\frac{d}{dT}(\Delta G^\circ) = \frac{d}{dT}[200 + 2T \log T - 15T]$$

$$\Delta S^\circ = -\left[0 + 2 \log T + \frac{2T}{T} - 15\right]$$

When $T = 100$ K,

$$\Delta S^\circ = -(2 \ \times 2 + 2 - 15) = 9 \text{ cal K}^{-1}$$

196. Nine (9)

$$\mu_{JT} = \left(\frac{\Delta T}{\Delta p}\right)$$

$$\therefore \Delta T = \mu_{JT} \Delta p$$

$$= 0.6375\,(6.0 - 20.12) \text{ K}$$

$$= -9.00 \text{ K}$$

■ Negative sign indicates decrease in temperature. Cooling takes place.

197. Two (2) Work done = area under the curve

$$= \frac{1}{2}(AB)\,(AC) = \frac{1}{2}(10)\,(20)$$

$$= 100 \text{ L atm}$$

$$= 100 \times 101.27 \text{ J} = 10127 \text{ J}$$

Heat absorbed $= 5 \times 10^4$ J

$$\therefore \eta = \frac{\text{work done}}{\text{heat absorbed}}$$

$$= \frac{10127}{5 \times 10^4} = 0.20$$

$$\therefore 10x = 0.20 \times 10 = 2.0$$

■ 1 L atm = 101.27 J

198. Four (4)

$$\Delta S_{\text{universe}} = (\Delta S)_{\text{system}} + (\Delta S)_{\text{surrounding}}$$

$$(\Delta S)_{\text{system}} = 2.303\,nR \log \frac{V_2}{V_1}$$

$$= 2.303 \times 0.5 \times 8.314 \ \log \frac{5}{1}$$

$$= 6.7 \text{ JK}^{-1}$$

$$(\Delta S)_{\text{surrounding}} = \frac{q_{\text{surrounding}}}{T}$$

Since, $\Delta E = q + W$

$$W = -p\,(V_2 - V_1)$$

$= -2(5-1) = -8$ L atm
$= -8 \times 101.27$ J $= -810.06$ J

$\therefore (\Delta S)_{surrounding} = -\dfrac{810.16 \text{ J}}{300 \text{ K}}$
$= -2.7$ JK^{-1}

$\Delta S_{universe} = (\Delta S)_{system} + (\Delta S)_{surrounding}$
$= 6.7 - 2.7 = 4.0$ JK^{-1}

■ 1 L atm = 101.27 J

199. Three (3)

$(\Delta S)_{rev} = 2.303\, nR \log\dfrac{V_2}{V_1} = 1.0$ JK^{-1}

$\therefore W_{rev} = -\Delta G = -T\Delta S$
$= 10 \times 298 = 2980$ J

$W_{irrev} = 1000$ J

$\therefore$ Ratio $= 2980/1000 = 2.98 \approx 3.0$

200. (– 13537.6)

$\Delta G° = \Delta H° - T\Delta S°$

and $\Delta H° = \Delta U° + \Delta n_g RT$

As $2A(g) \longrightarrow A_2(g)$

$\Delta Hg = 1 - 2 = -1$

$\therefore \Delta H° = -20 + (-1) \times 8.314 \times 10^{-3} \times 298$
$= -22.477$ kJ

$\therefore \Delta G° = -22.477 - 298 \times (-30 \times 10^{-3})$
$= -13.5376$ kJ
$= -13537.6$ J

201. Six (6) Intake $= 1.0 \times 10^7$ J day^{-1}

Output = 0.0374 HP
$= (0.0374 \times 746$ W) with 6 h day^{-1}
$= 0.0374 \times 746 \times 3600 \times 6$ J
$= 6.02 \times 10^5$ J day^{-1}

Thus, $\eta = \dfrac{\text{output}}{\text{input}} \times 100 = 6.0\%$

■ 1 W = 1 Js^{-1}, 1 h = 3600 s

202. Four (4) Formation of juice is a slow process thus reversible.

$W = -2.303\, nRT \log\dfrac{V_2}{V_1}$

n = number of moles of solute present in (pH = 1) solution in 1 dm^3

pH = 1, $[H^+] = 10^{-pH} = 10^{-1} = 0.1$ M

Thus, $x = 0.1$ mol

Concentration = mol L^{-1}

$\therefore \dfrac{C_1}{C_2} = \dfrac{V_2}{V_1}$

$C_1 = 10^{-pH} = 10^{-1} = 0.1$

$C_2 = 10^{-7.6021} = 2.5 \times 10^{-8}$

$\therefore \dfrac{C_1}{C_2} = \dfrac{2.5 \times 10^{-8}}{0.1} = 2.5 \times 10^{-7}$

$\therefore W = -2.303 \times 0.1 \times 8.314 \times 10^{-3} \times 326 \log 2.5 \times 10^{-7}$
$= 4.1 \approx 4.0$ kJ

203. Two (2)

$\Delta S = 2.303\, nR \log\dfrac{p_1}{p_2} + 2.303\, nC_p \log\dfrac{T_2}{T_1}$

Since, isoentropic, Hence $\Delta S = 0$

$\therefore -R \log\dfrac{p_1}{p_2} = C_p \log\dfrac{T_2}{T_1}$

$-R \log\dfrac{p_1}{p_2} = \dfrac{5}{2} R \log\dfrac{T_2}{T_1}$

$-\log\dfrac{1.36}{p_2} = 2.5 \log\dfrac{348}{298}$

$\log\dfrac{p_2}{1.36} = 0.1684$

$\dfrac{p_2}{1.36} = 1.47$

$p_2 = 1.47 \times 1.36$
$= 2.0$ bar

204. (–14.6)

Given

(i) $2Cu(s) + \frac{1}{2}O_2(g) \longrightarrow Cu_2O(s)$;

$\Delta G° = -78000$ J/mol $= -78$ kJ/mol

(ii) $H_2(g) + \frac{1}{2}O_2(g) \longrightarrow H_2O(g)$;

$\Delta G° = -178000$ J/mol $= -178$ kJ/mol

So, net reaction is (by (i)-(ii))

$2Cu(s) + H_2O(g) \longrightarrow Cu_2O(s) + H_2(g)$;

$\Delta G = 100000$ J/mol or 10^5 J/mol
$= 100$ kJ/mol

Now, for the above reaction

$$\Delta G = \Delta G° + RT \ln\left[\frac{p_{H_2}}{p_{H_2O}}\right]$$

and to prevent above reaction, $\Delta G \geq 0$

So, $\Delta G° + RT \ln\left[\dfrac{p_{H_2}}{p_{H_2O}}\right]$

After putting the values,

$10^5 + 8 \times 1250 \ln\left[\dfrac{p_{H_2}}{p_{H_2O}}\right] \geq 0$

or $10^5 + 10^4 \ln\left[\dfrac{p_{H_2}}{p_{H_2O}}\right] \geq 0$

or $10^4(\ln p_{H_2} - \ln p_{H_2O}) \geq -10^5$

or $\ln p_{H_2} \geq -10 + \ln p_{H_2O}$

or $\ln p_{H_2} \geq -10 + 2.3 \log(0.01)$ (as $p_{H_2O} = 1\%$)
$\geq -10 - 4.6$

so $\ln p_{H_2} \geq -14.6$

205. (+ 8500)

For the reaction,

$A(g) + B(g) \rightleftharpoons AB(g)$

Given $E_{a_b} = E_{a_f} + 2RT$

or $E_{a_b} - E_{a_f} = 2RT$

Further

$A_f = 4A_b$ or $\dfrac{A_f}{A_b} = 4$

Now, rate constant for forward reaction,

$K_f = A_f e^{-E_{a_f}/RT}$

Likewise, rate constant for backward reaction,

$K_b = A_b e^{-E_{a_b}/RT}$

At equilibrium,

Rate of forward reaction
= rate of backward reaction

i.e., $K_f = K_b$ or $\dfrac{K_f}{K_b} = K_{eq}$

so $K_{eq} = \dfrac{A_f e^{-E_{a_f}/RT}}{A_b e^{-E_{a_b}/RT}} = \dfrac{A_f}{A_b} e^{-(E_{a_f} - E_{a_b})/RT}$

After putting the given values,

$K_{eq} = 4e^2$ (as $E_{a_b} - E_{af} = 2RT$ and $\dfrac{A_f}{A_b} = 4$)

Now, $\Delta G° = -RT \ln K_{eq}$
$= -2500 \ln(4e^2)$
$= -2500(\ln 4 + \ln e^2)$
$= -2500(1.4 + 2)$
$= -2500 \times 3.4 = -8500$ J/mol

Absolute value = 8500 J/mol

206. Two (2) Work done along dashed line is irreversible $= \Sigma p\Delta V$

$W_d = 4(2 - 0.5) + 1(3 - 2) + 0.75(5.5 - 3)$
$= 4 \times 1.5 + 1 \times 1 + 0.75 \times 2.5$
$= 8.875$ L atm

Along solid line work is reversible

$p_1 = 4$ atm, $V_1 = 0.5$ L

$W_s = 2.303\, RT \log\dfrac{V_2}{V_1}$
$= 2.303 p_1 V_1 \log\dfrac{V_2}{V_1}$
$= 2.303 \times 2 \log\dfrac{5.5}{0.5} = 4.79$ L atm

$\dfrac{W_d}{W_s} = \dfrac{8.875}{4.79} \approx 2$

Type VI. Matrix Matching

207. (b) For an isobaric heating of an ideal gas, the process is considered to occur in two steps:

(I-II) : An isochoric heating

(II-III) : Isobaric, isothermal expansion

(I-II) $W = 0$

$$\Delta U = \int_{T_1}^{T_2} nC_V dT$$

When $C_p = \frac{7}{2}R, \quad \therefore C_V = \frac{5}{2}R$

$$\therefore \quad \Delta U = nC_V(T_2 - T_1)$$
$$= 2 \times \frac{5}{2} \times 8.314 \ (317 - 255)$$
$$= 2577 \text{ J}$$
$$\Delta H = \int_{T_1}^{T_2} nC_p \, dT$$
$$= nC_p (T_2 - T_1)$$
$$= 2 \times \frac{7}{2} \times 8.314(317 - 255)$$
$$= 3608 \text{ J}$$
$$W = -p_{ext}(V_2 - V_1)$$
$$= -1 \times 1 \text{ L bar} = -100 \text{ J}$$
$$q = \Delta U - W = 2577 - (-100)$$
$$= 2677 \text{ J}$$

Thus, (i) - (r)
(ii)-(p)
(iii)-(s)
(iv)-(q)

■ 1 L bar = 100 J

208. (a) (i) $\Delta H^\circ = \frac{2.303 \, RT_1T_2}{(T_2 - T_1)} \log \frac{K_2}{K_1}$

$$= \frac{2.303 \times 8.314 \times 10^{-3} \times 298 \times 373}{75} \log 10$$

$= 28.38 \text{ kJ mol}^{-1}$

Thus (i)—(s)

(ii) $\Delta G^\circ = -2.303 \, RT \log K_1$

$= -5.40 \text{ kJ mol}^{-1}$

Thus, (ii)—(p)

(iii) $\Delta G^\circ_{373} = -2.303 \, RT \log K_2$

$= -13.9 \text{ kJ mol}^{-1}$

Thus, (iii)—(q)

(iv) $\log \frac{K_2}{K_1} = \log 10 = 1$

Thus, (iv)—(r)

209. (c) For $MnO_4^- + 8H^+ + 5Fe^{2+}$

$$\longrightarrow Mn^{2+} + 5Fe^{3+} + 8H_2O$$

Electrons exchanged = 5

$$\log_{10} K = -\frac{2303(K)}{T} + 4.06$$

Thermodynamic equation is

$$\log_{10} K = -\frac{\Delta H^\circ}{2.303 \, RT} + \frac{\Delta S^\circ}{2.303 \, R}$$

(i) On comparison

$$\frac{\Delta S^\circ}{2.303 \, R} = 4.06$$

$$\therefore \quad \Delta S^\circ = 2.303 \times 4.06 \times R$$
$$= 2.303 \times 4.06 \times 8.314 \times 10^{-3} \text{kJ mol}^{-1} \text{K}^{-1}$$
$$= 0.078 \text{ kJ mol}^{-1}\text{K}^{-1}$$

Thus, (i)—(q)

(ii) $\frac{\Delta H^\circ}{2.303 \, R} = 2303$

$$\therefore \Delta H^\circ = 2.303 \times 2303 \times R$$
$$= 2.303 \times 2303 \times 8.314 \times 10^{-3} \text{kJ mol}^{-1}$$
$$= 44.1 \text{ kJ mol}^{-1}$$

Thus, (ii)—(r)

(iii) $\Delta G^\circ = \Delta H^\circ - T\Delta S$

$= 44.1 - 300 \times 0.078$

$= 20.7 \text{ kJ mol}^{-1}$

Thus, (iii)—(p)

(iv) Temperature coefficient of EMF of the cell reaction

$$\left(\frac{dE_{cell}}{dT}\right) = \frac{\Delta S^\circ}{nF} (\text{in J}) = \frac{0.078 \times 1000}{5 \times 96500}$$
$$= 1.62 \times 10^{-4} \text{ J}$$

$\therefore$ (iv) —(s)

210. (a) $W_1 = -p_{ext}(V_2 - V_1)$

$p_{ext} = 1.0 \text{ bar} = 1.0 \times 10^5 \text{ Pa}$

$\therefore \quad W_1 = -1.0 \times 10^5 (10.0 - 1.0) \text{ Pa m}^3$

$= -9.0 \times 10^5 \text{ J}$

Thus, (i)—(s)

■ 1 Pa x m³ = 1 J

(b) W_2 (by compression)

$$W_2 = -p_{ext}(V_2 - V_1)$$
$$= -10.0 \times 10^5 (1.0 - 10) \text{ Pa m}^3$$
$$= 9.0 \times 10^6 \text{ J}$$

Thus, (ii)—(q)

(iii) $W_{total} = W_1 + W_2$

$= -9.0 \times 10^5 + 9.0 \times 10^6$

$= -0.9 \times 10^6 + 9.0 \times 10^6$

$= 8.1 \times 10^6 \text{ J}$

$\therefore$ (iii)—(p)

(iv) It is carried out reversibly and isothermally to set maximum work.

$$W_4 = -2.303 \, n \, RT \log \frac{V_2}{V_1}$$
$$= -2.303 \times \left(\frac{pV}{RT}\right) RT \log \frac{V_2}{V_1}$$
$$= -2.303 \times pV \log \frac{V_2}{V_1}$$
$$= (-2.303 \times 10.0 \times 10^5 \times 1.0) \log \frac{1}{10}$$
$$= 2.303 \times 10^6 \text{ J}$$

Thus, (iv)—(r)

211. (d) (i) $H_2O(l, \text{ at } 263 \text{ K}) \longrightarrow H_2O(l, \text{ at } 273 \text{ K})$

$$\Delta S = 2.303 \, nC_p \log \frac{T_2}{T_1}$$
$$= 2.303 \times \frac{100}{18} \times 75.3 \log \frac{273.0}{263.0}$$
$$= 15.61 \text{ J K}^{-1}$$

Thus, (i)—(p)

(ii) $H_2O(l, \text{ at } 273 \text{ K}) \longrightarrow H_2O(s, \text{ at } 273 \text{ K})$

$$\Delta S = \frac{n\Delta H^\circ}{T} = -\frac{100}{18} \times \frac{6.00}{273} \text{ kJ K}^{-1}$$
$$= -0.122 \text{ kJ} = -122.0 \text{ J K}^{-1}$$

Thus (ii)—(s)

(iii) $H_2O(s, \text{ at } 273 \text{ K}) \longrightarrow H_2O(s, \text{ at } 263 \text{ K})$

$$\Delta S = 2.303 \, nC_p \log \frac{T_2}{T_1}$$
$$= 2.303 \times \frac{100}{18} \times 38 \log \frac{263}{273}$$
$$= -7.88 \text{ J K}^{-1}$$

Thus, (iii)—(r)

(iv) $\Delta S_{total} = \Delta S_1 + \Delta S_2 + \Delta S_3$

$= 15.61 - 122.0 - 7.88$

$= -114.27 \text{ J K}^{-1}$

Thus, (iv)—(q)

212. (b)

213. (b) (1) **Isothermal reversible process,**

By first law,

$$\Delta U = q + W$$
$$\therefore \quad q = \Delta U - W$$

Since, $a = 0$ as shown by equation (no force of attraction, hence no loss of internal energy U)

$$\therefore \quad \Delta U = 0$$

Also, $\Delta H = \Delta U + \Delta(pV)$

$$\therefore \quad \Delta H = \Delta(pV)$$

Since, $p = \frac{RT}{(V - b)}$

$$\therefore \quad pV = \frac{RTV}{(V - b)}$$

$$\therefore \Delta H = RT\left[\frac{V_2}{(V_2 - b)} - \frac{V_1}{(V_1 - b)}\right]$$
$$= RT\left[\frac{V_2 - b + b}{(V_2 - b)} - \frac{V_1 - b + b}{(V_1 - b)}\right]$$
$$= RT\left[1 + \frac{b}{(V_2 - b)} - 1 - \frac{b}{(V_1 - b)}\right]$$
$$= RTb\left[\frac{1}{(V_2 - b)} - \frac{1}{(V_1 - b)}\right]$$

$$= RTb\left[\frac{p_2}{RT} - \frac{p_1}{RT}\right] = b(p_2 - p_1)$$

Thus, (i)–(r).

■ $\frac{1}{(V-b)} = \frac{p}{RT}$ (given)

(ii) **Isobaric reversible process**

In isobaric reversible process, $dp = 0$

$$\Delta U = C_V(\Delta T) = C_V(T_2 - T_1)$$
$$= C_V\left[\frac{p(V_2 - b)}{R} - \frac{p(V_1 - b)}{R}\right]$$
$$= \frac{C_V p}{R}(V_2 - V_1)$$
$$\Delta H = \Delta U + \Delta(pV)$$
$$= \frac{C_V p}{R}(V_2 - V_1) + p(V_2 - V_1)$$
$$= p(V_2 - V_1)\left[\frac{C_V + R}{R}\right]$$

Thus, (ii)–(s)

(iii) **Isochoric reversible process**

$$V = \text{constant}$$
$$\therefore \quad dV = 0$$
$$\therefore \quad \Delta U = C_V\,\Delta T = C_V(T_2 - T_1)$$
$$= C_V\left[\frac{p_2(V-b)}{R} - \frac{p_1(V-b)}{R}\right]$$
$$= C_V\frac{(V-b)}{R}(p_2 - p_1)$$
$$\Delta H = \Delta U + p(\Delta V)$$
$$= \Delta U + p\Delta(RT + pb)/p$$
$$= \Delta U + R\Delta T + b\Delta p$$
$$\Delta H = C_V\frac{(V-b)}{R}(p_2 - p_1) + R(T_2 - T_1) + b(p_2 - p_1)$$
$$= \frac{C_V(V-b)}{R}(p_2 - p_1) + R\left[\frac{p_2(V-b)}{R} - \frac{p_1(V-b)}{R}\right] + b(p_2 - p_1)$$
$$= \frac{C_V(V-b)}{R}(p_2 - p_1) + (p_2 - p_1)(V-b) + b(p_2 - p_1)$$
$$= (p_2 - p_1)\left[\frac{C_V}{R}(V-b) + (V-b) + b\right]$$
$$= (p_2 - p_1)\left[\left(\frac{C_V + R}{R}\right)(V-b) + b\right]$$
$$= \frac{C_p}{R}(p_2 - p_1)(V-b) + (p_2 - p_1)b$$

Thus, (iii)–(q)

(iv) **Adiabatic irreversible process.**

$$q = 0, \quad \therefore \quad \Delta U = q + W = 0 + W$$

$$\Delta U = W = -p[(V_2 - b) - (V_1 - b)]$$
$$= -p(V_2 - V_1)$$
$$\Delta U = -p_2\left[\frac{RT_2}{p_2} - \frac{RT_1}{p_1}\right]$$

(p_2 is the external pressure $p = p_2$)

$$\therefore \quad \Delta U = -\left[RT_2 - \frac{RT_1p_2}{p_1}\right]$$

Proceeding as above

$$\boxed{\Delta H = C_p\,(T_2 - T_1) + b(p_2 - p_1)}$$

Thus, (iv)–(p)

214. (c) N_2 taken $= 28\text{ g} = \frac{28}{28} = 1\text{ mol}$

$$T_1 = 300\text{ K}$$
$$V_1 = 20\text{ dm}^3$$
$$V_2 = 10\text{ dm}^3$$

For adiabatic expansion :

$$\frac{T_2}{T_1} = \left(\frac{V_1}{V_2}\right)^{\gamma - 1}$$

$\gamma = 1.4$ for N_2 (diatomic gas)

$$\therefore \quad T_2 = 300\,(2)^{0.4}$$
$$= 300 \times 1.32\text{ K}$$
$$= 396\text{ K}$$

Also, $\frac{\Delta U}{\Delta T} = C_V$

$$\therefore \quad \Delta U = nC_V\Delta T\ (n = 1)$$
$$= \frac{5}{2}R\,(T_2 - T_1)$$
$$= \frac{5}{2} \times 8.314\,(396 - 300)$$
$$= 1995\text{ J}$$

Also, $\Delta U = q - W$

and $q = 0$ for adiabatic expansion

$$\therefore \quad \Delta U = -W = 1995\text{ J}$$
$$\frac{\Delta H}{\Delta T} = nC_p$$
$$\Delta H = nC_p(T_2 - T_1)$$
$$= 1 \times 3.5 \times 8.314 \times 96\text{ J}$$
$$\Delta H = 2794\text{ J}$$

Thus, (i)–(s) (ii)–(p)
(iii)–(q) (iv)–(q)
(v)–(r)

215. (c) **Step (a) It is isobaric**

$$C_p - C_V = R$$
$$\therefore \quad C_p = C_V + R$$
$$= 1.5R + R = 2.5R$$
$$\therefore \quad \frac{\Delta H}{\Delta T} = C_p$$
$$\Delta H_1 = C_p\Delta T$$
$$= C_p(T_2 - T_1)$$
$$= 2.5 \times 8.314\,(373 - 298)$$
$$= 1558.9\text{ J mol}^{-1}$$

Also, $q_1 = \Delta H = 1558.9\text{ J mol}^{-1}$

$$\Delta U_1 = C_V\Delta T$$
$$= 1.5R\,(T_2 - T_1)$$
$$= 1.5 \times 8.314 \times (378 - 298)$$
$$= 935.3\text{ J mol}^{-1}$$
$$W_1 = -p\Delta V$$
$$= \Delta U - \Delta H$$
$$= 935.3 - 1558.9$$
$$= -623.6\text{ J mol}^{-1}$$

Step (b) Isothermal reversible

$$V_1 = V \quad V_2 = 2V$$
$$\therefore \quad W_2 = -2.303RT\log\frac{V_2}{V_1}$$
$$= -2.303 \times 8.314 \times 373\log 2$$
$$= -2150.0\text{ J mol}^{-1}$$

Since, reversible, $\therefore\ \Delta U = 0$

and $\Delta H = 0$

and $q_2 = -W_2$

$$= +2150.0\text{ J mol}^{-1}$$

Step (c) Adiabatic reversible cooling

$$q_3 = 0$$
$$W_3 = \Delta U_3 = C_V(T_2 - T_1)$$
$$= 1.5 \times 8.314\,(308 - 373)$$
$$= -810.6\text{ J mol}^{-1}$$
$$\Delta H_3 = C_p(T_2 - T_1)$$
$$= 2.5 \times 8.314 \times (308 - 373)$$
$$= -3751.0\text{ J mol}^{-1}$$

Thus, net change of

$$q = 1558.9 + 2150.0 + 0$$
$$= 3708.9\text{ J}$$
$$= 3.71\text{ kJ mol}^{-1}$$

Thus, (i)-(q).

$$W = -623.6 - 2150 - 810.6$$
$$= -3584\text{ J mol}^{-1}$$
$$= -3.584\text{ kJ mol}^{-1}$$

Thus, (ii)-(s).

$$\Delta U = 935.3 + 0 - 810.6$$
$$= 124.75\text{ J mol}^{-1}$$
$$= 0.125\text{ kJ mol}^{-1}$$

Thus, (iii)-(p)

$$\Delta H = 1558.9 + 0 - 1351.0$$
$$= 207.9\text{ J}$$
$$= 0.208\text{ kJ mol}^{-1}$$

Thus, (iv)-(r)

Thermochemistry

Chapter Topics

- Thermochemical Standard States
- Enthalpy of Neutralisation and Enthalpy of Solution
- Bond Energy or Bond Enthalpy and Bond Dissociation Enthalpy
- Hess's Law of Constant Heat Summation
- Calorimetry

Thermochemical Standard States

Enthalpy change taking place in a reaction is studied under **thermochemistry.** The thermochemical standard state of a substance is its most stable state under **standard pressure** (one bar) and at some **specified temperature** (25°C or 298 K) unless otherwise specified. Under these conditions, any parameter is designated as $\Delta H°$, $\Delta E°$, $\Delta S°$ ... .

- For a pure substance in the liquid or solid phase, the standard state is pure liquid or solid.
- For a gas, the standard state is the gas at a pressure of one bar; in a mixture of gases, its partial pressure must be one bar.
- For a substance in solution, the standard state refers to one molar concentration (1 mol L^{-1}).

Different terms have been summarised below :

Different types of standard enthalpy changes (Based on IUPAC recommendations)

	Transition enthalpy	Definition	Example	Symbol
1.	Enthalpy of formation	Change of enthalpy when one mole of the compound formed from its elements	$Na(s) + \frac{1}{2}Cl_2(g) \longrightarrow NaCl(s)$	$\Delta_f H°$ or $\Delta H°_f$
2.	Enthalpy of combustion	Change of enthalpy when one mole of the compound (fuel) is burnt completely in oxygen (oxidation)	$CH_4(g) + 2O_2(g) \longrightarrow CO_2(g) + 2H_2O(l)$	$\Delta_C H°$ or $\Delta H°_C$
3.	Enthalpy of fusion	Change of enthalpy when one mole of the liquid is formed from the solid without a change in temperature	$H_2O(s) \longrightarrow H_2O(l)$	$\Delta_{fus} H°$ or $\Delta H°_{fus}$
4.	Enthalpy of vaporisation	Change of enthalpy when one mole of the vapour formed from the liquid without a change in temperature	$H_2O(l) \longrightarrow H_2O(g)$	$\Delta_{vap} H°$ or $\Delta H°_{vap}$
5.	Enthalpy of sublimation	Change of enthalpy when one mole of the vapour formed from the solid	$H_2O(s) \longrightarrow H_2O(g)$	$\Delta_{sub} H°$ or $\Delta H°_{sub}$
6.	Enthalpy of atomisation	Change of enthalpy when one mole of the substance broken into isolated atoms in the gas phase	$H_2(g) \longrightarrow 2H(g)$	$\Delta_{at} H°$ or $\Delta H°_{at}$

	Transition enthalpy	Definition	Example	Symbol
7.	Enthalpy of reaction	Change of enthalpy when taking place in a reaction	$A \longrightarrow B$	$\Delta_r H°$ or $\Delta H°_r$
8.	Enthalpy of neutralisation	Change of enthalpy when one mole of water formed by the neutralisation of an acid by a base	$HCl(aq) + NaOH(aq) \longrightarrow H_2O + NaCl(aq)$	$\Delta_n H°$ or $\Delta H°_n$
9.	Enthalpy of ionisation	Change of enthalpy when one mole of atom ionised, all species in gaseous phase	$Na(g) \longrightarrow Na^+(g) + e^-$	$\Delta_{ion} H°$ or $\Delta H°_{ion}$
10.	Electron gain enthalpy	Change of enthalpy when one mole of anions being formed, all species in the gaseous phase	$X(g) + e^- \longrightarrow X(g)$	$\Delta_{eg} H°$ or $\Delta H°_{eg}$
11.	Lattice enthalpy	Change of enthalpy when one mole of a crystal is completely separated into isolated particles in the gaseous phase	$K^+Cl^-(s) \longrightarrow K^+(g) + Cl^-(g)$	$\Delta_L H°$ or $\Delta H°_L$
12.	Bond dissociation enthalpy (bond $A—B$)	Change of enthalpy when one mole of bonds broken–all species in the gaseous phase	$AB(g) \longrightarrow A(g) + B(g)$	$\Delta H°_{A-B}$
13.	Enthalpy of solution	Change of enthalpy when one mole of the solute dissolved in excess of solvent so that further dilution produces no enthalpy change	$A(s) + H_2O(\text{excess}) \longrightarrow A(aq)$	$\Delta_{sol} H°$ or $\Delta H°_{sol}$
14.	Enthalpy of hydration	Change of enthalpy when one mole of the ion in gaseous phase is hydrated	$X^{\pm}(g) \longrightarrow X^{\pm}(aq)$	$\Delta_{hyd} H°$ or $\Delta H°_{hyd}$
15.	Enthalpy of mixing	Change of enthalpy when one mole each of the two or more substances is mixed	pure substances $\longrightarrow$ mixture	$\Delta_{mix} H°$ or $\Delta H°_{mix}$

Enthalpy of reaction ($\Delta_r H°$)

It is defined as "the heat change during a chemical reaction when the number of moles of reactants have reacted completely as indicated by balanced chemical equation."

$$\Delta_r H° = \Sigma H_P° - \Sigma H_R°$$
$$= \text{Sum of enthalpies of products} - \text{sum of enthalpies of reactants}$$

- If $H_P° = H_R°$, $\Delta_r H° = 0$, heat is neither absorbed nor evolved.
- If $H_P° > H_R°$, $\Delta_r H° = +$ ve, heat is absorbed (endothermic)

$$A + q \longrightarrow B, \qquad \Delta_r H° = q$$

- If $H_P° < H_R°$, $\Delta_r H° = -$ ve, heat is evolved (exothermic)

$$A - q \longrightarrow B, \qquad \Delta_r H° = -q$$

Factors affecting enthalpy of reaction

(i) **Physical states of the reactants and products**

Enthalpy of reaction is different for different physical states.

$$H_2(g) + \frac{1}{2}O_2(g) \longrightarrow H_2O(l), \quad \Delta H° = -285.9 \text{ kJ mol}^{-1}$$

$$H_2(g) + \frac{1}{2}O_2(g) \longrightarrow H_2O(g), \quad \Delta H° = -241.8 \text{ kJ mol}^{-1}$$

The difference in two $\Delta H°$ values arises due to different physical states of water.

Thus, $$H_2O(l) \longrightarrow H_2O(g), \quad \Delta H° = 44.1 \text{ kJ mol}^{-1}$$
(285.9 – 241.8)

This value of $\Delta H°$ represents molar enthalpy of vaporisation of water as $H_2O\ (l)$ is vaporised to $H_2O\ (g)$.

(ii) **Allotropic forms of the element**

$$C(\text{graphite}) + O_2(g) \longrightarrow CO_2(g), \quad \Delta H° = -393.5 \text{ kJ mol}^{-1}$$
$$C(\text{diamond}) + O_2(g) \longrightarrow CO_2(g), \quad \Delta H° = -380.4 \text{ kJ mol}^{-1}$$

Thus, $C(\text{diamond}) \longrightarrow C(\text{graphite}), \Delta H° = 13.1 \text{ kJ mol}^{-1}$

Thus, value of $\Delta H°$ arises due to different allotropes of carbon and is the molar enthalpy of transition of carbon.

(iii) **Reaction conditions** (at constant volume or at constant pressure)

$$\Delta H° = \Delta E° + \Delta n_g RT$$

$\Delta H°$ ↑ Heat change during reaction at constant pressure; $\Delta E°$ ↑ Heat change during reaction at constant volume

If a reaction involves only solids and liquids, then

$$\Delta H° = \Delta E° \quad \text{or} \quad \Delta H = \Delta E$$

If it involves gases also then, ΔH and ΔE are different.

Δn_g = (Number of gaseous products – Number of gaseous reactants)

If $\Delta n_g = 0$, $\Delta H° = \Delta E°$

if $\Delta n_g > 0$, if $\Delta n_g < 0$ } $\Delta H°$ and $\Delta E°$ are different

(iv) Effect of temperature Enthalpy of a substance increases with increase in temperature. It is due to the fact that, the heat capacity of the substance varies with temperature.

By Kirchhoff's equation at constant pressure,

$$\Delta H_2 = \Delta H_1 + \Delta C_p(T_2 - T_1)$$

and at constant volume

$$\Delta E_2 = \Delta E_1 + \Delta C_V (T_2 - T_1)$$

where, ΔC_p = [Heat capacities of products − heat capacities of reactants at constant p]

ΔC_V = [Heat capacities of products − heat capacities of reactants at constant V]

C_p and C_V for different gases

Gas	C_p	C_V	$C_p - C_V$
Monoatomic	$\frac{5}{2}R$	$\frac{3}{2}R$	R
Diatomic	$\frac{7}{2}R$	$\frac{5}{2}R$	R
Polyatomic	$4R$	$3R$	R

(v) Enthalpy is a state function, a change in enthalpy is independent of the path between two states.

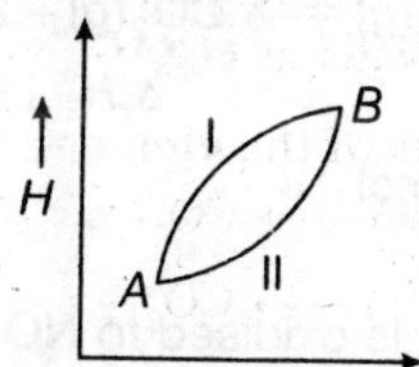

$$\Delta H_1 = \Delta H_2 = H_B - H_A$$

Enthalpy of formation ($\Delta_f H°$)

The enthalpy change which occurs when one mole of a compound is formed from its constituent elements is known as enthalpy of formation ($\Delta_f H$); (in standard state it is denoted by $\Delta_f H°$).

- **The standard enthalpies of formation of elements in their reference states are zero at all temperatures.**
- $\Delta_f H°$ (of a given substance) = its enthalpy

$$C(s) + O_2(g) \longrightarrow CO_2(g)$$

$$\Delta_f H°(CO_2) = H°(CO_2) - [H°(C) + H°(O_2)]$$
$$= H°(CO_2) - [0 + 0]$$

Thus, $\Delta_f H°(CO_2) = H°(CO_2)$

If $\Delta_f H°$ of CO_2, H_2O and CH_4 are x_1, x_2, and x_3 per mol of the product formed, then $\Delta_r H°$ of

$$CH_4 + 2O_2 \longrightarrow CO_2 + 2H_2O$$

$$\Delta_r H° = \Delta_f H°(CO_2) + 2\Delta_f H°(H_2O) - [\Delta_f H°(CH_4) + \Delta_f H°(O_2)]$$
$$= x_1 + 2x_2 - x_3$$

Enthalpy of combustion ($\Delta_C H°$)

The enthalpy decrease ($\Delta_C H°$ = −ve in exothermic change), that takes place when one mole of the substance is completely burnt in oxygen is called enthalpy of combustion ($\Delta_C H$); in standard state and it is denoted by ($\Delta_C H°$).

(i) $CH_4(g) + 2O_2(g) \longrightarrow CO_2(g) + 2H_2O(l)$

(ii) $C(s) + \frac{1}{2}O_2(g) \longrightarrow CO(g)$

Thermochemical equation (ii) represents $\Delta_f H°$ of CO but not the $\Delta_C H°$ of carbon, as CO can be further oxidised to CO_2.

- $\Delta_C H°$ of hydrocarbons, food materials, fuels, etc. can be converted into **calorific values**, which are measured per gram of the substance.

  If, $\Delta_C H°$ of $CH_4 = q$ kJ mol^{-1}, then calorific value of CH_4

$$= \left(\frac{q \text{ kJ}}{16}\right) \text{kJ g}^{-1}$$

- If $\Delta_C H°$ of the substance and its elements are known, $\Delta_f H°$ of that substance can be calculated as given below :

  If $\Delta_C H°$ of CH_4, C and H_2 are x_1, x_2 and x_3 respectively then $\Delta_f H°$ of CH_4 can be derived.

(i) $CH_4 + O_2 \longrightarrow CO_2 + 2H_2O, \Delta H_1 = x_1$

(ii) $C + O_2 \longrightarrow CO_2, \Delta H_2 = x_2$

(iii) $H_2 + \frac{1}{2}O_2 \longrightarrow H_2O, \Delta H_3 = x_3$

In Eq. (ii), CO_2 is formed. Also, it represents combustion of carbon.

Thus, $\Delta_f H°(CO_2) = \Delta_C H°(C) = H°(CO_2)$

Similarly, for Eq. (iii)

$$\Delta_f H°(H_2O) = \Delta_C H°(H_2) = H°(H_2O)$$

For Eq. (i)

$$\Delta H_1 = x_1 = [H°_{CO_2} + 2H°_{H_2O}] - [H°_{CH_4}]$$
$$= x_2 + 2x_3 - H°_{CH_4}$$

$$\therefore \quad H°_{CH_4} = (x_2 + 2x_3 - x_1)$$

$$H°_{CH_4} = \Delta_f H°(CH_4) = (x_2 + 2x_3 - x_1)$$

Solved Examples & Instant Practice

Example 6.1) For the reaction,

$$2H_2(g) + O_2(g) \longrightarrow 2H_2O(l),$$

$\Delta H^\circ = -136$ kcal at 298 K and at 1 bar.

What is standard enthalpy of H_2O ?

Sol. Standard enthalpy of the elements is taken as zero, thus standard enthalpy of formation of a given species is the standard enthalpy of that species.

$$\Delta H^\circ = (H_P^\circ - H_R^\circ)$$

Enthalpy of elements = 0

$$-136 \text{ kcal} = 2H^\circ_{H_2O} - [2H^\circ_{H_2} + H^\circ_{O_2}]$$

$$-136 = 2H^\circ_{H_2O} - [0 + 0]$$

$$\therefore \quad H^\circ_{H_2O} = -68 \text{ kcal mol}^{-1}$$

In the given reaction, 2 moles of H_2O are formed.

Thus, $\Delta_f H^\circ (H_2O) = -68$ kcal mol^{-1}

Also $\quad H^\circ_{H_2O} = \Delta_f H^\circ (H_2O)$

Immediate Test 1

Given,

$$H^\circ_{C_2H_4} = +52.5 \text{ kJ mol}^{-1}$$

$$H^\circ_{C_2H_6} = -83.8 \text{ kJ mol}^{-1}$$

What is ΔH° of the reaction

$$C_2H_4(g) + H_2(g) \longrightarrow C_2H_6(g)$$

Example 6.2) For the reaction,

$$CO + \frac{1}{2}O_2 \longrightarrow CO_2, \quad \Delta H^\circ = -68 \text{ kcal mol}^{-1}$$

If $H^\circ_{CO} = -26$ kcal mol^{-1}

What is $H^\circ_{CO_2}$?

Sol. Given, reaction represents combustion of CO. Thus, from the fact

$$\Delta H^\circ = H^\circ \text{(products)} - H^\circ \text{(reactants)}$$

and $\quad H^\circ$ (element) = 0

unknown data can be derived.

$$-68 = H^\circ_{CO_2} - [H^\circ_{(CO)} + \frac{1}{2}H^\circ_{(O_2)}] = H^\circ_{CO_2} - [(-26) + 0]$$

$$\therefore \quad H^\circ_{CO_2} = -94 \text{ kcal mol}^{-1}$$

Immediate Test 2

$\Delta_f H^\circ$ of PCl_3 and PCl_5 are x_1 and x_2 respectively. What is ΔH° of the reaction

$$PCl_3 + Cl_2 \longrightarrow PCl_5$$

Example 6.3) Given,

$$N(g) + 3H_2(g) \longrightarrow 2NH_3(g), \ \Delta_r H^\circ = -92.2 \text{ kJ at 298 K}$$

Calculate, $\Delta_r H^\circ_{348}$ at 338 K.

Also, calculate $\Delta_r E^\circ$ (or $\Delta_r U^\circ$) at both temperatures.

Sol. In this reaction, effect of temperature on the value of ΔH° is to be predicted by Kirchoff's equation, $\Delta H^\circ_{T_2} = \Delta H^\circ_{T_1} + \Delta C_p (T_2 - T_1)$

Also $\quad \Delta H^\circ_T = \Delta U^\circ_T + \Delta n_g RT$

$$\Delta C_p = C_p \text{ (products)} - C_p \text{ (reactants)}$$

$$\Delta C_p = 2C_p(NH_3) - [C_p(N_2) + 3C_p(H_2)]$$

$$= 2 \times 4R - \left[\frac{7}{2}R + 3 \times \frac{7}{2}R\right] = -6R$$

$$\therefore \quad \Delta_r H^\circ_{348} = \Delta_r H^\circ_{298} + \Delta C_p (T_2 - T_1)$$

$$= -92.2 + (-6) \times 8.314 \times 10^{-3} (50)$$

$$= -94.69 \text{ kJ mol}^{-1}$$

To calculate ΔU°

$$\Delta U^\circ_{298} = \Delta H^\circ_{298} - \Delta n_g RT$$

$$\Delta n_g = -2$$

$$\therefore \quad \Delta U^\circ_{298} = -92.2 - (-2) \times 8.314 \times 10^{-3} \times 298$$

$$= -87.24 \text{ kJ mol}^{-1}$$

$$\Delta U^\circ_{338} = -94.69 - (-2) \times 8.314 \times 10^{-3} \times 338$$

$$= -89.07 \text{ kJ mol}^{-1}$$

Immediate Test 3

At 298 K, $\Delta_f H^\circ$ of $H_2O(g)$, $CO_2(g)$, are -58, -94 kcal mol^{-1}.

Calculate $\Delta_f H^\circ$ of CH_4 at 398 K, if

$$CH_4(g) + 2O_2(g) \longrightarrow CO_2(g) + 2H_2O(g),$$

$$\Delta_r H^\circ_{298} = -260 \text{ kcal mol}^{-1}$$

C_p (graphite) = 8.53 J mol^{-1} K^{-1}

Example 6.4) NH_3 is oxidised to NO and H_2O. Calculate heat of combustion of NH_3, if standard enthalpy of formation of

$$NH_3 = -11.02 \text{ kcal mol}^{-1}$$

$$NO = -21.6 \text{ kcal mol}^{-1}$$

and $\quad H_2O = -68.0$ kcal mol^{-1}

When standard heat of combustion of a species is known and also the standard heat of formation of the oxidised products are also known, then, heat of formation of the combusted species can be derived.

Also, $\quad \Delta_f H^\circ (X) = H^\circ (X)$

Sol. $2NH_3(g) + 2.5O_2(g) \longrightarrow 2NO(g) + 3H_2O(l)$

$$\Delta_r H^\circ = \Sigma H^\circ \text{(products)} - \Sigma H^\circ \text{(reactants)}$$

$$= [2(-21.6) + 3(-68.0)] - 2[-11.02]$$

$$= -225.16 \text{ kcal for 2 mol } NH_3$$

$$\text{Thus, } \Delta_C H^\circ (NH_3) = -\frac{225.16}{2} = -112.58 \text{ kcal mol}^{-1}$$

Immediate Test 4

Standard heat of combustion of C_6H_6, C (graphite) and H_2 are $-x_1$, $-x_2$ and $-x_3$ kJ mol^{-1}. Calculate heat of formation of C_6H_6.

KNOWLEDGE CONFIRMATION Test 1

1 The enthalpy change for which of the following processes represents the enthalpy of formation of AgCl?

(a) $Ag^+(aq) + Cl^-(aq) \longrightarrow AgCl(s)$

(b) $Ag(s) + \frac{1}{2}Cl_2(g) \longrightarrow AgCl(s)$

(c) $Ag(s) + Cl(g) \longrightarrow AgCl(s)$

(d) $Ag(s) + AuCl(s) \longrightarrow Au(s) + AgCl(s)$

2 Which is not the correct notation of the given reaction?

(a) $C + O_2 \longrightarrow CO_2,\ \Delta_C H°(C), \Delta_f H°(CO_2)$

(b) $C + \frac{1}{2}O_2 \longrightarrow CO, \Delta_f, H°(CO)$

(c) $CO + \frac{1}{2}O_2 \longrightarrow CO_2, \Delta_f H°(CO_2)$

(d) $H_2 + \frac{1}{2}O_2 \longrightarrow H_2O, \Delta_f H°(H_2O)$

3 $\Delta_f H°$ of HgO is -21.7 kcal mol^{-1}. Mass of mercury which can be liberated from HgO at 298 K by the treatment of excess of HgO with 10.0 kcal of heat is (Hg = 206)

(a) 94.93 g (b) 447.02 g (c) 51.79 g (d) 69.72 g

4 In the above case, how much O_2 gas at NTP is formed in a closed vessel by the same heat?

(a) 1.12 L (b) 0.194 L (c) 11.2 L (d) 5.16 L

5 Given, $\Delta_f H°$ of $CaO(s) = -151.9$ kcal mol^{-1}

$\Delta_f H°$ of $CaC_2(s) = -14.2$ kcal mol^{-1}

$\Delta_f H°$ of $CO(g) = -26.4$ kcal mol^{-1}

Heat required to make 1.0 kg of CaC_2 from $CaO(s)$ and $C(s)$ is

$$CaO(s) + 3C(s) \longrightarrow CaC_2(s) + CO(g)$$

(a) 1739 kcal (b) -1739 kcal

(c) -14.2 kcal (d) $+14.2$ kcal

6 Given, $\Delta_f H°$ of $Al_2O_3 = -399.1$ kcal mol^{-1},

$CuO = -37.6$ kcal mol^{-1}

and $3CuO(s) + 2Al(s) \longrightarrow Al_2O_3(s) + Cu(s)$

Enthalpy change when 1 mole of CuO is reduced by Al is

(a) + 95.43 kcal (b) -95.43 kcal

(c) -286.3 kcal (d) + 286.3 kcal

7 The heat evolved in combustion of 1 g of starch $(C_6H_{10}O_5)_n$ into CO_2 and H_2O is 4.18 kcal

$\Delta_f H°(H_2O) = -68$ kcal

$\Delta_f H°(CO_2) = -94$ kcal

Thus, standard enthalpy of formation of 1 g of starch is

(a) 1.40 kcal (b) -1.40 kcal (c) 226.84 kcal (d) -226.84 kcal

8 Enthalpy of combustion of CO at 298 K is -68.0 kcal mol^{-1}. What is enthalpy of combustion of 100 g of CO at 398 K?

(a) -244 kcal (b) 68.32 kcal (c) + 244 kcal (d) -68.32 kcal

9 $\Delta_f H°(H_2O(g)) = -58.0$ kcal mol^{-1}

$\Delta_f H°(H_2O(l)) = -68.0$ kcal mol^{-1}

Thus, heat of vaporisation of $H_2O(l)$ per g at 298 K and 1 atm is

(a) 556 cal g^{-1} (b) -556 cal g^{-1}

(c) 7 kcal g^{-1} (d) -7 kcal g^{-1}

10 Given,

I. $C(\text{graphite}) + \frac{1}{2}O_2(g) \longrightarrow CO(g),\quad \Delta H = -26$ kcal

II. $CO(g) + \frac{1}{2}O_2(g) \longrightarrow CO_2(g),\quad \Delta H = -68$ kcal

Thus, incorrect statement is

(a) $\Delta_f H°(CO) = -26$ kcal mol^{-1} (b) $\Delta_f H°(CO_2) = -94$ kcal mol^{-1}

(c) $\Delta_f H°(CO_2) = -68$ kcal mol^{-1} (d) $\Delta_C H°(CO) = -68$ kcal mol^{-1}

11 $\Delta_f H°(O_3) = 143$ kJ mol^{-1}

Thus, enthalpy change for the following

$3O_2(g) \longrightarrow 2O_3(g)$, is

(a) 143 kJ (b) 286 kJ (c) 429 kJ (d) zero

12 2.7 g of Al reacts with stoichiometric amount of Fe_2O_3.

$2Al + Fe_2O_3 \longrightarrow 2Fe + Al_2O_3,\quad \Delta H° = -852$ kJ

Thus, enthalpy change is

(a) -85.2 kJ (b) -42.6 kJ

(c) + 85.2 kJ (d) + 42.6 kJ

13 Which of these species has standard enthalpy of formation equal to zero?

(a) $F_2(g)$ (b) $F(g)$ (c) $HF(aq)$ (d) $F^-(aq)$

14 Consider the following reactions :

I. $N_2 + O_2 \longrightarrow 2NO, \Delta H° = x_1$

II. $2CO + O_2 \longrightarrow 2CO_2, \Delta H° = x_2$

III. $2H_2O + O_2 \longrightarrow 2H_2O_2, \Delta H° = x_3$

IV. $PCl_3 + Cl_2 \longrightarrow PCl_5, \Delta H° = x_4$

In which case (s), $\Delta_f H° = \frac{\Delta H°}{2}$

(a) I, II, III (b) II and III

(c) Only I (d) Only III

15 Which of the following is a state function?

(a) Enthalpy (b) Internal energy

(c) Entropy (d) All of these

16 In the following reaction at 298 K,

$$F_2(g) + 2HCl(aq) \longrightarrow 2HF(aq) + Cl_2(g),$$
$$\Delta H^\circ = -84.4 \text{ kcal}$$

and $\Delta_f H^\circ(\text{HF}) = -64.2 \text{ kcal mol}^{-1}$ thus, $\Delta_f H^\circ(\text{HCl})$ is
(a) + 20.2 kcal mol^{-1} (b) – 22.0 kcal mol^{-1}
(c) – 20.2 kcal mol^{-1} (d) + 22.0 kcal mol^{-1}

17 Which of the following has the highest enthalpy content?
(a) $H_2O(s)$ (b) $H_2O(l)$ (c) $H_2O(g)$ (d) Equal

18 Heat of vaporisation of $A(l)$ is x_1 cal and heat of fusion of $A(s)$ is x_2 cal. Hence, heat of sublimation of $A(s)$ is
(a) $(x_1 - x_2)$ cal (b) $(x_2 - x_1)$ cal
(c) $(x_1 + x_2)$ cal (d) $-(x_1 + x_2)$ cal

19 For the following reaction,

$$A + B + x_1 \longrightarrow C + D + x_2$$

Select the correct statement.
(a) If $x_1 > x_2$, reaction is exothermic
(b) If $x_2 > x_1$, reaction is endothermic
(c) If $x_2 > x_1$, reaction is exothermic
(d) None of the above statement is correct

20 Heat of reaction is independent of
(a) temperature (b) pressure
(c) physical state (d) path adopted

21 Consider the following reactions :
I. $NH_4HS(s) \rightleftharpoons NH_3(g) + H_2S(g)$
II. $CaCO_3(s) \rightleftharpoons CaO(s) + CO_2(s)$
III. $PCl_5(g) \rightleftharpoons PCl_3(g) + Cl_2(g)$

In which case(s), $\Delta H - \Delta E = RT$
(a) I, II and III (b) I and II (c) II and III (d) I and III

22 Heat of combustion of CH_4, C_2H_6 and C_3H_8 are respectively, – 210, – 368.4 and – 526.3 kcal mol^{-1}. Hence, maximum calorific value (in kcal g^{-1}) is of
(a) C_3H_8 (b) C_2H_6 (c) CH_4 (d) C_2H_6 and C_3H_8

23 In the complete combustion of C_2H_6, 54 g of H_2O is formed and 370 kcal of heat is evolved. Thus, heat of combustion of C_2H_6 is
(a) + 370 kcal mol^{-1} (b) – 370 kcal mol^{-1}
(c) – 6.61 kcal mol^{-1} (d) + 6.61 kcal mol^{-1}

24 Which represents enthalpy of combustion?
(a) $C_6H_6(l) + 4.5O_2(g) \longrightarrow 6CO(g) + 3H_2O(l), \Delta H = -200$ kcal
(b) $C(g) + O_2(g) \longrightarrow CO_2(g), \Delta H = 94$ kcal
(c) $CH_4(g) + 2O_2(g) \longrightarrow CO_2(g) + 2H_2O(l), \Delta H = -210$ kcal
(d) $2C(s) + O_2(g) \longrightarrow 2CO(g), \Delta H = -52$ kcal

25 Heat of combustion of CH_4 at 298 K and 1 bar is – 210 kcal mol^{-1}. Thus, heat of combustion at constant volume is
(a) – 210 kcal mol^{-1} (b) – 198 kcal mol^{-1}
(c) – 208.8 kcal mol^{-1} (d) – 211.2 kcal mol^{-1}

26 The difference between ΔH and ΔU, $(\Delta H - \Delta U)$ when the combustion of one mole of heptane (l) is carried out at temperature T, is equal to ***[JEE Main 2019 (II) NTA]***
(a) $-4RT$ (b) $3RT$
(c) $4RT$ (d) $-3RT$

Enthalpy of Neutralisation and Enthalpy of Solution

Enthalpy of neutralisation

The enthalpy of neutralisation of an acid with an alkali is the enthalpy of reaction which takes place, when an amount of acid or alkali is neutralised to form one mole of water in dilute aqueous solution.

$$HCl(aq) + NaOH(aq) \longrightarrow NaCl(aq) + H_2O(l), \quad \Delta H = -57.3 \text{ kJ mol}^{-1}$$

$$H^+(aq) + Cl^-(aq) + Na^+(aq) + OH^-(aq) \longrightarrow Na^+(aq) + Cl^-(aq) + H_2O(l)$$

$$H^+(aq) + OH^-(aq) \longrightarrow H_2O(l), \quad \Delta H = -57.3 \text{ kJ mol}^{-1}$$

- **Heat of neutralisation of strong acid with strong base is constant and is – 57.3 kJ mol^{-1}.**
- **Thus, heat of neutralisation of a strong acid by a strong base is the enthalpy decrease in the formation of one mole of $H_2O(l)$ from $H^+(aq)$ and $OH^-(aq)$.**

By convention, $\Delta_f H^\circ(H^+) = 0$

- **If one of the electrolyte (acid or base) is weak, then some heat is absorbed in the ionisation of the weak electrolyte (to make it to behave as strong), hence heat of neutralisation of weak acid and strong base or strong acid and weak base or weak acid and weak base is less than 57.3 kJ mol^{-1}.**

■ $HF(aq) \longrightarrow H^+(aq) + F^-(aq)$ is exothermic.

Enthalpy of solution

The total energy released or absorbed when one mole of solute is dissolved in large excess of solvent, so that further addition of solvent does not produce further heat change, is called enthalpy of solution.

- $KCl(s) + H_2O(l) \rightleftharpoons KCl(aq); \Delta H° > 0$

It is an endothermic change as ionisation of KCl absorbs heat.

- $CaO(s) + H_2O(l) \rightleftharpoons Ca(OH)_2; \Delta H° < 0$

It is an exothermic change, as CaO is hydrated, heat is evolved.

(i) **Integral enthalpy of solution** is the enthalpy change per mole of solute when it is dissolved in pure solvent to give a solution of given concentration.

(ii) **Differential enthalpy of solution** is the enthalpy change when one mole of solute is dissolved in large volume of solution of known concentration, so that further dilution produces no enthalpy change.

(iii) **Enthalpy of dilution** is the enthalpy change when solution containing one mole of solute is diluted from one concentration to the other concentration.

Let ΔH be the enthalpy change when n_2 moles of solute are mixed with n_1 moles of solvent, then

$$\left(\frac{\Delta H}{\Delta n_2}\right)_{T_1, p_1, n_1} = \text{Differential enthalpy of solution}$$

$$\left(\frac{\Delta H}{\Delta n_1}\right)_{T_1, p_1, n_2} = \text{Differential enthalpy of dilution}$$

Enthalpy of hydration

Enthalpy of hydration is defined as the enthalpy change when one mole of solute is hydrated. It is generally (not always) an exothermic change.

$$\Delta H_{\text{solution}} = (\Delta H_{\text{hydration}} - \text{lattice energy})$$

Lattice energy is the energy required to dissociate one mole of lattice into its gaseous ions.

$$\underset{\text{Lattice}}{AB(s)} \rightleftharpoons A^+(g) + B^-(g), \qquad \Delta H = U$$

Reversely, lattice energy is the energy released when gaseous ions combine to form one mole of lattice.

$$A^+(g) + B^-(g) \longrightarrow \underset{\text{Lattice}}{AB(s)}, \qquad \Delta H = -U$$

- If $\Delta H_{\text{hydration}} > U$, solute dissolves in water.
- $\Delta H_{\text{hydration}} > U$, solute does not dissolve in water.
- If $\Delta H_{\text{hydration}} = U$, solute remains in equilibrium with the given solvent (H_2O).

Solved Examples & Instant Practice

Example 6.5) Heat of neutralisation of $CH_3COOH(aq)$ and $NaOH(aq)$ is -55.4 kJ mol^{-1}. Also, heat of neutralisation of $CH_3COOH(aq)$ and $NH_4OH(aq)$ is -50.4 kJ mol^{-1}. What is heat of neutralisation of $HCl(aq)$ and $NH_4OH(aq)$?

NH_4OH is a weak base. To derive the value of heat of neutralisation of NH_4OH and HCl, first we have to calculate the heat of ionisation of NH_4OH. From the first two sets of enthalpy value, heat of ionisation of NH_4OH is calculated.

Sol. I. $H^+(aq) + OH^-(aq) \rightleftharpoons H_2O(l); \quad \Delta H° = -57.3$ kJ mol^{-1}

II. $\underset{\text{Weak}}{CH_3COOH(aq)} + \underset{\text{Strong}}{NaOH(aq)} \rightleftharpoons CH_3COONa(aq) + H_2O(l);$

$\Delta H° = -55.4$ kJ mol^{-1}

This $\Delta H°$ is less than -57.3 kJ mol^{-1}.

Thus, heat of ionisation of $CH_3COOH = +1.9$ kJ mol^{-1}.

III. $CH_3COOH(aq) + NH_4OH(aq) \rightleftharpoons CH_3COONH_4(aq) + H_2O(l),$

$\Delta H° = -50.4$ kJ mol^{-1}

In this case, both are weak electrolytes.

Total enthalpy lost in the ionisation of weak acid and weak base $= -50.4 + 57.3 = 6.9$ kJ

This gives heat of ionisation of NH_4OH.

Thus, heat of neutralisation of NH_4OH and HCl can be evaluated.

From I and II,

As $\Delta H°_{\text{ionisation}}(CH_3COOH) = 1.9$ kJ mol^{-1}

$\therefore \quad \Delta H°_{\text{ionisation}}(NH_4OH) = 6.9 - 1.9$

$= 5.0$ kJ mol^{-1}

Thus, $NH_4OH(aq) + HCl(aq) \rightleftharpoons NH_4Cl(aq) + H_2O(l),$

ΔH = enthalpy of ionisation of NH_4OH + enthalpy of neutralisation of H^+ by OH^-.

$\Delta H = -57.3 + 5.0$

$= -52.3$ kJ mol^{-1}

Immediate Test 5

(i) What is enthalpy of neutralisation of 100 mL of 1M $Ca(OH)_2$ by 100 mL of 1 M H_2SO_4? Consider both as strong electrolyte.

(ii) Enthalpy of neutralisation of 100 mL of 1M HCN by 100 mL of 1M NaOH is 290 cal. What is enthalpy of ionisation of HCN, if enthalpy of ionisation of CH_3COOH is 1.3 kcal, compare acid strength of HCN and CH_3COOH?

Example 6.6) Hydration energies of Li^+ and Cl^- ions are – 499 and – 382 kJ mol^{-1} respectively. If lattice energy of LiCl is – 840 kJ mol^{-1}, what is enthalpy of solution of LiCl?

Sol. Hydration energy is the enthalpy change when one mole of the solute is hydrated. When a solute is dissolved, some heat is involved in the ionisation of lattice into gaseous state and then hydration take place.

$$Li^+(g) + Cl^-(g) \rightleftharpoons LiCl(s), \qquad \Delta H = -U$$

$$\Delta H^\circ_{solution} = \Delta H^\circ_{hydration} - \text{lattice energy.}$$

$$\Delta H_{hydration}(LiCl) = \Delta H_{hydration}(Li^+ + Cl^-)$$
$$= -499 - 382 = -881 \text{ kJ mol}^{-1}$$
$$\Delta H_{solution} = -881 - (-840)$$
$$= -41 \text{ kJ mol}^{-1}$$

(an exothermic change)

Example 6.7) A solution of composition $CuCl_2 + 10H_2O$ is diluted with x moles of water, the heat disengaged is given by

$$Q_V = -\left(\frac{x \times 5023}{x + 21.24}\right) \text{cal}$$

The enthalpy of solution of $CuCl_2$ in 100 moles of water is –11.08 kcal. Calculate enthalpy of solution of $CuCl_2$ in 10 moles of water.

Sol.

I. $CuCl_2 \cdot 10\,H_2O + 590 \longrightarrow CuCl_2 \cdot 600\,H_2O$

$$Q_V = -\left(\frac{590 \times 5023}{590 + 2124}\right) = 4848 \text{ cal}$$

$$\therefore \quad \Delta H_{solution}(I) = -4848 \text{ cal}$$

Also $= -4.848 \text{ kcal} \approx -4.85 \text{ kcal}$

II. $CuCl_2 + 600\,H_2O \longrightarrow CuCl_2 \cdot 600\,H_2O$

Thus, (II – I) given = – 11.08 kcal

$CuCl_2 + 10H_2O \longrightarrow CuCl_2 \cdot 10H_2O, \Delta H = -6.23$ kcal

Immediate Test 6

(i) Enthalpy of solution of $MgSO_4(s)$ is – 91.21 kJ mol^{-1} and that of $MgSO_4 \cdot 7H_2O(s)$ is + 13.81 kJ mol^{-1}, at 298 K. What is enthalpy of hydration of $MgSO_4(s)$?

(ii) Enthalpy of crystallisation $BaSO_4$ from $Ba^{2+}(aq)$ and $SO_4^{2-}(aq)$ ions is –4.5 kcal mol^{-1}. Also $\Delta_f H^\circ(BaSO_4) = -349$ kcal mol^{-1}. Calculate $\Delta_f H^\circ$ of Ba^{2+} ion if $\Delta_f H^\circ$ of SO_4^{2-} ion is –216 kcal mol^{-1}.

(iii) 100 g of anhydrous $CuSO_4$ when dissolved in excess of water produced 10 kcal of heat. The same amount of $CuSO_4 \cdot 5H_2O$ on dissolving in large excess of water absorbed 1.1 kcal. Calculate enthalpy of hydration of $CuSO_4$.

KNOWLEDGE CONFIRMATION Test 2

1 The constant pressure dissolution of NaCl can be represented by

$$NaCl(s) \xrightarrow{①} Na^+(g) + Cl^-(g) \xrightarrow{③} Na^+(aq) + Cl^-(aq); \quad NaCl(s) \xrightarrow{②} Na^+(aq) + Cl^-(aq)$$

Energies of processes (1), (2) and (3) are called respectively as

	(1)	(2)	(3)
(a)	lattice energy	enthalpy of solution	enthalpy of hydration
(b)	lattice energy	enthalpy of hydration	enthalpy of solution
(c)	dissociation energy	enthalpy of solution	enthalpy of hydration
(d)	dissociation energy	enthalpy of hydration	enthalpy of solution

2 $CO_3^{2-}(aq)$ is decomposed by $H^+(aq)$ to form $CO_2(g)$ and $H_2O(l)$. If $\Delta H = -0.7$ kcal, then $\Delta_f H^\circ(CO_3^{2-})$ is ($\Delta_f H^\circ(CO_2) = -94$ kcal mol^{-1}, $\Delta_f H^\circ(H_2O) = -68$ kcal mol^{-1})

(a) – 0.7 kcal mol^{-1} (b) –161.3 kcal mol^{-1}
(c) 0 kcal mol^{-1} (d) + 161.3 kcal mol^{-1}

3 If the enthalpy of HCl (g) and $Cl^-(aq)$ are – 92.3 kJ mol^{-1} and –167.44 kJ mol^{-1} respectively, then heat of solution of HCl(g) is

(a) –75.14 kJ mol^{-1} (b) + 75.14 kJ mol^{-1}
(c) –167.44 kJ mol^{-1} (d) 0 kJ mol^{-1}

4 Given, $\Delta H^\circ_{solution}$ of MX = 20 kJ mol^{-1} and that of $MX \cdot H_2O$ = 10 kJ mol^{-1}. Thus, hydration energy of MX is

(a) 10 kJ mol^{-1} (b) – 10 kJ mol^{-1}
(c) – 30 kJ mol^{-1} (d) + 30 kJ mol^{-1}

5 Enthalpy change when 1 mole of H_2SO_4 is completely neutralised by NaOH is

(a) – 13.7 kcal mol^{-1} (b) – 27.4 kcal mol^{-1}
(c) – 6.85 kcal mol^{-1} (d) + 27.4 kcal mol^{-1}

6 Given, $\Delta_f H^\circ(H_2O) = -286.20$ kJ mol^{-1} and $H^+(aq) + OH^-(aq) \longrightarrow H_2O(l), \Delta H^\circ = -57.32$ kJ mol^{-1} then $\Delta_f H^\circ(OH^-)$ is (in kJ mol^{-1})

(a) – 228.88 (b) + 228.88 (c) –343.52 (d) +343.52

7 Given, $HCl(aq) + NaOH(aq) \longrightarrow NaCl(aq) + H_2O(l)$,
1equiv 1 equiv $\Delta H° = -57.36$ kJ mol^{-1}

$HA(aq) + NaOH(aq) \longrightarrow NaA(aq) + H_2O(l)$,
1 equiv (weak) 1equiv $\Delta H° = -42.02$ kJ mol^{-1}

$HA(aq) \longrightarrow H^+(aq) + A^-(aq), \Delta H° = x$

Thus, x is
(a) – 97.38 kJ $equiv^{-1}$
(b) – 15.34 kJ $equiv^{-1}$
(c) + 15.34 kJ $equiv^{-1}$
(d) + 97.38 kJ $equiv^{-1}$

8 $Ca(OH)_2 + HCl \longrightarrow Ca(OH)Cl + H_2O, \Delta H_1$
$Ca(OH)Cl + HCl \longrightarrow CaCl_2 + H_2O, \Delta H_2$,
ΔH_1 and ΔH_2 for 1: 1 molar ratio of each reactant are
(a) – 6.85 kcal, –6.85 kcal
(b) – 13.7 kcal, –13.7 kcal
(c) – 27.4 kcal, – 27.4 kcal
(d) –6.85 kcal,–13.7 kcal

9 The dissolution of $CaCl_2 \cdot 6H_2O$ in large volume of water is endothermic to the extent of 3.5 kcal mol^{-1}. For the reaction, $CaCl_2(s) + 6H_2O(l) \longrightarrow CaCl_2 \cdot 6H_2O(s)$, $\Delta H = -23.2$ kcal. Hence, heat of solution of $CaCl_2$ (anhydrous) in a large volume of water is
(a) 26.7 kcal (b) – 26.7 kcal
(c) 19.7 kcal (d) – 19.7 kcal

10 ΔH_f° [HCl (g)] = – 22.1 kcal mol^{-1} and ΔH_f° [$Cl^-(aq)$] = – 40 kcal mol^{-1}, then enthalpy change in the standard state when HCl(g) is dissolved in excess of H_2O is
(a) – 17.9 kcal mol^{-1} (b) – 62.1 kcal mol^{-1}
(c) + 62.1 kcal mol^{-1} (d) + 17 .9 kcal mol^{-1}

11 Instant cold packs used to treat athletic injuries contain water and
(a) solid NH_4Cl (b) solid NH_4NO_3
(c) solid NH_4HCO_3 (d) solid $(NH_4)_2C_2O_4$

12 Lattice energy of NaCl(s) is 788 kJ mol^{-1} and enthalpy of hydration is – 784 kJ mol^{-1}. Hence, heat of solution of NaCl(s) is ***[JEE Main 2020 (II) NTA]***
(a) 4 kJ mol^{-1} (b) – 4 kJ mol^{-1}
(c) – 1572 kJ mol^{-1} (d) 1572 kJ mol^{-1}

13 ΔH_f° for chloride ion from the following data is

$\frac{1}{2}H_2(g) + \frac{1}{2}Cl_2(g) \longrightarrow HCl(g), \Delta H_f^\circ = -22.1$ kcal

$HCl(g) + nH_2O \longrightarrow H^+(aq) + Cl^-(aq)$,
$\Delta H^\circ_{298\,K} = -17.9$ kcal

(a) – 40.0 kcal (b) + 40.0 kcal
(c) +17.9 kcal (d) + 22.1 kcal

14 ΔH_f° [$K^+(aq)$], ΔH_f°[$Cl^-(aq)$] and ΔH_f°(KCl) are respectively – 60.04, – 40.0 and – 104.18 kcal.
Hence, $\Delta H°$ for the process at 25°C of dissolving 1.00 mole of KCl in large excess of water,
$KCl(s) \longrightarrow K^+(aq) + Cl^-(aq)$ is
(a) – 4.14 kcal (b) + 4.14 kcal
(c) + 20.04 kcal (d) – 20.04 kcal

15 Which of the following processes is/are exothermic ?
(a) $HF(aq) + OH^- \longrightarrow H_2O(l) + F^-(aq)$
(b) $HF(aq) \longrightarrow H^+(aq) + F^-(aq)$
(c) $CaO(s) + H_2O(l) \longrightarrow Ca(OH)_2(aq)$
(d) All of the above

16 The enthalpy of neutralisation for the first proton of H_2S is –33.7 kJ mol^{-1}. Thus, first ionisation energy of H_2S is
(a) –221 kJ mol^{-1} (b) +55.8 kJ mol^{-1}
(c) 11.1 kJ mol^{-1} (d) 22.1 kJ mol^{-1}

17 Given, $\Delta_f H°(S^{2-}, aq) = 33.1$ kJ mol^{-1}
$\Delta_f H°(OH^-, aq) = -230.0$ kJ mol^{-1}
$\Delta_f H°(H_2O, l) = -285.8$ kJ mol^{-1}
$\Delta_f H°(HS^-, aq) = -17.6$ kJ mol^{-1}
Then heat of neutralisation of second proton in H_2S is
(a) –5.1 kJ mol^{-1} (b) +5.1 kJ mol^{-1}
(c) +17.6 kJ mol^{-1} (d) 15.1 kJ mol^{-1}

18 Enthalpy of neutralisation of a polybasic weak acid when all of its protons are neutralised is –150.0 kJ mol^{-1}.
Also, acid $\rightleftharpoons nH^+$ + anion of the acid, $\Delta H° = 17.4$ kJ mol^{-1}
Thus, basicity of the acid is
(a) 1 (b) 2 (c) 3 (d) 4

19 In which of the following reaction, ΔH is maximum assume all acids and bases are strong electrolytes?
(a) $H^+ + OH^- \longrightarrow H_2O$
(b) $H_2SO_4 + OH^- \longrightarrow HSO_4^- + H_2O$
(c) $H_3PO_4 + OH^- \longrightarrow H_2PO_4^- + H_2O$
(d) Equal

20 Consider following cases of neutralisation of acids by bases:
I. $HCN(aq) \rightleftharpoons H^+(aq) + CN^-(aq), \Delta H° = 43.7$ kJ mol^{-1}
$H^+(aq) + OH^- \rightleftharpoons H_2O, \Delta H° = -55.8$ kJ mol^{-1}
II. $CH_3COOH + NH_4OH \rightleftharpoons CH_3COONH_4 + H_2O$,
$\Delta H° = -44.4$ kJ mol^{-1}
$NH_4OH + HCl \rightleftharpoons NH_4Cl + H_2O, \Delta H° = -49.8$ kJ mol^{-1}

Thus, pH of equimolar solutions of HCN, CH_3COOH and HCl will be in order
(a) HCl < HCN < CH_3COOH (b) HCl < CH_3COOH < HCN
(c) CH_3COOH < HCN < HCl (d) HCN < CH_3COOH < HCl

Bond Energy or Bond Enthalpy and Bond Dissociation Enthalpy

Average energy required to break all bonds of one type present in 1 mole of the gaseous covalent compound to form the gaseous atoms is called bond energy or bond enthalpy. It is a measure of strength of the bond i.e. the force with which the atoms are bonded together.

The energy required to break a given bond in some specific compound is the bond dissociation energy.

$$H_2O(g) \longrightarrow H(g) + OH(g); \quad \Delta H^\circ_{298} = 498 \text{ kJ mol}^{-1}$$

$$OH \longrightarrow H^+(g) + O(g); \quad \Delta H^\circ_{298} = 430 \text{ kJ mol}^{-1}$$

Based on above reactions

498 kJ mol^{-1} is the bond dissociation energy of (O—H) bond in H_2O. 430 kJ mol^{-1} is the bond dissociation energy of (O—H) bond in OH and $\left(\frac{498 + 430}{2}\right) = 464$ kJ mol^{-1} is the bond enthalpy of OH bond.

Enthalpy change on breaking one mole of bonds completely to obtain atoms in the gas phase is called **atomisation enthalpy.**

$$H_2(g) \longrightarrow 2H(g); \quad \Delta_a H^\circ = 435 \text{ kJ mol}^{-1}$$

Based on bond enthalpies

$$\Delta_r H^\circ = (BE)_{reactants} - (BE)_{products}$$

All species should be in the gaseous state.

$$H_2(g) + \frac{1}{2}O_2(g) \longrightarrow H_2O(l)$$

then,
$$\Delta_r H = \left[(BE)_{H—H} + \frac{1}{2}(BE)_{O=O}\right] - [\text{enthalpy of vaporisation of } H_2O(l) + 2(BE)_{O—H}]$$

In the above case, H_2O is in the liquid state. Thus, first it should be converted into gaseous state by enthalpy of vaporisation. Any species in solid state requires enthalpy of sublimation for conversion into gaseous state.

Similar case arises with resonance energy

Resonance energy of species (X) = [Experimental value of $\Delta_f H^\circ(X) - \Delta_f H^\circ$ based on bond enthalpies]

Solved Examples & Instant Practice

Example 6.8) The average bond enthalpy of the O—H bond in water is defined as one half of the enthalpy change for the reaction,

$$H_2O(g) \longrightarrow 2H(g) + O(g)$$

Given, at 298 K

$\Delta_f H^\circ$ of $H_2O(g) = -241.8$ kJ mol^{-1}

$\Delta_f H^\circ$ of H $(g) = 218.0$ kJ mol^{-1}

$\Delta_f H^\circ$ of O $(g) = 249.2$ kJ mol^{-1}

Determine average bond enthalpy (ΔH) and ΔU of the (O—H) bond in H_2O.

Atomisation energies of H_2 and O_2 are to be related to bond energy of (O—H) bond in H_2O.

$$H_2O(g) \longrightarrow 2H(g) + O(g)$$

This equation can be achieved by

$$H_2(g) + \frac{1}{2}O_2(g) \longrightarrow H_2O(g)$$

$$H_2(g) \longrightarrow 2H(g)$$

$$\frac{1}{2}O_2(g) \longrightarrow O(g)$$

Thus, bond enthalpy of (OH) bond can be derived.

Also, $\Delta H^\circ = \Delta U^\circ + \Delta n_g RT$

Sol.

	(kJ)
$H_2O(g) \longrightarrow H_2(g) + \frac{1}{2}O_2(g)$	$\Delta H_1 = 241.8$
$H_2(g) \longrightarrow 2H(g)$	$\Delta H_2 = 436.0$
$\frac{1}{2}O_2(g) \longrightarrow O(g)$	$\Delta H_3 = 249.3$
∴ $H_2O(g) \longrightarrow 2H(g) + O(g)$	$\Delta H = 927.0$

In $H_2O(g)$, two (O—H) bonds are cleaved.

Thus, bond enthalpy of (O—H) bond at constant pressure

$$= \frac{927.0}{2}$$

$$= 463.5 \text{ kJ mol}^{-1}$$

$$\Delta H^\circ = \Delta U^\circ + \Delta n_g RT$$

Δn_g = moles of gaseous products – moles of gaseous reactants

$$927.0 = \Delta U^\circ + 2 \times 8.314 \times 10^{-3} \times 298$$

$$\Delta U^\circ = 922.04$$

∴ Bond enthalpy of (O—H) bond at constant volume

$$= \frac{922.04}{2} = 461.02$$

Immediate Test 7

Estimate the average S—F bond energy in SF_6.

Given, $\Delta_f H^\circ (SF_6) = -1100 \text{ kJ mol}^{-1}$

$\Delta_f H^\circ (S, g) = 275 \text{ kJ mol}^{-1}$

$\Delta_f H^\circ (F, g) = 80 \text{ kJ mol}^{-1}$

Example 6.9) $\Delta_f H^\circ$ **of ethane, ethene and benzene from gaseous atoms are** -2839.2, -2275.2 **and** $-5506 \text{ kJ mol}^{-1}$ **respectively at 298 K. Calculate resonance energy of benzene, compared with one Kekule structure. The bond enthalpy of (C—H) bond is 410.87** kJ mol^{-1}**.**

$\Delta_f H^\circ$ *(element) = 0*

and $\Delta_f H^\circ = -$ *(Energy required to break all bonds in one mole). Also,* $\Delta_f H^\circ$ *of ethane and ethene are given. Thus, (C—C) and (C=C) bond enthalpies are calculated, since (C—H) bond enthalpy is given. From these values,* $\Delta_f H^\circ$ *of benzene is calculated.*

Resonance energy = (experimental $\Delta_f H^\circ -$ *calculated* $\Delta_f H^\circ$*)*

Sol. Since, $\Delta_f H^\circ$ (of any substance) $= -$ (B.E. of all types of bonds in 1 mole of it)

H H
H—C—C—H
H H

$\therefore \Delta_f H^\circ (C_2H_6) = -2839.2 \text{ kJ} = -[BE(C—C) + 6 \times BE(C—H)]$

$\therefore$ BE (C—C) $= 2839.2 - 6 \times 410.87 = 373.98 \text{ kJ mol}^{-1}$

Similarly, in ethene H—C(H)=C(H)—H

$\Delta_f H^\circ (C_2H_4) = -2275.2 = -[BE(C=C) + 4 \times BE(C—H)]$

$\therefore (BE)_{C=C} = 2275.2 - 4 \times 410.87 = 631.72 \text{ kJ mol}^{-1}$

In benzene (with 6(C—H), 3 (C = C) and 3 (C—C) bonds

$\Delta_f H^\circ (C_6H_6) = -[3 \times BE(C—C) + 3 \times BE(C=C) + 6BE(C—H)]$

$= -[3 \times 373.98 + 3 \times 631.72 + 6(410.87)]$

$= -5482.32 \text{ kJ mol}^{-1}$

$\therefore$ Resonance energy $= -5506 - (-5482.32) = -23.68 \text{ kJ mol}^{-1}$

Immediate Test 8

Calculate, resonance energy of N_2O from the following data.

$\Delta_f H^\circ (N_2O) = 82.0 \text{ kJ mol}^{-1}$

Assume structure as $\overset{\ominus}{N} = \overset{\oplus}{N} = O$

BE of (N ≡ N) bond $= 946 \text{ kJ mol}^{-1}$

(N = N) bond $= 418 \text{ kJ mol}^{-1}$

(O = O) bond $= 498 \text{ kJ mol}^{-1}$

(N = O) bond $= 607 \text{ kJ mol}^{-1}$

KNOWLEDGE CONFIRMATION **Test 3**

1 $\Delta_f H^\circ$ of $CH_4(g)$ from gaseous atoms is x. Thus, bond enthalpy of (C—H) bond is

(a) x (b) $\frac{x}{4}$ (c) $\frac{-x}{4}$ (d) $-x$

2 Bond enthalpy of $(N \equiv N) = x_1 \text{ kJ mol}^{-1}$; $(H—H) = x_2 \text{ kJ mol}^{-1}$ and $(N—H) = x_3 \text{ kJ mol}^{-1}$

Thus, $\Delta_f H^\circ$ of NH_3 is

(a) $(x_1 + x_2 - x_3)$ (b) $x + 3x_2 - 6x_3$

(c) $\left(\frac{x_1 + 3x_2 - 6x_3}{2}\right)$ (d) $\left(\frac{6x_3 - x_1 - 3x_2}{2}\right)$

3 For the isomerisation of $CH_3CH_2OH \rightleftharpoons CH_3OCH_3$ ΔH° is

if bond enthalpy of $(C—C) = x_1$; $(C—H) = x_2$; $(C—O) = x_3$; $(O—H) = x_4$

(a) $(x_1 + x_2 + x_3 + x_4)$ (b) $(x_1 - x_2 - x_3 + x_4)$

(c) $-(x_1 - x_2 - x_3 + x_4)$ (d) $-(x_1 + x_2 + x_3 + x_4)$

4 Given at 298 K

	$\Delta H^\circ (\text{kJ mol}^{-1})$
$H_2(g) + O_2(g) \longrightarrow 2OH(g)$	78.00
$H_2(g) \longrightarrow 2H(g)$	436.0
$O_2(g) \longrightarrow 2O(g)$	498.0

Thus, ΔH° for

$OH(g) \longrightarrow H(g) + O(g)$ is

(a) 428 kJ mol^{-1} (b) -428 kJ mol^{-1}

(c) 856 kJ mol^{-1} (d) 214 kJ mol^{-1}

5 For the reaction.

I. $CH_4(g) \longrightarrow C(g) + 4H(g)$, $\Delta H^\circ = x_1$

II. $C_2H_6(g) \longrightarrow 2C(g) + 6H(g)$, $\Delta H^\circ = x_2$

Thus, (C—C) bond energy is

(a) $x_1 - x_2$ (b) $x_2 - x_1$

(c) $x_2 + 1.5x_1$ (d) $x_2 - 1.5x_1$

6 $\Delta_r H°$ of the following reaction,

$2H_2(g) + O_2(g) \longrightarrow 2H_2O(l)$, is determined by

(a) bond enthalpies of (H—H) bond, (O=O) bond and (O—H) bond
(b) all the values in (a) and enthalpy of vaporisation of $H_2O(l)$
(c) $\Delta_f H°$ of H_2, O_2 and H_2O
(d) Both (b) and (c)

7 Given

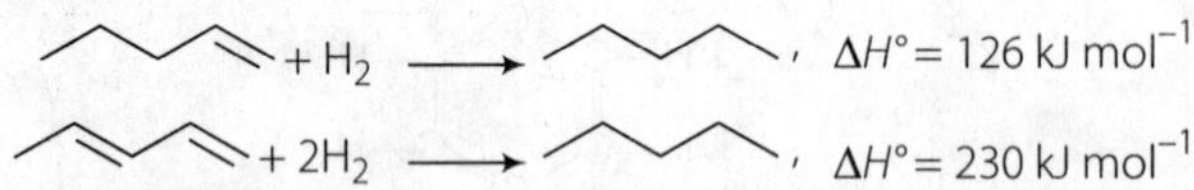

Thus, resonance (delocalisation) energy of 1,3-pentadiene is

(a) 22 kJ (b) 104 kJ (c) 252 kJ (d) 11 kJ

8 For the reaction,

$$O(g) + O_2(g) \longrightarrow O_3(g), \quad \Delta H° = -107.2 \text{ kJ}$$

Thus, average bond enthalpy in O_3 is (in kJ mol^{-1}) bond enthalpy of O=O bond is 498.8 kJ mol^{-1}).

(a) 606.0 (b) 107.2 (c) 391.6 (d) 303.0

9 Given, bond enthalpies,

H—H = 414 kJ mol^{-1}; O=O = 498 kJ mol^{-1};

H—O = 464 kJ mol^{-1}; O—O = 142 kJ mol^{-1}

$\Delta H^{\circ}_{vap}(H_2O_2) = 51.47$ kJ mol^{-1}

Then $\Delta_f H°[H_2O_2(l)]$ is

(a) −188.47 kJ mol^{-1} (b) 188.47 kJ mol^{-1}
(c) 137.0 kJ mol^{-1} (d) −137.00 kJ mol^{-1}

10 $\Delta_f H°(O) = 249$ kJ mol^{-1}, $\Delta_f H°(O_3) = 142.7$ kJ mol^{-1}

Thus, bond enthalpy of (O—O) bond in O_3 is

(a) 302.15 kJ mol^{-1} (b) 604.30 kJ mol^{-1}
(c) 201.4 kJ mol^{-1} (d) None of these

11 From bond enthalpies data, ($\Delta_f H°$) heat of formation of isoprene is 103.31 kJ mol^{-1}.

Also, $\Delta_c H°$ (isoprene, C_5H_8) = −3120 kJ mol^{-1}

$\Delta_f H°(H_2O) = -285.77$ kJ mol^{-1}

$\Delta_f H°(CO_2) = -393.71$ kJ mol^{-1}

Thus, resonance energy of isoprene is

($CH_2 = CH—CH_2—CH = CH_2$)

(a) −94.51 kJ mol^{-1} (b) +94.51 kJ mol^{-1}
(c) 8.8 kJ mol^{-1} (d) −8.8 kJ mol^{-1}

12 Given

$\Delta_f H°[C_2H_5—S—C_2H_5(g)] = -147.23$ kJ mol^{-1}

$\Delta_f H°[C_2H_5—S—S—C_2H_5(g)] = -201.92$ kJ mol^{-1}

and $S(s) \longrightarrow S(g)$, $\Delta H° = 222.80$ kJ mol^{-1}

Thus, bond enthalpy of (S—S) bond is.

(a) + 54.69 kJ mol^{-1} (b) 277.49 kJ mol^{-1}
(c) 223.20 kJ mol^{-1} (d) None of these

13 Given, $N_2H_2(g) + H_2(g) \longrightarrow N_2H_4(g)$;

$\Delta_r H^{\circ}_{298} = -108.76$ kJ mol^{-1}

B.E of (N—N) = 163.18 kJ mol^{-1}

B.E (H—H) = 435.89 kJ mol^{-1}

If N_2H_2 has structure as H—N=N—H, B.E of (N=N) bond is

(a) 200 kJ mol^{-1} (b) 400 kJ mol^{-1}
(c) 100 kJ mol^{-1} (d) 600 kJ mol^{-1}

14 The enthalpy of atomisation of PH_3 is 953.95 kJ mol^{-1} and that of P_2H_4 is 1.485×10^3 kJ mol^{-1}. Thus, bond enthalpy of (P—P) bond is

(a) 65.0 kJ mol^{-1} (b) 612.6 kJ mol^{-1}
(c) 671.0 kJ mol^{-1} (d) 213.4 kJ mol^{-1}

15 Given, $\Delta_f H°(O_3) = 142.7$ kJ mol^{-1}

and $\Delta_f H°(O) = 249.17$ kJ mol^{-1}

Thus, average bond enthalpy in ozone (O_3)

$O_3(g) \longrightarrow 3O(g)$ is

(a) 106.47 kJ mol^{-1} (b) 604.80 kJ mol^{-1}
(c) 302.40 kJ mol^{-1} (d) 445.10 kJ mol^{-1}

Hess's Law of Constant Heat Summation

For a chemical reaction that can be written as the sum of two or more steps, the enthalpy change for the overall equation is equal to the sum of the enthalpy change for the individual steps.

- Hess's law is a special case of first law of thermodynamics.

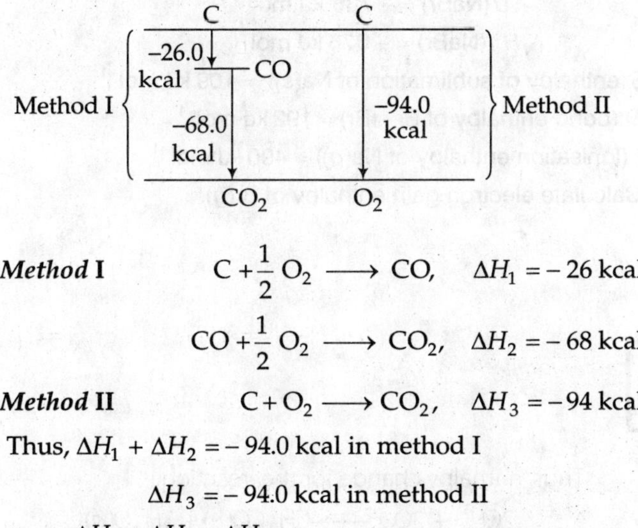

***Method* I** $\quad C + \frac{1}{2} O_2 \longrightarrow CO, \quad \Delta H_1 = -26$ kcal

$\quad CO + \frac{1}{2} O_2 \longrightarrow CO_2, \quad \Delta H_2 = -68$ kcal

***Method* II** $\quad C + O_2 \longrightarrow CO_2, \quad \Delta H_3 = -94$ kcal

Thus, $\Delta H_1 + \Delta H_2 = -94.0$ kcal in method I

$\Delta H_3 = -94.0$ kcal in method II

$\therefore \quad \Delta H_1 + \Delta H_2 = \Delta H_3$

- **Born-Haber Cycle** used to determine lattice energy is based on Hess's law.

Formation of NaCl (*s*) can be explained by **Born-Haber cycle.**

Method I direct: $Na(s) + \frac{1}{2} Cl_2(g) \xrightarrow[= Q]{\Delta H_1} NaCl(s)$

Method II in Steps

Sublimation S → $Na(g)$; Dissociation $D/2$ → $Cl(g)$

Ionisation I; Electongain $-E$; Q

$Na^+(g) + Cl^-(g)$ → $-U$ → $NaCl(s)$

$$\Delta H_2 = S + I + \frac{D}{2} - E - U$$

As $\quad \Delta H_1 = \Delta H_2 \quad \because \quad \boxed{Q = S + I + \frac{D}{2} - E - U}$

where, S = enthalpy sublimation,
I = ionisation enthalpy
D = dissociation enthalpy (bond-energy)
E = electron gain enthalpy (electron affinity)
U = lattice energy-released when one mole of lattice is formed from gaseous ions.

Solved Examples & Instant Practice

Example 6.10) For the following reactions,

I. $2Na(s) + \frac{1}{2} O_2(g) \longrightarrow Na_2O, \Delta H = x$

II. $Na_2O(s) + H_2O \longrightarrow 2NaOH\ (aq), \Delta H = -56$ kcal

III. $2Na(s) + 2H_2O(l) \longrightarrow 2NaOH(aq) + H_2(g),$
$\Delta H = -88$ kcal

IV. $H_2(g) + \frac{1}{2} O_2(g) \longrightarrow H_2O\ (l), \Delta H = -68$ kcal

Derive value of x.

Sol. Calculation is based on Hess's law. $Na_2O(s)$ has been formed in reaction (i), thus ($\Delta H = x$) is the enthalpy of formation of Na_2O. Reaction (ii) to (iv) can be arranged in such a way that net reaction gives (i).

We observe,

I + II = III + IV

Thus, x can be calculated.

Add I and II

$2Na + \frac{1}{2} O_2 + H_2O \longrightarrow 2NaOH, \quad \Delta H_1 = (x - 56)$ kcal

Add III and IV

$2Na + \frac{1}{2} O_2 + H_2O \longrightarrow 2NaOH, \quad \Delta H_2 = -156$ kcal

As both represent same chemical change

Thus, $\quad \Delta H_1 = \Delta H_2 \quad \Rightarrow x = -100$ kcal

Immediate Test 9

From the following data at 298 K. Calculate $\Delta_f H°$ of FeO(*s*) and $Fe_2O_3(s)$.

I. $Fe_2O_3(s) + 3C(\text{graphite}) \longrightarrow 2Fe(s) + 3CO(g),$
$\Delta H° = 492.6$ kJ mol^{-1}

II. $FeO(s) + C(\text{graphite}) \longrightarrow Fe(s) + CO(g),$
$\Delta H° = 155.8$ kJ mol^{-1}

III. $C(\text{graphite}) + O_2\ (g) \longrightarrow CO_2\ (g),$
$\Delta H° = -393.51$ kJmol^{-1}

IV. $C\ (\text{graphite}) + \frac{1}{2} O_2\ (g) \longrightarrow CO\ (g),$
$\Delta H° = -282.98$ kJmol^{-1}

Example 6.11) Make a Born-Haber cycle to calculate lattice energy of $MgBr_2(s)$.

Born-Haber cycle is based on the comparison of enthalpy of formation of a compound from its elements and the total enthalpy change involved in :

- *Sublimation of solid into gaseous state by sublimation enthalpy.*
- *Ionisation of the gaseous atom to cation by ionisation enthalpy.*
- *Dissociation of gas into gaseous atom by bond enthalpy.*
- *Converting gaseous ions into lattice by lattice enthalpy.*

Sol. (Lattice energy)

I. $Mg(s) + Br_2(l) \longrightarrow MgBr_2(s)\ \Delta H_1 = q$

II. $Mg(s) \xrightarrow{\text{Sublimation}} Mg(g),\ \Delta H = S$

$Mg(s) \xrightarrow{\text{Ionisation}} Mg^{2+}(g) + 2e^-,\quad \Delta H = I (= I_1 + II_2)$

$Br_2(l) \xrightarrow{\text{Vaporisation}} Br_2(g),\quad \Delta H = L$ (latent heat of vaporisation)

$Br_2(g) \xrightarrow{\text{Dissociation}} 2Br(g),\quad \Delta H = D$

$2Br(g) + 2e^- \xrightarrow{\text{Anion formation}} 2Br^-,\ \Delta H = -2E$

$Mg^{2+}(g) + 2Br^-(g) \xrightarrow{\text{Lattice formation}} MgBr_2(s),\ \Delta H = -U$

Add all steps in II

$$\Delta H_2 = (S + I + L + D - 2E - U) \Rightarrow \Delta H_1 = \Delta H_2$$

$$\therefore \quad q = S + I + L + D - 2E - U$$

$$\therefore \quad U = S + I + L + D - 2E - q$$

Immediate Test 10

Given,

$$U(\text{NaBr}) = -736 \text{ kJ mol}^{-1}$$

$$\Delta_f H^\circ (\text{NaBr}) = -376 \text{ kJ mol}^{-1}$$

S (enthalpy of sublimation of Na(s)) $= 109 \text{ kJ mol}^{-1}$

D (bond enthalpy of Br—Br) $= 192 \text{ kJ mol}^{-1}$

I (Ionisation enthalpy of Na(g)) $= 490 \text{ kJ mol}^{-1}$

Calculate electron gain enthalpy of Br(g).

KNOWLEDGE CONFIRMATION Test 4

1 What is enthalpy of sublimation of $I_2(s)$?

If $\Delta_f H^\circ(\text{NaI}(s)) = q$, other parameters being constants used in Born-Haber cycle.

(a) $2\left(q - S(\text{Na}) - \frac{D}{2} - I + E + U\right)$ (b) $\left(q - S(\text{Na}) + \frac{D}{2} - I + E + U\right)$

(c) $-\left(q - S(\text{Na}) + \frac{D}{2} - I + E + U\right)$ (d) None of these

2 $Mg(s) + Br_2(g) \longrightarrow MgBr_2(s)$,

ΔS (entropy change) $= x_1$ cal K^{-1} at temperature T

(in cal)

$Mg(s) \longrightarrow Mg(g),\quad \Delta H = S$

$Mg(s) \longrightarrow Mg^{2+}(g) + 2e^-,\quad \Delta H = I$

$Br_2(g) \longrightarrow 2Br(g),\quad \Delta H = D$

$2Br(g) + 2e^- \longrightarrow 2Br^-(g),\quad \Delta H = -2E$

$Mg^{2+}(g) + 2Br^-(g) \longrightarrow MgBr(s),\quad \Delta H = x_2$

Thus, x_2 is

(a) $x_1 + S + I + D - 2E$ (b) $x_1T - S - I - D + 2E$

(c) $-(x_1T + S + 2I + D - 2E)$ (d) $(x_1T + S + I - D - 2E)$

3 Given that, at 298K

$CH_4(g) + 2O_2(g) \longrightarrow CO_2 + 2H_2O(g),$

$\Delta H^\circ = -802.3 \text{ kJ mol}^{-1}$

$CH_2CO(g) + 2O_2(g) \longrightarrow 2CO_2 + H_2O(g)$

$\Delta H^\circ = -981.1 \text{ kJ mol}^{-1}$

Thus, enthalpy change for the reaction is

$2CH_4 + 2O_2 \longrightarrow CH_2CO(g) + 3H_2O(g)$

(a) -623.5 kJ (b) $+623.5$ kJ

(c) -178.8 kJ (d) $+802.3$ kJ

4 The enthalpy change for the following processes are given,

$Cl_2(g) \longrightarrow 2Cl(g),\ 242.3 \text{ kJ mol}^{-1}$

$I_2(g) \longrightarrow 2I(g),\ 151.0 \text{ kJ mol}^{-1}$

$ICl(g) \longrightarrow I(g) + Cl(g),\ 211.3 \text{ kJ mol}^{-1}$

$I_2(s) \longrightarrow I_2(g),\ 62.76 \text{ kJ mol}^{-1}$

Given that, the standard states of iodine and chlorine are $I_2(s)$ and $Cl_2(g)$, then $\Delta_f H^\circ(ICl(g))$ will be (in kJ mol^{-1})

(a) -14.6 (b) -16.73 (c) $+16.73$ (d) $+244.8$

5 $\Delta_f H^\circ(CO_2) = x_1$

$2C + O_2 \longrightarrow 2CO,\quad \Delta H = x_2$

$2CO + O_2 \longrightarrow 2CO_2,\quad \Delta H = x_3$

Thus,

(a) $x_1 = (x_2 + x_3)$ (b) $x_1 = -(x_2 + x_3)$

(c) $2x_1 = (x_2 + x_3)$ (d) $2x_1 = -(x_2 + x_3)$

6 Given,

$HA + NaOH \rightleftharpoons NaA + H_2O,\quad \Delta H = x_1$

$HCl + NaOH \rightleftharpoons NaCl + H_2O,\quad \Delta H = x_2$

$NH_4OH + HCl \rightleftharpoons NH_4Cl + H_2O,\quad \Delta H = x_3$

then for

$NH_4OH + HA \rightleftharpoons NH_4A + H_2O,\quad \Delta H = x_4$

thus, x_4 is related to x_1, x_2 and x_3 by

(a) $(3x_2 - x_1 - x_3)$ (b) $-(3x_2 - x_1 - x_3)$

(c) $(x_1 - x_2 + x_3)$ (d) $(2x_2 - x_1 - x_3)$

7 Given,

		kJ
I.	$N_2(g) + 3H_2(g) \longrightarrow 2NH_3(g)$,	$\Delta H^\circ = -91.8$
II.	$4NH_3(g) + 5O_2(g) \longrightarrow 4NO(g) + 6H_2O(g)$,	$\Delta H^\circ = -906.2$
III.	$2H_2(g) + O_2(g) \longrightarrow 2H_2O(g)$,	$\Delta H^\circ = -483.6$

Thus, ΔH° for $N_2(g) + O_2(g) \longrightarrow 2NO(g)$ is

(a) – 90.25 kJ (b) + 90.25 kJ

(c) – 180.50 kJ (d) +180.50 kJ

8 Based on following thermochemical data in gaseous phase, $\Delta_f H^\circ (NCl_3)$ is

		(ΔH)
I.	$NH_3 + 3Cl_2 \longrightarrow NCl_3 + 3HCl$,	$-\Delta H_1$
II.	$N_2 + 3H_2 \longrightarrow 2NH_3$,	$-\Delta H_2$
III.	$H_2 + Cl_2 \longrightarrow 2HCl$,	$+\Delta H_3$

(a) $-\left(\Delta H_1 - \frac{\Delta H_2}{2} + \frac{3}{2}\Delta H_3\right)$ (b) $\left(\Delta H_1 + \frac{\Delta H_2}{2} - \frac{3}{2}\Delta H_3\right)$

(c) $\left(\Delta H_1 - \frac{\Delta H_2}{2} - \frac{3}{2}\Delta H_3\right)$ (d) $\left(\Delta H_1 + \frac{\Delta H_2}{2} + \frac{3}{2}\Delta H_3\right)$

9 Given,

		ΔH° (kJ mol^{-1})
I.	$4B(s) + 3O_2(g) \longrightarrow 2B_2O_3(s)$	– 2546
II.	$2H_2(g) + O_2(g) \longrightarrow H_2O(l)$	– 572
III.	$H_2O(l) \longrightarrow H_2O(g)$	44
IV.	$2B(s) + 3H_2(g) \longrightarrow B_2H_6(g)$	36

Enthalpy change for the combustion of diborane (a potential rocket fuel) is (in kJ mol^{-1})

(a) – 36 (b) – 1237

(c) – 2035 (d) – 1639

10 Select correct statements.

(a) Hess's law is the limiting case of first law of thermodynamics

(b) Born-Haber cycle is used to determine electrongain enthalpy

(c) Enthalpy is a state function

(d) All of the above are correct statements

11 Lattice energies of KF, KCl, KBr and KI are respectively 826.4, 717.9, 689.0 and 645.0 kJ mol^{-1}. Thus,

(a) as interionic distance increases as size of anion increases, lattice energy decreases

(b) as interionic distance increases an size of cation increases, lattice energy decreases

(c) Both of the above are correct

(d) None of these is correct

12 If for the following reactions :

$C(s) \longrightarrow C(g)$; $\Delta H = 172$ kcal mol^{-1}

$\frac{1}{2}H_2(g) \longrightarrow H(g)$; $\Delta H = 52$ kcal mol^{-1}

$\Delta_f H^\circ (H_2O, l) = -68.0$ kcal mol^{-1}

$\Delta_f H^\circ (H_2O, g) = -94.0$ kcal mol^{-1}

$\Delta_c H^\circ (C_2H_6) = -372.0$ kcal mol^{-1}

$\Delta_c H^\circ (C_3H_8) = -530.0$ kcal mol^{-1}

there bond enthalpy of (C—C) and (C—H) bonds are respectively

	$\Delta H^\circ_{(C—C)}$ (kcal mol^{-1})	$\Delta H^\circ_{(C—H)}$ (kcal mol^{-1})
(a)	41.0	48.5
(b)	82.0	48.5
(c)	82.0	99.0
(d)	41.0	99.0

13 Bond enthalpies of (N≡N), (H—H), (N—N) and (N—H) bonds are respectively x_1, x_2, x_3 and x_4 (kJ mol^{-1}). Thus, $\Delta_f H^\circ$ of N_2H_4 is

(a) $x_1 + 2x_2 - x_3 - 4x_4$ (b) $x_3 + 4x_4 - x_1 - 2x_2$

(c) $x_1 + x_2 - x_3 - x_4$ (d) $(x_3 + x_4) - (x_1 + x_2)$

14 The bond dissociation enthalpies of $H_2(g)$ and $N_2(g)$ are + 436.0 kJ mol^{-1} and 942.0 kJ mol^{-1}. Thus, enthalpy of atomisation of $NH_3(g)$ is ($\Delta_f H^\circ (NH_3) = -46.0$ kJ mol^{-1})

(a) 1.92×10^3 kJ (b) 1.17×10^3 kJ

(c) 1.68×10^3 kJ (d) 1.79×10^3 kJ

15 Given

(i) C(graphite) + $O_2(g) \longrightarrow CO_2(g)$; $\Delta_r H^\circ = x$ kJ mol^{-1}

(ii) C(graphite) + $\frac{1}{2}O_2(g) \longrightarrow CO(g)$; $\Delta_r H^\circ = y$ kJ mol^{-1}

(iii) $CO(g) + \frac{1}{2}O_2(g) \longrightarrow CO_2(g)$; $\Delta_r H^\circ = z$ kJ mol^{-1}

Based on the above thermochemical equations, find out which one of the following algebraic relationships is correct ? ***[JEE Main 2019 (I) NTA]***

(a) $y = 2z - x$ (b) $x = y - z$

(c) $z = x + y$ (d) $x = y + z$

Calorimetry

In the laboratory, heat changes in physical and chemical processes are measured with a calorimeter which is a insulated (closed) container and is used specifically for this purpose. The process of measuring heat change is called calorimetry. Calorimetry is based on the knowledge of following concepts:

- **Specific heat (s)** is the amount of heat required to raise the temperature of one gram of the substance by one degree.
  Unit kJ $g^{-1}K^{-1}$
- **Heat capacity (C)** is the amount of heat required to raise the temperature of the given quantity of the substance by one degree.
  Unit kJ K^{-1}

$$\text{Heat capacity} = \text{mass} \times \text{specific heat}$$

Thus, $$q(\text{heat}) = ms\Delta T = C\Delta T$$

Constant volume calorimetry

- If some or all of the reactants or products are volatile, it is necessary to place the reaction mixture for which ΔU and ΔH are being measured, in a device called **bomb calorimeter**.
- Heat of combustion is usually measured by placing a known mass of a compound in a steel container called a constant volume bomb calorimeter, which is filled with O_2 at about 30 atm of pressure.This is immersed in known **amount of water.**
- On ignition of the sample electrically, heat is evolved which can be calculated accurately by recording the rise in temperature of water.

Heat lost by the sample = Heat gained by water

$$q_{\text{system}} = q_{\text{water}} + q_{\text{bomb}} + q_{\text{reaction}} = 0$$

$$\therefore \quad q_{\text{reaction}} = -(q_{\text{water}} + q_{\text{bomb}})$$

$$q_{\text{water}} = ms\,\Delta T$$

$$\Rightarrow \quad q_{\text{bomb}} = C_{\text{bomb}}\,\Delta T$$

Thus, $q_{\text{reaction}} = \Delta U$ (heat of reaction at constant volume)

To determine ΔU_{comb}, the heat capacity of the bomb calorimeter (C_{bomb}) must first be determined by carrying out a reaction for which q_{reaction} is already known.

Constant pressure calorimetry

Enthalpy change taking place in neutralisation process, dissolution process etc, is measured by constant pressure calorimetry.

$$q_p = \Delta H$$

Adiabatic flame temperature

Adiabatic flame temperature (T_f) is a temperature in which the system attains, if the changes in the system are carried out under adiabatic conditions.

- **At constant pressure**

$$T_f = \left[\frac{-\Delta_r H_T}{C_p(\text{products})} + T\right]$$

- **At constant volume**

$$T_f = \left[\frac{-\Delta_r U_T}{C_V(\text{products})} + T\right]$$

Solved Examples & Instant Practice

Example 6.12) On dissolving 1.420 g of $Na_2SO_4(s)$ in 100 g of H_2O (l), temperature increased by 0.037 K. What is standard enthalpy of solution of Na_2SO_4? Given specific heat of water = 4.184 J $g^{-1}K^{-1}$, calorimeter constant of constant pressure calorimeter = 342.5 JK^{-1}

When an anhydrous solution like Na_2SO_4 is dissolved in water, hydration takes place; being exothermic, temperature. Dissolution takes place in a constant pressure calorimeter, thus

$$\Delta H^\circ_{\text{cal}} = -C_p\ (\text{calorimeter}) \times \Delta T$$

$$\Delta H^\circ_{\text{solution}} = -ms\Delta T$$

Sol.

$$\Delta H^\circ_{\text{cal}} = -342.5\ JK^{-1} \times 0.037\ K = -12.6725\ J$$

$$\Delta H^\circ_{\text{solution}} = -mS\Delta T$$

$$= -100\ g \times 4.184\ Jg^{-1}K^{-1} \times 0.037\ K$$

$$= -15.4808\ J$$

$$\text{Total } \Delta H^\circ = \Delta H^\circ_{\text{cal}} + \Delta H^\circ_{\text{soln}} = (-12.6725 - 15.4808)\ J$$

$$= -28.1533\ J \text{ for } 1.420\text{ g of solute}$$

$$\text{Moles of } Na_2SO_4 = \frac{1.420}{142} = 0.01\ \text{mol}$$

$$\therefore \quad \Delta H^\circ = \frac{-28.1533\ J}{0.01\ \text{mol}} = -2815.33\ J\ mol^{-1}$$

Immediate Test 11

Two solutions, initially at 25.08°C were mixed in an insulated bottle. One contained 400 mL of 0.200 M weak monoprotic acid solution. The other contained 100 mL of a solution having 0.800M NaOH. After the mixing, the temperature increased by 1.17°.How much heat is evolved in the neutralisation of 1 mole of the acid. Assume that, the densities of all solutions are 1 g cm^{-3} and that their specific heat capacities are all 4.2 $Jg^{-1}K^{-1}$.

Example 6.13) A 1.250 g sample of benzoic acid was placed in a combustion bomb. The bomb was filled with an excess of O_2 at high pressure, sealed and immersed in a part of water which served as the calorimeter.

The heat capacity of the entire apparatus was found to be 2.422 kcal K^{-1}. On combustion, temperature increased by 3.256 K. What is ΔE_{comb} (enthalpy of combustion at constant volume) of benzoic acid?

When an acid is combusted in a bomb calorimeter, temperature increases, combustion being exothermic. Also, enthalpy change corresponds to data at constant volume. For the given amount, data can be converted for one mole.

Sol. Heat capacity = 2.422 kcal K^{-1}

$$\Delta T = 3.256 \text{ K}$$

$$\therefore \quad \Delta E = -C\Delta T = -2.422 \text{ kcal K}^{-1} \times 3.256 \text{ K}$$

$$= -7.886 \text{ kcal}$$

$$\text{Benzoic acid} = 1.250 \text{ g} = \frac{1.250 \text{ g}}{122 \text{ g mol}^{-1}} = 0.01 \text{ mol}$$

$$\therefore \quad \Delta E_{comb} = \frac{-7.886 \text{ kcal}}{0.01 \text{ mol}} = -788.6 \text{ kcal mol}^{-1}$$

- Benzoic acid (C_6H_5COOH).
  Molar mass $= 7 \times 12 + 6 \times 1 + 2 \times 16 = 122$ g mol^{-1}

Immediate Test 12

A quantity of 1.922 g of methanol (CH_3OH) was burnt in a constant volume bomb calorimeter. Consequently, temperature of the water raised by 4.2°. If the quantity of the surrounding, the calorimeter was 2000 g and the heat capacity of the bomb calorimeter was 2.02 kJ K^{-1}. Calculate the molar heat of combustion of methanol.

Specific heat of water = 4.184 $Jg^{-1}K^{-1}$.

Example 6.14)

(i) Calculate the adiabatic flame temperature for the following reaction carried out under constant pressure condition:

$$CH_4(g) + 2O_2(g) \longrightarrow CO_2(g) + 2H_2O(g);$$

$$\Delta H^\circ_{298} = -803.33 \text{ kJ mol}^{-1}$$

$$C_p(CO_2) = 36.29 \text{ JK}^{-1} \text{ mol}^{-1}$$

$$C_p(H_2O, g) = 33.58 \text{ JK}^{-1} \text{ mol}^{-1}$$

(ii) If the reaction is carried out under constant volume condition, what would be effect on the adiabatic temperature?

Sol. Adiabatic flame temperature can be calculated based on the relation,

$$T_f = -\frac{\Delta_r H_T}{C_p \text{ (products)}} + T$$

Products are gases CO_2 and H_2O.

Also, $\Delta n_g = 0$, hence

$$\Delta_r H^\circ = \Delta_r U^\circ$$

and $C_p - C_V = R$

Thus, adiabatic flame temperature under constant volume condition can be calculated.

$$\text{(i) } C_p(CO_2 + 2H_2O) = \frac{(36.29 + 2 \times 33.58)}{1000} \text{ kJ K}^{-1} \text{ mol}^{-1}$$

$$= 0.104 \text{ kJ K}^{-1} \text{ mol}^{-1}$$

$$T_f = \frac{+803.33 \text{ kJ mol}^{-1}}{0.104 \text{ kJ K}^{-1} \text{ mol}^{-1}} + 298 = 8048 \text{ K}$$

(ii) $\Delta n_g = 0$

$$\therefore \quad \Delta_r U^\circ = \Delta_r H^\circ = -803.33 \text{ kJ mol}^{-1}$$

$$C_V = C_p - R$$

$$\therefore \quad C_V(CO_2) = (36.29 - 8.314) \text{ JK}^{-1} \text{ mol}^{-1}$$

$$C_V(H_2O) = (33.58 - 8.314) \text{ JK}^{-1} \text{ mol}^{-1}$$

$$\therefore \quad C_V(CO_2 + 2H_2O) = (36.29 - 8.314) + (33.58 - 8.314) 2$$

$$= 78.51 \text{ J mol}^{-1} \text{ K}^{-1} = 0.0785 \text{ kJ mol}^{-1} \text{ K}^{-1}$$

$$T_f = \left[\frac{-\Delta_r U^\circ}{C_V} + T\right] = \frac{(-803.33)}{0.0785} + 298 = 10532 \text{ K}$$

Thus, T_f (constant volume) $> T_f$ (constant pressure)

Change = 10532 − 8048 = 2484 K higher

Immediate Test 13

Consider combustion of $CH_4(g)$ under constant volume condition using air (80% N_2 and 20% O_2).

$$CH_4(g) + 2O_2(g) \longrightarrow CO_2(g) + 2H_2O(g),$$

$$\Delta_r H^\circ_{298} = -803.33 \text{ kJ mol}^{-1}$$

Calculate, adiabatic flame temperature.

$$C_p(CO_2) = 36.29 \text{ JK}^{-1} \text{ mol}^{-1}$$

$$C_p(H_2O) = 33.58 \text{ J K}^{-1} \text{ mol}^{-1}$$

$$C_p(N_2) = 29.29 \text{ J K}^{-1} \text{ mol}^{-1}$$

KNOWLEDGE CONFIRMATION Test 5

1 Temperature of 12 g of a substance is raised from 20°C to 30°C by absorption of 240 kJ of heat. Thus, specific heat of the substance is

(a) $2\ kJ\ g^{-1}, K^{-1}$ (b) $24\ kJ\ g^{-1}, K^{-1}$
(c) $20\ kJ\ g^{-1}, K^{-1}$ (d) $240\ kJ\ g^{-1}, K^{-1}$

2 The formation of SO_3 from SO_2 and O_2 is exothermic by 97.03 kJ at 298 K and 1 atm pressure in a bomb calorimeter. The enthalpy of combustion of SO_2 at constant pressure is

(a) – 97.03 kJ (b) – 98.27 kJ
(c) + 97.03 kJ (d) + 98.27 kJ

3 The specific heat of water is 1 cal $g^{-1}K^{-1}$. 25 g of water absorbs 100 cal of heat. If final temperature is 317 K, then initial temperature is

(a) 321 K (b) 313 K (c) 309 K (d) 298 K

4 A bomb calorimeter has a heat capacity of 783 JK^{-1} and contains 254 g of water which has a specific heat of 4.184 J $g^{-1}K^{-1}$. Heat absorbed/evolved by a reaction when temperature changes from 23.73°C to 26.01°C is

(a) + 1.78 kJ (b) + 2.42 kJ
(c) –1.78 kJ (d) – 4.21 kJ

5 1 g of graphite is burnt in a calorimeter in excess of O_2 at 298 K and 1 atmospheric pressure. During the reaction, temperature increased by 1 K. Heat capacity of the bomb calorimeter is 20.7 kJ K^{-1}, thus enthalpy of combustion at constant pressure and constant volume can be :
(in kJ mol^{-1})

(a) – 248.4 , – 248.4 (b) – 248.4 , – 249.4
(c) – 248.4 , – 250.2 (d) + 248.4 , + 248.4

6 Assuming that 50% of the heat is useful, how many kg of water at 288 K can be heated to 368 K by burning 200 L of methane (CH_4) measured at STP.
Given $\Delta_c H° = -211$K cal mol^{-1}.

(a) 11.77 kg (b) 23.54 kg (c) 47.08 kg (d) 5.88 kg

7 8 g of NH_4NO_3 was dissolved in 400 g of water taken in a calorimeter (water equivalent of the calorimeter is 50 cal K^{-1}). A fall in temperature of 1.3°C was noted. Thus, enthalpy of solution is

(a) – 24.5 kJ mol^{-1} (b) + 24.5 kJ mol^{-1}
(c) 3.7 kJ mol^{-1} (d) – 3.7 kJ mol^{-1}

8 An adiabatic bomb calorimeter is commonly used to measure heat of combustion of substances under constant volume conditions. A 0.5421 g sample of benzoic acid was burnt in a calorimeter with a resulting temperature increase of 2.680 K. Thus, calorimeter constant is (Given $\Delta_C U$ (benzoic acid) = – 3227 kJ)

(a) 5.35 kJ K^{-1} (b) 14.34 kJ mol^{-1}
(c) 1.204×10^3 kJ K^{-1} (d) – 5.35 kJ mol^{-1}

9 Above calorimeter was used to combust 0.6521 g naphthalene ($C_{10}H_8$) when temperature increase was 1.173 K. Thus, $\Delta_C U°$ at 298 K is

$$C_{10}H_8(s) + 12O_2(g) \longrightarrow 10CO_2(g) + 4H_2O(l)$$

(a) – 1032 kJ mol^{-1} (b) – 1232 kJ mol^{-1}
(c) – 987 kJ mol^{-1} (d) – 787 kJ mol^{-1}

10 For the above case, $\Delta_C H°$ at 298 K is

(a) – 1232 kJ mol^{-1} (b) – 1237 kJ mol^{-1}
(c) – 1227 kJ mol^{-1} (d) – 1240 kJ mol^{-1}

11 A bomb calorimeter was constructed so that the contribution of the reaction products to the heat capacity is negligible. To calibrate this calorimeter, a 1.320 g sample of benzoic acid (C_6H_5COOH) was oxidised giving a temperature change of 5.88° C. If $\Delta_C U°$ (benzoic acid) = –26.26 kJ g^{-1}, then heat capacity of the calorimeter is

(a) 5.9 kJ K^{-1} (b) 4.5 kJ mol^{-1}
(c) 412.8 kJ K^{-1} (d) 179.2 kJ mol^{-1}

12 An oxygen bomb calorimeter was calibrated using a 0.325 g sample of benzoic acid
$\Delta_C U°$ (benzoic acid = – 105.02 kJ g^{-1})
which gave a change in temperature of 1.48°C. A 0.69 g sample of gasoline was oxidised in the calorimeter, resulting in the temperature change of 4.89°C.
Thus, $\Delta_C U°$ (gasoline) is

(a) – 29.1 kJ g^{-1} (b) – 40.8 kJ g^{-1}
(c) – 27.2 kJ g^{-1} (d) – 10.0 kJ g^{-1}

13 Consider a calorimeter which measures the heat of reaction by the amount of ice that is melted at 273 K.

$$\Delta H°_{fusion} \text{ (ice)} = 1436.3 \text{ cal mol}^{-1}$$

After correction for heat loss of the calorimeter, 0.251 g of ice melted in a particular reaction. Thus, the heat of reaction is (cal mol^{-1})

(a) 20.1 (b) 83.7 (c) –20.1 (d) – 83.7

14 Exactly 25 mL of 0.5 M HCl and 25 mL of 0.5 M NaOH were mixed in a solution calorimeter and a temperature increase of 3.015 K was observed.
Given, specific heat of the resulting NaCl solution is = 4.1 JK^{-1} g^{-1} and density = 1.0 g mL^{-1}
Thus, calorimeter constant is

(a) 30.1 J K^{-1} (b) 15.1 J K^{-1} (c) 19.2 J K^{-1} (d) 27.2 J K^{-1}

ACID TEST

For JEE Main

TYPE I MCQs with Only ONE Correct Alternate

1 As 1.00 g of $O_3(g)$ decomposed to form $O_2(g)$ under constant pressure conditions, 2.97 kJ was transferred to the surroundings. Thus, $\Delta_r H°$ for

$$2O_3(g) \longrightarrow 3O_2(g) \text{ is}$$

(a) 285.12 kJ mol^{-1} (b) – 285.12 kJ mol^{-1}
(c) 142.58 kJ mol^{-1} (d) – 142.58 kJ mol^{-1}

2 Assume that, a human requires '2500 cal' of energy each day for metabolic activity. What mass of sucrose ($C_{12}H_{22}O_{11}$) is needed to provide this energy?

$$C_{12}H_{22}O_{11} + 12\,O_2 \longrightarrow 12CO_2 + 11\,H_2O,$$
$$\Delta H = -5.647 \text{ kJ mol}^{-1}$$

(a) 342.0 g (b) 301.0 g (c) 633.5 g (d) 422.2 g

3 Hot carbon reacts with steam to produce an equimolar mixture of $CO(g)$ and $H_2(g)$, known as water gas.

$$C(s) + H_2O(g) \longrightarrow CO(g) + H_2(g)$$

Given, $\Delta_C H°(CO(g)) = -283.0 \text{ kJ mol}^{-1}$

$\Delta_C H°(H_2(g)) = -242.0 \text{ kJ mol}^{-1}$

What is the energy released if water gas is used as fuel?
(a) – 525.0 kJ (b) – 267.5 kJ (c) + 525.0 kJ (d) + 267.5 kJ

4 For the reaction at 298 K

$$4KClO_3(s) \longrightarrow 3KClO_4(s) + KCl(s)$$

$(\Delta_r H° - \Delta_r U°)$ is
(a) Zero (b) RT (c) $-RT$ (d) $-2RT$

5 For the following equilibrium at 298 K

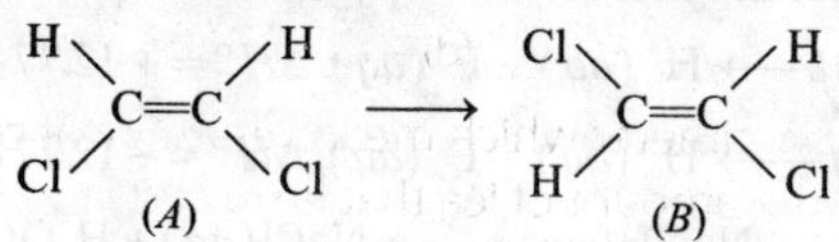

$$\Delta H° = 2.38 \text{ kJ mol}^{-1}$$

29% of the A-isomer is converted to B. Thus, enthalpy change is
(a) 2.38 kJ (b) 1.19 kJ (c) 1.93 kJ (d) 0.69 kJ

6 The enthalpy of solution of NaCl (s) is 4 kJ mol^{-1}, and enthalpy of hydration of its ions is – 784 kJ mol^{-1}. Thus, lattice energy of NaCl in kJ mol^{-1} is
(a) – 788 (b) + 4 (c) + 398 (d) + 780

7 Enthalpy change for the reaction

$$4H(g) \longrightarrow 2H_2(g) \text{ is } -869.6 \text{ kJ}.$$

Thus, dissociation enthalpy of H—H bond is
(a) 217.4 kJ (b) – 434.8 kJ (c) – 869.6 kJ (d) + 434.8 kJ

8 Given bond dissociation energies of XY, X_2 and Y_2 are in the ratio of 1 : 1 : 0.5.

Also, $\Delta_f H°(XY) = -200 \text{ kJ mol}^{-1}$

Thus, bond dissociation energy of (X—X) bond is
(a) 400 kJ mol^{-1} (b) 300 kJ mol^{-1}
(c) 200 kJ mol^{-1} (d) 800 kJ mol^{-1}

9 ΔH values are plotted against $(T_2 - T_1)$ when following straight line is obtained.

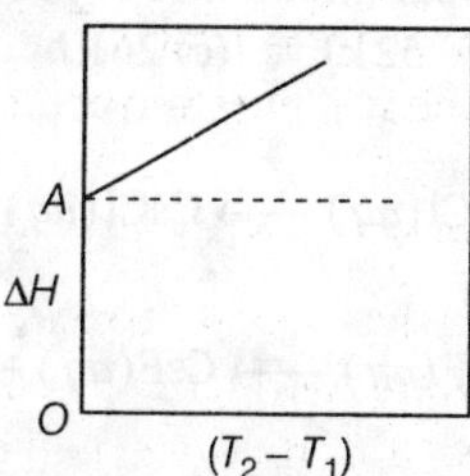

When $(T_2 - T_1) = 0$, then ΔH is equal to
(a) $\Delta H_1 = \Delta H_2$ (b) $\Delta H_1 > \Delta H_2$
(c) $\Delta H_2 > \Delta H_1$ (d) $\Delta H_1 = \Delta H_2 = 0$

10 Given, enthalpy of dissolution of $BaCl_2(s)$ and $BaCl_2 \cdot 2H_2O(s)$ are – 20.6 and 8.8 kJ mol^{-1} respectively. Thus, enthalpy of hydration of $BaCl_2$ is

$$BaCl_2(s) + 2H_2O(l) \longrightarrow BaCl_2 \cdot 2H_2O(s)$$

(a) 29.4 kJ mol^{-1} (b) – 29.4 kJ mol^{-1}
(c) – 11.8 kJ mol^{-1} (d) 38.2 kJ mol^{-1}

11 Given,

$$H_2O(l) \longrightarrow H_2O(g); \quad \Delta H^°_{vap} = 40.66 \text{ kJ at 1 atm}$$

then $\Delta U^°_{vap}$ at 1 atm is (in kJ mol^{-1}) (assume water vapour as an ideal gas)
(a) + 37.56 (b) – 43.76 (c) + 43.76 (d) + 40.66

12 To decompose 9 g of $H_2O(l)$ into H_2 and O_2, 142.5 kJ of heat is absorbed. Thus, $\Delta_f H°(H_2O(l))$ is
(a) + 285.0 kJ mol^{-1} (b) – 285.0 kJ mol^{-1}
(c) – 1425.5 kJ mol^{-1} (d) – 15.83 kJ mol^{-1}

13 Given,

I. $C(s) + O_2(g) \longrightarrow CO_2(g), \Delta H° = -94$ kcal
II. $2\,CO(g) + O_2(g) \longrightarrow 2CO_2(g), \Delta H° = -135.2$ kcal

Thus, $\Delta_f H°$ of $CO(g)$ is
(a) 26.4 kcal mol^{-1} (b) – 26.4 kcal mol^{-1}
(c) 41.2 kcal mol^{-1} (d) – 41.2 kcal mol^{-1}

14 Given, $\Delta_C H°$ (enthalpy of combustion) of

$$\text{Coke (carbon)} = -393.5\,\text{kJ mol}^{-1}$$
$$CO = -285\,\text{kJ mol}^{-1}$$
$$H_2 = -285\,\text{kJ mol}^{-1}$$

Thus, ratio of enthalpies liberated from combustion of 1 kg of coke and by burning water gas obtained from 1 kg of coke (100% carbon) is

(a) 0.79 : 1 (b) 0.69 : 1
(c) 0.86 : 1 (d) 0.96 : 1

15 In the following reaction,

$$4NO_2(g) + O_2(g) \longrightarrow 2N_2O_5(g),\ \Delta H° = -110\,\text{kJ}$$
$$4NO_2(g) + O_2(g) \longrightarrow 2N_2O_5(s),\ \Delta H° = -162\,\text{kJ}$$

Thus, enthalpy of sublimation of $N_2O_5(s)$ is

(a) 52 kJ (b) – 52 kJ (c) 26 kJ (d) –26 kJ

16 Given,

I. $CsOH(aq) + HCl(aq) \longrightarrow CsCl(aq) + H_2O(l)$, $\Delta H° = -13.4$ kcal

II. $CsOH(aq) + HF(aq) \longrightarrow CsF(aq) + H_2O(l)$, $\Delta H° = -16.4$ kcal

Thus, $\Delta H°$ of $HF(aq) \rightleftharpoons H^+(aq) + F^-(aq)$ is

(a) + 39.8 kcal (b) – 39.8 kcal
(c) – 3.0 kcal (d) + 3.0 kcal

17 Consider following reactions,

I. $C(g) + 4H(g) \longrightarrow CH_4(g)$, $\Delta_r H = x$ kJ mol^{-1}

II. C (graphite) + $2H_2(g) \longrightarrow CH_4(g)$, $\Delta_r H = y$ kJ mol^{-1}

Thus,

(a) $x = y$ (b) $x = 2y$
(c) $x > y$ (d) $x < y$

18 $\Delta_f H°(H_2O) = -68$ kcal mol^{-1}, thus, $\Delta_f H°(OH^-)$ is

(a) – 68 kcal mol^{-1} (b) – 54.3 kcal mol^{-1}
(c) 54.3 kcal mol^{-1} (d) – 71.7 kcal mol^{-1}

19 The standard heat of combustion of solid boron is equal to

(a) $\Delta_f H°(B_2O_3)$ (b) $\frac{1}{2}\Delta_f H°(B_2O_3)$
(c) $2\Delta_f H°(B_2O_3)$ (d) $-\frac{1}{2}\Delta_f H°(B_2O_3)$

20 Given,

I. $NaOH + HCl \rightleftharpoons NaCl + H_2O$, $\Delta H = x_1$

II. $NH_4OH + HCl \rightleftharpoons NH_4Cl + H_2O$, $\Delta H = x_2$

III. $NaOH + CH_3COOH \rightleftharpoons CH_3COONa + H_2O$, $\Delta H = x_3$

IV. $CH_3COOH + NH_4OH \rightleftharpoons CH_3COONH_4 + H_2O$, $\Delta H = x_4$

Thus, x_4 is equal to

(a) $(x_1 + x_2 + x_3)$ (b) $-(x_1 + x_2 + x_3)$
(c) $-(x_2 + x_3 - x_1)$ (d) $(x_2 + x_3 - x_1)$

21 Heat of ionisation of CH_3COOH is 0.005 kcal g^{-1}. Thus, enthalpy change when 1 mole of $Ca(OH)_2$ is completely neutralised by CH_3COOH is

(a) – 27.4 kcal (b) – 13.6 kcal
(c) – 26.8 kcal (d) – 27.1 kcal

22 For the ionisation of HS^-

$$HS^-(aq) \rightleftharpoons H^+(aq) + S^{2-}(aq),\ \Delta H° = 14.22\,\text{kcal mol}^{-1}$$

Thus, $\Delta H°$ of the reaction (in kcal mol^{-1}) is

$$HS^-(aq) + OH^-(aq) \longrightarrow S^{2-}(aq) + H_2O$$

(a) – 0.52 (b) + 0.52 (c) 14.22 (d) – 14.22

23 Given, $\Delta H°$ (kJ mol^{-1})

I. $F_2(g) \longrightarrow 2F(g)$, 156.9

II. $F^-(g) \longrightarrow F(g) + e^-$ 333.0

III. $F_2^-(g) \longrightarrow F_2(g) + e^-$ 290.0

Thus, bond enthalpy of $F_2^-(g)$ ion is (i.e. ΔH of $F_2^-(g) \longrightarrow F(g) + F^-(g)$)

(a) 446.9 kJ (b) 113.9 kJ (c) 779.9 kJ (d) 623.0 kJ

24 Given, $PH_3(g) \longrightarrow P(g) + 3H(g)$, $\Delta H° = 953$ kJ mol^{-1}

$$P_2H_4(g) \longrightarrow 2P(g) + 4H(g), \Delta H° = 1485\,\text{kJ mol}^{-1}$$

Thus, $\Delta H°$ of $P_2H_6 \longrightarrow 2P(g) + 6H(g)$ is

(a) 953 kJ mol^{-1} (b) 214.33 kJ mol^{-1}
(c) 1906 kJ mol^{-1} (d) 2120.33 kJ mol^{-1}

25 Given,

I. $HF(aq) + OH^-(aq) \longrightarrow H_2O(l) + F^-(aq)$, $\Delta H° = -68.6$ kJ mol^{-1}

II. $H^+(aq) + OH^-(aq) \longrightarrow H_2O(l)$, $\Delta H° = -55.83$ kJ mol^{-1}

Which is not the correct enthalpy change representation?

(a) $HF(aq) \longrightarrow H^+(aq) + F^-(aq)$, $\Delta H° = +12.77$ kJ mol^{-1}

(b) $HF(aq) \longrightarrow H^+(aq) + F^-(aq)$, $\Delta H° = -12.77$ kJ mol^{-1}

(c) $HCl(aq) + NaOH(aq) \longrightarrow NaCl(aq) + H_2O(l)$, $\Delta H° = -55.83$ kJ mol^{-1}

(d) $H_2SO_4(aq) + Ca(OH)_2(aq) \longrightarrow CaSO_4(aq) + 2H_2O(l)$, $\Delta H° = -111.66$ kJ mol^{-1}

26 Given, Bond energy (H—H) $= x_1$

Bond energy (O=O) $= x_2$

Bond energy (O—H) $= x_3$

and $\Delta H_{vap}[H_2O(l) \longrightarrow H_2O(g)] = x_4$

then $\Delta_f H°[H_2O(l)]$ is :

(a) $x_1 + \frac{x_2}{2} - x_3 + x_4$ (b) $2x_3 - x_1 - \frac{x_2}{2} - x_4$
(c) $x_1 + \frac{x_2}{2} - 2x_3 - x_4$ (d) $x_1 + \frac{x_2}{2} - 2x_3 + x_4$

27 Given, I. $Fe_2O_3(s) + 1.5C(s) \longrightarrow 1.5CO_2 + 2Fe(s)$, $\Delta H° = +234.1$ kJ mol^{-1}

II. $C(s) + O_2(g) \longrightarrow CO_2(g)$, $\Delta H° = -393.5$ kJ mol^{-1}

Thus, $\Delta_f H°[Fe_2O_3(s)]$ is

(a) + 356.15 kJ mol^{-1} (b) + 824.15 kJ mol^{-1}
(c) – 824.35 kJ mol^{-1} (d) – 627.60 kJ mol^{-1}

28 Consider following reaction.

Stage I 30 mL of 0.1 M NaOH + 10 mL of 0.1 M HCl

$\Delta H_1 = x_1$ kcal

Stage II 20 mL of 0.1 M HCl was further added after stage I.

$\Delta H_2 = x_2$ kcal

Thus, x_1 and x_2 are respectively

	x_1 (cal)	x_2 (cal)
(a)	−13.7	−13.7
(b)	−27.4	−13.7
(c)	−13.7	−27.4
(d)	−27.4	−27.4

29 If $HCl(g) + \underset{\text{Excess}}{H_2O(l)} \rightleftharpoons H^+(aq) + Cl^-(aq)$, $\Delta H°_{298\text{ K}} = -17.9$ kcal

and $\Delta_f H°[HCl(g)] = -22.1$ kcal

then, $\Delta_f H°(Cl^-)$ is

(a) −40.0 kcal (b) 40.0 kcal
(c) +17.9 kcal (d) +22.1 kcal

30 Given, $\Delta_f H°(NH_3) = -46.0$ kJ mol^{-1}

$\Delta_f H°$ (H_2 from atoms) = −436 kJ mol^{-1}

$\Delta_f H°$ (N_2 from atoms) = −712 kJ mol^{-1}

Thus average bond enthalpy of (N—H) bond in NH_3.

(a) – 1102 kJ mol^{-1} (b) + 352 kJ mol^{-1}
(c) + 1056 kJ mol^{-1} (d) – 964 kJ mol^{-1}

31 Given, at 298 K

$\Delta_{comb} H°$ of $H_2 = -241$ kJ mol^{-1}

$\Delta_{comb} H°$ of cyclohexane (C_6H_{12}) = – 3920 kJ mol^{-1}

$\Delta_{comb} H°$ of cyclohexene (C_6H_{10}) = – 3800 kJ mol^{-1}

In the hydrogenation of *x* g of cyclohexene to cyclohexane, 29.51 kJ of heat is liberated. Thus, *x* is

(a) 10 g (b) 20 g (c) 82 g (d) 41 g

32 The standard molar enthalpy of formation of molecular O_2 at 298 K is zero. Thus, its value at 315 K is $C_p^\circ(O_2) = 29.4$ J mol^{-1}.

(a) Zero (b) 0.5 kJ mol^{-1}
(c) – 0.5 kJ mol^{-1} (d) Cannot be predicted.

33 At 298 K, for CO $(\Delta_C H_{298} - \Delta_C U_{298})$ is

(a) 27 cal (b) 54 cal
(c) – 298 cal (d) 600 cal

34 The standard heat of combustion of propane is – 2220 kJ mol^{-1} at 298 K.

If $H_2O(l) \longrightarrow H_2O(g)$, $\Delta H° = 44.0$ kJ mol^{-1}

then, $\Delta H°$ of

$C_3H_8(g) + 5O_2(g) \longrightarrow 3CO_2 + 4H_2O(g)$ is

(a) – 2220.0 kJ (b) – 2044.0 kJ
(c) – 2396.0 kJ (d) – 2176.0 kJ

35 Given, $\Delta_f H°(NO) = 21.6$ kcal mol^{-1}. Thus,

(a) 43.2 kcal is absorbed when 1.0 g of N_2 reacts
(b) 43.2 kcal is absorbed when 1.0 g of O_2 reacts
(c) 43.2 kcal is absorbed when 1.0 mole of O_2 reacts
(d) 43.2 kcal is released when 2.0 moles of NO are formed

36 For the reaction,

$N_2H_4(g) + H_2(g) \longrightarrow 2NH_3(g)\ \Delta_f H = +187.6$ kJ

If $\Delta_f H°(N_2H_4) = 95.4$ kJ mol^{-1}, then $\Delta_f H°(NH_3)$ is

(a) – 46.1 kJ mol^{-1} (b) + 46.1 kJ mol^{-1}
(c) – 141.5 kJ mol^{-1} (d) – 233.7 kJ mol^{-1}

37 When 100 mL of 0.1 M $Ba(OH)_2$ is neutralised by 100 mL of 0.1 M H_2SO_4, temperature rise is ΔT_1. On neutralisation of 50 mL of 0.1 M $Ba(OH)_2$ by 100 mL of 0.1 M HCl, temperature rise is ΔT_2. Thus,

(a) $\Delta T_1 = \Delta T_2$ (b) $\Delta T_1 = 2\Delta T_2$
(c) $\Delta T_2 = 2\Delta T_1$ (d) $\Delta T_1 = 1.5\,\Delta T_2$

38 $\Delta_f H°(H_2O)(g) = -241.8$ kJ mol^{-1}. 90 g each of H_2 and O_2 are allowed to undergo reaction to form $H_2O(g)$. Thus, $\Delta_r H°$ of $H_2(g) + \frac{1}{2}O_2(g) \longrightarrow H_2O(g)$ is

(a) – 2.72×10^3 kJ (b) + 1.36×10^3 kJ
(c) – 1.36×10^3 kJ (d) + 2.72×10^3 kJ

39 When 5.6 g of Fe is allowed to react with O_2 to form $Fe_2O_3(s)$, 41 kJ of heat is liberated. Thus, $\Delta_f H°(Fe_2O_3)$ in standard state is

(a) – 41 kJ mol^{-1} (b) −82 kJ mol^{-1}
(c) – 410 kJ mol^{-1} (d) – 820 kJ mol^{-1}

40 Numerical value of $(\Delta H° - \Delta U°)$ is maximum for

(a) $PCl_5(g) \longrightarrow PCl_3(g) + Cl_2(g)$
(b) $N_2(g) + 3H_2(g) \longrightarrow 2NH_3(g)$
(c) $N_2(g) + O_2(g) \longrightarrow 2NO(g)$
(d) $2SO_2(g) + O_2(g) \longrightarrow 2SO_3(g)$

41 The combustion of benzene (*l*) gives $CO_2(g)$ and $H_2O(l)$. Given that heat of combustion of benzene at constant volume is – 3263.9 kJ mol^{-1} at 25°C, heat of combustion (in kJ mol^{-1}) of benzene at constant pressure and at 25°C will be ($R = 8.314$ J K^{-1} mol^{-1}) **[JEE Main 2018]**

(a) 3260 (b) – 3267.6 (c) 4152.6 (d) – 452.46

42 Given, $C(graphite) + O_2(g) \longrightarrow CO_2(g)$;

$$\Delta_r H° = -393.5 \text{ kJ mol}^{-1}$$

$$H_2(g) + \frac{1}{2}O_2(g) \longrightarrow H_2O(l); \ \Delta_r H° = -285.8 \text{ kJ mol}^{-1}$$

$$CO_2(g) + 2H_2O(l) \longrightarrow CH_4(g) + 2O_2(g);$$

$$\Delta_r H° = +890.3 \text{ kJ mol}^{-1}$$

Based on the above thermochemical equations, the value of $\Delta_r H°$ at 298 K for the reaction, **[JEE Main 2017]**

$$C\,(graphite) + 2H_2(g) \longrightarrow CH_4(g)$$

(a) + 78.8 kJ mol^{-1} (b) + 144.0 kJ mol^{-1}
(c) – 74.8 kJ mol^{-1} (d) – 144.0 kJ mol^{-1}

43 The heat of combustion of carbon and carbon monoxide are – 393.5 and – 283.5 kJ mol^{-1} respectively. The heat of formation (in kJ) of carbon monoxide per mole is **[JEE Main 2016]**

(a) 676.5 (b) – 676.5 (c) – 110.0 (d) 110.5

44 For the complete combustion of ethanol, $C_2H_5OH(l) + 3O_2(g) \longrightarrow 2\,CO_2(g) + 3H_2O(l)$, the amount of heat produced as measured in bomb calorimeter is 1364.47 kJ mol^{-1} at 25°C. Assuming ideality, the enthalpy of combustion, $\Delta_C H$ for the reaction will be
($R = 8.314$ J $K^{-1}mol^{-1}$) **[JEE Main 2014]**

(a) – 1366.95 kJ mol^{-1} (b) – 1361.95 kJ mol^{-1}
(c) – 1460.50 kJ mol^{-1} (d) – 1350.50 kJ mol^{-1}

45 The value of enthalpy change (ΔH) for the reaction, $C_2H_5OH(l) + 3O_2(g) \longrightarrow 2CO_2(g) + 3H_2O(l)$ at 27°C is – 1366.5 kJ mol^{-1}. The value of internal energy change for the above reaction at this temperature will be **[AIEEE 2011]**

(a) – 1371.5 kJ (b) – 1369.0 kJ
(c) – 1364.0 kJ (d) – 1361.5 kJ

46 Consider the reaction,

$$4NO_2(g) + O_2(g) \longrightarrow 2N_2O_5(g); \ \Delta_r H = -111 \text{ kJ}$$

If $N_2O_5(s)$ is formed instead of $N_2O_5(g)$ in the above reaction, the $\Delta_r H$ value will be
(Given, ΔH of sublimation for N_2O_5 is 54 kJ mol^{-1}) **[AIEEE 2011]**

(a) – 165 kJ (b) + 54 kJ (c) + 219 kJ (d) – 219 kJ

47 The standard enthalpy of formation of NH_3 is – 46.0 kJ mol^{-1}. If the enthalpy of formation of H_2 from its atoms is – 436 kJ mol^{-1} and that of N_2 is – 712 kJ mol^{-1}, the average bond enthalpy of N—H bond in NH_3 is **[AIEEE 2010]**

(a) – 964 kJ mol^{-1} (b) + 352 kJ mol^{-1}
(c) + 1056 kJ mol^{-1} (d) – 1102 kJ mol^{-1}

48 In a fuel cell, methanol is used as fuel and oxygen gas is used as an oxidiser. The reaction is

$$CH_3OH(l) + \frac{3}{2}O_2(g) \longrightarrow CO_2(g) + 2H_2O(l) \text{ at 298 K,}$$

standard Gibb's energies of formation for $CH_3OH(l)$, $H_2O(l)$ and $CO_2(g)$ are – 166.2, – 237.2 and – 394.4 kJ mol^{-1}, respectively. If standard enthalpy of combustion of methanol is – 726 kJ mol^{-1}, efficiency of the fuel cell will be **[AIEEE 2009]**

(a) 80% (b) 87%
(c) 90% (d) 97%

49 On the basis of the following thermochemical data $[\Delta_f H°(H^+, aq) = 0]$

$$H_2O(l) \longrightarrow H^+(aq) + OH^-(aq); \ \Delta H = 57.32 \text{ kJ}$$

$$H_2(g) + \frac{1}{2}O_2(g) \longrightarrow H_2O(l); \quad \Delta H = -286.20 \text{ kJ}$$

The value of enthalpy of formation of OH^- ion at 25°C is **[AIEEE 2009]**

(a) – 22.88 kJ (b) – 228.88 kJ
(c) + 228.88 kJ (d) –343.52 kJ

50 Oxidising power of chlorine in aqueous solution can be determined by the parameters indicated below.

$$\frac{1}{2}Cl_2(g) \xrightarrow{\frac{1}{2}\Delta_{diss}H°} Cl(g) \xrightarrow{\Delta E_a H°} Cl^-(g) \xrightarrow{\Delta_{hyd}H°} Cl^-(aq)$$

The energy involved in the conversion of $\frac{1}{2}Cl_2(g)$ to $Cl^-(aq)$.
(Using the data, $\Delta_{diss} H°_{Cl_2} = 240$ kJ mol^{-1}
$\Delta_{E_a} H°_{Cl} = -349$ kJ mol^{-1} $\Delta_{hyd} H°_{Cl} = -381$ kJ mol^{-1})
will be **[AIEEE 2008]**

(a) + 152 kJ mol^{-1} (b) – 610 kJ mol^{-1}
(c) – 850 kJ mol^{-1} (d) + 120 kJ mol^{-1}

51 $(\Delta H - \Delta E)$ for the formation of carbon monoxide (CO) from its elements at 298 K is ($R = 8.314$ J$K^{-1}mol^{-1}$) **[AIEEE 2006]**

(a) – 1238.78 J mol^{-1} (b) 1238.78 J mol^{-1}
(c) – 2477.57 J mol^{-1} (d) 2477.57 J mol^{-1}

52. The enthalpy changes for the following processes are listed below

$$Cl_2(g) = 2Cl(g), \ 242.3 \text{ kJ mol}^{-1}$$

$$I_2(g) = 2I(g), \ 151.0 \text{ kJ mol}^{-1}$$

$$ICl(g) = I(g) + Cl(g), \ 211.3 \text{ kJ mol}^{-1}$$

$$I_2(s) = I_2(g), \ 62.76 \text{ kJ mol}^{-1}$$

Given that, the standard states for iodine and chlorine are $I_2(s)$ and $Cl_2(g)$, the standard enthalpy of formation of $ICl(g)$ is **[AIEEE 2006]**

(a) $-14.6\,kJ\,mol^{-1}$ (b) $-16.7\,kJ\,mol^{-1}$

(c) $+16.7\,kJ\,mol^{-1}$ (d) $+244.8\,kJ\,mol^{-1}$

53 The standard enthalpy of formation (ΔH_f°) at 298 K for methane, $CH_4(g)$ is $-74.8\,kJ\,mol^{-1}$. The additional information required to determine the average energy for C—H bond formation would be **[AIEEE 2006]**

(a) the dissociation energy of H_2 and enthalpy of sublimation of carbon

(b) latent heat of vaporisation of methane

(c) the first four ionisation energies of carbon and electron gain enthalpy of hydrogen

(d) the dissociation energy of hydrogen molecule, H_2

54 Consider following transition:

	C(graphite) $\longrightarrow$	C (diamond)
Density	$2.25\,g\,cm^{-3}$	$3.51\,g\,cm^{-3}$

Pressure at which $(\Delta H - \Delta U)$ is equal to -1 kJ is ($1\,dm^3\,bar = 100\,J$)

(a) 5.2×10^3 bar (b) 5.2×10^2 bar

(c) 6.1×10^3 bar (d) 6.1×10^2 bar

55 Consider following reaction in which C_p values have been given below species the reaction:

$$O_3(g) + OH(g) \longrightarrow H(g) + 2O_2(g),$$

$$\Delta_r H^\circ_{298} = 36.3\,kJ$$

$C_p\,(JK^{-1}mol^{-1})$: 39.29 29.89 20.78 29.36

Thus, $\Delta_r H^\circ_{373}$ for this reaction is

(a) -37.1 kJ (b) $+37.1$ kJ

(c) -38.9 kJ (d) -38.9 kJ

56 Consider the following thermochemical equations:

	$\Delta_r H^\circ$ (kJ)
$Ag(s) \longrightarrow Ag^+(aq) + e^-$	105.6
$Cl_2(g) + 2e^- \longrightarrow 2Cl^-(aq)$	-334.4
$Br_2(l) + 2e^- \longrightarrow 2Br^-(aq)$	-243.1
$AgCl(s) \longrightarrow Ag^+(aq) + Cl^-(aq)$	65.5
$AgBr(s) \longrightarrow Ag^+(aq) + Br^-(aq)$	84.4

Thus out of

I. $Ag(s) + \frac{1}{2}Cl_2(g) \longrightarrow AgCl(s)$

II. $Ag(s) + \frac{1}{2}Br_2(l) \longrightarrow AgBr(s)$

(a) I is more endothermic than II

(b) II is more endothermic than I

(c) I is more exothermic than II

(d) II is more exothermic than I

57 Consider the dissolution process of methanol (CH_3OH) in water (H_2O) to consist of two steps :

I. $CH_3OH(l) \longrightarrow CH_3OH(g)$; $\Delta_{vap}H^\circ = 38.00\,kJ\,mol^{-1}$

II. $CH_3OH(g) + nH_2O \longrightarrow CH_3OH \cdot nH_2O$, $\Delta_{solv}H^\circ = ?$

Given that the enthalpy of solution is $-7.27\,kJ\,mol^{-1}$, then enthalpy of solvation of step II is

(a) $30.63\,kJ\,mol^{-1}$ (b) $-30.63\,kJ\,mol^{-1}$

(c) $45.27\,kJ\,mol^{-1}$ (d) $-45.27\,kJ\,mol^{-1}$

58 Consider conversion of $H_2O(s)$ to $H_2O(g)$ at 273 K and 6×10^{-3} bar pressure

$$H_2O(s) \longrightarrow H_2O(l) \longrightarrow H_2O(g)$$

Latent heat of fusion of ice = $6.0\,kJ\,mol^{-1}$ and latent heat of vaporisation of water = $40.0\,kJ\,mol^{-1}$ at 273 K

Thus, ΔH and ΔU in this conversion are respectively

	$\Delta H\,(kJ\,mol^{-1})$	$\Delta U\,(kJ\,mol^{-1})$
(a)	46.00	46.00
(b)	46.00	43.73
(c)	43.73	43.37
(d)	-46.00	-43.73

59 For a reaction of dimerisation of gaseous A into gaseous A_2 at 400 K

$$2A(g) \longrightarrow A_2(g);\ \Delta H^\circ_{400} = -60.0\,kJ\,mol^{-1}$$

If $\Delta C_p = 5.0 + 2.0\times10^{-2}\,T$

what is temperature at which $\Delta H_T = 0$?

(a) 320.6 K (b) 316.0 K

(c) 373.0 K (d) 305.4 K

60 Enthalpy of sublimation of iodine is 24 cal g^{-1} at 200°C. If specific heat of $I_2(s)$ and I_2(vap.) are 0.055 and 0.031 cal $g^{-1}K^{-1}$ respectively, then enthalpy of sublimation of iodine at 250°C in cal g^{-1} is **[JEE Main 2019 (II) NTA]**

(a) 2.85 (b) 5.7

(c) 22.8 (d) 11.4

ACID TEST
For JEE Advanced

TYPE I MCQs with Only ONE Correct Alternate

61 For two weak acids HA and HB, enthalpy of neutralisation with strong acids are given.

$$HA(aq) + NaOH(aq) \longrightarrow NaA(aq) + H_2O(l); \quad \Delta H = -54.0 \text{ kJ mol}^{-1}$$

$$HB(aq) + NaOH(aq) \longrightarrow NaB(aq) + H_2O(l); \quad \Delta H = -51.0 \text{ kJ mol}^{-1}$$

Which has higher pH of equimolar solution?

(a) HA (b) HB
(c) equal (d) insufficient data

62 Heat of atomisation of H_2 is 400 kJ mol^{-1}. Heat of atomisation of H_2, F_2 and HF are in the ratio of 2 : 1 : 3. Thus, $\Delta_f H$ of HF is

(a) -600 kJ mol^{-1} (b) -1200 kJ mol^{-1}
(c) -300 kJ mol^{-1} (d) None of these

63 In the following reaction,

$$NaOH(aq) + HCl(aq) \rightleftharpoons NaCl(aq)$$

Case I	1L, 1M	1L, 1M	$\Delta T = 10°C$
Case II	1L, 1M	2L, 0.5 M	$\Delta T = x°C$

Thus, x is

(a) 5° (b) 7° (c) 10° (d) 20°

64 $\Delta_f H°$ of Fe_2O_3 is x kJ mol^{-1} and $\Delta_f H°$ of FeO is y kJ mol^{-1}.

Thus, $\Delta_f H°$ of Fe_3O_4 is

(a) $x + y$ (b) $x - y$ (c) $2x - y$ (d) $x - 2y$

65 Heat of atomisation of NH_3 and N_2H_4 are p and q kJ mol^{-1} respectively. Thus, (N — N) bond energy is

(a) $\frac{3q - 4p}{3}$ (b) $\frac{4q - 3p}{3}$
(c) $\frac{2q - 3p}{3}$ (d) $\frac{4q - 3p}{4}$

66 For the following reaction,

$$H^+(aq) + OH^-(aq) \longrightarrow H_2O(l), \; \Delta H° = -13.7 \text{ kcal mol}^{-1}$$

Thus, enthalpy change when 50 mL of 0.01 M $Ca(OH)_2$ reacts with 25 mL of 0.01 M HCl is

(a) $\frac{-13.7}{4}$ cal (b) $\frac{-13.7}{2}$ cal (c) $\frac{-13.7}{4}$ kcal (d) $\frac{-13.7}{2}$ kcal

67 For the reaction at 300 K

$$C_6H_6(l) + 7.5O_2(g) \longrightarrow 6CO_2(g) + 3H_2O(l); \quad \Delta H° = -3.271 \times 10^3 \text{ kJ}$$

Thus, $\Delta E°$ at 300 K is

(a) -3.267×10^3 kJ (b) -4.9×10^3 kJ
(c) -4.9×10^3 kJ (d) -3.275×10^3 kJ

68 $\Delta_f H°$ of $C_8H_{18} = -250$ kJ mol^{-1}

$\Delta_f H°$ of $CO_2 = -394$ kJ mol^{-1}

$\Delta_f H°$ of $H_2O = -286$ kJ mol^{-1}

Thus, $\Delta H°$ of the following reaction is

$$C_8H_{18}(g) + 12.5O_2(g) \longrightarrow 8CO_2(g) + 9H_2O(l)$$

(a) -5310 kJ mol^{-1} (b) -5476 kJ mol^{-1}
(c) -5726 kJ mol^{-1} (d) -5726 kJ mol^{-1}

69 For the reaction,

$$CH_2{=}CHCH_3(g) + H_2(g) \longrightarrow CH_3CH_2CH_3 \quad \Delta H° = -124 \text{ kJ mol}^{-1}$$

$\Delta_C H°$ (propane) $= -2220$ kJ mol^{-1}

$\Delta_f H°(H_2O) = -286$ kJ mol^{-1}

Thus $\Delta_C H°$ (propene, C_3H_6) is

(a) $+2506$ kJ mol^{-1} (b) -2506 kJ mol^{-1}
(c) -1789 kJ mol^{-1} (d) -2058 kJ mol^{-1}

70 When 120 mg of $C_{10}H_8(s)$ (naphthalene) was burnt in a bomb calorimeter, the temperature rise by 3.05 K. By how much will the temperature rise when 150 mg of $C_6H_5OH(s)$, (phenol) is burnt in the calorimeter under identical conditions

$\Delta_C H°(C_{10}H_8) = -2720$ kJ mol^{-1}

$\Delta_C H°(C_6H_6O) = -3054$ kJ mol^{-1}

(a) 3.05 K (b) 2.70 K (c) 5.83 K (d) 1.90 K

71 Given, $P(s) + 1.5Cl_2(g) \longrightarrow PCl_3(g), \Delta H° = 306$ kJ mol^{-1}

$P(s) \longrightarrow P(g), \quad \Delta H° = 314$ kJ mol^{-1}

$\frac{1}{2}Cl_2(g) \longrightarrow Cl(g), \quad \Delta H° = 121$ kJ mol^{-1}

Thus, bond energy of (P — Cl) bond is

(a) 123.7 kJ mol^{-1} (b) 371 kJ mol^{-1}
(c) 19.0 kJ mol^{-1} (d) -371 kJ mol^{-1}

72 A 0.5421g sample of benzoic acid was burnt in a calorimeter with a resulting temperature increase of 2.680 K.

$$\Delta_C U^\circ \text{ (benzoic acid)} = -3227 \text{ kJ mol}^{-1}$$

If 0.6521 g of sample of naphthalene ($C_{10}H_8$) is used in the same calorimeter, combustion caused a 1.173 K increase in temperature.

Thus, $\Delta_C U^\circ$ for the reaction is

$$C_{10}H_8 + 12O_2 \longrightarrow 10CO_2 + 4H_2O$$

(a) $-1232 \text{ kJ mol}^{-1}$ (b) $-1027 \text{ kJ mol}^{-1}$

(c) $-3220 \text{ kJ mol}^{-1}$ (d) $-6310 \text{ kJ mol}^{-1}$

73 The polymerisation of ethylene to linear polyethylene is represented by the reaction.

$$n\, CH_2{=}CH_2 \longrightarrow {-}(CH_2{-}CH_2)_n{-}$$

where n is large integral values. Thus, enthalpy of polymerisation per mole of ethylene at 298 K is

Given, (C $=$ C) bond dissociation energy $= 590 \text{ kJ mol}^{-1}$ and that of (C—C) bond is $= 331 \text{ kJ mol}^{-1}$.

(a) 72 kJ mol^{-1} (b) $-72.0 \text{ kJ mol}^{-1}$

(c) $\frac{72}{n} \text{ kJ mol}^{-1}$ (d) $-\frac{72.0}{n} \text{ kJ mol}^{-1}$

74 For benzoic acid, $\Delta_C U^\circ = -3251 \text{ kJ mol}^{-1}$

A 0.825 g of benzoic acid ($C_7H_6O_2$) on combustion in a calorimeter gave a temperature increase of 1.94 K. A sample of 0.727 g of D-ribose ($C_5H_{10}O_5$) on combustion gave the temperature increase of 0.910 K. Thus, $\Delta_f U^\circ$ of D-ribose is

Given, $\Delta_f H^\circ(H_2O) = -286 \text{ kJ mol}^{-1}$

$$\Delta_f H^\circ(CO_2) = -394 \text{ kJ mol}^{-1}$$

(a) $+1272.8 \text{ kJ mol}^{-1}$ (b) $-1272.8 \text{ kJ mol}^{-1}$

(c) $+2127 \text{ kJ mol}^{-1}$ (d) $-2127.2 \text{ kJ mol}^{-1}$

75 How much heat (in kcal) is necessary to convert 100 g of ice at 273 K to water vapour (steam) at 373 K?

$$\Delta H_{\text{fusion}} = 80 \text{ kcal kg}^{-1}$$

$$\Delta H_{\text{vap}} = 540 \text{ kcal kg}^{-1}$$

Heat capacity $= 1.0 \text{ kcal kg}^{-1} \text{ K}^{-1}$

(a) 72.0 (b) 79.0 (c) 48.0 (d) 60.0

76 When 20 g of Al is heated from 90 to 115° C, 105 cal is required. Thus, molar heat capacity at constant pressure is

(a) $5.67 \text{ cal mol}^{-1} \text{ K}^{-1}$ (b) $0.21 \text{ cal mol}^{-1} \text{ K}^{-1}$

(c) $6.71 \text{ cal mol}^{-1} \text{ K}^{-1}$ (d) $0.71 \text{ cal mol}^{-1} \text{ K}^{-1}$

77 Combustion of 5.0 g of coke raised the temperature of 1.0 kg of water from 10°C to 47°C. Thus, calorific value of coke in kcal g^{-1} is

(a) 37 kcal g^{-1} (b) 7.4 kcal g^{-1}

(c) 9 kcal g^{-1} (d) 1.2 kcal g^{-1}

78 Propane gas is used as a fuel for household heating. Assuming no heat loss, then volume of propane gas measured at 298 K and 1 atm pressure, necessary to heat 4.0 kg of water from 50°C to 60°C is

$$\Delta_{\text{comb}} H^\circ \text{ (propane)} = -520.0 \text{ kcal mol}^{-1}$$

(a) 4.56 L (b) 2.70 L (c) 1.72 L (d) 1.88 L

79 The thermochemical equation for the dissociation of H_2 is

$$H_2 \longrightarrow 2H, \Delta H = 436 \text{ kJ mol}^{-1}$$

$$\Delta_f H^\circ(\underset{\text{Steam}}{H_2O}) = -242 \text{ kJ mol}^{-1}$$

Thus, ratio of energy yield on combustion of hydrogen atoms that of H_2 to form 1 mole of steam is

(a) 0.36 (b) 3.70 (c) 2.80 (d) 1.40

80 The commercial production of water gas utilises the reaction

$$C + H_2O(g) \longrightarrow \underbrace{CO(g) + H_2(g)}_{\text{Water gas}}$$

How many grams of carbon must be burnt to CO_2 to provide enough heat for the conversion of 100 g carbon to water gas.

$$\Delta_f H^\circ(CO) = -110.53 \text{ kJ mol}^{-1}$$

$$\Delta_f H^\circ(H_2O(g)) = -241.81 \text{ kJ mol}^{-1}$$

$$\Delta_f H^\circ(CO_2) = -393.51 \text{ kJ mol}^{-1}$$

(a) 16.68 g (b) 33.4 g

(c) 50.04 g (d) 12.0 g

81 When 1 mole of carbon reacted with O_2 to form CO and CO_2 at 298 K and constant pressure 75.0 kcal of heat was liberated with 100% efficiency. Thus, O_2 reacted, $\Delta_f H^\circ(CO) = -26 \text{ kcal}$, $\Delta_f H^\circ(CO_2) = -94 \text{ kcal}$

(a) 0.14 mol (b) 0.86 mol

(c) 0.50 mol (d) 1.00 mol

82 15.50 g of carbon is treated with 25.0 L of air (19% O_2) at 298 K and 5.50 atm pressure. If oxidation products are CO and CO_2, heat evolved will be

$$\Delta_f H^\circ(CO) = -26.0 \text{ kcal}$$

$$\Delta_f H^\circ(CO_2) = -94.0 \text{ kcal}$$

(a) -26.0 kcal (b) -94.0 kcal

(c) -94.74 kcal (d) -120.0 kcal

83 How many moles of Na_2CO_3 can be decomposed by HCl to liberated 4 kcal of heat under standard states.

$$\Delta_f H^\circ(CO_3^{2-}) = -161.6 \text{ kcal}$$

$$\Delta_f H^\circ(CO_2) = -94.0 \text{ kcal}$$

$$\Delta_f H^\circ(H_2O) = -68.0 \text{ kcal}$$

(a) 0.1 mol (b) 1.0 mol

(c) 10.0 mol (d) 0.01 mol

84 How many kJ of heat will be liberated in making 22.4 L at S.T.P of H_2S from FeS and dil. HCl (in kJ mol^{-1})?

$$\Delta_f H°(Fe^{2+}) = -87.9 \text{ kJ mol}^{-1}$$
$$\Delta_f H°(FeS) = -95.4 \text{ kJ mol}^{-1}$$
$$\Delta_f H°(H_2S) = -20.6 \text{ kJ mol}^{-1}$$

(a) −13.1 (b) +13.1 (c) −27.2 (d) −61.2

85 The solution of $CaCl_2 \cdot 6H_2O$ in a large volume of water is endothermic to the extent of 3.5 kcal mol^{-1}. Also,

$$CaCl_2(s) + 6H_2O(l) \longrightarrow CaCl_2 \cdot 6H_2O(s)$$
$$\Delta H° = -23.2 \text{ kcal mol}^{-1}$$

Thus, heat of solution of $CaCl_2(s)$ in a large volume of water is

(a) 19.7 kcal (b) −19.7 kcal
(c) 26.7 kcal (d) −26.7 kcal

86 Gaseous ozone is bubbled through water-ice mixture at 273 K. As the $O_3(g)$ decomposes to form $O_2(g)$, the enthalpy of reaction is absorbed by the resulting ice.

$$\Delta H°_{fusion}(ice) = 6.0 \text{ kJ mol}^{-1}$$

and $2O_3(g) \longrightarrow 3O_2(g)$, $\Delta H° = -285.4$ kJ

Thus, mass of ice that melts for each gram of O_3 that decomposes is

(a) 8.92 g (b) 0.50 g (c) 4.46 g (d) 17.84 g

87 Which oxidising agent will generate the greatest amount of energy for 0.1 g of oxidising agent ?

(a) $2H_2(g) + O_2(g) \longrightarrow 2H_2O(g) + 483.6$ kJ
(b) $3H_2(g) + O_3(g) \longrightarrow 3H_2O(g) + 868.2$ kJ
(c) $H_2(g) + H_2O_2(g) \longrightarrow 2H_2O(g) + 347.3$ kJ
(d) $3H_2(g) + N_2(g) \longrightarrow 2NH_3(g) + 92.11$ kJ

88 Hot carbon reacts with steam to produce an equimolar mixture of CO(g) and $H_2(g)$ known as water gas. Thus, energy released if water gas obtained from 1 kg coal is used as fuel with 50% efficiency is

$$\Delta_C H°(H_2) = -242 \text{ kJ mol}^{-1}$$
$$\Delta_C H°(CO) = -283 \text{ kJ mol}^{-1}$$

(a) -6×10^3 kJ (b) -43.750×10^3 kJ
(c) -10.937×10^5 kJ (d) -21.875×10^3 kJ

89 12.0 g of carbon is treated with steam to form water gas, $(CO + H_2)$. The water gas undergoes 'water gas shift' reaction at high temperature.

$$\Delta_C H°(CO) = -283.0 \text{ kJ}$$
$$\Delta_C H°(H_2) = -242.0 \text{ kJ}$$
$$\Delta_C H°(C) = -393.0 \text{ kJ}$$

Difference in the enthalpy change of combustion of water gas before and after 'water gas shift' is

(a) −41.0 kJ (b) +41.0 kJ (c) −110.0 kJ (d) −151 kJ

90 Ethanol (C_2H_5OH) can undergo decomposition to form two sets of products

$C_2H_5OH(g)$ —I→ $C_2H_4(g) + H_2O(g)$, $\Delta_r H° = 45.54$ kJ

$C_2H_5OH(g)$ —II→ $CH_3CHO(g) + H_2(g)$, $\Delta_r H° = 68.91$ kJ

If the molar ratio of C_2H_4 to CH_3CHO is 8 : 1 in a set of gaseous products, then enthalpy change involved in the decomposition process is

(a) 433.23 kJ (b) 48.14 kJ
(c) 114.45 kJ (d) 57.23 kJ

91 Pressure at which

$$(\Delta_r H° - \Delta_r U°) = -1 \text{ kJ}$$

for the reaction

$$C\text{ (graphite)} \longrightarrow C\text{ (diamond)}$$

density of graphite = 2.25 g cm^{-3}

density of diamond = 3.51 g cm^{-3}

(a) 2716 atm (b) 1000 atm
(c) 5416 atm (d) 1260 atm

92 For the reaction

$$2O_3(g) \longrightarrow 3O_2(g), \quad \Delta_r H° = -285.4 \text{ kJ}$$

Thus, work done is

(a) −2.5 kJ (c) +2.5 kJ (c) 0 (d) −7.5 kJ

93 Given,

$$H_2C_2O_4(aq) \rightleftharpoons 2H^+(aq) + C_2O_4^{2-}; \Delta H° = +3.2 \text{ kcal mol}^{-1}$$

Thus, heat of neutralisation of oxalic acid ($H_2C_2O_4$) is

(a) −10.5 kcal mol^{-1} (b) −24.2 kcal mol^{-1}
(c) −16.9 kcal mol^{-1} (d) −30.6 kcal mol^{-1}

94 Given, $\Delta_f H°(H_2S) = -20.1 \text{ kJ mol}^{-1}$

$$\Delta_f H°(H(g)) = +218.0 \text{ kJ mol}^{-1}$$
$$\Delta_f H°(S(g)) = +277.0 \text{ kJ mol}^{-1}$$

Bond dissociation energy of first (H—S) bond in $H_2S = 376.6 \text{ kJ mol}^{-1}$.

Thus, $\Delta_f H°(HS)$ is (in kJ mol^{-1})

(a) 138.5 (b) −138.5 (c) −501.1 (d) 515.1

95 If

$H_2(g) \longrightarrow 2H(g)$, $\Delta H° = x_1$
$O_2(g) \longrightarrow 2O(g)$, $\Delta H° = x_2$
$O—H(g) \longrightarrow O(g) + H(g)$, $\Delta H° = x_3$
$H_2O(l) \longrightarrow H_2O(g)$, $\Delta H° = x_4$

then $\Delta_f H°(H_2O(l))$ is

(a) $x_1 + \frac{x_2}{2} + x_3 — x_4$ (b) $x_1 + \frac{x_2}{2} - 2x_3 - x_4$
(c) $2x_3 + x_4 - x_1 - \frac{x_2}{2}$ (d) $2x_1 + x_2 - 4x_3 - 2x_4$

96 A sample containing 2 moles of graphite reacts completely with limited quantity of O_2 at 25°C and 1 bar pressure, producing 481 kJ of heat and a mixture of CO and CO_2.

$$\Delta_f H(CO) = -110.5\ kJ\ mol^{-1}$$
$$\Delta_f H(CO_2) = -393.5\ kJ\ mol^{-1}$$

Thus, CO and CO_2 are formed in

(a) 1 : 1 (b) 1 : 2 (c) 1 : 3 (d) 1.17 : 1

97 Quantity of heat (in kJ) liberated due to complete combustion of 1.65×10^4 L of CH_4 measured at 300 K and 1 bar pressure is $\Delta_C H°(CH_4) = -890\ kJ\ mol^{-1}$

(a) -5.89×10^5 (b) -14.68×10^5
(c) -1.79×10^5 (d) -6.79×10^5

98 Oxidising power of Cl_2 in aqueous solution can be determined by the parameters indicated below :

$$\frac{1}{2}Cl_2(g) \xrightarrow{\frac{1}{2}\Delta_{diss}H°} Cl(g),\ \frac{240}{2}\ kJ \quad (\Delta H°)$$
$$Cl(g) \xrightarrow{\Delta_{E_a}H°} Cl^-(g), -349\ kJ$$
$$Cl^-(g) \xrightarrow{\Delta_{hyd}H°} Cl^-(aq), -381\ kJ$$

Thus, total enthalpy change when $Cl_2(g)$ (0.5 mole) changes of $Cl^-(aq)$ is

(a) +152 kJ (b) −610 kJ
(c) −850 kJ (d) +120 kJ

99 The standard enthalpies of formation of $CO_2(g)$, $H_2O(l)$ and glucose (s) at 25°C are −400 kJ/mol, −300 kJ/mol and −1300 kJ/mol, respectively. The standard enthalpy of combustion per gram of glucose at 25°C is ***[JEE Adv. 2013]***

(a) + 2900 kJ (b) −2900 kJ
(c) −16.11 kJ (d) +16.11 kJ

100 Using the data provided, calculate the multiple bond energy (kJ mol^{-1}) of a C≡C bond C_2H_2. That energy is (take the bond energy of a C—H bond as 350 kJ mol^{-1}). ***[JEE Adv. 2012]***

$$2C(s) + H_2(g) \longrightarrow C_2H_2(g); \quad \Delta H = 225\ kJ\ mol^{-1}$$
$$2C(s) \longrightarrow 2C(g); \quad \Delta H = 1410\ kJ\ mol^{-1}$$
$$H_2(g) \longrightarrow 2H(g); \quad \Delta H = 330\ kJ\ mol^{-1}$$

(a) 1165 (b) 837 (c) 865 (d) 815

101 Based on this graph, values for N_2O_4 for different transitions

I. ΔH_{fusion} at 262 K
II. ΔH_{vap} at 262 K and
III. ΔH_{vap} at 400 K are respectively (in kJ mol^{-1})

(Melting point of N_2O_4 = 262 K)

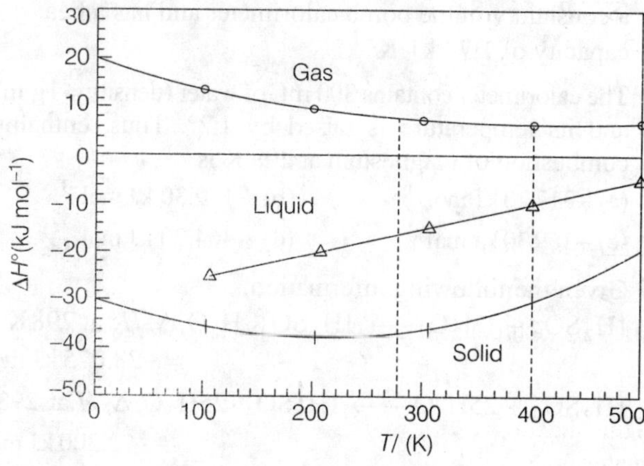

	I	II	III
(a)	14.7	20.9	30.7
(b)	14.7	33.4	26.0
(c)	20.9	30.9	31.8
(d)	14.2	16.3	18.9

102 The heat of combustion of methane to produce gaseous water at 298 K is −802.34 kJ mol^{-1} and to produce liquid water at the same temperature is −890.36 kJ mol^{-1}.
Thus, $\Delta_{vap}H°$ for water at 298 K is

(a) 88.02 kJ mol^{-1} (b) −88.02 kJ mol^{-1}
(c) + 44.01 kJ mol^{-1} (d) − 44.01 kJ mol^{-1}

103 The enthalpy of neutralisation of

I. $HS^-\ (aq) = -5.1\ kJ\ mol^{-1}$
II. $HCl\ (aq) = -57.2\ kJ\ mol^{-1}$

and enthalpy of formation of

III. $HS^-\ (aq) = -17.6\ kJ\ mol^{-1}$
IV. $H_2O(l) = -285.8\ kJ\ mol^{-1}$

Thus, enthalpy of formation $S^{2-}(aq)$ is

(a) + 61.0 kJ mol^{-1} (b) −61.0 kJ mol^{-1}
(c) −33.1 kJ mol^{-1} (d) 34.5 kJ mol^{-1}

104 Consider the formation of gaseous methanol from the gaseous species as:

$$C(g) + 4H(g) + O(g) \longrightarrow CH_3OH(g),$$
$$\Delta_f H°(CH_3OH, g) = -47.96\ kcal\ mol^{-1}$$
$$\Delta_f H°(C, g) = 171.29\ kcal\ mol^{-1}$$
$$\Delta_f H°(H, g) = 52.10\ kcal\ mol^{-1}$$
$$\Delta_f H°(O, g) = 59.60\ kcal\ mol^{-1}$$

Average B.E. of (C—H) bond = 415.9 kJ mol^{-1}
B.E. of (O—H) bond = 463.6 kJ mol^{-1}
Thus, B.E. of (C—O) bond is

(a) 314.2 kJ mol^{-1} (b) 169.3 kJ mol^{-1}
(c) 102.0 kJ mol^{-1} (d) 192.0 kJ mol^{-1}

105 A 0.24 g sample of magnesium (24.0 g mol^{-1}) is burnt in a constant volume bomb calorimeter and has a heat capacity of 1.77 kJ K^{-1}.
The calorimeter contains 300 mL of water (density = 1 g mL^{-1}) and its temperature is raised by 1.2°. Thus, enthalpy of combustion of magnesium at 298 K is
(a) −317.20 kJ mol^{-1} (b) − 179.30 kJ mol^{-1}
(c) −369.30 kJ mol^{-1} (d) − 364.20 kJ mol^{-1}

106 Given the following information:
$$1H_2SO_4 + 1H_2O \longrightarrow 1H_2SO_4 \cdot H_2O, \Delta_r H° \text{ at } 298\text{ K} = -28.075 \text{ kJ mol}^{-1}$$
$$1H_2SO_4 + 25H_2O \longrightarrow 1H_2SO_4 \cdot 25H_2O; \Delta_r H \text{ at } 298\text{ K} = -72.300 \text{ kJ mol}^{-1}$$
Temperature change when the following dilution takes place at 290 K is
$$1H_2SO_4 \cdot 1H_2O + 24H_2O \longrightarrow 1H_2SO_4 \cdot 25H_2O$$
(a) 19.3 K (b) 1.93 K (c) 23.5 K (d) 2.35 K

107 Consider following reaction of fusion of ice at 273 K and 1 bar.
$$H_2O(s) \xrightleftharpoons{273\text{ K}} H_2O(l);$$
$\Delta H = 6.0 \text{kJ mol}^{-1}$
Volume 0.0196 dm^3 mol^{-1} 0.0180 dm^3 mol^{-1}
Thus, ΔU of the process is approximately
(a) −6.0 kJ mol^{-1} (b) 5.70 kJ mol^{-1}
(c) 6.0 kJ mol^{-1} (d) −5.84 kJ mol^{-1}

TYPE II Statement Based Questions

Directions Answers of Q. Nos. (108-112) have been based on the following codes.
(a) Statement I is true; Statement II is true; Statement II is the correct explanation of Statement I.
(b) Statement I is true; Statement II is true; Statement II is not the correct explanation of Statement I.
(c) Statement I is true; Statement II is false.
(d) Statement I is false; Statement II is true.

108 **Statement I** Based on the following thermodynamic data.
$N_2(g) + O_2(g) \longrightarrow 2NO(g), \Delta_r H° = 180$ kJ
$2NO(g) + O_2(g) \longrightarrow 2NO_2(g), \Delta_r H° = -148$ kJ
NO_2 is more stable than NO.
Statement II NO(g) is an endothermic compound while NO_2 is an exothermic compound.

109 **Statement I** If bond energy of (H—H) bond x_1, that of (O=O) bond x_2, that of (H—O) bond is x_3 then $\Delta_f H°$ of $H_2O(l)$ is $\left[x_1 + \frac{x_2}{2} - 2x_3 - \Delta H_{vap}(H_2O)\right]$.
Statement II Additional heat is also required to vaporise $H_2O(l)$ to $H_2O(g)$.

110 **Statement I** C_V value of He is always $\frac{3}{2}R$ but C_V value of H_2 is $\frac{3}{2}R$ at low temperature; $\frac{5}{2}R$ at moderate temperature and more than $\frac{5}{2}R$ at higher temperature.
Statement II At low temperature, only translational degree of freedom contributes to heat capacity, while at higher temperature, rotational and vibrational degree of freedom also contribute to heat capacitiy. ***[IIT JEE 2003]***

111 **Statement I** If $\Delta_f H°$ of H is x from $H_2(g)$ then bond enthalpy of (H—H) bond is $2x$.
Statement II Formation of H(g) is an endothermic reaction.

TYPE III MCQs with ONE or MORE than ONE Correct Alternate

112 Choose the reaction(s) from the following options, for which the standard enthalpy of reaction is equal to standard enthalpy of formation. ***[JEE Adv. 2019]***
(a) $2C(g) + 3H_2(g) \longrightarrow C_2H_6(g)$
(b) $\frac{3}{2}O_2(g) \longrightarrow 2O_3(g)$
(c) $2H_2(g) + O_2(g) \longrightarrow 2H_2O(l)$
(d) $\frac{1}{8}S_8(s) + O_2(g) \longrightarrow SO_2(g)$

113 Consider following thermochemical reaction,
I. $C + \frac{1}{2}O_2 \longrightarrow CO, \Delta H° = x_1$
II. $2CO + O_2 \longrightarrow 2CO_2, \Delta H° = x_2$
III. $C + O_2 \longrightarrow CO_2, \Delta H° = x_3$
Select correct alternates.
(a) $\Delta_f H°$ of CO is x_1 and that of CO_2 is $\left(\frac{x_2}{2}\right)$
(b) $\left(x_1 + \frac{x_2}{2}\right) = x_3$
(c) $\Delta_f H°$ of CO_2 is x_3 or $\left(\frac{2x_1 + x_2}{2}\right)$
(d) $\Delta_C H°$ of carbon is x_3

114 $\Delta_f H°(H) = x_1$ from H_2
$\Delta_f H°(O) = x_2$ from O_2
bond energy (O—H) = x_3
$\Delta_{vap} H°(H_2O, (l) \longrightarrow H_2O, (g)) = x_4$
then
(a) bond energy of (H—H) = $2x_1$
(b) bond energy of (O=O) = x_2
(c) $\Delta_f H°[H_2O,(l)] = (2x_1 + x_2 - 2x_3 - x_4)$
(d) $\Delta_f H°[H_2O, g] = (x_1 + x_2 - 2x_3)$

115 Dissociation energy of $A_2(g)$ is x kJ, that of $B_2(g)$ is $x/2$ kJ and that of $(A—B)$ is $2x$ kJ. If $\Delta_f H°(AB)$ is -200 kJ mol^{-1}, then
(a) dissociation energy of $(A—B)$ is $+200$ kJ mol^{-1}
(b) dissociation energy of A_2 is $+160$ kJ mol^{-1}
(c) dissociation energy of $A—B$ is $+320$ kJ mol^{-1}
(d) $\Delta_f H°(A_2B)$ is -440 kJ mol^{-1}

116 Select correct alternates.
(a) If $C_p = 3 + 2 \times 10^{-2}\, T$ cal mol^{-1} K^{-1} then
$C_V = 1 + 2 \times 10^{-2}\, T$ cal mol^{-1} K^{-1}
(b) $\Delta H = C_p(T_2 - T_1)$
(c) $\Delta H = (C_V + R)(T_2 - T_1)$
(d) $\Delta E = (C_p - R)(T_2 - T_1)$

117 Select correct alternates.
(a) For per mole change $\frac{d(\Delta H)}{dT} = \frac{d(\Delta E)}{dT} + R$
(b) In the absence of force of attraction $\Delta E = \frac{C_V p}{R}(V_2 - V_1)$ for real gas.
(c) In the absence of force of attraction
$\Delta H = \left(\frac{C_V + R}{R}\right) p(V_2 - V_1)$ for real gas.
(d) For an ideal gas, $\Delta E = C_V(T_2 - T_1)$

118 Standard enthalpies of combustion of fumaric acid and maleic acid are -1336.0 kJ mol^{-1} and -1359.2 kJ mol^{-1} respectively.
Also, $\Delta_f H°(CO_2) = -393.5$ kJ mol^{-1}
$\Delta_f H°(H_2O) = -285.8$ kJ mol^{-1}.
Thus,
(a) heat is absorbed in the conversion of maleic acid to fumaric acid
(b) heat is absorbed in the conversion of fumaric acid to maleic acid
(c) maleic acid is more stable than furmaric acid
(d) fumaric acid is more stable than maleic acid

119 In a constant pressure calorimeter with heat capacity of 453 J K^{-1}, 200 mL of 0.862 M HCl and 200 mL of 0.431 M $Ba(OH)_2$ are mixed. (density = 1 g mL^{-1})
Initially, both solutions are at 20.48°C. Select correct statement.
(a) $\Delta_r H°$ is $-$ 9.69 kJ
(b) Final temperature is 25.07 °C
(c) Some HCl is left unreacted
(d) Some $Ba(OH)_2$ is left unreacted

120 For a given substance
$\Delta H_T^\circ = a + bT$; $\Delta H_{298}^\circ = 5$ kJ mol^{-1}
$\Delta H_{300}^\circ = 5.5$ kJ mol^{-1},
then,
(a) ΔH_{350}° is 18 kJ mol^{-1}
(b) C_p is 0.25 kJ K^{-1} mol^{-1}
(c) C_V is 0.25 kJ K^{-1} mol^{-1}
(d) ΔE_{300}° is 3.0 kJ mol^{-1} if $\Delta n_g = +1$

TYPE IV Passage Based MCQs (Comprehension)

Passage 1

When 1.0 mole of C_8H_{18} at 298 K is completely burnt at constant pressure, H_2O, CO and CO_2 (all gaseous products at 573 K) are formed and 90.20 kcal heat is lost to the surrounding.

kcal mol^{-1}

$\Delta_f H°(H_2O(l)) = -68.0$
$\Delta_f H°(H_2O(g)) = -58.0$
$\Delta_f H°(CO_2) = -94.0$
$\Delta_f H°(CO) = -26.0$
$\Delta_C H°(C_8H_{18}) = -1302.7$

121 The ratio of moles of CO and CO_2 formed in the above oxidation process is
(a) 1.33 (b) 0.75 (c) 0.33 (d) 1.67

122 Thus, work done is
(a) 0 J (b) -200.0 J
(c) -169.70 J (d) -275.83 J

Passage 2

H_2 can be oxidised to H_2O by O_2, O_3 and H_2O_2 in the following reactions.

	$\Delta H°$ (kJ)
I. $2H_2(g) + O_2(g) \longrightarrow 2H_2O(g)$	-483.6
II. $3H_2(g) + O_3(g) \longrightarrow 3H_2O(g)$	-886.2
III. $H_2(g) + H_2O_2(g) \longrightarrow 2H_2O(g)$	-347.3

123 Which oxidising agent will generate the greatest amount of energy for 1 mole of $H_2(g)$?
(a) O_2 (b) O_3 (c) H_2O_2 (d) equal

124 Which of the three reactions gives above will generate the greatest amount of energy on a total mass basis of reactants?
(a) I (b) II (c) III (d) equally

Passage 3

Assume human body of mass 75 kg as a closed system requiring "250 cal" of energy each day. Specific heat = 4 JK^{-1} g^{-1}.

125 What would be the temperature increase resulting from the energy intake?
(a) 12.27 K (b) 34.87 K
(c) 51.00 K (d) 27.28 K

126 If the body temperature is to be maintained at a constant value, by the evaporation of water, what mass of water must evaporate?

$$\Delta H_{vap}(H_2O) = 44 \text{ kJ mol}^{-1}$$

(a) 1.692 kg (b) 5.279 kg (c) 1.798 kg (d) 4.279 kg

Passage 4

Based on the following figure.

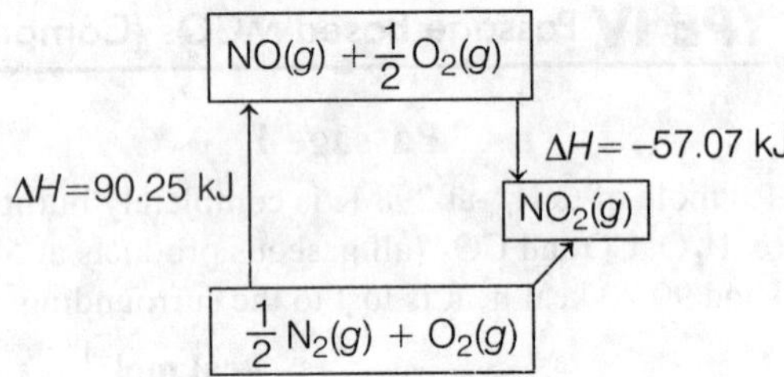

127 $\Delta_f H^\circ(NO_2)$ is

(a) 33.18 kJ mol^{-1} (b) –33.18 kJ mol^{-1}
(c) –57.07 kJ mol^{-1} (d) +57.07 kJ mol^{-1}

128 $\Delta_C H^\circ$ (enthalpy of combustion) of NO(g) is

(a) –90.25 kJ mol^{-1} (b) –57.07 kJ mol^{-1}
(c) –33.18 kJ mol^{-1} (d) None of these

Passage 5

Consider the following experiments :

Exp.	Reactions	ΔT	Specific heat (C_p)	Density	ΔH
I.	HCl + NaOH ⟶ 5mL 25 mL 0.5M 0.5 M	3.015 K	4.10 JK^{-1}g^{-1}	1.0 g mL^{-1}	–57.2 kJ mol^{-1} HCl
II.	CH_3COOH + NaOH ⟶ 25 mL 25 mL 0.5 m 0.5 m	2.934 K	4.10 JK^{-1} g^{-1}	1.0 g mL^{-1}	Q

129 Calorimeter constant of the calorimeter is

(a) C_p = 32.15 JK^{-1} (b) C_p = 3.21 JK^{-1}
(c) C_p = 12.60 JK^{-1} (d) C_p = 15.05 JK^{-1}

130 Enthalpy of neutralisation (Q) in experiment II is

(a) –57.2 kJ mol^{-1} (b) –55.7 kJ mol^{-1}
(c) –61.2 kJ mol^{-1} (d) –54.0 kJ mol^{-1}

Passage 6

When 100 mL of 1.0 M HCl was mixed with 100 mL of 1.0 M NaOH in an insulated beaker at constant pressure, a temperature increase of 5.7°C was measured for the beaker and its contents (Expt. 1). Because the enthalpy of neutralisation of a strong acid with a strong base is a constant (–57.0 kJ mol^{-1}), this experiment could be used to measure the calorimeter constant.

In a second experiment (Expt. 2), 100 mL of 2.0 M acetic acid ($K_a = 2.0 \times 10^{-5}$) was mixed with 100 mL of 1.0 M NaOH (under identical conditions to Expt. 1) where a temperature rise of 5.6° C was measured.

(Consider heat capacity of all solutions as 4.2 J g^{-1} K^{-1} and density of all solutions as 1.0 g mL^{-1}) ***[JEE Adv. 2015]***

131 Enthalpy of dissociation (in kJ mol^{-1}) of acetic acid obtained from the Expt. 2 is

(a) 1.0 (b) 10.0 (c) 24.5 (d) 51.4

132 The pH of the solution after experiment (2) is

(a) 2.8 (b) 4.7 (c) 5.0 (d) 7.0

TYPE V Numerical Skills

133 Exactly 3.00 g of carbon was burnt to CO_2 in a copper calorimeter.
(Specific heat of copper = 0.092 cal g^{-1} K^{-1}). The mass of the calorimeter is 1500 g and that of water (specific heat = 1 cal g^{-1} K^{-1}) inside it is 2000 g. Temperature of the water increased from 20°C to 31.3°C. Heat of combustion of carbon is $y \times 10^3$ cal g^{-1}. What is value of y?

134 x kJ of enthalpy is required to prepare 0.01 mole of (Cl^+Cl^-)—a plasma.

Given , $Cl(g) \longrightarrow Cl^+(g) + e^-$, $\Delta H^\circ = 1257.5$ kJ mol^{-1}

$Cl(g) + e^- \longrightarrow Cl^-(g)$, $\Delta H^\circ = -359.8$ kJ mol^{-1}

What is value of x?

135 The heat of combustion of ethane gas is 390 kcal mol^{-1}. Assuming that 60% of the heat is useful, how many m^3 of ethane measured at STP must be burnt to supply enough heat to convert 50.0 kg water at 10°C to steam at 100°C?
Specific heat of water = 1 cal g^{-1} K^{-1}
Heat of vaporisation of water = 540 cal g^{-1}

136 The combustion of 5.0 g of carbon raised the temperature of 1.00 kg of water from 10° to 35°C. Thus, heat value of coke in kcal g^{-1} is.

137 A new element 'X' forms a compound XCl_n with chlorine. XCl_n contains 1.455 g chlorine/g of X. The specific heat of 'X' is 0.050 cal g^{-1} K^{-1}. Thus, X is ...

138 Consider following two experiments :

I. 50 mL of 1 M HCl + 50 mL of 1 M NaOH, Δt = 2.85°
II. 50 mL of 1 M CH_3COOH + 50 mL of 1 M NaOH, Δt = 2.80°

Thus, enthalpy of ionisation of CH_3COOH is ..... kJ mol^{-1}.

139 $\Delta_C H^\circ$ of $(A) = -10$ kJ mol^{-1}
$\Delta_C H^\circ$ of $(B) = -15$ kJ mol^{-1}
A mixture of 3 moles of A and x moles of B released enthalpy of 105 kJ. What is the value of x?

140 The heat capacity of a calorimeter (called calorimeter constant) was determined by heating the calorimeter and its content using an electrical heater, if $\Delta T = 1.221\,K$. When 1.25 A of electricity of 3.26 V was passed through the heater immersed in 137.5 g of water in the calorimeter for 175 s, determine the calorimeter constant (in JK^{-1}). Specific heat of water at constant pressure is 75.291 JK^{-1} mol^{-1}.

141 The heat of combustion of ethane gas C_2H_6 is 368 kcal mol^{-1}. Assuming that 60.0% of the heat is useful, how many litres of ethane measured at STP must be burnt to supply enough heat to convert 50.0 kg of water at 10°C to steam at 100°C?
Specific heat of water 1 cal/g/°C.
Latent heat = 540 cal/g of vaporisation for $H_2O\,(l)$.

142 The heat of combustion of methane is 211 kcal mol^{-1}. Assuming that 50% of the heat is useful, how many kg of water at 15°C can be heated to 93.33°C by burning 200 L of methane measured at STP ?
Specific heat = 1 cal g^{-1} = (1 kcal kg^{-1})

143 A and B are two insulated bottles containing solutions as given at 25°C.

400 mL of 0.2 M CH_3COOH	+	100 mL of 0.8 M NaOH
A		B

On mixing temperature rises to 26.18°C; densities of the solutions are $1\,g/cm^3$ and specific heat capacities are $4.2\,J\,g^{-1}\,K^{-1}$. Thus, heat of neutralisation of weak acid per mole is ....kJ.

144 Given,

$$C_2H_4(g) + 3O_2(g) \longrightarrow 2CO_2(g) + 2H_2O(l);$$
$$\Delta H^\circ = -337.3\ \text{kcal mol}^{-1}$$

Assuming 70.0% efficiency, how many kg of water at 20°C can be converted into steam at 100°C by burning $1\,m^3$ of C_2H_4 gas at STP?
Specific heat of water = 1 kcal kg^{-1}
Latent heat of vaporisation of water = 540 kcal kg^{-1}

145 A 1.250 g sample of benzoic acid ($C_7H_6O_2$) was placed in a combustion bomb. The bomb was filled with an excess of oxygen at high pressure, sealed and immersed in a pail of water which served as a calorimeter.
The heat capacity of the entire apparatus was found to be 2422 cal K^{-1}. After complete combustion of the sample temperature raised by 3.258 K. What is ΔE (combustion) per mole of benzoic acid in kcal?
(Assume ΔE (combustion) is negative)

146 When molecular beams of $OH(g)$ and $H(g)$ at 25°C undergo reaction, the energy released cannot be dissipated quickly, so the product gases. $H_2O\,(g)$ and $H(g)$ are warmer than 25°C. Determine the temperature of the product gases, given
C_p for $H_2O\,(g) = 33.587\,J\,K^{-1}\,mol^{-1}$
C_p for $H(g) = 20.784\,J\,K^{-1}\,mol^{-1}$
$OH(g) + H_2(g) \longrightarrow H_2O(g) + H(g),\ \Delta_r H^\circ = -62.80\ \text{kJ}$

147 The heat of combustion of ethanol into CO_2 and H_2O is – 327 kcal mol^{-1} at constant pressure. The heat evolved (in cal) at constant volume and 27°C (if all gases behave ideally is ......) ($R = 2$ cal $mol^{-1}\,K^{-1}$)
[JEE Main 2020 (II) NTA]

148 Compare the heat of combustion of 1.00 kg of carbon with that of water gas obtained from 1.00 kg of carbon with 100% conversion efficiency.

$$\Delta_C H^\circ\,(C) = -94.0\ \text{kcal}$$
$$\Delta_C H^\circ\,(H_2) = -68.0\ \text{kcal}$$
$$\Delta_C H^\circ\,(CO) = -68.0\ \text{kcal}$$

149 A 1.00 L sample of mixture of methane gas and oxygen measured at 298 K and 740 Torr was allowed to react at constant pressure in a calorimeter which, together with contents had a heat capacity of 1260 cal K^{-1}. Due to combustion of methane temperature raised by 0.667 K. What is mole per cent of CH_4 in the original mixture ?

$$\Delta_C H^\circ\,(CH_4) = -210.8\ \text{kcal mol}^{-1}$$

150 What is the minimum mass in kg of the cooling water needed to remove the heat of reaction for each kilogram (kg) of C_2H_2 (acetylene) reacting with $HCl(g)$ to form vinyl chloride?

$$CH \equiv CH(g) + HCl(g) \longrightarrow CH_2 = CHCl(g),$$
$$\Delta_r H^\circ = -98.8\ \text{kJ mol}^{-1}$$

Assume that the inlet temperature of the cooling water is 25°C, outlet temperature is 35°C and $C_p = 75.291\,JK^{-1}\,mol^{-1}$.

151 The standard heat of formation ($\Delta_f H^\circ_{298}$) of ethane (in kJ mol^{-1}), if the heat of combustion of ethane, hydrogen and graphite are –1560, –393.5 and –286 kJ mol^{-1} respectively, is ....
[JEE Main 2020 (I) NTA]

152 It is estimated that an average human brain consumes the equivalents of 10g glucose per hour. Estimate the power output of the brain in Watts. ($1\,W = 1\,Js^{-1}$)

$$\Delta_f H^\circ\,(H_2O)\,(l) = -286\ \text{kJ mol}^{-1}$$
$$\Delta_f H^\circ\,(CO_2) = -394\ \text{kJ mol}^{-1}$$
$$\Delta_f H^\circ\,(\text{glucose})\,(aq) = -1260\ \text{kJ mol}^{-1}$$

153 150 mL of 0.4 N HCl is neutralised with excess of $NH_4OH\,(aq)$ in a dewar flask with a resulting rise in temperature of 2.36°. If the heat capacity of the flask and its content is 315 cal K^{-1}, calculate the heat of neutralisation in kcal equiv $^{-1}$.

154 The combustion of 0.875 g of benzoic acid (122 g mol^{-1}) in a bomb calorimeter at 298K caused a temperature rise of 2.28K, while combustion of 0.783 g of ethyl ethanoate (88 g mol^{-1}) caused a temperature rise of 1.95 K. Calculate the internal energy change of combustion of ethyl ethanoate.

$$\Delta_C U° \text{ (benzoic acid)} = -3251 \text{ kJ mol}^{-1}$$

155 A sample of 1 mole of H_2 and 0.5 mole of O_2 at 25°C in a sealed bomb calorimeter is ignited by an electric spark. Calculate the final temperature in Kelvin of the gaseous water produced.

$$\Delta_f H(H_2O)(g) = -58.0 \text{ kcal mol}^{-1}$$

$$C_p = 5.92 \text{ cal mol}^{-1} \text{ K}^{-1}$$

TYPE VI Matrix Matching

156 Consider the following reactions :

I. $C(s) + H_2O(g) \longrightarrow CO(g) + H_2(g)$

II. $CO(g) + H_2O(g) \longrightarrow CO_2(g) + H_2(g)$

III. $CH_4(g) + H_2O(g) \longrightarrow CO(g) + 3H_2(g)$

IV. $CH_4(g) + 2O_2(g) \longrightarrow CO_2(g) + 2H_2O(l)$

$$\Delta_C H°(C) = -393.50 \text{ kJ mol}^{-1}$$

$$\Delta_C H°(H_2) = -285.83 \text{ kJ mol}^{-1}$$

$$\Delta_C H°(CO) = -283.0 \text{ kJ mol}^{-1}$$

$$\Delta_C H°(CH_4) = -890.4 \text{ kJ mol}^{-1}$$

Match the combination of given reactions in Column I with the fuel value in Column II and select the answer from the codes given :

Column I	Column II
(i) Product of reaction I used as fuel	(p) −571.76 kJ
(ii) Product of reaction I and II used as fuel	(q) −890.4 kJ
(iii) Product of reaction III used as fuel	(r) −568.83 kJ
(iv) CH_4 gas used as fuel	(s) −1140.5 kJ

Codes

	(i)	(ii)	(iii)	(iv)
(a)	(r)	(p)	(q)	(s)
(b)	(r)	(q)	(s)	(p)
(c)	(r)	(p)	(s)	(q)
(d)	(p)	(s)	(q)	(r)

157 For the following reactions :

	$\Delta_r H°$(kJ)
A. $2H_2(g) + O_2(g) \longrightarrow 2H_2O(g)$	−483.6
B. $3H_2(g) + O_3(g) \longrightarrow 3H_2O(g)$	−868.2
C. $H_2(g) + H_2O_2(g) \longrightarrow 2H_2O(g)$	−347.3
D. $H_2(g) + CO(g) + O_2 \longrightarrow H_2O + CO_2$	−568.8

Match the reactants or part of reactants used as fuel given in Column I with their fuel values given in Column II and select the answer from the codes given.

Column I	Column II
(i) Maximum amount of energy for 1.00 g of oxidising agent	(p) −18.09 kJ
(ii) Maximum amount of energy for 1.00 mole of reducing agent	(q) −347.3 kJ
(iii) Maximum amount of energy released on total mass basis	(r) −9.64 kJ
(iv) Minimum amount of energy for 1.00 mole of oxidising agent	(s) −16.1 kJ

Codes

	(i)	(ii)	(iii)	(iv)
(a)	(p)	(r)	(q)	(s)
(b)	(p)	(r)	(s)	(q)
(c)	(q)	(r)	(p)	(s)
(d)	(q)	(p)	(s)	(r)

158 A quantity of 100 mL of 0.5 M NaOH is mixed with 100 mL of 0.5 M HCl in a constant pressure calorimeter that has a heat capacity of 335 J K^{-1}. The temperature increase due to mixing was 2.4°.

Density of solution = 1.0g mL^{-1}

Specific heat of solution = 4.184 Jg^{-1} K^{-1}

Match the enthalpy (in kJ) of various changes given in Column I with their values (in kJ) in Column II and select the answer from the codes given.

Column I	Column II
(i) Enthalpy of solution on mixing	(p) −2.812
(ii) Calorimeter constant	(q) −56.24
(iii) Enthalpy of reaction	(r) −2.008
(iv) Enthalpy of neutralisation (kJ mol^{-1})	(s) 0.804

Codes

	(i)	(ii)	(iii)	(iv)
(a)	(q)	(r)	(s)	(p)
(b)	(r)	(p)	(q)	(s)
(c)	(r)	(s)	(p)	(q)
(d)	(p)	(q)	(r)	(s)

159 Consider the following transformation of H_2O in different phases.

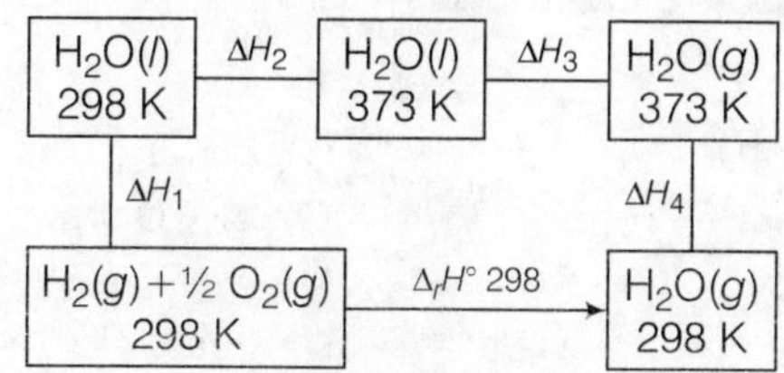

$\Delta_f H°(H_2O, l) = -285.83$ kJ mol^{-1}

$C_p (H_2O, l) = 75.291$ J K^{-1} mol^{-1}

$C_p (H_2O, g) = 33.577$ J K^{-1} mol^{-1}

$\Delta_{vap} H(H_2O) = 40.883$ J K^{-1} mol^{-1} at 1 atm (373 K)

Compare the parameters $\Delta H, \Delta H_2$ (in kJ) in Column I with the corresponding values in Column II and select the answer from the codes given.

Column I		Column II	
(i)	ΔH_1	(p)	−244.95
(ii)	ΔH_2	(q)	−285.83
(iii)	ΔH_3	(r)	5.65
(iv)	ΔH_4	(s)	40.883
(v)	$\Delta_f H(H_2O, g)$	(s)	−2.5183

Codes

	(i)	(ii)	(iii)	(iv)	(v)
(a)	(p)	(t)	(r)	(q)	(s)
(b)	(t)	(s)	(r)	(q)	(p)
(c)	(p)	(q)	(r)	(s)	(t)
(d)	(q)	(r)	(s)	(t)	(p)

160 Match the transformation in Column I with appropriate options in Column II. ***[IIT JEE 2011]***

Column I		Column II	
(i)	$CO_2(s) \longrightarrow CO_2(g)$	(p)	Phase transition
(ii)	$CaCO_3(s) \longrightarrow CaO(s) + CO_2(g)$	(q)	Allotropic change
(iii)	$2H(g) \longrightarrow H_2(g)$	(r)	$\Delta H > 0$
(iv)	P(white, *s*) $\longrightarrow$ P (red, *s*)	(s)	$\Delta S > 0$
		(t)	$\Delta S < 0$

Codes

	(i)	(ii)	(iii)	(iv)
(a)	(p,s)	(r)	(p,q)	(t)
(b)	(p,r,s)	(r,s)	(t)	(p, q, t)
(c)	(q)	(p)	(s)	(r, t)
(d)	(p,t)	(q)	(r)	(r)

HINTS & EXPLANATIONS

Immediate Tests

1. $H^\circ_{H_2} = 0$

$\therefore \Delta_r H^\circ = H^\circ_{C_2H_6} - (H^\circ_{C_2H_4} + H^\circ_{H_2})$

$= -83.8 - (52.5 + 0)$

$= -136.3$ kJ mol^{-1}

2. $\Delta_f H^\circ(PCl_3) = x_1 \Rightarrow H^\circ_{PCl_3} = x_1$

$\Delta_f H^\circ(PCl_5) = x_2 \Rightarrow H^\circ_{PCl_5} = x_2$

$\Delta_f H^\circ(Cl_2) = 0 \Rightarrow H^\circ_{Cl_2} = 0$

$\therefore \quad \Delta H^\circ = x_2 - (x_1 + 0) = (x_2 - x_1)$

3. At 298 K,

$\Delta_f H^\circ(H_2O) = -58$ kcal mol^{-1}

$\Rightarrow \quad H^\circ(H_2O) = -58$ kcal mol^{-1}

$\Delta_f H^\circ(CO_2) = -94$ kcal mol^{-1}

$\Rightarrow \quad H^\circ(CO_2) = -94$ kcal mol^{-1}

$\Delta_f H^\circ(CH_4) = ?$

$-260 = [H^\circ_{CO_2} + 2H^\circ_{H_2O}]$

$- [H^\circ_{CH_4} + 2H^\circ_{O_2}]$

$= -94 - 2 \times 58 - H^\circ_{CH_4}$

$\therefore \quad H^\circ_{CH_4} = -94 - 116 + 260$

$= +50$ kcal mol^{-1}

Since, 1 kcal $= \dfrac{8.3143 \times 10^{-3}}{1.987 \times 10^{-3}}$ kJ

$\therefore \quad$ 50 kcal = 209.21 kJ at 298 K

$C(\text{graphite}) + 2H_2(g) \longrightarrow CH_4(g)$

$\Delta C_p = C_p(CH_4) - [2C_p(H_2) + C_p(C)]$

$= 4R - \left[2 \times \dfrac{7}{2}R + 8.53 \text{ J}\right]$

$= 4 \times 8.314 - [7 \times 8.314 + 8.53]$

$= -33.472$ J mol^{-1} K^{-1}

$\therefore \Delta H^\circ_{398} = \Delta H^\circ_{298} + \Delta C_p (T_2 - T_1)$

$= 209.21 \times 10^3 - 33.472 \times 100$

$= 205.863 \times 10^3$ J

$= 205.863$ kJ mol^{-1}

4. (i) $C_6H_6(l) + 7.5O_2(g) \longrightarrow 6CO_2(g) + 3H_2O(l), \ \Delta H = -x_1$

(ii) $C(s) + O_2(g) \longrightarrow CO_2(g), \ \Delta H = -x_2$

(iii) $H_2(g) + \dfrac{1}{2}O_2(g) \longrightarrow H_2O(l), \quad \Delta H = -x_3$

From (ii), $CO_2(g)$ is formed from element.

Thus, $\Delta_C H^\circ(\text{carbon}) = \Delta_f H^\circ(CO_2) = H^\circ(CO_2)$

Similarly, from (iii)

$\Delta_C H^\circ(H_2) = \Delta_f H^\circ(H_2O) = H^\circ(H_2O)$

$H^\circ(O_2) = 0$

Thus, from (i)

$-x_1 = -6x_1 - 3x_2 - [H^\circ(C_6H_6)]$

$\therefore \ H^\circ(C_6H_6) = \Delta_f H^\circ(C_6H_6)$

$= -6x_1 - 3x_2 + x_1$

5. (i) $H_2SO_4(aq) \rightleftharpoons 2H^+(aq) + SO_4^{2-}(aq)$

$Ca(OH)_2(aq) \rightleftharpoons Ca^{2+}(aq) + 2OH^-(aq)$

$H^+ + OH^- \rightleftharpoons H_2O$

$\Delta H^\circ = -57.3$ kJ mol^{-1}

Hence, $\quad \Delta H^\circ = (-57.3 \times 2)$ kJ mol^{-1} of H_2SO_4 or $Ca(OH)_2$

$Ca(OH)_2 = H_2SO_4 = \dfrac{100 \times 1 \text{ M}}{1000} = 0.1$ mol

Thus, $\Delta H^\circ = -57.3 \times 2 \times 0.1$

$= -11.46$ kJ

■ $\dfrac{\text{Volume (in mL)} \times \text{molarity}}{1000} = \text{Moles}$

(ii) Moles of HCN $= \dfrac{100 \times 1}{1000} = 0.1$ mol

Moles of NaOH $= \dfrac{100 \times 1}{1000} = 0.1$ mol

$HCN(aq) + NaOH(aq) \longrightarrow NaCN(aq) + H_2O(l)$

ΔH (given) $= -290$ cal

$= -0.290$ kcal for 0.1 mol NaOH and 0.1 mol HCN

Thus, enthalpy of neutralisation of HCN by NaOH $= \dfrac{-0.290}{0.1} = -2.9$ kcal mol^{-1}

Also $H^+(aq) + OH^-(aq) \longrightarrow H_2O(l)$

$\therefore \Delta H^\circ = -13.7$ kcal mol^{-1}

Thus, $HCN(aq) \rightleftharpoons H^+(aq) + CN^-(aq)$

$\Delta H = -2.9 - (13.7)$

$= +10.8$ kcal mol^{-1}

Enthalpy of ionisation of CH_3COOH

$= 1.3$ kcal mol^{-1}

Thus, CH_3COOH is stronger than HCN as more heat is required to ionise HCN as compared to that of CH_3COOH.

6. (i) (a) $MgSO_4(s) + (aq) \longrightarrow MgSO_4 \cdot 7H_2O(aq)$,

$\Delta H_1 = 91.21$ kJ mol^{-1}

(b) $MgSO_4 \cdot 7H_2O(s) + (aq) \longrightarrow MgSO_4 \cdot 7H_2O(aq)$,

$\Delta H_2 = 13.81$ kJ mol^{-1}

Eq. (i) involves

(c) $MgSO_4(s) + 7H_2O(l) \longrightarrow MgSO_4 \cdot 7H_2O(s), \ \Delta H_3 = ?$

(d) $MgSO_4 \cdot 7H_2O(s) + (aq) \longrightarrow MgSO_4 \cdot 7H_2O(aq)$,

$\Delta H_2 = 13.81$ kJ mol^{-1}

Thus, $\quad$ (i) = (iii + ii)

$\therefore \quad \Delta H_1 = \Delta H_2 + \Delta H_3$

$\therefore \quad \Delta H_3 = \Delta H_1 - \Delta H_2$

$= -91.21 - 13.81$

$= -105.02$ kJ mol^{-1}

(ii) $Ba^{2+}(aq) + SO_4^{2-}(aq) \longrightarrow BaSO_4(s)$;

$\Delta H^\circ = -4.5$ kcal

$\Delta H^\circ = \Delta H^\circ_{f(BaSO_4)} - [\Delta H_{f(Ba^{2+})} + \Delta H_{f(SO_4^{2-})}]$

$-4.5 = -349 - [\Delta H^\circ_{(Ba^{2+})} - 216]$

$\therefore \Delta H^\circ_{Ba^{2+}} = -349 + 216 + 4.5$

$= -128.5$ kcal

(iii) $CuSO_4 = \dfrac{100}{159.5}$ mol $= 0.627$ mol

$CuSO_4 \cdot 5H_2O = \dfrac{100}{249.5}$ mol

$= 0.401$ mol

I. $CuSO_4(s) + H_2O$ (excess) $\longrightarrow CuSO_4 \cdot 5H_2O(aq)$

$\Delta H = -10.0$ kcal for 0.627 mol

$\therefore \Delta H^\circ_{\text{solution}}(CuSO_4) = \dfrac{-10.0}{0.627}$ kcal mol^{-1}

$= -15.95$ kcal mol^{-1}

II. $CuSO_4 \cdot 5H_2O(s)$ + (excess) $\longrightarrow CuSO_4 \cdot 5H_2O(aq)$

$= 1.1$ kcal for 0.401 mol

$\therefore \Delta H^\circ_{\text{solution}}(CuSO_4 \cdot 5H_2O)$

$= \dfrac{1.1}{0.401} = 2.743$ kcal mol^{-1}

(I–II) given,

$= -15.95 - 2.743 = -18.693$ kcal

7. $S(s) + 3F_2(g) \longrightarrow SF_6(g)$

$\Delta_f H^\circ(SF_6) = [\Delta_f H^\circ(S, g) + 6\Delta_f H^\circ(F) - 6(BE)_{S-F}]$

$-1100 = [275 + 6 \times 80] - 6x$

$\therefore \quad x = \dfrac{275 + 6 \times 80 + 1100}{6}$

$= 309.17$ kJ mol^{-1}

8. $N_2(g) + \dfrac{1}{2}O_2(g) \longrightarrow \overset{-}{N}{=}\overset{+}{N}{=}O$

$\Delta_f H^\circ = BE(N \equiv N) + \dfrac{1}{2}BE(O{=}O) - [BE(N{=}N) + BE(N{=}O)]$

$= \left[946 + \left(\dfrac{498}{2}\right)\right] - [418 + 607]$

$= 170$ kJ mol^{-1}

$\therefore$ Resonance energy $= 82.0 - 170.0$
$= -88 \text{ kJ mol}^{-1}$

9. V. $Fe(s) + \frac{1}{2}O_2 \longrightarrow FeO(s)$

III – II – IV gives V, $\Delta_f H° = ?$

$\therefore\ \Delta_f H°(FeO) = -393.51 - 155.8 + 282.98$
$= -266.33 \text{ kJ mol}^{-1}$

VI. $2Fe + \frac{3}{2}O_2 \longrightarrow Fe_2O_3,\ \Delta_f H° = ?$

3 (III) – (I) – 3(IV) gives (VI).

Thus, $\Delta_f H°(Fe_2O_3) = -824.2 \text{ kJ mol}^{-1}$

10. I. $Na(s) + \frac{1}{2}Br_2(g) \longrightarrow NaBr(s)$,

$\Delta_f H°(NaBr) = -376 \text{ kJ mol}^{-1}$

II. (a) $Na(s) \longrightarrow Na(g)$, $\Delta H = S$

(b) $\frac{1}{2}Br_2(g) \longrightarrow Br(g)$, $\Delta H = \frac{D}{2}$

(c) $Na(g) \longrightarrow Na^+(g) + e^-$, $\Delta H = I$

(d) $Br(g) + e^- \longrightarrow Br^-(g)$, $\Delta H = -E$

(e) $Na^+(g) + Br^-(g) \longrightarrow NaBr^-(s)$,

By adding (a) to (e) $\Delta H = -U$

$Na(s) + \frac{1}{2}Br_2(g) \longrightarrow NaBr(s)$,

I and II represent same chemical change.

$$\Delta_f H\,(NaBr) = \left(S + \frac{D}{2} + I - E - U\right)$$

$$\therefore\quad -376 = S + \frac{D}{2} + I - E - U$$
$$= 109 + \frac{192}{2} + 490 - E - 736$$
$$\therefore\quad E = 335 \text{ kJ mol}^{-1}$$

Thus, electron affinity of Br
$= -335 \text{ kJ mol}^{-1}$

11. Weak monoprotic acid

$$\frac{\text{Molarity} \times \text{Volume(mL)}}{1000} = \frac{400 \times 0.2}{1000} = 0.08 \text{ mol}$$

$$NaOH = \frac{100 \times 0.8}{1000} = 0.08 \text{ mol}$$

$$\text{Heat} = m \cdot s\Delta T$$
$$= (100 + 400)\text{g} \times 4.2 \text{ J g}^{-1}\text{K}^{-1} \times 1.17 \text{ K}$$
$$= 2457 \text{ J} = 2.457 \text{ kJ}$$

$$\therefore \text{ Heat of neutralisation } = -\frac{2.457}{0.08} \text{ kJ}$$
$$= -30.7125 \text{ kJ mol}^{-1}$$

12. $\Delta E_{comb} = -(\Delta E_{water} + \Delta E_{bomb})$

$\Delta E_{water} = m.s\Delta T$
$= 2000 \times 4.184 \times 4.2 = 35145.6 \text{ J}$
$= 35.1456 \text{ kJ}$

$\Delta E_{bomb} = c \times \Delta T$
$= 2.02 \times 4.2 = 8.484 \text{ kJ}$

$\therefore\ \Delta E_{comb} = -(35.1456 + 8.484)$
$= -43.6296 \text{ kJ}$

CH_3OH taken $= 1.922 \text{ g} = \frac{1.922}{32}$
$= 0.06 \text{ mol}$

$$\therefore\quad \Delta E_{comb} = \frac{-43.6296}{0.66}$$
$$= -727.16 \text{ kJ mol}^{-1}$$

13. When air (80% N_2, 20% O_2, i.e. 4 : 1 ratio) is used for combustion, every mol of $CH_4(g)$ uses two mol of $O_2(g)$. Thus, products also contain 8 mol of N_2.

$$CH_4(g) + 2O_2(g) \longrightarrow CO_2(g) + 2H_2O(g) + 8 \text{ mol } N_2$$

As, $C_V = C_p - R$

$C_V(CO_2, g) = 36.290 - 8.314$
$= 27.976 \text{ kJ mol}^{-1} \text{ K}^{-1}$

$C_V(CO_2, g) = 33.580 - 8.314$
$= 25.266 \text{ kJ mol}^{-1} \text{ K}^{-1}$

$C_V(N_2, 9) = 29.290 - 8.314$
$= 20.976 \text{ kJ mol}^{-1} \text{ K}^{-1}$

$\therefore C_V(\text{products}) = C_V(CO_2) + 2C_V(H_2O) + 8C_V(N_2)$
$= 27.967 + 2 \times 25.266 + 8 \times 20.976$
$= 246.316 \text{ J mol}^{-1} \text{ K}^{-1}$

$\therefore\ = 246.316 \times 10^{-3} \text{ kJ mol}^{-1} \text{ K}^{-1}$

$\Delta n_g = 0$

$\therefore\ \Delta_r U° = \Delta_r H°$

$$\therefore\quad T_f = \left(-\frac{\Delta_r U_T}{C_V} + T\right)$$
$$= \frac{-(-803.33)}{246.316 \times 10^{-3}} + 298$$
$$= 3559.4 \text{ K}$$

Knowledge Confirmation Test 1

1. (b) **2.** (c) **3.** (a) **4.** (d) **5.** (a) **6.** (b) **7.** (b) **8.** (d) **9.** (a) **10.** (c)
11. (b) **12.** (b) **13.** (a) **14.** (c) **15.** (d) **16.** (b) **17.** (c) **18.** (c) **19.** (c) **20.** (d)
21. (c) **22.** (c) **23.** (b) **24.** (c) **25.** (c) **26.** (a)

Knowledge Confirmation Test 2

1. (a) **2.** (b) **3.** (a) **4.** (a) **5.** (b) **6.** (a) **7.** (c) **8.** (b) **9.** (d) **10.** (a)
11. (b) **12.** (a) **13.** (a) **14.** (b) **15.** (d) **16.** (d) **17.** (a) **18.** (c) **19.** (d) **20.** (b)

Knowledge Confirmation Test 3

1. (c) **2.** (c) **3.** (b) **4.** (a) **5.** (d) **6.** (b) **7.** (a) **8.** (d) **9.** (a) **10.** (a)
11. (a) **12.** (b) **13.** (b) **14.** (d) **15.** (c)

Knowledge Confirmation Test 4

1. (a) **2.** (b) **3.** (a) **4.** (c) **5.** (c) **6.** (a) **7.** (d) **8.** (a) **9.** (c) **10.** (d)
11. (c) **12.** (c) **13.** (a) **14.** (c) **15.** (d)

Knowledge Confirmation Test 5

1. (a) **2.** (b) **3.** (b) **4.** (d) **5.** (a) **6.** (a) **7.** (b) **8.** (a) **9.** (b) **10.** (b)
11. (a) **12.** (b) **13.** (c) **14.** (a)

Acid Test for JEE Main

Type I. MCQs with Only ONE Correct Alternate

1. (b) $2O_3(g) \longrightarrow 3O_2(g)$

For 1g O_3, $\Delta H°=2.97$ kJ

Thus, for 96 g O_3 (1 mol),

$$\Delta H° = 2.97 \times 96 g\ O_3 = 285.12 kJ\ mol^{-1}$$

Since, heat is transferred to the surroundings.

Hence, $\Delta_r H° = -285.12$ kJ mol^{-1}

2. (c) The 'calorie' used in nutrition is actually a kilocalorie.

As 1 kcal = 4.184 kJ

$\therefore$ 2500 kcal = 2500×4.184 kJ
$= 10460$ kJ

$\Delta_C H°(C_{12}H_{22}O_{11}) = -5.647$ MJ
$= -5.647 \times 10^6$ J
$= -5.647 \times 10^3$ kJ

Molar mass of $C_{12}H_{22}O_{11}$
$= 12 \times 12 + 22 \times 1 + 11 \times 16$
$= 342$ g mol^{-1}

5.647×10^3 kJ is from= 342 g$(C_{12}H_{22}O_{11})$

$\therefore$ 10646 kJ is from = $\frac{342 \times 10646}{5.647 \times 10^3}$
$= 633.5$ g

3. (a) CO and H_2 in 1:1 molar ratio are the contents of water gas. Thus, their $\Delta_C H$ is the total heat.

$\Delta H = \Delta_C H°(CO) + \Delta_C H°(H_2)$
$= -283.0 + (-242.0) = -525$ kJ

4. (a) $\Delta n_g = 0$ (gaseous species)

$\therefore \Delta H° = \Delta U° + \Delta n_g RT$

$\therefore (\Delta H° - \Delta U°) = 0$

5. (d) $\Delta H° = 2.38$ kJ mol^{-1}
$= 2.38 \times 0.29$ mol $= 0.69$ kJ

6. (a) $\Delta H°_{sol} = \Delta H°_{hydration} - \Delta H_{lattice}$

$4 = -784 - \Delta H_{lattice}$

$\therefore \Delta H_{lattice} = -784 - 4 = -788$ kJ mol^{-1}

- $Na^+(g) + Cl^-(g) \longrightarrow NaCl(s)$;

$\Delta H°_{lattice} = -788$ kJ mol^{-1}

$NaCl(s) \longrightarrow Na^+(g) + Cl^-(g)$

$\Delta H°_{lattice} = 788$ kJ mol^{-1}

7. (d) $2H_2(g) \longrightarrow 4H(g), \Delta H° = +869.6$ kJ

$H_2 \longrightarrow 2H(g)$,

$\Delta H° = +\frac{869.6}{2} = 434.8$ kJ

- Dissociation enthalpy is the energy required to break (H – H) bond.

8. (d) $X_2 + Y_2 \longrightarrow 2XY$

$\Delta H° = 2\Delta_f H°(XY) = -400$ kJ mol^{-1}

Let bond energy of $X_2 = a$ kJ mol^{-1}

$Y_2 = \frac{a}{2}$ kJ $mol^{-1} \Rightarrow XY = a$ kJ mol^{-1}

$\therefore$ By bond energies values,

$-400 = \left(a + \frac{a}{2}\right) - 2a = -\frac{a}{2}$

$a = 800$ kJ mol^{-1}

Thus, bond energy of ($X — X$) bond
$= 800$ kJ mol^{-1}

9. (a) By Kirchhoff's equation, giving variation of ΔH with temperature.

$\Delta H_2 = \Delta H_1 + \Delta C_p(T_2 - T_1)$

when, $(T_2 - T_1) = 0$

$\Delta H_1 = \Delta H_2$

10. (b) $BaCl_2(s) + aq \longrightarrow BaCl_2 \cdot 2H_2O(aq)$;

$\Delta H = -20.6$ kJ mol^{-1}

$BaCl_2 \cdot 2H_2O(s) + aq \longrightarrow BaCl_2 \cdot 2H_2O(aq)$;
$\Delta H = -8.8$ kJ mol^{-1}

Adding $\therefore$ $BaCl_2(s) \longrightarrow BaCl_2 \cdot 2H_2O(s)$

$\Delta H = -20.6 - 8.8 = -29.4$ kJ mol^{-1}

11. (a) Boiling point of water at 1atm
$= 100°C = 373$ K

$H_2O(l) \longrightarrow H_2O(g), \quad \Delta n_g = +1$

$\therefore \Delta H°_{vap} = \Delta U°_{vap} + \Delta n_g RT$

$40.66 = \Delta U°_{vap} + 1 \times 8.314 \times 10^{-3} \times 373$

$\therefore \Delta U°_{vap} = 37.56$ kJ mol^{-1}

12. (b) $H_2 + \frac{1}{2}O_2 \longrightarrow H_2O(l), \quad \Delta_f H° = ?$

$\underset{18g}{H_2O} \longrightarrow H_2 + \frac{1}{2}O_2$

9g is decomposed by = 142.5 kJ mol^{-1}

$\therefore$ 18g is decomposed by = 285.0 kJ mol^{-1}

As formation of water is reverse of decomposition,

$\therefore \Delta_f H°(H_2O) = -285.0$ kJ mol^{-1}

13. (b) From eq (I),

$\Delta_f H°(CO_2) = -94$ kcal mol^{-1}

From Eq. (II),

$\Delta H = -135.2 = 2\Delta_f H°(CO_2)$
$- [2\Delta_f H°(CO) + \Delta_f H°(O_2)]$

$2\Delta_f H°(CO) = -2 \times 94 + 135.2$

$\therefore \Delta_f H°(CO) = -26.4$ kcal mol^{-1}

$\Delta_f H(O_2) = 0$

14. (b) 1 kg carbon (coke) = $\frac{1000}{12}$ mol

$\therefore \Delta_{comb} H_1$ of 1 kg coke = $\left(393.5 \times \frac{1000}{12}\right)$ kJ

$C + H_2O(g) \longrightarrow CO + H_2$

CO from 1 kg carbon = $\left(\frac{1000}{12}\right)$ mol

H_2 from 1 kg carbon = $\left(\frac{1000}{12}\right)$ mol

($CO + H_2$) is called water gas.

Thus, enthalpy of $\left(\frac{1000}{12}\right)$ mol of water gas

$\Delta H_2 = \frac{1000}{12}(285) + \frac{1000}{12}(285)$

$= \frac{1000}{12} \times 570$

$\therefore \frac{\Delta H_1}{\Delta H_2} = \frac{393.5}{570} = 0.69 : 1$

15. (c) On subtracing,

$2N_2O_5(s) \longrightarrow 2N_2O_5(g), \Delta H = 52$ kJ

$\therefore \Delta_{sub} H° = \frac{52}{2} = 26$ kJ mol^{-1}

16. (c) $H^+(aq) + OH^-(aq) \longrightarrow H_2O$,

$\Delta H° = -13.7$ kcal

From I : $\Delta H°$ (ionisation of CsOH)
$= +0.3$ kcal

From II : $CsOH \rightleftharpoons Cs^+ + OH^-$,

$\Delta H = +0.3$ kcal

$HF \rightleftharpoons H^+ + F^-; \Delta H = q$

$H^+ + OH^- \rightleftharpoons H_2O; \Delta H = -13.7$

$CsOH + HF \rightleftharpoons CsF + H_2O$;

$\Delta H = 0.3 + q - 13.7 = -16.4$

$\therefore q = -3.0$ kcal

- Ionisation of HF(aq) is an exothermic process.

17. (d) C(graphite) $\longrightarrow$ C(g), $\Delta H = x_1$

$2H_2(g) \longrightarrow 4H(g), \quad \Delta H = x_2$

C (graphite) $+ 2H_2(g) \rightarrow CH_4$, $C(g) + 4H(g) \rightarrow CH_4$

$\Delta H = x \qquad \Delta H = y$

thus, $(x < y)$, $(y - x) = (x_1 + x_2)$

18. (b) $H^+ + OH^- \longrightarrow H_2O, \Delta H° = -13.7$ kcal

$-13.7 = \Delta_f H°(H_2O)$
$-[\Delta_f H°(H^+) + \Delta_f H°(OH^-)]$

$\therefore = -68.0 - [0 + \Delta_f H°(OH^-)]$

$\therefore \Delta_f H°(OH^-) = (-68.0 + 13.7)$
$= -54.3$ kcal mol^{-1}

- Heat of neutralisation of 1 equivalent of H^+ by 1 equivalent of OH^- is constant and = –13.7 kcal

19. (b) $4B + 3O_2 \longrightarrow 2B_2O_3$

$2B + \frac{3}{2}O_2 \longrightarrow B_2O_3, \Delta_f H°(B_2O_3) = x$

$B + \frac{3}{4}O_2 \longrightarrow \frac{1}{2}B_2O_3, \Delta_C H°(B) = y$

thus, $y = \frac{x}{2}$

20. (d) NH_4OH is a weak base and CH_3COOH is a weak acid, hence ionisation involves absorption of heat.

I : $OH^- + H^+ \rightleftharpoons H_2O$; $\Delta H = x_1$

II: $NH_4OH \rightleftharpoons NH_4^+ + OH^-$; $\Delta H = y$

$OH^- + H^+$ (from HCl) $\longrightarrow H_2O$; $\Delta H = x_1$

$\therefore NH_4OH + H^+ \rightleftharpoons NH_4^+ + H_2O$;

$(y + x_1) = x_2$

$\therefore \quad y = (x_2 - x_1)$

III : $CH_3COOH \rightleftharpoons CH_3COO^- + H^+$, $\Delta H = z$

As above, $z = (x_3 - x_1)$

$\therefore$ IV: $NH_4OH \rightleftharpoons NH_4^+ + OH^-$; $\Delta H = (x_2 - x_1)$

$CH_3COOH \rightleftharpoons CH_3COO^- + H^+$; $\Delta H = (x_3 - x_1)$

$H^+ + OH^- \rightleftharpoons H_2O$; $\Delta H = x_1$

$\therefore \Delta H = x_2 - x_1 + x_3 - x_1 + x_1 = x_2 + x_3 - x_1$

21. (c) $CH_3COOH \rightleftharpoons CH_3COO^- + H^+$

(a weak acid)

$\Delta H° = 0.005\ \text{kcal g}^{-1}$

$= 0.005 \times 60\ \text{kcal mol}^{-1}$

$= 0.3\ \text{kcal mol}^{-1}$

$Ca(OH)_2 \rightleftharpoons Ca^{2+} + 2OH^-$

$2CH_3COOH + \underset{1\ \text{mol}}{Ca(OH)_2} \longrightarrow (CH_3COO)_2Ca + H_2O$

$-27.4 + 0.6 = -26.8$ kcal

■ $H^+ + OH^- \longrightarrow H_2O$; $\Delta H° = -13.7$ kcal

$Ca(OH)_2 \equiv 2OH^-$

22. (b) $HS^-(aq) \rightleftharpoons H^+(aq) + S^{2-}(aq)$,

$\Delta H° = 14.22$ kcal

$H^+(aq) + OH^-(aq) \longrightarrow H_2O(l)$,

$\Delta H° = -13.70$ kcal

$HS^-(aq) + OH^-(aq) \longrightarrow S^{2-}(aq) + H_2O(l)$

$\therefore \Delta H° = 14.22 - 13.70 = 0.52\ \text{kcal mol}^{-1}$

23. (b) $F_2^-(g) \longrightarrow F(g) + F^-(g)$

can be obtained by

Eq. I + Eq. III – Eq. II

$\therefore \Delta H° = 156.9 + 290 - 333 = 113.9$ kJ

24. (d) $PH_3(g) \longrightarrow P(g) + 3H(g)$;

$\Delta H° = 953\ \text{kJ mol}^{-1}$

$\therefore$ Bond Energy (P—H) $= \dfrac{953}{3}\ \text{kJ mol}^{-1}$

$P_2H_4(g) \longrightarrow 2P(g) + 4H(g)$

$(\text{Bond energy})_{P-P} + 4(\text{Bond energy})_{P-H} = 1485$ kJ

$\therefore (\text{Bond energy})_{P-P} = 1485 - 4\left(\dfrac{953}{3}\right)$

$= 214.33$ kJ

$P_2H_6(g) \longrightarrow 2P(g) + 6H(g)$

ΔH = Bond energy (P—P) + 6 Bond energy (P—H)

$= 214.33 + 6 \times \dfrac{953}{3}$

$= 214.33 + 1906 = 2120.33$ kJ

25. (a) $HF(aq) \longrightarrow H^+(aq) + F^-(aq)$,

$\Delta H° = x$ kJ

$H^+(aq) + OH^-(aq) \longrightarrow H_2O(l)$,

$\Delta H° = -55.83$ kJ

$\therefore HF(aq) + OH^-(aq) \longrightarrow H_2O(l) + F^-(aq)$,

$\Delta H° = (x - 55.83)$

Given, $(x - 55.83) = -68.6$ kJ

$x = -12.77\ \text{kJ mol}^{-1}$

Thus, enthalpy change in (a) is incorrect.

■ Dissociation always absorbs heat (endothermic), but ionisation of HF is exothermic, as F^- is hydrated to the extent that

$\Delta H_{\text{hydration}} > \Delta H_{\text{ionisation}}$

Hydration is exothermic.

26. (c) $H—H(g) + \dfrac{1}{2}(O{=}O)(g) \longrightarrow H—O—H(l)$

$\Delta_f H°(H_2O)$

$= \left[(\text{Bond energy})_{H-H} + \dfrac{1}{2}(\text{Bond energy})_{O=O}\right]$

$-[\Delta H°_{\text{vap}}(H_2O) + 2(\text{Bond energy})_{O-H}]$

$= x_1 + \dfrac{x_2}{2} - [x_4 + 2x_3] = \left[x_1 + \dfrac{x_2}{2} - 2x_3 - x_4\right]$

27. (c) $2Fe(s) + 1.5O_2(g) \longrightarrow Fe_2O_3(s)$,

$\Delta H° = ?$

Operate

(1.5 Eq. (II) – Eq. I) gives above equation

$\therefore -(393.5)1.5 - 234.1 = -824.35$ kJ

28. (c) In stage I, $M \times V(\text{mL})/1000 = \text{mol}$

$NaOH = \dfrac{30 \times 0.1}{1000}\ \text{mol} = 3 \times 10^{-3}$ mol

$HCl = \dfrac{10 \times 0.1}{1000} = 1 \times 10^{-3}$ mol

In stage II, $NaOH = 2 \times 10^{-3}$ mol

$HCl = 2 \times 10^{-3}$ mol

as 10 mL of each of NaOH and HCl already neutralised in stage I.

Since, $NaOH + HCl \longrightarrow NaCl + H_2O$,

$\Delta H = -13.7\ \text{kcal mol}^{-1}$

Hence, in stage I :

1×10^{-3} mol of HCl is neutralised.

Thus, $\Delta H_1 = x_1 = -13.7 \times 10^{-3}$ kcal

$= -13.7$ cal

In stage II :

Mixture contains 20 mL of 0.1M NaOH and 20 mL of 0.1M HCl

$\therefore \Delta H_2 = x_2 = -13.7 \times 2 \times 10^{-3}$ kcal

$= -27.4$ cal

29. (a) H_2O is in excess and thus

$\Delta H = -17.9 = \Delta_f H°(H^+) + \Delta_f H°(Cl^-) - \Delta_f H°(HCl)$

$-17.9 = 0 + \Delta_f H°(Cl^-) - (-22.1)$

$\Delta_f H°(Cl^-) = -40.0$ kcal

$\Delta_f H(H^+) = 0$

30. (b) $N_2(g) + 3H_2(g) \longrightarrow 2NH_3(g)$

$\Delta H° = 2\Delta_f H°(NH_3) = -92\ \text{kJ mol}^{-1}$

Given, $\Delta_f H°$ (H_2 from atoms)

$= -436\ \text{kJ mol}^{-1}$

$2H \longrightarrow H_2$

and $\Delta_f H°$ (N_2 from atoms) $= -712\ \text{kJ mol}^{-1}$

$2N \longrightarrow N_2$

Thus, Bond energy (H—H) $= 436\ \text{kJ mol}^{-1}$

Bond energy (N≡N) $= 712\ \text{kJ mol}^{-1}$

Based on BE, $\Delta H° = (BE)_R - (BE)_P$

$\therefore -92 = BE(N{\equiv}N) + 3BE(H—H) - 6BE(N—H)$

$= 712 + 3 \times 436 - 6x$

$\therefore \quad x = \dfrac{712 + 3 \times 436 + 92}{6} = 352\ \text{kJ mol}^{-1}$

31. (b) I. $H_2 + \dfrac{1}{2}O_2 \longrightarrow H_2O$,

$\Delta H° = -241\ \text{kJ mol}^{-1}$

II. $\underset{C_6H_{12}}{\text{(cyclohexane)}} + 9O_2 \longrightarrow 6CO_2 + 6H_2O$,

$\Delta H° = -3920\ \text{kJ mol}^{-1}$

III. $\underset{C_6H_{10}}{\text{(cyclohexene)}} + 8.5O_2 \longrightarrow 6CO_2 + 5H_2O$,

$\Delta H° = -3800\ \text{kJ mol}^{-1}$

IV. (cyclohexene) $+ H_2 \longrightarrow$ (cyclohexane)

(Hydrogenation of cyclohexene)

On rearranging,

$\therefore \quad$ IV = I + III – II

$\Delta H° = -241 - 3800 + 3920$

$= -121\ \text{kJ mol}^{-1}$

121 kJ of heat is released in the hydrogenation of = 1 mole (= 82 g) of cyclohexene.

29.51 kJ of heat is released in the hydrogenation of $= \dfrac{82}{121} \times 29.51$ g

= 20 g cyclohexene.

32. (b) $\Delta H_2 = \Delta H_1 + \Delta C_p(T_2 - T_1)$

$= 0 + 29.4(315 - 298)$

$= 499.8\ \text{J mol}^{-1}$

$= 0.5\ \text{kJ mol}^{-1}$

33. (c) $CO(g)+\frac{1}{2}O_2(g) \longrightarrow CO_2(g)$,

$$\Delta n_g = -\frac{1}{2}$$

$$\therefore \quad \Delta_C H^\circ = \Delta_C U^\circ + \Delta n_g RT$$

$$\Delta_C H^\circ - \Delta_C U^\circ = \Delta n_g RT$$

$$= -\frac{1}{2} \times 2 \text{ cal mol}^{-1} \text{K}^{-1} \times 298$$

$$= -298 \text{ cal}$$

34. (b) $C_3H_8(g)+5O_2(g) \longrightarrow 3CO_2(g)+4H_2O(l)$, $\Delta H^\circ = -222.0 \text{ kJ mol}^{-1}$

$4H_2O(l) \longrightarrow 4H_2O(g)$, $\Delta H^\circ = 4 \times 44 \text{ kJ}$

$\therefore \; C_3H_8(g)+5O_2(g) \longrightarrow 3CO_2(g)+4H_2O(g)$

$$\Delta H^\circ = (-2220+176) \text{ kJ} = -2044 \text{ kJ}$$

35. (c) $\Delta_f H(NO) = 21.6 \text{ kcal mol}^{-1}$,

$\Delta H^\circ > 0$, endothermic

$\therefore \frac{1}{2}N_2(g)+\frac{1}{2}O_2(g) \longrightarrow NO(g)$

0.5 mol	0.5 mol	$\Delta H^\circ = 21.6$ kcal
1.0 mol	1.0 mol	$\Delta H^\circ = 43.2$ kcal

36. (a) $\Delta H = -187.6 = 2\Delta_f H(NH_3) - [\Delta_f H^\circ(N_2H_4) + \Delta_f H^\circ(H_2)]$

$$= 2\Delta_f H(NH_3) - [95.4 + 0]$$

$$\therefore \; 2\Delta_f H^\circ(NH_3) = -187.6 + 95.4 = -92.2$$

$$\therefore \; \Delta_f H^\circ(NH_3) = -46.1 \text{ kJ mol}^{-1}$$

37. (b) 100 mL of 0.1 M $Ba(OH)_2$

$$= \frac{100 \times 0.1}{1000} = 0.01 \text{ mol}$$

100 mL of 0.1 M H_2SO_4 = 0.01 mol

100 mL of 0.1 M HCl = 0.01 mol

50 mL of 0.01 M $Ba(OH)_2$ = 0.005 mol

***Case* I** Temperature is rise ΔT_1 when 0.01 mol of $Ba(OH)_2$ is neutralised by 0.01 mol of H_2SO_4.

$$Ba(OH)_2 \equiv 2OH^-$$

$$H_2SO_4 \equiv 2H^+$$

***Case* II** Temperature rise is ΔT_2 when 0.005 mol of $Ba(OH)_2$ is neutralised by 0.01 mol of HCl.

$$HCl = H^+$$

Case	**$[H^+]$**	**$[OH^-]$**	**Rise in temp.**
I	0.02 mol	0.02 mol	ΔT_1
II	0.01 mol	0.01 mol	ΔT_2

Thus, $\Delta H_1 > \Delta H_2$

hence, $\Delta T_1 > \Delta T_2$ and $\Delta T_1 = 2\Delta T_2$

38. (c) $H_2 = O_2 = 90 \text{ g} \Rightarrow H_2 = 45 \text{ mol}$

$$O_2 = \frac{90}{32} \text{ mol}$$

$H_2(g) + \frac{1}{2}O_2(g) \longrightarrow H_2O(l)$

1 mol	0.5 mol
45 mol	90/32 mol

Thus, O_2 is in limiting quantity

$$\Delta H^\circ \text{ due to } \frac{90}{32} \text{ mol} = -241.8 \times 2 \times \frac{90}{32}$$

$$= -1.36 \times 10^3 \text{ kJ}$$

39. (d) $2Fe(s) + \frac{3}{2}O_2(g) \longrightarrow Fe_2O_3(s)$

5.6 g	$\Delta H = -41$ kJ
112 g	?

In the formation of 1 mol Fe_2O_3, 2 mol Fe(= 112 g) are used

$\therefore \Delta H_f{}^\circ(Fe_2O_3)$ from 112 g

$$\text{Fe} = -\frac{41}{5.6} \times 112 = -820 \text{ kJ}$$

40. (b) $\Delta H^\circ - \Delta U^\circ = \Delta n_g RT$

Greater the value of Δn_g, larger the difference.

(a) $\Delta n_g = 1$

(b) $\Delta n_g = -2$

(c) $\Delta n_g = 0$

(d) $\Delta n_g = -1$

41. (b) $C_6H_6(l) + 7.5O_2(g) \longrightarrow 6CO_2(g) + 3H_2O(l)$
Benzene

ΔE (Heat of combustion at constant volume $= -3263.9 \text{ kJ mol}^{-1}$)

$\therefore \; \Delta n_g$ = (Moles of gaseous products − moles of gaseous reactants)

$$\Delta n_g = 6 - 7.5 = -1.5$$

$$\therefore \; \Delta H = \Delta E + \Delta n_g RT$$

$$= -3263.9 - 1.5 \times 8.314 \times 10^{-3} \times 298$$

$$= -3267.6 \text{ kJ mol}^{-1}$$

42. (c) $C_{(graphite)} + O_2(g) \longrightarrow CO_2(g)$;

$$\Delta_r H_1^\circ = -393.5 \text{ kJ mol}^{-1} \quad \ldots(i)$$

$H_2(g) + \frac{1}{2}O_2(g) \longrightarrow H_2O(l)$;

$$\Delta_r H_2^\circ = -285.8 \text{ kJ mol}^{-1} \quad \ldots(ii)$$

$CO_2(g) + 2H_2O(l) \longrightarrow CH_4(g) + 2O_2(g)$;

$$\Delta_r H_3^\circ = +890.3 \text{ kJ mol}^{-1} \quad \ldots(iii)$$

$C_{(graphite)} + 2H_2(g) \longrightarrow CH_4(g)$;

$$\Delta_r H_4^\circ = ? \quad \ldots(iv)$$

On multiplying Eq. (ii) by 2

$$2H_2(g) + O_2(g) \longrightarrow 2H_2O(l) \quad \ldots(v)$$

$$\Delta_r H_5^\circ = 2 \times -285.8 \text{ kJ mol}^{-1}$$

$$= -571.6 \text{ kJ mol}^{-1}$$

Now, on adding Eq. (i), (iii) and (v), we get Eq. (iv)

$$\therefore \Delta_r H_4^\circ = \Delta_r H_1^\circ + \Delta_r H_3^\circ + \Delta_r H_5^\circ$$

$$= -393.5 \text{ kJ mol}^{-1} + 890.3 \text{ kJ mol}^{-1} + (-571.6 \text{ kJ mol}^{-1})$$

$$= (-496.8 + 571.6) \text{ kJ mol}^{-1}$$

$$= -74.8 \text{ kJ mol}^{-1}$$

43. (c) I. $C(s) + O_2(g) \longrightarrow CO_2(g)$;

$$\Delta_C H^\circ = -393.5 \text{ kJ mol}^{-1}$$

II. $CO(g) + \frac{1}{2}O_2(g) \longrightarrow CO_2(g)$;

$$\Delta_C H^\circ = -283.5$$

(I – II) gives a reaction in which 1 mol CO formed.

$C(s) + \frac{1}{2}O_2(g) \longrightarrow CO(g)$;

$$\Delta_f H^\circ(CO) = -393.5 + 283.5$$

$$= -110.0 \text{ kJ mol}^{-1}$$

44. (a) $C_2H_5OH(l) + 3O_2(g) \longrightarrow 2CO_2(g) + 3H_2O(l)$

Amount of heat produced in bomb calorimeter, at constant volume and at 298 K is ΔU.

$$\Delta U = -1364.47 \text{ kJ mol}^{-1}$$

Enthalpy of a combustion reaction is

$$\Delta H = \Delta U + \Delta n_g RT$$

where, ΔU = internal energy (Heat of reaction at constant volume)

Δn_g = moles of gaseous (products − reactants)

$$\Delta n_g = 2 - 3 = -1$$

Thus, $\Delta H = -1364.47 + \left[\frac{(-1) \times 8.314 \times 298}{1000}\right]$

$$\Delta H = -1364.47 - 2.477$$

$$= -1366.947 \text{ kJ mol}^{-1}$$

45. (c) Relation between ΔH (enthalpy change) and ΔE (internal energy change) is

$$\Delta H = \Delta E + \Delta n_g RT$$

where,

Δn_g = (moles of gaseous products − moles of gaseous reactants)

$$\Delta n_g = 2 - 3 = -1$$

$$-1366.5 = \Delta E - 1 \times 8.314 \times 10^{-3} \times 300$$

$$\therefore \quad \Delta E = -1364.0 \text{ kJ mol}^{-1}$$

46. (d) $4NO_2(g) + O_2(g) \longrightarrow 2N_2O_5(g)$;

$$\Delta_r H = -111 \text{ kJ}$$

$N_2O_5(g) \longrightarrow N_2O_5(s)$; $\Delta_r H = -108$ kJ

$4NO_2(g) + O_2(g) \longrightarrow 2N_2O_5(s)$; $\Delta_r H = -219$ kJ

Since, $N_2O_5(s) \xrightarrow{\text{Sublimation}} N_2O_5(g)$,

$$\Delta H_{sub} = +54 \text{ kJ mol}^{-1}$$

47. (b) $\frac{1}{2}N_2(g) + \frac{3}{2}H_2(g) \longrightarrow NH_3(g)$;

$$\Delta_r H = -46 \text{ kJ mol}^{-1}$$

$2H(g) \longrightarrow H_2(g)$;

$$\Delta_f H^\circ = -436 \text{ kJ mol}^{-1}$$

Hence, bond energy (H—H) = 436 kJ mol^{-1}

Similarly, bond energy ($N \equiv N$) = + 712 kJ mol^{-1}

$$\Delta_r H = \left[\frac{1}{2}\text{Bond energy }(N_2) + \frac{3}{2}\text{Bond energy }(H_2)\right] - 3\text{ Bond energy (N—H)}$$

$$-46 = \left[\frac{1}{2}\times 712 + \frac{3}{2}\times 436\right] - 3\text{ Bond energy (N—H)}$$

$$-46 = (356 + 654) - 3\text{ Bond energy (N—H)}$$

3 Bond energy (N—H) = 1056 kJ

Bond energy (N—H) = 352 kJ mol^{-1}

48. (d) Percentage efficiency of the fuel cell

$$= \frac{\Delta G^\circ}{\Delta H^\circ} \times 100$$

The concerned reaction is

$$CH_3OH(l) + \frac{3}{2}O_2(g) \longrightarrow CO_2(g) + 2H_2O(l)$$

$$\Delta G_r{}^\circ = \Delta G^\circ(\text{products}) - \Delta G^\circ(\text{reactants})$$

$$\Delta G^\circ_r = [\Delta G^\circ_f(CO_2, g) + 2\Delta G^\circ_f[(H_2O, l)] \;[-\Delta G^\circ_f(CH_3OH, l) - \frac{3}{2}\Delta G^\circ_f(O_2, g)]$$

$$= -394.4 + 2(-237.2) - (-166.2) - 0$$

$$= -394.4 - 474.4 + 166.2$$

$$= -702.6 \text{ kJ mol}^{-1}$$

$$\text{Percentage efficiency} = \frac{702.6}{726} \times 100 = 96.78\% = 97\%$$

49. (b) Consider the heat of formation of H_2O

$$H_2(g) + \frac{1}{2}O_2(g) \longrightarrow H_2O(l);$$

$$\Delta H = -286.20 \text{ kJ}$$

$$\Delta H_f(H_2O, l) = -286.20 \text{ kJ mol}^{-1}$$

Now, consider the ionisation of H_2O

$$H_2O(l) \longrightarrow H^+(aq) + OH^-(aq);$$

$$\Delta H = 57.32 \text{ kJ}$$

$$\Delta H_r = \Delta H_f(H^+, aq) + \Delta H_f(OH^-, aq) - \Delta H_f(H_2O, l)$$

$$57.32 = 0 + \Delta H_f(OH^-, aq) - (-286.20)$$

$$\text{Thus, } \Delta H_f(OH^-, aq) = 57.32 - 286.20 = -228.88 \text{ kJ mol}^{-1}$$

50. (b) $\frac{1}{2}Cl_2(g) + aq \longrightarrow Cl^-(aq)$ can be written in steps

	ΔH°/kJ
$\frac{1}{2}Cl_2(g) \xrightarrow{\text{Dissociation}} Cl(g)$	240/2
$Cl(g) + e^- \xrightarrow{\text{Electron gain}} Cl^-(g)$	−349
$Cl^-(g) + aq \xrightarrow{\text{Hydration}} Cl^-(aq)$	−381

$$\therefore \Delta H = \frac{1}{2}\Delta H_{\text{diss}(Cl_2)} + \Delta H_{E_a(Cl)} + \Delta H_{\text{hyd}(Cl^-)}$$

$$= \frac{240}{2} - 349 - 381$$

$$= -610 \text{ kJ mol}^{-1}$$

51. (b) $C(s) + \frac{1}{2}O_2(g) \longrightarrow CO(g);$

$$\Delta n_g = 1 - \frac{1}{2} = \frac{1}{2}$$

Calculate $\Delta H - \Delta E$ by using the formula,

$$\Delta H - \Delta E = \Delta n_g RT = \frac{1}{2} \times 8.314 \times 298$$

$$= 1238.78 \text{ J mol}^{-1}$$

52. (c) $\frac{1}{2}I_2(s) + \frac{1}{2}Cl_2(g) \longrightarrow ICl(g)$

$$\Delta H = \left[\frac{1}{2}\Delta H_{\text{sub}} + \frac{1}{2}\Delta H_{\text{diss}}(Cl_2) + \frac{1}{2}\Delta H_{\text{diss}}(I_2)\right] - \Delta H_{ICl}$$

$$= \left(\frac{1}{2}\times 62.76 + \frac{1}{2}\times 242.3 + \frac{1}{2}\times 151.0\right) - 211.3$$

$$= (228.03 - 211.3) \text{ kJ}$$

$$\Delta H = 16.73 \text{ kJ mol}^{-1}$$

53. (a) Carbon is found in solid state. The state of substance affects the enthalpy change.

$$C(s) \longrightarrow C(g) \text{ (sublimation)},$$

$$\text{and } H_2(g) \longrightarrow 2H(g) \text{ (dissociation)}$$

Thus, sublimation enthalpy of C(s) and dissociation enthalpy of $H_2(g)$ are required to determine the average energy for C—H bond formation.

54. (a)

$$\Delta H = \Delta U + p\Delta V$$

$$\Delta H - \Delta U = p\Delta V$$

$$\therefore \quad p = \frac{\Delta H - \Delta U}{\Delta V}$$

Density = Mass/Volume

$$\text{For diamond, molar volume} = \frac{12}{3.51} \text{ cm}^3$$

$$\text{For graphite, molar volume} = \frac{12}{2.25} \text{ cm}^3$$

$$\therefore \quad \Delta V = \left(\frac{12}{3.51} - \frac{12}{2.25}\right) \text{cm}^3$$

$$= -1.91 \text{ cm}^3$$

$$= -1.91 \times 10^{-3} \text{ dm}^3$$

$$\Delta H - \Delta U = -1 \text{ kJ} = -1000 \text{ J}$$

$$= -\frac{1000 \text{ J}}{100 \text{ J (dm}^3\text{ bar}^{-1})}$$

$$= -10 \text{ dm}^3 \text{ bar}$$

$$\therefore \quad p = \frac{-10 \text{ dm}^3 \text{bar}}{-1.91 \times 10^{-3} \text{ dm}^3}$$

$$= 5236 \text{ bar} = 5.236 \times 10^3 \text{ bar}$$

55. (b) By Kirchoff's equation,

$$\Delta_r H^\circ_{373} = \Delta_r H^\circ_{298} + \Delta C_p (T_2 - T_1)$$

$$\Delta C_p = [C_p(H) + 2C_p(O_2)] - [C_p(O_3) + C_p(OH)]$$

$$= [20.78 + 2 \times 29.36] - [39.29 + 29.89]$$

$$= 10.32 \text{ JK}^{-1} = 10.32 \times 10^{-3} \text{ kJ K}^{-1}$$

$$\therefore \quad \Delta_r H^\circ_{373} = 36.3 \text{ kJ} + 10.32 \times 10^{-3}(373 - 298)$$

$$= 36.3 + 0.8 \text{ kJ} = +37.1 \text{ kJ}$$

56. (c) Using Hess's law for each desired thermochemical equation,

$$Ag(s) \longrightarrow Ag^+(aq) + e^-, \quad \Delta_r H^\circ = 105.6 \text{ kJ}$$

$$\frac{1}{2}Cl_2(g) + e^- \longrightarrow Cl^-(aq), \quad \Delta_r H^\circ = -167.2 \text{ kJ}$$

$$Ag^+(aq) + Cl^-(aq) \longrightarrow AgCl(s), \quad \Delta_r H^\circ = -65.5 \text{ kJ}$$

$$Ag(s) + \frac{1}{2}Cl_2(g) \longrightarrow AgCl(s), \quad \Delta_r H^\circ = -127.1 \text{ kJ}$$

Similarly for II

$$Ag(s) + \frac{1}{2}Br_2(l) \longrightarrow AgBr(s), \quad \Delta_r H^\circ = -100.4 \text{ kJ}$$

Both are exothermic reactions and I is more exothermic than II.

57. (d) Adding (I + II) gives,

$$CH_3OH(l) + nH_2O(l) \longrightarrow CH_3OH \text{ in } n\, H_2O$$

$$\Delta_{\text{solution}} H^\circ = \Delta_{\text{vapour}} H^\circ + \Delta_{\text{solv}} H^\circ$$

$$-7.27 = 3800 + \Delta_{\text{solv}} H^\circ$$

$$\therefore \quad \Delta_{\text{solv}} H^\circ = -38.0 - 7.27$$

$$= -45.27 \text{ kJ mol}^{-1}$$

58. (b) $\Delta H_{(\text{Total})} = \Delta H_{\text{fusion}} + \Delta H_{\text{vap}}$

$$= (6.0 + 40.0) = 46.0 \text{ kJ mol}^{-1}$$

$$p\Delta V = p[V(\text{vapour}) - V(\text{ice})]$$

$$= p\left(\frac{nRT}{p} - 0\right)$$

(Volume of ice is negligible)

$$= nRT = 1 \times 8.314 \times 273$$

$$= 2270 \text{ J} = 2.27 \text{ kJ mol}^{-1}$$

$$\therefore \quad \Delta U = \Delta H - p\Delta V$$

$$= 46 - 2.27 = 43.73 \text{ kJ mol}^{-1}$$

59. (d) By Kirchoff's equation,

$$\Delta H^\circ_T = \Delta H^\circ_{300} + \Delta C_p \int_{300}^{T} dt$$

$$0 = -60.0 + \int_{300}^{T} (5.0 + 2.0 \times 10^{-2} T) dt$$

$$0 = -60.0 + \left[5T + \frac{2.0 \times 10^{-2}}{2} T^2\right]_{300}^{T}$$

$$0 = -60 + 5(T - 300) + 0.01[T^2 - 300^2]$$

$$60 = 5T - 1500 + 0.01\, T^2 - 900$$

$$0.01\, T^2 + 5T - 2460 = 0$$

$$T = \frac{-5 + \sqrt{25 + 98.4}}{0.02} = 305.4 \text{ K}$$

60. (c) $I_2(s) \longrightarrow I_2(g)$

By Kirchhoff's equation,

$$\Delta H_{T_2} = \Delta H_{T_1} + \Delta C_p\ (T_2 - T_1)$$

Given,

$$\Delta H_{473} = 24 \text{ cal g}^{-1}$$
$$\Delta C_p = C_p(I_2(g)) - C_p(I_2(s))$$
$$= 0.031 - 0.055$$
$$= -0.024 \text{ cal g}^{-1}\text{ K}^{-1}$$
$$T_1 = 473 \text{ K}$$
$$T_2 = 523 \text{ K}$$
$$(T_2 - T_1) = 50 \text{ K}$$
$$\Delta H_{523} = 24 + (-0.024) \times 50$$
$$= 22.8 \text{ cal g}^{-1}$$

Acid Test for JEE Advanced

Type I. MCQs with Only ONE Correct Alternate

61. (b) Smaller the value of enthalpy of neutralisation, weaker the acid.

Thus, HB is weaker acid than HA

Thus, (H^+) in $HB < (H^+)$ in HA

Since, $pH = -\log[H^+]$

Hence, pH of $HB >$ pH of HA of equal molar concentration.

62. (c) $H_2 \longrightarrow 2H, \qquad \Delta H = 400 \text{ kJ mol}^{-1}$

Bond energies of H_2, F_2 and HF are in the ratio of 2 : 1 : 3.

Thus, bond energy of H—H bond

$$= 400 \text{ kJ mol}^{-1}$$

$$\text{Bond energy of } F_2 = \frac{1}{2} \text{ bond energy of } H_2$$
$$= 200 \text{ kJ mol}^{-1}$$
$$\text{Bond energy of HF} = \frac{3}{2} \text{ bond energy of } H_2$$
$$= 600 \text{ kJ mol}^{-1}$$

Reaction showing formation of one mol HF

$$\frac{1}{2}H_2 + \frac{1}{2}F_2 \longrightarrow HF$$

$$\Delta H = \frac{1}{2}(\text{bond energy})_{H-H} + \frac{1}{2}(\text{bond energy})_{F-F} - (\text{bond energy})_{H-F}$$
$$= 200 + 100 - 600 = -300 \text{ kJ mol}^{-1}$$
$$= \frac{400}{2} + \frac{1}{2}\left(400 \times \frac{1}{2}\right) - \frac{400}{2} \times 3$$
$$= 200 + 100 - 600 = -300 \text{ kJ}$$
$$\Delta_f H(\text{HF}) = -300 \text{ kJ mol}^{-1}$$

63. (c) In both cases,

1 mole of NaOH is neutralised by 1 mole of HCl. Thus, ΔT (change in temperature) is identical.

$$\frac{MV(\text{litre})}{1000} = \text{mol}$$

64. (a) $2Fe + \frac{3}{2}O_2 \longrightarrow Fe_2O_3,$

$$\Delta_f H° = x \text{ kJ mol}^{-1}$$

$Fe + \frac{1}{2}O_2 \longrightarrow FeO, \ \Delta_f H° = y \text{ kJ mol}^{-1}$

$3Fe + 2O_2 \longrightarrow Fe_3O_4, \ (Fe_2O_3 + FeO);$

$$\Delta_f H° = z \text{ kJ mol}^{-1} = ?$$

Thus, $(x + y) = z$

65. (a) $NH_3 \longrightarrow N + 3H, \ \Delta H = p$ (thus, N—H bonds are cleaved)

Thus, bond energy of (N—H) bond = $p/3$

$$\underset{\substack{| \\ H}}{H—N}—\underset{\substack{| \\ H}}{N}—H \longrightarrow 2N + 4H, \quad \Delta H = q$$

One (N—N) bond and four (N—H) bonds are cleaved.

q = bond energy of one N—N bond + bond energy of four N—H bonds.

$$q = x + \frac{4p}{3}$$
$$\therefore \quad x = q - \frac{4p}{3} = \left(\frac{3q - 4p}{3}\right)$$

66. (a) $50 \times 0.01 \text{M Ca(OH)}_2$

$$= \frac{50 \times 0.01}{1000} \text{ mol Ca(OH)}_2$$
$$= 5 \times 10^{-4} \text{ mol Ca(OH)}_2$$

as 1 mol $Ca(OH)_2$ = 2 mol OH^-

$$= 1 \times 10^{-3} \text{ mol } (OH^-)$$
$$25 \times 0.01 \text{ M HCl} = \frac{25 \times 0.01}{1000} \text{ mol HCl}$$
$$= 0.25 \times 10^{-3} \text{ mol HCl}$$

Thus, HCl is completely neutralised.

$\Delta H°$ for 0.25×10^{-3} mol HCl

$$= -13.7 \times 0.25 \times 10^{-3} \text{ kcal}$$
$$= -\frac{13.7}{4} \times 10^{-3} \text{ kcal} = -\frac{13.7}{4} \text{ cal}$$

67. (a) $\Delta H° = \Delta E° + \Delta n_g RT$

$$\Delta n_g = 6 - 7.5 = -1.5$$
$$-3.271 \times 10^3 = \Delta E° - 1.5 \times 8.314 \times 10^{-3} \times 300$$
$$\therefore \ \Delta E° = -3.271 \times 10^3 + 1.5 \times 8.314 \times 10^{-3} \times 300$$
$$= -3.267 \times 10^3 \text{ kJ}$$

68. (b) $\Delta_f H°$(of species X) = enthalpy (of species X) and enthalpy of elements = 0

Thus,

$$\Delta H° = 8\Delta_f H°(CO_2) + 9\Delta_f H°(H_2O) - \Delta_f H°(C_8H_{18}) - 125\Delta_f H°(O_2)$$
$$= 8 \times 394 - 9 \times 286 - (-250) - 12.5 \times 0$$
$$= -5476 \text{ kJ mol}^{-1}$$

69. (d) I. $CH_3CH{=}CH_2 + H_2 \longrightarrow CH_3CH_2CH_3,$

$$\Delta H° = -124 \text{ kJ}$$

II. $CH_3CH_2CH_3 + 5O_2 \longrightarrow 3CO_2 + 4H_2O,$

$$\Delta H° = -2220 \text{ kJ}$$

III. $H_2O \longrightarrow H_2 + \frac{1}{2}O_2, \ \Delta H° = +286 \text{ kJ}$

IV. $CH_3CH_2{=}CH_2 + \frac{9}{2}O_2 \longrightarrow 3CO_2 + 3HO_2, \ \Delta H° = ?$

I + II + III = IV

IV. represents combustion of propene

$$\therefore \ \Delta_C H°(CH_3CH{=}CH_2) = -2058 \text{ kJ mol}^{-1}$$

70. (c) $C_{10}H_8 + O_2 \longrightarrow 10\,CO_2 + 4H_2O,$

$$\Delta H = -2720 \text{ kJ mol}^{-1}$$
$$C_{10}H_8 = \frac{120 \times 10^{-3}}{128} \text{ mol}$$
$$C_6H_6O = \frac{150 \times 10^{-3}}{94} \text{ mol}$$

$C_p \Delta T$ = Heat released in the combustion

$$C_p \times 3.05 = -2720 \times \frac{120 \times 10^{-3}}{128} \text{ for } C_{10}H_8$$
$$C_p \times \Delta T = -3054 \times \frac{150 \times 10^{-3}}{94} \text{ for phenol}$$
$$\therefore \quad \Delta T = 5.83 \text{ K}$$

71. (b) Based on bond energy value

$$P(s) + 1.5\,Cl_2(g) \longrightarrow PCl_3(g)$$

306 = $\Delta H°$ [of atomisation of P(s) to P(g)] + 1.5 bond energy of (Cl—Cl) bond − 3 (bond energy) of (P—Cl) bond.

$$306 = 314 + 242 \times \frac{3}{2} - 3x$$
$$\therefore \quad 3x = 314 + 363 - 306$$
$$= 371 \text{ kJ mol}^{-1}$$

72. (a) Moles of benzoic acid $(C_7H_6O_2)$

$$= \frac{0.5421}{122}$$

$$\text{Heat due to} \left(\frac{0.5421}{122}\right) \text{mol of benzoic acid}$$
$$= -3227 \times \frac{0.5421}{122}$$
$$= -14.34 \text{ kJ}$$
$$C_p \text{ (calorimeter constant)} = \frac{14.34 \text{ kJ}}{2.680 \text{ K}} \text{ kJ}$$
$$= 5.351 \text{ kJ K}^{-1}$$
$$\text{For naphthalene } (C_{10}H_8) = \frac{0.6521}{128} \text{ mol}$$

Heat due to combustion = $C_p\Delta T$

$= 5.351 \times 1.173 = 6.2767$ kJ

$\therefore \quad \Delta_c U° = \frac{6.2767}{0.6521} \times 128$

$= - 1232$ kJ mol^{-1}

73. (b) C=C ⟶ C—C

One π bond is cleaved; Two new σ bonds are formed

ΔH = (bond energy)$_{C=C}$ − 2(bond energy)$_{C—C}$

$= 590 - 2 \times 331 = - 72$ kJ

74. (b) For benzoic acid, mol $= \frac{0.825}{122}$

$\Delta_C U = -3251$ kJ mol^{-1}

Heat capacity × $\Delta T = q$

$C \times 1.94$ K $= 3251 \times \frac{0.825}{122}$ kJ

$C = 3251 \times \frac{0.825}{122 \times 1.94}$ kJ K^{-1}

$= 11.332$ kJ K^{-1}

For D-ribose, moles $= \frac{0.727}{150}$ mol

Thus, heat liberated

$C \times \Delta T = 11.332 \times 0.910 = 10.31$ kJ

$\therefore \Delta_c U°$(D-ribose) $= \frac{-10.31}{0.727} \times 150$

$= - 2127.2$ kJ mol^{-1}

$C_5H_{10}O_5 + 5O_2 \longrightarrow 5CO_2 + 5H_2O$

Since, $\Delta_f H°$= enthalpy

$- 2127.2 = 5\Delta_f H°(CO_2) + 5\Delta_f H°(H_2O) - \Delta_f H°(C_5H_{10}O_5)$

$\therefore \Delta_f H°(C_5H_{10}O_5) = - 1272.8$ kJ

75. (a) m = 100 g = 0.1 kg water

100 g H_2O (*s*) at 273 K $\xrightarrow{\Delta H_1}$ 100 g H_2O (*l*) at 273 K

(T = constant)

100 g H_2O (*l*) at 273 K $\xrightarrow{\Delta H_2}$ 100 g H_2O (*l*) at 373 K

100 g H_2O (*l*) at 373 K $\xrightarrow{\Delta H_3}$ 100 g H_2O (*g*) at 373 K

(T = constant)

$\therefore \Delta H_1 = \Delta H_{fusion} \times m$

$= 80$ kcal kg$^{-1} \times 0.1$ kg $= 8.0$ kcal

$\Delta T = 373 - 273 = 100$ K

$\Delta H_2 = ms\Delta T$

$= 0.1 \times 1 \times 100 = 10.0$ kcal

$\Delta H_3 = \Delta H_{vap} \times m = 540 \times 0.1 = 54.0$ kcal

$\therefore \Delta H_{total} = 72.0$ kcal

76. (a) Al = 20 g $= \frac{20}{27}$ mol, $\Delta T = 25$ K

Molar heat capacity = C_p

$\therefore nC_p\,\Delta T = q$

$\therefore \quad C_p = \frac{q}{n\Delta T} = \frac{105}{\left(\frac{20}{27}\right)25}$

$= 5.67$ cal K^{-1} mol^{-1}

77. (b) $q = m.s\Delta T$

$= 1000$ g $\times 1.0$ cal g^{-1} K$^{-1} \times 37$ K

$= 37000$ cal $= 37$ kcal

Calorific value $= \frac{37 \text{ kcal}}{5 \text{ g}} = 7.4$ kcal g^{-1}

78. (d) s = 1 cal g^{-1} K^{-1}for H_2O

$q = m.s\Delta T$

$= 4000 \times 1.0 \times 10 = 40{,}000$ cal

$= 40$ kcal

Moles of propane required

$= \frac{40 \text{ kcal}}{520.0 \text{ kcal mol}^{-1}} = 0.077$ mol

For ideal gas, $pV = nRT$

$\therefore \; V = \frac{nRT}{p} = \frac{0.077 \times 0.0821 \times 298}{1}$

$= 1.88$ L

79. (c) I. $H_2 \longrightarrow 2H, \Delta H° = + 436$ kJ mol^{-1}

II. $H_2 + \frac{1}{2}O_2 \longrightarrow H_2O,$

$\Delta H = - 242$ kJ mol^{-1}

(II – I) gives combustion of H to form 1 mol H_2O (*g*)

$2H + \frac{1}{2}O_2 \longrightarrow H_2O,$

$\Delta H = - 678$ kJ mol^{-1}

Thus,

$\frac{\text{Enthalpy of combustion of } H_2 \text{ to form 1 mol } H_2O\,(g)}{\text{Enthalpy of combustion of H-atoms to form 1 mole } H_2O}$

$= \frac{-678}{-242} = 2.8$

80. (b) $C + H_2O(g) \longrightarrow CO(g) + H_2(g)$

$\Delta H° = \Delta_f H°(CO) - \Delta_f H\,(H_2O)$

$= - 110.53 + 241.81$

$= - 131.28$ kJ mol^{-1}

Thus, enthalpy due to 100 g carbon

$= \frac{100}{12}$ mol $= \frac{131.28 \times 100}{12} = - 1094$ kJ

$C + O_2 \longrightarrow CO_2, \quad \Delta_f H° = - 393.51$ kJ

Thus, carbon required for 1094 kJ heat

$= \frac{1094 \text{ kJ}}{393.51 \text{ kJ mol}^{-1}} = 2.78$ mol

$= 2.78$ mol $\times 12$ g mol^{-1} $= 33.36$ g

81. (b) I. $C + O_2 \longrightarrow CO_2,$

$\Delta H° = - 94$ kcal

II. $C + \frac{1}{2}O_2 \longrightarrow CO, \; \Delta H° = - 26$ kcal

Let carbon used in reaction I = x mol

$\Delta H = - 94x$ kcal

and carbon used in reaction II

$= (1 - x)$ mol

$\Delta H = -26(1 - x)$ kcal

$\therefore$ Total $\Delta H = - 94\,x - 26\,(1 - x)$

$= - 75$

$94x + 26 - 26x = 75$

$\therefore \quad x = \frac{49}{68} = 0.72$ mol

Thus, O_2 used in I = 0.72 mol

O_2 used in II = 0.14 mol

Total = 0.86 mol

82. (c) Carbon = 15.50 g $= \frac{15.5}{12.0} = 1.2917$ mol

$n(\text{air}) = \frac{pV}{RT} = \frac{5.50 \times 25.0}{0.0821 \times 298} = 5.62$ mol

O_2 in air (19%) $= 5.62 \times 0.19$

$= 1.0678$ mol

$C + \frac{1}{2}O_2 \longrightarrow CO$

If CO formed = x mol − $\frac{x}{2}$ mol O_2 used

$C + O_2 \longrightarrow CO_2$

then CO_2 formed = $(1.2917 - x)$ mol

$= (1.2917 - x)$ mol O_2

$\frac{x}{2} + (1.2917 - x) = 1.0678$

$x = 0.448$ mol CO formed

$\Delta H = 0.448 \times (-26)$ kcal

$(1.2917 - x) = 0.844$ mol CO_2 formed

$\Delta H = 0.844(-94)$ kcal

Thus, total $\Delta H = 0.448 \times (-26) + 0.844\,(-94)$

$= - 94.74$ kcal

83. (c) $CO_3^{2-}(aq) + 2H^+(aq) \longrightarrow CO_2(g) + H_2O(l)$

$\Delta H° = [\Delta_f H°(CO_2) + \Delta_f H°(H_2O)] - [\Delta_f H°(CO_3^{2-}) + 2\Delta_f H°(H^+)]$

$= [- 94 - 68] - [- 161.6 + 2 \times 0]$

$= - 0.4$ kcal (exothermic)

0.4 kcal is liberated from = 1 mol CO_3^{2-}

4 kcal is liberated from = 10 mol CO_3^2

84. (a) $FeS\,(s) + 2H^+(aq) \longrightarrow Fe^{2+}(aq) + H_2S\,(g)$

22.4 L at STP = 1 mol H_2S

$\Delta H° = [\Delta_f H°(H_2S) + \Delta_f H°(Fe^{2+})] - [\Delta_f H°(FeS) + 2\,\Delta_f H°(H^+)]$

$= [-20.6 - 87.9] - [-95.4 + 0]$
$= -108.5 + 95.4 = -13.1 \text{ kJ mol}^{-1}$

85. (b) $CaCl_2.6H_2O(s) \longrightarrow Ca^{2+}(aq) + 2Cl^-(aq) + 6H_2O$ (excess), $\Delta H° = 3.5$ kcal

$CaCl_2(s) + 6H_2O(s) \longrightarrow CaCl_2.6H_2O$, $\Delta H° = -23.2$ kcal

Adding

$CaCl_2 \xrightarrow{H_2O} Ca^{2+}(aq) + 2Cl^-(aq)$, $\Delta H° = -19.7$ kcal

86. (a) $2O_3(g) \longrightarrow 3O_2(g)$, $\Delta H° = -285.4 \text{ kJ mol}^{-1}$

Thus, ΔH due to 1 g $O_3 = \dfrac{-285.4 \times 1}{96} = -2.973$ kJ

ΔH_{fusion} (ice) $= 6.0 \text{ kJ mol}^{-1}$

If ice melts $= w$ gram $= \dfrac{w}{18}$ mol

Then $\dfrac{w}{18} \times 6 = 2.973$

$\therefore \quad w = \dfrac{2.973 \times 18}{6} = 8.92$ g

87. (b)

(a) $\Delta H = \dfrac{-483.6}{32} \text{ kJ g}^{-1} = -15.11$ kJ

(b) $\Delta H = \dfrac{-868.2}{48} \text{ kJ g}^{-1}$
$= -18.08$ kJ (max)

(c) $\Delta H = \dfrac{-347.3}{34} \text{ kJ g}^{-1} = -10.21$ kJ

(d) $\Delta H = \dfrac{-92.11}{28} \text{ kJ g}^{-1} = -3.29$ kJ

■ In (c), oxidising agent is H_2O_2 and (d) it is N_2.
All reactions are exothermic

88. (d) $C(s) + \underset{\text{Steam}}{H_2O(g)} \longrightarrow CO(g) + H_2(g)$

Carbon $= 1000 \text{ g} = \dfrac{1000}{12}$ mol

$[CO(g) = H_2(g)]$ from 1kg carbon (50% reaction)

$= \dfrac{1000}{12} \times \dfrac{50}{100} = \dfrac{125}{3}$ mol

Since, $\Delta_C H°(CO) = -283 \text{ kJ mol}^{-1}$

$\therefore \Delta H°$ from $\dfrac{125}{3}$ mol $CO = -283 \times \dfrac{125}{3}$ kJ

Since, $\Delta_C H°(H_2) = -242 \text{ kJ mol}^{-1}$

$\therefore \quad \Delta H°$ from $\dfrac{125}{3}$ mol H_2

$= -242 \times \dfrac{125}{3}$ kJ

Total $= -(283 + 242)\dfrac{125}{3}$ kJ.
$= -21.875 \times 10^3$ kJ

89. (a) Carbon $= 12.0 \text{ g} = \dfrac{12.0}{12} = 1.0$ mol

$\underset{1 \text{ mol}}{C} + H_2O \text{ (steam)} \longrightarrow \underbrace{\underset{1 \text{ mol}}{CO} + \underset{1 \text{ mol}}{H_2}}_{\text{Water gas}}$

$CO + \dfrac{1}{2}O_2 \longrightarrow CO_2$, $\Delta H° = -283.0$ kJ

$H_2 + \dfrac{1}{2}O_2 \longrightarrow H_2O$, $\Delta H° = -242.0$ kJ

Total $\Delta H° = -525.0$ kJ from 1 mol carbon

'Water gas shift' reaction converts the $CO(g)$ in water gas to $CO_2(g)$ and $H_2(g)$.

$CO(g) + H_2O(g) \longrightarrow CO_2(g)$ and $H_2(g)$

Thus, total $H_2 = 2$ mol, after water gas shift reaction.

CO_2 is already in combusted form

$\Delta H°$ due to 2 mol of H_2
$= -242 \times 2 = -484$ kJ

$\therefore$ Difference $= -525 + 484 = -41.0$ kJ

90. (b) $n(C_2H_4) = 8$ mol

$n(CH_3CHO) = 1$ mol

$\therefore$ Total mol $= 9$

$\therefore \quad \chi_{C_2H_4} = 8/9$, $\chi_{CH_3CHO} = 1/9$

Enthalpy change in set I $= \dfrac{8}{9} \times 45.54$ kJ

Enthalpy change in set II $= \dfrac{1}{9} \times 68.91$ kJ

Total $\Delta H = \left(\dfrac{8}{9} \times 45.54 + \dfrac{1}{9} \times 68.91\right)$ kJ
$= 48.14$ kJ

91. (c) For 1 mole of the species

$(\Delta_r H° - \Delta_r U°) = p\Delta V$
$= p(V_2 - V_1) = -1$ kJ

For diamond, density $= 3.51 \text{ g cm}^{-3}$

$\dfrac{\text{Mass}}{\text{Volume}} = \text{Density}$

$\therefore V_2 = \dfrac{\text{Mass}}{\text{Density}} = \dfrac{12}{3.51} \text{ cm}^3 = \dfrac{12}{3.51} \times 10^{-3}$ L

Similarly, for graphite $V_1 = \dfrac{12}{2.25} \times 10^{-3}$ L

$1 \text{ kJ} = 1000 \text{ J} = \dfrac{1000 \times 0.0821}{8.314}$ L-atm

$\therefore \quad p\left(\dfrac{12}{3.51} \times 10^{-3} - \dfrac{12 \times 10^{-3}}{2.25}\right) = \dfrac{-1000 \times 0.0821}{8.314}$

$p\left(\dfrac{2.25 - 3.51}{2.25 \times 3.51}\right) 12 \times 10^{-3} = \dfrac{-1000 \times 0.0821}{8.314}$

$p = 5416$ atm

■ 0.0821 L atm = 8.314 J

$\therefore$ 1 L atm $= \dfrac{8.314}{0.0821}$ J or 1 J $= \dfrac{0.0821}{8.314}$ L atm

92. (a) $\Delta_r H° - \Delta_r U° = -p\Delta V = W = \Delta n_g RT$

$\therefore \; W = -p\Delta V = \Delta_r H° - \Delta_r U°$

$\Delta_r U° = \Delta_r H° - \Delta n_g RT$
$= -285.4 - (+1) \times 8.314 \times 10^{-3} \times 298$
$= -287.88$ kJ

$\therefore \; \Delta_r H° - \Delta_r U° = -285.4 - (-287.9)$
$= 2.5$ kJ

$\therefore W = -p\Delta V = -2.5$ kJ

93. (b) $H_2C_2O_4(aq) \rightleftharpoons 2H^+(aq) + C_2O_4^{2-}$
$\Delta H° = +3.2 \text{ kcal mol}^{-1}$

$2H^+(aq) + 2OH^-(aq) \longrightarrow 2H_2O(l)$
$\Delta H° = -(13.7 \times 2) = -27.4$ kcal

$\therefore \; H_2C_2O_4(aq) + 2OH^-(aq) \longrightarrow 2H_2O(l) + C_2O_4^{2-}(aq)$
$\Delta H° = -24.2 \text{ kcal mol}^{-1}$

■ $H_2C_2O_4$ is a dibasic acid.

$H^+ + OH^- \longrightarrow H_2O \; \Delta H° = -13.7$ kcal

$\therefore$ For dibasic acid, $\Delta H° = -27.4$ + enthalpy of ionisation

94. (a) $H—S—H \longrightarrow HS + H$

$\Delta H° = 376.6 \text{ kJ mol}^{-1}$

$\therefore \; \Delta_r H° = \Delta_f H°(HS) + \Delta_f H°(H) - \Delta_f H°(H_2S)$

$+376.6 = \Delta_f H°(HS) + 218.0 + 20.1$

$\therefore \; \Delta_f H°(HS) = 376.6 - 238.1$
$= +138.5 \text{ kJ mol}^{-1}$

95. (b) $H_2(g) + \dfrac{1}{2}O_2(g) \longrightarrow H_2O(g)$

$\Delta_f H°[H_2O(g)]$ = Bond energy (H—H) $+ \dfrac{1}{2}$ bond energy (O=O) $- 2$ bond energy (O—H)

$= \left(x_1 + \dfrac{x_2}{2} - 2x_3\right)$

$H_2O(l) \longrightarrow H_2O(g), \Delta H° = x_4$

$\therefore \; \Delta_f H°[H_2O(g)] - \Delta_f H°[H_2O(l)]$, $\Delta H° = x_4$

$\therefore \Delta_f H°[H_2O(l)] = \Delta_f H°[H_2O(g)] - x_4$

$= \left(x_1 + \dfrac{x_2}{2} - 2x_3 - x_4\right)$

96. (d) If carbon changing to $CO = x$ mol thus, carbon changing to $CO_2 = (2 - x)$ mol

$\therefore \; C + \dfrac{1}{2}O_2 \longrightarrow CO$,
$\Delta H° = (-110.5\,x)$ kJ

$C + O_2 \longrightarrow CO_2$,
$\Delta H° = (2 - x)(-393.5)$ kJ

Total $\Delta H = -[110.5x + (2 - x) \times 393.5]$

$\therefore \; -110.5\,x + (2 - x)(-393.5) = 481$

$110.5x + 393.5 \times 2 - 393.5x = 481$

$x = 1.08$ mol

Thus, CO formed = 1.08 mol

CO_2 formed = 0.92 mol

Ratio = 1.08 / 0.92 = 1.17 / 1

97. (a) Moles of $CH_4 = \frac{pV}{RT} = \frac{1 \times 1.65 \times 10^4}{0.0831 \times 300}$

$= 661.853$ mol

$\Delta_C H°(CH_4) = -890$ kJ mol^{-1}

$\therefore \quad \Delta H° = -890 \times 661.853$

$= -5.89 \times 10^5$ kJ

98. (b) By adding $\frac{1}{2}Cl_2(g) \longrightarrow Cl^-(aq)$

$\Delta H° = +\frac{240}{2} - 349 - 381 = -610$ kJ

99. (c) We make use of concept that heat of formation is the enthalpy of any species

$\Delta_f H°(x) = H_x^\circ$

$\underset{\text{Glucose}}{C_6H_{12}O_6(s)} + 6O_2(g) \longrightarrow 6CO_2(g) + 6H_2O(l)$

$\Delta_C H°(C_6H_{12}O_6) = [6\Delta_f H°(CO_2)] + 6\Delta_f H°(H_2O)] - [\Delta_f H°(C_6H_{12}O_6) + 6\Delta_f H°(O_2)]$

$= -6 \times 400 - 6 \times 300 - (-1300 + 0)$

$= -2900$ kJ mol^{-1}

Thus, $\Delta_C H° = -\frac{2900}{180}$ kJ g^{-1}

$= -16.11$ kJg^{-1}

Molar mass of glucose ($C_6H_{12}O_6$) = 180 g mol^{-1}

100. (d) $2C(s) + H_2(g) \longrightarrow H{-}C \equiv C{-}H$

$\Delta_f H°(C_2H_2) = 225 = [2\Delta H_{sub}(C(s)) + \text{bond energy (H—H)}] - (2\,\text{bond energy(C—H)} + C \equiv C)]$

$225 = [(1 \times 1410) + 330] - (350 \times 2 + x)]$

$\because x = 1410 + 330 - 700 - 225$

$= 815$ kJ mol^{-1}

- While, calculating ΔH based on (B.E.) values, all species should be in gaseous state. If solid, enthalpy of sublimation should be added. ΔH = (BE of reactants – BE of products).

101. (b) Fusion of N_2O_4 is

$N_2O_4(s) \rightleftharpoons N_2O_4(l)$

From graph,

At 262 K,

$\Delta H(N_2O_4, s) = -36.1$ kJ mol^{-1}

$\Delta H(N_2O_4, l) = -21.4$ kJ mol^{-1}

$\therefore \quad \Delta H_{fusion}$ (at 262 K) $= -21.4 - (-36.1)$

$= 14.7$ kJ mol^{-1}

Vaporisation of N_2O_4 at 202 K

$N_2O_4(l) \rightleftharpoons N_2O_4(g)$

$\Delta H(N_2O_4, g) = 12.0$ kJ mol^{-1}

$\therefore \quad \Delta H_{vap}$ (at 262) $= 12.0 - (-21.4)$

$= 33.4$ kJ mol^{-1}

Vaporisation of N_2O_4 at 400 K

$N_2O_4(l, 400\text{ K}) \rightleftharpoons N_2O_4(g, 400\text{ K})$

$\Delta H(N_2O_4, l)$ at 400 K $= -14.0$ kJ mol^{-1}

$\Delta H(N_2O_4, g)$ at 400 K $= 12.0$ kJ mol^{-1}

$\therefore \Delta H_{vap}$ (at 400 K) $= 12 - (-14.0)$

$= 26$ kJ mol^{-1}

102. (c) Given,

$CH_4(g) + 2O_2(g) \longrightarrow CO_2(g) + 2H_2O(l)$, $\Delta H° = -802.34$ kJ mol^{-1}

$CH_4(g) + 2O_2(g) \longrightarrow CO_2(g) + 2H_2O(l)$, $\Delta H° = -890.36$ kJ mol^{-1}

$\therefore \quad 2H_2O(l) \longrightarrow 2H_2O(l)$,

$\Delta H° = 890.36 - 802.34 = 88.02$ kJ

$\therefore \quad \Delta H°_{vap}$ (at 298 K) $= \frac{88.02\text{ kJ}}{2}$

$= 44.01$ kJ mol^{-1}

103. (d) Given,

I. $HS^-(aq) + OH^-(aq) \longrightarrow H_2O(l) + S^{2-}(aq)$, $\Delta H = -5.1$ kJ mol^{-1}

II. $HCl(aq) + OH^-(aq) \longrightarrow H_2O(l) + Cl^-(aq)$, $\Delta H = -57.2$ kJ mol^{-1}

or $H^+(aq) + OH^-(aq) \longrightarrow H_2O(l)$

From II,

$\Delta H = -57.2 = \Delta_f H°(H_2O, l) - \Delta_f H°(H^+) - \Delta_f H°(OH^-)$

$-57.2 = -285.8 - 0 - \Delta_f H°(OH^-)$

$\Delta_f H°(OH^-) = (-285.8 + 57.2)$ kJ mol^{-1}

$= -228.6$ kJ mol^{-1}

From I,

$\Delta H = -5.1 = \Delta_f H°(H_2O, l) + \Delta_f H°(S^{2-}, aq) - [\Delta_f H°(HS^-) + \Delta_f H°(OH^-)]$

$-5.1 = -285.8 + \Delta_f H°(S^{2-}) - [-17.6 - 228.6]$

$= -285.8 + \Delta_f H°(S^{2-}) + 246.2$

$\therefore \Delta_f H°(S^{2-}) = 285.8 - 246.2 - 5.1$

$= 34.5$ kJ mol^{-1}

104. (a) For the reaction,

$C(g) + 4H(g) + O(g) \longrightarrow CH_3OH(g)$

$\Delta H = \Delta_f H(CH_3OH) - [\Delta_f H(C, g) + 4\Delta_f H(H, g) + \Delta_f H(O)]$

$= -47.96 - [171.29 + 4 \times 52.10 + 59.60]$

$= -487.25$ kcal mol^{-1}

$= -2025.5$ kJ mol^{-1}

Based on B.E. values

$-2025.5 = (0 + 0 + 0) - [3BE(C{-}H) + BE(O{-}H)]$

$= (3 \times 415.9 + 463.6 + \text{B.E. (C—O)})$

$\therefore$ BE (C—O) $= -3 \times 415.9 - 463.6 + 2025.5$

$= 314.2$ kJ mol^{-1}

- 1 kcal = 4.157 kJ

105. (d) Water = 300 mL = 300 × 1 = 300 g

$\therefore \quad q_{water} = mS\Delta T$

$= 300\text{ g} \times 4.184\text{ Jg}^{-1}\text{K}^{-1} \times 1.2\text{ K}$

$= 1506\text{ J} = 1.506$ kJ

$q_{bomb} = C_{bomb}\Delta T$

$= 1.77 \times 1.2\text{ kJ} = 2.124$ kJ

$q_{comb} = -(q_{water} + q_{bomb})$

$= -1.506 - 2.124 = -3.63$ kJ

$\Delta_c U = \frac{q}{\text{moles of Mg}} = -\frac{3.63\text{ kJ}}{\frac{0.24}{24.0}\text{ mol}}$

$= -363.0$ kJ mol^{-1}

$Mg(s) + \frac{1}{2}O_2(g) \longrightarrow MgO(s)$

$\therefore \quad \Delta n_g = -0.5$

$\therefore \quad \Delta_c H = \Delta_c U + \Delta n_g RT$

$= -363.0 - \frac{1}{2} \times 8.314 \times 10^{-3} \times 298$

$= -364.20$ kJ mol^{-1}

106. (a)

I. $1\,H_2SO_4 + 1\,H_2O \longrightarrow H_2SO_4 \cdot H_2O$

II. $H_2SO_4 + 25H_2O \longrightarrow H_2SO_4 \cdot 25H_2O$

(II – I) gives,

$1H_2SO_4 \cdot 1H_2O + 24H_2O \longrightarrow 1H_2SO_4 \cdot 25H_2O$

$\Delta_r H = -72.300 + 28.075$

$= -44.225$ kJ mol^{-1}

Heat capacity = 4.184 J g^{-1} K^{-1}

Total mass of solution of 25 mol H_2O and 1 mol H_2SO_4

$= 25 \times 18 + 98 = 548$ g

$m \times S \times \Delta T = 44.225$

$548 \times \frac{4.184}{1000}\text{kJ} \times \Delta T = 44.225$

$\therefore \quad \Delta T = 19.3$ K

107. (c) $\Delta H = \Delta U + p\Delta V$

$p\Delta V = 1\text{ bar} \times (0.0180 - 0.0196)\text{ dm}^3$

$= -1.6 \times 10^{-3}\text{dm}^3\text{ bar mol}^{-1}$

$= -1.6 \times 10^{-3} \times 100\text{ J mol}^{-1}$

$= -0.16$ J mol^{-1}

$\therefore \Delta U = \Delta H - p\Delta V = 6000\text{ J} + 0.16$

$= 6000.16$ J mol^{-1}

≈ 6.0 kJ mol^{-1}

Type II. Statement Based Questions

108. (c) **109.** (a) **110.** (a) **111.** (b)

Type III. MCQs with More than One Correct Alternate

112. (b, d) Standard enthalpy of formation of a substance is the standard enthalpy change when one mole of the substance is formed from its elements in their standard and stable state.

Enthalpy of the element is taken as zero.

(a) In this C(g) is not the element in stable and standard state. Standard state of carbon is graphite.

(b) One mole of $O_3(g)$ is formed from O_2. Thus correct.

(c) H_2 and O_2 are elements but given reaction give enthalpy change of the formation of two moles of H_2O. Thus incorrect.

(d) $S_8(s)$ and $O_2(g)$ are elements, one mole of SO_2 is formed. Thus correct.

113. (b, c, d) In I, CO is formed from its elements

thus, $\Delta_f H°(CO) = x_1$

In III, CO_2 is formed from its elements.

then $\Delta_f H°(CO_2) = x_3$

Thus, (a) is incorrect.

Also, $\left(I + \frac{II}{2}\right)$: $C + O_2 \longrightarrow CO_2$

then $\left(x_1 + \frac{x_2}{2}\right) = x_3$

then, (b) is correct.

thus (c) is also correct.

C is combusted to CO_2 in III, then

$\Delta_C H°(\text{carbon}) = x_3$

Thus, (d) is also correct.

114. (a, c, d) $\frac{1}{2}H_2(g) \longrightarrow H(g), \quad \Delta H = x_1$

then, bond energy of (H—H) $= 2x_1$

$\frac{1}{2}O_2(g) \longrightarrow O(g), \Delta H = x_2$

$\therefore$ Bond energy of (O═O) $= 2x_2$

$H_2(g) + \frac{1}{2}O_2 \longrightarrow H_2O(g)$

$\Delta_f H°(H_2O, g) =$ bond energy (H—H) $+ \frac{1}{2}$ bond energy (O═O) $- 2$ bond energy (O—H)

$= 2x_1 + x_2 - 2x_3$

Thus, (d) is correct.

$H_2O(g) \longrightarrow H_2O(l), \quad \Delta H = -x_4$

$\therefore \Delta_f H°(H_2O, l) = 2x_1 + x_2 - 2x_3 - x_4$

115. (b, c, d) $A_2 + B_2 \longrightarrow 2AB$

$\frac{1}{2}A_2(g) + \frac{1}{2}B_2(g) \longrightarrow AB(g)$

$\Delta_f H°(AB) = -200$

$= \left[\frac{1}{2}(\text{bond energy})A_2 + \frac{1}{2}(\text{bond energy})B_2\right] - \text{bond energy }(AB)$

$-200 = \frac{x}{2} + \frac{x}{4} - 2x$

$-200 = -1.25\,x$

$\therefore \quad x = 160 \text{ kJ mol}^{-1}$

Thus,

bond energy $(A—A) = 160 \text{ kJ mol}^{-1}$

Thus, (b) is correct and bond energy $(A — B) = 320 \text{ kJ mol}^{-1}$

Thus, (c) is correct but (a) is incorrect.

$A_2(g) + \frac{1}{2}B_2(g) \longrightarrow A - B - A$

$\Delta_f H°(A_2B) = \left(160 + \frac{160}{4}\right) - 2 \times 320$

$= 200 - 640 = -440 \text{ kJ mol}^{-1}$

Thus, (d) is correct.

116. (a, b, c, d)

(a) $C_p = 3 + 2 \times 10^{-2}\,T$

$C_p - C_V = R$

$\therefore \quad C_V = C_p - R = 3 + 2 \times 10^{-2}\,T - 2$

$= 1 + 2 \times 10^{-2}T.$

Thus, (a) is correct.

(b) $\left(\frac{\Delta H}{\Delta T}\right)_p = C_p$

$\therefore \quad \Delta H = C_p \Delta T = C_p(T_2 - T_1)$

Thus, (b) is correct

(c) $C_p - C_V = R$

$C_p = C_V + R$

$\therefore \quad \Delta H = C_p \Delta T = (C_V + R)(T_2 - T_1)$

Thus, (c) is correct.

(d) Since $\left(\frac{\Delta E}{\Delta T}\right)_V = C_V$

$\therefore \quad \Delta E = C_V \Delta T = C_V(T_2 - T_1)$

$C_p - C_V = R$

$\therefore \quad C_V = C_p - R$

$\therefore \quad (\Delta E) = C_V \Delta T = (C_p - R)(T_2 - T_1)$

Thus (d) is correct.

117. (a, b, c, d)

(a) $\Delta H = \Delta E + \Delta n_g RT$

$\therefore \quad d\frac{(\Delta H)}{dT} = \frac{d(\Delta E)}{dT} + \Delta n_g R$

For per mol change, $(\Delta n_g = 1)$

$\frac{d(\Delta H)}{dT} = \frac{d(\Delta E)}{dT} + R$

Thus, (a) is correct.

(b) $\Delta E = C_V \Delta T = C_V(T_2 - T_1)$

When attractive forces are neglected

$a/V^2 = 0$

Then van der Waals, equation for real gas

$\left(p + \frac{a}{V^2}\right)(V - b) = RT$ changes to,

$p(V - b) = RT$

$\therefore \quad T = \frac{p(V - b)}{R}$

$\therefore (T_2 - T_1) = \frac{p(V_2 - b)}{R} - \frac{p(V_1 - b)}{R}$

$= \frac{p}{R}(V_2 - V_1)$

$\therefore \quad \Delta E = C_V(T_2 - T_1)$

$= \frac{C_V p}{R}(V_2 - V_1)$

Thus, (b) is correct.

(c) $\Delta H = \Delta T\, C_p = C_p(T_2 - T_1)$

As in (b)

$(T_2 - T_1) = \frac{p}{R}(V_2 - V_1)$

$\therefore \quad \Delta H = \frac{C_p p}{R}(V_2 - V_1)$

Since, $C_p - C_V = R$

$\therefore \quad C_p = (C_V + R)$

$\therefore \quad \Delta H = \left(\frac{C_V + R}{R}\right)p(V_2 - V_1)$

Thus, (c) is correct.

(d) $\left(\frac{\Delta E}{\Delta T}\right)_V = C_V$

$\therefore \quad \Delta E = C_V(T_2 - T_1)$

Thus, (d) is correct.

118. (b, d) Fumaric acid $\begin{matrix} \text{CHCOOH} \\ \| \\ \text{HOOCCH} \end{matrix}$

trans-isomer $-(A)$

Maleic acid $\begin{matrix} \text{CHCOOH} \\ \| \\ \text{CHCOOH} \end{matrix}$

cis-isomer$-(B)$

$A + O_2 \longrightarrow 4\,CO_2 + 2H_2O$

$\Delta H° = -1336.0 \text{ kJ mol}^{-1}$

$B + O_2 \longrightarrow 4CO_2 + 2H_2O$

$\Delta H° = -1359.2 \text{ kJ mol}^{-1}$

$\therefore \quad B \longrightarrow A, \ \Delta H° = -23.2$ exothermic

$A \longrightarrow B, \Delta H° = +23.2$ endothermic

Thus, (b) is correct.

$\Delta_f H°(A)$

$-1336 = 4\Delta_f H°(CO_2) + 2\Delta_f H°(H_2O) - \Delta_f H°(A)$

$\therefore \Delta_f H°(A) = -809.6 \text{ kJ mol}^{-1}$

$\Delta_f H°(B) = -786.4 \text{ kJ mol}^{-1}$

Thus, A is more exothermic, hence more stable than B.

119. (a,b) $H^+(aq) + OH^-(aq) \longrightarrow H_2O(l),$

$\Delta H° = -56.2 \text{ kJ mol}^{-1}$

$\frac{MV \text{ (mL)}}{1000} = \text{mol}$

Moles of HCl $= \frac{200 \times 0.862}{1000}$ mol

$= 0.1724 \text{ mol } [H^+]$

Moles of $Ba(OH)_2 = \frac{200 \times 0.431}{1000}$ mol

$= 0.0862 \text{ mol } Ba(OH)_2$

$= 0.1724 \text{ mol } [OH^-]$

Thus, $[H^+] = [OH^-]$, hence no reactant is left unreacted.

$\Delta_r H°$ for 0.1724 mol H^+ or OH^- ion

$= -0.1724 \times 56.2 = -9.69$ kJ

Thus, (a) is correct.

$$\Delta H_{calorimeter} = C_p\ \Delta T = 435\ \text{J K}^{-1}\ \Delta T\ \text{K}$$
$$= 435\ \Delta T \text{J} = 0.435\ \Delta T\ \text{kJ}$$
$$\Delta H_{solution} = m.s\ \Delta T = 400 \times 4.184\ \Delta T\ \text{J}$$
$$= 1673.6\ \Delta T\ \text{J} = 1.6736\ \Delta T\ \text{kJ}$$
$$\Delta H_{Total} = (0.435\Delta T + 1.6736\Delta T)\text{kJ}$$
$$\therefore\ 9.69 - [0.435 + 1.6736]\ \Delta T$$
$$\Delta T = 4.59°$$
$$(T_2 - T_1) = 4.59°$$
$$\therefore\ T_2 = T_1 + 4.59 = 20.48 + 4.59$$
$$= 25.07°\text{ C}$$

Thus, (b) is correct.

120. (a, b, d) $\Delta H_T^\circ = a + bT$

$$\Delta H_{300}^\circ = a + 300b = 5.5$$
$$\Delta H_{298}^\circ = a + 298b = 5.0$$
$$\therefore\ 2b = 0.5$$
$$b = 0.25$$
$$\therefore\ a = -69.5$$
$$\therefore\ \Delta H_{350}^\circ = -69.5 + 350 \times 0.25 = 18\ \text{kJ mol}^{-1}$$

Thus, (a) is correct.

$$\Delta H° = a + bT$$

As, $\dfrac{d(\Delta H°)}{dT} = C_p$

$$\therefore\ \frac{d(\Delta H°)}{dT} = b = 0.25 = C_p$$
$$C_p = 0.25\ \text{kJ K}^{-1}\ \text{mol}^{-1}$$

Thus, (b) is correct.

Since, $C_p - C_V = R$

$$\therefore\ C_V = (C_p - R)$$
$$= (0.25 - 8.314 \times 10^{-3})$$
$$= 0.24\ \text{kJ mol}^{-1}$$

Thus, (c) is incorrect.

$$\Delta H_T^\circ = \Delta E_T^\circ + \Delta n_g RT$$
$$\Delta H_{300}^\circ = \Delta E_T^\circ + \Delta n_g RT$$
$$5.5 = \Delta E_T^\circ + 1 \times 8.314 \times 10^{-3} \times 300$$
$$\Delta E_T^\circ = 3.0\ \text{kJ mol}^{-1}$$

Thus, (d) is correct.

Type IV. Pasage Based MCQs (Comprehension)

Passage 1

If C_8H_{18} is completely oxidised to CO_2 and H_2O at 298K

$$C_8H_{18}(g) + 12.5O_2 \longrightarrow 8CO_2 + 9H_2O(l)$$
$$\Delta_C H = -1302.7 = 8\Delta_f H°(CO_2) + 9\Delta_f H°(H_2O) - \Delta_f H°(C_8H_{18})$$
$$\Delta_f H°(C_8H_{18}) = -8 \times 94.0 - 9 \times 68 + 1302.7$$
$$\Delta_f H°(C_8H_{18}) = -61.3\ \text{kcal}$$

0.1 mol of C_8H_{18} having 8 carbon atoms will yield total of 0.8 mol of CO and CO_2.

If CO formed = x mol

then CO_2 formed = $(0.8 - x)$ mol

$$\underset{0.1}{C_8H_{18}} + O_2 \longrightarrow \underset{x}{CO} + \underset{(0.8-x)}{CO_2} + \underset{0.9}{9H_2O}$$
$$\Delta H = -90.2 = x(-26.0) + (0.8 - x)(-94) + (0.9)(-58.0) - 0.1(-61.3)$$
$$-90.2 = -26x + 94x + 0.8(-94) - 0.9 \times 58 + 6.13$$
$$68x = 31.07 \Rightarrow x = 0.457\ \text{mol}$$
$$\therefore\ CO = 0.457\ \text{mol}$$
$$CO_2 = (0.8 - 0.457) = 0.343\ \text{mol}$$
$$\therefore\ \text{Ratio} = \frac{0.457}{0.343} = 1.33$$

Work done $= -p\Delta V = p(V_2 - V_1)$

Initial moles of O_2 = 0.343 due to $CO_2 + \dfrac{0.457}{2}$ due to CO = 0.5715 mol

Final moles of gaseous products

= (0.8 mol CO and CO_2) + 0.9 mol H_2O

= 1.7 mol

$$\therefore\ V_1 = \frac{nRT}{p}$$
$$= \frac{0.5715 \times 0.0821 \times 298}{p}\text{L} = \left(\frac{13.98}{p}\right)\text{L}$$
$$V_2 = \frac{1.7 \times 0.0821 \times 573}{p} = \frac{79.97}{p}\text{L}$$
$$\therefore\ w = \left[\frac{79.97 - 13.98}{p}\right]p$$
$$= -65.99\ \text{L-atm} = -65.99 \times 4.18\ \text{J} = -275.83\ \text{J} \quad (\because 1\ \text{L-atm} = 4.18\ \text{J})$$

121. (a)

122. (d)

Passage 2

For 1 mol of H_2 from reactions I, II and III

$$\text{In I} = \frac{-483.6}{2} = -241.8\ \text{kJ}$$
$$\text{In II} = \frac{-886.2}{3} = -295.4\ \text{kJ}$$
$$\text{In III} = \frac{-347.3}{1} = -347.3\ \text{kJ (maximum)}$$

Total mass in I

= 2 moles H_2 + 1 mole

O_2 = 4 + 32 = 36 g

II = 3 moles H_2 + 1 mole

O_3 = 6 + 48 = 54 g

III = 1 mole H_2 + 1 mole

H_2O_2 = 2 + 34 = 36 g

Thus, heat generated per gram of total mass of reactants in I

$$= -\frac{483.6}{36} = -13.43\ \text{kJ}$$
$$\text{II} = \frac{-886.2}{54} = -16.41\ \text{kJ (maximum)}$$
$$\text{III} = -\frac{347.3}{36} = -9.65\ \text{kJ}$$

123. (c)

124. (b)

Passage 3

The 'calorie' used in nutrition is actually a kilocalorie,

$$2500\ \text{kcal} \times 4.184\ \text{kJ / kcal} = 10460\ \text{kJ day}^{-1}$$
$$4\ \text{JK}^{-1}\text{g}^{-1} = 4 \times 10^{-3}\ \text{kJ K}^{-1}\text{g}^{-1}$$

For 75 kg body,

$$m.s.\Delta T = 10460$$
$$75\ \text{kg} \times 10^3\ \text{g} \times 4 \times 10^{-3}\text{kJ g}^{-1} \times \Delta T = 10460\ \text{kJ day}^{-1}$$
$$\therefore\ \Delta T = 34.87\ \text{K}$$

Let mass of water required to maintain the body temperature $= m\ \text{g} \dfrac{m \times g}{18\text{g mol}^{-1}} 44\ \text{kJ mol}^{-1} = 10460\ \text{kJ}$

$$\therefore\ m = 4279\ \text{g} = 4.279\ \text{kg}$$

125. (b)

126. (d)

Passage 4

I. $\dfrac{1}{2}N_2(g) + \dfrac{1}{2}O_2(g) \longrightarrow NO,$ $\quad \Delta H = +90.25$ kJ

II. $NO(g) + \dfrac{1}{2}O_2(g) \longrightarrow NO_2,$ $\quad \Delta H = -57.07$ kJ

III. $\dfrac{1}{2}N_2(g) + O_2(g) \longrightarrow NO_2,$ $\quad \Delta H = +33.18$ kJ

(I + II ≡ III)

NO_2 is formed in (III) from its elements

Thus, $\Delta_f H°(NO_2) = +33.18\ \text{kJ mol}^{-1}$

NO is oxidised to NO_2 in II.

Thus, $\Delta_C H°(NO) = -57.07\ \text{kJ mol}^{-1}$

127. (a)

128. (b)

Passage 5

In experiments I and II reactants are in stoichiometric amounts, thus neutralisation takes place.

I. $\quad HCl = NaOH = \dfrac{25 \times 0.5}{1000}$ mol

$= 0.0125$ mol

II. $CH_3COOH = NaOH = \dfrac{25 \times 0.5}{1000}$ mol

$= 0.0125$ mol

Thus, in experiment I

ΔH for 0.0125 mol HCl or NaOH

$= -57.2 \times 0.0125 = 0.715$ kJ = 715 J

$\Delta T = 3.015$ K

50 mL solution = 50.0 g

$$C_p \text{ calorimeter} = \frac{\Delta H}{\Delta T} - mS$$

$$= \frac{715}{3.015} - 50 \times 4.1$$

$$= 32.15 \text{ JK}^{-1}$$

In experiment II

Solution = 50 mL = 50.0 g

$$\Delta H = [C_p(\text{calorimeter}) + mS]\Delta T$$

$$= [32.15 + 50 \times 4.1]\ 2.934$$

$$= 695.8 \text{ J}$$

$$\therefore\ Q \text{ (per mol of } CH_3COOH) = -\frac{695.85 \text{ J}}{0.0125 \text{ mol}}$$

$$= -55.7 \times 10^3 \text{ J mol}^{-1}$$

$$= -55.7 \text{ kJ mol}^{-1}$$

129. (a)

130. (b)

Passage 6

$$\frac{MV(\text{mL})}{1000} = \text{moles}$$

$$\therefore\ 100 \text{ mL of } 1.0 \text{ M HCl} = \frac{100 \times 1}{1000} = 0.1 \text{ mol}$$

$$\text{and } 100 \text{ mL of } 1.0 \text{ M NaOH} = 100 \times \frac{1}{1000}$$

$$= 0.1 \text{ mol}$$

HCl is completely neutralised by NaOH.

Thus, enthalpy decreases $= -57.0 \times 0.1 = -5.7$ kJ

For experiment I,

$\Delta T \times$ heat capacity = 5.7 kJ

$\therefore$ 5.7°C × heat capacity = 5.7 kJ

$$\text{Heat capacity} = \frac{5.7 \text{ kJ}}{5.7°\text{C}} = 1.0 \text{ kJ/°C}$$

In experiment II ,

$$CH_3COOH = 100 \times \frac{2}{1000} = 0.2 \text{ mol}$$

$$\text{NaOH} = \frac{100 \times 1}{1000} = 0.1 \text{ mol}$$

	CH_3COOH +	NaOH $\longrightarrow$	CH_3COONa +	H_2O
Initial (mol)	0.2	0.1	0	0
At equilib. (mol)	0.1	0	0.1	0.1

0.1 mol CH_3COOH is left unreacted and mixture of CH_3COOH and CH_3COONa is a buffer.

Enthalpy decrease for neutralisation of 0.1 mol CH_3COOH by 0.1 mol NaOH.

$= \Delta T \times$ heat capacity

$= -5.6°\text{C} \times 1 \text{ kJ / °C}$

$= -5.6$ kJ

Thus, enthalpy of dissociation of

$CH_3COOH = -5.6 - (-5.7)$

$= 0.1$ for 0.1 mol kJ

$= 1.0 \text{ kJ mol}^{-1}$

By Handerson equation for pH of basic buffer

$$\text{pH} = pK_a + \log\frac{[CH_3COONa]}{[CH_3COOH]}$$

$$= pK_a + \log\frac{0.1}{0.1}$$

$$= pK_a = -\log 2 \times 10^{-5} = 4.7$$

131. (a)

132. (b)

Type V. Numerical Skills

133. Eight (8) $\Delta T = 31.3 - 20.0 = 11.3°$

q(calorimeter)

$= [m_1c_1(\text{Cu}) + m_1c_2(H_2O)]\Delta T$

$= [0.092 \times 1500 + 1 \times 2000]11.3$

$= 24.159 \times 10^3$ cal

Heat value of carbon

$$= \frac{24.159 \times 10^3}{3}$$

$$= 8.05 \times 10^3 \approx 8 \times 10^3 \text{ cal g}^{-1}$$

Thus $y = 3$

134. Nine (9)

	$\Delta H°$
$Cl(g) \longrightarrow Cl^+(s) + e^-$	1257.5 kJ
$Cl(g) + e^- \longrightarrow Cl^-(g)$	−359.8 kJ
$2Cl(g) \longrightarrow Cl^+\ Cl^-$	$897.7 \text{ kJ mol}^{-1}$

Thus, for 0.01 mole (Cl^+Cl^-),

$\Delta H = 8.977\text{kJ} \approx 9.0$ kJ

135. Three (3)

ΔH to convert 50.0 kg of water at 10°C to $H_2O(g)$ at 100°C.

$\Delta H = \Delta H_1 + \Delta H_2$

ΔH_1 = Heat to convert 50.0 kg $H_2O(l)$ at 10° C to 50.0 kg $H_2O(l)$ at 100°C

$= m.s.\Delta T$

$= 50 \times 10^3 \times 1 \times 90$ cal

ΔH_2 = Heat to convert $H_2O(l)$ at 100° C to $H_2O(g)$ at 100° C

$= m.\Delta H_v = 50 \times 10^3 \times 540$ cal

$\therefore$ Total heat $= 50 \times 10^3[540 + 90]$ cal

$= 630 \times 50 \times 10^3$ cal

$= 630 \times 50$ kcal

$\Delta_C H°$ (ethane) = 390 kcal mol^{-1}

$= 390 \times 0.6$ kcal mol^{-1}

if efficiency is 60%

Thus, moles of ethane required

$$= \frac{630 \times 50 \text{ kcal}}{390 \times 0.6 \text{ kcal mol}^{-1}} = 134.6 \text{ mol}$$

Since, $pV = nRT$

$$\therefore\quad V = \frac{nRT}{p} \text{ (at STP)}$$

$$= \frac{134.6 \times 0.0821 \times 273}{1}$$

$$= 3017 \text{ L} = 3.017 \text{ m}^3 \approx 3.0\text{m}^3$$

■ (1 L = 1 dm^3) = 1000 cm^3

$$= \frac{1000}{10^6} \text{m}^3 = 1 \times 10^{-3} \text{ m}^3$$

136. Seven (7)

q = mass × heat capacity × ΔT

$= 1 \times 10^3 \text{ g} \times 1\text{cal g}^{-1}\text{ K}^{-1} \times 35 \text{ K}$

$= 35000$ cal = 35 kcal

Thus, heat value (in kcal g^{-1})

$$= \frac{35}{5} = 7 \text{ kcal g}^{-1}$$

137. Five (5)

By Dulong and Petit law,

Atomic weight × specific heat

$= 6 \text{ cal mol}^{-1}\text{K}^{-1}$

$\therefore$ Atomic weight of X

$$= \frac{6 \text{ cal mol}^{-1}\text{K}^{-1}}{0.050 \text{ cal g}^{-1}\text{K}^{-1}}$$

$$= 120 \text{ g mol}^{-1}$$

Chlorine present in 120 g of X

$= 120 \times 1.455 = 174.6$ g

$n \times 35.5 = 174.6$

Thus, chlorine in one mole X

$$= \frac{174.6}{35.5} = 5$$

Thus, $X = 5$

138. One (1)

I. $H^+(aq) + OH^-(aq) \longrightarrow H_2O(l)$,

$\Delta H° = -57.0 \text{ kJ mol}^{-1}$ (standard value)

$$\frac{M \times V(\text{mL})}{1000} = \text{mol}$$

$\therefore$ HCl = NaOH = 0.05 mol

Thus, enthalpy of neutralisation of 0.05 mol

HCl by 0.05 mol NaOH $= -57.0 \times 0.05$

$= -2.85$ kJ

Also, heat capacity × ΔT = 2.85

$$\text{Heat capacity} = \frac{2.85\text{kJ}}{\Delta T \text{ K}} = \frac{2.85}{2.85} = 1 \text{ kJ K}^{-1}$$

II. q = Heat capacity × ΔT

$= 1.0 \text{ kJ K}^{-1} \times 2.8 \text{ K} = 2.8$ kJ

Thus, heat of neutralisation of CH_3COOH by NaOH

$$= \frac{2.8 \text{ kJ}}{0.05 \text{ mol}} = 56.0 \text{ kJ mol}^{-1}$$

This is less than the standard value of heat of neutralisation of strong acid by strong base. Difference is used in the ionisation of weak acid.

Thus, enthalpy of ionisation of CH_3COOH (weak acid)

$= 57.0 - 56.0 = 1.0$ kJ mol^{-1}

139. Five (5)

$(-10 \times 3) + (-15 \times x) = -105$

$30 + 15x = 105 \Rightarrow x = 5$

140. Nine (9)

$C_p(\text{calorimeter}) = C_p(\text{content}) - C_p(H_2O)$

$= \left(\frac{\Delta H}{\Delta T}\right)_p - C_p$

$\Delta H = \text{A.t.}V = 1.25 \times 175 \times 3.26 \text{ A s V}$

$= 713.125 \text{ J } (\because 1 \text{ A s V} = 1 \text{ J})$

$C_p \text{ (content)} = \frac{137.5 \text{ g}}{18 \text{ g mol}^{-1}}$

$\times 75.291 \text{ JK}^{-1}\text{mol}^{-1}$

$= 575.14 \text{ JK}^{-1}$

$\therefore C_p \text{ (calorimeter)} = \left(\frac{\Delta H}{\Delta T}\right) - C_p (H_2O)$

$= \frac{713.125}{1.221 \text{ K}} - 575.14 \text{ JK}^{-1}$

$= 8.91 \approx 9.0 \text{ J K}^{-1}$

141. (3166)

Heat required to convert 50.0 kg of water at 10°C to steam at 100°C.

$= \Delta H_1 + \Delta H_2$

ΔH_1 = Heat required to convert 50 kg of $H_2O(l)$ at 10°C to $H_2O(l)$ at 100°C.

ΔH_2 = Heat required to convert 50 g $H_2O(l)$ at 100°C to 50 g $H_2O(g)$ at 100°C

$\therefore \Delta H = (50 \times 10^3 \text{ g}) \times 1 \text{ cal / g/°C} \times 90°\text{C}$

$+ 50 \times 10^3 \text{ g} \times 540 \text{ cal/g}$

$= 3.15 \times 10^7 \text{ cal} = 3.15 \times 10^4 \text{ kcal}$

Heat supplied by C_2H_6 = 368 kcal mol^{-1} if 100% efficient

$= 368 \times 0.6$ kcal mol^{-1} if 60% efficient

$= 220.8$ kcal mol^{-1}

Thus, C_2H_6 required for 3.15×10^4 kcal heat

$= \frac{3.15 \times 10^4}{220.8}$ mol

$= 142.663$ mol

At STP, 1 mol = 22.4 L

$\therefore$ 142.663 mol = 22.4×142.663

$= 3196$ L

142. (0012)

At STP, 22.4 L = 1 mol

$\therefore 200 \text{ L} = \frac{200}{22.4} = 8.93 \text{ mol}$

Heat due to 8.923 mol methane

$= 8.93 \times 211 \times 0.50$ kcal

(being 50% efficient) = 942.12 kcal

$q = m.C.\Delta T$

$\therefore \text{Mass} = \frac{q}{C \times \Delta T} = \frac{942.12 \text{ kcal}}{1 \times 78.33} = 12.0 \text{ kg}$

143. (31)

Total volume = 400 + 100 = 500 mL

Mass = 500 g

Heat change = $m.s.\Delta T$

$= 500 \times 4.2 \times 1.18$

$= 2.478 \times 10^3$ J

As $\frac{M \times V(\text{mL})}{1000}$

$\therefore CH_3COOH \text{ taken} = \frac{400 \times 0.2}{1000} = 0.08 \text{ mol}$

$\text{NaOH taken} = \frac{100 \times 0.8}{1000} = 0.08 \text{ mol}$

Thus, heat of neutralisation per mol is

$= \frac{2.478 \times 10^3}{0.08} \text{ J} = 30.975 \times 10^3 \text{ J} = 31 \text{ kJ}$

144. (17)

$1 \text{m}^3 C_2H_4 = 10^6 \text{cm}^3 = 10^3 \text{ L}$

As 22.4 L at STP = 1 mol

$\therefore 10^3 \text{ L at STP} = \frac{1000}{22.4} = 44.6428 \text{ mol}$

Heat due to 44.6428 mol C_2H_4 with 70% efficiency

$= 337.3 \times 44.6428 \times 0.7$

$= 10540.6$ kcal

$\underset{\text{at 20° C}}{H_2O(l)} \longrightarrow \underset{\text{at 100°C}}{H_2O(l)}, \ \Delta H_1 = m.s.\Delta T$

$= 1 \times 1 \times 80$

$= 80 \text{ kcal kg}^{-1}$

$\underset{\text{at 100° C}}{H_2O(l)} \longrightarrow \underset{\text{at 100° C}}{H_2O(g)}, \quad \Delta H_2 = m\,L$

$= 1 \times 540 \text{ kcal kg}^{-1}$

Total heat = 620 kcal kg^{-1}

Thus, kg of water that can be converted into steam

$= \frac{10540.6 \text{ kcal}}{620 \text{ kcal kg}^{-1}} = 17.00 \text{ kg}$

145. (770)

$q \text{ (acid)} = -q \text{ (calorimeter)}$

at constant volume $\times \Delta T$

$= -2422 \times 3.258$

$= -7890.876$ cal

Benzoic acid (C_7H_6O, 122 g mol^{-1})

$= (1.250 / 122)$ mol

$\therefore \Delta E \text{ (combustion)} = \frac{-7890.876 \text{ cal}}{(1.250/122) \text{ mol}}$

$= 770000$ cal mol^{-1}

$= 770$ kcal mol^{-1}

146. (1453)

The heat capacity of the product gases

$= C_p (H_2O) + C_p (H)$

$= 33.587 + 20.784$

$= 54.371 \text{ J K}^{-1}\text{mol}^{-1}$

$\Delta H = C_p \int_{T_1}^{T_2} dT = C_p \Delta T$

$\therefore \Delta T = \frac{\Delta H}{C_p} = \frac{62.8 \times 10^3 \text{ J mol}^{-1}}{54.371 \text{ J K}^{-1}\text{mol}^{-1}}$

$= 1155$ K

$\therefore$ Temperature of the product

$= 1155 + 298 \text{ K} = 1453$ K

147. (–326400)

$C_2H_5OH(l) + 3O_2(g) \longrightarrow 2CO_2(g) + 3H_2O(l)$

$\Delta n_g = 2 - 3 = -1$

$\Delta H = \Delta U + \Delta n_g RT$

$-327 = \Delta U - 1 \times 2 \times 10^{-3} \times 300$

$\therefore \Delta U = -327 + 0.6$

$= -326.4 \text{ kcal} = -326400 \text{ cal}$

148. (0.69)

$C + O_2 \longrightarrow CO_2, \quad \Delta_C H° = -94.0 \text{ kcal mol}^{-1}$

1 kg carbon = 1000 g carbon

$= \frac{1000}{12}$ mol carbon

$\therefore \Delta_C H_1^{\circ}$ (of 1 kg carbon)

$= \frac{1000}{12} (-94)$ kcal

$C + H_2O \longrightarrow CO + H_2$

CO from 1 kg carbon $= \frac{1000}{12}$ mol

H_2 from 1 kg carbon $= \frac{1000}{12}$ mol

$\therefore \Delta_C H° \text{ (CO) due to } \frac{1000}{12}$ mol carbon

$= \frac{1000}{12} (-68)$ kcal

$\Delta_C H° (H_2) \text{ due to } \frac{1000}{12}$ mol carbon

$= \frac{1000}{12} (-68)$ kcal

ΔH_2° = total ΔH of water gas

$= \frac{2000}{12} (-68)$ kcal

$\therefore \frac{\Delta H_1^{\circ}}{\Delta H_2} = \frac{-94}{-136} = 0.69$

149. Ten (10)

Heat generated in the calorimeter = $C.\Delta T$

$= 1260 \times 0.667 = 840.42$ cal

$\Delta_C H° (CH_4) = -210.8$ kcal

$\therefore$ Moles of CH_4 used

$$= \frac{840.42 \text{ cal}}{210.8 \times 10^3 \text{cal mol}^{-1}}$$

$$= 3.986 \times 10^{-3}$$

Total moles taken $n = \frac{pV}{RT} = \frac{\left(\frac{740}{760}\right)(1)}{0.0821 \times 298}$

$= 0.398$ mol

Mole percentage of CH_4

$$= \frac{3.986 \times 10^{-3}}{0.0398} \times 100 = 10.0\%$$

150. (90.85)

$n(C_2H_2) = 1 \text{ kg} = \frac{1000}{26}$ mol

ΔH due to $\frac{1000}{26}$ mol of C_2H_2

$$= 98.8 \times \frac{1000}{26} \text{ kJ} = -3800 \text{ kJ}$$

If water needed m g $\left(= \frac{m}{18} \text{mol}\right)$ then

$$\Delta H = m.C.\ \Delta T = \frac{m}{18} \times 75.291 \times 10 \text{ J}$$

$$\frac{m}{18} \times 75.291 \times 10 = 3800 \times 10^3$$

$$\therefore m = \frac{3800 \times 10^3 \times 18}{75.291 \times 10} = 90.847 \times 10^3 \text{ g}$$

$= 90.847 \text{ kg} \approx 90.85$ kg

151. (–192.5)

$\Delta_f H°(C_2H_6) = \Delta H°(C_2H_6)$

$C(\text{graphite}) + O_2(g) \longrightarrow CO_2(g),$

$\Delta_C H° = -286 \text{ kJ mol}^{-1}$

$H°(CO_2) = -286 \text{ kJ mol}^{-1}$

$H_2(g) + \frac{1}{2} O_2(g) \longrightarrow H_2O(l),$

$\Delta_C H° = -393.5 \text{ kJ mol}^{-1}$

$\therefore \quad H°(H_2O) = -393.5 \text{ kJ mol}^{-1}$

$C_2H_6(g) + O_2 g) \longrightarrow 2CO_2(g) + 3H_2O(l)$

$\Delta_C H° = -1560 \text{ kJ mol}^{-1}$

$\therefore \Delta_C H°(C_2H_2) = [2H°_{CO_2} + 3H°_{H_2O}] - [H°_{C_2H_6} + H°_{O_2}]$

$-1560 = 2 \times (-286) + 3 \times (-393.5) - [H°_{C_2H_6} + 0]$

$\therefore \quad H°_{C_2H_6} = -572 - 1180.5 + 1560$

$= -$ **192.5 kJ mol^{-1}**

152. (43.53)

$C_6H_{12}O_6(aq) + 6O_2(g) \longrightarrow 6CO_2(g) + 6H_2O(l)$

$\therefore \Delta_c H°(C_6H_{12}O_6) = 6\Delta_f H°(CO_2) + 6\Delta_f H°(H_2O) - \Delta_f H°(C_6H_{12}O_6)$

$$= -2820 \text{ kJ mol}^{-1} = -\frac{2820}{180} \text{kJ g}^{-1}$$

Thus, $\Delta_c H°$ (glucose) for 10 g

$$= \frac{-2820}{180} \times 10 = -156.7 \text{ kJ per hour}$$

$$= -\frac{156.7 \times 10^3}{3600} \text{ Js}^{-1}$$

$= 43.53 \text{ Js}^{-1} = -43.53$ W

153. (12.4)

$\frac{MV(\text{mL})}{1000} = $ mol = equation (for HCl)

HCl = 150 mL of 0.4 N

$$= \frac{150 \times 0.4}{1000} \text{ equivalent}$$

$= 0.06$ equivalent

$Q =$ Heat capacity $\times \Delta T$

$= 315 \text{ cal K}^{-1} \times 2.36$

$= 743.4$ cal

$$\therefore \Delta H^{\circ}_{\text{neutralisation}} = \frac{-743.4 \text{ cal}}{0.06 \text{ equiv}}$$

$= 12390 \text{ cal equiv}^{-1}$

$= 12.39 \text{ kcal equiv}^{-1}$

≈ 12.40

154. (2241)

ΔT_1 (benzoic acid) $= 2.28$ K

ΔT_2 (ethyl ethanoate) $= 1.95$ K

Benzoic acid $= \frac{0.875}{122}$ mol

Heat capacity of the calorimeter (C) $\times \Delta T = \Delta_C U$ for benzoic acid for

$\frac{0.875}{122}$ mol benzoic acid $C \times \Delta T_1$

$$= \frac{3251}{122} \times 0.875 \text{ kJ}$$

For $\left(\frac{0.783}{88}\right)$ mol ethyl ethanoate

$$C \times \Delta T_2 = \Delta_C U \times \frac{0.783}{88}$$

$$\frac{\Delta T_2}{\Delta T_1} = \Delta_C U \times \frac{0.783}{88} \times \frac{122}{3251 \times 0.875}$$

$$\frac{1.95}{2.28} = \frac{\Delta_C U \times 0.783 \times 122}{88 \times 3251 \times 0.875}$$

$\therefore \quad \Delta_C U = 2241.2 \text{ kJ mol}^{-1}$

155. (15018)

$H_2(g) + \frac{1}{2} O_2(g) \longrightarrow H_2O(g)$

$\Delta_r H°$ (for 1 mole H_2O) $= -58.0$ kcal

In a closed system, V is constant

thus, $q = \Delta E$

$\Delta H = \Delta E + \Delta n_g RT$

$-58.0 = \Delta E + (-0.5) \times 2 \times 10^{-3} \times 298$

$\therefore \quad \Delta E = -57.702$ kcal

$C_p - C_V = R$

$\therefore \quad C_V = C_p - R = 5.92 - 2.0$

$= 3.92 \text{ cal mol}^{-1} \text{ K}^{-1}$

$\therefore \quad q = n.C_V.\Delta T$

$57.702 \times 10^3 = 1 \times 3.92 \times \Delta T$

$$\therefore \quad \Delta T = \frac{57.702 \times 10^3}{3.92} \text{K} = 14720 \text{ K}$$

Final temperature = 14720 + 289 K

= 15018 K

Type VI. Matrix Matching

156. (c)

(i) If products of reaction (I), (CO, H_2) are used as fuel, then

$CO(g) + \frac{1}{2} O_2 \longrightarrow CO_2,$

$\Delta H° = -283.0$ kJ

$H_2(g) + \frac{1}{2} O_2 \longrightarrow H_2O,$

$\Delta H° = -285.83$ kJ

Total = –568.83 kJ

Thus, (i) - (r)

(ii) If products of reactions (I) and (II) are used as fuel, then CO is oxidiser. Only H_2 is left as fuel.

Total moles of $H_2 = 2$

$\therefore \Delta_c H°(H_2) = 2(-285.83)$

$= -571.46$ kJ

Thus, (ii)-(p)

(iii) $CO(g)$ and $H_2(g)$ in 1 : 3 mole ratio are the products of reaction (III)

$\therefore \quad \Delta H = -283.0 + 3(-285.83)$

$= -1140.5$ kJ

Thus, (iii)-(s)

(iv) If CH_4 is used as fuel then, $\Delta H° = -890.4$ kJ

Thus, (iv)-(q)

157. (b) (i)

Reaction	Oxidising agent	$\Delta H°$ per grams of oxidising agent (kJ)
A	O_2	$-\frac{483.6}{32} = -15.11$
B	O_3	$\frac{-868.2}{48} = -18.09$ (max)
C	H_2O_2	$\frac{-347.3}{34} = -10.21$
D	O_2	$\frac{-568.8}{32} = -17.78$

Thus, (i)-(p)

(ii)

Reaction	Reducing agent	$\Delta H°$ per mole of H_2 (kJ)
A	2 moles H_2	–241.8
B	3 moles H_2	–289.4
C	1 moles H_2	–347.3 (max)
D	1 mole H_2 and 1 mole CO	–284.4

Thus, (ii)-(r)

(iii)

Reaction	Total mass of reactants	ΔH° per gram of total mass (kJ)
A	36 g	$\frac{-483.6}{36} = -13.4$
B	54 g	$\frac{-868.2}{54} = -16.1$
C	36 g	$-\frac{347.3}{36} = -9.64$
D	62 g	$\frac{-568.8}{62} = -9.17$

Thus, (iii)-(s)

(iv) Minimum energy released per mol of oxidising agent is in (C)

Thus, (iv)-(q)

158. (c) $\Delta H_{system} = \Delta H_{sol} + \Delta H_{calorimeter} + \Delta H_{reaction} = 0$

$\therefore \Delta H_{reaction} = -(\Delta H_{sol} + \Delta H_{calorimeter})$

$\Delta H_{sol} = m.s.\Delta T$

$= (200 \text{ mL} \times 1) \times 4.184 \times 2.4$

$= 2008.32$

$= 2.008 \text{ kJ}$

$\Delta H_{calorimeter} = C \times \Delta T$

$= 335 \times 2.40 = 804 \text{ J}$

$= 0.804 \text{ kJ}$

$\therefore \Delta H_{reaction} = -(2.008 + 0.809)$

$= -2.812 \text{ kJ}$

$\text{NaOH} = \text{HCl} = \frac{100 \times 0.5}{1000} = 0.05 \text{ mol}$

$\therefore \Delta H_{neutralisation} = \frac{-2.812 \text{ kJ}}{0.05 \text{ mol}}$

$= -56.24 \text{ kJ mol}^{-1}$

Thus, (i)-(r)

(ii)-(s)

(iii)-(p)

(iv)-(q)

159. (d) (i) $\Delta H_1 = \Delta_f H^\circ(H_2O, l)$

$= -285.83 \text{ kJ}$

Thus, (i)-(q)

(ii) ΔH_2 = enthalpy change to convert 1 mol $H_2O(l)$ at 298 K to $H_2O(g)$ at 373 K

$= n.C_p.\Delta T$

$= 1 \times 75.291 \times 10^{-3} \times 75$

$= 5.647 \text{ kJ}$

Thus, (ii)-(r)

(iii) $\Delta H_3 = \Delta_{vap} H^\circ$ of $H_2O(l)$ at 373 K $\longrightarrow$ $H_2O(g)$ at 373 K

$= 40.883 \text{ kJ mol}^{-1}$

Thus, (iii)-(s)

(iv) ΔH_4 = enthalpy change for conversion of 1 mol $H_2O(g)$ at 373 K to 1 mol H_2O (l) at 298 K (being exothermic, $\Delta H^\circ < 0$)

$= -n.C_p(H_2O, g).\Delta T$

$= -1 \times 33.577 \times 75$

$= -2518 \text{ J}$

$= -2.518 \text{ kJ}$

Thus, (iv)-(t)

$\Delta H = \text{kJ mol}^{-1}$

(v) $H_2(g) + \frac{1}{2}O_2(g) \rightarrow H_2O(l) \quad -285.83$

$H_2O(l) \longrightarrow H_2O(g) \quad +40.883$

$H_2(g) + \frac{1}{2}O_2(g) \longrightarrow H_2O(g)$

$\therefore \Delta_f H(H_2O, g) = -244.95 \text{ kJ mol}^{-1}$

Thus, (v)-(p)

160. (b)

Chemical Equilibrium

Chapter Topics

- State of Equilibrium
- Types of Equilibria
- Relation between Vapour Density and Degree of Dissociation
- Le-Chatelier's Principle
- Thermodynamics of Chemical Equilibrium

State of Equilibrium

When a reaction takes place in a closed vessel under given conditions, a stage is reached when there is no change in the concentration of the reactants and products. This represents **a reaction in equilibrium**.

This state of equilibrium is not **static** but **dynamic** in nature, as **reaction does not stop actually** but proceed in both the directions with equal rate.

Physical equilibrium

Process	Property that becomes constant at equilibrium
I. Solid $\rightleftharpoons$ liquid e.g. Ice $\rightleftharpoons H_2O(l)$	Melting point or freezing point at constant pressure.
II. Liquid $\rightleftharpoons$ vapour e.g. $H_2O(l) \rightleftharpoons H_2O(g)$	Vapour pressure (pressure of vapours above liquid) at constant temperature. A point where vapour pressure is equal to atmospheric pressure is called boiling point.
III. Solute $(s) + H_2O(l) \rightleftharpoons$ solution	Solubility (or concentration) of the solid solute at constant temperature.
IV. Gas $(g) + H_2O(l) \rightleftharpoons$ gas (aq)	Solubility of the gas at constant pressure and temperature.

Chemical equilibrium

Like physical process, equilibrium in a chemical process occurs when opposing processes takes place in a chemical reaction. Such reactions are called **reversible reactions**.

$$P + Q \underset{\text{backward}}{\overset{\text{forward}}{\rightleftharpoons}} R + S$$

At the start of reaction, reactants undergo reaction to form products. After formation of the products, backward reaction also starts. With time, rate of forward reaction decreases and that of backward reaction increases and at a time both rates become equal i.e.

$$\left(\frac{dx}{dt}\right)_{\text{forward}} = \left(\frac{dx}{dt}\right)_{\text{backward}}$$

This represents **dynamic equilibrium.**

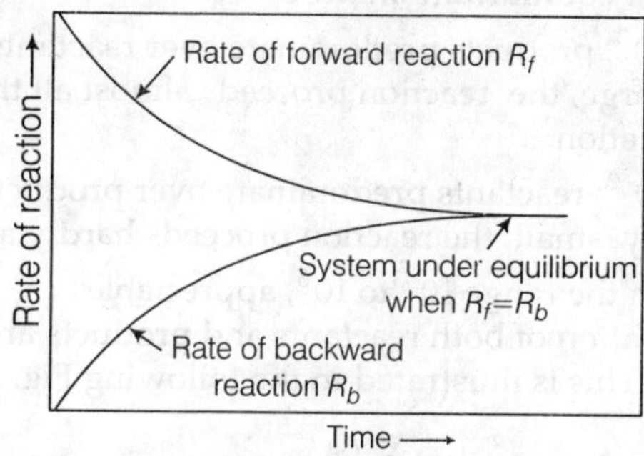

When system attains equilibrium, concentration of the reactants (P, Q) and that of the products (R, S), no longer changes.

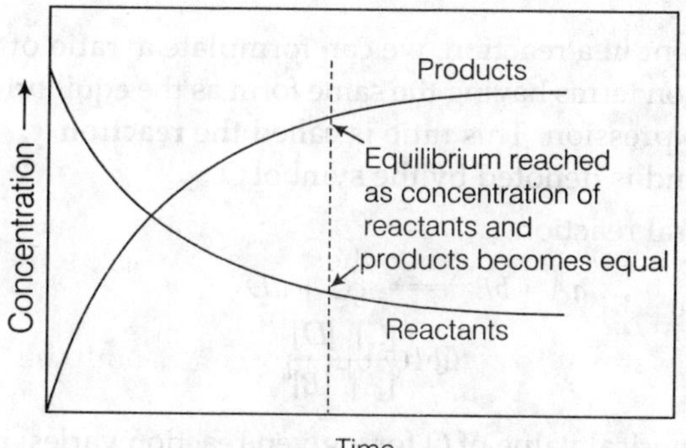

Thus,
$$\left(\frac{dx}{dt}\right)_f = \left(\frac{dx}{dt}\right)_b$$

$$-\frac{d[\text{reactant}]}{dt} = \frac{d[\text{product}]}{dt}$$

Negative sign indicates that concentration of the reactants decreases with time.

Dynamic nature of chemical equilibrium

The equilibrium state is a dynamic balance between the forward and the backward reaction. For the reaction,

$$N_2 + 3H_2 \rightleftharpoons 2NH_3$$

a dynamic equilibrium is attained when the rate of formation of NH_3 (in the forward side) is equal to the rate of formation of N_2 and H_2 in the backward side.

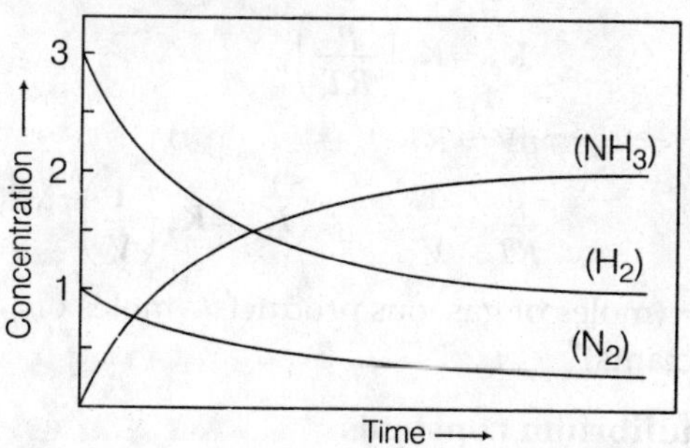

Law of mass action and equilibrium constant (Guldberg and Waage-1864)

The rate at which a substance reacts is proportional to its active mass and the rate of a chemical reaction is proportional to the product of the active masses of the reacting substances.

Active mass (or activity) $= \frac{\text{moles}}{\text{litre}}$ or molar concentration.

In a reversible reaction,

$$aA + bB \rightleftharpoons cC + dD$$

For the forward reaction,

$$\frac{-d[A]}{dt} \propto [A]^a \text{ and } \frac{-d[B]}{dt} \propto [B]^b$$

$$\text{Rate}\left(\frac{dx}{dt}\right)_f = k_f [A]^a [B]^b$$

where, k_f is the rate constant of forward reaction.

Similarly, for the backward reaction

$$\left(\frac{dx}{dt}\right)_b = k_b [C]^c [D]^d$$

k_b is the rate constant of backward reaction

$$\left(\frac{dx}{dt}\right)_{\text{net}} = \left(\frac{dx}{dt}\right)_f - \left(\frac{dx}{dt}\right)_b = k_f [A]^a [B]^b - k_b [C][D]^d$$

At dynamic equilibrium,

$$\left(\frac{dx}{dt}\right)_f = \left(\frac{dx}{dt}\right)_b \Rightarrow K_c = \frac{k_f}{k_b} = \frac{[C]^c[D]^d}{[A]^a[B]^b}$$

K_c is called equilibrium constant and this equation represents **law of chemical equilibrium.**

In terms of partial pressure, equilibrium constant is K_p.

$$K_p = \frac{p_C^c \, p_D^d}{p_A^a \, p_B^b}$$

In terms of mole fraction, equilibrium constant is K_χ.

$$K_\chi = \frac{\chi_C^c \, \chi_D^d}{\chi_A^a \, \chi_B^b}$$

K_c, K_p or K_χ varies with temperature.

Relation between K_p, K_c and K_χ

$$K_p = K_c\,(RT)^{\Delta n_g} \Rightarrow K_p = K_\chi (p)^{\Delta n_g}$$

$$K_c = K_\chi \left(\frac{p}{RT}\right)^{\Delta n_g}$$

Since, $\quad pV = RT$

$\therefore \quad \frac{p}{RT} = \frac{1}{V} \qquad \therefore\; K_c = K_\chi \left(\frac{1}{V}\right)^{\Delta n_g}$

where, Δn_g = (moles of gaseous products – moles of gaseous reactants)

Units of equilibrium constants

Δn_g	K_p	K_c	K_χ	Example
0	Unitless	Unitless	Unitless	$N_2 + O_2 \rightleftharpoons 2NO$
+1	bar	mol L^{-1}	Unitless	$PCl_5 \rightleftharpoons PCl_3 + Cl_2$
–1	bar^{-1}	L mol^{-1}	Unitless	$2NO_2 \rightleftharpoons N_2O_4$
+2	bar^2	$mol^2\,L^{-2}$	Unitless	$2NH_3 \rightleftharpoons N_2 + 3H_2$

- The standard state for a pure gas is 1 bar and partial pressure with respect to standard state is measured by dividing the given pressure by 1 bar. Thus, a pressure of 2 bar with respect to standard state is 2 bar/1 bar = 2 which is thus a dimensionless quantity.
- Molar concentration of pure substance in standard state is 1 M (1 mol L^{-1}) and thus 2 M solution with respect to standard state is 2 which is again a dimensionless quantity.
- K_p and K_C are dimensionless quantities but have different numerical values due to different standard states.

Characteristics of equilibrium constant

- If you reverse a reaction, equilibrium constant is also reversed.

$$A + B \rightleftharpoons C + D, \qquad \text{if } K_C = K$$

then $\quad C + D \rightleftharpoons A + B; \qquad K_C' = \frac{1}{K}$

- If you multiply each of the coefficients by a factor m, the new equilibrium constant is raised to the same factor.

$$A + B \rightleftharpoons C + D, \qquad \text{if } K_C = K$$

Then, $\quad mA + mB \rightleftharpoons mC + mD, \qquad K_C' = K^m$

- Similarly, for the division by a factor m

$$K_C' = (K)^{1/m}$$

- If you add two or three consecutive reactions, equilibrium constant is obtained by multiplying the equilibrium constants of the stepwise reactions.

$$A \rightleftharpoons B \qquad K = K_1$$

$$B \rightleftharpoons C \qquad K = K_2$$

$$C \rightleftharpoons D \qquad K = K_3$$

Then for $\quad A \rightleftharpoons D \qquad K = K_1K_2K_3$

- Similarly for substraction

$$A \rightleftharpoons B \qquad K = K_1$$

$$A \rightleftharpoons C \qquad K = K_2$$

Then for $\quad B \rightleftharpoons C \qquad K = \frac{K_2}{K_1}$

Judging the extent and direction of reactions

We can make the following generalisations concerning the composition of equilibrium mixture.

(i) If $K_C > 10^3$, products predominate over reactants. If K_C is very large, the reaction proceeds almost all the way to completion.

(ii) If $K_C < 10^{-3}$, reactants predominate over products. If K_C is very small, the reaction proceeds hardly at all.

(iii) If K_C is in the range 10^{-3} to 10^3, appreciable concentration of both reactants and products are present. This is illustrated in the following Fig.

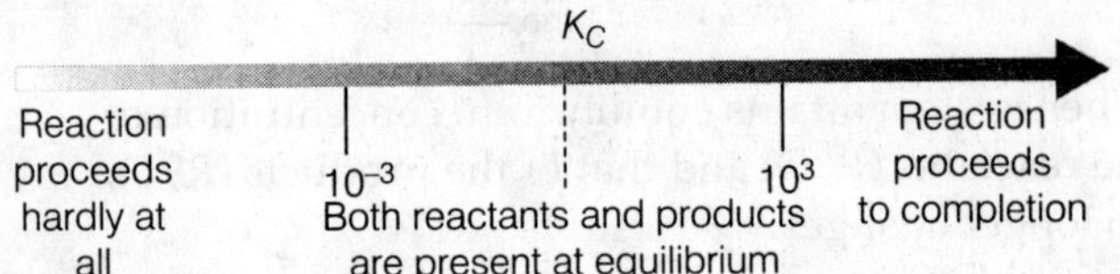

At each point in a reaction, we can formulate a ratio of concentration terms having the same form as the equilibrium constant expression. This ratio is called the **reaction quotient** and is denoted by the symbol Q.

For a general reaction,

$$aA + bB \rightleftharpoons cC + dD$$

$$Q = \frac{[C]^c\,[D]^d}{[A]^a\,[B]^b}$$

- The numerical value of Q for a given reaction varies; it depends on the concentration of products and reactants present at the time when Q is determined.
- At the very start when the reactants are mixed, there is no product. Thus, at this instant $Q = 0$.
- As the reaction proceeds, the value of Q increases as the concentration of the products increases and the concentration of the reactants simultaneously decreases.
- When the reaction reaches equilibrium, the value of the reaction quotient no longer changes because the concentration no longer changes.
- Reaction quotient has the same value at all points after equilibrium is attained. This constant value is called **equilibrium constant.**

$$Q = K_C = \frac{[C]^c\,[D]^d}{[A]^a\,[B]^b}$$

where molar concentrations represent equilibrium constant.

- The reaction quotient Q_C is useful in predicting the direction of reaction by comparing its value with K_C. Thus, we can make following generalisation regarding the direction of reaction.

Reactants ⟶ Products

Equilibrium

Reactants ⟵ Products

- To predict the direction of any chemical reaction, we simply calculate the value of Q (reaction quotient) from the given values of molar concentration and compare the value of Q and K.
  (i) If $Q < K$, the reaction goes from left to right.
  (ii) If $Q > K$, the reaction goes from right to left.
  (iii) If $Q = K$, the reaction mixture is already in equilibrium, and no net reaction occurs.

Solved Examples & Instant Practice

Example 7.1) For the following reaction in equilibrium, $N_2O_4(g) \rightleftharpoons 2NO_2$, $K_C = 0.25$ mol L^{-1} at 300K. If rate constant of forward reaction is 1.25×10^{-2} s^{-1}, what is rate constant of the backward reaction?

Sol. When equilibrium is attained,

$$\left(\frac{dx}{dt}\right)_f = \left(\frac{dx}{dt}\right)_b$$

Equilibrium constant $(K_C) = \dfrac{K_f}{K_C}$ $\quad\therefore\ K_b = \dfrac{K_f}{K_C}$

Rate constant of backward reaction

$$= \frac{\text{Rate constant of forward reaction}}{\text{Equilibrium constant}}$$

$$K_b = \frac{1.25 \times 10^{-2}\ \text{s}^{-1}}{0.25\ \text{mol L}^{-1}} = 5 \times 10^{-2}\ \text{L mol}^{-1}\text{s}^{-1}$$

Immediate Test 1

For the reaction,

$$A \longrightarrow B + C$$

$$\text{rate} = \left(\frac{dx}{dt}\right)_f = k[A]$$

If rate is 0.05 mol L^{-1}h^{-1}at $[A] = 0.120$ mol L^{-1}and $K_C = 0.5$ mol L^{-1}, what is rate constant of backward reaction?

Example 7.2) In the following gaseous phase, equilibrium in 2 L flask at 300 K,

$$2SO_3(g) \rightleftharpoons 2SO_2(g) + O_2(g), \quad K_C = 1.0 \times 10^{-6}$$

moles of SO_2 and SO_3 are equal. Calculate the number of moles of O_2 at equilibrium.

Moles of SO_2 and SO_3 are equal.
Thus, $n_{SO_2} = n_{SO_3}$

$$\therefore \quad [SO_2] = [SO_3] = \frac{n}{2}\ \text{mol L}^{-1}$$

Thus, number of moles of O_2 can be calculated.

Sol. $K_C = \dfrac{[SO_2]^2\,[O_2]}{[SO_3]^2} = 1.0 \times 10^{-6}$

Let, $SO_2 = SO_3 = n$ mol

and $O_2 = x$ mol

Then, $\dfrac{\left(\frac{n}{2}\right)^2 \left(\frac{x}{2}\right)}{\left(\frac{n}{2}\right)^2} = 1.0 \times 10^{-6}$

$\therefore \quad x = 2.0 \times 10^{-6}$ mol

Immediate Test 2

PCl_5 dissociates into PCl_3 and Cl_2 in a 2 L flask at 800 K. At equilibrium, mixture is found to contain 1 mole of PCl_5 and 2 moles each of PCl_3 and Cl_2. Calculate equilibrium constants of forward and backward reaction.

Example 7.3) Equilibrium mixture of the following reaction,

$$N_2O_4 \rightleftharpoons 2NO_2$$

contains 0.5 mole of N_2O_4 and 1.5 mole of NO_2 in 5 L flask at 5 bar and 300 K. Calculate

(i) K_p, K_C and K_χ

(ii) K_C for $NO_2 \rightleftharpoons \frac{1}{2}N_2O_4$

$$K_p = \frac{\textit{partial pressure of products}}{\textit{partial pressure of reactants}}$$

$$p_i = p\left(\frac{n_i}{n_{\text{total}}}\right) = p\chi_i$$

$$K_C = \frac{[\textit{Product}]}{[\textit{Reactant}]}$$

$K_\chi = \dfrac{\chi_{\text{product}}}{\chi_{\text{reactant}}}$ *(Concentrations are in mole fraction)*

Sol. At equilibrium total moles of NO_2 and N_2O_4 $= 1.5 + 0.5 = 2.0$

	$N_2O_4 \rightleftharpoons$	$2NO_2$
Mole fraction	$\frac{0.5}{2.0} = 0.25$	$\frac{1.5}{2.0} = 0.75$
Partial pressure	(0.25×5) bar	(0.75×5) bar
Active mass	$\frac{0.5}{5} = 0.1$M	$\frac{1.5}{5} = 0.3$M

(i) $K_p = \frac{p^2_{NO_2}}{p_{N_2O_4}} = \frac{(0.75 \times 5)^2}{(0.25 \times 5)} = 11 \cdot 25$

$K_C = \frac{[NO_2]^2}{[N_2O_4]} = \frac{(0.3)^2}{0.1} = 0.9$

$K_\chi = \frac{\chi^2_{NO_2}}{\chi_{N_2O_4}} = \frac{(0.75)^2}{0.25} = 2.25$

(ii) $2NO_2 \rightleftharpoons N_2O_4$ $\quad K'_C = \frac{1}{K_C}$

$NO_2 \rightleftharpoons \frac{1}{2}N_2O_4$ $\quad K''_C = \sqrt{K'_C} = \sqrt{\frac{1}{K_C}} = \sqrt{\frac{1}{0.9}} = 1.05$

Immediate Test 3

For the equilibrium,

$2NOCl(g) \rightleftharpoons 2NO(g) + Cl_2(g)$, $K_c = 3.75 \times 10^{-6}$ at 1069 K.

Calculate the value of K_p at this temperature. ***[NCERT]***

Example 7.4) Calculate the equilibrium constant for the reaction.

I. $CO(g) + H_2O(g) \rightleftharpoons CO_2(g) + H_2(g)$

if the equilibrium constant for reactions are:

II. $2CO(g) + O_2(g) \rightleftharpoons 2CO_2(g)$, $K = 4.0 \times 10^{-2}$

III. $2H_2(g) + O_2(g) \rightleftharpoons 2H_2O(g)$, $K = 0.36$

If reactions are added, net equilibrium constant $= K_1 K_2 \ldots\ldots K_n$

If net reaction is obtained by subtraction

$$K = \frac{K_1}{K_2}$$

and if divided by n, then $K = \left(\frac{K_1}{K_2}\right)^{1/n}$

For this case,

$\frac{1}{2}(\text{II} - \text{III}) = I$

Thus, $K_{\text{I}} = \sqrt{\frac{K_{\text{II}}}{K_{\text{III}}}}$

Sol. Subtract III from II then

$2CO(g) + 2H_2(g) \rightleftharpoons 2CO_2(g) + 2H_2O(g)$

$\therefore \quad K = K_{\text{II}} / K_{\text{III}} = \frac{4.0 \times 10^{-2}}{0.36}$

Thus, to get reaction (I) divide the above equation by 2

$CO(g) + H_2O(g) \rightleftharpoons CO_2(g) + H_2(g)$

$\therefore \quad K_{\text{I}} = \sqrt{\frac{4 \times 10^{-2}}{0.36}} = 0.33$

Immediate Test 4

(i) If equilibrium constant for $CH_3COOH + H_2O \rightleftharpoons CH_3COO^- + H_3O^+$ is 1.8×10^{-5}, calculate equilibrium constant for

$CH_3COOH + OH^- \rightleftharpoons CH_3COO^- + H_2O$

Also given,

$2H_2O \rightleftharpoons H_3O^+ + OH^-$, $K = 1.0 \times 10^{-14}$

(ii) Calculate equilibrium constant for $NH_3 + H_2O \rightleftharpoons NH_4^+ + OH^-$, if equilibrium constants for $NH_4OH + H^+ \rightleftharpoons NH_4^+ + H_2O$ and $H_2O \rightleftharpoons H^+ + OH^-$ are respectively 1.8×10^9 and 1.0×10^{-14}.

Example 7.5) For the equilibrium, $2SO_2(g) + O_2(g) \rightleftharpoons 2SO_3(g)$, calculate the temperature at which $K_p = K_C$, under a pressure of 1 bar.

$K_p = K_C\,(RT)^{\Delta n_g}$

If, $K_p = K_C \Rightarrow (RT)^{\Delta n_g} = 1$

Thus, T is calculated.

Sol. $K_p = K_C\,(RT)^{\Delta n_g} \Rightarrow \Delta n_g = -1$

$\therefore \quad K_p = K_C (RT)^{-1} \Rightarrow K_p = \frac{K_C}{RT}$

If, $\quad K_p = K_C \Rightarrow (RT) = 1$

$T = \frac{1}{R} = \frac{1}{0.0831} = 12.03$ K

Immediate Test 5

Calculate the temperature at which

(a) $K_p = K_C$ under a pressure of 1 bar.

(b) $K_p = K_\chi$, for the gaseous phase equilibrium taking place in 10 L flask.

$N_2 + 3H_2 \rightleftharpoons 2NH_3$

Example 7.6) A mixture of 4.2 moles of N_2, 2.0 moles of H_2 and 10.0 moles of NH_3 is introduced into 20.0 L reaction vessel at 500 K.

$N_2(g) + 3H_2(g) \rightleftharpoons 2NH_3(g)$, $K_C = 1.7 \times 10^2$

(i) Is the reaction mixture in equilibrium?

(ii) If not, what is the direction of the reaction?

Let, $Q =$ *reaction quotient based on given quantity.*

$= \frac{[NH_3]^2}{[N_2][H_2]^3}$

If,

(i) $Q = K_C$, *system is in equilibrium.*

(ii) $Q < K_C$, *system shifts in the direction, so that [product] increases, [reactant] decreases till* $Q = K_C$ *i.e. reaction moves in the forward direction.*

(iii) $Q > K_C$, *system shifts in backward side, till* $Q = K_C$

Sol.

(i) $[N_2]=\left(\frac{4.2\text{ mol}}{20\text{ L}}\right)=0.21\text{ M}$

$[H_2]=\left(\frac{2.0}{20}\right)=0.10\text{ M} \Rightarrow [NH_3]=\left(\frac{10.0}{20}\right)=0.50\text{ M}$

$\therefore \quad Q=\frac{[NH_3]^2}{[N_2][H_2]^3}=\frac{(0.50)^2}{(0.21)(0.10)^3}=1.19\times 10^3$

$K_C=1.7\times 10^2$

Thus, $Q>K_C$, hence reaction mixture is not in equilibrium.

(ii) To make $Q=K_C$, reaction moves in the backward side.

Immediate Test 6

(i) For the following reaction,

$$PCl_5 \rightleftharpoons PCl_3+Cl_2, K_C=0.2$$

if 0.4 mole of PCl_5, 0.2 mole of PCl_3 and 0.6 mole of Cl_2 are taken in 1 L flask, predict the direction in which reaction proceeds.

(ii) For the equilibrium,

$$A+2B \rightleftharpoons 2C, \; K_C=8.4\times 10^{-2}$$

if 1.0 mole of A, 2.0 moles of B and 3.0 moles of C are placed in a 1.02 L vessel, predict the direction of the equilibrium.

KNOWLEDGE CONFIRMATION **Test 1**

1 Consider the reaction,

$$2SO_2(g)+O_2(g) \rightleftharpoons 2SO_3(g)$$

The equilibrium K_p is related to K_C by

(a) $K_p=K_C$ (b) $K_c=K_C(RT)$ (c) $K_C=K_p(RT)$ (d) $K_p=K_C(RT)^2$

2 K_p is expressed in the unit of bar for the equilibrium

(a) $2NO_2(g) \rightleftharpoons N_2O_4(g)$

(b) $PCl_5(g) \rightleftharpoons PCl_3(g)+Cl_2(g)$

(c) $N_2(g)+3H_2(g) \rightleftharpoons 2NH_3(g)$

(d) $H_2(g)+Br_2(g) \rightleftharpoons 2HBr(g)$

3 PCl_5 dissociates into PCl_3 and Cl_2 in a 2 L flask at 800 K. At equilibrium mixture is found to contain 1 mole PCl_5 and 2 moles each of PCl_3 and Cl_2. Thus, K_C and K_χ are respectively,

(a) 2, 0.8 (b) 0.8, 2 (c) 0.8, 0.8 (d) 2, 2

4 Water-gas 'shift' reaction is

$$CO(g)+H_2O(g) \rightleftharpoons CO_2(g)+H_2(g)$$

At 473 K, $p_{CO_2}=0.2$ bar, $p_{H_2O}=0.01$ bar,

$p_{H_2}=0.1$ bar, $p_{CO}=2.0$ bar

Thus, K_C is

(a) 2 (b) 1 (c) 4 (d) 0.2

5 H_2 is produced industrially by the steam hydrocarbon reforming process as given by

$$H_2O(g)+CH_4(g) \rightleftharpoons CO(g)+3H_2(g)$$

If, $K_C=3.8\times 10^{-3}$ at 1000 K, then K_p is

$(R=0.0831\text{ L bar mol}^{-1}\text{ K}^{-1})$

(a) 3.8×10^{-3} (b) 2.63×10^2 (c) 26.24 (d) 3.9×10^{-2}

6 If for the equilibria,

$C_6H_5COOH(aq) \rightleftharpoons C_6H_5COO^-(aq)+H^+(aq)$, $K_1=2\times 10^{-5}$

$H_2O(l) \rightleftharpoons H^+(aq)+OH^-(aq)$, $K_2=1\times 10^{-14}$

$C_6H_5COO^-(aq)+H_2O(l) \rightleftharpoons C_6H_5COOH(aq)+OH^-(aq)$, $K_3=?$

thus, K_3 is

(a) 5.0×10^{-10} (b) 5.0×10^5

(c) 2.0×10^{-9} (d) 2.0×10^9

7 $2A+3B \rightleftharpoons nC$, $K_C=1.2\times 10^{-2}\text{ L mol}^{-1}$. Thus, n is equal to

(a) 2 (b) 3 (c) 4 (d) 1

8 0.01 M each of A, B, C and D are present in the following equilibria at 300 K.

I. $A+B \rightleftharpoons C+D$ II. $A+2B \rightleftharpoons C+D$

III. $2A+B \rightleftharpoons 2C+D$ IV. $A+B \rightleftharpoons C+2D$

Extent of reaction is in order,

(a) I < II < III = IV (b) I > II > III = IV

(c) IV > III = I > II (d) IV < III = I < II

9 For a reaction, $2NO+O_2 \rightleftharpoons 2NO_2$

$$\left(\frac{dx}{dt}\right)_1=2.6\times 10^3[NO]^2[O_2] \Rightarrow \left(\frac{dx}{dt}\right)_2=4.10[NO_2]^2$$

Thus, equilibrium constant of

$$NO+\frac{1}{2}O_2 \rightleftharpoons NO_2 \text{ is}$$

(a) 25.18 (b) 6.34×10^2 (c) 1.58×10^{-3} (d) 3.97×10^{-2}

10 Equilibrium constants for

$$2CO+O_2 \rightleftharpoons 2CO_2, K=4.0\times 10^{-2}$$

$$2H_2+O_2 \rightleftharpoons 2H_2O, K=3.6\times 10^{-1}$$

Thus, for the equilibrium

$$CO+H_2O \rightleftharpoons CO_2+H_2, K \text{ is}$$

(a) 0.111 (b) 0.333 (c) 9.0 (d) 3.00

11 Following equilibrium is set up in 5 L flask at 300 K

$$N_2+3H_2 \rightleftharpoons 2NH_3$$

If, $K_p=0.4\text{ bar}^{-2}$, then K_χ (in terms of mole fraction) is

$(RT=24.93)$

(a) 9.92 (b) 0.10 (c) 98.41 (d) 0.01

12 Equilibrium constant of $Hg_2Cl_2(s)$ in terms of active mass is
(a) $[Hg^+]^2[Cl^-]^2$ (b) $[Hg_2^{2+}][Cl^-]^2$
(c) $[Hg^{2+}][Cl^-]^2$ (d) $[Hg^{2+}][Cl^-]$

13 For the following reversible reaction

$$A + B \rightleftharpoons C + D$$

$$\left(\frac{dx}{dt}\right)_{net} = 1\times10^{-5}\,[A][B] - 1\times10^{-7}\,[C][D]$$

Thus, equilibrium constant is
(a) 0.01 (b) 100 (c) 1×10^{-12} (d) 1×10^{12}

14 For the following gaseous phase reaction
$PCl_5 \rightleftharpoons PCl_3 + Cl_2$, K_p is found to be equal to K_χ.
This is attained when pressure is :
(a) 1 atm (b) 0.5 atm
(c) 2 atm (d) 4 atm

15 For the reaction in equilibrium

$$A \rightleftharpoons B$$

$$\frac{[B]}{[A]} = 4.0\times10^8, \frac{-d[A]}{dt} = 2.3\times10^6\ s^{-1}\,[A], \frac{-d[B]}{dt} = K[B]$$

Thus, K is
(a) $1.1\times10^{-15}\ s^{-1}$ (b) $5.8\times10^{-3}\ s^{-1}$
(c) $9.2\times10^{14}\ s^{-1}$ (d) $1.74\times10^2\ s^{-1}$

16 Following gaseous phase reaction is taking place at 400 K in a 5 L flask.

$$N_2 + 3H_2 \rightleftharpoons 2NH_3$$

For this
(a) $K_C = K_\chi$ (b) $K_C = 25K_\chi$ (c) $K_\chi = 25K_C$ (d) $K_C = 5K_\chi$

17 For the following reaction,

$$H_2(g) + I_2 \underset{K_b}{\overset{K_f}{\rightleftharpoons}} 2HI(g), K_C = 57 \text{ at } 700\text{ K}$$

Thus,
(a) rate constant K_f for the formation of HI is smaller than that of rate constant K_b for the dissociation of HI.
(b) $K_f > K_b$
(c) Addition of catalyst increases value of K_C
(d) Addition of catalyst decreases value of K_C

18 For which of the following reactions will the equilibrium mixture contains an appreciable concentration of both reactants and products ?
(a) $Cl_2(g) \rightleftharpoons 2Cl(g)$, $K_C = 6.4\times10^{-39}$
(b) $Cl_2(g) + 2NO(g) \rightleftharpoons 2NOCl(g)$, $K_C = 3.7\times10^8$
(c) $Cl_2 + 2NO_2(g) \rightleftharpoons 2NO_2Cl(g)$, $K_C = 1.8$
(d) All of the above

19 The position of the equilibrium for a system when $K_C = 4.6\times10^{-15}$ can be described as being favoured to ...(X)..., concentration of the products is relatively ...(Y)....
Blanks (X) and (Y) are
(a) the right, larger (b) the left, small
(c) the left, larger (d) the right, small

20 For the following equilibria

$$M + L \rightleftharpoons ML, K_1 = \beta_1$$
$$ML + L \rightleftharpoons ML_2, K_2 = \beta_2$$
$$ML_2 + L \rightleftharpoons ML_3, K_3 = \beta_3$$

then for the formation of ML_3 from M and L, K_4 is
(a) $K_4 = \beta_1 + \beta_2 + \beta_3$ (b) $\frac{1}{K_4} = \frac{1}{\beta_1} + \frac{1}{\beta_2} + \frac{1}{\beta_3}$
(c) $\log K_4 = \log\beta_1 + \log\beta_2 + \log\beta_3$ (d) $pK_4 = \log\beta_1 + \log\beta_2 + \log\beta_3$

21 For the following equilibrium at 400 K

$$CaCO_3(s) \rightleftharpoons CaO(s) + CO_2(g)$$

K_C is found to be 4×10^{-3} mol dm^{-3} thus, K_p is
(a) 4×10^{-3} bar (b) 7.52 bar (c) 1×10^{-2} bar (d) 0.133 bar

22 For the decomposition of NH_3 into N_2 and H_2 at 800 K
$2NH_3(g) \rightleftharpoons N_2(g) + 3H_2(g)$, K_p is 7.0×10^{-2} when pressures as in the unit of bar. Thus, K_C is
(a) 1.6×10^{-5} (b) 1.6×10^5 (c) 6.3×10^3 (d) 2.0×10^{-4}

23 For the reaction,
$N_2(g) + 3H_2(g) \rightleftharpoons 2NH_3(g)$, $K_p = 41$ bar^{-2} at 400 K
Arrange the values of K_p for the following equilibrium in increasing order :
I. $2NH_3(g) \rightleftharpoons N_2(g) + 3H_2(g)$, K_1
II. $\frac{1}{2}N_2(g) + \frac{3}{2}H_2(g) \rightleftharpoons NH_3(g)$, K_2
III. $2N_2(g) + 6H_2(g) \rightleftharpoons 4NH_3(g)$, K_3
(a) $K_1 < K_2 < K_3$ (b) $K_1 = K_2 = K_3$ (c) $K_1 < K_3 < K_2$ (d) $K_3 < K_2 < K_1$

24 For the equilibrium, $2CO(g) + O_2(g) \rightleftharpoons 2CO_2(g)$ the ratio of K_p/K_c is
(a) $(RT)^{-2}$ (b) $(RT)^{-1}$ (c) $(RT)^2$ (d) (RT)

25 For the above equilibria relation between K_p, K_c and K_x is
(a) $K_p = K_c(RT)^{-1} = K_x(V)$ (b) $K_p(RT) = K_c = K_x(RT)^2/p$
(c) Both of these (d) None of these

26 Consider the following reversible chemical reactions,

$$A_2(g) + B_2(g) \overset{K_1}{\rightleftharpoons} 2AB(g),$$
$$6AB(g) \overset{K_2}{\rightleftharpoons} 3A_2(g) + 3B_2(g)$$

[JEE Main 2019 (I) NTA]

The relation between K_1 and K_2 is
(a) $K_2 = K_1^3$ (b) $K_1K_2 = 3$ (c) $K_2 = K_1^{-3}$ (d) $K_1K_2 = 1/3$

27 In which one of the following equilibria, $K_p \neq K_c$? **[JEE Main 2019 (II) NTA]**
(a) $2C(s) + O_2(g) \rightleftharpoons 2CO(g)$
(b) $2HI(g) \rightleftharpoons H_2(g) + I_2(g)$
(c) $NO_2(g) + SO_2(g) \rightleftharpoons NO(g) + SO_3(g)$
(d) $2NO(g) \rightleftharpoons N_2(g) + O_2(g)$

28 The values of K_p/K_c for the following reactions at 300 K are respectively. (At 300 K, $RT = 24.62$ dm^3 atm mol^{-1})
I. $N_2(g) + O_2(g) \rightleftharpoons 2NO(g)$
II. $N_2O_4(g) \rightleftharpoons 2NO(g)$

III. $N_2(g) + 3H_2(g) \rightleftharpoons 2NH_3(g)$ **[JEE Main 2019 (I) NTA]**

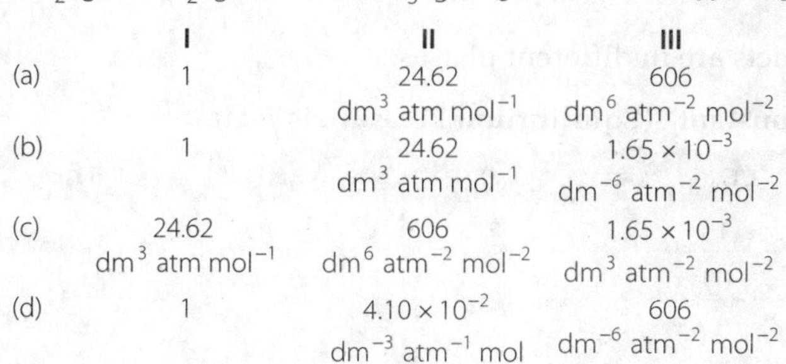

	I	II	III
(a)	1	24.62 $dm^3\ atm\ mol^{-1}$	606 $dm^6\ atm^{-2}\ mol^{-2}$
(b)	1	24.62 $dm^3\ atm\ mol^{-1}$	1.65×10^{-3} $dm^{-6}\ atm^{-2}\ mol^{-2}$
(c)	24.62 $dm^3\ atm\ mol^{-1}$	606 $dm^6\ atm^{-2}\ mol^{-2}$	1.65×10^{-3} $dm^3\ atm^{-2}\ mol^{-2}$
(d)	1	4.10×10^{-2} $dm^{-3}\ atm^{-1}\ mol$	606 $dm^{-6}\ atm^{-2}\ mol^{-2}$

29 For the equilibrium, $A \rightleftharpoons B$, the variation of the rate of the forward (*a*) and reverse (*b*) reaction with time is given by **[JEE Main 2020 (II) NTA]**

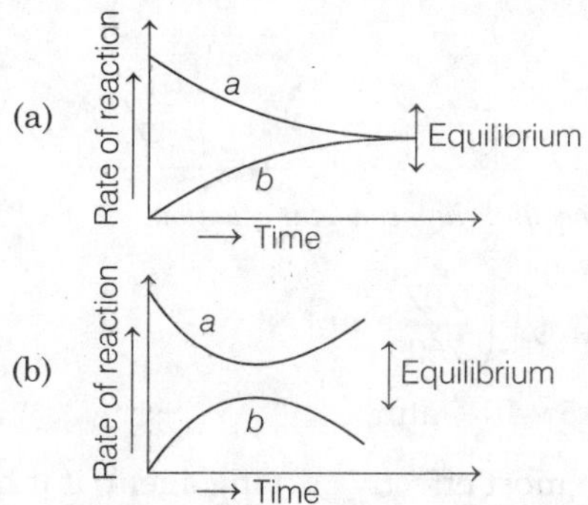

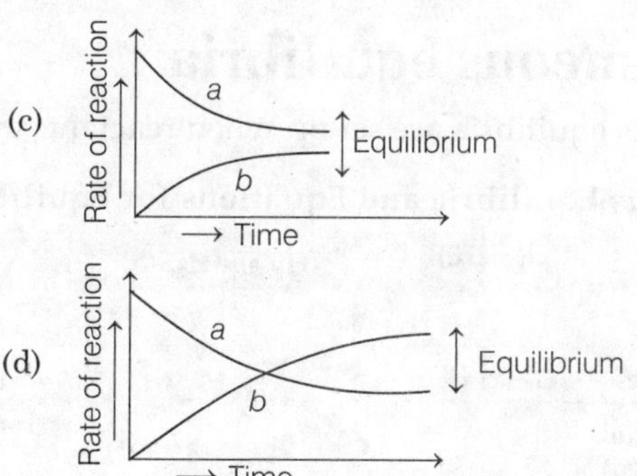

30 If the equilibrium constant for $A \rightleftharpoons B + C$ is $K_{eq}^{(1)}$ and that of $B + C \rightleftharpoons P$ is $K_{eq}^{(2)}$, the equilibrium constant for $A \rightleftharpoons P$ is **[JEE Main 2020 (II) NTA]**

(a) $K_{eq}^{(1)}/K_{eq}^{2}$ (b) $K_{eq}^{(1)} + K_{eq}^{(2)}$ (c) $K_{eq}^{(1)} K_{eq}^{(2)}$ (d) $K_{eq}^{(2)} - K_{eq}^{(1)}$

31 The value of K_C is 64 at 800 K for the reaction,

$$N_2(g) + 3H_2(g) \rightleftharpoons 2NH_3(g)$$

The value of K_C for the following reaction is

$$NH_3(g) \rightleftharpoons \frac{1}{2}N_2(g) + \frac{3}{2}H_2(g)$$

[JEE Main 2020 (II) NTA]

(a) $\frac{1}{64}$ (b) 8 (c) $\frac{1}{4}$ (d) $\frac{1}{8}$

Types of Equilibria

Homogeneous equilibria

Homogeneous equilibria are set up when reactants and products are in same phases.

Homogeneous Equilibria and Equations for Equilibrium Constant (Equilibrium Pressure is *p* atm in a *V* Litre Flask)

	$H_2(g) + I_2(g) \rightleftharpoons 2HI(g)$			$N_2(g)$ +	$3H_2(g) \rightleftharpoons 2NH_3(g)$		$PCl_5(g) \rightleftharpoons PCl_3(g) + Cl_2(g)$		
Initial moles	a	b	0	1	3	0	1	0	0
Equilibrium moles	$(a-x)$	$(b-x)$	$2x$	$(1-x)$	$(3-3x)$	$2x$	$(1-x)$	x	x
Total moles at equilibrium		$(a+b)$			$(4-2x)$			$(1+x)$	
Active masses (mol L^{-1})	$\left(\frac{a-x}{V}\right)$	$\left(\frac{b-x}{V}\right)$	$\left(\frac{2x}{V}\right)$	$\left(\frac{1-x}{V}\right)$	$3\left(\frac{1-x}{V}\right)$	$\left(\frac{2x}{V}\right)$	$\left(\frac{1-x}{V}\right)$	$\left(\frac{x}{V}\right)$	$\left(\frac{x}{V}\right)$
Mole fraction	$\left(\frac{a-x}{a+b}\right)$	$\left(\frac{b-x}{a+b}\right)$	$\left(\frac{2x}{a+b}\right)$	$\frac{1-x}{2(2-x)}$	$\frac{3}{2}\left(\frac{1-x}{2-x}\right)$	$\frac{x}{(2-x)}$	$\left(\frac{1-x}{1+x}\right)$	$\left(\frac{x}{1+x}\right)$	$\left(\frac{x}{1+x}\right)$
Partial pressure	$p\left(\frac{a-x}{a+b}\right)$	$p\left(\frac{b-x}{a+b}\right)$	$p\left(\frac{2x}{a+b}\right)$	$p\left(\frac{1-x}{2(2-x)}\right)$	$p\left(\frac{3(1-x)}{2(2-x)}\right)$	$\frac{px}{(2-x)}$	$p\left(\frac{1-x}{1+x}\right)$	$p\left(\frac{x}{1+x}\right)$	$p\left(\frac{x}{1+x}\right)$
K_C		$\frac{4x^2}{(a-x)(b-x)}$			$\frac{4x^2V^2}{27(1-x)^4}$			$\frac{x^2}{(1-x)V}$	
K_p		$\frac{4x^2}{(a-x)(b-x)}$			$\frac{16x^2(2-x)^2}{27(1-x)^4 p^2}$			$\frac{px^2}{(1-x^2)}$	

■ For $N_2O_4(g) \rightleftharpoons 2NO_2(g)$, $K_C = \frac{4x^2}{(1-x)V}$, $K_p = \frac{4px^2}{(1-x^2)}$

Heterogeneous equilibria

Heterogeneous equilibria are set up when reactants and products are in different phases.

Heterogeneous Equilibria and Equations for Equilibrium Constant* (Equilibrium Pressure is p atm)

	$NH_4HS(s) \rightleftharpoons$	$NH_3(g)+$	$H_2S(g)$	$C(s)$ +	$CO_2(g) \rightleftharpoons$	$2CO(g)$	$NH_2CO_2NH_4(s) \rightleftharpoons$	$2NH_3(g)+$	$CO_2(g)$
Initial moles	1	0	0	1	1	0	1	0	0
Equilibrium moles	$(1-x)$	x	x	$(1-x)$	$(1-x)$	$2x$	$(1-x)$	$2x$	x
Total moles at equil. (solid not included)		$2x$			$(1+x)$			$3x$	
Mole fraction		$\frac{x}{2x}=\frac{1}{2},$	$\frac{1}{2}$		$\left(\frac{1-x}{1+x}\right)$	$\left(\frac{2x}{1+x}\right)$		$\frac{2}{3}$	$\frac{1}{3}$
Partial pressure		$\frac{p}{2}$	$\frac{p}{2}$		$p\left(\frac{1-x}{1+x}\right)$	$p\left(\frac{2x}{1+x}\right)$		$\frac{2p}{3}$	$\frac{p}{3}$
K_p		$\frac{p^2}{4}$			$\frac{4px^2}{(1-x^2)}$			$\frac{4p^3}{27}$	

Concentration terms (active mass or partial pressure) of pure solid and pure liquid are not written in equilibrium constant equation.

As a general rule, as stated earlier also,the concentration of pure solids and pure liquids are not included when writing an equilibrium equation.

Thus, $MgCO_3(s) \rightleftharpoons MgO(s) + CO_2(g)$

$$K_C = [CO_2], \; K_p = p_{CO_2}$$

$MgCO_3(s)$ and $MgO(s)$ being pure solids, their active masses and partial pressures are not included in equilibrium equation relating K_p or K_c.

Similarly, for the equilibrium

$$Fe_2O_3(s) + 3CO(g) \rightleftharpoons 3CO_2(g) + 2Fe(l)$$

$$K_C = \frac{[CO_2]^3}{[CO]^3} \Rightarrow K_p = \frac{p^3_{CO_2}}{p^3_{CO}}$$

Dew point and relative humidity

- The moisture content of a gas is often expressed in terms of the **dew point** which is the temperature to which a gas must be cooled before it becomes saturated with water vapours.
- At this temperature, water or ice (depending on the temperature) will be deposited on a solid surface. Dew point of H_2O is 43°C at which vapour pressure of ice formed is 0.07 Torr.

$$CaCl_2 \cdot 2H_2O(s) \rightleftharpoons CaCl_2(s) + 2H_2O(g)$$

- $CaCl_2(s)$ has its desiccating properties (water absorbing properties) due to the formation of $CaCl_2 \cdot 2H_2O(s)$

$$K_p = p^2_{H_2O} = \left(\frac{0.07}{760}\text{atm}\right)^2$$

$$= 8.5 \times 10^{-9} \text{ atm}^2$$

- A substance is the most effective drying agent, if it has the lowest vapour pressure of water in equilibrium with it.
- A hydrated salt will lose water (a property called **efflorescent**) below vapour pressure of water at that temperature.

$$Na_2SO_4 \cdot 10H_2O(s) \rightleftharpoons Na_2SO_4(s) + 10H_2O(g)$$

At 0°C, $K_p = 4.08 \times 10^{-25}$, $K_p = p^{10}_{H_2O}$

$$p_{H_2O} = (4.08 \times 10^{-25})^{1/10}$$

$$= 3.64 \times 10^{-3} \text{atm}$$

$$= 2.77 \text{ Torr}$$

Hence, $Na_2SO_4 \cdot 10H_2O$ will efflorescence at a vapour pressure below 3.64×10^{-3}atm at 0°C, or below relative humidity of 60.5%.

Vapour pressure of H_2O at 0°C is 4.58 Torr.

$$\text{Relative humidity} = \frac{\text{partial pressure of } H_2O}{\text{vapour pressure of } H_2O} \times 100$$

An anhydrous salt (Na_2SO_4) will absorb water above relative humidity 60.5%.

Solved Examples & Instant Practice

Example 7.7) One mole each of PCl_5, PCl_3 and Cl_2 are taken in 1 L flask at 400 K. When equilibrium is attained, molar concentration of Cl_2 is found to be 1.5 M. Calculate equilibrium constant K_p and K_C for

$$PCl_5(g) \rightleftharpoons PCl_3(g) + Cl_2(g)$$

From the moles of Cl_2 (initial and final), degree of dissociation can be calculated. Thus, K_C hence K_p is calculated.

$$K_p = K_C(RT)^{\Delta n_g} \Rightarrow \Delta n_g = 1$$

Sol.

	$PCl_5(g)$	$\rightleftharpoons$	$PCl_3(g)$	+	$Cl_2(g)$
Initial mole	1		1		1
At equilibrium	$(1-x)$		$(1+x)$		$(1+x)$

Given, $\dfrac{(1+x)}{V} = 1.5\text{ M} \quad (V = 1\text{ L})$

$(1+x) = 1.5\text{ mol} \Rightarrow x = (0.5)\text{ mol}$

$\therefore \quad [PCl_5] = \left(\dfrac{1-x}{1}\right) = 0.5\text{ M} \Rightarrow [Cl_2] = [PCl_3] = \left(\dfrac{1+x}{1}\right) = 1.5\text{ M}$

$\therefore K_C = \dfrac{[PCl_3][Cl_2]}{[PCl_5]} = \dfrac{1.5 \times 1.5}{0.5} = 4.5$

$K_p = K_C(RT)^{\Delta n_g} = K_C(RT) = 4.5\,(0.0821 \times 400) = 147.78$

Example 7.8) A weak monoprotic acid (HA) is ionised 5% in 0.1 M aqueous solution. What is equilibrium constant for its ionisation?

$$HA(aq) + H_2O(l) \rightleftharpoons H_3O^+(aq) + A^-(aq)$$

Sol. $H_2O(l)$ is taken as pure liquid, hence its active mass = 1 mol L^{-1}, and is not taken in expression for K_C or K_p.

	$HA(aq) + H_2O(l)$	$\rightleftharpoons$	$H_3O^+(aq)$	+	$A^-(aq)$
Initial	0.1 M		0		0
Change	$-\left(0.1 \times \dfrac{5}{100}\right)$		$+\left(\dfrac{0.1 \times 5}{100}\right)$		$+\left(\dfrac{0.1 \times 5}{100}\right)$
At equilibrium	$(0.1 - 5 \times 10^{-3})$ = 0.095 M		5×10^{-3} M		5×10^{-3} M

$\therefore \quad K_C = \dfrac{[H_3O^+][A^-]}{[HA]} = \dfrac{(5 \times 10^{-3})^2}{0.095} = 2.63 \times 10^{-4}$

■ K_C is also the ionisation constant of weak acid.

Immediate Test 7

(i) Determine the value of the equilibrium constant for the reaction

$$A + B \rightleftharpoons 2C$$

if 1.0 mole of A, 1.4 mole of B and 0.50 mole of C are placed in a 1.0 L vessel and allowed to come to equilibrium. The final concentration of C is 0.75 mol L^{-1}.

(ii) At a certain temperature, 1.0 mole of $PCl_3(g)$ and 2.0 mole of $Cl_2(g)$ were placed in a 3.00 L flask. When equilibrium was established, only 0.70 mole of PCl_3 remained. Calculate equilibrium constant of

$$PCl_5(g) \rightleftharpoons PCl_3(g) + Cl_2(g)$$

Example 7.9) Calculate the equilibrium concentration of T after 1.0 mole of G, 2.0 moles of J and 0.50 mole of D are put into a 1.0 L vessel and allowed to come to equilibrium.

$$2G + J \rightleftharpoons D + 2T, K = 1.5 \times 10^{-3}$$

From the given molar concentration and equilibrium constant, molar concentration at equilibrium can be calculated by taking approximation.

Sol.

	$2G$	+	J	$\rightleftharpoons$	D	+	$2T$
Initial mole	1.0		2.0		0.5		
At equilibrium	$(1-2x) \approx 1$		$(2-x) \approx 2$		$(0.5+x) \approx 0.5$		$2x$

$\therefore \quad K_C = 1.5 \times 10^{-3}$

$\therefore \quad K_C = \dfrac{[D][T]^2}{[G]^2[J]}$

$1.5 \times 10^{-3} = \dfrac{(0.5)(2x)^2}{1 \times 2}$

$\therefore \quad x^2 = 1.5 \times 10^{-3} \Rightarrow x = 0.039$

$\therefore \quad 2x = 0.078\text{ mol} \quad \therefore \quad [T] = 0.078\text{ mol L}^{-1} = 0.078\text{ M}$

Immediate Test 8

Exactly 1 mole each of H_2 and I_2 are heated in a 30 L evacuated chamber to 470°C.

$$H_2(g) + I_2(g) \rightleftharpoons 2HI(g),\ K_C = 50$$

(i) How many moles of I_2 remains unreacted when equilibrium is established?

(ii) Total pressure in the chamber.

(iii) Partial pressures of each species.

Example 7.10) 1 mole each of I_2 and H_2 react in 1 L flask to form HI. Equilibrium mixture required 100 mL of 1 M $Na_2S_2O_3$ to completely react with unreacted I_2. Calculate equilibrium constant K_C for

$$H_2 + I_2 \rightleftharpoons 2HI$$

I_2 can oxidise $Na_2S_2O_3$ to $Na_2S_4O_6$ thus unreacted I_2 is known.

$$H_2 + I_2 \rightleftharpoons 2HI$$
$$2Na_2S_2O_3 + I_2 \longrightarrow 2NaI + Na_2S_4O_6$$

Moles of $Na_2S_2O_3 = \dfrac{\text{molarity} \times \text{volume}}{1000}$

$\therefore \quad$ *Moles of* $I_2 = \left(\dfrac{\text{moles of } Na_2S_2O_3}{2}\right)$

Thus, equilibrium molar concentration of H_2, I_2 and HI are known.

Sol.

	H_2	+	I_2	$\rightleftharpoons$	$2HI$
Initial mol	1		1		0
At equilibrium	$(1-x)$		$(1-x)$		$2x$

$Na_2S_2O_3$ used $= \dfrac{100 \times 1}{1000} = 0.1\text{ mol}$

$\therefore \quad I_2$ unreacted $= \dfrac{0.1}{2} = 0.05 = (1-x)\text{ mol} \quad \therefore \quad x = 0.95\text{ mol}$

$\therefore \quad [H_2] = (1 - x) = 0.05 \text{ mol L}^{-1}$

$[I_2] = (1 - x) = 0.05 \text{ mol L}^{-1}$

$[HI] = 2x = 0.95 \times 2 = 1.9 \text{ mol L}^{-1}$

$$\therefore \quad K_C = \frac{[HI]^2}{[H_2][I_2]} = \frac{(1.9)^2}{(0.05)(0.05)} = 1.444 \times 10^3$$

Immediate Test 9

Following equilibrium is studied by taking 1 mole of N_2 and 3 moles of H_2 in 1L flask at 300 K.

$$N_2(g) + 3H_2(g) \rightleftharpoons 2NH_3(g)$$

NH_3 formed at equilibrium is neutralised by 100 mL of 1 M HCl. Calculate equilibrium constant K_C.

Example 7.11) Determine the value of the equilibrium constant for the reaction

$$A + 2B \rightleftharpoons 2C$$

if 1.0 mole of A, 2.0 moles of B and 3.0 moles of C are placed in 1.0 L vessel and allowed to come to equilibrium. The final concentration of C is 1.4 mol L^{-1}.

Sol. $[C]_{\text{initial}} = \frac{3.0}{1} = 3 \text{ mol L}^{-1}$

$[C]_{\text{final}} = 1.4 \text{ mol L}^{-1}$

Thus, reaction takes place reversely.

	$2C$	$\rightleftharpoons$ A	+ $2B$
Initial mole	3	1	2
Change	$-2x$	$+x$	$+2x$
At equilibrium	$(3-2x)$	$(1+x)$	$2(1+x)$
Active mass (mol L^{-1})	$(3-2x)$	$(1+x)$	$2(1+x)$

Given, $(3 - 2x) = 1.4 \text{ mol L}^{-1}$

Thus, x is known

$$K_C = \frac{[A][B]^2}{[C]^2} = \frac{(1+x)[2(1+x)]^2}{(3-2x)^2} = \frac{4(1+x)^3}{(3-2x)^2}$$

$(3 - 2x) = 1.4 \text{ mol L}^{-1}$ (given)

$$\therefore \quad x = \frac{3 - 1.4}{2} = 0.8 \text{ mol L}^{-1}$$

$$\therefore \quad K_C = \frac{4(1.8)^3}{(1.4)^2} = 11.902$$

$\therefore \ K'_C$ for $A + 2B \rightleftharpoons 2C$

$$= \frac{1}{K_C} = \frac{1}{11.902} = 8.4 \times 10^{-2}$$

Immediate Test 10

1 mole each of N_2, H_2 and NH_3 are placed at 300 K in a 5 L flask. At equilibrium, partial pressure of NH_3 was found to be 2.493 bar. Calculate equilibrium constant K_C.

$$N_2 + 3H_2 \rightleftharpoons 2NH_3$$

Example 7.12) If we start with 60 g of CH_3COOH and 46 g C_2H_5OH in presence of dil. HCl, 49 g of $CH_3COOC_2H_5$ is formed. Calculate amount of $CH_3COOC_2H_5$, if we start with 120 g of CH_3COOH with same amount of C_2H_5OH under identical experimental conditions.

Sol. $CH_3COOH + C_2H_5OH \overset{H^+}{\rightleftharpoons} CH_3COOC_2H_5 + H_2O$

Under identical conditions (at constant temperature), two sets are studied. Thus, equilibrium constant remains unchanged. Also, convert given quantities into moles.

	Set I	Set II
CH_3COOH	60 g = 1 mol	120 g = 2 mol
CH_3CH_2OH	46 g = 1 mol	46 g = 1 mol
$CH_3COOC_2H_5$	88 g = 0.5 mol	?

		CH_3COOH	+ C_2H_5OH	$\overset{H^+}{\rightleftharpoons}$ $CH_3COOC_2H_5$	+ H_2O
Set-I	Initial	1 mol	1 mol	0	0
	At equilibrium	$(1-x)$	$(1-x)$	x	x
Set-II	Initial	2 mol	1 mol	0	0
	At equilibrium	$(2-y)$	$(1-y)$	y	y

$$\therefore \quad K_C = \frac{[CH_3COOC_2H_5][H_2O]}{[CH_3COOH][C_2H_5OH]} = \frac{x^2}{(1-x)^2} = \frac{y^2}{(2-y)(1-y)}$$

Since, $x = 0.5$ mol (given)

$$\text{Hence,} \quad \frac{(0.5)^2}{(0.5)^2} = \frac{y^2}{(2-y)(1-y)} \Rightarrow y^2 = 2 + y^2 - 3y$$

$$\therefore \quad y = \frac{2}{3} \text{ mol} = \frac{2}{3} \text{ mol} \times 88 \text{ g mol}^{-1} = 58.67 \text{ g}$$

■ % of CH_3COOH converted into ester

$$= \frac{\frac{2}{3} \text{ mol formed}}{2 \text{ mol acid}} \times 100 = 33.33\%$$

Immediate Test 11

If we start with 1 mole of A and 1 mole of B in 5 L flask, 0.5 mole of C is formed in the equilibrium of

$$A + B \rightleftharpoons C + D$$

What is molar concentration of each species, if the reaction is carried with 2 moles of A and 1 mole of B in 5 L flask at the same temperature?

Example 7.13) At 320 K, equilibrium constant (K_p) for the gaseous phase reaction

$$N_2O_4 \rightleftharpoons 2NO_2$$

is 0.66. Compute the partial pressures of N_2O_4 and NO_2 at equilibrium and at a total pressure of 0.5 bar. Also, calculate equilibrium constant K_C.

$$N_2O_4(g) \rightleftharpoons 2NO_2(g), \ K_p = \frac{p^2_{NO_2}}{p_{N_2O_4}}$$

Also, $\quad p_{\text{total}} = p_{N_2O_4} + p_{NO_2}$

For the values of K_p, p_{total}, partial pressures p_{NO_2} and $p_{N_2O_4}$ are calculated.

$$K_p = K_C(RT)^{\Delta n_g}$$

Sol. $p_{\text{total}} = p_{N_2O_4} + p_{NO_2}$

Let $\quad p_{NO_2} = p$ bar then, $p_{N_2O_4} = (0.50 - p)$

$$\therefore \quad K_p = 0.66 = \frac{p^2}{(0.50 - p)} \Rightarrow p^2 + 0.66p - 0.33 = 0$$

$$p = \frac{-0.66 + \sqrt{(0.66)^2 + 4 \times 0.330}}{2} = 0.3324 \text{ bar}$$

$\therefore \quad p_{NO_2} = 0.3324 \text{ bar} \Rightarrow p_{N_2O_4} = 0.5 - 0.3324 = 0.167 \text{ bar}$

$K_p = K_C(RT)^{\Delta n_g}, \Delta n_g = 1$

$$\therefore \quad K_C = \frac{K_p}{(RT)^{\Delta n_g}} = \frac{0.66}{(0.0831 \times 320)} = 0.025$$

Example 7.14) Some solid NH_4HS is placed in a flask containing 0.5 atm of NH_3. Upon heating following equilibrium is attained.

$$NH_4HS(s) \rightleftharpoons NH_3(g) + H_2S(g), \quad K_p = 0.11$$

Calculate partial pressure of each species at equilibrium.

$NH_4HS(s)$ *is in the solid state and others are gaseous species. Thus, pressure set up is due to* NH_3 *and* H_2S*. From* K_p*, partial pressure of each species is calculated.*

Sol. $NH_4HS(s) \rightleftharpoons NH_3(g) + H_2S(g)$

	$NH_4HS(s)$	$NH_3(g)$	$H_2S(g)$
Initial	1 atm	0.5 atm	0
At equilibrium	$(1-x)$	$(0.5+x)$	x

$K_p = p_{NH_3} \cdot p_{H_2S} \Rightarrow 0.11 = (0.5 + x)x \quad \therefore x^2 + 0.5x - 0.11 = 0$

$$x = \frac{-0.5 + \sqrt{(0.5)^2 + 0.44}}{2} = 0.17 \text{ atm}$$

$\therefore \quad p_{NH_3} = 0.50 + 0.17 = 0.67 \text{ atm} \Rightarrow p_{H_2S} = 0.17 \text{ atm}$

$p_{total} = 0.84 \text{ atm}$

Immediate Test 12

$Ca(HCO_3)_2$ is strongly heated and after equilibrium is attained, temperature is reduced to 298 K.

$$Ca(HCO_3)_2(s) \rightleftharpoons CaO(s) + H_2O(l) + 2CO_2(g)$$

If $K_p = 36 \text{ atm}^2$, calculate partial pressure of CO_2.

Example 7.15) N_2O_4 is 25% dissociated at 310 K and at a pressure of 1 bar. Calculate

(i) K_p and

(ii) per cent dissociation of N_2O_4 at 0.1 bar and 310 K.

$N_2O_4 \rightleftharpoons 2NO_2$

$$K_p = \frac{p^2_{NO_2}}{p_{N_2O_4}} = \frac{4x^2p}{(1-x^2)}$$

(From table of homogeneous equilibria)
Thus, K_p *is calculated.*
Also, under approximation

$$K_p = 4x^2p \quad \therefore x = \sqrt{\frac{K_p}{4p}} = \frac{1}{2}\sqrt{\frac{K_p}{p}}$$

Thus, degree of dissociation is dependent on pressure

$$\frac{x_2}{x_1} = \sqrt{\frac{p_1}{p_2}}$$

Sol. (i) $K_p = \frac{4x^2p}{(1-x^2)} = \frac{4(0.25)^2 \times 1}{[1-(0.25)^2]} \Rightarrow K_p = 0.267$

(ii) Degree of dissociation, when $p = 0.1$ bar

$$x = \frac{1}{2}\sqrt{\frac{0.267}{0.1}} = 0.81$$

■ $K_p = \frac{4x^2p}{(1-x^2)} \approx \frac{4x^2p}{1} \Rightarrow x = \frac{1}{2}\sqrt{\frac{K_p}{p}}$

Since, K_p is constant.

$$\therefore \quad \frac{x_2}{x_1} = \sqrt{\frac{p_1}{p_2}} \Rightarrow x_2 = x_1\sqrt{\frac{p_1}{p_2}} = 0.25\sqrt{\frac{1}{0.1}} = 0.79 \approx 0.80$$

In short $\quad x \propto \left(\frac{1}{p}\right)^{\Delta n_g/2}, \Delta n_g = +1, x \propto \sqrt{\frac{1}{p}}$

Immediate Test 13

The equilibrium constant K_p for the reaction

$$N_2O_4(g) \rightleftharpoons 2NO_2(g)$$

is 636 mm Hg at 770 K.

(a) If the pressure of the gas mixture is 158 mm Hg, calculate the percentage dissociation of N_2O_4.

(b) At what pressure, will it be half dissociated?

Example 7.16) For the reaction,

$$CaCO_3(s) \rightleftharpoons CaO(s) + CO_2(g)$$

$K_p = 1.16$ atm at 1000 K. If 25.0 g of $CaCO_3$ was put into a 10.0 L container and heated to 1000 K, what per cent of the $CaCO_3$ would remain unreacted at equilibrium?

$$CaCO_3(s) \rightleftharpoons CaO(s) + CO_2(g)$$

Only gaseous species is CO_2*. Thus,*

$$K_p = p_{CO_2} = \frac{nRT}{V}$$

Thus, number of moles of CO_2 *formed (n) or number of moles of* $CaCO_3$ *decomposed is calculated.*

Sol. $K_p = p_{CO_2} = 1.16 \text{ atm}$

$$\therefore \quad p = \frac{nRT}{V}$$

$$\therefore \quad n(CO_2) = \frac{pV}{RT} = \frac{1.16 \times 10}{0.0821 \times 1000} = 0.141 \text{ mol}$$

$CO_2 \equiv CaCO_3$

Thus, $CaCO_3$ decomposed = 0.141 mol

$CaCO_3$ initially present $= \frac{25}{100} = 0.250$ mol

Thus, unreacted $CaCO_3 = 0.250 - 0.141 = 0.109$ mol

$$\% = \frac{0.109}{0.25} \times 100 = 43.6\%$$

Example 7.17) For $CaCl_2 \cdot 2H_2O$ at 300 K

$$CaCl_2 \cdot 2H_2O(s) \rightleftharpoons CaCl_2(s) + 2H_2O(g)$$

partial pressure of $H_2O(g)$ is 0.07 Torr.

Calculate

(i) K_p (equilibrium constant)

(ii) R_H (relative humidity of vapour pressure of water is 23.8 Torr).

(iii) Under what condition, will $CaCl_2 \cdot 2H_2O$ be efflorescent at 300 K?

Sol. $K_p = p^2_{H_2O}$ other being in solid state.

$$\text{Relative humidity } (R_H) = \frac{\text{Partial pressure of } H_2O}{\text{Vapour pressure of } H_2O} \times 100$$

$CaCl_2 \cdot 2H_2O$ will be efflorescent when R_H is less than the calculated value.

(i) $K_p = p^2_{H_2O} = \left(\frac{0.07}{760}\right)^2 \text{ atm}^2 = 8.48 \times 10^{-9} \text{ atm}^2$

(ii) $R_H = \frac{0.07}{23.8} \times 100 = 0.2941$

(iii) Below (R_H) of 0.2941, it will lose water.

Immediate Test 14

For $Na_2SO_4 \cdot 10H_2O$ (Glauber's salt)

$$Na_2SO_4 \cdot 10H_2O(s) \rightleftharpoons Na_2SO_4(s) + 10H_2O(g)$$

(pressure is in Torr) $K_p = 4.08 \times 10^{-25}$ at 273 K.

Vapour pressure of water at 273 K = 0.07 Torr. Calculate relative humidity due to $Na_2SO_4 \cdot 10H_2O$.

Example 7.18) A saturated solution of iodine in water contains 0.330 g I_2/L. More than this can dissolve in a KI solution because of the following equilibrium:

$$I_2(aq) + I^-(aq) \rightleftharpoons I_3^-(aq)$$

A 0.100 M I^- solution dissolves 12.5 g I_2/L, most of which is converted to I_3^-. Assuming that the concentration of I_2 in all saturated solutions is the same, calculate the equilibrium constant for the above reaction. (I = 127)

$I_2(aq)$ is soluble in I^- forming I_3^-. Equilibrium concentration of I_2 has been given from which $[I_3^-]$ and $[I^-]$ can be determined hence, the value of K_C.

Sol. $I_2(aq) + I^-(aq) \rightleftharpoons I_3^-(aq)$

	$I_2(aq)$	$I^-(aq)$	$I_3^-(aq)$
	1 mol	1 mol	1 mol
	a	b	0
	$(a-x)$	$(b-x)$	(x)

$$0.330 \text{ g } I_2 = \frac{0.330}{254} = 1.30 \times 10^{-3} \text{ mol } I_2$$

I_2 taken

$$a = 12.5 \text{ g } I_2 = \frac{12.5}{254} = 0.0492 \text{ mol } I_2$$

$(a - x)$ = At equilibrium, $[I_2] = 1.30 \times 10^{-3}$ M,

$x = [I_3^-] = (0.0492 - 1.30 \times 10^{-3})$ M = 0.0479 M

$(b - x) = [I^-] = (0.100 - 0.0479)$
= 0.0521 M

$$\therefore \quad K_C = \frac{[I_3^-]}{[I_2][I^-]} = \frac{0.0479}{(1.30 \times 10^{-3})(0.0521)} = 707.22$$

KNOWLEDGE CONFIRMATION Test 2

1 In the following equilibrium,

$$A + 2B \rightleftharpoons 2C$$

a 10 L flask contains 1 mole each of *A*, *B* and *C*. At equilibrium, molar concentration of *A* is 0.14 mol L^{-1}. Thus, equilibrium constant of the above equilibrium reaction is (check reverse reaction is favoured)

(a) 11.34 (b) 1.41×10^{-2} (c) 6.75 (d) 1.12×10^{-2}

2 In the following equilibrium, initial moles of *A* is twice of *B*.

$$A + 2B \rightleftharpoons 3C + D$$

At equilibrium, moles of *B* and *C* are equal. Thus, degree of dissociation of *A* is

(a) 5.0% (b) 10.0% (c) 20.0% (d) 25.0%

3 For $H_2(g) + I_2(g) \rightleftharpoons 2HI(g)$,

equilibrium constant K_C and degree of dissociation are related by equation

(a) $\frac{\sqrt{K_C}}{2+\sqrt{K_C}}$ (b) $\frac{2+\sqrt{K_C}}{\sqrt{K_C}}$ (c) $\sqrt{K_C}[2+\sqrt{K_C}]$ (d) $\frac{\sqrt{K_C}}{1+\sqrt{K_C}}$

4 PCl_5 is 10% dissociated at 1 atm and 300 K. Thus, its K_p is

(a) 5.0×10^{-2} (b) 5.0×10^{-3} (c) 1.1×10^{-2} (d) 1.1×10^{-3}

5 N_2O_4 is 20% dissociated at a total pressure of 1 bar. Thus, percentage dissociation at 0.5 bar is

(a) 27.7% (b) 15.0% (c) 14.5% (d) 13.6%

6 In the following equilibrium,

$$Ca(HCO_3)_2(s) \rightleftharpoons CaO(s) + 2CO_2(g) + H_2O(l)$$

when temperature is set at 298 K after decomposition, total pressure was found to be 4 bar. What is K_p of the reaction?

(a) 4 (b) 2 (c) 16 (d) 0.25

7 In the above equilibrium in Q.6 at 400 K, K_p is 4 when pressure is in bar unit. Thus, partial pressure of CO_2 and H_2O are respectively.

	p_{CO_2}	p_{H_2O}		p_{CO_2}	p_{H_2O}
(a)	2 bar	1 bar	(b)	2 bar	2 bar
(c)	1 bar	2 bar	(d)	1 bar	1 bar

8 Ammonium carbamate $(NH_2CO_2NH_4)$ decomposes into $NH_3(g)$ and $CO_2(g)$:

$$NH_2CO_2NH_4(s) \rightleftharpoons 2NH_3(g) + CO_2(g)$$

K_p in terms of pressure is

(a) $\frac{p^2}{4}$ (b) $\frac{4p^3}{27}$ (c) $\frac{p^3}{27}$ (d) $\frac{4p^2}{3}$

9 For the following equilibrium,

$$CO(g) + Cl_2(g) \rightleftharpoons COCl_2(g), K_C = 4$$

one mole of $CO(g)$, 2 moles of Cl_2 and 1 mole of $COCl_2(g)$ are placed in 1 L flask. When equilibrium is set up $[COCl_2]$ formed is

(a) 0.75 M (b) 0.25 M (c) 2.25 M (d) 1.68 M

10 For the reaction,

$CO(g) + H_2O(g) \rightleftharpoons CO_2(g) + H_2(g), K_C = 4.24$ at 800 K

equilibrium concentration of $CO_2(g)$ at 800 K is, when $[CO] = [H_2O] = 0.10$ M at start, ***[NCERT]***

(a) 0.050 M (b) 0.033 M (c) 0.067 M (d) 0.01 M

11 3.0 moles of PCl_5 in 1 L flask was allowed to attain equilibrium at 380 K. Thus, mole fraction of PCl_5 at equilibrium is ***[NCERT]***

$$PCl_5 \rightleftharpoons PCl_3 + Cl_2, K_C = 1.80$$

(a) 0.11 (b) 0.45 (c) 0.22 (d) 0.78

12 In each of the following, total pressure set up at equilibrium is assumed to be equal and is 1 atm with equilibrium constants given (assume 50% dissociation)

I. $CaCO_3(s) \rightleftharpoons CaO(s) + CO_2(g), K_1$

II. $NH_4HS(s) \rightleftharpoons NH_3(g) + H_2S(g), K_2$

III. $C(s) + CO_2(g) \rightleftharpoons 2CO(g), K_3$

IV. $NH_2CO_2NH_4(s) \rightleftharpoons 2NH_3(g) + CO_2(g), K_4$

Thus,

(a) $K_1 = K_2 = K_3 = K_4$ (b) $K_1 < K_2 < K_3 < K_4$
(c) $K_4 < K_3 < K_2 < K_1$ (d) $K_4 < K_2 < K_1 < K_3$

13 For the following equilibrium,

$CuSO_4 \cdot 5H_2O(s) \rightleftharpoons CuSO_4 \cdot 3H_2O(s) + 2H_2O(g)$

$K_p = 1.086 \times 10^{-4}$ atm^2 at 298 K

vapour pressure of water at 298 K = 23.8 torr. $CuSO_4 \cdot 5H_2O$ loses water when relative humidity is

(a) less than 33.3% (b) above 33.3%
(c) less than 66.6% (d) above 66.6%

14 For the equilibrium in gaseous phase

$$2SO_2 + O_2 \rightleftharpoons 2SO_3$$

One starts with 2 moles of SO_2 and 1 mole of O_2 at 3 atm. When equilibrium is attained, pressure changes to 2.5 atm. Hence, K_p is

(a) 3 atm^{-1} (b) 2.5 atm^{-1} (c) 2 atm^{-1} (d) 0.5 atm^{-1}

15 The equilibrium constant for the following reaction is 1.6×10^5 at 1024 K.

$$H_2(g) + Br_2(g) \rightleftharpoons 2HBr(g)$$

$HBr(g)$ at 10.0 bar is introduced into a sealed container at 1024 K. Thus, partial pressure of H_2 and Br_2 together is

(a) 10 bar (b) 0.05 bar (c) 0.025 bar (d) 0.10 bar

16 For the following equilibrium taking place in 1 L flask at 300 K

$$PCl_5(g) \rightleftharpoons PCl_3(g) + Cl_2(s), \quad K_C = 4$$

Thus, degree of dissociation x is

(a) $(2\sqrt{2} - 1)$ (b) $2(\sqrt{2} - 1)$ (c) $2(\sqrt{2} + 1)$ (d) $-2(\sqrt{2} + 1)$

17 For the following equilibrium at 400 K in 10 L flask

$Na_2SO_4 \cdot 10H_2O(s) \rightleftharpoons Na_2SO_4 \cdot 8H_2O(s) + 2H_2O(g)$

$K_p = 1 \times 10^{-4}$ bar^2

Thus, number of moles of H_2O in vapour state is

(a) 0.010 (b) 0.003 (c) 0.002 (d) 0.001

18 For the equilibrium,

$C(s) + CO_2(g) \rightleftharpoons 2CO(g), K_p = 63$ atm at 1000 K

If at equilibrium $p_{CO} = 10p_{CO_2}$, then, total pressure is

(a) 6.3 atm (b) 0.63 atm (c) 6.93 atm (d) 69.3 atm

19 For the equilibrium,

α-(D) glucose $\rightleftharpoons$ β-(D) glucose, $K_C = 1.8$

Thus, percentage of α-(D) glucose at equilibrium is

(a) 35.7 (b) 40.2 (c) 91.0 (d) 27.2

20 For the reaction, $AB(g) \rightleftharpoons A(g) + B(g)$, AB is 33% dissociated at 300 K and at a pressure p. Thus,

(a) $p = K_p$ (b) $p = 3K_p$ (c) $p = 4K_p$ (d) $p = 8K_p$

21 A flask containing $F_2(g)$ at 2.00 bar and 1000 K is allowed to equilibrate with $F(g)$

$$F_2(g) \longrightarrow 2F(g) \quad K_p = 9.59 \times 10^{-3}$$

Thus, partial pressure of F_2 and $F(g)$ are

	p_{F_2}	p_F		p_{F_2}	p_F
(a)	1.93 bar	0.135 bar	(b)	1.93 bar	0.965 bar
(c)	1.93 bar	1.93 bar	(d)	0.965 bar	0.965 bar

22 For the above equilibrium, K_c and K_χ at 1000K are

	K_c	K_χ		K_c	K_χ
(a)	1.153×10^{-4}	1.135×10^{-4}	(b)	1.153×10^{-4}	4.63×10^{-3}
(c)	4.63×10^{-3}	4.63×10^{-3}	(d)	4.63×10^{-3}	1.153×10^{-3}

23 A 0.100 mol of NO_2 was placed in a 10.0 L container and heated to 750 K. The total pressure of equilibrium mixture as a result of the decomposition

$$2NO_2(g) \rightleftharpoons 2NO(g) + O_2(g)$$

was 0.827 bar. Thus, equilibrium constant K_p is

(a) 0.704 (b) 1.42 (c) 2.02 (d) 1.42

24 A mixture containing 1.25 bar of H_2 and 0.75 bar of C_2H_2 reacted to form C_2H_4

$C_2H_2(g) + H_2(g) \rightleftharpoons C_2H_4(g), K_p = 5.14 \propto 10^{24}$

Thus, partial pressures of $C_2H_4(g)$ is

(a) 2.9×10^{-25} bar (b) 0.50 bar
(c) 0.75 bar (d) 5.14×10^{24} bar

25 $CO(g)$ reduces $FeO(s)$ to $Fe(s)$ and following equilibrium is attained at 1300 K

$$FeO(s) + CO(g) \rightleftharpoons Fe(s) + CO_2(g); \quad K_p = 0.5$$

$CO(g)$ at a pressure of 1 bar and excess of $FeO(s)$ are placed in a container at 1300 K. Thus, pressures of CO and CO_2 are respectively.

	p_{CO} (bar)	p_{CO_2} (bar)		p_{CO} (bar)	p_{CO_2} (bar)
(a)	0.50	0.50	(b)	0.33	0.67
(c)	0.67	0.33	(d)	0.67	0.67

Relation between Vapour Density and Degree of Dissociation

Degree of dissociation can be defined as the fraction that undergoes dissociation in a reaction.

$$x \text{ (degree of dissociation)} = \frac{\text{Number of moles dissociated}}{\text{Initial number of moles}}$$

Vapour density of a substance is defined as the mass of a certain volume of a substance divided by the mass of the same volume of hydrogen.

$$\text{Vapour density} \times 2 = \text{Molar mass}$$

If D = Theoretical vapour density in the absence of dissociation
d = Observed vapour density due to dissociation

then, $$x = \frac{D-d}{(y-1)d}$$

where, y = number of moles of products (ions, molecules) from one mole reactant.

Note $$x = \frac{D-d}{(y-1)d}$$

$\therefore$ $$\frac{D}{d} - 1 = (y-1)x$$

$\therefore$ $$\frac{D}{d} = 1 + (y-1)x$$

$\frac{D}{d}$ is also called **van't Hoff factor** (class XII).

For

I. $PCl_5 \rightleftharpoons PCl_3 + Cl_2$, $y = 2$, $\therefore x = \left(\frac{D-d}{d}\right)$

II. $N_2O_4 \rightleftharpoons 2NO_2$ as in I

III. $2NO_2 \rightleftharpoons N_2O_4$, $y = \frac{1}{2}$, $x = \frac{2(d-D)}{d}$

Solved Examples & Instant Practice

Example 7.19) For the following equilibrium in the gaseous phase:

$$PCl_5 \rightleftharpoons PCl_3 + Cl_2$$

vapour density of the gaseous mixture is found to be 100, when 1 mole of PCl_5 is taken in 10 L flask at 300 K. Calculate

(i) percentage dissociation of PCl_5

(ii) equilibrium pressure at 300 K

Due to dissociation number of moles increases, hence vapour density decreases.

$$x \text{ (degree of dissociation)} = \frac{D-d}{(y-1)d}$$

where, D is the theoretical vapour density and d is the experimental vapour density.

y = number of moles of the products from one mole reactant.

Sol. (i) $D = \frac{\text{molar mass of } PCl_5}{2} = \frac{208.5}{2} = 104.25$

$d = 100$ (given)

$y = 2$

$\therefore$ $$x = \frac{D-d}{(y-1)d} = \frac{104.25-100}{(2-1)\,100} = 0.0425$$

(ii)

	PCl_5	$\rightleftharpoons$	PCl_3	+	Cl_2
Initial	1		0		0
At equilibrium	$(1-x)$		x		x

Total moles at equilibrium = $(1+x)$ = 1.0425

$\therefore$ $$p = \frac{n}{V}RT = \frac{1.0425 \times 0.0821 \times 300}{10}$$

$= 2.568$ atm

Immediate Test 15

(i) In the following equilibrium.

NO_2 is found to 50% of the total volume:

$$N_2O_4(g) \rightleftharpoons 2NO_2(g)$$

Calculate

(a) degree of dissociation of N_2O_4

(b) abnormal molar mass

(c) van't Hoff factor which is $i = 1 + (y-1)x$

(ii) Following equilibrium is set up at 298 K starting with equal moles of N_2O_4 and NO_2 in 1L flask.

At equilibrium, average molar mass of the mixture was found to be 61.34.

$$N_2O_4(g) \rightleftharpoons 2NO_2(g)$$

Calculate

(a) degree of dissociation (b) initial moles (c) K_C

Example 7.20) $N_2O_4(g) \rightleftharpoons 2NO_2(g)$

$K_p = 0.66$ at 1 atm pressure

Calculate vapour density at equilibrium.

Sol. $$N_2O_4 \rightleftharpoons 2NO_2$$

$$K_p = \frac{4x^2 p}{(1-x^2)} \Rightarrow 0.66 = \frac{4x^2}{(1-x^2)}$$

$0.66 - 0.66x^2 = 4x^2 \quad \therefore \quad 4.66x^2 = 0.66 \quad \therefore \quad x = 0.38$

$$x = \frac{D-d}{d} = \frac{D}{d} - 1 \quad \therefore \quad \frac{D}{d} = 1 + x = 1.38$$

$\therefore$ d (vapour density of the mixture) $= \frac{D}{1.38} = \frac{46}{1.38} = 33.33$

Example 7.21) CH_3COOH forms dimer in benzene

$$CH_3COOH \rightleftharpoons \frac{1}{2}(CH_3COOH)_2$$

If, $K_C = 1$ at 298 K, starting with 1 M CH_3COOH solution, calculate abnormal molar mass of CH_3COOH.

Sol.

$$CH_3COOH \rightleftharpoons \frac{1}{2}(CH_3COOH)_2 \text{ (dimer)}$$

Initial	1 M	0
At equilibrium	$(1-x)$	$x/2$

$$\therefore \quad K_C = \frac{[(CH_3COOH)_2]^{1/2}}{[CH_3COOH]}$$

$$1 = \frac{\sqrt{x/2}}{(1-x)}$$

$$\Rightarrow \quad \frac{x}{2} = (1-x)^2$$

$$\Rightarrow 1 + x^2 - 2x = \frac{x}{2} \Rightarrow x^2 - 2.5x + 1 = 0$$

$$\therefore \quad x = \frac{2.5 - \sqrt{(2.5)^2 - 4}}{2} = 0.314$$

Thus, dimer formation is 31.4%.

$$x = \frac{D-d}{d(y-1)}$$

Here, $\quad y = \frac{1}{2}$

$$\therefore \quad x = \frac{D-d}{d\left(\frac{1}{2}-1\right)} \Rightarrow x = \left(\frac{d-D}{d}\right)2 \Rightarrow x = 0.314 \text{ (above)}$$

$$0.314 = \left(1 - \frac{D}{d}\right)2 \qquad \therefore \quad \frac{D}{d} = \left(1 - \frac{0.314}{2}\right) = 0.843$$

$$\therefore \quad d = \frac{D}{\left(1 - \frac{0.314}{2}\right)} = \frac{30(\text{V.D})}{0.843} = 35.6$$

$\therefore$ Abnormal molar mass $= 35.6 \times 2 = 71.2 \text{ g mol}^{-1}$

KNOWLEDGE CONFIRMATION **Test 3**

1 In the following equilibrium in the gas phase

$$O_3 \rightleftharpoons \frac{3}{2}O_2$$

vapour density of the gaseous mixture is 20. Thus, degree of dissociation of O_3 into O_2 is

(a) 4% (b) 40% (c) 20% (d) 2%

2 $H_2(g)$ dissociates into $H(g)$ as given

$$H_2(g) = 2H(g)$$

$K_p = 0.04$ at 1 atm. Thus, vapour density of the mixture of $H_2(g)$ and $H(g)$ is

(a) 0.91 (b) 0.091 (c) 1.00 (d) 1.091

3 For the following equilibrium

$$N_2O_4(g) \rightleftharpoons 2NO_2(g)$$

NO_2 is 80% of the total volume.

Thus, vapour density of the mixture of NO_2 and N_2O_4 is

(a) 25.56 (b) 23.0 (c) 28.20 (d) 27.60

4 If $i = [1 + (y-1)x]$ is van't Hoff factor, what is van't Hoff factor for the 50% dimer formation of A into A_2.

$$2A(g) \rightleftharpoons A_2(g)$$

(a) 0.75 (b) 1.50 (c) 2.00 (d) 1.75

5 For the following,

$$PCl_5 \rightleftharpoons PCl_3 + Cl_2$$

van't Hoff factor is 1.5. Thus, vapour density of the gaseous mixture is

(a) 69.5 (b) 156.75 (c) 104.5 (d) 139.00

6 Degree of dissociation (x) varies with the ratio $\left(\frac{D}{d}\right)$ by the graph for $N_2O_4 \rightleftharpoons 2NO_2$

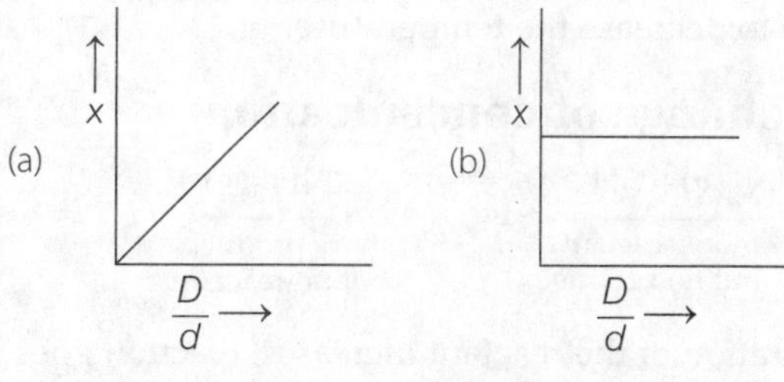

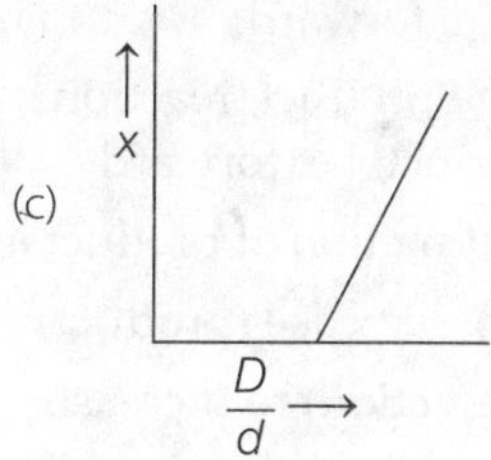

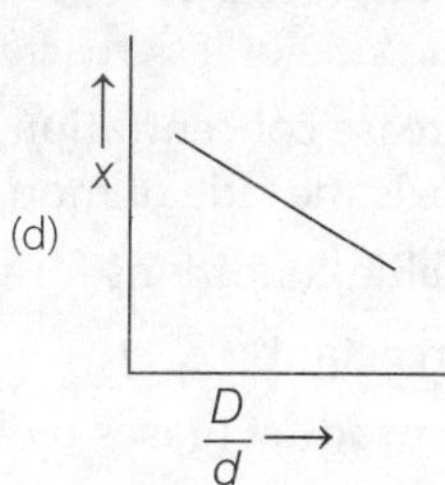

7 For the reaction,

$$PCl_5 \rightleftharpoons PCl_3 + Cl_2$$

$$\left(\frac{dx}{dt}\right) = 0.09\,[PCl_5] - 0.01\,[PCl_3]\,[Cl_2]$$

The reaction takes place in 1L flask. Thus, vapour density of the gaseous mixture is

(a) 104.5 (b) 100.2
(c) 54.71 (d) 69.7

8 $C_6H_5COOH \rightleftharpoons \frac{1}{2}(C_6H_5COOH)_2$

$K_C = 2$, starting with 1M C_6H_5COOH. Thus, abnormal molar mass of benzoic acid is

(a) 122 g mol^{-1} (b) 244 g mol^{-1}

(c) 175.5 g mol^{-1} (d) 187.2 g mol^{-1}

9 In the following equilibrium

$$A \rightleftharpoons \frac{1}{2}A_2$$

(molar mass of A=100 g mol^{-1})

vapour density of the mixture is 75. Thus, starting with 1M solution of A, K_C will be

(a) 0.577 (b) 0.73

(c) 1.57 (d) 1.73

10 For the two equilibria :

I : $A \rightleftharpoons 2B, K_1$ II: $A \rightleftharpoons \frac{1}{2}(A_2), K_2$

degree of dissociation in I = degree of association in II = 4%. Then, starting with 1M of A, K_1 and K_2 are related as

(a) $K_1 = K_2$ (b) $K_1 = 4.5 \times 10^{-2} K_2$

(c) $K_2 = 15.62 K_2$ (d) $K_1 K_2 = 1$

Le-Chatelier's Principle

If a stress is applied to a reaction mixture at equilibrium, reaction occurs in that direction that minimises the stress.

Stress means a change in concentration, pressure, volume or temperature that disturbs the original equilibrium.

It means,

- if you increase concentration of the reactants, reaction goes in the direction that tends to decrease concentration.
- if you increase pressure (or decrease volume), reaction goes in the direction that tends to decrease pressure.
- if you increase temperature, reaction goes in the direction that tends to decrease the temperature.

Effect of change of concentration

$$\underbrace{N_2(g) + 3H_2(g)}_{\text{more reactant but no product}} \rightleftharpoons \underbrace{2NH_3(g)}_{\text{more product but no reactant}}$$

- If concentration of the reactant increases, reaction goes towards the side of less reactant, i.e. forward.
- If you decrease concentration of the product, reaction goes towards the side of more product, i.e. forward.

Thus, favourable conditions for the formation of product are

(i) increase (reactant) (ii) decrease (product)

Thus, isolate product (gases by liquefaction) to increase yield.

Effect of change of pressure

$$pV = nRT \Rightarrow p \propto n$$

Thus, if number of moles changes, pressure also changes. For gaseous phase equilibrium,

$$aA + bB \rightleftharpoons cC + dD$$
$$\Delta n_g = (c+d) - (a+b)$$

- If $\Delta n_g = 0$, no change in pressure, thus, no effect of pressure.
- If $\Delta n_g > 0$, pressure increases thus, increase in pressure takes the reaction towards lower pressure.

$$\underbrace{PCl_5(g)}_{\substack{\text{1 mol} \\ \text{low } p}} \rightleftharpoons \underbrace{PCl_3(g) + Cl_2(g)}_{\substack{\text{2 mol} \\ \text{high } p}}$$

Increase in pressure shifts the reaction in backward side.

- If $\Delta n_g < 0$, pressure decreases thus, increase in pressure takes the reaction towards lower pressure (in which number of moles decreases)

$$\underbrace{N_2(g) + 3H_2(g)}_{\substack{\text{4 mol} \\ \text{high } p}} \rightleftharpoons \underbrace{2NH_3(g)}_{\substack{\text{2 mol} \\ \text{low } p}}$$

If pressure is increased, formation of NH_3 increases.

- If x = quantity of product, then, $x \propto (1/p)^{\Delta n_g/2}$

Thus, for

$$PCl_5 \rightleftharpoons PCl_3 + Cl_2, \Delta n_g = +1, x \propto \sqrt{1/p}$$
$$2SO_2 + O_2 \rightleftharpoons 2SO_3, \Delta n_g = -1, x \propto \sqrt{p}$$
$$N_2 + 3H_2 \rightleftharpoons 2NH_3, \Delta n_g = +1, x \propto p$$

Effect of change of temperature

***Case* I Exothermic reaction** Here system releases heat, thus system gets heated.

$$\underset{\text{low heat}}{A - q} \rightleftharpoons \underset{\text{high heat}}{B}$$

Increase in temperature takes the reaction towards the side of low heat, i.e. backward.

Thus, exothermic reactions are favoured at low temperature.

***Case* II Endothermic reaction** Here system absorbs heat, thus system cools down.

$$\underset{\substack{\text{high heat} \\ \text{high temperature}}}{A + q} \rightleftharpoons \underset{\substack{\text{low heat} \\ \text{low temperature}}}{B}$$

Thus, if temperature is increased, reaction goes in the direction of low heat, i.e. forward.

Thus, endothermic reactions are favoured at high temperature.

- Boiling point increases and freezing point is lowered on increasing pressure.
- Solubility of a gas in water increases on increasing pressure.
- Solubility of solute in a solvent increases (if $\Delta H > 0$), decreases (if $\Delta H < 0$) on increasing temperature.

Effect of catalyst

It lowers the energy of activation of both (forward and backward) sides equally hence no effect on the, composition of the equilibrium mixture.

Activation energy is the energy required to take the reactants to the transition state where they can react and give the final product.

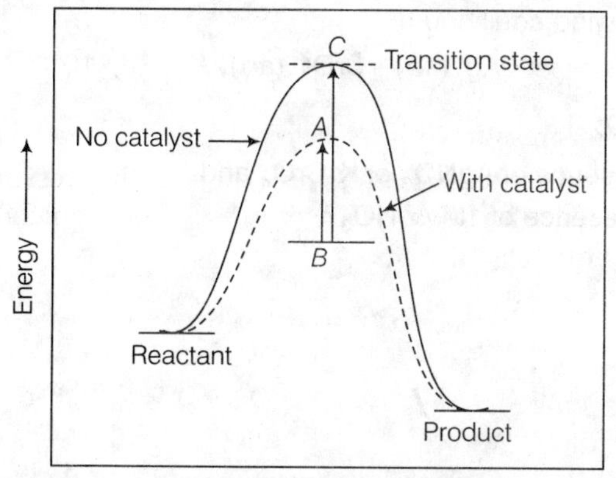

AC = Energy of activation without catalyst $= E_a$

AB = Energy of activation with catalyst $= E_a'$

$$E_a' < E_a$$

The effect of varying conditions on the equilibrium

$$aA + bB \rightleftharpoons cC + dD$$

$$\Delta n_g = [c + d] - [a + b]$$

Change imposed on the system in equilibrium	Equilibrium position moves	Equilibrium constant	Any other points
Concentration of A or B increased	To right	No change	—
Concentration of C or D increased	To left	No change	—
Pressure is increased	To right if $(c+d) < (a+b)$ i.e. $\Delta n_g = -$ ve	No change	Very little effect, if any, of in liquid solution
	To left if $(c+d) > (a+b)$ i.e. $\Delta n_g = +$ ve	No change	
	No change if $(c+d) = (a+d)$, i.e. $\Delta n_g = 0$	No change	
T is increased	To left if $\Delta H = -$ve (exothermic)	Value decreased	Equilibrium achieved faster
	To right if $\Delta H = +$ve (endothermic)	Value increased	
Addition of catalyst	No change	No change	Equilibrium achieved faster

To study the favourable conditions for the specific direction for the given equilibrium

Equilibrium reaction	Δn_g	Direction of changing p		ΔH	Direction on changing T		Direction of changing concentration		Favourable conditions for forward direction
		$p\uparrow$	$p\downarrow$		$T\uparrow$	$T\downarrow$	Reaction ↑	Product ↑	
$N_2(g) + 3H_2(g) \rightleftharpoons 2NH_3(g) + Q$	−2	→	←	−ve	←	→	→	←	High p, low T and isolation of NH_3 by liquefaction
$PCl_5(g) + Q \rightleftharpoons PCl_3(g) + Cl_2(g)$	+1	←	→	+ve	→	←	→	←	Low p, high T and isolation of PCl_3 and Cl_2
$2HI(g) + Q \rightleftharpoons H_2(g) + I_2(g)$	0	No effect	No effect	+ve	→	←	→	←	High T and isolation of product formed
$H_2O(l) + Q \rightleftharpoons H_2O(g)$	+1	←	→	+ve	→	←	→	←	Increase in p causes liquefaction of H_2O (g), hence boiling point of H_2O (l) is increased
$NH_3(g) + H_2O(l) - Q \rightleftharpoons NH_4OH(l)$	−1	→	←	− ve	←	→	→	←	Any gas is dissolved in water under high p

Solved Examples & Instant Practice

Example 7.22) For a weak acid H*A*, equilibrium constant (K_a) is 4×10^{-5}.

$$CH_3COOH \rightleftharpoons CH_3COO^- + H^+$$

$$K_a = \frac{[CH_3COO^-][H^+]}{[CH_3COOH]}$$

Calculate percentage decrease in the degree of ionisation of 0.1 M CH_3COOH in presence of 1M CH_3COONa.

$$CH_3COONa \rightleftharpoons CH_3COO^- + Na^+$$

In presence of CH_3COONa*, concentration of one of the products* (CH_3COO^-) *is increased, hence, by Le-Chatelier's principle, ionisation of* CH_3COOH *is decreased.*

Sol. $CH_3COOH \rightleftharpoons CH_3COO^- + H^+$

	CH_3COOH	CH_3COO^-	H^+
Initial	C	0	0
At equilibrium	$C-Cx$	Cx	Cx

Ionisation constant of weak acid K_a is

$$\therefore \quad K_a = \frac{[CH_3COO^-][H^+]}{[CH_3COOH]} = \frac{Cx^2}{(1-x)} \approx Cx^2$$

$$\therefore \quad x = \sqrt{\frac{K_a}{C}} = \sqrt{\frac{4\times10^{-5}}{0.1}} = 2\times10^{-2}$$

In presence of CH_3COONa

$[CH_3COO^-] = 1\,M$

$$\therefore \quad 4\times10^{-5} = \frac{1[H^+]}{0.1}, \quad \therefore [H^+] = 4\times10^{-6}$$

But $[H^+] = Cx'$

(x'= degree of ionisation in presence of CH_3COONa)

$$\therefore \quad x' = \frac{4\times10^{-6}}{0.1} = 4\times10^{-5}$$

$$x\,(\%) = 2\times10^{-2}\times100 = 2\%$$

$$x'(\%) = 4\times10^{-5}\times100 = 0.004\%$$

$$\text{Decrease} = 2 - 0.004 = 1.996\%$$

- Effect of decreasing degree of ionisation of a weak electrolyte in presence of common in is called common-ion effect.

Immediate Test 16

For the following equilibrium

$$Ag_2CrO_4(s) \rightleftharpoons 2Ag^+(aq) + CrO_4^{2-}(aq), \; K_{eq} = 4\times10^{-18}$$

What is $[CrO_4^{2-}]$

(a) in the absence of $AgNO_3$ or K_2CrO_4 and

(b) in the presence of 1M $AgNO_3$?

KNOWLEDGE CONFIRMATION Test 4

1 The equilibrium which is not affected by volume change at constant temperature is

(a) $H_2(g) + I_2(g) \rightleftharpoons 2HI(g)$
(b) $N_2O_4(g) \rightleftharpoons 2NO_2(g)$
(c) $N_2(g) + 3H_2(g) \rightleftharpoons 2NH_3(g)$
(d) $PCl_5(g) \rightleftharpoons PCl_3(g) + Cl_2(g)$

2 Ionisation of a weak acid (H*A*) is decreased in presence of

(a) NaOH (b) Na*A*
(c) NH_4OH (d) All of these

3 Formation of $SO_3(g)$ can be increased by

$$2SO_2 + O_2 \rightleftharpoons 2SO_3$$

(a) adding more $SO_3(g)$ (b) decreasing SO_2
(c) decreasing O_2 (d) adding $H_2O(l)$

4 Ionisation of NH_4OH is decreased in qualitative analysis of cations by addition of

(a) NaCl (b) NH_4Cl
(c) $(NH_4)_2SO_4$ (d) NH_4NO_3

5 Soap is formed by saponification of fat.

Fat + NaOH $\rightleftharpoons$ glycerol + *R*COONa (soap)

Soap is separated from glycerol by

(a) addition of NaCl (b) passing HCl gas into mixture
(c) Both (a) and (b) (d) None of the these

6 $2NO_2(g) \rightleftharpoons N_2O_4(g)$

Dimer formation is 10% at 300 K and 20% at 250 K. Thus, dimerisation is favoured at

(a) low temperature, low pressure
(b) low temperature, high pressure
(c) high temperature, high pressure
(d) high temperature, low pressure

7 Solubility of gas in water can be increased by

(a) increasing pressure (b) decreasing pressure
(c) liquefaction (d) adding inert gas

8 Solubility of Ag_2CrO_4 in water can be decreased by addition of

(a) $AgNO_3$ (b) K_2CrO_4
(c) Both (a) and (b) (d) None of these

9 Ni (s)+$H_2(g)$ $\rightleftharpoons$ H_2 gas adsorbed on nickel surface with evolution of heat.

Extent of adsorption can be increased on

(a) increasing pressure
(b) decreasing temperature
(c) increasing pressure and decreasing temperature
(d) increasing both pressure and temperature

10 In which case, increase in temperature will increase the quantity of the product?

(a) 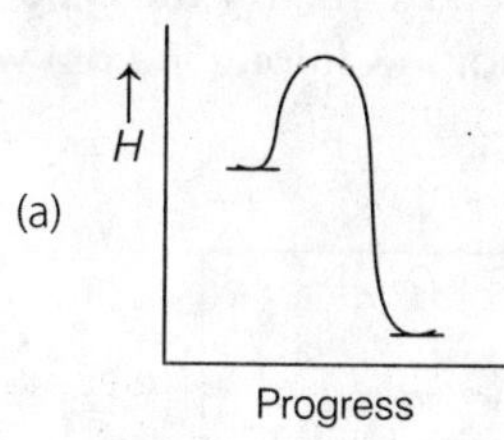

(b) 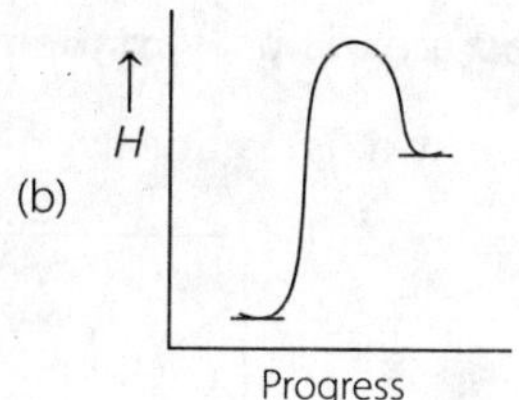

(c) 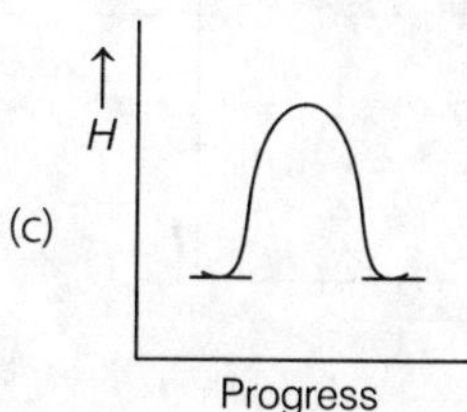

(d) In all cases

11 If pressure is made four times of the initial value, which equilibrium is most favoured in forward side?

(a) $PCl_5(g) \rightleftharpoons PCl_3(g) + Cl_2(g)$
(b) $2NH_3(g) \rightleftharpoons N_2(g) + 3H_2(g)$
(c) $N_2(g) + 3H_2(g) \rightleftharpoons 2NH_3(g)$
(d) $2SO_2(g) + O_2(g) \rightleftharpoons 2SO_3(g)$

12 For a reaction, $aA \rightleftharpoons bB$, $x \propto (p)^{-2}$

Thus, $(a-b)$ is equal to

(a) 2 (b) 3 (c) 4 (d) −4

13 In the following equilibrium, amount of $CO(g)$ can be decreased by

$$2CO(g) + O_2(g) \rightleftharpoons 2CO_2(g)$$

(a) decreasing volume at constant temperature
(b) adding argon gas
(c) adding O_2 gas (d) All of the above

14 On increasing temperature, yield of the reactant is increased. When pressure is made four times, yield becomes half. This equilibrium can be represented as

(a) $A + q \rightleftharpoons 3B$ (b) $A + q \rightleftharpoons 2B$
(c) $A - q \rightleftharpoons 3B$ (d) $A - q \rightleftharpoons 2B$

15 Ionisation of H_2S (a weak dibasic acid) in qualitative analysis of group II (copper group) can be decreased by the addition of

(a) HCl (b) H_2SO_4 (c) HNO_3 (d) CH_3COOH

16 For the reaction, $2SO_2(g) + O_2(g) \rightleftharpoons 2SO_3(g)$

$\Delta H = -57.2$ kJ mol^{-1} and $K_C = 1.7 \times 10^{16}$

Which of the following statement is incorrect?

[JEE Main 2019 (II) NTA]

(a) The equilibrium constant decreases as the temperature increases
(b) The addition of inert gas at constant volume will not affect the equilibrium constant
(c) The equilibrium will shift in forward direction as the pressure increases
(d) The equilibrium constant is large suggestive of reaction going to completion and so no catalyst is required

Thermodynamics of Chemical Equilibrium

Spontaneity

A spontaneous or natural process is a process that occurs in a system left to right itself once started, no action from outside the system (external action) is necessary to make the process continue.

$$C(s) + O_2(g) \longrightarrow CO_2(g)$$

After carbon is ignited, further burning takes place itself, thus spontaneous.

Criterion of spontaneity

$$\boxed{\Delta G = \Delta H - T\Delta S}$$

ΔG = Change in free energy G, ΔH = Change in enthalpy H
ΔS = Change in entropy S (randomness)

Sign of ΔG is taken as the true criterion for deciding spontaneous nature of the reaction at constant temperature and pressure.

(i) $\Delta G < 0$ (if $T\Delta S > \Delta H$)
the process is spontaneous, i.e. randomness (disorder) is more predominant.

(ii) $\Delta G > 0$ (if $T\Delta S > \Delta H$)
i.e. heat content is more predominant.

(iii) $\Delta G = 0$ (i.e. $T\Delta S = \Delta H$)
i.e. randomness is balanced by heat content.

Thus, ΔG is the driving force based on $T\Delta S$ and ΔH.

Criterion for spontaneous change, $\Delta G = \Delta H - T\Delta S$

Case	ΔH	ΔS	ΔG	Result	Example
1.	–	+	–	Spontaneous at all temperature	$2N_2O(g) \longrightarrow 2N_2(g) + O_2(g)$
2.	–	–	–	Spontaneous at low temperature	$H_2O(l) \longrightarrow H_2O(g)$
	–	–	+	Non-spontaneous at high temperature	
3.	+	+	+	Non-spontaneous at low temperature	$2NH_3(g) \longrightarrow N_2(g) + 3H_2(g)$
			–	Spontaneous at high temperature	
4.	+	–	+	Non-spontaneous at all temperature	$3O_2(g) \longrightarrow 2O_3(g)$
5.	$T\Delta S = \Delta H$		0	Equilibrium	$A \rightleftharpoons B$

Relation between $\Delta G°$, ΔG, K_{eq} and Q

(Reaction quotient)

ΔG for a reaction under any set of conditions is related to its value for standard conditions, that is $\Delta G°$ by equation

$$\Delta G = \Delta G° + 2.303\ RT \log Q$$

Under equilibrium condition,

$$Q = K_p = K_C = K \quad \text{and} \quad \Delta G = 0,$$

$$\Delta G° = -2.303\ RT \log K \Rightarrow \Delta G° = -RT \log_e K$$

$$\therefore \quad \boxed{K = e^{-\Delta G°/RT}}$$

If $\Delta G°<0$, $\dfrac{-\Delta G°}{RT}$ is positive and $e^{-\Delta G°/RT} > 1$.

Thus $K>1$ hence spontaneous.

- If $\Delta G°>0$, $\dfrac{-\Delta G°}{RT}$ is negative and $e^{-\Delta G°/RT} < 1$.

Thus, $K<1$, hence non-spontaneous.

We have replaced K_p or K_c by K called thermodynamic equilibrium constant. For a general reaction,

$$aA + bB \rightleftharpoons cC + dD$$

$$K = \frac{[a_C]^c[a_D]^d}{[a_A]^a[a_B]^b}$$

where the symbol a represents the activity of the reactants and products. It is actually a ratio of the equilibrium activity of a substance to its activity in its standard state. Thus, equilibrium constant is unitless quantity, a being also unitless.

(i) For pure solids and liquids, $a = 1$

(ii) For gases ideal behaviour is considered and the activity of a gas is equal to its pressure in bar.

(iii) For components in solution, a = molar concentration

Effect of temperature on equilibrium constant

$$\Delta G = \Delta G° + 2.303 RT \log Q$$

At equilibrium, $Q = K$ (thermodynamic equilibrium constant), and $\Delta G = 0$

$$\therefore \quad \Delta G° = -2.303 RT \log_{10} K$$

Also, $$\Delta G° = \Delta H° - T\Delta S°$$

$$\therefore \quad -2.303 RT \log K = \Delta H° - T\Delta S°$$

$$\therefore \quad \boxed{\log_{10} K = -\frac{\Delta H°}{2.303\ RT} + \frac{\Delta S°}{2.303\ R}}$$

This is called van't Hoff equation.

- $\Delta H°$ and $\Delta S°$ are temperature independent in the given temperature range.
- Above equation represents a straight line (of the type $y = -mx + c$). Thus, variation of $\log_{10} K$ (along y-axis) with $\dfrac{1}{T}$ (along x-axis) is linear.

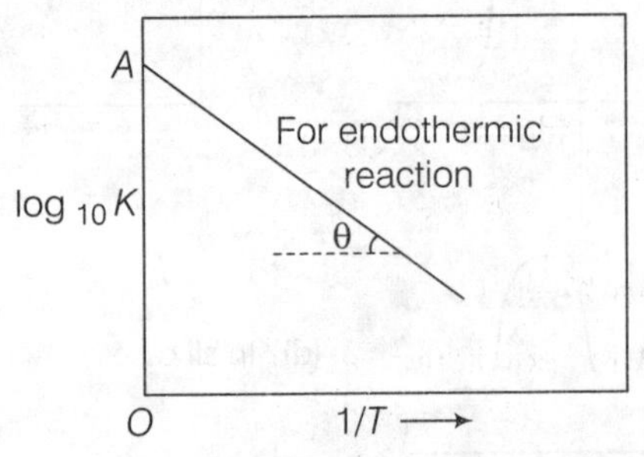

$$\text{Slope} = -\frac{\Delta H°}{2.303\ R} \text{ and } OA = \Delta S°/2.303\ R$$

If K_1 = equilibrium constant at temperature T_1 and K_2 = equilibrium constant at temperature T_2 then,

$$\frac{\Delta H°}{2.303\ R}\left[\frac{1}{T_1} - \frac{1}{T_2}\right] = \log_{10}\frac{K_2}{K_1}$$

$$\therefore \quad \Delta H° = \frac{2.303\ R\ T_1 T_2}{(T_2 - T_1)} \log \frac{K_2}{K_1}$$

(i) If $K_2 > K_1$, when $T_2 > T_1$ then $\Delta H°>0$ thus, endothermic.

(ii) If $K_2 < K_1$, when $T_2 > T_1$ then $\Delta H°<0$ thus, exothermic.

- In this case, K decreases with increase in temperature.

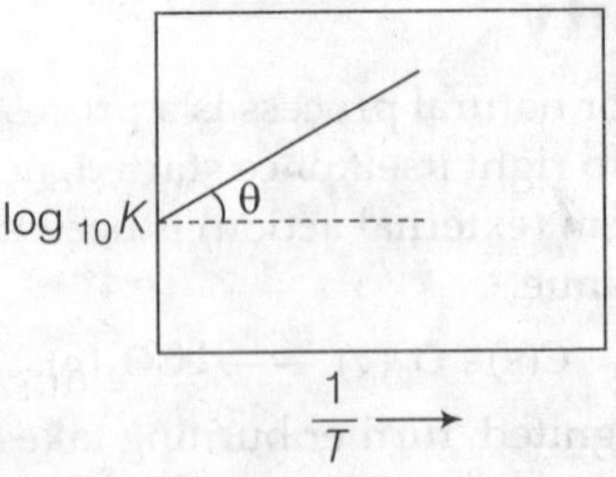

$\Delta G°$ is also related to EMF of a cell $E°$, $\Delta G° = -nFE°$

n = number of electrons

F = Faraday's of electricity = 96500 C

$$\therefore \quad E° = \frac{2.303\ RT}{nF} \log K$$

At 298K, $$\frac{2.303\ RT}{F} = \frac{2.303 \times 8.314 \times 298}{96500} = 0.0591\ \text{V}$$

Solved Examples & Instant Practice

Example 7.23) Phosphorylation of glucose is non-spontaneous reaction at 300 K, $\Delta G°$ is found to be $14.0\,\text{kJ mol}^{-1}$. Calculate the thermodynamic equilibrium constant. ($R = 8.314 \times 10^{-3}\text{kJ mol}^{-1}\text{K}^{-1}$)

Sol. $$\Delta G = \Delta G° + 2.303RT\log_{10}K$$

At equilibrium, $\Delta G = 0$

$$\therefore \quad \Delta G° = -2.303RT\log_{10}K$$

Thus, K is calculated.

$$\Delta G° = -2.303RT\log_{10}K$$

$$14 = -2.303 \times 8.314 \times 10^{-3} \times 300\log_{10}K$$

$$\therefore \quad \log_{10}K = -\frac{14 \times 10^3}{2.303 \times 8.314 \times 300} = -2.437$$

$$\therefore \quad K = 3.66 \times 10^{-3}$$

Immediate Test 17

For the following equilibrium at 300 K

$$A + B \rightleftharpoons C + D, \qquad \Delta G° = 460\text{ cal}$$

If two moles each of A and B were allowed to come equilibrium at 300 K, calculate ratio of molar concentration of $[C]$ to $[A]$ at equilibrium.

Example 7.24) For the following equilibrium at 400 K,

$$CaCO_3(s) \rightleftharpoons CaO(s) + CO_2(g)$$

$$\Delta H° = 20.0\text{ kJ mol}^{-1}, \quad p_{CO_2} = 0.12\text{ bar}$$

Calculate

(i) K_p (ii) $\Delta G°$(iii) $\Delta S°$

Sol. Species in gaseous state is CO_2,

thus, $K_p = p_{CO_2} \Rightarrow \Delta G° = -2.303RT\log K$

Thus, $\Delta G°$ is known

Also, $$\Delta G° = \Delta H° - T\Delta S°$$

Thus, $\Delta S°$ is calculated.

$$K_p = p_{CO_2} = 0.12\text{ bar}$$

$$\therefore \quad \Delta G° = -2.303 \times 8.314 \times 10^{-3} \times 400\log 0.12 = 7.052\text{kJ}$$

$$\therefore \quad \Delta G° = \Delta H° - T\Delta S°$$

$$\therefore \quad \Delta S° = \frac{\Delta H° - \Delta G°}{T} = \frac{20 - 7.052}{400} = 0.03237\text{kJ mol}^{-1}\text{K}^{-1}$$

$$= 32.37\text{ J mol}^{-1}\text{K}^{-1}$$

Immediate Test 18

For the reaction at 298 K

$$A(g) + B(g) \rightleftharpoons C(g) + D(g)$$

$$\Delta H° = -29.8\text{kcal mol}^{-1}$$

$$\Delta S° = -100\text{ cal mol}^{-1}\text{ K}^{-1}$$

calculate $\Delta G°$ and equilibrium constant.

Example 7.25) Variation of equilibrium constant K_{eq} with temperature T (K) is given by van't Hoff equation.

$$\log K_{eq} = \log A - \frac{\Delta H°}{2.303RT}$$

A graph between $\log K_{eq}$ and T^{-1} is linear as shown below.

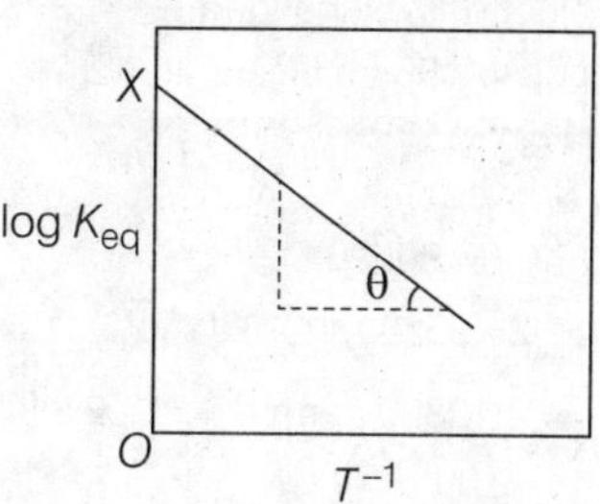

$$\tan^{-1} = 0.5 \quad \text{and} \quad OX = 10$$

Calculate,

(i) $\Delta H°$ (standard heat of reaction at 298 K).

(ii) K_{eq} at 298 K

(iii) K_{eq} at 798 K, if $\Delta H°$ is temperature independent in the given temperature range.

Sol. Variation of $\log K_C$ with T^{-1} is linear and can be compared to a straight line

$$y = c - mx \Rightarrow m = \text{slope} = \frac{\Delta H°}{2.303R}$$

Also, $$\Delta H° = \frac{2.303RT_1T_2}{(T_2 - T_1)}\log\frac{K_2}{K_1}$$

If T_1, T_2, K_1 are known, K_2 can be calculated.

(i) Slope = $\tan\theta = 0.5$

$$\therefore \quad \frac{\Delta H°}{2.303R} = 0.5 \Rightarrow \Delta H° = 2.303 \times 0.5 \times 2\text{ cal} = 2.303\text{ cal mol}^{-1}$$

(ii) $\log K_{eq} = 10 - \frac{0.5}{298} = 9.9983 \qquad K_{eq} = 9.96 \times 10^9$

(iii) K_{eq} at 798K

$$\Delta H° = \frac{2.303RT_1T_2}{(T_2 - T_1)}\log\frac{K_2}{K_1}$$

$$\frac{\Delta H°}{2.303R} = \frac{T_1T_2}{(T_2 - T_1)}\log\frac{K_2}{K_1}$$

$$0.5 = \frac{298 \times 798}{500}\log\frac{K_2}{9.96 \times 10^9}$$

$$\therefore \quad \log\left(\frac{K_2}{9.96 \times 10^9}\right) = \frac{0.5 \times 500}{298 \times 798} = 1.05 \times 10^{-3} \quad \therefore K_2 = 9.98 \times 10^9$$

Immediate Test 19

The vapour pressure of $H_2(g)$ over LiH(s) is 0.278m bar at 400 K and 27.8m bar at 900 K.

Calculate $\Delta H°$ in the given temperature range.

$$LiH(s) \rightleftharpoons Li(l) + \frac{1}{2}H_2(g)$$

Example 7.26) EMF of a cell with cell reaction

$$Zn + Cu^{2+} \rightleftharpoons Zn^{2+} + Cu$$

$$E^\circ_{cell} = 1.10\,V \text{ at } 298\,K$$

Calculate (i) ΔG°

(ii) equilibrium constant K_{eq}

Sol. Problem is based an electrochemical cell for which

$$\Delta G^\circ = -nFE^\circ_{cell}$$

where, n = number of electrons exchanged,

F = Faraday's constant

Also, $\Delta G^\circ = -2.303RT\log K_{eq}$

If ΔG° is known K_{eq} is derived

(i) $n = 2,\ F = 96500\,C$

$$\Delta G^\circ = -2 \times 96500 \times 1.10\text{ J mol}^{-1}$$

$$= -212300\text{ J mol}^{-1} = -212.3\text{ kJ mol}^{-1}$$

(ii) $\Delta G^\circ = -2.303RT\log K_{eq}$

$$-212.3 = -2.303 \times 8.314 \times 10^{-3} \times 298\log K_{eq}$$

$$\log K_{eq} = 37.2074 \Rightarrow K_{eq} = 1.6123 \times 10^{37}$$

■ If R in joules T in K and F = 96500 then $\frac{RT}{F}$ in volts.

Immediate Test 20

For an electrochemical cell with cell reaction

$$Zn + 2Ag^+(1\,M) \rightleftharpoons 2Ag + Zn^{2+}(1\,M)$$

$$K_{eq} = 6.2 \times 10^{52} \text{ at } 298\,K$$

Calculate (i) E°_{cell}, (ii) ΔG°

(Given at 298K, $\frac{2.303\,RT}{F} = 0.0591\,V$)

Example 7.27) At what minimum temperature, following reaction will be spontaneous?

$$2\,KClO_3 \longrightarrow 2KCl + 3O_2$$

Given, $\Delta H^\circ = 25\text{ kcal mol}^{-1},\ \Delta S^\circ = 50\text{ cal K}^{-1}$

Sol. A spontaneous reaction goes to completion after it is initiated,

$$\Delta G^\circ = \Delta H^\circ - T\Delta S^\circ$$

Reaction will be spontaneous, if

$\Delta G^\circ < 0$ i.e. $T\Delta S^\circ > \Delta H^\circ$

i.e. $T > \frac{\Delta H^\circ}{\Delta S^\circ} \Rightarrow T > \frac{25 \times 1000\text{ cal}}{50\text{ cal K}^{-1}} \Rightarrow > 500\text{K}^{-1}$

Immediate Test 21

The standard reaction enthalpy of

$$Zn(s) + H_2O(g) \longrightarrow ZnO(s) + H_2(g) \text{ is}$$

224 kJ mol^{-1} in the temperature range 920 K to 1280 K. If $\Delta G^\circ = 33\text{ kJmol}^{-1}$ at 1280 K. Calculate temperature at which the equilibrium constant becomes greater than 1.

Example 7.28) For the following reaction

$$A \rightleftharpoons B + C$$

$$\left(\frac{dx}{dt}\right) = 1.2 \times 10^{-3}\text{s}^{-1}[A] - 2.4 \times 10^{-2}\text{m}^{-1}\text{s}^{-1}[B][C] \text{ at } 400\,K$$

and $\left(\frac{dx}{dt}\right) = 1.0 \times 10^{-2}\text{s}^{-1}[A] - 2.0 \times 10^{-2}\text{m}^{-1}\text{s}^{-1}[B][C]$ at 500 K.

Calculate ΔH° in the given temperature range.

Sol. $\frac{dx}{dt} = K_f\text{ [reactant]} - K_b\text{ [product]}$

$$\Rightarrow K_C = \frac{K_f}{K_b}$$

Thus, at two temperatures equilibrium constants are known.

Thus, $\Delta H = \frac{2.303RT_1T_2}{(T_2 - T_1)}\log\frac{K_2}{K_1}$

$$K_1\text{ (at 400 K) } K_f / K_b = \frac{1.2 \times 10^{-3}}{2.4 \times 10^{-2}} = 0.05$$

$$K_2\text{ (at 500 K)} = \frac{1.0 \times 10^{-2}}{2.0 \times 10^{-2}} = 0.50$$

$\therefore$ $\frac{K_2}{K_1} = \frac{0.50}{0.05} = 10$

$\therefore$ $\Delta H^\circ = \frac{2.303 \times 8.314 \times 400 \times 500}{100}\log 10$

$$= 38294\text{ Jmol}^{-1}$$

$$= 38.294\text{ kJ mol}^{-1}$$

Example 7.29) For the following reactions

$$A \rightleftharpoons B + C,\ \Delta G_1^\circ, K_1,$$

$$B + C \rightleftharpoons D,\quad \Delta G_2^\circ, K_2$$

$$A \rightleftharpoons D,\quad \Delta G_3^\circ, K_3$$

What is relation between ΔG_1°, ΔG_2° and ΔG_3° and K_1, K_2 and K_3 for the reaction ?

When a net reaction is obtained by addition, equilibrium constants are multiplied but ΔG are added.

Sol.

$$A \rightleftharpoons B + C,\ K_1$$

$$B + C \rightleftharpoons D,\ K_2$$

$$A \rightleftharpoons D,\ K_3 = K_1K_2$$

$\therefore$ $\boxed{\log K_3 = \log K_1 + \log K_2}$

$\therefore$ $-\log K_3 = -\log K_1 - \log K_2$

Since, $\Delta G = -2.303RT\log K$

$\therefore$ $\frac{\Delta G_3}{2.303RT} = \frac{\Delta G_1}{2.303RT} + \frac{\Delta G_2}{2.303RT}$

$\therefore$ $\boxed{\Delta G_3 = \Delta G_1 + \Delta G_2}$

Example 7.30) In the following equilibrium

$$N_2O_4(g) \rightleftharpoons 2NO_2(g)$$

when 5 moles of each species are taken at 298 K, total pressure was found to be 20 bar.

Given, $\Delta G°(N_2O_4) = 100$ kJ mol^{-1}

$\Delta G°(NO_2) = 50$ kJ mol^{-1}

What is $\Delta G°$ of the reaction?

Predict the direction of the reaction.

Sol. $p_{total} = 20$ bar

Total moles of N_2O_4 and $NO_2 = 10$

$$\chi_{N_2O_4} = \chi_{NO_2} = \frac{5}{10} = 0.5$$

$\therefore$ $p_{N_2O_4} = p_{NO_2} = 0.5 \times 20 = 10$ bar

$\therefore$ Reaction quotient of

$$N_2O_4(g) \rightleftharpoons 2NO_2(g)$$

$$Q = \frac{p^2_{NO_2}}{p_{NO_4}} = \frac{100}{10} = 10$$

$$\Delta G = \Delta G° + 2.303RT\log Q$$

$$\Delta G° = 2\Delta G°(NO_2) - \Delta G°(N_2O_4) = 2 \times 50 - 100 = 0$$

$\therefore$ $\Delta G = 2.303RT\log 10 = +\text{ve}$

Thus, non-spontaneous.

KNOWLEDGE CONFIRMATION **Test 5**

1 In the following thermodynamic relation,

$$\log_{10} K = -1.04 - \frac{1088\ K}{T}$$

(a) entropy change is – 4.8 cal mol^{-1}K^{-1}

(b) enthalpy change is 5.01 kcal mol^{-1}

(c) equilibrium constant is 1×10^{-6} at 219.4 K

(d) All of the above are correct

2 For a reaction, $A \rightleftharpoons B$

variations of $\log_{10} K$ with $\frac{1}{T}$ can be represented graphically as

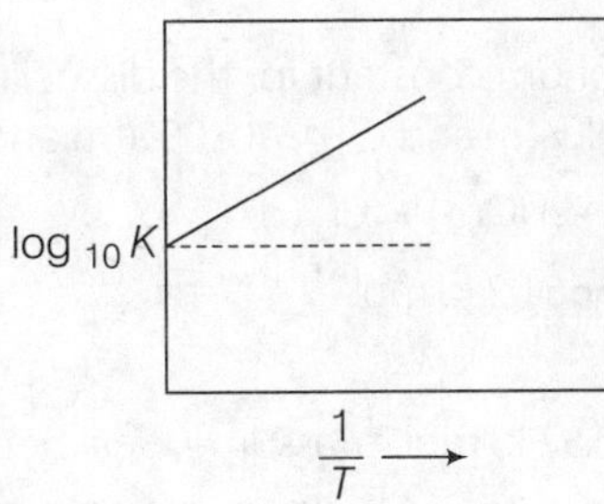

Thus,

(a) reaction is exothermic

(b) reaction is favoured at low temperature

(c) formation of NH_3 can be represented thermodynamically by this graph

(d) All of the above are correct

3 For a thermodynamic reaction in equilibrium

$A \rightleftharpoons B \quad \Delta G_1°, K_1$

$B \rightleftharpoons C \quad \Delta G_2°, K_2$

$A \rightleftharpoons C \quad \Delta G_3°, K_3$

then,

(a) $\log K_1 + \log K_2 = \log K_3$

(b) $\Delta G_1° + \Delta G_2° = \Delta G_3°$

(c) Both of the above are correct

(d) None of the above is correct

4 Which of the following is not the correct relation?

(a) $\Delta G° = -nFE°$ (b) $\Delta G = \Delta G° + 2.303RT\log Q$

(c) $\Delta G° = 2.303RT\log K_{eq}$ (d) $E° = \frac{0.0591}{n}\log K_{eq}$ at 298 K

5 If the equilibrium constant for a reaction is very small (say 1×10^{-20}), what would be the value of $\Delta G°$ expected to be?

(a) A small positive number (b) A large positive number

(c) A small negative number (d) A large negative number

6 Consider the following equilibria at 300 K and 400 K with their equilibrium constants.

		300 K	400 K
I.	$A(g) \rightleftharpoons 2B(g)$;	$K_{eq} = 10$	$K_{eq} = 5$
II.	$C(g) \rightleftharpoons D(g)$;	$K_{eq} = 2$	$K_{eq} = 5$

Thus,

(a) I is endothermic, II is exothermic

(b) I is exothermic, II is endothermic

(c) I and II both are endothermic

(d) I and II both are exothermic

7 For the following equilibrium at 298 K, starting with 1 mole of A and B, in 1L flask

$$2A + B \rightleftharpoons 2C + D$$

ratio of molar concentration of C and A at equilibrium is 2 : 1. Thus, $\Delta G°$ at 298 K is

(a) $-298\,R\log 4$ (b) $+298\,R\log 4$

(c) $-298\,R\log 2$ (d) $+298\,R\log 2$

8 van't Hoff isochore equation is

(a) $\log_{10} K = -\dfrac{\Delta H°}{2.303\ RT} + \dfrac{\Delta S°}{2.303R}$

(b) $\dfrac{d \log_{10} K}{dT} = \dfrac{\Delta H°}{2.303\ RT^2}$

(c) Both (a) and (b)

(d) None of the above

9 If ΔH and ΔG are negative and ΔS is positive, then reaction is

(a) spontaneous at all temperature

(b) non- spontaneous at all temperature

(c) spontaneous at low temperature and non-spontaneous at high temperature

(d) in equilibrium

10 For the following equilibrium at 298 K,

$$CO(g) + H_2O(g) \rightleftharpoons CO_2(g) + H_2(g)$$

($\Delta G°$ kcal mol^{-1}) −32.81 −54.64 −94.26 0.0

Thus, percentage of CO(g) converted into products is

(a) ≈ 100% (b) ≈ 50%

(c) ≈ 40% (d) ≈ 20%

11 At 1 atmospheric pressure, N_2O_4 is 50% dissociated at 300 K and 80% dissociated at 400 K.

$$N_2O_4(g) \rightleftharpoons 2NO_2(g)$$

Thus, $\Delta H°$ of the above equilibrium is

(a) $1200\ R \ln\left(\dfrac{16}{3}\right)$ (b) $400\ R \ln 3$

(c) $300\ R \ln 4$ (d) $1200\ R \ln\left(\dfrac{3}{16}\right)$

12 $\Delta G°$ at 25°C for the reaction,

$$\frac{1}{2} N_2\ (g) + \frac{3}{2} H_2(g) \rightleftharpoons NH_3(g)$$

is − 16.5 kJ mol^{-1}. Hence, thermodynamic equilibrium constant is

(a) 1.08 (b) 7.80×10^2

(c) 4.57×10^6 (d) 7.98×10^{34}

13 What are the signs for ΔH, ΔS and ΔG for the freezing of liquid water at −10°C?

(a) + − + (b) − − 0

(c) − + 0 (d) − − −

14 If the $E°_{cell}$ for a given reaction has a negative value, which gives the correct relationship for the values of $\Delta G°$ and K_{eq}?

(a) $\Delta G° > 0; K_{eq} < 1$ (b) $\Delta G° > 0; K_{eq} > 1$

(c) $\Delta G° < 0; K_{eq} > 1$ (d) $\Delta G° < 0; K_{eq} < 1$

15 For an isomerisation reaction $A \rightleftharpoons B$, the temperature dependence of equilibrium constant is given by

$$\log_e K = 4.0 - \frac{2000}{T}$$

The value of $\Delta S°$ at 400 K is , therefore

(a) $4R$ (b) $5R$ (c) $400R$ (d) $2000\ R$

16 For the equilibrium,

$$Cu^{2+}(aq) + 4NH_3(aq) \rightleftharpoons [Cu(NH_3)_4]^{2+}(aq)$$

$$[Cu^{2+}] = [NH_3] = [Cu(NH_3)_4]^{2+} = 0.01 M$$

$$\Delta G°_{298} = -70.54 \text{ kJ, thus } \Delta G_{298} \text{ is}$$

(a) −70.54 kJ (b) +24.89 kJ

(c) −24.89 kJ (d) +70.54 kJ

17 For the reaction

$$CaCO_3(s) \rightleftharpoons CaO(s) + CO_2(g)$$

$\Delta G°_{1000} = 2290$ kJ

Thus, pressure of CO_2 over a sample of $CaCO_3$ at 1000 K is

(a) 6.37×10^{-2} atm (b) 6.37×10^{-3} atm

(c) 1.73×10^{-3} atm (d) 2.06×10^{-3} atm

18 For the following equilibrium :

Glycerol + HPO_4^{2-} ⟶ DL-glycerol-1-phosphate + H_2O

$K = 0.0228$ at 25 °C and $K = 0.0122$ at 37°C

$\Delta G°_{298} = 9.37$ kJ

Thus, $\Delta S°$ at 298 K is

(a) +165.8 J K^{-1} (b) −165.8 J K^{-1}

(c) 134.5 J K^{-1} (d) −134.5 J K^{-1}

19 What is equilibrium constant for the dissociation of NOCl (g) into NO (g) and Cl(g) at 1.00 atm and 298 K ?

$$2\,NOCl\ (g) \longrightarrow 2NO(g) + Cl_2(g)$$

$\Delta_f G°(NOCl) = 66.07$ kJ mol^{-1}

$\Delta_f G°(Cl_2) = 0$

$\Delta_f G°(NO) = 86.57$ kJ mol^{-1} (assume ideal behaviour)

(a) 2.55×10^{-4} (b) 6.52×10^{-8}

(c) 1.30×10^{-7} (d) 1.70×10^{-14}

20 Based on above data, what is percent dissociation NOCl (g) at 1.00 atm ?

$$NOCl(g) \rightleftharpoons NO(g) + \frac{1}{2} Cl_2(g)$$

(a) 6.20% (b) 3.84% (c) 0.51% (d) 1.02%

ACID TEST

For JEE Main

TYPE I MCQs with Only ONE Correct Alternate

1 When 3.00 moles of A and 1.00 mole of B are mixed in a 1.00 L flask at 300 K, following equilibrium is set up

$$A(g) + 2B(g) \rightleftharpoons 2C(g)$$

The equilibrium mixture contains 0.50 mole of C. Thus, K_C is

(a) 0.12 (b) 0.72 (c) 0.36 (d) 0.48

2 Two moles of NO and an undetermined amount of O_2 are placed in a 1 L flask at 460°C. When following equilibrium is attained

$$2NO(g) + O_2(g) \rightleftharpoons 2NO_2(g),$$

equilibrium mixture contained 0.00156 mole O_2 and 0.500 mole of NO_2. Thus, equilibrium constant K_C is

(a) 4.42 (b) 40.1
(c) 71.2 (d) 214.0

3 Equilibrium constant of an exothermic reaction is expressed in the unit of $mol^{-2} L^2$. Product concentration can be increased by

I. increasing temperature
II. decreasing temperature
III. increasing pressure
IV. decreasing pressure

Select the correct option.

(a) I, II (b) II, III
(c) I, III (d) II, IV

4 For the heterogeneous equilibrium set up in a 6.50 L flask

$$CaCO_3(s) \rightleftharpoons CaO(s) + CO_2(g),$$
$$K_C = 0.02 \text{ mol L}^{-1}$$

What is minimum mass of $CaCO_3$ so that it decomposes completely to establish this equilibrium?

(a) 0.02 g (b) 2.0 g
(c) 0.13 g (d) 13.0 g

5 Consider following gaseous phase equilibrium

I. $PCl_5 \rightleftharpoons PCl_3 + Cl_2$
II. $2HI \rightleftharpoons H_2 + I_2$
III. $N_2 + 3H_2 \rightleftharpoons 2NH_3$
IV. $2SO_2 + O_2 \rightleftharpoons 2SO_3$

Molar concentration of each species in equilibrium is 0.01 M. Thus, extent of the reactions taking place is

(a) I < II < III < IV (b) I < II < IV < III
(c) IV < III < II < I (d) III < IV < II < I

6 5.1 g of NH_4SH is introduced in 3.0 L evacuated flask at 327°C. 30% of solid NH_4SH decomposed to NH_3 and H_2S as gases. The K_p of the reaction at 327°C is ($R = 0.082 \text{ atm mol}^{-1} \text{K}^{-1}$) ***[JEE Main 2019 (I) NTA]***

(a) 0.242×10^{-4} atm^2 (b) 0.242 atm^2
(c) 4.9×10^{-3} atm^2 (d) 1×10^{-4} atm^2

7 For the following equilibrium in gaseous phase,

$$3A + B \rightleftharpoons 2C, K_C = 9.0$$

volume of the flask in which 2.0 moles each of A, B and C can be placed in equilibrium is

(a) 10 L (b) 9 L (c) 6 L (d) 5 L

8 At 650 K, following equilibrium is set up by taking 0.25 mole each of CO_2 and H_2,

$$CO_2(g) + H_2(g) \rightleftharpoons CO(g) + H_2O(g), \ K_p = 0.16$$

At equilibrium, mole per cent of CO is

(a) 7.14 (b) 28.57 (c) 14.28 (d) 33.33

9 For the following equilibrium,

$$3A(g) + B(g) \rightleftharpoons 2C(g) + D(g),$$

initial moles of B is twice of A. At equilibrium moles of A and C are equal. Thus, per cent conversion of B is

(a) 5% (b) 10% (c) 20% (d) 40%

10 For the following equilibria :

	Equilibrium constant
I : $A + 2B \rightleftharpoons C$	K_1
II : $C + D \rightleftharpoons 3A$	K_2
III : $6B + D \rightleftharpoons 2C$	K_3

Thus,

(a) $3K_1 / K_2 = K_3$ (b) $\dfrac{K_1^3}{K_2} = K_3$
(c) $3K_1 / K_2^2 = K_3$ (d) $K_1^3 / K_3 = K_2$

11 $O_2(g) \rightleftharpoons 2O(g), K_p = 1.2 \times 10^{-10}$ at 1800 K.

Starting with 1 mole O_2 gas in a 10.0 L flask at 1800 K, number of O-atoms in the flask will be

(a) 1.71×10^{16} (b) 3.42×10^{18}
(c) 0.855×10^{18} (d) 1.71×10^{18}

12 For the following equilibrium,

$$C(s) + CO_2(g) \rightleftharpoons 2CO(g)$$
$$K_p = 3.00 \text{ at } 1000 \text{ K}.$$

If $p_{CO_2} = 0.48$ bar initially, p_{CO} at equilibrium will be

(a) 0.15 bar (b) 0.66 bar (c) 0.24 bar (d) 0.12 bar

13 For the following gaseous equilibria X, Y and Z at 300 K.

$X: 2SO_2 + O_2 \rightleftharpoons 2SO_3$

$Y: PCl_5 \rightleftharpoons PCl_3 + Cl_2$

$Z: 2HI \rightleftharpoons H_2 + I_2$

ratio of K_p and K_C $\left(\text{i.e.} \dfrac{K_p}{K_C}\right)$ in the increasing order is

(a) $X = Y = Z$ (b) $X < Y < Z$
(c) $X < Z < Y$ (d) $Z < Y < X$

14 $N_2 + 3H_2 \rightleftharpoons 2NH_3$ is a gaseous phase equilibrium reaction taking place in a 5 L flask at 400 K. For this,

(a) $K_C = K_\chi$ (b) $K_C = 25K_\chi$
(c) $K_\chi = 25K_C$ (d) $K_C = 5K_c$

15 Consider following equilibria :

I : $CaCO_3(s) \rightleftharpoons CaO(s) + CO_2(g)$, $p_{CO_2} = 2$ atm

II : $CO_2(g) + C(s) \rightleftharpoons 2CO(g)$, $K_p = 6$ atm

III : $CaCO_3(s) + C(s) \rightleftharpoons CaO(s) + 2CO(g)$, $K_p' = ?$

Thus, K_p' is

(a) 8 (b) 4 (c) 12 (d) 3

16 $N_2O_4 \rightleftharpoons 2NO_2$, $K_C = 4$. This reversible reaction is studied graphically as shown in the given figure. Select the correct statements out of I, II and III.

I. Reaction quotient has maximum value at point A.

II. Reaction proceeds left to right at a point when $[N_2O_4] = [NO_2] = 0.1$ M

III. $K_C = Q$ when point D or F is reached.

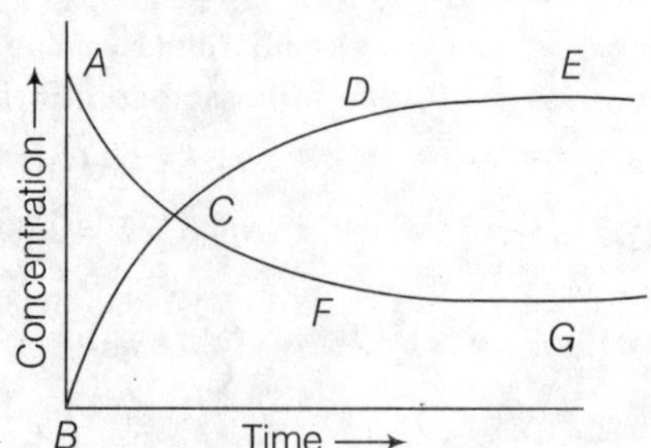

(a) I, II (b) II, III (c) I, III (d) I, II, III

17 Consider the reaction,

$$N_2(g) + 3H_2(g) \rightleftharpoons 2NH_3(g)$$

The equilibrium constant of the above reaction is K_p. If pure ammonia is left to dissociate, the partial pressure of ammonia at equilibrium is given by (Assume that $p_{NH_3} << p_{total}$ at equilibrium) ***[JEE Main 2019 (I) NTA]***

(a) $\dfrac{3^{3/2} K_p^{1/2} p^2}{4}$ (b) $\dfrac{3^{3/2} K_p^{1/2} p^2}{16}$

(c) $\dfrac{K_p^{1/2} p^2}{16}$ (d) $\dfrac{K_p^{1/2} p^2}{4}$

18 In the equilibrium, $PCl_5 \rightleftharpoons PCl_3 + Cl_2$ starting with 2 moles of PCl_5 in 5 L flask at 350 K, there is 80% dissociation. Hence, equilibrium pressure is

(a) 11.50 atm (b) 32.2 atm (c) 20.7 atm (d) 13.8 atm

19 In which case(s), vapour density remains unchanged on dissociation?

(a) $N_2O_4(g) \rightleftharpoons 2NO_2(g)$
(b) $N_2(g) + O_2(g) \rightleftharpoons 2NO(g)$
(c) $PCl_5(g) \rightleftharpoons PCl_3(g) + Cl_2(g)$
(d) In all of the above cases

20 For the reversible reaction,

$$2NO(g) + O_2(g) \rightleftharpoons 2NO_2(g).$$

Net rate is $\left(\dfrac{dx}{dt}\right)_{net} = 2.6 \times 10^3 [NO]^2[O_2] - 4.1[NO_2]^2$

In a reaction vessel, $[NO] = [O_2] = 0.01$ mol L^{-1} and $[NO_2] = 0.1$ mol L^{-1} then above reaction is

(a) shifted in forward direction
(b) shifted in backward direction
(c) in equilibrium
(d) not predictable in the absence of required data

21 $CO_2(g)$ can be dissolved in H_2O as given by

$$CO_2(g) + H_2O(l) \rightleftharpoons CO_2(aq)$$

Solubility of CO_2 in H_2O can be increased by

(a) increasing pressure (b) decreasing pressure
(c) decreasing volume of H_2O (d) increasing $CO_2(g)$

22 The following pictures represent the composition equilibrium mixture of the reaction, $A + B \rightleftharpoons AB$ at 300 K and 400 K.

at 300 K
at 400 K
A ●
B ○
AB ●○

This represents that it is

(a) an exothermic reaction
(b) an endothermic reaction
(c) a non-thermodynamic reaction with $\Delta H° =$ zero
(d) nothing can be predicted

23 Minimum temperature at which following reaction will be spontaneous is

$A \rightleftharpoons B, \Delta H = 50$ kcal mol^{-1}; $\Delta S = 100$ cal K^{-1}mol^{-1}

(a) 490 K (b) 500 K (c) 501 K (d) 500.1 K

24 A mixture was prepared with

$$[SO_3] = 0.50\text{ M}, [SO_2] = 0.00\text{ M}, [O_2] = 0.35\text{ M}$$

for the equilibrium at 600 K.

$$2SO_2(g) + O_2(g) \rightleftharpoons 2SO_3(g); \quad K_C = 4.00$$

At equilibrium $[O_2]$ is

(a) 0.045 M (b) 0.035 M
(c) 0.350 M (d) 0.45 M

25 Given the equilibrium constant values,

I. $N_2(g)+\frac{1}{2}O_2(g) \rightleftharpoons N_2O(g)$; $K_C = 2.7\times 10^{-18}$

II. $N_2O_4(g) \rightleftharpoons 2NO_2(g)$, $K_C = 4.6\times 10^{-3}$

III. $\frac{1}{2}N_2(g)+O_2(g) \rightleftharpoons NO_2(g)$; $K_C = 4.1\times 10^{-9}$

Thus, for the reaction,

$2N_2O(g)+3O_2(g) \rightleftharpoons 2N_2O_4(g)$, K_C is

(a) 5.46×10^{7} (b) 5.46×10^{-7}
(c) 1.832×10^{6} (d) 1.832×10^{-6}

26 1, 3-butadiene and 1-butyne exist in equilibrium in gaseous phase at 296 K.

$CH_2{=}CH{-}CH{=}CH_2(g) \rightleftharpoons CH_3CH_2C{\equiv}CH(g)$

$\Delta G°$ 152.41 kJ mol^{-1} 201.7 (kJ mol^{-1})

Ratio of their partial pressures at 298 K is

(a) 2×10^{-9} (b) 1×10^{-9}
(c) 8×10^{-7} (d) 8×10^{-6}

27 Variation of $\log K_p$ with temperature (T) is given by for the equilibrium :

$NH_4HS(s) \rightleftharpoons NH_3(g)+H_2S(g)$

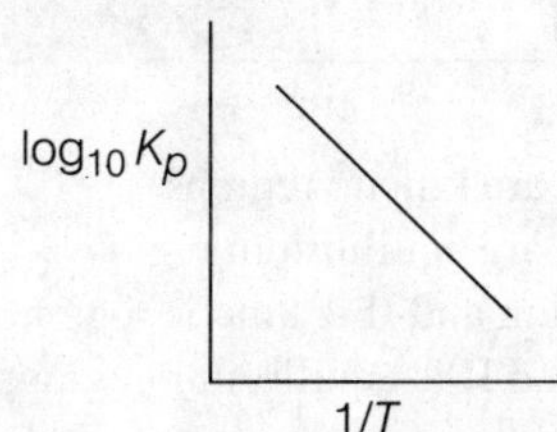

The equilibrium is displaced in forward side on
(a) increasing temperature and decreasing pressure
(b) increasing temperature and pressure both
(c) decreasing temperature and pressure both
(d) decreasing temperature and increasing pressure

28 Which of the following reaction almost goes to the completion?

(a) $2Cu(s)+O_2(g) \rightleftharpoons CuO(s)$, $K_C = 4\times 10^{45}$
(b) $H_3PO_4(aq) \rightleftharpoons H_2PO_4^-(aq)+H^+(aq)$, $K_C = 7.5\times 10^{-3}$
(c) $2HBr(g) \rightleftharpoons H_2(g)+Br_2(g)$, $K_C = 2\times 10^{-19}$
(d) $Cl_2(g) \rightleftharpoons 2Cl(g)$, $K_C = 6.4\times 10^{-39}$

29 For the following equilibrium reaction,

$N_2O_4(g) \rightleftharpoons 2NO_2(g)$

NO_2 is 50% of the total volume at a given temperature. Hence, vapour density of the equilibrium mixture is

(a) 34.5 (b) 25.0
(c) 23.0 (d) 20.0

30 There is 50% dimer formation of benzoic acid (C_6H_5COOH) in benzene solution

$2C_6H_5COOH \rightleftharpoons (C_6H_5COOH)_2$

Hence, abnormal molecular weight of benzoic acid (theoretical value = 122 g mol^{-1}) is

(a) 61 g mol^{-1} (b) 244 g mol^{-1}
(c) 163 g mol^{-1} (d) 81 g mol^{-1}

31 For the equilibrium,

$N_2O_4(g) \rightleftharpoons 2NO_2(g)$

$x = \frac{D-d}{d}$ where, d is experimental vapour density and D is theoretical vapour density. Thus, for the equilibrium

$NO_2(g) \rightleftharpoons \frac{1}{2}N_2O_4(g)$, x is

(a) $\frac{d}{D-d}$ (b) $\frac{1}{2}\frac{d}{(D-d)}$
(c) $2\left(\frac{d-D}{D}\right)$ (d) $2\left(\frac{d-D}{d}\right)$

32 In the following equilibrium at 400 K in 1 dm^3 flask,

$COCl_2(g) \rightleftharpoons CO(g)+Cl_2(g)$

ratio of theoretical and experimental vapour density is 1.4. Thus, equilibrium constant K_C is

(a) 0.267 (b) 3.75 (c) 1.00 (d) 0.667

33 $A(g)$ is 100% converted into B according to the reaction,

$A(g) \rightleftharpoons 3B(g)$

Value of $\left(\frac{D}{d}\right)$ at this point is

(a) 1.0 (b) 2.0 (c) 2.5 (d) 3.0

34 Equilibrium constant for the following equilibrium

$3ClO^-(aq) \rightleftharpoons 2Cl^-(aq)+ClO_3^-(aq)$

is 1.0×10^{28} at a temperature at which $RT = 2500$ J mol^{-1}. Gibbs free energy change ($\Delta G°$) is

(a) – 70.0 kJ mol^{-1} (b) + 30.395 kJ mol^{-1}
(c) – 161.21 kJ mol^{-1} (d) + 371.24 kJ mol^{-1}

35 For the reaction at 298 K,

$D_2O(l) \rightleftharpoons D_2O(g)$; $\Delta_r G°_{298} = 8.904$ kJ

Thus, vapour pressure of D_2O at 298 K is

(a) 2.75×10^{-2} bar (b) 760 torr
(c) 1.00 bar (d) 0.0821 atm

36 Naphthalene, a white solid used to make mothballs, has a vapour pressure of 0.10 mmHg at 27°C. Hence, K_p (atm) and K_C (mol L^{-1}) for the equilibrium are respectively

$C_{10}H_8(s) \rightleftharpoons C_{10}H_8(g)$

(a) 0.10, 0.10 (b) 0.10, 4.1×10^{-3}
(c) 1.32×10^{-4}, 5.36×10^{-6} (d) 5.36×10^{-6}, 1.32×10^{-4}

37 For the following equilibrium, $N_2O_4(g) \rightleftharpoons 2NO_2(g)$ K_p (in atm) is found to be equal to K_C (in mol L^{-1}). This is attained when

(a) $T = 1$ K (b) $T = 12.18$ K
(c) $T = 27.3$ K (d) $T = 273$ K

38 Aerated water contains CO_2 dissolved in water

$$CO_2(g) + H_2O(l) \rightleftharpoons H_2CO_3(aq)$$

Variation of solubility (S) with pressure (p) is shown by

(a) (b)

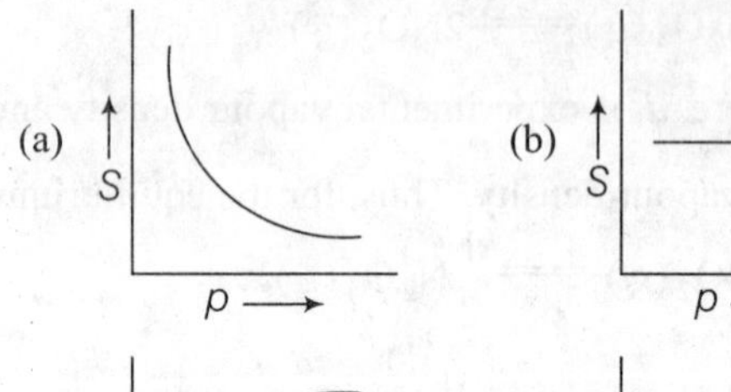

(c) (d)

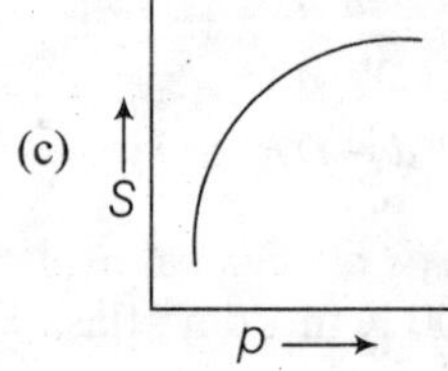

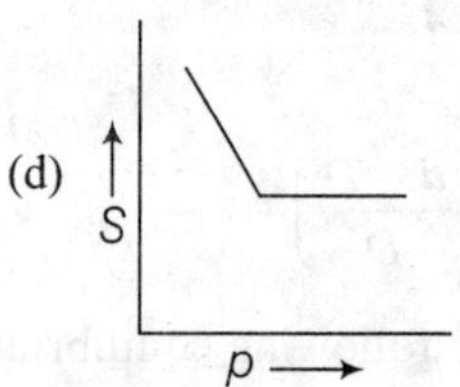

39 For the following equilibrium at 373 K,

$$H_2O(l) \rightleftharpoons H_2O(g)$$

$\Delta G°$ is

(a) $-2.303\,RT$ (b) $+2.303\,RT$
(c) 0.00 (d) 1.00

40 ΔG at 298 K for the following equilibrium is

$$H_2O(l) \rightleftharpoons H^+(aq) + OH^-(aq)$$

(Given $\Delta_r G° = 79.885$ kJ)

(a) -79.885 kJ (b) $+79.885$ kJ
(c) 0.00 kJ (d) -39.941 kJ

41 $CCl_4(g)$ dissociates 50% into gaseous free radicals at 1000 K and at equilibrium experimental vapour density is found to be 38.5. Thus, $CCl_4(g)$ dissociates under the given conditions to

(a) $CCl_3(g)$, $Cl(g)$ (b) $CCl_2(g)$, $Cl(g)$
(c) $C(g)$, $Cl(g)$ (d) $CCl(g)$, $Cl(g)$

42 0.578 g $N_2O_4(g)$ dissociates in a 1 dm^3 flask at 308 K and gives a pressure of 24.12 kPa.

$$N_2O_4(g) \rightleftharpoons 2NO_2(g)$$

Thus, degree of dissociation of N_2O_4 is

(a) 10% (b) 20.2% (c) 40.5% (d) 50.0%

43 $SO_3(g)$ is partially dissociated into $SO_2(g)$ and $O_2(g)$ at 900 K and 1 atm as

$$SO_3(g) \rightleftharpoons SO_2(g) + \frac{1}{2}O_2(g)$$

The density of the equilibrium mixture was found to be 0.866 g dm^{-3}. Thus, degree of dissociation of $SO_3(g)$ is

(a) 20% (b) 25% (c) 50% (d) 75%

44 For the equilibrium,

α-(D) glucose $\rightleftharpoons$ β-(D) glucose $K_C = 1.8$

The percentage of α-(D)-glucose at equilibrium in the mixture is

(a) 35.7 (b) 40.2
(c) 91.0 (d) 27.2

45 In the reaction

$$AB(g) \rightleftharpoons A(g) + B(g)$$

at 303 K, $K_p = 2.56 \times 10^{-2}$ bar

At equilibrium, total pressure is 1 bar. Thus, percentage dissociation of AB is

(a) 87% (b) 16%
(c) 13% (d) 6%

46 Variation of the concentration of the reactant (X) and the product (Y) is shown in the figure. Select the correct statement(s).

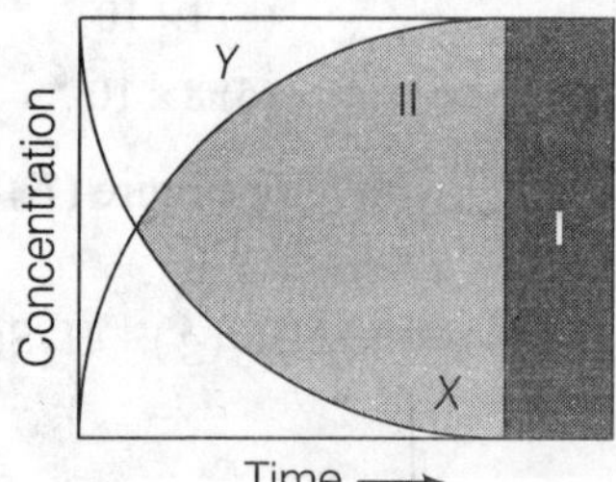

(a) I and II both are kinetic regions
(b) I and II both are equilibrium regions
(c) I is equilibrium and II is kinetic regions
(d) I is kinetic and II is equilibrium regions

47 Given exothermic reaction,

$$CoCl_4^{2-}(aq) + 6H_2O(l) \rightleftharpoons [Co(H_2O)_6]^{2+} + 4Cl^-$$

Which one of the following will decrease the equilibrium concentration of $CoCl_4^{2-}$?

(a) Addition of HCl
(b) Addition of $Co(NO_3)_2$
(c) The solution is diluted with water
(d) The temperature is increased

48 $Ca(HCO_3)_2(s)$ decomposes as

$$Ca(HCO_3)_2(s) \longrightarrow CaCO_3(s) + H_2O(g) + CO_2(g)$$

Total pressure at equilibrium is found to be 0.12 bar. Thus, K_p is

(a) 0.24 (b) 0.06
(c) 0.0036 (d) 0.0144

49 Select the incorrect statement.

(a) There is no change in the concentration of the reactants and products at equilibrium.
(b) Equilibrium is always dynamic.
(c) Equilibrium can be approached from either of the sides.
(d) Catalyst can alter the state of equilibrium.

50 Which of the following relative value of K_f (rate constant of forward reaction) and K_b (rate constant of backward reaction) results in an equilibrium mixture that contain large amount of reactant and small amounts of products?
(a) $K_f > K_b$ (b) $K_f = K_b$
(c) $K_f < K_b$ (d) None of these

51 When hydrochloric acid is added to cobalt (II) nitrate solution at room temperature, the following reaction takes place.

$$\underset{\text{Pink}}{[Co(H_2O)_6]^{2+}} + 4Cl^-(aq) \rightleftharpoons \underset{\text{Blue}}{[CoCl_4]^{2+}(aq)} + 6H_2O(l)$$

The solution is blue at room temperature. It turns pink when cooled in a freezing mixture. Thus, for the forward reaction
(a) $\Delta H > 0$ (b) $\Delta H < 0$
(c) $\Delta H = 0$ (d) Not predictable

52 Two moles each of reactant A and B are taken in a 5L reaction flask. They react as

$$A(g) + B(g) \rightleftharpoons C(g) + D(g)$$

when equilibrium is attained, concentration of C is triple of B. Thus, K_C is
(a) 4.5 (b) 6 (c) 9 (d) $\frac{1}{6}$

53 Consider the reaction for which $K_p = 0.497$ bar at 500 K

$$PCl_5(g) \rightleftharpoons PCl_3(g) + Cl_2(g)$$

If the three gases are mixed in a closed vessel so that $p_{PCl_5} = p_{Cl_2} = p_{Cl_3} = 1$ bar select the correct statement.
(a) More PCl_5 will be produced.
(b) More PCl_3 will be produced.
(c) Equilibrium will be established when 50% reaction is complete.
(d) None of the above

54 $\Delta_f G°$ at 500 K for a substance 'S' in liquid state and gaseous state are + 100.7 kcal mol^{-1} and + 103 kcal mol^{-1} respectively.

$$S(l) \rightleftharpoons S(g)$$

Vapour pressure of liquid 'S' at 500 K is approximately ($R = 2$ cal mol^{-1} K^{-1}) **[JEE Main 2018]**
(a) 100 atm (b) 1 atm (c) 10 atm (d) 0.1 atm

55 At 320 K, a gas A_2 is 20% dissociated to $A(g)$. The standard free energy change at 320 K and 1 atm in J mol^{-1} is **[JEE Main 2018]**
(a) 4763 (b) 2068 (c) 4281 (d) 1844

56 The equilibrium constant at 298 K for a reaction $A + B \rightleftharpoons C + D$ is 100. If the initial concentration of all the four species were 1 M each, then equilibrium concentration of D (in mol L^{-1}) will be **[JEE Main 2016]**
(a) 0.818 (b) 1.818 (c) 1.182 (d) 0.182

57 The increase of pressure on (ice $\rightleftharpoons$ water) system at constant temperature will lead to **[JEE Main 2015]**
(a) no effect on the equilibrium
(b) a decrease in the entropy of the system
(c) a shift of the equilibrium in the forward direction
(d) an increase in the Gibbs energy of the system

58 The standard Gibbs energy change at 300 K for the reaction $2A \longrightarrow B + C$, is 2494.2 J mol^{-1}. At a given time, the composition of the reaction mixture is

$$[A] = \frac{1}{2}, [B] = 2 \text{ and } [C] = \frac{1}{2}$$

The reaction proceeds in the **[JEE Main 2015]**
(a) forward direction because $Q > K_C$
(b) reverse direction because $Q > K_C$
(c) forward direction because $Q < K_C$
(d) reverse direction because $Q < K_C$

59 For the reaction, $SO_2(g) + \frac{1}{2}O_2(g) \rightleftharpoons SO_3(g)$, if $K_p = K_C(RT)^x$ where the symbols have usual meanings then, the value of x is (assuming ideality), **[JEE Main 2014]**
(a) -1 (b) $-\frac{1}{2}$ (c) $\frac{1}{2}$ (d) 1

60 The equilibrium constant (K_C) for the reaction, $N_2(g) + O_2(g) \longrightarrow 2NO(g)$ at temperature T is 4×10^{-4}. The value of K_C for the reaction $NO(g) \longrightarrow \frac{1}{2}N_2(g) + \frac{1}{2}O_2(g)$ at the same temperature is **[AIEEE 2012]**
(a) 0.02 (b) 2.5×10^2 (c) 4×10^{-4} (d) 50.0

61 A vessel at 1000 K contains CO_2 with a pressure of 0.5 atm. Some of the CO_2 is converted into CO on the addition of graphite; if the total pressure at equilibrium is 0.8 atm, the value of K_p is **[AIEEE 2011]**
(a) 1.8 atm (b) 3 atm (c) 0.3 atm (d) 0.18 atm

62 For the following three reactions, I, II and III, equilibrium constants are given
I. $CO(g) + H_2O(g) \rightleftharpoons CO_2(g) + H_2(g)$, K_1
II. $CH_4(g) + H_2O(g) \rightleftharpoons CO(g) + 3H_2(g)$, K_2
III. $CH_4(g) + 2H_2O(g) \rightleftharpoons CO_2(g) + 4H_2(g)$, K_3
Which of the following relations is correct? **[AIEEE 2008]**
(a) $K_1\sqrt{K_2} = K_3$ (b) $K_2K_3 = K_1$
(c) $K_3 = K_1K_2$ (d) $K_3K_2^3 = K_1^2$

63 The equilibrium constants K_{p_1} and K_{p_2} for the reactions $X \rightleftharpoons 2Y$ and $Z \rightleftharpoons P + Q$, respectively are in the ratio of 1 : 9. If the degree of dissociation of X and Z be equal, then the ratio of total pressure at these equilibria is **[AIEEE 2008]**
(a) 1 : 36 (b) 1 : 1 (c) 1 : 3 (d) 1 : 9

64 The equilibrium constant K_C for the reaction,

$$SO_3(g) \rightleftharpoons SO_2(g) + \frac{1}{2}O_2(g)$$

is 4.9×10^{-2}. The value of K_C for the reaction $2SO_2(g) + O_2(g) \rightleftharpoons 2SO_3(g)$ will be ***[AIEEE 2006]***

(a) 416 (b) 2.40×10^{-3} (c) 9.8×10^{-2} (d) 4.9×10^{-2}

65 Phosphorus pentachloride dissociates as follows, in a closed reaction vessel

$$PCl_5(g) \rightleftharpoons PCl_3(g) + Cl_2(g)$$

If the total pressure at equilibrium of the reaction mixture is p and degree of dissociation of PCl_5 is x, the partial pressure of PCl_3 will be ***[AIEEE 2006]***

(a) $\left(\frac{x}{x+1}\right)p$ (b) $\left(\frac{2x}{1-x}\right)p$ (c) $\left(\frac{x}{x-1}\right)p$ (d) $\left(\frac{x}{1-x}\right)p$

66 An amount of solid NH_4HS is placed in a flask already containing ammonia gas at a certain temperature and 0.50 atm pressure. Ammonium hydrogen sulphide decomposes to yield NH_3 and H_2S gases in the flask. When the decomposition reaction reaches equilibrium, the total pressure in the flask rises to 0.84 atm. The equilibrium constant for the decomposition of NH_4HS at this temperature is ***[AIEEE 2005]***

(a) 0.11 (b) 0.17 (c) 0.18 (d) 0.30

67 For the reaction,

$$2NO_2(g) \rightleftharpoons 2NO(g) + O_2(g)$$

$[K_C = 1.8 \times 10^{-6}$ at 184°C, $R = 0.00831$ kJ/(mol K)]

When K_p and K_C are compared at 184°C it is found that ***[AIEEE 2005]***

(a) whether K_p is greater than, less than or equal to K_C depends upon the total gas pressure

(b) $K_p = K_C$

(c) K_p is less than K_C

(d) K_p is greater than K_C

68 The following data for the equilibrium composition of the reaction :

$$2Na(g) \rightleftharpoons Na_2(g)$$

at 1.0×10^3 Pa pressure and 1480 K have been obtained.

Mass % of Na (monomer gas) = 71.3

Mass % of Na_2 (dimer gas) = 28.7

Thus, K_p is

(a) 2.43×10^{-4} (b) 4.8×10^{-4}

(c) 2.43×10^3 (d) 2.43×10^{-3}

69 For the following equilibrium in gaseous phase at 400 K and a total pressure 11.5 bar,

$PCl_5 \rightleftharpoons PCl_3 + Cl_2$, $K_p = 0.25$

Thus, volume per cent of Cl_2 at equilibrium is

(a) 2.74% (b) 0.274%

(c) 27.4% (d) None of these

70 Solid NH_4I dissociates at 400K and HI formed dissociates into H_2 and I_2.

I. $NH_4I(s) \rightleftharpoons NH_3(g) + HI(g), K_p = 36$

II. $2HI(g) \rightleftharpoons H_2(g) + I_2(g), K_2 = ?$

If both the equilibria exist simultaneously and partial pressure of $I_2(g)$ is 2 atm, and then K_2 is

(a) 0.12 (b) 0.21 (c) 10.0 (d) 0.01

71 If $\left(\frac{d \log_e K_p}{dT}\right) = \frac{\Delta H°}{RT^2}$ then $\left(\frac{d \log_e K_C}{dT}\right)$ is equal to

(a) $-\frac{\Delta U°}{RT^2}$ (b) $\frac{\Delta U°}{RT^2}$ (c) $\frac{\Delta U°}{RT}$ (d) $-\frac{\Delta U°}{RT} + \frac{\Delta n_g}{T}$

72 At 1400K, for the reactions in equilibrium :

I. $3H_2(g) + SO_2(g) \rightleftharpoons H_2S(g) + 2H_2O(g)$, $K_{p_1} = 1.8 \times 10^4$

II. $H_2(g) + \frac{1}{2}S_2(g) \rightleftharpoons H_2S(g), K_{p_2} = 0.80$

Thus, K_{p_3} for the equilibrium

III. $4H_2(g) + 2SO_2(g) \rightleftharpoons S_2(g) + 4H_2O(g)$ is

(a) 2.25×10^{-3} (b) 5.06×10^{-8}

(c) 5.00×10^8 (d) 2.25×10^3

73 In a system , the equilibrium reaction

$$\frac{1}{2}N_2(g) + \frac{3}{2}H_2(g) \rightleftharpoons NH_3(g)$$

was studied from pure NH_3. At 0.1325 bar pressure and 673K, gaseous mixture contained 3.85 mol% of NH_3. Thus K_x (in terms of mole fraction) is

(a) 0.128 (b) 0.256 (c) 0.064 (d) 0.512

74 At 298K, $\Delta G°$ for the reaction, $N_2O_4(g) \rightleftharpoons 2NO_2(g)$ is 5.74 kJ mol^{-1}. Thus, degree of dissociation at a pressure of 10 bar and 298K is (RT= 2.48 kJ mol^{-1})

(a) 0.025 (b) 0.01 (c) 0.05 (d) 0.10

75 In a closed vessel containing ammonium carbamate (NH_2COONH_4) in equilibrium with its vapour, NH_3 is added such that the partial pressure of NH_3 now equals the original total pressure. Thus, the ratio of the total pressure to, the original pressure is

$$NH_2COONH_4(s) \rightleftharpoons CO_2(g) + 2NH_3(g)$$

(a) 31 :27 (b) 27 : 31 (c) 1 :1 (d) 31 :9

76 For the following equilibrium in gaseous phase at 298 K.

$$2A(g) + B(g) \rightleftharpoons A_2B(g) \quad \Delta G° = -5.0 \text{ kJ mol}^{-1}$$

Total pressure required to convert 60% of B into A_2B when the reactants in the stoichiometric ratio are used, is (RT = 2.48 kJ mol^{-1})

(a) 0.01 atm (b) 1.00 atm

(c) 1.60 atm (d) 0.10 atm

ACID TEST
For JEE Advanced

TYPE I MCQs with Only ONE Correct Alternate

77 4.86 g of $Ca(HCO_3)_2$ is heated at 400 K in 1 L flask and after equilibrium is attained, temperature is reduced to 298 K.

$$Ca(HCO_3)_2(s) \rightleftharpoons CaO(s) + 2CO_2(g) + H_2O(l), \quad K_p = 0.25$$

(pressure is in the unit of bar)

Percentage of $Ca(HCO_3)_2$ remained unreacted is

(a) 33.33% (b) 66.66% (c) 50.00% (d) 25.00%

78 For the following equilibrium,

$$CaCO_3(s) \rightleftharpoons CaO(s) + CO_2(g)$$

experiments carried out between 850°C and 950°C lead to set of K_p values following the equation :

$$\log K_p = 7.282 - \frac{8500\,K}{T}$$

If the reaction is carried out in quiet air, what temperature would be predicted for the complete decomposition of $CaCO_3$?

(a) 1123 K (b) 1223 K
(c) 1167 K (d) 1173 K

79 For the following equilibrium,

$$N_2O_4(g) \rightleftharpoons 2NO_2(g), \quad K_C = 0.67$$

If we start with 3 moles of NO_2 and 1 mole of N_2O_4 in 1 L flask, then NO_2 present at equilibrium is

(a) 1.51 mol (b) 2.02 mol
(c) 1.17 mol (d) 0.85 mol

80 13.8 g of N_2O_4 was placed in 1 L reaction vessel at 400 K and total pressure at equilibrium was found to be 9.15 bar.

$$N_2O_4 \rightleftharpoons 2NO_2$$

Thus, K_p is

(a) 83.10 (b) 9.385
(c) 2.586 (d) None of these

81 At 90° C, the following equilibrium is established

$$H_2(g) + S(s) \rightleftharpoons H_2S(g), K = 6.8 \times 10^{-2}$$

If 0.20 mole of H_2 and 1.0 mole of sulphur are heated to 90°C in a 1.0 L vessel, partial pressure of H_2S at equilibrium will be

(a) 0.42 bar (b) 0.38 bar
(c) 1.27 bar (d) 0.27 bar

82 If 1.0 mole of A, 2.0 moles of B and 3.0 moles of C are placed in a 1.0 L flask and allowed to come to equilibrium, the final concentration of C is 1.4 mol L^{-1}. Thus, equilibrium constant is for the equilibrium

$$A + 2B \rightleftharpoons 2C$$

(a) 11.90 (b) 0.84 (c) 0.084 (d) 1.19

83 One mole of $Ca(HCO_3)_2$ is decomposed in a 10 L flask at 400 K and when equilibrium is set up temperature was restored at 298 K.

$$Ca(HCO_3)_2(s) \rightleftharpoons CaO(s) + H_2O(g) + 2CO_2(g)$$

CO_2 formed required 200 mL of 5 M KOH to absorb it. Thus, K_p at 298 K is

(a) 1.06 (b) 0.95 (c) 0.66 (d) 1.53

84 Fe^{2+} complexed with CN^- forms $[Fe(CN)_6]^{4-}$

$$Fe^{2+} + 6CN^- \rightleftharpoons [Fe(CN)_6]^{4-}, \quad K = 1 \times 10^{24}$$

Fe^{2+} in equilibrium with $[Fe(CN)_6]^{4-}$ when 75.0 mL of 0.03 M $FeSO_4$ is mixed with 125.0 mL of 0.20 M KCN is

(a) 6.0×10^{-19} M (b) 1.2×10^{-18} M
(c) 3.0×10^{-19} M (d) 6.0×10^{-18} M

85 1 mole N_2 and 3 moles H_2 are taken in a closed vessel. When equilibrium is set up,

$$N_2 + 3H_2 \rightleftharpoons 2NH_3$$

partial pressure of N_2 is $\frac{p}{3}$. If total pressure is $2p$, then K_p is

(a) $1.33\, p^2$ (b) $1.33\, p^{-2}$
(c) $0.33\, p^{-2}$ (d) None of these

86 For the reaction in equilibrium at 1400 K in a 10 L flask

$$CH_4(g) + 2H_2S(g) \rightleftharpoons CS_2(g) + 4H_2(g), \quad (K_C = 2.5 \times 10^{-3})$$

3.0 moles each of CS_2 and H_2, 4.0 moles of H_2S and 2.00 moles of CH_4 are taken. For such case

(a) reaction proceeds towards left to attain equilibrium
(b) reaction proceeds towards right to attain equilibrium
(c) reaction is in equilibrium
(d) given data is insufficient to decide the direction

87 Following equilibrium is set up in a 10 L flask at 2000 K and at 8 atm

$$2O_3(g) \rightleftharpoons 3O_2(g) \quad \Delta G° = -534.52\,kJ$$

Thus, partial pressure of O_2 is found to be

(a) 9.71×10^{-2} atm (b) 9.71×10^{-4} atm
(c) 2.40×10^{-6} atm (d) 8.0×10^{-6} atm

88 Following equilibria take place in a closed vessel simultaneously.

$$PCl_5(g) \rightleftharpoons PCl_3(g) + Cl_2(g)$$
$$COCl_2(g) \rightleftharpoons CO(g) + Cl_2(g)$$

After decomposition of PCl_5, some $CO(g)$ is added. Thus, equilibrium concentration of

(a) PCl_5 decreases (b) PCl_5 increases
(c) Cl_2 increases (d) PCl_3 decreases

89 Under the given conditions of temperature T K, $K_p = K_C$ for the following equilibrium in gaseous phase

$$N_2 + 3H_2 \rightleftharpoons 2NH_3$$

Thus, temperature T is

(a) 273 K (b) 546 K (c) 1 K (d) 12.2 K

90 Following equilibrium is set up by taking 1 mole of N_2 and 3 moles of H_2 in a closed container at a pressure of 4 atm.

$$N_2 + 3H_2 \rightleftharpoons 2NH_3$$

After equilibrium is set up, pressure falls by 1 atm. Thus, equilibrium constant K_p for the following equilibrium is

$$2NH_3 \rightleftharpoons N_2 + 3H_2$$

(a) 1.6875 (b) 0.1875 (c) 3.3750 (d) 5.3333

91 Consider following equilibria in aqueous alkaline solution

I. $S + S^{2-} \longrightarrow S_2^{2-}$, $K_1 = 12$

II. $2S + S^{2-} \longrightarrow S_3^{2-}$, $K_2 = 132$

III. $S_2^{2-} + S \longrightarrow S_3^{2-}$, $K_3 = ?$

Thus, K_3 is

(a) 11 (b) 12 (c) 132 (d) 0.091

92 Degree of dissociation x of the following gaseous phase reaction is related to equilibrium constant K_p by

$$2HI \rightleftharpoons H_2 + I_2$$

(a) $\sqrt{0.5 + K_p}$ (b) $0.5 + \sqrt{K_p}$

(c) $\sqrt{\dfrac{K_p}{0.5 + K_p}}$ (d) $\dfrac{\sqrt{K_p}}{0.5 + \sqrt{K_p}}$

93 Following equilibrium was studied in the presence of inert gas Ne.

$$2NH_3(g) \rightleftharpoons N_2(g) + 3H_2(g)$$

At equilibrium at 700 K and 10 atm, the equilibrium gaseous mixture contains 10 mole % each of $N_2(g)$ and $NH_3(g)$. Thus, K_p is

(a) 4.32×10^2 (b) 8.64×10^2
(c) 6.92×10^2 (d) 9.7×10^2

94 For the following equilibrium,

$$C(\text{diamond}) \rightleftharpoons C(\text{graphite}), \Delta H = 13.1 \text{ kJ mol}^{-1}$$

density (g mL^{-1}) 3.5 2.3

Thus, favourable conditions for the formation of diamond are

(a) high pressure, low temperature
(b) low pressure, low temperature
(c) high pressure, high temperature
(d) low pressure, high temperature

95 N_2O_5 dissociates in the following steps

$$N_2O_5(g) \rightleftharpoons N_2O_3 + O_2, K_C = 2.5$$
$$N_2O_3 \rightleftharpoons N_2O + O_2$$

4 moles of N_2O_5 in a 1 L flask are allowed to attain equilibrium. O_2 formed was 2.5 M. Thus, equilibrium concentration of N_2O is

(a) 1.00 M (b) 1.50 M (c) 0.35 M (d) 2.17 M

96 For the following gaseous phase reaction

$$A(g) + 2B(g) \rightleftharpoons C(g), \quad K_C = 0.25\,(\text{mol L}^{-1})^{-1}$$

Amount of A that must be mixed with 4 moles of B in a 5 L flask to get 1 mole of C at equilibrium is

(a) 3 mol (b) 2.6 mol (c) 26 mol (d) 5.2 mol

97 For the equilibrium reaction,

$$CO(g) + H_2O(g) \rightleftharpoons CO_2(g) + H_2(g), K_p = 3 \text{ at } 500 \text{ K}.$$

If 80 g of water gas (equimolar mixture of $CO(g)$ and $H_2(g)$ and 90 g of $H_2O(g)$ (steam) are taken in a 2 L vessel, then equilibrium molar concentration of H_2 is

(a) 3.50 (b) 1.75 (c) 1.50 (d) 0.75

98 For the following gaseous phase equilibrium

$$X \rightleftharpoons 2Y, \quad K_{p_1}$$
$$Z \rightleftharpoons P + Q, \quad K_{p_2}$$

If K_{p_1} and K_{p_2} are in the ratio of 1 : 9 when degree of dissociation of X and Z are equal, then ratio of total pressures of these equilibria is

(a) 1:1 (b) 1:3 (c) 1:9 (d) 1 : 36

99 $Na_2SO_4 \cdot 10H_2O(s)$ is efflorescent at when vapour pressure of water is below (p is in atm)

$$Na_2SO_4 \cdot 10H_2O(s) \rightleftharpoons Na_2SO_4(s) + 10H_2O(g);$$
$$K_p = 2.56 \times 10^{-20}$$

(a) 1.1×10^{-2} atm (b) 1.2×10^{-4} atm
(c) 1.457×10^{-6} atm (d) 2.2×10^{-2} atm

100 Given, the reactions, $A + B \rightleftharpoons C + D$ if one mole each of A and B are taken in 5 L flask at 300 K, 0.7 mole of C are formed. Molar concentration of each species at equilibrium, when one mole of each are taken initially is

	[A]	[B]	[C]	[D]
(a)	0.7	0.7	0.3	0.3
(b)	0.12	0.12	0.28	0.28
(c)	0.40	0.40	1.40	1.40
(d)	0.40	0.40	0.40	0.40

101 The binding of oxygen of haemoglobin (Hb), giving oxyhaemoglobin (HbO_2), is partially regulated by the concentration of H_3O^+ and dissolved CO_2 in blood.

$$HbO_2 + H_3O^+ + CO_2 \rightleftharpoons H^+—Hb—CO_2 + O_2 + H_2O$$

Release of O_2 is favoured when there is
(a) production of lactic acid during excretion
(b) production of CO_2 during excretion
(c) Both (a) and (b)
(d) None of the above

102 In the following equilibrium amount of $CO(g)$ can be decreased by

$$2CO(g) + O_2(g) \rightleftharpoons 2CO_2(g)$$

(a) decreasing volume at constant temperature
(b) adding argon gas
(c) adding O_2 gas
(d) All of the above

103 A container, whose volume is V, contains an equilibrium mixture that consists of 2 mol each of PCl_5, PCl_3 and Cl_2 gases at a pressure of 3 bar and temperature T. A certain amount of Cl_2 (g) is now introduced, keeping the pressure and temperature constant, until the equilibrium volume is 2V. Thus K_p and amount of Cl_2 added are respectively

	K_p (bar)	Cl_2 added (mol)
(a)	1	0.67
(b)	2	0.67
(c)	1	6.67
(d)	3	6.67

104 Variation of $\log_{10} K$ with $1/T$ is shown by the following graph in which straight line is at 45°, hence $\Delta H°$ is

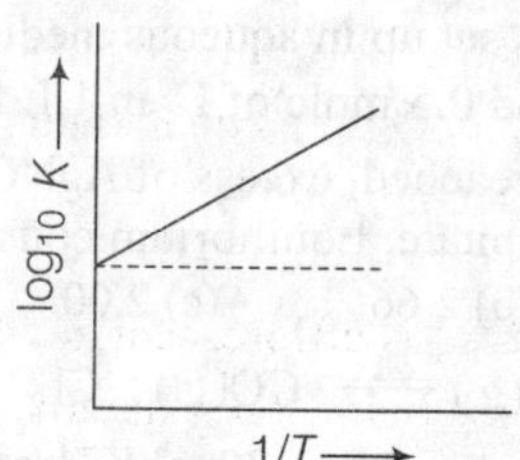

(a) + 4.606 cal (b) – 4.606 cal
(c) 2 cal (d) – 2 cal

105 For the following reaction through stages I, II and III

$$A \xrightarrow{\text{I}} B \xrightarrow{\text{II}} C \xrightarrow{\text{III}} D$$

quantity of the product formed (x) varies with temperature (T) as given

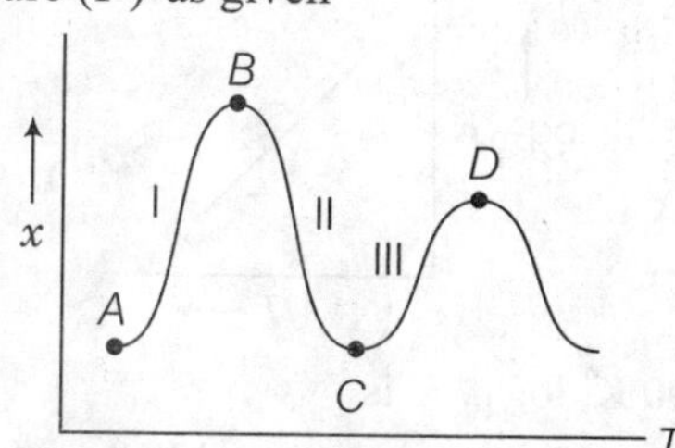

Select the correct statement.
(a) Stages I and III are endothermic but II is exothermic
(b) Stages I and III are exothermic but II is endothermic
(c) Stages II and III are exothermic but I is endothermic
(d) Stage I is exothermic but stages II and III endothermic

106 When NH_3 is heated in a 0.50 L flask at 700 K and 100 atm pressure, it decomposes into N_2 and H_2 and their equilibrium moles are given below.

$$\underset{0.30}{2NH_3(g)} \rightleftharpoons \underset{0.30}{N_2(g)} + \underset{0.90}{3H_2(g)}$$

Which of the pairs given represents correct value?

	Initial moles of NH_3	K_C for NH_3 formation
(a)	0.80	9.720
(b)	0.90	9.720
(c)	0.80	0.103
(d)	0.90	0.103

107 For the reaction in equilibrium,

I. $CO(g) + \frac{1}{2}O_2(g) \rightleftharpoons CO_2(g)$

II. $2CO(g) + O_2(g) \rightleftharpoons 2CO_2(g)$

Equilibrium constant	Free energy change
K_1	ΔG_1
K_2	ΔG_2

Then,
(a) $K_1 = 2K_2, \Delta G_1 = 2\Delta G_2$ (b) $K_2 = 2K_1, \Delta G_2 = 2\Delta G_1$
(c) $K_2 = K_1^2, \Delta G_2 = 2\Delta G_1$ (d) $K_2 = K_1^2, \Delta G_2 = \Delta G_1^2$

108 Conversion factor for converting partial pressures (in K_p) to active masses (in K_C) is
(a) nRT (b) $\frac{1}{RT}$ (c) $(RT)^2$ (d) $\frac{1}{(RT)^2}$

109 0.1 mol H_2 and 0.2 mol CO_2 are introduced in an evacuated flask at 723 K and following reaction occurs to give an equilibrium pressure of 50.0 kPa.

$$H_2(g) + CO_2(g) \overset{K_1}{\rightleftharpoons} H_2O(g) + CO(g) \quad ...(1)$$

Analysis of the mixture shows that it contains 10 mol % H_2O. A mixture of CoO (s) and Co (s) is then introduced such that the additional equilibria (2) and (3) are established.

$$CoO(s) + H_2(g) \overset{K_2}{\rightleftharpoons} Co(s) + H_2O(g) \quad ...(2)$$

$$Co(s) + CO_2(g) \overset{K_3}{\rightleftharpoons} CoO(g) + CO(g) \quad ...(3)$$

Analysis of the new equilibrium mixture, thus obtained is found to contain 30 mol% of H_2O. Thus equilibrium constants K_1, K_2 and K_3 are.

	K_1	K_2	K_3
(a)	0.075	0.818	9.0
(b)	13.33	9.0	0.111
(c)	0.075	9.0	1.222
(d)	0.075	9.0	0.818

110 Under standard state (at 1 bar and 298 K), K_p for the equilibrium

$$N_2O_4(g) \rightleftharpoons 2NO_2(g) \text{ is } 0.146$$

What is ΔG under the given condition when $p_{N_2O_4} = 10$ bar and $p_{NO_2} = 1$ bar

(a) 0.37 kJ mol^{-1} (b) + 0.85 kJ mol^{-1}
(c) – 0.37 kJ mol^{-1} (d) – 0.85 kJ mol^{-1}

111 At equilibrium, at 298 K, NO formed is x% by volume

$$N_2(g) + O_2(g) \rightleftharpoons 2NO(g)$$

If $x = \sqrt{Kab} \cdot \dfrac{K(a+b)}{4}$ in the mixture with a and b volume percentage of N_2 and O_2 initially, then maximum yield of NO is formed when

(a) $a = b$ (b) $a = 2b$ (c) $a = \dfrac{b}{3}$ (d) $a = \dfrac{1}{b}$

112 For the equilibrium,

$$2FeSO_4(s) \rightleftharpoons Fe_2O_3(s) + SO_2(g) + SO_3(g)$$

total gas pressure is 0.9 bar at 929 K. Equilibrium pressure under the given condition is ....when $SO_2(g)$ at 0.6 bar is also added initially.

(a) 0.64 bar (b) 0.24 bar (c) 1.28 bar (d) 1.08 bar

113 In the following equilibrium,

$$A(g) + B(g) \rightleftharpoons C(g) + D(g)$$

initial mole fraction of $A(g)$ is 0.40 in 5 L flask mole fraction of A decreased to 0.30 at equilibrium.

Thus, K_χ is

(a) $\dfrac{1}{10}$ (b) $\dfrac{1}{12}$ (c) $\dfrac{1}{14}$ (d) $\dfrac{1}{15}$

114 In the dissociation of Ag_2CO_3 at 1200 K in 1 L closed vessel total pressure set-up is p atm.

$$Ag_2CO_3(s) \rightleftharpoons 2Ag(s) + CO_2(g) + \frac{1}{2}O_2(g)$$

Thus, equilibrium constant K_p is

(a) $2\left(\dfrac{p}{3}\right)^{3/2}$ (b) $\left(\dfrac{2p}{3}\right)^{3/2}$ (c) $\left(\dfrac{p}{3}\right)^{3/2}$ (d) $\left(\dfrac{2p}{3}\right)^{1/2}$

115 For the equilibrium $PCl_5(g) \rightleftharpoons PCl_3(g) + Cl_2(g)$

$$K_{eq} = 100 \text{ and } \Delta G° = -20.0 \text{ kJ mol}^{-1}$$

at a given temperature. For the equilibrium

$$\frac{1}{2}PCl_3(g) + \frac{1}{2}Cl_2 \longrightarrow \frac{1}{2}PCl_5(g)$$

equilibrium constant K'_{eq} and $\Delta G'°$ respectively are

	K'_{eq}	$\Delta G'°$ (kJ mol^{-1})
(a)	0.01	– 10.0
(b)	0.10	– 10.0
(c)	0.10	+ 10.0
(d)	0.01	+ 10.0

116 Benzoic acid (C_6H_5COOH, 122 g mol^{-1}) forms dimer in benzene solvent

$$\underset{A}{C_6H_5COOH} \rightleftharpoons \underset{B}{\frac{1}{2}(C_6H_5COOH)_2}$$

vapour density of a mixture of A and B is found to be 91.5. If initially $[A] = 1.0$ M, K_C at equilibrium is

(a) 1.74 (b) 0.534 (c) 0.33 (d) 3.03

117 $Ca(HCO_3)_2$ decomposes at 400 K as

$$Ca(HCO_3)_2(s) \longrightarrow CaO(s) + 2CO_2(g) + H_2O(g)$$

pressure set-up is 7.5 bar. It is then cooled to 298 K. $\Delta H°$ in the given temperature range is

(a) – 8.9 kJ mol^{-1} (b) 2.14 kJ mol^{-1}
(c) – 2.14 kJ mol^{-1} (d) 8.9 kJ mol^{-1}

118 20 g of sample of $CaCO_3(s)$ of 50% impurity is placed in a sealed vessel of 1L capacity at 400 K when 50% dissociation takes place. If CO_2 gas at 0.5 atm is already present, per cent dissociation of $CaCO_3$ is

$$CaCO_3(s) \rightleftharpoons CaO(s) + CO_2(g)$$

(a) 25.0% (b) 28.7% (c) 40.0% (d) 34.8%

119 In the following equilibrium,

$A(g) \rightleftharpoons B(g)$, fraction (f) of B is defined as

$$(f) = \frac{[B]}{[A]+[B]}$$

If $(f) = 0.33$, equilibrium constant K_C is

(a) 0.50 (b) 0.33 (c) 0.66 (d) 0.25

120 $I_2 + I^- \rightleftharpoons I_3^-$

This reaction is set up in aqueous medium. We start with 1 mole of I_2 and 0.5 mole of I^- in 1 L flask. After equilibrium is reached, excess of $AgNO_3$ gave 0.25 mole of yellow precipitate. Equilibrium constant is

(a) 1.33 (b) 2.66 (c) 2.00 (d) 3.00

121 Given, $COCl_2(g) \rightleftharpoons CO(g) + Cl_2(g)$

$K_p = 8 \times 10^{-9}$ atm; $\Delta S° = 30$ cal K^{-1} at 373 K.

Temperature at which phosgene will be 0.1% dissociated at 2 atm ($R = 2$ cal mol^{-1}K^{-1}) is

(a) 373 K (b) 413 K (c) 446 K (d) 512 K

122 A plot of $\log_{10} K$ and $1/T$ is linear with a slope, – 6720 K and intercept + 9.72 for $H_2O(l) \rightleftharpoons H^+ + OH^-$

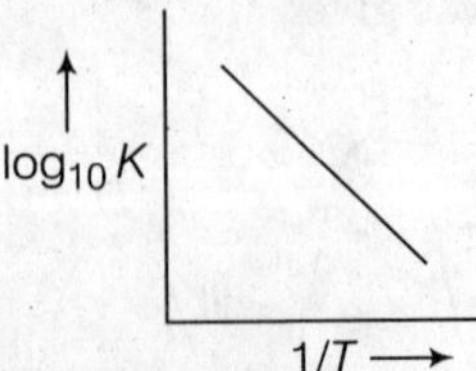

Thus, at 300 K, $\log_{10} K$ is

(a) 12.08 (b) 2.96 (c) – 12.68 (d) – 2.96

123 In the following reaction, $A(g) \underset{k_2}{\overset{k_1}{\rightleftharpoons}} B(g)$

$\frac{-d[A]}{dt} = k_1[A]$ for the forward reaction

$\frac{-d[B]}{dt} = k_2[B]$ for the backward reaction

Half-life period of the forward reaction is 10 min and that of backward reaction is 1 min. Thus, equilibrium constant is

(a) 0.693 (b) 0.0693 (c) 0.1 (d) 10.0

124 The equilibrium constants for the reaction H_3BO_3 + glycerine $\rightleftharpoons$ (H_3BO_3 · glycerine) is 0.90. Glycerine present per litre of 0.1 MH_3BO_3 to convert 60% of H_3BO_3 into (H_3BO_3 · glycerine) is

(a) 0.167 M (b) 1.67 M
(c) 0.0167 M (d) 10.67 M

125 At 273 K and 1 atm, 1 L of $N_2O_4(g)$ decomposes to $NO_2(g)$ as given,

$$N_2O_4(g) \rightleftharpoons 2NO_2(g)$$

At equilibrium, original volume is 25% less than the existing volume. Percentage decomposition of $N_2O_4(g)$ is thus,

(a) 25% (b) 50% (c) 66.66% (d) 33.33%

126 $H_2S(g)$ initially at a pressure of 10.0 atm and a temperature of 800 K, dissociates as

$$2H_2S(g) \rightleftharpoons 2H_2(g) + S_2(g)$$

At equilibrium, the partial pressure of S_2 vapour is 0.020 atm. Thus, K_p is

(a) 3.23×10^{-7} (b) 6.45×10^{-7}
(c) 1.55×10^{6} (d) 6.20×10^{7}

127 At 700 K and 350 bar, a 1:3 mixture of $N_2(g)$ and $H_2(g)$ reacts to form an equilibrium mixture containing $\chi(NH_3) = 0.50$. Assuming ideal behaviour K_p for the equilibrium reaction, $N_2(g) + 3H_2(g) \rightleftharpoons 2NH_3(g)$ is

(a) 2.03×10^{-4} (b) 3.55×10^{-3}
(c) 1.02×10^{-4} (d) 3.1×10^{-4}

128 A gaseous phase reaction taking place in 1L flask at 400 K is given, $N_2(g) + 3H_2(g) \rightleftharpoons 2NH_3(g)$.

Starting with 1 mole N_2 and 3 moles H_2, equilibrium mixture required 250 mL of 1 M H_2SO_4. Thus, K_C is

(a) 0.006 (b) 0.08 (c) 0.029 (d) 2.05

129 For the following equilibrium starting with 2 moles SO_2 and 1 mole O_2 in 1L flask,

$$2SO_2(g) + O_2(g) \rightleftharpoons 2SO_3(g)$$

equilibrium mixture required 0.4 mole MnO_4^- in acidic medium. Hence, K_C is

(a) 2.0 (b) 0.4 (c) 1.6 (d) 2.6

130 For the equilibrium,

$$C(s) + CO_2(g) \rightleftharpoons 2CO(g); K_p = 63 \text{ atm}$$

at 1000 K; if at equilibrium $p_{CO} = 10 p_{CO_2}$ then total pressure at equilibrium is

(a) 6.30 atm (b) 0.63 atm (c) 6.93 atm (d) 69.3 atm

131 Equilibrium constant can also be expressed in terms of K_χ, when concentrations of the species are taken in mole fraction.

$$F_2(g) \rightleftharpoons 2F(g); \; K_\chi = \frac{\chi_F^2}{\chi_{F_2}}$$

For the above equilibrium mixture, average molar mass at 1000 K was 36.74 g mol^{-1}. Thus, K_χ is

(a) 4.7×10^{-3} (b) 2124×10^2
(c) 7.1×10^2 (d) 14.08

132 For the following equilibrium $A(g) \rightleftharpoons B(g)$

$$K_p = 25 \text{ at } 300 \text{ K and } K_p = 10 \text{ at } 400 \text{ K}$$

Thus, backward reaction will have energy of activation

(a) equal to that of forward reaction
(b) less than that of forward reaction
(c) greater than that of forward reaction
(d) data is incomplete to predict

133 For the reversible reaction at equilibrium

$$N_2(g) + O_2(g) \rightleftharpoons 2NO(g)$$

$C = C_o e^{-2.1 \times 10^{-3} t}$ for the forward reaction and

$C = C_o e^{-4.2 \times 10^{-4} t}$ for the backward reaction. Thus, K_C is

(a) 5.0 (b) 2.0 (c) 0.5 (d) 0.2

134 For the following reaction, $A \longrightarrow B + C$, given that

(A)	$-\frac{d[A]}{dt}$
0.10 M	1×10^{-2} mol L^{-1}s^{-1}
0.20 M	2×10^{-2} mol L^{-1}s^{-1}

If this sets in equilibrium and $K_C = 10$ mol L^{-1}, then rate constant of the backward reaction is

(a) 1×10^{-2} L mol^{-1}s^{-1} (b) 1×10^{-3} L mol^{-1}s^{-1}
(c) 1×10^{2} L mol^{-1}s^{-1} (d) 1×10^{3} L mol^{-1}s^{-1}

135 At 800 K, $\Delta G°$ for the reaction $NiO(s) + H_2(g) \rightleftharpoons Ni(s) + H_2O(g)$ is -9.0 kcal. Thus, ratio of pressures of water vapours and hydrogen in equilibrium with NiO and Ni at 800 K in terms of logarithm is

(a) 2.44 (b) 1.06 (c) 5.63 (d) -2.44

136 In the following equilibrium, $AB \rightleftharpoons A^+ + B^-$

AB is 10% dissociated, when $[AB] = 1$M

What is the per cent dissociation if 1 M AB is dissociated in the presence of 1 M A^+?

(a) 5.2% (b) 6.0% (c) 1.1% (d) 10.0%

137 For the gaseous phase reaction,

$$CO(g) + 2H_2(g) \rightleftharpoons CH_3OH(g)$$

H_2 gas is introduced into a 5 L flask at 600 K containing 0.2 mole of $CO(g)$ and a catalyst, until the pressure is 4.92 atm. At this point 0.1 mole of $CH_3OH(g)$ is formed. Thus, K_p is

(a) 1.03 (b) 2.500×10^3 (c) 5.72 (d) 6.80

138 In the following equilibrium,

$$N_2(g) + O_2(g) \rightleftharpoons 2NO(g)$$

$K_C = 2.1 \times 10^{-3}$ at 2500 K

At equilibrium, $X_{NO} = 0.018$. Thus, X_{N_2} initially in the mixture of air (N_2 and O_2) is

(a) 0.74 (b) 0.26 (c) 0.50 (d) 0.25

139 In 1 L flask, 2 moles N_2, and 4 moles of H_2 are taken at constant temperature. At equilibrium, 2 moles of NH_3 are formed at equilibrium pressure of 1 bar. Thus, for the equilibrium constant, K_p, K_c and K_χ are respectively.

$$N_2(g) + 3H_2(g) \rightleftharpoons 2NH_3(g)$$

	K_p	K_C	K_χ
(a)	4	4	4
(b)	64	64	64
(c)	64	4	64
(d)	4	64	64

140

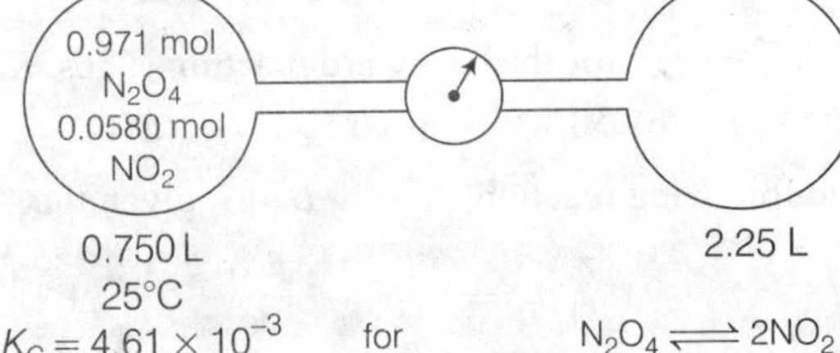

$K_C = 4.61 \times 10^{-3}$ for $N_2O_4 \rightleftharpoons 2NO_2$

The N_2O_4 and NO_2 equilibrium mixture in the flask on the left is allowed to expand into the evacuated flask on the right. Thus, when final equilibrium is established, NO_2 in the mixture is

(a) 0.950 mol (b) 0.100 mol
(c) 0.971 mol (d) 0.058 mol

141 $Ca(HCO_3)_2$ decomposes as

$$Ca(HCO_3)_2(s) \rightleftharpoons CaCO_3(s) + H_2O(g) + CO_2(g)$$

Equilibrium pressure is 0.12 bar. If reaction mixture also contains $H_2O(g)$ at 0.20 bar, then partial pressure of CO_2 is

(a) 0.20 bar (b) 0.0167 bar (c) 0.040 bar (d) 0.10 bar

142 For the following equilibrium at a

$$H_2O(l) \rightleftharpoons H_2O(g)$$

given temperature 298 K

$$\Delta_f G°(H_2O(g)) = 10 \text{ kJ mol}^{-1}$$

$$\Delta_f G°(H_2O(l)) = 9.9917 \text{ kJ mol}^{-1}$$

Thus, vapour pressure of water at 298 K is ($R = 8.3 \times 10^{-3}$ kJ mol^{-1}K^{-1})

(a) 1.0 atm (b) 0.5 atm (c) 0.1 atm (d) 0.01 atm

143 $Ag^+ + NH_3 \rightleftharpoons [Ag(NH_3)]^+$; $K_1 = 3.5 \times 10^{-3}$

$[Ag(NH_3)]^+ + NH_3 \rightleftharpoons [Ag(NH_3)_2]^+$

$K_2 = 1.74 \times 10^{-3}$ then the formation constant of $[Ag(NH_3)_2]^+$ is **[IIT JEE 2006]**

(a) 6.09×10^{-6} (b) 6.09×10^6
(c) 6.09×10^{-9} (d) None of these

144 $N_2 + 3H_2 \rightleftharpoons 2NH_3$

Which is correct statement if N_2 is added at equilibrium condition? **[IIT JEE 2006]**

(a) The equilibrium will shift to forward direction because according to second law of thermodynamics, the entropy must increases in the direction of spontaneous reaction.
(b) The condition for equilibrium is, $G(N_2) + 3G(H_2) = 2G(NH_3)$, where G is Gibb's free energy per mole of the gaseous species measured at that partial pressure. The condition of equilibrium is unaffected by the use of catalyst, which increases the rate of both forward and backward reactions to the same extent.
(c) The catalyst will increase the rate of forward reaction by α and that of backward reaction by β.
(d) Catalyst will not alter the rate of either of the reactions.

145 Consider the following equilibrium in a closed container,

$$N_2O_4(g) \rightleftharpoons 2NO_2(g)$$

At a fixed temperature, the volume of the reaction container is halved. For this change, which of the following statements hold true regarding the equilibrium constant (K_p) and degree of dissociation (α)? **[IIT JEE 2002]**

(a) Neither K_p nor α changes
(b) Both K_p and α changes
(c) K_p changes but α does not change
(d) K_p does not change but α changes

146 The decomposition reaction, $N_2O_4 \rightleftharpoons 2NO_2$, is expressed by $K_p = \dfrac{4x^2 p}{(1-x^2)}$, where p = pressure, x = extent of decomposition. Which one of the following statements is true? **[IIT JEE 2001]**

(a) K_p increases with increase of p
(b) K_p increases with increase of x
(c) K_p increases with decrease of x
(d) K_p remains constant with change in p and x

147 For the reversible reaction,

$$N_2(g) + 3H_2(g) \rightleftharpoons 2NH_3(g)$$

at 500° C, the value of K_p is 1.44×10^{-5} when partial pressure is measured in atmosphere. The corresponding value of K_C with concentration in mol/L is **[IIT JEE 2008]**

(a) $\frac{1.44\times 10^{-5}}{(0.082\times 500)^{-2}}$ (b) $\frac{1.44\times 10^{-5}}{(8.314\times 773)^{-2}}$

(c) $\frac{1.44\times 10^{-5}}{(0.082\times 773)^{2}}$ (d) $\frac{1.44\times 10^{-5}}{(0.082\times 773)^{-2}}$

148 $COCl_2$ gas dissociates according to the equation :

$$COCl_2 \rightleftharpoons CO + Cl_2$$

At 724 K and at 1bar, density is found to be 1.162 g dm^{-3}; Thus, $\Delta G°$ of the reaction is

(a) -7.213 kJ mol^{-1} (b) -9.416 kJ mol^{-1}

(c) 7.213 kJ mol^{-1} (d) 9.416 kJ mol^{-1}

149 The density of an equilibrium mixture N_2O_4 and NO_2 at 1.0 bar is 3.62 g dm^{-3} at 288 K and 1.84 g dm^{-3} at 348 K. Thus. enthalpy change of the reaction :

$$N_2O_4\,(g) \rightleftharpoons 2NO_2\,(g)$$

is

(a) -22.93 kJ mol^{-1} (b) 79.05 kJ mol^{-1}

(c) $+22.93$ kJ mol^{-1} (d) -79.05 kJ mol^{-1}

150 Hot copper turnings can be used as an **"oxygen getter"** for inert gas supplies by slowly passing the gas over the turnings at 600 K.

$$2Cu(s)+\frac{1}{2}O_2\,(g) \longrightarrow Cu_2O(s);\ \Delta_f G° = -124.944 \text{ kJ}$$

Thus, number of O_2 molecules left in 1L of the gas supply after equilibrium is reached is

(a) 2.20 L^{-1} (b) 1.90 L^{-1} (c) 1.00 L^{-1} (d) 2.14 L^{-1}

151 The vapour pressure of H_2 over LiH(*s*) is 0.278 mbar as at 800 K and 6.19 mbar at 900 K. Thus, $\Delta_r H°$ of the reaction is

$$LiH(s) \longrightarrow Li(l)+\frac{1}{2}H_2\,(g)$$

(a) -92.89 kJ (b) 92.89 kJ

(c) -188.80 kJ (d) 188.80 kJ

152 At a pressure of 1.00 bar, an equilibrium exists at 2000 K between 0.250 mol of Br_2 (*g*), 0.750 mol of F_2 (*g*) and 0.50 mol of BrF_3 (*g*) at 2000 K.

$$Br_2\,(g)+3F_2\,(g) \longrightarrow 2BrF_3\,(g)$$

For this equilibrium.

(a) $K_p = 5.33$

(b) If pressure is increased to 2.0 bar, reaction quotient is decreased and more BrF_3 (*g*) is formed

(c) Both of the above are correct

(d) None of the above is correct

153 For the following equilibrium

$$Br_2\,(g)+Cl_2\,(g) \longrightarrow 2BrCl(g)$$

taking *x* moles of Br_2 (*g*) and *y* moles of Cl_2 (*g*) maximum yield of the product occurs when

(a) $x = y$ (b) $x = 2y$ (c) $2x = y$ (d) $x = 3y$

154 The disproportionation of $Cu^{2+}(aq)$ was studied electrochemically at 298 K.

$$2Cu^+(aq) \longrightarrow Cu(s)+Cu^{2+}(aq)$$

Thus, equilibrium constant is given by

(a) 2.84×10^6 (b) 1.7×10^6 (c) 1.7×10^{12} (d) 2.84×10^{12}

155 For a reaction,

$$NH_3\,(g) \rightleftharpoons \frac{1}{2}N_2\,(g)+\frac{3}{2}H_2\,(g)$$

fraction of $NH_3\,(g)$ dissociated at a total pressure *p* is given by

(a) $\alpha = \left[1+\frac{3\sqrt{3}\,(p)}{4\ K_p}\right]^{-1/2}$ (b) $\alpha = \left[1+\frac{3\sqrt{3}\,(p)}{4\ K_p}\right]^{1/2}$

(c) $\alpha = \left[1+\frac{3\sqrt{3}\,(p)}{4\ K_p}\right]^{-1}$ (d) None of these

TYPE II Statement Based Questions

Directions (Q. No. 156-169) The following 4 items consists of two statements. One labelled as the 'Statement' (I) and other as 'Statement' (II). You are to examine these two statements carefully and select the correct answers to these items using the codes given below:

(a) Both statements (I) and (II) are true and statement (II) is the correct explanation of statement (I).

(b) Both statements (I) and (II) are true, but statement (II) is not the correct explanation of statement (I).

(c) Statement (I) is true, but (II) is false.

(d) Statement (I) is false, but (II) is true.

156 Statement I If for the series of reaction I, II and III

$$A \rightleftharpoons B$$
$$B \rightleftharpoons C$$
$$C \rightleftharpoons D$$

equilibrium constants are K_1, K_2 and K_3 then for the net reaction

$$A \longrightarrow D$$
$$K = K_1 + K_2 + K_3$$

Statement II $\Delta G° = \Delta G_1° + \Delta G_2° + \Delta G_3°$

157 Statement I Aerated bottles (CO_2 in H_2O) are filled at high pressure.

$$CO_2\,(g)+H_2O(l) \rightleftharpoons H_2CO_3\,(aq)$$

Statement II Solubility of gas increases due to increase in pressure.

158 Statement I Degree of dissociation of

$$N_2O_4\,(g) \rightleftharpoons 2NO_2\,(g)$$

is dependent on pressure

$$x = \sqrt{\frac{K_p}{K_p + 4p}}$$

Statement II For the equilibrium in gaseous phase

$$A \rightleftharpoons nB$$

$$x \propto \left(\frac{1}{p}\right)^{\frac{\Delta n_g}{2}}$$

159 **Statement I** A reaction mixture contains 1 mole N_2, 2 moles NH_3 and 3 moles H_2 in 10 L flask at 300 K, then $K_C = 14.8$ for $N_2 + 3H_2 \rightleftharpoons 2NH_3$

Statement II If H_2O is added, K_c remains unchanged.

160 **Statement I** Decomposition of ammonium carbonate is favoured at high temperature and high pressure

$$NH_2COONH_4(s) \rightleftharpoons 2NH_3(g) + CO_2(g)$$

Statement II Reaction is endothermic and proceeds with increase in pressure.

161 **Statement I** Intensity of red colour decreases on addition of oxalic acid.

$$Fe^{3+}(aq) + SCN^-(aq) \rightleftharpoons \underset{\text{Deep red}}{[Fe(SCN)]^{2+}(aq)}$$

Statement II Oxalic acid reacts with Fe^{3+} ions to form the stable complex ion, thus decreasing the concentration of free Fe^{3+} ions.

162 **Statement I** For a spontaneous reaction $\Delta G < 0$.

Statement II When equilibrium is attained reaction quotient $Q = K_C$ and $\Delta G° = -2.303\,RT \log K_C$.

163 **Statement I** A catalyst does not alter the equilibrium constant.

Statement II The forward reaction and backward reaction are affected to the same extent.

164 **Statement I** In the following graph, showing variation of G with number of moles.

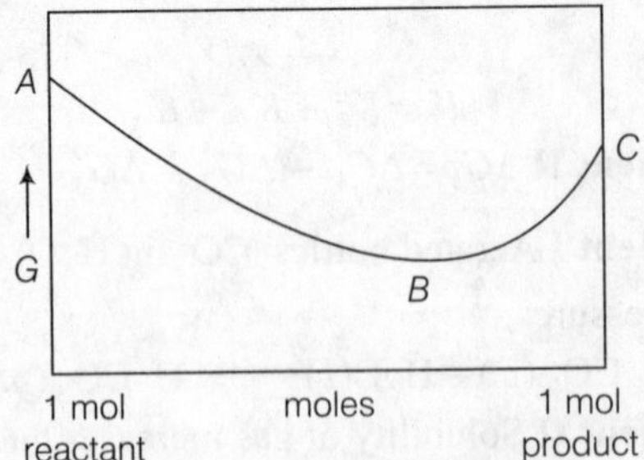

Forward reaction is spontaneous, when $\Delta G < 0$ and and $K_C > Q$.

Statement II Reverse reaction is spontaneous, when $\Delta G > 0$ and $Q > K$

(Q is reactant quotient)

165 **Statement I** A reaction is in equilibrium when $\Delta G = 0$

Statement II Under equilibrium condition $\Delta G° = -2.303\,RT \log K$ (K = thermodynamic equilibrium constant)

166 **Statement I** ΔG and $\Delta G°$ are related by equation $\Delta G = \Delta G° + 2.303\,RT \log Q$.

Statement II At equilibrium, $\Delta G° = 0$, so that $\Delta G = -2.303\,RT \log Q$.

167 **Statement I** Sign of ΔG is the true criterion of deciding spontaneity of a reaction.

Statement II $\Delta G = \Delta H - T\Delta S$

168 **Statement I** For $H_2 + I_2 \rightleftharpoons 2HI$ $\quad K_p = K_C = K_\chi$

Statement II $\Delta n_g = 0$

169 **Statement I** A reaction is spontaneous if $T\Delta S° > \Delta H°$

Statement II $\Delta G°$ is the driving force.

TYPE III MCQs with ONE or MORE than ONE Correct Alternate

170 Which represent(s) variation of K_{eq} with temperature?

(a) $\log_e K_{eq} = \text{constant} - \frac{\Delta H}{RT}$

(b) $\log_{10} K_{eq} = \text{constant} - \frac{\Delta H}{RT}$

(c) $\frac{d[\log_{10} K_{eq}]}{dT} = \frac{\Delta H}{RT^2}$ (d) $\frac{d[\log_e K_{eq}]}{dT} = +\frac{\Delta H}{RT^2}$

171 For the following type of reversible reaction

$$N_2O_4(g) \rightleftharpoons 2NO_2(g)$$

(a) equilibrium is possible in a closed system at a given temperature

(b) both the reactions, forward and backward, occur at the same rate and there is dynamic but stable condition

(c) equilibrium is represented graphically as

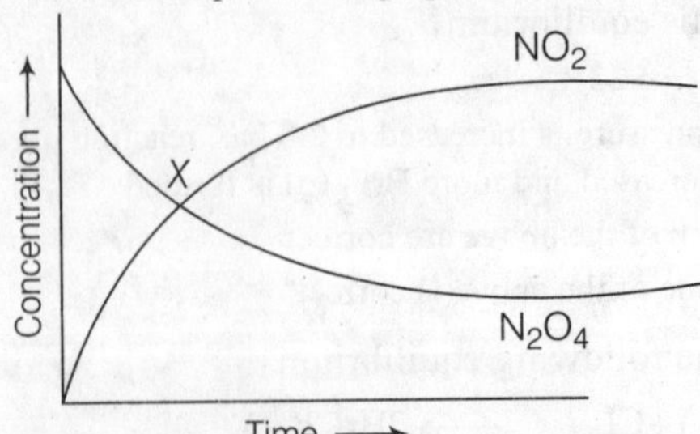

(d) in the above graph, (X) represents point of dynamic equilibrium

172 Select the correct statement(s) about the following equilibrium.

$$H_2O(l) \rightleftharpoons H_2O \text{ (vapour)}$$

(a) At constant vapour pressure, number of molecules leaving the liquid equals the number returning to the liquid from vapour
(b) This does not represent static equilibrium
(c) This represents dynamic equilibrium and the rates of the forward and backward reactions become equal
(d) This represents dynamic as well as static equilibrium

173 Combustion of $CO(g)$ to $CO_2(g)$

$$2CO(g) + O_2(g) \rightleftharpoons 2CO_2(g)$$

can be increased by
(a) decreasing volume at constant temperature
(b) adding argon gas
(c) adding O_2 gas
(d) decreasing pressure at constant temperature

174 Which of the following on the addition will cause deep red colour to disappear?

$$\underset{\text{Pale yellow}}{Fe^{3+}(aq)} + \underset{\text{Colourless}}{SCN^-(aq)} \rightleftharpoons \underset{\text{Deep red}}{[Fe(SCN)]^{2+}(aq)}$$

(a) $AgNO_3$ (b) $HgCl_2$
(c) H_2O (d) $H_2C_2O_4$

175 Which is/are correct relation(s) for thermodynamic equilibrium constant?
(a) $\Delta G° = -2.303\, RT \log K$
(b) $\Delta G = \Delta G° + 2.303\, RT \log K$
(c) $E°_{cell} = \frac{0.0591}{n} \log K$ at 298 K for the reaction $A \rightleftharpoons A^{n+} + ne^-$
(d) $E = E° - \frac{0.0591}{n} \log K$

176 $Ca(HCO_3)_2$ is heated in a closed vessel as $Ca(HCO_3)_2(s) \rightleftharpoons CaCO_3(s) + CO_2(g) + H_2O(g)$ and at 298 K, $p_{total} = 6$ bar
Then,
(a) $K_p = 6$ (b) $K_p = 9$
(c) $p_{CO_2} = p_{H_2O} = 3$ bar (d) $K_p = 3$

177 For the following reactions in gaseous phases,

		Free energy change
I.	$CO + 2H_2 \rightleftharpoons CH_3OH$	ΔG_1°
II.	$2CO + 4H_2 \rightleftharpoons C_2H_5OH + H_2O$	ΔG_2°
III.	$2CH_3OH \rightleftharpoons C_2H_5OH + H_2O$	ΔG_3°

then
(a) $\Delta G_3^\circ = 2\Delta G°_1 - \Delta G°_2$ (b) $\Delta G_3^\circ = \Delta G°_2 - \Delta G°_1$
(c) $\Delta G_3^\circ = \Delta G°_1 - \Delta G°_2$ (d) $\Delta G_3^\circ = \Delta G°_2 - 2\Delta G°_1$

178 Sulphuric acid (H_2SO_4) is manufactured through $SO_3(g)$ by the following equilibrium,

$$2SO_2(g) + O_2(g) \rightleftharpoons 2SO_3(g) + Q$$

equilibrium is displaced towards the formation of $SO_3(g)$, if
(a) some H_2O is added
(b) inert gas (as helium) is passed into the mixture
(c) temperature is lowered
(d) SO_3 is passed into the mixture

179 Solubility of NH_3 in H_2O is increased

$$NH_3(g) + H_2O(l) \rightleftharpoons NH_4OH(aq)$$

if
(a) pressure is increased (b) H_2O is added
(c) NH_3 is liquefied (d) pressure is decreased

180 Solubility of $CaO(s)$ in H_2O is increased if,
(a) pressure is increased (b) temperature is lowered
(c) water is added (d) volume is decreased

181 For the following equilibrium,

$$NH_4HS(s) \rightleftharpoons NH_3(g) + H_2S(g)$$

partial pressure of NH_3 will increase
(a) if NH_3 is added after equilibrium is established
(b) if H_2S is added after equilibrium is established
(c) temperature is increased
(d) volume of the flask is decreased

182 For a reaction, $A \rightleftharpoons P$, the plots of $[A]$ and $[P]$ with time at temperatures T_1 and T_2 are given below.

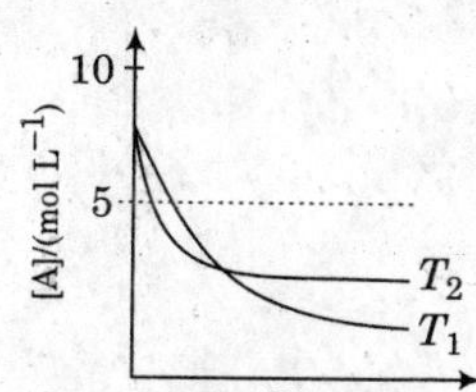

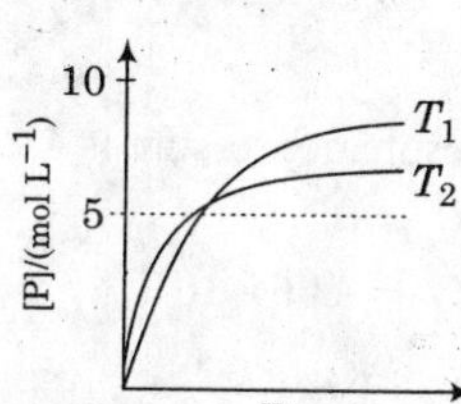

If $T_2 > T_1$, the correct statement(s) is are
(Assume $\Delta H^\ominus$ and $\Delta S^\ominus$ are independent of temperature and ratio of ln K at T_1 to ln K at T_2 is greater than T_2 / T_1. Here H, S, G and K are enthalpy, entropy, Gibbs energy and equilibrium constant, respectively.) **[JEE Adv. 2018]**
(a) $\Delta H^\ominus < 0, \Delta S^\ominus < 0$ (b) $\Delta G^\ominus < 0, \Delta H^\ominus > 0$
(c) $\Delta G^\ominus < 0, \Delta S^\ominus < 0$ (d) $\Delta G^\ominus < 0, \Delta S^\ominus > 0$

183 $H_2O(l) \rightleftharpoons H_2O(s)$; $\Delta H = -q$
Application of pressure on this equilibrium
(a) causes formation of more ice
(b) causes fusion of ice
(c) has no effect
(d) lower the melting point

184 $AgCl(s)$ is sparingly soluble salt,

$$AgCl(s) \rightleftharpoons Ag^+(aq) + Cl^-(aq)$$

There is
(a) increase in solubility if $NH_3(aq)$ is added
(b) increase in solubility if NaCl or $AgNO_3$ is added
(c) decrease in solubility if KCl is added
(d) decrease in solubility if H_2O is added

185 Variation of equilibrium constant (K) with temperature, (T) is given by van't Hoff equation.

$$\log_{10} K = \log A - \frac{\Delta H^\circ}{2.303RT}$$

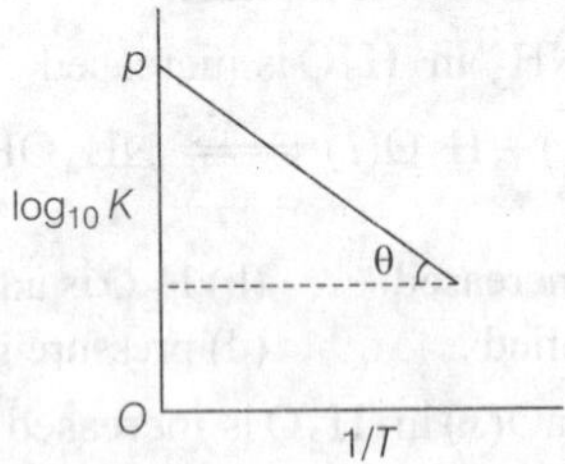

Graphically, it is shown as given, $\theta = \tan(0.5)$ and $OP = 10$.

Thus,

(a) pre-exponential factor is 10

(b) pre-exponential factor is 10^{10}

(c) heat of reaction is 2853 J mol^{-1} at 298 K

(d) heat of reaction is 9.574 J mol^{-1} at 298 K

186 One mole of $N_2O_4(g)$ at 300 K is kept in a closed container under one atmosphere. It is heated to 600 K when 20% by mass of $N_2O_4(g)$ decomposes to NO_2.

$$N_2O_4(g) \rightleftharpoons 2NO_2(g)$$

Thus,

(a) resultant pressure is 1.2 atm

(b) $K_p = 0.2$

(c) $K_C = 4.06 \times 10^{-3}$

(d) $K_p / K_C = 0.28$

187 For the gas phase reactions carried in a closed vessel,

$$C_2H_4 + H_2 \rightleftharpoons C_2H_6 \quad (\Delta H = -136 \text{ kJ mol}^{-1})$$

equilibrium concentration of C_2H_4 can be increased by

(a) increasing the temperature (b) decreasing the pressure

(c) removal of some H_2 (d) adding some C_2H_6

188 In the following endothermic equilibrium,

$$2NaNO_3(s) \rightleftharpoons 2NaNO_2(s) + O_2(g)$$

(a) addition of $NaNO_2$ favours reverse reaction

(b) addition of $NaNO_3$ favours forward reaction

(c) increasing temperature favours forward reaction

(d) increasing pressure favours forward reaction

189 The equilibrium, $SO_2Cl_2(g) \rightleftharpoons SO_2(g) + Cl_2(g)$ is attained at 298 K in a closed container and an inert gas helium is introduced. Which of the following statements is/are correct?

(a) Concentration of each species changes

(b) More Cl_2 is formed

(c) SO_2 decreases

(d) Both SO_2 and Cl_2 increases

190 For the reaction, $PCl_5(g) \rightleftharpoons PCl_3(g) + Cl_2(g)$ the forward reaction at constant temperature is favoured by

(a) introducing an inert gas at constant volume

(b) introducing Cl_2 gas at constant volume

(c) introducing an inert gas at constant pressure

(d) introducing PCl_5 at constant volume

191 Consider the following equilibria,

I. $A(s) \rightleftharpoons A'(g) + NH_3(g)$, $p_{eq} = 10$ cmHg

II. $B(s) \rightleftharpoons B'(g) + NH_3(g)$, $p_{eq} = 24$ cmHg

Thus,

(a) $K_I = 25\ cm^2$ (b) $K_{II} = 144\ cm^2$

(c) $p_{total} = 34$ cmHg when decomposed together

(d) $p_{total} = 26$ cmHg when decomposed together

192 At 1700 K and 1.10 atm, 1g of chlorine occupies 1.96 L in the following equilibrium,

$$\frac{1}{2}Cl_2(g) \rightleftharpoons 2Cl(g)$$

If gas behaves ideally, then,

(a) $K_p = K_C = K_\chi$ (b) $K_\chi = 0.187$

(c) $K_p = 0.196\ atm^{1/2}$ (d) $K_C = 0.0165\ (mol\ L^{-1})^{1/2}$

193 For the equilibrium,

$$Cl_2(g) \rightleftharpoons 2Cl(g)$$

degree of dissociation of Cl_2 is 0.071 at 1 atm and 1600K. Thus,

(a) $\chi_{Cl_2} > \chi_{Cl}$ (b) $K_\chi = 0.0204$

(c) $K_p = 0.0204$ atm (d) $K_C = 1.55 \times 10^{-4}$ mol L^{-1}

194 For the reaction, $2SO_3(g) \rightleftharpoons 2SO_2(g) + O_2(g)$ when 2 moles of SO_3 are taken in a flask of 10.0 L at 350 K, at equilibrium ratio of SO_2 to SO_3 is 0.663.

Thus,

(a) $K_{eq} = 0.0176$ mol L^{-1} (b) $\Delta G^\circ = 11.76$ kJ mol L^{-1}

(c) $[O_2] = 0.04$ mol L^{-1} (d) $[SO_3] = 0.12$ mol L^{-1}

195 Select the correct relationships for the given equilibria.

(a) $N_2(g) + O_2(g) \rightleftharpoons 2NO(g)$; $K_{eq} = K_1$

$NO(g) \rightleftharpoons \frac{1}{2}N_2(g) + \frac{1}{2}O_2(g)$; $K_{eq} = K_2$ thus,

$$K_1K_2^2 = 1$$

(b) Free energy changes is ΔG_1° for

$2NO_2(g) \rightleftharpoons N_2O_4(g)$ and ΔG_2° for

$\frac{1}{2}N_2O_4(g) \rightleftharpoons NO_2(g)$, then $2\Delta G_2^\circ + \Delta G_1^\circ = 0$

(c) van't Hoff equation is, $\Delta_r H^\circ\left(\frac{1}{T_2} - \frac{1}{T_1}\right) = \frac{\Delta_r G_2^\circ}{T_2} - \frac{\Delta_r G_1^\circ}{T_1}$

(d) For the equilibrium, $A(g) \rightleftharpoons 2B(g)$

$$x = \sqrt{\frac{K_p}{K_p + 4p}} \quad (x = \text{degree of dissociation})$$

196 $\frac{\partial}{\partial T}\left(\frac{\Delta G^\circ}{T}\right) = -\frac{\Delta H^\circ}{T^2}$ can be expressed as

(a) $\frac{\partial \ln K}{\partial T} = \frac{\Delta H^\circ}{RT^2}$ (b) $\frac{\partial \ln K}{\partial T} = -\frac{\Delta H^\circ \partial}{R \partial T}\left(\frac{1}{T}\right)$

(c) $\ln K = \frac{-\Delta H}{RT} + \text{constant}$ (d) $\ln \frac{K_2}{K_1} = \frac{\Delta H^\circ}{R}\left(\frac{1}{T_1} - \frac{1}{T_2}\right)$

(at two different temperatures T_1 and T_2 having equilibrium constant K_1 and K_2)

197 For the equilibrium,

$$A \rightleftharpoons nB$$

degree of dissociation x can be

(a) $\frac{D-d}{(n-1)d}$ (D = vapour density if no dissociation, d = vapour density if dissociation)

(b) $\frac{p_i - p}{(n-1)p}$ (p_i = initial pressure)

(c) $\frac{d-D}{(n-1)d}$

(d) $\frac{(n-1)(p-p_i)}{p_i}$

198 For the equilibrium,

$$COCl_2(g) \rightleftharpoons CO(g) + Cl_2(g)$$

(a) $K_p = \frac{px^2}{(1-x^2)}$ (x = degree of dissociation)

(b) $x = \sqrt{\frac{K_p}{p+K_p}}$

(c) $K_C = \frac{x^2V}{(1-x)}$

(d) $K_C = \frac{x^2}{(1-x)V}$

199 Variation of $\log K_p$ with temperature is shown graphically for the decomposition of NH_3

$$2NH_3(g) \rightleftharpoons N_2(g) + 3H_2(g)$$

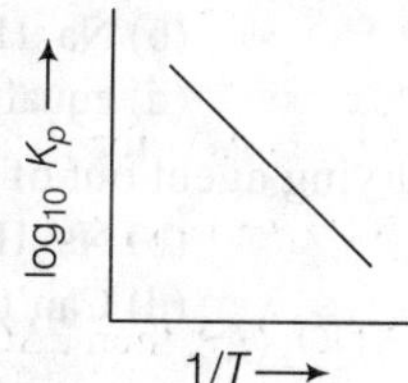

Decomposition can be prevented by
(a) lowering the temperature
(b) increasing the pressure
(c) isolation of N_2 and H_2 gases
(d) adding H_2 gas

200 The % yield of ammonia as a function of time in the reaction $N_2(g) + 3H_2(g) \rightleftharpoons 2NH_3(g)$, $\Delta H < 0$ at (p, T_1) is given below,

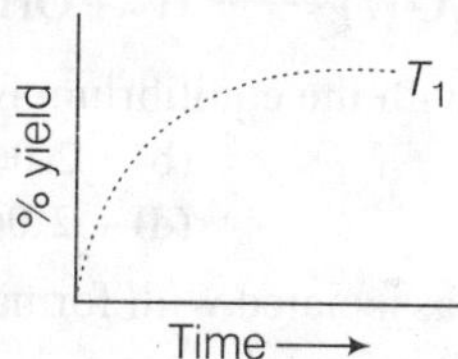

If this reaction is conducted at (p, T_2), with $T_2 > T_1$, the % yield of ammonia as a function of time is represented by **(JEE Adv. 2015)**

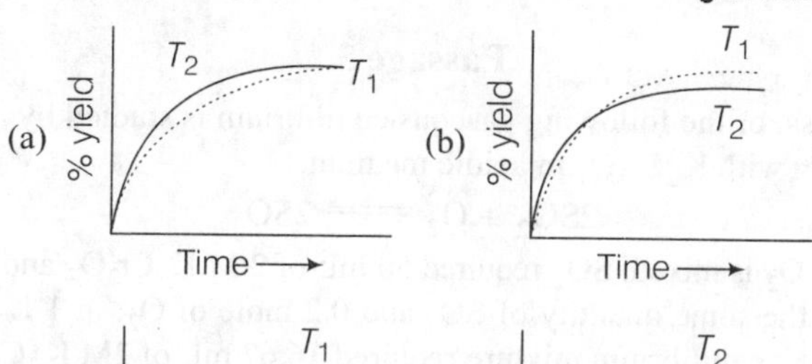

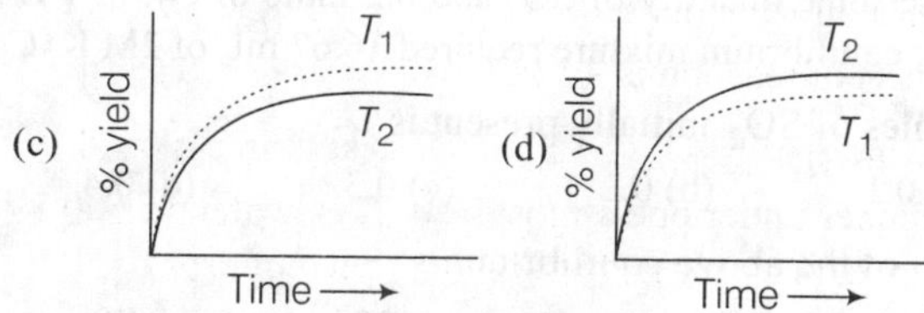

201 The thermal dissociation of equilibrium of $CaCO_3(s)$ is studied under different conditions.

$$CaCO_3(s) \rightleftharpoons CaO(s) + CO_2(g)$$

For this equilibrium, correct statement(s) is/are **[JEE Adv. 2013]**
(a) ΔH is dependent on T
(b) K is independent of initial amount $CaCO_3$
(c) K is dependent on the pressure of CO_2 at a given T
(d) ΔH is independent of the catalyst, if any

202 The equilibrium $2Cu^+ \rightleftharpoons Cu + Cu^{2+}$ in aqueous medium at 25°C shifts towards the left in the presence of **(IIT JEE 2011)**
(a) NO_3^- (b) Cl^- (c) SCN^- (d) CN^-

TYPE IV Passage Based MCQs (Comprehension)

Passage 1

When 1.00 mole of pure ethanol (C_2H_5OH) is mixed with 1.00 mole of ethanoic acid (CH_3COOH) at 298 K, the equilibrium mixture contains $\frac{2}{3}$ mole each of ester and water.

203 ΔG° of the reaction is
(a) – 3.44 kJ (b) – 0.826 kJ (c) + 3.44 kJ (d) + 0.826 kJ

204 How many moles of ester is formed at equilibrium when 3 moles of ethanol and 1 mole of ethanoic acid are mixed?
(a) 4.4 mol (b) 0.9 mol (c) 0.5 mol (d) 0.75 mol

Passage 2

Dissociation of H_2O in H^+ and OH^- is endothermic at 298 K

$$H_2O(l) \rightleftharpoons H^+ + OH^- \quad \Delta H° = +13.7\,kcal$$

205 $\Delta G°$ associated with the equilibrium is
(a) -19.2 kcal (b) -2.06 kcal
(c) $+19.2$ kcal (d) $+2.06$ kcal

206 Entropy change associated with formation of H_2O from H^+ and OH^- ions is
(a) 110.4 cal $mol^{-1}K^{-1}$ (b) -110.4 cal $mol^{-1}K^{-1}$
(c) $+18.46$ cal $mol^{-1}K^{-1}$ (d) -18.46 cal $mol^{-1}K^{-1}$

Passage 3

Progress, of the following gaseous equilibrium is studied by reaction with $K_2Cr_2O_7$ in acidic medium.

$$2SO_2 + O_2 \rightleftharpoons 2SO_3$$

Before O_2 is mixed, SO_2 required 50 mL of 2 M $K_2Cr_2O_7$ and after taking the some quantity of SO_2 and 0.2 mole of O_2, in 1 L flask at 300 K, equilibrium mixture required 16.67 mL of 2M $K_2Cr_2O_7$.

207 Moles of SO_2 initially present is
(a) 0.1 (b) 0.2 (c) 0.3 (d) 0.4

208 K_C of the above equilibrium is
(a) 10 (b) 20 (c) 30 (d) 40

Passage 4

3 moles each of N_2 and H_2 are taken in 10 L flask at 300 K when following equilibrium is set up.

$$N_2(g) + 3H_2(g) \rightleftharpoons 2NH_3(g)$$

At equilibrium, reaction mixture required 100 mL of 5 M HCl.

209 Equilibrium constant (K_p) is
(a) 1.283×10^{-3} bar^{-2} (b) 2.417×10^{-2} bar^{-2}
(c) 1.697×10^{-3} bar (d) 1.283×10^{-3} bar^2

210 If 5 L of H_2O is added in the reaction mixture, partial pressure of H_2 and N_2 are respectively (in bar).

	p_{H_2}	p_{N_2}
(a)	2.75	2.25
(b)	5.50	5.50
(c)	11.22	13.71
(d)	13.71	11.22

Passage 5

Rate of disappearance of the reactant A at two different temperatures is given

$$A \rightleftharpoons B$$

$$\frac{-d[A]}{dt} = 2 \times 10^{-2}\,s^{-1}[A] - 4 \times 10^{-3}\,s^{-1}[B] \text{ at 300 K}$$

$$\frac{-d[A]}{dt} = 4 \times 10^{-2}\,s^{-1}[A] - 16 \times 10^{-4}\,s^{-1}[B] \text{ at 400 K}$$

211 Select correct statement about equilibrium constant K.
(a) $K_{300} > K_{400}$ thus reaction is endothermic
(b) $K_{300} > K_{400}$ thus reaction is exothermic
(c) $K_{300} < K_{400}$ thus reaction is exothermic
(d) $K_{300} < K_{400}$ thus reaction is endothermic

212 $\Delta H°$ (heat of reaction) in the given temperature range is
(a) -3.86 kcal mol^{-1} (b) 3.86 kcal mol^{-1}
(c) 3.86×10^3 kcal mol^{-1} (d) -3.86×10^3 kcal mol^{-1}

Passage 6

Glauber salt ($Na_2SO_4.10H_2O$) exists as following equilibrium at 273 K.

$$Na_2SO_4.10H_2O(s) \rightleftharpoons Na_2SO_4(s) + 10H_2O(g), \quad K_p = 4.08 \times 10^{-25}$$

The vapour pressure of water at 273 K = 4.358 Torr.

213 At what relative humidities will $Na_2SO_4.10H_2O$ be efflorescent when exposed to air at 273 K?
(a) Above 60.5% (b) Below 60.5%
(c) Above 39.5% (d) Below 39.5%

214 At what relative humidities will Na_2SO_4 be deliquescent (i.e. absorb moisture) when exposed to air at 273 K ?
(a) Above 60.5% (b) Below 60.5%
(c) Above 39.5% (d) Below 39.5%

Passage 7

Equilibrium constants are given (in atm) for the following reactions at 273 K.

I. $SrCl_2 \cdot 6H_2O(s) \rightleftharpoons SrCl_2 \cdot 2H_2O(s) + 4H_2O(g), \quad K_p = 6.89 \times 10^{-12}$

II. $Na_2HPO_4 \cdot 12H_2O(s) \rightleftharpoons Na_2HPO_4 \cdot 7H_2O(s) + 5H_2O(g), \quad K_p = 5.25 \times 10^{-13}$

III. $CuSO_4 \cdot 5H_2O(s) \rightleftharpoons CuSO_4 \cdot 3H_2O(s) + 2H_2O(g), \quad K_p = 1.086 \times 10^{-4}$

Vapour pressure of water at 273 K = 4.358 torr

215 Vapour pressure of water in equilibrium with air is maximum in case of
(a) $SrCl_2 \cdot 6H_2O$ (b) $Na_2HPO_4 \cdot 12H_2O$
(c) $CuSO_4 \cdot 5H_2O$ (d) equal

216 Which is the best drying agent out of
(a) $SrCl_2 \cdot 6H_2O$ (b) $Na_2HPO_4 \cdot 12H_2O$
(c) $CuSO_4 \cdot 5H_2O$ (d) Can't be predicted

Passage 8

The equilibrium constant for the reaction

$$2C_3H_6(g) \rightleftharpoons C_2H_4(g) + C_4H_8(g)$$

is found to fit the expression between 300 K and 600 K.

$$\log_e K = -1.04 - \frac{1088\,K}{T}$$

217 ΔH° and ΔS° of the given reaction are respectively

	ΔH° (kcal mol^{-1})	ΔS° (cal mol^{-1}K^{-1})
(a)	2.176	− 2.08
(b)	− 2.176	+ 2.08
(c)	− 2.176	− 2.08
(d)	+ 2.176	+ 2.08

218 ΔG° associated with the above equilibrium (in kcal mol^{-1}) at 400 K is

(a) − 3.008 (b) 3.008 (c) 1.760 (d) − 1.760

Passage 9

The complexion of Fe^{2+} with the chelating agent dipyridyl (abbreviated dipy) has been studied kinetically in both the forward and backward directions. For the complex ion reaction

$$Fe^{2+}(aq) + 3\text{dipy} \longrightarrow [Fe(\text{dipy})_3]^{2+}(aq)$$

the rate of the formation of the complex at 298 K is given by rate $= (1.45 \times 10^{13}\ L^3 mol^{-3} s^{-1})[Fe^{2+}][\text{dipy}]^3$ and for the reverse reaction, the rate of disappearance of the complex is

$$\text{rate} = (1.22 \times 10^{-4} s^{-1})\ [Fe(\text{dipy})_3^{2+}]$$

219 What is equilibrium constant for the equilibrium ?

$$Fe^{2+}(aq) + 3\text{dipy} \rightleftharpoons [Fe(\text{dipy})_3^{2+}](aq)$$

(a) 8.4138×10^{-18} (b) 2.3770×10^{17}

(c) 1.1885×10^{17} (d) 5.9426×10^{6}

220 If half-life period of the backward reaction is $\dfrac{0.693}{k}$ (k = rate constant), then half-life period is about

(a) 95 min (b) 5680 seconds

(c) 0.85 min (d) None of these

Passage 10

Following equilibrium is set up at 300 K.

$$N_2O_4(g) \rightleftharpoons 2NO_2(g)$$

221 Degree of dissociation (x) is related to equilibrium constant K_p and pressure by

(a) $\sqrt{\dfrac{K_p}{K_p + 4p}}$ (b) $\sqrt{\dfrac{K_p + 4p}{K_p}}$

(c) $\sqrt{\dfrac{K_p}{K_p + p}}$ (d) $\sqrt{\dfrac{K_p + p}{K_p}}$

222 Fraction of NO_2 in terms of K_p and p is given by

(a) $\sqrt{4K_p} / \sqrt{K_p + 4p} + \sqrt{K_p}$

(b) $\dfrac{2}{\sqrt{1 + \dfrac{4p}{K_p}} + 1}$

(c) Both are correct

(d) None of the above is correct

Passage 11

Thermal decomposition of gaseous X_2 to gaseous X at 298 K takes place according to the following equation,

$$X_2(g) \rightleftharpoons 2X(g)$$

The standard reaction Gibbs energy, $\Delta_r G^\circ$, of this reaction is positive. At the start of the reaction, there is one mole of X_2 and no X. As the reaction proceeds, the number of moles of X formed is given by β. Thus, $\beta_{\text{equilibrium}}$ is the number of moles of X formed at equilibrium. The reaction is carried out at a constant total pressure of 2 bar.

Consider the gases to behave ideally.

(Given, $R = 0.083$ L bar K^{-1} mol^{-1}) ***[JEE Adv. 2016]***

223 The equilibrium constant K_p for this reaction at 298K, in terms of $\beta_{\text{equilibrium}}$ is

(a) $\dfrac{8\beta^2_{\text{equil.}}}{2 - \beta_{\text{equil.}}}$ (b) $\dfrac{8\beta^2_{\text{equil.}}}{4 - \beta^2_{\text{equil.}}}$ (c) $\dfrac{4\beta^2_{\text{equil.}}}{2 - \beta_{\text{equil.}}}$ (d) $\dfrac{4\beta^2_{\text{equil.}}}{4 - \beta^2_{\text{equil.}}}$

224 The incorrect statement among the following for this reaction is

(a) decrease in the total pressure will result in the formation of more moles of gaseous X

(b) at the start of the reaction, dissociation of gaseous X_2 takes place spontaneously

(c) $\beta_{\text{equilibrium}} = 0.7$

(d) $K_C < 1$

Passage 12

Two solids compounds A and B dissociate into gaseous products at 298K :

$$\text{I} : A(s) \rightleftharpoons A'(g) + H_2S(g),\ K_\text{I}$$

$$\text{II} : B(s) \rightleftharpoons B'(g) + H_2S(g),\ K_\text{II}$$

At 298, vapour pressure over excess solid A is 50 mm and that of over excess solid B is 68 mm.

225 Dissociation constants of A (s) and B (s) are respectively

	K_I	K_II
(a)	1.08×10^{-3} atm^2	2.0×10^{-3} atm^2
(b)	1.08×10^{-3} atm^2	1.08×10^{-3} atm^2
(c)	2.0×10^{-3} atm^2	2.0×10^{-3} atm^2
(d)	6.5×10^{-2} atm^2	8.0×10^{-2} atm^2

226 Total pressure of gases exerted over solids A and B is

(a) 1.01 atm (b) 0.11 atm

(c) 1.10 atm (d) 0.011 atm

TYPE V Numerical Skills

227 2 moles of SO_2 and 1 mole of O_2 are taken in 1 L flask at 298 K, when following equilibrium is set up

$$2SO_2(g) + O_2(g) \rightleftharpoons 2SO_3(g)$$

equilibrium mixture required 0.33 mole of $Cr_2O_7^{2-}$ in the acidic medium. Thus, equilibrium constant K_C is ......

228 For the reaction,

$$CaCO_3(s) \rightleftharpoons CaO(s) + CO_2(g)$$

$K_p = 1.16$ atm at 800°C. If 220 g of $CaCO_3$ was put into a 10.0 L container and heated to 800°C, what per cent of the $CaCO_3$ would decompose at equilibrium?

229 7.07 g NH_4HS (s) is placed in 1 dm^3 flask at 300 K, when following equilibrium is set up

$$NH_4HS(s) \rightleftharpoons NH_3(g) + H_2S(g),\ K_p = 0.25\ atm^2.$$

How much $NH_4HS(s)$ (in grams) is left in the flask after equilibrium is set up?

230 Consider the reaction $A \rightleftharpoons B$ at 1000 K. At time t', the temperature of the system was increased to 2000 K and the system was allowed to reach equilibrium. Throughout this experiment the partial pressure of A was maintained at 1 bar. Given below is the plot of the partial pressure of B with time. What is the ratio of the standard Gibbs energy of the reaction at 1000 K to that at 2000 K? ***[JEE Adv. 2020]***

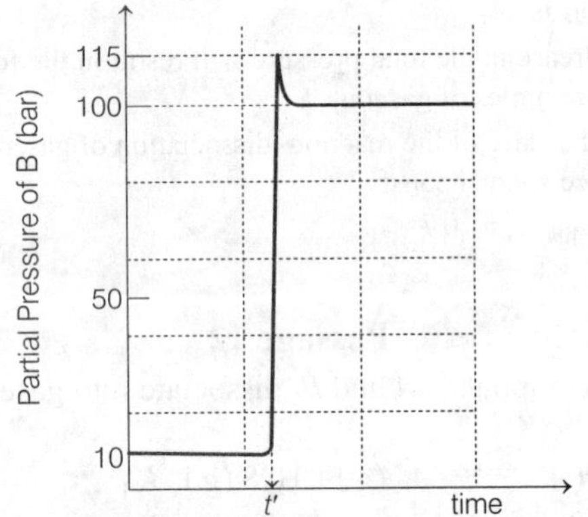

231 For the reversible reaction,

$$A \underset{K_2}{\overset{K_1}{\rightleftharpoons}} B$$

$$K_1 = 10^{15} e^{-2000/T}\ s^{-1}$$

$$K_2 = 10^{12} e^{-2000/T}\ s^{-1}$$

What is the value of $\left(-\dfrac{\Delta G°}{2.303\,RT}\right)$?

232 Consider following equilibrium :

$$A(g) \rightleftharpoons 4B(g)$$

values of $\left(\dfrac{D}{d}\right)$ taken along y-axis have been plotted *versus* α (along x-axis) where, α is the degree of dissociation.

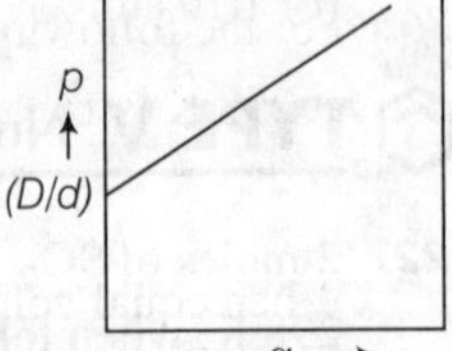

What is the value of $\left(\dfrac{D}{d}\right)$ at the point corresponding to 100% dessication 1A ?

233 2 moles of SO_2 and 1 mole of O_2 are taken in 2 L flask at 3 atm. When equilibrium is set up, pressure decreases by 0.5 atm. Hence, equilibrium constant K_C is ......

234 What is the value of K_p for the equation.

$$2Cl(g) \rightleftharpoons Cl_2(g)$$

when the system contains equal number of $Cl(g)$ atoms and $Cl_2(g)$ molecules at 1 bar and 300 K?

235 For the following equilibrium at constant temperature.

$$PCl_5(g) \rightleftharpoons PCl_3(g) + Cl_2(g)$$

Variation of $\log \dfrac{[PCl_3]}{[PCl_5]}$ with $\log (Cl_2)$ is shown below:

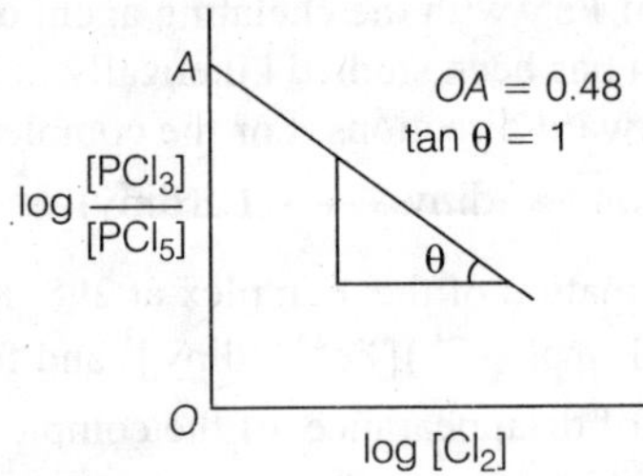

What is the equilibrium constant K_C?

236 For the reaction,

$$A(g) + B(g) \rightleftharpoons C(g) + D(g) + E(g)$$

Internal energy change $(\Delta E°) = -90.0$ kcal

Entropy change $(\Delta S°) = 100$ cal K^{-1} at -14°C

Thermodynamic equilibrium constant is

$$\log_{10} K = 10^n$$

What is value of n?

237 For the following gaseous phase equilibrium.

$$A(g) + xB(g) \rightleftharpoons yC(g)$$

molar concentrations vary with time as shown below :

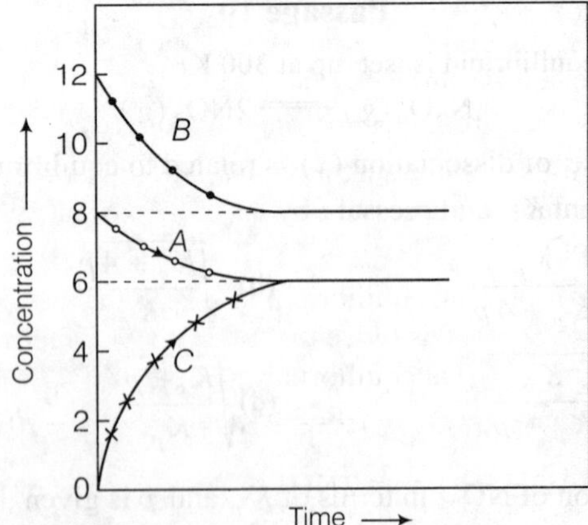

What is the value of $(x + y)$?

238 $[Ag^+]$ in a solution made by dissolving both Ag_2CrO_4 and $Ag_2C_2O_4$ as until saturation is reached with respect to both salts is $y \times 10^{-4}$ M. What is the value of y?

$$K_{sp}(Ag_2CrO_4) = 9.0 \times 10^{-12}$$

$$K_{sp}(Ag_2C_2O_4) = 6.0 \times 10^{-12}$$

239 One litre solution was prepared containing 0.005 mole of silver (Ag^+) and 1.00 mole of NH_3. K_f for $[Ag(NH_3)_2]^+$ is 1.0×10^8. Free $[Ag^+]$ in the solution at equilibrium is $y \times 10^{-11}$ mol L^{-1}. What is the value of y?

240 75.0 mL of 0.03 M $FeSO_4$ is mixed with 125.0 mL of 0.20 M KCN to form $K_4[Fe(CN)_6]$.
Given, $Fe^{2+} + 6CN^- \rightleftharpoons [Fe(CN)_6]^{4-}$, $K_{eq} = 1 \times 10^{24}$

Unreacted Fe^{2+} in equilibrium with complex is $x \times 10^{-19}$ M, thus $x =$ ......?

241 In the following reversible reaction in a closed container, n moles of H_2 and 2 moles of N_2 are allowed to attain equilibrium.

$$N_2(g) + 3H_2(g) \rightleftharpoons 2NH_3(g)$$

Partial pressure of NH_3 in the mixture is 4/9 times the total initial pressure. What is value of n, if N_2 content at equilibrium is 4/3 mole?

242 For a reaction,

$$X + 2Y \rightleftharpoons 2Z$$

0.1 mol of X, 1.5 mole of Y and 0.5 mole of Z, were taken in a 1 L vessel and allowed to react. At equilibrium, the concentration of Z was 1.0 mol L^{-1}. The equilibrium constant of the reaction is $\left(\frac{x}{15}\right)$. The value of x is ......

[JEE Main 2020 (II) NTA]

243 One mole of a mixture of N_2, NO_2 and N_2O_4 has average molar mass 48.5 g mol^{-1}. On heating, all the N_2O_4 dissociates into NO_2 and molar mass of the mixture is lowered by 9.7 g mol^{-1}. Number of moles of N_2O_4 in the mixture is $\frac{1}{n}$. What is value of n?

244 For the equilibrium,

$$AB(g) \rightleftharpoons A(g) + B(g),$$

the equilibrium pressure at which one-third of AB is dissociated, is n times of equilibrium constant. What is value of n?

245 For the following equilibrium in a 10 L flask at 298 K, moles of $SO_3(g)$ is twice that of $SO_2(g)$. Determine the moles of O_2 (g) at equilibrium.

$$2SO_2(g) + O_2(g) \rightleftharpoons 2SO_3(g), \; K_C = 10 \text{ L mol}^{-1}$$

246 $N_2(g) + 3H_2(g) \rightleftharpoons 2NH_3(g)$ is a gaseous phase equilibrium reaction taking place at 400 K in a 5 L flask.

For this, $\frac{K_C}{K_\chi} = (n)^2$

What is the value of n?

247 For the following equilibrium starting with 2 moles of SO_2 and 1 mole O_2 in 1 L flask.

$$2SO_2(g) + O_2(g) \rightleftharpoons 2SO_3(g)$$

equilibrium mixture required 0.4 mole of MnO_4^- in acidic medium. Thus, equilibrium constant $K_C = ?$

248 $Ca(HCO_3)_2$ is strongly heated and after equilibrium is attained, temperature changed to 298 K.

$$Ca(HCO_3)_2(s) \rightleftharpoons CaCO_3(s) + CO_2(g) + H_2O(g)$$
$$K_p = 36 \text{ (pressure taken in atm)}$$

Thus, pressure set up due to CO_2 is ...... atm.

249 At 1 atmospheric pressure, N_2O_4 is 50% dissociated at 300 K and 80% dissociated at 400 K as given :

$$N_2O_4(g) \rightleftharpoons 2NO_2(g)$$

The enthalpy of dissociation is x kcal mol^{-1}. Thus, x is ......

250 At 298 K, ΔG for the following equilibrium

$$H_2O(l) \rightleftharpoons H^+(aq) + OH^-(aq)$$

is x kJ if $\Delta G°$ is 79.882 kJ. What is the value of x?

251 For the equilibrium at 2 bar

$$N_2(g) + 3H_2(g) \rightleftharpoons 2NH_3(g)$$
$$\left[\frac{\partial(\log K_\chi)}{\partial p}\right] = \ldots$$

where, K_χ is equilibrium constant when concentration is in mole fraction.

252 Fraction $f(P)$ of the product (P) in the reaction $R \rightarrow P$ is defined by $\frac{[P]}{[P]+[R]}$

If $\Delta G°$ is 6.22 kJ mol^{-1} at 300 K, calculate the value of 100 $f(P)$.

253 For the equilibrium,

$$NH_3(g) \rightleftharpoons \frac{1}{2}N_2(g) + \frac{3}{2}H_2(g)$$

degree of dissociation is ...... % at 1 bar if $K_p = 0.00782$.

254 In the following sublimation equilibrium of ammonium carbamate

$$NH_2COONH_4(s) \rightleftharpoons 2NH_3(g) + CO_2(g)$$

total pressure is 3 atm at 298 K. What is equilibrium constant K_p?

255 For the following reaction, the equilibrium constant K_C at 298 K is 1.6×10^{17}.

$$Fe^{2+}(aq) + S^{2-}(aq) \rightleftharpoons FeS(s).$$

When equal volumes of 0.06 M $Fe^{2+}(aq)$ and 0.2 M $S^{2-}(aq)$ solutions are mixed, the equilibrium concentration of $Fe^{2+}(aq)$ is found to be $Y \times 10^{-7}$ M.

The value Y is ......

[JEE Adv. 2019]

256 At 1000 K, pressure of CO_2 in equilibrium with CaO and CO_2 is 2.105 atm.

$$CaCO_3(s) \rightleftharpoons CaO(s) + CO_2(g)$$

The equilibrium constant for the reaction

$$C(s) + CO_2(s) \rightleftharpoons 2\,CO(g)$$

is 1.9 is at the same temperature when pressure is in atm. Solid C, CaO and $CaCO_3$ are mixed and allowed to come to equilibrium at 1000 K in a closed vessel. What is the pressure of $CO(g)$ in atm when equilibrium is attained?

257 Consider the following reversible reaction,

$$A(g) + B(g) \rightleftharpoons AB(g)$$

The activation energy of the backward reaction exceeds that of the forward reaction by $2RT$ (in J mol^{-1}). If the pre-exponential factor of the forward reaction is 4 times that of the reverse reaction, the absolute value of $\Delta G^{\ominus}$ (in J mol^{-1}) for the reaction at 300 K is ....

(Given ; $\ln(2) = 0.7$, $RT = 2500$ J mol^{-1} at 300 K and G is the Gibbs energy) ***[JEE Adv. 2018]***

TYPE VI Matrix Matching

Directions (Q. Nos. 258-261) are based on the matching of Columns (1), (2) and (3).

In each case, 1 mole each of reactants and 2 moles each of products have been taken in 10 L flask at the condition where

$$2.303\,RT = 1.4 \text{ kcal mol}^{-1}$$

Column 1		Column 2 Equilibrium Constant		Column 3 $\Delta G° = -2.303RT \log K$
(I) $H_2(g) + I_2(g) \rightleftharpoons 2HI(g)$	(i)	0.008	(p)	0.56
(II) $PCl_5(g) \rightleftharpoons PCl_3(g) + Cl_2(g)$	(ii)	40.0	(q)	2.94
(III) $2SO_2(g) + O_2(g) \rightleftharpoons 2SO_3(g)$	(iii)	0.4	(r)	− 0.84
(IV) $NH_2COONH_4(s) \rightleftharpoons 2NH_3(g) + CO_2(g)$	(iv)	4.0	(s)	− 2.24

258 Degree of dissociation $x = \sqrt{\dfrac{K_p}{K_p + p}}$

(a) (I) - (i) - (p) (b) (II) - (iii) - (p)
(c) (II) - (iii) - (r) (d) (I) - (iii) - (q)

259 Degree of dissociation is independent of pressure.

(a) (I) - (iv) - (r) (b) (I) - (iv) - (q)
(c) (II) - (iv) - (q) (d) (I) - (iii) - (r)

260 For this equilibrium,

$$p = 3\left(\frac{K_p}{4}\right)^{1/3}$$

(a) (IV) - (iii) - (s) (b) (IV) - (ii) - (r)
(c) (IV) - (i) - (q) (d) (IV) - (i) - (r)

261 For this equilibrium, if pressure is made four times, degree of dissociation is doubled.

(a) (IV) - (i) - (r) (b) (IV) - (ii) - (s)
(c) (III) - (ii) - (q) (d) (III) - (ii) - (s)

Directions (Q. Nos. 262-265) are based on the matching of columns (1), (2) and (3). In each case, number of reactants are stoichiometric coefficients.

Column 1 (Equilibria)		Column 2 (x = degree of dissociation)		Column 3 (Spontaneous nature)
(I) $\underset{(g)}{N_2O_4} \rightleftharpoons \underset{(g)}{2NO_2} - q$	(i)	$\sqrt{\dfrac{K_p}{4p^2 + K_p}}$	(p)	at low temperature, low pressure
(II) $\underset{(g)}{PCl_5} + q \rightleftharpoons \underset{(g)}{PCl_3} + \underset{(g)}{Cl_2}$	(ii)	$\sqrt{\dfrac{K_p}{4p + K_p}}$	(q)	at low temperature, high pressure
(III) $\underset{(s)}{C} + \underset{(g)}{CO_2} \rightleftharpoons \underset{(g)}{2CO} - q$	(iii)	$\sqrt{\dfrac{K_p}{p + K_p}}$	(r)	at high temperature, low pressure
(IV) $\underset{(g)}{N_2} + \underset{(g)}{3H_2} \rightleftharpoons \underset{(g)}{2NH_3} + q$	(iv)	$\dfrac{p}{8}\sqrt{27K_p}$ if $x << 1$ or 2	(s)	at high temperature, high pressure

262 Diamagnetic nature of gas changes to paramagnetic nature.

(a) (I) - (iii) - (q) (b) (I) - (iii) - (s)
(c) (I) - (ii) - (q) (d) (I) - (ii) - (r)

263 Hybridisation state of the central atom changes when products are formed.

(a) (II) - (iii) - (p) (b) (II) - (iii) - (r)
(c) (II) - (ii) - (r) (d) (II) - (ii) - (q)

264 Non-flammable gas changes to flammable gas.

(a) (I) - (iii) - (s) (b) (I) - (ii) - (r)
(c) (III) - (ii) - (r) (d) (III) - (ii) - (q)

265 Odourless gas changes to pungent gas and quantity of product formed is proportional to pressure applied.

(a) (IV) - (iv) - (q) (b) (IV) - (iv) - (r)
(c) (IV) - (iii) - (s) (d) (III) - (iii) - (q)

266 The hydrogenation of pyridine (C_5H_5N) to piperidine ($C_5H_{11}N$)

$$C_5H_5N(g) + 3H_2(g) \rightleftharpoons C_5H_{11}N(g)$$

is an equilibrium process whose equilibrium constant (K_p) is given by

$$\log_{10} K_p = -20.281 + \frac{10.560\,K}{T}$$

Match the thermodynamics parameters in column I with their respective values in column II and select the answer from the codes given.

Column I	Column II
(i) $\log_{10} K_p$ at 500 K	(p) − 388.32
(ii) $\Delta H°$ (in J)	(q) − 20.26
(iii) $\Delta S°$ (in J)	(r) 193.96×10^3
(iv) $\Delta G°$ at 500 K (in J)	(s) − 202.19

Codes

	(i)	(ii)	(iii)	(iv)
(a)	(q)	(s)	(r)	(p)
(b)	(q)	(s)	(p)	(r)
(c)	(q)	(p)	(r)	(s)
(d)	(p)	(s)	(r)	(q)

267 In the following equilibrium, $H_2(g) + I_2(g) \rightleftharpoons 2HI(g)$ is set up at 298 K in a 5 L flask. Experiment is carried by taking 0.1 mole each of $H_2(g)$ and $I_2(g)$.
After equilibrium is attained, $I_2(g)$ was dissolved in KI and required 100 mL of 0.1 M $Na_2S_2O_3$ solution.
Match the values given in column II with the respective terms in column I, and select the answer from the codes given.

Column I		Column II
(i) HI (mole) formed at equilibrium.	(p)	0.005
(ii) H_2 (mole) at equilibrium.	(q)	0.01
(iii) $Na_2S_2O_3$ (mole) reacted.	(r)	1.00
(iv) $\frac{K_C}{K_p}$	(s)	0.19

Codes

	(i)	(ii)	(iii)	(iv)
(a)	(s)	(p)	(r)	(q)
(b)	(s)	(q)	(p)	(r)
(c)	(s)	(p)	(q)	(r)
(d)	(p)	(s)	(q)	(r)

268 Given, at 298 K

I : $Fe_2O_3(s) + 3H_2(g) \rightleftharpoons 2Fe(s) + 3H_2O(l)$, $K_p^{I} = 4.0 \times 10^{-6}$

II : $CO_2(g) + H_2(g) \rightleftharpoons CO(g) + H_2O(l)$, $K_p^{II} = 3.2 \times 10^{-4}$

III : $Fe_2O_3(s) + 3CO(g) \rightleftharpoons 3CO_2(g) + 2Fe(s)$, $K_p^{III} = ?$

Match the parameters given in column I with their respective values in column II and select the answer from the codes given.

Column I	Column II
(i) K_p^{III}	(p) 3.2×10^{-6}
(ii) $\frac{p_{CO}}{p_{CO_2}}$ at equilibrium in III	(q) 0.063×10^3
(iii) p_{H_2} at equilibrium in I	(r) 2×10^{-2}
(iv) $\frac{p_{CO}}{p_{H_2}}$ in II, when $p_{CO_2} = 1 \times 10^2$ bar	(s) 1.2207×10^5

Codes

	(i)	(ii)	(iii)	(iv)
(a)	(s)	(r)	(q)	(p)
(b)	(s)	(r)	(p)	(q)
(c)	(s)	(p)	(q)	(r)
(d)	(p)	(r)	(s)	(q)

269 For the reaction,

$$Br_2(g) \longrightarrow 2Br(g)$$

$$K_C = 38.4 \text{ at } 2400 \text{ K}$$

$$K_C = 84.7 \text{ at } 2600 \text{ K}.$$

Match the thermodynamic parameter in Column I with their values in Column II and select the answer from the codes given.

Column I	Column II
(i) $\Delta_r H°$ in the given temperature range (in kJ)	(p) 58.0
(ii) K_C at 2500 K	(q) 116.0
(iii) $-\Delta_r G°$ at 2500K (in kJ)	(r) 205.0
(iv) $-\Delta_r S°$ at 2500K (in JK^{-1})	(s) 84.4

Codes

	(i)	(ii)	(iii)	(iv)
(a)	(p)	(q)	(r)	(s)
(b)	(r)	(s)	(p)	(q)
(c)	(r)	(p)	(s)	(q)
(d)	(r)	(s)	(q)	(p)

270 Formation of $SO_3(g)$ in contact process is exothermic.

$$SO_2(g) + \frac{1}{2}O_2(g) \rightleftharpoons SO_3(g)$$

Match the effects as applied in Column I and the direction in Column II in which equilibrium is displaced and select the answer from the codes given.

Column I	Column II
(i) Pressure of the system is increased without addition of inert gas	(p) Forward
(ii) Inert gas added keeping the volume of the system constant	(q) Backward
(iii) Inert gas added keeping pressure of the system constant	(r) No effect
(iv) Temperature is increased	(s) Cannot be predicted.

Codes

	(i)	(ii)	(iii)	(iv)
(a)	(p)	(r)	(s)	(q)
(b)	(p)	(q)	(s)	(r)
(c)	(p)	(r)	(q)	(q)
(d)	(r)	(s)	(p)	(q)

HINTS & EXPLANATIONS

Immediate Tests

1. $\left(\frac{dx}{dt}\right) = K_f\,[A]^3$

$$\therefore\ K_f = \frac{\left(\frac{dx}{dt}\right)}{[A]} = \frac{0.05\text{ mol L}^{-1}\text{ h}^{-1}}{0.120\text{ mol L}^{-1}}$$

$$= 0.417\text{ h}^{-1}$$

Also, $K_C = \frac{K_f}{K_b}$

$$\therefore\ K_b = \frac{K_f}{K_C} = \frac{0.417\text{ h}^{-1}}{0.50\text{ mol L}^{-1}}$$

$$= 0.83\text{ L mol h}^{-1}$$

- It can be concluded that forward reaction is of first-order and backward reaction is of second order based on units of rate constant.
  For nth order unit of rate constant
  $= (\text{conc.})^{1-n}\text{time}^{-1}$

2.
$$PCl_5 \rightleftharpoons PCl_3 + Cl_2$$

Equilibrium moles: 1, 2, 2

Active mass: $\left(\frac{1}{2}\right)$M, $\left(\frac{2}{2}\right)$M, $\left(\frac{2}{2}\right)$M

$$\therefore\ K_C = \frac{[PCl_3][Cl_2]}{[PCl_5]} = \frac{1\times 1}{0.5} = 2$$

For $PCl_3 + Cl_2 \rightleftharpoons PCl_5$

$$K_C' = \frac{1}{K_C} = \frac{1}{2} = 0.5$$

3. $K_p = K_C(RT)^{\Delta n_g}$

$\Delta n_g = 3 - 2 = 1$

$\therefore\ K_p = 3.75\times 10^{-6}\ (0.0831\times 1069)^1$

$= 3.34\times 10^{-4}$

- $R = 0.0831\text{ L bar mol}^{-1}\text{ K}^{-1}$

4. (i) $H_2O + H_2O \rightleftharpoons H_3O^+ + OH^-,$

$$K_1 = 1\times 10^{-14}$$

$CH_3COOH + OH^- \rightleftharpoons$

$CH_3COO^- + H_2O,\ K_2 = ?$

$CH_3COOH + H_2O \rightleftharpoons CH_3COO^- + H_3O^+,$

$$K_3 = 1.8\times 10^{-5}$$

$K_1K_2 = K_3$ (due to addition)

$$\therefore\ K_2 = \frac{K_3}{K_1} = \frac{1.8\times 10^{-5}}{1\times 10^{-14}} = 1.8\times 10^9$$

(ii) I. $(NH_3 + H_2O) \rightleftharpoons NH_4^+ + OH^-,\ K_1$

II. $NH_4OH + H^+ \rightleftharpoons NH_4^+ + H_2O,$

$$K_2 = 1.8\times 10^9$$

III. $H_2O \rightleftharpoons H^+ + OH^-,\ K_3 = 1.0\times 10^{-14}$

On adding II and III, I is obtained

$$\text{I} = \text{II} + \text{III}$$

$$K_1 = K_2K_3 = 1.8\times 10^{-5}$$

5. $N_2(g) + 3H_2(g) \rightleftharpoons 2NH_3(g)$

$$\Delta n_g = -2$$

(a) $K_p = K_C\,(RT)^{-2} = \frac{K_C}{(RT)^2}$

If, $K_p = K_C$

$(RT)^2 = 1 \qquad (0.0831\times T)^2 = 1$

$$\therefore\ T^2 = \left(\frac{1}{0.0831}\right)^2 \Rightarrow T = 12.03\text{ K}$$

(b) $K_p = K_\chi(p)^{\Delta n_g}$

If $K_p = K_\chi$, then $(p)^{\Delta n_g} = 1$

$pV = RT$

$$\therefore\ p = \left(\frac{RT}{V}\right)$$

Since, $\Delta n_g = -2$

$$\therefore\ \left(\frac{V}{RT}\right)^{-2} = 1$$

$$\left(\frac{RT}{V}\right)^2 = 1$$

$$\therefore T = \frac{V}{R} = \frac{10}{0.0831} = 120.3\text{ K}$$

6. (i) $[PCl_5] = \frac{0.4\text{ mol}}{1\text{L}} = 0.4\text{ M}$

$$[PCl_3] = \frac{0.2\text{ mol}}{1\text{L}} = 0.2\text{ M}$$

$$[Cl_2] = \frac{0.6\text{ mol}}{1\text{L}} = 0.6\text{ M}$$

$$[PCl_5] \rightleftharpoons PCl_3 + Cl_2$$

Reaction quotient, $Q = \frac{[PCl_3][Cl_2]}{[PCl_5]}$

$$= \frac{0.2\times 0.6}{0.4} = 0.3$$

$$K_C = 0.2$$

Thus, $\qquad Q > K_C.$

Reaction moves right to left.

(ii) $[A] = \frac{1.0}{1.0} = 1.0\text{ M}$

$[B] = 2.0\text{ M}$

$[C] = 3.0\text{ M}$

$$Q = \frac{[C]^2}{[A][B]^2}$$

$$= \frac{(3)^2}{(1)\,(2)^2} = 2.25 >> K_C\text{ (given)}$$

Hence, reaction proceeds right to left.

7. (i)

	A	+	B	$\rightleftharpoons$	$2C$
Initial	$\left(\frac{1.0}{1}\right)$ = 1.0 M		$\left(\frac{1.4}{1}\right)$ = 1.4 M		$\left(\frac{0.5}{1}\right)$ = 0.5 M
Change	$-x$		$-x$		$+2x$
Equilibrium conc.	$(1.0-x)$ M		$(1.4-x)$ M		$(0.5+2x)$ M

Given, $[C]_{eq} = (0.5 + 2x) = 0.75\text{ M}$

$$\therefore\quad x = \frac{0.25}{2}\text{ M} = 0.125\text{ M}$$

$[A]_{eq} = (1.0 - 0.125) = 0.875\text{ M}$

$[B]_{eq} = (1.4 - 0.125) = 1.275\text{ M}$

$[C]_{eq} = 0.75\text{ M}$

$$\therefore\ K_C = \frac{[C]^2}{[A][B]} = \frac{(0.75)^2}{(0.875)(1.275)} = 0.504$$

(ii)

	$PCl_3(g)$ +	$Cl_2(g)$ $\rightleftharpoons$	$PCl_5(g)$
Initial mol	1.0	2.0	0
Change	$-x$	$-x$	$+x$
Equilibrium	$(1-x)$	$(2-x)$	x
Active mass (mol L^{-1})	$\left(\frac{1-x}{3}\right)$	$\left(\frac{2-x}{3}\right)$	$\left(\frac{x}{3}\right)$

Given, $\qquad (1-x) = 0.7$

$\therefore \qquad x = 0.3$

$$\therefore\ K_C = \frac{[PCl_5]}{[PCl_3][Cl_2]} = \frac{\left(\frac{0.3}{3}\right)}{\left(\frac{0.7}{3}\right)\left(\frac{1.7}{3}\right)} = 0.756$$

$\therefore$ For $PCl_5(g) \rightleftharpoons PCl_3(g) + Cl_2(g),$

$$K_C' = \frac{1}{K_C} = 1.322$$

8. (i)

	$H_2(g)$ +	$I_2(g)$ $\rightleftharpoons$	$2HI(g)$
Initial mol	1	1	0
At equili.	$(1-x)$	$(1-x)$	$2x$

$$K_C = \frac{4x^2}{(1-x)^2} = 50$$

$$\therefore\ \left(\frac{x}{1-x}\right) = \left(\frac{50}{4}\right)^{1/2} = 3.54$$

$$x = 0.78$$

$\therefore\ I_2$ unreacted $= (1-x) = 0.22$ mol

$\therefore$ Total moles at equilibrium

$= (1-x) + (1-x) + 2x = 2$

(ii) $p = \frac{n}{V}RT = \frac{2\times 0.0821\times 743}{30}$

$= 4.1$ atm

(iii) $p_{HI} = x_{HI}\ p_{total} = \left(\frac{1-x}{2}\right)p_{total}$

$$= \left(\frac{0.22}{2}\right)4.1 = 0.451\text{ atm}$$

$$p_{HI} = x_{HI}p_{total} = 0.78\times 4.1 = 3.2\text{atm}$$

9. $NH_3 + HCl \rightleftharpoons NH_4Cl$

$NH_3 \equiv HCl$

Moles of HCl $= \frac{100 \times 1}{1000} = 0.1$ mol

$\therefore$ NH_3 at equilibrium = 0.1

	N_2 +	$3H_2$ $\rightleftharpoons$	$2NH_3$
Initial mol	1	3	0
At equil	$(1-x)$	$3(1-x)$	$2x$

$2x = 0.1 \quad \therefore x = 0.05$

$\therefore \quad [N_2] = (1-x) = 0.95$ M

$[H_2] = 3(1-x) = 3(0.95)$ M

$[NH_3] = 2x = 0.1$ M

$$K_c = \frac{[NH_3]^2}{[N_2][H_2]^3} = \frac{(0.1)^2}{(0.95)\,27(0.95)^3}$$

$$= 4.54 \times 10^{-4}$$

10. $N_2 + 3H_2 \rightleftharpoons 2NH_3$

$$p_{NH_3} = \frac{nRT}{V}$$

$$2.493 \text{ bar} = \frac{n \times 0.0831 \times 300}{5}$$

$\therefore \quad n(NH_3) = 0.5$ mol

$n(NH_3)$ taken initially = 1.0 mol

Thus, reverse reaction takes place.

	$2NH_3$ $\rightleftharpoons$	N_2 +	$3H_2$
Initial mol	1	1	1
Change mol	$-2x$	$+x$	$+3x$
At equil.	$(1-2x)$	$(1+x)$	$(1+3x)$

Total moles at equilibrium = $(3 + 2x)$

$$p_{NH_3} = 2.493 \text{ bar} = (1-2x)\frac{RT}{V}$$

$$\therefore \quad (1-2x) = \frac{2.493 \times 5}{0.0831 \times 300} = 0.5$$

$\therefore \quad x = 0.25$

$$\therefore \quad [NH_3] = \left(\frac{1-2x}{V}\right) = \frac{0.5}{5} = 0.1 \text{ M}$$

$$[N_2] = \frac{1+x}{5} = \frac{1.25}{5} = 0.25 \text{ M}$$

$$[H_2] = \frac{(1+3x)}{V} = \frac{1.75}{5} = 0.35 \text{ M}$$

Thus, for $2NH_3 \rightleftharpoons N_2 + 3H_2$

$$K_C = \frac{[N_2][H_2]^3}{[NH_3]^2} = \frac{(0.25)(0.35)^3}{(0.1)^2} = 1.072$$

$\therefore$ K_C' for $N_2 + 3H_2 \rightleftharpoons 2NH_3$

$$K_C' = \frac{1}{K_C} = 0.933$$

11. Solution

	A +	B $\rightleftharpoons$	C +	D
Case I : Initial :	1	1	0	0 mol
Change :	$-x$	$-x$	$+x$	$+x$
			$x = 0.5$	
At equil :	$(1-x)$	$(1-x)$	x	x
Case II : Initial :	2	1	0	0
Change :	$-y$	$-y$	$+y$	$+y$
At equil :	$(2-y)$	$(1-y)$	y	y

$$\therefore K_C = \frac{[C][D]}{[A][B]} = \frac{x^2}{(1-x)(1-x)}$$

$$= \frac{y^2}{(2-y)(1-y)}$$

Putting the value of x,

$$K_C = \frac{\left(\frac{1}{2}\right)^2}{\left(\frac{1}{2}\right)\left(\frac{1}{2}\right)} = \frac{y^2}{(2-1)(1-y)}$$

$$\frac{y^2}{(2-y)(1-y)} = 1$$

$$y^2 = [2 + y^2 - 3y]$$

$$y = \frac{2}{3} \text{ mol}$$

$$[A] = \frac{\text{mol}}{\text{L}} = \frac{2 - \frac{2}{3}}{5} = \frac{4}{15} = 0.267 \text{ M}$$

$$[B] = \frac{1 - \frac{2}{3}}{5} = \frac{1}{15} = 0.067 \text{ M}$$

$$[C] = \frac{2}{15} = 0.133 \text{ M}$$

$$[D] = \frac{2}{15} = 0.133 \text{ M}$$

12. H_2O is liquid at 298 K, only gaseous species is CO_2.

$\therefore \quad K_p = p^2_{CO_2}$

$\therefore \quad p^2_{CO_2} = 36 \text{ atm}^2$

$\therefore \quad p_{CO_2} = 6$ atm

13. (a) $K_p = \dfrac{4x^2\,p}{(1-x^2)} = 636$

$$\frac{4x^2 \times 158}{(1-x^2)} = 636$$

$$\therefore \quad \frac{x^2}{1-x^2} = \frac{632}{158} = 4$$

$$\therefore \quad x^2 = 4 - 4x^2$$

$$5x^2 = 4$$

$$x^2 = \frac{4}{5}$$

$\therefore \quad x = 0.89$, i.e. 89%

(b) When, $x = 0.5$

$$\frac{4(0.5)^2\,p}{[1-(0.5)^2]} = 636$$

$$\frac{4(0.25)p}{0.75} = 636$$

$\therefore \quad p = 636 \times 0.75 = 477$ mm Hg

14. $K_p = (p_{H_2O})^{10} = 4.08 \times 10^{-25}$

$\therefore \quad p_{H_2O} = 3.64 \times 10^{-3}$ Torr

Vapour pressure of $H_2O = 0.07$ Torr

Thus,

$$R_H = \frac{\text{Partial pressure of } H_2O \times 100}{\text{Vapour pressure of } H_2O}$$

$$= \frac{3.64 \times 10^{-3}}{0.07} \times 100 = 5.2\,\%$$

15. (i) (a)

	$N_2O_4(g)$ $\rightleftharpoons$	$2NO_2(g)$
Initial mol	1	0
At equil.	$(1-x)$	$2x$

Total mol = $(1 + x)$

Since, mol $\propto$ volume

Hence, % by volume means % by mol

NO_2 = 50 % by volume

$$\therefore \quad \left(\frac{2x}{1+x}\right) \times 100 = 50$$

$$\therefore \quad \frac{2x}{1+x} = \frac{1}{2}$$

$$4x = 1 + x$$

$$\therefore \quad x = \left(\frac{1}{3}\right)$$

(b) $\quad x = \dfrac{D-d}{d(y-1)}$

$$\left[\because D = \frac{\text{Molar mass}}{2} = 46\right]$$

$$\frac{1}{3} = \frac{46}{d} - 1 \quad (y = 2)$$

$$\frac{4}{3} = \frac{46}{d}$$

$$\therefore \quad d = \frac{46 \times 3}{4} = 34.5$$

$\therefore$ Abnormal molar mass

$= 34.5 \times 2 = 69$ g mol^{-1}

(c) $i = 1 + (2-1)\frac{1}{3} = \left(\frac{4}{3}\right)$

(ii)

	$N_2O_4(g)$ $\rightleftharpoons$	$2NO_2(g)$
Initial	n	n
At equil.	$(n-x)$	$(n+2x)$

Total moles = $(2n + x)$

$$\chi_{N_2O_4} = \frac{n-x}{(2n+x)}$$

$$\chi_{NO_2} = \frac{n+2x}{(2n+x)}$$

Also, vapour density of mixture

$$= \frac{\text{Average molar mass}}{2} = \frac{61.34}{2}$$

$$d = 30.67$$

(a) x is related to vapour density

$$x = \frac{D-d}{d} = \frac{D}{d} - 1 = \frac{46}{30.67} - 1 = 0.5$$

(b) Also, $M_{av} = \dfrac{\chi_1 M_1 + \chi_2 M_2}{\chi_1 + \chi_2}$

$$61.35 = \frac{n-0.5}{(2x+0.5)} \times 92 + \frac{n+1}{(2n+0.5)} \times 46$$

$\therefore \quad n = 2$, Total moles = 4

(c) $K_C = \frac{[NO_2]^2}{[N_2O_4]}$

$= \frac{(n+2x)^2}{(n-x)} = \frac{(3)^2}{(1.5)} = 6.0$

16. (a) $Ag_2CrO_4\ (s) \rightleftharpoons 2Ag^+\ (aq) + CrO_4^{2-}\ (aq)$

$K = [Ag^+]^2 [CrO_4^{2-}] = 4 \times 10^{-18}$

If $[CrO_4^{2-}] = x$M

then, $[Ag^+] = 2x$

$\therefore\ (2x)^2(x) = 4 \times 10^{-18}$

$4x^3 = 4 \times 10^{-18}$

$x = 1 \times 10^{-6}$ M

$\therefore [CrO_4^{2-}] = 1 \times 10^{-6}$ M

in the absence of $AgNO_3$ or K_2CrO_4.

(b) In the presence of 1 M $AgNO_3$

$[Ag^+] = 1$ M

$\therefore\ (1)^2 [CrO_4^{2-}] = 4 \times 10^{-18}$

$\therefore\ [CrO_4^{2-}] = 4 \times 10^{-18}$M

■ $[CrO_4^{2-}]$ in presence of 1 M of $AgNO_3$ is 4×10^{-18} M. Thus, solubility of Ag_2CrO_4 in presence of common ion is decreased.

17. $\Delta G° = -2.303\ RT\ \log K$

$460 = -2.303 \times 2 \times 300 \log K$

$\log K = -0.333$

$\therefore\ K = 0.465$

$A + B \rightleftharpoons C + D$

At equilibrium $[A] = [B]$ and $[C] = [D]$

$K = \frac{[C][D]}{[A][B]} = \frac{[C]^2}{[A]^2} = 0.465$

$\therefore\ \frac{[C]}{[A]} = 0.682$

18. $\Delta G° = \Delta H° - T\Delta S$

$= -29.8 - 298 \times \frac{(-100)}{1000}$

$= -29.8 + 29.8 = 0$

$\Delta G° = -2.303\ RT\ \log K$

$\therefore\ K = 1$

19. $LiH\ (s) \longrightarrow Li(l) + \frac{1}{2}H_2(g)$

Gaseous species is H_2

$\therefore\ K_p = \sqrt{p_{H_2}}$

$\therefore\ \frac{K_{p_2}\ (900\ K)}{K_{p_1}\ (400\ K)} = \sqrt{\frac{27.8}{0.278}} = 10$

$\therefore\ \Delta H° = \frac{2.303 \times 8.314 \times 400 \times 900}{500} \log 10$

$= 13786$ J mol^{-1}

$= 13.786$ kJ mol^{-1}

20. (i) $\Delta G° = -nFE°_{cell}$

Also, $\Delta G° = -2.303\ RT\ \log K_{eq}$

$\therefore\ E°_{Cell} = \frac{2.303\ RT}{nF} \log K_{eq}$

$= \frac{0.0591}{2} \log 6.2 \times 10^{52} = 1.56$V

(ii) $\Delta G° = -nFE°_{cell}$

$= -2 \times 96500 \times 1.56$

$= -301080$ J mol^{-1}

$= -301.08$ kJ mol^{-1}

21. $\Delta G° = -2.303\ RT\ \log K_{eq}$

If $K_{eq} > 1$

then $\Delta G° = -$ ve

$\Delta G° = \Delta H° - T\Delta S°$

Thus, $T\Delta S° > \Delta H°$

$\therefore\ T > \frac{\Delta H°}{\Delta S°}$

Also, $\Delta G° = \Delta H° - T\Delta S°$

$33 = 224 - 1280\ \Delta S°$

$\therefore\ \Delta S° = 0.15$ kJ mol^{-1} K^{-1}

$\therefore\ T > \frac{224\ \text{kJ mol}^{-1}}{0.15\ \text{kJ mol}^{-1}\text{K}^{-1}} = 1493$ K

Knowledge Confirmation Test 1

1. (c) **2.** (b) **3.** (a) **4.** (b) **5.** (c) **6.** (a) **7.** (c) **8.** (d) **9.** (a) **10.** (b)
11. (a) **12.** (b) **13.** (b) **14.** (a) **15.** (b) **16.** (b) **17.** (b) **18.** (b) **19.** (b) **20.** (c)
21. (d) **22.** (c) **23.** (a) **24.** (b) **25.** (c) **26.** (c) **27.** (a) **28.** (b) **29.** (a) **30.** (c)
31. (d)

Knowledge Confirmation Test 2

1. (b) **2.** (b) **3.** (a) **4.** (c) **5.** (a) **6.** (c) **7.** (a) **8.** (b) **9.** (d) **10.** (c)
11. (a) **12.** (d) **13.** (a) **14.** (c) **15.** (b) **16.** (b) **17.** (b) **18.** (c) **19.** (a) **20.** (d)
21. (a) **22.** (b) **23.** (a) **24.** (c) **25.** (c)

Knowledge Confirmation Test 3

1. (b) **2.** (a) **3.** (d) **4.** (a) **5.** (a) **6.** (c) **7.** (c) **8.** (d) **9.** (d) **10.** (b)

Knowledge Confirmation Test 4

1. (a) **2.** (b) **3.** (d) **4.** (b) **5.** (a) **6.** (b) **7.** (a) **8.** (c) **9.** (b) **10.** (c)
11. (c) **12.** (d) **13.** (d) **14.** (d) **15.** (a) **16.** (d)

Knowledge Confirmation Test 5

1. (d) **2.** (d) **3.** (c) **4.** (c) **5.** (b) **6.** (b) **7.** (c) **8.** (c) **9.** (a) **10.** (a)
11. (a) **12.** (b) **13.** (b) **14.** (a) **15.** (a) **16.** (c) **17.** (a) **18.** (b) **19.** (b) **20.** (b)

Acid Test for JEE Main

Type I. MCQs with Only ONE Correct Alternate

1. (c) $A(g) + 2B(g) \rightleftharpoons 2C(g)$

Initial 3 1 0

At equil. $(3-x)$ $(1-2x)$ $2x$

Given, $2x = 0.5$

$x = 0.25$ mol

$\therefore [A] = (3-x) = 2.75 \text{ mol L}^{-1}$

$[B] = (1-2x) = 0.50 \text{ mol L}^{-1}$

$[C] = 0.5 \text{ mol L}^{-1}$

$$K_C = \frac{[C]^2}{[A][B]^2} = \frac{(0.5)^2}{(2.75)(0.5)^2} = 0.36$$

2. (c) $2NO(g) + O_2(g) \rightleftharpoons 2NO_2(g)$

Initial 2 mol

At equil. $(2-2x)$ 0.00156 mol $2x$

$NO_2 = 2x = 0.50$ mol

$x = 0.25$ mol

$$\therefore [O_2]_{eq} = \left(\frac{0.00156}{1}\right) = 0.00156 \text{ M}$$

$[NO] = (2-2x) = (2-0.5) = 1.5\text{M}$

$[NO_2] = 2x = 0.50$ M

$$K_C = \frac{[NO_2]^2}{[NO]^2[O_2]} = \frac{(0.50)^2}{(1.5)^2(0.00156)}$$

$= 71.2$

3. (b) Exothermic, $\Delta H = -q$

Thus, reaction is favoured at low temperature.

$xA \rightleftharpoons yB$

$$K_c = \frac{[B]^y}{[A]^x}(\text{mol L}^{-1})^{y-x}$$

$(\text{mol L}^{-1})^{y-x} = (\text{mol L}^{-1})^{-2}$

thus, $y - x = -2 \Rightarrow y < x$

Thus, number of moles decreases $\Delta n_g < 0$.

$$(\text{product}) \propto \left(\frac{1}{p}\right)^{\Delta n_g/2}$$

$(\text{product}) \propto p$

Hence, reaction is favoured at high pressure.

4. (d) $CaCO_3(s) \rightleftharpoons CaO(s) + CO_2(g)$

$K_C = [CO_2] = 0.02 \text{ mol L}^{-1}$

$[CO_2] = [CaCO_3] = 0.02 \text{ mol L}^{-1}$

$\therefore [CaCO_3] = 0.02 \times 100 \text{ g L}^{-1} = 2 \text{ g L}^{-1}$

$= 2 \times 6.5$ g in 6.5 L flask $= 13.0$ g

5. (b) $$K_I = \frac{[PCl_3][Cl_2]}{[PCl_5]} = \frac{0.01 \times 0.01}{0.01}$$

$= 1 \times 10^{-2}$

$K_{II} = 1$

$$K_{III} = \frac{(0.01)^2}{(0.01)(0.01)^3} = 1 \times 10^4$$

$K_{IV} = 1 \times 10^2$

Thus, extent of reaction is I < II < IV < III.

6. (b) $NH_4SH(s) \rightleftharpoons NH_3(g) + H_2S(g)$

Initial mol n 0 0

At equil. $(n-x)$ x x

$K_C = [NH_3][H_2S]$

(solid is not considered)

$$NH_4SH = 5.1 \text{ g} = \frac{5.1}{51} = 0.1 \text{ mol}$$

$$x = 0.1 \times \frac{30}{100} = 0.03$$

$$\therefore [NH_3] = \frac{x}{V} = \frac{0.03}{3} = 0.01 \text{ mol L}^{-1}$$

$$[H_2S] = \frac{x}{V} = 0.01 \text{ mol L}^{-1}$$

$\therefore K_C = (0.01)^2 = 1 \times 10^{-4} \text{ mol}^2 \text{ L}^{-2}$

$T = 327 + 273 = 600$ K

Δn_g = moles of gaseous products − moles of gaseous reactants

$= 2$

$K_p = K_C(RT)^{\Delta n_g}$

$\therefore K_p = (1 \times 10^{-4} \text{ mol}^2 \text{ L}^{-2})$

$(0.082 \text{ L atm mol}^{-1} \text{ K}^{-1} \times 600 \text{ K})^2$

$= 0.242 \text{ atm}^2$

7. (c) $$K_C = \frac{\left(\frac{2}{V}\right)^2}{\left(\frac{2}{V}\right)^3\left(\frac{2}{V}\right)} = 9.0$$

$$\frac{V^2}{4} = 9 \Rightarrow V = 6 \text{ L}$$

8. (c) $CO_2(g) + H_2(g) \rightleftharpoons CO(g) + H_2O(g)$

Initial 0.25 0.25 0 0

At equil. $(0.25-x)$ $(0.25-x)$ x x

Total moles at equilibrium

$= (0.25-x) + (0.25-x) + x + x$

$= 0.50$

Since, $\Delta n_g = 0$

$\therefore K_p = K_C$

$$\therefore \frac{x^2}{(0.25-x)^2} = 0.16$$

$$\therefore \frac{x}{0.25-x} = 0.4 = \frac{2}{5}$$

$\therefore 5x = 0.5 - 2x$

$7x = 0.5$

$$x = \frac{5}{70} = \frac{1}{14}$$

$$\% \text{ of CO} = \left(\frac{1/14}{0.50}\right) \times 100 = 14.28\%$$

9. (b) $3A + B \rightleftharpoons 2C + D$

Initial 1 2 0 0

At equil. $(1-3x)$ $(2-x)$ $2x$ x

Given, $A = C$

$(1-3x) = 2x$ (given)

$\therefore x = 0.2$

$$\text{Thus, \% of } B \text{ reacted} = \frac{0.2}{2} \times 100 = 10\%$$

10. (d) $$K_1 = \frac{[C]}{[A][B]^2} \Rightarrow K_2 = \frac{[A]^3}{[C][D]}$$

$$K_3 = \frac{[C]^2}{[B]^6[D]}$$

Eq. (III) = (I) × 3 + (II)

$3A + 6B + C + D \rightleftharpoons 3C + 3A$

$\therefore 6B + D \rightleftharpoons 2C$

$\therefore K_3 = K_1^3 K_2$

$$\therefore \frac{K_1^3}{K_3} = K_2$$

11. (d) $O_2(g) \rightleftharpoons 2(O)$

Initial 1 0

At equil. $(1-x)$ $2x$

$$\therefore K_C = \frac{4x^2}{(1-x)V} = \frac{4x^2}{(1-x)10}$$

$$K_C = \frac{K_p}{(RT)^{\Delta n_g}} = \frac{1.2 \times 10^{-10}}{(0.0831 \times 1800)}$$

$= 8.0 \times 10^{-13}$

$$\therefore 8.0 \times 10^{-13} = \frac{4x^2}{(1-x)10}$$

Since, $K_C <<< 1$

$\therefore (1-x) \approx 1$

$$\therefore 8.0 \times 10^{-13} = \frac{4x^2}{10}$$

$\therefore x = 1.41 \times 10^{-6}$ mol

$\therefore$ O-atoms $= 2x = 2.82 \times 10^{-6}$ mol

$= 2.82 \times 6.02 \times 10^{23}$ atoms

$= 1.71 \times 10^{18}$ atoms

12. (b) $C(s) + CO_2(g) \rightleftharpoons 2CO(g)$

Initial 0.48 0 bar

At equil. $(0.48-x)$ $2x$ bar

$$\therefore K_p = \frac{4x^2}{(0.48-x)} = 3.0$$

$4x^2 + 3x - 1.44 = 0$

$$x = \frac{-3 + \sqrt{9 + 16 \times 1.44}}{8} = 0.33$$

$p_{CO} = 2x = 0.66$ bar

13. (c) $$X : \frac{K_p}{K_C} = (RT)^{-1} = \frac{1}{RT} = \frac{1}{300R}$$

$$Y : \frac{K_p}{K_C} = (RT) = 300R$$

$$Z : \frac{K_p}{K_C} = 1$$

$\therefore X < Z < Y$

14. (b) Relation between K_p and K_C is

$K_p = K_C(RT)^{\Delta n_g}$

Relation between K_p and K_χ is

$K_p = K_\chi(p)^{\Delta n_g}$

$\Delta n_g = -2 \Rightarrow pV = RT$

$\therefore\ p = \frac{RT}{V} = \left(\frac{0.0831 \times 400}{5}\right) = 6.05$

$K_C(RT)^{\Delta n_g} = K_\chi(p)^{\Delta n_g}$

$K_c(0.0831 \times 400)^{-2} = K_\chi(6.65)^{-2}$

$\therefore\ K_C = K_\chi\left(\frac{6.65}{0.0831 \times 400}\right)^{-2}$

$K_C = K_\chi \times 25$

$\therefore\ K_C = 25K_\chi$

15. (c) $K_p = p_{CO_2} = 2$ atm from (I)

$K_p = \frac{p_{CO}^2}{p_{CO_2}} = 6$ atm from (II)

$\therefore\ p_{CO}^2 = 6p_{CO_2} = 12$ from III

$K_p' = p_{CO}^2 = 12$ atm

16. (b) I. $Q = \frac{[NO_2]^2}{[N_2O_4]}$

Since, $[NO_2]$ is maximum and $[N_2O_4]$ is minimum at point A, hence Q is minimum at this point. Thus, false.

II. $Q = \frac{(0.1)^2}{(0.1)} = 0.1 < K_C$

Thus, reaction proceeds left to right. Thus, true.

III. $K_C = Q$ when equilibrium is reached at point D or F. Thus, true.

17. (b) $N_2(g) + 3H_2(g) \rightleftharpoons 2NH_3(g)$

If : $p_{N_2} = p, p_{H_2} = 3p, p_{NH_3} = 2p$

$\Rightarrow\ p_{(total)} = p_{N_2} + p_{NH_3} \simeq p_{N_2} + p_{H_2}$

$[\because p_{(total)} >> p_{NH_3}]$

$= p + 3p = 4p$

Now, $K_p = \frac{p_{NH_3}^2}{p_{N_2} \times p_{H_2}^3} = \frac{p_{NH_3}^2}{p \times (3p)^3}$

$= \frac{p_{NH_3}^2}{27 \times p^4} = \frac{p_{NH_3}^2}{27 \times \left(\frac{P}{4}\right)^4}$

$[\because p = 4p]$

$K_p = \frac{p_{NH_3}^2 \times 4^4}{3^2 \times 3 \times P^4}$

$p_{NH_3}^2 = \frac{3^2 \times 3 \times p^4 \times K_p}{4^4}$

$p_{NH_3} = \frac{3 \times 3^{1/2} \times p^2 \times K_p^{1/2}}{4^2}$

$= \frac{3^{3/2} \times p^2 \times K_p^{1/2}}{16}$

18. (c) $PCl_5 \rightleftharpoons PCl_3 + Cl_2$

	PCl_5	PCl_3	Cl_2
Initial	2	0	0 mol
At equil.	$(2-x)$	x	x mol

Total moles at equilibrium $= n = (2 + x)$ mol

$x = 2 \times \frac{80}{100} = 1.6$ mol

$\therefore n = 2 + 1.6 = 3.6$ mol

$p = \frac{n}{V}RT$

$= \frac{3.6 \text{ mol}}{5 \text{ L}} \times 0.0821 \text{ L atm mol}^{-1} \text{ K}^{-1} \times 350 \text{ K}$

$= 20.7$ atm

19. (b) For which $\Delta n_g = 0$

20. (b) $\left(\frac{dx}{dt}\right)_{net} = 2.6 \times 10^3 [NO]^2[O_2] - 4.1\ [NO]^2$

$\therefore$ Velocity constant of forward reaction $= K_f = 2.6 \times 10^3$

and that of back reaction $= K_b = 4.1$

$K_C = \frac{K_f}{K_b} = \frac{2.6 \times 10^3}{4.1} = 6.341 \times 10^2$

Q (reaction quotient) $= \frac{[NO_2]^2}{[NO]^2[O_2]}$

$= \frac{(0.1)^2}{(0.01)^2(0.01)} = 10{,}000 > K_C$

Hence, shifted in backward direction to attain equilibrium.

21. (a) Pressure decreases when CO_2 is dissolved in water. Hence, increase in pressure increases solublility.

22. (a) $A + B \rightleftharpoons AB;\ K_C = \frac{[AB]}{[A][B]}$

	A	B	AB	
At 300 K	2	2	7	$K_1 = \frac{7}{4}$
At 400 K	5	5	4	$K_2 = \frac{4}{25}$

on increasing temperature, K_C decreases, thus it is an exothermic reaction.

23. (d) $\Delta G = \Delta H - T\Delta S$

At equilibrium, $\Delta G = 0$

and for spontaneous reaction, $\Delta G < 0$

Thus, $T\Delta S > \Delta H$

$T > \frac{\Delta H}{\Delta S} > \frac{50 \times 1000 \text{ cal mol}^{-1}}{100 \text{ cal mol}^{-1} \text{ K}^{-1}}$

$\Rightarrow\ T > 500$ K

Thus, minimum temperature is 500.1 K.

24. (d) Since, $[SO_2] = 0.00$ M, hence reverse reaction takes place

$2SO_3(g) \rightleftharpoons 2SO_2(g) + O_2(g)$

	$2SO_3(g)$	$2SO_2(g)$	$O_2(g)$
Initial	0.50 M	0	0.35 M
At equilibrium	$(0.50 - 2x)$	$2x$	$(0.35 + x)$

$K_c' = \frac{1}{4} = \frac{[SO_2]^2\ [O_2]}{[SO_3]^2}$

$\frac{1}{4} = \frac{(2x)^2\ (0.35 + x)}{(0.50 - 2x)^2}\ (x < 0.25)$

on solving

$x = 0.1$

$\therefore\ [O_2] = 0.35 + 0.10 = 0.45$ M

25. (c) Required final reaction is obtained by $4 \times$ Eq. III $-$ 2 [Eq. I + Eq. II]

$K = \frac{K_{III}^4}{K_I^2\ K_{II}^2}$

$= \frac{(4.1 \times 10^{-9})^4}{(2.7 \times 10^{-18} \times 4.6 \times 10^{-3})^2}$

$= 1.832 \times 10^6$

26. (a) $\Delta G°(\text{net}) = \Delta G°(R) - \Delta G°(L)$

$= 201.7 - 152.4 = 49.3$ kJ mol^{-1}

$\Delta G° = -2.303\ RT \log K$

$= -2.303\ RT \log\left(\frac{p_2}{p_1}\right)$

where, p_2 = pressure of 1-butyne

p_1 = pressure of 1, 3-butadiene

$\therefore\ \log\frac{p_2}{p_1} = \left(-\frac{\Delta G°}{2.303\ RT}\right)$

$= \frac{-49.3 \text{ kJ mol}^{-1}}{2.303 \times 8.314 \times 10^{-3} \text{kJ mol}^{-1}\text{K}^{-1} \times 296 \text{ K}}$

$= -8.6986$

$\therefore\ \frac{p_2}{p_1} = 2.0 \times 10^{-9}$

27. (a) $\log K$ decreases as $\frac{1}{T}$ increases or (T decreases) thus, $\Delta H > 0$ (endothermic). Hence, increase in temperature displaces equilibrium in forward side.

$\Delta n_g = +1$ (gaseous)

Thus $x \propto \left(\frac{1}{p}\right)^{\Delta n_g/2} \Rightarrow x \propto \sqrt{\frac{1}{p}}$

If p decreases, x increases (forward side).

- If $\Delta n_g = 0$, no effect of p
  $\Delta n_g > 0$, equilibrium is displaced in backward side on increasing p and $\Delta n_g < 0$, it is displaced in forword side on increasing p.

28. (a) For which K_C is maximum.

29. (a) $N_2O_4(g) \rightleftharpoons 2NO_2(g)$

	$N_2O_4(g)$	$2NO_2(g)$
Initial	1	0 mol
At equilibrium	$(1-x)$	$2x$ mol

Total moles at equilibrium $= 1 - x + 2x = (1 + x)$

Since, $n \propto$ volume

if volume of 1 mole $= V$ L

then volume of $2x$ moles $= 2xV$ L

and volume of $(1 + x)$ mole $= (1 + x)\ V$ L

Thus, $NO_2 = 50\% = \frac{2x\ V}{(1 + x)\ V} \times 100$

$\therefore \quad \frac{2x}{1+x} = \frac{1}{2}$

$\therefore \quad x = \frac{1}{3} \Rightarrow x = \frac{D-d}{d}$

where, D = theoretical vapour density
d = observed vapour density

$D = \frac{92}{2} = 46 \text{ g mol}^{-1}$

$\therefore \quad x = \frac{46-d}{d} = \frac{1}{3}$

$d = 34.5 \text{ g mol}^{-1}$

30. (c) $2C_6H_5COOH \rightleftharpoons (C_6H_5COOH)_2$

$C_6H_5COOH \rightleftharpoons \frac{1}{2}(C_6H_5COOH)_2$

$y = \frac{1}{2}$

where, y = number of moles of product from 1 mole reactant

x (degree of dimer formation) $= \frac{D-d}{(y-1)\,d}$

D (theoretical vapour density)

$= \frac{\text{Molecular weight}}{2} = \frac{122}{2} = 61$

$\therefore \quad 0.50 = \frac{61-d}{\left(\frac{1}{2}-1\right)d} = \frac{61-d}{d}$

$\Rightarrow \quad 0.50\,(-0.50) = \frac{61-d}{d}$

$\therefore \quad 0.25 = \frac{d-61}{d} = 1 - \frac{61}{d}$

$\Rightarrow \quad d = \frac{61}{0.75} = 81.33$

$\therefore$ Abnormal molecular weight

$= 2 \times d = 162.66 \text{ g mol}^{-1}$

31. (d) $NO_2(g) \rightleftharpoons \frac{1}{2}N_2O_4(g)$

Initial mol $\quad 1 \quad 0$
At equilibrium $\quad (1-x) \quad x/2$

Total moles $= \left(1-x+\frac{x}{2}\right) = \left(1-\frac{x}{2}\right)$

Let volume of 1 mole $= V$

Volume of $\left(1-\frac{x}{2}\right)$ mole $= \left(1-\frac{x}{2}\right)V$

Density $= \frac{\text{Mass}}{\text{Volume}} \Rightarrow D = \frac{m}{V}$

and $\quad d = \frac{m}{\left(1-\frac{x}{2}\right)V}$

$\Rightarrow \quad \frac{D}{d} = \left(1-\frac{x}{2}\right)$

$\Rightarrow \quad \frac{x}{2} = 1 - \frac{D}{d} = \frac{d-D}{d}$

$\therefore \quad x = 2\frac{(d-D)}{d}$

■ y = number of moles of product from 1 mole reactant $= \frac{1}{2}$

thus $x = \frac{D-d}{(y-1)d} \Rightarrow x = 2\frac{(d-D)}{d}$

32. (a) $COCl_2(g) \rightleftharpoons CO(g) + Cl_2(g)$

Initial moles $\quad 1 \quad 0 \quad 0$
Moles at equil. $\quad (1-x) \quad x \quad x$

$x = \frac{D-d}{(y-1)d}$

$y = 2$

$x = \frac{D-d}{d}$

$\frac{D}{d} = 1 + x = 1.4$

$\therefore \quad x = 0.4$

$\therefore [COCl_2] = \frac{1-x}{1} = 0.6 \text{ mol dm}^{-3}$

$[CO] = [Cl_2] = \frac{x}{1} = 0.4 \text{ mol dm}^{-3}$

Thus,

$K_c = \frac{[CO]\,[Cl_2]}{[COCl_2]} = \frac{0.4 \times 0.4}{0.6} = 0.267$

33. (d) $x = \frac{D-d}{(y-1)\,d}$

Here, $y = 3$ (mole of product from one mole reactant)

$\therefore \quad x = \frac{D-d}{2d} \Rightarrow 2x = \frac{D-d}{d} = \frac{D}{d} - 1$

$\therefore \quad \frac{D}{d} = (1+2x)$

when $x = 1$, (100% dissociation)

$\frac{D}{d} = 1 + 2 = 3.0$

34. (c) $\Delta G° = -2.303\,RT \log K_p$

$= -2.303 \times 2500 \text{ J mol}^{-1} \log 1.0 \times 10^{28}$

$= -161.21 \times 10^3 \text{ J mol}^{-1}$

$= -161.21 \text{ kJ mol}^{-1}$

35. (a) $\Delta G° = -2.303\,RT \log K$

$= -2.303\,RT \log p_{D_2O}$

$D_2O(l) \rightleftharpoons \underbrace{D_2O\,(g)}$

Vapour pressure is due to $D_2O\,(g)$ only

$8.904 \text{ kJ mol}^{-1} = -2.303 \times 8.314 \times 10^{-3} \text{ kJ mol}^{-1}\text{ K}^{-1} \times 298 \text{ K} \log p_{D_2O}$

$\therefore \quad p_{D_2O} = 2.75 \times 10^{-2}$ bar

■ When R in J or kJ, pressure is in bar.

36. (c) $C_{10}H_8\,(s) \rightleftharpoons C_{10}H_8\,(g)$

$K_p = p_{C_{10}H_8} = 0.10$ mmHg

$= \frac{0.10}{760}$ atm $= 1.32 \times 10^{-4}$ atm

$\Delta n_g = +1 \Rightarrow K_p = K_C(RT)^{\Delta n_g}$

$\therefore \; K_c = \frac{K_p}{(RT)^{\Delta n_g}} = \frac{K_p}{RT}$

$= \frac{1.32 \times 10^{-4} \text{ atm}}{0.0821 \text{ L atm mol}^{-1}\text{K}^{-1} \times 300 \text{ K}}$

$= 5.36 \times 10^{-6} \text{ mol}^{-1}$

37. (b) $\Delta n_g = +1$

$K_p = K_C(RT)$

$\therefore$ If $K_p = K_C$, then, $T = \frac{1}{R}$

$K_p = K_C(RT)$

atm = mol L^{-1} (0.0821 L atm mol^{-1}K^{-1}) T

$\therefore \quad T = \frac{1}{0.0821}$ K $= 12.18$ K.

38. (c) $\Delta n_g = -1$ (gaseous species)

$x \propto \left(\frac{1}{p}\right)^{\Delta n_g/2} \quad \therefore \quad x \propto \sqrt{p}$

Thus, on increasing pressure, solubility increases.

39. (c) $\Delta G° = -2.303\,RT \log K_p$

$= -2.303\,RT \log p_{H_2O\,(g)}$

At 373 K, (boiling point of water)

$p_{H_2O\,(g)} = 1$ atm

$\therefore \quad \Delta G° = 0.00$

40. (c) $H_2O\,(l) \rightleftharpoons H^+\,(aq) + OH^-\,(aq)$

$K = K_w = [H^+]\,[OH^-]$

■ K_w is called ionic product of water.

$K_w = [H^+]\,[OH^-] = 1 \times 10^{-14}$ at 298 K

$\Delta G = \Delta G° + 2.303\,RT \log K_w$

$= 79.885 \text{ kJ mol}^{-1} + 2.303 \times 8.314 \times 10^{-3} \text{kJ mol}^{-1}\text{ K}^{-1} \times 298 \text{ K} \log 1 \times 10^{-14}$

$= 79.885 - 79.885 = 0$

■ Without calculation, $\Delta G = 0$ at equilibrium.

41. (b) $x = 0.50 = \frac{D-d}{(y-1)\,d}$

where, y = number of species from 1 mol $CCl_4(g)$

molar mass of $CCl_4 = 12 + 142$

$= 154 \text{ g mol}^{-1}$

D = theoretical vapour density $= \frac{154}{2} = 77$

d = experimental vapour density = 38.5

Thus, $\frac{1}{2} = \frac{77\;38.5}{38.5\,(y-1)} = \frac{1}{(y-1)}$

$y = 3$

(a) $CCl_4(g) \rightleftharpoons CCl_3(g) + Cl(g)$, $y = 2$
(b) $CCl_4(g) \rightleftharpoons CCl_2(g) + 2Cl(g)$, $y = 3$
(c) $CCl_4(g) \rightleftharpoons C(g) + 4Cl(g)$, $y = 5$
(d) $CCl_4(g) \rightleftharpoons CCl(g) + 3Cl(g)$, $y = 4$.

42. (d) $N_2O_4(g) \rightleftharpoons 2NO_2(g)$

Initial moles: 1, 0
Moles at equilibrium: $(1-x)$, $2x$

Total moles at equilibrium
$= 1 - x + 2x = (1 + x)$
1 mol changes to $= (1 + x)$ mol

$$\text{Moles of } N_2O_4 = \frac{0.578 \text{ g}}{92 \text{ g mol}}$$

$$p = \frac{n}{V}RT = \frac{w}{mV}RT$$

$$1 \text{ dm}^3 = 1 \times 10^{-3} \text{m}^3$$
$$R = 8.314 \text{ Pa m}^3\text{mol}^{-1} \text{K}^{-1}$$
$$p = 24.12 \times 10^3 \text{ Pa}$$

$$\therefore 24.12 \times 10^3 = \frac{0.578(1 + x) \times 8.314 \times 308}{92 \times 1 \times 10^{-3}}$$

$$\therefore \quad x = 0.50$$

Thus, 50% dissociation.

■ 1 Pa m^3 = 1 J

43. (c) $SO_3(g) \rightleftharpoons SO_2(g) + \frac{1}{2}O_2(g)$

y = number of moles of products from one mole reactant = 1.5

$$x = \frac{D-d}{d(y-1)} = \frac{D-d}{0.5\,d}$$

D = vapour density before dissociation

$$= \frac{\text{molar mass}}{2} = \frac{80}{2} = 40$$

d = vapour density after dissociation

$$pV = nRT = \frac{w}{m}RT$$

m (molar mass of mixture)

$$= \frac{wRT}{Vp} = \frac{\rho RT}{p}$$
$$= \frac{0.866 \times 0.0821 \times 900}{1}$$
$$= 64.0 \text{ g mol}^{-1}$$
$$\therefore \quad d = 32.0 \text{ g mol}^{-1}$$
$$\therefore \quad x = \frac{D-d}{0.5\,d} = \frac{40 - 32}{0.5 \times 32} = 0.5$$

Thus, 50% dissociation.

44. (a) α-(D) glucose $\rightleftharpoons$ β-(D) glucose
(A $\quad$ B)

$$K_C = \frac{[B]}{[A]}$$

Fraction of A in the mixture of A and B

$$f[A] = \frac{[A]}{[B] + [A]} = \frac{[A]/[A]}{\frac{[B]}{[A]} + \frac{[A]}{[B]}} = \frac{1}{K + 1}$$

$$f[A] = \frac{1}{1.8 + 1} = \frac{1}{2.8} = 0.357$$

Thus, 35.7%.

45. (b) $AB(g) \rightleftharpoons A(g) + B(g)$

Initial: 1, 0, 0
At equil.: $(1-x)$, x, x

$$K_p = px^2(1 - x^2)$$

$$2.56 \times 10^{-2} = \frac{x^2}{(1 - x^2)} (p = 1 \text{ bar})$$

$$\therefore \; 0.0256(1 - x^2) = x^2$$

$$\therefore \quad x^2 = \frac{0.0256}{1.0256} = 0.025 \Rightarrow x = 0.16$$

Thus, 16% dissociation.

46. (c) In I, equilibrium is attained and in II rate changes.

47. (c) H_2O as reactant will react with $[CoCl_4]^{2-}$ thus, concentration of $[CoCl_4]^{2-}$ is decreased.

48. (c) $Ca(HCO_3)_2(s) \longrightarrow CaCO_3(s) + CO_2(g) + H_2O(g)$

Total pressure is due to $CO_2(g)$ and $H_2O(g)$, molar ratio being equal.

Thus, $p_{CO_2} = p_{H_2O}$
and $p_{CO_2} + p_{H_2O} = 0.12$
$\therefore$ $p_{CO_2} = p_{H_2O} = 0.06$ bar
$\therefore$ $K_p = p_{CO_2} \cdot p_{H_2O} = 0.0036$

49. (d) Catalyst equally affects forward and backward reaction.

50. (c) If (reactant) > product
then $K_C < 1$
thus, $K_f < K_b$
So, that $\frac{K_f}{K_b} (= K_C) < 1$.

51. (a) As temperature is lowered, equilibrium is displaced in backward side, thus on increasing temperature, forward reaction is favoured.
Hence, $\Delta H > 0$.

52. (c) $A(g) + B(g) \rightleftharpoons C(g) + D(g)$

2, 2, 0, 0 mol
$(2-x)$, $(2-x)$, x, x mol

$[C] = 3[B]$ (given)
$x = 3(2 - x)$
$x = 1.5$

$$K_C = \frac{[C][D]}{[A][B]} = \frac{1.5 \times 1.5}{0.5 \times 0.5}$$
$$K_C = 9$$

53. (a) $Q = \frac{p_{Cl_2} \cdot p_{PCl_3}}{p_{Cl_5}} = 1, Q > K_C$

Thus, backward side.

54. (d) $\Delta G° = \Delta_f G°$(gaseous S) $- \Delta_f G°$ (liquid S)

$= 103 - 100.7 = 2.3$ kcal mol^{-1}

Also, $S(l) \rightleftharpoons S(g)$

$$K_p = p_{S(g)}$$
$$\therefore \quad \Delta G° = -2.303\,RT \log K_p$$
$$2.3 = -2.303 \times 2 \times 10^{-3} \times 500 \log K_p$$
$$\therefore \quad \log K_p = -0.9986 \approx -1.000$$
$$K_p = 0.1 \text{ atm}$$

55. (a) $A_2(g) \rightleftharpoons 2A(g)$

$$K_p = \frac{4x^2 p}{(1 - x^2)}$$
$$x = 0.2 \text{ (given)}$$
$$K_p = \frac{4(0.2)^2 \times 1}{[1 - (0.2)^2]} = 0.167$$
$$\therefore \quad \Delta G° = -2.303\,RT \log K$$
$$= 2.303 \times 8.314 \times 320 \log 0.167$$
$$= 4763 \text{ J mol}^{-1}$$

56. (b) $A + B \rightleftharpoons C + D$

1 M, 1 M, 1 M, 1 M
$(1-x)$ M, $(1-x)$ M, $(1+x)$ M, $(1+x)$ M

$$K_{eq} = 100 = \frac{[C][D]}{[A][B]} \Rightarrow 100 = \frac{(1 + x)^2}{(1 - x)^2}$$
$$\therefore \quad 10 = \left(\frac{1+x}{1-x}\right)$$
$$\therefore \quad x = \frac{9}{11}$$
$$\therefore \quad [D] = 1 + x = 1 + \frac{9}{11} = \frac{20}{11} = 1.818 \text{ M}$$

57. (c) On increasing pressure, freezing point is lowered, hence ice melts. Equilibrium shifts in forward side.

58. (b) $\Delta G = -2.303\,RT \log K$

$$\log_{10} K = -\frac{\Delta G}{2.303\,RT}$$
$$= \frac{-2494.2 \text{ J mol}^{-1}}{2.303 \times 8.314 \text{ J mol}^{-1}\text{K}^{-1} \times 300 \text{ K}}$$
$$\log_{10} K = -0.4342 \Rightarrow K = 0.37$$

$$\text{Reaction quotient } Q = \frac{[B][C]}{[A]^2}$$
$$= \frac{(2)\left(\frac{1}{2}\right)}{\left(\frac{1}{2}\right)^2} = 4 \Rightarrow Q > K_C,$$

Hence, reaction proceeds in reverse direction to make $Q = K_C$.

59. (b) By using this formula, equilibrium constant, $K_p = K_C\,(RT)^{\Delta n_g}$

where, Δn_g = (number of moles of products) − (number of moles of reactants)

For the given reaction,

$$SO_2(g) + \frac{1}{2}O_2(g) \rightleftharpoons SO_3(g)$$

$$\Delta n_g = 1 - \left[\frac{1}{2} + 1\right] = 1 - \left[\frac{3}{2}\right] = -\frac{1}{2}$$

60. (d) $N_2(g) + O_2(g) \longrightarrow 2NO(g)$

$$K_C = \frac{[NO]^2}{[N_2][O_2]} = 4 \times 10^{-4}$$

For the reverse reaction,

$$2NO(g) \longrightarrow N_2(g) + O_2(g)$$

$$K_C' = \frac{1}{K_C} = \frac{[N_2][O_2]}{[NO]^2} = \frac{1}{4 \times 10^{-4}} = \frac{10^4}{4}$$

On dividing the reverse reaction by 2

$$NO(g) \longrightarrow \frac{1}{2}N_2(g) + \frac{1}{2}O_2(g)$$

$$K_C'' = \frac{[N_2]^{1/2}[O_2]^{1/2}}{[NO]} = \sqrt{K_C'}$$

$$= \sqrt{\frac{10^4}{4}} = \frac{100}{2} = 50$$

61. (a) $CO_2(g) + C(s) \rightleftharpoons 2CO(g)$

	$CO_2(g)$	$2CO(g)$
Initial	0.5 atm	—
At equil.	$0.5 - p$	$2p$ atm

This is a case of heterogeneous equilibrium. C (s) being solid is not considered. Total pressure of CO_2 and CO gases.

$$p_{CO_2} + p_{CO} = p_{total}$$

$\Rightarrow$ $(0.5 - p) + 2p = 0.8,$
$p = 0.3$atm

$\therefore$ $p_{CO_2} = 0.5 - 0.3 = 0.2$ atm

$\Rightarrow$ $p_{CO} = 2p = 0.6$ atm

$$K_p = \frac{p^2_{CO}}{p_{CO_2}} = \frac{0.6 \times 0.6}{0.2} = 1.8 \text{ atm}$$

62. (c) As equation 'III' is obtained on adding equation I and equation II,

so $K_3 = K_1 K_2$

63. (a) $X \rightleftharpoons 2Y$

	X	$2Y$
At equil.	1	0
Mole fraction	$(1-\alpha)$	2α
Mole fraction	$\left(\frac{1-\alpha}{1+\alpha}\right)$,	$\left(\frac{2\alpha}{1+\alpha}\right)$
Partial pressure	$\frac{(1-\alpha)p}{(1+\alpha)}$	$\frac{2\alpha p_1}{(1+\alpha)}$

$$K_{p_1} = p_Y^2 / p_X = \frac{4\alpha^2 p_1}{(1-\alpha^2)}$$

$Z \rightleftharpoons P + Q$

	Z	P	Q
Initial	1	0	0
At equil.	$(1-\alpha)$	α	α
Mole fraction	$\left(\frac{1-\alpha}{1+\alpha}\right)$	$\frac{\alpha}{1+\alpha}$	$\frac{\alpha}{1+\alpha}$
Partial pressure	$\frac{(1-\alpha)p_2}{(1+\alpha)}$	$\frac{\alpha p_2}{(1+\alpha)}$	$\frac{\alpha p_2}{(1+\alpha)}$

$$K_{p_2} = \frac{p_P p_Q}{p_Z} = \frac{\alpha^2 p_2}{(1-\alpha^2)}$$

$$\Rightarrow \quad \frac{K_{p_1}}{K_{p_2}} = \frac{4p_1}{p_2} \Rightarrow \frac{1}{9} = \frac{4p_1}{p_2}$$

$$\therefore \quad \frac{p_1}{p_2} = \frac{1}{36}$$

64. (a) Equilibrium constant for the reaction,

$$SO_2(g) + \frac{1}{2}O_2(g) \rightleftharpoons SO_3(g)$$

$$K_C = \frac{1}{4.9 \times 10^{-2}}$$

and for $2SO_2(g) + O_2(g) \rightleftharpoons 2SO_3(g)$

$$K_C' = K_C^2 = \left(\frac{1}{4.9 \times 10^{-2}}\right)^2 = \frac{10^4}{(4.9)^2}$$

$$= 416.490 \approx 416$$

65. (a) $PCl_5(g) \rightleftharpoons PCl_3(g) + Cl_2(g)$

	$PCl_5(g)$	$PCl_3(g)$	$Cl_2(g)$
Initial	1	0	0
At equil.	$(1-x)$	x	x

Total number of moles at equilibrium

$$= (1 - x) + x + x = 1 + x$$

$$\chi_{PCl_3} = \frac{x}{1+x}$$

$$p_{PCl_3} \chi_{PCl_3} = \left[\frac{x}{1+x}\right] p$$

66. (a) $NH_4HS(s) \rightleftharpoons NH_3(g) + H_2S(g)$

	$NH_4HS(s)$	$NH_3(g)$	$H_2S(g)$
Initial	1	0.5 atm	0
At equil.	$(1-x)$	$(0.5+x)$ atm	x atm

Total pressure at equilibrium

$$= p_{NH_3} + p_{H_2S}$$
$$= (0.5 + x + x) \text{ atm}$$
$$= 0.84 \text{ atm}$$

$\therefore$ $x = 0.17$ atm

$\therefore$ $p_{NH_3} = 0.50 + 0.17 = 0.67$ atm

$\Rightarrow$ $p_{H_2S} = 0.17$ atm

$\therefore K_p = p_{NH_3} \cdot p_{H_2S} = 0.67 \times 0.17$
$= 0.114$ atm

67. (d) $2NO_2(g) \rightleftharpoons 2NO(g) + O_2(g)$

$K_C = 1.8 \times 10^{-6}$ at 184°C (= 457 K)

$R = 0.00831 \text{ kJ mol}^{-1}\text{K}^{-1}$

$\Rightarrow K_p = K_C(RT)^{\Delta n_g}$

where, Δn_g = (gaseous products – gaseous reactants)

$= 3 - 2 = 1$

$\therefore$ $K_p = 1.8 \times 10^{-6} \times 0.00831 \times 457$

$= 6.836 \times 10^{-6} > 1.8 \times 10^{-6}$

Thus, $K_p > K_C$.

68. (a) At equilibrium

$$2Na(g) \rightleftharpoons Na_2(g)$$

	$2Na(g)$	$Na_2(g)$
Mass %	71.3 g	28.7 g
Mol %	3.1 mol	0.624 mol

Total mol = 3.10 + 0.624 = 3.724 mol

$$\therefore \quad \chi_{Na} = \frac{3.1}{3.724} = 0.832$$

$$X_{Na_2} = \frac{0.624}{3.724} = 0.168$$

$\therefore$ $p_{Na} = 0.832 \times 1.0 \times 10^3$ Pa
$= 8.32 \times 10^2$ Pa

$p_{Na_2} = 0.168 \times 1 \times 10^3 = 1.68 \times 10^2$ Pa

$$\therefore K_p = \frac{p_{Na_2}}{p^2_{Na}} = \frac{1.68 \times 10^2}{(8.32 \times 10^2)^2}$$

$$= 2.43 \times 10^{-4}$$

69. (c) $PCl_5(g) \rightleftharpoons PCl_3(g) + Cl_2(g)$

	$PCl_5(g)$	$PCl_3(g)$	$Cl_2(g)$
Initial	1	0	0
At equil.	$(1-x)$	x	x

Total mol $= (1 + x)$

Mole fraction	$\left(\frac{1-x}{1+x}\right)$	$\left(\frac{x}{1+x}\right)$	$\left(\frac{x}{1+x}\right)$
Partial pressure	$\left(\frac{1-x}{1+x}\right)p$	$\left(\frac{xp}{1+x}\right)$	$\left(\frac{xp}{1+x}\right)$

$$K_p = \frac{p_{PCl_3} \cdot p_{Cl_2}}{p_{Cl_5}}$$

$$K_p = \frac{x^2 p}{(1-x^2)}$$

$$\therefore \quad 0.25 = \frac{x^2 \times 1.5}{(1-x^2)}$$

$$0.25 - 0.25x^2 = 1.5x^2$$

$$1.75x^2 = 0.25$$

$$x^2 = \frac{0.25}{1.75}$$

$$\therefore \quad x = 0.378$$

$$\text{Mole fraction of } Cl_2 = \left(\frac{x}{1+x}\right) = \left(\frac{0.378}{1.378}\right)$$
$$= 0.274$$

Thus, mole % = 27.4 %

Since, volume $\propto$ mole.

$\therefore$ Volume % = 27.4%

70. (b) $NH_4I(s) \rightleftharpoons NH_3(g) + HI(g)$

HI decomposes into H_2 and I_2 at the same moment. Thus, pressure of HI decreases but that of due to NH_3 remains unchanged.

$$2HI \rightleftharpoons H_2 + I_2$$

	$2HI$	H_2	I_2
Initial	p	0	0
At equil.	$(p - 2x)$	x	x

Given x (due to I_2) = 2 atm

$\therefore$ $x = 2$ atm

$\therefore K_p$ of equilibrium I $= p_{NH_3} p_{HI}$

$$p(p - 2x) = 36$$
$$p(p - 4) = 36$$
$$p^2 - 4p - 36 = 0$$

$$\therefore \quad p = \frac{4 \pm \sqrt{16 + 144}}{2} = 8.32 \text{ atm}$$

$$K_p(\text{II}) = K_2 = \frac{p_{H_2} p_{I_2}}{p^2_{HI}} = \frac{x^2}{(p - 2x)^2}$$

$$= \frac{(2)^2}{(8.32 - 4)^2} = 0.214$$

71. (b) Given, $\frac{d[\log_e K_p]}{dT} = \frac{\Delta H°}{RT^2}$

Also $K_p = K_C(RT)^{\Delta n}$

and $\Delta H° = \Delta U° + \Delta nRT$

$$\frac{d[\log K_C(RT)^{\Delta n}]}{dT} = \frac{\Delta U° + \Delta nRT}{RT^2}$$

$$\frac{d[\log K_C]}{dT} + \frac{\Delta nR}{RT} = \frac{\Delta U° + \Delta nRT}{RT^2}$$

$$\frac{d[\log K_C]}{dT} + \frac{\Delta n}{T} = \frac{\Delta U°}{RT^2} + \frac{\Delta n}{T}$$

$$\therefore \quad \frac{d(\log K_C)}{dT} = \frac{\Delta U°}{RT^2}$$

72. (c) 2[I-II] given III

$$\therefore K_{p_3} = \left(\frac{K_{p_1}}{K_{p_2}}\right)^2 = \left(\frac{1.8 \times 10^4}{0.8}\right)^2$$

$$= 5.00 \times 10^8$$

73. (a) $\frac{1}{2}N_2(g) + \frac{1}{2}H_2(g) \rightleftharpoons NH_3(g)$

$$X_{NH_3} = 0.0385$$

Also $X_{N_2} + X_{H_2} = 1 - 0.0385$

$$= 0.9615$$

Also molar ratio of N_2 and H_2 is 1 : 3.

Hence, $X_{N_2} = \frac{0.9615}{4} = 0.2404$

$$X_{H_2} = \frac{3}{4}(0.9615) = 0.7211$$

$$\therefore \quad K_X = \frac{X_{NH_3}}{X_{N_2}^{1/2} X_{H_2}^{3/2}}$$

$$= \frac{0.0385}{(0.2404)^{1/2}(0.7211)^{3/2}} = 0.128$$

74. (c) $\Delta G° = -2.303\, RT \log K_p$

$$5.74 \text{ kJ mol}^{-1} = -2.303 \times 2.48 \text{ kJ mol}^{-1} \log K_p$$

$\therefore \log K_p = -1.00$

$\therefore \quad K_p = 0.1$

For $\quad N_2O_4 \rightleftharpoons 2NO_2$

$$K_p = \frac{4x^2 p}{(1-x^2)}$$

$$0.1 = \frac{4x^2 \times 10}{(1-x^2)}$$

$$\therefore \frac{1-x^2}{x^2} = \frac{40}{0.1} = 400 \Rightarrow \frac{1}{x^2} - 1 = 400$$

$$x^2 = \frac{1}{401} \Rightarrow x^2 = 2.5 \times 10^{-3}$$

$$x = 0.05$$

75. (a)

	$NH_2COONH_4(s) \rightleftharpoons$	$2NH_3(g)$ +	$CO_2(s)$
Initial	1	0	0
At equil.	$(1-x)$	$2x$	x

If $\quad p_{CO_2} = x$

Then $\quad p_{NH_3} = 2x$

Total pressure $= x + 2x = 3x$

and $\quad K_p = p_{NH_3}^2 \cdot p_{CO_2}$

$$= (2x)^2 \cdot (x) = 4x^3$$

It NH_3 is added, partial pressure of $NH_3 = 3x$

To keep K_p constant, pressure of CO_2 decreases.

Let $p_{CO_2} = y$ them $K_p = p_{NH_3}^2 p_{CO_2}$

$$4x^3 = (3x)^2(y)$$

$$4x^3 = 9x^2 y$$

$$\therefore \quad y = \frac{4x}{9}$$

Thus, total pressure after NH_3 is added

$$= 3x + y = 3x + \frac{4x}{9} = \frac{31x}{9}$$

Thus, ratio

$$= \frac{\text{total pressure after } NH_3 \text{ is added}}{\text{original pressure}}$$

$$= \frac{31x}{9} / 3x = 31 : 27$$

76. (b) $\Delta G° = -2.303 RT \log K_p$

$$5.0 = -2.303 \times 2.48 \log K_p$$

$$\log K_p = \frac{5.0}{2.303 \times 2.48}$$

$$\log K_p = 0.8754$$

$$\therefore \quad K_p = 7.506$$

	$2A(g)$ +	$B(g) \rightleftharpoons$	$A_2B(g)$
Initial	2	1	0
At equil	$(2-2x)$	$(1-x)$	x
	$(2-1.2)$	$(1-0.6)$	0.6
	$(x = 0.60)$		
∴ Mole fraction	$\left(\frac{0.8}{1.8}\right)$	$\frac{0.4}{1.8}$	$\left(\frac{0.6}{1.8}\right)$
Partial pressure	$\frac{4p}{9}$	$\frac{2p}{9}$	$\frac{p}{3}$

(Total moles $= 0.8 + 0.4 + 0.6 = 1.8$)

$$\therefore \quad K_p = \frac{p_{A_2B}}{p_A^2 p_B} = \frac{p/3}{\left(\frac{4p}{9}\right)^2\left(\frac{2p}{9}\right)}$$

$$7.506 = 7.594/p^2$$

$$p^2 = \frac{7.594}{7.506} = 1.011$$

$$\therefore \quad p = 1.0 \text{ atm}$$

Acid Test for JEE Advanced

Type I. MCQs with Only ONE Correct Alternate

77. (b) At 298 K, H_2O is in the liquid form (pure state), thus, it is not a part of the concentration factor in K_p.

$$K_p = p_{CO_2}^2 = 0.25$$

$\therefore \quad p_{CO_2} = 0.5$ bar

Thus, number of moles of CO_2 formed

$$n_{CO_2} = \frac{pV}{RT} = \frac{0.5 \times 1}{0.0831 \times 298} = 0.02\text{mol}$$

Thus, $Ca(HCO_3)_2$ reacted = 0.01 mol

$Ca(HCO_3)_2 \longrightarrow$	$2CO_2$
1 mol	2 mol
0.01 mol	0.02 mol

$$Ca(HCO_3)_2 \text{ taken} = \frac{4.86 \text{ g}}{162 \text{ g mol}^{-1}}$$

$$= 0.03 \text{ mol}$$

$$Ca(HCO_3)_2 \text{ unreacted} = 0.03 - 0.01$$

$$= 0.02 \text{ mol}$$

$$\% \text{ of unreacted } Ca(HCO_3)_2 = \frac{0.02}{0.03} \times 100$$

$$= 66.66\%$$

78. (c) If the $CaCO_3$ can decompose to yield CO_2 at 1.00 atm (to push back the air), thus $K_p = 1$ atm

$$\therefore \quad \log K_p = 7.282 - \frac{8500 \text{ K}}{T}$$

$$\log (1) = 7.282 - \frac{8500}{T}$$

$$\therefore \quad T = \frac{8500}{7.282} = 1167 \text{ K}$$

79. (d) Reaction quotient of the given amount

$$Q = \frac{[NO_2]^2}{[N_2O_4]} = \frac{\left(\frac{3}{1}\right)^2}{\left(\frac{1}{1}\right)} = 9$$

$$Q > K_C(0.67)$$

Thus, equilibrium is displaced in backward side.

	$2NO_2(g) \rightleftharpoons$	$N_2O_4(g)$
Initial	3	1
At equil.	$(3-2x)$	x

$$\therefore \quad K'_C = \frac{1}{K_C} = \frac{1}{0.67} = \frac{[N_2O_4]}{[NO_2]^2}$$

$$\frac{3}{2} = \frac{x}{(3-2x)^2}$$

$$3(9 + 4x^2 - 12x) = 2x$$

$$12x^2 - 38x + 27 = 0$$

$$x = \frac{38 - \sqrt{(38)^2 - (27 \times 12) \times 4}}{24}$$

$$= 1.076$$

$$\therefore [NO_2]_{equil.} = 3 - 2x$$

$$= (3 - 2 \times 1.076) = 0.85 \text{ mol}$$

80. (a)

	$N_2O_4 \rightleftharpoons$	$2NO_2$
Initial	a	0
At equil.	$(a-x)$	$2x$

$$a = \frac{13.8 \text{ g L}^{-1}}{92 \text{ g mol}^{-1}} = 0.15 \text{ mol L}^{-1}$$

Total moles at equilibrium $= (a + x)$

$\therefore \quad p = \frac{n}{V}RT$

$9.15 = \left(\frac{a+x}{1}\right) \times 0.0831 \times 400$

$(a + x) = 0.275$

$\therefore \quad x = 0.275 - 0.150 = 0.125$

$K_C = \frac{4x^2}{(a-x)V} = \frac{4(0.125)^2}{(0.15-0.125)1} = 2.5$

$\therefore \; K_p = K_C(RT)^{\Delta n_g}$

$= 2.5 \times 0.0831 \times 400 = 83.10$

81. (b) $H_2(g) + S(s) \rightleftharpoons H_2S(g)$

Initial	0.20	1.0	0
At equil.	(0.20 – x)		x

$\therefore \quad [H_2]_{equil.} = \left(\frac{0.20 - x}{1}\right)$

$= (0.20 - x)\text{ mol L}^{-1}$

$[H_2S]_{equil.} = \left(\frac{x}{1}\right) = x\text{ mol L}^{-1}$

$K_C = 6.8 \times 10^{-2} = \frac{[H_2S]}{[H_2]}$

$0.068 = \frac{x}{(0.20 - x)}$

$0.0136 = 1.068\,x$

$\therefore \quad x = 0.0127\text{ mol}$

$p_{H_2S} = \frac{nRT}{V} = \frac{0.0127 \times 0.0831 \times 363}{1}$

$= 0.38\text{ bar}$

82. (c) $[C]_{equil.} < [C]_{initial}$

thus reaction takes place reversely.

$2C \rightleftharpoons A + 2B$

Initial	3	1	2
At equil.	(3 – 2x)	(1 + x)	(2 + 2x)

$(3 - 2x) = 1.4$

$\therefore \quad x = 0.8\text{ mol L}^{-1}$

$\therefore \quad [C] = 1.4\text{ mol L}^{-1}$

$[A] = (1 + x) = 1.8\text{ mol L}^{-1}$

$[B] = 2 + 2x = 3.6\text{ mol L}^{-1}$

$\therefore \; K_C = \frac{[C]^2}{[A][B]^2} = \frac{(1.4)^2}{(1.8)(3.6)^2} = 0.084$

83. (d) $Ca(HCO_3)_2(s) \rightleftharpoons CaO(s) + H_2O(g) + 2CO_2(g)$

At 400 K, $H_2O(g)$ is formed but at 298 K it is condensed to $H_2O(l)$. Pressure set up is due to CO_2 only.

$K_p = (p_{CO_2})^2$

$2KOH + CO_2 \longrightarrow K_2CO_3 + H_2O$

KOH required = 200 mL of 5 M KOH

$= \frac{200 \times 5}{1000} = 1\text{ mol}$

Thus, $\quad CO_2 = \frac{1}{2}KOH = 0.5\text{ mol}$

$p_{CO_2} = \frac{nRT}{V} = \frac{0.5 \times 0.083 \times 298}{10}$

$= 1.2364\text{ bar}$

$\therefore \; K_p = [p_{CO_2}]^2 = (1.2367)^2 = 1.53\text{ bar}^2$

84. (c) Large value of K indicates that all the Fe^{2+} is complexed.

Let $[Fe^{2+}] = x$ in equilibrium with complex.

Total volume of solution

$= 200\text{ mL} = 0.200\text{ L}$

$Fe^{2+} = 75 \times 0.03$ millimol

$= \frac{75 \times 0.03}{1000}\text{ mol} = 2.25 \times 10^{-3}\text{ mol}$

$\therefore \quad [Fe^{2+}] = \frac{2.25 \times 10^{-3}\text{ mol}}{0.2\text{ L}}$

$= 0.01125\text{ M}$

KCN = 125 × 0.2 millimol

$= \frac{125 \times 0.2}{1000}\text{ mol} = 0.025\text{ mol}$

$\therefore \; [CN^-] = \frac{0.025\text{ mol}}{0.200\text{ L}} = 0.125\text{ mol}$

$[CN^-]$ reacted with $Fe^{2+} = 0.01125 \times 6$

$= 0.0675\text{ M}$

$[CN^-]$ unreacted $= 0.125 - 0.0675$

$= 0.0575\text{ M}$

$\therefore \quad K = \frac{[Fe(CN)_6]^{4-}}{[Fe^{2+}][CN^-]^6}$

$K = \frac{[0.01125]}{(x)[0.0575]^6} = 1 \times 10^{24}$

$\therefore \quad x = 3.0 \times 10^{-19}\text{ M}$

85. (b) $N_2 + 3H_2 \rightleftharpoons 2NH_3$

Total pressure $= 2p$

$p_{NH_3} + p_{N_2} + p_{H_2} = 2p$

$p_{N_2} = \frac{p}{3}$ (given)

$\therefore \; p_{H_2} = 3p_{N_2} = p$

$\therefore \quad p_{NH_3} = 2p - \frac{p}{3} - p = \frac{2p}{3}$

$\therefore \quad K_p = \frac{(p_{NH_3})^2}{(p_{N_2})(p_{H_2})^3} = \frac{\left(\frac{2p}{3}\right)^2}{\left(\frac{p}{3}\right)(p)^3}$

$= \frac{4}{3p^2} = 1.33p^{-2}$

86. (a) Reaction quotient (Q)

$Q = \frac{[CS_2][H_2]^4}{[CH_4][H_2S]^2} = \frac{\left(\frac{3}{10}\right)\left(\frac{3}{10}\right)^4}{\left(\frac{2}{10}\right)\left(\frac{4}{10}\right)^2}$

$= 7.59 \times 10^{-2}$

$Q(7.59 \times 10^{-2}) > K_C(2.5 \times 10^{-3})$

Thus, to attain equilibrium, reaction proceeds from right to left.

87. (c) $-\Delta G° = 2.303\,RT \log K$

$534.52 = -2.303 \times 8.314 \times 10^{-3} \times 2000 \log K$

$\therefore \quad \log K = +23.264$

$K = 9.08 \times 10^{13}$

K is very high indicating that O_3 is very small

$p_{O_2} + p_{O_3} = 8$

$\therefore \quad p_{O_2} = 8$ if p_{O_3} is very small.

To keep it in equilibrium, let

$p_{O_3} = x$

$\therefore \quad K_p = \frac{(p_{O_2})^3}{(p_{O_3})^2}$

$9.08 \times 10^{13} = \frac{(8)^3}{(p_{O_3})^2}$

$p_{O_3} = 2.37 \times 10^{-6}\text{ atm} \approx 2.40 \times 10^{-6}\text{ atm}$

88. (a) $CO(g)$ added will combine with $Cl_2(g)$

$CO(g) + Cl_2(g) \rightleftharpoons COCl_2(g)$

Thus, PCl_5 dissociates to a greater extent and PCl_5 decreases.

89. (d) $K_p = K_C(RT)^{\Delta n_g}$

If $K_p = K_C$, then

$(RT)^{\Delta n_g} = 1$

but $\quad \Delta n_g = -2$

$(RT)^{-2} = 1$

$\frac{1}{(RT)^2} = 1 \Rightarrow \frac{1}{RT} = 1$

$\therefore \quad RT = 1$

$\therefore \quad T = \frac{1}{R} = \frac{1}{0.0821} = 12.2\text{ K}$

90. (a) $N_2(g) + 3H_2(g) \rightleftharpoons 2NH_3(g)$

Initial	1	3	0 mol
At equil.	(1 – x)	(3 – 3x)	2x mol

Total moles at equilibrium = (4 – 2x)

Initial pressure of 4 mol = 4 atm

$\therefore$ Equilibrium pressure of (4 – 2x) mol = 3 atm

$\because \quad x = 0.5$

$\therefore$ Total mol = (4 – 2 × 0.5) = 3

$\therefore \quad p_{N_2} = \left(\frac{1-x}{4-2x}\right) \cdot p$

$= \frac{0.5 \times 3}{3} = 0.5\text{ atm}$

$p_{H_2} = 1.5\text{ atm}$

$p_{NH_3} = 1.0\text{ atm}$

$\therefore \quad K_p = \dfrac{p^2_{NH_3}}{p_{N_2} \cdot p^3_{H_2}} = \dfrac{1}{(0.5)(1.5)^3}$

$\therefore \quad K'_p$ for $2NH_3 \rightleftharpoons N_2 + 3H_2$

$= \dfrac{1}{K_p} = 1.6875$

91. (a) (II-I) gives III.

$\therefore \quad K_3 = \dfrac{K_2}{K_1} = \dfrac{132}{12} = 11$

92. (d) $2HI \rightleftharpoons H_2 + I_2$

Initial	1	0	0 mol
At equil.	$(1-x)$	$\frac{x}{2}$	$\frac{x}{2}$ mol

$K_p = \dfrac{x^2}{4(1-x)^2}$

$\dfrac{x}{(1-x)} = \sqrt{4K_p} = 2\sqrt{K_p}$

$x = 2\sqrt{K_p} - 2x\sqrt{K_p}$

$x[1 + 2\sqrt{K_p}] = 2\sqrt{K_p}$

$x = \dfrac{2\sqrt{K_p}}{1 + 2\sqrt{K_p}}$

$x = \dfrac{\sqrt{K_p}}{0.5 + \sqrt{K_p}}$

93. (c) $2NH_3(g) \rightleftharpoons N_2(g) + 3H_2(g)$

Initial	1	0	0
At equil.	$(1-2x)$	x	$3x$

Total moles at equilibrium = $(1 + 2x)$

(Ne remains unreacted throughout)

Given, $\left(\dfrac{1-2x}{1+2x}\right) = \dfrac{1}{10}$

$\therefore \quad 10 - 20x = 1 + 2x$

$\therefore \quad 9 = 22x \Rightarrow x = \dfrac{9}{22}$

$\therefore \quad p_{NH_3} = \left(\dfrac{1-2x}{1+2x}\right)p$

$= \dfrac{1}{10} \times 10 = 1$ atm

$p_{N_2} = \left(\dfrac{x}{1+2x}\right)10 = \left[\dfrac{\frac{9}{22} \times 10}{1 + 2\left(\frac{9}{22}\right)}\right] = \dfrac{9}{4}$ atm

$p_{H_2} = \left(\dfrac{3x}{1+2x}\right) \times 10 = \dfrac{\left(3 \times \frac{9}{22}\right) \times 10}{1 + \frac{18}{22}}$

$1 = \dfrac{27}{4}$ atm

$\therefore \quad K_p = \dfrac{p_{N_2}(p_{H_2})^3}{p^2_{NH_3}} = \dfrac{\left(\frac{9}{4}\right)\left(\frac{27}{4}\right)^3}{(1)^2}$

$= 692 = 6.92 \times 10^2$

94. (c) Endothermic, favoured at low temperature towards formation of graphite. High temperature favours formation of diamond density $= \dfrac{m}{V}$

Thus, density $\propto p$.

Hence, when graphite is formed, pressure increased. Low pressure favours formation of graphite, high pressure favours formation of diamond.

95. (c) $N_2O_5(g) \rightleftharpoons N_2O_3 + O_2$

Initial	4	0	0 mol
At equil	$(4-x)$	x	x mol

$V = 1$ L

$K_C = 2.5 = \dfrac{[N_2O_3][O_2]}{[N_2O_5]} = \dfrac{x^2}{(4-x)}$

$10 - 2.5x = x^2$

$\therefore \quad x^2 + 2.5x - 10 = 0$

$\therefore \quad x = \dfrac{-2.5 + \sqrt{(2.5)^2 + 40}}{2} = 2.15$ M

Thus, N_2O_3 formed initial = 2.15 M

O_2 formed = 2.15 M

Total O_2 formed = 2.5 M

$N_2O_3 \longrightarrow N_2O + O_2$

Thus, O_2 from N_2O_3 = 2.50 – 2.15

= 0.35 M

Thus, N_2O formed = 0.35 M

96. (c) $A + 2B \rightleftharpoons C$

Initial	n	4	0
At equil.	$(n-x)$	$(4-2x)$	x

$x = 1$ (given)

$\therefore \quad [A] = \dfrac{(n-1)}{5}$

$[B] = \left(\dfrac{2}{5}\right) = 0.4$

$[C] = \left(\dfrac{1}{5}\right) = 0.2$

$\therefore \quad K_C = \dfrac{[C]}{[A][B]^2}$

$0.25 = \dfrac{0.2}{\frac{(n-1)}{5}(0.4)^2}$

$\therefore \quad n = 26$ mol

97. (a) $CO + H_2 = 60$ g

(1 : 1 molar ratio)

If CO = x g = $\dfrac{x}{28}$ mol

then $H_2 = \dfrac{60-x}{2}$ mol

Given $\dfrac{x}{28} = \dfrac{60-x}{2}$

$x = 56$

thus, CO = 2 mol

H_2 = 2 mol

H_2O = 90 g = 5 mol

$CO(g) + H_2O(g) \rightleftharpoons CO_2(g) + H_2(g)$

Initial	2	5	0	2 mol
At equil.	$(2-x)$	$(5-x)$	x	$(2+x)$ mol

$\Delta n_g = 0$

$K_p = K_C = \dfrac{[CO_2][H_2]}{[CO][H_2O]}$

$3.0 = \dfrac{x(2+x)}{(2-x)(5-x)}$

This gives $x = 1.5$ mol

$\therefore$ H_2 at equilibrium = $2 + x$ = 3.50 mol

98. (d) $X \rightleftharpoons 2Y$

Initial	1	0
At equil.	$(1-\alpha_1)$	$2\alpha_1$

Total pressure = p_1,

then $K_{p_1} = \dfrac{4\alpha_1^2 p_1}{(1-\alpha_1^2)}$

$Z \rightleftharpoons P + Q$

Initial	1	0	0
At equil.	$(1-\alpha_2)$	α_2	α_2

Total pressure = p_2

$\therefore \quad K_{p_2} = \dfrac{\alpha_2^2 p_2}{1-\alpha_2^2} = \dfrac{\alpha_1^2 p_2}{1-\alpha_1^2}$

Since, $(\alpha_1 = \alpha_2)$

$\therefore \quad \dfrac{K_{p_1}}{K_{p_2}} = \dfrac{1}{9} = \dfrac{4p_1}{p_2}$

$\therefore \quad p_1 : p_2 = 1 : 36$

99. (a) $K_p = (p_{H_2O})^{10}$

$2.56 \times 10^{-20} = (p_{H_2O})^{10}$

$\log (2.56 \times 10^{-20}) = 10 \log p_{H_2O}$

$p_{H_2O} = 0.011$ atm

$\Rightarrow \quad p_{H_2O} = 1.1 \times 10^{-2}$ atm

(only water is in gaseous state)

100. (b) $A + B \rightleftharpoons C + D$

***Case* I :**	Initial	1	1	0	0
	At equil.	$(1-x)$	$(1-x)$	x	x
					$x = 0.7$
***Case* II :**	Initial	1	1	1	1
	At equil.	$(1-y)$	$(1-y)$	$(1+y)$	$(1+y)$

$K_C = \dfrac{[C][D]}{[A][B]} = \dfrac{x^2}{(1-x)^2} = \dfrac{(1+y)^2}{(1-y)^2}$

$\therefore \quad \dfrac{x}{1-x} = \dfrac{1+y}{(1-y)} \Rightarrow \dfrac{0.7}{0.3} = \dfrac{1+y}{(1-y)}$

$7 - 7y = 3 + 3y \Rightarrow y = 0.4$

$\therefore \quad [A] = [B] = \dfrac{1-y}{5} = 0.12$ mol L^{-1}

$[C] = [D] = \dfrac{1+y}{5} = \dfrac{1.4}{5} = 0.28$ mol L^{-1}

101. (a) If lactic acid is produced, H_3O^+ is formed in excess, hence equilibrium is displaced in forward side releasing O_2 gas.

102. (d) $\Delta n_g = -1$

$$x \propto \left(\frac{1}{p}\right)^{\Delta n_g/2} \Rightarrow x \propto \sqrt{p}$$

(a) Thus, on decreasing volume, pressure is increased.
Thus, formation of product is increased (and thus decreasing CO).
(b) Addition of argon (inert gas) increases pressure thus as in (a).
(c) O_2 (reactant) will react with CO hence amount of CO decreases.

103. (c)

	$PCl_5 \rightleftharpoons$	PCl_3 +	Cl_2
Initial at equil	2 mol	2 mol	2 mol
			Total mol = 6
χ	$\frac{2}{6}$	$\frac{2}{6}$	$\frac{2}{6}$
Partial pressure	$\frac{2}{6}p$	$\frac{2}{6}p$	$\frac{2}{6}p$
	1 bar	1 bar	1 bar

$$\therefore K_p = \frac{p_{Cl_2} \cdot p_{PCl_3}}{p_{PCl_5}} = \frac{1 \times 1}{1} = 1$$

If Cl_2 added be = y mol
Then reaction quotient is increased, hence reaction is displaced in backward side.

	PCl_3 +	$Cl_2 \rightleftharpoons$	PCl_5
After y mol	2	2	2
Cl_2 added	2	$(2 + y)$	2
At equilibrium	$(2 - x)$	$(2 + y) - x$	$(2 + x)$

Initial volume = V, Final volume = $2V$
Initial mol = 6, Since, $V \propto n$
hence, total modes = 12

$\therefore \quad 2 + 2 + y + 2 = 12$

$\therefore \quad y = 6$ mol

Thus, Cl_2 added = 6 mol
At equilibrium total moles of PCl_3 and PCl_5 = 4
$\therefore$ Cl_2 at equilibrium = 12 – 4 = 8 mol

$$\therefore p_{PCl_3} = \left(\frac{2-x}{12}\right) \times 3 = \left(\frac{2-x}{4}\right) \text{bar}$$

$$p_{PCl_5} = \left(\frac{2+x}{12}\right) \times 3 = \left(\frac{2+x}{4}\right) \text{bar}$$

$$p_{Cl_2} = \left(\frac{8}{12} \times 3\right) = 2 \text{ bar}$$

$$\therefore \quad K_p = \frac{p_{PCl_3} \cdot p_{Cl_2}}{p_{PCl_5}} = \frac{\left(\frac{2-x}{4}\right) \times 2}{\left(\frac{2+x}{4}\right)} = 1$$

$2(2 - x) = (2 + 4) \Rightarrow 4 - 2x = 2 + x$

$\therefore \quad 3x = 2 \Rightarrow x = 0.67$

Thus, Cl_2 added = 6 + 0.67 = 6.67 mol

104. (b) $\log_{10} K = + \frac{\Delta H°}{2.303\, RT} + \frac{\Delta S°}{2.303 R}$

(Since, $\log_{10} K$ increases as $\frac{1}{T}$ increases (or T decreases), given reaction is exothermic).

On comparison ; $\frac{\Delta H°}{2.303 R} = \tan 45° = 1$

$\therefore \quad \Delta H° = 2.303\, R = 2.303 \times 2$
$= 4.606 \text{ cal mol}^{-1}$

Since, it is exothermic.
$\Delta H° = -4.606 \text{ cal mol}^{-1}$

105. (a) $A \xrightarrow{\text{I}} B$, x increases on increasing T thus, endothermic.
$B \xrightarrow{\text{II}} C$, x decreases on increasing T thus, exothermic.
$C \xrightarrow{\text{III}} D$ as in I thus, endothermic.

106. (d)

	$2NH_3(g) \rightleftharpoons$	$N_2(g)$ +	$3H_2(g)$
Initial	a	0	0
At equil.	$(a - 2x)$	x	$3x$

$x = 0.30$

$\therefore \quad a - 2x = 0.30$

$\therefore \quad a = 0.90$

Thus, initial moles of NH_3 = 0.90 mol

$$K_C = \frac{[N_2]\,[H_2]^3}{[NH_3]^2} = \frac{\left(\frac{0.30}{0.50}\right)\left(\frac{0.90}{0.50}\right)^3}{\left(\frac{0.30}{0.50}\right)^2} = 9.72$$

Thus, K_C for NH_3 formation

$N_2(g) + 3H_2(g) \rightleftharpoons 2NH_3(g)$

$$= \frac{1}{9.72} = 0.103$$

107. (c) $K_1 = \frac{[CO_2]}{[CO]\,[O_2]^{1/2}}$

$$\Rightarrow K_2 = \frac{[CO_2]^2}{[CO]^2[O_2]} = K_1^2$$

$\Delta G_1 = -2.303\, RT \log K_1$
$\Delta G_2 = -2.303\, RT \log K_2$
$= -2.303\, RT \log K_1^2$
$= +2 \times (-2.303\, RT \log K_1)$
$= 2\Delta G_1.$

108. (b) $pV = nRT$

$$\because \quad p = \frac{n}{V} RT$$

$$\text{Partial pressure} = \left(\frac{\text{mol}}{\text{litre}}\right) RT$$

$$\therefore \quad (\text{mol L}^{-1}) = (\text{partial pressure}) \times \frac{1}{RT}$$

109. (d)

	$H_2(g)$ +	$CO_2(g) \rightleftharpoons$	$H_2O(g)$ +	$CO(g)$
Initial	0.1	0.2	0	0
At equil.	$(0.1 - x)$	$(0.2 - x)$	x	x

Total moles at equilibrium = 0.3

$$\chi_{H_2O} = \frac{x}{0.3} = \frac{10}{100} = 0.1 \text{ (given)}$$

$\therefore \quad x = 0.3 \times 0.1 = 0.03$

At equilibrium

$\therefore \quad [H_2O] = 0.03$ M

$[CO] = 0.03$ M
$[H_2] = 0.1 - x = 0.10 - 0.03 = 0.07$ M
$[CO_2] = (0.2 - x) = 0.20 - 0.03 = 0.17$ M

$$\therefore \quad K_1 = \frac{[H_2O][CO]}{[H_2][CO_2]} = \frac{0.03 \times 0.03}{0.07 \times 0.17} = 0.075$$

Equilibrium (2)

	$CoO(s) + H_2(g) \rightleftharpoons$	$Co(s) + H_2O(g)$
Initial	0.07	0.03
At equil.	$(0.07 - y)$	$(0.03 + y)$

	$Co(s) + CO_2(g) \rightleftharpoons$	$CoO(s) + CO(g)$
Initial	0.17	0.03
At equil	$(0.17 - y)$	$(0.03 + y)$

Total moles in (2) and (3) at equil.
$= (0.07 - y) + (0.03 + y) + (0.03 + y) + (0.17 - y)$
$= 0.30$ mol

$$X_{H_2O} = \frac{(0.03 + y)}{0.30} = \frac{30}{100} = 0.3 \text{ (given)}$$

$\therefore \quad 0.03 + y = 0.09$

$\therefore \quad y = 0.06$

$$\therefore K_2 = \frac{[H_2O]}{[H_2]} = \frac{(0.03 + 0.06)}{(0.07 + 0.06)} = 9.0$$

$$K_3 = \frac{(0.03 + 0.06)}{(0.17 - 0.06)} = \frac{0.09}{0.11} = 0.818$$

Thus, $K_1 = 0.075$
$K_2 = 9.0$
$K_3 = 0.818$

110. (d) $\Delta G = \Delta G° + 2.303\, RT \log K_p$

$$= -2.303\, RT \log (K_p)_{\text{standard}} + 2.303\, RT \log \frac{p^2_{NO_2}}{p_{N_2O_4}}$$

$$= -2.303\, RT \left[\log 0.141 - \log \frac{1}{10}\right]$$

$= (-2.303 \times 8.314 \times 10^{-3} \text{ kJ mol}^{-1}\text{K}^{-1} \times 298 \text{ K}) \log 1.41$
$= -0.85 \text{ kJ mol}^{-1}$

111. (a) $N_2(g) + O_2(g) \rightleftharpoons 2NO(g)$

$$x = \sqrt{Kab}\, \frac{K(a + b)}{4}$$

For maximum yield of NO

$$\frac{dx}{da} = 0 \text{ and } \frac{dx}{db} = 0$$

$$\Rightarrow \quad \left(\frac{dx}{da}\right) = \sqrt{Kb}\, \frac{1}{2\sqrt{a}}\, \frac{K}{4} = 0$$

$$\left(\frac{dx}{ab}\right) = \sqrt{Ka} \cdot \frac{1}{2\sqrt{b}}\, \frac{K}{4} = 0$$

$$\Rightarrow \quad \frac{\sqrt{Kb}}{2\sqrt{a}}\, \frac{K}{4} = \frac{\sqrt{Ka}}{2\sqrt{b}}\, \frac{K}{4}$$

$\therefore \quad a = b$

112. (d) $K_p = p_{SO_2} \cdot p_{SO_3}$

(others are in solid state)

Given, $p_{SO_2} + p_{SO_3} = 0.9$ bar

$\therefore \quad p_{SO_2} = p_{SO_3} = 0.45$ bar

$\therefore \quad K_p = 0.45 \times 0.45 = 0.2025 \text{ bar}^2$

If $SO_2(g)$ is also present initially let degree of dissociation be $= x$

then $p_{SO_2} = (0.6 + x)$ and $p_{SO_3} = x$

$\therefore \quad K_p = p_{SO_2} \cdot p_{SO_3}$

$\therefore \quad 0.2025 = x(0.6 + x)$

$x^2 + 0.6x - 0.2025 = 0$

$x = 0.24$ bar

$\therefore \quad p_{\text{total}} = x + (0.6 + x)$

$2x + 0.60 = 1.08$ bar

113. (d) $\chi_A + \chi_B = 1.0$

If $\chi_A = 0.40, \chi_B = 0.60$

	$A(g)$	$+ \; B(g)$	$\longrightarrow C(g)$	$+ \; D(g)$
Initial	0.40	0.60	0	0
At equil.	$(0.40 - \alpha)$	$(0.60 - \alpha)$	0	α

$0.40 - \alpha = 0.30$

$\alpha = 0.10$

$$\therefore K_\chi = \frac{\chi_C \cdot \chi_D}{\chi_A \cdot \chi_B} = \frac{0.1 \times 0.1}{0.30 \times 0.50} = \frac{1}{15}$$

114. (a) $Ag_2CO_3(s) \rightleftharpoons 2Ag(s) + CO_2(g) + \frac{1}{2}O_2(g)$

	$Ag_2CO_3(s)$	$2Ag(s)$	$CO_2(g)$	$O_2(g)$
Initial	1	0	0	0
At equil.	$(1 - x)$	x	x	$\frac{x}{2}$
Mole fraction			$\frac{2}{3}$	$\frac{1}{3}$
Partial pressure			$\frac{2p}{3}$	$\frac{p}{3}$

$$\therefore K_p = p_{CO_2} \cdot p_{O_2}^{1/2} = \left(\frac{2p}{3}\right)\left(\frac{p}{3}\right)^{1/2}$$

$$= 2\left(\frac{p}{3}\right)\left(\frac{p}{3}\right)^{1/2} = 2\left(\frac{p}{3}\right)^{3/2}$$

■ Only gaseous species considered.

115. (c) $PCl_5(g) \rightleftharpoons PCl_3(g) + Cl_2(g)$;

$K_{eq} = 100$

$\therefore \quad \Delta G° = -2.303\, RT \log K$

$= -20.0 \text{ kJ mol}^{-1}$ (given)

For $PCl_3(g) + Cl_2(g) \rightleftharpoons PCl_5(g)$;

$K_{eq} = \frac{1}{100}$ and for

$\frac{1}{2}PCl_3(g) + \frac{1}{2}Cl_2(g) \rightleftharpoons \frac{1}{2}PCl_5(g)$;

$$K_{eq} = \sqrt{\frac{1}{100}} = \frac{1}{10} = 0.1$$

$$\Delta G° = -2.303\, RT \log (\sqrt{K_{eq}})^{-1}$$

$$= +\frac{2.303\, RT \log K_{eq}}{2}$$

$$= -\frac{\Delta G°}{2} = \frac{+20}{2} = +10 \text{ kJ mol}^{-1}$$

116. (a) $C_6H_5COOH \rightleftharpoons \frac{1}{2}(C_6H_5COOH)$

	C_6H_5COOH	$\frac{1}{2}(C_6H_5COOH)$
Initial	1.0 M	0
At equil.	$(1 - x)$ M	$\frac{x}{2}$ M

(D) = Vapour density of

$$C_6H_5COOH = \frac{\text{molecular weight}}{2}$$

$$= \frac{122}{2} = 61 \text{ g mol}^{-1}$$

(d) = Vapour density due to association

$= 91.5 \text{ g mol}^{-1}$

$$x = \frac{D - d}{(y - 1)\, d}$$

where, $y = \frac{1}{2}$ = number of product from one mol reactant

$$x = \frac{61 - 91.5}{\left(\frac{1}{2} - 1\right)91.5} = 0.666$$

$$K_C = \frac{[C_6H_5COOH]^{1/2}}{[C_6H_5COOH]}$$

$$= \frac{\left(\frac{x}{2}\right)^{1/2}}{(1 - x)} = \frac{\left(\frac{0.666}{2}\right)^{1/2}}{(0.333)} = 1.74$$

117. (d) $Ca(HCO_3)_2(s) \rightleftharpoons CaO(s) + 2CO_2(g) + H_2O(g)$

Take only gaseous species

$p_{\text{total}} = p_{CO_2} + p_{H_2O}$ at 400 K

$\Rightarrow 7.5 \text{ bar} = 2p + p = 3p$

$\therefore \quad p = 2.5$ bar

$\therefore \quad p_{CO_2} = 5.0 \text{ bar} \Rightarrow p_{H_2O} = 2.5$ bar

$\therefore \quad K_p(400 \text{ K}) = p_{CO_2}^2\, p_{H_2O}$

$= 25 \times 2.5 = 62.5$ bar

■ At 298 K, $H_2O(g)$ is condensed to $H_2O(l)$ and pressure set-up is due to CO_2 only.

$\therefore p_{CO_2}$(at 298 K) = 5.0 bar

$\therefore \quad K_p(298 \text{ K}) = p_{CO_2}^2 = 25.0$

$$\therefore \quad \frac{K_p(400)}{K_p(298)} = \frac{62.5}{25} = 2.5$$

$$\Delta H° = \frac{2.303 RT_1T_2}{(T_2 - T_1)} \log \frac{K_p(400)}{K_p(298)}$$

$$= \frac{2.303 \times 8.314 \times 10^{-3} \text{ kJ mol}^{-1}\text{K}^{-1} \times 298 \text{ K} \times 400 \text{ K}}{(400 - 298 \text{ K})} \log 2.5$$

$= 8.9 \text{ kJ mol}^{-1}$

118. (d) Pure $CaCO_3 = 20 \times \frac{50}{100} = 10$ g

$= 0.1$ mol

***Case* I** $CaCO_3(s) \rightleftharpoons CaO(s) + CO_2(g)$

	$CaCO_3(s)$	$CaO(s)$	$CO_2(g)$
Initial	0.1	0	0 mol
At equil.	$(0.1 - x)$	x	x mol

$x = 0.05$ mol (50% of 0.1 mol)

$$p_{CO_2} = \frac{n}{V}RT = \frac{0.05}{1} \times 0.0821 \times 400$$

$= 1.642$ atm

Thus, $K_p = p_{CO_2} = 1.642$ atm

***Case* II** $CaCO_3(s) \rightleftharpoons CaO(s) + CO_2(g)$

	$CaCO_3(s)$	$CaO(s)$	$CO_2(g)$
Initial	0.1 mol	0	0.5 atm
At equil.	$(0.1 - y)$	y	$0.5 + y$

$K_p = (0.5 + y) = 1.642$

$\therefore \quad y = 1.142 \Rightarrow p = \frac{nRT}{V}$

$$1.142 \text{ atm} = \frac{n \times 0.0821 \times 400}{1}$$

$n = 0.0348$ (dissociated)

$$\text{Thus, percentage} = \frac{0.0348}{0.1} \times 100 = 34.8\%$$

■ It is a case of Le-Chatelier's principle

119. (a) $A(g) \rightleftharpoons B(g)$

$$(f) = \frac{[B]}{[A] + [B]}, K_C = \frac{[B]}{[A]} = \frac{[B]/[A]}{\frac{[A]}{[A]} + \frac{[B]}{[A]}}$$

$$0.33 = \frac{K}{1 + K} = \frac{1}{3}$$

$\therefore \quad 1 + K = 3K$

$\therefore \quad K = 0.50$

120. (a) $I_2 + I^- \rightleftharpoons I_3^-$

	I_2	I^-	I_3^-
Initial	1	0.5	0 mol
At equil.	$(1 - x)$	$(0.5 - x)$	x mol

$Ag^+ + I^- \longrightarrow AgI$

$[Ag^+] \equiv [I^-] \equiv 0.25$ mol

$\therefore \quad 0.5 - x = 0.25$

Thus, $x = 0.25$

$$\therefore K_C = \frac{[I_3^-]}{[I_2][I^-]} = \frac{x/V}{\left(\frac{1 - x}{V}\right)\left(\frac{0.5 - x}{V}\right)}$$

$$= \frac{0.25}{(0.75)(0.25)} = \frac{1}{0.75} = 1.33$$

121. (c) ***Step* I** Calculation of $\Delta G°$

$\Delta G° = -2.303\, RT \log K_p$

$= -2.303 \times 2 \times 373 \log 8 \times 10^{-9}$

$= +13910.8$ cal

***Step* II** Calculation of $\Delta H°$

$\Delta G° = \Delta H° - T\Delta S°$

$\Delta H° = \Delta G° + T\Delta S°$

$= 13910.8 + 373 \times 30$

$= 25100.8$ cal

***Step* III** Calculation of K_2 (at temperature T_2 having 0.1% dissociation)

$$\alpha = \frac{0.1}{100} = 1 \times 10^{-3}$$

$$K_2 = \frac{p\alpha^2}{(1 - \alpha^2)} = \frac{2(1 \times 10^{-3})^2}{[1 - (1 \times 10^{-3})^2]}$$

$\approx 2 \times 10^{-6}$

***Step* IV** $\Delta H^\circ = \frac{2.303\, RT_1T_2}{(T_2 - T_1)} \log \frac{K_2}{K_1}$

$$\frac{T_2 - T_1}{T_1T_2} = \frac{2.303R}{\Delta H^\circ} \log \frac{K_2}{K_1}$$

$$\frac{1}{T_1} - \frac{1}{T_2} = \frac{2.303 \times 2}{25100.8} \log \frac{2 \times 10^{-6}}{8 \times 10^{-9}}$$

$$\frac{1}{373} - \frac{1}{T_2} = 4.4 \times 10^{-4}$$

$$\Rightarrow \quad \frac{1}{T_2} = \frac{1}{373} - 4.4 \times 10^{-4}$$

$$T_2 = 446 \text{ K}$$

$$\Delta E^\circ = -2.303RT \log K$$

Also $\Delta G^\circ = \Delta H^\circ - T\Delta S^\circ$

122. (c) $\Delta G^\circ = -2.303RT \log K$

Also, $\Delta G^\circ = \Delta H^\circ - T\Delta S^\circ$

$$\therefore \quad \log_{10} K = -\frac{\Delta H^\circ}{2.303\, RT} + \frac{\Delta S^\circ}{2.303\, R}$$

This is linear of the type of $= -mx + c$

$$\text{Slope } (m) = -\frac{\Delta H^\circ}{2.303\, R} = -6720$$

$$\text{Intercept } (c) \frac{\Delta S^\circ}{2.303\, R} = -9.72$$

$$\log_{10} K = -\frac{6720}{300} + 9.72$$

$$\Rightarrow \quad \log_{10} K = -12.68$$

123. (c) $A(g) \rightleftharpoons B(g)$

$-\frac{d[A]}{dt} = k_1[A]$ thus first-order kinetics,

$-\frac{d[A]}{dt} = k_2[A]$ thus first order kinetics

For first order kinetics

$$T_{50} \text{ (half-life period)} = \frac{0.693}{k}$$

$$k_1 = \frac{0.693}{T_{50}} = \frac{0.693}{10} \text{ min}^{-1}$$

$$\Rightarrow \quad k_2 = \frac{0.693}{T_{50}} = \frac{0.693}{1} \text{ min}^{-1}$$

$$\therefore \quad K_C = \frac{k_1}{k_2} = 0.1$$

■ For first order kinetics

$$k = \frac{2.303}{t} \log \frac{C_0 \text{(initial)}}{C \text{ (at time } t)}$$

If $C = \frac{C_0}{2}$ (50% reaction), $t = T_{50}$

$$\therefore \; T_{50} = \frac{2.303}{k} \log 2 = \frac{2.303 \times 0.3010}{k}$$

$$= 0.693/k$$

124. (b) H_3BO_3 + glycerine $\rightleftharpoons$ (H_3BO_3.glycerine)

$[H_3BO_3]$ taken = 0.1 M

60% of $[H_3BO_3]$ is converted into product

$\therefore [H_3BO_3]_{\text{equil.}} = 0.1 - 0.1 \times 0.6 = 0.04$ M

and $[H_3BO_3$.glycerine] M

$$K = 0.90 = \frac{[H_3BO_3 \,.\, \text{glycerine}]}{[H_3BO_3]\,[\text{glycerine}]}$$

$$= \frac{0.06}{0.04 \times [\text{glycerine}]}$$

[glycerine] = 1.67 M

125. (d) $pV = nRT \Rightarrow V = \frac{nRT}{p}$

$\therefore$ $V \propto n$ at constant p and T.

Thus, moles can be expressed in terms of volume.

	$N_2O_4(g) \rightleftharpoons$	$2NO_2(g)$
Initial volume	1	0
At equil	$(1 - x)$	$2x$

Total volume at equilibrium

$$= 1 - x + 2x = (1 + x)$$

Given,

$$\frac{75}{100}(1 + x) = 1 \text{ (25\% less)}$$

$$x = \frac{1}{3} = 0.3333$$

Thus, 33.33% dissociation.

126. (a)

	$2H_2S(g) \rightleftharpoons$	$2H_2(g)$ +	$S_2(g)$
Initial	10 atm	0	0
At equil.	$(10 - 2x)$ atm	$2x$	x

$x = 0.020$ atm (given)

$$\because p_{H_2S} = 10 - 2x = 10 - 0.02 \times 2 = 9.96 \text{ atm}$$

$$p_{H_2} = 2x = 0.04 \text{ atm} \Rightarrow p_{S_2} = x = 0.02$$

$$K_p = \frac{p_{S_2} \times p^2_{H_2}}{p^2_{H_2S}} = \frac{0.02 \times (0.04)^2}{(9.96)^2}$$

$$= 3.23 \times 10^{-7} \text{ atm}$$

127. (d) $N_2(g) + 3H_2(g) \rightleftharpoons 2NH_3(g)$

Mole fraction of $NH_3 = \chi_{(NH_3)} = 0.50$

Also, $\chi_{(N_2)} + \chi_{(H_2)} + \chi_{(NH_3)} = 1.0$

$\chi_{(N_2)} + \chi_{(H_2)} = 0.50$

Also, $\chi_{(H_2)} = 3 \times (N_2)$

$\therefore$ $4\chi_{(N_2)} = 0.50$

$$\Rightarrow \chi_{(N_2)} = \frac{0.50}{4} \Rightarrow \quad \chi_{(H_2)} = \frac{1.5}{4}$$

$$p_{\text{(total)}} = 350 \text{ bar}$$

$$\therefore \quad p_{NH_3} = 350 \times \frac{1}{2} = 175 \text{ bar,}$$

$$p_{N_2} = 350 \times \frac{0.50}{4} \text{ bar}$$

$$p_{H_2} = 350 \times \frac{1.5}{4} \text{ bar}$$

$$K_p = \frac{p^2_{NH_3}}{p_{N_2} \cdot p^3_{H_2}}$$

$$= \frac{(175)^2}{\left(350 \times \frac{0.5}{4}\right)\left(\frac{350 \times 1.50}{4}\right)^3}$$

$$= 3.1 \times 10^{-4}$$

128. (c)

	$N_2(g) + 3H_2(g) \rightleftharpoons$		$2NH_3(g)$
Initial	1	3	0 mol
At equil.	$(1 - x)$	$3(1 - x)$	$2x$ mol

$$2NH_3 + H_2SO_4 \rightleftharpoons (NH_4)_2SO_4$$

$$\text{Moles of } H_2SO_4 \text{ required} = \frac{MV}{1000}$$

$$= \frac{250 \times 1}{1000} = 0.250 \text{ mol}$$

■ Molarity (mol L^{-1}) × mL = millimoles

Since, 1 $H_2SO_4 \equiv 2NH_3$

Thus, $NH_3 = 0.500$ mol

$\therefore$ $2x = 0.500 \Rightarrow x = 0.250$ mol

$(1 - x) = (1 - 0.250) = 0.750$ mol

$$K_C = \frac{[NH_3]^2}{[N_2]\,[H_2]^3} = \frac{\left(\frac{2x}{1}\right)^2}{\frac{(1-x)}{1}\left(\frac{1-x}{1}\right)^3 (3)^3}$$

$$= \frac{(0.50)^2}{(0.750)^4\,(27)} = 0.029$$

129. (a)

	$2SO_2(g) + O_2(g) \rightleftharpoons$		$2SO_3(g)$
Initial	2	1	0 mol
At equil.	$(2 - 2x)$	$(1 - x)$	$2x$ mol

$SO_2(g)$ reduces MnO_4^- to Mn^{2+}

$$5SO_2(g) + 2MnO_4^-(aq) + H^+ \longrightarrow 2Mn^{2+}(aq) + 5\,SO_4^{2-}(aq)$$

$$2MnO_4^- = 5\,SO_2$$

$$\therefore \; 0.4 \text{ MnO}_4^- = \frac{5}{2} \times 0.4 = 1.0 \text{ mol } SO_2$$

Thus, $2 - 2x = 1 \Rightarrow 2x = 1$

$$x = 0.5$$

$$[SO_2] = \frac{2 - 2x}{1} = 1 \text{ mol L}^{-1}$$

$$[O_2] = \frac{(1 - x)}{1} = 0.5 \text{ mol L}^{-1}$$

$$[SO_3] = \frac{2x}{1} = \frac{1}{1} \text{ mol L}^{-1}$$

$$\therefore \; K_C = \frac{[SO_3]}{[SO_2]^2\,[O_2]} = \frac{(1)^2}{(1)^2\,(0.5)} = 2.0$$

130. (c) $C(s) + CO_2(g) \rightleftharpoons 2CO(g)$

$$K_p = \frac{(p_{CO})^2}{(p_{CO_2})} = 63 \text{ atm}$$

Given $p_{CO} = 10\, p_{CO_2}$

If $p_{CO_2} = x$

Then $p_{CO} = 10x \Rightarrow \frac{(10x)^2}{x} = 63$

$100x = 63 \Rightarrow x = 0.63$ atm

$\therefore$ $p_{CO_2} = 0.63$ atm

$\Rightarrow$ $p_{CO} = 10 p_{CO_2} = 6.3$ atm

$p_{\text{(total)}} = 6.93$ atm

131. (a) Let, $F_2(g) = \chi$ (mole fraction), molar mass = 38.0 g mol^{-1}

$F(g) = (1 - \chi)$,

Molar mass = 19.0 g mol^{-1}

$\therefore$ Average molar mass

$$= \frac{M_1\chi_1 + M_2\chi_2}{\chi_1 + \chi_2}$$

$$36.74 = 38\chi + 19\,(1 - \chi)$$

$\therefore$ $\chi = 0.9337$ (mol fraction of F_2)

$(1 - \chi) = 0.0663$ (mol fraction of F)

$$\therefore\ K_\chi = \frac{\chi_F^2}{\chi_{F_2}} = \frac{(0.0663)^2}{0.9337} = 4.708 \times 10^{-3}$$

132. (c) $\Delta H^\circ = \dfrac{2.303\,RT_1T_2}{(T_2 - T_1)} \log\,(K_2 / K_1)$

$$= \frac{2.303 \times 2\ \text{cal mol}^{-1}\ \text{K}^{-1} \times 300\ \text{K} \times 400\ \text{K}}{(400 - 300)} \log\frac{10}{25}$$

= negative

- Since, $K_2 < K_1$, $T_2 > T_1$.
  Thus, reaction is exothermic.
  E_a' (backward) $> E_a$ (forward)

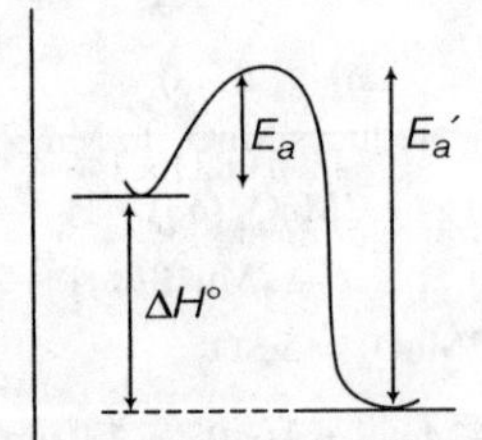

E_a'(backward) $> E_a$(forward)

$\Delta H° > 0$, E_a(forward) $> E_a$(backward)

$\Delta H° < 0$, E_a (forward) $< E_a$(backward)

133. (a) By kinetics for first order reaction

$$k\ \text{(rate constant)} = \frac{1}{t} \log\left(\frac{C_0}{C}\right)$$

$$\therefore \quad C = C_0 e^{-kt}$$

Then $K_f = 2.1 \times 10^{-3}$

$\Rightarrow$ $K_b = 4.2 \times 10^{-4}$

$$\therefore\ K_C = \frac{K_f}{K_b} = \frac{2.1 \times 10^{-3}}{4.2 \times 10^{-4}} = 5.0$$

- For first order kinetics rate constant
  $$k = \frac{1}{t}\log_e \frac{C_0\,\text{(initial)}}{C\ \text{(at time } t)}$$

134. (a) $\dfrac{-d[A]}{dt} = K\,[A]^n$

On doubling $[A]$, rate is doubled.

Hence, $n = 1$

$$\therefore\ K_f = \frac{-d\,[A]/\,dt}{[A]} = \frac{1 \times 10^{-2}\text{mol L}^{-1}\text{s}^{-1}}{0.1\ \text{mol L}^{-1}}$$

$$= 0.1\ \text{s}^{-1} \Rightarrow K_c = \frac{K_f}{K_b}$$

$$\therefore\quad K_b = \frac{K_f}{K_c} = \frac{0.1\ \text{s}^{-1}}{10\ \text{mol L}^{-1}}$$

$$= 1 \times 10^{-2}\ \ \text{L mol}^{-1}\text{s}^{-1}$$

135. (a) $K_p = \dfrac{p_{H_2O}}{p_{H_2}}$

$$\Delta G° = -\,2.303RT \log K_p$$

$$-9.0 = -\,2.303 \times 0.002 \times 800 \log K_p$$

$$\therefore \quad \log K_p = 2.44$$

$$\therefore \quad \log\left(\frac{p_{H_2O}}{p_{H_2}}\right) = 2.44$$

136. (c) *Case* I $K_C = \dfrac{x^2}{(1 - x)}$

$$= \frac{(0.1)^2}{(1 - 0.1)} = \frac{0.01}{0.90} = \frac{1}{90}$$

Case II $AB \rightleftharpoons A^+ + B^-$

	AB	A^+	B^-
Initial	1	1	0
At equil.	$(1 - y)$	$(1 + y)$	y

$$K_c = \frac{[A^+][B^-]}{[AB]}$$

$$\frac{1}{90} = \frac{(1 + y)y}{(1 - y)}$$

$$y^2 + y = (1 - y)\frac{1}{90}$$

$$y^2 + \frac{91y}{90} - \frac{1}{90} = 0$$

$$y = \frac{-\dfrac{91}{90} + \sqrt{\left(\dfrac{91}{90}\right)^2 + \dfrac{4}{90}}}{2} = 0.0108$$

Thus, % dissociation = 1.08% $\approx$ 1.10%

137. (a) Let H_2 taken be = n mol

$$CO(g) + 2H_2(g) \rightleftharpoons CH_3OH(g)$$

	$CO(g)$	$2H_2(g)$	$CH_3OH(g)$
Initial mol	0.2	n	0
At equil.	$(0.2 - x)$	$(n - 2x)$	x

Given, $x = 0.1$ mol CH_3OH

Pressure set up due to H_2 and CO before equilibrium is attained

$= 4.92$ atm

$$\therefore \quad pV = (0.2 + n)RT$$

$$(0.2 + n) = \frac{pV}{RT} = \frac{4.92 \times 5}{0.0821 \times 600} = 0.5$$

$\therefore$ $n = 0.3$ mol = H_2 taken initially

Total moles at equilibrium

$$= (0.2 - x) + (n - 2x) + x$$

$$= (0.2 + n - 2x)$$

$$= 0.2 + 0.3 - 0.2 = 0.3\ \text{mol}$$

Thus, equilibrium pressure due to gaseous mixture

$$= \frac{4.92 \times 0.3}{0.5} = 2.952\ \text{atm}$$

	CO	H_2	CH_3OH
$\chi =$	1/3	1/3	1/3
Partial pressure	$\dfrac{2.925}{3}$	$\dfrac{2.952}{3}$	$\dfrac{2.952}{3}$

$$K_p = p_{CH_3OH} / p_{CO}\,p_{H_2}^2$$

$$= \left(\frac{3}{2.952}\right)^2 = 1.03$$

138. (a) Let N_2 = a mole

then O_2 = $(100 - a)$ mol

	N_2	+ O_2	$\rightleftharpoons$ 2NO
Initia	a	$(100 - a)$	0 mol
At equil.	$(a - x)$	$(100 - a - x)$	$2x$ mol

$$\chi_{NO} = 0.018\ \text{(given)}$$

$$\%\ NO = \frac{2x \times 100}{100} = 1.8$$

$$x = 0.9$$

$$[N_2] = (a - 0.9)$$

$$[O_2] = (100 - a - 0.9)$$

$$= (99.1 - a)$$

$$\therefore \quad [NO] = 2x = 1.8$$

$$K_C = \frac{[NO]^2}{[N_2][O_2]}$$

$$= \frac{(1.8 / V)^2}{\left(\dfrac{a - 0.9}{V}\right)\left(\dfrac{99.1 - a}{V}\right)}$$

$$\therefore \quad a = 74.46\%$$

139. (c)

	N_2	+ $3H_2$	$\rightleftharpoons$ $2NH_3$
Initial mol	2	4	0
At equil.	$(2 - x)$	$(4 - 3x)$	$2x = 2$,
			$\therefore x = 1$
Active mass	$\left(\dfrac{2 - x}{1}\right)$	$\left(\dfrac{4 - 3x}{1}\right)$	$\left(\dfrac{2x}{1}\right)$
Mole fraction	$\dfrac{1}{4}$	$\dfrac{1}{4}$	$\dfrac{2}{4}$
Partial pressure	$\left(1 \times \dfrac{1}{4}\right)$	$\left(1 \times \dfrac{1}{4}\right)$	$\left(1 \times \dfrac{2}{4}\right)$

$$\therefore \quad K_C = \frac{(2)^2}{(1)\,(1)^3} = 4$$

$$K_p = \frac{\left(\dfrac{1}{2}\right)^2}{\left(\dfrac{1}{4}\right)\left(\dfrac{1}{4}\right)^3} = 64$$

$$K_\chi = \frac{\left(\dfrac{1}{2}\right)^2}{\left(\dfrac{1}{4}\right)\left(\dfrac{1}{4}\right)^3} = 64$$

140. (b)

N_2O_4	$\rightleftharpoons$ $2NO_2$
0.971 mol	0.058 mol

$$K_c = 4.61 \times 10^{-3}$$

$$\therefore \quad [N_2O_4] = \frac{0.971}{0.750}\ \text{mol L}^{-1}$$

$$[NO_2] = \frac{0.058}{0.750}\ \text{mol L}^{-1}$$

$\therefore$ Q (reaction quotient) $= \dfrac{[NO_2]^2}{[N_2O_4]}$

$$= \dfrac{\left(\dfrac{0.058}{0.750}\right)^2}{\left(\dfrac{0.971}{0.750}\right)} = 4.61 \times 10^{-3}$$

$Q = K_C$ thus system is in equilibrium.

If volume of the right hand side is 2.25 L,

$$\text{then } Q = \dfrac{\left(\dfrac{0.058}{2.25}\right)^2}{\left(\dfrac{0.971}{2.25}\right)} = 1.54 \times 10^{-3} << K_C$$

Thus, equilibrium is spontaneous in forward side.

$$N_2O_4 \rightleftharpoons 2NO_2$$

	N_2O_4	$2NO_2$
	0.971	0.058 mol
	$(0.971 - x)$	$(0.058 + 2x)$

$\therefore$ $K_C = 4.61 \times 10^{-3}$

$$= \dfrac{\left(\dfrac{0.058 + 2x}{2.25}\right)^2}{\left(\dfrac{0.971 - x}{2.25}\right)}$$

$\therefore$ $x = 0.021$

$[NO_2] = (0.058 + 0.042) = 0.100$ mol

141. (b) $Ca(HCO_3)_2(s) \rightleftharpoons CaCO_3(s)$

	$Ca(HCO_3)_2(s)$	$CaCO_3(s)$
Initial	1	0
At equil.	$(1 - x)$	x

$+ H_2O(g) + CO_2(g)$

	$H_2O(g)$	$CO_2(g)$
Initial	0	0
At equil.	x	x

only gaseous species

$$\therefore K_p = p_{H_2O} \cdot p_{CO_2} = \dfrac{p^2}{4} = \dfrac{(0.12)^2}{4}$$

If $H_2O(g)$ is also present and degree of decomposition is y then

$H_2O(g) = (0.20 + y)$

$CO_2(g) = y$

$$\therefore \quad (0.20 + y)y = \left(\dfrac{0.12}{4}\right)^2$$

$y = 0.0167$ bar

142. (a) $\Delta G^\circ = \Delta G^\circ(H_2O \text{ gas}) - \Delta G^\circ(H_2O \text{ liquid})$

$= 10 - 9.9917$

$= 8.3 \times 10^{-3}$ kJ mol^{-1}

$\Delta G^\circ = -2.303\, RT \log K_p$

$8.3 \times 10^{-3} = -2.303 \times 8.3 \times 10^{-3} \times 298 \log K_p$

$\log K_p = -1.46 \times 10^{-3}$

$K_p = 0.9964 \text{ atm} \approx 1.0 \text{ atm}$

143. (a) $Ag^+ + NH_3 \rightleftharpoons [Ag(NH_3)]^+$; K_1

$[Ag(NH_3)]^+ + NH_3 \rightleftharpoons [Ag(NH_3)_2]^+$; K_2

$Ag^+ + 2NH_3 \rightleftharpoons [Ag(NH_3)_2]^+$; K_3

K_3 is formation constant of $[Ag(NH_3)_2]^+$

$$K_1 = \dfrac{[Ag(NH_3)]^+}{[Ag^+][NH_3]}$$

$$\Rightarrow K_2 = \dfrac{[Ag(NH_3)_2]^+}{[Ag(NH_3)]^+[NH_3]}$$

$$\text{and } K_3 = \dfrac{[Ag(NH_3)_2]^+}{[Ag^+][NH_3]^2} = K_1K_2$$

$= 3.5 \times 10^{-3} \times 1.74 \times 10^{-3}$

$= 6.09 \times 10^{-6}$

144. (b) At equilibrium, $\Delta G = 0$

$\therefore$ ΔG (product) $- \Delta G$ (reactants)

145. (d) K_p is dependent on temperatures.

When volume is halved, K_p remains constant but (α) degree of dissociation changes.

$\Rightarrow$ α (degree of dissociation)

$$\propto \left(\dfrac{1}{p}\right)^{\Delta n_g/2} \propto (V)^{\Delta n_g/2}$$

where, Δn_g = moles of (gaseous products – gaseous reactants)

$\Delta n_g = 1$

$\therefore$ α is proportional to $\sqrt{V}$.

146. (d) K_p is dependent on temperature.

147. (d) $K_p = K_C(RT)^{\Delta n_g}$

$$\therefore K_C = K_p/(RT)^{\Delta n_g} = \dfrac{1.44 \times 10^{-5}}{(0.0821 \times 773)^{-2}}$$

148. (d) $COCl_2(g) \rightleftharpoons CO(g) + Cl_2(g)$

	$COCl_2(g)$	$CO(g)$	$Cl_2(g)$
Initial	n	0	0
At equili.	$(n - nx)$	nx	nx

Molar mass of $COCl_2$ = 99 g mol^{-1}

Total moles at equilibrium

$= n - nx + nx + nx = n(1 + x)$

$$= \dfrac{w}{m}(1 + x) = \dfrac{w(1 + x)}{99}$$

$$\therefore \quad p = \dfrac{n}{Vx}RT = \dfrac{w(1 + x)}{99V}RT_{288}$$

But $\dfrac{w}{V}$ = density (d)

$$\therefore \quad p = \dfrac{d(1 + x)}{99}RT$$

$$\because (1 + x) = \dfrac{99p}{RT\ d} = \dfrac{99 \times 1.0}{0.0831 \times 724 \times 1.162}$$

$(1 + x) = 1.416$

$\therefore$ $x = 0.416$

$$\text{Also, } K_p = \dfrac{x^2p}{(1 - x^2)} = \dfrac{(0.416)^2}{[1 - (0.416)^2]} \times 1$$

$K_p = 0.2093$

$\therefore$ $\Delta G^\circ = -2.303\, RT \log K_p$

$= -2.303 \times 8.314 \times 10^{-3} \times 724 \log 0.2093$

$= 9.416$ kJ mol^{-1}

149. (b) $N_2O_4(g) \rightleftharpoons 2NO_2(g)$

	$N_2O_4(g)$	$2NO_2(g)$
Initial	n	0
At equil.	$(n - nx)$	$2nx$

Total moles at equilibrium $= n(1 + x)$

Molar mass of N_2O_4 = 92 g mol^{-1}

$$\therefore \quad n(1 + x) = \dfrac{w}{m}(1 + x) = \dfrac{w(1 + x)}{92}$$

$$\text{Also} \quad p = \dfrac{n}{V}RT + p = \dfrac{w(1 + x)}{92V}RT$$

But $\dfrac{w}{V}$ = density d

$$\therefore \quad p = \dfrac{d(1 + x)}{92}RT$$

$$\therefore \quad (1 + x) = \dfrac{92p}{dRT}$$

$$\therefore \quad x = \left(\dfrac{92p}{dRT} - 1\right)$$

At 288 K,

$d = 3.62\text{g dm}^{-3}$

$$\therefore x_1 = \left(\dfrac{92 \times 1}{3.62 \times 0.0831 \times 288} - 1\right) = 0.062$$

At 348 K,

$$x_2 = \left(\dfrac{92 \times 1}{1.84 \times 0.0831 \times 348} - 1\right) = 0.730$$

K_p for the equilibrium

$N_2O_4(g) \rightleftharpoons 2NO_2(g)$

$$K_p = \dfrac{4x^2p}{(1 - x^2)}$$

$$\therefore \quad K_{288} = \dfrac{4(0.062)^2 \times 1}{[1 - (0.062)^2]} = 0.0154$$

$$K_{348} = \dfrac{4(0.730)^2}{[1 - (0.730)^2]} = 4.563$$

$$\Delta H^\circ = \dfrac{2.303RT_1T_2}{(T_2 - T_1)}\log\dfrac{K_2}{K_1}$$

$$= \dfrac{2.303 \times 8.314 \times 10^{-3} \times 288 \times 348}{(348 - 288)} \log\dfrac{4.563}{0.0154}$$

$= 79.05$ kJ mol^{-1}

150. (d) $\Delta G^\circ = -2.303\, RT \log K_{eq}$

$-124.944 = -2.303 \times 8.314 \times 10^{-3} \times 600 \log K_{eq}$

$\log K_{eq} = 10.876$

$\therefore$ K_{eq} = Antilog of 10.876

$= 7.516 \times 10^{10}$

Also Cu(s) and $Cu_2O(s)$ are in solid state

$\therefore K_{eq} = (p_{O_2})^{-1/2} = 7.516 \times 10^{10}$

$\therefore p_{O_2} = 1.77 \times 10^{-22}$ bar

If number of molecules of O_2 left = N

$$\text{Then } n, \text{(moles)} = \dfrac{N}{N_0} = \dfrac{N}{6.02 \times 10^{23}}$$

$\therefore \quad p_{O_2} = \frac{nRT}{V}$

$\therefore \quad n = \frac{p_{O_2} V}{RT} = \frac{1.77 \times 10^{-22} \times 1}{0.0831 \times 600}$

$\therefore \quad N = N_0 \; n$

$= \frac{6.02 \times 10^{23} \times 1.77 \times 10^{-22}}{0.0831 \times 600}$

$= 2.14$ molecules L^{-1}

151. (b) $LiH(s) \longrightarrow Li(l) + \frac{1}{2}H_2(g)$

$K_p = p_{H_2}^{1/2}$

$\therefore \quad \frac{K_{900}}{K_{800}} = \frac{\sqrt{6.19 \text{ m bar}}}{\sqrt{0.278 \text{ m bar}}}$

By using equation

$\Delta_r H° = \frac{2.303 R T_1 T_2}{T_2 - T_1} \log \frac{K_{900}}{K_{800}}$

$= \frac{2.303 \times 8.314 \times 10^{-3} \times 800 \times 900}{100} \log \sqrt{\frac{6.19}{0.278}}$

$= 92.89$ kJ

152. (c) $Br_2(g) + 3F_2(g) \longrightarrow 2BrF_3(g)$

	Br_2	F_2	BrF_3
At equili moles	0.250	0.750	0.500
total moles = 1.5			
Mole fraction	$\chi_{Br_2} = \frac{0.250}{1.500} = \frac{1}{6}$	$\chi_{F_2} = \frac{0.750}{1.500} = \frac{1}{2}$	$\frac{0.500}{1.500} = \frac{1}{3}$
Partial pressure	$\frac{1}{6}$ bar	$\frac{1}{2}$ bar	$\frac{1}{3}$ bar

$\therefore \; K_p = \frac{(p_{BrF_3})^2}{(p_{Br_2})(p_{F_2})} = \frac{\left(\frac{1}{3}\right)^2}{\left(\frac{1}{6}\right)\left(\frac{1}{2}\right)^3} = 5.33$

If pressure is increased to 2 bar

$p_{BrF_3} = \frac{1}{3} \times 2 = \frac{2}{3}$ bar,

$p_{Br_2} = \frac{1}{3}$ bar, $p_{F_2} = 1$ bar

$Q_D = \frac{\left(\frac{2}{3}\right)^2}{\left(\frac{2}{2}\right)^3\left(\frac{2}{6}\right)}$

$Q_p = 1.33, \quad Q_p < K_p$

Thus, reaction quotient is decreased from 5.33 to 1.33 and more BrF_3 is formed.

153. (a) Let at equilibrium

$p_{Cl_2} / p_{Br_2} = z$ (ratio)

$\therefore \quad p_{a_2} = z \; p_{Br_2}$

Thus total pressure

$p_t = p_{Cl_2} + p_{Br_2} + p_{BrCl}$

$= z p_{Br_2} + p_{Br_2} + p_{BrCl}$

$p_t = (z+1) p_{Br_2} + p_{BrCl}$

$\therefore \quad p_{B_2} = \frac{p_t - p_{BrCl}}{(z+1)}$

$p_{Cl_2} = z \frac{(p_t - p_{BrCl})}{(z+1)}$

$\therefore \quad K_p = \frac{p_{BrCl}^2}{p_{Cl_2} \; p_{Br_2}}$

$K_p = \frac{(p_{BrCl})^2}{z\left[\frac{p_t - p_{BrCl}}{(z+1)}\right]\left[\frac{p_t - p_{BrCl}}{z+1}\right]}$

$K_p = \frac{p_{BrCl}^2 (z+1)^2}{z(p_t - p_{BrCl})^2}$

$\log K_p = 2 \log p_{BrCl} + 2 \log(z+1) - \log z - 2\log(p_t - p_{BrCl})$

For maximum yield,

$\left[\frac{\partial p_{BrCl}}{\partial z}\right] = 0$

$\therefore \quad \frac{\log K_p}{\partial z} = 0 + \frac{2}{z+1} - \frac{1}{2} + 0$

$\therefore \quad 2z = z + 1$

$\therefore \quad z = 1$

$\therefore \quad \frac{p_{Br_2}}{p_{Cl_2}} = 1$

$\therefore \quad p_{Br_2} = p_{Cl_2}$

$\therefore \quad x = y$

154. (d) $\Delta G° = -2.3403 \, RT \log K_{eq}$

and $\Delta G° = -nFE°$

$\therefore \quad E° = \frac{2.303RT}{nF} \log K_{eq}$

$E° = \frac{0.0591}{n} \log K_{eq}$

$n = 2$ (electrons)

$\therefore \quad \log K_{eq} = \frac{0.368 \times 2}{0.0591}$

$\log K_{eq} = 12.45$

$\therefore \quad K_{eq} = 2.84 \times 10^{12}$

155. (a) $NH_3(g) \rightleftharpoons \frac{1}{2}N_2(g) + \frac{3}{2}H_2(g)$

	NH_3	N_2	H_2	
Total moles at $t = 0$	n	0	0	
At equil.	$n(1-\alpha)$	$\frac{n}{2}\alpha$	$\frac{3}{2}n\alpha$	$n(1+\alpha)$
Mole fraction	$\frac{(1-\alpha)}{(1+\alpha)}$	$\frac{\alpha}{2(1+\alpha)}$	$\frac{3\alpha}{2(1+\alpha)}$	
Partial pressure	$\frac{(1-\alpha)p}{(1+\alpha)}$	$\frac{\alpha p}{2(1+\alpha)}$	$\frac{3(\alpha)}{2(1+\alpha)} p$	

$K_p = \frac{p_{N_2}^{1/2} \; p_{H_2}^{3/2}}{p_{NH_3}}$

$= \frac{\left[\frac{\alpha p}{2(1+\alpha)}\right]^{1/2}\left[\frac{3(\alpha)}{2(1+\alpha)}\right]^{3/2}}{\left(\frac{1-\alpha}{1+\alpha}\right)p}$

$K_p = \frac{3\sqrt{3}\,\alpha^2 p}{4(1-\alpha^2)}$

$\frac{1-\alpha^2}{\alpha^2} = \frac{3\sqrt{3}p}{4K_p}$

$\frac{1}{\alpha^2} = \left(1 + \frac{3\sqrt{3}p}{4K_p}\right)$

$\frac{1}{\alpha} = \left(1 + \frac{3\sqrt{3}p}{4K_p}\right)^{1/2}$

$\alpha = \left(1 + \frac{3\sqrt{3}p}{4K_p}\right)^{-1/2}$

Type II. Statement Based Questions

156. (d) **157.** (a) **158.** (b) **159.** (c)
160. (d) **161.** (a) **162.** (b) **163.** (a)
164. (b) **165.** (b) **166.** (c) **167.** (b)
168. (a) **169.** (b)

Type III. MCQs with One or More than One Correct Alternate

170. (a, d) $\log_e K_{eq} = \frac{\Delta S°}{R} - \frac{\Delta H°}{RT}$

$\log_e K_{eq} = \text{constant} - \frac{\Delta H°}{RT}$

$\therefore \quad \frac{d[\log_e K_{eq}]}{dT} = + \frac{\Delta H}{RT^2}$

$\log_{10} K_{eq} = \text{constant} - \frac{\Delta H°}{2.303\,RT}$

$\therefore \quad \frac{d[\log K_{eq}]}{dT} = + \frac{\Delta H}{2.303\,RT^2}$

Thus, (a) and (d).

171. (a, b, c) Point (X) does not represent dynamic equilibrium.

172. (a, b, c)

173. (a, b, c) as per Le-chatelier's rule.

174. (a, b, d) Any species that can remove Fe^{3+} or SCN^- will prevent complex formation hence deep red colour will disappear.

$Ag^+ + SCN^- \longrightarrow (AgSCN)\downarrow$

$Hg^{2+} + 2SCN^- \longrightarrow Hg(SCN)_2 \downarrow$

$Fe^{3+} + 3C_2O_4^{2-} \longrightarrow [Fe(C_2O_4)_3]^{3-}$

175. (a, b, c, d) ΔG, $\Delta G°$ and K are related by

$\Delta G = \Delta G° + 2.303\,RT \log K$

At equilibrium $\Delta G = 0$

$\therefore \quad \Delta G° = -2.303\,RT \log K$

In an electrochemical cell

$A \longrightarrow A^{n+} + ne^-$

$K = [A^{n+}], \; \Delta G° = -nFE°_{cell}$

and $\quad \Delta G° = -nFE°_{cell}$

$-nFE°_{cell} = -2.303\,RT \log K$

$E°_{cell} = \frac{2.303\,RT}{nF} \log K$

At 298 K, $\frac{2.303RT}{F} = 0.0591\text{V}$

$\therefore \quad E^\circ_{cell} = \frac{0.0591}{n}\log K$

$\Delta G = \Delta G^\circ + 2.303RT\log K$

$-nFE_{cell} = -nFE^\circ_{cell} + 2.303RT\log K$

$\therefore \quad E_{cell} = E^\circ_{cell} - \frac{0.0591}{n}\log K$

176. (a) At high temperature, H_2O is in gaseous state but at 298 K it is condensed to liquid state thus

$$K_p = p_{CO_2} = 6 \text{ bar}$$

177. (d) Eq. (III) = Eq. (II) − Eq. [I] ×2

$\therefore \quad K_3 = \frac{K_2}{K_1^2}$

$\log K_3 = \log K_2 - \log K_1^2$

$= \log K_2 - 2\log K_1$

$$-\frac{\Delta G_3^\circ}{2.303RT} = -\frac{\Delta G_2^\circ}{2.303RT} - \left(-\frac{2\Delta G_1^\circ}{2.303RT}\right)$$

$\therefore \quad \Delta G_3^\circ = \Delta G_2^\circ - 2\Delta G_1^\circ$

178. (a, b, c) (a) H_2O added will dissolve SO_3, thus equilibrium is displaced towards formation of more SO_3.

(b) Amount of $SO_3(x) \propto \left(\frac{1}{p}\right)^{\Delta n_g/2}$

$\Delta n_g = -1 \quad \therefore \quad x \propto \sqrt{p}$

Thus, addition of inert gas will increase pressure, hence formation of SO_3 is favoured.

(c) $\Delta H = -Q$, exothermic.

Exothermic reactions are favoured at low temperature.

179. (a, b) (a) Solubility $\propto p$

(b) H_2O added results in the formation of NH_4OH, thus solubility is increased.

180. (b, c) Dissolution of CaO in water is an exothermic process. Thus, lowering of temperature will dissolve more CaO. Also, addition of H_2O lower the temperature. Hence, solubility is increased.

181. (a, b, c) Addition of NH_3 and H_2S will increase total pressure, hence partial pressure of NH_3 will increase.

Increase in temperature favours dissociation hence, partial pressure of $NH_3\left(p \propto \frac{RT}{V}\right)$ increases.

182. (a, c) For the reaction,

$$A \rightleftharpoons P$$

Given, $T_1 < T_2$

$$\frac{\ln K_1}{\ln K_2} > \frac{T_2}{T_1} \quad \text{...(i)}$$

It shows, on increasing the temperature, K decreases so reaction is exothermic. i.e.

$$\Delta H^\circ < 0$$

Besides, graph shows $K > 1$

So, $\quad \Delta G^\circ < 0$

Now from equation (i)

$$T_1 \ln K_1 > T_2 \ln K_2$$

$$-\Delta G^\circ_1 > -\Delta G^\circ_2$$

Likewise

$$(-\Delta H^\circ + T_1\Delta S^\circ) > (-\Delta H^\circ + T_2\Delta S^\circ)$$

or simply

$$T_1\Delta S^\circ > T_2\Delta S^\circ$$

So, $\quad \Delta S^\circ < 0$

In other words, increase of ΔG with increase in temperature is possible only when $\Delta S^\circ < 0$.

Hence, option (a) and (c) are correct.

183. (b, d)

184. (a, c) (a) AgCl dissolves in NH_3 forming $[Ag(NH_3)_2]Cl$

(c) In presence of Cl^- (common ion) solubility of AgCl is decreased.

Addition of H_2O increases solubility.

185. (a, d) $\log K = \log A - \frac{\Delta H^\circ}{2.303RT}$

It is a straight line of the type

$$y = c - mx$$

on comparison

$\log A = c = OP$ (intercept on y-axis) = 10

$\therefore \quad A = 10^{10}$

Slope $= m = \frac{\Delta H^\circ}{2.303R} = \tan\theta = 0.5$

$\therefore \Delta H = 2.303 \times 8.314 \times \frac{1}{2} = 9.574 \text{ J mol}^{-1}$

186. (a, b, c) $\quad N_2O_4 \rightleftharpoons 2NO_2$

	N_2O_4	$2NO_2$	
Initial(mol)	1	0	
At equil.	$(1-x)$	$2x$	(Total moles at equil. = $1+x$)
Mole fraction	$\left(\frac{1-x}{1+x}\right)$	$\left(\frac{2x}{1+x}\right)$	
Partial pressure	$p\left(\frac{1-x}{1+x}\right)$	$p\left(\frac{2x}{1+x}\right)$	(p = 1 atm)

1 mol N_2O_4 = 92 g,

x = 20% of 92 by mass =

$$92 \times \frac{20}{100} = 18.4\text{g} = \frac{18.4}{92} = 0.2 \text{ mol}$$

Total mol at equilibrium = $1 + x$ = 1.2

$$p \propto n$$

Thus, resultant pressure = 1.2 atm

$$\therefore K_p = \frac{4x^2p}{(1-x^2)} = \frac{4(0.2)^2 \times 1.2}{(1-0.04)} = 0.2$$

$$K_p = K_C(RT)^{\Delta n_g},\ \Delta n_g = 1$$

$$= K_C(RT)$$

$$\therefore K_C = \frac{K_p}{RT} = \frac{0.2}{0.0821 \times 600} = 4.06 \times 10^{-3}$$

187. (a, b, c, d)

$C_2H_4(g) + H_2(g) \rightleftharpoons C_2H_6(g)$;

$\Delta H = -136 \text{ kJmol}^{-1}$

(a) Reaction is exothermic, thus increase in temperature favours backward reaction in which C_2H_4 and H_2 are formed.

(b) Quantity of product $x \propto \left(\frac{1}{p}\right)^{\Delta n_g/2}$

$$\Delta n_g = -1$$

$$\therefore \quad x \propto \left(\frac{1}{p}\right)^{-\frac{1}{2}} \propto \sqrt{p}$$

Thus, if pressure is decreased, $C_2H_6(g)$ decreases. It means reaction is favoured in backward side.

(c, d) Removal of H_2 or addition of C_2H_6 will increase amount of C_2H_4.

188. (a, b, c)

If pressure is increased backward reaction is favoured.

189. (a, c)

190. (c, d)

191. (a, b, d)

(a) For I : $p_{eq} = 10$ cm Hg

$\therefore \quad p_{A'} = \frac{10}{2} = 5$ cm Hg

$p_{NH_3} = 5$ cmHg

$\therefore \quad K_1 = 5 \times 5 = 25 \text{ cm}^2$

(b) For II : Similarly $K_2 = 144 \text{ cm}^2$

(d) When placed together pressure of each gaseous species in

I = x cmHg and in II = y cmHg

$p_{A'} = x$

$p_{B'} = y$

$p_{NH_3} = (x + y)$

$\therefore x(x + y) = 25$

$y(x + y) = 144$

Adding, $(x + y)(x + y) = 169$

$(x + y) = 13$

$\therefore$ Total pressure $= p_{A'} + p_{B'} + p_{NH_3}$

$= x + y + x + y$

$= 2(x + y) = 26$ cm Hg

192. (b, c, d) $pV = nRT$

$$\therefore \quad n \text{ (Total)} = \frac{pV}{RT}$$

$$= \frac{1.1 \text{ atm} \times 1.96 \text{ L}}{0.0821 \text{ L atm mol}^{-1}\text{ K}^{-1} \times 1700 \text{ K}}$$

$$= 0.0154 \text{ mol}$$

If $Cl_2 = y\text{ g} = \frac{y}{71}$ mol

Then, $Cl = (1-y)\,g = \frac{1-y}{35.5}$ mol

$\therefore \quad \frac{y}{71} + \frac{1-y}{35.5} = 0.0154$

$\Rightarrow \quad y + 2 - 2y = 1.0934$

$\therefore \quad y = 0.9066$ g

	Amount	Mole	Mole fraction
Cl_2	0.9066 g	0.0128 mol	0.8292
Cl	0.0934 g	2.63×10^{-3}	0.1708

$$K_\chi = \frac{\chi_{Cl}}{\sqrt{\chi_{Cl_2}}} = \frac{0.1708}{\sqrt{0.8292}} = 0.187$$

$$K_p = K_\chi p^{\Delta n_g} = 0.187\,(1.10)^{1/2}$$

$$= 0.196 \text{ atm}^{1/2}$$

$$K_C = K_p (RT)^{-1/2}$$

$$= \frac{K_p}{\sqrt{RT}} = \frac{0.196}{\sqrt{0.0821 \times 1700}}$$

$$= 0.0165 \,(\text{mol L}^{-1})^{1/2}$$

193. (a, b, c, d) $\quad Cl_2 \rightleftharpoons 2Cl$

	Cl_2	$2Cl$
Initial	1	0 mol
At equili.	$(1-x)$	$2x$

$x = 0.071$

$\therefore \quad Cl_2 = (1-x) = 1 - 0.071 = 0.929$ mol

$Cl = 0.142$ mol

$n_{total} = 0.929 + 0.142 = 1.071$ mol

$\therefore \chi_{Cl_2} = \frac{0.929}{1.071}, \chi_{Cl} = \frac{0.142}{1.071}$

Thus, $\chi_{Cl_2} > \chi_{Cl}$.

$$K_\chi = \frac{\chi^2_{Cl}}{\chi_{Cl_2}} = \frac{(0.142/1.071)^2}{(0.929/1.071)} = 0.0204$$

$$K_p = K_\chi (p)^{\Delta n_g} = K_\chi = 0.0204 \text{ atm}$$

$$K_C = \frac{K_p}{RT} = \frac{0.0204}{0.0821 \times 1600}$$

$$= 1.55 \times 10^{-4} \text{mol L}^{-1}$$

194. (a, b, c, d)

$$2SO_3(g) \rightleftharpoons 2SO_2(g) + O_2(g)$$

	$2SO_3(g)$	$2SO_2(g)$	$O_2(g)$
Initial	2 mol	0	0
At equil.	$(2-2x)$	$2x$	x
Molar conc.	$\frac{2(1-x)}{10} M$	$\frac{2x}{10} M$	$\frac{x}{10} M$

Given, $\frac{[SO_2]}{[SO_3]} = \frac{2x}{2(1-x)} = 0.663$

$x = 0.4$

$$\therefore \quad K_{eq} = \frac{[SO_2]^2[O_2]}{[SO_3]^2} = (0.663)^2 \left(\frac{0.4}{10}\right)$$

$$= 0.0176 \text{ mol L}^{-1}$$

$$\Delta G° = -2.303 RT \log K_{eq}$$

$$= -2.303 \times 8.314 \times 10^{-3} \times 350 \log 0.0176$$

$$= 11.76 \text{ kJ mol}^{-1}$$

$$[O_2] = \frac{x}{10} = \frac{0.4}{10} = 0.04 \text{ mol L}^{-1}$$

$$[SO_3] = \frac{2(1-x)}{10} = 0.12 \text{ mol L}^{-1}$$

195. (a, b, c, d)

(a) $N_2(g) + O_2(g) \rightleftharpoons 2NO(g)$

$$K_1 = \frac{[NO]^2}{[N_2][O_2]}$$

$$NO(g) \rightleftharpoons \frac{1}{2}N_2(g) + \frac{1}{2}O_2(g)$$

$$K_2 = \frac{[N_2]^{1/2}[O_2]^{1/2}}{[NO]}$$

$$\Rightarrow \quad K_2^2 = \frac{[N_2][O_2]}{[NO]^2}$$

Thus, $K_1 K_2^2 = 1$

Thus, (a) is correct.

(b) Free energy can be obtained by algebraic summation.

$$2NO_2(g) \rightleftharpoons N_2O_4(g);\ \Delta G_1°$$

$$NO_2(g) \rightleftharpoons \frac{1}{2}N_2O_4(g);\ \frac{\Delta G_1°}{2}$$

$$\frac{1}{2}N_2O_4(g) \rightleftharpoons NO_2(g);\ -\frac{\Delta G_1°}{2}$$

Thus, $\quad \Delta G_2° = -\frac{\Delta G_1°}{2}$

$\Rightarrow \quad 2\Delta G_2° + \Delta G_1° = 0$

Thus, (b) is correct.

$$\text{(c)}\ \Delta_r H° = \frac{2.303\,RT_1T_2}{(T_2 - T_1)} \log \frac{K_2}{K_1}$$

$$\text{or}\quad \Delta_r H° \frac{(T_2 - T_1)}{T_1T_2} = 2.303\,R \log K_2 - 2.303\,R \log K_1$$

$$\Delta_r H° \left[\frac{1}{T_1} - \frac{1}{T_2}\right] = \frac{2.303\,R\,T_2 \log K_2}{T_2} - \frac{2.303\,RT_1}{T_1} \log K_1$$

But, $2.303\,RT \log K = -\Delta_r G°$

$$\therefore \Delta_r H° \left[\frac{1}{T_1} - \frac{1}{T_2}\right] = -\frac{\Delta_r G_2°}{T_2} \left(\frac{\Delta G_1°}{T_1}\right)$$

$$\Delta_r H° \left[\frac{1}{T_2} - \frac{1}{T_1}\right] = \frac{\Delta_r G_2°}{T_2} - \frac{\Delta_r G_1°}{T_1}$$

Thus, (c) is correct.

(d) $\quad A(g) \rightleftharpoons 2B(g)$

	$A(g)$	$2B(g)$
Initial	1	0
At equil.	$(1-x)$	$2x$

Total moles $= (1+x)$

Partial pressure $p_A = \left(\frac{1-x}{1+x}\right)p$

$$p_B = \frac{2xp}{(1+x)}$$

$$K_p = p_B^2 / p_A$$

$$K_p = \frac{4x^2p}{(1-x^2)} \Rightarrow \frac{x^2}{(1-x^2)} = \frac{K_p}{4p}$$

On solving $\quad x = \sqrt{\frac{K_p}{K_p + 4p}}$

Thus, (d) is correct.

196. (a, b, c, d) $\frac{\partial}{\partial T}\left(\frac{\Delta G°}{T}\right) = -\frac{\Delta H°}{T_2}$

Since, $\Delta G° = -RT \ln K$

$$\therefore \quad \frac{\partial}{\partial T}\left(\frac{-RT \ln K}{T}\right) = -\frac{\Delta H°}{T^2}$$

$$\therefore \quad \frac{\partial}{\partial T}(\ln K) = \frac{\Delta H°}{RT^2}$$

Thus, (a) is correct.

$$\text{or} \quad \partial \frac{\ln K}{\partial T} = -\frac{\Delta H°}{R} \frac{\partial}{\partial T}\left(\frac{1}{T}\right)$$

Thus, (b) is correct.

$$\partial(\ln K) = \frac{\Delta H°}{RT^2} \partial T$$

$$\therefore \quad \int \partial(\ln K) = \frac{\Delta H°}{R} \int \frac{\partial T}{T^2}$$

$$\therefore \quad \ln K = \text{constant} - \frac{\Delta H°}{RT}$$

Thus, (c) is correct.

At temperature T_1 and T_2

$$\ln K_2 = \text{constant} - \frac{\Delta H°}{RT_2}$$

$$\text{and } \ln K_1 = \text{constant} - \frac{\Delta H°}{RT_1}$$

$$\therefore \quad \ln \frac{K_2}{K_1} = \frac{\Delta H°}{R}\left[\frac{1}{T_1} - \frac{1}{T_2}\right]$$

Thus, (d) is correct

197. (a,b) $\quad A \rightleftharpoons nB$

A	nB
1	0
$(1-x)$	nx

Total moles at equilibrium $= 1 - x + nx$

$= 1 + x(n-1)$

Initial mole $= 1$

Thus, volume $\propto$ moles and volume after dissociation $\propto [1 + x(n-1)]$.

$$D \propto \frac{1}{V} \Rightarrow d \propto \frac{1}{[1 + x(n-1)]V}$$

$$\frac{D}{d} = 1 + x(n-1)$$

$$\therefore \quad \frac{D - d}{(n-1)d} = x$$

Thus, (a) as correct.

Also, $\quad pV = nRT = \frac{w}{m}RT$

$$\therefore \quad p = \frac{w}{V}mRT = \frac{d}{m}RT$$

$$\therefore \quad d = \frac{pm}{RT}$$

$$\text{Thus,} \quad D = \frac{p_i m}{RT} \Rightarrow x = \frac{p_i - p}{(n-1)p}$$

Thus, (b) is correct.

198. (a, b, d)

$$K_p = \frac{px^2}{(1-x^2)} \text{ and } K_C = \frac{x^2}{(1-x)V}$$

$$K_p(1-x^2) = px^2$$

$$K_p = K_p x^2 + px^2 = x^2(K_p + p)$$

$$\therefore x = \sqrt{\frac{K_p}{K_p + p}}$$

199. (a, b, d)

As $\frac{1}{T}$ increases (T decreases, K_p decreases)

Hence, K_p increases with increase in temperature. Thus, endothermic.

(a) If T is lowered, decomposition is lowered.

(b) If p is increased, reaction is displaced in backward side. Thus, true.

(d) If H_2 is added, more NH_3 is formed.

200. (c) $N_2(g) + 3H_2(g) \rightleftharpoons 2NH_3(g)$

$\Delta H < 0$ (exothermic)

For exothermic reaction, high temperature favours the reaction in backward direction, i.e. yield of reaction decreases.

■ $\Delta H < 0, T \uparrow$, backward;
$\Delta H < 0, T \downarrow$, forward
$\Delta H > 0, T \uparrow$, forward;
$\Delta H > 0, T \downarrow$, backward

201. (a, b, c, d)

(a) ΔH (Heat of reaction) varies with temperature as given by Kirchhoff's equation

$$\Delta H_{T_2} = \Delta H_{T_1} + \Delta C_p (T_2 - T_1)$$

where, ΔC_p = (Heat capacity of products – Heat capacity of reactants)

Thus, (a) is correct.

(b) K_p does not depend on the amount of $CaCO_3$, but dependent on pressure of CO_2.

$$K_p = p_{CO_2}$$

Thus, (b) is correct.

(c) Thus (c) is correct.

(d) Catalyst lowers E_a (activation energy)

$$\Delta H = (H_P - H_R)$$

Thus, catalyst does not affect ΔH.

202. (b, c, d) $Cu^+ + Cl^- \longrightarrow CuCl\downarrow$ (White ppt.)

$Cu^+ + CN^- \longrightarrow CuCN\downarrow$ (White ppt.)

$Cu^+ + SCN^- \longrightarrow CuSCN\downarrow$ (White ppt.)

Thus, Cl^-, SCN^- and CN^- removes Cu^+ from reaction mixture and thus equilibrium shifts towards left.

■ All nitrates are water soluble.

Type IV. Passage Based MCQs (Comprehension)

Passage 1

$$CH_3COOH(l) + C_2H_5OH(l) \rightleftharpoons CH_3COOC_2H_5(l) + H_2O(l)$$

	CH_3COOH	C_2H_5OH	$CH_3COOC_2H_5$	H_2O
Case I Initial	1	1	0	0
At equil.	$(1-x)$,	$(1-x)$	x	x

$$x = \frac{2}{3}$$

	CH_3COOH	C_2H_5OH	$CH_3COOC_2H_5$	H_2O
Case II Initial	1	3	0	0
At equil.	$(1-y)$	$(3-y)$	y	y

***Case* I or *Case* II**

$$K_C = \frac{[CH_3COOC_2H_5][H_2O]}{[CH_3COOH][C_2H_5OH]}$$

$$= \frac{x^2}{(1-x)^2} = \frac{(2/3)^2}{(1/3)^2} = 4$$

$$\Delta G° = -2.303\,RT \log K$$

$$= -2.303 \times 8.314 \times 10^{-3} \times 298 \log 4$$

$$= -3.44 \text{ kJ}$$

■ R is 8.314×10^{-3} kJ mol^{-1} K^{-1}.

***Case* II** Since, temperature is constant, K_C remains as 4.

$$K_c = 4 = \frac{y^2}{(3-y)(1-y)}$$

$$4(3-y)(1-y) = y^2$$

$$3y^2 - 16y + 12 = 0$$

$$y = \frac{16 \pm \sqrt{(16)^2 - 144}}{6}$$

$$= 0.90 \text{ (or 4.43 neglected as } y = 1)$$

203. (a)

204. (b)

Passage 2

$$H_2O(l) \rightleftharpoons H^+ + OH^-$$

$$K_{eq} = K_w = [H^+][OH^-] = 1 \times 10^{-14} \text{ at 298 K}$$

$$\therefore \quad \Delta G° = -2.303\,RT \log K_w$$

$$= -2.303 \times 0.002 \times 298 \log 1 \times 10^{-14}$$

$$= 19.2 \text{ kcal mol}^{-1}$$

$$H^+ + OH^- \rightleftharpoons H_2O$$

$$\Delta G° = -19.2 \text{ kcal mol}^{-1}$$

$$\Delta H° = -13.7 \text{ kcal mol}^{-1} \text{ (standard value)}$$

$$\therefore \quad \Delta G° = \Delta H° - T\Delta S°$$

$$\therefore \quad \Delta S° = \frac{\Delta H° - \Delta G°}{T}$$

$$\therefore \quad = \frac{-13.7 + 19.2}{298}$$

$$= 0.01846 \text{ kcal mol}^{-1}\text{K}^{-1}$$

$$= 18.46 \text{ cal mol}^{-1}\text{K}^{-1}$$

205. (c)

206. (c)

Passage 3

$$3SO_2 + Cr_2O_7^{2-} + 2H^+ \longrightarrow 3SO_4^{2-} + 2Cr^{3+} + H_2O$$

$Cr_2O_7^{2-}$ required = 50 mL of 2 M

= 50 × 2 millimol = 0.1 mol

Thus, SO_2 taken = 3 × mol of $Cr_2O_7^{2-}$

= 0.3 mol

	$2SO_2$	+ O_2	$\rightleftharpoons 2SO_3$
Initial.	0.3	0.2	0 mol
At equil.	$(0.3-2x)$	$(0.2-x)$	$2x$ mol

$(K_2Cr_2O_7)$ required by SO_2

$$= \frac{16.67 \times 2}{1000} \text{ mol} = 0.0333 \text{ mol}$$

$$1 \text{ mol } Cr_2O_7^{2-} = 3 \text{ mol } SO_2$$

$$\therefore \quad 0.0333 \text{ mol } Cr_2O_7^{2-} = 0.0999 \text{ mol} = 0.1 \text{ mol } SO_2$$

$\therefore$ $[SO_2]$ at equilibrium

$= (0.3 - 2x) = 0.1$ mol L^{-1}

$[O_2]$ at equilibrium

$= (0.2 - 0.1) = 0.1$ mol L^{-1}

$[SO_3]$ at equilibrium

$= 2x = 0.2$ mol L^{-1}

$$K_C = \frac{[SO_3]^2}{[SO_2]^2[O_2]} = \frac{(0.2)^2}{(0.1)^2 \times 0.1} = 40$$

207. (c)

208. (d)

Passage 4

	$N_2(g)$	+ $3H_2(g)$	$\rightleftharpoons 2NH_3(g)$
Initial mol	3	3	0
At equil.	$(3-x)$	$(3-3x)$	$2x$
(Calculated below)	$(3-0.25)$	$(3-0.75)$	0.50
$x = 0.25$	= 2.75	= 2.25	= 0.50

At equilibrium $NH_3 \equiv HCl$

$$\text{Thus, HCl} = \frac{100 \times 5}{1000} = 0.5 \text{ mol}$$

Thus, NH_3 formed = 0.5 mol = $2x$

$\therefore x = 0.25$ mol

$\therefore$ Total moles of reactants and products at equilibrium = 5.50

$$\therefore \text{Total pressure} = \frac{nRT}{V}$$

$$= \frac{5.50 \times 0.0831 \times 300}{10}$$

$$= 13.71 \text{ bar}$$

$(R = 0.0831$ L bar mol^{-1}K$^{-1})$

$$\therefore \quad p_{N_2} = \left(\frac{2.75}{5.50}\right) 13.71 = 6.855 \text{ bar}$$

$$p_{H_2} = \left(\frac{2.25}{5.50}\right) 13.71 = 5.609 \text{ bar}$$

$$p_{NH_3} = \left(\frac{0.50}{5.50}\right) 13.71 = 1.246 \text{ bar}$$

$$\therefore \quad K_p = \frac{p^2_{NH_3}}{p_{N_2}\, p^3_{H_2}} = \frac{(1.246)^2}{(6.853)(5.609)^3}$$

$$= 1.283 \times 10^{-3} \text{ bar}^{-2}$$

If H_2O is added, all the NH_3 is dissolved in it and its gaseous form changes to aqueous form.

Also, available volume for exerting pressure = (10 − 5) L = 5 L

$$n_{N_2} + n_{H_2} = 5.0$$

$$p = \frac{nRT}{V} = \frac{5 \times 0.0831 \times 300}{5}$$

$$= 24.93 \text{ bar}$$

$$\therefore \quad p_{N_2} = \left(\frac{2.75}{5.00}\right) 24.93 \text{ bar} = 13.71 \text{ bar}$$

$$p_{H_2} = 24.93 - p_{N_2} = 11.22 \text{ bar}$$

209. (a)

210. (c)

Passage 5

$A \longrightarrow B$

Net rate = $K_f[A] - K_b[B]$

and $K_C = K_f / K_b$

$$\text{At 300K,} \quad K_C = \frac{K_f}{K_b} = \frac{2 \times 10^{-2}}{4 \times 10^{-3}} = 5$$

$$\text{At 400K} \quad K_C = \frac{k_f}{k_b} = \frac{4 \times 10^{-2}}{16 \times 10^{-4}} = 25$$

K_C at 400 K > K_C at 300 K

On increasing temperature, K_C increases. It means reaction is spontaneous in forward side. Thus, reaction is endothermic.

Heat of reaction

$$\Delta H^\circ = \frac{2.303\, RT_1T_2}{(T_2 - T_1)} \log \frac{K_C(400)}{K_C(300)}$$

$$= 3.86 \text{ kcal mol}^{-1}$$

211. (d)

212. (b)

Passage 6

$$K_p = (p_{H_2O})^{10} = 4.08 \times 10^{-25}$$

$$\therefore p_{H_2O} = 3.64 \times 10^{-3} \text{ atm}$$

$$= 3.64 \times 10^{-3} \times 760 \text{ Torr}$$

$$= 2.77 \text{ Torr}$$

The hydrate $Na_2SO_4.10H_2O$ will lose water (efflorescence) below 2.77 Torr ($= 3.64 \times 10^{-3}$ atm)

vapour pressure of H_2O at 273 K = 4.58 Torr.

$$\therefore \text{Relative humidity} = \frac{2.77}{4.58} \times 100 = 60.5\%$$

Thus, below 60.5%.

Alternately

Na_2SO_4 (anhydrous salt) will absorb moisture above 60.5% relative humidity.

213. (b)

214. (a)

Passage 7

I. $K_p = (p_{H_2O})^4 = 6.89 \times 10^{-12}$

$\therefore p_{H_2O} = 1.62 \times 10^{-3}$ atm (minimum)

II. $K_p = (p_{H_2O})^5 = 5.25 \times 10^{-13}$

$\therefore p_{H_2O} = 3.5 \times 10^{-3}$ atm

III. $K_p = (p_{H_2O})^2 = 1.086 \times 10^{-4}$

$\therefore p_{H_2O} = 1.04 \times 10^{-2}$ atm (maximum)

Salt with minimum value of equilibrium vapour pressure has maximum capacity to absorb moisture, hence best drying agent.

215. (c)

216. (a)

Passage 8

$$\Delta G^\circ = \Delta H^\circ - T\Delta S^\circ$$

$$-2.303\, RT \log_{10} K = \Delta H^\circ - T\Delta S^\circ$$

$$\therefore \quad \log_{10} K = -\frac{\Delta H^\circ}{2.303\, RT} + \frac{\Delta S^\circ}{2.303\, R}$$

$$\text{or } \log_e K = -\frac{\Delta H^\circ}{RT} + \frac{\Delta S^\circ}{R}$$

$$\log_e K = -\frac{1088\text{K}}{T} - 1.04$$

$$\text{On comparison,} \quad \frac{\Delta H^\circ}{R} = 1088\text{K}$$

$$\therefore \Delta H^\circ = 1088\text{K} \times R$$

$$= 1088\text{K} \times 2 \times 10^{-3} \text{ kcal mol}^{-1}\text{K}^{-1}$$

$$= 2.176 \text{ kcal}$$

$$\frac{\Delta S^\circ}{R} = -1.04$$

$$\Delta S^\circ = -1.04 \times R$$

$$= -1.04 \times 2 \text{ cal mol}^{-1}\text{K}^{-1}$$

$$= -2.08 \text{ cal mol}^{-1}\text{K}^{-1}$$

$$\text{Also, } \Delta G^\circ = \Delta H^\circ - T\Delta S^\circ$$

$$= 2.176 - 400\,(-2.08 \times 10^{-3})$$

$$= 3.008 \text{ kcal mol}^{-1}$$

217. (a)

218. (b)

Passage 9

$$\left(\frac{dx}{dt}\right)_f = (1.45 \times 10^{13} \text{ L}^3 \text{ mol}^{-3} \text{ s}^{-1})\,[Fe^{2+}]\,[\text{dipy}]^3$$

$$\left(\frac{dx}{dt}\right)_b = (1.22 \times 10^{-4} \text{ s}^{-1})\,[Fe(\text{dipy})_3^{2+}]$$

When equilibrium is attainted

$$\left(\frac{dx}{dt}\right)_f = \left(\frac{dx}{dt}\right)_b$$

$$\therefore 1.45 \times 10^{13} \text{ L}^3\text{mol}^{-3}\text{s}^{-1}$$

$$[Fe^{2+}][\text{dipy}]^3 = 1.22 \times 10^{-4} \text{ s}^{-1}[Fe(\text{dipy})]^{2+}$$

$\therefore$ Equilibrium constant of the complex

$$\frac{[Fe(\text{dipy})^{2+}]}{[Fe^{2+}][\text{dipy}]^3} = \frac{1.45 \times 10^{13}}{1.22 \times 10^{-4}} \text{L}^3\text{mol}^{-3}$$

$$= 1.1885 \times 10^{17} \text{ (mol L}^{-1})^{-3}$$

For backward reaction

K_b (rate constant) = 1.22×10^{-4} s^{-1}

$$\therefore \quad t_{50} \text{ (half-life)} = \frac{0.693}{k}$$

$$= \frac{0.693}{1.22 \times 10^{-4} \text{ s}^{-1}} = 5680 \text{ s} = 95 \text{ min}$$

For first-order kinetics

$$k = \frac{2.303}{t} \log \frac{C_0}{C}$$

When 50% reaction $t = t_{50}$

$$k = \frac{2.303 \log 2}{t_{50}}$$

219. (c)

220. (a), (b)

Passage 10

	$N_2O_4 \rightleftharpoons$	$2NO_2$
Initial (mol)	1	0
At equil.	$(1 - x)$	$2x$ (Total moles = $1 + x$)
Mole fraction	$\left(\frac{1-x}{1+x}\right)$	$\left(\frac{2x}{1+x}\right)$

$$\therefore \quad K_p = \frac{4x^2 p}{(1 - x^2)}$$

$$\therefore \quad 4x^2 p = K_p - x^2 K_p$$

$$\therefore \quad 4x^2 p + x^2 K_p = K_p$$

$$x^2 (4p + K_p) = K_p$$

$$x = \sqrt{\frac{K_p}{K_p + 4p}}$$

$$\text{Fraction of } NO_2 \text{ in the mixture} = \frac{2x}{1 + x}$$

$$= \frac{2\sqrt{\frac{K_p}{K_p + 4p}}}{1 + \sqrt{\frac{K_p}{K_p + 4p}}}$$

$$= \frac{\sqrt{4K_p}}{\sqrt{K_p + 4p} + \sqrt{K_p}} = \frac{2}{\sqrt{1 + \frac{4p}{K_p}} + 1}$$

221. (a)

222. (c)

Passage 11

$$X_2(g) \rightleftharpoons 2X(g)$$

At $t = 0$	1	0
At equil.	$\left(1-\frac{x}{2}\right)$	x
Mole fraction	$\frac{(1-x/2)}{\left(1+\frac{x}{2}\right)}$	$\frac{x}{\left(1+\frac{x}{2}\right)}$
Partial pressure	$p\frac{\left(1-\frac{x}{2}\right)}{\left(1+\frac{x}{2}\right)}$	$\frac{px}{\left(1+\frac{x}{2}\right)}$

Total moles $= \left(1+\frac{x}{2}\right)$ and $p = 2$ bar

When $x = \beta_{equil}$ = moles of product at equilibrium

$\therefore K_p = p_\chi^2 / p_{\chi_2}$

$$= \left[px\left(1+\frac{x}{2}\right)\right]^2 / \frac{p\left(1-\frac{x}{2}\right)}{\left(1+\frac{x}{2}\right)} = \frac{px^2}{\left(1-\frac{x^2}{4}\right)}$$

$$= \frac{4px^2}{(4-x^2)}$$

$$K_p = \frac{4 \times 2(\beta_{equil}^2)}{4-\beta_{equil}^2} = \frac{8\beta_{equil}^2}{(4-\beta_{equil}^2)}$$

(a) $K_p = \frac{4px^2}{(4-x^2)} \approx 4px^2 = x \propto \sqrt{\frac{1}{p}}$

If p decreases, x increases, equilibrium is shifted in the forward side.

Thus, statement (a) is correct.

(b) At the start of the reaction, $Q = 0$

where, Q is the reaction quotient

$$\Delta G = \Delta G° + 2.303\, RT \log Q$$

Since, $\Delta G° > 0$, ΔG is thus –ve, hence dissociation takes place spontaneously.

(c) If we use $x = 0.7$ and $p = 2$ bar

then $K_p = \frac{4 \times 2\,(0.7)^2}{(4-(0.7)^2)} = 1.16 > 1$

Thus, (c) is incorrect.

(d) At equilibrium, $\Delta G = 0$

$\therefore \quad \Delta G° = -\,2.303\,RT\,\log K_p$

Since, $\Delta G° = +$ ve

hence, $K_p < 1 \Rightarrow K_C = \frac{K_p}{(RT)}$

Thus, $K_C < 1$,

Thus, (d) is also correct.

223. (b)

224. (c)

Passage 12

I. $A(s) \rightleftharpoons A'(g) + H_2S(g)$

Vapour pressure of $A'(g)$ and $H_2S(g)$ over solid $A = 50$ mm

$\therefore p_{A'} = p_{H_2S} = 25.0$ mm

$\therefore K_I = p_{A'}\, p_{H_2S} = 25 \times 25 = 625\ \text{mm}^2$

$$= \frac{625}{(760)^2}\ \text{atm}^2 = 1.08 \times 10^{-3}\ \text{atm}^2$$

II. $B(s) \rightleftharpoons B'(g) + H_2S(g)$

Total vapour pressure of $B'(g)$ and $H_2S(g) = 68$ mm

$K_{II} = p_{B'}\, p_{H_2S} = (34)^2\ \text{mm}^2$

$\therefore \quad K_{II} = \frac{(34)^2}{(760)^2} = 8.0 \times 10^{-3}\ \text{atm}^2$

If both solids are considered, let vapour pressure of $A'(g)$ in I $= x$

and that of $B'(g)$ in II $= y$

$\therefore \quad H_2S = (x+y)$

$\therefore \quad K_I = x(x+y) = (25)^2 = 625$

$K_{II} = y(x+y) = (34)^2 = 1156$

$\therefore \quad \frac{x}{y} = \frac{625}{1156} \quad \therefore x = \left(\frac{625}{1156}y\right)$

$\therefore \quad \frac{625\,y}{1156}\left[\frac{625}{1156}y + y\right] = 625$

$$y^2\left[\frac{625+1156}{(1156)^2}\right] = 1$$

$y = 27.39$ mm

$x = \frac{625}{1156} \times 27.39 = 14.81$ mm

$\therefore$ Total vapour pressure at equilibrium over the solids. A and B

$p_{A'} + p_{B'} + p_{H_2S} = x + y + (x+y)$

$= 2(x+y)$

$= 2(14.81 + 27.39)$

$= 84.4$ mm

$= \frac{84.4}{760} = 0.11$ atm

225. (a)

226. (b)

Type V. Numerical Skills

227. **Two (2)**

$$2SO_2(g) + O_2(g) \rightleftharpoons 2SO_3(g)$$

Initial mol	2	1	0
At equil.	$(2-2x)$	$(1-x)$	$2x$
Active mass	$\frac{(2-2x)}{1}$	$\left(\frac{1-x}{1}\right)$	$\frac{2x}{1}$

$$Cr_2O_7^{2-} + 3SO_2 + 2H^+ \longrightarrow 2Cr^{3+} + H_2O + 3SO_4^{2-}$$

3 mol $SO_2 \equiv 1$ mol CrO_7^{2-}

$2(1-x)$ mol $SO_2 = \frac{2(1-x)}{3}$ mol (given) $Cr_2O_7^{2-}$

$$\frac{2(1-x)}{3} = \frac{1}{3}$$

$\therefore \quad x = 0.5$

$\therefore \quad [SO_2] = 1\ \text{mol L}^{-1}$

$[SO_3] = 1\ \text{mol L}^{-1}$

$[O_2] = 0.5\ \text{mol L}^{-1}$

$\therefore K_C = \frac{[SO_3]^2}{[SO_2]^2[O_2]} = \frac{[1]^2}{(1)^2(0.5)} = 2$

228. **Six (6)**

$CaCO_3(s) \rightleftharpoons CaO(s) + CO_2(g)$

$K_p = p_{CO_2} = 1.16$ atm

$n(CO_2) = n(CaCO_3$ decomposed$)$

$= \frac{pV}{RT} = \frac{1.16 \times 10.0}{0.0821 \times 1073} = 0.132$ mol

$CaCO_3$ taken $= 220\ \text{g} = \frac{220}{100} = 2.20$ mol

Thus, percentage of $CaCO_3$ reacted

$= \frac{0.132 \times 100}{2.2} = 6.0\,\%$

229. **Five (5)**

$NH_4HS(s) \rightleftharpoons NH_3(g) + H_2S(g)$

Let $p = p_{NH_3} = p_{H_2S}$, when equilibrium is set up.

$\therefore \quad K_p = p^2 = 0.25\ \text{atm}^2$

$\therefore \quad p = 0.5$ atm

Thus, total pressure $= 0.5 + 0.5 = 1.0$ atm

Also $pV = nRT$

$\therefore \quad n = \frac{pV}{RT}$

$= \frac{1 \times 1}{0.0821 \times 300} = 0.0406$ mol

$\therefore$ NH_4HS decomposed $= 0.0406$ mol

$= 0.0406 \times 51\ \text{g} = 2.07$ g

NH_4HS left unreacted

$= 7.07 - 2.07 = 5.0$ g

230. **(0.25)**

Given : $A \rightleftharpoons B$ (Pa = 1 bar)

Using $\Delta G = \Delta G^0 + RT \ln K_p$

At equilibrium : $\Delta G^0 = -RT \ln K_p$

$\Delta G_1^0 = -RT \ln K_{p_1}$ ... (1)

$\Delta G_2^0 = -RT \ln K_{p_2}$ ... (2)

$$\frac{\Delta G_1^0}{\Delta G_2^0} = \frac{T_1}{T_2} \times \frac{\ln K_{p_1}}{\ln K_{p_2}} = \frac{1000}{2000} \times \frac{\ln(10)}{\ln(100)}$$

$\Rightarrow \quad \frac{1}{4} \Rightarrow 0.25$

231. **Three (3)** Equilibrium constant $(K) = \frac{K_1}{K_2}$

$= \frac{\text{rate constant of forward reaction}}{\text{rate constant of backward reaction}}$

$\frac{10^{15}}{10^{12}} = 10^3$

$\Delta G° = -2.303\, RT \log K$

$\therefore \frac{-\Delta G°}{2.303\, RT} = \log K = \log 10^3$

$= 3 \log 10 = 3$

232. **Four (4)** $A(g) \rightleftharpoons 4B(g)$

	$A(g)$	$4B(g)$
Initial	1	0
At equil.	$(1-\alpha)$	4α

Total moles at equilibrium

$= 1 - \alpha + 4\alpha = (1 + 3\alpha)$

$\text{Density} = \frac{\text{mass}}{\text{volume}}$

and volume $\propto n$ (moles)

$D \propto \frac{1}{V}$ and $d \propto \frac{1}{(1+3\alpha)V}$

$\therefore \frac{D}{d} = (1 + 3\alpha)$

when $\alpha = 1$ (100% dissociation) $\frac{D}{d} = 4$

■ If volume of 1 mole = V L
then volume of $(1 + 3\alpha)$ moles
$= (1 + 3\alpha)$ V L

233. **Four (4)**

$2SO_2(g) + O_2(g) \rightleftharpoons 2SO_3(g)$

	$2SO_2(g)$	$O_2(g)$	$2SO_3(g)$
Initial mol	2	1	0
At equil.	$(2-2x)$	$(1-x)$	$2x$

Total moles at equilibrium = $(3 - x)$

Since, $p \propto n$

Hence, $\frac{p_{\text{initial}}}{p_{\text{equil.}}} = \frac{n_{\text{initial}}}{n_{\text{equil.}}}$

$\frac{3.0}{2.5} = \frac{3}{(3-x)}$

$x = 0.5$

$\therefore [SO_2] = \left(\frac{2-2x}{2}\right) = 0.5 \text{ mol L}^{-1}$

$[O_2] = \frac{x}{2} = 0.25 \text{ mol L}^{-1}$

$[SO_3] = \frac{2(1-x)}{2} = 0.5 \text{ mol L}^{-1}$

$\therefore K_C = \frac{[SO_3]^2}{[SO_2]^2[O_2]} = \frac{(0.5)^2}{(0.5)^2\,(0.25)} = 4$

234. **Two (2)** $2Cl(g) \rightleftharpoons Cl_2(g)$

$n_{Cl_2} = n_{Cl}$

$\chi_{Cl_2} = 0.5$

$\chi_{Cl} = 0.5$

$\therefore p_{Cl_2} = \chi_{Cl_2}\, p = 0.5 \times 1 = 0.5$ bar

$p_{Cl} = 0.5$ bar

$\therefore K_p = \frac{p_{Cl_2}}{p_{Cl}^2} = \frac{0.5}{0.5 \times 0.5} = 2.0$

235. **Three (3)**

$PCl_5(g) \rightleftharpoons PCl_3(g) + Cl_2(g)$

$K_C = \frac{[PCl_3][Cl_2]}{[PCl_5]}$

$\therefore \log K_C = \log \frac{[PCl_3]}{[PCl_5]} + \log[Cl_2]$

$\log \frac{[PCl_3]}{[PCl_5]} = \log K_C - \log[Cl_2]$

When $\log[Cl_2]$ increases, $\log \frac{[PCl_3]}{[PCl_5]}$ decreases.

$\therefore \quad OA = \log K_C = 0.48$

$\therefore \quad K_C = 3.0$

236. **Two (2)** $\Delta n_g = 3 - 2 = 1$

$\Delta H° = \Delta E° + \Delta n_g RT$

$= -90 + 1 \times 2 \times 10^{-3} \times 259$

$= -89.482$ kcal

$\Delta G° = \Delta H° - T\Delta S°$

$= -89.482 - 259 \times 100 \times 10^{-3}$

$= -115.382$ kcal

Also, $\Delta G° = -2.303\, RT \log K$

$\therefore \quad \log K = 96.71 \approx 100 = 10^2$

$\log K = 10^2 = 10^n$

$\therefore \quad n = 2$

237. **Five (5)** Initial concentration of A = 8 M

Initial concentration of B = 12 M

$A(g) + xB(g) \rightleftharpoons yC(g)$

	$A(g)$	$xB(g)$	$yC(g)$
Initial	8 M	12 M	0
At equil.	$(8-\alpha)$	$(12-x\alpha)$	$y\alpha$

At equilibrium $[A] = 6$ M

$\therefore \quad (8 - \alpha) = 6$

$\therefore \quad \alpha = 2$ M

$\therefore$ Also, $B_{\text{equilibrium}} = (12 - x\alpha) = 8$ M

$12 - 2x = 8$

$x = 2$

Also, $[C]_{eq} = 6$ M

$\therefore \quad y\alpha = 6$

$2y = 6$

$\therefore \quad y = 3$

$\therefore \quad (x + y) = 5$

238. **Three (3)** K_{sp} are of approximately same order.

$Ag_2CrO_4 \rightleftharpoons 2Ag^+ + CrO_4^{2-}$

$Ag_2C_2O_4 \rightleftharpoons 2Ag^+ + C_2O_4^{2-}$

$[CrO_4^{2-}] = \frac{1}{2}[Ag^+]$

$[C_2O_4^{2-}] = \frac{1}{2}[Ag^+]$

$[Ag^+][CrO_4^{2-}] = K_{sp}$

$\therefore$ In Ag_2CrO_4, $[CrO_4^{2-}] = \frac{9.0 \times 10^{-12}}{[Ag^+]^2}$

and in $Ag_2C_2O_4$, $[C_2O_4^{2-}] = \frac{6.0 \times 10^{-12}}{[Ag^+]^2}$

$[Ag^+]_{\text{total}} = 2[CrO_4^{2-}] + 2[C_2O_4^{2-}]$

$\therefore$ or $0.5\,[Ag^+] = [CrO_4^{2-}] + [C_2O_4^{2-}]$

$= \frac{9.0 \times 10^{-12}}{[Ag^+]^2} + \frac{6.0 \times 10^{-12}}{[Ag^+]^2}$

$\therefore \quad 0.5\,[Ag^+]^3 = 1.5 \times 10^{-11}$

$\therefore \quad [Ag^+] = 3.1 \times 10^{-4} \text{M} \approx 3.0 \times 10^{-4}$ M

$\therefore \quad y = 3$

239. **Five (5)**

$Ag^+ + 2NH_3 \rightleftharpoons [Ag(NH_3)_2]^+$

	Ag^+	$2NH_3$	$[Ag(NH_3)_2]^+$
Initial	0.005	1.00	0 mol
At equil.	$(0.005 - x)$	$(1.00 - 2x)$	x mol $\approx$ 1.00 M

Since, $K_f\,[Ag(NH_3)_2]^+$ is very high, it is assumed that all the Ag^+ is complexed as $[Ag(NH_3)_2]^+$.

Thus, $[Ag(NH_3)_2]^+ = [Ag^+]$taken

$K_f = \frac{[Ag(NH_3)_2]^+}{[Ag^+][NH_3]^2}$

$1.0 \times 10^8 = \frac{[0.005]}{[Ag^+][1]^2}$

$\therefore [Ag^+] = 0.005 \times 1 \times 10^{-8}$ M

$= 5 \times 10^{-11}$M

$= y \times 10^{-11}$M

$\therefore \quad y = 5$

240. **Three (3)** Total volume = 200 mL

$\therefore \quad [Fe^{2+}]$ in mixture

$= \frac{75 \times 0.03 \times 10^{-3}}{0.200\,\text{L}} \text{ mol L}^{-1}$

$[Fe^{2+}] = 0.01125$ M

$[CN^-]$ in mixture

$= \frac{125 \times 0.2 \times 10^{-3}}{0.2\text{ L}}$ mol

$= 0.125$ M

$Fe^{2+} + 6CN^- \rightleftharpoons [Fe(CN)_6]^{4-}$

	Fe^{2+}	$6CN^-$	$[Fe(CN)_6]^{4-}$
Initial	0.01125 M	0.125 M	
At equil.	α M	$(0.125 - 0.01125 \times 6)$ = 0.0575 M	0.01125 M

Large value of K_{eq} indicate that, all the Fe^{2+} is complexed and to keep the equilibrium, unreacted $[Fe^{2+}] = \alpha$

$\therefore \quad K_{eq} = \frac{[Fe(CN)_6]^{4-}}{[Fe^{2+}][0.0575]^6}$

$1 \times 10^{24} = \frac{0.01125}{[\alpha]\,(0.0575)^6}$

$\therefore\ \alpha = 3.1 \times 10^{-19} \approx 3.0 \times 10^{-19}$ M

$= x \times 10^{-19}$ M

Thus, $x = 3$

■ $\frac{MV(\text{mL})}{1000} = \text{mol}$

241. One (1)

$$N_2(g) + 3H_2(g) \rightleftharpoons 2NH_3(g)$$

Initial	2	n	mol
At equil.	$(2-x)$	$(n-3x)$	$2x$ mol

Total moles at equilibrium

$= 2 - x + n - 3x + 2x$

$= 2 + n - 2x$

Let initial pressure of $(2+n)$ moles be $= p_i$ then pressure of $(2+n-2x)$ moles at equilibrium

$$= \frac{p_i\,(2+n-2x)}{(2+n)}$$

Mole fraction of $NH_3 = \frac{2x}{(2+n-2x)}$

Partial pressure of $NH_3 = p\chi_{NH_3}$

$$= \frac{p_i\,(2+n-2x)}{(2+n)} \cdot \frac{2x}{(2+n-2x)}$$

$$= \frac{2xp_i}{(2+n)}$$

Given, $p_{NH_3} = \frac{4}{9} p_i$

$$\frac{2xp_i}{(2+n)} = \frac{4}{9} p_i$$

$$\frac{x}{(2+n)} = \frac{2}{9} \Rightarrow 9x = 4 + 2n$$

Also, N_2 content at equilibrium

$(2-x) = \frac{4}{3}$ (given)

$\therefore\ x = 2 - \frac{4}{3} = \frac{2}{3}$

$\therefore\ 9 \times \frac{2}{3} = 4 + 2n \Rightarrow n = 1$

242. (20)

$$X + 2Y \rightleftharpoons 2Z$$

Initial	1.0	1.5	0.5 mol
At equil.	$(1.0-\alpha)$	$(1.5-2\alpha)$	$(0.5+2\alpha)$ mol L^{-1}
Active mass	$\frac{(1.0-\alpha)}{1}$,	$\frac{(1.5-2\alpha)}{1}$,	$\frac{(0.5+2\alpha)}{1}$ mol L^{-1}

Given, $(0.5 + 2\alpha) = 1.0$

$\alpha = 0.25$ mol L^{-1}

$\therefore\ [X] = (1.0 - 0.25) = 0.75$ mol L^{-1}

$[Y] = (1.5 - 0.5) = 1.0$ mol L^{-1}

$[Z] = 1.0$ mol L^{-1}

$$K_{eq} = \frac{[Z]^2}{[X][Y]^2}$$

$$= \frac{(1)^2}{(0.75)(1.0)^2} = \frac{100}{75} = \frac{20}{15} = \frac{x}{15}$$

Thus, $x = 20$

243. Four (4) Let N_2O_4 be $= x$ mol

NO_2 be $= y$ mol then $N_2 = (1 - x - y)$ mol

$$N_2O_4 \rightleftharpoons 2NO_2$$

Initial	1	2 mol
At equil.	x	$2x$ mol

Average molar mass $\overline{m}$

$$= \frac{92x + 46y + 28(1-x-y)}{1}$$

$48.5 = 46[2x + y] + 28[1 - x - y]$

After decomposition $N_2O_4 = 0$

$NO_2 = (2x + y)$ and $N_2 = (1 - x - y)$

Total moles $= 2x + y + 1 - x - y = (1 + x)$

Thus, average molar mass (48.5–9.7)

$= 38.8$ g mol^{-1}

$$\therefore\ 38.8 = \frac{46(2x+y) + 28(1-x-y)}{(1+x)}$$

$$38.8 = \frac{48.5}{(1+x)}$$

$$\therefore\ (1+x) = \left(\frac{48.5}{38.8}\right) = 1.25$$

$$x = 0.25 = \frac{1}{4} = \frac{1}{n}$$

$\therefore\ n = 4$

244. Eight (8)

$$AB(g) \rightleftharpoons A(g) + B(g)$$

Initial	1	0	0 mol
At equil.	$\left(1-\frac{1}{3}\right)$	$\frac{1}{3}$	$\frac{1}{3}$
	$\frac{2}{3}$	$\frac{1}{3}$	$\frac{1}{3}$

Total moles $= \frac{2}{3} + \frac{1}{3} + \frac{1}{3} = \frac{4}{3}$

Thus,	Mole fraction	Partial pressure
$AB(g)$	$\frac{2/3}{4/3} = \frac{1}{2}$	$\frac{p}{2}$
$A(g)$	$\frac{1/3}{4/3} = \frac{1}{4}$	$\frac{p}{4}$
$B(g)$	$\frac{1/3}{4/3} = \frac{1}{4}$	$\frac{p}{4}$

$$\therefore\ K_p = \frac{p_A \cdot p_B}{p_{AB}} = \frac{p^2/16}{p/2} = \frac{p}{8}$$

$\therefore\ p = 8K_p$

$\therefore\ n = 8$

245. Four (4)

$$2SO_2(g) + O_2(g) \rightleftharpoons 2SO_3(g)$$

If $SO_2 = x$ mol

$\therefore\ [SO_2] = \left(\frac{x}{10}\right)$ mol L^{-1}

$SO_3 = 2x$ mol

$\therefore\ [SO_3] = \left(\frac{2x}{10}\right)$ mol L^{-1}

$O_2 = y$ mol

$\therefore\ [O_2] = \left(\frac{y}{10}\right)$ mol L^{-1}

$$\therefore\ K_C = \frac{[SO_3]^2}{[SO_2]^2[O_2]}$$

$$10 = \frac{\left(\frac{2x}{10}\right)^2}{\left(\frac{x}{10}\right)^2\left(\frac{y}{10}\right)} = \frac{40}{y}$$

$\therefore\ y = 4$ mol

246. Five (5) Relation between K_C, K_p and K_χ is

$$K_p = K_\chi\,(p)^{\Delta n_g}$$

and $K_p = K_C\,(RT)^{\Delta n_g}$

$\therefore\ K_\chi(p)^{\Delta ng} = K_c\,(RT)^{\Delta n_g}$

$\therefore\ K_C = K_\chi\left(\frac{p}{RT}\right)^{\Delta n_g}$

$\therefore\ pV = RT$

$\therefore\ \frac{p}{RT} = \frac{1}{V}$

$\therefore\ K_C = K_\chi\left(\frac{1}{V}\right)^{\Delta n_g}$

$\Delta n_g = -2$

$K_C = K_\chi\left(\frac{1}{5}\right)^{-2} = K_\chi\,(5)^2$

$\frac{K_C}{K_\chi} = (5)^2$

Thus, $n = 5$

247. Two (2)

$$2SO_2(g) + O_2(g) \rightleftharpoons 2SO_3(g)$$

Initial	2	1	0 mol
At equil.	$(2-2x)$	$(1-x)$	$2x$ mol

MnO_4^- oxidises SO_2 to SO_4^{2-} in acidic medium

$$5SO_2 + 2MnO_4^- + H^+ \rightleftharpoons Mn^{2+} + 5SO_4^{2-}$$

5 mol $SO_2 \equiv 2$ mole MnO_4^-

$\therefore\ (2 - 2x)$ mol

$SO_2 \equiv 0.4\,(2 - 2x)$ mol MnO_4^-

$0.4\,(2 - 2x) = 0.4$ (given)

$\therefore\ x = 0.5$

$\therefore\ [SO_2] = \frac{2-2x}{1} = 1$ mol L^{-1}

$[O_2] = 0.5$ mol L^{-1}

$[SO_3] = 1$ mol L^{-1}

$\therefore\ K_C = 2$

248. Six (6) Decomposition takes place at high temperature but at 298 K, H_2O (g) is condensed to liquid H_2O.

Thus, pressure is due to CO_2 only

$\therefore\ K_p = p^2_{CO_2} = 36$

$\therefore\ p_{CO_2} = 6$ atm

249. **Four (4)**

$$\Delta H = 2.303 \frac{RT_1T_2}{T_2 - T_1} \log \frac{K_2(\text{at } T_2)}{K_1(\text{at } T_1)}$$

$$N_2O_4(g) \rightleftharpoons 2NO_2(g)$$

	$N_2O_4(g)$	$2NO_2(g)$
Initial mol	1	0
At equil.	$(1-\alpha)$	2α

$$\therefore \quad K_p = \frac{4\alpha^2 p}{(1-\alpha^2)}$$

$$K_p\ (300\text{ K}) = \frac{4(0.5)^2\ 1}{(1-0.25)} = \frac{4}{3}$$

$$K_p\ (400\text{ K}) = \frac{4(0.8)^2\ 1}{(1-0.64)} = \frac{64}{9}$$

$$\Delta H = \frac{2.303 \times 2 \times 10^{-3} \times 300 \times 400}{(400-300)} \log \frac{64/9}{4/3}$$

$$= 4.02 \text{ kcal} \approx 4.0 \text{ kcal}$$

250. **Zero (0)**

$$H_2O(l) \rightleftharpoons H^+(aq) + OH^-(aq)$$

$$K_{eq} = K_w = 1 \times 10^{-14} \text{ at } 298 \text{ K}$$

$$\text{and} \Delta G = \Delta G° + 2.303\ RT \log K$$

$$= 79.882 + 2.303 \times 8.3143 \times 10^{-3} \times 298 \log 1 \times 10^{-14}$$

$$= 79.882 - 79.882 = 0.00 \text{ kJ}$$

251. **One (1)** $K_p = K_\chi\ (p)^{\Delta n_g}$

$$\log K_p = \log K_\chi + \Delta n_g \log p$$

$$\frac{\partial}{\partial p}(\log K_p) = \frac{\partial \log K_\chi}{\partial p} + \frac{\partial}{\partial p}(\Delta n_g \log p)$$

$$0 = \frac{\partial \log K_\chi}{\partial p} + \frac{\partial n_g}{p}$$

$$\therefore \quad \frac{\partial \log K_\chi}{\partial p} = -\frac{\Delta n_g}{p}$$

here, $\Delta n_g = 2 - 4 = -2$

$p = 2$ bar

$$\therefore \quad \frac{\partial \log K_\chi}{\partial p} = -\frac{(-2)}{2} = 1$$

252. **Eight (8)** $\Delta G° = -2.303\ RT \log K$

$$6.22 \text{ kJ mol}^{-1} = -2.303 \times 8.314 \times 10^{-3} \text{ kJ mol}^{-1}\text{ K}^{-1} \times 300 \text{ K} \log K$$

$$\therefore \quad \log K = -1.083$$

$$\therefore \quad K = 0.083$$

$$R \rightleftharpoons P$$

$$K = \frac{[R]}{[P]}$$

$$f(P) = \frac{[P]}{[P]+[R]} = \frac{[P]/[R]}{\frac{[P]}{[R]} + \frac{[R]}{[R]}}$$

$$= \frac{K}{K+1} = \frac{0.083}{1.083}$$

$$f(P) = 0.08$$

$$\therefore \quad 100\ f(P) = 8$$

253. **Eight (8)**

$$NH_3(g) \rightleftharpoons \frac{1}{2}N_2(g) + \frac{3}{2}H_2(g)$$

	$NH_3(g)$	$\frac{1}{2}N_2(g)$	$\frac{3}{2}H_2(g)$
Initial	1	0	0 mol
At equil.	$(1-x)$	$\frac{x}{2}$	$\frac{3}{2}x$ mol
Mole fraction	$\frac{1-x}{(1+x)}$	$\frac{x}{2(1+x)}$	$\frac{3x}{2(1+x)}$
Partial pressure	$\frac{(1-x)p}{(1+x)}$	$\frac{xp}{2(1+x)}$	$\frac{3px}{2(1+x)}$

■ Total moles at equilibrium = $(1+x)$

$$K_p = \frac{(p_{N_2})^{1/2}(p_{H_2})^{3/2}}{(p_{NH_3})} = \frac{1.3x^2}{(1-x^2)}$$

$$x = \left(\frac{K_p}{1.3 + K_p}\right)^{1/2} = \frac{0.00782}{(1.3 + 0.00782)} = 0.08$$

Percentage $= 0.08 \times 100 = 8\%$

254. **Four (4)**

$$NH_2COONH_4(s) \rightleftharpoons 2NH_3(g) + CO_2(g)$$

	$NH_2COONH_4(s)$	$2NH_3(g)$	$CO_2(g)$
Initial mol	1	0	0
At equil.	$(1-x)$	$2x$	x
Mole fraction (only gaseous species are taken)		$\frac{2}{3}$	$\frac{1}{3}$
Partial pressure		$\left(\frac{2}{3}p\right)$	$\left(\frac{p}{3}\right)$

$$K_p = p^2_{NH_3}\ p_{CO_2} = \frac{4p^3}{27} = \frac{4(3)^3}{27} = 4$$

255. **(8.93)**

When equal volume are mixed,

$$Fe^{2+}(aq) = 0.03 \text{ M}$$

$$S^{2-}(aq) = 0.1 \text{ M}$$

$$Fe^{2+}(aq) + S^{2-}(aq) \rightleftharpoons FeS(s)$$

	$Fe^{2+}(aq)$	$S^{2-}(aq)$
Initial :	0.06 M	0.2 M
In mixture	0.03 M	0.1 M
Reacted	0.03 M	0.03 M
After reaction	?	(0.10 – 0.03) M = 0.07 M

Since equilibrium exists, hence some $Fe^{2+}(aq)$ remains unreacted

$$\therefore \quad K_C = \frac{1}{[Fe^{2+}][S^{2-}]}$$

$$1.6 \times 10^{17} = \frac{1}{[Fe^{2+}](0.07)}$$

$$\therefore\ [Fe^{2+}(aq)] = 0.07 \times 1.0 \times 10^{17}$$

$$= 8.93 \times 10^{-17}$$

Thus $Y = 8.93$

■ For FeS (s) $\rightleftharpoons Fe^{2+}(aq) + S^{2-}(aq)$

$$K_{SP} = \frac{1}{K_C} = \frac{1}{16 \times 10^{17}}$$

256. **Two (2)**

$$CaCO_3(s) \rightleftharpoons CaO(s) + CO_2(g)$$

$$K_p = p_{CO_2} = 2.105 \text{ atm}$$

$$C(s) + CO_2(g) \rightleftharpoons 2CO(g),\ K_p = 1.9$$

$$K_p = \frac{p^2_{CO}}{p_{CO_2}} = 1.9$$

$$p^2_{CO} = p_{CO_2} \times 1.9 = 2.105 \times 1.9 = 4.0$$

$$\therefore\ p_{CO} = 2.0 \text{ atm}$$

257. **(–8500)**

$$A(g) + B(g) \rightleftharpoons AB(g)$$

$E_a(f)$ activation energy of forward reaction

$E_a(b)$ = activation energy of backward reaction

$$= E_a(f) + 2RT$$

E_a is related to rate constant (k) and pre-exponential factor by Arrhenius equation.

$$K = Ae^{-E_a/RT}$$

$$\therefore \quad K_f = A_f e^{-E_a(f)/RT}$$

$$\text{and} \quad K_b = A_b\ e^{-E_a(b)/RT}$$

At equilibrium : $(\text{rate})_f = (\text{rate})_b$

$$\therefore \quad k_f[A][B] = k_b[AB]$$

$$\therefore \quad K_c = \frac{k_f}{k_b} = \frac{[AB]}{[A][B]}$$

where, K_C is the equilibrium constant.

Also $A_f = 4A_b$

$$K_C = \frac{K_f}{K_b} = \frac{A_f e^{-E_a(f)/RT}}{A_b e^{-E_a(b)/RT}}$$

$$= 4\frac{e^{-E_a(f)/RT}}{e^{-(Ea(f)/2RT)/RT}} = 4e^2$$

$$\Delta G° = -RT \ln K_c = -2500 \ln(4e^2)$$

$$= -2500[\ln 4 + \ln e^2] = -2500\ (2 \ln 2 + 2 \ln e)$$

$$= -2500\,[2 \times 0.7 + 2] = -8500 \text{ J mol}^{-1}$$

Type VI. Matrix Matching

258. (b) For $PCl_5 \rightleftharpoons PCl_3 + Cl_2$

$$K_p = \frac{px^2}{(1-x^2)}$$

$$\therefore \quad x = \sqrt{\frac{K_p}{K_p + p}}$$

$$K_C = \frac{[PCl_3][Cl_2]}{[PCl_5]} = \frac{\left(\frac{2}{10}\right)\left(\frac{2}{10}\right)}{\left(\frac{1}{10}\right)} = 0.4$$

$$\therefore\ \Delta G° = -2.303\ RT \log K_c$$

$$= -1.4 \log 0.4 = +\ 0.56 \text{ kcal mol}^{-1}$$

Thus, (II) - (iii) - (p).

259. (a) $H_2 + I_2 \rightleftharpoons 2HI$

$$K_C = \frac{4x^2}{(1-x)^2}$$

Thus, x is independent of pressure.

$$K_C = \frac{[HI]^2}{[H_2][I_2]} = \frac{\left(\frac{2}{10}\right)^2}{\left(\frac{1}{10}\right)\left(\frac{1}{10}\right)} = 4.0$$

$\therefore \quad \Delta G° = -2.303\ RT \log K_c$
$= -1.4 \log 4$
$= -0.84$ kcal mol^{-1}

Thus, (I)-(iv)-(r).

260. (c) For

$$NH_2COONH_4(s) \rightleftharpoons 2NH_3(g) + CO_2(g)$$

Initial 1 0 0
At equil. $(1-x)$ $2x$ x

$\therefore \quad p_{NH_3} = \frac{2p}{3}$

$p_{CO_2} = \frac{p}{3}$

$\therefore \quad K_p = (p_{NH_3})^2 (p_{CO_2})$

$= \left(\frac{2p}{3}\right)^2\left(\frac{p}{3}\right) = \frac{4p^3}{27}$

$\therefore p = \left(\frac{27}{4}K_p\right)^{1/3} = 3\left(\frac{K_p}{4}\right)^{1/3}$

$K_C = [NH_3]^2[CO_2] = \left(\frac{2}{10}\right)^2\left(\frac{2}{10}\right)^2$

$= \frac{8}{1000} = 0.008$

$\Delta G° = -2.303\ RT \log K_c$
$= -1.4 \log 0.008 = 2.94$ kJ

Thus, (IV)-(i)-(q).

261. (d) Degree of dissociation increases two times of pressure is increased four times, it means

$x \propto \sqrt{p}$

For $2SO_2 + O_2 \rightleftharpoons 2SO_3$

$-x \propto \left(\frac{1}{p}\right)^{\Delta n_g/2}$

$\Delta n_g = -1$

$\therefore \quad x \propto \sqrt{p}$

$$K_C = \frac{[SO_3]^2}{[SO_2]^2[O_2]} = \frac{\left(\frac{2}{10}\right)^2}{\left(\frac{1}{10}\right)^2\left(\frac{1}{10}\right)} = 40$$

$\Delta G° = -2.303\ RT \log K_C$
$= -1.40 \log 40 = -2.24$

Thus, (III)-(ii)-(s).

262. (d) N_2O_4 is diamagnetic and NO_2 is paramagnetic.

$$N_2O_4\ (g) \rightleftharpoons 2NO_2\ (g)$$

$K_p = \frac{4x^2p}{(1-x^2)}$

$\therefore \quad x = \sqrt{\frac{K_p}{4p + K_p}}$

Being endothermic, reaction is favoured at high temperature.

Also, $\Delta n_g = +1$, hence favoured at low pressure.

x (product) $\propto \left(\frac{1}{p}\right)^{\Delta n_g/2} \propto \sqrt{\frac{1}{p}}$

Thus, (I)-(ii)-(r).

263. (b) $PCl_5 \longrightarrow PCl_3 + Cl_2$
$\uparrow$ sp^3d $\quad \uparrow$ sp^3

$K_p = \frac{px^2}{(1-x^2)}$

$\therefore \quad x = \sqrt{\frac{K_p}{p + K_p}}$

Endothermic, $\Delta n_g = +1$

Thus, favoured at low pressure and high temperature.

Thus, (II)-(iii)-(r).

264. (c) CO_2 is non-flammable, CO is flammable

$C(s) + CO_2(g) \longrightarrow 2CO(g)$

$K_p = \frac{4x^2p}{(1-x^2)}$

$\therefore \quad x = \sqrt{\frac{K_p}{4p + K_p}}$

$\Delta n_g = +1$, endothermic

Thus, favoured at low pressure , high temperature.

$\therefore$ (III)-(ii)-(r).

265. (a) N_2, H_2 are odourless gases, NH_3 is pungent in smell,

$N_2 + 3H_2 \rightleftharpoons 2NH_3$

$K_p = \frac{16x^2(2-x)^2}{27(1-x)^4p^2} \approx \frac{64x^2}{27p^2}$

$\therefore \quad x = \frac{p}{8}\sqrt{27K_p}$

$\Delta n_g = -2$, exothermic, thus favoured at high p and low temperature.

Thus, (IV)-(iv)-(q).

266. (b) $\log_{10} K_p = \frac{-\Delta H°}{2.303\ RT} + \frac{\Delta S°}{2.303R}$

Given, $\log_{10} K_p = +\frac{10.560\ K}{T} - 20.281$

On comparison, $\frac{-\Delta H}{2.303R} = 10.56$

$\therefore \Delta H° = -10.56 \times 2.303 \times R$
$= -10.56 \times 2.303 \times 8.314$ J mol^{-1}K^{-1}K
$= -202.19$ J

Thus, (ii) $\rightarrow$ (s).

$\frac{\Delta S°}{2.303R} = -20.281$

$\therefore \Delta S° = -20.281 \times 8.314$ J mol^{-1} K^{-1} $\times 2.303$
$= -388.32$ J mol^{-1}K^{-1}

Thus, (iii) $\rightarrow$ (p).

At 500 K,

$\log_{10} K_p = -20.281 + \frac{10.560}{500} = -20.26$

Thus, (i) $\rightarrow$ (q).

Also, $\Delta G° = \Delta H° - T\Delta S°$
$= -2.303\ RT \log K_p$
$= -2.303 \times 8.314 \times 500 \times (-20.26)$
$= 193.96 \times 10^3$ J

Thus, (iv) $\rightarrow$ (r).

267. (c) $H_2(g) + I_2(g) \rightleftharpoons 2HI(g)$

Initial 0.1 0.1 0 mol
At equil. $(0.1-x)$ $(0.1-x)$ $2x$ mol

Unreacted $I_2 = (0.1-x) = 100$ mL of 0.1 M $Na_2S_2O_3$

$I_2 + 2Na_2S_2O_3 \longrightarrow 2NaI + Na_2S_4O_6$

$\frac{MV(\text{mL})}{1000} = $ mol

$Na_2S_2O_3$ reacted $= \frac{100 \times 0.1}{1000}$ mol
$= 0.01$ mol

2 mol $Na_2S_2O_3 \equiv 1$ mol I_2

$\therefore$ 0.01 mol $Na_2S_2O_3 = \frac{0.01}{2}$
$= 0.005$ mol I_2

Thus, H_2 at equilibrium $= 0.005$ mol

Also, $0.005 = (0.1 - x)$

$\therefore \quad x = 0.095$

$\therefore \quad HI = 2x = 0.095 \times 2 = 0.19$ mol

$K_p = K_C(RT)^{\Delta n_g}$

But $\Delta n_g = 0 \quad \therefore \quad \frac{K_c}{K_p} = 1$

Thus, (i) $\longrightarrow$ (s), (ii) $\longrightarrow$ (p), (iii) $\longrightarrow$ (q), (iv) $\longrightarrow$ (r).

268. (a) Eq. (I) – Eq. (II) $\times$ 3 = Eq. (III)

Thus, $K_p^{III} = \frac{K_p^{I}}{(K_p^{II})^3} = \frac{4.0 \times 10^{-6}}{(3.2 \times 10^{-4})^3}$
$= 1.2207 \times 10^5$

From III, $\left(\frac{p_{CO_2}}{p_{CO}}\right)^3 = 1.2207 \times 10^5$

$\frac{p_{CO_2}}{p_{CO}} = (1.2207 \times 10^5)^{\frac{1}{3}} = 49.606$

$\Rightarrow \quad \frac{p_{CO}}{p_{CO_2}} = 0.02$

From I, $K_p^I = \frac{1}{p_{H_2}^3} = 4.0 \times 10^{-6}$

$\Rightarrow \quad \frac{1}{p_{H_2}} = (4.0 \times 10^{-6})^{\frac{1}{3}} = 0.01587$

$\Rightarrow \quad p_{H_2} = 63.0$ bar

From II, $K_p^{II} = \dfrac{p_{CO}}{p_{CO_2} \cdot p_{H_2}} = 3.2 \times 10^{-4}$

$$\frac{p_{CO}}{p_{H_2}} = 3.2 \times 10^{-4} \times p_{CO_2}$$

$$= 3.2 \times 10^{-4} \times 1 \times 10^{-2}$$

$$= 3.2 \times 10^{-6}$$

Thus, (i) ⟶ (s), (ii) ⟶ (r),
(iii) ⟶ (q), (iv) ⟶ (p)

269. (c) (i) $\Delta_r H^\circ = \dfrac{2.303 RT_1T_2}{T_2 - T_1} \log \dfrac{K_{T_2}}{K_{T_1}}$

$$= \frac{2.303 \times 8.314 \times 10^{-3} \times 2400 \times 2600}{200}$$

$$\log \frac{84.7}{38.4} = 205 \text{ kJ}$$

Thus, (i) – (r)

(ii) $\Delta H^\circ = \dfrac{2.303 RT_1T_2}{(T_2 - T_1)} \log \dfrac{K_{T_2}}{K_{T_1}}$

$$= \frac{2.303 RT_1T_3}{(T_3 - T_1)} \log \frac{K_{T_3}}{K_{T_1}}$$

$$\frac{2600}{200} \log \frac{84.7}{38.4} = \frac{2500}{10.0} \log \frac{K_{T_3}}{38.4}$$

$\therefore \quad \log \dfrac{K_{T_3}}{38.4} = 0.1784 \Rightarrow \dfrac{K_{T_3}}{38.4} = 1.51$

$$K_{T_3} = 57.98 \approx 58.0$$

Thus, (ii) – (p).

(iii) $\Delta G^\circ = -2.303\, RT \log K_{T_3} = -2.303 \times 8.314 \times 10^{-3} \times 2500 \log 58.0$

$$= -84.4 \text{ kJ}$$

$\therefore \; -\Delta G^\circ = 84.4$ kJ

Thus, (iii) – (s).

(iv) $\Delta G^\circ = \Delta H^\circ - T\Delta S^\circ$

$\therefore \; T\Delta S^\circ = \Delta H^\circ - \Delta G^\circ$

$$\Delta S^\circ = \frac{\Delta H^\circ - \Delta G^\circ}{T} = \frac{250 - (-84.4)}{2500}$$

$$= 0.11576 \text{ kJ K}^{-1} = 115.76 \text{ J K}^{-1}$$

$$\approx 116 \text{ JK}^{-1}$$

Thus, (iv) – (q).

270. (c) (i) If pressure is increased by compressing the system without addition of gas from outside, more SO_3 is produced from the combination of SO_2 and O_2 (as K_p is constant).

Also quantity of the product (x)

$$x \propto \left(\frac{1}{p}\right)^{\Delta n_g/2}$$

$$\Delta n_g = -\frac{1}{2}$$

$$x \propto \left(\frac{1}{p}\right)^{-1/4}$$

$\therefore \quad x \propto (p)^4$

Thus, equilibrium is in forward side.

∴ Then (i) ...(p)

(ii) If an inert gas is added at constant volume, both n_{Total} and p increase in the same ratio .

Thus no effect an equilibrium

Then (ii) ...(r)

(iii) If an inert gas is added at constant pressure n_{Total} is increased while p remains constant.

Thus, extent of conversion of SO_2 and O_2 to SO_3 decreases and equilibrium is displaced in backward side.

Thus, (iii) ...(q)

(iv) Since reaction is exothermic, hence by Le-chatelier's principle, increase in temperature displaces equilibrium in backward side.

Thus, (iv) ...(q)

Ionic Equilibrium

Chapter Topics
- Acids and Bases
- pH-Scale
- Ostwald's Dilution Law
- Buffer Solutions
- Hydrolysis of Salts
- Common Ion Effect and Solubility Product
- Indicators—Their Use in Acid-Base Titrations

Acids and Bases

The Arrhenius concept

- An acid is a substance which ionises in water to produce H^+ ion (or the hydronium, H_3O^+ ion).

$$\underset{\text{Acid}}{HA(aq)} \rightleftharpoons H^+(aq) + A^-(aq)$$

H^+ ion is a proton and is hydrated to give H_3O^+.

$$H^+(aq) + H_2O(l) \rightleftharpoons H_3O^+(aq)$$

- A base is a substance which ionises in water to produce OH^- ion.

$$\underset{\text{Base}}{BOH(aq)} \rightleftharpoons B^+(aq) + OH^-(aq)$$

- Equilibrium established between ionised and non-ionised species is called **ionic equilibrium** and is set up in species that are weakly ionised in their solutions. Such substances are called **weak electrolytes** (NH_4OH, CH_3COOH etc).
- The substances that are ionised almost completely in aqueous solutions are called **strong electrolytes** (HCl, KOH, KCl, etc).

α **(degree of ionisation of weak electrolyte)**

$$= \frac{\textbf{amount of ionised}}{\textbf{amount taken}}$$

If 0.02 mole of CH_3COOH is ionised out of 2 moles taken then $\alpha = \frac{0.02}{2.0} = 0.01$.

Thus, 1% ionisation.

- The reaction product of an acid and a base is called a **salt.**

$$HCl + NaOH \longrightarrow NaCl + H_2O$$

- A neutralisation reaction involves the combination of H^+ and OH^- ions to form H_2O.

$$H^+(aq) + OH^-(aq) \rightleftharpoons H_2O\ (l)$$

Limitations of Arrhenius Concept

- Restricted to aqueous solution.
- Not applicable to substances that do not contain OH^- ion but are basic in aqueous solution (CaO, BaO, NH_3).

$$CaO + H_2O \longrightarrow \underset{\text{Basic}}{Ca(OH)_2}$$

- Not applicable to substances that do not contain H^+ ion but are acidic in aqueous solution (CO_2, SO_3, SO_2).

$$SO_3 + H_2O \longrightarrow H_2SO_4$$

The Bronsted-Lowry protonic concepts

(Proton transfer theory)

- An acid is a proton donor and a base is a proton acceptor.
- HCl, HNO_3, CH_3COOH, etc., are **acids** as they furnish H^+ ion in aqueous solution.

$$HCl \longrightarrow H^+ + Cl^-$$

$$HNO_3 \longrightarrow H^+ + NO_3^-$$

$$CH_3COOH \longrightarrow H^+ + CH_3COO^-$$

- Cl^-, NO_3^- and CH_3COO^- ions are now proton acceptor and, thus are **bases**.

$$Cl^- + H^+ \longrightarrow HCl$$

$$NO_3^- + H^+ \longrightarrow HNO_3$$

All bases accept protons and there is no need for them to contain OH^- ions.

- For a molecule or ion to accept a proton, it must have at least one unshared pair of electrons that it can use for bonding to proton.

$$H-\ddot{\underset{|}{O}}{:}\ + H^+ \longrightarrow H_3O^+$$
$$\quad H$$

Conjugate acid-base pairs

Chemical species that differ in composition by a single proton are called '**conjugate pair**'.

$$\underset{\text{Acid}}{HCl} \underset{H^+\text{ gained}}{\overset{H^+\text{ lost}}{\rightleftarrows}} \underset{\text{Base}}{Cl^-}$$

Acid is converted into a base by loss of H^+ and Cl^- is converted into acid by gain of H^+ ion.

HCl and Cl^- differ by a proton and such acid-base pair formed by exchange of H^+ ion is called conjugate **acid-base pair**.

$$\underset{\substack{\text{Acid}_1\\(H^+\text{ ion donor})}}{HA} + \underset{\substack{\text{Base}_2\\(H^+\text{ ion acceptor})}}{B} \rightleftharpoons \underset{\substack{\text{Acid}_2\\(H^+\text{ ion donor})}}{BH^+} + \underset{\substack{\text{Base}_1\\(H^+\text{ ion}\\\text{acceptor})}}{A^-}$$

Conjugate acid-base pair

Amphiprotic species

Species (as water) which can donate proton (thus act as acids) and can also accept proton (thus act as bases) are called **amphiprotic species.**

In the following reaction, H_2O is a base.

$$\underset{\text{Acid}_1}{CH_3COOH} + \underset{\text{Base}_2}{H_2O} \rightleftharpoons \underset{\text{Acid}_2}{H_3O^+} + \underset{\text{Base}_1}{CH_3COO^-}$$

and in the following reaction, it is an acid.

$$\underset{\text{Base}_1}{NH_3} + \underset{\text{Acid}_2}{H_2O} \rightleftharpoons \underset{\text{Base}_2}{OH^-} + \underset{\text{Acid}_1}{NH_4^+}$$

$$\underset{\text{Acid}_1}{H_2O} + \underset{\text{Base}_2}{H_2O} \rightleftharpoons \underset{\text{Acid}_2}{H_3O^+} + \underset{\text{Base}_1}{OH^-}$$

$$\underset{\text{Base}_1}{NH_3} + \underset{\text{Acid}_2}{NH_3} \rightleftharpoons \underset{\text{Base}_2}{NH_2^-} + \underset{\text{Acid}_1}{NH_4^+}$$

$$\underset{\text{Base (Proton acceptor)}}{HCO_3^-} + H_2O \rightleftharpoons H_2CO_3 + OH^-$$

$$\underset{\text{Acid (Proton donor)}}{HCO_3^-} + H_2O \rightleftharpoons CO_3^{2-} + H_3O^+$$

- Amphoteric species are different from amphiprotic species. Amphoteric species are soluble in alkali and acids both.

(i) $Al_2O_3 + 2NaOH \longrightarrow 2NaAlO_2 + H_2O$

(ii) $Al_2O_3 + 6HCl \longrightarrow 2AlCl_3 + 3H_2O$

In (i), Al_2O_3 is soluble in NaOH, thus it is an acidic oxide.

In (ii), Al_2O_3 is soluble in HCl, thus is a basic oxide.

Factors affecting acid strength

- **Bond strength and electronegativity** When strength of H—*A* bond decreases i.e. the energy required to break the bond decreases, *HA* becomes a stronger acid. Also, when the *HA* bond becomes more polar i.e. electronegativity difference between the atoms H and *A* increases and there is marked charge separation, cleavage of the bond becomes easier thereby increasing the acidic strength.

	H—F	H—Cl	H—Br	H—I
Bond strength ←	max			
Acid strength →				max

	C	N	O	F (max)
Electronegativity →				
	CH_4	NH_3	H_2O	HF (max)
Acid strength →				

- **Four factors which affect the acidity of H—*A*.**

(i) Elements effects (ii) Inductive effects
(iii) Resonance effects (iv) Hybridisation effects

In case of $H^+—X^-$ (X = F, Cl, Br, I), size of X^- increases down the group. As size of X^- increases, stability of X^- also increases in the order :

$$F^- < Cl^- < Br^- < I^-$$

Thus, acid strength increases in the order

$$HF < HCl < HBr < HI$$

- Size and not the electronegativity determines acidity as we move down a column. In case of acids along a period. i.e.

	C N O F
Electronegativity	Increases →
Tendency to withdraw shared bonding electrons	Increases →
Ionisation of H—*A*	Increases →
Acid strength	$CH_4 < NH_3 < H_2O < HF$ →

- **For oxoacids**

HOI < HOBr < HOCl (based on electronegativity)

$\underset{+1}{HClO} < \underset{+3}{HClO_2} < \underset{+5}{HClO_3} < \underset{+7}{HClO_4}$ (based on number of O-atoms or oxidation number of central atom)

Greater the number of O-atoms, greater the delocalisation of negative charge of and, thus higher the stability of the ion. Thus, strength acid is increased.

Lewis acids and Lewis bases

Lewis acid is an electron deficient species (duplet or octet incomplete) in the form of ion or molecule and can accept a pair of electrons in the formation of coordinate bond and, thus duplet or octet is completed. They are also called **electrophiles** (electron-loving).

BF_3 (one electron pair short in B)
$AlCl_3$ (one electron pair short in Al)
H^+ (one electron pair short in H^+)

- Neutral molecules with vacant *d*-orbitals can accept a pair of electrons thus are Lewis acids (PCl_3, PCl_5, SF_4, $ZnCl_2$, etc).
- If central atom is bonded to more electronegative atom by multiple bonds, are Lewis acids (CO_2, CH_3COCH_3).

Lewis base is an electron rich species (have unshared electron pair) and can donate electrons to electron-deficient species (Lewis acid). These are also called **nucleophiles** (nucleus-loving).

NH_3 one pair of extra electrons
H_2O two pairs of extra electrons

- Electron-pair is always transferred from nucleophiles to electrophiles.

$\underset{\text{Nucleophile (Lewis base)}}{H_3N:} \longrightarrow \underset{\text{Electrophile (Lewis acid)}}{H^+}$ or $[H_3N \rightarrow H]^+$

Coordinate bond joining Lewis base to Lewis acid

- All Lewis bases are Bronsted-Lowry bases and *vice-versa*.

Thus, NH_3 is a Lewis base as it is lone-pair donor and NH_3 is also Bronsted-Lowry base as it accepts H^+ ion.

Strength of Lewis acids and Lewis Bases

- Greater the nuclear charge on the central atom, larger is Lewis acidic strength ($Li^+ < Be^{2+} < B^{3+}$).
- More the number of electronegative atoms attached, more is the acidic strength $HClO_4 > HClO_3 > HClO_2$.
- Larger the positive charge on the ion, greater is its Lewis strength.

Thus, $Fe^{3+} > Fe^{2+} > Fe$ and $Sn^{4+} > Sn^{2+}$

- If charges are same on two or more species, acidic strength increases as size decreases.

Li^+ Na^+ K^+ → Size increases
← Lewis acid strength (Max)

- Smaller the size of the central atom, smaller the tendency to donate electron-pair, hence smaller the Lewis base strength.

For	NH_3, PH_3, AsH_3, SbH_3, BiH_3
size of central atom	N < P < As < Sb < Bi
Lewis base strength	NH_3 PH_3 AsH_3 SbH_3 BiH_3 → (Max)

- Also if acid is weak, its conjugate base is strong.

HF < HCl < HBr < HI (Max) → Acidic strength
(Max) $F^- > Cl^- > Br^- > I^-$ ← Lewis base

Ionisation constants of acids and bases

Strength of an acid or a base is expressed in terms of dissociation constant or ionisation constant.

For an acid $HA \rightleftharpoons H^+ + A^-$

K_a (dissociation constant of an acid) $= \dfrac{[H^+][A^-]}{[HA]}$

For a base $A^- + H_2O \rightleftharpoons HA + OH^-$

K_b (dissociation constant of a base) $= \dfrac{[HA][OH^-]}{[A^-]}$

(HA and A^-) is a conjugate acid-base pair.

Thus, for a conjugate acid-base pair, K_a(for an acid) K_b(for its conjugate base) $= [H^+][OH^-]$.

$$\therefore \quad \boxed{K_aK_b = [H^+][OH^-] = K_w}$$

K_w is called ionic-product of water (refer next part).

An acid-base reaction is favoured in the direction from **(stronger acid + stronger base) to (weaker base + weaker acid) or from (stronger H^+ ion donor + stronger H^+ ion acceptor) to (weaker H^+ ion donor + weaker H^+ ion acceptor).**

Ionic product of water

H_2O is amphiprotic

$$\underset{\text{Acid}}{H_2O(l)} \rightleftharpoons H^+(aq) + OH^-$$

$$\underset{\text{Base}}{H_2O(l)} + H^+(aq) \rightleftharpoons H_3O^+(aq)$$

Thus, $H_2O(l) + H_2O(l) \rightleftharpoons H_3O^+(aq) + OH^-(aq)$

$$\therefore K_C \text{ (equilibrium constant)} = \frac{[H_3O^+][OH^-]}{[H_2O]^2}$$

or $$K_C = \frac{[H_3O^+][OH^-]}{[H_2O][H_2O]}$$

$$K_C[H_2O] = \frac{[H_3O^+][OH^-]}{[H_2O]}$$

At 298 K, $[H_3O^+] = [OH^-] = 1 \times 10^{-7}$ M

and $[H_2O] = 1 \text{ g mL}^{-1} = 1000 \text{ g L}^{-1} = \frac{1000}{18} = 55.55 \text{ mol L}^{-1}$

If H_2O is an acid, $K_a = \frac{[H^+][OH^-]}{[H_2O]}$

$$K_a = \frac{1 \times 10^{-14}}{55.55} = 1.8 \times 10^{-16} \text{ (for } H_2O)$$

As, $[H_2O]$ remains constant

$$K_a[55.55] = 1 \times 10^{-14}$$

$$K_w = [H^+][OH^-] = 1 \times 10^{-14} \text{ at 298 K.}$$

K_w is called **ionic-product** of water or **autoionisation constant** or **autoprotolysis constant** of water.

On increasing the temperature, ionisation increases, hence K_w also increases with increasing temperature, but in all cases

$$[H^+] = [OH^-] = \sqrt{K_w}$$

This type of autoprotolysis constant can be taken for any amphiprotic solvent.

$$NH_3 + NH_3 \longrightarrow NH_4^+ + NH_2^-$$

$$K_{solv} = [NH_4^+][NH_2^-]$$

$$2CH_3COOH \rightleftharpoons CH_3COO^- + CH_3COOH_2^+$$

$$K_{solv} = [CH_3COO^-][CH_3COOH_2^+]$$

$[H_3O^+]$ and $[OH^-]$ in a mixture

- **In a mixture of strong acids**

$$[H_3O^+] = \frac{\Sigma NV}{\Sigma V} = \frac{N_1V_1 + N_2V_2 + \ldots}{V_1 + V_2 + \ldots}$$

- **In a mixture of strong bases**

$$[OH^-] = \frac{\Sigma NV}{\Sigma V}$$

- **In a mixture of strong acid and strong base**

(i) If N_1V_1 (acid) $= N_2V_2$ (base)

mixture is neutral, $[H_3O^+] = [OH^-] = 1 \times 10^{-7}$ M

(ii) If N_1V_1 (acid) $> N_2V_2$ (base)

mixture is acidic, $[H_3O^+]_{mix} = \frac{N_1V_1 - N_2V_2}{(V_1 + V_2)}$

(iii) If N_1V_1 (acid) $< N_2V_2$ (base)

mixture is basic, $[OH^-]_{mix} = \left(\frac{N_2V_2 - N_1V_1}{V_1 + V_2}\right)$

Solved Examples & Instant Practice

Example 8.1) In the following acid-base reactions, identify acid and base in terms of Bronsted-Lowry concept. Also, label conjugate acid-base pair.

(a) $CH_3NH_2 + H_2O \rightleftharpoons OH^- + CH_3\overset{+}{N}H_3$

(b) $HCO_3^- + OH^- \rightleftharpoons H_2O + CO_3^{2-}$

(c) $HCO_3^- + HCl \rightleftharpoons Cl^- + H_2CO_3$

H^+ ion donor is a Bronsted-Lowry acid and H^+ ion acceptor is a Bronsted-Lowry base. Species formed by exchange of H^+ ion are conjugate acid-base pairs. Acid is converted into conjugate base and base is converted to conjugate acid.

Sol.

(a)

$$CH_3NH_2 + H_2O \rightleftharpoons OH^- + CH_3\overset{+}{N}H_3$$

CH_3NH_2: H^+ ion acceptor (base$_2$); H_2O: H^+ ion donor (acid$_1$); OH^-: (Base$_1$); $CH_3\overset{+}{N}H_3$: (Acid$_2$)

(b) $\underset{\text{Acid}_1}{HCO_3^-} + \underset{\text{Base}_2}{OH^-} \rightleftharpoons \underset{\text{Acid}_2}{H_2O} + \underset{\text{Base}_1}{CO_3^{2-}}$

HCO_3^- donates a proton, thus it is an acid. OH^- accepts a proton, thus it is a base.

HCO_3^- changes to CO_3^{2-} (conjugate base) and OH^- changes to H_2O (conjugate acid).

(c) $\underset{Base_2}{HCO_3^-} + \underset{Acid_1}{HCl} \rightleftharpoons \underset{Base_1}{Cl^-} + \underset{Acid_2}{H_2CO_3}$

HCl (H^+ ion donor) is converted to Cl^- (a conjugate base) and HCO_3^- (H^+ ion acceptor) is a base and is converted to H_2CO_3 (a conjugate acid).

■ HCO_3^- is thus amphiprotic, being H^+ ion donor in (b) and H^+ ion acceptor in (c).

Immediate Test 1

In the following reactions, select conjugate acid-base pair.

(a) $HCO_3^- + H_2O \longrightarrow CO_3^{2-} + H_3O^+$

(b) $CH_3COOH + NH_3 \longrightarrow NH_4^+ + CH_3COO^-$

(c) $HSO_4^- + H_2O \longrightarrow H_3O^+ + SO_4^{2-}$

(d) $HSO_4^- + H_2O \longrightarrow OH^- + H_2SO_4$

Example 8.2) If you mix equal concentration of reactants and products which of the following reactions proceed to the right and which proceed to the left?

(a) $HI(aq) + OH^-(aq) \rightleftharpoons H_2O(l) + I^-(aq)$

(b) $HCO_3^-(aq) + Br^-(aq) \rightleftharpoons HBr(aq) + CO_3^{2-}(aq)$

A Bronsted-Lowry acid-base reaction is always favoured in the direction from the stronger to the weaker acid/base combination.

Sol.

(a)

$$\underset{\text{Strong acid}}{HI(aq)} + \underset{\text{Strong base}}{OH^-(aq)} \rightleftharpoons \underset{\text{Weak acid}}{H_2O(l)} + \underset{\text{Weak base}}{I^-(aq)}$$

HI is the strongest acid of the HX family thus, I^- is the weakest conjugate base.

If H_2O is a weak acid (very feebly ionised), OH^- is a stronger base. Thus, reaction (a) is spontaneous in forward side, as going from stronger acid-base combination to weaker acid-base combination.

(b) $\underset{\substack{Acid_1\\ weak}}{HCO_3^-(aq)} + \underset{\substack{Base_2\\ weak}}{Br^-(aq)} \rightleftharpoons \underset{\substack{Acid_2\\ strong}}{HBr(aq)} + \underset{\substack{Base_1\\ strong}}{CO_3^{2-}(aq)}$

This reaction proceeds towards left.

HBr is a stronger acid, thus its conjugate base (Br^-) is weak base. HCO_3^- is a weak acid and its conjugate base (CO_3^{2-}) is a weak base.

Immediate Test 2

(i) Predict the direction of the following equilibria:

(a) $HCl(aq) + H_2O(l) \longrightarrow H_3O^+(aq) + Cl^-(aq)$

(b) $HF(aq) + H_2O(l) \longrightarrow H_3O^+(aq) + F^-(aq)$

(c) $O^{2-}(aq) + H_2O(l) \longrightarrow OH^-(aq) + OH^-(aq)$

(d) $H_2SO_4(aq) + NH_3(aq) \longrightarrow NH_4^+(aq) + HSO_4^-(aq)$

(e) $HCO_3^-(aq) + SO_4^{2-}(aq) \longrightarrow HSO_4^-(aq) + CO_3^{2-}(aq)$

(ii) CH_3COOH is a proton donor and $C_2H_5O^-$ is a proton acceptor. In which direction, following equilibrium is favoured?

$CH_3COOH + C_2H_5O^- \rightleftharpoons CH_3COO^- + C_2H_5OH$

Example 8.3) Compare the acid strength of H_3PO_2, H_3PO_3 and H_3PO_4.

Sol. In the oxyacids with same central atom, comparison is based on:

Rule I Greater the number of oxygen atoms attached to central atom, greater the acid strength.

Rule II Greater the oxidation number of the central atom, greater the acid strength.

	H_3PO_2	H_3PO_3	H_3PO_4
Rule I	Two O-atoms attached to P	Three O-atoms attached to P	Four O-atoms attached to P
Rule II	O.N of P = +1	O.N. of P = +3	O.N. of P = +5

Thus, acid-strength is $H_3PO_2 < H_3PO_3 < H_3PO_4$.

■ H attached to P directly indicates reducing behaviour. Thus, reducing behaviour :
$H_3PO_2 > H_3PO_3 > H_3PO_4$ (none)
O.N. of H = 1 and that of O is –2.

Immediate Test 3

(i) Compare the basic strength of NO_2^- and NO_3^-.

(ii) Compare the acidic strength of H_2SO_4 and H_2SO_3.

Example 8.4) Identify Lewis acids and Lewis bases in the following reactions.

(a) $SO_3 + H_2O \longrightarrow H_2SO_4$

(b) $CO_2 + H_2O \longrightarrow H_2CO_3$

(c) $Cu^{2+} + 4NH_3 \longrightarrow [Cu(NH_3)_4]^{2+}$

(d) $Ni + 4CO \longrightarrow Ni(CO)_4$

(e) $C_6H_6 + CH_3Cl \xrightarrow{AlCl_3} C_6H_5CH_3 + HCl$

Lone-pair acceptor (electron deficient) is a Lewis acid and lone-pair donor (electron rich) is a Lewis base.

Sol.

	Lewis acid	Lewis base
(a)	SO_3	H_2O
(b)	CO_2	H_2O
(c)	Cu^{2+}	NH_3
(d)	Ni	CO
(e)	$AlCl_3$	CH_3Cl

NH_3 (Lewis base) is coordinated to Cu^{2+} (Lewis acid).

$$\left[\begin{array}{ccc} & NH_3 & \\ & \downarrow & \\ NH_3 \longrightarrow & Cu & \longleftarrow NH_3 \\ & \uparrow & \\ & NH_3 & \end{array}\right]^{2+}$$

Similarly, in $Ni(CO)_4$

- $CH_3Cl + AlCl_3 \longrightarrow AlCl_4^- + \overset{+}{C}H_3$

$\overset{+}{C}H_3$ causes replacement of H of benzene in electrophilic substitution reaction.

Immediate Test 4

(i) Identify Lewis acids and Lewis bases in the following reactions.

(a) $CO_2 + OH^- \longrightarrow HCO_3^-$

(b) $B(OH)_3 + OH^- \longrightarrow B(OH)_4^-$

(c) $AlCl_3 + Cl^- \longrightarrow AlCl_4^-$

(d) $Cr^{3+} + 6H_2O \longrightarrow [Cr(H_2O)_6]^{3+}$

(ii) Out of the following :

$H_2PO_4^-$, SO_3^{2-}, ClO^-, Fe^{3+} and BCl_3 select

(a) Bronsted-Lowry acid (b) Bronsted-Lowry base

(c) Lewis acid (d) Lewis base

Example 8.5) Ionisation constant of HCN is 4.9×10^{-10} at 298 K. Calculate ionisation constant of CN^-.

HA and A^- is a conjugate acid-base pair.
If ionisation constant of weak acid is K_a, then ionisation of its conjugate base is

$$K_b = \frac{K_w}{K_a} = \frac{1 \times 10^{-14}}{K_a}$$

Sol. Conjugate base of a weak acid is a source of OH^- in aqueous solution.

I. $HCN + H_2O \rightleftharpoons H_3O^+ + CN^-$ II. $CN^- + H_2O \rightleftharpoons HCN + OH^-$

From I : $K_a = \dfrac{[CN^-][H_3O^+]}{[HCN]}$

From II : $K_b = \dfrac{[HCN][OH^-]}{[CN^-]}$

$\therefore$ $K_a K_b = [H_3O^+][OH^-] = K_w$

$K_a(HCN) = 4.9 \times 10^{-10}$ at 298 K

$$K_b = \frac{K_w}{K_a} \quad \therefore \quad K_b(CN^-) = \frac{1.0 \times 10^{-14}}{4.9 \times 10^{-10}} = 2.041 \times 10^{-5}$$

Immediate Test 5

(i) Ionisation constant of CH_3COOH is 1.8×10^{-5}. Calculate ionisation constant of

$$CH_3COO^- + H_2O \rightleftharpoons CH_3COOH + OH^-$$

(ii) For the equilibrium

$$(CH_3)_3NH^+ + H_2O \rightleftharpoons (CH_3)_3N + H_3O^+$$

ionisation constant is 1.54×10^{-10}. Calculate ionisation constant of

$$(CH_3)_3N + H_2O \rightleftharpoons (CH_3)_3\overset{\oplus}{N}H + OH^-$$

Example 8.6) 100 mL of 0.01 M H_2SO_4 is mixed with 100 mL of $Ca(OH)_2$ solution giving resultant (OH^-) in the mixture equal to 5×10^{-3} M. What is the molar concentration of $Ca(OH)_2$ in the original solution?

Sol. If an acid is mixed with a base, the resultant solution will be acidic, basic or neutral, depending on the number of moles of acid and base.

Also, $\dfrac{M(\text{Molarity}) \times \text{volume (mL)}}{1000} = \text{mol}$

If acid and base differ in number of H^+ and OH^-, then number of moles of acid and base should be converted to number of H^+ and OH^-.

1 mol HCl ≡ 1 mol H^+, 1 mol $Ca(OH)_2$ ≡ 2 mol OH^-

1 M $Ca(OH)_2$ = 2N (OH^-), 1 M H_2SO_4 ≡ 2N (H^+)

If $Ca(OH)_2 = M_1$ (molarity) then, $Ca(OH)_2 = 2M_1$ (normality)

H_2SO_4 = 0.01 M = 0.02 N

$$\text{Resultant } [OH^-] = \frac{N_1V_1(\text{base}) - N_2V_2(\text{acid})}{V_1 + V_2}$$

$$5 \times 10^{-3} = \frac{2M_1 \times 100 - 0.02 \times 100}{200} \Rightarrow M_1 = 0.015\,M$$

Immediate Test 6

What is the normality of the resulting solutions (acidic/basic/neutral), when following solutions are mixed?

I. 0.1 M H_2SO_4 II. 0.1 M HCl

III. 0.1 M $Ca(OH)_2$ IV. 0.1 M NaOH

(a) I and II in 1:1 volume (b) I and II in 1:2 volume

(c) I and IV in 1:2 volume (d) I and III in 1:1 volume

(e) II and III in 1:1 volume (f) II and III in 2:1 volume

(g) II and IV in 1:2 volume

Example 8.7) Self-ionisation constant for pure formic acid is 10^{-6} at 298 K. What percentage of formic acid molecules in pure formic acid, HCOOH are converted to formate ion? Density of formic acid is 1.22 g cm^{-3}.

A protic solvent as H_2O, NH_3, etc. undergoes self-ionisation giving a cation (by gain of proton) and an anion (by loss of proton).

$$2HCOOH \rightleftharpoons HCOO^- + HCOOH_2^+$$

$$K_{solv} = [HCOO^-][HCOOH_2] = 1 \times 10^{-6}$$

Since, $[HCOO^-] = [HCOO\overset{+}{H}_2] = \sqrt{1 \times 10^{-6}}$

thus, $[HCOO^-]$ *is known. From density, molar concentration of* HCOOH *is calculated and thus percentage of* $HCOO^-$ *in* HCOOH.

Sol. $[HCOOH] = 1.22\text{ g cm}^{-3} = 1.22 \times 10^3 \text{ g L}^{-1}$

$$= \frac{1.22 \times 10^3 \text{ g L}^{-1}}{46 \text{ g mol}^{-1}} = 26.52 \text{ mol L}^{-1}$$

$[HCOO^-][HCOOH_2^+] = K_{solv} = 1 \times 10^{-6}$

$\therefore$ $[HCOO^-] = [HCOOH_2^+] = \sqrt{1 \times 10^{-6}} = 1 \times 10^{-3}$ M

Fraction of $HCOO^-$ in HCOOH $= \dfrac{1 \times 10^{-3}}{26.52}$

% of HCOOH converted to $HCOO^-$ $= \dfrac{1 \times 10^{-3}}{26.52} \times 100 = 3.77 \times 10^{-3}\%$

Immediate Test 7

Self-ionisation constant for water is 10^{-14} at 298 K. Density of water at 298 K is 1000 kg m^{-3}. Calculate percentage of $[H_3O^+]$ in water.

KNOWLEDGE CONFIRMATION Test 1

1 Electronegativity (EN) values of

$$\underset{2.5}{C}\quad\underset{3.0}{N}\quad\underset{3.5}{O}\quad\underset{4.0}{F}\longrightarrow$$

Thus, strongest conjugate base is

(a) CH_3^- (b) NH_2^- (c) OH^- (d) F^-

2 H—*X* bond strength of halogen acids are

	H—F	H—Cl	H—Br	H—I
kJ mol^{-1}	567	431	366	299

Strongest acid and strongest conjugate base are respectively

(a) H—F, I^- (b) H—I, F^- (c) H—I, I^- (d) H—F, F^-

3 In which case, I is stronger Lewis acid than II

	I	II
(a)	BH_3	BF_3
(b)	SO_3	SO_2
(c)	Sn^{2+}	Sn^{4+}
(d)	CH_4	$\overset{+}{C}H_3$

4 Which is the strongest acid?

(a) $HBrO_3$ (b) $HBrO_2$ (c) HBrO (d) $HBrO_4$

5 CH_3COOH is a weak acid in aqueous solution but is a strong acid in

(a) HF (b) NH_3 (c) H_2O (d) HNO_3

6 100 mL of 2 M HCl is mixed with 200 mL of 1 M HCl. Hence, resultant $[Cl^-]$ is

(a) 3.0 M (b) 1.5 M (c) 1.33 M (d) 2.66 M

7 $[H_3O^+]$ in 0.5 M H_2SO_4 is

(a) 1.0 M (b) 0.5 M (c) 0.25 M (d) 1.5 M

8 In aqueous solution, HCl exists as

(a) Cl^- (b) H_3O^+ (c) HCl^- (d) $H_3O^+Cl^-$

9 Conjugate bases of H_2 and HO_2^- are respectively

(a) H^+, O_2^{2-} (b) H^-, O_2^{2-} (c) H_3^+, H_2O_2 (d) H^+, H_2O_2

10 Strongest acid-base pair is

(a) H_3O^+, H_2O (b) H_3O^+, OH^- (c) H_2O, H_3O^+ (d) OH^-, H_3O^+

11 A carbocation ($\overset{\oplus}{C}H_3$) is

(a) a Lewis acid (b) an electrophilic reagent
(c) Both (a) and (b) (d) None of these

12 Out of

I. $\overset{-}{C}H_3$ (carbanion); II. $\overset{\oplus}{C}H_5$ (carbonium ion)

III. $\overset{\oplus}{C}H_3$ (carbenium ion)

Lewis acid can be

(a) II, III (b) I, III (c) I, II (d) III

13 Relative strength cannot be compared in aqueous solution of the following pair :

(a) $HClO_4$ and HBr (b) $HClO_4$ and HNO_3
(c) H_2SO_4 and HNO_3 (d) All of these

14 For HPO_4^{2-} and NH_4^+, select the correct statement(s).

(a) Both behave as Bronsted-Lowry acid
(b) HPO_4^{2-} is a Lewis base as well as Bronsted-Lowry base
(c) HPO_4^{2-} is amphiprotic
(d) All of the above are correct

15 Out of $NaH_2PO_2, Na_2HPO_3, NaHCO_3, Na_2HPO_4$ and NaH_2PO_4 acid salts is/are

(a) all except $NaHCO_3$
(b) all except NaH_2PO_2, Na_2HPO_3
(c) all except $NaH_2PO_2, Na_2HPO_3, Na_2HPO_4$
(d) All are acid salts

16 Consider the following reactions:

I. $\underset{A}{[Al(OH)_3(H_2O)_3]} + H_3O^+ \rightleftharpoons [Al(OH)_2(H_2O)_4]^+ + H_2O$

II. $\underset{A}{[Al(OH)_3(H_2O)_3]} + OH^- \rightleftharpoons [Al(OH)_4(H_2O)_2]^- + H_2O$

Select the correct statement.

(a) *A* is a base in I and *A* is an acid in II.
(b) *A* is an acid in I and *A* is a base in II.
(c) *A* is a base in I and II both.
(d) *A* is an acid in I and II both.

17 For the following reactions, dissociation constant (DC) < 0 (proceeding in forward side).

$$CH_3COOH + H_2O \rightleftharpoons CH_3COO^- + H_3O^+$$
$$CH_3COOH + HF \rightleftharpoons F^- + CH_3COOH_2^+$$
$$HNO_2 + HF \rightleftharpoons H_2F^+ + NO_2^-$$

Thus, increasing order of K_a values of the acids is

(a) $H_2O < CH_3COOH < HF < HNO_2$
(b) $H_2O < CH_3COOH < HNO_2 < HF$
(c) $H_2O < HF < CH_3COOH < HNO_2$
(d) $HNO_2 < HF < CH_3COOH < HF$

18 For the reaction,

$$\underset{A}{[Al(H_2O)_6]^{3+}} + \underset{B}{HCO_3^-} \rightleftharpoons \underset{C}{[Al(H_2O)_5OH]^{2+}} + \underset{D}{H_2CO_3}$$

A, *B*, *C*, *D* are designated as

	A	B	C	D
(a)	$(acid)_1$	$(base)_1$	$(acid)_2$	$(base)_2$
(b)	$(acid)_1$	$(base)_2$	$(base)_1$	$(acid)_2$
(c)	$(acid)_1$	$(base)_1$	$(base)_2$	$(acid)_2$
(d)	$(base)_1$	$(base)_2$	$(acid)_1$	$(acid)_2$

19 For the equilibrium,

$$H_2PO_4^- + H_2O \rightleftharpoons HPO_4^{2-} + H_3O^+$$

equilibrium constant is K_1, and for the equilibrium

$$HPO_4^{2-} + H_2O \rightleftharpoons H_2PO_4^- + OH^-$$

equilibrium constant is K_2, then

(a) $K_1K_2 = K_w$ (b) $\frac{K_1}{K_2} = K_w$ (c) $K_1K_2K_w = 1$ (d) $\frac{K_2}{K_1} = K_w$

20 For the successive ionisation of H_3PO_4, ionisation constants are given

$H_3PO_4 + H_2O \rightleftharpoons H_2PO_4^- + H_3O^+, K_1$

$H_2PO_4^- + H_2O \rightleftharpoons HPO_4^{2-} + H_3O^+, K_2$

$HPO_4^{2-} + H_2O \rightleftharpoons PO_4^{3-} + H_3O^+, K_3$

and overall, $H_3PO_4 + 3H_2O \longrightarrow PO_4^{3-} + 3H_3O^+, K$ then

(a) $K = K_1 + K_2 + K_3$ (b) $K = K_1K_2K_3$
(c) $K = (K_1K_2K_3)^{-1}$ (d) $K = (K_1 + K_2 + K_3)^{-1}$

21 Density of CH_3CH_2OH is 0.920 g cm^{-3}. If $CH_3CH_2O^-$ content is 1.35×10^{-5} g dm^{-3}, ion product $[CH_3CH_2O^-][CH_3CH_2OH_2^+]$ is

(a) 1.82×10^{-10} (b) 9×10^{-14}
(c) 1.35×10^{-5} (d) 3×10^{-7}

22 At 220 K, ion product of NH_3 is 1×10^{-30}. Thus, number of NH_4^+ ions present per dm^3 of pure liquid ammonia is

(a) 1.0×10^{-15} (b) 6.0×10^{8}
(c) 6.0×10^{-8} (d) 6.0×10^{-7}

23 In the formation of $S_2O_3^{2-}$ from S and SO_3^{2-},

(a) S is Lewis base and SO_3^{2-} is a Lewis acid
(b) S is Lewis base as well as Lewis acid
(c) S is Lewis acid and SO_3^{2-} is a Lewis base
(d) SO_3^{2-} is a Lewis acid as well as Lewis base

24 H_3PO_3 is a dibasic acid. Its overall ionisation constant is 4×10^{-5}. If second ionisation constant is 2.5×10^{-3}, its first ionisation constant is

(a) 6.25 (b) 1×10^{-7}
(c) 1.0×10^{7} (d) 1.6×10^{-2}

25 Density of water is 1.0 kg dm^{-3} at 298 K. Its ion product is 1×10^{-14}. Thus, fraction of H_2O converted to OH^- ion is

(a) 1.0×10^{-7} (b) 1.8×10^{-7}
(c) 1.8×10^{-9} (d) 1.8×10^{-14}

26 With which of the following bases will the ionisation of CH_3COOH proceed furthest toward completion (to the right) (or for with which $\Delta G°$ is most negative?

(a) H_2O (b) NH_3 (c) Cl^- (d) NO_3^-

27 Consider following acid-base equilibria :

I. $NH_4^+ + OH^- \rightleftharpoons H_2O + NH_3$

II. $HSO_4^- + NO_3^- \rightleftharpoons HNO_3 + SO_4^{2-}$

III. $CH_3OH + CH_3COO^- \rightleftharpoons CH_3COOH + CH_3O^-$

Directions of the above equilibria are

	I	II	III		I	II	III
(a)	→	→	←	(b)	→	←	→
(c)	←	←	→	(d)	→	←	←

28 $HClO_3$ is stronger acid than H_3PO_4 due to the fact:

(a) $HClO_3$ has three O-atoms attached to Cl, while H_3PO_4 has four O-atoms attached to P
(b) Oxidation number of Cl in $HClO_3$ is higher than that of P in H_3PO_4
(c) Electronegativity of Cl is higher than that of P
(d) None of the above

pH-Scale

The term pH is derived from the French word. 'Puissance of hydrogen' (power of hydrogen) and refers to the power of 10 (the exponent) used to express molar H_3O^+ concentration.

$$[H_3O^+] = 10^{-pH}$$

$$\therefore \quad pH = -\log[H_3O^+] = \log\frac{1}{[H_3O^+]}$$

Similarly,

$$pOH = -\log[OH^-]$$

In water

$$[H_3O^+][OH^-] = K_w$$

Take logarithm,

$$\therefore \quad \log[H_3O^+] + \log[OH^-] = \log K_w$$

$$-\log[H_3O^+] - \log[OH^-] = -\log K_w$$

$$\therefore \quad \boxed{pH + pOH = pK_w = 14 \text{ (at 298 K)}}$$

At 298 K, $[H_3O^+][OH^-] = 1 \times 10^{-14}$

- If solution is **neutral**.

$$[H_3O^+] = [OH^-] = 1 \times 10^{-7} \text{ M (at 298 K)}$$

$$pH = pOH = 7$$

It is a case of neutral solutions.

- If solution is **acidic**.

$$[H_3O^+] > 10^{-7}M \text{ and } [OH^-] < 10^{-7}M$$

Thus, pH < 7 and pOH > 7

Thus, acidic solutions have

$$0 \le pH < 7$$

- If solution is **basic**.

$$[OH^-] > 10^{-7}M$$
$$[H_3O^+] < 10^{-7}M$$

$\therefore$ pH > 7 and pOH < 7

Thus, basic solutions have

$$7 < pH \le 14$$

- pH can also be negative, as in 2 M HCl

$$[H_3O^+] = 2\text{ M}$$

$\therefore$ $pH = -\log 2 = -0.3010$

- As solution becomes more acidic, its $[H_3O^+]$ increases, hence pH decreases.
- As solution becomes more basic, its $[OH^-]$ increases, $[H_3O^+]$ decreases, hence pH increases.

pH of strong acids and strong bases

- In strong acids,

$$[H_3O^+] = \text{basicity} \times \text{molarity} = \text{normality}$$

- In strong bases,

$$[OH^-] = \text{acidicity} \times \text{molarity} = \text{normality}$$

- In mixture of strong acids

$$N_{mix} = [H_3O^+] = \frac{\Sigma NV}{\Sigma V}$$

- In mixture of strong bases

$$N_{mix} = [OH^-] = \frac{\Sigma NV}{\Sigma V}$$

- In a mixture of strong acids and strong bases

If N_1V_1 (acid) > N_2V_2 (base)

$$N(H_3O^+) = \frac{N_1V_1 - N_2V_2}{(V_1 + V_2)}$$

If N_1V_1 (acid) < N_2V_2 (base)

$$N(OH^-) = \frac{N_2V_2 - N_1V_1}{(V_1 + V_2)}$$

■ In all cases, if molarity is given, convert these values to normality.

pH of very dilute solutions

If　[Acid] < 10^{-6} M

or　[Base] < 10^{-6} M

Then $[H_3O^+] = [OH^-] = 1 \times 10^{-7}$ M of water must be added to acid or base concentration to calculate total $[H_3O^+]$ or $[OH^-]$

e.g. (i) In case of [HCl] = 10^{-6}M

Then $[H^+]$ from HCl = 10^{-6}M

$$H_2O \rightleftharpoons H^+ + OH^-$$

	H_2O	H^+	OH^-
Initial	C	0	0
After dissociation	$(C - x)$	x	x

Thus, $[H_3O^+]_{HCl} = (10^{-6} + x)$

$$[OH^-] = x$$

$\therefore$ $[H_3O^+][OH^-] = K_w = 1 \times 10^{-14}$

$$(10^{-6} + x)x = 1 \times 10^{-14} ;\ x^2 + 10^{-6}x = 1 \times 10^{-14}$$

Thus, given $x = 1 \times 10^{-8}$ M

$\therefore$ $[H_3O^+] = 10^{-6} + 10^{-8} = 101 \times 10^{-8}$

$$pH = -\log(101 \times 10^{-8}) = 5.9956$$

Exact pH = 5.9956

pH = 6.0 (approx.)

(ii) In case of HCl = 10^{-7}M HCl, pH ≠ 7 as it is acidic solution

$$[H_3O^+] = (10^{-7} + x)$$
$$[OH^-] = x$$

$\therefore$ $x^2 + 10^{-7}x - 1 \times 10^{-14} = 0$

$$x = 0.62 \times 10^{-7}\text{ M}$$

$\therefore$ $[H_3O^+] = 1 \times 10^{-7} + 0.62 \times 10^{-7} = 1.62 \times 10^{-7}$

$$pH = 6.79 < 7$$

■ You may avoid tedious calculation as explained below:

(iii) In case of 10^{-8} M HCl, $[H^+]_{total} = [H^+]_{HCl} + [H^+]_{H_2O}$

$$= 10^{-8} + 10^{-7}$$
$$= 11 \times 10^{-8}$$

$\therefore$ $= pH = 8 - \log 11$

$$= 8 - 1.04 = 6.96$$

pH based on exact calculation = 6.98 ≈ 6.96

- In case of weak acids, $[H_3O^+]$ or in case weak bases $[OH^-]$ is less than the molar concentration of the given solute due to smaller extent of ionisation. In such cases, we take help of **Ostwald's dilution law** (discussed in next section).

Solved Examples & Instant Practice

Example 8.8) The concentration of hydrogen ion in a sample of soft drink is 3.8×10^{-3} M. What is its pH? ***[NCERT]***

Sol. In cold drinks, acidity arises due to dissolved CO_2 in H_2O

$$CO_2 + H_2O \rightleftharpoons H_2CO_3$$
$$H_2CO_3 \rightleftharpoons H^+ + HCO_3^-$$

and $\quad pH = -\log [H_3O^+]$

$$[H_3O^+] = 3.8 \times 10^{-3} \text{ M}$$

$\therefore \quad pH = -\log[H_3O^+] = -\log (3.8 \times 10^{-3})$

$$= 3 - \log 3.8 = 3 - 0.58 = 2.42$$

Immediate Test 8

(i) At 298 K, 0.10 g of NaOH is dissolved in 250 mL of a solution. What is its pH?

(ii) Calculate pH of 0.05×10^{-2} M $Ba(OH)_2$ solution taking it as strong electrolyte.

(iii) Calculate pH of each of the following solutions.

(a) A sample of sea water that has $[OH^-] = 1.60 \times 10^{-6}$M

(b) A sample of acid that has $[H_3O^+] = 6.0 \times 10^{-6}$ M

(c) 1 M HCl

(d) a solution containing 0.56 g CaO in 100 mL solution

Example 8.9) In aqueous NaOH solution, $[NaOH] = 4 \times 10^{-7}$ M, calculate its pH.

It is case of very dilute solution.

$[NaOH] = 4 \times 10^{-7}$ M

pOH = 7 − log 4 if calculated directly

If $[OH^-]$ of H_2O is also taken, then pH would be slightly different.

Sol. $[OH^-]$ of water is not considered.

then $[OH^-]$ from NaOH $= 4 \times 10^{-7}$ M

$\therefore \quad pOH = -\log[OH^-]$

$$= 7 - \log 4 = 7 - 0.602 = 6.398 \approx 6.4$$
$$pH = 7.6$$

$[OH^-]$ of water is also considered

$$\underset{x}{H_2O} \rightleftharpoons \underset{x}{H^+} + OH^-$$

$$[H_3O^+] = x$$
$$[OH^-] = (x + 4 \times 10^{-7})$$

$\therefore \quad [H_3O^+][OH^-] = 1 \times 10^{-14}$

$$x(x + 4 \times 10^{-7}) = 1 \times 10^{-14}$$

$\therefore \quad x^2 + 4 \times 10^{-7}x - 1 \times 10^{-14} = 0$

$$x = \frac{-4 \times 10^{-7} + \sqrt{(4 \times 10^{-7})^2 + 4 \times 10^{-14}}}{2} = 2.36 \times 10^{-8} \text{ M}$$

$\therefore \quad [OH^-] = (2.36 \times 10^{-8} + 4 \times 10^{-7}) = 4.23 \times 10^{-7}$

$$pOH = 6.373$$
$$pH = 7.63 \approx 7.6$$

Hence, quite similar in both cases.

Immediate Test 9

(i) Calculate pH of 1×10^{-8} M NaOH.

(ii) 10 mL of 1×10^{-6} M HCl is diluted by adding 100 mL H_2O. What is pH of dilute solution?

(iii) Calculate pH of

(a) 10^{-2} M H_2SO_4 (b) 10^{-2} N H_2SO_4

(c) 10^{-2} M $Ca(OH)_2$ (d) 10^{-2}N $Ca(OH)_2$

Example 8.10) Human blood has a pH of 7.4. Calculate concentration of H_3O^+ and OH^- ions.

Sol. Blood is alkaline in nature. From the pH (and therefore pOH) $[H_3O^+]$ and $[OH^-]$ can be calculated.

$$pH = -\log_{10} [H_3O^+]$$

$\therefore \quad [H_3O^+] = 10^{-pH}$ = antilog of [− pH]

$$[OH^-] = K_w / [H_3O^+]$$
$$pH = 7.4 = -\log [H_3O^+]$$

$\therefore \quad \log [H_3O^+] = -7.4 = \bar{8}.6$

$\therefore \quad [H_3O^+] = 4.0 \times 10^{-8}$

As $\quad [H_3O^+][OH^-] = 1 \times 10^{-14}$

$\therefore \quad [OH^-] = \dfrac{1 \times 10^{-14}}{4.0 \times 10^{-8}} = 2.5 \times 10^{-7}$ M

Example 8.11) What amount of H_2SO_4 (in terms of millimoles) should be dissolved in 100 mL solution to have a pH = 4.0?

Sol. H_2SO_4 is dibasic acid. Hence, every mol of H_2SO_4 gives 2 mol of H^+ ions. Thus, from the pH, $[H_3O^+]$ is calculated, hence number of millimoles.

$$pH = -\log [H_3O^+]$$
$$[H_3O^+] = 10^{-pH} \text{ N}$$
$$[H_2SO_4] = \left(\frac{10^{-pH}}{2}\right) \text{M (mol L}^{-1}\text{)}$$

Thus, amount in 100 mL can be calculated.

$$pH = 4.0$$

$\therefore \quad [H_3O^+] = 10^{-4}$M

$$H_2SO_4 \rightleftharpoons 2H^+ + SO_4^{2-}$$

Every H_2SO_4 furnished $2H^+$ ions,

Thus, $[H_2SO_4] = \left(\dfrac{10^{-4}}{2}\right)$ m $= 5 \times 10^{-5}$ M H_2SO_4

$$= 5 \times 10^{-5} \text{ mol L}^{-1} = 5 \times 10^{-5} \times 10^3 \text{ millimol}$$
$$= 5 \times 10^{-2} \text{ millimol L}^{-1}$$
$$= \frac{5 \times 10^{-2}}{10} \text{ millimol in 100 mL} = 5 \times 10^{-3} \text{ millimol}$$

Immediate Test 10

(i) Calculate millimoles of $Ca(OH)_2$ in 100 mL solution of pH 12.

(ii) What amount of SO_3 gas should be dissolved in 1L of aqueous solution to have a pH of 2?

Example 8.12) Equal volumes of two solutions of pH = 6 and pH = 8 are mixed. What is the pH of the resultant mixture?

Sol. pH = 6, means acidic solution.

pH = 8, means basic solution.

Thus, mixture contains equal volumes of acid and base.

Compare N_1V_1 (acid) and N_2V_2 (base) and calculate pH.

pH	$[H_3O^+]$	$[OH^-]$	Volume
6	$(10^{-6}M)$		V
8	$(10^{-8}\ M)$	$(10^{-6}\ M)$	V

N_1V_1 (acid) $= 10^{-6}V$

N_2V_2 (base) $= 10^{-6}\ V$

$\therefore$ $N_1V_1 = N_2V_2$ thus, neutral

$\therefore$ pH $= 7$

Immediate Test 11

(i) What will be the resultant pH, when 700 mL of an aqueous solution of HCl (pH = 2) is mixed with 300 mL of an aqueous solution of NaOH of pH = 12?

(ii) 40 mL of 0.4 M HNO_3 and 40 mL of 0.4 M $Ca(OH)_2$ solutions were mixed and diluted to 500 mL. Calculate the pH of the resultant solution.

(iii) Calculate the pH of an aqueous solution i.e. 3.00% KOH by mass and has density 1.0242 g mL^{-1}.

(iv) 248 mL of HCl gas at 1 bar and 298 K is passed into aqueous solution and diluted to 1 L. What is pH of solution?

KNOWLEDGE CONFIRMATION Test 2

1 1 mL of HCl of pH 5 is dilute to 1000 mL. Thus, pH of the final solution is

(a) 8.0 (b) 5.0 (c) 6.96 (d) 7.0

2 How many moles of NaOH must be added to 1 L of aqueous solution to change its pH from 12 to 13?

(a) 4.0 g (b) 0.4 g
(c) 3.6 g (d) 3.0 g

3 Which of the following mixtures will have pH closer to 1?

(a) 75 mL of 0.2 N HCl + 25 mL of 0.2 N NaOH
(b) 10 mL of 0.1 N HCl + 90 mL of 0.1 N NaOH
(c) 55 mL of 0.1 N HCl + 45 mL of 0.1 N NaOH
(d) 100 mL of 0.1 N HCl + 100 mL of 0.1 N NaOH

4 Which has maximum pH?

(a) 0.01 M H_2SO_4 (b) 0.01 M HCl
(c) 0.01 M $Ca(OH)_2$ (d) 0.01 M NaOH

5 In a basic solution, pH is 12.3. Hence, $[OH^-]$ is

(a) 2×10^{-2} M (b) 5×10^{-3} M
(c) 3×10^{-12} M (d) 4×10^{-10}M

6 In the calculation of pH of a solution, $[H_3O^+]$ or $[OH^-]$ of water is also considered in the following.

(a) 10^{-5} M HCl (b) 10^{-5} M NaOH
(c) 10^{-8} M NaOH (d) 10^{-6} M $Ca(OH)_2$

7 pH of a neutral solution increases to 12.0 at 298 K. The increase in $[OH^-]$ is .... times.

(a) 5 (b) 10^3 (c) 10^5 (d) 4

8 The hydrogen ion concentration of the ocean water is about 2×10^{-9}M. Thus, its pH is

(a) 8.85 (b) 9.3 (c) 7.85 (d) 8.7

9 A basic solution of pH = 9, is 1000 times more basic than the original solution. Thus, pH of the original solution is

(a) 6 (b) 9 (c) 10 (d) 12

10 Number of equivalents of H_2SO_4 present in 500 mL solution of pH = 2 is

(a) 5×10^{-3} (b) 1×10^{-3}
(c) 1×10^{-2} (d) 5×10^{-2}

11 H_2A is a strong diprotic acid. Thus, pH of its 0.01 N and 0.01 M solutions are respectively

(a) 2, 2 (b) 2, 1.7 (c) 1.7, 2 (d) 1.7, 1.7

12 10 mL of NaOH solution of pH = 9 is diluted to 1000 mL. Thus, pH of the diluted NaOH solution is

(a) 7.0 (b) between 7 and 8
(c) 12.0 (d) between 8 and 9

13 5.6 g KOH and 4.9 g H_2SO_4 are dissolved in water and solution is diluted to 1 L. Thus, pH of the resulting solution is

(a) 7.0 (b) 1.0 (c) 2.0 (d) 8.0

14 At 90°C, K_w $(H_2O) = 1\times10^{-12}$. If 100 mL of 0.2 M HCl is added to 200 mL of 0.1 NaOH at 90°C, then resulting solution is

(a) neutral (b) basic
(c) acidic (d) can not be determined

15 25 mL of 0.10 M HCl is titrated with 0.10 M NaOH. pH will be maximum at the point when NaOH added is

(a) 10 mL (b) 15 mL
(c) 20 mL (d) 25 mL

16 4.9×10^{-2} g H_2SO_4 is dissolved in 500 mL of solution. Thus, $[H^+]$ and $[SO_4^{2-}]$ are respectively.

	$[H^+]$	$[SO_4^{2-}]$
(a)	1×10^{-3} M	1×10^{-3} M
(b)	2×10^{-3} M	1×10^{-3} M
(c)	2×10^{-3} M	2×10^{-3} M
(d)	1×10^{-3} M	2×10^{-3} M

17 On increasing the temperature of water
(a) pH increases, pOH decreases
(b) pH decreases, pOH increases
(c) Both pH and pOH decreases
(d) Both pH and pOH increases

18 0.24 g of Mg reacts with 80 mL of HCl of pH (– 0.30). pH after reaction complete, is ($\log 7 = 0.8450$)
(a) 0.30 (b) – 0.30
(c) – 0.24 (d) 0.24

19 In dilute H_2SO_4 aqueous solution, pH is –0.3010. Thus, H_2SO_4 is
(a) 2.0 M (b) 1.0 M (c) – 0.05 M (d) 0.05 M

20 How many times a solution of pH = 2, has higher acidity than the solution of pH = 6?
(a) 400 (b) 800 (c) 1200 (d) 10000

21 If ionic products of water are compared at 290 K and 350 K, then
(a) pOH (290 K) = pOH (350 K) (b) pOH (290 K) > pOH (350 K)
(c) pOH (290 K) < pOH (350 K) (d) can not be predicted

22 On dilution pH of a strong acid changes from 3 to 5. Thus, dilution made is
(a) $\frac{5}{3}$ times (b) $\frac{3}{5}$ times (c) 10^2 times (d) 10^{-3} times

23 At 298 K 0.01 mole of NaOH is dissolved in 10 L of water. Thus, pH of water changes by
(a) 4 units (b) 3 units (c) 11 units (d) 0 units

24 Equal volumes of pH = 1 and pH = 2 solutions are mixed. pH of the resultant solution will be
(a) 1.76 (b) 1.26 (c) 0.76 (d) 2.26

25 At 298 K, pH of water is 7. On heating water to 350 K,
(a) pH will decrease and solution becomes acidic
(b) pH will increase and solution becomes basic
(c) pH will remain constant as 7
(d) pH will decrease but solution will be neutral

26 In 0.015 M HCl, $[OH^-]$ is
(a) 5×10^{-12} M (b) 6.7×10^{-13} M
(c) 2.0×10^{-5} M (d) 5×10^{-2} M

27 Variation of pH, pOH or pK_w with temperature is shown for H_2O.

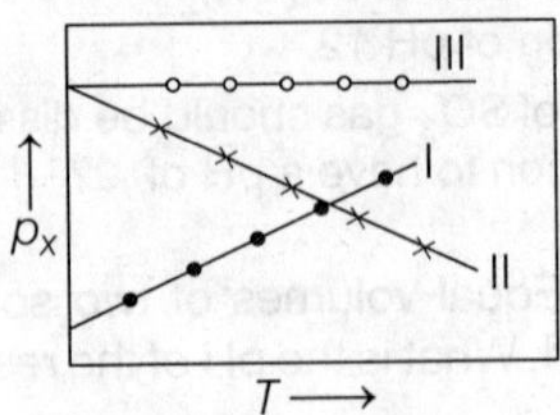

Variation is shown by line
(a) I (b) II
(c) III (d) None of these

28 For NaOH, pH = 13, and density is 1 g mL^{-1}. Thus, mole fraction of NaOH in solution is
(a) 1.80×10^{-3} (b) 5.57×10^{-2}
(c) 0.1 (d) None is correct

29 4 g NaOH is dissolved in 360 mL H_2O ($d = 1$ g mL^{-1}). How much water should be added to make pH = 13 (assume negligible volume of solute)
(a) 360 g (b) 640 g (c) 644 g (d) 636 g

30 In what ratio solutions of pH = 3 and pH = 6 should be mixed so that mixture has pH = 4?
(a) 1 : 9.09 (b) 9.09 : 1 (c) 1 : 2 (d) 2 : 1

31 What is pH of a solution obtained by dissolving 200 mL HCl (*g*) measured at 300 K and 1 bar pressure in 4.0 L water solution?
(a) 2.70 (b) 2.50 (c) 1.30 (d) 1.79

32 How many millilitres of concentrated HCl(*aq*), (which is 36.0% HCl by mass and density, $d = 1.18$ g mL^{-1}) are required to produce 12.5 L of solution with pH = 2.10?
(a) 1.60 mL (b) 7.90 mL
(c) 0.85 mL (d) 8.50 mL

33 H_2SO_4, a strong dibasic acid has a pH of –2.3010. Thus, number of SO_4^{2-} ions per mL of solution is
(a) 1.20×10^{26} (b) 6.02×10^{25}
(c) 3.01×10^{25} (d) None of these

34 In which of the following mixtures, pH is very close to 4?
(a) 100 mL of 1×10^{-4} M HCl + 100 mL of 1×10^{-8} M NaOH
(b) 200 mL of 4×10^{-4} M HCl + 200 mL of 4×10^{-4} M NaOH
(c) 200 mL of 3×10^{-4} M HCl + 100 mL of 3×10^{-4} M NaOH
(d) 100 mL of 3×10^{-4} M HCl + 200 mL of 3×10^{-4} M NaOH

35 25 mL of a $HNO_3(aq)$ solution with a pH of 2.00 is mixed with 25 mL of KOH(*aq*) solution with a pH 11.00. Thus, pH of the final solution is
(a) 2.35 (b) 2.10 (c) 9.70 (d) 6.8

Ostwald's Dilution Law

Ostwald's dilution law states "for a weak electrolyte, degree of ionisation increases with dilution and is inversely proportional to the square root of molar concentration or directly proportional to square root of dilution."

For weak acid

$$HA + H_2O \rightleftharpoons H_3O^+ + A^-$$

Initial (mol^{-1})	C	0	0
After ionisation	$(C - Cx)$	Cx	Cx

where, x is the degree of ionisation.

$\therefore$ Ionisation constant, $K_a = \dfrac{[H_3O^+][A^-]}{[HA]}$

$$K_a = \frac{Cx^2}{(1-x)}$$

- **Limiting case**

If $x << 1$

$K_a \approx Cx^2$

$$x \approx \sqrt{\frac{K_a}{C}}$$

Thus, $x \propto \sqrt{\dfrac{1}{C}}$

Since, $C = \dfrac{\text{Mol}}{\text{L}} = \dfrac{n}{V}$

$\therefore$ $x \propto \sqrt{V}$

Thus,

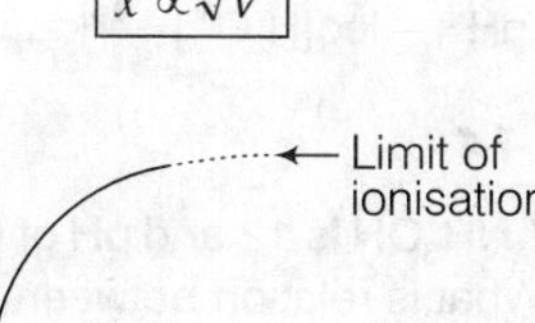

- **In weak acids,**

$$[H_3O^+] = Cx = C\sqrt{\frac{K_a}{C}} = \sqrt{K_aC}$$

$$[H_3O^+] = \sqrt{K_aC}$$

- **Relative extent of ionisation in two weak acids**

Since, $x = \sqrt{\dfrac{K_a}{C}}$

hence, for two weak acids

$$\frac{x_1}{x_2} = \sqrt{\frac{K_1 C_2}{K_2 C_1}}$$

- **Relative strength** (in terms of H_3O^+) **in two weak acids**

$$\frac{[H_3O^+]_1}{[H_3O^+]_2} = \sqrt{\frac{K_1C_1}{K_2C_2}}$$

- **pH of a weak acid**

Since, $[H_3O^+] = \sqrt{K_aC}$

$\therefore$ $$\text{pH} = -\log[H_3O^+] = \frac{1}{2}[pK_a - \log C]$$

- **$[H_3O^+]$ in a mixture of weak acid and a strong acid**

If C_1 is the molar concentration of weak acid having ionisation constant K_a and C_2 is the molar concentration of strong acid, then

$$[H_3O^+] = (C_2 + C_1x) = [C_2 + \sqrt{K_aC_1}]$$

- **$[H_3O^+]$ in a mixture of two weak acids**

$$[H_3O^+] = \sqrt{K_1C_1 + K_2C_2}$$

Similarly, for weak base (BOH)

$$x = \sqrt{\frac{K_b}{C}}$$

$$[OH^-] = \sqrt{K_bC}$$

$$\text{pOH} = \frac{1}{2}[pK_b - \log C]$$

Thus, $\text{pH} = 14 - \text{pOH} = 14 - \dfrac{1}{2}[pK_b - \log C]$

- **Extent of ionisation in two weak bases**

$$\frac{x_1}{x_2} = \sqrt{\frac{K_1C_2}{K_2C_1}}$$

- **Relative strength** (in terms of OH^-) **of two weak bases**

$$\frac{[OH^-]_1}{[OH^-]_2} = \sqrt{\frac{K_1C_1}{K_2C_2}}$$

- **$[OH^-]$ in a mixture of two weak bases**

$$[OH] = \sqrt{K_1C_1 + K_2C_2}$$

Solved Examples & Instant Practice

Example 8.13) Given, 0.02 M CH_3COOH

$$CH_3COOH + H_2O \rightleftharpoons CH_3COO^- + H_3O^+, K_a = 1.8 \times 10^{-5}$$

Calculate

(a) $[H_3O^+]$ (b) % ionisation and (c) pH

Weak acid is feebly ionised, hence (H_3O^+) is calculated using Ostwald's dilution law.
For a weak acid, we assume $x << 1$, such that

$$x = \sqrt{\frac{K_a}{C}}$$

$$[H_3O^+] = \sqrt{K_a C} \quad \text{and} \quad pH = \frac{1}{2}[pK_a - \log C]$$

When $pK_a = -\log K_a$

Sol.

(a) $[H_3O^+] = \sqrt{K_a C} = \sqrt{1.8 \times 10^{-5} \times 0.02} = 6 \times 10^{-4}$ M

(b) $x = \sqrt{\frac{K_a}{C}} = \sqrt{\frac{1.8 \times 10^{-5}}{0.02}} = 0.03$

Thus, 3% ionisation.

(c) $pH = -\log[H_3O^+] = -\log 6 \times 10^{-4}$

$\therefore$ $pH = 4 - \log 6 = 3.22$

Immediate Test 12

Calculate

(a) percentage ionisation and

(b) pH of 0.010 M HCN solution. K_a (HCN) $= 6.2 \times 10^{-10}$

Example 8.14) A solution is 0.2 M in HCOOH ($K_a = 1.8 \times 10^{-4}$) and 0.2 M in CH_3COOH ($K_a = 1.8 \times 10^{-5}$). Calculate $[H_3O^+]$ and pH of the solution.

Given mixture is of weak acids. Thus, $[H_3O^+]$ is calculated by Ostwald's dilution law.
$[H_3O^+]$ in a mixture of two weak acids.

$$[H_3O^+] = \sqrt{K_1C_1 + K_2C_2}$$

Thus, $pH = -\log[H_3O^+]$

Sol.

	K_a	C
HCOOH	1.8×10^{-4}	0.2
CH_3COOH	1.8×10^{-5}	0.2

$\therefore$ $[H_3O^+] = \sqrt{1.8 \times 10^{-4} \times 0.2 + 1.8 \times 10^{-5} \times 0.2} = 6.3 \times 10^{-3}$ M

$\therefore$ $pH = -\log[H_3O^+] = -\log 6.3 \times 10^{-3} = 2.2$

Immediate Test 13

A solution is 0.01 M in NH_4OH ($K_b = 1.8 \times 10^{-5}$) and 0.01 M in RNH_3OH ($K_b = 3.0 \times 10^{-7}$). Calculate pH of the solution.

Example 8.15) At 298 K, $K_a(HA) = K_b(BOH)$
It is found that pH of 0.01 M *BOH* solution is 12. Calculate pH of 0.1 M *HA* solution.

From pH of 0.01 M BOH, K_b is calculated. Since, $K_a = K_b$, thus K_a is known. Hence, pH of weak acid is calculated.

$$pOH = \frac{1}{2}[pK_b - \log C]$$

$$pH = \frac{1}{2}[pK_a - \log C]$$

Sol. For weak base, pH = 12

$$pOH = 2$$

$\therefore$ $pOH = \frac{1}{2}[pK_b - \log C] \Rightarrow 2 = \frac{1}{2}[pK_b - \log 0.01]$

$$4 = pK_b + 2 \Rightarrow pK_b = 2$$

$\therefore$ $pK_a = pK_b = 2$

Thus, $pH\,(HA) = \frac{1}{2}[pK_a - \log C] = \frac{1}{2}[2 - \log 0.1] = \frac{1}{2}[2 + 1] = 1.5$

As $pK_a = 2$

$\therefore$ $K_a = 10^{-2}$ indicates that acid is not fairly weak.

$$HA \rightleftharpoons H^+ + A^-$$

$\therefore$ $K_a = \frac{Cx^2}{(1-x)} \Rightarrow 10^{-2} = \frac{0.1\,x^2}{(1-x)}$

$$0.01 - 0.01x = 0.1x^2$$

$\therefore$ $x^2 + 0.1x - 0.1 = 0$

$$x = -0.1 \pm \frac{\sqrt{(0.1)^2 + 0.4}}{2} = 0.27$$

$\therefore$ $[H_3O^+] = Cx = 0.1 \times 0.27 = 0.027$

$\therefore$ $pH = -\log[H_3O^+] = -\log(0.027) = 1.568$ (exact)

Immediate Test 14

pH of 0.01 M $CH_3CH_2NH_3OH$ is 12 and pH of 0.001 M CH_3CH_2COOH is 5. What is relation between $K_b(CH_3CH_2NH_3OH)$ and $K_a(CH_3CH_2COOH)$?

Example 8.16) 50 mL of 0.2 M HCl is mixed with 50 mL of 0.2 M CH_3COOH ($K_a = 1.8 \times 10^{-5}$). What is pH of the resulting solution ?

It is a mixture of strong acid and weak acid. Concentration should be considered taking dilution factor into account.

$$[H_3O^+] = C_2(HCl) + \sqrt{C_1K_a}$$

Sol. Total volume of mixture = 50 + 50 = 100 mL

C_2 (HCl) = 0.1 M in mixture (using, $M_1V_1 = M_2V_2$

C_1 (CH_3COOH) = 0.1 M in mixture

$\therefore$ $[H_3O^+] = 0.1 + \sqrt{0.1 \times 1.8 \times 10^{-5}} = 0.101 \Rightarrow pH = 1.0$

■ Check, it is pH of 0.1 M HCl(*aq*) solution.

Immediate Test 15

Calculate pH of a mixture of 0.01 M KOH and 0.01 M NH_4OH.
$K_b(NH_4OH) = 1.8 \times 10^{-5}$

Example 8.17) For a weak acid, variation of $\log[H_3O^+]$ with degree of ionisation x in terms of $\log\left(\frac{1-x}{x}\right)$ can be expressed by graph. What is degree of ionisation of weak acid HA when pH is 5?

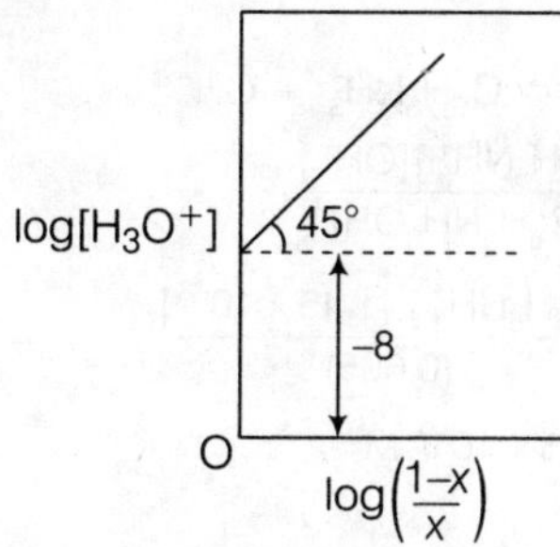

Ostwald's dilution law has been given in the form of graphical study.

$$\begin{array}{lcll} HA + H_2O & \rightleftharpoons & H_3O^+ + & A^- \\ C & & 0 & 0 \\ C(1-x) & & ? & Cx \end{array}$$

$$K_a = \frac{[H_3O^+][A^-]}{[HA]}$$

$$[H_3O^+] = K_a \frac{[HA]}{[A^-]} = K_a \frac{(1-x)}{x}$$

$$\therefore \quad \log[H_3O^+] = \log\left(\frac{1-x}{x}\right) + \log K_a$$

$$y = mx + c$$

Thus, $c = \log K_a$

If $pH = -\log[H_3O^+]$ is known, x can be calculated.

Sol. From graph, intercept on y-axis is

$$C = \log K_a = -8$$

When pH = 5

$$-\log[H_3O^+] = -\log K_a - \log\frac{(1-x)}{x}$$

$$pH = -\log K_a + \log\left(\frac{x}{1-x}\right)$$

$$5 = 8 + \log\left(\frac{x}{1-x}\right) \Rightarrow -3 = \log\left(\frac{x}{1-x}\right)$$

$$\therefore \quad \frac{x}{(1-x)} = 10^{-3} \qquad \therefore \quad x = 10^{-3} - x \times 10^{-3}$$

$$x + x \times 10^{-3} = 10^{-3} \qquad \therefore \quad x = 1 \times 10^{-3}$$

Immediate Test 16

(i) (a) For a weak acid, pH = 6 and pK_a = 8. Calculate mole fraction of conjugate base of HA.
(b) What is pH of 1×10^{-3} M HCOOH?
$K_a = 1.8 \times 10^{-4}$

(ii) Compare degree of ionisation in 0.2 M CH_3COOH?
(a) if solution is very dilute and $(1-x) \approx 1$
(b) if solution is such that $(1-x) \neq 1$
$K_a\ (CH_3COOH) = 1.8 \times 10^{-5}$

Example 8.18) What is $[HCOO^-]$ in a solution i.e. both 0.015 M HCOOH and 0.020 M HCl?

$$K_a(HCOOH) = 1.8 \times 10^{-4}$$

In presence of strong acid, its H^+ is much higher than that of due to weak acid. Thus, total $[H^+] = [H^+]$ of strong acid

Sol. $HCOOH \rightleftharpoons HCOO^- + H^+$

$$K_a = \frac{[HCOO^-][H^+]}{[HCOOH]}$$

HCl completely ionises to give 0.02 M H^+. Thus, $[HCOO^-]$ can be calculated.

$$[HCOO^-] = K_a \frac{[HCOOH]}{[H^+]}$$

$$= 1.8 \times 10^{-4} \frac{(0.015)}{0.02} = 1.35 \times 10^{-4}\ M$$

> ■ If HCl is not taken
> $$[H_3O^+] = [HCOO^-] = \sqrt{K_a C} = \sqrt{1.8 \times 10^{-4} \times 0.02} = 1.9 \times 10^{-3}$$
> Thus, in presence of HCl ionisation of HCOOH is decreased. In next part, we shall discuss it under "common-ion effect".

Immediate Test 17

What is $[NH_4^+]$ in 0.01 M $NH_3(aq)$ in presence of 0.001 M KOH?
$K_b(NH_3) = 1.8 \times 10^{-5}$

Example 8.19) Calculate the molar concentration of OH^- ion in a solution made by dissolving 0.005 mol each of ammonia and pyridine (C_5H_5N) in enough water to make 0.200 dm³ of solution?
Also calculate $[NH_4^+]$ and $[C_5H_5NH^+]$, the pyridinium ion

$$K_b[NH_3] = 1.8 \times 10^{-5}$$
$$K_b(C_5H_5N) = 1.52 \times 10^{-9}$$

$K_b\ (C_5H_5N) << K_b\ (NH_3)$
Thus, $[OH^-]$ from NH_4OH will affect ionisation of C_5H_5NHOH.

Sol. Initially $[NH_4OH] = [C_5H_5NHOH]$

$$= \frac{0.005}{02} = 0.025\ M$$

In NH_4OH

$$[NH_4^+] = [OH^-] = \sqrt{K_b C}$$
$$= \sqrt{1.8 \times 10^{-5} \times 0.025} = 6.71 \times 10^{-4}\ M$$

In C_5H_5NHOH

$$[C_5H_5NH^+] = [OH^-] = \sqrt{1.52 \times 10^{-9} \times 0.025}$$
$$= 6.16 \times 10^{-6}\ M.$$

Thus, $[OH^-]_{NH_4OH} > [OH^-]_{C_5H_5NHOH}$

Hence, ionisation of C_5H_5NHOH is taken in presence of $[OH^-]$ of NH_4OH

$$C_5H_5N + H_2O \rightleftharpoons C_5H_5\overset{+}{N}H + OH^-$$

$$K_b = \frac{[C_5H_5\overset{+}{N}H][OH^-]}{[C_5H_5NHOH]}$$

$$1.52 \times 10^{-9} = \frac{[C_5H_5\overset{+}{N}H][6.71 \times 10^{-4}]}{[0.025]}$$

$$\therefore \quad [C_5H_5\overset{+}{N}H] = 5.66 \times 10^{-8}\ M$$

Example 8.20) 0.01 mole each of CH_3NH_2 and $C_6H_5NH_2$ were dissolved is 0.50 dm³ solution. Calculate molar concentration of $CH_3\overset{\oplus}{N}H_3$ and $C_6H_5\overset{\oplus}{N}H_3$.

$$K_b(CH_3NH_2) = 4.2 \times 10^{-4}$$
$$K_b(C_6H_5NH_2) = 4.2 \times 10^{-10}$$

Sol. $K_b(CH_3NH_2) > K_b(C_6H_5NH_2)$

Hence, ionisation of $C_6H_5NH_3^+OH^-$ in aqueous solution is affected by $[OH^-]$ of $CH_3NH_3^+OH^-$.

In (CH_3NH_3OH)

$$CH_3NH_2 + H_2O \rightleftharpoons CH_3NH_3^+ + OH^-$$

$\therefore$ By Ostwald's dilution law,

$$[CH_3NH_3^+] = [OH^-] = \sqrt{K_bC}$$
$$= \sqrt{4.2 \times 10^{-4} \times 0.005} = 1.45 \times 10^{-3}\ M$$

In $(C_6H_5NH_3OH)$

$$C_6H_5NH_3OH \rightleftharpoons C_6H_5NH_3^+ + OH^-$$

$$K_b = \frac{[C_6H_5NH_3^+][OH^-]}{[C_6H_5NH_3OH]}$$

$$4.2 \times 10^{-10} = \frac{[C_6H_5NH_3^+][1.45 \times 10^{-3}]}{(0.005)}$$

$$\therefore \quad [C_6H_5NH_3^+] = 1.45 \times 10^{-9}\ M$$

KNOWLEDGE CONFIRMATION Test 3

1 For a weak monoprotic acid, HA $K_a = 4 \times 10^{-8}$. Thus, $[H_3O^+]$ in 0.25 M HA is
(a) 0.25 M (b) 1.0×10^{-4} M
(c) 2×10^{-3} M (d) 1.0×10^{-10} M

2 Per cent dissociation of 0.01 M BOH having $K_b = 10^{-4}$ is
(a) 9.5% (b) 10.0%
(c) 17.0% (d) 1.0%

3 For HCN, $(K_a = 1 \times 10^{-9})$ degree of ionisation at 0.1 M and 0.001 M are respectively α_1 and α_2. Thus, (α_1/α_2) is
(a) 1 (b) 0.1 (c) 10 (d) 0.01

4 CH_3COOH is 1% dissociated at 0.18 M. Thus, its ionisation constant is
(a) 1.8×10^{-5} (b) 1.8×10^{-3}
(c) 1.8×10^{-7} (d) 5.56×10^{-4}

5 A weak base BOH has pH = 9 at 0.01 M. Thus, ionisation constant of the weak base is
(a) 1×10^{-9} (b) 2×10^{-8} (c) 1×10^{-7} (d) 1×10^{-8}

6 For a decimolar monoprotic acid (HA), degree of dissociation is 0.01. Thus, pK_a of the acid is
(a) 7 (b) 5 (c) 3 (d) 2

7 6.0 g of HA (molar mass = 60.0 g mol⁻¹, $K_a = 10^{-5}$) is dissolved in 1 dm³ of solution. Thus, pH of the solution is
(a) 3 (b) 4 (c) 5 (d) 6

8 At 298 K, $K_a(HA) = K_b(HB)$. pH of 0.01 M (HA) is 5.0. Thus, pOH of 10^{-4} M (BOH) solution is
(a) 4.5 (b) 5.5 (c) 6.0 (d) 6.5

9 If degree of ionisation of a weak acid is α, then
(a) $pH = \log K_a + \log\left(\frac{\alpha}{1-\alpha}\right)$ (b) $pH = \log\left(\frac{1}{K_a}\right) + \log\frac{\alpha}{1-\alpha}$
(c) $pH = \log\left(\frac{1}{K_a}\right) + \log\left(\frac{1-\alpha}{\alpha}\right)$ (d) $pH = \log K_a + \log[\alpha(1-\alpha)]$

10 Variation of $\log[H^+]$ with $\log\left(\frac{1-x}{x}\right)$ is given by

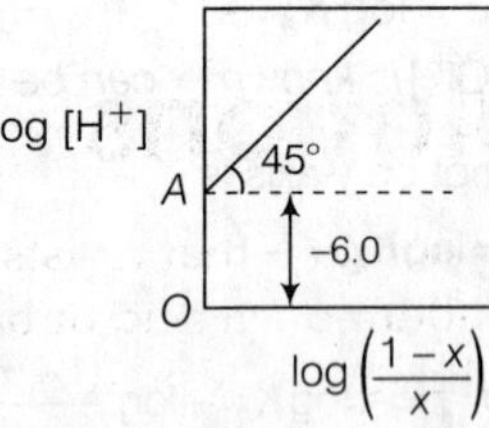

Thus, pH of a solution of weak acid at 1% ionisation is
(a) 4.0 (b) 6.0 (c) 2.0 (d) 3.0

11 A weak monoprotic acid is 1% ionised at 1 M. Thus, its per cent ionisation at 4 M is
(a) 4% (b) 5% (c) 0.5% (d) 0.2%

12 For water, a weak acid, $[H_3O^+] = 1.0 \times 10^{-7}$ M at 298 K. Thus, its pK_a is (molar concentration of water = 55.55 M)
(a) 7.0 (b) 15.74 (c) 14.0 (d) 12.68

13 For the weak base,

$$BOH \rightleftharpoons B^+ + OH^-$$

pH was found to be 12. If pK_b of BOH is 3, degree of ionisation of weak base is
(a) 0.1 (b) 0.01 (c) 0.05 (d) 0.005

14 The value of K_w of the physiological temperature (310 K) is 2.4×10^{-14}. What is pH at this temperature for neutral point?
(a) 7.0 (b) 6.81 (c) 9.0 (d) 7.19

15 pH of 7.0×10^{-8} M HCl is
(a) 6.77 (b) 5.95 (c) 7.15 (d) 8.05

16 Ionisation constant of a weak acid is 1.0×10^{-4}. Thus, equilibrium constant for the reaction is

$$A^- + H_3O^+ \rightleftharpoons HA + H_2O$$

(a) 10^4 (b) 10^{-4} (c) 10^{-10} (d) 10^{10}

17 For formic acid, HCOOH, $K_a = 1.8 \times 10^{-4}$. Percentage ionisation of 0.001 M HCOOH solution is
(a) 42.43% (b) 34.37%
(c) 4.243% (d) 3.437%

18 Concentration of CH_3COOH needed to give $[H_3O^+] = 3.5 \times 10^{-4}$ M is $[K_a(CH_3COOH) = 1.8 \times 10^{-5}$ M]
(a) 6.8×10^{-3} M (b) 3.6×10^{-3} M
(c) 1.8×10^{-5} M (d) 1.8×10^{9} M

19 In 1.0 dm^3 solution, 0.1 mole of NH_3 is present. If 0.00135 mole of NH_3 dissociates into NH_4^+ and OH^-, then ionisation constant of the base is
(a) 2.0×10^{-5} (b) 1.84×10^{-4}
(c) 1.84×10^{-5} (d) 3.68×10^{-4}

20 What is $[NH_4^+]$ in a solution that is 0.02 M in NH_3 and 0.01 M KOH? ($K_b = 1.8 \times 10^{-5}$)
(a) 1.8×10^{-5} M (b) 3.6×10^{-4} M
(c) 0.01 M (d) 3.6×10^{-5} M

21 A 0.30 M solution of fluoroacetic acid has a pH of 1.70. Thus, ionisation constant of the acid is

$$CH_2FCOOH(aq) + H_2O \rightleftharpoons H_3O^+(aq) + CH_2FCOO^-(aq)$$

(a) 1.33×10^{-3} (b) 1.33×10^{-4}
(c) 2.66×10^{-2} (d) 1.33×10^{-2}

22 A saturated aqueous solution of *o*-nitrophenol $OH\,C_6H_4NO_2$ has a pH = 4.53. Thus, solubility of *o*-nitrophenol (in gL^{-1}) is

$$OHC_6H_4NO_2 + H_2O \rightleftharpoons H_3O^+ + \bar{O}\,C_6H_4NO_2,$$

($pK_a = 7.23$)

(Molar mass of *o*-nitrophenol = 123.0 g mol^{-1})
(a) 0.182 gL^{-1} (b) 1.82 gL^{-1}
(c) 1.82×10^{-3} gL^{-1} (d) None of these

23 In a mixture of two weak monobasic acids *HX* (degree of dissociation α_1) and *HY* (degree of dissociation α_2) with concentration C_1 and C_2 and dissociation constants K_1 and K_2, select correct statement(s).
(a) $K_1 = \frac{[C_1\alpha_1 + C_2\alpha_2]C_1\alpha_1}{C_1(1-\alpha_1)}$ (b) $K_2 = \frac{[C_1\alpha_1 + C_2\alpha_2]C_2\alpha_2}{C_2(1-\alpha_2)}$
(c) Both of the above are correct (d) None of these

24 $K_a(CH_3COOH) = K_b(NH_4OH)$. Thus, pH of the aqueous 1M CH_3COOH would be, if pH of the aqueous 1M NH_4OH solution be 10.8.
(a) 10.8 (b) 3.2 (c) 4.2 (d) 7.0

25 A solution is 0.10 M in HCl and 0.10 M $CHCl_2 \cdot COOH$. ($K_a = 1.0 \times 10^{-2}$). Thus, pH of the solution
(a) 1.0 (b) 0.88 (c) –0.88 (d) 1.5

Buffer Solutions

A buffer is defined as a solution that resists any change in its pH when a small amount of an acid or base is added or when the solution is diluted.

In order for a solution to act as a buffer, it must have two components

(i) one of which is able to neutralise acids.
(ii) other of which is able to neutralise bases.

Two types of buffers

- **Acidic buffer** is a mixture of weak acid (*HA*) and its conjugate base (A^-) or one of its salts.

$$HA \rightleftharpoons H^+ + A^-$$

(i) CH_3COOH — $CH_3COO^-(Na^+)$
(ii) C_6H_5COOH — $C_6H_5COO^-(Na^+)$
(iii) HCO_3^- — CO_3^{2-}

pH of acidic buffer is given by Henderson-Hasselbalch equation

$$pH = pK_a + \log\frac{[\text{Conjugate base}]}{[\text{Acid}]}$$

$$pH = pK_a + \log\frac{[A^-]}{[HA]} \Rightarrow pH = pK_a + \log\frac{[\text{Proton acceptor}]}{[\text{Proton donor}]}$$

- **Basic buffer** is a mixture of weak base and its conjugate acid (or one of its salts).

$$BOH(\text{weak base}) \rightleftharpoons B^+(\text{salt})$$

NH_4OH — $NH_4^+(NH_4Cl)$
$Cu(OH)_2$ — $Cu^{2+}(CuSO_4)$

Or

B (base) — BH^+ (conjugate acid)
$NH_3(aq)$ — NH_4^+
CH_3NH_2 — $CH_3NH_3^+$

pH of basic buffer is given by Henderson-Hasselbalch equation,

$$pOH = pK_b + \log\frac{[\text{conjugate acid}]}{[\text{weak base}]}$$

$$pOH = pK_b + \log\frac{[\text{proton donor}]}{[\text{proton acceptor}]}$$

$$pH = 14 - pOH$$

Also, for basic buffer

$$pH = pK_a[BH^+] + \log\frac{[B]}{[BH^+]}$$

$$pH = pK_a\,(\text{conjugate acid}) + \log\frac{[\text{base}]}{[\text{conjugate acid}]}$$

Buffer action (in acidic buffer)

Effect of addition of acid or base on pH of acidic buffer

(i) **If OH^- ion is added to the acidic buffer,** equivalent amount of the acid is neutralised, thus decreasing the concentration of the acid and increasing the concentration of its conjugate base, thus increasing pH.

$$HA + OH^- \rightleftharpoons A^- + H_2O$$

	HA	OH^-	A^-	
Initially	C_1		C_2	mol L^{-1}
Added		x		mol L^{-1}
After	$(C_1 - x)$	0	$(C_2 + x)$	mol L^{-1}

$$pH = pK_a + \log\frac{[A^-]}{[HA]}$$

$$pH = pK_a + \log\left(\frac{C_2}{C_1}\right) \text{ (if no } OH^- \text{ is added)}$$

$$pH' = pK_a + \log\frac{(C_2 + x)}{(C_1 - x)} \text{ (if } OH^- \text{ is added)}$$

$$pH' > pH$$

if $pH' \approx pH$, then buffer action is appreciable.

(ii) **If H^+ is added to the acidic buffer,** equivalent amount of the conjugate base is converted to the acid thus, decreasing pH.

$$A^- + H^+ \rightleftharpoons HA$$

	A^-	H^+	HA	
Initially	C_2		C_1	mol L^{-1}
Added		x		mol L^{-1}
After	$(C_2 - x)$	0	$(C_1 + x)$	mol L^{-1}

$$pH'' = pK_a + \log\frac{(C_2 - x)}{(C_1 + x)'} \Rightarrow (pH'' < pH)$$

if $pH'' \approx pH$, then buffer action is appreciable.

Effect of dilution on pH

(i) Dilution of a buffer solution does not affect the pH since, both components of the buffer are affected to the same extent by dilution.

(ii) At the half neutralisation point of the acid, where $[HA] = [A^-]$

$$\text{then, } pH = pK_a + \log\frac{[HA]}{[A^-]} = pK_a + \log 1$$

$$pH = pK_a$$

Buffer action (in basic buffer)

Effect of addition of acid or base on basic buffer on pH.

(i) Addition of H^+ ion into the basic buffer will decrease pH due to increase in the concentration of conjugate acid BH^+.

$$BOH + H^+ \rightleftharpoons B^+ + H_2O$$

	BOH	H^+	B^+	
Initially	C_1		C_2	mol L^{-1}
Added			x	mol L^{-1}
After	$(C_1 - x)$		$(C_2 + x)$	mol L^{-1}

(ii) Addition of OH^- ion into the basic buffer will increase pH due to increase in the concentration of base BOH.

$$B^+ + OH^- \rightleftharpoons BOH$$

	B^+	OH^-	BOH	
Initially	C_2		C_1	mol L^{-1}
Added			x	mol L^{-1}
After	$(C_2 - x)$		$(C_1 + x)$	mol L^{-1}

(iii) At half-neutralisation of the base, where $[BOH] = [B^+]$, $pOH = pK_b$, $pH = 14 - pK_b$

(iv) Due to dilution, there is no effect on pH.

Buffer index and buffer capacity

The buffer index can be defined as the differential ratio of the increase in the amount of strong acid or base added to pH variation.

The buffer capacity is numerically expressed to be equal with the minimum concentration of acid or base which causes the variation of buffer's pH with one unit.

$$\text{Buffer index } (\beta) = \frac{d(n)}{d(pH)}$$

where $d(n)$ is the number of moles of strong acid or base added to one litre of buffer and $d(pH)$ is the corresponding change in pH.

- Buffer capacity of an acidic buffer is maximum when
$$pH = pK_a$$
For this, [acid] = [conjugate base]
- Buffer capacity of a basic buffer is maximum, when
$$pOH = pK_b$$
Thus, [base] = [conjugate acid]
- A solution of weak acid and its conjugate base is regarded as an acidic buffer only when
$$pH = pK_a \pm 1 \text{ or } \frac{1}{10} \le \frac{[\text{salt}]}{[\text{acid}]} \le 10$$

- A solution of a weak base and its conjugate acid is regarded as basic buffer only when

$$pOH = pK_b \pm 1 \text{ or } \frac{1}{10} < \frac{[\text{salt}]}{[\text{base}]} \le 10$$

Importance of Buffer Solutions

- Many biological reactions occur in the pH range of 6 to 8.
- A number of specified enzyme reactions may occur in the pH range of 4 to 10 and even higher.
- Biological systems of some phosphate buffers

$$H_3PO_4 + H_2PO_4^-, \quad H_2PO_4^- + HPO_4^{2-}$$
$$HPO_4^{2-} + PO_4^{3-}$$

The best buffering capacity is within ± pH unit of respective pK_a values.

- Controlling the pH of the blood is necessary as decrease in pH of blood (from 7.4) lead to **acidosis** which may cause heart failure or kidney failure. On the other hand, **alkalosis** which causes increase in pH of blood, may lead to vomiting, over-breathing etc.
- The normal pH value of blood plasma is 7.4 and is controlled by HCO_3^- / H_2CO_3 buffer.

$$H_2CO_3 + H_2O \xrightleftharpoons{K_{a_1} = 4.2 \times 10^{-7}} HCO_3^- + H_3O^+,$$

$$HCO_3^- + H_2O \xrightleftharpoons{K_{a_2} = 5.6 \times 10^{-11}} CO_3^{2-} + H_3O^+$$

Since, $K_{a_2} << K_{a_1}$, hence H_2CO_3 / HCO_3^- equilibrium is important in controlling pH of blood.

Solved Examples & Instant Practice

Example 8.21) A buffer is 0.02 M in CH_3COOH and 0.01 M CH_3COONa. $pK_a(CH_3COOH) = 4.74$
What is pH of the buffer ?

Sol. It is an acidic buffer. pH can be calculated by Henderson-Hasselbalch equation.

$$pH = pK_a + \log\frac{[\text{conjugate base}]}{[\text{weak acid}]}$$

$$pH = 4.74 + \log\frac{0.01}{0.02}$$

$$= 4.74 - \log 2 = 4.74 - 0.30 = 4.44$$

■ Since, ($pH = pK_a \pm 1$), its buffer action is within range.

Example 8.22) 500 mL of a solution contains 7.4 g CH_3CH_2COOH and 5.6 g of CH_3CH_2COOK. pK_a of CH_3CH_2COOH is 5. Calculate pH of the mixture.

Sol. It is an acidic buffer.

Convert given amount in molar concentration

$$[CH_3CH_2COOH] = \frac{7.4 \text{ g}/74 \text{ g mol}^{-1}}{0.5 \text{ L}} = 0.2 \text{ mol L}^{-1}$$

$$[CH_3CH_2COOK] = \frac{5.6/112}{0.5} = 0.1 \text{ mol L}^{-1}$$

By Henderson- Hasselbalch equation,

$$\therefore \quad pH = 5 + \log\frac{0.1}{0.2} = 5 - 0.3 = 4.7$$

Immediate Test 18

(i) Calculate the pH of a solution containing 0.1 M H_3BO_3 and 0.15 M NaH_2BO_3.
K_a of ($H_3BO_3 \rightleftharpoons H^+ + H_2BO_3^-$) is 7.3×10^{-10}

(ii) Calculate the pH of 0.01M CH_3COOH, ($pK_a = 4.74$). How much CH_3COONa should be added to 50 mL of CH_3COOH, so that its pH increases by 1 unit?

Example 8.23) Calculate pH of a solution prepared by mixing 50.0 mL of 0.200 M CH_3COOH and 50 · 0 mL of 0.100 M NaOH. $pK_a(CH_3COOH) = 4.74$

On comparison, moles of CH_3COOH > *moles of NaOH*
Thus, NaOH will react with CH_3COOH *and* CH_3COONa *(equal to NaOH) will be formed. Thus, mixture will be a buffer of* CH_3COOH *and* CH_3COONa.

Sol. $CH_3COOH = 50 \times 0.20 = 10$ millimol

$NaOH = 50 \times 0.10 = 5$ millimoles

	CH_3COOH +	$NaOH$ ⇌	CH_3COONa +	H_2O
Initial (millimol)	10	5		
After reaction	5	0	5	

Thus, $[CH_3COOH] = 5$ millimoles in 100 mL = 0.05 M

Similarly, $[CH_3COONa] = 0.05$ M

By Henderson-Hasselbalch equation,

$$\therefore \quad pH = pK_a + \log\frac{[CH_3COONa]}{[CH_3COOH]} = 4.74 + \log\frac{0.05}{0.05} = 4.74$$

Immediate Test 19

Calculate the pH of a solution containing 75 mL of 0.01 M HCl and 50 mL of 0.02 M CH_3COONa. $pK_a(CH_3COOH) = 4.74$.

Example 8.24) Calculate the pH of a solution made by mixing 50.0 mL of 0.20 M NH_4Cl and 75.0 mL of 0.1 M NaOH. [$pK_b(NH_4OH) = 4.74$]

Sol. $NH_4Cl + NaOH \rightleftharpoons NH_4OH + NaCl$

Part of NH_4Cl is converted to NH_4OH on reaction with limiting reagent NaOH. Thus, mixture is a buffer.

$NH_4Cl = 50 \times 0.20 = 10$ millimol

$NaOH = 75 \times 0.10 = 7.5$ millimol

Total volume = 125 mL = 0.125 L

$$NH_4Cl + NaOH \rightleftharpoons NH_4OH + NaCl$$

	NH_4Cl	$NaOH$	NH_4OH
Initial (millimol)	10	7.5	
At equilibrium	2.5	0	7.5

$$[NH_4Cl] = \frac{2.5 \times 10^{-3}}{0.125} = 0.02\text{ M} \Rightarrow [NH_4OH] = \frac{7.5 \times 10^{-3}}{0.125} = 0.06\text{ M}$$

Thus, by Henderson-Hasselbalch equation,

$$pOH = pK_b + \log\frac{[NH_4Cl]}{[NH_4OH]} = 4.74 + \log\frac{1}{3} = 4.26$$

$$\therefore \quad pH = 14 - 4.26 = 9.74$$

Immediate Test 20

Calculate the pH of a solution which results from the mixing of 50.0 mL of 0.30 M HCl with 50.0 mL of 0.40 M NH_3. ($pK_a(NH_4^+) = 9.26$)

Example 8.25) The base imidazole has $K_b = 9.8 \times 10^{-8}$.

(a) In what amounts should 0.02 M HCl and 0.02 M imidazole be mixed to make 100 mL of buffer at pH 7.00?

(b) If the resulting buffer is diluted to 1 L, what is the pH of the diluted buffer.

Sol.

(a) Let imidazole be shown as = Im

$$Im + H_2O \rightleftharpoons ImH^+ + OH^-$$

Let volume of 0.02 M HCl be = V mL = 0.02 V millimol

and that of 0.02 m imidazole be = $(100 - V)$ mL

= 0.02 $(100 - V)$ millimol

$$Im + HCl \rightleftharpoons ImH^+ + Cl^-$$

	Im	HCl	ImH^+
Initial millimol	$0.02(100 - V)$	$0.02V$	
After	$0.02(100 - V) - 0.02V$ $[2 - 0.04V]$	0	$0.02V$

$$K_b = \frac{[ImH^+][OH^-]}{[Im]} = 9.8 \times 10^{-8}$$

$$\frac{0.02\,V \times 1 \times 10^{-7}}{2\,[1 - 0.02V]} = 9.8 \times 10^{-8} \Rightarrow \frac{0.01\,V}{(1 - 0.02\,V)} = 0.98$$

$$0.0296\,V = 0.98 \Rightarrow V = 33.1\text{ mL}$$

$\therefore$ HCl required = 33.1 mL

(b) Since, both are equally diluted, hence no effect on pH.

Immediate Test 21

To prepare 100 mL of a buffer of pH 9, calculate volume of 0.1 M NH_4OH and 0.1 M HCl solution. $pK_b(NH_4OH) = 4.74$

Example 8.26) The pH inside most cells is maintained at around 7.4 by a phosphate buffer made from the $H_2PO_4^-(aq)$ ion and its conjugate base $HPO_4^{2-}(aq)$. For the equilibrium

$$H_2PO_4^-(aq) + H_2O(l) \rightleftharpoons HPO_4^{2-}(aq) + H_3O^+(aq),$$

$$pK_a = 7.2$$

A typical value for the total phosphate concentration in a cell is 0.02 M. Calculate $[HPO_4^{2-}]$ and $[H_2PO_4^-]$ inside the cell.

Total concentration of the acid and conjugate base is known. Thus, from the pH and pK_a values, amount of each component can be calculated by Henderson-Hasselbalch equation.

Sol. Let $HPO_4^{2-} = x$ mol L^{-1}

then $H_2PO_4^- = (0.02 - x)$ mol L^{-1}

By Henderson-Hasselbalch equation,

$$pH = pK_a + \log\frac{[HPO_4^{2-}]}{[H_2PO_4^-]}$$

$$7.4 = 7.2 + \log\left(\frac{x}{0.02 - x}\right)$$

$$\log\left(\frac{x}{0.02 - x}\right) = 0.2 \Rightarrow \frac{x}{(0.02 - x)} = 1.585$$

$$\therefore \quad x = 1.226 \times 10^{-2}\text{ M}$$

Thus, $[HPO_4^{2-}] = 1.226 \times 10^{-2}$ M

and $[H_2PO_4^-] = 7.74 \times 10^{-3}$ M

Immediate Test 22

pH of a buffer of $NaHSO_4$ and Na_2SO_4 is 2. If pK_a of HSO_4^- is 2.0, what is molar concentration of $NaHSO_4$ and Na_2SO_4, if total concentration is 0.2 M?

Example 8.27) For the $[HCO_3^- / H_2CO_3]$ buffer that controls pH of the blood, variation of pH with $\log([HCO_3^-]/[H_2CO_3])$ is shown

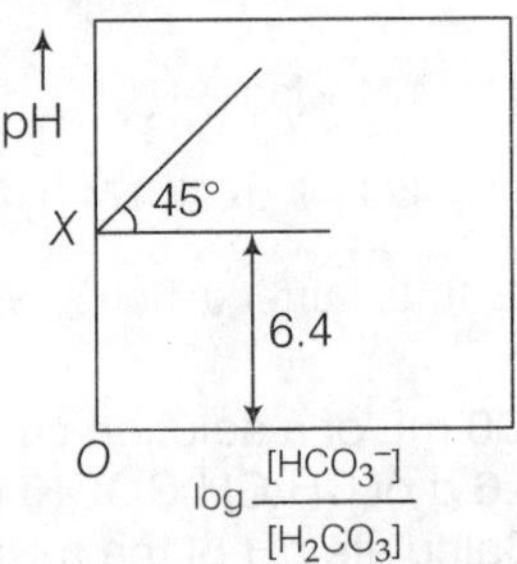

What is pH of the buffer when $[CO_2(aq)]$ and $[HCO_3^-]$ are in 1 : 10 molar ratio?

Aqueous CO_2 (CO_2 in H_2O) acts like a buffer of H_2CO_3 and HCO_3^-.

Given, graph is for Henderson-Hasselbalch equation and is a straight line, $y = mx + c$. On comparison, pK_a is derived, thus pH is known.

Sol. Based on Henderson-Hasselbalch equation, graph is linear with OX = Intercept on pH axis.

$$pH = pK_a + \log\frac{[HCO_3^-]}{[H_2CO_3]}$$

$$y = mx + c \Rightarrow pK_a = c = 6.4$$

Given, $[HCO_3^-]/[H_2CO_3] = [10/1]$

$$\therefore \quad pH = 6.4 + \log 10 = 7.4$$

Immediate Test 23

For the basic buffer $[NH_4OH + NH_4Cl]$ variation of pH with $\log \frac{[NH_3]}{[NH_4^+]}$ is shown

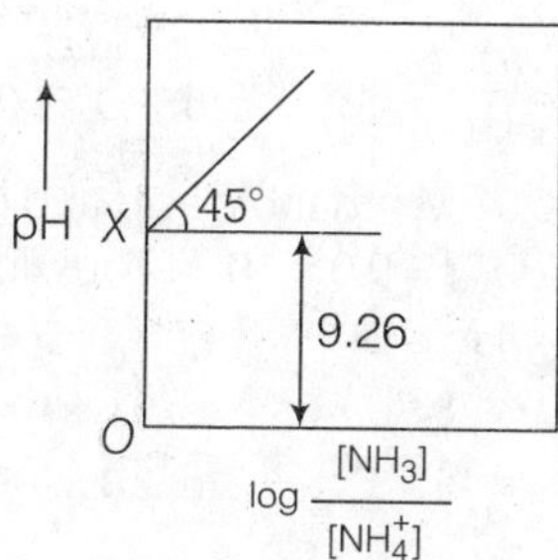

Calculate pH when 100 mL of 0.1 M NH_4OH is treated with 50 mL of 0.1 M HCl.

Example 8.28) pH of an acidic buffer of Na_2HPO_4 and NaH_2PO_4 is 4.7. If pK_a of $H_2PO_4^-$ is 5.0, calculate mole fraction of $H_2PO_4^-$ in the buffer.

$$pH = pK_a + \log \frac{[HPO_4^{2-}]}{[H_2PO_4^-]}$$

pH and pK_a *are known. Thus,* $\frac{[HPO_4^{2-}]}{[H_2PO_4^-]}$ *is also known.*

Hence, mole fraction is calculated.

Sol. *If* $H_2PO_4^-$ *is* y mol L^{-1} *and* HPO_4^{2-} *is* x mol L^{-1}.

$$pH = pK_a + \log \frac{[HPO_4^{2-}]}{[H_2PO_4^-]}$$

$$4.7 = 5.0 + \log \frac{(x)}{(y)}$$

$$-0.3 = \log\left(\frac{x}{y}\right) \Rightarrow \log\left(\frac{y}{x}\right) = 0.3$$

Take antilog,

$$\therefore \quad \frac{y}{x} = \frac{2}{1}$$

Thus, $(y + x) = 3$

$\therefore$ Mole fraction of $H_2PO_4^- = \frac{y}{x+y} = \frac{2}{3}$

Immediate Test 24

For the basic buffer, pyridine and pyridine hydrochloride, mole fraction of pyridine is 0.4. What is value of $(pOH - pK_b)$ of this buffer?

Example 8.29) Calculate the pH of a solution resulting from the addition of 50 mL of 0.10 M HCl to 50.0 mL of a solution containing 0.15 M CH_3COOH and 0.20 M CH_3COONa. $[pK_a(CH_3COOH) = 4.74]$

Problem deals with effect of addition of acid to acidic buffer.

$$CH_3COO^- + H^+ \rightleftharpoons CH_3COOH$$

When HCl is added to this buffer, $[CH_3COO^-]$ *decreases and* $[CH_3COOH]$ *increases equal to the amount of HCl added. Thus, pH decreases.*

Sol. HCl added $= 50 \times 0.1 = 5.0$ millimol

$CH_3COOH = 50 \times 0.15 = 7.5$ millimol

$CH_3COONa = 50 \times 0.20 = 10.0$ millimol

	CH_3COO^-	+ H^+	$\rightleftharpoons CH_3COOH$	
Initial	10.0		7.5	millimol
Added		5.0		millimol
After reaction	(10.0 – 5.0)	(5.0 – 5.0)	(7.5 + 5.0)	millimol
At equilibrium	5.0	0	12.5	millimol

Thus, $pH = pK_a + \log \frac{[CH_3COO^-]}{[CH_3COOH]}$

$$pH = 4.74 + \log\left(\frac{5.0}{12.5}\right)$$

$$= 474 + \log 0.4 = 4.74 - 0.40 = 4.34$$

- If HCl is not added,

$$pH = 4.74 + \log\left(\frac{0.20}{0.15}\right) = 4.75 + 0.125 = 4.865$$

Thus, buffer capacity is within ±1.

Immediate Test 25

Determine the pH of a solution after 0.10 mole of NaOH is added to 1.00 L of a solution containing 0.15 M CH_3CH_2COOH and 0.20 M CH_3CH_2COONa.

$[pK_a(CH_3CH_2COOH) = 5.0]$

Example 8.30) A basic buffer contains 0.01 M pyridine (C_5H_5N) and 0.02 M pyridinium chloride (C_5H_5NHCl). If one drop of NaOH is added to one litre of a buffer making [NaOH] = 0.005 M, what is change in pOH?

Sol.

	$C_5H_5\overset{\oplus}{N}H$	+ $\overset{-}{O}H$	$\longrightarrow C_5H_5N$	+ H_2O
Initial	0.02 M		0.01 M	
Added		0.005 M		
At equilibrium	(0.02 – 0.005) M = (0.015) M		(0.01 + 0.005) M = (0.015 M)	

$$pOH\ (\text{before adding } OH^-) = pK_b + \log\left(\frac{0.02}{0.01}\right) = pK_b + \log 2$$

$$p'OH\ (\text{after adding } OH^-) = pK_b + \log\left(\frac{0.015}{0.015}\right) = pK_b$$

$$\therefore \quad (pOH - p'OH) = \log 2 = 0.3010$$

Immediate Test 26

10 mL of 0.01 M HCl is added to 90 mL of a buffer of 0.01 M NH_4OH and 0.01 M NH_4Cl. $pK_b(NH_4OH) = 4.74$. Calculate change in pH.

KNOWLEDGE CONFIRMATION **Test 4**

1 For the equilibrium,

$$H_2CO_3 + H_2O \rightleftharpoons HCO_3^- + H_3O^+, \quad pK_a = 6.38$$

For controlling pH of blood, (7.40), $\log\frac{[HCO_3^-]}{[H_2CO_3]}$ is

(a) 1.02 (b) – 1.02 (c) 0.9803 (d) – 0.9803

2 For $CH_3COOH + H_2O \rightleftharpoons CH_3COO^- + H_3O^+$,

$$pK_a = 4.74$$

Buffer capacity is maximum at pH

(a) 4.74 (b) 9.26 (c) 5.74 (d) 3.74

3. For $NH_4OH \rightleftharpoons NH_4^+ + OH^-$, $pK_b = 4.74$

Buffer capacity is maximum at pH

(a) 4.74 (b) 9.26 (c) 2.37 (d) 4.63

4 20 mL of 0.2 M NaOH is added to 50 mL of 0.2 M CH_3COOH. Thus, $(pH - pK_a)$ is

(a) $\log\frac{3}{2}$ (b) $\log\frac{2}{3}$ (c) log 2 (d) 2log 2

5 pH of the mixture of 50 mL of 0.3 M HCl and 50 mL of 0.4 M NH_3 solution is $[pK_a(NH_4^+) = 9.26]$

(a) 5.22 (b) 1.30 (c) 8.78 (d) 12.70

6 75 mL of 0.1 M NaOH is added to 50 mL of 0.2 M NH_4Cl solution at 298 K. If $pK_b(NH_3)$ is 4.74, pH of the mixture is

(a) 4.74 + log 3 (b) 4.74 – log 3
(c) 9.26 + log 3 (d) 9.26 – log 3

7 A buffer is 0.1 M CH_3CH_2COOH and 0.05 M $(CH_3CH_2COO)_2Ba$. pK_a of CH_3CH_2COOH is 5.0. Thus, pH of the buffer is

(a) 5.3 (b) 4.7 (c) 5.0 (d) 4.0

8 One or more of the following operations will not change pH of acidic buffer *R*COONa and *R*COOH.

I. diluting the mixture ten times
II. adding some HCl
III. adding some NaOH
IV. adding equal moles each of *R*COONa and *R*COOH

Select the correct alternate.

(a) II and III (b) I and II (c) III and IV (d) I and IV

9 A weak acid *HA* has degree of dissociation *x*. Thus, $(pH - pK_a)$ is

(a) p_x (b) p_{1-x} (c) $p_{1-x} + p_x$ (d) $p_{1-x} - p_x$

10 A basic buffer of pH = 9.26 is to be prepared from 2.0 M NH_4Cl and 1.0 M $NH_3(aq)$. In one litre of buffer, volume of 2.0 M NH_4Cl solution is $(pK_b(NH_3) = 4.74)$

(a) 400 mL (b) 200 mL (c) 800 mL (d) 333 mL

11 Important diagnostic analysis in the blood is

(a) $[H_2PO_4^-]/[HPO_4^{2-}]$ (b) $[HCO_3^-]/[CO_2]$
(c) $[CO_3^{2-}]/[HCO_3^-]$ (d) $[PO_4^{3-}]/[HPO_4^{2-}]$

12 In a buffer of 0.01 M ethanoic acid and 0.01 M calcium ethanoate, $[H_3O^+] = 9.0 \times 10^{-6}$. Thus, ionisation constant of ethanoic acid is

(a) 1.8×10^{-5} (b) 9.0×10^{-6}
(c) 5.55×10^{-10} (d) 2.0×10^{-9}

13 pK_a of CH_3COOH is 4.74. Thus, buffer range of CH_3COOH and CH_3COONa buffer is

(a) 4.74 to 6.74 (b) 3.74 to 4.74
(c) 3.74 to 5.74 (d) 1.0 to – 1.0

14 In the following variation of pH with $\log\frac{[A^{-1}]}{[HA]}$ of acidic buffer [*HA* and A^-], graph is the type. To make pH = 4, ratio $\frac{[HA]}{[A^-]}$ should be

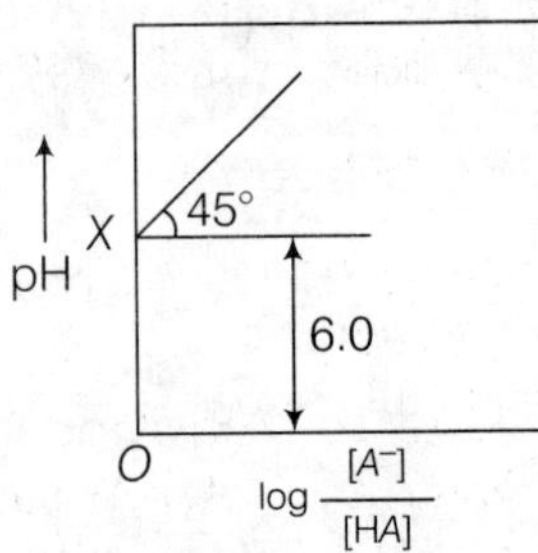

(a) 1 : 2 (b) 2 : 1 (c) 1 : 100 (d) 100 : 1

15 20.0 g of NaOH is added to 0.5 L of 1.5 M NH_4Cl solution. If $pK_b(NH_4OH)$ is 4.74, pH of the resultant solution is

(a) 9.56 (b) 4.49 (c) 7.00 (d) 7.80

16 For the equilibrium,

$$H_2PO_4^- + H_2O \rightleftharpoons HPO_4^{2-} + H_3O^+, \quad pK_a = 7.10$$

pH of the blood (which is 7.40) is controlled by $H_2PO_4^-$ and HPO_4^{2-}. What is ratio of $[H_2PO_4^-]/[HPO_4^{2-}]$ in the blood?

(a) 2 : 1 (b) 1 : 2 (c) 3 : 1 (d) 1 : 3

17 1 M NH_4OH and 1 M HCl are mixed to make total volume of 300 mL. If pH of the mixture is 9.26 and $pK_a(NH_4^+) = 9.26$, then volume ratio of NH_4OH and HCl will be:

(a) 1 : 1 (b) 1 : 2 (c) 2 : 1 (d) 3 : 1

18 *x* mole of $(NH_4)_2SO_4$ is added to 500 mL of 0.01 M NH_4OH to prepare a buffer of pH 8.26. $[pK_a(NH_4^+) = 9.26]$, thus *x* is

(a) 0.05 mol (b) 0.025 mol
(c) 0.10 mol (d) 0.005 mol

19 100 mL of 0.01 M benzoic acid ($pK_a = 4.20$) is titrated using 0.01 M KOH. pH at the point when benzoic acid is 50% neutalised is
(a) 4.20 (b) $4.20 + \log 2$
(c) $4.20 - \log 2$ (d) 4.0

20 1.20 mole of CH_3NH_2 ($pK_b = 3.3$) is added to 0.08 mole of HCl and solution is diluted to 1 dm^3. Thus, pH of the resulting solution is
(a) 11.32 (b) 10.70 (c) 10.42 (d) 11.85

21 Buffer index of buffer of 0.1 M NH_4OH and 0.1 M NH_4Cl is
(a) 0.052 (b) 0.115 (c) 0.025 (d) 0.230

22 Number of $[OH^-]$ ions present per mm^3 of buffer solution of 0.15 M CH_3COONa and 1.5 M CH_3COOH($pK_a = 5.0$).
(a) $10^{-10} N_0$ (b) $10^{-4} N_0$
(c) $10^{-3} N_0$ (d) $10^{-6} N_0$

23 On adding 1 mL of HCl (= 0.05 M in the solution) pH of the buffer of 0.10 M CH_3COOH and 0.10 M CH_3COONa will be ($\Delta V = 0$)
(a) $pK_a + \log 1$ (b) $pK_a + \log 3$
(c) $pK_a - \log 3$ (d) $pK_a + \log 2$

24 On adding 1 mL of HCl (0.05 M in the solution) to a buffer of 1 M NH_4OH and 1M NH_4Cl (pK_b (NH_4OH) = 4.74)
(a) pH increases from 4.74 to 5.04
(b) pH decreases from 4.74 to 4.44
(c) pH increases from 9.26 to 9.30
(d) pH decreases from 9.26 to 9.22

25 Given 50 mL of 0.20 M solution of the acid *HA* ($K_a = 1.0 \times 10^{-5}$) and 50 mL of Na*A* solution. Thus, in a buffer of pH 4, molar concentration of Na*A* is
(a) 1.0×10^{-2} M (b) 2.0×10^{-2} M
(c) 1.0×10^{-5} M (d) 2.0×10^{-5} M

26 pH of 0.01 M CH_3COOH is 3.37. Amount of NaOH that should be added to 1 dm^3 of CH_3COOH, so that pH of the resulting solution be 4.74, is [pK_a (CH_3COOH)] = 4.74
(a) 0.4 g (b) 0.1 g
(c) 0.05 g (d) 0.2 g

27 pH of a buffer of *HA*($pK_a = 5$) and A^- is 4. Thus, mole fraction of *HA* in the buffer mixture is
(a) $\frac{1}{11}$ (b) $\frac{10}{11}$ (c) $\frac{1}{10}$ (d) $\frac{9}{10}$

28 *HA* is 50% ionised. pOH of an aqueous solution of *HA* and A^- (in a buffer) is [$pK_a(HA) = 4.5$]
(a) 4.5 (b) 2.5
(c) 9.5 (d) 7.0

29 CH_3NH_2 (0.1 mol, $K_b = 5 \times 10^{-4}$) is added to 0.08 mole of HCl and the solution is diluted to 1L. Resulting hydrogen ion concentration is
(a) 1.6×10^{-11} (b) 8×10^{-11}
(c) 5×10^{-5} (d) 8×10^{-2}

30 Aqueous solutions of HNO_3, KOH, CH_3COOH and CH_3COONa of identical concentrations are provided. The pair(s) of solution which form a buffer upon mixing is (are)
(a) HNO_3, CH_3COOH (b) KOH, CH_3COONa
(c) HNO_3, CH_3COONa (d) CH_3COOH, CH_3COONa

31 Which of the following will raise the pH of 1.00 L of 0-50 M HCl to the greatest extent.
(a) 0.40 mol NaOH (b) 0.50 mol CH_3COOH
(c) 0.60 mol CH_3COONa (d) 0.70 mol NaOH

32 A 25.00 mL of 0.01 M C_6H_5COOH (benzoic acid)($pK_a = 4.2$) is titrated with 0.01 M $Ba(OH)_2$. Thus, pH of the solution after 6.25 mL of 0.01 M $Ba(OH)_2$ has been added is
(a) 2.96 (b) 5.22 (c) 4.60 (d) 4.20

33 Above solution can be made of pH = 7 after the addtion of
(a) 25mL of $Ba(OH)_2$
(b) 12.5 mL of $Ba(OH)_2$
(c) 6.25 mL of $Ba(OH)_2$
(d) Can't be made benzoic acid being weak acid

34 When 0.80 mol of acid is added to 250 mL of a buffer solution, pH decreases by 0.2 units. Thus, buffer capacity of the buffer is
(a) 0.2 (b) 0.3 (c) 0.4 (d) 0.5

35 In which of the following buffer pH = pK_a
(a) 25 mL of 1 M HCl solution added to 50 mL of 1 M CH_3COONa
(b) 1 L of solution containing 0.1 M NH_3 and 13.2 g of $(NH_4)_2SO_4$
(c) 100 mL of 0.1M H_2CO_3 and 100 mL of 0.1 M $NaHCO_3$
(d) In all of the above cases

36 20 mL of 0.1 M H_2SO_4 solution is added to 30 mL of 0.2 M NH_4OH solution. The pH of the resultant mixture is (pK_b of NH_4OH = 4.7) ***[JEE Main 2019(I) NTA]***
(a) 9.3 (b) 5.0 (c) 9.0 (d) 5.2

37 Consider the following statements.
(A) The pH of a mixture containing 400 mL of 0.1 M H_2SO_4 and 400 mL of 0.1 M NaOH will be approximately 1.3.
(B) Ionic product of water is temperature dependent.
(C) A monobasic acid with $K_a = 10^{-5}$ has a pH = 5. The degree of dissociation of this acid is 50%.
(D) The Le-Chatelier's principle is not applicable to common-ion effect statement are. ***[JEE Main 2019 (II) NTA]***

The correct statements are
(a) (A), (B) and (D) (b) (B) and (C)
(c) (A) and (B) (d) (A), (B), (C)

Hydrolysis of Salts

Interaction of cation or anion or both of a salt with water to give acidic or basic or neutral solution is termed as **salt hydrolysis.** Hydrolysis will occur only if a chemical reaction can produce a **weak acid** or **weak base.**

Type I. Salt of strong acid and strong base

$$\underset{\text{Salt}}{NaCl} + H_2O \rightleftharpoons \underset{\text{SB}}{NaOH\,(aq)} + \underset{\text{SA}}{HCl\,(aq)}$$

$$Na^+\,Cl^- + H_2O \rightleftharpoons Na^+ + OH^- + H^+ + Cl^-$$

Net $\boxed{H_2O \rightleftharpoons H^+ + OH^-}$

- Their is no interaction of salt with H_2O. Thus, no hydrolysis of salt of strong acid and strong base.
- No effect on litmus or turmeric paper.
- Being neutral, pH = 7 at 298 K.

Type II. Salt of weak acid and strong base

$$\underset{\text{Salt}}{CH_3COONa} + H_2O \rightleftharpoons \underset{\text{WA}}{CH_3COOH} + \underset{\text{SB}}{NaOH}$$

$$CH_3COO^- + Na^+ + H_2O \rightleftharpoons CH_3COOH + Na^+ + OH^-$$

Net : $\boxed{CH_3COO^- + H_2O \rightleftharpoons CH_3COOH + OH^-}$

$$CO_3^{2-} + 2H_2O \rightleftharpoons H_2CO_3 + 2OH^-$$

- Anion of the salt (or conjugate base of weak acid) is hydrolysed.
- Hydrolysis results in the formation of free OH^- ions.

  Number of (OH^-) = Charge on anion

  Thus, larger the charge, greater the number of (OH^-) ions and thus, larger the pH.
- Solution is basic, pH > 7
  - such solutions turn red litmus blue.
  - such solutions turn turmeric paper brown.

$$A^- + H_2O \rightleftharpoons HA + OH^-$$

$$\text{Hydrolysis constant, } K_h = \frac{[HA][OH^-]}{[A^-]} = \frac{Cx^2}{(1-x)} \approx Cx^2$$

$$\therefore \quad \boxed{x = \sqrt{\frac{K_h}{C}}}$$

where x = degree of hydrolysis

$$HA \rightleftharpoons H^+ + A^+$$

$$\therefore \quad K_a = \frac{[H^+][A^-]}{[HA]}$$

$$\therefore \quad K_h \cdot K_a = \frac{[HA][OH^-]}{[A^-]}\frac{[A^-][H^+]}{[HA]} = [H^+][OH^-] = K_w$$

$$\therefore \quad \boxed{K_h = \frac{K_w}{K_a}}$$

$$\therefore \quad x = \sqrt{\frac{K_w}{K_a\,C}}$$

$$\boxed{pH = 7 + \frac{1}{2}[pK_a + \log C]}$$

- Hydrolysis constant of anion of salt of weak acid and strong base is also the ionisation constant of conjugate base of weak acid.

$$\boxed{\begin{array}{c} A^- + H_2O \rightleftharpoons HA + OH^- \\ K_b = K_h = \dfrac{[HA]\,[OH^-]}{[A^-]} = \dfrac{K_w}{K_a} \end{array}}$$

Type III. Salt of weak base and strong acid

$$\underset{\text{Salt}}{NH_4\,Cl} + H_2O \rightleftharpoons \underset{\text{WB}}{NH_4\,OH} + \underset{\text{SA}}{HCl}$$

$$NH_4^+Cl^- + H_2O \rightleftharpoons NH_4OH + H^+ + Cl^-$$

Net $\boxed{NH_4^+ + H_2O \rightleftharpoons NH_4OH + H^+}$

$$Cu^{2+} + 2H_2O \rightleftharpoons Cu(OH)_2 + 2H^+$$

$$Al^{3+} + 3H_2O \rightleftharpoons Al(OH)_3 + 3H^+$$

- Cation of the salt (or conjugate acid of weak base) is hydrolysed.
- Hydrolysis results in the formation of free H^+ ions.

  Number of H^+ ions = Charge on cation

  Thus, larger the charge, greater the number of H^+ ions and thus, smaller the pH.

  Solution is acidic, pH < 7
  - such solutions turn blue litmus red.

$$\text{Hydrolysis constant, } K_h = \frac{K_w}{K_b} = \frac{Cx^2}{(1-x)} \approx Cx^2$$

$$\therefore \quad \boxed{x = \sqrt{\frac{K_h}{C}} = \sqrt{\frac{K_w}{K_b C}}}$$

and $\boxed{pH = 7 - \frac{1}{2}[pK_b + \log C]}$

Hydrolysis constant K_h of cation of salt of weak base and strong acid is also the ionisation constant of conjugate acid of the weak base.

$$NH_4^+ + H_2O \rightleftharpoons NH_4OH + H^+$$

$$K_a = \frac{[NH_4OH][H^+]}{[NH_4^+]} = K_h = \frac{K_w}{K_b}$$

Type IV. Salt of weak acid and weak base

$$\underset{\text{Salt}}{CH_3COONH_4} + H_2O \rightleftharpoons \underset{\text{WA}}{CH_3COOH} + \underset{\text{WB}}{NH_4OH}$$

$$CH_3COO^- + NH_4^+ + H_2O \rightleftharpoons CH_3COOH + NH_4OH$$

- Cation and anion both are hydrolysed.
- $K_h = \frac{x^2}{(1-x)^2} = \frac{K_w}{K_a\ K_b}$

$$\therefore \quad \left(\frac{x}{1-x}\right) = \sqrt{K_h} = \sqrt{\frac{K_w}{K_a\ K_b}}$$

If $x << 1$

$$\boxed{x = \sqrt{K_h} = \sqrt{\frac{K_w}{K_a\ K_b}}}$$

Thus, degree of hydrolysis is independent of concentration of salt.

$$\boxed{pH = 7 + \frac{1}{2}[pK_a - pK_b]}$$

– If $K_a = K_b$, $pK_a = pK_b$ then pH = 7 (neutral)

– If $K_a > K_b$, $pK_a < pK_b$

$$(pK_a - pK_b) = y$$

then $\quad pH = 7 - \left(\frac{y}{2}\right)$

thus, $\quad pH < 7$ (acidic)

– If $K_a < K_b$, $pK_a > pK_b$

$$(pK_a - pK_b) = y$$

then, $\quad pH = 7 + \left(\frac{y}{2}\right)$,

$pH > 7$ (thus basic solution).

Type V. Hydrolysis of amphiprotic anions

Amphiprotic anions are **proton donor** as well as proton acceptor.

$$\underset{\text{Acid}}{HCO_3^-} + H_2O \rightleftharpoons CO_3^{2-} + H_3O^+$$

$$\underset{\text{Base}}{HCO_3^-} + H_2O \rightleftharpoons H_2CO_3 + OH^-$$

Thus, HCO_3^- is amphiprotic

$$H_2CO_3 \rightleftharpoons H^+ + HCO_3^-,\ K_{a_1}$$

$$HCO_3^- \rightleftharpoons H^+ + CO_3^{2-},\ K_{a_2}$$

$$\boxed{pH = \frac{pK_{a_1} + pK_{a_2}}{2}}$$

For **polyprotic salts**, take K_a values of the steps involved

$$H_3PO_4 \rightleftharpoons H_2PO_4^- + H^+\ K_{a_1}$$

$$H_2PO_4^- \rightleftharpoons HPO_4^{2-} + H^+\ K_{a_2}$$

$$HPO_4^{2-} \rightleftharpoons PO_4^{3-} + H^+\ K_{a_3}$$

For $H_2PO_4^-$, take K_{a_1} and K_{a_2}

For HPO_4^{2-}, take K_{a_2} and K_{a_3}

Thus, $\quad pH(H_2PO_4^-) = \left(\frac{pK_{a_1} + pK_{a_2}}{2}\right)$

$$pH[HPO_4^{2-}] = \frac{pK_{a_2} + pK_{a_3}}{2}$$

If anion is amphiprotic and cation is also hydrolysed as in NH_4HCO_3.

(HCO_3^- is amphiprotic and NH_4^+ is hydrolysed)

then $\quad \boxed{[H_3O^+] = \sqrt{K_{a_1} K_{a_2} + \frac{K_w K_{a_1}}{K_b}}}$

K_b is the ionisation constant of base. K_{a_1} and K_{a_2} are stepwise ionisation constants of acid.

$$H_2A \rightleftharpoons H^+ + \underset{\text{Amphiprotic}}{HA^-},\ K_{a_1}$$

$$HA^- \rightleftharpoons H^+ + A^{2-},\ K_{a_2}$$

e.g. For PO_4^{3-} in one step hydrolysis

$$PO_4^{3-} + H_2O \rightleftharpoons HPO_4^{2-} + OH^-$$

$$pH = 7 + \frac{1}{2}[pK_{a_3} + \log C]$$

PO_4^{3-} is like a weak base.

Solved Examples & Instant Practice

Example 8.31) Calculate pH of 1 M PO_4^{3-} solution.

$$pK_b(PO_4^{3-}) = 1.62$$

Sol. Aqueous solution of PO_4^{3-} is alkaline due to hydrolysis

$$PO_4^{3-} + H_2O \rightleftharpoons HPO_4^{2-} + OH^- \text{ and thus pH} > 7,$$

For such cases

$$pH = 7 + \frac{pK_b}{2} + \frac{\log C}{2}$$

$$pH = 7 + \frac{1.02}{2} + \frac{\log 1}{2} = 7 + 0.81 + 0 = 7.81$$

■ PO_4^{3-} behaves as a base in aqueous solution. Thus, $K_b = K_h$ (hydrolysis constant of PO_4^{3-})

$$x \text{ (degree of hydrolysis)} = \sqrt{\frac{K_h}{C}} = \sqrt{\frac{K_w}{K_b C}}$$

$$[OH^-] = C\alpha = C\sqrt{\frac{K_w}{K_b C}} = \sqrt{\frac{K_w C}{K_b}}$$

$$\therefore \quad pOH = \frac{1}{2}[pK_w - \log C - pK_b]$$

$$\therefore \quad pOH = (14 - pOH) = \frac{1}{2}[pK_w + pK_b + \log C]$$

$$= 7 + \frac{pK_b}{2} + \frac{\log C}{2}$$

Immediate Test 27

Calculate pH of 0.005 M $(NH_4)_2SO_4$.
Given, $pK_a(NH_4^+) = 9.26$

Example 8.32) What is pH of 0.02 M aqueous $CuSO_4$ solution?

$$Cu^{2+}(aq) + 2H_2O(l) \rightleftharpoons [Cu(OH)]^+(aq) + H_3O^+(aq), \quad K_a = 5 \times 10^{-9}$$

Sol. $CuSO_4$ is a salt of weak base $[Cu(OH)]^+$ and strong acid H_2SO_4. Thus, its aqueous solution is acidic due to hydrolysis of Cu^{2+}.

$$pH < 7$$

$$pH = 7 - \frac{pK_b}{2} - \frac{\log C}{2}$$

Also, $\quad K_a K_b = K_w$

If $\quad K_a(Cu^{2+}) = 5 \times 10^{-9}$

then, $\quad K_b[Cu(OH)^+] = \dfrac{K_w}{K_a} = \dfrac{1 \times 10^{-14}}{5 \times 10^{-9}} = 2 \times 10^{-6}$

$$\therefore \quad pK_b = (6 - \log 2)$$

$$pH = 7 - \left[\frac{6 - \log 2}{2}\right] - \frac{\log 0.02}{2}$$

$$pH = 7 - 3 + \frac{\log 2}{2} + \frac{2}{2} - \frac{\log 2}{2} = 5.0$$

■ If aqueous solution of Cu^{2+} is acidic, then by Ostwald's dilution law, $pH = \frac{1}{2}(pK_a - \log C)$

Immediate Test 28

For $Ni^{2+}(aq)$ solution,

$$Ni^{2+}(aq) + H_2O(l) \rightleftharpoons [Ni(OH)]^+(aq) + H_3O^+(aq)$$

$[H_3O^+] = 4.5 \times 10^{-6}$ in 0.04 M aqueous solution.

(a) calculate ionisation constant (K_a) of the above reaction. Also, calculate
(b) hydrolysis constant and
(c) degree of hydrolysis.

Example 8.33) 100 mL of 0.01 M CH_3CH_2COOH ($K_a = 1 \times 10^{-5}$) is treated with 0.02 M NaOH. Calculate pH after
(a) 25 mL of NaOH is added. (b) 50 mL of NaOH is added.

Before CH_3CH_2COOH is completely neutralised mixture is a buffer and

$$pH = pK_a + \log\frac{[CH_3CH_2COO^-]}{[CH_3CH_2COOH]}$$

After complete reaction of CH_3CH_2COOH stoichiometrically with NaOH, CH_3CH_2COONa is formed but its aqueous solution is alkaline due to hydrolysis and pH > 7.

$$\therefore \quad pH = 7 + \frac{pK_a}{2} + \frac{\log C}{2}$$

■ Concentration of the salt is taken after dilution.

Sol. MV (mL) = millimol.

100 mL of 0.01 M CH_3CH_2COOH = 1 millimol
25 mL 90.02 M NaOH = 0.5 millimol
50 mL 90.0 M NaOH = 1 millimol

	CH_3CH_2COOH +	NaOH ⇌	CH_3CH_2COONa +	H_2O
Initial	1 millimol	0	0	0
Stage I. (NaOH added)		0.5 millimol		
At equili.	0.5		0.5	
	Buffer			
Stage II. (NaOH added)		1 millmol		
After reaction	0	0	1 millmol	

1 millimol in 150 mL solutions

$$\therefore \quad [CH_3CH_2COONa] = \frac{1 \times 10^{-3} \text{mol}}{0.150 \text{ L}} = 6.67 \times 10^{-3} \text{ M}$$

(a) pH of the buffer

$$pH = pK_a + \log\frac{[CH_3CH_2COONa]}{[CH_3CH_2COOH]} = 5.0 + \log 1 = 5.0$$

(b) Due to hydrolysis,

$$pH = 7 + \frac{pK_a}{2} + \frac{\log C}{2} = 7 + \frac{5.0}{2} + \left[\frac{\log 6.67 \times 10^{-3}}{2}\right]$$

$$= 9.50 - 1.09 = 8.41$$

Immediate Test 29

50 mL of 0.001 M $CH_3CH_2NH_2$ ($K_b = 1 \times 10^{-5}$) is titrated using 0.005 M HCl. Calculate pH after
(a) 5 mL of HCl is added. (b) 10 mL of HCl is added.

Example 8.34) A 0.25 M solution of pyridinium chloride $C_5H_4NH^+Cl^-$ was found to have pH of 2.89. What is K_b for the basic dissociation of C_5H_5N?

Aqueous solution of $C_5H_5NH^+$ is acidic due to its hydrolysis.

$$C_5H_5NH^+ + H_2O \rightleftharpoons C_6H_5N + H_3O^+$$

Thus, hydrolysis constant K_h is known. Also, $C_5N_5NH^+$ is behaving like a weak acid. Thus, it is also ionisation constant of $C_5H_5NH^+$.

Sol. $K_h\ (C_5H_5NH) = K_a$

Also, $K_aK_b = K_w$

$\therefore$ $K_b\ (C_5H_5N) = \dfrac{K_w}{K_a} = \dfrac{K_w}{K_h}$

$pH = 2.89$

$\therefore$ $[H_3O^+] = 10^{-2.89} = 10^{-3.0}\ 10^{0.11} = 1288 \times 10^{-3}$ M

$\therefore$ $K_h = K_a = \dfrac{[C_5H_5N]\ [H_3O^+]}{[C_5H_5NH^+]} = \dfrac{(1288 \times 10^{-3})^2}{025}$

$= 6.636 \times 10^{-6}$

$\therefore$ $K_b(C_5H_5N) = \dfrac{1 \times 10^{-14}}{6.636 \times 10^{-6}} = 1.51 \times 10^{-9}$

Immediate Test 30

For the equilibrium giving hydrolysis of Fe^{3+}

$Fe^{3+} + 2H_2O \rightleftharpoons [Fe(OH)]^{2+} + H_3O^+,\ K_a = K_h = 6.5 \times 10^{-3}$

What is the maximum pH value which could be used so that at least 95% of the total iron (III) in a dilute solution exists as Fe^{3+}?

Example 8.35) Calculate pH of 0.01 M $NaHCO_3$

$K_{a_1} = 4.2 \times 10^{-7}, K_{a_2} = 5.6 \times 10^{-11}$.

Sol. HCO_3^- is amphiprotic, it is thus H^+ ion acceptor as well as H^+ ion donor.

$$\underset{\text{Base}}{HCO_3^-} + H_2O \rightleftharpoons H_2CO_3 + OH^-$$

$$\underset{\text{Acid}}{HCO_3^-} + H_2O \rightleftharpoons CO_3^{2-} + H_3O^+$$

For amphiprotic species,

$pH = \left(\dfrac{pK_{a_1} + pK_{a_2}}{2}\right) \Rightarrow K_{a_1} = 4.2 \times 10^{-7}$

$\therefore$ $pK_{a_1} = 6.38$ $\therefore K_{a_2} = 5.6 \times 10^{-11}$

$pK_{a_2} = 10.25$

$\therefore$ $pH = \dfrac{pK_{a_1} + pK_{a_2}}{2} = \dfrac{6.38 + 1025}{2} = 8.32$

Immediate Test 31

Calculate pH of 0.01 M aqueous solution each of

(a) PO_4^{3-} (b) HPO_4^{2-} (c) $H_2PO_4^-$

Given for H_3PO_4 $\begin{bmatrix} pK_{a_1} = 2.15 \\ pK_{a_2} = 7.20 \\ pK_{a_3} = 12.35 \end{bmatrix}$

Example 8.36) 25 mL of a dilute aqueous solution of H_2A is titrated with NaOH(*aq*). The solution has pH = 5.0 when 8.0 mL of 0.02 M NaOH has been added and pH = 8.0 when 16.0 mL of 0.02 M NaOH has been added (the equivalent point). Calculate pK_{a_1} and pK_{a_2} of the dibasic acid H_2A.

H_2A being a dibasic acid is neutralised in two stages:

I. $H_2A + NaOH \longrightarrow NaHA + H_2O$

II. $NaHA + NaOH \longrightarrow Na_2A + H_2O$

In stage I, H_2A is monobasic acid and at half neutralisation

$$[H_2A] = [NaHA]$$

Thus, it is buffer.

$\therefore$ $pH = pK_{a_1} + \log \dfrac{[NaHA]}{[H_2A]}$

NaHA formed is amphiprotic. It is proton donor as well as proton acceptor.

Thus, $pH = \left(\dfrac{pK_{a_1} + pK_{a_2}}{2}\right)$

Thus, pK_{a_1} and pK_{a_2} are calculated.

Sol. Equivalent point is reached after addition of NaOH = 16.0 mL. Thus, when 8.0 mL NaOH is added, H_2A is 50%. neutralised upto HA^-. Thus, by Henderson-Hasselbalch equation.

Stage I $5 = pK_{a_1} + \log \dfrac{[NaHA]}{[H_2A]}$

Since, $[NaHA] = [H_2A]$ at 50% reaction

hence, $pK_{a_1} = 5$

Stage II NaHA is amphiprotic, thus

$pH = \dfrac{pK_{a_1} + pK_{a_2}}{2} \Rightarrow 8 = \left(\dfrac{5 + pK_{a_2}}{2}\right)$ $\therefore pK_{a_2} = 11$

Immediate Test 32

0.02 M aqueous solution of [*A*] is titrated with 0.02 M NaOH

OH

(*A*)

COOH

	NaOH added	pH
I.	8.12 mL	4.60
II.	16.24 mL	8.00

Calculate, pK_{a_1} and pK_{a_2} of [*A*].

Example 8.37) Variation of pH of salt of weak base ($CH_3CH_2NH_2$) and strong acid ($CH_3CH_2NH_3^+Cl^-$) with log*C* is shown:

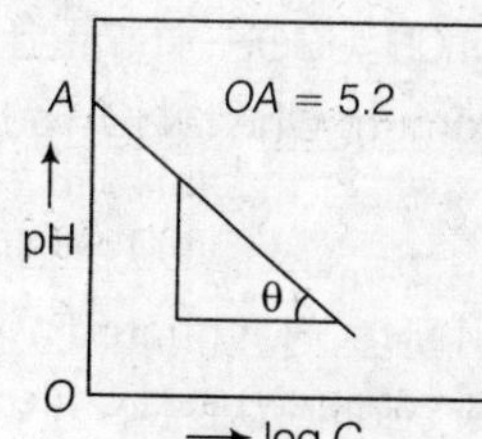

Calculate pH of 0.01 M ($CH_3CH_2NH_3^+Cl^-$).

Sol. For salt of weak base and strong acid, due to hydrolysis of cation

$$pH = 7 - \frac{pK_b}{2} - \frac{\log C}{2} \Rightarrow = \left(7 - \frac{pK_b}{2}\right) - \frac{\log C}{2}$$

If can be compared to a straight line, $y = c - mx$,

when $C = 1$, $\log C = 0$, pH = OA.

$$\text{Slope} = \frac{1}{2}$$

$$\text{Intercepts } OA = \left(7 - \frac{pK_b}{2}\right)$$

From intercept pK_b is known, hence pH is calculated.

$$OA = 5.2 = \left(7 - \frac{pK_b}{2}\right) \quad \therefore \quad \frac{pK_b}{2} = 7 - 5.2 = 1.8 \Rightarrow pK_b = 3.6$$

$$\therefore \quad pH = \left(7 - \frac{3.6}{2}\right) - \frac{\log 0.01}{2} = 5 - 2 + 1 = 6.2$$

Immediate Test 33

For CH_3COONa (salt of weak acid and strong base), variation of pH with $\log C$ is given.

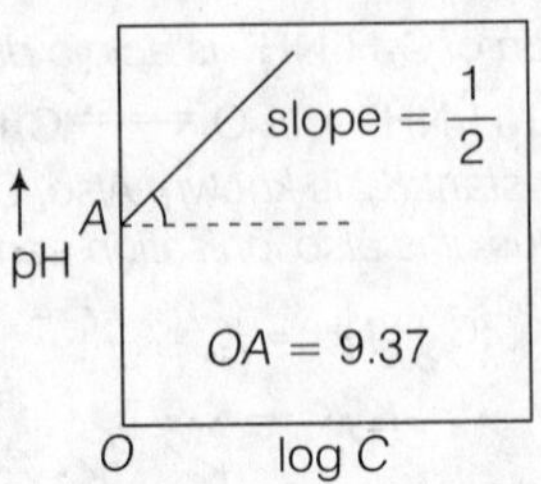

Calculate pH of 0.001 M CH_3COONa solution.

KNOWLEDGE CONFIRMATION Test 5

1 In the following equilibrium, $B^+ + H_2O \rightleftharpoons BOH + H^+$ equilibrium constant is

(a) K_w / K_b (b) $K_h(B^+)$
(c) Both of these (d) None of these

2 In the following equilibrium, $A^- + H_2O \rightleftharpoons HA + OH^-$ equilibrium constant is

(a) $\frac{K_w}{K_a}$ (b) $K_h(A^-)$
(c) Both of these (d) None of these

3 pH of 0.01 M $NaHCO_3$ solution is given

$$H_2CO_3 \rightleftharpoons H^+ + HCO_3^-, pK_{a_1} = x_1$$

$$HCO_3^- \rightleftharpoons H^+ + CO_3^{2-}, pK_{a_2} = x_2$$

(a) $\left(\frac{x_1 + x_2}{2}\right) + 1$ (b) $\left(\frac{x_1 + x_2}{2}\right) - 1$
(c) $(x_1 + x_2) + 1$ (d) $\left(\frac{x_1 + x_2}{2}\right)$

4 pH of the following is not affected by dilution

I. $NaHSO_3$ II. NaHS
III. $NaHCO_3$ IV. NaH_2PO_2

(a) I, II, III (b) I, II (c) I, III (d) I, II, III, IV

5 100 mL of 0.01 M CH_3COOH is titrated using 0.01 M NaOH. pH is maximum when NaOH added is

(a) 50 mL (b) 75 mL
(c) 90 mL (d) 100 mL

6 100 mL of 0.01 M NH_4OH is titrated using 0.01 M HCl. pH is maximum after addition of HCl

(a) 50 mL (b) 75 mL (c) 100 mL (d) 90 mL

7 Due to hydrolysis of CH_3COONa, pH may change with concentration as given .

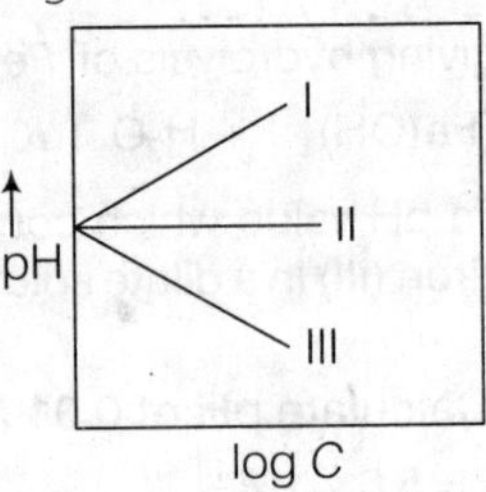

Which is the correct variation?

(a) I (b) II
(c) III (d) can not be predicted

8 For the salt NH_4Cl, pH changes with concentration as given

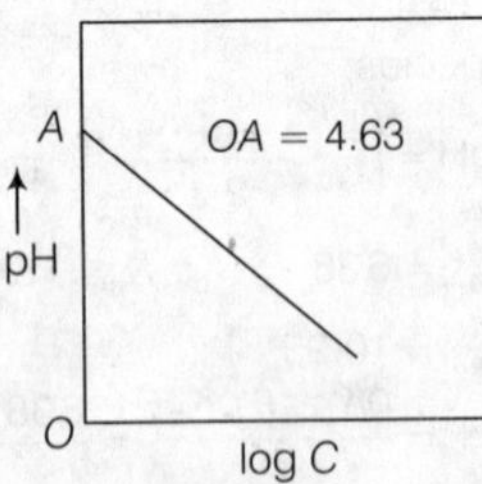

Thus, pH of 0.01 M NH_4Cl is

(a) 4.63 (b) 5.63 (c) 5.74 (d) 2.0

9 HX, HY and HZ are three weak acids. pH of 0.01 M solution of NaX, NaY and NaZ are respectively 8, 9 and 10. Thus, pK_a values of

(a) $HX < HY < HZ$ (b) $HZ < HY < HZ$
(c) $HX = HY = HZ$ (d) can not be said

10 pH of 100 mL 0.01 M CH_3COOH ($pK_a = 4.74$) at the points when

I. 50 mL of 0.01 M NaOH and

II. 100 mL of 0.01 M NaOH have been added are

	I	II		I	II
(a)	4.74	4.74	(b)	4.74	7.00
(c)	7.00	4.74	(d)	4.74	8.22

11 pH of 50 mL of 0.02 M NH_4OH ($pK_b = 4.74$) at the points when

I. 25 mL of 0.02 M HCl and

II. 50 mL of 0.02 M HCl has been added are

	I	II		I	II
(a)	4.74	7.0	(b)	9.26	7.0
(c)	9.26	5.63	(d)	4.74	5.63

12 $CuSO_4$ solution on reaction with $NaHCO_3$ gives

(a) H_2 gas (b) SO_2 gas (c) CO_2 gas (d) SO_3 gas

13 Degree of hydrolysis of a salt of strong acid and weak base (when degree of hydrolysis is very small) is

(a) $\sqrt{\frac{K_wK_a}{C}}$ (b) $\sqrt{\frac{K_w}{K_bC}}$ (c) $\sqrt{\frac{K_wC}{K_b}}$ (d) $\sqrt{\frac{K_wK_b}{C}}$

14 Ionisation constant of HOCl is 3.0×10^{-8}. Thus, hydrolysis constant of OCl^- ion is

(a) 3.0×10^{-8} (b) 3.33×10^{9}

(c) 3.33×10^{-7} (d) 3.33×10^{7}

15 For

$$C_6H_5OH + H_2O \rightleftharpoons C_6H_5O^- + H_3O^+, K = 1.0 \times 10^{-10}$$

Thus, pH of 0.10 M $C_6H_5O^-$ is

(a) 11.50 (b) 10.51 (c) 11.04 (d) 12

16 For 0.1 M RNH_3Cl, degree of hydrolysis is 1.0%. Thus, degree of hydrolysis when concentration is made four times is

(a) 0.01% (b) .0001% (c) 0.2% (d) 0.5%

17 For weak acid (CH_3COOH), $K_a = 1.8 \times 10^{-5}$ and weak base (NH_4OH), $K_b = 1.8 \times 10^{-5}$. Thus, per cent hydrolysis of 0.1M CH_3COONH_4

(a) 0.55 (b) 7.63 (c) 0.055 (d) 0.0763

18 pH of 0.05 M calcium acetate solution is [pK_a (CH_3COOH) = 4.74]

(a) 8.72 (b) 8.87 (c) 7.00 (d) 1.30

19 pK_b of NH_3 is 4.74 and pK_b of A^-, B^-, C^- are 4, 5, 6 respectively. Aqueous solution of 0.01 M has pH in the increasing order as :

(a) $NH_4A < NH_3B < NH_4C$

(b) $NH_4C < NH_3B < NH_4A$

(c) $NH_4C < NH_4A < NH_4B$

(d) All have equal pH being salt of weak acid and weak base

20 Given, $H_2CO_3 \rightleftharpoons H^+ + HCO_3^-$, $pK_1 = 6.38$

$HCO_3^- \rightleftharpoons H^+ + CO_3^{2-}$, $pK_2 = 10.26$

Thus, pH of 1.0 M and 0.1 M solutions of $NaHCO_3$ are respectively

	1.0	0.1 M		1.0	0.1 M
(a)	8.32	7.32	(b)	7.32	8.32
(c)	8.32	8.32	(d)	7.32	7.32

21 Consider the following salts :

I. NH_4CN II. NH_4HCO_3

III. NaHS IV. $CH_3NH_3^+Cl^-$

V. NaH_2PO_2

pH of the following are independent of concentration.

(a) All (b) All except IV and V

(c) All except III and V (d) All except I, II

22 pK_a of CH_3COOH is 4.74. Thus, pK_b of CH_3COO^- and pK_h of CH_3COO^- are respectively ($pK_h = -\log K_h$, K_h is hydrolysis constant)

(a) 4.74, 9.26 (b) 9.26, 4.74 (c) 4.74, 4.74 (d) 9.26, 9.26

23 For NH_3, pK_b (4.74) thus pK_a and pK_h of NH_4^+ ion are respectively

(a) 4.74, 9.26 (b) 4.74, 4.74 (c) 9.26, 9.26 (d) 9.26, 4.47

24 Consider the salt of weak acid *HA* and weak base *BOH*

pK_a (*HA*) = 6

pK_b (*BOH*) = 6

Thus, pH and degree of hydrolysis of 0.01 M *BA* would be

	pH	% degree of hydrolysis
(a)	7	1%
(b)	7	10%
(c)	6	1%
(d)	4.5	10%

25 pH of aqueous 0.1 M $FeCl_3$ solution at 298 K is given by

$$[Fe(H_2O)_6]^{3+} + H_2O(l) \rightleftharpoons [Fe(H_2O)_6OH]^{2+} + H_3O^+, \quad K = 1.0 \times 10^{-3}$$

(a) 2.00 (b) 2.50 (c) 2.30 (d) 2.02

26 0.100 g of NH_4Cl and KCl mixture in 1 L solution has a pH of 6.13. pK_a of NH_4^+ is 9.26. Thus, NH_4Cl in the mixture is

(a) 53.5% (b) 46.5%

(c) 50.00% (d) 25.00 %

27 20 mL of 0.1 M CH_3COOH is titrated with 0.1 M NaOH. pH of the mixture will be more than 7, when [pK_a (CH_3COOH) = 4.74]

(a) 25 mL of 0.1 M NaOH added (b) 20 mL of 0.1 M NaOH added

(c) Both of the thase (d) None of these

28 Phenolphthalein gives pink colour in basic solution and is colourless in acidic solution. Select correct statement(s).

At the equivalent point in the titration of

(a) weak acid with strong base, colourless solution with phenolphthalein changes to pink.
(b) weak base with strong acid, pink colour is never restored
(c) Both of the above are correct
(d) None of the above is correct

29 Which of the following solutions containing weak acid and salt of its conjugate base has maximum buffer capacity?

(a) (salt) = (acid) (b) (salt) > (acid)
(c) (salt) < (acid) (d) (salt) + (acid) is minimum

30 Sodium phenate is hydrolysed to the extent of 3% in 0.1 M solution at 298 K. Also, K_a (phenol) $= 1.3 \times 10^{-10}$.

Thus, ionic product of water at 298 K is

(a) 1.095×10^{-7}
(b) 1.2×10^{-14}
(c) 1.00×10^{-14}
(d) 1.00×10^{-7}

Common Ion Effect and Solubility Product

Common ion effect

In presence of common ion, (from a strong electrolyte) degree of ionisation of weak electrolyte is decreased. This is called **common ion effect**.

- Ionisation of CH_3COOH (weak acid) is decreased by the addition of CH_3COONa (CH_3COO^- being the common ion)

$$CH_3COOH \rightleftharpoons CH_3COO^- + H^+ \quad ...(A)$$

$$CH_3COONa \rightleftharpoons CH_3COO^- + Na^+$$

In the presence of CH_3COO^-, equilibrium (A) shifts in backward direction.

- Ionisation of H_2S (weak acid) is decreased by the addition of HCl (H^+ being the common ion)

$$H_2S \rightleftharpoons 2H^+ + S^{2-}$$

$$HCl \rightleftharpoons H^+ + Cl^-$$

- Ionisation of NH_4OH (weak base) is decreased by the addition of NH_4Cl, (NH_4^+ being the common ion)

$$NH_4OH \rightleftharpoons NH_4^+ + OH^-$$

$$NH_4Cl \rightleftharpoons NH_4^+ + Cl^-$$

- Solubility of a sparingly soluble salt is decreased by the addition of common ion. Presence of $AgNO_3$ or KCl, decreases the solubility of AgCl.

$$AgCl(s) \rightleftharpoons Ag^+(aq) + Cl^-(aq)$$

$$AgNO_3(aq) \rightleftharpoons \underset{\text{Common ion}}{Ag^+(aq)} + NO_3^-(aq)$$

$$KCl(aq) \rightleftharpoons K^+(aq) + \underset{\text{Common ion}}{Cl^-(aq)}$$

The common ion effect is, thus based on Le-Chatelier's principle in which the stress on the equilibrium that results from raising one of the products concentration is relieved by shifting the equilibrium to the left.

Explanation Consider the case of ionisation of weak acid (HA)

$$HA \rightleftharpoons H + A^- \quad ...(B)$$

$$HCl \rightleftharpoons Cl^- + H^+$$

In the presence of strong acid (like HCl), with H^+ as common ion, H^+ of HCl combines with A^- to form HA and thus, equilibrium (B) is displaced towards HA side and as a result of it, ionisation is decreased.

Solubility product

- A solution which remains in contact with excess of solute is said to be **saturated.**
- The amount of a solute, dissolved in a given volume of a solvent (in 100 mL or in 1 L) to form a saturated solution, at a given temperature, is termed as the **solubility** of the solute in that solvent.
- For a sparingly soluble salts (like AgCl, $BaSO_4$, PbS ...), ionisation is very small and concentration of the salt may be considered as constant.

Thus, for AgCl

$$AgCl(s) \rightleftharpoons Ag^+(aq) + Cl^-(aq), \quad K_C = [Ag^+][Cl^-]$$

[AgCl(s)] is not included in expression of K_C.

Instead of writing K_c, we write constant as K_{sp} called the **solubility product constant**, for the equilibrium between undissolved solute and its ions in a saturated solution.

Thus, $K_{sp} = [Ag^+][Cl^-]$

If S represents solubility of AgCl (in mol L^{-1}), then

$$[Ag^+] = [Cl^-] = S \text{ mol } L^{-1}$$

$$K_{sp} = [Ag^+][Cl^-] = S^2$$

$$S = \sqrt{K_{sp}}$$

(i) For $BaSO_4$ (solute giving two ions)

$$BaSO_4(s) \rightleftharpoons \underset{S}{Ba^{2+}(aq)} + \underset{S}{SO_4^{2-}(aq)}$$

$$K_{sp} = [Ba^{2+}][SO_4^{2-}] = S^2$$

$$S = \sqrt{K_{sp}}$$

(ii) For PbI_2 (solute giving three ions)

$$PbI_2(s) \rightleftharpoons \underset{S}{Pb^{2+}(aq)} + \underset{2S}{2I^-(aq)}$$

$$K_{sp} = [Pb^{2+}][I^-]^2 = (S)(2S)^2 = 4S^3$$

$$\therefore \quad S = \left(\frac{K_{sp}}{4}\right)^{1/3}$$

(iii) For $Al(OH)_3$ (solute giving four ions)

$$Al(OH)_3(s) \rightleftharpoons \underset{S}{Al^{3+}(aq)} + \underset{3S}{3OH^-(aq)}$$

$$K_{sp} = [Al^{3+}][OH^-]^3 = (S)(3S)^3 = 27S^4$$

$$S = \left(\frac{K_{sp}}{27}\right)^{1/4}$$

(iv) For a solute A_xB_y, (giving $(x+y)$ ions)

$$A_xB_y(s) \rightleftharpoons \underset{xS}{xA^{y+}} + \underset{yS}{yB^{x-}}$$

$$K_{sp} = [A^{y+}]^x[B^{x-}]^y = [xS]^x[yS]^y = x^x y^y [S]^{x+y}$$

$$\therefore \quad S = \left[\frac{K_{sp}}{x^x y^y}\right]^{\frac{1}{x+y}}$$

K_{sp} of A_xB_y (any insoluble salt) can also be expressed in logarithm form and hence in terms pK_{sp},

$$K_{sp} = x^x y^y S^{x+y}$$

Taking log on both sides.

$$\log K_{sp} = x \log x + y \log y + (x+y) \log S$$

$$-\log K_{sp} = -[x \log x + y \log y + (x+y) \log S]$$

$$pK_{sp} = xp_x + yp_y + (x+y)p_S$$

A_xB_y	x	y	pK_{sp}
AgCl	1	1	$2p_S$
PbI_2	1	2	$2p_2 + 3p_S$
Ag_2CrO_4	2	1	$2p_2 + 3p_S$
$Al(OH)_3$	1	3	$3p_3 + 4p_S$

■ $p_1 = -\log 1 = 0$

- K_{sp} corresponds to a saturated solution.
- K_{sp} is temperature dependent. On increasing temperature, solubility increases, forward reaction is favoured thus K_{sp} increases on increasing the temperature.

- For any solute (say AB)

$$AB \rightleftharpoons A^+ + B^-$$

$$Q = [A^+][B^-]$$

  – When $Q = K_{sp}$, solution is in equilibrium and is the stage of start of precipitation.
  – When $Q < K_{sp}$, solution is unsaturated and precipitation cannot occur.
  – When $Q > K_{sp}$, solution is said to be supersaturated and precipitation takes place.

Applications

- A solute AB is precipitated in aqueous solution, if

$$[A^+][B^-] > K_{sp}$$

Any possible dilution that may occur on mixing two solutions, must be considered before the criterion for precipitation is applied.

Completeness of precipitation is favoured by small value of K_{sp} and high concentration of common ion.

- **Solubility of a salt of strong acid and strong base. (as AgCl) in presence of common ion (as Cl^-)**

If KCl is added in AgCl(s), solubility is decreased due to common ion Cl^-.

Let solubility of AgCl(s) in presence of 1M KCl $= x$ mol L^{-1}

$$\underset{1\,M}{KCl} \rightleftharpoons K^+ + \underset{1\,M}{Cl^-}$$

$$AgCl(s) \rightleftharpoons \underset{x}{Ag^+(aq)} + \underset{x}{Cl^-(aq)}$$

$$\text{Total } [Ag^+] = x \text{ M}$$

$$\text{Total } [Cl^-] = (x+1)\text{ M} \approx 1 \text{ M}$$

$$\therefore \quad K_{sp}(AgCl) = [Ag^+][Cl^-] = x \times 1 = x$$

$$\text{Thus,} \quad K_{sp}(AgCl) = x$$

- **Solubility of a sparingly soluble salt in an acidic buffer**

$$CH_3COOAg(s) \rightleftharpoons CH_3COO^-(aq) + Ag^+(aq), \quad K_1 = K_{sp}$$

$$CH_3COO^-(aq) + \underset{\text{(from buffer)}}{H^+(aq)} \rightleftharpoons CH_3COOH(aq), \quad K_2 = \frac{1}{K_a}$$

$$CH_3COOAg(s) + H^+(aq) \rightleftharpoons CH_3COOH(aq) + Ag^+(aq)$$

$$K_3 = \frac{K_{sp}}{K_a} = K_1K_2$$

If solubility $= x$ in presence of H^+

$$\therefore \quad = \frac{xx}{[H^+]} = \frac{x^2}{[H^+]}$$

Thus, x is calculated.

- **Solubility of a solute in presence of basic buffer**

  Solubility of $Al(OH)_3$, $Mg(OH)_2$ etc., is affected in presence of basic buffer.

- **Simultaneous solubility**

  Solubility of a mixture of two sparingly soluble salts is affected in presence of common ion of the salt.

  e.g. Solubility of AgBr and AgCl mixture is affected by common ion Ag^+.

  If solubility of AgCl $= x$ and that of AgBr $= y$

  then, $[Ag^+] = [x + y]$

  $[Cl^-] = x \Rightarrow [Br^-] = y$

  $\therefore \quad K_{sp}(AgCl) = (x + y)x$

  $K_{sp}(AgBr) = (x + y)y$

  Thus, x and y are calculated.

- **Analysis and separation of cations into qualitative groups based on the K_{sp} values and common ion effect.**

  Group I AgCl, Hg_2Cl_2 and $PbCl_2$ have low K_{sp} values thus, precipitated by addition of HCl.

  Group II Cu^{2+}, Cd^{2+}, Pb^{2+}, Hg^{2+}, Bi^{3+}, As^{3+}, Sb^{3+}, Sn^{2+} are precipitated as sulphides. ($\overset{II}{M}S$, $\overset{III}{M_2}S_3$) by passing H_2S gas in presence of HCl. K_{sp} of MS, M_2S_3 are very small and they are precipitated by low $[S^{2-}]$ which is feasible in presence of H^+ (common ion of H_2S and HCl).

  Group III Al^{3+}, Cr^{3+}, Fe^{3+} are precipitated as hydroxides by NH_4OH in presence of NH_4Cl (NH_4^+ being common ion).

Solved Examples & Instant Practice

Example 8.38) Solubility of AgCl(*s*) in aqueous solution is 1×10^{-5} M. Calculate its

(a) solubility product and

(b) solubility in presence of 0.01 M $AgNO_3$.

Sol. $AgCl(s) \rightleftharpoons \underset{(S)}{Ag^+(aq)} + \underset{(S)}{Cl^-(aq)}$

Let solubility in aqueous solution be $= S$ mol L^{-1} then $K_{sp} = S^2$. In presence of $AgNO_3$ (common ion Ag^+), solubility is decreased.

(a) $AgCl(s) \rightleftharpoons Ag^+(aq) + Cl^-(aq)$

$S = 1\times 10^{-5}$ M

Thus $\quad K_{sp} = [Ag^+][Cl^-] = (1\times 10^{-5})^2 = 1\times 10^{-10}$

(b) In presence of 0.01 M $AgNO_3$, let solubility be x ($<<1\times 10^{-5}$ M)

$AgCl(s) \rightleftharpoons \underset{xM}{Ag^+(aq)} + \underset{xM}{Cl^-(aq)}$

$AgNO_3(aq) \rightleftharpoons \underset{0.01\,M}{Ag^+(aq)} + NO_3^-(aq)$

$\therefore \quad [Ag^+]_{total} = (x + 0.01)\,M \approx 0.01\,M$

(as $x << 1\times 10^{-5}$ due to common ion effect)

$[Cl^-] = x$ M

$\therefore \quad K_{sp} = [Ag^+][Cl^-]$

$1\times 10^{-10} = (0.01)(x)$

$\therefore \quad x = 1\times 10^{-8}$ M

Thus, solubility of AgCl in presence of 0.01M $AgNO_3$ $= 1\times 10^{-8}$ M

■ Solubility of AgCl is thus decreased is presence of common ion (in this case Ag^+) and also Cl^- ion (from NaCl or KCl).

If $[Ag^+] = 1$ M, then solubility $= 1\times 10^{-10}$ M

If $[Ag^+] = 0.1$ M, then solubility $= 1\times 10^{-9}$ M

If $[Ag^+] = 0.01$ M, then solubility $= 1\times 10^{-8}$ M

Thus, larger the solubility of the common ion , smaller the solubility of the sparingly soluble salt. Thus, it is always advisable to wash the precipitate with the electrolyte with common ion and not with water.

Immediate Test 34

Solubility product of $BaSO_4$ is 1.1×10^{-10}. Calculate its solubility in

(a) water (b) 0.1 M $BaCl_2$ (c) 0.01 M K_2SO_4

Example 8.39) A particular saturated solution of silver chromate has

$[Ag^+] = 5\times 10^{-5}$ M and $[CrO_4^{2-}] = 4.4\times 10^{-4}$ M

(a) Calculate solubility product of silver chromate.

(b) Compare solubility of silver chromate in aqueous solution, 0.1 M $AgNO_3$ and 0.1 M K_2CrO_4.

For a sparingly soluble salt, A_xB_y

$K_{sp} = x^x y^y (S)^{x+y}$

$Ag_2CrO_4 \rightleftharpoons 2Ag^+ + CrO_4^{2-}$

$\therefore \quad K_{sp} = [Ag^+]^2[CrO_4^{2-}]$

Since, $[Ag^+]$ and $[CrO_4^{2-}]$ are known, K_{sp} is calculated.

Also, $\quad K_{sp} = 4S^3$

Thus, S (solubility in aqueous solution) is derived.

In presence of 0.1 M $AgNO_3$ (common ion Ag^+) and K_2CrO_4 (common ion CrO_4^{2-}) solubility is decreased.

Sol.

(a) Given, $[Ag^+] = 5 \times 10^{-5} M$

$[CrO_4^{2-}] = 4.4 \times 10^{-4}$ M

$K_{sp} = [Ag^+]^2 [CrO_4^{2-}]$

$= (5 \times 10^{-8})^2 (4.4 \times 10^{-4}) = 1.1 \times 10^{-18}$

(b) I. If solubility in aqueous solution = S then, $K_{sp} = 4S^3$

$\therefore \quad S = \sqrt[3]{\left(\frac{K_{sp}}{4}\right)} = \sqrt[3]{\frac{1.1 \times 10^{-18}}{4}} = 6.5 \times 10^{-7}$ M

II. Let solubility in 0.1 M $AgNO_3$ be = x mol L^{-1} then,

$$Ag_2CrO_4(s) \rightleftharpoons \underset{2x}{2Ag^+(aq)} + \underset{x}{CrO_4^{2-}}$$

$$AgNO_3 \rightleftharpoons \underset{0.1\,M}{Ag^+(aq)} + \underset{0\,M}{NO_3^-(aq)}$$

$\therefore \quad [Ag^+]_{total} = (2x + 0.1) \approx 0.1$ M

$[CrO_4^{2-}] = x$

$\therefore \quad K_{sp} = [Ag^+]^2 [CrO_4^{2-}]$

$1.1 \times 10^{-18} = [0.1]^2 [x]$

$\therefore \quad x = 1.18 \times 10^{-16}$ M

III. Let solubility in 0.1 M K_2CrO_4 be = y mol L^{-1}

then $\quad [Ag^+] = 2y$ M

and $\quad [CrO_4^{2-}] = (y + 0.1) \approx 0.1$ M

$\therefore \quad K_{sp} = [Ag^+]^2 [CrO_4^{2-}]$

$1.1 \times 10^{-18} = (2y)^2 (0.1)$

$4y^2 = 1.1 \times 10^{-17}$

$y = 1.66 \times 10^{-9}$ M

On comparison of solubility in water

$>$ in K_2CrO_4 $>$ in $AgNO_3$

■ Thus, for washing precipitate of Ag_2CrO_4, $AgNO_3$ is the best reagent out of H_2O, $AgNO_3$ and K_2CrO_4.

Immediate Test 35

Calculate the solubility of A_2X_3 in pure water assuming that neither kind of ions reacts with water.

$K_{sp}(A_2X_3) = 1.1 \times 10^{-23}$ ***[NCERT]***

Example 8.40) K_{sp} of $Al(OH)_3$ is 1.0×10^{-15}. At what pH does 1.0×10^{-3} M Al^{3+} precipitate on the addition of buffer of NH_4Cl and NH_4OH?

Basic buffer (NH_4Cl and NH_4OH) controls pH for the precipitation of $Al(OH)_3$. It is a part of qualitative analysis of Al^{3+} of group III (basic radicals).

$$Al(OH)_3(s) \rightleftharpoons Al^{3+}(aq) + 3OH^+(aq)$$

$Al(OH)_3$ is precipitated, if

$$[Al^{3+}][OH^-]^3 > K_{sp}$$

Sol. Given, $[Al^{3+}] = 1.0 \times 10^{-3}$ M

$K_{sp} = 1.0 \times 10^{-15}$

$\therefore \quad [Al^{3+}][OH^-]^3 = 1.0 \times 10^{-15}$

$(1.0 \times 10^{-3})[OH^-]^3 = 1.0 \times 10^{-15}$

$\therefore \quad [OH^-]^3 = 1.0 \times 10^{-12}$

$[OH^-] = 1.0 \times 10^{-4}$ M

Thus, $\quad$ pOH = 4

Since, pH + pOH = 14

$\therefore \quad$ pH = 14 − 4 = 10.0

Immediate Test 36

(i) K_{sp} of $Fe(OH)_3$ is 2.6×10^{-39}. What is its pH?

(ii) Calculate the molar solubility of $Fe(OH)_3$ in a buffer of 0.1 M NH_4Cl and 0.1 M NH_4OH. $K_b(NH_3) = 1.8 \times 10^{-5}$, $K_{sp}[Fe(OH)_3] = 2.6 \times 10^{-39}$.

Example 8.41) What is minimum volume of water required to dissolve 1 g of calcium sulphate?

$K_{sp}[CaSO_4] = 9.1 \times 10^{-6}$

$$CaSO_4(s) \rightleftharpoons \underset{S}{Ca^{2+}(aq)} + \underset{S}{SO_4^{2-}(aq)}$$

$$K_{sp} = [Ca^{2+}][SO_4^{2-}]$$

Thus, solubility S (mol L^{-1}) is known.

S × molar mass = Solubility in g L^{-1}

Thus, volume can be calculated.

Sol. $[Ca^{2+}][SO_4^{2-}] = 9.1 \times 10^{-6}$

$S^2 = 9.1 \times 10^{-6}$

$S = \sqrt{9.1 \times 10^{-6}}$ mol L^{-1}

$= 3.017 \times 10^{-3}$ mol L^{-1}

$= 3.017 \times 10^{-3}$ mol $L^{-1} \times 136$ g mol^{-1}

$= 0.4102$ g L^{-1}

0.4102 g is dissolved in = 1 L

$\therefore$ 1 g $CaSO_4$ is dissolved in $= \frac{1}{0.4102}$ L = 2.437 L

■ Molar mass of $CaSO_4$ = 40 + 32 + 64 = 136 g mol^{-1}

Immediate Test 37

A 100 mL sample is removed from solution saturated with $CaSO_4$ at 298 K. On evaporation of water completely, residue left was 0.24 g. What is K_{sp} of $CaSO_4$?

Example 8.42) Calculate percentage ionisation of 0.01 M CH_3COOH in presence of 0.001 M HCl. $K_a(CH_3COOH) = 1.8 \times 10^{-5}$ M.

$$CH_3COOH(aq) \rightleftharpoons CH_3COO^-(aq) + H^+(aq)$$

HCl (a strong acid), decreases ionisation of CH_3COOH by common ion effect, which is also based on Le-Chatelier's principle.

Sol. Let $(CH_3COOH) = C$ mol L^{-1}

$$CH_3COOH(aq) \rightleftharpoons CH_3COO^-(aq) + H^+(aq)$$

Initial conc. C 0 0

After ionisation $(C - Cx)$ Cx (0.001M) from HCl

$\therefore \quad K_a = \dfrac{[CH_3COO^-][H^+]}{[CH_3COOH]} \Rightarrow 1.8 \times 10^{-5} = \dfrac{Cx[0.001]}{C[1-x]}$

$\therefore \quad \left(\dfrac{x}{1-x}\right) = 1.8 \times 10^{-2} = 0.018$

$x = 0.0177$

Thus, % ionisation = 0.0177 × 100 = 1.77%

- If HCl is not added, by Ostwald's dilution law,

$$x = \sqrt{\frac{K_a}{C}} = \sqrt{\frac{1.8 \times 10^{-5}}{0.01}} = 0.0424 >> 0.0177$$

Immediate Test 38

(i) Calculate percentage ionisation of 0.1 M C_5H_5N in presence of 0.001 M NaOH. $K_b(C_5H_5N) = 5.0 \times 10^{-6}$

(ii) Calculate the molar solubility of $Ni(OH)_2$ in 0.1 M NaOH. K_{sp} of $Ni(OH)_2$ is 2.0×10^{-15}. ***[NCERT]***

Example 8.43) A mixture of solid $SrSO_4$ and solid $BaSO_4$ is shaken up with water until saturation equilibrium is established. Given, $K_{sp}(BaSO_4) = 1.5 \times 10^{-9}$ and $K_{sp}(SrSO_4) = 7.5 \times 10^{-7}$

Calculate the concentration of Sr^{2+}, Ba^{2+} and SO_4^{2-} ions.

SO_4^{2-} as common ion causes common ion effect on the solubility of $SrSO_4$ and $BaSO_4$ depending on their K_{sp} values.

Sol. Let $[BaSO_4] = x$ M and $[SrSO_4] = y$ M

$\therefore \quad [Ba^{2+}] = x$ M

$[Sr^{2+}] = y$ M and $[SO_4^{2-}] = (x + y)$ M

$\therefore \quad [Ba^{2+}][SO_4^{2-}] = K_{sp} = 1.5 \times 10^{-9}$

$x(x + y) = 1.5 \times 10^{-9}$ ...(i)

and $[Sr^{2+}][SO_4^{2-}] = K_{sp} = 7.5 \times 10^{-7}$

$y(x + y) = 7.5 \times 10^{-7}$ ...(ii)

Divide (i) by (ii),

$\therefore \quad \dfrac{x}{y} = \dfrac{1.5 \times 10^{-9}}{7.5 \times 10^{-7}} = 2 \times 10^{-3} \quad \therefore x = (2 \times 10^{-3})y$

For $BaSO_4$ from (i),

$(2 \times 10^{-3})y\,[2 \times 10^{-3}y + y] = 1.5 \times 10^{-9}$

$2.004 \times 10^{-3}y^2 = 1.5 \times 10^{-9} \Rightarrow y = 8.65 \times 10^{-4}$ M

$\therefore \quad [Sr^{2+}] = 8.65 \times 10^{-4}$ M

and $[Ba^{2+}] = x = 2 \times 10^{-3} \times 8.65 \times 10^{-4} = 1.73 \times 10^{-6}$ M

and $[SO_4^{2-}] = x + y = 8.67 \times 10^{-4}$ M

Immediate Test 39

Calculate the molar concentration of Ag^+, Br^- and CNS^- in a mixture of AgBr and AgCNS.

Given, $K_{sp}(AgBr) = 5 \times 10^{-13}$ and $K_{sp}(AgCNS) = 1 \times 10^{-12}$

Example 8.44) Will a precipitate of $BaCO_3$ form by mixing equal volumes of the following solutions? $[K_{sp}(BaCO_3) = 2.6 \times 10^{-9}]$

(a) 3×10^{-3} M $BaCl_2$ and 2×10^{-3} M Na_2CO_3

(b) 1×10^{-5} M $Ba(NO_3)_2$ and 4×10^{-5} M Na_2CO_3.

$$Ba^{2+} + CO_3^{2-} \longrightarrow BaCO_3 \downarrow$$

$BaCO_3$ is precipitated when $[Ba^{2+}][CO_3^{2-}] > K_{sp}$

Due to mixing of two solutions, volume changes, hence molar concentration also changes.

$$M_1V_1 = M_2V_2$$

When equal volumes are taken, volume of solution is doubled and concentration is halved.

Sol. Using $(M_1V_1)_{initial} = (M_2V_2)_{mix} \Rightarrow V_2 = 2V_2, (M_2)_{mix} = (M_1/2)$

(a) 3×10^{-3} M $BaCl_2 = 1.5 \times 10^{-3}$ M $[Ba^{2+}]_{mix}$

2×10^{-3} M $Na_2CO_3 = 1.0 \times 10^{-3}$ M $[CO_3^{2-}]_{mix}$

1×10^{-5} M $Ba(NO_3)_2 = 5 \times 10^{-6}$ M $[Ba^{2+}]_{mix}$

4×10^{-5} M $Na_2CO_3 = 2 \times 10^{-5}$ M $[CO_3^{2-}]_{mix}$

$[Ba^{2+}][CO_3^{2-}] = 1.5 \times 10^{-3} \times 1.0 \times 10^{-3}$

$= 1.5 \times 10^{-6} > K_{sp}\ (2.0 \times 10^{-9})$

Thus, $BaCO_3$ is precipitated

(b) $[Ba^{2+}][CO_3^{2-}] = 5 \times 10^{-6} \times 2 \times 10^{-5}$

$= 1 \times 10^{-10} < K_{sp}\ (2.0 \times 10^{-9})$

Thus, $BaCO_3$ is not precipitated.

Immediate Test 40

Should $Mg(OH)_2$ precipitate from a solution that is 0.010 M $MgCl_2$, if the solution is also made 0.1 M in $NH_3(aq)$? $K_{sp}[Mg(OH)_2] = 1.8 \times 10^{-11}$ and $K_b(NH_4OH) = 1.8 \times 10^{-5}$

Example 8.45) The ionisation constant of benzoic acid is 6.46×10^{-5} and K_{sp} for silver benzoate is 2.5×10^{-13}. How many times is silver benzoate more soluble in a buffer of pH 3.19 compared to its solubility in pure water? ***[NCERT]***

In the absence of buffer, solubility = $\sqrt{K_{sp}}$

In presence of acidic buffer, $C_6H_5COO^-$ changes to C_6H_5COOH, thus, solubility is increased.

Sol. Let solubility of C_6H_5COOAg in buffer = x mol L^{-1}

$$C_6H_5COOAg(s) \rightleftharpoons C_6H_5COO^-(aq) + Ag^+(aq), \quad K_1 = K_{sp}$$

$$C_6H_5COO^-(aq) + \underset{\text{Buffer}}{H^+(aq)} \rightleftharpoons C_6H_5COOH(aq), \quad K_2 = \frac{1}{K_a}$$

$$C_6H_5COOAg(s) + H^+(aq) \rightleftharpoons \underset{x}{C_6H_5COOH(aq)} + \underset{x}{Ag^+(aq)},$$

$$K_3 = \frac{K_{sp}}{K_a}$$

$K_1 = K_{sp} = [CH_3COO^-][Ag^+]$

$K_2 = \dfrac{1}{K_a} = [C_6H_5COOH]/[C_6H_5COO^-][H^+]$

If solubility in buffer = x
then,

$$K_3 = \frac{[C_6H_5COOH]\,[Ag^+]}{[H^+]} = \frac{K_{sp}}{K_a} = \frac{x^2}{[H^+]} = \frac{2.5\times10^{-13}}{6.46\times10^{-5}}$$

For pH = 3.19, $[H^+] = 10^{-3.19} = 6.46\times10^{-4}$ M

$$\therefore \quad \frac{x^2}{6.46\times10^{-4}} = \frac{2.5\times10^{-13}}{6.46\times10^{-5}}$$

$$x^2 = 2.5\times10^{-12} \Rightarrow x = 1.58\times10^{-6}\text{ M}$$

Solubility in the absence of buffer

$$y = \sqrt{K_{sp}} = \sqrt{2.5\times10^{-13}} = 5\times10^{-7}\text{ M}$$

$$\therefore \quad \frac{x}{y} = \frac{1.58\times10^{-6}\text{ M}}{5\times10^{-7}\text{ M}} = 3.16\text{ times}$$

Immediate Test 41

Calculate solubility of $CaF_2(s)$ in a buffer solution with pH = 3.00.
$K_{sp}(CaF_2) = 5.3\times10^{-9}$ and $K_a(HF) = 6.7\times10^{-4}$

Example 8.46) What concentration of free CN^- must be maintained in a solution that is 1.8 M $AgNO_3$ and 0.327 M NaCl to prevent AgCl(*s*) from precipitating?
Given, $K_{sp}[AgCl] = 1.8\times10^{-10}$

$$Ag^+(aq) + 2CN^-(aq) \rightleftharpoons [Ag(CN)_2]^-, \quad K_f = 5.6\times10^{18}$$

CN^- forms soluble complex with Ag^+ and, thus prevents its precipitation if NaCl is added to $AgNO_3$. In the absence of CN^-, AgCl is precipitated.
Formation constant (K_f) of the complex $[Ag(CN)_2]^-$ is very high indicating that all the Ag^+ ion has been complexed as $[Ag(CN)_2]^-$ = 1.8 M
Thus, $[CN^-]$ can be evaluated.

Sol. $AgCl(s) \rightleftharpoons Ag^+(aq) + Cl^-(aq),\ K_1 = K_{sp}$
$Ag^+(aq) + 2CN^-(aq) \rightleftharpoons [Ag(CN)_2]^-(aq),\ K_2 = K_f$

$AgCl(s) + 2CN^-(aq) \rightleftharpoons [Ag(CN)_2]^-(aq) + Cl^-(aq)$

$K_1 = K_{sp} = [Ag^+][Cl^-]$
$K_2 = K_f$ (formation constant)

$$= \frac{[Ag(CN)_2]}{[Ag^+][CN^-]^2}$$

$$K_3 = K_1K_2 = K_{sp}K_f$$

$$K_3 = \frac{[Ag(CN)_2]^-[Cl^-]}{[CN^-]^2} = K_{sp}K_f$$

Given, $[Cl^-] = [NaCl] = 0.327$ M

$$\therefore \quad \frac{(1.8)\,(0.327)}{[CN^-]^2} = 1.8\times10^{-10}\times5.6\times10^{18}$$

$$\therefore \quad [CN^-]^2 = 5.84\times10^{-10}$$

$$\therefore \quad [CN^-] = 2.42\times10^{-5}\text{ M}$$

Immediate Test 42

What is molar solubility of AgCl(*s*) in 0.100 M $NH_3(aq)$?
$K_{sp}(AgCl) = 1.8\times10^{-10}$, and $K_f[Ag(NH_3)_2] = 1.6\times10^7$

Example 8.47) $K_{sp}(AgCl) = 1.8\times10^{-10}$
and $K_f[Ag(NH_3)_2^+] = 1.6\times10^7$
0.10 mole sample of $AgNO_3$ is dissolved in 1.0 L of 1.00 M NH_3. If 0.01 mole of NaCl is added to this solution, will AgCl(*s*) precipitate?

AgCl is soluble in NH_3.
Value of $K_f[Ag(NH_3)_2^+] = 1.6\times10^7$, indicates that all the Ag^+ has been complexed, only very small amount of Ag^+ remains to maintain equilibrium.
AgCl is precipitated, if

$$[Ag^+]\,[Cl^-] > K_{sp}$$

Sol.

	Ag^+	+	$2NH_3$	$\rightleftharpoons$	$[Ag(NH_3^+)_2]$
Initial	0.1 M		1.00 M		0
At equilibrium	x		(1.00 – 0.2) M		0.10 M

$$K_f = \frac{[Ag(NH_3)_2^+]}{[Ag^+]\,[NH_3]^2} \Rightarrow \frac{0.10}{x(0.80)^2} = 1.6\times10^7$$

$$x = 9.8\times10^{-9}$$

Thus, undissolved $[Ag^+] = 9.8\times10^{-9} \Rightarrow [Cl^-]$ added = 0.01 M

$$\therefore \quad [Ag^+]\,[Cl^-] = 9.8\times10^{-9}\times0.01$$
$$= 9.8\times10^{-11} < 1.8\times10^{-10}\ (K_{sp})$$

Ionic product $[Ag^+][Cl^-]$ is less than K_{sp} thus, AgCl is not precipitated.

Immediate Test 43

What is minimum concentration of NH_3 required to prevent AgCl(*s*) from precipitating from 1.00 L of a solution containing 0.10 mol $AgNO_3$ and 0.01 mol NaCl?
$K_{sp}[AgCl] = 1.8\times10^{-10}$, $K_f[Ag(NH_3)_2^+] = 1.6\times10^7$

Example 8.48) An aqueous solution of metal bromide MBr_2(0.05 M) is saturated with H_2S. What is the minimum pH at which *MS* will precipitate?

$$K_{sp}(MS) = 6.0\times10^{-21},\ [H_2S]_{Saturated} = 0.1\text{ M}$$
$$K_{a_1}(H_2S) = 1\times10^{-7},\ K_{a_2}(H_2S) = 1.3\times10^{-13}$$

From the given values of K_{a_1} and K_{a_2}, $[S^{2-}]$ is calculated, thus $[H^+]$ and pH is calculated.

Sol. $H_2S \rightleftharpoons H^+ + HS^-,\ K_{a_1} = \dfrac{[H^+]\,[HS^-]}{[H_2S]}$

$HS^- \rightleftharpoons H^+ + S^{2-},\ K_{a_2} = \dfrac{[H^+]\,[S^{2-}]}{[HS^-]}$

$H_2S \rightleftharpoons 2H^+ + S^{2-}$

$$\therefore \quad K = K_{a_1}K_{a_2} = \frac{[H^+]^2\,[S^{2-}]}{[H_2S]} \quad ...(1)$$

At equilibrium, $[M^{2+}]\,[S^{2-}] = K_{sp}$
Then [*MS*] is precipitated from 0.05 M MBr_2

$$[M^{2+}]\,[S^{2-}] > K_{sp}$$

$$\therefore \quad [S^{2-}] > \frac{6.0\times10^{-21}}{[0.05]} > 1.2\times10^{-19}\text{ M}$$

This is minimum concentration of S^{2-} to precipitate MS.

$$\therefore \quad \frac{[H^+]^2\,[1.2\times 10^{-19}]}{0.1} = 1.0\times 10^{-7}\times 1.3\times 10^{-13}$$

$$\therefore \quad [H^+]^2 = 0.0108$$

$$[H^+] = 0.104 \text{ M}$$

$$\therefore \quad \text{pH} = 0.98 \text{ M}$$

Immediate Test 44

K_{sp} of CdS $= 8.0\times 10^{-27}$

K_{sp} of ZnS $= 1.6\times 10^{-24}$

K_{sp} of MnS $= 2.5\times 10^{-13}$

Which of the above ions each of 1.0×10^{-6} M in 0.01 M HCl is precipitated, if 0.05 M H_2S in passed into their aqueous solutions? For H_2S

$$K_{a_1} = 1.0\times 10^{-7} \Rightarrow K_{a_2} = 1.0\times 10^{-14}$$

Example 8.49) For the sparingly soluble salt $M(OH)_2$,

$$\log[M^{2+}] = \log K_{sp} + 2\,\text{pOH}$$

Graphically, variation is shown as :

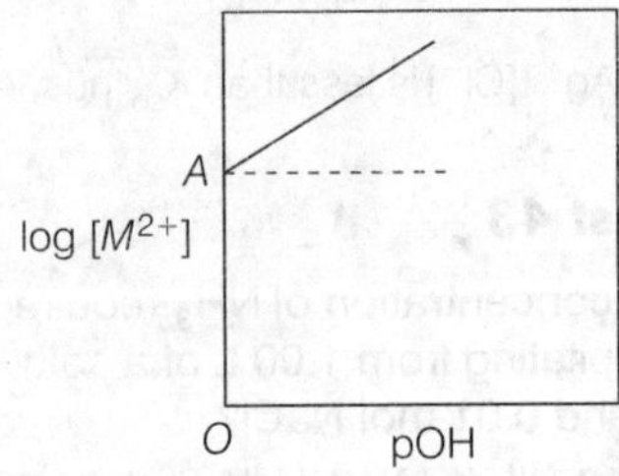

If $OA = -6$, what is $[M^{2+}]$ at pH 9. Also, calculate K_{sp}.

Sol.

$$K_{sp} = [M^{2+}]\,[OH^-]^2$$

$$\log K_{sp} = \log [M^{2+}] + 2\log [OH^-]$$

$$\therefore \quad \log [M^{2+}] = \log K_{sp} - 2\log [OH^-] = \log K_{sp} + 2\,\text{pOH}$$

Equation of K_{sp} has been converted into logarithm form which is a linear equation.

$$y = c + mx,$$

On comparison, $OA = c = \log K_{sp}$

$$c = OA = \log K_{sp} = -6$$

$$\therefore \quad K_{sp} = 10^{-6}$$

$$\text{pH} + \text{pOH} = 14$$

$$\log[M^{2+}] = -6 + 2\,[14 - \text{pH}]$$

$$= -6 + 2[14 - 9]$$

$$= -6 + 2\times 5 = 4$$

$$\therefore \quad [M^{2+}] = 10^4 \text{ M}$$

Immediate Test 45

For the sparingly soluble salt $Mg(OH)_2$, variation of $\log [Mg^{2+}]$ with pOH is shown

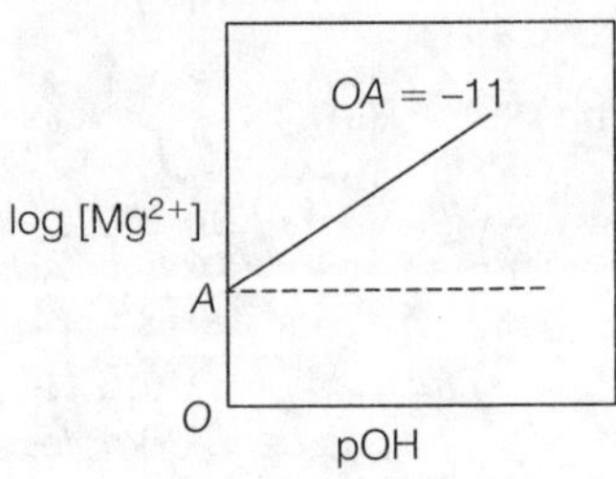

What is pH when $[Mg^{2+}] = 10^{-3}$ M?

KNOWLEDGE CONFIRMATION Test 6

1 K_{sp} of $M_2S_3 = 2.7\times 10^{-26}$. $[S^{2-}]$ to precipitate 0.001 M MCl_3 as M_2S_3 is

(a) 1.6×10^{-10} M (b) 5.2×10^{-12} M
(c) 2.7×10^{-24} M (d) 3.0×10^{-7} M

2 A saturated solution of aluminium phosphate has $[Al^{3+}] = 3\times 10^{-4}$ M and $[PO_4^{3-}] = 3\times 10^{-4}$ M. Thus, solubility product of aluminium phosphate is

(a) 9×10^{-8} (b) 27×10^{-8}
(c) 1.08×10^{-8} (d) 1.08×10^{-6}

3 K_{sp} of $Cu(OH)_2$ is 2.5×10^{-19}. At what pH, will 1×10^{-6} M $CuSO_4$ be precipitated as $Cu(OH)_2$?

(a) 5.0 (b) 7.7 (c) 10.2 (d) 11.7

4 K_{sp} of $Fe(OH)_2$ is 8.0×10^{-16}. Its solubility in a buffer of pH 12 is

(a) 8.0×10^{-4} M (b) 8.0×10^{4} M
(c) 8.0×10^{-12} M (d) 8.0×10^{12} M

5 Molar solubility of $Mn(OH)_2$ in a buffer of 0.01 M NH_4OH and 0.01 M NH_4Cl is 1.4×10^{-4} M. Thus, K_{sp} of $Mn(OH)_2$ is $[K_b\,(NH_4OH) = 1.8\times 10^{-5}]$

(a) 1.1×10^{-11} (b) 1.96×10^{-8}
(c) 2.7×10^{-12} (d) 4.5×10^{-14}

6 Solubility of a sparingly soluble salt MCl_2 in water is 1.0×10^{-4}. Thus, its solubility in 0.01 M HCl is

(a) 1.0×10^{-8} M (b) 4.0×10^{-8} M
(c) 1.0×10^{-10} M (d) 4.0×10^{-10} M

7 Based on above data, solubility of MCl_2 in 0.01 M $M(NO_3)_2$ is
(a) 2.0×10^{-5} M (b) 4.0×10^{-8} M
(c) 1.0×10^{-10} M (d) 4.0×10^{-10} M

8 If K_{sp} of $Fe(OH)_2$ is 1×10^{-15}, then
(a) $p_{Fe} + p_{OH} = 15$ (b) $p_{Fe} = p_H = 15$
(c) $p_{Fe} + 2p_{OH} = -15$ (d) $p_{Fe} + 2p_{OH} = 15$

9 For AgOH, $K_{sp} = 1 \times 10^{-12}$

Then,
(a) $p_{Ag} + p_{OH} = 12$ (b) $p_{Ag} + 2 = p_H$
(c) Both (a) and (b) (d) None of these

10 For AgCl, variation of p_{Ag} with p_{Cl} is shown

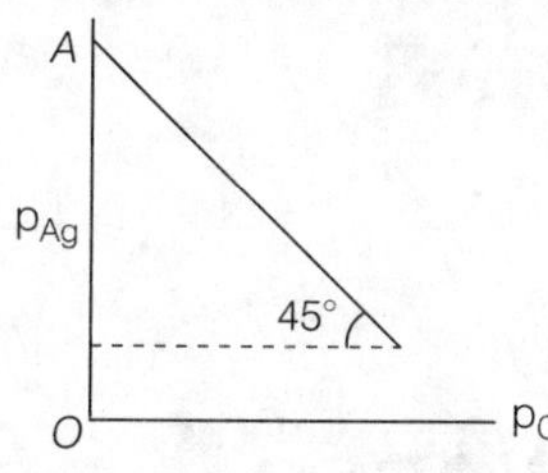

$OA = 10.0$

Thus, for $AgCl(s) \rightleftharpoons Ag^+(aq) + Cl^-(aq)$, K is
(a) 10^{10} (b) 10 (c) 10^{-10} (d) 10^{-20}

11 Solubility product of

$MS = 1 \times 10^{-6}$

$MS_2 = 4 \times 10^{-9}$

$MS_3 = 27 \times 10^{-12}$

Thus, solubility of these salts in aqueous solution is in the order :
(a) $MS < MS_2 < MS_3$ (b) $MS_3 < MS_2 > MS$
(c) $MS_2 < MS_3 < MS$ (d) $MS = MS_2 = MS_3$

12 For H_2S, $K_{a_1} K_{a_2} = 1 \times 10^{-20}$ and $K_{sp}(ZnS) = 1 \times 10^{-21}$ Minimum pH required to prevent the precipitation of ZnS in a solution that is 0.01 M $ZnCl_2$ and 0.10 M H_2S is
(a) 0 (b) 1 (c) 2 (d) 4

13 Equal volumes of 0.001 M $AgNO_3$ and following salts are mixed separately.

0.001 M KCl
0.001 M K_2CrO_4
0.001 M Na_3PO_4

Which is precipitated out of
(a) $AgCl(K_{sp} = 1.8 \times 10^{-10})$ (b) $Ag_2CrO_4(K_{sp} = 1.1 \times 10^{-12})$
(c) $Ag_3PO_4(K_{sp} = 1.8 \times 10^{-18})$ (d) All are precipitated

14 Per cent ionisation of 0.01 M CH_3NH_2 in presence of 0.01 M NaOH is ($K_b(CH_3NH_2) = 4.0 \times 10^{-5}$)
(a) 4.0% (b) 0.4% (c) 0.004% (d) 0.04%

15 Solubility of Ag_2CrO_4 is decreased in presence of
(a) $AgNO_3$ (b) AgCl
(c) $BaCrO_4$ (d) $PbCrO_4$

16 Expression for K_{sp} for mercurous nitrate $Hg_2(NO_3)_2$ is
(a) $[Hg^+]^2 [NO_3^-]^2$ (b) $[Hg^+][NO_3^-]$
(c) $[Hg_2^{2+}][NO_3^-]^2$ (d) $[Hg^{2+}][NO_3^-]^2$

17 K_{sp} of H_2S is 1×10^{-22}. $[S^{2}]$ in a buffer of pH = 7 is
(a) 1×10^{-15} M (b) 1.0×10^{-8} M
(c) 1×10^{-29} M (d) 1.0×10^{-22} M

18 K_{sp} of CdS $= 8 \times 10^{-27}$ and that of $H_2S = 1 \times 10^{-22}$. 1.0×10^{-14} M $CdCl_2$ solution is precipitated on passing H_2S at pH about
(a) 4 (b) 6
(c) 5 (d) 7

19 Minimum loss of Ag_2CrO_4 precipitate ($K_{sp} = 1.1 \times 10^{-12}$) in washing takes place, if it is washed with
(a) 0.01 M K_2CrO_4 (b) 0.01 M $AgNO_3$
(c) water (d) HNO_3

20 Solubility product of AgCl $= 1.8 \times 10^{-10}$, when 50 mL of 0.1 M HCl is added to $AgNO_3$ solution, AgCl just precipitates when final volume is 200 mL.
Thus, molar concentration of $AgNO_3$ is
(a) 2.4×10^{-8} M (b) 1.8×10^{-8} M
(c) 1.2×10^{-9} M (d) 9.6×10^{-9} M

21 K_{sp} of Ag_2CO_3 is 8.39×10^{-12}. Thus, $[Ag^+]$ in saturated solution is
(a) 1.28×10^{-4} M (b) 2.56×10^{-4} M
(c) 0.64×10^{-4} M (d) 2.89×10^{-6} M

22 Solubility of $Mg(OH)_2$ in a particular buffer is found to 4.8×10^{-3} g L^{-1}. Thus, pH of the buffer is [K_{sp} of $Mg(OH)_2$ 4.8×10^{-3}
(a) 4 (b) 6
(c) 8 (d) 10

23 K_{sp} of a salt A_xB is 2.7×10^{-15} and its solubility is 1×10^{-4} M. Thus, value of x is
(a) 1 (b) 2
(c) 3 (d) 4

24 Solubility of sparingly soluble salt, AB, AB_2 and AB_3 is same as 1×10^{-3} M. Thus, solubility products of these salts are
(a) 1×10^{-6} each
(b) $1 \times 10^{-6}, 4 \times 10^{-6}, 27 \times 10^{-6}$
(c) $1 \times 10^{-6}, 4 \times 10^{-9}, 2.7 \times 10^{-11}$
(d) $1 \times 10^{-6}, 4 \times 10^{-8}, 2.7 \times 10^{-8}$

25 For the sparingly soluble salt $M(OH)_3$ $\log[M^{3+}]$ varies with pOH as given, $[M^{3+}]$ at pH = 12 is

X
log $[M^{3+}]$
OX = −9
O
pOH

(a) 10^{-3} M (b) 10^{-2} M
(c) 10^{-4} M (d) 10^{-1} M

26 Solubility product of PbI_2 is 1.39×10^{-8} at 298 K. Its PbI_2 is 90% dissociated in a saturated solution, then solubility of the salt is
(a) 1.68×10^{-3} M (b) 1.36×10^{-3} M
(c) 1.5×10^{-3} M (d) None of these

27 $AgNO_3(aq)$ is slowly added to a solution with $[Cl^-] = 0.115$ M and $[Br^-] = 0.204$ M. What per cent of Br^- remains unprecipitated at the point at which AgCl(*s*) begins to precipitate? [K_{sp}(AgCl) $= 1.8 \times 10^{-10}$, K_{sp}(AgBr) $= 5.0 \times 10^{-13}$]
(a) 0.24% (b) 0.12% (c) 1.20% (d) 2.40%

28 Pure water is saturated with slightly soluble PbI_2. Which of these is a correct statement concerning the lead ion concentration in the solution?
(a) $[Pb^{2+}] = [I^-]$ (b) $[Pb^{2+}] = K_{sp}$ of PbI_2
(c) $[Pb^{2+}] = \sqrt{K_{sp}}$ (d) $(Pb^{2+}) = 0.5\,[I^-]$

29 A 25.00 mL sample of clear saturated solution of PbI_2 requires 12.5 mL of a certain $AgNO_3(aq)$ for its titration. $K_{sp}(PbI_2) = 1.40 \times 10^{-8}$. Thus, molarity of $AgNO_3$ solution is
(a) 2.0×10^{-3} M (b) 4.0×10^{-3} M
(c) 6.0×10^{-3} M (d) 1.0×10^{-3} M

30 A 0.15 M Na_2SO_4 solution also saturated with Ag_2SO_4 has $[Ag^+] = 9.7 \times 10^{-3}$ M. Thus, K_{sp} of Ag_2SO_4 is
(a) 1.40×10^{-5} (b) 1.46×10^{-3}
(c) 2.12×10^{-6} (d) 5.64×10^{-5}

Indicators–Their Use in Acid-Base Titrations

Indicator is generally a weak acid or weak base. End point of an acid-base titration can be detected by change of colour using a suitable indicator. The colour of the ionised form is markedly different from that of unionised form. One form may be colourless, but the other form must be coloured. Ionisation takes place during the titration and unionised form changes to ionised form or *vice-versa*.

Indicator is a weak acid HIn

$$\underset{\text{Colourless}}{\text{HIn}} \rightleftharpoons H^+ + \underset{\text{Coloured}}{In^-}$$

$$K_{In} = \frac{[H^+][In^-]}{[HIn]} \Rightarrow pH = pK_{In} + \log\frac{[In^-]}{[HIn]}$$

The indicator changes colour over a pH range. In the indicators, in which both forms (HIn and In^-) are coloured, one colour is observed, if the ratio of concentrations of the two forms is 10:1.

Case I If $\frac{[In^-]}{[HIn]} = \frac{1}{10}$ then $pH = pK_a - 1$

Case II If $\frac{[In^-]}{[HIn]} = \frac{10}{1}$ thus, $pH = pK_a + 1$

Thus, if pH changes from $(pK_a - 1)$ to $(pK_a + 1)$, indicator shows a colour change.

Thus, $\Delta pH = 2$ units

Case III $[In^-] = [HIn]$ then, $H = pK_a$

Thus, pK_a of the indicator should be close to the pH of the equivalence point.

- **Indicator is a weak base**

$$InOH \rightleftharpoons In^+ + OH^-$$

$$K_{In} = \frac{[In^+][OH^-]}{[InOH]} \Rightarrow pOH = pK_{In} + \log\frac{[In^+]}{[InOH]}$$

For this also colour changes if pOH changes from $(pK_{In} + 1)$ to $(pK_{In} - 1)$

$$\Delta pOH = 2 \text{ units}$$

pH transition ranges and colours of some common indicators

Indicator	pH range	acid solution	Colour in alkaline solution
Thymol blue (acid)	1.2-2.8	red	yellow
Bromo phenol blue	3.1-4.6	yellow	purple
Methyl orange	3.1-4.5	red	yellow
Methyl red	4.2-6.3	red	yellow
Bromo thymol blue	6.0-7.5	orange	blue
Phenol red	6.4-8.2	yellow	red
Thymol blue (base)	8.1-9.6	yellow	blue
Phenolphthalein	8.0-9.8	colourless	pink
Thymophthalein	9.3-10.5	colourless	blue
Alizarin yellow R	10.1-12.1	yellow	lilac

Theories of indicators

Ostwald's theory

There is equilibrium between ionised and unionised forms of an indicator. Due to pH change, one form changes to other, hence colour changes.

Some popular indicators are discussed below :

- **Phenolphthalein** (PhH– a weak acid)

$$\underset{\text{Colourless in acid}}{PhH} \rightleftharpoons \underset{\text{Pink in base}}{Ph^-} + H^+$$

In presence of NaOH (strong base), Ph^- (pink) form is obtained, hence colourless solution changes to pink (pH> 7). Since, it behaves as a weak acid, it is not convenient to use it in the titration of weak base as it cannot shift equilibrium towards the ionised form. Also, Ph^- is hydrolysed back to PhH.

- **Methyl orange** (MeOH– a weak base)

$$\underset{\text{Yellow in alkali}}{MeOH} \rightleftharpoons \underset{\text{Reddish orange in acid}}{Me^+} + OH^-$$

When acid is added in the solution containing methyl orange, ionised form is obtained, hence colour change appears due to change in pH. Since, it behaves as a weak base, this indicator is not suitable in the titration of weak acid as it cannot shift equilibrium towards the ionised form completely. Also, Me^+ is hydrolysed back to MeOH.

Quinonoid theory

An indicator exits in two forms;

Quinonoid coloured ⇌ Benzenoid colourless or light colour

when the value of pH changes, one form changes to the other hence colour change appears.

Acid-base titrations

An acid-base titration involves a neutralisation reaction in which an acid is reacted with an equivalent amount of a base. By constructing a titration curve, we can easily explain, how the end points of these titrations can be detected.

A titration curve is constructed by plotting the pH of the solution as a function of the volume of titrant added. **The titrant is always a strong acid or a strong base. The analyte may be either a strong base or acid or a weak base or acid.**

Titration of strong acid *versus* strong base

A plot showing the variation of pH with the amount of added base is called a **titration curve**. The general shape of this curve is identical for all the titrations of strong acids with strong bases.

The pH is low at the start of the titration and it changes slowly with added base until near the equivalent point when it rises sharply. This rise continues beyond the equivalence point to a high pH, after which the rate of increase in pH becomes much slower.

The equivalence point occurs at the steepest part of the curve, which is at pH for a titration of strong acid with a strong base.

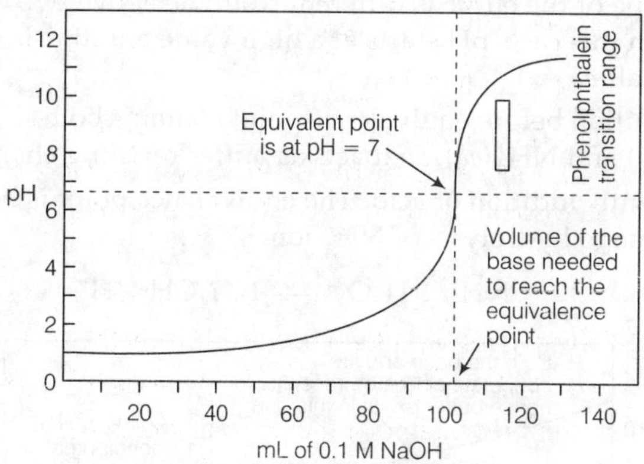

■ As molar concentration of acid decreases, pH increases, hence steep part (of the equivalence point) of the titration curves becomes shorter. The equivalence point is always at pH 7 regardless of the concentration of the acid base used.

Titration of weak acid *versus* strong base

If weak acid is titrated against a strong base, the same volume of base is needed to reach the equivalence point as would be the case if the acid were a strong acid of the same molar concentration.

There is difference in the shape of titration curve before neutralisation as compared to above case but after the equivalence point, the titration curve has the same shape. In case of weak acid, there is less ionisation, thus initial pH is higher. Also, before neutralisation, the system acts as a buffer.

$$CH_3COOH + OH^- \rightleftharpoons CH_3COO^- + H_2O$$

Buffer

Thus, change in pH is very small. Also, after neutralisation, anion formed is hydrolysed releasing OH^- ion. Thus, equivalence point is at higher pH than that of the equivalence point of strong acid and strong base.

$$CH_3CO\bar{O} + H_2C \rightleftharpoons CH_3COOH + O\bar{H}$$

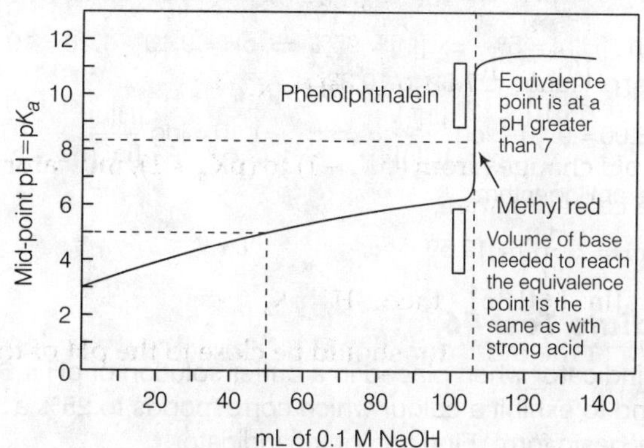

Titration of weak base *versus* strong acid

In this case, HCl (*aq*) is added to the $NH_3(aq)$ solution so the shape of the curve is different from the above two cases. In this case, pH starts at a high value and finishes at a low value.

The solution before equivalence point contains both $NH_3(aq)$ and $NH_4^+(aq)$, so it acts as buffer resisting change in pH with addition of acid. The equivalence point is below pH 7 due to hydrolysis of NH_4^+ ion.

$$NH_4^+ + H_2O \rightleftharpoons NH_4OH + H^+$$

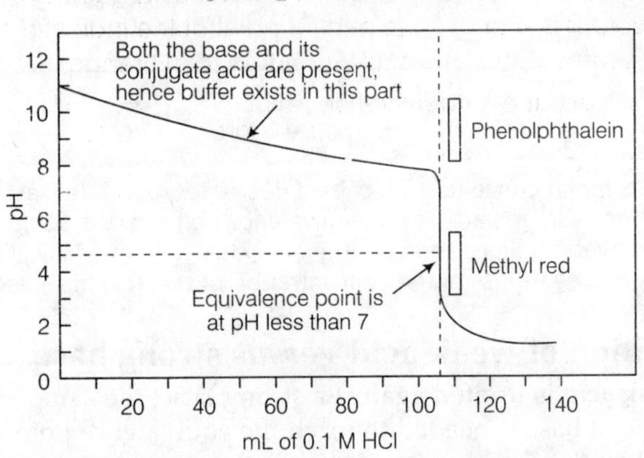

Indicators in acid-base titrations

	Acid-base titrations	Indicators
1.	Strong acid *vs* strong base	Bromothymol blue, phenolphthalein methyl orange, thymophthalein
2.	Strong acid *vs* weak base	Methyl orange, methyl red, bromo cresol green
3.	Weak acid *vs* strong base	Phenolphthalein, thymophthalein
4.	Weak acid *vs* weak base	Phenol red

Phenolphthalein cannot be used in the titration of Na_2CO_3 or $NaHCO_3$ with strong acid as it does not indicate colour after $NaHCO_3$ is formed.

$$Na_2CO_3 + HCl \longrightarrow NaHCO_3 + NaCl$$

$$NaHCO_3 + HCl \longrightarrow \text{No colour indication by phenolphthalein}$$

However, with methyl orange, complete reaction is indicated. Thus, if V = volume of acid used with titration Na_2CO_3 using phenolphthalein as indicator then $2V$ = volume of acid used with same titration using methyl orange as indicator.

Solved Examples & Instant Practice

Example 8.50) The pK_a of phenolphthalein is 9.10.

(a) Over what pH range does this indicator change from 95 per cent HIn to 95 per cent In^- form?

(b) What is the ratio of non-ionised form to the ionised form of the indicator at pH 8.00?

$$HIn \rightleftharpoons H^+ + In^-$$

$$K_a = \frac{[H^+][In^-]}{[HIn]} \Rightarrow pH = pK_a + \log\frac{[In^-]}{[HIn]}$$

$[In^-]$ and [HIn] percentages have been given, thus pH range is derived.

Sol. (a) When [HIn] = 95%, $[In^-]$ = 5%

then $\quad pH = 9.10 + \log\left(\frac{5}{19}\right) = 9.10 - 1.28 = 7.82$

when [HIn] = 5% ⇒ [In] = 95% ⇒ pH = 9.10 + 1.28 = 10.38

Thus, pH range is 7.82 to 10.38.

(b) $8.00 = 9.10 + \log\frac{[In^-]}{[HIn]} \Rightarrow +1.10 = \log\frac{[HIn]}{[In^-]}$

Take antilogarithm

$$\therefore \quad \frac{[HIn]}{[In^-]} = 12.59$$

Immediate Test 46

A given indicator when placed in a buffer solution of pH 4.63 was found to exhibit a colour which corresponds to 25% acid and 75% basic form. Find pK_a of the indicator.

Example 8.51) At what pH will a 1.0×10^{-3} M solution with an indicator with $K_b = 1 \times 10^{-10}$ changes colour?

Sol. It is a basic indicator.

$$In + H_2O \rightleftharpoons InH^+ + OH^-$$

$$K_b = \frac{[InH^+][OH^-]}{[In]}$$

Colour change occurs when $[InH^+]$ = [In]

$$\therefore \quad [OH^-] = K_b = 1 \times 10^{-10} m$$

$$pOH = 10 \quad \therefore \quad pH = 14 - 4 = 10$$

Example 8.52) 50.0 mL of 0.1 M HCN is titrated with 0.10 M NaOH. Calculate pH at the equivalence point. Select suitable indicator based on pH.

HCN is a weak acid and methyl orange cannot be used as the indicator.

Also, at the equivalence point 50 mL *of* 0.1 M HCN ≡ 50 mL *of* 0.1 M NaOH

$$[NaCN]_{\text{equivalence point}} = \frac{0.1 \times 50}{100} = 0.05\,M$$

NaCN *is a salt of weak acid and strong base, thus hydrolysed to give alkaline solution, hence* pH > 7.

$$pH = 7 + \frac{pK_a}{2} + \frac{\log C}{2}$$

Sol. M_1V_1 (HCN) = M_2V_2 (NaOH)

$$V_2(\text{NaOH}) = \frac{M_1V_1}{M_2} = \frac{0.1 \times 50}{0.1} = 50 \text{ mL}$$

Total volume after titration = 50 mL

Thus, [NaCN] = 0.05 M (due to dilution in mixture)

$$CN^- + H_2O \rightleftharpoons \underset{\text{Alkaline}}{HCN + OH^-}$$

$$pH = 7 + \frac{pK_a}{2} + \frac{\log C}{2} = 7 + \frac{9.21}{2} + \frac{\log 0.05}{2}$$

$$= 7 + 4.605 - 0.651 = 10.954$$

Thymophthalein is the suitable indicator.

Example 8.53) **Bromophenol blue is an indicator with K_a value of 5.84×10^{-5}. What percentage of this indicator is in its basic form at pH of 4.84 ?**

Let bromophenol blue be represented as HBb

$$HBb + H_2O \rightleftharpoons Bb^- + H_3O^+$$

$$K_a = \frac{[Bb^-][H_3O^+]}{[HBb]}$$

From pH and K_a, ratio $\frac{[Bb^-]}{[HBb]}$ is known thus, percentage of $[Bb^-]$ is calculated.

Sol. pH = 4.84

$$[H^+] = 10^{-4.84} = 10^{-5}\, 10^{0.16} = 1.45 \times 10^{-5}$$

$$5.84 \times 10^{-5} = \frac{[Bb^-]}{[HBb]} \times 1.45 \times 10^{-5}$$

$$\therefore \quad \frac{[Bb^-]}{[HBb]} = \frac{4.04}{1} \Rightarrow [Bb^-] + [HBb] = 5.04$$

$$\therefore \quad [Bb^-] = \frac{4.04}{5.04} \times 100 = 80.16\%$$

Immediate Test 47

(i) An acid-base indicator has K_a of 3.0×10^{-5}. The acid form of the indicator is red and the basic form is blue. By how much must the pH change in order to change the indicator from 75% red to 75% blue?

(ii) Phenolphthalein is colourless in acidic solution and pink in basic solution. At what pH, indicator is 10% in colourless form?
pK_a(indicator) = 9.4

Example 8.54) **An indicator is a weak acid and pH range of its colour is 4 to 6. If the neutral point of the indicator lies in the centre of the (H^+) corresponding to pH range, then calculate pH at the equivalence point.**

$$pH = 10^{-pH}$$

$$[H^+] \textit{ at the centre} = \left(\frac{[H^+]_1 + [H^+]_2}{2}\right)$$

Thus, pH is calculated.

Sol.

pH	$[H^+]$
4	10^{-4} M
6	10^{-6} M

$$\text{Thus, } [H^+] \text{ at the equivalence point} = \left(\frac{10^{-4} + 10^{-6}}{2}\right) \text{M}$$

$$= \left(\frac{101 \times 10^{-6}}{2}\right) \text{M} = 50.5 \times 10^{-6} \text{ M}$$

$$\therefore \quad pH = -\log [H^+]$$

$$= -\log (50.5 \times 10^{-6}) = 4.3$$

KNOWLEDGE CONFIRMATION **Test 7**

1 For an acid indicator $K_a = 1 \times 10^{-5}$. The range of the pH for change of colour is

(a) 3-5 (b) 4-6
(c) 5-7 (d) 6-8

2 Which form is coloured due to change in pH?

(a) 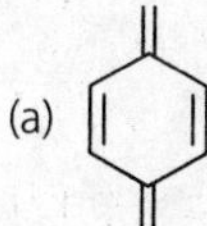 (b) 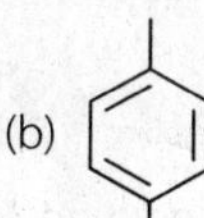

(c) Both (a) and (b) (d) None of these

3 Phenolphthalein is not suitable in the titration of

(a) Na_2CO_3 with HCl (b) NH_4OH with HCl
(c) $NaHCO_3$ with HCl (d) All of these

4 Methyl orange is not suitable in the titration of

(a) NaOH with CH_3COOH (b) NaOH with HCl
(c) Both (a) and (b) (d) None of these

5 In the titration of Na_2CO_3 with HCl, indicator used is

(a) phenolphthalein (b) methyl red
(c) Both (a) and (b) (d) None of the above

6 pK_b of an indicator is 5. At the equivalence point, pH is

(a) 5 (b) 7 (c) 9 (d) 10

7 Consider following observations of different indicators in different pH.

	Indicator	Colour in	
		acid	base
I.	Phenolphthalein	pink	colourless
II.	Phenolphthalein	colourless	pink
III.	Methyl orange	red	yellow
IV.	Methyl orange	yellow	red

Select correct observations.

(a) I, III (b) II, IV
(c) II, III (d) None of these

8 Select the correct statements about indicators :

(a) Near the equivalence point pH = pK_a for acid indicators and pH = $(14 - pK_b)$ for base indicators

(b) Most indicators have a transition range of two pH units.

(c) Methyl orange exists in following equilibrium at different pH

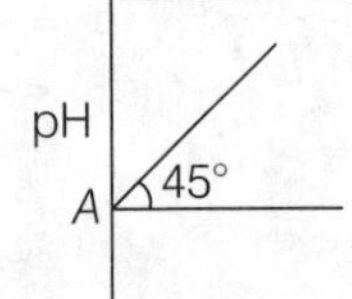

(d) All of the above statements are correct

9 An indicator is a weak acid and pH range of its colour is 3 to 5. If the neutral point of the indicator lies in the centre of the $[H^+]$ corresponding to given pH range then pH at the equivalence point is

(a) 3.3 (b) 4.0 (c) 7.0 (d) 5.0

10 For an acid indicator, pH varies with log*x*, when $\left(x = \frac{[\text{basic form}]}{[\text{acidic form}]}\right)$ as given

If *OA*=4.7, then pH at the point when indicator is 66.66% in basic form is

pH, A, 45°, O, log *x*

(a) 4.7 (b) 3.7 (c) 5.7 (d) 5.0

11 For phenolphthalein, pK_{In} = 9.7. The indicator can be used from 8.2 to 10. Thus, the ratio of $\frac{[In^-]}{[HIn]}$ for the lower and upper limits of the range is

	Lower limit	**Upper limit**
(a)	31.62	0.50
(b)	0.05	31.62
(c)	0.032	0.50
(d)	0.05	0.032

12 In the tiration of CH_3COOH with NaOH, phenolphthalein indicates ...... colour at the equivalent point (neutral point).

(a) colourless (b) pink
(c) orange (d) blue

13 In the titration of NH_4OH wih strong acid, phenolphthalein (PhH) can not be used as an indicator as

(a) NH_4^+ ion is hydrolysed back to NH_4OH and excess of NH_4OH is required to achieve end point.

(b) Ph^- is hydrolysed back to PhH thus, pink colour due to Ph^- disappears.

$$Ph^- + H_2O \rightleftharpoons PhH + OH^-$$

(c) Both of the above are correct.

(d) None of the above is correct.

14 In the titration of weak acid with a strong base, graph between pH and volume of NaOH added is of the type :

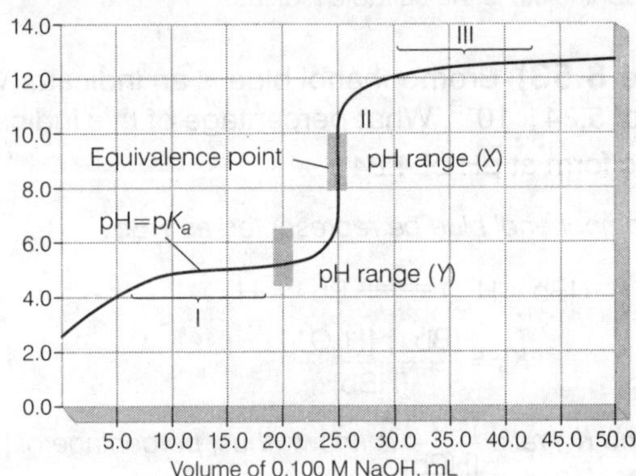

In this,

(a) point *X* is the pH range for phenolphthalein and point *Y* is the pH range for methyl red

(b) point *X* is the pH range for methyl red and point *Y* is the pH range for phenolphthalein.

(c) Both point (*X* and *Y*) are for phenolphthalein

(d) Both point (*X* and *Y*) are for methyl orange

15 In the above graph :

(a) Buffer solution appears in the **region I**

(b) Hydrolysis of salt of weak acid and strong base appears in the **region II**

(c) Region of part III is due to when all the acid is neutralised.

(d) All of the above are correct.

16 In an acid-base titration, 0.1 M HCl solution was added to the NaOH solution of unknown strength. Which of the following correctly shows the change of pH of the titration mixture in this experiment? ***[JEE Main 2019 (II) NTA]***

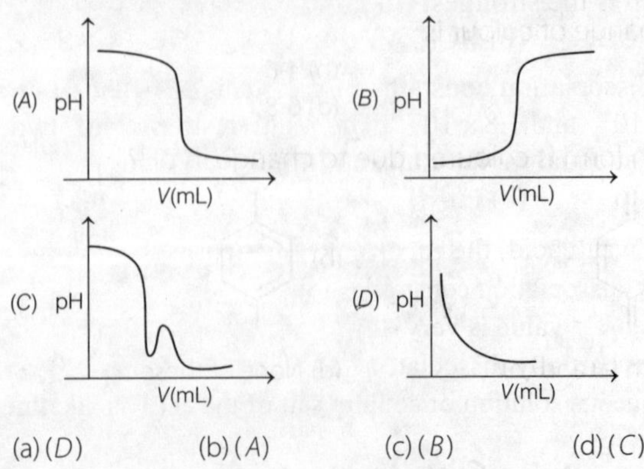

(a) (*D*) (b) (*A*) (c) (*B*) (d) (*C*)

ACID TEST
For JEE Main

TYPE I MCQs with Only ONE Correct Alternate

1 MY and NY_3, two nearly insoluble salts have the same K_{sp} values of 6.2×10^{-13} at room temperature. Which statement would be true in regard of MY and NY_3?

(a) The molar solubility of MY in water is less than that of NY_3
(b) The salts MY and NY_3 are more soluble in 0.5 M KY than that in pure water
(c) The addition of the salt of KY to solution of MY and NY_3 will have no effect on their solubilities
(d) The molar solubilities of MY and NY_3 in water are identical

2 Boric acid is an acid because its molecule

(a) contains replaceable H^+ ion
(b) gives a proton
(c) accept OH^- from water releasing proton
(d) combines with proton from water molecule

3 The K_{sp} of Ag_2CrO_4, AgCl, AgBr and AgI are respectively, 1.1×10^{-12}, 1.8×10^{-10}, 5.0×10^{-13}, 8.3×10^{-17}. Which one of the following salts will precipitate last if $AgNO_3$ solution is added to the solution containing equal moles of NaCl, NaBr, NaI and Na_2CrO_4?

(a) AgI (b) AgCl (c) AgBr (d) Ag_2CrO_4

4 What is the pH of the resulting solution when equal volumes of 0.1 M NaOH and 0.01 M HCl are mixed?

(a) 12.65 (b) 2.0 (c) 7.0 (d) 1.04

5 Using the Gibbs energy change, $\Delta G° = +63.3$ kJ for the following reaction:

$$Ag_2CO_3(s) \rightleftharpoons 2Ag^+(aq) + CO_3^{2-}(aq)$$

The K_{sp} of $Ag_2CO_3(s)$ in water at 25°C is

(a) 3.2×10^{-26} (b) 8.0×10^{-12}
(c) 2.9×10^{-3} (d) 7.9×10^{-2}

6 Which is the strongest acid in the following?

(a) H_2SO_4 (b) $HClO_3$ (c) $HClO_4$ (d) H_2SO_3

7 The dissociation constants of two acids HA_1 and HA_2 are 3.0×10^{-4} and 1.8×10^{-5}. The relative strength of two acids at equal molar concentration is

(a) 1 : 16 (b) 1 : 4 (c) 4 : 1 (d) 16 : 1

8 For a weak acid, the incorrect statement is

(a) its dissociation constant is low
(b) its pK_a value is very low
(c) it is partially dissociated
(d) aqueous solution of sodium salt of the acid is alkaline in nature

9 A solution of pH 9.0 is 1000 times as basic as a solution A. The pH of this solutions A is

(a) 9 (b) 8 (c) 7 (d) 6

10 The solubility product of a binary weak electrolyte is 4×10^{-10} at 298 K. Its solubility in mol dm^{-3} is

(a) 4×10^{-5} (b) 2×10^{-5} (c) 8×10^{-2} (d) 16×10^{-20}

11 A weak acid HX has K_a value of 1×10^{-5}. It forms a salt NaX with NaOH. The degree of hydrolysis of 0.1M solution of NaX is

(a) 0.0001% (b) 0.01% (c) 0.10% (d) 0.15%

12 Which of the following is not a conjugate acid-base pair?

I. $H_2PO_2^-$, HPO_2^- II. H_3PO_4, $H_2PO_4^-$
III. HPO_4^{2-}, PO_4^{3-} IV. HPO_3^{2-}, PO_3^{3-}

(a) I, IV (b) II, III (c) I, III (d) II, IV

13 pH of a saturated solution of $Ba(OH)_2$ is 12. Thus, K_{sp} of $Ba(OH)_2$ is

(a) 3.3×10^{-7} (b) 5.0×10^{-7}
(c) 4.0×10^{-6} (d) 5.0×10^{-6}

14 0.01 M ammonium acetate is diluted to 0.001 M solution. Thus, change in pH is

(a) 5 (b) 10 (c) 9 (d) 0

15 Equal volume of two solutions of pH 2 and 12 are mixed. Thus pH of the resulting mixture is

(a) 7.0 (b) 5.0 (c) 6.0 (d) 8.7

16 Buffer solutions have constant acidity and alkalinity, because

(a) they give unionised acid or base on reaction with added acid or alkali
(b) acids and alkalis in these solutions are shielded from attack by other ions
(c) they have large excess of H^+ or OH^- ions
(d) they have fixed value of pH

17 In the following cases,

(a) 20 mL of 0.1M CH_3COOH + 10 mL of 0.1 M NaOH
$pH = pK_a$
(b) 10 mL of 0.1M NH_4OH + 10 mL of 0.05 M $(NH_4)_2SO_4$
$pH = (14 - pK_b)$
(c) 20 mL of 0.1 M NH_4OH + 10 mL of 0.1 M HCl
$pH = (14 - pK_b)$
(d) All of the above are correct

18 pH of 0.005 M HA acid is 5. Thus, percentage ionisation of this acid is

(a) 2 (b) 0.2 (c) 0.5 (d) .25

19 Which of the following fluoro compounds is most likely to behave as a Lewis base?
(a) BF_3 (b) PF_3 (c) CF_4 (d) SiF_4

20 For a weak acid, H*A*, percentage ionisation is given as
(a) $100\sqrt{\frac{K_a}{C}}$ (b) $\frac{100}{1+10^{(pH-pK_a)}}$
(c) Both (a) and (b) (d) None of these

21 4.0 g of NaOH and 4.9 g of H_2SO_4 are dissolved in water and volume is made upto 250 mL. The pH of this solution is
(a) 7.0 (b) 1.0 (c) 2.0 (d) 12.0

22 Given K_a (HCN) $=4.8\times10^{-10}$
$K_a(NH_4^+)=5.76\times10^{-10}$
Thus, equilibrium constant of the following reaction is
$$NH_4^+ + CN^- \rightleftharpoons NH_3 + HCN$$
(a) 0.83 (b) 1.2
(c) 8.0×10^{-11} (d) 2.76×10^{-9}

23 Given , $HCN \rightleftharpoons H^+ + CN^-$; $\Delta H° = 45\text{ kJ mol}^{-1}$
$CH_3COOH \rightleftharpoons CH_3COO^- + H^+$; $\Delta H° = 2.1\text{ kJ mol}^{-1}$
Thus,
(a) pK_a (HCN) = pK_a (CH_3COOH)
(b) pK_a (HCN) > pK_a (CH_3COOH)
(c) pK_a (HCN) < pK_a (CH_3COOH)
(d) can not be compared

24 $[HCOO^-]$ in a solution of 0.01 M HCOOH in presence of 0.01 M HCl is $[K_a(HCOOH)=1.8\times10^{-4}]$
(a) 1.8×10^{-3} M (b) 1.0×10^{-2} M
(c) 1.8×10^{-4} M (d) 1×10^{-4} M

25 For four weak acids H*A*, H*B*, H*C*, and H*D*, heat of neutralisation with NaOH are −13, −12, −11 and −10 kJ mol^{-1}. Thus, the salt which is maximum hydrolysed is
(a) 1 M Na*A* (b) 1 M Na*B* (c) 1 M Na*C* (d) 1M Na*D*

26 The pH of a solution containing 0.4 M HCO_3^- and 0.2 M CO_3^{2-} is
$$pK_{a_1}=6.4,\ pK_{a_2}=10.4$$
(a) 10.4 (b) 10.1 (c) 6.1 (d) 10.7

27 The pH of the resultant solution of 20 mL of 0.1 M H_3PO_4 and 20 mL of 0.1 M Na_3PO_4 is
(a) $pK_{a_1}+\log 2$ (b) pK_{a_1}
(c) pK_{a_2} (d) $\left(\frac{pK_{a_1}+pK_{a_2}}{2}\right)$

28 The salt of which one of the following weak acids will be most hydrolysed ?
(a) H*A* : $K_a=1\times10^{-8}$ (b) H*B* : $K_a=1\times10^{-6}$
(c) H*C* : $K_a=3\times10^{-8}$ (d) H*D* : $K_a=1\times10^{-10}$

29 Which of the following when mixed will give a solution with pH greater than 7 ?
(a) 100 mL of 0.2 M H_2SO_4 + 100 mL of 0.3 M NaOH
(b) 100 mL of 0.1 M CH_3COOH + 100 mL of 0.1 M NaOH
(c) 50 mL of 0.1 M HCl + 50 mL of 0.1 M CH_3COONa
(d) 25 mL of 0.1 M HNO_3 + 25 mL of 0.1 NH_3

30 0.150 mole of CH_3COONH_4 is dissolved in water to make 1 L of solution. Then $[NH_3]$ is
$[pK_b(NH_3)=pK_a(CH_3COOH)=4.74]$
(a) 8.3×10^{-4} M (b) 1.8×10^{-5} M
(c) 1.0×10^{-7} M (d) 1.8×10^{-9}M

31 For H_2S, $K_{a_1}K_{a_2}=1.0\times10^{-21}$
Thus, $[S^{2-}]$ in a solution that is 0.05 M H_2S and 0.01 M HCl is
(a) 1.0×10^{-19}M (b) 5.0×10^{-19} M
(c) 5.0×10^{-17}M (d) 1.0×10^{-17}M

32 $[SO_4^{2-}]$ in 0.15 M H_2SO_4 is (assume 100% ionisation in first step and $K_2=0.0102$)
(a) 8.9×10^{-3} (b) 1.2×10^{-3}
(c) 1.02×10^{-4} (d) 1.5×10^{-2}

33 pH at which 1×10^{-3}M solution of an indicator with $K_b=1.0\times10^{-10}$ changes colour is
(a) 10.0 (b) 4.0 (c) 3.0 (d) 5.0

34 The ionisation constant of HCOOH is 1.80×10^{-4}. Thus, per cent ionisation of 0.001M solution of this acid is
(a) 42% (b) 34% (c) 4.2% (d) 3.4%

35 What molar concentration of NH_3 provides a $[OH^-]$ $=1.5\times10^{-3}$ M? $[K_b(NH_3)=1.8\times10^{-5}]$
(a) 0.125 M (b) 0.0015 M
(c) 0.1265 M (d) 0.1235 M

36 Consider a solution of a monoprotic weak acid of acidity constant K_a. What is the minimum concentration, (C) in terms of K_a, such that the concentration of the undissociated acid can be equated to C within a 10% limit of error?
(a) $C=9K_a$ (b) $10C=K_a$
(c) $C=10K_a$ (d) $C=90K_a$

37 Select the correct statement(s).
(a) When pH of blood rises above about 7.45, alkalosis occurs
(b) When pH of blood falls below about 7.35, acidosis occurs
(c) Respiratory alkalosis is caused by hyperventilation, or excessive respiration
(d) All of the above are correct statements

38 At 25°C the solubility product of Hg_2Cl_2 in water is 3.2×10^{-17} mol^3 dm^{-9}. What is the solubility of Hg_2Cl_2 in water at 25° C ?
(a) 12×10^{-12} M (b) 3.0×10^{-6} M
(c) 2×10^{-6}M (d) 12×10^{-16} M

39 Which of the molecular hydrides acts as a Lewis acid?
(a) CH_4 (b) H_2O (c) NH_3 (d) B_2H_6

40 pH of a saturated solution of $Ba(OH)_2$ is 12. The value of its K_{sp} is
(a) 5.00×10^{-7} (b) 4.00×10^{-6}
(c) 4.00×10^{-7} (d) 5.00×10^{-6}

41 0.023 g of sodium metal is reacted with 100 cm^3 of water. The pH of the resulting solution is
(a) 10 (b) 11 (c) 9 (d) 12

42 0.1 M HCl and 0.1 M H_2SO_4 each of volume 2 mL are mixed and volume is made upto 6 mL by adding 2 mL of 0.01N NaCl. The pH of the resulting mixture is
(a) 1.17 (b) 1.0
(c) 0.3 (d) log 2 – log 3

43 The solubility product of a salt having formula M_2X_3 is 2.2×10^{-20}. If the solubility of an another salt having formula M_2X is twice the molar solubility of M_2X_3, then solubility product of M_2X is
(a) 3×10^{-12} (b) 9.16×10^{-5}
(c) 4.58×10^{-5} (d) 2.76×10^{-18}

44 K_a of HCN and CH_3COOH are respectively 4.5×10^{-10} and 1.5×10^{-5} at 298 K. Thus, equilibrium constant for
$CN^- + CH_3COOH \rightleftharpoons CH_3COO^- + HCN$ would be
(a) 3.1×10^5 (b) 3.2×10^{-5}
(c) 3.3×10^{-4} (d) 3.3×10^4

45 At 4° C, $K_w = 1 \times 10^{-16}$. A solution with pH = 7.5 at 4°C will
(a) turns blue litmus red
(b) turns red litmus blue
(c) turns turmeric paper brown
(d) be neutral to litmus

46 1 M NH_4OH and 1 M HCl are mixed to make total volume of 300 mL. If pH of the mixture is 9.26 and pK_a $(NH_4^+) = 9.26$ then volume ratio of NH_4OH and HCl will be
(a) 1 : 1 (b) 1 : 2 (c) 2 : 1 (d) 3 : 1

47 Solution of aniline hydrochloride is X due to hydrolysis of Y, X and Y are
(a) basic, $C_6H_5NH_3^+$ (b) acidic, $C_6H_5NH_3^+$
(c) basic, Cl^- (d) acidic, Cl^-

48 pH of aqueous NaCl solution after electrolysis
(a) increases (b) decreases
(c) remains unchanged (d) can not be predicted

49 A 50.00 mL sample of 0.0100 M $Ba(OH)_2$ is titrated with 0.0100 M HCl. The solution at the equivalence point is
(a) 3.33×10^{-3} M $BaCl_2$ (b) 5.00×10^{-3}M $BaCl_2$
(c) 2.50×10^{-3} M $BaCl_2$ (d) 100×10^{-2} M $BaCl_2$

50 40 mL of 0.025 M solution of the protonated form of the amino acid phenylalanine (H_2A^+) is treated with 10 mL of 0.1 M NaOH. pH at this stage is
$(pK_{a_1} = 182, pK_{a_2} = 9.13$ of $H_2A^+)$
(a) 5.48 (b) 7.00
(c) 1.82 (d) 9.13

51 A buffer solution of pH 9.80 is to be prepared from 1 M NH_4Cl and 1 M NH_3 solution. pK_b of NH_3 is 4.74. In 1 L of the buffer solution, volume of NH_4Cl is
[log (0.288) = – 0.54]
(a) 200 mL (b) 775 mL
(c) 500 mL (d) 225 mL

52 HA is 50% ionised. pOH of an aqueous solution of HA and A^- (in a buffer) is [pK_a $(HA) = 4.5$]
(a) 4.5 (b) 2.5 (c) 9.5 (d) 7.0

53 pH of 0.01 M calcium acetate solution is
(pK_a of $CH_3COOH = 4.74$)
(a) 7.00 (b) 9.26
(c) 8.52 (d) 4.74

54 The pK_a of a weak acid HA is 4.80. The pK_b of a weak base BOH is 4.78. The pH of an aqueous solution of the 0.01 M salt BA, is
(a) 9.58 (b) 4.79
(c) 7.01 (d) 9.22

55 Phenolphthalein can't be used in the titration of
(a) HCl with NaOH (b) CH_3COOH with NaOH
(c) HCl with NH_4OH (d) H_2SO_4 with NH_4OH

56 A mixture contains 0.1 M HCOOH ($K_a = 1.8 \times 10^{-4}$) and 0.1 M HOCN ($K_a = 3.3 \times 10^{-4}$). Thus, molar concentration of H_3O^+ is
(a) 7.14×10^{-3} M (b) 4.1×10^{-4} M
(c) 0.20 M (d) 4.1×10^{-3}M

57 Indicator can exist in two forms depending on the medium.

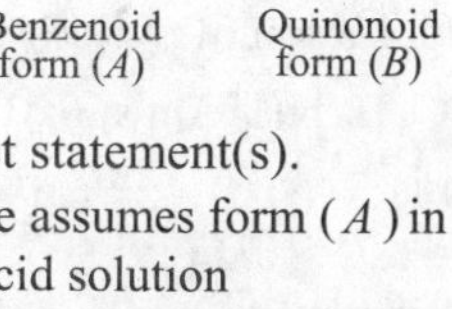

Benzenoid form (A)   Quinonoid form (B)

Select the correct statement(s).
(a) Methyl orange assumes form (A) in alkaline solution and form (B) in acid solution
(b) Phenolphthalein assumes form (A) in acid solution and form (B) in alkaline solution
(c) Thymophthalein assumes form (A) in acid solution and form (B) in alkaline solution
(d) All of the above

58 For any weak acid indicator (HIn) ionising as

$$HIn \rightleftharpoons H^+ + In^-$$

colour of the unionised form (HIn) is observed when

(a) $\frac{[In^-]}{[HIn]} = \frac{1}{10}$ (b) $pH = pK_a - 1$
(c) Both (a) and (b) (d) None of these

59 pK_b of phenolate ion is 4.0. Thus, pH of 0.01M sodium phenolate solution is
(a) 10.0 (b) 9.0 (c) 8.0 (d) 11.0

60 The solubility in water of a sparingly soluble salt AB_2 is 1.0×10^{-5} mol^{-1}L^{-1}. Its solubility in presence of 0.1 M A^{2+} ion is
(a) 2.0×10^{-7}M (b) 1.0×10^{-7}M
(c) 2.0×10^{-14} M (d) 4.0×10^{-15} M

61 The solubility product of the salt $Al(OH)_3$ in water at 298 K is 2.7×10^{-11}. The concentration of Al^{3+} in saturated aqueous solution of the salt is
(a) 2.7×10^{-6}M (b) 2.7×10^{-4}M
(c) 10×10^{-4} M (d) 1.0×10^{-3} M

62 Which of the following solutions will have pH close to 1.0? ***[JEE Main 2018]***
(a) 100 mL of 0.1 M HCl + 100 mL of 0.1 M NaOH
(b) 55 mL of 0.1 M HCl + 45 mL of 0.1 M KOH
(c) 10 mL of 0.2 M HCl + 90 mL of 0.1 M KOH
(d) 75 mL of 0.2 M HCl + 25 mL of 0.2 M NaOH

63 Which of the following when mixed, will give a solution with pH greater than 7 ?
(a) 25 mL of 0.1 M HNO_3 + 25 mL of 0.1 M NaOH
(b) 100 mL of 0.1 M CH_3COOH + 100 mL of 0.1 M KOH
(c) 100 mL of 0.2 M H_2SO_4 + 100 mL of 0.3 M NaOH
(d) 50 mL of 0.1 M HCl + 50 mL of 0.2 M NaCl

64 In a solution of C_6H_5COOK and C_6H_5COOH the ratio of conjugate base to acid is increased by 100 times. Thus change in pH will be
(a) +2 (b) −2 (c) +1 (d) −1

65 The pH of a neutral solution increases to 12.0 on making it alkaline. The increase in $[OH^-]$ is .... times.
(a) 5 (b) 10^3 (c) 10^5 (d) 4

66 The percentage ionisation of pyridine(C_5H_5N) that forms pyridinium ion ($C_5H_5NH^+$) in a 0.10 M aqueous pyridine solution is
(K_b for $C_5H_5N = 1.7 \times 10^{-9}$)
(a) 16% (b) 0.77% (c) 0.006% (d) 0.013 %

67 Consider oxoacids of N, S and Cl
I. $HNO_2, HNO_3, H_2N_2O_2$
II. $H_2SO_3, H_2SO_4, H_2S_2O_3$
III. $HClO, HClO_2, HClO_3, HClO_4$

Strongest acid in each case is

	I	II	III
(a)	HNO_3	H_2SO_3	$HClO_3$
(b)	$H_2N_2O_2$	$H_2S_2O_3$	$HClO$
(c)	HNO_3	H_2SO_4	$HClO_4$
(d)	HNO_3	H_2SO_3	$HClO_3$

68 Out of $H_2O, OH^-, H_3O^+, H_2SO_4, HSO_4^-, HCl, H^+$ strongest acid and strongest base are

	Strongest acid	Strongest base
(a)	H_2SO_4	OH^-
(b)	HCl	Cl^-
(c)	H_2O	OH^-
(d)	H_3O^+	OH^-

69 The pH of 0.1 M solution of a weak monobasic acid is 3. Thus, its ionisation constant K_a is
(a) 3×10^{-1} (b) 1×10^{-3}
(c) 1×10^{-5} (d) 1×10^{-7}

70 20.0 g of NaOH is added to 0.5 L of 1.5 M NH_4Cl solution. If pK_b (NH_3) is 4.74, pH of the resultant mixture is
(a) 9.56 (b) 4.44
(c) 7.00 (d) 7.80

71 pH of the blood (which is 7.40) is controlled by $H_2PO_4^-$ and HPO_4^{2-}. pK_a of $H_2PO_4^-$ is 7.10. What is the ratio of $\frac{[H_2PO_4^-]}{[HPO_4^{2-}]}$ in the blood?
(a) 2 : 1 (b) 1 : 2 (c) 3 : 1 (d) 1 : 3

72 If the equilibrium constant of reaction of weak acid H*A* and strong base is 10^9, then pH of 0.1 M Na*A* is
(a) 5 (b) 7 (c) 8 (d) 9

73 In the following reaction,

$$\underset{(A)}{[Cu(H_2O)_3(OH)^+]} + \underset{(B)}{[Al(H_2O)_6^{3+}]} \longrightarrow \underset{(C)}{[Cu(H_2O)_4^{2+}]} + \underset{(D)}{[Al(H_2O)_5(OH)^{2+}]}$$

(a) (*A*) is a base and (*B*) the acid
(b) (*C*) is the conjugate acid of (*A*) and (*D*) is the conjugate base of (*B*)
(c) Both (a) and (b) are correct
(d) None of the above is correct

74 Buffer index of a buffer of 0.1 M NH_4OH and 0.1 M NH_4Cl is
(a) 0.082 (b) 0.115
(c) 0.025 (d) 0.230

75 pK_a of a weak acid H*A* is 4.0. Effective range of a buffer of H*A* and A^- is about pH
(a) 3 to 4 (b) 3 to 6
(c) 3 to 5 (d) 4 to 5

76 pK_a of BH^+ is 8.0. A buffer of B and BH^+ has effective range of about pH
(a) 5 to 6 (b) 6 to 8
(c) 6 to 7 (d) 7 to 9

77 Which of the hydrates species can exist?
I. $H_5O_2^+$ II. H_3O^+
III. $H_3O_2^-$ IV. $H_5O_3^-$
Select the correct alternate.
(a) Only II (b) Both I and II
(c) I, II and III (d) I, II, III and IV

78 The pH of a solution resulting when 50 mL of 0.2 M HCl is mixed with 50 mL of 0.20 M AcOH ($K_a = 1.8 \times 10^{-5}$) is
(a) 0.70 (b) 0.30
(c) 1.00 (d) 2.00

79 pK_{a_1} and pK_{a_2} of H_2SO_3 are 1.82 and 7.20. pH after 20 mL of 0.160 M NaOH is added to 40 mL of 0.080 M H_2SO_3 is
(a) 7.00 (b) 1.82
(c) 8.80 (d) 4.51

80 The acid ionisation (hydrolysis) constant of Zn^{2+} is 1×10^{-9}. Hence, pH of 0.001 M solution of $ZnCl_2$ is
(a) 9.0 (b) 3.0 (c) 6.0 (d) 7.0

81 How many times a solution of pH = 2 has higher acidity than the solution of pH = 6?
(a) 400 (b) 800 (c) 1200 (d) 10000

82 The K_a for formic acid is 2.0×10^{-4} mol L^{-1}, then K_h for $HCOO^-$ is
(a) 2×10^{-5} mol L^{-1} (b) 4×10^{-7} mol L^{-1}
(c) 5×10^{-11} mol L^{-1} (d) 5×10^{-5} mol L^{-1}

83 0.1 mole of CH_3NH_2 ($K_b = 5 \times 10^{-4}$) is mixed with 0.08 mole of HCl and diluted to 1 L. What will be the H^+ concentration in the solution?
(a) 8×10^{-2} M (b) 8×10^{-11} M
(c) 16×10^{-11} M (d) 8×10^{-5} M

84 An acid indicator is ....% ionised in its basic form at pH of 5 ($K_a = 1 \times 10^{-5}$)
(a) 20% (b) 40%
(c) 50% (d) 100%

85 For the reaction $Hg^{2+} + 2Cl^- \rightleftharpoons HgCl_2$,
$K = 1.65 \times 10^{13}$ concentration of Hg^{2+} at the equivalence point in the titration of 2.0 mmol of Hg^{2+} with Cl^- when final volume is 100 mL, is
(a) 8.25×10^{14} M (b) 1.65×10^{13} M
(c) 2.87×10^{6} M (d) 6.72×10^{-6} M

86 It is desired to prepare 100 mL of a buffer of pH 5.00. Acetic ($pK_a = 4.74$), benzoic ($pK_a = 4.18$) and formic acids ($pK_a = 3.68$) and their salts are available for use. Which acid should be used for maximum effectiveness against increase or decrease in pH?
(a) Acetic acid (b) Benzoic acid
(c) Formic acid (d) Any one of these

87 Molar solubility of $Fe(OH)_3$ in a solution containing 0.10 M $C_2O_4^{2-}$ is
K_{sp} $[Fe(OH)_3] = 4 \times 10^{-38}$, K_f $[Fe(C_2O_4)_3^{3-}] = 2 \times 10^{20}$
(a) 1.78×10^{-6} M (b) 3.02×10^{-6} M
(c) 3.80×10^{-6} M (d) 4.15×10^{-6} M

88 To precipitate as $Ag_2S(s)$ all the Ag^+ present in 338 mL of saturated solution, of $AgBrO_3$ requires 30.4 mL of $H_2S(g)$ measured at 296 K and 748 mmHg.
$$2Ag^+(aq) + H_2S(g) \longrightarrow Ag_2S(s) + 2H^+(aq)$$
Thus, K_{sp} of $AgBrO_3$ is
(a) 7.26×10^{-3} (b) 3.63×10^{-3}
(c) 5.27×10^{-5} (d) 1.32×10^{-5}

89 What mass of CH_3COOH must be dissolved per kg of aqueous solution if the solution is to have same freezing point as 0.15 molal $CH_2ClCOOH$?
K_a (CH_3COOH: 1.8×10^{-5}; $CH_2ClCOOH$: 1.4×10^{-3}
K_f (H_2O: 1.86° mol^{-1} kg)
[**Hint** ΔT_f = molality $\times K_f \times i$
i = van't Hoff factor = $(1 + x)$] for monobasic acid
(a) 9.87 g (b) 9.77 g
(c) 9.42 g (d) 9.56 g

90 What is the pH of 0.05 M potassium hydrogen phthalate $KHC_8H_4O_4$?
For phthalic acid,
$C_6H_4(COOH)_2$ (benzene ring with two adjacent –COOH groups) $K_{a_1} = 1.1 \times 10^{-3}$, $K_{a_2} = 3.7 \times 10^{-6}$
(a) 4.2 (b) 7.8
(c) 8.4 (d) 4.8

91 How many drops of 10.0 M HCl or 10.0 M NH_3 to bring the pH of 0.50 mL of 0.5 M $NH_4Cl(aq)$ solution to 7? (1 drop = 0.05 mL) and pK_b of NH_3 = 4.74
(a) 2 drops of NH_3 (b) 3 drops of NH_3
(c) 2 drops of HCl (d) 5 drops of HCl

92 A particular water sample saturated with CaF_2 ($K_{sp} = 5.3 \times 10^{-9}$) is found to have a Ca^{2+} content of 115 ppm. Thus, F^- content in the water sample is :
(a) 1.36×10^{-3} mol L^{-1} (b) 0.02584 gL^{-1}
(c) 25.84 ppm (d) All of the above

93 A 25.00 mL sample of clear saturated solution of PbI_2 requires 13.3 mL of certain $AgNO_3(aq)$ for its titration. K_{sp} $(PbI_2) = 7.1 \times 10^{-9}$. Thus, molarity of $AgNO_3$ solution is

(a) 4.55×10^{-2} M (b) 4.55×10^{-3} M
(c) 2.28×10^{-3} M (d) None of these

94 The solubility of $Mg(OH)_2$ in a particular buffer solution is found to be 0.65 g L^{-1}. Thus, pH of the buffer solution is $K_{sp} = [Mg(OH)_2 = 1.8 \times 10^{-11}]$

(a) 11.95 (b) 10.20
(c) 9.60 (d) 12.05

95 A particular water sample has 131 ppm of $CaSO_4$. If this water is boiled in a tea kettle, approximately what fraction of the water must be evaporated before $CaSO_4(s)$ begins to precipitate (no effect on solubility of $CaSO_4$ in the temperature range 0°C to 100°C.
$K_{sp}(CaSO_4 = 9.1 \times 10^{-6})$

(a) 0.50 (b) 0.68
(c) 0.46 (d) 0.32

96 Solubility product of barium oxalate is 2.2×10^{-7} at 300 K. Thus, solubility of barium oxalate in 0.05 M sodium oxalate is

(a) 4.2×10^{-4} M (b) 3.0×10^{-6} M
(c) 4.4×10^{-6} M (d) 1.2×10^{-6} M

97 Solubility of AgCN in a buffer of pH 3 is
(K_{sp} of AgCN $= 1.2 \times 10^{-16}$ K_a of HCN $= 4.8 \times 10^{-10}$)

(a) 1.6×10^{-5} M
(b) 1.9×10^{-5} M
(c) 2.7×10^{-6} M
(d) 1.6×10^{-10} M

98 An aqueous solution of a metal bromide MBr_2 (0.05M) is saturated with H_2S. Thus, minimum pH at which MS will precipitate is (K_{sp} of $MS = 6.0 \times 10^{-21}$
$K_{a_1} K_{a_2}$ $(H_2S) = 1.3 \times 10^{-20}$, $[H_2S] = 0.1$ M

(a) 1.263 (b) 3.169
(c) 0.983 (d) 4.200

99 Given, $H_2SO_4(aq) \rightleftharpoons H^+(aq) + HSO_4^-$, $K_1 = 1$
$HSO_4^-(aq) \rightleftharpoons H^+(aq) + SO_4^{2-}(aq)$, $K_2 = 1.26 \times 10^{-2}$
Thus, $[H_3O^+]$ in 0.36 M H_2SO_4 is

(a) 0.0118 M (b) 0.0236 M
(c) 0.3600 M (d) 0.3718 M

100 Which of the following salts is most basic in aqueous solution? *[JEE Main 2018]*

(a) $FeCl_3$ (b) $Pb(CH_3COO)_2$
(c) $Al(CN)_3$ (d) CH_3COOK

101 An alkali is titrated against an acid with methyl orange as an indicator. Which of the following is a correct combination? *[JEE Main 2018]*

	Base	Acid	End point
(a)	Weak	Strong	Yellow to pinkish red
(b)	Strong	Strong	Pink to colourless
(c)	Weak	Strong	Colourless to pink
(d)	Strong	Strong	Pinkish red to yellow

102 An aqueous solution contains an unknown concentration of Ba^{2+}. When 50 mL of a 1M solution of Na_2SO_4 is added, $BaSO_4$ just begins to precipitate. The final volume is 500 mL. The solubility product (K_{sp}) of $BaSO_4$ is 1×10^{-10}. What is the original concentration of Ba^{2+}? *[JEE Main 2018]*

(a) 1.1×10^{-9} M (b) 1.0×10^{-10} M
(c) 5.0×10^{-9} M (d) 2.0×10^{-9} M

103 An aqueous solution contains 0.10 M H_2S and 0.20 M HCl. If the equilibrium constant for the formation of HS^- from H_2S is 1.0×10^{-7} and that of S^{2-} from HS^- ions is 1.2×10^{-13}, then the concentration of S^{2-} ions in aqueous solution is *[JEE Main 2018]*

(a) 6.0×10^{-21} (b) 5.0×10^{-19}
(c) 5×10^{-8} (d) 3×10^{-20}

104 pK_a of a weak acid (HA) and pK_b of a weak base (BOH) are 3.2 and 3.4 respectively. The pH of their salt (BA) solution is *[JEE Main 2017]*

(a) 7.2 (b) 6.9
(c) 7.0 (d) 1.0

105 How many litres of water must be added to 1 L of an aqueous solution of HCl with a pH of 1 to create an aqueous solution with pH of 2? *[JEE Main 2014]*

(a) 0.1 L (b) 0.9 L
(c) 2.0 L (d) 9.0 L

106 The pH of a 0.1 M solution of the acid HQ is 3. The value of the ionisation constant K_a of the acid is *[AIEEE 2011]*

(a) 3×10^{-1} (b) 1×10^{-3}
(c) 1×10^{-5} (d) 1×10^{-7}

107 The K_{sp} for $Cr(OH)_3$ is 1.6×10^{-30}. The molar solubility of this compound in water is *[AIEEE 2011]*

(a) $\sqrt[2]{1.6 \times 10^{-30}}$ (b) $\sqrt[4]{1.6 \times 10^{-30}}$
(c) $\sqrt[4]{1.6 \times 10^{-30} / 27}$ (d) $1.6 \times 10^{-30} / 27$

108 An acid HA ionises as $HA \rightleftharpoons H^+ + A^-$. The pH of 1.0 M solution is 5. Its dissociation constant would be *[AIEEE 2011]*

(a) 1×10^{-10} (b) 5
(c) 5×10^{-8} (d) 1×10^{-5}

109 Three reactions involving $H_2PO_4^-$ are given below: ***[AIEEE 2010]***

I. $H_3PO_4 + H_2O \longrightarrow H_3O^+ + H_2PO_4^-$

II. $H_2PO_4^- + H_2O \longrightarrow HPO_4^{2-} + H_3O^+$

III. $H_2PO_4^- + OH^- \longrightarrow H_3PO_4 + O^{2-}$

In which of the above $H_2PO_4^-$ acts as an acid?

(a) Only II (b) I and II
(c) Only III (d) Only I

110 In aqueous solution, the ionisation constants for carbonic acid are $K_1 = 4.2 \times 10^{-7}$ and $K_2 = 4.8 \times 10^{-11}$

Select the correct statement for a saturated 0.034 M solution of the carbonic acid. ***(AIEEE 2010)***

(a) The concentration of CO_3^{2-} is 0.034 M
(b) The concentration of CO_3^{2-} is greater than that of HCO_3^-
(c) The concentration of H^+ and HCO_3^- are approximately equal
(d) The concentration of H^+ is double that of CO_3^{2-}

111 Solubility product of silver bromide is 5.0×10^{-13}. The quantity of potassium bromide (molar mass taken as 120 g mol^{-1}) to be added to 1L of 0.05 M solution of silver nitrate to start the precipitation of AgBr is ***[AIEEE 2010]***

(a) 1.2×10^{-10} g (b) 1.2×10^{-9} g
(c) 6.2×10^{-5} g (d) 5.0×10^{-8} g

112 At 25°C, the solubility product of $Mg(OH)_2$ is 1.0×10^{-11}. At which pH, will Mg^{2+} ions start precipitating in the form of $Mg(OH)_2$ from a solution of 0.001 M Mg^{2+} ions? ***[AIEEE 2010]***

(a) 9 (b) 10
(c) 11 (d) 8

113 Solid $Ba(NO_3)_2$ is gradually dissolved in a 1.0×10^{-4} M Na_2CO_3 solution. At what concentration of Ba^{2+}, a precipitate will begin to form? (K_{sp} for $BaCO_3 = 5.1 \times 10^{-9}$) ***[AIEEE 2010]***

(a) 4.1×10^{-5} M (b) 5.1×10^{-5} M
(c) 8.1×10^{-8} M (d) 8.1×10^{-7} M

114 Four species are listed below:

I. HCO_3^- II. H_3O^+ III. HSO_4^- IV. HSO_3F

Which one of the following is the correct sequence of their acidic strength? ***[AIEEE 2008]***

(a) IV< II < III < I (b) II < III < I < IV
(c) I < III < II < IV (d) III < I < IV < II

115 The pK_a of a weak acid HA is 4.80. The pK_b of a weak base BOH is 4.78. The pH of an aqueous solution of the corresponding salt BA will be ***[AIEEE 2008]***

(a) 9.58 (b) 4.79
(c) 7.01 (d) 9.22

116 In a saturated solution of the sparingly soluble strong electrolyte $AgIO_3$ (molecular mass = 283) the equilibrium which sets is

$$AgIO_3(s) \rightleftharpoons Ag^+(aq) + IO_3^-(aq)$$

If the solubility product constant K_{sp} of $AgIO_3$ at a given temperature is 1.0×10^{-8}, what is the mass of $AgIO_3$ contained in 100 mL of its saturated solution? ***[AIEEE 2007]***

(a) 28.3×10^{-2} g (b) 2.83×10^{-3} g
(c) 1.0×10^{-7} g (d) 1.0×10^{-4} g

117 The pK_a of a weak acid (HA) is 4.5. The pOH of an aqueous buffered solution of HA in which 50% of acid ionised, is ***[AIEEE 2007]***

(a) 4.5 (b) 2.5 (c) 9.5 (d) 7.0

118 The first and second dissociation constants of an acid H_2A are 1.0×10^{-5} and 5.0×10^{-10}, respectively.The overall dissociation constant of the acid will be ***[AIEEE 2007]***

(a) 5.0×10^{-5} (b) 5.0×10^{15}
(c) 5.0×10^{-15} (d) 0.2×10^{5}

119 An acidic buffer is obtained on mixing ***[JEE Main 2020 (II) NTA]***

(a) 100 mL of 0.1 M CH_3COOH and 100 mL of 0.1 M NaOH
(b) 100 mL of 0.1 M HCl and 200 mL of 0.1 M NaCl
(c) 100 mL of 0.1 M CH_3COOH and 200 mL of 0.1 M NaOH
(d) 100 mL of 0.1 M HCl and 200 mL of 0.1 M CH_3COONa

120 The solubility product of a salt having general formula MX_2, in water is 4×10^{-12}. The concentration of M^{2+} ions in the aqueous solution of the salts, is ***[AIEEE 2005]***

(a) 4.0×10^{-10} M (b) 1.6×10^{-4} M
(c) 1.0×10^{-4} M (d) 2.0×10^{-6} M

121 The stoichiometry and solubility product of a salt with solubility curve given below are respectively

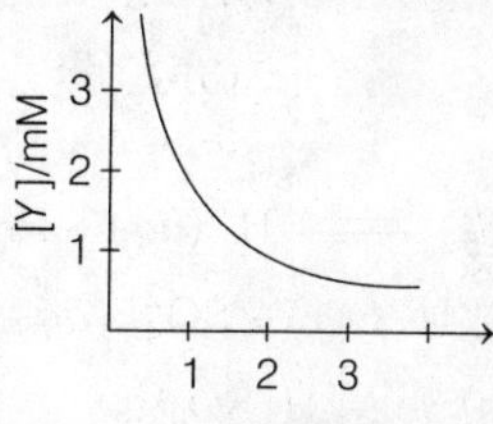

[JEE Main 2020 (I) NTA]

	Stoichiometry	**Solubility Product**
(a)	X_2Y,	2×10^{-9} M^3
(b)	XY,	2×10^{-6} M^3
(c)	XY_2,	1×10^{-9} M^3
(d)	XY_2,	4×10^{-9} M^3

122 100 mL of 0.1M HCl is taken is a beaker and to it 100 mL of 0.1 M NaOH is added in steps of 2 mL and the pH continuously measured. Which of the following graphs correctly depicts the change in pH? ***[JEE Main 2020 (II) NTA]***

(a) 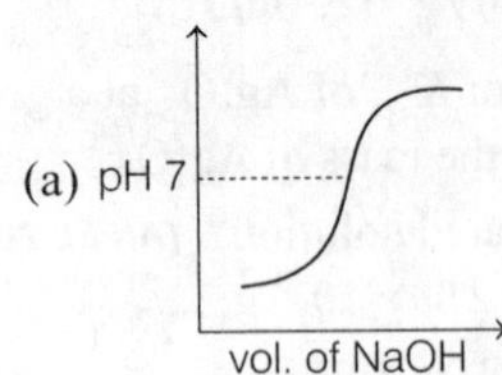

(b) 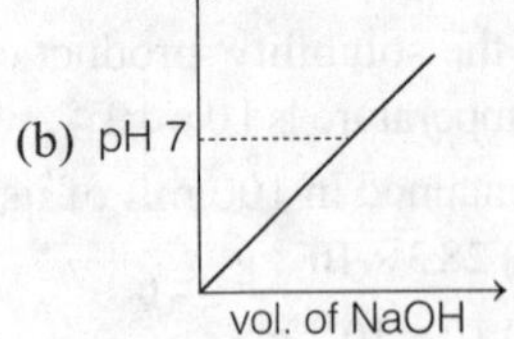

(c) 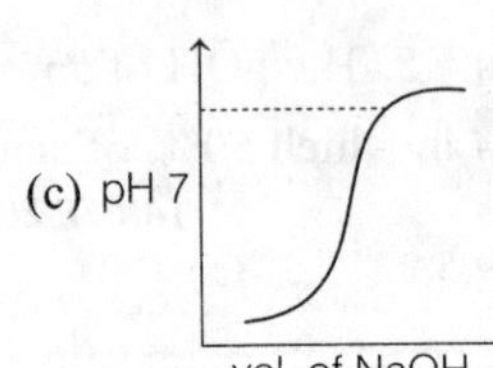

(d) 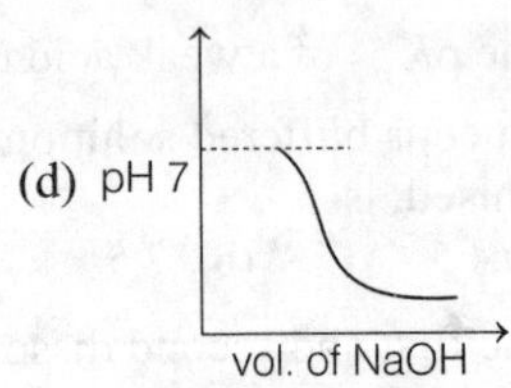

123 If solubility product of $Zr_3(PO_4)_4$ is denoted by K_{sp} and its molar solubility is denoted by S, then which of the following relations between S and K_{sp} is correct? ***[JEE Main 2019 (II) NTA]***

(a) $S = \left(\dfrac{K_{sp}}{144}\right)^{1/6}$ (b) $S = \left(\dfrac{K_{sp}}{6912}\right)^{1/7}$

(c) $S = \left(\dfrac{K_{sp}}{929}\right)^{1/9}$ (d) $S = \left(\dfrac{K_{sp}}{216}\right)^{1/7}$

124 Which one of the following substances has the highest proton affinity? ***[AIEEE 2003]***

(a) H_2O (b) H_2S (c) NH_3 (d) PH_3

125 The solubility in water of a sparingly soluble salt AB_2 is 1.0×10^{-5} mol L^{-1}. Its solubility product will be ***[AIEEE 2003]***

(a) 4×10^{-15} (b) 4×10^{-10}

(c) 1×10^{-15} (d) 1×10^{-10}

126 Which one of the following statements is not true? ***[AIEEE 2003]***

(a) The conjugate base of $H_2PO_4^-$ is HPO_4^{2-}

(b) pH + pOH = 14 for all aqueous solutions

(c) The pH of 1×10^{-8} M HCl is 8

(d) 96500 C of electricity when passed through a $CuSO_4$ solution deposits 1 g equivalent of copper at the cathode

127 Which one of the following species acts as both Bronsted acid and base? ***[AIEEE 2002]***

(a) $H_2PO_2^-$

(b) HPO_3^{2-}

(c) HPO_4^{2-}

(d) All of the above

128 If K_{sp} of Ag_2CO_3 is 8×10^{-12}, the molar solubility of Ag_2CO_3 in 0.1 M $AgNO_3$ is ***[AIEEE 2002]***

(a) 8×10^{-12} M

(b) 8×10^{-13} M

(c) 8×10^{-10} M

(d) 8×10^{-11} M

129 The pH of 0.02 M NH_4Cl solution will be ($K_b(NH_4OH) = 10^{-5}$) and log 2 = 0.3.10 ***[JEE Main 2019 (II) NTA]***

(a) 4.65 (b) 2.65

(c) 5.35 (d) 4.35

130 What is the molar solubility of $Al(OH)_3$ in 0.2 M NaOH solution? Given that, solubility product of $Al(OH)_3 = 2.4 \times 10^{-24}$ ***[JEE Main 2019 (II) NTA]***

(a) 3×10^{-19}

(b) 12×10^{-21}

(c) 3×10^{-22}

(d) 12×10^{-23}

ACID TEST

For JEE Advanced

TYPE I MCQs with Only ONE Correct Alternate

131 pK_a of $CH_3COOH = 4.74$, pK_a of $ClCH_2COOH = 2.88$. Thus, difference in pH of 0.01 M solution of CH_3COOH and $ClCH_2COOH$ solution is

(a) 0.93 (b) 1.86 (c) 3.72 (d) 4.00

132 Percentage ionisation of 0.02 M dimethyl amine ($(CH_3)_2NH$) in the presence of 1 M NaOH, is ($K_b = 5.4 \times 10^{-4}$)

(a) 0.54% (b) 0.17% (c) 0.054% (d) 0.0017%

133 Out of the following amphoteric as well as amphiprotic species is/are

I. H_2O, II. $H_2PO_2^-$,

III. HPO_3^{2-} IV. HPO_4^{2-}

(a) I, II, III and IV (b) I, II, III

(c) I (d) IV

134 Titration curve, if a strong base is titrated with strong acid is

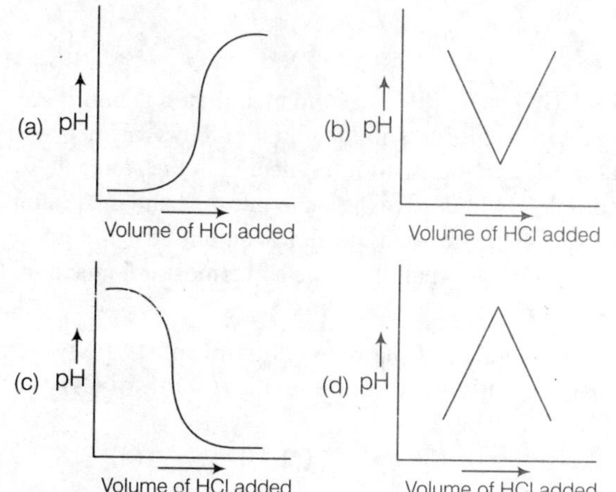

135 Auto-ionisation of liquid NH_3 is $2NH_3 \rightleftharpoons NH_4^+ + NH_2^-$ with $K_{NH_3} = [NH_4^+][NH_2^-] = 10^{-30}$ at $-50°C$

Number of amide ion NH_2^-, present per mm^3 of pure liquid NH_3 is

(a) 600 (b) 300 (c) 200 (d) 100

136 H*X* is a weak acid. It forms salt Na*X* on reacting with caustic soda. If K_a of H*X* is 1×10^{-5}, degree of hydrolysis of 0.1 M Na*X* solution is

(a) 0.01% (b) 0.001%

(c) 0.1% (d) 0.5%

137 Given,

$$H_2S + H_2O \rightleftharpoons H_3O^+ + HS^-, K_{a_1} = 1.0 \times 10^{-7}$$

$$HS^- + H_2O \rightleftharpoons H_3O^+ + S^{2-}, K_{a_2} = 1.2 \times 10^{-13}$$

Thus, $[S^{2-}]$ in the presence of 0.2 M HCl due to 0.1 M H_2S is

(a) 1.10×10^{-20} M (b) 1.32×10^{-6} M

(c) 1.02×10^{-27} M (d) 3.0×10^{-20} M

138 A solution is a mixture of 0.05 M NaCl and 0.05 M NaI. The concentration of iodide ion in the solution when AgCl starts precipitating is equal to

$[K_{sp}(AgCl) = 1 \times 10^{-10}, K_{sp}(AgI) = 4 \times 10^{-16}]$

(a) 4×10^{-6} M (b) 2×10^{-8} M

(c) 2×10^{-7} M (d) 8×10^{-15} M

139 Assuming 100% ionisation which will have maximum pH?

(a) 0.01 M NH_4Cl (b) 0.01 M $(NH_4)_2SO_4$

(c) 0.01 M $(NH_4)_3PO_4$ (d) Equal

140 If solubility of AgCl(*s*) in water, 0.05 M $AgNO_3$, 0.05 M NaCl and 0.01 M $CaCl_2$ are respectively S_1, S_2, S_3 and S_4 then ($K_{sp} = 1 \times 10^{-10}$)

(a) $S_1 = S_2 = S_3 = S_4$ (b) $S_2 < S_1 = S_3 < S_4$

(c) $S_4 < S_3 < S_2 < S_1$ (d) $S_2 = S_3 < S_4 < S_1$

141 An acid base indicator has $K_a = 3.0 \times 10^{-8}$. The acid form of the indicator changes as

$$\underset{\text{Red}}{HIn} = H^+ + \underset{\text{Blue}}{In^-}$$

Change in $[H^+]$ required to change the indicator from 75% red to 75% blue is

(a) 3×10^{-8} M (b) 8×10^{-8} M

(c) 9×10^{-8} M (d) 1×10^{-8}M

142 200 mL of an aqueous solution of HCl (pH = 2) is mixed with 300 mL of an aqueous solution of NaOH (pH = 12). Thus, pH of the resultant mixture is
(a) 14.0 (b) 10.2 (c) 7.9 (d) 11.3

143 Vessel A contains 100 mL of HCl of pH = 2 and vessel B contains 100 mL of NaOH of pH = 12. Al_2O_3 is added in each vessel. Molar ratio of Al_2O_3 required by A and B is
(a) 1 : 2 (b) 2 : 1 (c) 1 : 3 (d) 3 : 1

144 H_2SO_4 solution (density = 1.8 gm L^{-1}) is 500 m. Thus, its pH is (m = molality)
(a) 2.70 (b) −2.70 (c) −1.26 (d) −1.56

145 0.24 g sample of Mg reacts with 80.0 mL of HCl solution whose pH is – 0.30. pH after all Mg has reacted is
(a) 0.30 (b) – 0.30
(c) – 0.24 (d) 0.24

146 For the equilibrium at 298 K,

$$NH_4OH \rightleftharpoons NH_4^+ + OH^-; \quad \Delta H° = 4.4 \text{ kJ mol}^{-1}$$

and $\Delta S° = -76.53 \times 10^{-3}$ kJ K^{-1} mol^{-1}.

Thus, pK_b of NH_4OH is
(a) 4.77 (b) 9.23 (c) −4.77 (d) 7.00

147 At 298 K, K_w of water is 1×10^{-14}. Thus, ionisation constant of water is
(a) 1×10^{-14} (b) 5.55×10^{-15}
(c) 1.8×10^{-16} (d) 55.5×10^{-10}

148 K_a of CH_3COOH is 1.8×10^{-5}. Its 0.1 M solution should be diluted .... times so that pH is doubled. (Assume $x <<< 1$)
(a) four (b) 5.55×10^4
(c) 5.55×10^6 (d) 0.01

149 The atmospheric SO_2 concentration over a certain region is 0.12 ppm by volume. Assuming 100% ionisation as

$$H_2O + SO_2 \rightleftharpoons H^+ + HSO_3^-$$

pH of rain water (acid rain) due to this pollution is
(a) 5.73 (b) 3.92 (c) 8.27 (d) 10.08

150 Calcium lactate is salt of a weak acid represented as $Ca(Lac)_2$. Its saturated solution contain 0.13 mole in 0.50 L solution and pH is 8.4. Assume complete dissociation of the salt, pK_a of the lactic acid is
(a) 6.16 (b) 3.085 (c) 10.92 (d) 5.80

151 Solubility product of silver bromide is 5.0×10^{-13}. The quantity of potassium bromide (120 g mol^{-1}) to be added to 1 L of 0.05 M solution of silver nitrate to start the precipitation of AgBr, is
(a) 1.2×10^{-10} g (b) 1.2×10^{-9} g
(c) 6.2×10^{-5} g (d) 5.0×10^{-8} g

152 Solid $Ba(NO_3)_2$ is gradually dissolved in a 1.0×10^{-4} M Na_2CO_3 solution. At what concentration of Ba^{2+} will a precipitate begin to form? (K_{sp} of $BaCO_3 = 5.1 \times 10^{-9}$)
(a) 4.1×10^{-5} M (b) 5.1×10^{-5} M
(c) 8.1×10^{-8} M (d) 8.1×10^{-7} M

153 The silver ion in a solution is precipitated by the adding chloride ion.

$$Ag^+(aq) + Cl^-(aq) \rightleftharpoons AgCl(s), \; K = 1 \times 10^{10}$$

The final volume of the solution is 500 mL. At a point when not more than 0.10 mg of Ag^+ ion remains unprecipitated $[Cl^-]$ ion is
(a) 5.4×10^{-5} M (b) 1.9×10^{-6} M
(c) 5.4×10^{-4} M (d) 1.9×10^{-7} M

154 In a saturated solution of the sparingly soluble $AgIO_3$ (283 g mol^{-1}), the equilibrium which sets in is

$$AgIO_3(s) \rightleftharpoons Ag^+(aq) + IO_3^-(aq)$$

Given, K_{sp} ($AgIO_3 = 1.0 \times 10^{-8}$)

Mass of $AgIO_3$ present in 100 mL of saturated solution is
(a) 28.3×10^{-2} g (b) 2.83×10^{-3} g
(c) 10×10^{-7} g (d) 10×10^{-4} g

155

$$\text{Aspirin (HO–C(=O)–C}_6\text{H}_4\text{–O–C(=O)–CH}_3) + H_2O \rightleftharpoons {}^-\text{O–C(=O)–C}_6\text{H}_4\text{–O–C(=O)–CH}_3 + H_3O^+$$

Aspirin

$pK_a = 3.5$

The pH of gastric juice in human stomach is about 2.3 and that in small intestine is about 8. Thus, aspirin will be
(a) unionised in the small intestine and in the stomach
(b) completely ionised in the small intestine and in the stomach
(c) ionised in the stomach and almost unionised in the intestine
(d) ionised in the small intestine and almost unionised in the stomach

156 What is the value of pH when 200 mL of 0.01 M $Ca(OH)_2$ solution is saturated with 100 mL of CO_2 gas at 29°C and 0.1 bar?
(a) 12.2 (b) 1.8 (c) 7.0 (d) – 18

157 Freezing point of 0.01 M aqueous solution of a monobasic acid is lowered by 0.205°.
K_f (molal depression constant) = 1.86° mol^{-1} kg.

Assume molality = molarity, ionisation constant of weak acid is
(a) 1.11×10^{-3} (b) 2.0×10^{-3}
(c) 1.7×10^{-4} (d) 1.8×10^{-5}

158 The acid ionisation (hydrolysis constant) of Zn^{2+} is 1.0×10^{-9}. Thus pH of 0.001 M $ZnCl_2$ (*aq*) solution is
(a) 6.0 (b) 8.0 (c) 2.0 (d) 9.0

159 The acid ionisation constant of Al^{3+} is 1.0×10^{-12}. Thus, basic dissociation constant of $Al(OH)^{2+}$ is
(a) 1.0×10^{12} (b) 1.0×10^{-2}
(c) 1.0×10^{2} (d) 1.0×10^{-26}

160 pH of a mixture of 100.0 mL of 0.4 M HCl and 100.0 mL of 0.4 M NH_3 is $[pK_b(NH_3)=4.74]$
(a) 0.40 (b) 0.70 (c) 4.98 (d) 9.04

161 K_a for the acid ionisation of Fe^{3+} to $[Fe(OH)^{2+}]$ and H^+ is 6.5×10^{-3}. The maximum pH value which could be used so that at least 95% of total iron (III) in a dilute solution exists as Fe^{3+} is
(a) 0.91 (b) 2.00 (c) 1.95 (d) 6.05

162 $[S^{-2}]$ in a saturated 0.1 M H_2S $(K_{a_1}K_{a_2}=1\times 10^{-21})$ to which enough HCl has been added to produce $[H^+]$ of 2×10^{-4} M is
(a) 5.0×10^{-17}M (b) 5.0×10^{-15} M
(c) 5.0×10^{-21} M (d) 2.5×10^{-15} M

163 K_{a_1} and K_{a_2} for oxalic acid $H_2C_2O_4$ are 5.6×10^{-2} and 5.4×10^{-5}. Thus, pH of 0.005 M solution of $Na_2C_2O_4$ is
(a) 6.02 (b) 7.98
(c) 7.00 (d) 12.02

164 0.005 M CrO_4^{2-} is hydrolysis to $HCrO_4^-$ to the extent of 0.26%. Thus, ionisation constant of

$$HCrO_4^- + H_2O \rightleftharpoons CrO_4^{2-} + H_3O^+$$ is

(a) 3.0×10^{-7} (b) 6.2×10^{-7}
(c) 1.1×10^{-6} (d) 2.2×10^{-6}

165 pH of 0.01 M H_3PO_4 $(K_{a_1}=7.1\times 10^{-3})$ is
(a) 2.07 (b) 2.25
(c) 9.70 (d) 11.93

166 $[CO_3^{2-}]$ in 0.001 M Na_2CO_3 after hydrolysis is completed is $[K_{a_2}(H_2CO_3)=4.7\times 10^{-11}]$
(a) 6.3×10^{-4} M (b) 3.7×10^{-4} M
(c) 1.0×10^{-4} M (d) 2.1×10^{-4} M

167 If 0.005 mole $NaHCO_3$ is added to a large volume of a solution buffered at pH 8.00, then $\frac{[H_2CO_3]}{[CO_3^{2-}]}$ is
$(K_1=4.5\times 10^{-7}, K_2=4.7\times 10^{-11})$
(a) 4.73 (b) 0.214
(c) 2.2×10^{-2} (d) 4.73×10^{-3}

168. For which of the following acid indicator with $K_{In}=4\times 10^{-4}$, is not suitable for the titrations involving
(a) $CH_3COOH+NaOH$ (b) NH_3+HCl
(c) NaOH + HCl (d) All of these

169 The solubility of ML_2 (formula weight 60.0 g mol^{-1}) in water is 2.4×10^{-5} g/100 mL solution. Thus, K_{sp} of ML_2 is
(a) 5.8×10^{-10} (b) 4.0×10^{-7}
(c) 1.6×10^{-16} (d) 2.6×10^{-18}

170 If 50.0 mL of a solution containing 0.001 mol Ag^+ ion is mixed with 50.0 mL of 0.10 M HCl solution, Ag^+ ion remained in solution is $[K_{sp}(AgCl)=1\times 10^{-10}]$
(a) 1.0×10^{-10} mol (b) 2.5×10^{-10} mol
(c) 1.0×10^{-5} mol (d) 2.5×10^{-9} mol

171 50 mL of 0.20 M $Pb(NO_3)_2$ is mixed with 50 mL of 1.5 M NaCl solution. Thus, Pb^{2+} remained in solution is (Pb = 206) $K_{sp}(PbCl_2)=1.7\times 10^{-4}$
(a) 6.0 mg (b) 12.0 mg
(c) 9.0 mg (d) 7.0 mg

172 pH of a solution when 100 mL of 0.1 M $MgCl_2$ is added to 100 mL of 0.2 M NaOH is $[K_{sp}(Mg(OH)_2)=1.2\times 10^{-11}]$
(a) 3.54 (b) 9.72
(c) 10.46 (d) 4.28

173 A mixture of water and AgCl is shaken until a saturated solution is obtained. 100 mL of filtrate is added to 100 mL of 0.03 M NaBr.

$$K_{sp}(AgCl)=1.0\times 10^{-10}$$
$$K_{sp}(AgBr)=5.0\times 10^{-13}$$

Then,
(a) AgCl is precipitated
(b) AgBr is precipitated
(c) AgCl remains in equilibrium with Ag^+ and Cl^-.
(d) AgBr remains in equilibrium with Ag^+ and Br^-.

174 Ag_2SO_4 and $SrSO_4$ are both shaken up with pure water. $K_{sp}(Ag_2SO_4)=1.5\times 10^{-5}$ and $K_{sp}(SrSO_4)=2.8\times 10^{-7}$, $[Sr^{2+}]$ in the saturated mixture is
(a) 3.1×10^{-2} M (b) 1.55×10^{-2} M
(c) 1.8×10^{-5} M (d) None of these

175 A saturated solution of silver benzoate has a pH of 8.63. K_a (benzoic acid) $=6.5\times 10^{-5}$ $(pK_a=4.19)$ Thus, K_{sp} of silver benzoate is
(a) 6.0×10^{-12} (b) 1.4×10^{-4}
(c) 3.0×10^{-6} (d) 1.4×10^{-2}

176 Given, H_2S ($K_{a_1} = 1.0\times 10^{-7}$, $K_{a_2} = 1.0\times 10^{-14}$) $K_{sp}(Ag_2S) = 1.6\times 10^{-49}$. Maximum possible $[Ag^+]$ in a saturated H_2S (0.1 M) from which precipitation of Ag^+ as Ag_2S does not occur is

(a) 4.0×10^{-18} M (b) 1.0×10^{-14} M
(c) 1.0×10^{-7} M (d) 1.0×10^{-21} M

177 0.10 M $CuSO_4$ solution is saturated with 0.1 M H_2S until no further change takes place. Thus, $[Cu^{2+}]$ in saturated solution is $K_{sp}(CuS) = 8.5\times 10^{-36}$ and

$K_{a_1}K_{a_2}(H_2S) = 1.0\times 10^{-21}$

(a) 1.7×10^{-8} M (b) 2.9×10^{-18} M
(c) 3.4×10^{-15} M (d) 8.5×10^{-18} M

178. NaCl combine with AgCl to form $NaAgCl_2$. Assuming, no change in volume, amount of NaCl that can dissolve 0.010 mole AgCl in 100 L solution is

$K_{sp}(AgCl) = 1.0\times 10^{-10}$

$K_f(AgCl_2^-) = 3.0\times 10^5$

(K_f is formation constant of $AgCl_2^-$)

(a) 1.948 kg (b) 19.48 kg (c) 194.8 kg (d) 0.1948 kg

179 Minimum quantity of ammonia which must be added to 1.0 L of solution in order dissolve 0.10 mole AgCl by forming $[Ag(NH_3)_2]^+$

$K_{sp}(AgCl) = 1.0\times 10^{-10}$

$K_f[Ag(NH_3)_2]^+ = 1.0\times 10^8$

(a) 1.0 M (b) 0.5 M (c) 2.0 M (d) 0.01 M

180 How much NH_3 must be added to 0.004 M Ag^+ solution to just prevent the precipitation of AgCl when $[Cl^-]$ reaches 0.001 M ? $K_{sp}(AgCl) = 1.0\times 10^{-10}$

$K_f[Ag(NH_3)]^+ = 1.0\times 10^8$

(K_f is formation constant)

(a) 0.2 M (b) 0.02 M
(c) 2.0 M (d) 1.0 M

181 For AgCl, variation of p_{Ag} with p_{Cl} is given

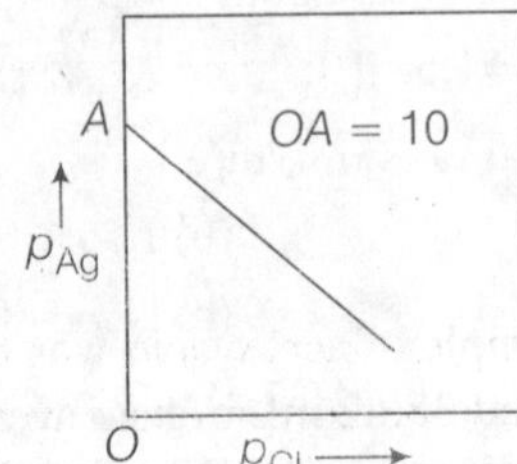

Thus, solubility of AgCl in presence of 0.01 M $AgNO_3$ is

(a) 1×10^{-4} M (b) 1×10^{-5} M
(c) 1×10^{-8} M (d) 1×10^{-10} M

182 For a salt of strong acid and weak base (NH_4X) pH varies with concentration as shown.

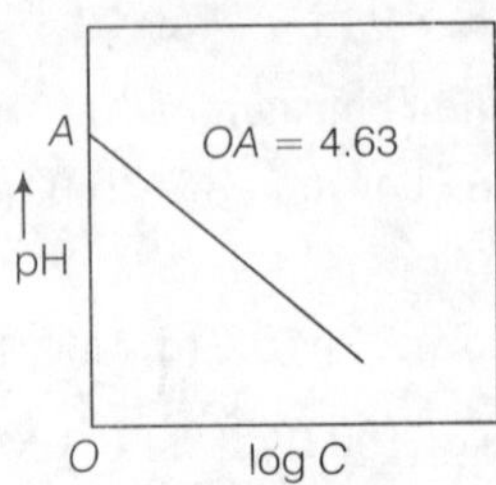

Thus pH of 0.01 M NH_4X solution is

(a) 4.63 (b) 5.63 (c) 6.63 (d) 7.00

183 Which is the incorrect variation of pH with log (C).

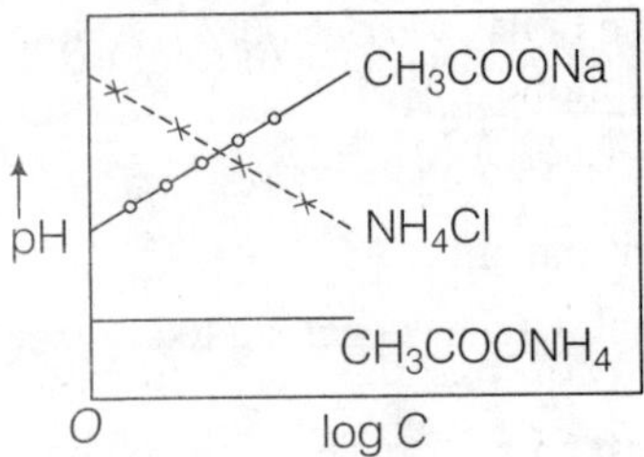

(a) CH_3COONa (b) NH_4Cl
(c) CH_3COONH_4 (d) None of these

184 At 298 K, $K_w = [H_3O^+][OH^-] = 1\times 10^{-14}$. Thus, total number of $[H_3O^+]$ and $[OH^-]$ ions present per mm^3 of pure water at 298 K is

(a) 6.02×10^{16} (b) 12.04×10^{16}
(c) 12.04×10^{10} (d) 6.02×10^{10}

185 How much (in moles) of calcium acetate must be added to 1 L of 0.01 M CH_3COOH to increase its pH by 2.37 units? pK_a (CH_3COOH) = 4.74

(a) 0.1 mol (b) 0.05 mol
(c) 0.2 mol (d) 0.01 mol

186 0.005 mol each of ammonia and pyridine (C_5H_5N) is dissolved in enough water to make 0.200 dm^3 solution. $K_b(NH_3) = 1.8\times 10^{-5}$, $K_b(C_5H_5N) = 1.5\times 10^{-9}$. Thus,

(a) ionisation of $NH_3(aq)$ is decreased due to presence of $C_5H_5N(aq)$
(b) ionisation of $C_5H_5N(aq)$ is decreased due to the presence of $NH_3(aq)$
(c) Both have their independent existence
(d) $[C_5H_5NH^+] = [NH_4^+]$ in aqueous solution

187 A solution is 0.03 M in a weak acid HA ($K_a = 1.38\times 10^{-4}$) and 0.10 M in phenol C_6H_5OH ($K_a = 1.05\times 10^{-10}$). Thus, $[C_6H_5O^-]$ in the solution is

(a) 3.24×10^{-6} M (b) 2.0×10^{-3} M
(c) 5.20×10^{-9} M (d) 1.0×10^{-10} M

188 $[H_3O^+]$ in a solution that is 0.1 M HCOOH and 0.1 M HOCN is

$K_a(HCOOH) = 1.8 \times 10^{-4}$
$K_a(HOCN) = 3.3 \times 10^{-4}$

(a) 4.2×10^{-3} M (b) 5.7×10^{-3} M
(c) 9.9×10^{-3} M (d) 7.1×10^{-3} M

189 What is change in pH of 0.01 M HCl when its one litre of solution is mixed with 0.02 mole of CH_3COONa? $[pK_a(CH_3COOH) = 4.74]$
(a) 1.74 (b) 1.00
(c) 2.74 (d) 2.00

190 How many moles of NaOH can be added to 1.00 L of a solution of 0.10 M in NH_3 and 0.10 M in NH_4Cl without changing the pOH by more than 1.00 unit (assume no change in volume)?

$K_b(NH_3) = 1.8 \times 10^{-5}$, $pK_b = 4.74$

(a) 0.182 (b) 0.082
(c) 0.200 (d) 0.282

191 The solubility of $Mg(OH)_2$ in a particular buffer solution is found to be 0.65 g L^{-1}. Thus, pH of the buffer solution is $[K_{sp}$ of $Mg(OH)_2 = 1.8 \times 10^{-11}]$
(a) 9.6 (b) 5.3 (c) 4.4 (d) 8.7

192 A 0.15 M Na_2SO_4 solution saturated with Ag_2SO_4 has $[Ag^+] = 9.7 \times 10^{-3}$ M. Thus, K_{sp} of Ag_2SO_4 is
(a) 3.65×10^{-6} (b) 9.40×10^{-5}
(c) 1.41×10^{-5} (d) 6.30×10^{-4}

193 A particular water sample has 136 ppm $CaSO_4$ ($K_{sp} = 9.0 \times 10^{-6}$). If 1 L of this water is boiled in a tea kettle, how much water must be evaporated before $CaSO_4(s)$ begins to precipitate? (Assume, solubility is temperature independent in working stage)
(a) 500 mL (b) 200 mL
(c) 667 mL (d) 340 mL

194 To precipitate as $Ag_2S(s)$, all the Ag^+ ions present in 338 mL of a saturated solution of $AgBrO_3$ requires 30.4 mL of $H_2S(g)$ measured at 23° C and 748 mm Hg. Thus, K_{sp} of $AgBrO_3$ is

$$2Ag^+(aq) + H_2S(g) \longrightarrow Ag_2S(s) + 2H^+(aq)$$

(a) 5.3×10^{-5} (b) 6.0×10^{-6}
(c) 7.3×10^{-3} (d) 2.5×10^{-3}

195 Solubility of $Mg(OH)_2$ in 0.1 M CH_3COONa is $[K_{sp}$ of $Mg(OH)_2 = 1.8 \times 10^{-11}$, $K_a(CH_3COOH) = 1.8 \times 10^{-5}$, $pK_a = 4.74]$
(a) 0.33 M (b) 0.66 M
(c) 1.0×10^{-2} M (d) 1.8×10^{-3} M

196 Given, $H_2CO_3 \rightleftharpoons H^+ + HCO_3^-$, $K_{a_1} = 4.3 \times 10^{-7}$ and $HCO_3^- \rightleftharpoons H^+ + CO_3^{2-}$, $K_{a_2} = 4.8 \times 10^{-11}$
Thus, fraction of carbonate present as H_2CO_3 in the solution of pH 10.00 is
(a) 3.2×10^{-4} (b) 4.6×10^{-4}
(c) 2.3×10^{-4} (d) 1.6×10^{-4}

197 A volume of 50.00 mL of weak monobasic acid of unknown concentration is titrated with 0.10 M solution of NaOH. The equivalence point is reached after 39.30 mL of NaOH solution has been added. At the half-equivalence point (19.65 mL), the pH is 4.85. Thus, initial concentration of the acid and its pK_a values are

	$[HA]_{initial}$	pK_a
(a)	0.1 M	4.85
(b)	0.079 M	4.85
(c)	0.1 M	3.70
(d)	0.079 M	2.93

198 pH of 0.01 M NH_4HCO_3 solution is :

$K_{a_1}, (H_2CO_3) = 4.57 \times 10^{-7}$
$K_{a_2}, (H_2CO_3) = 4.57 \times 10^{-11}$
$K_b(NH_3) = 1.8 \times 10^{-5}$

(a) 7.78 (b) 5.54
(c) 9.42 (d) 6.42

199 In dilute H_2SO_4 aqueous solution, mole fraction of H_2SO_4 is 0.01. Assume density of solution as 1 g mL^{-1}, pH of the dilute H_2SO_4 solution is
(a) 0.05 (b) −0.05
(c) 12 (d) 2.0

200 Given, $H_2S(aq) + H_2O(l) \rightleftharpoons H_3O^+(aq) + HS^-(aq)$; $K = 9.1 \times 10^{-8}$ and for
$FeS(s) + H_2O(l) \rightleftharpoons Fe^{2+}(aq) + HS^-(aq) + OH^-(aq)$; $K = 5 \times 10^{-19}$
Thus, molar solubility of FeS(s) in a buffer solution of pH = 3.0 in which $[H_2S]$ is fixed at 0.1 M, is
(a) 5.5×10^{-3} M
(b) 1.2×10^{-2} M
(c) 9.1×10^{-8} M
(d) 7.9×10^{-7} M

201 A 50.00 mL sample of acetic acid was titrated with 0.12 M KOH and 38.62 mL of base were required to reach the equivalence point. What was the pH of the titration mixture, when 19.31 mL of base has been added? $[pK_a(\text{acetic acid}) = 4.74]$
(a) 2.94 (b) 3.54
(c) 4.74 (d) 5.74

202 Following is the titration curve of CH_3COOH against NaOH added with phenolphthalein as the indicator.

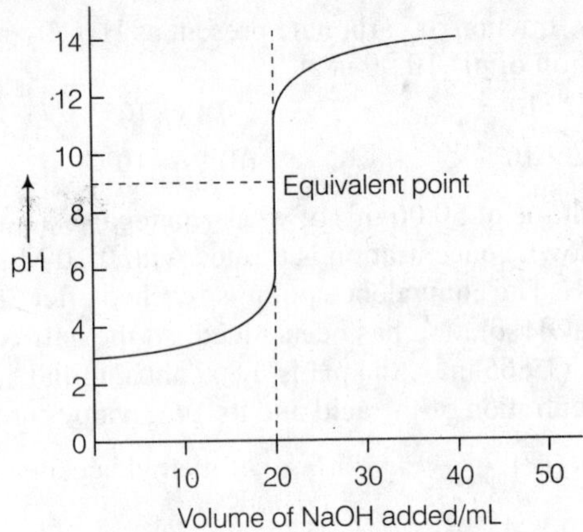

K_{In} value of phenolphthalein is 4.0×10^{-10}. Thus, incorrect statement is

(a) it begins to change colour from the pH 9.4
(b) it begins to change colour from acid colourless at pH 8.4 to the base form (reddish pink) at pH 10.4
(c) phenolphthalein is suitable indicator for CH_3COOH—NaOH titration.
(d) phenolphthalein is a weak acid

203 Select the correct statements.

(a) Red colour of methyl red is due to the structure

H_3C, H_3C >N– (pyridine ring, =N–) –C(=O)–O–H   I

(b) Yellow colour of methyl red is due to the structure

H_3C, H_3C >N– (pyridine ring, –N–) –C(=O)–$O^{\ominus}$ II

(c) $pH = pK_{In}$ when I and II have equal concentrations
(d) All of the above are correct statements

204 A solution is 0.1 M with respect to Ag^+, Ca^{2+}, Mg^{2+} and Al^{3+}. Which will precipitate at lowest concentration of $[PO_4^{3-}]$ when solution of Na_3PO_4 is added?

(a) $Ag_3PO_4 (K_{sp} = 1 \times 10^{-6})$
(b) $Ca_3(PO_4)_2 \ (K_{sp} = 1 \times 10^{-33})$
(c) $Mg_3(PO_4)_2 \ (K_{sp} = 1 \times 10^{-24})$
(d) $AlPO_4 \ (K_{sp} = 1 \times 10^{-20})$

205 H_2S is passed into 1 dm^3 of a solution containing 0.1 mole of Zn^{2+} and 0.01 mole of the Cu^{2+} till the sulphide ion concentration reaches 8.1×10^{-19} mole. Which one of the following statements is true?
[K_{sp} of ZnS and CuS are 3×10^{-22} and 8×10^{-36}, respectively].

(a) Only ZnS precipitates
(b) Both CuS and ZnS precipitate
(c) Only CuS precipitate
(d) No precipitation occurs

206 A handbook states that the solubility of $RNH_2(g)$ in water at 1 atm and 298 K is 959 volumes of $RNH_2(g)$ per volume of water, $pK_b(RNH_2) = 3.4$. Thus, maximum pH that can be attained by dissolving RNH_2 in water is

(a) 8.2 (b) 10.9
(c) 12.4 (d) 13.1

207 For a sparingly soluble salt A_pB_q, the relationship of its solubility product K_{sp} with solubility (*S*), (in mol L^{-1}) is

(a) $K_{sp} = S^{p+q} \ p^p p^q$ (b) $K_{sp} = S^{p+q} \ p^q p^p$
(c) $K_{sp} = S^{pq} \ p^p q^q$ (d) $K_{sp} = S^{pq} \ (pq)^{p+q}$

208 Number of moles of NH_4Cl required to prevent $Mg(OH)_2$ from precipitating in a litre of solution containing 0.02 mole of NH_3 and 0.001 mole of Mg^{2+} is
[$K_{sp} Mg(OH)_2 = 1 \times 10^{-11}$, $K_b(NH_4OH) = 1.8 \times 10^{-5}$]

(a) 4.1×10^{-4} mol (b) 3.6×10^{-3} mol
(c) 2×10^{-2} mol (d) 0.1 mol

209 The $Al(OH)_3$ is involved in the following two equilibrium

$$Al(OH)_3(s) + OH^- \rightleftharpoons [Al(OH)_4^-], \quad K_1$$
$$Al(OH)_3(s) \rightleftharpoons Al^{3+} + 3OH^-, \ K_2$$

At which $[OH^-]$ solubility of $Al(OH)_3$ in NaOH is minimum?

(a) $[OH^-] = \left(\frac{K_2}{K_1}\right)^{\frac{1}{3}}$ (b) $[OH]^- = \left(\frac{K_1}{K_2}\right)^{\frac{1}{4}}$
(c) $[OH^-] = \left(\frac{3K_2}{K_1}\right)^{\frac{1}{4}}$ (d) None of these

210 Molar solubility of AgCl in 0.100 M $NH_3(aq)$
[K_{sp} (AgCl) $= 1.8 \times 10^{-10}$,
$K_f[(Ag(NH_3)_2)^+] = 1.6 \times 10^7$.

(a) 4.85×10^{-3} M (b) 2.88×10^{-3} M
(c) 1.60×10^{-5} M (d) 4.90×10^{-5} M

211 What minimum concentration of thiosulphate ion ($S_2O_3^{2-}$) should be present in 0.10 M $AgNO_3$ so that AgCl(*s*) does not precipitate when the solution is also made 0.10 M in Cl^-

$$K_{sp}\ (AgCl) = 1.8 \times 10^{-10}$$
$$K_f\ [Ag(S_2O_3)_2^{3-}] = 1.7 \times 10^{13}$$

(a) 3.27×10^{-7} M (b) 1.90×10^{-6} M
(c) 5.72×10^{-4} M (d) 6.30×10^{-4} M

212 What mass of benzoic acid (122 g mol^{-1}) must be dissolved per kg of aqueous solution, if the solution is to have the same freezing point as 0.10 molal (mol kg^{-1}), acetic acid (50 g mol^{-1})
K_a benzoic acid : 6.3×10^{-5}; acetic acid $= 1.8 \times 10^{-5}$
$K_f(H_2O) = 1.86°$ mol^{-1} kg, [ΔT_f = molality $\times K_f \times i$ (van't Hoff factor), $i = (1+x), x$ = degree of ionisation of weak monobasic acid]
(a) 11.6 g (b) 12.2 g (c) 10.9 g (d) 6.3 g

213 When 200 mL of 0.35 M $K_2CrO_4(aq)$ is added to 200 mL of 0.01 M $AgNO_3(aq)$, percent of Ag^+ that is left unprecipitated (i.e., that remains soluble) is :

$$[K_{sp}\ (Ag_2CrO_4) = 1.1 \times 10^{-12}]$$

Also, assume that $[CrO_4^{2-}]$ remains constant during the precipitation.
(a) 0.052% (b) 0.52% (c) 5.20% (d) 2.60%

214 Solubility of MnS in a buffer solution that is 0.1 M CH_3COOH and 0.5 M CH_3COONa is
[$K_a(CH_3COOH) = 1.8 \times 10^{-5}$, K_{sp} (MnS) $= 3 \times 10^{-14}$
$[H_3O^+]$ = constant in the buffer)
(a) 5.012 gL^{-1} (b) 1.926 gL^{-1}
(c) 0.1715 gL^{-1} (d) 1.715 gL^{-1}

215 The solubility of AgCN(*s*) in 0.200 M $NH_3(aq)$ is 8.8×10^{-6} mol L^{-1}. Thus, K_{sp} for AgCN is
$[K_f[Ag(NH_3)_2^+)] = 1.6 \times 10^7$
(a) 1.9×10^{-16} (b) 1.2×10^{-16}
(c) 2.0×10^{-16} (d) 1.4×10^{-10}

216 Solubility product of $Ca(OH)_2$ at 298 K is 4.2×10^{-5}. A 500 mL of saturated $Ca(OH)_2$ solution is mixed with equal volume of 0.4 M NaOH. Thus, $Ca(OH)_2$ which is precipitated is
(a) 0.816 g (b) 0.783 g (c) 0.987 g (d) 0.742 g

217 For H_2O, $H_2O + H_2O \rightleftharpoons H_3O^+ + OH^-$,
$$\Delta H = 56.6 \text{ kJ mol}^{-1}$$
In the given temperature range, if $K_w = 1 \times 10^{-14}$ at 300 K, K_w at 1 atm is
(a) 2.0×10^{-13} (b) 9.7×10^{-13}
(c) 1.0×10^{-12} (d) 8.4×10^{-13}

218 If a very small amount of phenolphthalein were added to decinormal solution of sodium acetate at 298 K, then fraction of the indicator that would exist in the coloured form is [K_a (CH_3COOH) $= 1.8 \times 10^{-5}$, K_a (Phenolphthalein) $= 3.16 \times 10^{-10}$]
(a) 0.234 (b) 1.234 (c) 0.19 (d) 4.27

219 If the final volume is to be one litre, moles of HCl to be added to 500 mL of 0.1 M Na_2CO_3 solution in order to adjust the pH 10.0 is : ($K_{a_1} = 4.52 \times 10^{-7}$ and $K_{a_2} = 4.67 \times 10^{-11}$ for H_2CO_3)
(a) 1.034 mol (b) 0.034 mol
(c) 2.107 mol (d) 0.468 mol

220 The initial rate of hydrolysis of methyl acetate (1M) by a weak acid (*HA*, 1M) is 1/100th of that of strong acid (*HX*, 1 M) at 25° C. The K_a (*HA*) is ***[JEE Adv. 2013]***
(a) 1×10^{-4} (b) 1×10^{-5} (c) 1×10^{-6} (d) 1×10^{-3}

221 The K_{sp} of Ag_2CrO_4 is 1.1×10^{-12} at 298 K. The solubility (in mol/L) of Ag_2CrO_4 in a 0.1 M $AgNO_3$ solution, is ***[JEE Adv. 2013]***
(a) 1.1×10^{-11} (b) 1.1×10^{-10}
(c) 1.1×10^{-12} (d) 1.1×10^{-9}

222 2.5 mL of $\frac{2}{5}$ M weak monoacidic base ($K_b = 1 \times 10^{-12}$ at 25° C) is titrated with $\frac{2}{15}$ M HCl in water at 25° C. The concentration of H^+ at equivalence point is ($K_w = 1 \times 10^{-14}$ at 25° C) ***[JEE Adv. 2008]***
(a) 3.7×10^{-13} M (b) 3.2×10^{-7} M
(c) 3.2×10^{-2} M (d) 2.7×10^{-2} M

223 Solubility product constant (K_{sp}) of salts of types *MX*, MX_2 and M_3X at temperature *T* are 4.0×10^{-8}, 3.2×10^{-14} and 2.7×10^{-15}, respectively. Solubilities (mol dm^{-3}) of the salts at temperature *T* are in the order ***[JEE Adv. 2008]***
(a) $MX > MX_2 > M_3X$ (b) $M_3X > MX_2 > MX$
(c) $MX_2 > M_3X > MX$ (d) $MX > M_3X > MX_2$

224 The species present in solution when CO_2 is dissolved in water are ***[JEE Adv. 2006]***
(a) CO_2, H_2CO_3, HCO_3^-, CO_3^{2-}
(b) H_2CO_3, CO_3^{2-}
(c) HCO_3^-, CO_3^{2-}
(d) CO_2, H_2CO_3

225 CH_3NH_2 (0.1 mol, $K_b = 5 \times 10^{-4}$) is added to 0.08 mole of HCl and the solution is diluted to one litre, resulting hydrogen ion concentration is ***[JEE Adv. 2005]***
(a) 1.6×10^{-11} M (b) 8×10^{-11} M
(c) 5×10^{-5} M (d) 8×10^{-2} M

TYPE II Statement Based Questions

Directions Answers of Q. Nos. (226-236) have been based on the following codes.

(a) Statement I is true; Statement II is true; Statement II is the correct explanation of Statement I
(b) Statement I is true; Statement II is true; Statement II is not the correct explanation of Statement I
(c) Statement I is true; Statement II is false
(d) Statement I is false; Statement II is true

226 **Statement I** Methyl orange is not a suitable indicator for the titration of strong base with weak acid.
Statement II When equivalence point is reacted, salt formed is hydrolysed to form basic solution.

227 **Statement I** A solution containing a mixture of CH_3COOH and CH_3COONa maintains a constant value of pH on the addition of small amounts of acid or alkali.
Statement II Mixture acts as a buffer solution around pH 4.75. *(NCERT Exemplar)*

228 **Statement I** In an acid-base titration involving a strong base and a weak acid, methyl orange can be used as an indicator.
Statement II Methyl orange changes its colour in the pH range 3 to 5.

229 **Statement I** Sodium carbonate cannot be titrated by strong acid using phenolphthalein as the indicator.
Statement II Phenolphthalein indicates 50% of the reaction of Na_2CO_3 upto $NaHCO_3$ stage.

230 **Statement I** If H_2S gas is passed into aqueous $ZnCl_2$ solution, ZnS is not precipitated.
Statement II HCl formed decreases ionisation of H_2S, thus $[S^{2-}]$ is not sufficient to precipitate ZnS of high K_{sp} value.

231 **Statement I** Increasing order of acidity of hydrogen halide are

$$HF < HCl < HBr < HI$$

Statement II While, comparing acid strength formed by the elements belonging to the same group of periodic table, H—A bond strength is more important factor in determining acidity of an acid than the polar nature of the bond. *(NCERT Exemplar)*

232 **Statement I** If 10 mL of 1 M HCl is required to titrate 20 mL of 1 M Na_2CO_3 using phenolphthalein indicator then 20 mL of 1 M HCl is required to titrate same volume of Na_2CO_3, using methyl orange indicator.
Statement II Phenolphthalein fails to indicate colour change after $NaHCO_3$ is formed.

233 **Statement I** $NaNH_2$ is a strong base and NH_4Cl is a strong acid in liquid NH_3.
Statement II NH_3 undergoes autoprotolysis to form NH_4^+ and NH_2^-.

234 **Statement I** Lewis acid strength of $Li^+ < Be^{2+} < B^{3+}$.
Statement II Greater the charge of the central atom, larger is the Lewis acid strength.

235 **Statement I** When Cu(II) and sulphide ions are mixed, they react together extremely quickly to give a solid.
Statement II The equilibrium constant of

$$Cu^{2+}(aq) + S^{2-}(aq) \rightleftharpoons CuS(s)$$

is high because the solubility product is low. *[JEE Main 2020 (II) NTA]*

236 **Statement I** The pH of water increases with increase in temperature.
Statement II The dissociation of water into H^+ and OH^- ions is an endothermic reaction. *[JEE Main 2020 (I) NTA]*

TYPE III MCQs with ONE or MORE than ONE Correct Alternate

237 Which of the following compounds/ions can act as Bronsted-Lowry acid as well as Bronsted-Lowry base?
(a) HCO_3^- (b) $H_2PO_2^-$
(c) $H_2PO_3^-$ (d) HSO_4^-

238 Which of the following statement(s) is /are correct?
(a) pH of 1.0×10^{-7} M NaOH is 7
(b) The conjugate base of $H_2PO_2^-$ is HPO_2^{2-}
(c) Autoprotolysis constant of water increases with temperature.
(d) When CH_3COOH is titrated against NaOH, at the half neutralisation point pH=pK_a

239 For the buffer($CH_3COONa + CH_3COOH$),
(a) pH decreases on the addition of HCl
(b) pH increases on the addition of NaOH
(c) pH is controlled by CH_3COO^- when HCl is added
(d) pH is controlled by CH_3COOH when NaOH is added.

240 pH of which of the following is not affected by dilution?
(a) Buffer solutions of C_6H_5COOH and C_6H_5COONa
(b) Buffer solutions of NH_4OH and NH_4Cl
(c) Aqueous solution of sodium benzoate
(d) Aqueous solution of ammonium benzoate

241 Which of the following will function as buffer solutions?
(a) $Na_2B_4O_7 + H_3BO_3$ (b) $NaH_2PO_4 + Na_2HPO_4$
(c) $NaHCO_3 + H_2CO_3$ (d) NaOH+ NaCl

242 Given $K_{sp}(AgCl) = 1 \times 10^{-10}$ and $p_x = -\log x$, select the correct statement(s).
(a) $p_{Ag} + p_{Cl} = 10$
(b) $p_{Cl} = 8$ in 0.01 M Ag^+
(c) $p_{Ag} + p_{Cl} < 10$ in the presence of Ag^+
(d) $p_{Ag} = p_{Cl} = 5$ in saturated AgCl solution

243 Some or more species given below have pH less than 7.
(a) 10^{-8} M HCl
(b) 10^{-8} M NaOH
(c) 10 mL of 10^{-6} M HCl diluted to 100 mL
(d) 10 mL of 0.01 M CH_3COOH at the end point by titration using 0.01 M NaOH

244 In the following mixtures of equal volumes of each component.
(a) 0.01 M $(NH_4)_2SO_4$ and 0.02 M NH_4OH, pOH=pK_b
(b) 0.01 M $(CH_3COO)_2Ca$ and 0.01 M CH_3COOH pH>pK_a
(c) 0.01 M NH_4OH and 0.01 M H_2SO_4 pH=7
(d) 0.01 M $Ca(OH)_2$ and 0.01 M H_2SO_4 pH=7

245 Select the correct statement(s).
(a) NH_4Cl is a strong acid in liquid NH_3
(b) $NaNH_2$ is a strong base in liquid NH_3
(c) CH_3COOH is a base in H_2SO_4
(d) H_3O^+ is the strongest acid that can exist in aqueous solution.

246 For the acid indicator phenolphthalein

$$\underset{\text{Colourless}}{PhH} \rightleftharpoons \underset{\text{Pink}}{Ph^-} + H^+$$

(a) solution appears colourless when $\frac{[Ph^-]}{[PhH]} = \frac{1}{10}$
(b) solution appears pink when $\frac{[Ph^-]}{[PhH]} = 10$
(c) solution changes colourless to pink when pH changes from $(pK_a - 1)$ to $(pK_a + 1)$
(d) solution changes pink to colourless when pH changes from $(pK_a - 1)$ to $(pK_a + 1)$

247 $NH_3(g)$ is a base as defined by
(a) Arrhenius theory (b) Bronsted-Lowry
(c) Lewis (d) Henderson

248 Select the correct fact(s) about H_3BO_3.
(a) It is a weak monobasic acid
(b) It ionises as $H_3BO_3 \rightleftharpoons H^+ + H_2BO_3^-$
(c) It is a tribasic acid
(d) It does not donate proton, but accepts OH^-, thus it is a Lewis acid

$$B(OH)_3 + 2H_2O \rightleftharpoons [B(OH)_4]^- + H_3O^+$$

249 Which of the following are amphiprotic species?
(a) Glycine (b) Salicylic acid
(c) Sulphanilic acid (d) Anthranilic acid

250 Given,

Species	K_{sp}
LiOH	1×10^{-6}
$Mg(OH)_2$	1×10^{-12}
$Al(OH)_3$	1×10^{-27}
$Si(OH)_4$	1×10^{-28}

Thus,
(a) pH(LiOH)= $8 + p_{Li}$ (b) pH[$Mg(OH)_2$]= $8 + p_{Mg}$
(c) pH[$Al(OH)_3$]=$\frac{p_{Al}}{3} + 5$ (d) pH[$Si(OH)_4$]=$7 + \frac{p_{Si}}{4}$

251 For the following equilibrium:

$$HONO(aq) + CN^-(aq) \rightleftharpoons HCN(aq) + ONO^-(aq),$$
$$K = 1.1\times10^6$$

Thus,
(a) CN^- is a stronger base than ONO^-
(b) HCN is a stronger acid than HONO
(c) the conjugate base of HONO is ONO^-
(d) $\Delta G = 0$

252 Based on Ostwald's theory of acid-base indicators,
(a) ionised and unionised forms have different colours
(b) colour change is due to conversion of unionised form to ionised form and *vice-versa* when pH changes
(c) Benzenoid form changes to quinonoid form and *vice-versa* due to change in pH
(d) ionised and unionised forms have same colour

253 CrO_4^{2-} ion is being titrated with Ag^+ ion,

$$2Ag^+ + CrO_4^{2-} \longrightarrow Ag_2CrO_4(s)$$

At the equivalence point
(a) $p_{Ag} + 2p_{CrO_4} = pK_{sp}$ (b) $3p_{CrO_4} = pK_{sp} + 2\log 2$
(c) $3p_{Ag} + 2\log 2 = pK_{sp}$ (d) $p_{Ag} = p_{CrO_4} - \log 2$

254 $Al(OH)_3(H_2O)_3$ can interact with OH^- as well as H_3O^+ as

I. $[Al(OH)_3(H_2O)_3] + OH^- \rightleftharpoons [Al(OH)_4(H_2O)_2]^- + H_2O$

II. $[Al(OH)_3(H_2O)_3] + H_3O^+ \rightleftharpoons [Al(OH)_2(H_2O)_4]^+ + H_2O$

Thus,
(a) $[Al(OH)_3(H_2O)_3]$ is an amphiprotic species
(b) $[Al(OH)_3(H_2O)_3]$ is a Bronsted-Lowry acid
(c) H_2O (products) is an acid in I and a base in II
(d) $[Al(OH)_3(H_2O_3)]$ is an acid in I and II

255 K_{sp} of $BaSO_4$ is 1.1×10^{-10}. Thus, $BaSO_4$ is precipitated of
(a) 100 mL of 4×10^{-3} M $BaCl_2$ is mixed with 300 mL of 6.0×10^{-4} M Na_2SO_4
(b) 100 mL of 4×10^{-4} M $BaCl_2$ is mixed with 300 mL of 6.0×10^{-8} M Na_2SO_4
(c) 300 mL of 4×10^{-4} M $BaCl_2$ is mixed with 100 mL of 6.0×10^{-8} M Na_2SO_4
(d) 300 mL of 4×10^{-4} M $BaCl_2$ is mixed with 300 mL of 6.0×10^{-4} M Na_2SO_4

256 If following equilibrium has $\Delta G° < 0$,

$HA + HB \rightleftharpoons H_2A^+ + B^-$ then
(a) $pK_a(HA) < pK_a(HB)$ (b) $pK_a(HA) < pK_a(HB)$
(c) $pK_b(HA) = pK_a(HB)$ (d) $pK_b(A^-) < pK_b(B^-)$

257 Consider the titration of 0.01 M phthalic acid (dibasic acid) with 0.01 M NaOH,

$$\underset{A}{C_6H_4(COOH)_2} \xrightarrow{OH^-} \underset{B}{C_6H_4(COO^-)(COOH)} \xrightarrow{OH^-} \underset{C}{C_6H_4(COO^-)_2}$$

$pK_{a_1} = 2.89, \quad pK_{a_2} = 5.41$

Select correct alternate(s).

(a) pH at the first half-equivalence point is 2.89
(b) pH at the first equivalence point is 4.15
(c) pH at the second half-equivalence point is 5.41
(d) pH at the second equivalence point is 8.47

258 The concentration of sulphide ion in 0.1 M HCl solution saturated with H_2S is 1.0×10^{-19} M. 10 mL of this solution is added to 5 mL of 0.04 M solution of the following.

$MnCl_2$	K_{sp} of MnS	2.5×10^{-13}
$ZnCl_2$	K_{sp} of ZnS	1.6×10^{-21}
$CdCl_2$	K_{sp} of CdS	8.0×10^{-27}
$CuSO_4$	K_{sp} of CuS	6.3×10^{-36}

In which of these solutions precipitation will take place?

(a) Mn^{2+} (b) Zn^{2+} (c) Cd^{2+} (d) Cu^{2+}

259 Aqueous solutions of HNO_3, KOH, CH_3COOH and CH_3COONa of identical concentrations are provided. The pair(s) of solution when will form a buffer upon mixing is/are *(IIT JEE 2010)*

(a) HNO_3 and CH_3COOH
(b) KOH and CH_3COONa
(c) HNO_3 and CH_3COONa
(d) CH_3COOH and CH_3COONa

260 Effectiveness of a buffer is measured in terms of buffer capacity (β). Select correct statement(s) about buffer capacity.

(a) $\beta = \frac{d[\text{Base}]}{d[\text{pH}]}$

(b) $\beta = \frac{-d[\text{Base}]}{-d[\text{pH}]}$

(c) β is maximum for an acidic buffer at pH=pK_a
(d) If pH $= pK_a \pm 1$, then it is most effective range for a buffer.

261 0.10 mole of Na_3PO_4 is dissolved in 1.0 L of solution.

For H_3PO_4, $K_1 = 7.1\times 10^{-3}$
$K_2 = 6.3\times 10^{-7}$
$K_3 = 4.5\times 10^{-13}$

Thus,

(a) $[OH^-] = 4.71\times 10^{-2}$ M due to hydrolysis
(b) $[H_3PO_4]$ formed due to hydrolysis is 6.0×10^{-18} M
(c) stepwise hydrolysis constants are respectively 2.22×10^{-2}, 1.60×10^{-7} and 1.4×10^{-12}.
(d) only $[OH^-]$ from first step is significant.

TYPE IV Passage Based MCQs (Comprehension)

Passage 1

K_{sp} of $CaF_2 = 3.4\times 10^{-11}$

K_{sp} of $SrF_2 = 2.9\times 10^{-9}$

262 Simultaneous solubility of CaF_2 is

(a) 2.04×10^{-4} M (b) 1.02×10^{-4} M
(c) 4.08×10^{-4} M (d) 1.05×10^{-5} M

263 Simultaneous solubility of

(a) CaF_2 is supressed by the common ion F^- from SrF_2
(b) SrF_2 is supressed by the common ion of F^- from CaF_2
(c) CaF_2 and SrF_2 is equally affected by F^-
(d) CaF_2 and SrF_2 is not affected by common ion effect

Passage 2

After solid $SrCO_3$ was equilibrated with a pH 8.60 buffer, the solution was found to have $[Sr^{2+}] = 2.2\times 10^{-4}$ M. Given, hydrolysis of CO_3^{2-} also occurs

$HCO_3^- + H_2O \rightleftharpoons H_3O^+ + CO_3^{2-}, \quad K = 4.7\times 10^{-11}$

$CO_3^{2-} + H_2O \rightleftharpoons HCO_3^- + OH^-$

264 Percentage of HCO_3^- formed due to hydrolysis is

(a) 98.16% (b) 9.816%
(c) 0.9816% (d) 0.09816%

265 K_{sp} of $SrCO_3$ is

(a) 4.2×10^{-10} (b) 8.9×10^{-10}
(c) 1.78×10^{-10} (d) 1.78×10^{-8}

Passage 3

K_{sp} of $CaCO_3$ is 1.0×10^{-8}, $K_a[HCO_3^-] = 4.7\times 10^{-11}$. It is placed in a buffer of pH 8.00. Assume hydrolysis of CO_3^{2-} takes place.

266 $[CO_3^{2-}]$ present due to hydrolysis is

(a) 95.3% (b) 4.7% (c) 99.53% (d) 0.47%

267 Solubility of $CaCO_3$ in the buffer is

(a) 2.13×10^{-6} M (b) 1.0×10^{-4} M
(c) 1.45×10^{-3} M (d) 1.0×10^{-6} M

Passage 4

Given that 0.001 mole each of Cd^{2+} and Fe^{2+} is contained in 1.0 L of 0.022 M HCl and this solution is saturated with 0.1 M H_2S

$K_{a_1}K_{a_2}(H_2S) = (1.0\times 10^{-21})$

$K_{sp}(CdS) = 8\times 10^{-27}$

$K_{sp}(FeS) = 3.7\times 10^{-19}$

268 Which ion is precipitated under given condition?

(a) Fe^{2+} (b) Cd^{2+}
(c) Both of these (d) None of these

269 How much $[Cd^{2+}]$ remains in solution at equilibrium?

(a) 4.0×10^{-8} M (b) 2.0×10^{-8} M
(c) 8×10^{-25} M (d) 8×10^{-24} M

Passage 5

For the equilibrium :

$Al(OH)_3(s) \rightleftharpoons Al^{3+}(aq)+3OH^-(aq), K_{sp}=1.3\times10^{-33}$

270 What is the minimum pH at which $Al(OH)_3$ will precipitate from a solution that is 0.075 M in Al^{3+} ?

(a) 7.80 (b) 3.41
(c) 6.20 (d) 10.58

271 What is the maximum quantity of CH_3COONa that can be added to 250.0 mL of solution containing 0.075 M Al^{3+} and 1.00 M CH_3COOH? [pK_a (CH_3COOH) = 4.74]

(a) 0.96 g (b) 0.048 g
(c) 1.96 g (d) 0.096 g

Passage 6

Freshly prepared $Al(OH)_3$ and $Mg(OH)_2$ are stirred vigorously in a buffer containing 0.25 M NH_4Cl and 0.05 M NH_4OH.

$K_b[NH_4OH]=1.8\times10^{-5}$

$K_{sp}[Mg(OH)_2]=8.9\times10^{-12}$

$K_{sp}[Al(OH)_3]=6.0\times10^{-32}$

272 Select correct statement(s)

(a) Solubility of $Al(OH)_3$ is larger than that of $Mg(OH)_2$ in the buffer
(b) Solubility of $Mg(OH)_2$ is larger than that of $Al(OH)_3$ in the buffer
(c) Both are equally soluble
(d) None of the above is correct

273 In the absence of buffer, ratio of solubilities of $Mg(OH)_2$ and $Al(OH)_3$ is

(a) 1.9×10^4 (b) 5.26×10^{-5}
(c) 3.8×10^4 (d) 2.63×10^5

Passage 7

A solution is 0.01M in Ag^+ ion and 0.02 M Ba^{2+} ion. A 0.1M Na_2CrO_4 solution is gradually added to this solution.
K_{sp} : $Ag_2CrO_4=9\times10^{-12}$, $BaCrO_4=2\times10^{-10}$

274 Molar concentrations of Na_2CrO_4 required to precipitate Ag^+ and Ba^{2+} ions separately are

	For Ag^+ ion	For Ba^{2+} ion
(a)	9×10^{-8} M	1×10^{-8} M
(b)	9×10^{-8} M	9×10^{-8} M
(c)	1×10^{-8} M	9×10^{-8} M
(d)	1×10^{-8} M	9×10^{-8} M

275 Species precipitated first is and its concentration when the precipitation of the second ion starts is :

(a) Ba^{2+}, 60.0% (b) Ag^+, 60%
(c) Ag^+, 89% (d) Ba^{2+}, 89%

Passage 8

Neutralisation of *p*-hydroxybenzoic acid (*A*) takes place in two stages:

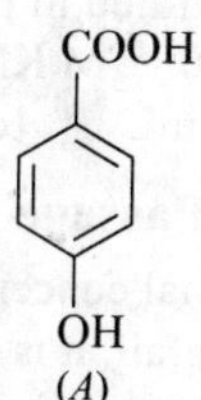

(*A*)

25 mL of dilute aqueous solution of (*A*) is titrated with 0.02 M NaOH.

pH = 4.57, when 8.12 mL of NaOH has been added

pH = 7.02, when 16.24 mL of NaOH has been added (equivalence point).

276 What is the value of pK_a of the acid (*A*) at first ionisation stage?

(a) 9.43 (b) 7.00 (c) 4.57 (d) 2.30

277 What is value of pK_a of the acid (*A*) at second ionisation stage?

(a) 9.47 (b) 4.53 (c) 7.00 (d) 10.00

Passage 9

20 mL of H_3PO_4 is neutralised by 10 mL of 0.01 M NaOH upto NaH_2PO_4 stage and then by 20 mL of 0.01 M NaOH upto Na_2HPO_4 stage.

For H_3PO_4, $pK_{a_1}=2.12$, $pK_{a_2}=7.22$
$pK_{a_3}=12.32$

278 What is pH of H_3PO_4 assuming to be a monobasic acid?

(a) 2.21 (b) 7.22 (c) 12.32 (d) 7.00

279 What is pH of NaH_2PO_4 solution?

(a) 7.00 (b) 9.77 (c) 4.67 (d) 7.22

Passage 10

The magnesium ion concentration in sea water is about 0.059 M. It is maintained at pH=11.30. $K_{sp}[Mg(OH)_2]=1.8\times10^{-11}$.

280 What will be $[Mg^{2+}]$ remaining in solution when precipitation is complete at pH 11.30 ?

(a) 4.5×10^{-6} M (b) 9.0×10^{-9} M
(c) 3.6×10^{-14} M (d) 1.8×10^{-4} M

281 Percentage of Mg^{2+} remained in sea water sample after this treatment is

(a) 4.5 % (b) 4.5×10^{-4} %
(c) 7.6×10^{-3} % (d) 3.6×10^{-3} %

Passage 11

One litre of saturated CaC_2O_4 solution required 200 mL of 1×10^{-4} M $KMnO_4$ in acidic medium.

282 What is K_{sp} of CaC_2O_4?
(a) 4.0×10^{-10} (b) 5.0×10^{-5}
(c) 3.0×10^{-9} (d) 2.5×10^{-9}

283 If same solution is titrated in presence of 1×10^{-3} M $CaCl_2$ solution, 1×10^{-4} M $KMnO_4$ required is
(a) 10 mL (b) 20 mL (c) 30 mL (d) 100 mL

Passage 12

Acid rain is an environmental concern all over the world. In assessing the acidity of rainfall, it is important to have an idea of the acidity of natural rain water. Assuming that, natural rain water (i.e., rain water contaminated with HNO_3 and H_2SO_4) is in equilibrium with 3.6×10^{-4} atm CO_2.

$$K_{a_1}(H_2CO_3)=4.3\times10^{-7}$$

K_H(Henry's law constant of CO_2) $=1.25\times10^6$ Torr

284 What is pH of natural rain water?
(a) 5.64 (b) 5.70 (c) 7.00 (d) 7.40

285 If SO_2 content, in the atmosphere is 0.12 ppm by volume, pH of rain water (assume 100% ionisation of acid rain as monobasic acid) is
(a) 5.73 (b) 5.62 (c) 5.41 (d) 2.00

Passage 13

pH of saturated solution of $Mg(OH)_2$ is 10.42. 0.05 M Mg^{2+} solution is shaken with 0.05 M NH_3. (log 3.8 = 0.58)

286 What is K_{sp} of $Mg(OH)_2$?
(a) 1.73×10^{-8} (b) 2.76×10^{-7}
(c) 6.91×10^{-8} (d) 9.0×10^{-12}

287 What molar concentration of NH_4Cl should be maintained required to prevent the formation of $Mg(OH)_2$ in solution?

$$K_b(NH_4OH)=1.8\times10^{-5}$$

(a) 14.92 M (b) 7.46 M (c) 0.067 M (d) 0.670 M

Passage 14

A solution is 0.10 M in Ag^+ and also 0.10 M in Hg^{2+}.

$$K_{sp}(AgI)=8.5\times10^{-17}$$
$$K_{sp}(HgI_2)=2.5\times10^{-26}$$

288 Maximum concentration of iodide ion at which
(a) Ag^+ is precipitated as AgI when $[I^-]=5\times10^{-13}$ M
(b) Hg^{2+} is precipitated as HgI_2 when $[I^-]=8.5\times10^{-16}$ M
(c) Ag^+ and Hg^{2+} both are precipitated simultaneously
(d) None of them is precipitated

289 Percentage of metal ion precipitated is
(a) Hg^{2+}, 0.17% (b) Ag^+, 0.17%
(c) Hg^{2+}, 99.83% (d) Ag^+, 99.83

Passage 15

A solution is prepared by dissolving 0.10 mole of Na_3PO_4 in sufficient water to make 1.00 L solution.

For H_3PO_4

$$K_{a_1}=7.1\times10^{-3}$$
$$K_{a_2}=6.3\times10^{-8}$$
$$K_{a_3}=4.5\times10^{-13}$$

290 $[OH^-]$ due to hydrolysis is
(a) 4.71×10^{-2} M (b) 1.0×10^{-7} M
(c) 1.0×10^{-12} M (d) 2.2×10^{-12} M

291 H_3PO_4 formed due to hydrolysis is
(a) 1.6×10^{-7} M (b) 4.8×10^{-18} M
(c) 4.5×10^{-13} M (d) 7.1×10^{-3} M

Passage 16

You have been provided with 0.05 M H_2S solution.

$$K_{a_1}=1.0\times10^{-7}$$
$$K_{a_2}=1.0\times10^{-14}$$

292 $[H_3O^+]$ in the above solution is
(a) 1.7×10^{-6} M (b) 7.1×10^{-14} M
(c) 2.9×10^{-7} M (d) 7.1×10^{-5} M

293 $[S^{2-}]$ in the above solution is
(a) 1.0×10^{-14} M (b) 1.0×10^{-7} M
(c) 1.0×10^{-21} M (d) 1.0×10^{-5} M

Passage 17

Equal volumes of 1.0 M Na_2CO_3 and 1.0 M HCl are mixed.

$$K_{a_1}(H_2CO_3)=4.5\times10^{-7}$$
$$K_{a_2}(H_2CO_3)=4.7\times10^{-11}$$

294 pH of the solution is
(a) 6.93 (b) 4.37 (c) 8.34 (d) 7.00

295 $[CO_3^{2-}]$ at equilibrium is
(a) 4.1×10^{-6} M (b) 1.0×10^{-3} M
(c) 7.0×10^{-7} M (d) 5.0×10^{-3} M

Passage 18

When 100 mL of 1.0 M HCl was mixed with 100 mL of 1.0 M NaOH in an insulated beaker at constant pressure, a temperature increase of 5.7° C was measured for the beaker and its contents (Expt. 1). Because the enthalpy of neutralisation of a strong acid with a strong base is a constant (– 57.0 kJ mol^{-1}), this experiment could be used to measure the calorimeter constant. In a second experiment (Expt. 2), 100 mL of 2.0 M acetic acid ($K_a=2.0\times10^{-5}$) was mixed with 100 ml of 1.0 M NaOH (under identical conditions to Expt. 1) where a temperature rise of 5.6° C was measured.

(Consider heat capacity of all solutions as 4.2 $Jg^{-1}K^{-1}$ and density of all solutions as 1.0 g mL^{-1}). ***[JEE Adv. 2015]***

296 Enthalpy of dissociation (in kJ mol^{-1}) of acetic acid obtained from the Expt. 2 is
(a) 1.0 (b) 10.0 (c) 24.5 (d) 51.4

297 The pH of the solution after Expt. 2 is ***[JEE Adv. 2015]***
(a) 2.8 (b) 4.7 (c) 5.0 (d) 7.0

TYPE V Numerical Skills

298 5.00 mL of 0.10 M oxalic acid solution taken in a conical flask is titrated against NaOH from a burette using phenolphthalein indicator. The volume of NaOH required for the appearance of permanent faint pink color is tabulated below for five experiments. What is the concentration, in molarity, of the NaOH solution?

Exp. No.	Vol. of NaOH (mL)
1	12.5
2	10.5
3	9.0
4	9.0
5	9.0

[JEE Adv. 2020]

299 For a basic buffer containing base B and conjugate acid BH^+; $(pH - pK_a) = 0.7$. What is the value of ratio of $\frac{[B]}{[BH^+]}$?

300 The pH at the half-equivalence point of titration of the Zwitter ion (A), valine 9.714 with NaOH and 2.286 with HCl. Thus, its isoelectric pH is ....

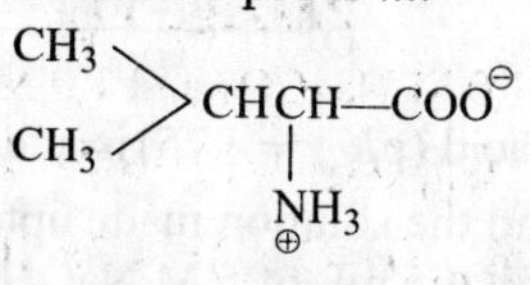

$$(CH_3)_2CH{-}\underset{\overset{|}{\overset{\oplus}{NH_3}}}{CH}{-}COO^{\ominus}$$

301 pH of 10 mL solution of a strong monobasic acid increases by 1 unit on mixing $10x$ mL of H_2O. What is value of x?

302 A solution of 0.1 M weak base (B) is titrated with 0.1 M of a strong acid (HA). The variation of pH of the solution with the volume of HA added is shown in the figure below. What is the pK_b of the base? The neutralization reaction is given by

$$B + HA \longrightarrow BH^+ + A^-.$$

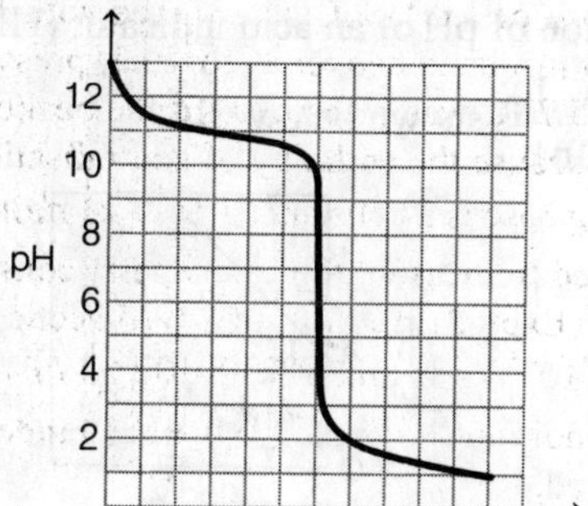

pH (axis: 2, 4, 6, 8, 10, 12)
0 2 4 6 8 10 12
Volume of HA (mL)

[JEE Adv. 2020]

303 A weak acid (HA) is 1% ionised at 0.01 M. What is its pH when 100 mL of this acid is treated with 25 mL of 0.01 M $Ca(OH)_2$?

304 10 mL of 0.05 M H_2SO_4 is neutralised by a mixture of 1 mL of 0.1 M KOH and x mL of 0.1 M NaOH. What is the value of x?

305 Aqueous solutions of HCOOH and CH_3COOH each have equal pH, when ratio of molar concentration is 0.25. What is ratio of their ionisation constants. K_a (HCOOH)/ K_a (CH_3COOH)?

306 A soft drink was bottled with a partial pressure of CO_2 of 3 bar over the liquid at room temperature. The partial pressure of CO_2 over the solution approaches a value of 30 bar when 44 g of CO_2 is dissolved in 1 kg of water at room temperature. The approximate pH of the soft drink is ..... $\times 10^{-1}$. (First dissociation constant of $H_2CO_3 = 4.0 \times 10^{-7}$, $\log 2 = 0.3$; density of the soft drink $= 1\text{ g mL}^{-1}$) ***[JEE Main 2020 (II) NTA]***

307 K_{sp} of H_2S is 1×10^{-22} and that of CdS is 8.0×10^{-27}. 1×10^{-14} M $CdCl_2$ solution is precipitated at pH$=x$. What is value of x?

308 In 1 litre saturated solution of AgCl, 0.1 mole of CuCl is added. The resultant concentration of Ag^+ in the solution is 1.6×10^{-x} M. The value of x is .....
$[K_{sp}(AgCl) = 1.6 \times 10^{-10}, K_{sp}(CuCl) = 1.0 \times 10^{-6}]$ ***(IIT JEE 2011)***

309 The total number of diprotic acids among the following is H_2CO_3, $H_2S_2O_7$, H_2CrO_4, H_2SO_3, H_3BO_3, H_3PO_2, H_3PO_4, H_2SO_4, H_3PO_3. ***(IIT JEE 2010)***

310 Amongst the following, the total number of compounds whose aqueous solution turns red litmus paper to blue is KCN, K_2SO_4, $(NH_4)_2C_2O_4$, NaCl, $Zn(NO_3)_2$, $FeCl_3$, K_2CO_3, NH_4NO_3 and LiCN. ***[IIT JEE 2010]***

311 Liquid ammonia ionises to a slight extent. At 230 K, its ion product is 10^{-30}. There are $x \times 10^2$ NH_2^- (amide) ions per mm^3 of pure liquid NH_3. What is value of x.

312 If the solubility product of AB_2 is 3.20×10^{-11} M^3, then the solubility of AB_2 in pure water is ... $\times 10^4$ mol L^{-1}. [Assuming that neither kind of ion reacts with water] ***[JEE Main 2020 (II) NTA]***

313 What is the per cent error in the hydronium ion concentration made by neglecting the ionisation of water in 1.0×10^{-6} M NaOH?

314 If $K_a(HA) = K_b(BOH)$ at 298 K, and pH of 10^{-4} M BOH is 8.0, then pH of 10^{-2} MHA will be ....

315 For a weak acid (HA), variation of log $[H^+]$ with $\log\left(\frac{1-x}{x}\right)$ is given. Thus, pH of the solution when HA is 1% ionised is ....

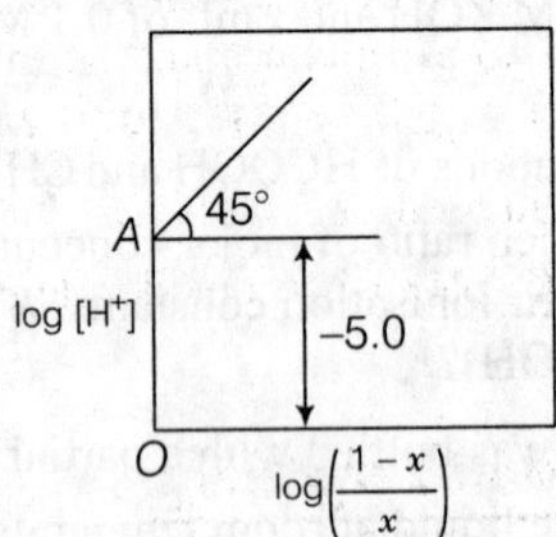

316 For water at 310 K, $K_w = 1.11 \times 10^{-14}$, and its ionisation constant is $x \times 10^{-16}$. What is value of x?

317 In a buffer of HA and NaA, mole fraction of HA is 0.2. What is pH of this buffer (K_a (HA) $= 4 \times 10^{-5}$)?

318 Solubility of sparingly soluble salt A_2X_3 in water is $y \times 10^{-5}$ mol L^{-1}. If $K_{sp}(A_2X_3)$ is 1.1×10^{-23}, what is value of y?

319 For the salt of CH_3CH_2COONa, variation of pH with log C is shown.

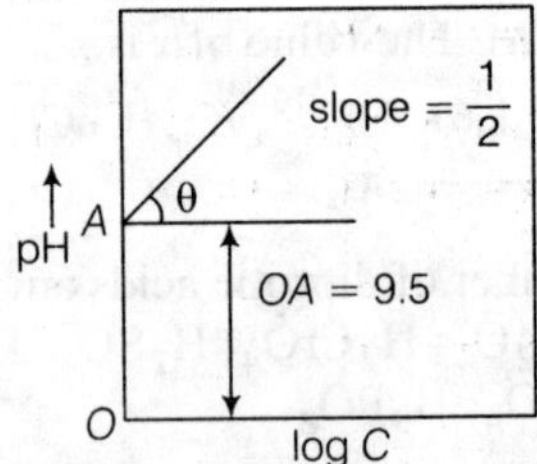

Thus, pH of 0.001 M CH_3CH_2COONa solution is ....

320 How many of the following will turn blue litmus red in aqueous solutions? $KHSO_4$, $FeCl_3$, $AlCl_3$, $CuSO_4$, $NaHCO_3$, CH_3NH_3Cl, $C_5H_5NHHSO_4$, C_6H_5COONa, Na_2CO_3, $[Zn(H_2O)_4]Cl_2$.

321 The solubility of $Mg(OH)_2$ in a particular buffer is found to be 0.18 mol L^{-1}. What is the pH of the buffer? $K_{sp}[Mg(OH)_2] = 1.8 \times 10^{-11}$

322 A 25.0 mL sample of saturated PbI_2 requires 15.13 mL of a certain $AgNO_3(aq)$ for its titration.

$$K_{sp}(PbI_2) = 7.1 \times 10^{-9}$$

$$PbI_2(s) \rightleftharpoons Pb^{2+}(aq) + 2I^-(aq)$$

Molarity of $AgNO_3$ solution is $y \times 10^{-3}$M. What is value of y?

323. In the following graph,

$$OA = +9.7448$$

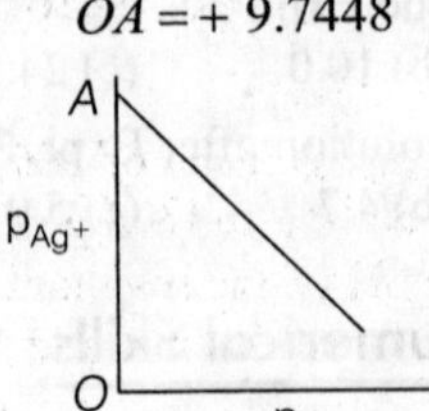

If antilog of 0.2552 = 1.8, 3.6×10^{-5} M $AgNO_3$ is required to precipitate $x \times 10^{-6}$ M KCl. What is valued x?

324 K_{sp} of $Mg(OH)_2$ is 1.0×10^{-12}. 01 M $Mg(OH)_2$ will precipitate at the limiting pH ......

325 K_{sp} of ZnS is 1.0×10^{-21}. For H_2S, $K_{a_1}K_{a_2} = 1 \times 10^{-20}$. Minimum pH required to prevent precipitation of $ZnCl_2$ solution as ZnS by 0.10 M H_2S is 1. If $[ZnCl_2] = C$ mol L^{-1}. What is value of p_C ?

326 For the sparingly soluble salt $M(OH)_3$, variation of $\log[M^{3+}]$ with pOH is shown in the graph, OA = − 16. What is pH when $[M^{3+}] = 10^{-1}$ M?

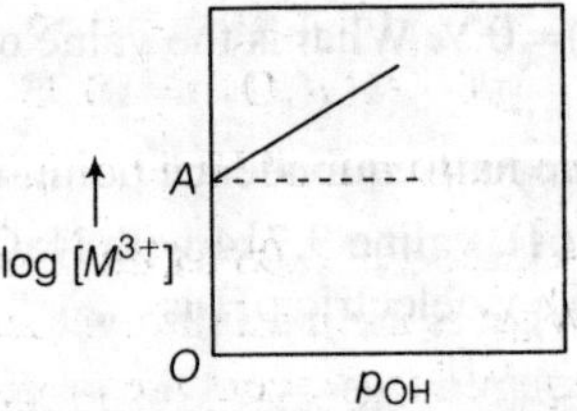

327 3 g of acetic acid ($pK_a = 4.75$) is added to 250 mL of 0.1 M HCl and the solution made upto 500 mL. To 20 mL of this solution 0.5 mL of 5 M NaOH is added. The pH of the solution is .... **[JEE Main 2020 (I) NTA]**

328 For an acid-base indicator $K_a = 3.0 \times 10^{-4}$. Its acid form is orange and base form is yellow. If pH changes by log x, the indicator changes from 75 orange to 75% yellow. What is value of x?

329 An indicator has K_a value of 4.0×10^{-5}. Its basic form is 10x% at pH = 5. What is value of x?

330 Variation of pH of an acid indicator (HIn) with log y

$$y = \frac{[In^-]}{[HIn]}$$ is shown below

What is value of y when pH is 5.4? (Given, log 2 = 0.3)

331 K_{sp} of HgI_2 is 2.5×10^{-26}. $[I^-]$ required to precipitate 0.1 M $Hg(NO_3)_2$ as HgI_2 is $y\times10^{-13}$ M. Thus, y is ....

332 Two solutions, A and B, each of 100 L were made by dissolving 4 g of NaOH and 9.8 g of H_2SO_4 in water respectively. The pH of the resultant solution obtained from mixing 40 L of solution A and 10 L of solution B is .... **[JEE Main 2020 (I) NTA]**

333 10 mL of 0.1 M of a weak acid HA is titrated against 0.1 M NaOH. If pK_a $(HA) = 5.3$, pH at the equivalence point is .....

334 This solubility of a salt of weak acid (AB) at pH 3 is $Y\times10^{-3}$ mol L^{-1}. The value of Y is ....

(Given that the value of solubility product of AB $[K_{sp}) = 2\times10^{-10}$ and the value of ionisation constant of $HB(K_a) = 1\times10^{-8}]$

335 0.3 mole of C_5H_5NHCl is added to 1 dm^3 of 0.2 M C_5H_5N solution. K_b(pyridine, C_5H_5N) $= 1.5\times10^{-9}$. Thus pH of the solution is ....

336 50 mL of 0.05 M K_2CO_3 is titrated against 0.1 M HCl.

$$pK_{a_1}(H_2CO_3) = 6.35$$
$$pK_{a_2}(H_2CO_3) = 10.33$$

What is pH when 40 mL of HCl has been added.

337 An acidified solution of 0.05 M Zn^{2+} is saturated with 0.1 M H_2S. What is the minimum molar concentration (M) of H^+ required to prevent the precipitation of ZnS? Use K_{sp} (ZnS) $= 1.25\times10^{-22}$ and overall dissociation constant of H_2S, $K_{Net} = K_1K_2 = 1\times10^{-21}$. **[JEE Adv. 2020]**

338 For a sparingly soluble salt A_2B, $K_{sp} = 1\times10^{-16}$. What is the value of (OY) when graph between p_A $(= -\log A)$ and p_B $(= -\log B)$ is linear as shown

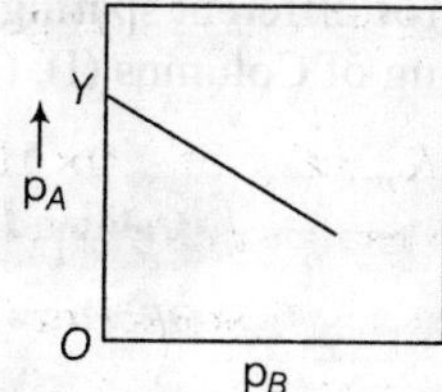

339 A buffer is 0.25 M in CH_3COOH and 0.56 M in CH_3COONa. 0.006 mole of HCl is added to 0.300 L of this buffer. What is the pH of the resultant solution $[pK_a(CH_3COOH) = 4.74]$

340 K_{sp} of NiC_2O_4 and K_{sp} of Na_3AlF_6 are equal to 4×10^{-10}. Molar solubility of Na_3AlF_6 is 10^n times higher than that of NiC_2O_4. What is value of n?

341 $y\times10^{-3}$ mole of NaOH must be added to 1.0 L of 0.01 M, H_3BO_3 solution to make a buffer solution of pH 10.10. pK_a (H_3BO_3—a monobasic acid) $= 9.14$. What is value of y?

342 The molar conductivity of a solution of a weak acid HX (0.01 M) is 10 times smaller than the molar conductivity of a solution of a weak acid HY (0.01 M). If $\lambda^0_{X^-} \approx \lambda^0_{Y^-}$, the difference in their pK_a values, $pK_a(HX) - pK_a(HY)$, is (consider degree of ionisation of both acids to be << 1) **[JEE Adv. 2015]**

TYPE VI Matrix Matching

343 The following thermodynamic quantities are given at 298 K.

Reaction	$\Delta H°$ (kJ mol^{-1})	$\Delta S°$ (JK^{-1} mol^{-1})
$NH_3 + H^+ \longrightarrow NH_4^+$	− 52.2	+ 1.67
$H_2O \longrightarrow H^+ + OH^-$	56.6	− 78.20

Match the parameters given in Column I with their respective values given in Column II.

Column I	Column II
(i) pK_b for NH_4OH	(p) − 0.0765
(ii) $\Delta H°$ (in kJ mol^{-1}) for $NH_4OH \rightleftharpoons NH_4^+ + OH^-$	(q) 4.77
(iii) $\Delta G°$ (in kJ mol^{-1}) for $NH_4OH \rightleftharpoons NH_4^+ + OH^-$	(r) 4.4
(iv) $\Delta S°$ (in kJ $mol^{-1}K^{-1}$ for $NH_4^+OH \rightleftharpoons NH_4^+ + OH^-$	(s) 27.21

Codes

	(i)	(ii)	(iii)	(iv)
(a)	(p)	(q)	(r)	(s)
(b)	(s)	(q)	(p)	(r)
(c)	(p)	(s)	(r)	(q)
(d)	(q)	(r)	(s)	(p)

344 100 mL of 0.01 M CH_3COOH is titrated with 0.01 M KOH. Match the pH of the solution mixture in given Column II with the stages of addition of KOH given in Column I. $[pK_a(CH_3COOH) = 4.74]$

Column I	Column II
(i) 25 mL	(p) 8.22
(ii) 50 mL	(q) 4.26
(iii) 75 mL	(r) 4.74
(iv) 100 mL	(s) 5.22

Codes

	(i)	(ii)	(iii)	(iv)
(a)	(p)	(s)	(r)	(q)
(b)	(s)	(p)	(q)	(r)
(c)	(s)	(p)	(r)	(q)
(d)	(q)	(r)	(s)	(p)

345 pK_a of different acids are given below

Acid	pK_a
NH_4^+	9.26
CH_3COOH	4.74
C_6H_5COOH	4.20
HCN	9.21
$C_6H_5NH_3^+$	4.62

Match the species (salt) given in Column I with their corresponding pH of 0.1 M solutions given in Column II.

Column I	Column II
(i) CH_3COONH_4	(p) 8.6
(ii) C_6H_5COOK	(q) 11.1
(iii) $C_6H_5NH_3^+Cl^-$	(r) 7.00
(iv) NaCN	(s) 2.81

Codes

	(i)	(ii)	(iii)	(iv)
(a)	(r)	(q)	(p)	(s)
(b)	(r)	(p)	(s)	(q)
(c)	(p)	(q)	(r)	(s)
(d)	(s)	(r)	(q)	(p)

346 Match the pH values in Column I of different sparingly soluble salts given in Column II and select the answer from the codes. ($p_m = -\log M^{n+}$)

Column I	Column II
(i) LiOH ($K_{sp} = 1 \times 10^{-6}$)	(p) $\left(\frac{p_m + 16}{2}\right)$
(ii) $Mg(OH)_2$ ($K_{sp} = 1 \times 10^{-12}$)	(q) $\left(\frac{p_m + 28}{4}\right)$
(iii) $Al(OH)_3$ ($K_{sp} = 1 \times 10^{-27}$)	(r) $(p_m + 8)$
(iv) $Si(OH)_4$ ($K_{sp} = 1 \times 10^{-28}$)	(s) $\left(\frac{p_m + 15}{3}\right)$

Codes

	(i)	(ii)	(iii)	(iv)
(a)	(p)	(r)	(q)	(s)
(b)	(s)	(r)	(q)	(p)
(c)	(r)	(q)	(p)	(s)
(d)	(r)	(p)	(s)	(q)

347 For a salt of weak acid (*HA*) and strong base (*M*OH) variation of pH with log *C* (*C* is molar concentration) is given.

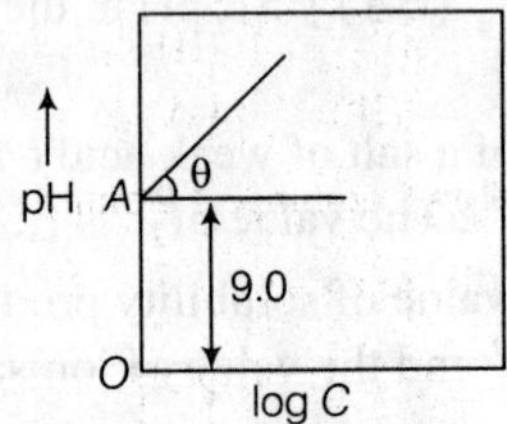

Match the parameter in Column I with their values in Column II

Column I	Column II
(i) pK_a of the weak acid	(p) 8.0
(ii) pH of 0.01 M salt	(q) 10.0
(iii) pH of 0.01 M *HA*	(r) 4.0
(iv) Per cent ionisation of the 0.01 M weak acid	(s) 3.0

Codes

	(i)	(ii)	(iii)	(iv)
(a)	(r)	(q)	(p)	(s)
(b)	(s)	(r)	(q)	(p)
(c)	(r)	(p)	(s)	(q)
(d)	(p)	(q)	(s)	(r)

348 Given graph is based on the graphical variation of $\log K_{sp}$ with log(*s*) of different sparingly soluble salt (A_xB_y) and matching of Columns (I), (II) and (II) (*s* = molar solubility).

Column I		Column II		Column III	
	K_{sp}		*OP*		$(x+y)\log(s)$
(i) Ag(OH)	1×10^{-10}	(I)	1.4314	(p)	− 16
(ii) $Mg(OH)_2$	4×10^{-12}	(II)	2.4083	(q)	−12
(iii) $Al(OH)_3$	2.7×10^{-15}	(III)	0.6020	(r)	−10
(iv) $Si(OH)_4$	2.56×10^{-18}	(IV)	0	(s)	− 20

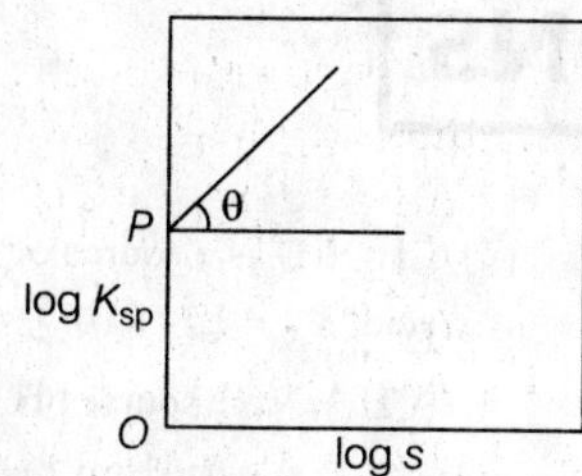

	(i)	(ii)	(iii)	(iv)
(a)	(IV-r)	(III-q)	(I-p)	(II-s)
(b)	(IV-r)	(III-p)	(I-q)	(II-s)
(c)	(I-r)	(II-q)	(IV-p)	(III-s)
(d)	(I-r)	(III-s)	(II-q)	(IV-p)

(Q. 349 to 352) are based on matching of Columns (I), (II) and (III).

100 mL of 0.01 M phthalic acid (*A*)

$$C_6H_4(COOH)_2$$

is being titrated with 0.02 M KOH

$$pK_{a_1} = 289, pK_{a_2} = 5.41$$

Column I	Column II	Column III
(i) First half equivalent point	(I) 100 mL of 0.01 M $Ca(OH)_2$	(p) 8.55
(ii) First equivalent point	(II) 75 mL of 0.01 M $Ca(OH)_2$	(q) 5.41
(iii) Second half equivalent point	(III) 50 mL of 0.02 M KOH	(r) 4.15
(iv) Second equivalent point	(IV) 25 mL of 0.02 M KOH	(s) 2.89

349 This point is achieved in Column (I) when KOH added in Column (II) to give a pH in Column (III).

Codes

(a) (i)-(IV)-(s)
(b) (i)-(II)-(p)
(c) (i)-(III)-(p)
(d) (i)-(II)-(q)

350 This species formed is amphiprotic and is formed when KOH added in Column (II) to give a pH in Column (III).

Codes

(a) (ii)-(IV)-(p)
(b) (ii)-(III)-(r)
(c) (ii)-(IV)-(s)
(d) (ii)-(III)-(q)

351 This point is achieved when 75% of *A* is neutralised by KOH in Column (II) to give a pH in Column (III).

Codes

(a) (iii)-(III)-(s)
(b) (iii)-(II)-(r)
(c) (iii)-(II)-(q)
(d) (iii)-(I)-(p)

352 100% of *A* is converted into salt by KOH in Column (II) to give a solution of pH in Column (3).

Codes

(a) (iv)-(II)-(r)
(b) (iv)-(II)-(s)
(c) (iv)-(II)-(q)
(d) (iv)-(I)-(p)

353 Dilution processes of different aqueous solutions, with water, are given in List-I. The effects of dilution of the solution on $[H^+]$ are given in List-II.

(**Note** Degree of dissociation (α) of weak acid and weak base is << 1; degree of hydrolysis of salt << 1; $[H^+]$ represents the concentration of H^+ ions)

List-I	List-II
P. (10 mL of 0.1 M NaOH + 20 mL of 0.1 M acetic acid) diluted to 60 mL	(i) the value of $[H^+]$ does not change on dilution
Q. (20 mL of 0.1M NaOH + 20 mL of 0.1 M acetic0 acid) diluted to 80 mL	(ii) the value of $[H^+]$ changes to half of its initial value on dilution.
R. (20 mL of 0.1 M HCl + 20 mL of 0.1 ammonia solution) diluted to 80 mL	(iii) the value of $[H^+]$ changes to two times of its initial value on dilution.
S. 10 mL saturated solution of $Ni(OH)_2$ in equilibrium with excess solid $Ni(OH)_2$ is diluted to 20 mL (solid $Ni(OH)_2$ is still present after diluton)	(iv) the value of $[H^+]$ changes to $\frac{1}{\sqrt{2}}$ times of its initial value on dilution.
	(v) the value of $[H^+]$ changes to $\sqrt{2}$ times of its initial value on dilution.

Match each process given in List-I with one or more effect(s) in List-II. The correct option is

(a) P → (iv); Q → (ii); R → (iii); S → (i)
(b) P → (iv); Q → (iii); R → (ii); S → (iii)
(c) P → (i); Q → (iv); R → (v); S → (iii)
(d) P → (i); Q → (v); R → (iv); S → (i)

HINTS & EXPLANATIONS

Immediate Tests

1. (a) $\underset{\text{Acid}_1}{HCO_3^-} + \underset{\text{Base}_2}{H_2O} \longrightarrow \underset{\text{Acid}_2}{H_3O^+} + \underset{\text{Base}_1}{CO_3^{2-}}$

(b) $\underset{\text{Acid}_1}{CH_3COOH} + \underset{\text{Base}_2}{NH_3} \longrightarrow \underset{\text{Acid}_2}{NH_4^+} + \underset{\text{Base}_1}{CH_3COO^-}$

(c) $\underset{\text{Acid}_1}{HSO_4^-} + \underset{\text{Base}_2}{H_2O} \longrightarrow \underset{\text{Acid}_2}{H_3O^+} + \underset{\text{Base}_1}{SO_4^{2-}}$

(d) $\underset{\text{Base}_1}{HSO_4^-} + \underset{\text{Acid}_2}{H_2O} \longrightarrow \underset{\text{Base}_2}{OH^-} + \underset{\text{Acid}_1}{H_2SO_4}$

■ Based on (c) and (d), HSO_4^- is amphiprotic.

2. (i) (a) $\underset{\text{Strong acid}}{HCl(aq)} + \underset{\text{Strong base}}{H_2O(l)} \longrightarrow \underset{\text{Weak acid}}{H_3O^+(aq)} + \underset{\text{Weak base}}{Cl^-(aq)}$

Towards right

(b) $\underset{\text{Weak acid}}{HF(aq)} + \underset{\text{Weak base}}{H_2O(l)} \longrightarrow \underset{\text{Strong acid}}{H_3O^+} + \underset{\text{Strong base}}{F^-(aq)}$

Toward left

(c) $O^{2-}(aq) + H_2O(l) \longrightarrow 2OH^-(aq)$

Towards right

(d) Towards right

(e) Towards left

(ii) Towards right.

$CH_3COOH + C_2H_5O^- \rightleftharpoons \underset{\text{Weaker base}}{CH_3COO^-} + \underset{\text{Weaker acid}}{C_2H_5OH}$

3. (i) NO_2^- is the conjugate base of HNO_2 and NO_3^- is the conjugate base of HNO_3.

$$\begin{array}{lcc} & HNO_2 & HNO_3 \\ & \uparrow & \uparrow \\ \text{O.N.} & +3 & +5 \end{array}$$

Thus, HNO_3 is stronger acid than HNO_2. If acid is strong, its conjugate base is weak. Thus, NO_3^- (conjugate base of stronger HNO_3) is a weaker base than NO_2^-. (Conjugate base of weaker acid HNO_2). Also in NO_3^-, negative charge is localised to greater extent than in NO_2^-.

(ii)

$$\begin{array}{lcc} & H_2SO_4 > & H_2SO_3 \\ & \uparrow & \uparrow \\ \text{O.N.} & +6 & +4 \end{array}$$

Thus, H_2SO_4 is stronger acid than H_2SO_3. Number of O-atoms attached to S in H_2SO_4 is four compared to H_2SO_3 in which three O-atoms are attached to S-atoms. Negative charge on SO_4^{2-} is delocalised to greater extent than in SO_3^{2-}.

4. (i)

	Lewis acid	Lewis base
(a)	CO_2	OH^-
(b)	$B(OH)_3$	OH^-
(c)	$AlCl_3$	Cl^-
(d)	Cr^{3+}	H_2O

■ CO_2 by electron transfer gets positive charge on carbon atom on which OH^- is attached.

$O{=}C{=}O \rightleftharpoons O{=}\overset{\oplus}{C}{-}\overset{\ominus}{O} \xrightarrow{OH^-} O{=}C(OH){-}O^{\ominus}$

(ii) (a) $H_2PO_4^-$

(b) SO_3^{2-}, $H_2PO_4^-$, ClO^-

($H_2PO_4^-$ is amphiprotic)

(c) Fe^{3+}, BCl_3

(d) $H_2PO_4^-$, SO_3^{2-}, ClO^-

■ $\underset{\text{Acid}}{H_2PO_4^-} \rightleftharpoons H^+ + \underset{\text{Base}}{HPO_4^{2-}}$

$\underset{\text{Base}}{H_2PO_4^-} + H^+ \rightleftharpoons \underset{\text{Acid}}{H_3PO_4}$

Thus, $H_2PO_4^-$ is amphiprotic, SO_3^{2-} is a Lewis base as well as Lowry-Bronsted base.

5. (i) $\underset{\text{Acid}}{CH_3COOH} + H_2O \rightleftharpoons CH_3COO^- + H_3O^+$

$$K_a = \frac{[CH_3COO^-][H_3O^+]}{[CH_3COOH]}$$

$\underset{\text{Base}}{CH_3COO^-} + H_2O \rightleftharpoons CH_3COOH + OH^-$

$$K_b = \frac{[CH_3COOH][OH^-]}{[CH_3COO^-]}$$

$\therefore\ K_a \cdot K_b = [H_3O^+][OH^-] = K_w$

$$\therefore\ K_b(CH_3COO^-) = \frac{K_w}{K_a} = \frac{1\times10^{-14}}{1.8\times10^{-5}} = 5.55\times10^{-10}$$

(ii) $CH_3NH_3^+$ is a source of H^+, thus acts as an acid, $K_a = 1.54\times10^{-10}$

$(CH_3)_3N$ is a source of OH^-, thus is a base.

$$K_b = \frac{1\times10^{-14}}{1.54\times10^{-10}} = 6.49\times10^{-5}$$

6. (a) 0.1 M H_2SO_4 = 0.2 N H_2SO_4

$$N_{\text{Acid mixture}} = \frac{\Sigma NV}{\Sigma V} = \frac{0.2\times V + 0.1\ V}{V+V}$$

$[H^+]_{\text{Mix}} = 0.15$ M

(b) $$[H^+]_{\text{Mix}} = \frac{0.2\ V + 0.1\times 2V}{V+2V} = \frac{0.4}{3} = 0.133\ \text{M}$$

(c) **Acid-base** **Mixture**

0.1 M H_2SO_4 = 0.2 N H_2SO_4

0.1 M NaOH = 0.1 N NaOH

$\therefore\ N_1V_1(\text{acid}) = 0.2\times1$

$N_2V_2(\text{base}) = 0.1\times2$

$N_1V_1 = N_2V_2$

Thus, neutral.

(d) Neutral as N_1V_1 (acid) = N_2V_2 (base)

(e) 0.1 M $Ca(OH)_2$ = 0.2 N

0.1 M HCl = 0.1 N

$N_1V_1(\text{acid}) = 0.1\times1$

$N_2V_2(\text{base}) = 0.2\times1$

$N_2V_2 > N_1V_1$

Thus, basic.

$$N(OH)^- = \frac{0.2-0.1}{2} = \frac{0.1}{2} = 0.05\ \text{M}$$

(f) Neutral

(g) Basic $$N(OH^-) = \frac{0.1\times2 - 0.1\times1}{2+1} = \frac{0.1}{3} = 0.033\ \text{M}$$

7. Density of water = 1000 kg m^{-3}

$= 10^6\ g\ m^{-3} = 10^3\ g\ dm^{-3}$

$\therefore$ Molar concentration of H_2O

$$= \frac{10^3\ g\ dm^{-3}}{18\ g\ mol^{-1}} = 55.55\ g\ dm^{-3}$$

Also $H_2O + H_2O \rightleftharpoons H_3O^+ + OH^-$

$[H_3O^+][OH^-] = 1\times10^{-14}$

$\therefore\ [H_3O^+] = \sqrt{1\times10^{-14}} = 1\times10^{-7}$ M

Thus, $[H_3O^+]$ in pure water

$$= \frac{1\times10^{-7}}{55.55} = 1.8\times10^{-9}$$

Percentage $= 1.8\times10^{-9}\times100$

$= 1.8\times10^{-7}\%$

8. (i) 0.10 g NaOH$=\dfrac{0.10\text{g}}{40\text{ g mol}^{-1}}$

$=2.5\times10^{-3}$ mol

$\therefore\ [M]_{NaOH}=\dfrac{\text{mol}}{\text{L}}=\dfrac{2.5\times10^{-3}}{0.250\text{ L}}$ mol

$=0.01\text{ mol L}^{-1}$

NaOH being a strong electrolyte,

$[OH^-]=0.01\text{M}$

$\therefore$ pOH$=-\log 1\times10^{-2}=2$

Since, pH+ pOH=14

$\therefore$ pH= 14 − 2 = 12

(ii) $Ba(OH)_2=0.05\times10^{-2}$ M

$Ba(OH)_2 \rightleftharpoons Ba^{2+}+2OH^-$

$\therefore [OH^-]=2[Ba(OH)_2]=1\times10^{-3}$ M

$\therefore$ pOH= 3 $\therefore$ pH=11

(iii) (a) $[OH^-]=1.6\times10^{-6}$ M

$\therefore$ pOH$=-\log(1.6\times10^{-6})$

$=6-\log 1.6$

$=6-0.2730=5.2220$

(c) 1 M HCl = 1 M $[H_3O^+]$

$\therefore$ pH$=-\log 1=0$

(d) $CaO+H_2O \rightleftharpoons Ca(OH)_2$

$\therefore$ CaO = 0.56 g in 100 mL

$=\left(\dfrac{0.56}{56}\right)$ mol in 0.1 L

$\therefore\ [CaO]=\dfrac{0.01}{0.10}=0.1$ M

$\therefore\ [OH^-]=2[CaO]=0.2$ M

$\therefore$ pOH$=-\log 0.2=\log 5=0.6990$

$\therefore$ pH= 14 − pOH= 13.3010

9. (i) $[OH^-]=1\times10^{-8}$ M

pOH= 8

pH= 6 ⇐ It is incorrect.

Since, NaOH is basic and pH>7.

Method I Thus, $[OH^-]$ of water is also considered.

$[OH^-]_{NaOH}=1\times10^{-8}$ M

$[OH^-]_{H_2O}=1\times10^{-7}\text{ M}=10\times10^{-8}$ M

$[OH^-]_{total}=11\times10^{-8}$ M

$\therefore$ pOH= 8 − log 11

$\therefore$ pH=6 + log 11 = 7.04

$\therefore$ pH > 7

Method II If calculated, exactly

$H_2O \rightleftharpoons H^+ + OH^-$

	H_2O	H^+	OH^-
Initial	1	0	0
At equil.	$(1-x)$	x	x

$[OH^-]$ = from NaOH + from H_2O

$=1\times10^{-8}+x$

$[H_3O^+]=x$

$\therefore\ x^2+1\times10^{-8}x-1\times10^{-14}=0$

we apply formula, $x=\dfrac{-b\pm\sqrt{b^2-4ac}}{2a}$

$x=\dfrac{-1\times10^{-8}+\sqrt{1\times10^{-16}+4\times10^{-14}}}{2}$

$=9.51\times10^{-8}$ M

$\therefore\ [OH^-]=(1.0\times10^{-8}+9.51\times10^{-8})$

$=1.05\times10^{-7}$

pOH= 6.98

pH= 7.02 ≈ 7.04

■ Thus, avoid tedious calculation and proceed as in method I.

(ii) 10 mL of 10^{-6} M HCl = 100 mL of N_1-HCl.

$\therefore\ N_1$(dilute) $=1\times10^{-7}$ M

$[H_3O^+]_{HCl}=1\times10^{-7}$ M

Since acidic, pH<7. Thus, proceed as given in text.

$[H_3O^+]_{H_2O}=1\times10^{-7}$ M

Total $[H^+]=2\times10^{-7}$ M

pH= 7 − 0.30= 6.70

(iii) (a) 10^{-2} M $H_2SO_4=2\times10^{-2}$ N $[H^+]$;

pH= 1.7

(b) 10^{-2} N $H_2SO_4=1\times10^{-2}$ N(H^+);

pH= 2.0

(c) 10^{-2} M $Ca(OH)_2=2\times10^{-2}$ N(OH^-);

pOH= 1.7, pH=12.3

(d) 10^{-2} N $Ca(OH)_2=1\times10^{-2}$ N (OH^-);

pOH=2, pH=12

■ In calculation of pH, $[H^+]_{Acid}$ = basicity × molarity = normality.

10. (i) $Ca(OH)_2 \rightleftharpoons Ca^{2+}+2OH^-$

pH= 12.0

$\therefore$ pOH=2.0

$\therefore\ [OH^-]=10^{-2}$ M

$\therefore [Ca(OH)_2]=\dfrac{1}{2}\times10^{-2}\text{M}=5\times10^{-3}$ M

$=5\times10^{-3}\text{ mol L}^{-1}$

$=5.0\text{ millimol L}^{-1}$

$=\dfrac{5.0}{10}$ millimol in 100 mL

$=0.5$ millimol

(ii) $SO_3+H_2O \rightleftharpoons H_2SO_4$

Aqueous solution of SO_3 is H_2SO_4

$H_2SO_4 \rightleftharpoons 2H^+ + SO_4^{2-}$

pH= 2

$\therefore\ [H^+]=10^{-2}$ M

$\therefore\ [H_2SO_4]=[SO_3]=\dfrac{10^{-2}\text{ M}}{2}$

$=5\times10^{-3}$ M (mol L^{-1})

$=5\times80\times10^{-3}\text{ g L}^{-1}$

$=0.4$ g SO_3 in 1 L solution

11. (i)

	pH	N_A	Volume
HCl	2	$N_1(H^+)=10^{-2}$N	V_1= 700 mL
NaOH	12		
	pOH = 2	$N_2[OH^-]=10^{-2}$ N	V_2 = 300 mL

N_1V_1 (Acid)= 7

N_2V_2 (Base) = 3

$N_1V_1>N_2V_2$,

Thus, mixture is acidic.

$N(H^+)=\dfrac{N_1V_1-N_2V_2}{V_1+V_2}$

$N(H^+)=\dfrac{7-3}{1000}=4\times10^{-3}$ M

$\therefore$ pH = 3 − log 4 = 2.4

(ii) $HNO_3=0.4\text{ M}=0.4$ N

$Ca(OH)_2=0.4\text{ M}=0.8$ N

$\therefore\ N_1V_1$ (acid) $=0.4\times40=16$

N_2V_2(base) $=0.8\times40=32>16$

Thus, mixture is basic.

$N(OH^-)$ in mixture $=\dfrac{N_2V_2-N_1V_1}{V_1+V_2}$

$=\dfrac{32-16}{80}=\dfrac{16}{80}$

$=\dfrac{1}{5}=0.2$ N

Total volume = 80 mL

80 mL of 0.2 N$[OH^-]$ is diluted to 500 mL.

$\therefore\ 80\times0.2=N_2'(OH)\times500$

$\therefore\ N_2'(OH^-)=\dfrac{16}{500}\text{ N}=0.032$ N

$\therefore$ pOH$=-\log(0.032)=1.5$

pH=12.5

(iii) KOH= 3.0 g in 100 g solution.

$=3.0$ g in $\left(\dfrac{100}{1.0242}\right)$ mL solution.

$\therefore\ [KOH]=\dfrac{\frac{3}{56}\text{ mol}}{\left(\frac{0.1}{1.0242}\right)\text{L}}=0.549$ M

$\therefore$ [OH] = 0.549

pOH$=-\log[OH^-]=0.26$

$\therefore$ pH=13.74

(iv) $HCl+H_2O \rightleftharpoons H_3O^+ + Cl^-$

$n(HCl)=\dfrac{pV}{RT}$

$=\dfrac{1\text{ bar}\times0.248\text{ L}}{0.08314\text{ bar L mol}^{-1}\text{K}^{-1}\times298\text{ K}}$

$=0.01\text{ mol L}^{-1}$

$\therefore$ $[HCl] = 0.01\ M = [H_3O^+]$

$\therefore$ pH = 2

12. $x = \sqrt{\frac{K_a}{C}} = \sqrt{\frac{6.2\times10^{-10}}{0.01}} = 2.5\times10^{-4}$

(a) Thus, percentage ionisation

$= 2.5\times10^{-4}\times100 = 0.025$

(b) $pH = \frac{1}{2}[[pK_a - \log C]$

$= \frac{1}{2}[-\log 6.2\times10^{-10} - \log 0.01]$

$= \frac{1}{2}[9.21 + 2.0] = 5.6$

Or $[H_3O^+] = \sqrt{K_aC} = \sqrt{6.2\times10^{-10}\times0.01}$

$= 2.5\times10^{-6}$

$\therefore$ pH = 5.6

13. For mixture of weak bases,

$[OH^-]_{mix} = \sqrt{K_1C_1 + K_2C_2}$

$= \sqrt{1.8\times10^{-5}\times0.01 + 3.0\times10^{-7}\times0.01}$

$= 4.28\times10^{-4}$ M

$\therefore$ $pOH - \log[OH^-] = 3.37$

Since, pH + pOH = 14

$\therefore$ pH = 14 − 3.37 = 10.63

14. $pOH(\text{weak base}) = \frac{1}{2}[pK_b - \log C]$

$2 = \frac{1}{2}[pK_b - \log 0.01]$

$4 = pK_b + 2$

$pK_b = 2$

$\therefore$ $K_b = 10^{-2}$

$pH(\text{weak acid}) = \frac{1}{2}[pK_a - \log C]$

$5 = \frac{1}{2}[pK_a - \log 0.001]$

$= \frac{1}{2}[pK_a + 3]$

$pK_a = 7.\ K_a = 10^{-7}$

$\therefore$ $\frac{K_b}{K_a} = \frac{10^{-2}}{10^{-7}} = 10^5$

15. For a mixture of weak base and strong base.

$[OH^-] = C_1(\text{strong base}) + C_2\alpha\,(\text{weak base})$

But, $\alpha = \sqrt{\frac{K_b}{C}}$

$\therefore$ $[OH^-] = C_1 + \sqrt{C_2K_b}$

$= 0.01 + \sqrt{0.01\times1.8\times10^{-5}}$

$= 0.01 + 4.243\times10^{-4} = 0.0104$

$\therefore$ pOH = 1.982

$\therefore$ pH = 12.018 ≈ 12

■ If acid or base is too weak. Total $[OH^-]$ or $[H^+]$ = conc. of base or acid

Thus, pOH of a mixture = pOH of strong base = 2

$\therefore$ pH = 12

16. (i) (a)

	HA	$\rightleftharpoons$	H^+	+	A^-
Initial mole	1		0		0
At equil.	$(1-x)$		x		x

A^- is the conjugate base of HA.

Mole fraction of $A^- = \frac{x}{(1+x)}$

$pH = pK_a + \log\frac{x}{(1-x)}$

$6 = 8 + \log\left(\frac{x}{1-x}\right) \Rightarrow -2 = \log\left(\frac{x}{1-x}\right)$

$\therefore$ $\frac{x}{(1-x)} = 10^{-2}$

$\therefore$ $x = 0.0099$

$\therefore$ Mole fraction of $A^- = \frac{0.0099}{1+0.0099}$

$= 9.8\times10^{-3}$

(b) $HCOOH + H_2O \rightleftharpoons HCOO^- + H_3O$

$K_a = \frac{Cx^2}{(1-x)} = 1.8\times10^{-4}$

$\frac{1\times10^{-3}(x^2)}{(1-x)} = 1.8\times10^{-4}$

$\frac{x^2}{(1-x)} = 0.18$

Thus x can not be neglected as compared to 1

$\therefore$ $x = 0.3437$

$\therefore$ $[H_3O^+] = Cx = 1\times10^{-3}\times0.3437$

$= 3.437\times10^{-4}$

$\therefore$ pH = 3.46

■ If approximation is made

$pH = \frac{1}{2}[pK_a - \log C] = \frac{3.74+3}{2} = 3.37$

(ii) (a) $K_a = \frac{Cx^2}{(1-x)} \approx Cx^2$

$\therefore$ $x = \sqrt{\frac{K_a}{C}} = \sqrt{\frac{1.8\times10^{-5}}{0.2}} = 9.48\times10^{-3}$

(b) $K_a = \frac{Cx^2}{(1-x)} = 1.8\times10^{-5}$

$\frac{0.2x^2}{(1-x)} = 1.8\times10^{-5}$

$\therefore$ $\frac{x^2}{(1-x)} = 9.0\times10^{-5}$

$x = \frac{-9\times10^{-5} + \sqrt{(9.0\times10^{-5})^2 + 36\times10^{-5}}}{2}$

$= 9.44\times10^{-3} \approx 9.48\times10^{-3}$

Thus, degree of ionisation in both cases is approximately same.

17. $NH_4OH \rightleftharpoons NH_4^+ + OH^-$

$KOH \rightleftharpoons K^+ + OH^-$

$[OH^-]$ of KOH is taken

$K_b = \frac{[NH_4^+][OH^-]}{[NH_4OH]}$

$[NH_4^+] = \frac{K_b[NH_4OH]}{[OH^-]}$

$= \frac{1.8\times10^{-5}(0.01)}{(0.001)} = 1.8\times10^{-4}$

18. (i) $H_3BO_3 \rightleftharpoons H^+ + H_2BO_3^-$

$K_a = \frac{[H^+][H_2BO_3^-]}{[H_3BO_3]}$

$7.3\times10^{-10} = \frac{[H^+](0.15)}{(0.10)}$

$\therefore$ $[H^+] = \frac{7.3\times10^{-10}\times0.10}{0.15}$

$= 4.87\times10^{-10}$

$pH = -\log[H^+] = -\log 4.87\times10^{-10}$

$\therefore$ pH = 9.31

(ii) $pH = \frac{1}{2}[pK_a - \log C]$

$= \frac{1}{2}[4.74 - \log 0.01]$

$= \frac{1}{2}[4.74 + 2] = 3.37$

pH of buffer = 4.37 (increase by one unit)

$\therefore$ If x mole CH_3COONa is added in 50 mL,

then, $[CH_3COONa] = \frac{x}{0.050}\ M = 20x\ M$

By Henderson -Hasselbalch (H-H) equation,

$\therefore$ $pH = pK_a + \log\frac{[CH_3COONa]}{[CH_3COOH]}$

$4.37 = 4.74 + \log\left(\frac{20x}{0.01}\right)$

$-0.37 = \log\left(\frac{20x}{0.01}\right)$

$\frac{20x}{0.01} = 0.4266$

$x = 2.133\times10^{-4}$ mol

19. $CH_3COONa = 50\times0.02 = 1$ millimol

$HCl = 75\times0.01 = 0.75$ millimol

	CH_3COONa	+ HCl	$\rightleftharpoons$ CH_3COOH	+ NaCl
Initial (mmol)	1.0	0.75		
At equil.	$(1-0.75) = 0.25$	0	0.75	

By (H-H) equation,

$\therefore$ $pH = pK_a + \log\frac{[CH_3COONa]}{[CH_3COOH]}$

$= 4.74 + \log\frac{0.25}{0.75} = 4.74 - 0.48 = 4.26$

20. $NH_3 = 50 \times 0.40 = 20$ millimol

$HCl = 50 \times 0.30 = 15$ millimol

$pK_b = 14 - pK_a = 14 - 9.26 = 4.74$

	NH_3 +	$HCl \rightleftharpoons$	NH_4Cl
Initial (mmol)	20	15	
After reaction	(20 – 15)	(15 – 15)	15
	5 mmol	0	15 mmol

By (H-H) equation,

$$pOH = pK_b + \log\frac{[NH_4Cl]}{[NH_4OH]}$$

$= 4.74 + \log(15/5)$

$= 4.74 + 0.48 = 5.22$

$\therefore$ pH = 14 – 5.22 = 8.78

21. $NH_4OH + HCl \rightleftharpoons NH_4Cl + H_2O$

If $NH_4OH = V$ mL $= 0.1\,V$ millimol

then $HCl = (100 - V)$ mL

$= 0.1(100 - V)$ millimol

$NH_4Cl = HCl = 0.1(100 - V)$ millimol

and NH_4OH left $= [0.1\,V - 0.1(100 - V)]$

$= [0.2\,V - 10]$ millimol

By (H-H) equation,

$$pOH = pK_b + \log\frac{[NH_4Cl]}{[NH_4OH]}$$

$$5 = 4.74 + \log\frac{[0.2\,V - 10]}{0.1\,(100 - V)}$$

$$0.26 = \log\frac{0.2\,V - 10}{(10 - 0.1\,V)}$$

$$1.82 = \frac{0.2V - 10}{(10 - 0.1\,V)}$$

$18.2 - 0.182\,V = 0.2\,V - 10$

$0.382V = 28.2$

$V = 73.8$ mL

Then $NH_4OH = 73.8$ mL

and $HCl = 26.2$ mL

22. $HSO_4^- \rightleftharpoons H^+ + SO_4^{2-}$

Let $[HSO_4^-] = x$ mol L^{-1}

then $[SO_4^{2-}] = (0.2 - 4)$ mol L^{-1}

By (H-H) equation,

$$pH = pK_a + \log\frac{[SO_4^{2-}]}{[HSO_4^-]}$$

$$2 = 2 + \log\left[\frac{0.2 - x}{x}\right]$$

$$\therefore \quad \frac{0.2 - x}{x} = 1$$

$x = 0.1$ M

Thus, $[HSO_4^-] = 0.1$ M and

$[SO_4^{2-}] = 0.1\,M = (0.2 - 0.1)$

23. It is a case of basic buffer.

By (H-H) equation,

$$pOH = pK_b + \log\frac{[NH_4^+]}{[NH_3]}$$

But $pOH = 14 - pH$

and $pK_a = 14 - pK_b$

$$\therefore \quad pH = [14 - pK_b] - \log\frac{[NH_4^+]}{[NH_3]}$$

$$pH = pK_a + \log\frac{[NH_3]}{[NH_4^+]}$$

$y = c + mx = \tan 45° = 1$

Thus, $pK_a[NH_4^+] = 9.26$

$[NH_4^+] = [NH_3] = 0.05$ M

Since, 50 mL of 0.1 M HCl converts equivalent amount of NH_4OH into NH_4Cl.

$[NH_4^+] = [NH_3] = 0.05$ M

$$pH = 9.26 + \log\left(\frac{0.05}{0.05}\right)$$

pH = 9.26

24. (pyridine, *A*) $+ H_2O \rightleftharpoons$ (pyridinium, N–H, *B*) $+ OH^{\ominus}$

$$pOH = pK_b + \log\frac{[B]}{[A]}$$

Let $[A] = x$ mol L^{-1}

and $[B] = y$ mol L^{-1}

then x_A (pyridine) $= \dfrac{x}{x + y} = 0.4$ (given)

$$\frac{x}{(x + y)} = \frac{2}{5}$$

$\therefore$ $y = 3 = [B]$ and $x = 2 = [A]$

$\therefore$ $(pOH - pK_b) = \log\dfrac{3}{2} = 0.1761$

25. [NaOH] = 0.1 mol in 1 L = 0.1 M

Addition of NaOH will increase $[CH_3CH_2COONa]$ and will decrease $[CH_3CH_2COOH]$.

Thus, pH is affected.

	CH_3CH_2COOH +	$OH^- \rightleftharpoons$	$CH_3CH_2COO^-$
Initial	0.15 M		0.20 M
Added	—	0.10 M	—
After reac.	(0.15 – 0.10) M	0	(0.20 + 0.10)
	= (0.05) M	0	= 0.30 M

$$\therefore \quad pH = 5.0 + \log\frac{0.30}{0.05}$$

$= 5.0 + \log 6 = 5.0 + 0.48 = 5.48$

26. $[HCl] = 10 \times 0.01 = 0.1$ millimol

$[NH_4OH] = 90 \times 0.01 = 0.9$ millimol

$[NH_4Cl] = 90 \times 0.01 = 0.9$ millimol

	NH_4OH +	$HCl \rightleftharpoons$	NH_4Cl +	H_2O
Initial	0.9 mmol		0.9 mmol	
Added			0.1 mmol	
At equil.	0.8 mmol		1.0 mmol	

pOH (before HCl is added)

$$= pK_b + \log\frac{0.01}{0.01} = pK_b$$

pOH (after HCl is added)

$$= pK_b + \log\frac{1.0}{0.8} = pK_b + 0.097$$

Change in pOH = 0.097 unit

$\therefore$ Change in pH = 0.097 unit

27. $(NH_4)_2SO_4$ is a salt of weak base and strong acid.

$NH_4^+ + H_2O \rightleftharpoons NH_4OH + H^+$; $pK_a = 9.26$

Aqueous solution of NH_4^+ ion is acidic due to hydrolysis.

$$\text{Thus, } pH = 7 - \frac{pK_b}{2} - \frac{\log C}{2}$$

If $pK_a(NH_4^+) = 9.26$

then $pK_b(NH_3) = 14.0 - 9.26 = 4.74$

$[(NH_4)_2SO_4] = 2NH_4^+$

$(NH_4^+) = 2 \times 0.005 = 0.01$ M

$$\therefore \quad pH = 7 - \frac{4.74}{2} - \frac{\log 0.01}{2}$$

$= 7 - 2.37 + 1 = 5.63$

28. (a) $K_a = \dfrac{[Ni(OH^+)][H_3O^+]}{[Ni^{2+}(aq)]}$

Since, $[H_3O^+] = [Ni(OH)^+]$

$$\therefore \quad K_a = \frac{(4.5 \times 10^{-6})^2}{(0.04)} = 5.06 \times 10^{-10}$$

(b) Given reaction is also hydrolysis reaction of Ni^{2+}, thus

$K_h = K_a = 5.06 \times 10^{-10}$

(c) Degree of hydrolysis

$$\alpha = \sqrt{\frac{K_h}{C}} = \sqrt{\frac{5.06 \times 10^{-10}}{0.04}}$$

$= 1.125 \times 10^{-4} = 0.01125\%$

29. $CH_3CH_2NH_2 + HCl \rightleftharpoons CH_3CH_2\overset{+}{N}H_3Cl^-$

	$CH_3CH_2NH_2$	HCl	$CH_3CH_2\overset{+}{N}H_3Cl^-$
Initial (mmol)	0.05	0	0
Stage I HCl added		0.025	
At equil.	0.025	0	0.025
		Buffer	
Stage II HCl added (mmol)		0.05	
At equil.	0	0	0.05

Aq. solution of $CH_3CH_2NH_3^+$ is acidic due to hydrolysis.

(a) pH of the buffer

$$pOH = pK_b + \log\frac{[CH_3CH_2NH_3^+]}{[CH_3CH_2NH_2]}$$

$$= 5 + \log\frac{0.025}{0.025} = 5.0$$

(b) $CH_3CH_2NH_3^+ + H_2O \rightleftharpoons CH_3CH_2NH_3OH + H^+$,

pH < 7

$[CH_3CH_2NH_3^+]_{mix} = 0.05$ mL in 60 mL

$$\therefore \quad = \frac{0.05 \times 10^{-3}\ \text{mol}}{0.060\ \text{L}} = 8.33 \times 10^{-4}\ \text{M}$$

$$\therefore\ \text{pH} = 7 - \frac{\text{p}K_b}{2} - \frac{\log C}{2}$$

$$= 7 - 2.50 - \frac{\log 8.33 \times 10^{-4}}{2}$$

$$= 7 - 2.50 + 1.54 = 6.04$$

■ $\text{p}K_b = -\log K_b$

30. $Fe^{3+} + 2H_2O \rightleftharpoons [Fe(OH)]^{2+} + H_3O^+$

If $[Fe^{3+}] = \frac{95}{100} = 0.95\ \text{M}$

then $[Fe(OH)]^{2+} = 0.05\ \text{M}$

$$\therefore \quad K_h = K_a = 6.5 \times 10^{-3}$$

$$= \frac{[Fe(OH)]^{2+}[H_3O^+]}{[Fe^{3+}]}$$

$$= \left(\frac{0.05}{0.95}\right)[H_3O^+]$$

$\therefore\ [H_3O^+] = 0.1235\ \text{M}$

$$\text{pH} = -\log[H_3O^+] = 0.91$$

31. (a) For 0.01 M PO_4^{3-}

$PO_4^{3-} + H_2O \rightleftharpoons HPO_4^{2-} + OH^-$

Solution is basic and HPO_4^{2-} and PO_4^{3-} ions are involved.

$$\therefore\ \text{pH} = 7 + \frac{\text{p}K_{a_3}}{2} + \frac{\log C}{2}$$

$$= 7 + \frac{12.35}{2} + \frac{\log 0.01}{2} = 12.18$$

(b) For HPO_4^{2-}

It is amphiprotic

$HPO_4^{2-} + H_2O \rightleftharpoons H_3O^+ + PO_4^{3-}$,

$HPO_4^{2-} + H_2O \rightleftharpoons H_2PO_4^- + OH^-$,

Thus, $\text{pH} = \frac{\text{p}K_{a_2} + \text{p}K_{a_3}}{2}$

$$= \frac{7.20 + 12.35}{2} = 9.78$$

(c) For $H_2PO_4^-$

It is also amphiprotic,

$H_2PO_4^- + H_2O \rightleftharpoons H_3O^+ + HPO_4^{2-}$

$H_2PO_4^- + H_2O \rightleftharpoons H_3PO_4 + OH^-$

$$\therefore\ \text{pH} = \frac{\text{p}K_{a_1} + \text{p}K_{a_2}}{2} = \frac{2.15 + 7.20}{2}$$

$$= 4.68$$

32. (I)

$$\underset{(A)}{HO-C_6H_4-COOH} + OH^- \rightleftharpoons \underset{(B)}{HO-C_6H_4-COO^-} + H_2O$$

In stage I, 50% of (A) is converted into (B). Thus,

$$[A] = [B]$$

It is now a buffer

$$\therefore\ \text{pH} = \text{p}K_{a_1} + \log\frac{[B]}{[A]}$$

$$4.60 = \text{p}K_{a_1} + \log 1 = \text{p}K_{a_1}$$

$$\therefore\ \text{p}K_{a_1} = 4.60$$

(II) B is amphiprotic

$$\underset{\text{Base}}{HO-C_6H_4-COO^-} + H_2O \rightleftharpoons HO-C_6H_4-COOH + OH^-$$

$$\underset{\text{Acid}}{HO-C_6H_4-COO^-} + H_2O \rightleftharpoons {}^-O-C_6H_4-COO^- + H_3O^+$$

Then, $\text{pH} = \frac{\text{p}K_{a_1} + \text{p}K_{a_2}}{2}$

$$8.0 = (4.60 + \text{p}K_{a_2})/2$$

$$\therefore\ \text{p}K_{a_2} = 11.40$$

33. For a salt of weak acid and strong base

$$\text{pH} = 7 + \frac{\text{p}K_a}{2} + \frac{\log C}{2}$$

$$\text{pH} = \left[7 + \frac{\text{p}K_a}{2}\right] + \frac{1}{2}\log C$$

We compare it by equation

$$y = c + mx$$

$$\text{Slope} = \frac{1}{2} = \tan\theta$$

and intercept, $c = OA = 9.37$

$$\therefore\quad 7 + \frac{\text{p}K_a}{2} = 9.37$$

$$\text{p}K_a = 4.74$$

$$\therefore\quad \text{pH} = 9.37 + \frac{1}{2}\log(0.001)$$

$$= 9.37 + \frac{1}{2}(-3)$$

$$= 9.37 - 1.50 = 7.87$$

34. $BaSO_4(s) \rightleftharpoons Ba^{2+}(aq) + SO_4^{2-}(aq)$

$$K_{sp} = [Ba^{2+}][SO_4^{2-}]$$

(a) In water, solubility $= x$

then $1.1 \times 10^{-10} = x.x = x^2$

$$\therefore\quad x = \sqrt{1.1 \times 10^{-10}}\ \text{M}$$

$$= 1.05 \times 10^{-5}\ \text{M}$$

(b) In 0.1 M $BaCl_2$, solubility be $= y\ \text{mol L}^{-1}$

$y << x$ (due to common ion effect)

$\therefore\ BaSO_4(s) \rightleftharpoons Ba^{2+}(aq) + SO_4^{2-}(aq)$

$$\underset{0.1\ \text{M}}{BaCl_2(aq)} \rightleftharpoons Ba^{2+}(aq) + 2Cl^-(aq)$$

$$[Ba^{2+}]_{\text{total}} = (y + 0.1)\ \text{M} \approx 0.1\ \text{M}$$

$$[SO_4^{2-}] = y\ \text{M}$$

$$\therefore\ [Ba^{2+}][SO_4^{2-}] = K_{sp}$$

$$0.1 \times y = 1.1 \times 10^{-10}$$

$$\therefore\ y = 1.1 \times 10^{-9}\ \text{M}$$

(c) In 0.01 M K_2SO_4, solubility be $= z\ \text{mol L}^{-1}$

$$[Ba^{2+}] = z$$

$$[SO_4^{2-}] = (0.01 + z) \approx 0.01\ \text{M}$$

$$\therefore\ [Ba^{2+}][SO_4^{2-}] = K_{sp}$$

$$z\,(0.01) = 1.1 \times 10^{-10}$$

$$\therefore\quad z = 1.1 \times 10^{-8}\ \text{M}$$

35. Assume solubility $= S$ mol L^{-1}

$$A_2X_3(s) \rightleftharpoons \underset{(2S)}{2A^{3+}(aq)} + \underset{(3S)}{3X^{2-}(aq)}$$

$$K_{sp} = [A^{3+}]^2[X^{2-}]^3$$

$$= (2S)^2(3S)^3$$

$$1.1 \times 10^{-23} = 108\,S^5$$

$$\frac{1.1 \times 10^{-23}}{108} = S^5$$

$$1 \times 10^{-25} = S^5$$

$$\therefore\quad S = 1.0 \times 10^{-5}\ \text{mol L}^{-1}$$

36. (i) $Fe(OH)_3(s) \rightleftharpoons \underset{(S)}{Fe^{3+}(aq)} + \underset{(3S)}{3OH^-(aq)}$

$$K_{sp} = [Fe^{3+}][OH^-]^3 = (S)(3S)^3$$

$$2.6 \times 10^{-39} = 27S^4$$

$$\therefore\quad S = 9.9 \times 10^{-11}\ \text{M}$$

$$\therefore\quad [OH^-] = 3S = 3 \times 9.9 \times 10^{-11}\ \text{M}$$

$$= 2.97 \times 10^{-10}\ \text{M}$$

$$\therefore\quad \text{pOH} = -\log[OH^-] = 9.53$$

Since, pH + pOH = 14

$\therefore$ pH = 14.00 − 9.53 = 4.47

■ Aqueous solution of Fe^{3+} is acidic due to hydrolysis. Thus, pH < 7.

(ii) For a weak base,

$$NH_4OH(aq) \rightleftharpoons NH_4^+(aq) + OH^-(aq)$$

$$\therefore\quad K_b = \frac{[NH_4^+][OH^-]}{[NH_4OH]}$$

$$1.8 \times 10^{-5} = \frac{0.1[OH^-]}{0.1}$$

$$\therefore\ [OH^-]_{\text{buffer}} = 1.8 \times 10^{-5}\ \text{M}$$

$$Fe(OH)_3(s) \rightleftharpoons Fe^{3+}(aq) + 3OH^-(aq)$$

$$\therefore\ K_{sp}[Fe(OH)_3] = [Fe^{3+}][OH^-]^3$$

$$2.6 \times 10^{-39} = [Fe^{3+}][1.8 \times 10^{-5}]^3$$

$\therefore \quad [Fe^{3+}] = \frac{2.6 \times 10^{-39}}{(1.8 \times 10^{-5})^3} M$

$= 4.46 \times 10^{-25}$ M

- In the absence of buffer, molar solubility of $Fe(OH)_3 = S$ mol L^{-1}

$Fe(OH)_3(s) \rightleftharpoons Fe^{3+}(aq) + 3OH^-(aq)$
$\quad S \quad 3S$

$K_{sp} = [Fe^{3+}][OH^-]^3 = (S)(3S)^3 = 27S^4$

$= 4\sqrt{\frac{K_{sp}}{27}} = \left(\frac{2.6 \times 10^{-39}}{27}\right)^{1/4}$

$= 9.9 \times 10^{-11}$ M

Thus, due to common ion effect of OH^- (from buffer) solubility of $Fe(OH)_3$ is decreased.

37. Saturated solution of $CaSO_4$ has $CaSO_4$

$= 0.24$ g per 100 mL $= 2.4$ g L^{-1}

$= \frac{2.4}{136}$ mol L^{-1}

$\therefore [Ca^{2+}] = [SO_4^{2-}] = \frac{2.4}{136}$ M

$\therefore \quad K_{sp} = [Ca^{2+}][SO_4^{2-}] = \left(\frac{2.4}{136}\right)^2$

$= 3.11 \times 10^{-4}$

38.(i) $C_5H_5N + H_2O \rightleftharpoons C_5H_5NH^+ + OH^-$

C	0	0 M
$(C - Cx)$	Cx	0.001 M

$\therefore \quad K_b = \frac{[C_5H_5NH^+][OH^-]}{[C_5H_5N]}$

$5 \times 10^{-6} = \frac{(Cx)(10^{-3})}{C(1-x)}$

$\therefore \quad \left(\frac{x}{1-x}\right) = 5 \times 10^{-3} = 0.005$

$x = 0.00497 \approx 0.005$

$(x << 1$, thus $(1 - x) \approx 1)$

(ii) This is a case of common ion effect.

$K_{sp} = [Ni^{2+}][OH^-]^2$

$2.0 \times 10^{-15} = [Ni^{2+}](0.1)^2$

$\therefore \quad [Ni^{2+}] = 2.0 \times 10^{-13}$ M

39. Let $[AgBr] = x$ mol L^{-1}

$\therefore \quad [Ag^+] = [Br^-] = x$ M

and $[Ag^+][CNS^-] = y$ mol L^{-1}

$\therefore \quad [Ag^+] = [CNS^-] = y$ M

$\therefore$ In mixture, $[Ag^+] = (x + y)$ M

$[Br^-] = x$ M

and $[CNS^-] = y$ M

For AgBr : $[Ag^+][Br^-] = 5 \times 10^{-15}$

For AgCNS : $[Ag^+][CNS^-] = 1 \times 10^{-12}$

$\therefore \quad (x + y)x = 5 \times 10^{-13}$ ...(i)

and $(x + y)y = 1 \times 10^{-12}$ ...(ii)

$\therefore \quad \frac{x}{y} = 5 \times 10^{-1} = 0.5 \Rightarrow x = 0.5y$

From (i),

$1.5y^2 = 5 \times 10^{-13}$

$\therefore \quad y = 5.77 \times 10^{-7}$ M

and $\quad x = 2.89 \times 10^{-7}$ M

and $\quad (x + y) = 8.66 \times 10^{-7}$ M

Thus $\quad [Ag^+] = 8.66 \times 10^{-7}$ M

$[Br^-] = 2.89 \times 10^{-7}$ M

and $\quad [CNS^-] = 5.77 \times 10^{-7}$ M

40. $[Mg^{2+}] = 0.01$ M

$[OH^-]$ in $NH_4OH = \sqrt{K_bC}$ by Ostwald's dilution law.

$= \sqrt{1.8 \times 10^{-5} \times 0.1}$

$= 1.34 \times 10^{-3}$ M

$\therefore [Mg^{2+}][OH^-]^2 = 0.01 \times (1.34 \times 10^{-3})^2$

$= 1.80 \times 10^{-8} > K_{sp}[Mg(OH)_2]$

Thus, $Mg(OH)_2$ is precipitated.

41. $CaF_2(s) \rightleftharpoons Ca^{2+}(aq) + 2F^-(aq)$, $\quad K_1 = K_{sp}$

$2F^-(aq) + 2H^+(aq) \rightleftharpoons 2HF(aq)$, $\quad K_2 = \frac{1}{K_a^2}$

$CaF_2(s) + 2H^+(aq) \rightleftharpoons Ca^{2+}(aq) + 2HF(aq)$, $\quad K_3 = \frac{K_{sp}}{K_a^2}$
(1×10^{-3}) M $\quad x \quad 2x$

$K_1 = K_{sp} = [Ca^{2+}][F^-]^2$

$K_2 = \frac{1}{K_a^2} = \frac{[HF]^2}{[H^+]^2[F^-]^2}$

$K_3 = \frac{[Ca^{2+}][HF]^2}{[H^+]^2} = \frac{K_{sp}}{(K_a)^2}$

$\therefore \quad \frac{(x)(2x)^2}{(1 \times 10^{-3})^2} = \frac{5.3 \times 10^{-9}}{(6.7 \times 10^{-4})^2}$

$\therefore \quad x = 1.43 \times 10^{-3}$ M

Thus, molar solubility of CaF_2 in a buffer of pH = 3 is 1.43×10^{-3} M.

42. $AgCl(s) \rightleftharpoons Ag^+(aq) + Cl^-(aq)$, $\quad K_1 = K_{sp}$

$Ag^+(aq) + 2NH_3(aq) \rightleftharpoons [Ag(NH_3)_2]^+(aq)$, $\quad K_2 = K_f$

$AgCl(s) + 2NH_3(aq) \rightleftharpoons [Ag(NH_3)_2]^+(aq) + Cl^-(aq)$

Initial	0.10 M	0	0
At equli.	(0.10 – 2x)	x	x

$K_1 = K_p = [Ag^+][Cl^-]$

$K_2 = K_f = [Ag(NH_3]_2 / [Ag^+][NH_3]^2$

$K_3 = K_{sp}K_f$

$K_3 = \frac{[Ag(NH_3)_2^+][Cl^-]}{[NH_3]^2}$

$= \frac{x^2}{(0.10 - 2x)^2}$

$= 1.8 \times 10^{-10} \times 1.0 \times 10^7$

$\frac{x}{(0.10 - 2x)} = \sqrt{0.00288} = 0.0536$

$x = 4.8 \times 10^{-3}$ M

43. If AgCl is not precipitated

$[Ag^+][Cl^-] \le K_{sp}$

Given $\quad [Cl^-] = 0.01$ M

$\therefore \quad [Ag^+](0.01) \le 1.8 \times 10^{-10}$

$\therefore \quad [Ag^+] \le 1.8 \times 10^{-8}$ M

$Ag^+ + 2NH_3 \rightleftharpoons [Ag(NH_3]_2^+]$

$K_f = \frac{[Ag(NH_3)_2^+]}{[Ag^+][NH_3]^2}$

Large value of K_f indicates that all the Ag^+ ion is complexed.

$\therefore \quad 1.6 \times 10^7 = \frac{0.1}{(1.8 \times 10^{-8})[NH_3]^2}$

$\therefore \quad [NH_3]^2 = 0.3472$

$[NH_3] = 0.59$ M

44. HCl decreases ionisation of H_2S and HS^- due to common ion effect. In HCl,

$[H_3O^+] = 0.01$ M

$K_{a_1} = 1.0 \times 10^{-7} = \frac{[H_3O^+][HS^-]}{[H_2S]}$

$\therefore 1.0 \times 10^{-7} = \frac{(0.01)[HS^-]}{0.05}$

$[HS^-] = 5 \times 10^{-7}$ M

$K_{a_2} = \frac{[H^+][S^{2-}]}{[HS^-]}$

$1.0 \times 10^{-14} = \frac{(0.01)[S^{2-}]}{[5 \times 10^{-7}]}$

$\therefore \quad [S^{2-}] = 5 \times 10^{-21}$ M

$[MS]$ is precipitate of $[M^{2+}][S^{2-}] > K_{sp}$

$[M^{2+}][S^{2-}] = 5 \times 10^{-27}$

MS	$[M^{2+}][S^{2-}]$	K_{sp}	ppt
CdS	5×10^{-27}	8×10^{-27}	$K_{sp} > [M^{2+}][S^{2-}]$
ZnS	5×10^{-27}	1.6×10^{-24}	No
MnS	5×10^{-27}	2.5×10^{-13}	No

45. $\quad K_{sp} = [Mg^{2+}][OH^-]^2$

$\log K_{sp} = \log[Mg^{2+}] + 2\log[OH^-]$

$\log[Mg^{2+}] = \log K_{sp} - 2\log[OH^-]$

$\log[Mg^{2+}] = \log K_{sp} + 2pOH$

On comparing,

$$y = c + mx$$
$$c = \log K_{sp} = OA = -11$$
$$\therefore \log[Mg^{2+}] = -11 + 2\,pOH$$
$$= -11 + 2[14 - pH]$$
$$\log[10^{-3}] = -11 + 2[14 - pH]$$
$$-3 = -11 + 28 - 2pH$$
$$2pH = 28 - 11 + 3 = 20$$
$$2pH = 20$$
$$\therefore pH = 10$$

46. $\underset{\substack{\text{Acid form} \\ 25\%}}{HIn} \rightleftharpoons H^+ + \underset{\substack{\text{Base form} \\ 75\%}}{In^-}$

$$pH = pK_{In} + \log\frac{[In^-]}{[HIn]}$$
$$4.63 = pK_{In} + \log\left(\frac{75}{25}\right)$$
$$= pK_{In} + 0.48$$
$$\therefore pK_{In} = 4.15$$

47. (i) $\underset{\substack{\text{Acid} \\ \text{(Red)}}}{HIn} \rightleftharpoons \underset{\substack{\text{Base} \\ \text{(Blue)}}}{In^-} + H^+$

$$K_a = \frac{[In^-][H^+]}{[HIn]}$$
$$K_a = \frac{[Base]}{[Acid]}[H^+]$$
$$[H^+] = K_a\frac{[Acid]}{[Base]}$$

Case **I** $[H^+]_I = 3.0 \times 10^{-5}\left(\frac{75}{25}\right)$

$$[H^+]_I = 9.0 \times 10^{-5}$$
$$\therefore pH = 5 - \log 9$$

Case **II**

$$[H^+]_{II} = 3.0 \times 10^{-5}\left(\frac{25}{75}\right) = 1 \times 10^{-5}$$
$$pH = 5.0$$
$$\therefore \text{Change} = 5.0 - (5 - \log 9)$$
$$= \log 9 = 0.95$$

(ii) Phenolphthalein is a weak acid

$$\underset{\substack{\text{Acid} \\ \text{Colourless}}}{HIn} \rightleftharpoons \underset{\substack{\text{Base} \\ \text{Pink}}}{In^-} + H^+$$
$$K_a = \frac{[In^-][H^+]}{[HIn]} = \frac{(pink)[H^+]}{[colourless]}$$
$$[H^+] = K_a\frac{(colourless)}{(pink)}$$
$$= K_a \times \left(\frac{10}{90}\right)$$
$$\therefore \log[H^+] = \log K_a + \log\left(\frac{1}{9}\right)$$
$$-\log[H^+] = -\log K_a - \log\left(\frac{1}{9}\right)$$
$$\therefore pH = pK_a + \log 9$$
$$= 9.40 + 0.95$$
$$= 10.35$$

Knowledge Confirmation Test 1

1. (a)	**2.** (b)	**3.** (b)	**4.** (d)	**5.** (b)	**6.** (c)	**7.** (a)	**8.** (d)	**9.** (b)	**10.** (b)
11. (c)	**12.** (d)	**13.** (d)	**14.** (d)	**15.** (b)	**16.** (a)	**17.** (a)	**18.** (b)	**19.** (a)	**20.** (b)
21. (b)	**22.** (b)	**23.** (c)	**24.** (d)	**25.** (c)	**26.** (b)	**27.** (d)	**28.** (c)		

Knowledge Confirmation Test 2

1. (c)	**2.** (c)	**3.** (a)	**4.** (c)	**5.** (a)	**6.** (c)	**7.** (c)	**8.** (d)	**9.** (d)	**10.** (a)
11. (b)	**12.** (b)	**13.** (a)	**14.** (b)	**15.** (d)	**16.** (b)	**17.** (c)	**18.** (c)	**19.** (b)	**20.** (d)
21. (b)	**22.** (c)	**23.** (a)	**24.** (b)	**25.** (d)	**26.** (b)	**27.** (b)	**28.** (a)	**29.** (b)	**30.** (a)
31. (a)	**32.** (d)	**33.** (b)	**34.** (c)	**35.** (a)					

Knowledge Confirmation Test 3

1. (b)	**2.** (a)	**3.** (b)	**4.** (a)	**5.** (d)	**6.** (b)	**7.** (a)	**8.** (c)	**9.** (b)	**10.** (a)
11. (c)	**12.** (b)	**13.** (a)	**14.** (b)	**15.** (a)	**16.** (a)	**17.** (b)	**18.** (a)	**19.** (c)	**20.** (d)
21. (a)	**22.** (b)	**23.** (c)	**24.** (b)	**25.** (b)					

Knowledge Confirmation Test 4

1. (a)	**2.** (a)	**3.** (b)	**4.** (b)	**5.** (c)	**6.** (c)	**7.** (c)	**8.** (d)	**9.** (d)	**10.** (d)
11. (b)	**12.** (a)	**13.** (c)	**14.** (d)	**15.** (a)	**16.** (b)	**17.** (c)	**18.** (b)	**19.** (a)	**20.** (d)
21. (b)	**22.** (a)	**23.** (c)	**24.** (d)	**25.** (b)	**26.** (d)	**27.** (b)	**28.** (c)	**29.** (b)	**30.** (d)
31. (c)	**32.** (d)	**33.** (d)	**34.** (c)	**35.** (d)	**36.** (a)	**37.** (a)			

Knowledge Confirmation Test 5

1. (c)	**2.** (c)	**3.** (d)	**4.** (a)	**5.** (d)	**6.** (a)	**7.** (a)	**8.** (b)	**9.** (a)	**10.** (d)
11. (c)	**12.** (c)	**13.** (b)	**14.** (c)	**15.** (a)	**16.** (d)	**17.** (a)	**18.** (b)	**19.** (b)	**20.** (c)
21. (b)	**22.** (d)	**23.** (c)	**24.** (b)	**25.** (a)	**26.** (a)	**27.** (c)	**28.** (c)	**29.** (a)	**30.** (b)

Knowledge Confirmation Test 6

1. (d)	**2.** (a)	**3.** (b)	**4.** (c)	**5.** (d)	**6.** (b)	**7.** (a)	**8.** (d)	**9.** (c)	**10.** (c)
11. (d)	**12.** (b)	**13.** (d)	**14.** (b)	**15.** (a)	**16.** (c)	**17.** (b)	**18.** (c)	**19.** (b)	**20.** (d)
21. (b)	**22.** (d)	**23.** (c)	**24.** (c)	**25.** (a)	**26.** (a)	**27.** (b)	**28.** (d)	**29.** (c)	**30.** (a)

Knowledge Confirmation Test 7

1. (b)	**2.** (a)	**3.** (d)	**4.** (a)	**5.** (b)	**6.** (c)	**7.** (c)	**8.** (d)	**9.** (a)	**10.** (d)
11. (a)	**12.** (b)	**13.** (c)	**14.** (a)	**15.** (d)	**16.** (b)				

Acid Test for JEE Main

Type I. MCQs with Only ONE Correct Alternate

1. (a) $MY \rightleftharpoons M^+ + Y^-$

$K_{sp} = S_1^2 = 6.2 \times 10^{-13}$

$\therefore \quad S_1 = 7.87 \times 10^{-7}$ M

$NY_3 \rightleftharpoons N^{3+} + 3Y^-$

$K_{sp} = 27S_2^4 = 6.2 \times 10^{-13}$

$S_2 = 3.89 \times 10^{-4}$ M

$S_2 > S_1$

Thus, (a) is correct.

2. (c) Boric acid is an acid because its molecules accept OH^- from water releasing proton. Reaction is given below:

$B[OH]_3 + H_2O \rightleftharpoons B[OH^-]_4 + H^+$

3. (d)

Salt	K_{sp}	Solubility
(a) AgI	8.3×10^{-17}	$S = \sqrt{K_{sp}} = 9.11 \times 10^{-9}$ M
(b) AgCl	1.8×10^{-10}	$S = \sqrt{K_{sp}} = 1.34 \times 10^{-5}$ M
(c) AgBr	5.0×10^{-13}	$S = \sqrt{K_{sp}} = 7.07 \times 10^{-7}$ M
(d) Ag_2CrO_4	1.1×10^{-12}	$S = \left(\frac{K_{sp}}{4}\right)^{1/3} = 6.50 \times 10^{-5}$ M

The salt which has maximum solubility will be precipitated last.

4. (a) V mL of 0.1 M NaOH $= \frac{V}{10}$ millimol

V mL of 0.01 M HCl $= \frac{V}{100}$ millimol

$\frac{V}{10} > \frac{V}{100}$, Thus, solution is alkaline.

$M[OH^-] = \frac{V/10 - V/100}{V + V} = \frac{0.09}{2}$

$\therefore \quad = 0.045$ M

$pOH = -\log[OH^-]$

$= -\log 0.045 = 1.35$

$pH = 12.65$

5. (b) $\Delta G° = -2.303\, RT \log K_{sp}$

63.3 kJ mol^{-1} $= -2.303 \times 8.3143$

$\times 10^{-3}$ kJ mol^{-1} K^{-1} $\times 298$ K $\log K_{sp}$

$\therefore \quad \log K_{sp} = -11.09$

$\therefore \quad K_{sp} = 8.00 \times 10^{-12}$

6. (c)

	H_2SO_4	H_2SO_3
	↑	↑
O.N.	+6	+4
	$HClO_3$	$HClO_4$
	↑	↑
O.N.	+5	+7

In ($HClO_4 \rightleftharpoons ClO_4^- + H^+$) oxidation number of Cl is maximum. Also negative charge is delocalised on four O-atoms. Thus, maximum resonance stabilised.

7. (c) Relative strength is measured in terms of$[H^+]$

By Ostwald's dilution law,

$[H^+] = \sqrt{K_a C}$

$\therefore \quad \frac{[H^+]_{HA_1}}{[H^+]_{HA_2}} = \sqrt{\frac{K_1 C_1}{K_2 C_2}}$

$= \sqrt{\frac{K_1}{K_2}}$, where $C_1 = C_2$

$= \sqrt{\frac{3.0 \times 10^{-4}}{1.8 \times 10^{-5}}} = 4.08 : 1$ or $4 : 1$

8. (b) If acid is weak, its K_a value is very low and pK_a $(= -\log K_a)$ is high.

9. (d) pH = 9, pOH = 5

Thus, $[OH^-] = 10^{-5}$

$10^{-5} = 1000 \times [OH^-]_A$

$[OH^-] = 1 \times 10^{-8}$

$\therefore \quad [pOH]_A = 8 \Rightarrow [pH]_A = 6$

10. (b) Binary electrolyte means (AB) type

$\therefore S = \sqrt{K_{sp}} = \sqrt{4 \times 10^{-10}} = 2 \times 10^{-5}$ M

11. (b) Hydrolysis of NaX is given by

$X^- + H_2O \rightleftharpoons HX + OH^-$

$x = \sqrt{\frac{K_h}{C}} = \sqrt{\frac{K_w}{K_a C}}$

$= \sqrt{\frac{1 \times 10^{-14}}{1 \times 10^{-5} \times 0.1}} = 1 \times 10^{-4}$

$\therefore$ % hydrolysis $= 1 \times 10^{-4} \times 100 = 0.01\%$

12. (a) H_3PO_2 is a monobasic acid

Thus, $\quad H_3PO_2 \rightleftharpoons H_2PO_2^-$

H_3PO_3 is a dibasic acid.

Thus,

$H_3PO_3 \rightleftharpoons H_2PO_3^- \rightleftharpoons HPO_3^{2-}$

Thus, HPO_2^{2-} and PO_3^{3-} are not formed.

13. (b) $\quad$ pH = 12

$\therefore \quad$ pOH = 2

$\therefore \quad [OH^-] = 1 \times 10^{-2}$ M

$Ba(OH)_2 \rightleftharpoons Ba^{2+} + 2OH^-$

$\therefore \quad [Ba^{2+}] = \frac{1}{2}[OH^-] = \left(\frac{1 \times 10^{-2}}{2}\right)$ M

$\therefore \quad K_{sp} = [Ba^{2+}][OH^-]^2$

$= \left(\frac{1 \times 10^{-2}}{2}\right)(1 \times 10^{-2})^2$

$= 5.0 \times 10^{-7}$

14. (d) When 0.01 M ammonium acetate is diluted to 0.001 M solution, then there is no change in the pH value.

Change in pH = 0

15. (a) pH = 2 (acidic) $\quad \therefore [H^+] = 1 \times 10^{-2}$

pH = 12 (basic)

$\therefore$ pOH = 2 $\quad \therefore [OH^-] = 1 \times 10^{-2}$ M

Thus, $[H^+] = [OH^-]$ in equal volumes

Thus, neutral solution pH = 7

16. (d) $A^- + H^+ \rightleftharpoons HA$

(Added; Weak acid)

HA and A^- are parts of buffer

$B^+ + OH^- \rightleftharpoons BOH$

(Added; Weak base)

BOH and B^+ are parts of buffer.

Thus, pH remains almost constant.

17. (d) 20 mL of 0.1 M CH_3COOH + 10 mL of 0.1 M NaOH

50% of CH_3COOH is converted to CH_3COONa.

Thus, $\quad [CH_3COOH] = [CH_3COONa]$

$\therefore \quad pH = pK_a + \log\frac{[CH_3COO^-]}{[CH_3COOH]} = pK_a$

Thus, correct.

10 mL of 0.05 M$(NH_4)_2SO_4$

$= 10$ mL of 0.1 M NH_4^+

10 mL of 0.1 M NH_4OH + 10 mL of 0.05 M $(NH_4)_2SO_4$

10 mL0.1 M NH_4^+

$pOH = pK_b + \log\frac{[NH_4^+]}{[NH_4OH]} = pK_b$

$\therefore \quad pH = (14 - pK_b)$

Thus, correct. Similarly (c).

18. (b) pH = 5

By Ostwald's dilution law,

$\therefore [H^+] = 10^{-5}$ M $= Cx$

$x = \frac{[H^+]}{(C)} = \frac{10^{-5}}{0.005} = 2 \times 10^{-3}$

$\therefore \quad \% = 0.2\%$

19. (a) BF_3 is electron deficient, thus lone-pair acceptor, thus Lewis acid. P, C, Si, have complete octet in fluorocompounds.

20. (c) $HA \rightleftharpoons H^+ + A^-$

By Ostwald's dilution law,

$K_a = \frac{Cx^2}{(1-x)} \approx Cx^2$

$\therefore \quad x = \sqrt{\frac{K_a}{C}}$

% ionisation $= 100\sqrt{\frac{K_a}{C}}$

Also, $HA \rightleftharpoons H^+ + A^-$

$C \quad 0 \quad 0$

$(C - Cx) \quad ? \quad Cx$

$$K_a = \frac{[H^+][A^-]}{[HA]}$$

$$\therefore [H^+] = K_a \frac{[HA]}{[A^-]}$$

$$= K_a \frac{C(1-x)}{Cx} = K_a\left(\frac{1-x}{x}\right)$$

$$\therefore \log[H^+] = \log K_a + \log\left(\frac{1}{x} - 1\right)$$

$$-\log[H^+] = -\log K_a + \log\left(\frac{1}{x} - 1\right)$$

$$pH = pK_a + \log\left(\frac{1}{x} - 1\right)$$

$$\log\left(\frac{1}{x} - 1\right) = (pH - pK_a)$$

$$\left(\frac{1}{x} - 1\right) = 10^{(pH - pK_a)}$$

$$\frac{1}{x} = 1 + 10^{(pH - pK_a)}$$

$$\therefore x = \frac{1}{1 + 10^{(pH - pK_a)}}$$

$$\text{Percent ionisation} = \frac{100}{1 + 10^{(pH - pK_a)}}$$

21. (a) $[NaOH] = \frac{4/40 \text{ mol}}{0.250 \text{ L}} = 0.4 \text{ M} = 0.4 \text{ N}$

$$[H_2SO_4] = \frac{4.9/98 \text{ mol}}{0.250 \text{ L}} = 0.2 \text{ M}$$

$$= 0.4 \text{ N}$$

Equivalent of NaOH ≡ Equivalent of H_2SO_4

Thus, neutral pH = 7

22. (b) $CN^- + H^+ \rightleftharpoons HCN,$

$$K_1 = \frac{1}{K_a(HCN)}$$

$$NH_4^+ \rightleftharpoons NH_3 + H^+, \quad K_2 = K_a(NH_4^+)$$

$$CN^- + NH_4^+ \rightleftharpoons NH_3 + HCN,$$

$$K_3 = K_1K_2$$

$$K_3 = \frac{[NH_3][HCN]}{[CN^-][NH_4^+]}$$

$$K_3 = \frac{5.76 \times 10^{-10}}{4.8 \times 10^{-10}} = 1.2$$

23. (b) $\Delta H°(HCN) > \Delta H°(CH_3COOH)$

Thus, CH_3COOH is stronger acid than HCN

$K_a(CH_3COOH) > K_a(HCN)$

$pK_a(CH_3COOH) < pK_a(HCN)$

24. (c) HCl causes common ion effect on HCOOH

$HCOOH \rightleftharpoons H^+ + HCOO^-$

$$K_a = \frac{[H^+][HCOO^-]}{[HCOOH]}$$

$$1.8 \times 10^{-4} = \frac{0.01[HCOO^-]}{0.01}$$

$$\therefore [HCOO^-] = 1.8 \times 10^{-4} \text{ M}$$

25. (d) Acid with least heat of neutralisation is the weakest acid, order being

$HA > HB > HC > HD$

$K_a \quad HA > HB > HC > HD$

$$\text{Degree of hydrolysis } (x) = \sqrt{\frac{K_w}{K_aC}}$$

$$\text{Thus,} \quad x \propto \sqrt{\frac{1}{K_a}}$$

Hence, weakest acid is maximum hydrolysed.

26. (b) $HCO_3^- \rightleftharpoons H^+ + CO_3^{2-}$

It is a buffer.

$$pH = pK_{a_2} + \log\frac{[CO_3^{2-}]}{[HCO_3^-]}$$

$$= 10.4 + \log\frac{0.2}{0.4} = 10.4 - \log 2$$

$$= 10.4 - 0.3 = 10.1$$

27. (c) Following equilibrium is set up on mixing. PO_4^{3-} is a proton acceptor and H_3PO_4 is a proton donor.

$PO_4^{3-} + H_3PO_4 \rightleftharpoons HPO_4^{2-} + H_2PO_4^-$

Mixture formed is a buffer of 0.05 M HPO_4^{2-} and 0.05 M $H_2PO_4^-$

$H_2PO_4^- \rightleftharpoons HPO_4^{2-} + H^+$

Second ionisation constant of H_3PO_4 (K_{a_2}) is involved.

$$\text{Thus, } pH = pK_{a_2} + \log\frac{[HPO_4^{2-}]}{[H_2PO_4^-]} = pK_{a_2}$$

28. (d) Degree of hydrolysis, $x = \sqrt{\frac{K_h}{C}}$

$$\text{and } K_h \text{ (hydrolysis constant)} = \frac{K_w}{K_a}$$

$$\therefore \quad x = \sqrt{\frac{K_w}{K_aC}}$$

$$\text{Thus,} \quad x \propto \sqrt{\frac{1}{K_a}}$$

Smaller the value of K_a, larger the degree of hydrolysis

Thus, [(b) < (a) < (c) < (d)].

29. (b) (a) 100 mL of 0.2 M (= 0.4 N) H_2SO_4 >100 mL of 0.3 N NaOH

Thus, acidic (pH < 7)

(b) 100 mL of 0.1 M CH_3COOH = 100 mL of 0.1 N NaOH.

At neutral point CH_3COONa is formed which is hydrolysed to basic solution. (pH > 7)

$CH_3COO^- + H_2O \rightleftharpoons CH_3COOH + OH^-$

(c) $CH_3COONa + HCl \rightleftharpoons CH_3COOH + NaCl$ (pH < 7)

(d) NH_4NO_3 is formed which is hydrolysed to form acidic solution. (pH < 7).

$NH_4^+ + H_2O \rightleftharpoons NH_4OH + H^+$

30. (a) Since, $pK_a = pK_b$, hence pH = 7

Thus $K_a = K_b = 1.8 \times 10^{-5}$

At any state of hydrolysis

$[NH_4^+] + [NH_3] = 0.150$ M

If, $\quad [NH_3] = x$

then $\quad [NH_4^+] = (0.150 - x)$ M ≈ 0.150 M

$NH_4^+ + H_2O \rightleftharpoons NH_3 + H_3O^+$

$\therefore \quad NH_4OH \rightleftharpoons NH_4^+ + OH^-$

$$K_b = \frac{[NH_4^+][OH^-]}{[NH_4OH]}$$

$$\text{and} \quad K_w = [H_3O^+][OH^-] = 1 \times 10^{-14}$$

$$K_h = \frac{[NH_3][H_3O^+]}{[NH_4^+]} = \frac{K_w}{K_b}$$

$$\frac{x \times 10^{-7}}{0.150} = \frac{1 \times 10^{-14}}{1.8 \times 10^{-5}}$$

$$x = 8.3 \times 10^{-4} \text{ M}$$

31. (b) $H_2S \rightleftharpoons H^+ + HS^-, \quad K_{a_1}$

$HS^- \rightleftharpoons H^+ + S^{2-}, \quad K_{a_2}$

$\therefore H_2S \rightleftharpoons 2H^+ + S^{2-}, \quad K = K_{a_1}K_{a_2}$

$$K = \frac{[H^+]^2[S^{2-}]}{[H_2S]} = K_{a_1}K_{a_2}$$

$$\therefore \quad [S^{2-}] = \frac{K_{a_1}K_{a_2}}{[H^+]^2}[H_2S]$$

$$= \frac{1.0 \times 10^{-21} \times 0.05}{(0.01)^2}$$

$$= 5.0 \times 10^{-19} \text{ M}$$

32. (a) $H_2SO_4 \rightleftharpoons H^+ + HSO_4^-,$

$[H_2SO_4] = [HSO_4^-] = 0.15$ M

$[H^+]$ due ot H_2SO_4 = 0.15 M

	HSO_4^-	$\rightleftharpoons$	SO_4^{2-}	$+ H^+$
Initial	0.15		0	0 mol L^{-1}
At equil.	(0.15 − x)		x	x mol L^{-1}

$[H^+]$ due to $HSO_4^- = x$ M

Total $[H^+]$ at equilibrium = (0.15 + x)

$$K_2 = \frac{[SO_4^{2-}][H^+]}{[HSO_4^-]}$$

$$0.0102 = \frac{(x)(0.15 + x)}{(0.15 - x)}$$

$$x = 8.9 \times 10^{-3} \text{ M}$$

$$= [SO_4^{2-}]$$

33. (b) Given, indicator with $K_b = 1.0 \times 10^{-10}$ is basic in nature.

At this state,

[ionised form] = [unionised form]

$\therefore$ pOH $= pK_b + \log\frac{[\text{ionised form}]}{[\text{unionised form}]}$

$\therefore$ pOH $= pK_b = 10$

$\therefore$ pH $= 14 - $ pOH $= 4$

34. (b) $HCOOH \rightleftharpoons H^+ + HCOO^-$

Initial C 0 0

At equil. $(C - Cx)$ Cx Cx

$$K_a = \frac{Cx^2}{(1-x)}$$

$$1.8 \times 10^{-4} = \frac{(0.001)(x^2)}{(1-x)}$$

$$\frac{x^2}{(1-x)} = 0.18$$

Thus, x can not be neglected.

$\therefore$ $x^2 + 0.18x - 0.18 = 0$

$$x = \frac{-0.18 + \sqrt{(0.18)^2 + 0.72}}{2} \Rightarrow x = 0.34$$

Thus, 34%

35. (c) $NH_3 + H_2O \rightleftharpoons NH_4^+ + OH^-$

Initial (mol L^{-1}) C 0 0

At equil. $(C - Cx)$ Cx Cx

Due to dissolution,

$[NH_4^+] = [OH^-] = Cx = 1.5 \times 10^{-3}$ M $= Cx$

$$K_b = \frac{[NH_4^+][OH^-]}{[NH_3]_{eq}}$$

$$\because \quad [NH_3]_{eq} = \frac{[NH_4^+][OH^-]}{K_b}$$

$$= \frac{(1.5 \times 10^{-3})^2}{1.8 \times 10^{-5}} = 0.125 \text{ M}$$

$\therefore$ $(C - Cx) = 0.125$

Total $[NH_3] = C = [NH_3]_{eq} + Cx$

$= 0.125 + 1.5 \times 10^{-3}$

$= 0.1265$ M

36. (d) Let, C = minimum initial concentration

$HA + H_2O \rightleftharpoons H_3O^+ + A^-$

Initial C 0 0

At equil. $(C - Cx)$ Cx Cx

$$K_a = \frac{Cx^2}{(1-x)}$$

We generally assume that $(1 - x) \approx 1$

but, we assume $(1 - x) \approx 0.9$

$\therefore$ $x = 0.1$

$$\therefore \quad K_a = \frac{C(0.1)^2}{(0.9)} = \frac{C \times 0.1 \times 0.1}{0.9}$$

$\therefore$ $C = 90\, K_a$

37. (d)

38. (c) $Hg_2Cl_2(s) \rightleftharpoons Hg_2^{2+} + 2Cl^-$

(S) $(2S)$

$K_{sp} = 4S^3$

$$S = \sqrt[3]{\frac{K_{sp}}{4}} = \sqrt[3]{\frac{3.2 \times 10^{-17}}{4}}$$

$= 2 \times 10^{-6}$ M

39. (d) B_2H_6 is electron-deficient in boron.

40. (a) pH = 12

pOH = 2

$[OH^-] = 10^{-2}$ M

$Ba(OH)_2 \rightleftharpoons Ba^{2+} + 2OH^-$

$$[Ba^{2+}] = \left(\frac{10^{-2}}{2}\right) \text{M}$$

$$K_{sp} = [Ba^{2+}][OH^-]^2$$

$$= \left(\frac{10^{-2}}{2}\right)(10^{-2})^2$$

$= 5.0 \times 10^{-7}$

41. (d) $Na + H_2O \rightleftharpoons NaOH + \frac{1}{2}H_2$

1 mol 1 mol

$$0.023 \text{ g} = \frac{0.023}{23} \text{ mol}$$

$= 0.001$ mol in 100 cm^3

$$[NaOH] = [OH^-] = \frac{0.001 \text{ mol}}{0.1 \text{ L}} = 0.01 \text{ M}$$

pOH = 2 $\Rightarrow$ pH = 12

42. (b) NaCl has no acidic nature, it only dilutes mixture.

$0.1 \text{ M } H_2SO_4 \equiv 0.2 \text{ N } H_2SO_4$

$$N(H^+)_{mix} = \frac{N_1V_1 + N_2V_2}{V_1 + V_2}$$

$$= \frac{0.1 \times 2 + 0.2 \times 2}{6} = 0.1 \text{ N}$$

pH $= -\log[H^+] = 1$

43. (a) $M_2X_3 \rightleftharpoons 2M^{3+} + 3X^{2-}$

$2S$ $3S$

(where, S = solubility)

$K_{sp} = (2S)^2 . (3S)^3 = 108S^5$

$2.2 \times 10^{-20} = 108S^5$

$S = 4.59 \times 10^{-5}$ M

For M_2X,

$M_2X \rightleftharpoons 2M^+ + X^{2-}$

$2S$ S

$K_{sp} = (2S)^2.(S)$

$K_{sp} = 4S^3$ M

$K_{sp} = 4(2 \times 4.59 \times 10^{-5})^3$

[$\because$ Solubility of M_2X = 2 × solubility of M_2X_3]

$= 3 \times 10^{-12}$

44. (d) $HCN \rightleftharpoons H^+ + CN^-$,

$K_a = 4.5 \times 10^{-10}$

$CH_3COOH \rightleftharpoons H^+ + CH_3COO^-$,

$K_a' = 1.5 \times 10^{-5}$

$CN^- + H^+ = HCN$, $K_a'' = \frac{1}{K_a}$

$CH_3COOH + CN^- \rightleftharpoons HCN + CH_3COO^-$,

$K_{eq} = K_a' . K_a''$

$$= 1.5 \times 10^{-5} \times \frac{1}{4.5 \times 10^{-10}} = 3.3 \times 10^4$$

45. (a) $K_w = [H_3O^+][OH^-] = 1 \times 10^{-16}$

$\therefore$ $[H_3O^+] = [OH^-] = 1 \times 10^{-8}$ M

$\therefore$ pH + pOH = 16

At pH = 8 (neutral)

pH < 8 acidic

pH > 8 basic

pH = 7.5 is acidic, turns blue litmus red.

46. (c) pH = 9.26 indicates $[NH_4OH] > [HCl]$ and thus mixture is a buffer since HCl will react with equivalent amount of NH_4OH forming NH_4Cl.

$M \times V$ = millimol

Let, x mL of 1 M HCl = x mL

$= 1 \times x = x$ mmol

$NH_4OH = (300 - x)$ mL

$= (300 - x)$ mmol

NH_4Cl formed = x mmol

NH_4OH unreacted

$= (300 - x) - x = (300 - 2x)$ mmol

pOH = 14 − 9.26 = 4.74

$pK_b = 14 - 9.26 = 4.74$

By Henderson-Hasselbalch equation,

$$\text{pOH} = pK_b + \log\frac{[NH_4^+]}{[NH_4OH]}$$

$$4.74 = 4.74 + \log\frac{x}{(300 - 2x)}$$

$$\Rightarrow \frac{x}{300 - 2x} = 1$$

$x = 100$ mL= volume of HCl

$(300 - x) = 200$ mL

= volume of NH_4OH, hence ratio is = 2 :1

47. (b) $C_6H_5NH_3^+ + H_2O \rightleftharpoons C_6H_5NH_3^+OH^- + H^+$

Y ... (acidic) X

Here, X is (acidic) and Y is $(C_6H_5NH_3^+)$

48. (a) $NaCl(aq) \rightleftharpoons Na^+(aq) + Cl^-(aq)$

Neutral (pH = 7)

At anode $Cl^- \longrightarrow \frac{1}{2}Cl_2 + e^-$

At cathode $Na^+ + e^- \longrightarrow Na$

$2Na + 2H_2O \longrightarrow NaOH + H_2$ basic (pH > 7)

49. (a) 0.01 M $Ba(OH)_2$ = 0.02 N $(Ba(OH)_2)$

$\therefore$ 50 mL of 0.02 N $Ba(OH)_2$

$\equiv V$ mL of 0.01 N HCl

$\therefore$ $V = 100$ mL

Total volume of mixture after neutralisation = 150 mL

$Ba(OH)_2$ = 50 mL of 0.1 M

$$= \frac{50 \times 0.01}{1000} = 5 \times 10^{-4} \text{ mol}$$

HCl = 100 mL of 0.01 M

$$= \frac{100 \times 0.01}{1000} = 1 \times 10^{-3} \text{ mol}$$

$$\underset{\substack{1\text{ mol} \\ 5\times10^{-2}\text{ mol}}}{Ba(OH)_2} + \underset{\substack{2\text{ mol} \\ 1\times10^{-3}\text{ mol}}}{2HCl} \longrightarrow \underset{\substack{1\text{ mol} \\ 5\times10^{-4}\text{ mol}}}{BaCl_2} + 2H_2O$$

$\therefore$ $BaCl_2$ formed

$= 5 \times 10^{-4}$ mol in 150 mL solution

$$\therefore [BaCl_2] = \frac{5 \times 10^{-4} \text{ mol}}{0.150 \text{ L}}$$

$$= 3.33 \times 10^{-3} \text{ M}$$

50. (a) Phenylalanine (amino acid) is proton acceptor as well as proton donor. Thus, it is amphiprotic. pH of this salt is given by

$$\text{pH} = \frac{pK_{a_1} + pK_{a_2}}{2} = \frac{1.82 + 9.13}{2}$$

$$= \frac{10.95}{2} = 5.48$$

51. (d) Buffer is mixture of V mL of 1 M NH_4Cl and $(1000 - V)$ mL of 1 M NH_4OH

pH = 9.8

$\therefore$ pOH = 4.2

$$\therefore \text{pOH} = pK_b + \log\frac{[NH_4Cl]}{[NH_4OH]}$$

$\because$ MV = millimol

$\therefore$ $[NH_4Cl] = V$ millimol

and $[NH_4OH] = (1000 - V)$ millimol

$$\therefore 4.20 = 4.74 + \log\frac{(V)}{(1000 - V)}$$

$$-0.54 = \log\left(\frac{V}{1000 - V}\right)$$

$$\log 0.28 = \log\left(\frac{V}{1000 - V}\right)$$

$$\therefore \frac{V}{1000 - V} = 0.288$$

$$V = 288 - 0.288\,V$$

$$\therefore V = 225 \text{ mL}$$

52. (c) $HA \rightleftharpoons H^+ + A^-$

$$\begin{matrix} 1 & 0 & 0 \\ (1-x) & x & x \end{matrix}$$

$x = 0.5$

$$\therefore \frac{[A^-]}{[HA]} = 1$$

$$\text{pH} = pK_a + \log\frac{[A^-]}{[HA]} = 4.5$$

$\therefore$ pOH = 14 − pH = 9.5

53. (c) It is a salt of strong base and weak acid

$$\underset{0.01\text{ M}}{(CH_3COO)_2Ca} \rightleftharpoons \underset{0.02\text{ M}}{2CH_3COO^-} + Ca^{2+}$$

$$\therefore \text{pH} = 7 + \frac{pK_a}{2} + \frac{\log C}{2}$$

$$= 7 + 2.37 + \frac{\log 0.02}{2}$$

$$= 9.37 - 0.85 = 8.52$$

54. (c) BA is a salt of weak acid and weak base.

$pK_a > pK_b$

$$\text{Thus, pH} = 7 + \left(\frac{pK_a - pK_b}{2}\right)$$

$$= 7 + \left(\frac{4.80 - 4.78}{2}\right)$$

$$= 7 + \frac{0.02}{2} = 7.01$$

55. (c) $\underset{\text{Colourless}}{PhH} + OH^- \rightleftharpoons \underset{\text{Pink}}{Ph^-} + H_2O$

In the titration of an acid by a base, pink colour is formed at the end point. This pink colour is due to Ph^- (quinonoid form). If base is weak (as NH_4OH), excess amount (other than equivalent point is to be added to reach equivalent point. Also Ph^- formed at the equivalent point, is hydrolysed back to PhH (colourless).

$Ph^- + H_2O \rightleftharpoons PhH + OH^-$

Thus, pink colour disappears.

56. (a) For mixture of weak acids

$$[H_3O^+] = \sqrt{K_1C_1 + K_2C_2}$$

$$= \sqrt{1.8 \times 10^{-4} \times 0.1 + 3.3 \times 10^{-4} \times 0.1}$$

$$= 7.14 \times 10^{-3} \text{ M}$$

57. (d) Refer theory of indicator.

58. (c) $\underset{\substack{\text{Colourless} \\ \text{(or light colour)}}}{HIn} \rightleftharpoons \underset{\text{Coloured}}{H^+ + In^-}$

$$\text{pH} = pK_a + \log\frac{[In^-]}{[HIn]}$$

When colour of the unionised form is observed.

$$\frac{[In^-]}{[HIn]} = \frac{1}{10}$$

$$\therefore \text{pH} = pK_a - 1$$

- When colour of the ionised form is observed

$$\frac{[In^-]}{[HIn]} = 10$$

$$\text{pH} = pK_a + 1$$

59. (d) (phenolate, O^-) + H_2O $\rightleftharpoons$ (phenol, OH) + OH^-

Solution is basic, pK_b (phenolate) = 4

$\therefore$ pK_a (phenol) = 10

$$\text{pH} = 7 + \frac{pK_a}{2} + \frac{\log C}{2}$$

$$= 7 + \frac{10}{2} + \log\frac{0.01}{2}$$

$$= 7 + 5 - 1 = 11$$

or (d) (phenolate, O^-) + H_2O $\rightleftharpoons$ (phenol, OH) + OH^-

if it is like as base, they by ostwalds dilution law,

$$\text{pOH} = \frac{1}{2}[pK_b - \log C] = \frac{1}{2}[4 - \log 0.01]$$

$$= \frac{1}{2}[4 + 2] = 3$$

pH = 3

Since, pH + pOH = 14

pH + 3 = 14

$\therefore$ pH = 11

60. (a) $AB_2(s) \rightleftharpoons \underset{S}{A^{2+}(aq)} + \underset{2S}{2B^-(aq)}$

$$K_{sp} = [A^{2+}][B^-]^2 = (S)(2S)^2 = 4S^3$$

$$= 4\,(1.0 \times 10^{-5})^3 = 4 \times 10^{-15}$$

In the presence of 0.1 M A^{2+}, solubility is decreased due to common ion effect.

$$[A^{2+}][B^-]^2 = 4 \times 10^{-15}$$

$$(0.1)[B^-]^2 = 4 \times 10^{-15}$$

$$[B^-] = 2.0 \times 10^{-7} \text{ M}$$

61. (d) $Al(OH)_3(s) \rightleftharpoons Al^{3+}(aq) + 3OH^-(s)$

Solubility = S mol L^{-1}

$$K_{sp} = [Al^{3+}][OH^-]^3 = (S)(3S)^3$$

$$27 \times 10^{-11} = 27S^4 \Rightarrow S^4 = 10^{-12}$$

$$S = 10^{-3} \text{ mol L}^{-1}$$

$$[Al^{3+}] = 1.0 \times 10^{-3} \text{ mol L}^{-1}$$

62. (d) pH = 1 means acidic solution.

and $[H^+]_{mix} = 0.1$ M, pH < 7

(a) N_1V_1 (acid) = N_2V_2 (base),

Thus, neutral.

$$\text{(b) } N(H^+) = \frac{55 \times 0.1 - 45 \times 0.1}{100}$$

$$[H^+] = \frac{5.5 - 4.5}{100} = 0.01 \text{ M}$$

pH = 2

(c) N_2V_2 (base) > N_1V_1 (acid)

alkaline solution, pH > 7

(d) $N(H^+) = \dfrac{75 \times 0.2 - 25 \times 0.2}{100}$

$= \dfrac{15 - 50}{100} = 0.1\,M$

pH = 1.0

63. (b) $CH_3COOH + KOH \rightleftharpoons CH_3COOK + H_2O$

but $CH_3COOH \equiv KOH$

CH_3COOK formed is hydrolysed to form alkaline solution

then, pH > 7

$pH = 7 + \dfrac{pK_a}{2} + \dfrac{\log C}{2}$

64. (a) $pH = pK_a + \log\dfrac{[\text{Conjugate base}]}{[\text{Acid}]}$

When ratio is 1 : 1

$pH = pK_a$

When ratio is 100 : 1

$pH' = pK_a + 2$

Thus, $pH' - pH = +2$

65. (c) pH (neutral) = 7

$\therefore$ pOH = 7

$\therefore$ $[OH^-]_1 = 10^{-7}$

pH = 12, pOH = 2

$\therefore$ $[OH^-]_2 = 10^{-2}$

Thus, $\dfrac{[OH^-]_2}{[OH^-]_1} = \dfrac{10^{-2}}{10^{-7}} = 10^5$

66. (d) $C_5H_5N + H_2O \rightleftharpoons C_5H_5NH^+ + OH^-$

$\alpha = \sqrt{\dfrac{K_b}{C}} = \sqrt{\dfrac{1.7 \times 10^{-9}}{0.10}} = 1.3 \times 10^{-4}$

$\therefore$ % $\alpha = 1.3 \times 10^{-4} \times 100 = 0.013\%$

67. (c) Larger the oxidation number of central atom, stronger the acid. Also, greater the delocalisation of negative charge, greater the acid strength.

68. (d) H_2O is the weakest acid and OH^- is the strongest base. H_2O is the weakest base and thus, H_3O^+ is the strongest acid.

69. (c) For weak monobasic acid

$pH = \dfrac{1}{2}(pK_a - \log C)$

$3 \times 2 = pK_a - \log(0.1) = pK_a + 1$

$pK_a = 5$

$\therefore$ $K_a = 1.0 \times 10^{-5}$

70. (a) 20.0 g NaOH is added to 0.5 L

$NaOH = \left(\dfrac{20}{40}\right) = 0.50$ mol

1.5 M NH_4Cl in 0.5 L = 1.5×0.5

= 0.75 mol

	NH_4Cl +	OH^- ⟶	NH_4OH +	Cl^-
Initial mol	0.75	0.5	0	0
At equil.	0.25	–	0.5	

Mixture is a buffer containing 0.25 mol NH_4Cl and 0.5 mol NH_4OH is 0.5 L solution.

$\therefore$ $pOH = pK_a + \log\dfrac{[NH_4Cl]}{[NH_4OH]}$

$= 4.74 + \log\dfrac{0.25}{0.50}$

$pOH = 4.74 + \log(1/2) = 4.44$

$\therefore$ pH = 14 – pOH

= 14 – 4.44 = 9.56

71. (b) $pH = pK_a + \log\dfrac{[HPO_4^{2-}]}{[H_2PO_4^{2-}]}$

$\because$ $7.40 = 7.10 + \log\dfrac{[HPO_4^{2-}]}{[H_2PO_4^{2-}]}$

$\therefore$ $\log\dfrac{[HPO_4^{2-}]}{[H_2PO_4^-]} = 0.30$

$\dfrac{[HPO_4^{2-}]}{[H_2PO_4^-]} = \dfrac{2}{1}$ (Antilog of 0.3 = 2.0)

$\therefore$ $\dfrac{[H_2PO_4^{2-}]}{[HPO_4^{2-}]} = \dfrac{1}{2}$ or 1: 2

72. (d) $HA + OH^- \rightleftharpoons H_2O + A^-$, $K_1 = 10^9$

$\therefore$ $A^- + H_2O \rightleftharpoons HA + OH^-$, $K_1' = 10^{-9}$

It is also K_b of A^- (base)

$\therefore$ $pK_b = 9\ (= -\log K_b)$

Solution is alkaline and $pK_a(HA) = 5$

$\therefore$ $pH = 7 + \dfrac{pK_a}{2} + \dfrac{\log C}{2}$

$= 7 + \dfrac{5}{2} + \dfrac{\log 0.1}{2}$

$= 9.5 - 0.5 = 9.0$

■ For a weak acid (HA) and its conjugate base (A^-)

$K_a K_b = 1 \times 10^{-14} = K_w$

$pK_a + pK_b = 14 = pK_w$

73. (c) *A* is proton acceptor, thus a base and changes to *C* (conjugate acid of (*A*).
(*B*) is proton donor and, thus a conjugate base is formed.

74. (a) It is a basic buffer,

$pOH = pK_b + \log\dfrac{[NH_4^+]}{[NH_3]}$

If minimum amount of strong acid $= x$ mol L^{-1} then

	NH_3 +	H^+ ⇌	NH_4^+
Initially	0.10 M		0.10 M
H^+ added		x M	
at equil.	(0.10 – x) M		(0.10 + x) M

For buffer capacity, *d*(pH) or *d*(pOH)

Due to increase in $[NH_4^+]$, pOH increases

$\therefore$ $(pOH + 1) = pK_b + \log\left(\dfrac{0.10 + x}{0.10 - x}\right)$ ... (ii)

From Eqs. (i) and (ii),

$\therefore$ $1 = \log\left(\dfrac{0.10 + x}{0.10 - x}\right)$

$\therefore$ $\left(\dfrac{0.10 + x}{0.10 - x}\right) = 10$

$\therefore$ $x = 0.082$

Thus, buffer capacity $= \dfrac{x}{d(pOH)} = 0.082$

75. (c) $pH = pK_a \pm 1$

76. (d) $pH = pK_a \pm 1$

77. (d) OH^- and H^+ are hydrated

$OH^- + H_2O \longrightarrow H_3O_2^- \xrightarrow{H_2O} H_5O_3^-$

$H^+ + H_2O \longrightarrow H_3O^+ \xrightarrow{H_2O} H_5O_2^+$

78. (c) In a mixture of weak acid (resultant concentration C_1 mol L^{-1} and ionisation constant K_1) and a strong acid (resultant concentration C_2 mol L^{-1}) total $[H_3O^+]$ is

$[H_3O^+] = \dfrac{C_2 + \sqrt{C_2^2 + 4K_1C_1}}{2}$

Due to dilution by one another

$C_1(AcOH) = \dfrac{0.2}{2} = 0.1\,M$

$C_2(HCl) = \dfrac{0.2}{2} = 0.1\,M$

$\therefore$ $[H_3O^+] = \dfrac{(0.1) + \sqrt{(0.1)^2 + 4 \times 1.8 \times 10^{-5} \times 0.1}}{2}$

= 0.1 M

$\therefore$ $pH = -\log[H_3O^+] = 1.00$

■ Alternately AcOH is a weak acid.Its $[H_3O^+] <<< 0.2$ M.

It simply cause dilution of HCl.

Resultant [HCl] due to dilution

$= \dfrac{0.2 \times 50}{100} = 0.1\,M$

79. (d) $H_2SO_3 + NaOH \rightleftharpoons NaHSO_3 + H_2O$

20 mL of 0.160 M NaOH = 3.2 millimol

NaOH 40 mL of 0.080 M H_2SO_3

= 3.2 millimol H_2SO_3

Thus, H_2SO_3 is converted into $NaHSO_3$ and HSO_3^- is amphiprotic

(H^+ is ion donor as well as acceptor)

$\underset{\text{Acid}}{HSO_3^-} \rightleftharpoons H^+ + SO_3^{2-}$

$\underset{\text{Base}}{HSO_3^-} + H^+ \rightleftharpoons H_2SO_4$

$$pH = \frac{pK_{a_1} + pK_{a_2}}{2}$$
$$= \frac{1.82 + 7.20}{2} = 4.51$$

80. (c) $Zn^{2+} + H_2O \rightleftharpoons Zn(OH)^+ + H^+$

$K_h = 1 \times 10^{-9}$

$K_w = 1 \times 10^{-14}$

$\Rightarrow \quad K_h = \frac{K_w}{K_b(Zn(OH)_2)}$

$\therefore \quad K_b = \frac{K_w}{K_h} = \frac{1\times10^{-14}}{1\times10^{-9}} = 1 \times 10^{-5}$

$pK_b = 5$

$\therefore \quad pH = 7 - \left(\frac{pK_b + \log C}{2}\right)$

$= 7 - \frac{(5-3)}{2} = 6.0$

Or Zn^{2+} furnishes H^+, thus is a weak acid.

By Ostwald's dilution law,

$[H^+] = \sqrt{K_a C}$

$= \sqrt{1\times10^{-9} \times 10^{-3}} = 1\times10^{-6}$ M

$\therefore$ pH = 6

81. (d) pH = 2, $[H^+]_1 = 10^{-2}$ M

pH = 6, $[H^+]_2 = 10^{-6}$ M

$\therefore \quad \frac{[H^+]_1}{[H^+]_2} = \frac{10^{-2} \text{ M}}{10^{-6} \text{ M}} = 10^4$ times = 10000

82. (c) $HCOO^- + H_2O \rightleftharpoons HCOOH + OH^-$

$K_h = \frac{K_w}{K_a} = \frac{1\times10^{-14}}{2\times10^{-4}} = 5\times10^{-11}$

83. (b) $CH_3NH_2 + H^+Cl^- \rightleftharpoons CH_3NH_3^+ + Cl^-$

Initial	0.1	0.08	0
Final	0.02	—	0.08 M

$CH_3NH_2 + H_2O \rightleftharpoons CH_3NH_3^+ + OH^-$

$K_b = \frac{[CH_3NH_3^+][OH^-]}{[CH_3NH_2]}$

$\Rightarrow \quad 5\times10^{-4} = \frac{(0.08)[OH^-]}{(0.02)}$

$[OH^-] = 1.25\times10^{-4}$ M

$[H^+] = \frac{K_w}{[OH^-]} = \frac{1\times10^{-14}}{1.25\times10^{-4}}$

$= 8\times10^{-11}$ M

84. (c) $K_a = 1\times10^{-5}$

$\therefore pK_a = 5$

$HIn \rightleftharpoons H^+ + In^-$

$pH = pK_a + \log\frac{[In^-]}{[HIn]}$

$\Rightarrow \quad 5 = 5 + \log\frac{[In^-]}{[HIn]}$

$\therefore \quad \frac{[In^-]}{[HIn]} = 1$

Thus, $[In^-] = [HIn]$

Thus, 50% ionisation.

85. (d) $[Hg^{2+}] = 2.0$ millimol in 100 mL solution

$= \frac{2\times10^{-3}\text{ mol}}{0.1 \text{ L}} = 2\times10^{-2}$ M

$= 0.02$ M

Since, stability constant of $HgCl_2$ is large (1.65×10^{13}) and $[Hg^{2+}]$ should be small.

At the end point

$[Cl^-] = 2[Hg^{2+}]$

$[HgCl_2] = 0.020 - [Hg^{2+}]$

≈ 0.02 M

$\therefore \quad \frac{[HgCl_2]}{[Hg^{2+}][Cl^-]^2} = 1.65\times10^{13}$

$\frac{0.02}{[Hg^{2+}][2Hg^{2+}]^2} = 1.65\times10^{13}$

$\therefore \quad 4[Hg^{2+}]^3 = \frac{0.02}{1.65\times10^{13}}$

$\therefore \quad [Hg^{2+}] = 6.72\times10^{-6}$ M

86. (a) pH of a buffer should be within ($pK_a \pm 1$).

87. (d) $Fe(OH)_3(s) \rightleftharpoons Fe^{3+}(aq) + 3OH^-(aq)$, $K_1 = K_{sp}$

$Fe^{3+}(aq) + 3C_2O_4^{2-}(aq) \rightleftharpoons [Fe(C_2O_4)_3]^{3-}(aq)$, $K_2 = K_f$

$Fe(OH)_3(s) + 3C_2O_4^{2-}(aq) \rightleftharpoons [Fe(C_2O_4)_3^{3-}](aq) + 3OH^-(aq)$;

Initial	0.10	0	0
Change	$-3x$	x	$3x$

$K_3 = K_{sp}K_f$

$\therefore \quad K_3 = \frac{[Fe(C_2O_4)_3^{3-}][OH^-]^3}{[C_2O_4^{2-}]^3}$

$4\times10^{-38}\times2\times10^{20} = \frac{x\times(3x)^3}{(0.10-3x)^3}$

$8\times10^{-18} = \frac{27x^4}{(0.1-3x)^3} \approx \frac{27x^4}{(0.1)^3}, x<<1$

$\therefore \quad 27x^4 = 8\times10^{-21}$

$x^4 = \frac{8\times10^{-21}}{27}$

$x = 4.15\times10^{-6}$ M

88. (c) Moles of $[H_2S] = \frac{pV}{RT}$

$= \frac{\left(\frac{748}{760}\right)\left(\frac{30.4}{1000}\right)}{0.0821\times296}$

$= 1.23\times10^{-3}$ mol in 338 mL solution

$\therefore \quad [H_2S] = \frac{1.23\times10^{-3}}{0.338}$ mol L^{-1}

$= 3.63\times10^{-3}$ M

Thus, solubility of $H_2S = 3.63\times10^{-3}$ M

$\therefore \quad [Ag^+] = (3.63\times10^{-3})\times2$

$K_{sp} = [Ag^+][BrO_3^-] = S^2$

$= (3.63\times10^{-3}\times2)^2$

$= 5.27\times10^{-5}$

89. (b) Depression in freezing point

For $ClCH_2COOH$,

$HA \rightleftharpoons H^+ + A^-$

$\Delta T_f = mK_f(i)$, i = vant' Hoff factor

$= 0.15\times1.86(1+x)$

By Ostwald's dilution law,

$x = \sqrt{\frac{K_a}{C}} = \sqrt{\frac{1.4\times10^{-3}}{0.15}} = 0.0966$

$\therefore \quad \Delta T_f = 0.15\times1.86\times1.0966$

$= 0.306°$

For CH_3COOH, let molality be $= m$ mol kg^{-1}

$\Delta T_f = 0.306°$

Let degree of ionisation of $CH_3COOH = \alpha$

then, $\Delta T_f = mK_f(1+\alpha)$

$0.306 = m\times1.86\times(1+\alpha)$

$m = \frac{0.306}{1.86(1+\alpha)}$

Also, by Ostwald's dilution law,

$\alpha = \sqrt{\frac{K_a}{C}} = \sqrt{\frac{K_a}{m}}$

$\alpha = \sqrt{\frac{1.8\times10^{-5}\times1.86(1+\alpha)}{0.306}}$

$\alpha^2 = 1.094\times10^{-4}(1+\alpha)$

$\alpha^2 - 1.094\times10^{-4}\alpha - 1.094\times10^{-4} = 0$

$\therefore \alpha = \frac{1.094\times10^{-4} + \sqrt{(1.094\times10^{-4})^2 + 4\times1.094\times10^{-4}}}{2}$

$= 0.0104$

$\therefore$ Molality of CH_3COOH

$= \frac{0.306}{1.86\times(1+\alpha)} = \frac{0.306}{1.86\times1.0104}$

$= 0.1628$ mol kg^{-1}

$= 9.77$ g kg^{-1}

90. (a) $C_6H_4(COOH)(COO^-)$ is amphiprotic

$C_6H_4(COOH)(COO^-)$ (Acid) $+ H_2O \rightleftharpoons C_6H_4(COO^-)(COO^-) + H_3O^+$

$C_6H_4(COOH)(COO^-)$ (Base) $+ H_2O \rightleftharpoons C_6H_4(COOH)_2 + OH^-$

$\therefore \quad [H_3O^+] = \sqrt{K_{a_1}K_{a_2}}$

$= \sqrt{(1.1 \times 10^{-3})(3.7 \times 10^{-6})}$

$= 6.4 \times 10^{-5}$

$\therefore \quad pH = -\log [H_3O]^+$

$= -\log (6.4 \times 10^{-5}) = 4.2$

91. (b) NH_4Cl solution is acidic due to hydrolysis.

$NH_4^+ + H_2O \rightleftharpoons NH_4OH + H^+$

$pH = 7 - \frac{pK_b}{2} - \frac{\log C}{2}$

$= 7 - \frac{4.74}{2} - \frac{\log 0.5}{2} = 4.78$

pH is to be increased from 4.78 to 7.00. Thus, NH_3 is to be added.

By Henderson-Hasselbalch equation,

$pH = pK_b + \log \frac{[NH_4^+]}{[NH_3]}$

$7 = 4.74 + \log \frac{0.5}{[NH_3]}$

$\log \frac{0.5}{[NH_3]} = 2.26$

$\frac{0.5}{[NH_3]} = 181.97$

$\therefore \quad [NH_3] = \frac{0.5}{181.97}$

$= 2.75 \times 10^{-3}$ M (mol L^{-1})

$= \frac{2.75 \times 10^{-3}}{2}$ = in 0.5 L

$= 1.375 \times 10^{-3}$ mol

Provided $[NH_3] = 10$ M

Thus, 1.375×10^{-3} mol NH_3 is in

$= \frac{1000}{10} \times 1.375 \times 10^{-3}$ mL NH_3

≈ 0.15 mL $= 0.05 \times n$ drops

$\therefore \quad n = 3$ drops of NH_3

92. (d) $[Ca^{2+}] = 115$ ppm

$= 115$ g in 10^6 mL water

$= \left(\frac{115}{40}\right)$ mol in 10^6 mL

$\therefore \quad = \frac{115}{40} \times 10^{-3}$ mol L^{-1}

$= 2.875 \times 10^{-3}$ mol L^{-1}

Also, $[Ca^{2+}][F^-]^2 = K_{sp}$

$\therefore \quad [F^-]^2 = \frac{K_{sp}}{[Ca^{2+}]}$

$[F^-] = \sqrt{\frac{K_{sp}}{[Ca^{2+}]}}$

$= \sqrt{\frac{5.3 \times 10^{-9}}{2.875 \times 10^{-3}}}$

$= 1.36 \times 10^{-3}$ M (mol L^{-1})

$= 1.36 \times 10^{-3} \times 19$ g L^{-1}

$= 0.02584$ g L^{-1}

$= \frac{0.02584 \times 10^6}{10^3}$ g in 10^6 mL

$= 25.84$ ppm

93. (b) I^- (from PbI_2) $+ Ag^+(aq) \longrightarrow AgI(s)$

$PbF_2(s) \rightleftharpoons Pb^{2+}(aq) + 2I^-(aq)$

$[Pb^{2+}][I^-]^2 = K_{sp}$

$(S)(2S)^2 = 7.1 \times 10^{-9}$

$\therefore \quad S = \sqrt[3]{\frac{7.1 \times 10^{-9}}{4}}$

$= 1.21 \times 10^{-3}$ M

$\therefore \quad [I^-]$ in $PbI_2 = 2S = 2.42 \times 10^{-3}$ M

By titration,

$\underset{AgNO_3}{M_1V_1} = \underset{I^-}{M_2V_2}$

$M_1(13.3) = 2.42 \times 10^{-3} \times 25$

$\therefore \quad M_1 = 4.55 \times 10^{-3}$ M

94. (c) $Mg(OH)_2(s) \rightleftharpoons Mg^{2+}(aq) + 2OH^-(aq)$

$[Mg^{2+}][OH^-]^2 = K_{sp}$

Solubility of $Mg(OH)_2$

= Solubility of Mg^{2+}

$= \frac{0.65}{58}$ mol L^{-1}

$\therefore \quad [OH^-]^2 = \frac{1.8 \times 10^{-11} \times 58}{0.65}$

$[OH^-] = 4.0 \times 10^{-5}$

$\therefore \quad pOH = 4.4$

$pH = 14 - pOH = 9.60$

95. (b) $CaSO_4(s) \rightleftharpoons Ca^+(aq) + SO_4^{2-}(aq)$

$K_{sp} = [Ca^{2+}][SO_4^{2-}]$

$9.1 \times 10^{-6} = S^2$

$\therefore$ S(solubility of $CaSO_4$) $= \sqrt{9.1 \times 10^{-6}}$

$= 3.017 \times 10^{-3}$ M

3.017×10^{-3} M $= 3.017 \times 10^{-3} \times 136$ g L^{-1}

$= \frac{3.017 \times 10^{-3} \times 136 \times 10^6}{10^3}$ ppm

$= 410.3$ ppm

131 parts is in $= 10^6$ parts

Thus, 416.3 parts is in $= \frac{10^6 \times 410.3}{131}$

$= 3.132 \times 10^6$ parts

Thus, water to be evaporated

$= 3.132 \times 10^6 - 1.0 \times 10^6$

$= 2.132 \times 10^6$ parts

Thus, fraction of water to be evaporated.

$= \frac{2.132 \times 10^6}{3.132 \times 10^6} = 0.68$

96. (c) $BaC_2O_4(s) \rightleftharpoons \underset{S}{Ba^{2+}(aq)} + \underset{S}{C_2O_4^{2-}(aq)}$

$\underset{0.5\text{ M}}{Na_2C_2O_4(aq)} \rightleftharpoons 2Na^+(aq) + C_2O_4^{2-}(aq)$

Total $[C_2O_4^{2-}] = (S + 0.05) \approx 0.05$ M

$[Ba^{2+}] = S$

$S \times 0.05 = K_{sp} = 2.2 \times 10^{-7}$

$\therefore \quad S = \frac{2.2 \times 10^{-7}}{0.05} = 4.4 \times 10^{-6}$ M

97. (a) Let solubility of AgCN(s) in buffer $= x$ mol L^{-1}

$AgCN(s) \rightleftharpoons Ag^+(aq) + CN^-(aq)\ K_1 = K_{sp}$

$CN^-(aq) + H^+(aq) \rightleftharpoons HCN \cdot K_2 = \frac{1}{K_a}$

$\therefore \quad AgCN(s) + H^+(aq) \rightleftharpoons \underset{x}{Ag^+(aq)} + \underset{x}{HCN}$

Buffer (pH = 3)

$\therefore \quad K_3 = \frac{[Ag^+][HCN]}{[H^+]} = \frac{x^2}{10^{-3}} = \frac{K_{sp}}{K_a}$

$x^2 = \frac{1.2 \times 10^{-16} \times 10^{-3}}{4.8 \times 10^{-10}}$

$x = 1.60 \times 10^{-5}$ M

98. (c) $MS(s) \rightleftharpoons M^{2+}(aq) + S^{2-}(aq)$;

$K_{sp} = [M^{2+}][S^{2-}]$

$\therefore \quad [S^{2-}] = \frac{K_{sp}}{[M^{2+}]} = \frac{6.0 \times 10^{-21}}{(0.05)}$

$= 1.2 \times 10^{-19}$

Also, $H_2S \rightleftharpoons 2H^+ + S^{2-}$, $K_a = K_1K_2$

$= 1.3 \times 10^{-20}$

$\therefore \quad [S^{2-}][H^+]^2 = K_{a_1}K_{a_2}[H_2S]$

$(1.2 \times 10^{-19})[H^+]^2 = 1.3 \times 10^{-20} \times 0.1$

$\therefore \quad [H^+]^2 = 0.01083$

$\therefore \quad [H^+] = 0.104$

$\therefore \quad pH = -\log[H^+] = 0.983$

99. (d) $[H_3O^+]$ due to H_2SO_4 in first step

$= 0.36$ M

	$HSO_4^-(aq)$	$\rightleftharpoons$	$H^+(aq)$	+	$SO_4^{2-}(aq)$
Initial	0.36		0		0
At equil.	$(0.36 - x)$		x		x

Total $[H^+] \rightleftharpoons (x + 0.36)$M

$\therefore \quad K_2 = \frac{[H^+][SO_4^{2-}]}{[HSO_4^-]}$

$$1.26 \times 10^{-2} = \frac{(0.36 + x)(x)}{(0.36 - x)}$$

$$1.26 \times 10^{-2}(0.36 - x) = 0.36x + x^2$$

$$0.004536 - 1.26 \times 10^{-2}x = 0.36x + x^2$$

$$\therefore \; x^2 + 0.3726x - 0.0045 = 0$$

$$x = \frac{-0.3726 + \sqrt{(0.3726)^2 + 4 \times 0.0045}}{2}$$

$$= 0.0118 \text{ M}$$

Thus, total $[H_3O^+]$

$$= 0.36 + 0.0118 = 0.3718 \text{ M}$$

100. (d) Salt of weak acid and strong base is most basic due to hydrolysis of anion.

$$CH_3COOK(aq) + H_2O(l) \rightleftharpoons CH_3COOH(aq) + KOH(aq)$$

$$\Downarrow \qquad \Downarrow$$

$$CH_3COO^-(aq) + K^+(aq) + H_2O(l) \rightleftharpoons CH_3COOH(aq) + K^+(aq) + OH^-(aq)$$

$$\text{Net}: CH_3COO^-(aq) + H_2O(l) \rightleftharpoons \underset{\text{Weak acid}}{CH_3COOH(aq)} + \underset{\text{Free } (OH^-) \text{ ion}}{OH^-(aq)}$$

$FeCl_3$ is a salt of strong acid and weak base-acidic.

$Pb(CH_3COO)_2$ is a salt of weak acid and weak base-neutral.

$Al(CN)_3$ is a salt of weak acid and weak base-neutral.

101. (a) Methyl orange behaves like a weak base

$$\underset{\text{Yellow in base}}{MeOH} \rightleftharpoons \underset{\text{Red}}{Me^+ + OH^-}$$

In presence of base, equilibrium is in left hand side, hence it is yellow in colour. When strong acid is added equilibrium is displaced towards right giving red colour in acid.

$$MeOH + H^+ \rightleftharpoons \underset{\text{Red in acid}}{Me^+} + H_2O$$

Thus, colour changes from yellow to pinkish red.

102. (a) $Ba^+(aq) + SO_4^{2-}(aq) \longrightarrow BaSO_4(s) \downarrow$

$[SO_4^{2-}]_{mix}$ from Na_2SO_4

When 50 mL of 1 M is diluted to 500 mL

$$[SO_4^{2-}] = \frac{50 \times 1}{500} = 0.1 \text{ M}$$

Thus, $[Ba^{2+}]$ when it begins to precipitate

$$= \frac{K_{sp}}{[SO_4^{2-}]} = \frac{1 \times 10^{-10}}{0.1}$$

$$= 1.1 \times 10^{-9} \text{ M}$$

Volume of $[Ba^{2+}] = 500 - 50 = 450$ mL

Thus, 450 mL of $M'Ba^{2+}$ is diluted to 500 mL of 1×10^{-9} M.

$$\therefore \quad 450 \times M' = 500 \times 1 \times 10^{-9}$$

$$M'(Ba^{2+}) = \frac{500}{450} \times 10^{9}$$

$$= 1.1 \times 10^{-9} \text{ M}$$

103. (d) $H_2S(aq) \overset{K_{a_1}}{\rightleftharpoons} HS^-(aq) + H^+(aq)$

$$HS^-(aq) \overset{K_{a_2}}{\rightleftharpoons} S^{2-}(aq) + H^+(aq)$$

$$K_{a_1} = \frac{[HS^-][H^+]}{[H_2S]}$$

$$K_{a_2} = \frac{[S^{2-}][H^+]}{[HS^-]}$$

$$\therefore \quad K_{a_1}K_{a_2} = \frac{[H^+]^2 [S^{2-}]}{[H_2S]}$$

$$1.0 \times 10^{-7} \times 1.2 \times 10^{-13} = \frac{(0.20)^2 [S^{2-}]}{0.10}$$

$$[S^{2-}] = 3 \times 10^{-20} \text{ M}$$

104. (b) $\text{pH} = 7 + \left(\frac{pK_a - pK_b}{2}\right)$

$$= 7 + \left(\frac{3.2 - 3.4}{2}\right) = 6.9$$

BA is a salt of weak acid and weak base.

105. (d) pH = 1

$$\therefore \; [H^+] = 10^{-1} = 0.1 \text{ M}$$

$$\text{pH} = 2$$

$$\therefore \; [H^+] = 10^{-2} = 0.01 \text{ M}$$

For dilution of HCl,

$$M_1V_1 = M_2V_2$$

$$0.1 \times 1 = 0.01 \times V_2$$

$$V_2 = 10 \text{ L}$$

Volume of water to be added

$$= 10 - 1 = 9.0 \text{ L}$$

106. (c) $HQ = H^+ + Q^-$

$[H^+] = \sqrt{K_aC}$ (by Ostwald's dilution law)

$$[H^+] = 10^{-pH} = 10^{-3} \text{ M}$$

$$C = 0.1 \text{ M}$$

$$\text{Thus,} \quad 10^{-3} = \sqrt{K_a \times 0.1}$$

$$10^{-6} = K_a \times 0.1$$

$$\therefore \quad K_a = 1 \times 10^{-5}$$

107. (c) Let molar solubility of $Cr(OH)_3$ $= S$ mol L^{-1}

$$Cr(OH)_3(s) \rightleftharpoons \underset{S}{Cr^{3+}(aq)} + \underset{3S}{3OH^-(aq)}$$

$$K_{sp} = 1.6 \times 10^{-30} = [Cr^{3+}][OH^-]^3$$

$$(S)(3S)^3 = 27S^4$$

$$\therefore \quad S^4 = \frac{1.6 \times 10^{-30}}{27}$$

$$S = \sqrt[4]{\frac{1.6 \times 10^{-30}}{27}}$$

108. (a) pH of solution = 5

For a weak monobasic acid,

$$\text{pH} = \frac{1}{2}(pK_a - \log C)$$

$$5 = \frac{1}{2}(pK_a - \log 1)$$

$$pK_a = 10 \quad \therefore K_a = 1 \times 10^{-10}$$

or proceed as in Q-106.

109. (a) Only in reaction (II), $H_2PO_4^-$ gives H^+ to H_2O. Thus, behaves as an acid.

110. (c) $H_2CO_3 \rightleftharpoons H^+ + HCO_3^-$;

$$K_1 = 4.2 \times 10^{-7}$$

$$HCO_3^- \rightleftharpoons H^+ + CO_3^{2-};$$

$$K_2 = 4.8 \times 10^{-11}$$

$$\therefore \; [H^+] = [HCO_3^-] \qquad K_1 >> K_2$$

$$K_2 = \frac{[H^+][CO_3^{2-}]}{[HCO_3^-]}$$

$$\text{So, } [CO_3^{2-}] = K_2 = 4.8 \times 10^{-11}$$

111. (b) $[AgNO_3] = [Ag^+] = 0.05$ M

$$K_{sp}[AgBr] = [Ag^+][Br^-]$$

$$[Br^-] = \frac{K_{sp}[AgBr]}{[Ag^+]} = \frac{5.0 \times 10^{-13}}{0.05}$$

$$= 10^{-11} \text{ M (mol L}^{-1})$$

Moles of KBr needed to precipitate $AgBr = [Br^-] \times V$

$$= 10^{-11} \text{ mol L}^{-1} \times 1 \text{ L} = 10^{-11} \text{ mol}$$

Therefore, amount of KBr needed to precipitate AgBr

$$= 10^{-11} \text{ mol} \times 120 \text{ g mol}^{-1} = 1.2 \times 10^{-9} \text{ g}$$

112. (b) $Mg(OH)_2 \rightleftharpoons Mg^{2+} + 2OH^-$;

$$K_{sp} = [Mg^{2+}][OH^-]^2$$

$$[OH^-] = \sqrt{\frac{K_{sp}}{[Mg^{2+}]}}$$

$$= \sqrt{\frac{1 \times 10^{-11}}{0.001}} = 1 \times 10^{-4} \text{ M}$$

$$\text{pOH} = -\log[OH^-] = -\log[10^{-4}]$$

$$\text{pOH} = 4$$

$$\therefore \quad \text{pH} = 14 - \text{pOH} = 14 - 4 = 10$$

113. (b) $Na_2CO_3 \rightleftharpoons 2Na^+ + CO_3^{2-}$

$$[Na_2CO_3] = [CO_3^{2-}] = 1 \times 10^{-4} \text{ M}$$

$$BaCO_3 \rightleftharpoons Ba^{2+} + CO_3^{2-}$$

$$K_{sp}(BaCO_3) = [Ba^{2+}][CO_3^{2-}]$$

$$[Ba^{2+}] = \frac{K_{sp}(BaCO_3)}{[CO_3^{2-}]} = \frac{5.1 \times 10^{-9}}{1 \times 10^{-4}}$$

$$[Ba^{2+}] = 5.1 \times 10^{-5} \text{ M}$$

Hence, at 5.1×10^{-5} M concentration of Ba^{2+}, a precipitate will begin to form.

114. (c) Conjugate bases of the given species are :

Species	Conjugate base
HCO_3^-	CO_3^{2-}
H_3O^+	H_2O
HSO_4^-	SO_4^{2-}
HSO_3F	FSO_3^-

Since, strong acid has a weak conjugate base. Thus, the basic strength of the conjugate bases of the given acid is opposite to their acidic strength. The basic strength of the conjugate bases of the given acids follows the order :

$$FSO_3^- < H_2O < SO_4^{2-} < CO_3^{2-}$$

Hence, the acidic strength follows the order :

$$HSO_3F > H_3O^+ > HSO_4^- > HCO_3^-$$

115. (c) For salt of weak acid and weak base,

$$= 7 + \left(\frac{pK_a - pK_b}{2}\right)$$

$$= 7 + \left(\frac{4.80 - 4.78}{2}\right) = 7.01$$

116. (b) $AgIO_3(s) \rightleftharpoons Ag^+(aq) + IO_3^-(aq)$

Let the solubility of $AgIO_3$ be S.

$$K_{sp} = [Ag^+][IO_3^-]$$

$$1.0 \times 10^{-8} = S^2$$

or $\quad S = 1 \times 10^{-4}$ mol L^{-1}

In 1000 mL $AgIO_3$ dissolved

$$= 1 \times 10^{-4} \text{ mol}$$

In 100 mL $AgIO_3$ dissolved

$$= 1 \times 10^{-5} \text{ mol}$$

Mass of $AgIO_3$ in 100 mL

$$= 1 \times 10^{-5} \text{ mol} \times 283 \text{ g mol}^{-1}$$

$$= 2.83 \times 10^{-3} \text{ g}$$

117. (c) When HA is 50% ionised.

$$[HA] = [A^-]$$

Buffer solution of weak acid $HA \rightarrow$ acidic buffer

$$pH = pK_a + \log\frac{[A^-]}{[HA]} \text{ or } pH = pK_a = 4.5$$

$$pOH = pK_w - pH \text{ or}$$

$$pOH = 14 - 4.5 = 9.5$$

118. (c) The overall dissociation constant of the acid is

$$K = K_1 \times K_2 = 1.0 \times 10^{-5} \times 5.0 \times 10^{-10}$$

$$= 5 \times 10^{-15}$$

119. (d) $CH_3COONa + HCl \longrightarrow CH_3COOH$

Initial : 200 mL of 0.1 M $\quad$ 100 mL of 0.1 M

after : 100 mL of 0.1M $\quad$ 100 mL of 0.1 M + NaCl

Thus, mixture obtained is a buffer containing 100 mL of 0.1 M CH_3COOH and 100 mL of 0.1 M CH_3CONa.

120. (c) $MX_2(s) \rightleftharpoons \underset{S}{M^{2+}(aq)} + \underset{2S}{2X^-(aq)}$

$$K_{sp} = [M^{2+}][X^-]^2$$

If solubility be S, then

$$K_{sp} = (S)(2S)^2 = 4S^3$$

$$4S^3 = 4 \times 10^{-12}$$

$$\therefore \quad S = 1 \times 10^{-4} \text{ M}$$

$$\therefore \quad [M^{2+}] = S = 1 \times 10^{-4} \text{ M}$$

121. (d) From graph, when

$$[X] = 1 \text{ mM} = 1 \times 10^{-3} \text{ M}$$

$$[Y] = 2 \text{ mM} = 2 \times 10^{-3} \text{ M}$$

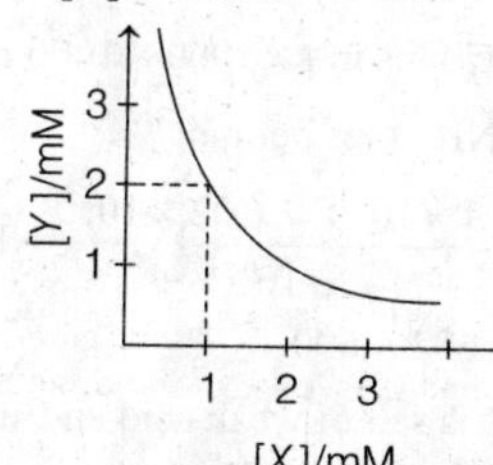

Thus, salt is XY_2

$$XY_2 \rightleftharpoons X^{2+} + 2Y^-$$

$$K_{sp} = [X^{2+}][Y^-]^2$$

$$= (1 \times 10^{-3})(2 \times 10^{-3})^2$$

$$= 4 \times 10^{-9} \text{ M}^3$$

122. (a) Strong acid is neutralised by strong base. As NaOH is added, HCl is neutralised and pH increases. At the neutral point pH is 7. Thus, graph (a) correctly depicts the change in pH.

123. (b) K_{sp} of A_xB_y in terms of solubility (S) is

$$K_{sp} = x^x y^y (S)^{x+y}$$

For $Zr_3(PO_4)_4$,

$$x = 3, \; y = 4$$

$$\therefore \quad K_{sp} = (3)^3(4)^4(S)^7$$

$$\therefore \quad S = \left(\frac{K_{sp}}{6912}\right)^{1/7}$$

124. (c) The tendency to accept the proton by the donation of their lone pair of electrons is called proton affinity. This proton affinity is also called basicity. Therefore, the molecule which donates their lone pair electrons more readily, is said to be more basic. Since, N can easily donate their lone pair of electrons than O, S and P due to their smaller size and low electronegativity. Thus, NH_3 possess the highest proton affinity. On the other hand, due to higher electronegativity of O, it cannot donate their electron pair easily, while P possess a larger size, becomes less basic in nature.

125. (a) $AB_2 \rightleftharpoons \underset{S}{A^{2+}} + \underset{2S}{2B^-}$

$$S = (1 \times 10^{-5})$$

$$K_{sp} = [A^{2+}][B^-]^2 = (S)(2S)^2 = 4S^3$$

$$= 4(1 \times 10^{-5})^3 = 4 \times 10^{-15}$$

126. (c) H_3PO_4 is a tribasic acid, ionising in three steps:

Thus,

$$H_3PO_4 \rightarrow H_2PO_4^- \rightarrow HPO_4^{2-} \rightarrow PO_4^{3-}$$

Hence, HPO_4^{2-} is the conjugate base of H_2PO_4. H_3PO_3 is a dibasic acid.

H_3PO_2 is a monobasic acid.

$$[HCl] = 1 \times 10^{-8} \text{ M}$$

It is very dilute solution and being an acid, pH should be less than 7.

$$[H^+]_{H_2O} = 1 \times 10^{7} \text{ M}$$

Thus, $[H^+]$ of water cannot be neglected.

$$[H^+]_{total} = [H^+]_{HCl} + [H^+]_{H_2O}$$

$$= 1 \times 10^{-8} \text{ M} + 1 \times 10^{-7} \text{ M}$$

$$= 11 \times 10^{-8} \text{ M}$$

$$pH = -\log(11 \times 10^{-8})$$

$$= 8 - \log 11 = 8 - 1.04 = 6.96$$

127. (c) According to Bronsted-Lowry concept of acids and bases, acid is a proton donor, whereas a base is a proton acceptor. Thus, according to this concept, HPO_4^{2-} can easily donate a proton and also accept a proton on reaction with water.

$$\underset{\text{Acid}}{HPO_4^{2-}} + H_2O \rightleftharpoons PO_4^{3-} + H_3O^+$$

$$\underset{\text{Base}}{HPO_4^{2-}} + H_2O \rightleftharpoons H_2PO_4^{2-} + OH^-$$

128. (c)

$$Ag_2CO_3(s) \rightleftharpoons 2Ag^+(aq) + CO_3^{2-}(aq)$$

$$K_{sp} = [Ag^+]^2[CO_3^{2-}]$$

$$8 \times 10^{-12} = (0.1)^2 (S)$$

$$\therefore \quad S = 8 \times 10^{-10} \text{ M}$$

129. (c) NH_4Cl aqueous solution is acidic due to hyrolysis of NH_4^+ ion :

$$NH_4^+(aq) + 2H_2O(l) \rightleftharpoons NH_4OH(aq) + H_3\overset{+}{O}(aq)$$

$$pH = 7 - \frac{pK_b}{2} - \frac{\log C}{2}$$

Given $K_b = 1 \times 10^{-5}$

$$\therefore \quad pK_b = -\log K_b = 5.0$$

$$\log C = \log 0.02 = \log 2 - \log 100$$

$$= 0.30 - 2.00 = -1.70$$

$$\therefore \quad pH = 7 - \frac{5.0}{2} - \left(\frac{-1.70}{2}\right) = 5.35$$

130. (c) $Al(OH)_3 \rightleftharpoons Al^{3+} + 3OH^-$

$K_{sp} = [Al^{3+}][OH^-]^3$

If solubility $= S$ mol L^{-1}

then $2.4 \times 10^{-24} = (S)(0.2)^3$

$\therefore \quad S = \dfrac{2.4 \times 10^{-24}}{(0.2)^3}$

$= 3.0 \times 10^{-22}$ mol L^{-1}

Acid Test for JEE Advanced

Type I. MCQs with Only ONE Correct Alternate

131. (a) By Ostwald's dilution law,

$[H_3O^+] = \sqrt{K_a C}$

$pH = \dfrac{1}{2}[pK_a - \log C]$

$pH = \dfrac{1}{2}[pK_a - \log 0.01]$,

$pH\ (CH_3COOH) = \dfrac{1}{2}[4.74 + 2]$

$pH(ClCH_2COOH) = \dfrac{1}{2}[2.88 + 2]$

$\therefore$ Difference $= 2.37 - 1.44 = 0.93$

132. (c) $(CH_3)_2NH + H_2O \rightleftharpoons (CH_3)_2\overset{+}{N}H_2 + \overset{-}{O}H$

$K_b = \dfrac{[(CH_3)_2NH_2^+][OH^-]}{[(CH_3)_2NH]}$

$5.4 \times 10^{-4} = \dfrac{[(CH_3)_2NH_2^+]}{0.02} \times 1$

$[(CH_3)_2NH_2^+] = \dfrac{5.4 \times 10^{-4} \times 0.02}{1}$

$= 1.08 \times 10^{-5}$

$[(CH_3)_2NH_2^+] = Cx$

$1.08 \times 10^{-5} = 0.02x$

$\therefore \quad x = 5.4 \times 10^{-4}$

$\therefore$ Percentage ionisation

$= 5.4 \times 10^{-2} = 0.054\%$

133. (c) Amphoteric species react with acid as well as with base and amphiprotic species are proton donor as well as proton acceptor. H_2O simply dissolves acid and base but no reaction. Thus it is not amphoteric. However, it is amphiprotic.

$\underset{Acid_1}{H_2O} + \underset{Base_2}{H_2O} \rightleftharpoons \underset{Acid_2}{H_3O^+} + \underset{Base_1}{OH^-}$

H_3PO_2 is monobasic acid, thus $H_2PO_2^-$ does not further ionise H_3PO_3 is dibasic acid, thus HPO_3^{2-} does not further ionise.

$\underset{Acid}{HPO_4^{2-}} + \underset{Base}{OH^-} \longrightarrow H_2O + PO_4^{3-}$

$\underset{Base}{HPO_4^{2-}} + \underset{Acid}{H_2O} \longrightarrow \underset{Acid}{H_2PO_4^-} + \underset{Base}{OH^-}$

$HPO_4^{2-} + H_2O \rightleftharpoons PO_4^{3-} + H_3O^+$

Thus, HPO_4^{2-} is amphiprotic as well as amphoteric.

134. (c)

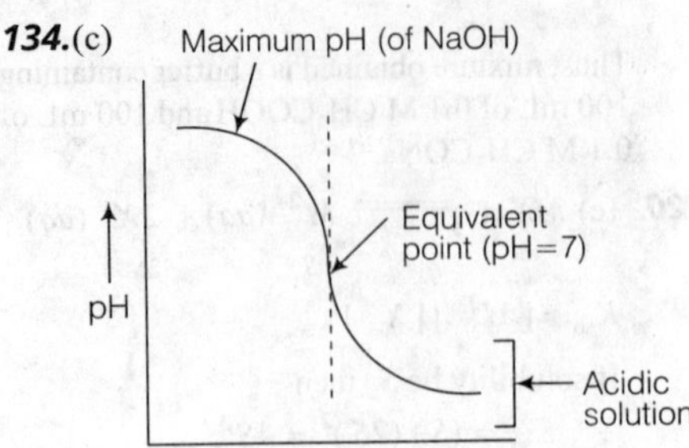

135. (a) $[NH_4^+] = [NH_2^-] = \sqrt{10^{-30}}$

$[NH_2^-] = 1 \times 10^{-15}$ M

$= 1 \times 10^{-15}$ mol in 1L

$= 1 \times 10^{-15} \times 6.02 \times 10^{23}$

NH_2^- ions in 1 L $= 1 \times 10^{-15} \times 6.02 \times 10^{23}$

(or NH_2^- ions in $1 \times 1000 \times 1000$ mm^3)

Thus, NH_2^- ions per mm^3

$= \dfrac{1 \times 10^{-15} \times 6.02 \times 10^{23}}{10^6}$ NH_2^- ions

$= 602 \approx 600$

136. (a) NaX is salt of weak acid and strong base.

$X^- + H_2O \rightleftharpoons HX + OH^-$

We can consider X^- as a base.

$K_b(X^-) = \dfrac{K_w}{K_a} = \dfrac{1 \times 10^{-14}}{1 \times 10^{-5}} = 1 \times 10^{-9}$

then,

By Ostwald's dilution law,

$x = \sqrt{\dfrac{K_b}{C}} = \sqrt{\dfrac{1 \times 10^{-9}}{0.1}}$

$= 1 \times 10^{-4}$ M

Thus, percentage $= 1 \times 10^{-4} \times 100 = 0.01\%$

Alternate

$X^-(aq)$ is basic due to hydrolysis degree of hydrolysis

$x = \sqrt{\dfrac{K_w}{K_a C}}$

$= \sqrt{\dfrac{1 \times 10^{-14}}{1 \times 10^{-5} \times 0.1}} = 1 \times 10^{-4}$

Thus, % $= 1 \times 10^{-4} \times 100 = 0.01\%$

137. (d) $H_2S(aq) \rightleftharpoons HS^-(aq) + H^+(aq)$, K_{a_1}

$HS^-(aq) \rightleftharpoons S^{2-}(aq) + H^+(aq)$, K_{a_2}

Adding, $\quad H_2S(aq) \rightleftharpoons S^{2-} + 2H^+$

$K_a(\text{net}) = \dfrac{[S^{2-}][H^+]^2}{[H_2S]} = K_{a_1}K_{a_2}$

$\dfrac{[S^{2-}][0.2]^2}{0.1} = 1.0 \times 10^{-7} \times 1.2 \times 10^{-13}$

$\therefore \quad [S^{2-}] = 3.0 \times 10^{-20}$ M

138. (c) $K_{sp}(AgCl) > K_{sp}(AgI)$

Hence, precipitation of AgI starts first.

$[Ag^+]$ required to precipitate

$[Cl^-] = \dfrac{1 \times 10^{-10}}{0.05} = 2 \times 10^{-9}$ M

$[I^-]$ at this stage $= \dfrac{K_{sp}[AgI]}{[Ag^+]}$

$= \dfrac{4.0 \times 10^{-16}}{2.0 \times 10^{-9}}$

$= 2 \times 10^{-7}$ M

139. (a) $pH(NH_4^+) = 7 - \dfrac{pK_b}{2} - \dfrac{\log C}{2}$

Thus larger the concentration, smaller the pH.

(a) 0.01 M NH_4Cl = 0.01 M NH_4^+

$pH = 7 - 2.37 + 1 = 5.63$ (maximum)

(b) 0.01 M $(NH_4)_2SO_4$ = 0.02 M NH_4^+

$pH = 7 - 2.37 - \dfrac{\log(0.02)}{2} = 5.48$

(c) $0.01M(NH_4)_3PO_4 \rightleftharpoons 0.03M\ NH_4^+$

$pH = 7 - 2.37 - \dfrac{\log(0.03)}{2} = 5.39$

140. (d) $S_1(\text{In } H_2O) = \sqrt{1 \times 10^{-10}} = 1 \times 10^{-5}$ M

In the presence of common ion,

$S = \dfrac{K_{sp}}{[\text{Common ion}]}$

$S_2(\text{In } 0.05\ M\ AgNO_3) = \dfrac{1 \times 10^{-10}}{0.05}$

$= 2 \times 10^{-9}$ M

S_3 (In 0.05 M NaCl) $= \dfrac{1 \times 10^{-10}}{0.05}$

$= 2 \times 10^{-9}$ M

$S_4(\text{In } 0.01\ M\ CaCl_2) = \dfrac{1 \times 10^{-10}}{0.02}$

$= 5 \times 10^{-9}$ M

Thus, $S_2 = S_3 < S_4 < S_1$

■ In 0.01 M $CaCl_2$, $[Cl^-] = 0.02$ M

141. (b) $\underset{\substack{Red \\ 75\%}}{HIn} \rightleftharpoons H^+ + \underset{\substack{Blue \\ 25\%}}{In^-}$

$K_a = \dfrac{[H^+][In^-]}{[HIn]}$

$[H^+] = K_a \dfrac{[HIn]}{[In^-]} = 3.0 \times 10^{-8} \times \dfrac{75}{25}$

$[H^+]_{75\%\ red} = 9.0 \times 10^{-8}$ M

$\underset{25\%\ Red}{HIn} \rightleftharpoons \underset{75\%\ Blue}{H^+ + In^-}$

$[H^+]_{75\%\ Blue} = 3.0 \times 10^{-8} \times \dfrac{25}{75}$

$= 1.0 \times 10^{-8}$ M

Change in $[H^+] = 9.0 \times 10^{-8} - 1.0 \times 10^{-8}$

$= 8.0 \times 10^{-8}$ M

142. (d) pH[HCl] = 2.0

$\therefore \quad [H^+] = 10^{-2}$ M

$[HCl] = 10^{-2}$ M

Volume = 200 mL

pH[NaOH] = 12.0

pOH = 2.0

$[OH^-] = 10^{-2}$ M

$[NaOH] = 10^{-2}$ M

Volume = 300 mL

N_1V_1 (acid) $= 200 \times 10^{-2} = 2$ millimol

N_2V_2(base) $= 300 \times 10^{-2} = 3$ millimol

$N_2V_2 > N_1V_1$

Thus, resultant mixture is basic.

$$N(OH^-) = \frac{N_2V_2 - N_1V_1}{V_1 + V_2} = \frac{3-2}{500} = 2 \times 10^{-3} \text{ M}$$

pOH $= -\log(2 \times 10^{-3}) = 2.7$

$\therefore$ pH = 14 − pOH = 14 − 2.7 = 11.3

143. (c)

	pH	$[H^+]$	$[OH^-]$
A	2	10^{-2} M	—
B	12	10^{-12} M	10^{-2} M

$$\text{Moles of HCl} = \frac{100 \times 10^{-2}}{1000} = 10^{-3} \text{ mol}$$

$$\text{Moles of NaOH} = \frac{100 \times 10^{-2}}{1000} = 10^{-3} \text{ mol}$$

$Al_2O_3 + 6HCl \longrightarrow 2AlCl_3 + 3H_2O$

6 mol HCl ≡ 1 mol Al_2O_3

$$1 \times 10^{-3} \text{ mol HCl} = \frac{1 \times 10^{-3}}{6} \text{ mol } Al_2O_3$$

$Al_2O_3 + 2NaOH \longrightarrow 2NaAlO_2 + H_2O$

2 mol NaOH ≡ 1 mol Al_2O_3

$$1 \times 10^{-3} \text{ mol NaOH} = \frac{1 \times 10^{-3}}{2} \text{ mol } Al_2O_3$$

Molar ratio of Al_2O_3 required by HCl and NaOH solutions

$$= \frac{1 \times 10^{-3}}{6} \times \frac{2}{1 \times 10^{-3}} = 1:3$$

144. (d) Molality of solution H_2SO_4 is 500 molal.

Step I 1000 g of H_2O has

= 500 mol H_2SO_4

1000 g of H_2O has = (500 × 98) g H_2SO_4

(1000 + 500 × 98) g solution has H_2SO_4

= 500 × 98 g

$d = 1.8$ g mL^{-1}

$$\frac{1000 + 500 + 98}{1.8} \text{ mL of solution has}$$

H_2SO_4 = 500 × 98 g

$$\frac{500(2 + 98)}{1.8} \text{ mL of solution has } H_2SO_4$$

= 500 × 98 g

$$\frac{100}{1.8} \text{ mL of solution has } H_2SO_4 = 98 \text{ g}$$

= 1 mol

1000 mL of solution has H_2SO_4 = 18 mol

$\therefore$ Molarity = 18 M

■ **Direct method**

$$\text{Molality} = \frac{1000\,M}{(1000d - Mm_1)}$$

M = Molarity, d = Density,

m_1 = Molar mass of solute

Step II pH of solution

$H_2SO_4 \rightleftharpoons 2H^+ + SO_4^{2-}$

H_2SO_4 is dibasic acid

$[H^+] = 18 \times 2 = 36$ M

$\therefore$ pH $= -\log[H^+] = -\log 36 = -1.56$

145. (c) $Mg + 2HCl \longrightarrow MgCl_2 + H_2$

1 mol 2 mol

$$[Mg] = 0.24 \text{ g} = \frac{0.24}{24} = 0.01 \text{ mol}$$

$[H^+]_{HCl} = 10^{-pH} = 10^{-0.30} = 2.0$ M

Volume of HCl = 80 mL

Millimoles of HCl = 80 × 2.0

= 160 millimol.

$$\text{Moles of HCl} = \frac{160}{1000} = 0.160 \text{ mol}$$

HCl required for 0.01 mol Mg = 0.02 mol

HCl unreacted = 0.160 − 0.02

= 0.140 mol in 80 mL

$$[HCl] \text{ after reaction} = \frac{0.140 \times 1000}{80}$$

= 1.75 M

$[H^+]$ = 1.75 M

pH $= -\log[H^+]$

$= -\log 1.75 = -0.24$

146. (a) $\Delta G° = -2.303\,RT \log K_b$

$$-\log K_b = \frac{\Delta G°}{2.303\,RT}$$

$$pK_b = \frac{\Delta G°}{2.303\,RT} = \frac{\Delta H° - T\Delta S°}{2.303\,RT}$$

$$= \frac{4.4 - (-76.53 \times 10^{-3} \times 298)}{2.303 \times 8.314 \times 10^{-3} \times 298}$$

= 4.77

147. (c) $H_2O + H_2O \rightleftharpoons H_3O^+ + OH^-$,

$K_w = [H_3O^+][OH^-] = 1 \times 10^{-14}$

Since, $[H_3O^+] = [OH^-]$

Hence, $[H_3O^+]^2 = 1 \times 10^{-14}$

$[H_3O^+] = 1 \times 10^{-7}$ M

For H_2O density = 1 g mL^{-1} = 1000 g L^{-1}

$$\text{Thus, molar concentration} = \frac{1000}{18} \text{ mol L}^{-1}$$

By Ostwald's dilution law,

$[H_3O^+] = \sqrt{K_aC}$

$$1 \times 10^{-7} = \sqrt{K_a \times \frac{1000}{18}}$$

$$\Rightarrow 1 \times 10^{-14} = K_a \times \frac{1000}{18}$$

$$\therefore \quad K_a = \frac{18 \times 10^{-14}}{1000}$$

$\Rightarrow \quad K_a = 1.8 \times 10^{-16}$

148. (c) pH of a weak acid is given by

I. pH $= \frac{1}{2}[pK_a - \log C]$ at C = 0.1 M

II. 2pH $= \frac{1}{2}[pK_a - \log C']$ at C' = ?

$\therefore$ 4pH $= pK_a - \log C'$

2pH $= pK_a - \log C$

$$2\text{pH} = \log C - \log C' = \log\frac{0.1}{C'}$$

From I. pH $= \frac{1}{2}[4.74 - \log 0.1]$

$= \frac{1}{2}[4.74 + 1.0] = 2.87$

$$\therefore \; 2 \times 2.87 = \log\frac{0.1}{C'}$$

$$\therefore \quad \frac{0.1}{C'} = 5.55 \times 10^5$$

$$\text{Thus, dilution } \frac{1}{C'} = \frac{5.55 \times 10^5}{0.1}$$

$= 5.55 \times 10^6$ times

149. (a) SO_2 is pollutant of acid-rain. SO_2 dissolved in H_2O forming H_2SO_3 (sulphurous acid) which is ionised 100% as H^+ and HSO_3^-.

Thus, 0.12 ppm = 0.12 g per 10^6 mL

$$= \frac{0.12}{64} \text{ mol per } 10^6 \text{ mL}$$

$$= \left(\frac{0.12 \times 1000}{64 \times 10^6}\right) \text{mol L}^{-1}$$

$= 1.875 \times 10^{-6}$ M

$[H^+] = 1.875 \times 10^{-6}$ M

pH $= -\log[H^+]$

$= -\log(1.875 \times 10^{-6}) = 5.73$

150. (b) $Ca(Lac)_2 \rightleftharpoons 2Lac^- + Ca^{2+}$

Lactic acid is a weak acid.

$$[\text{Salt}] = \frac{0.13 \text{ mol}}{0.50 \text{ L}} = 0.26 \text{ mol L}^{-1}$$

$\therefore$ [Lactate] = 0.26 × 2 = 0.52 M

Solution is alkaline due to hydrolysis of lactate ion

pH > 7

$$Lac^- + H_2O \rightleftharpoons HLac + \overline{O}H$$

$$pH = 7 + \frac{pK_a}{2} + \frac{\log C}{2}$$

$$8.4 = 7 + \frac{pK_a}{2} + \frac{\log 0.52}{2}$$

$$= 7 + \frac{pK_a}{2} + \left(\frac{-0.284}{2}\right)$$

$$pK_a = 3.085$$

151. (b) $KBr \rightleftharpoons K^+ + Br^-$

$$[Ag^+][Br^-] = K_{sp}$$

$$\therefore \quad [Br^-] = \frac{K_{sp}}{[Ag^+]} = \frac{5.0 \times 10^{-13}}{0.05\,M}$$

$$[Br^-] = 1.0 \times 10^{-11}\ mol\ L^{-1}$$

$$\therefore \text{ KBr to be added} = 1.0 \times 10^{-11} \times 120$$

$$= 1.2 \times 10^{-9}\ g$$

152. (b) $[Ba^{2+}][CO_3^{2-}] = K_{sp} = 5.1 \times 10^{-9}$

$$[Ba^{2+}][1.0 \times 10^{-4}] = 5.1 \times 10^{-9}$$

$$\therefore \quad [Ba^{2+}] = 5.1 \times 10^{-5}\ M$$

153. (a) $Ag^+(aq) + Cl^-(aq) \rightleftharpoons AgCl(s),$

$$K = 1 \times 10^{10}$$

$$AgCl(s) \rightleftharpoons Ag^+(aq) + Cl^-(aq)$$

Thus, K_{sp} of AgCl $= 1 \times 10^{-10}$

$[Ag^+] = 0.10$ mg in 0.5 L

$= 0.10 \times 10^{-3}$ g in 0.5 L

$= \frac{0.10 \times 10^{-3}}{108}$ mol in 0.5 L

$$\text{Thus, } [Ag^+] = \frac{9.26 \times 10^{-7}}{0.5}$$

$$= 1.85 \times 10^{-6}\ M$$

Also, $[Ag^+][Cl^-] = 1 \times 10^{-10}$

$$\text{Thus, } [Cl^-] = \frac{1 \times 10^{-10}}{[Ag^+]} = \frac{1 \times 10^{-10}}{1.85 \times 10^{-6}}$$

$$= 5.4 \times 10^{-5}\ M$$

154. (b) $K_{sp} = [Ag^+][IO_3^-] = S^2$

$$\therefore \quad S = \sqrt{K_{sp}} = 1.0 \times 10^{-4}\ mol\ L^{-1}$$

$$= 1.0 \times 10^{-4} \times 283\ g\ mol^{-1}\ mol\ L^{-1}$$

$$= 283 \times 10^{-4}\ g\ L^{-1}$$

$$= \frac{283 \times 10^{-4} \times 100}{1000}\ g \text{ in } 100\ mL$$

$$= 2.83 \times 10^{-3}\ g$$

155. (d)

(Structure: benzene ring with $OCOCH_3$ and $\underset{\|}{C}$–OH (C=O) groups) + $H_2O \rightleftharpoons$ (benzene ring with $OCOCH_3$ and CO^- (C=O) groups) $+ H_3O^+$

Unionised (A) Ionised (B)

$$pH = pK_a + \log\frac{[B]}{[A]}$$

In stomach (pH = 2.3) $< pK_a$

Hence, $[A] > [B]$

Thus, in stomach it exists as unionised form.

In small intestine, (pH = 8) $> pK_a$

Hence, $[B] > [A]$

Thus, ionised in small intestine.

156. (a) $Ca(OH)_2 + CO_2 \longrightarrow CaCO_3 \downarrow + H_2O$

$$n(CO_2) = \frac{pV}{RT}$$

$$= \frac{0.1\ bar \times 0.1\ L}{0.083\ bar\ L\,mol^{-1}K^{-1} \times 302\ K}$$

$$= 4 \times 10^{-4}\ mol$$

$Ca(OH)_2 = 200$ mL of 0.01 M = 2 millimol

$= 2 \times 10^{-3}$ mol

CO_2 is the limiting reactant.

$Ca(OH)_2$ reacted $= 4 \times 10^{-4}$ mol

$Ca(OH)_2$ unreacted

$= (2 \times 10^{-3}) - (4 \times 10^{-4})$

$= 16 \times 10^{-4}$ mol

$[OH^-] = 2 \times 16 \times 10^{-4}$ mol in 200 mL

(CO_2 is in gaseous state and its volume is not added)

$$\therefore [OH^-] = \frac{32 \times 10^{-4}\ mol}{0.2\ L} = 0.016\ M$$

$$pOH = -\log(0.016) = 1.8$$

$$\therefore \quad pH = 14.0 - 1.8 = 12.2$$

157. (a)

	$HA \rightleftharpoons$	H^+	$+ A^-$
Initial	C	0	0
At equilibrium	$(C - Cx)$	Cx	Cx

$$K_a = \frac{Cx^2}{(1-x)}$$

i = van't Hoff factor

$= [1 + (y - 1)x] = (1 + x)$

y = total ion from one mole

x = degree of ionisation

ΔT_f = depression in freezing point

$\Delta T_f = K_f \times$ molality $\times i$

$0.205 = 1.86 \times 0.1\,(1 + x)$

$x = 0.1$

$$\therefore K_a = \frac{0.1\,(0.1)^2}{(1 - 0.1)} = 1.11 \times 10^{-3}$$

158. (a) $Zn^{2+} + H_2O \rightleftharpoons Zn(OH)^+ + H^+$

$$\text{thus, } [H^+] = \sqrt{K_aC} = \sqrt{1.0 \times 10^{-9} \times 0.001}$$

$$= 1 \times 10^{-6}\ M$$

$$\text{thus, } pH = -\log[H^+] = -\log(1 \times 10^{-6})$$

$$= 6.0$$

159. (b) $Al^{3+} + H_2O \rightleftharpoons Al(OH)^{2+} + H^+,$

$$K_a = 1 \times 10^{-12}$$

$$Al(OH)^{2+} \rightleftharpoons Al^{3+} + OH^-,$$

$$K_b = ?$$

$$H_2O \rightleftharpoons H^+ + OH^-,$$

$$K_w = 1 \times 10^{-14}$$

$$\therefore \quad K_w = K_aK_b$$

$$\therefore \quad K_b = \frac{K_w}{K_a} = \frac{1 \times 10^{14}}{1 \times 10^{-12}} = 1.0 \times 10^{-2}$$

160. (c) $NH_3 + HCl \rightleftharpoons NH_4Cl$

Millimoles of $NH_3 = 100 \times 0.4 = 40$

Millimoles of $HCl = 100 \times 0.4 = 40$

Total 40 millimoles of NH_4Cl in 200 mL solution.

$$\text{Then } [NH_4Cl] = \frac{40 \times 10^{-3}}{0.2}\frac{mol}{L} = 0.2\ M$$

NH_4Cl solution is acidic due to hydrolysis.

$$NH_4^+ + H_2O \rightleftharpoons NH_4OH + \underset{\text{(Acidic)}}{H^+}$$

$$pH = 7 - \frac{pK_b}{2} - \frac{\log C}{2} = \log 0.2$$

$$= 7 - \frac{4.74}{2} - \frac{\log 0.2}{2} = 4.98$$

161. (a) $Fe^{3+} + H_2O \rightleftharpoons Fe(OH)^{2+} + H^+$

$$K_a = 6.5 \times 10^{-3} = \frac{[Fe(OH)^{2+}][H^+]}{[Fe^{3+}]}$$

Given $[Fe^{3+}] = 0.95$ M

$[Fe[OH]^{2+}] = 0.05$ M

$$\therefore \ 6.5 \times 10^{-3} = \frac{0.05[H^+]}{0.95}$$

$$\therefore \quad [H^+] = 0.1235\ M$$

$$\therefore \quad pH = -\log[H^+] = 0.91$$

162. (d) $H_2S \rightleftharpoons 2H^+ + S^{2-}$

$$K_{a_1}K_{a_2} = \frac{[H^+]^2[S]^{2-}}{[H_2S]}$$

$$[S^{2-}] = \frac{K_{a_1}K_{a_2}[H_2S]}{[H^+]^2} = \frac{1 \times 10^{-21}\,(0.1)}{(2 \times 10^{-4})^2}$$

$$= 2.5 \times 10^{-15}\ M$$

163. (b) Since $K_{a_1} >> K_{a_2}$, hydrolysis of $HC_2O_4^-$ is decreased by hydrolysis of $C_2O_4^{2-}$

$$C_2O_4^{2-} + H_2O \rightleftharpoons HC_2O_4^- + OH^-$$

$$[OH^-] = Cx = C\sqrt{\frac{K_h}{C}} = \sqrt{C\frac{K_w}{K_{a_2}}}$$

$$= \sqrt{\frac{0.05 \times 1 \times 10^{-14}}{5.4 \times 10^{-5}}}$$

$$= 9.6 \times 10^{-7}\ M$$

$$\therefore pOH = -\log[OH^-] = 6.02$$

$$\therefore \quad pH = 14 - 6.02 = 7.98$$

164. (a) $CrO_4^{2-} + H_2O \rightleftharpoons HCrO_4^- + OH^-$

$x\text{ (degree of hydrolysis)} = \sqrt{\frac{K_h}{C}} = \sqrt{\frac{K_w}{K_aC}}$

$x = \frac{0.26}{100} \quad \therefore x^2 = \frac{K_w}{K_aC}$

$\therefore \quad K_a = \frac{K_w}{x^2C}$

$K_a = \frac{1\times10^{-14}}{\left(\frac{0.26}{100}\right)^2(0.005)} = 3.0\times10^{-7}$

165. (b) $H_3PO_4 + H_2O \rightleftharpoons H_2PO_4^- + H_3O^+$

$K_{a_1} = 7.1\times10^{-3}, C = 0.01\,M$

$K_{a_1} = \frac{Cx^2}{(1-x)}$

(Approximation is not made as K_{a_1} is large)

$7.1\times10^{-3} = \frac{0.01\,x^2}{(1-x)}$

$\frac{x^2}{(1-x)} = 0.71$

$x^2 = 0.71 - 0.71x$

$x^2 + 0.71x - 0.71 = 0$

$x = \frac{-0.71 + \sqrt{(0.71)^2 + 4\times0.71}}{2}$

$= 0.5593$

$\therefore \quad [H_3O^+] = Cx = 0.01\times0.5593$

$= 5.593\times10^{-3}\,M$

$\therefore \quad pH = -\log[H_3O^+] = 2.25$

166. (a) $CO_3^{2-} + H_2O \rightleftharpoons HCO_3^- + OH^-$

$C \quad\quad 0 \quad\quad 0$

$(C - Cx) \quad\quad Cx \quad\quad Cx$

$K_h = \frac{Cx^2}{(1-x)} = \frac{K_w}{K_{a_2}}$

$\frac{0.001\,x^2}{(1-x)} = \frac{1\times10^{-14}}{4.7\times10^{-11}}$

$\frac{x^2}{(1-x)} = 0.2127$

$x^2 + 0.2127x - 0.2127 = 0$

$x = \frac{-0.2127 + \sqrt{(0.2127)^2 + 4\times0.2127}}{2}$

$= 0.367$

$\therefore \quad [CO_3^{2-}] = C(1-x)$

$= 0.001\,(1 - 0.367)$

$= 6.33\times10^{-4}\,M$

167. (a) $HCO_3^- + H_2O \rightleftharpoons H_2CO_3 + OH^-$

HCO_3^- is a base.

$K_h = \frac{K_w}{K_{a_1}} = \frac{[H_2CO_3][OH^-]}{[HCO_3^-]}$

$\therefore$ Given, pH = 8

$\therefore \quad pOH = 6$

$\therefore \quad [OH^-] = 10^{-6}\,M$

$\therefore \quad \frac{1\times10^{-14}}{4.5\times10^{-7}} = \frac{[H_2CO_3]}{[HCO_3^-]}\times10^{-6}$

$\therefore \quad \frac{[H_2CO_3]}{[HCO_3^-]} = \frac{1}{45} \quad \ldots(i)$

$HCO_3^- + H_2O \rightleftharpoons CO_3^{2-} + H_3O^+$

HCO_3^- is an acid

$K_{a_2} = \frac{[CO_3^{2-}][H_3O^+]}{[HCO_3^-]}$

$\frac{[CO_3^{2-}]}{[HCO_3^-]} = \frac{K_{a_2}}{[H_3O^+]} = \frac{4.7\times10^{-11}}{1\times10^{-8}}$

$= 4.7\times10^{-3}$

or $\quad \frac{[HCO_3^-]}{[CO_3^{2-}]} = 212.77 \quad \ldots(ii)$

Thus, (i) × (ii) gives

$\frac{[H_2CO_3]}{[CO_3^{2-}]} = \frac{212.77}{45} = 4.73$

168. (a) $K_{In} = 4\times10^{-4}$

Indicator changes colour when

$[In^-] = [HIn]$

$pH = pK_a + \log\frac{[In^-]}{[HIn]}$

then, $pH = pK_a = (4 - \log 2) < 7$

In (a), CH_3COONa formed at the equivalence point is hydrolysed back to basic solution. Thus, pH > 7 and this indicator will not work in the acidic range of the indicator.

169. (d) $ML_2 \rightleftharpoons M^{2+} + 2L^-$

$\quad\quad\quad S \quad\quad 2S$

Solubility, $S = 2.4\times10^{-5}$ g/100 mL

$= 2.4\times10^{-4}\text{ g L}^{-1}$

$= \frac{2.4\times10^{-4}}{60}\text{ mol L}^{-1}$

$= 4\times10^{-6}\,M$

$K_{sp}[M^{2+}][L^{-2}] = 4S^3 = 4\,(4\times10^{-6})^3$

$= 2.6\times10^{-18}$

170. (b) $[Ag^+] = \frac{0.001\times1000}{50} = 0.02\text{ mol L}^{-1}$

$[Cl^-] = 0.10\text{ mol L}^{-1}$

Total volume = 100 mL

On mixing $[Ag^+] = \frac{0.02}{2} = 0.01\text{ mol L}^{-1}$

and $[Cl^-] = \frac{0.10}{2} = 0.05\text{ mol L}^{-1}$

	Ag^+	+ Cl^-	$\rightleftharpoons$ AgCl
Initial	0.01	0.05	0
Reacted	0.01	0.01	
At equilibrium	x	0.04	0.01

■ $[Ag^+] = x$ is taken to keep the system in equilibrium

$\therefore \quad K_{sp} = [Ag^+][Cl^-]$

$1.0\times10^{-10} = [Ag^+]\times0.04$

$\therefore \quad [Ag^+] = \frac{1\times10^{-10}}{0.04} = 2.5\times10^{-9}\,M$

Thus, $[Ag^+]$ in 100 mL solution

$= 2.5\times10^{-10}$ mol

171. (b) $Pb^{2+} = 50\times0.2 = 10$ millimol

$Cl^- = 50\times1.5 = 75$ millimol

$Pb^{2+} + 2Cl^- \longrightarrow PbCl_2$

Assume $[Pb^{2+}]$ at equilibrium = x millimol

$[Pb^{2+}]$ reacted = 10 millimol

$[Cl^-]$ reacted = 20 millimol

$[Cl^-]$ at equilibrium = 75 − 20

= 55 millimol

$[Cl^-] = 55\times10^{-3}$ mol in 100 mL

$= 55\times10^{-2}$ mol in 1000 mL

$\therefore \quad [Cl^-] = 55\times10^{-2}\,M$

$K_{sp} = [Pb^{2+}][Cl^-]^2$

$1.7\times10^{-4} = (x)\,(55\times10^{-2})^2$

$x\text{ (soluble } Pb^{2+}) = 5.62\times10^{-4}\text{ mol L}^{-1}$

$= 5.62\times10^{-4}\times206\text{ g L}^{-1}$

$= 5.62\times10^{-4}\times206\times0.1$ g in 100 mL

$= 0.0116\text{ g} = 11.6\text{ mg} \approx 12.0\text{ mg}$

172. (c) 100 mL of 0.1 M $MgCl_2$ = 10 millimol

100 mL of 0.2 M NaOH = 20 millimol

$MgCl_2$	+ 2NaOH	$\longrightarrow$ $Mg(OH)_2$
1 mol	2 mol	1 mol
10 millimol	20 millimol	10 millimol

Thus, $Mg[OH]_2$ is formed.

Solution is basic due to equilibrium

$Mg(OH)_2 \rightleftharpoons Mg^{2+} + 2OH^-$

$\quad\quad\quad (S) \quad\quad (2S)$

$K_{sp} = [Mg^{2+}][OH^-]^2$

$K_{sp} = 4S^3 = 1.2\times10^{-11}$

$\therefore \quad S = 1.44\times10^{-4}\,M$

$\therefore \quad [OH^-] = 2S = 2.88\times10^{-4}\,M$

$\therefore \quad pOH = -\log[OH^-] = 3.54$

$\therefore \quad pH = 14 - pOH$

$= 14 - 3.54 = 10.46$

173. (b) $[Ag^+]$ in AgCl $= \sqrt{K_{sp}\,(AgCl)}$

$= \sqrt{1\times10^{-10}}$

$= 1\times10^{-5}\,M$

$[Br^-]$ in NaBr = 0.03 M

When 100 mL of each one is mixed

$$[Ag^+]_{mix} = \frac{1\times10^{-5}}{2} M$$

$$[Br^-]_{mix} = \frac{0.03}{2} M$$

$$\therefore [Ag^+][Br^-] = \frac{1\times10^{-5}\times0.03}{4}$$

$$= 7.5\times10^{-8} > K_{sp}[AgBr]$$

Thus, AgBr is precipitated.

174. (c) $[SO_4^{2-}]$ in Ag_2SO_4 >> $[SO_4^{2-}]$ in $SrSO_4$

Thus, $[SO_4^{2-}]$ from Ag_2SO_4 decreases solubility of $SrSO_4$ due to common ion effect

Solubility of $Ag_2SO_4 = x$ mol L^{-1}

$$\underset{}{Ag_2SO_4} \rightleftharpoons \underset{2x}{2Ag^+} + \underset{x}{SO_4^{2-}}$$

$$K_{sp}(Ag_2SO_4) = 4x^3 = 1.5\times10^{-5}$$

$$\therefore \quad x = 1.55\times10^{-2} M$$

$$\therefore [SO_4^{2-}] \text{ from } Ag_2SO_4 = 1.55\times10^{-2} M$$

$$SrSO_4 \rightleftharpoons \underset{y}{Sr^{2+}} + \underset{y}{SO_4^{2-}}$$

Solubility of $SrSO_4 = y$ mol L^{-1}

$$\text{Total } SO_4^{2-} = (y + 1.55\times10^{-2}) \approx 1.55\times10^{-2} M$$

$$K_{sp}(SrSO_4) = 2.8\times10^{-7} = y(1.55\times10^{-2})$$

$$y = 1.8\times10^{-5} M$$

175. (d) Solution of silver benzoate is alkaline due to hydrolysis.

$$C_6H_5COO^- + H_2O \rightleftharpoons C_6H_5COOH + OH^-$$

$$pH = 7 + \frac{pK_a}{2} + \frac{\log C}{2}$$

$$8.63 = 7 + \frac{4.19}{2} + \frac{\log C}{2}$$

$$\therefore \quad \log C = -0.93$$

$$\therefore \quad C = 0.117 M$$

$$\therefore [C_6H_5COO^-] = 0.117 M = [Ag^+]$$

$$C_6H_5COOAg(s) \rightleftharpoons C_6H_5COO^-(aq) + Ag^+(aq)$$

$$K_{sp} = [C_6H_5COO^-][Ag^+]$$

$$= (0.117)^2 = 1.37\times10^{-2}$$

176. (a) Saturated $[H_2S] = 0.1 M$

Since, $K_{a_1} >> K_{a_2}$,

$$H_2S + H_2O \rightleftharpoons H_3O^+ + HS^-$$

$$K_{a_1} = \frac{[H_3O^+][HS^-]}{[H_2S]}$$

$$\therefore [H_3O^+][HS^-] = 1.0\times10^{-7}\times0.1$$

Since, $[H_3O^+] = [HS^-]$

$$\therefore \quad [H_3O^+] = [HS^-] = \sqrt{1.0\times10^{-8}}$$

$$= 1.0\times10^{-4} M$$

$$\therefore HS^- + H_2O \rightleftharpoons H_3O^+ + S^{2-}$$

$$K_{a_2} = \frac{[H_3O^+][S^{2-}]}{[HS^-]}$$

$$\therefore \quad [S^{2-}] = K_{a_2} = 1.0\times10^{-14}$$

$$[Ag^+]^2[S^{2-}] = 1.6\times10^{-49}$$

$$[Ag^+]^2[1.0\times10^{-14}] = 1.6\times10^{-49}$$

$$\therefore \quad [Ag^+] = 4\times10^{-18} M$$

177. (c) $Cu^{2+} + 2H_2O + H_2S \rightleftharpoons CuS + 2H_3O^+$

If $[Cu^{2+}] = 0.1 M$

initially, $[H_3O^+] = 0.2 M$

$$H_2S \rightleftharpoons 2H + S^{2-}$$

$$\therefore K_{a_1}K_{a_2} = \frac{[H^+]^2[S^{2-}]}{[H_2S]}$$

$$1.0\times10^{-21} = \frac{(0.2)^2[S^{2-}]}{(0.1)}$$

$$\therefore \quad [S^{2-}] = 2.5\times10^{-21}$$

Since, $[Cu^{2+}][S^{2-}] = 8.8\times10^{-36}$

$$\therefore [Cu^{2+}] = \frac{8.5\times10^{-36}}{2.5\times10^{-21}} = 3.4\times10^{-15} M$$

178. (b) $AgCl + Cl^- \rightleftharpoons AgCl_2^-$

thus, $[AgCl_2^-] = [AgCl]$ taken

$$[AgCl_2^-] = 0.01 \text{ mol in } 100 L$$

$$= 1\times10^{-4} M$$

Formation constant K_f of $AgCl_2^-$

$$K_f(AgCl_2^-) = \frac{[AgCl_2^-]}{[Ag^+][Cl^-][Cl^-]}$$

$$3.0\times10^5 = \frac{1\times10^{-4}}{1\times10^{-10}[Cl^-]}$$

$$\therefore \quad [Cl^-] = 3.33 M$$

Thus, NaCl in 100 L = 3.33 × 100 mol

= 3.33 × 100 × 58.5 g

= 19.48 kg

179. (a) $AgCl(s) \rightleftharpoons Ag^+ + Cl^-$, $\quad K_1 = K_{sp}$

$$Ag^+ + 2NH_3 \rightleftharpoons [Ag(NH_3)_2]^+, \quad K_2 = K_f$$

$$AgCl + 2NH_3 \rightleftharpoons [Ag(NH_3)_2]^+ + Cl^-, \quad K = K_{sp}K_f$$

$$K = \frac{[Ag(NH_3)_2^+]^+[Cl^-]}{[NH_3]^2}$$

$$= 1.0\times10^{-10}\times1.0\times10^8 = 0.01$$

Due to complexation,

$$[Cl^-] = [AgCl] = [Ag^+] = 0.1 M$$

$$\therefore [Ag(NH_3)_2]^+ = 0.1 M$$

thus, $\quad [NH_3] = 1.0 M$

180. (b) $[Ag^+][Cl^-] = 1.0\times10^{-10}$

$$[Ag^+](0.001) = 1.0\times10^{-10}$$

$$\therefore \quad [Ag^+] = 1.0\times10^{-7} M$$

$$[Ag^+] \text{ taken} = 0.004 M$$

Thus, $[Ag(NH_3)_2]^+ = 0.004 M$

(assume all the Ag^+ is complexed)

$$Ag^+ + 2NH_3 \rightleftharpoons [Ag(NH_3^+)_2]$$

$$\therefore \quad K_f = \frac{[Ag(NH_3)_2^+]}{[Ag^+][NH_3]^2}$$

$$1.0\times10^8 = \frac{0.004}{(1.0\times10^{-7})[NH_3]^2}$$

$$\therefore \quad [NH_3] = 0.02 M$$

181. (c) $AgCl \rightleftharpoons Ag^+ + Cl^-$

$$K_{sp} = [Ag^+][Cl^-]$$

$$\log K_{sp} = \log[Ag^+] + \log[Cl^-]$$

As $\quad pK = -\log K$

$$\therefore \quad pK_{sp} = p_{Ag} + p_{Cl}$$

$$p_{Ag} = pK_{sp} - p_{Cl}$$

This represents a straight line.

$$y = c - mx$$

Thus, intercept $OA = c = pK_{sp} = 10$

$$\therefore \quad K_{sp} = 10^{-10}$$

$$\therefore [Ag^+][Cl^-] = 1\times10^{-10}$$

where, $\quad [Ag^+] = 0.01 M$

$$\therefore \quad [Cl^-] = \frac{1\times10^{-10}}{0.01} = 1\times10^{-8} M$$

Thus, solubility of AgCl is presence of 0.01 M $AgNO_3$ is 1×10^{-8} M.

182. (b) For such type of salt, as NH_4^+ solution is acidic, due to hydrolysis of NH_4^+.

$$NH_4^+ + H_2O \rightleftharpoons NH_4OH + H^+ \quad (pH < 7)$$

$$pH = \left(7 - \frac{pK_b}{2}\right) - \frac{\log C}{2}$$

$$= (\text{Constant}) - \left(\frac{\log C}{2}\right)$$

pH decreases as $\log C$ increases.

Slope $= \frac{1}{2}$,

$$OA = \text{intercept} = \text{constant} = \left(7 - \frac{pK_b}{2}\right)$$

$$= 4.63$$

$$\therefore pH = 4.63 - \frac{\log 0.01}{2}$$

$$= 4.63 + \frac{2}{2} = 5.63$$

183. (d) (a) For CH_3COONa

$$pH = \left(7 + \frac{pK_a}{2}\right) + \frac{\log C}{2}$$

Thus, pH increases with log C.

Thus (a) is correct. (b) For NH_4Cl

$$pH = \left(7 - \frac{pK_a}{2}\right) - \frac{\log C}{2}$$

Thus, pH decrease with log C
Thus (b) is correct.
(c) For CH_3COONH_4, pH is independent of concentration.

$$pH = 7 + \left(\frac{pK_a - pK_b}{2}\right)$$

Thus, (c) is correct.
Hence, none is incorrect. (all correct)

184. (c) $H_2O + H_2O \rightleftharpoons [H_3O^+][OH^-]$

$[H_3O^+][OH^-] = 1\times10^{-14}$ at 298 K

Also, $[H_3O^+] = [OH^-] = 1\times10^{-7}$ M

$= 1\times10^{-7}$ mol/dm^3

$= 1\times10^{-7}$ mol in 10^6 mm^3 H_2O

$= 1\times10^{-13}$ mol in 1 mm^3

$= 1\times10^{-13}\times6.02\times10^{23}$ ions each of $[H_3O^+]$

and $[OH^-]$ per mm^3 of $H_2O = 6.02\times10^{10}$

Thus, $[H_3O^+] + [OH^-] = 12.04\times10^{10}$ ions per mm^3.

■ 1 dm^3 = 1 L = 1000 cm^3
= $10^3\times10^3$ mm^3 = 10^6 mm^3

185. (b) $(CH_3COO)_2Ca \rightleftharpoons 2CH_3COO^- + Ca^{2+}$
x mol → $2x$ mol

pH of 0.01 M CH_3COOH

$$pH = \frac{1}{2}[pK_a - \log C]$$

$$= \frac{1}{2}[4.74 - \log 0.01] = 3.37$$

New pH = 3.37 + 2.37 = 5.74
Mixture is now a buffer.

$$pH = pK_a + \log\frac{[CH_3COO^-]}{[CH_3COOH]}$$

$$5.74 = 4.74 + \log\frac{2x}{0.01}$$

$$\log\frac{2x}{0.01} = 1.00$$

$$\frac{2x}{0.01} = 10$$

$$x = \frac{10\times0.01}{2} = 0.05 \text{ mol}$$

186. (b) If $NH_3(aq)$ and $C_5H_5N(aq)$ were present separately, then

$NH_3 + H_2O \rightleftharpoons NH_4^+ + OH^-$

$[NH_4^+] = [OH^-] = \sqrt{K_bC}$

$$= \sqrt{1.8\times10^{-5}\times\frac{0.005}{0.200}}$$

$= 6.7\times10^{-4}$ M

$C_5H_5N + H_2O \rightleftharpoons C_5H_5\overset{+}{N}H + OH^-$

$[C_5H_5NH^+] = [OH^-]$

$$= \sqrt{1.5\times10^{-9}\times\frac{0.005}{0.200}}$$

$= 1.93\times10^{-5}$ M $<< 6.7\times10^{-4}$

Thus, presence of $[OH^-]$ due to NH_3 decreases ionisation of $C_5H_5N(aq)$,

$C_5H_5N + H_2O \rightleftharpoons C_5H_5NH^+ + OH^-$

$$K_b = \frac{[C_5H_5NH^+][OH^-]}{[C_5H_5N]}$$

$$1.5\times10^{-9} = \frac{[C_5H_5NH^+](6.7\times10^{-4})}{\left(\frac{0.005}{0.200}\right)}$$

$\therefore [C_5H_5NH^+] = 5.6\times10^{-5}$ M $< 1.93\times10^{-5}$ M

Thus, ionisation of $C_5H_5N(aq)$ is decreased due to presence of $NH_3(aq)$.

187. (c) $K_a(HA) >> K_a(C_6H_5OH)$

Thus, $[H^+]$ of HA decreases ionisation of C_6H_5OH.

$[H^+]$ in $HA = \sqrt{K_aC} = \sqrt{1.38\times10^{-4}\times0.03}$

$= 2.03\times10^{-3}$ M

$C_6H_5OH \rightleftharpoons C_6H_5O^- + H^+$

$$K_a = \frac{[C_6H_5O^-][H^+]}{[C_6H_5OH]}$$

$$1.05\times10^{-10} = \frac{[C_6H_5O^-](2.03\times10^{-3})}{0.10}$$

$\therefore [C_6H_5O^-] = 5.17\times10^{-9}$ M

$\approx 5.20\times10^{-9}$ M

188. (d) $[H_3O^+] = \sqrt{K_1C_1 + K_2C_2}$ in two weak acids

$= \sqrt{1.8\times10^{-4}\times0.1 + 3.3\times10^{-4}\times0.1}$

$= 7.1\times10^{-3}$ M

■ In this case, K_1 and K_2 are approximately same, thus common ion effect cannot be taken.

189. (c) pH of 0.01 M HCl

$= -\log[H^+]$

$= -\log 10^{-2} = 2$

$$HCl = \frac{1000\times0.01}{1000} = 0.01 \text{ mol}$$

	CH_3COONa +	HCl ⇌	CH_3COOH +	NaCl
Initial	0.02	0.01	0	0 mol
After reac.	0.01	—	0.01	mol

Thus, mixture is a buffer,

$$\therefore \quad pH = pK_a + \log\frac{[CH_3COONa]}{[CH_3COOH]}$$

$$= 4.74 + \log\left(\frac{0.01}{0.01}\right) = 4.74$$

Thus, ΔpH = 4.74 − 2.00 = 2.74

190. (b) Initially, in the buffer of 0.10 M NH_3 and 0.10 M NH_4Cl

$$pOH = pK_b + \log\frac{[NH_4^+]}{[NH_3]}$$

$$pOH = 4.74 + \log\left(\frac{0.1}{0.1}\right) = 4.74$$

$\therefore$ pH = 14 − 4.74 = 9.26

pH after addition of NaOH should not be more than 10.26 (NaOH increases pH).

Thus, pOH = 3.74

$$\text{Thus,} \quad 3.74 = 4.74 + \log\frac{[NH_4^+]}{[NH_3]}$$

$$\log\frac{[NH_4^+]}{[NH_3]} = -1.0 \Rightarrow \frac{[NH_4^+]}{[NH_3]} = \frac{1}{10}$$

or $[NH_4^+] = 0.1[NH_3]$

Thus, if NaOH is added to buffer, ratio of $[NH_4^+]$ to $[NH_3]$ is 0.1.

Initially,

$[NH_3] + [NH_4^+] = 0.1 + 0.1 = 0.2$ M

$\therefore [NH_3] + 0.1[NH_3] = 0.2$ M

$1.1[NH_3] = 0.2$ M

$\therefore [NH_3] = 0.182$ M

$\therefore [NH_4^+] = 0.2 - 0.182 = 0.018$ mol

Thus, NaOH to be added = 0.1 − 0.018
= 0.082 mol L^{-1}

191. (a) $[Mg(OH)_2] = 0.65$ g L^{-1} $= \frac{0.65}{58}$ mol L^{-1}

$\therefore [Mg^{2+}] = \frac{0.65}{58}$ M

$[Mg^{2+}][OH^-]^2 = K_{sp} = 1.8\times10^{-11}$

$\therefore [OH^-]^2 = 1.8\times10^{-11}\times\frac{58}{0.65}$

$= 1.606\times10^{-9}$

$[OH^-] = 4.0\times10^{-5}$ M

$\Rightarrow$ pOH = 4.4

pH = 14 − 4.4 = 9.6

192. (c) $[SO_4^{2-}] = 0.15$ M

$[Ag^+] = 9.7\times10^{-3}$ M

$\therefore K_{sp} = [Ag^+]^2[SO_4^{2-}]$

$= (9.7\times10^{-3})^2(0.15)$

$= 1.41\times10^{-5}$

193. (c) $CaSO_4$ = 136 ppm

= 136 g in 10^6 mL solution

= 0.136 g in 1000 mL solution

$= \frac{0.136}{136} = 1\times10^{-3}$ mol L^{-1}

$K_{sp} = [Ca^{2+}][SO_4^{2-}] = 9\times10^{-6}$

Maximum solubility, ($CaSO_4$)

$= \sqrt{9\times10^{-6}} = 3\times10^{-3}$ M.

Thus, $CaSO_4$ will precipitate in water sample.

3×10^{-3} mol is present = 1000 mL

1×10^{-3} mol is present $=\frac{1000}{3}$ mL

Thus, water evaporated

$= 1000-\frac{1000}{3} = 667$ mL

194. (a) $AgBrO_3(s) \rightleftharpoons Ag^+(aq) + BrO_3^-(aq)$

Ag^+ is precipitated by H_2S

$$pV = nRT$$

$$\therefore n(H_2S) = \frac{pV}{RT}$$

$$= \frac{\left(\frac{748}{760}\right)\text{atm} \times \left(\frac{30.4}{1000}\right)\text{L}}{[0.0821 \text{ L atm mol}^{-1}\text{K}^{-1} \times 296 \text{ K}]}$$

$$= 1.23\times10^{-3} \text{ mol}$$

$$2Ag^+(aq) + S^{2-}(aq) \longrightarrow Ag_2S(s)$$

Thus, $[Ag^+] = 2\times H_2S$

$= 2.46\times10^{-3}$ mol in 338 mL

$$\therefore [Ag^+] = \frac{2.46\times10^{-3}\times1000}{338}$$

$$\therefore K_{sp} = [Ag^+][BrO_3^-] = [Ag^+]^2$$

$$= (7.28\times10^{-3})^2 = 5.3\times10^{-5}$$

195. (a) Aqueous solution of CH_3COONa is basic due to hydrolysis of CH_3COO^-.

$$CH_3COO^-(aq) + H_2O \rightleftharpoons CH_3COOH(aq) + OH^-(aq)$$

$$pH = 7 + \frac{pK_a}{2} + \frac{\log C}{2}$$

$$= 7 + \frac{4.74}{2} + \frac{\log 0.1}{2}$$

$$= 8.87$$

$$\therefore pOH = 14 - 8.87 = 5.13$$

$$[OH^-] = 10^{-pOH} = 10^{-5.13}$$

$$= 10^{-6}\,10^{0.87} = 7.4\times10^{-6} \text{ M}$$

Let solubility of $Mg(OH)_2 = x$ in 0.1 M CH_3COONa

$$Mg(OH)_2(s) \rightleftharpoons Mg^{2+}(aq) + 2OH^-(aq),$$

$$K_{sp} = [Mg^{2+}][OH^-]^2$$

$$1.8\times10^{-11} = (x)(7.4\times10^{-6})^2$$

$$x = 0.33 \text{ M}$$

196. (d) $H_2CO_3 \rightleftharpoons H^+ + HCO_3^-$

$$K_{a_1} = \frac{[H^+][HCO_3^-]}{[HCO_3]}$$

$\Rightarrow$ pH = 10, $[H^+] = 10^{-10}$

$$\therefore 4.3\times10^{-7} = 1\times10^{-10}\frac{[HCO_3^-]}{[H_2CO_3]}$$

$$\therefore \frac{[HCO_3^-]}{[H_2CO_3]} = \frac{4.3\times10^{-7}}{1\times10^{-10}} = 4.3\times10^3 \;\ldots\text{(i)}$$

$$HCO_3^- \rightleftharpoons H^+ + CO_3^{2-}$$

$$K_{a_2} = \frac{[H^+][CO_3^{2-}]}{[HCO_3^-]}$$

$$4.8\times10^{-11} = 1\times10^{-10}\frac{[CO_3^{2-}]}{[HCO_3^-]}$$

$$\frac{[CO_3^{2-}]}{[HCO_3^-]} = \frac{4.8\times10^{-11}}{1\times10^{-10}} = 0.48 \;\ldots\text{(ii)}$$

Fraction of $[H_2CO_3]$

$$= \frac{[H_2CO_3]}{[H_2CO_3] + [HCO_3^-] + [CO_3^{2-}]}$$

$$= \frac{\frac{[H_2CO_3]}{[HCO_3^-]}}{\frac{[H_2CO_3]}{[HCO_3^-]} + 1 + \frac{[CO_3^{2-}]}{[HCO_3^-]}}$$

From (i) and (ii),

$$= \frac{\left(\frac{1}{4.3\times10^3}\right)}{\left(\frac{1}{4.3\times10^{-3}}\right) + 1 + 0.48} = 1.6\times10^{-4}$$

197. (b) $\underset{\text{Acid}}{M_1V_1} = \underset{\text{Base}}{M_2V_2}$

$$M_1 \times 50.0 = 0.10\times39.30$$

$$M_1 = \frac{0.10\times39.30}{50} = 0.0786 \text{ M}$$

Thus, initial (acid) = 0.079 M

then half-equivalence point is reached

$$[HA] = [A^-]$$

$$pH = pK_a + \log\frac{[A^-]}{[HA]}$$

$$pH = pK_a = 4.85$$

198. (a) HCO_3^- is amphiprotic and NH_4^+ is also hydrolysed.

$$HCO_3^- \rightleftharpoons H^+ + CO_3^{2-}$$

$$HCO_3^- + H^+ \rightleftharpoons H_2CO_3$$

$$NH_4^+ + H_2O \rightleftharpoons NH_4OH + H^+$$

$$\therefore [H_3O^+] = \sqrt{K_{a_1}\left(\frac{K_w}{K_b} + K_{a_2}\right)}$$

$$= 1.66\times10^{-8} \text{ M}$$

$$\therefore \quad pH = 7.78$$

199. (b) Mole fraction of H_2SO_4 = 0.01

Mole fraction of H_2O = 0.99

Thus, moles of H_2SO_4 = 0.01

Moles of H_2O = 0.99

0.99 mol H_2O = 0.99 ×18 g = 17.82 g

= 17.82 mL = 0.01782 L.

$$\text{Thus, } [H_2SO_4] = \frac{0.01 \text{ mol}}{0.0782 \text{ L}} = 0.56 \text{ M}$$

$$H_2SO_4 = 2H^+ + SO_4^{2-}$$

$$\therefore \quad [H^+] = 2\times0.56 = 1.12 \text{ M}$$

$$pH = -\log 1.12 = -0.05$$

200. (a) pH = 3, pOH = 11

$$\therefore \quad [OH^-] = 1.0\times10^{-11} \text{ M}$$

$$H_2S + H_2O \rightleftharpoons H_3O^+ + HS^-$$

$$K_a = \frac{[H_3O^+][HS^-]}{[H_2S]}$$

$$9.1\times10^{-8} = \frac{(1\times10^{-3})[HS^-]}{0.1}$$

$$[HS^-] = 9.1\times10^{-6} \text{ M}$$

$$FeS(s) + H_2O(l) \rightleftharpoons Fe^{2+}(aq) + HS^-(aq) + OH^-(aq),$$

$$K = [Fe^{2+}][HS^-][OH^-]$$

$$[Fe^{2+}][HS^-][OH^-] = 5\times10^{-19}$$

$$[Fe^{2+}] = \frac{5\times10^{-19}}{9.1\times10^{-6}\times1\times10^{-11}}$$

$$= 5.5\times10^{-3} \text{ M}$$

201. (c) When 19.31 mL of base added, CH_3COOH is neutralised 50%

Thus, $[CH_3COOH] = [CH_3COONa]$

$$\therefore \quad pH = pK_a + \log\frac{[CH_3COONa]}{[CH_3COOH]}$$

$$pH = pK_a$$

202. (a) $pK_{In} = -\log K_{In}\,(4\times10^{-10})$

$= 10 - \log 4 = 9.4$

$$HIn \rightleftharpoons H^+ + In^-$$

$$pH = pK_{In} + \log\frac{[In^-]}{[HIn]}$$

At equivalent point, $[In^-] = [HIn]$

Thus, it is equivalent point. pH colour change starts from $(pK_{In} - 1)$ and completes at $(pK_{In} + 1)$.

Thus, (a) is incorrect.

203. (d) Non-ionised form I of methyl red is red in acid. In presence of base, form II is formed which is yellow. At the equivalent point, I = II and pH = pK_{In}

204. (d) (a) $Ag_3PO_4 \rightleftharpoons 3Ag^+ + PO_4^{3-}$,

$$K_{sp} = [Ag^+]^3[PO_4^{3-}]$$

$$[PO_4^{3-}] = \frac{K_{sp}}{(0.1)^3} = \frac{1\times10^{-6}}{10^{-3}} = 10^{-3}$$

(b) $Ca_3(PO_4)_2 \rightleftharpoons 3Ca^{2+} + 2PO_4^{3-}$

$$K_{sp} = [Ca^{2+}]^3[PO_4^{3-}]^2$$

$$10^{-33} = (0.1)^3[PO_4^{3-}]^2$$

$$[PO_4^{3-}]^2 = \frac{10^{-33}}{10^{-3}}$$

$[PO_4^{3-}]^2 = 10^{-30}$

$[PO_4^{3-}] = 1 \times 10^{-15}$ M

(c) $Mg_3(PO_4)_2 \rightleftharpoons 3Mg^{2+} + 2PO_4^{3-}$

as in (b) $[PO_4^{3-}]^2 = \frac{10^{-24}}{10^{-3}}$

$[PO_4^{3-}] = 3.16 \times 10^{-11}$ M

(d) $AlPO_4 \rightleftharpoons Al^{3+} + PO_4^{3-}$

$[PO_4^{3-}] = \frac{K_{sp}}{0.1} = \frac{10^{-20}}{0.1} = 10^{-19}$ M

Thus, $[PO_4^{3-}]$ is minimum to precipitate Al^{3+}.

205. (b) $[Zn^{2+}][S^{2-}] = 10^{-1} \times 8.1 \times 10^{-19}$

$= 8.1 \times 10^{-20} > K_{sp}$ of ZnS(3×10^{-22})

$[Cu^{2+}][S^{2-}] = 10^{-2} \times 8.1 \times 10^{-19}$

$= 8.1 \times 10^{-21} > K_{sp}$ of CuS (8×10^{-36})

Hence, both ions are precipitated as sulphides.

■ Precipitation occurs when ionic product $> K_{sp}$.

206. (d) $RNH_2 + H_2O \rightleftharpoons R\overset{+}{N}H_3 + OH^-$

It is a weak base.

Moles of $RNH_2 = \frac{pV}{RT} = \frac{1 \times 959}{0.0821 \times 298}$

$= 39.2$ mol L^{-1}

$\therefore \quad pOH = \frac{1}{2}[pK_b - \log C]$

$\frac{1}{2}[3.4 + \log 39.2] = \frac{1}{2}[3.4 - 1.59] = 0.9$

$\therefore \quad pH = 14 - 0.9 = 13.1$

207. (a) $A_pB_q \rightleftharpoons pA^{q+} + qB^{p-}$

$\quad\quad pS \quad\quad qS$

$K_{sp} = [A^{q+}]^p[B^{p-}]^q$

$= (pS)^p (qS)^q$

$= p^p S^p q^q S^q = p^p q^q S^{p+q}$

208. (b) $[Mg^{2+}][OH^-]^2 = 1 \times 10^{-11}$

$\therefore \ [OH^-] = \sqrt{\frac{1 \times 10^{-11}}{0.001}} = 1 \times 10^{-4}$ M

$NH_4OH \rightleftharpoons NH_4^+ + OH^-$

$\therefore \quad K_b = \frac{[NH_4^+][OH^-]}{[NH_4OH]}$

$1.8 \times 10^{-5} = \frac{[NH_4^+] \times 10^{-4}}{(0.02)}$

$\therefore \ [NH_4^+] = \frac{1.8 \times 10^{-5} \times 0.02}{1 \times 10^{-4}}$ M

$= 3.6 \times 10^{-3}$ mol L^{-1}

209. (c) $Al(OH)_3$ is present as Al^{3+} as well $Al(OH)_4^-$.

Thus, solubility (S)

$= [Al^{3+}] + [Al(OH)_4^-]$

$[Al^{3+}][OH^-]^3 = K_2$

$\therefore \quad [Al^{3+}] = \frac{K_2}{[OH^-]^3}$

and $[Al(OH)_4^-] = K_1[OH^-]$

$\therefore \quad S = \frac{K_2}{[OH^-]^3} + K_1[OH^-]$

For minimum solubility,

$\frac{dS}{d[OH^-]} = 0$

$\therefore \quad \frac{dS}{d[OH^-]} = 0 = -\frac{3K_2}{[OH^-]^4} + K_1$

$\therefore \quad \frac{3K_2}{[OH^-]^4} = K_1$

$\therefore \quad [OH^-]^4 = \frac{3K_2}{K_1}$

$\therefore \quad [OH^-] = \left(\frac{3K_2}{K_1}\right)^{1/4}$

210. (a) (a) $AgCl(s) \rightleftharpoons Ag^+(aq) + Cl^-(aq)$, $\quad K_1 = K_{sp}$

$Ag^+(aq) + 2NH_3(aq) \rightleftharpoons [Ag(NH_3)_2^+](aq)$, $\quad K_2 = K_f$

$AgCl(s) + 2NH_3(aq) \rightleftharpoons [Ag(NH_3)_2^+](aq) + Cl^-(aq)$, K_3

Initial change	0.1 M	0	0
	$-2x$	$+x$	$+x$
At Equil.	$(0.1 - 2x)$	x	x

$K_3 = K_1K_2 = K_{sp}.K_f$

$1.8 \times 10^{-10} \times 1.6 \times 10^7 = \frac{[Ag(NH_3)_2^+][Cl^-]}{[NH_3]^2}$

$2.88 \times 10^{-3} = \frac{x^2}{(0.1 - 2x)^2}$

$\therefore \frac{x}{(0.1 - 2x)} = 0.0537$

$(0.00537 - 0.1074x) = x$

$1.1074x = 0.00537$

$\therefore \quad x = 4.85 \times 10^{-3}$ M

211. (c) $AgCl(s) \rightleftharpoons Ag^+(aq) + Cl^-(aq)$, $\quad K_1 = K_{sp}$

$Ag^+(aq) + 2S_2O_3^{2-}(aq) \rightleftharpoons [Ag(S_2O_3)^2]^{3-}$, $\quad K_2 = K_f$

$AgCl(s) + 2S_2O_3^{2-}(aq) \rightleftharpoons [Ag(S_2O_3)_2^{3-}] + Cl^-$, $\quad K_3 = K_{sp}K_f$

$K_3 = K_{sp}K_f = \frac{[Ag(S_2O_3)_2^{3-}][Cl^-]}{[S_2O_3^{2-}]^2}$

Large value of $K_f([Ag(S_2O_3)_2^{3-}]$ indicates that all the Ag^+ ion is complexed. Thus, $[Ag^+] = [Ag(S_2O_3)_2^{3-}] = 0.10$ M

$\therefore 1.8 \times 10^{-10} \times 1.7 \times 10^{13} = \frac{[(0.10)(0.01)]}{[S_2O_3^{2-}]^2}$

$\therefore \ [S_2O_3^{2-}]^2 = 3.27 \times 10^{-7}$

$[S_2O_3^{2-}] = 5.72 \times 10^{-4}$ M

■ To keep all the Ag^+ ion in the complex form, maximum $[S_2O_3^{2-}] = 0.2$ M $= 2[Ag^+]$

212. (b) For acetic acid,

$CH_3COOH \rightleftharpoons CH_3COO^- + H^+$

$\Delta T_f = \text{Molality} \times K_f \times i$

$= 0.10 \times 1.86 \times (1 + x)$

For CH_3COOH, by Ostwald's dilution law,

$x = \frac{\sqrt{K_a}}{C} = \sqrt{\frac{1.8 \times 10^{-5}}{0.1}} = 0.0134$

$\therefore \quad \Delta T_f = 0.10 \times 1.86 \times 1.0134 = 0.19°$

For benzoic acid,

$C_6H_5COOH \rightleftharpoons C_6H_5COO^- + H^+$

Let degree of ionisation be $= \alpha$

then, $\quad \alpha = \sqrt{\frac{K_a}{C}} = \sqrt{\frac{6.3 \times 10^{-5}}{C}}$

Also, $\quad \Delta T_f = \text{molality} \times 1.86 \times (1 + \alpha)$

$0.19° = \text{molality} \times 1.80 \times (1 + \alpha)$

$\therefore \quad \text{molality} = \frac{0.19}{1.88(1 + \alpha)} = C$

$\therefore \quad \alpha = \sqrt{\frac{6.3 \times 10^{-5} \times 1.86 \times (1 + \alpha)}{0.19}}$

$\therefore \quad \alpha^2 = 6.17 \times 10^{-4}(1 + \alpha)$

$\therefore \quad \alpha^2 - 6.17 \times 10^{-4}\alpha - 6.17 \times 10^{-4} = 0$

$\therefore \quad \alpha = \frac{6.17 \times 10^{-4} + \sqrt{(6.17 \times 10^{-4})^2 + 4 \times 6.17 \times 10^{-4}}}{2}$

$= 0.025$

$\therefore$ Molality (benzoic acid) $= \frac{0.19}{1.86 \times 1.025}$

$= 0.10$ molal

$\therefore$ Amount in 1 kg water $= 122 \times 0.1$

$= 12.2$ g

213. (c)

$Ag_2CrO_4(s) \rightleftharpoons 2Ag^+(aq) + CrO_4^{2-}(aq)$

$K_{sp} = [Ag^+]^2[CrO_4^{2-}]$

$= 4S^3$ (S = solubility)

$\therefore \quad 4S^3 = 1.1 \times 10^{-12}$

$\therefore \quad S = 6.5 \times 10^{-5}$ M

Thus, solubility of Ag^+ ion $= 2S$

$= 2 \times 6.5 \times 10^{-5}$ M $= 1.3 \times 10^{-4}$ M

$[Ag^+]$ present in 400 mL total mixture

$= 1.3 \times 10^{-4} \times 400$ millimol

$[Ag^+]$ actually taken

$= 200 \times 0.005$ millimol

Thus, fraction of Ag^+ ion in solution

$$= \frac{1.3\times10^{-4}\times400}{200\times0.005} = 0.052$$

Thus, % of Ag^+ in solution (unprecipitated) $= 0.052\times100 = 5.2\%$

■ Due to dilution (on mixing)

$$[Ag^+] = \frac{200\times0.01}{400} = 0.005\ M$$

214. (d) $CH_3COOH \rightleftharpoons CH_3COO^- + H^+$

$$K_a = \frac{[CH_3COO^-][H^+]}{[CH_3COOH]}$$

$$\therefore [H^+] = K_a\frac{[CH_3COOH]}{[CH_3COO^-]} = \frac{1.8\times10^{-5}\times0.1}{0.5} = 3.6\times10^{-6}\ M$$

$$MnS(s) \rightleftharpoons Mn^{2+}(aq) + S^{2-}(aq);\quad K_1 = K_{sp}$$

$$2H^+ + S^{2-} \rightleftharpoons H_2S;\ K_2 = \frac{1}{K_{a_1}K_{a_2}}$$

$$MnS(s) + 2H^+ \rightleftharpoons Mn^{2+} + H_2S;\quad K_3 = K_1K_2 = \frac{K_{sp}}{K_{a_1}K_{a_2}}$$

$$\frac{[Mn^{2+}][H_2S]}{[H^+]^2} = \frac{3\times10^{-14}}{1\times10^{-21}}$$

$$\frac{x^2}{(3.6\times10^{-6})} = 3\times10^7$$

$$x^2 = 3\times10^7\times(3.6\times10^{-6})^2 = 3.888\times10^{-4}$$

$$x = 0.0197\ mol\ L^{-1} = 0.0197\times87\ g\ L^{-1} = 1.715\ g\ L^{-1}$$

215. (b) $AgCN(s) \rightleftharpoons Ag^+(aq) + CN^-(aq),\quad K_1 = K_{sp}$

$$Ag^+(aq) + 2NH_3(aq) \rightleftharpoons [Ag(NH_3)_2^+](aq),\quad K_2 = K_f$$

$$AgCN(s) + 2NH_3(aq) \rightleftharpoons [Ag(NH_3)_2^+] + CN,\quad K_3 = K_{sp}K_f$$

Initial	0.20 M	0	0
At equil.	(0.20 − 2x)	x	x

$$K_3 = K_{sp}K_f = \frac{[Ag(NH_3)_2^+][CN^-]}{[NH_3]^2}$$

$$K_{sp}\times1.6\times10^7 = \frac{x^2}{(0.20-2x)^2}$$

$$x = 8.8\times10^{-6}\ mol\ L^{-1}$$

$$K_{sp} = \frac{(8.8\times10^{-6})^2}{(0.20-2\times8.8\times10^{-6})^2\ 1.6\times10^7} = 1.2\times10^{-16}$$

216. (d) If NaOH is not added, then solubility

$$Ca(OH)_2(s) \rightleftharpoons Ca^{2+}(aq) + 2OH^-(aq);\quad K_{sp} = [Ca^{2+}][OH^-]^2$$

$$4.42\times10^{-5} = (S)(2S)^2$$

$$\therefore 4S^3 = 4.42\times10^{-5}$$

$$\therefore S = \sqrt[3]{\frac{4.42\times10^{-5}}{4}} = 0.0223\ mol\ L^{-1}$$

$$= \frac{0.0223}{2}\ mol\ in\ 500\ mL = \frac{0.0223}{2}\times74\ g\ in\ 500\ mL = 0.824\ g$$

In the presence of NaOH

Due to mixing, total volume is (1000 mL)

$$\text{Hence, } [NaOH]_{mix} = \frac{0.40}{2} = 0.20\ M$$

$$\therefore \text{Solubility } \frac{K_{sp}}{[OH^-]^2} = \frac{4.42\times10^{-5}}{(0.2)^2} = 1.105\times10^{-3}\ mol\ L^{-1}$$

$$= 1.105\times10^{-3}\times74\ g\ L^{-1} = 0.0818\ g$$

Thus, $Ca(OH)_2$ that is precipitated $= 0.824 - 0.0818 = 0.742$ g

217. (d) By van't Hoff equation,

$$\Delta H = \frac{2.303RT_1T_2}{(T_2-T_1)}\log\frac{(K_w)_{T_2}}{(K_w)_{T_1}}$$

B.P. at 1 atm = 373 K for H_2O

$$56.5 = \frac{2.303\times8.314\times10^{-3}\times300\times373}{(373-300)}\times\log\frac{(K_w)T_2}{1\times10^{-14}}$$

$$\therefore \log\frac{(K_w)_{T_2}}{1\times10^{-14}} = 1.925$$

$$\frac{(K_w)_{T_2}}{(K_w)_{300}} = 84.145$$

$$\therefore (K_w)_{T_2} = 84.145\times1\times10^{-14} = 8.41\times10^{-13}$$

218. (c) CH_3COONa solution is alkaline due to hydrolysis of CH_3COO^- ion.

$$CH_3COO^- + H_2O \rightleftharpoons CH_3COOH + OH^-$$

$$K_a(CH_3COOH) = 1.8\times10^{-5}$$

$$\therefore pK_a = -\log1.8\times10^{-5} = 4.74$$

pH of CH_3COONa due to hydrolysis

$$pH = 7 + \frac{pK_a}{2} + \frac{\log C}{2} = 7 + \frac{4.74}{2} + \frac{\log0.1}{2} = 7 + 2.37 - 0.5 = 8.87$$

$$\therefore [H_3O^+] = -\log pH = 10^{-pH} = 10^{-8.87} = 1.35\times10^{-9}$$

For phenolphthalein, ionic form is coloured and molecular form is colourless.

$$PhH \rightleftharpoons Ph^- + H^+$$

$$\therefore K_a = \frac{[Ph^-][H^+]}{[PhH]} \Rightarrow \frac{[Ph^-]}{[PhH]} = \frac{K_a}{[H^+]}$$

$$\frac{\text{Coloured form}}{\text{Colourless form}} = \frac{3.16\times10^{-10}}{1.35\times10^{-9}} = 0.234$$

Total part of coloured and colourless forms $= 1 + 0.234 = 1.234$

$$\text{Thus, fraction in coloured form} = \frac{0.234}{1.234} = 0.19$$

219. (b) Reaction of HCl with Na_2CO_3 takes place in two stages :

I: $CO_3^{2-} + H^+ \rightleftharpoons HCO_3^-$;

$$K_{a_1} = 4.52\times10^{-7},\quad pK_{a_1} = 6.34$$

II. $HCO_3^- + H^+ \rightleftharpoons H_2CO_3$

$$K_{a_2} = 4.67\times10^{-11},\quad pK_{a_2} = 10.33$$

pH at the half neutralisation point is

$$pH = \frac{pK_{a_1} + pK_{a_2}}{2} = \frac{6.34 + 10.33}{2} = 8.34$$

In the present case, pH is to be adjusted at 10.0. Thus, resultant solution should be a salt of weak acid and strong base (HCO_3^- and CO_3^{2-}).

$$HCO_3^-(aq) \rightleftharpoons CO_3^{2-} + H^+$$

$$\therefore pH = pK_{a_2} + \log\frac{[CO_3^{2-}]}{[HCO_3^-]}$$

$$10 = 10.33 + \log\frac{[CO_3^{2-}]}{[HCO_3^-]}$$

$$-0.33 = \log\frac{[CO_3^{2-}]}{[HCO_3^-]}$$

Due to total volume,

$$[CO_3^{2-}]_{mix} = \frac{0.10}{2} = 0.05\ M$$

Let HCl added to be $= x$ mol L^{-1}

	CO_3^{2-}	$+ H^+ \rightleftharpoons$	HCO_3^-
Inital	0.05 M	0	0
$[H^+]$ added	—	x	—
At equil.	(0.05 − x)	0	x

$$\therefore -0.33 = \log\left(\frac{0.05-x}{x}\right)$$

$$\frac{0.05-x}{x} = 0.468$$

$$0.05 - x = 0.468x$$

$$\therefore x = \frac{0.05}{1.468} = 0.034\ mol\ HCl$$

220. (a) Hydrolysis of ester (catalysed by H^+) follows first-order kinetics.
Acidic strength is dependent on rate/rate constant of the hydrolysis reaction.

$$\frac{[H^+] \text{ of strong acid } (HX)}{[H^+] \text{ of weak acid } (HA)} = \frac{\text{rate constant } k(HX)}{\text{rate constant } k(HA)} = \frac{\text{rate of reaction with } HX}{\text{rate of reaction with } HA} = \frac{R}{R'}$$

But $R' = \frac{1}{100}R$

$$\therefore \frac{[H^+] \text{ of } HX}{[H^+] \text{ of } HA} = 100$$

$[H^+]$ of HX (strong acid) $= [HX] = 1\,M$

$\therefore$ $[H^+]$ of $HA = \frac{1}{100} = 0.01\,M$

For weak acid,

$$HA \rightleftharpoons H^+ + A^-$$

Initial	1	0	0
After ionisation	$(1-x)$	x	x

$[H^+] = [A^-] = 0.01\,M$

$[HA] = (1-x) = 1 - 0.01 = 0.99$

$$\therefore K_a = \frac{[H^+][A^-]}{[HA]} = \frac{(0.01)(0.01)}{0.99} = 1.01 \times 10^{-4}$$

221. (b) In presence of common ion (in this case Ag^+ ion, solubility of sparingly soluble salt is decreased.

Let solubility of Ag_2CrO_4 in presence of 0.1 M $AgNO_3 = x$

$$\underset{}{Ag_2CrO_4} \rightleftharpoons \underset{2x}{2Ag^+} + \underset{x}{CrO_4^{2-}}$$

$$AgNO_3 \rightleftharpoons \underset{0.1}{Ag^+} + \underset{0.1}{NO_3^-}$$

Total $[Ag^+] = (2x + 0.1)\,M$

$\approx 0.01\,M$ as $x <<< 0.1\,M$

$[CrO_4^{2-}] = x\,M$

Thus, $[Ag^+]^2[CrO_4^{2-}] = K_{sp}$

$(0.1)^2(x) = 1.1 \times 10^{-12}$

$x = 1.1 \times 10^{-10}\,M$

222. (c) $BOH + H^+ \rightleftharpoons B^+ + H_2O$

Solution of B^+ is acidic due to hydrolysis

$$B^+ + H_2O \rightleftharpoons BOH + H^+$$

For titration,

$$\underset{\text{Base}}{M_1V_1} = \underset{\text{HCl}}{M_2V_2}$$

$$\frac{2}{5} \times 2.5 = \frac{2}{15} \times V$$

$V = 7.5$ mL

Total volume of solution

$= 2.5 + 7.5 = 10$ mL

$$[B^+]_{\text{dilute}} = \frac{2.5}{10} \times \frac{2}{5} = 0.1\,M$$

pH of B^+ due to hydrolysis

$(pK_b = -\log C \times 10^{-12} = 12)$

$$pH = 7 - \frac{pK_b}{2} - \frac{\log C}{2}$$

$$= 7 - \frac{12}{2} - \frac{\log 0.1}{2} = 1.5$$

$\therefore$ $[H^+] = 10^{-1.5} = 10^{-2}10^{0.5}$

$= 3.16 \times 10^{-2}\,M = 3.2 \times 10^{-2}\,M$

223. (d) $MX : K_{sp} = S^2 = 4 \times 10^{-8}$

$S = 2 \times 10^{-4}\,M$

$MX_2 : K_{sp} = 4S^3 = 3.2 \times 10^{-14}$

$S = 2 \times 10^{-5}\,M$

$M_3X : K_{sp} = 27S^4 = 2.7 \times 10^{-15}$

$S = 10^{-4}\,M$

Order of solubility is : $MX > M_3X > MX_2$

224. (a) When CO_2 is dissolved in water, following equilibria are established.

$$H_2O + CO_2 \rightleftharpoons H_2CO_3$$
$$H_2CO_3 \rightleftharpoons H^+ + HCO_3^-$$
$$HCO_3^- \rightleftharpoons H^+ + CO_3^{2-}$$

Therefore, in solution, all of the above mentioned species exist.

225. (b)

$$CH_3NH_2 + HCl \longrightarrow CH_3NH_3^+ + Cl^-$$

	CH_3NH_2	HCl	$CH_3NH_3^+$
Initial	0.10 M	0.08 M	0
Final	0.02 M	0 M	0.08 M

Mixture is a buffer

$$pOH = pK_b + \log\frac{[CH_3NH_3^+]}{[CH_3NH_2]}$$

$$= -\log(5 \times 10^{-4}) + \log\frac{0.08}{0.02} = 3.9$$

$pH = 14 - pOH = 10.1$

$[H^+] = 8 \times 10^{-11}\,M$

Type II. Statement Based Questions

226. (a) **227.** (b) **228.** (d) **229.** (a)
230. (a) **231.** (a) **232.** (a) **233.** (b)
234. (a)

235. (b) $Cu^{2+} + S^{2-}(aq) \longrightarrow Cu(s)$

When H_2S gas is passed into $Cu^{2+}(aq)$ solution, black precipitate of CuS are formed, as solubility product of CuS is low.

$$K_{sp} = [Cu^{2+}][S^{2-}]$$

and $$K_{eq} = \frac{1}{[Cu^{2+}][S^{2-}]}$$

Due to immediate reaction, K_{eq} is high, hence K_{sp} is low.

Thus, statements I and II are correct but statement II is not the correct explanation of statement I.

236. (d) $H_2O(l) \rightleftharpoons H^+(aq) + OH^-(aq)$

is an endothermic reaction. Due to increase in temperature, number of H^+ ions increases, thus pH decreases as

$$pH = -\log[H^+]$$

Thus, statement I is incorrect but statement II is correct.

Type III. MCQs with ONE or More than One Correct Alternate

237. (a, c, d) H^+ ion donor as well as H^+ ion acceptor are Bronsted-Lowry acid and base. These are also amphiprotic in nature.

$$H_2CO_3 \xleftarrow{H^+} HCO_3^- \xrightarrow[-H^+]{} CO_3^{2-}$$

$$H_3PO_4 \xleftarrow{H^+} H_2PO_4^- \xrightarrow[-H^+]{} HPO_4^{2-}$$

$$H_2SO_4 \xleftarrow{H^+} HSO_4^- \xrightarrow[-H^+]{} SO_4^{2-}$$

H_3PO_2 is monobasic acid hence, $H_2PO_2^-$ is not further ionised.

238. (c, d)

(a) pH of 1×10^{-7} M NaOH > 7 being basic in nature.
Thus, (a) is incorrect.

(b) $H_2PO_2^-$ does not further ionic thus, HPO_2^{2-} is not formed,
Thus, (b) is incorrect.

(c) $K_w = [H_3O^+][OH^-]$,
As temperature increases, ionisation of water increases, hence K_w increases.

(d) At half neutralisation point,
$[CH_3COOH] = [CH_3COONa]$
Thus, it makes buffer.

$$\therefore pH = pK_a + \log\frac{[CH_3COO^-]}{[CH_3COOH]}$$

$$pH = pK_a$$

239. (a, b, c, d)

$CH_3COO^- + H^+ \longrightarrow CH_3COOH$

CH_3COO^- controls pH when H^+ is added

$CH_3COOH + OH^- \longrightarrow CH_3COO^-$

CH_3COOH controls pH when OH^- is added.

$$pH = pK_a + \log\frac{[CH_3COO^-]}{[CH_3COOH]}$$

On addition of HCl, CH_3COOH increases thus, pH decreases.
On addition of NaOH, CH_3COO^- increases, hence pH increases.

240. (a, b, d)

(a) When a buffer solution is diluted, both parts are equally affected hence, pH remains unchanged.

Thus, (a) is correct.

(b) As in (a),

Thus, (b) is correct.

(c) Aqueous solution of sodium benzoate is basic in nature and is dependent on concentration.

$$pH = 7 + \frac{pK_a}{2} + \frac{\log C}{2}$$

(d) For ammonium benzoate (salt of weak acid and weak base)

$$pH = 7 + \left(\frac{pK_a - pK_b}{2}\right)$$

pH is independent of concentration.

241. (a, b, c) Each is a mixture of weak acid and its salt with strong base.

242. (a, b, d) $K_{sp} = [Ag^+][Cl^-] = 1 \times 10^{-10}$

$\therefore \log[Ag^+] + \log[Cl^-]$

$= \log(1 \times 10^{-10}) = -10$

$-\log[Ag^+] - \log[Cl^-] = 10$

$\therefore \quad p_{Ag} + p_{Cl} = 10.$

Thus, (a) is correct

In 0.01 M $[Ag^+]$

$(0.01)[Cl^-] = 1 \times 10^{-10}$

$[Cl^-] = 1 \times 10^{-10}/0.01 = 1 \times 10^{-8}$

$\log Cl = -8$

$-\log Cl = 8$

$\therefore \quad p_{Cl} = 8,$

Thus, (b) is correct.

In presence of Ag^+, solubility is decreased, but

$p_{Ag} + p_{Cl} = 10.$

Thus, (c) is incorrect.

Also, $[Ag^+] = [Cl^-]$

$= \sqrt{10^{-10}}$ in saturated AgCl

$\log[Ag^+] = \log[Cl^-] = -5$

$-\log[Ag^+] = -\log[Cl^-] = 5$

$\therefore \quad p_{Ag} = p_{Cl} = 5$

Thus, (d) is correct.

243. (a, c) (a) 10^{-8} M HCl, being acidic, $pH < 7$

(b) 10^{-8} M NaOH, being basic, $pH > 7$

(c) In diluted HCl, $HCl = 10^{-7}$M, but being acidic, $pH < 7$

(d) At the end point, CH_3COONa is formed and solution is basic due to hydrolysis.

$$CH_3COO^- + H_2O \longrightarrow CH_3COOH + OH^-$$

244. (a, b, d)

(a) In 0.01 M $(NH_4)_2SO_4$,

$[NH_4^+] = 0.02$ M

$$\therefore \quad p_{OH} = pK_b + \log\frac{[NH_4^+]}{[NH_4OH]}$$

$\therefore \quad p_{OH} = pK_b$

Thus, (a) is correct.

(b) 0.01 M $(CH_3COO)_2Ca$ = 0.02 M CH_3COO^-

$$\therefore \quad pH = pK_a + \log\frac{[CH_3COO^-]}{[CH_3COOH]}$$

$= pK_a + \log 2$

thus $pH > pK_a$,

thus (b) is correct.

(c) 0.01 M NH_4OH = 0.01 N NH_4OH

0.01 M H_2SO_4 = 0.02 N H_2SO_4

Thus, H_2SO_4 is not completely neutralised

Thus, $pH < 7$.

Thus, (c) is incorrect.

(d) 0.01 M $Ca(OH)_2$ = 0.02 N $Ca(OH)_2$

0.01 M H_2SO_4 = 0.02 N H_2SO_4

Thus, completely neutralisation.

Also, $CaSO_4$ is not hydrolysed

Thus, neutral, pH = 7

Thus, (d) is correct.

245. (a, b, c, d)

(a) $NH_3 + NH_3 \rightleftharpoons NH_4^+ + NH_2^-$

Species which gives cation of a solvent is a strong acid.

Thus, (a) is correct.

(b) Species which gives anion of the solvent is a strong base.

Thus (b) is correct

(c) $\underset{Base_1}{CH_3COOH} + \underset{Acid_2}{H_2SO_4} \rightleftharpoons \underset{Acid_1}{CH_3COOH_2^+} + \underset{Base_2}{HSO_4^-}$

H_2SO_4 is much stronger than CH_3COOH. Thus CH_3COOH is a base. Thus (c) is correct.

(d) H_2O is weak base, thus H_3O^+ is the strongest acid. Thus, (d) is correct.

246. (a, b, c)

(a) When $[Ph^-] < [PhH]$, equilibrium is in left side, thus solution appears colourless. Thus, (a) is correct

(b) It is reverse of (a).

Thus, (b) is correct.

(c) When $\frac{[Ph^-]}{[PhH]} = \frac{1}{10}$

$pH = (pK_a - 1)$, colourless

When $\frac{[Ph^-]}{[PhH]} = \frac{10}{1}$

$pH = (pK_a + 1)$, pink.

Thus, (c) is correct.

247. (b, c) $\underset{\text{Bronsted-Lowry base}}{NH_3} + H^+ \longrightarrow NH_4^+$

NH_3 is H^+ ion acceptor, thus Bronsted-Lowy base.

NH_3 is lone pair donor thus, Lewis base.

- NH_3 is a base in aqueous solution.

$NH_4OH \rightleftharpoons NH_4^+ + OH^-$

Thus, it is Arrhenius base in aqueous solution.

248. (a, d) H_3BO_3 is a weak monobasic acid and ionises in aqueous solution.

249. (a, c, d)

(a) $CH_2 - COOH \leftarrow$ Acidic

$|$

$NH_2 \leftarrow$ Basic

(b)

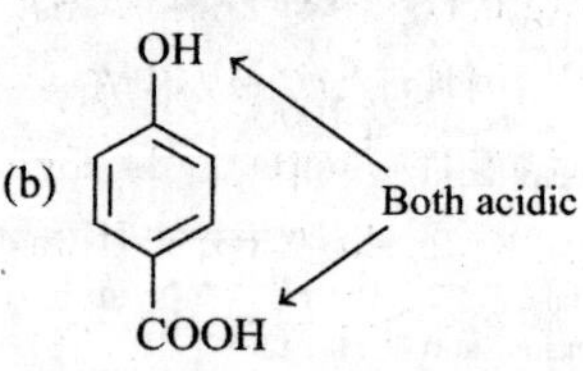

- Phenol is acidic in nature.

(c)

(d)

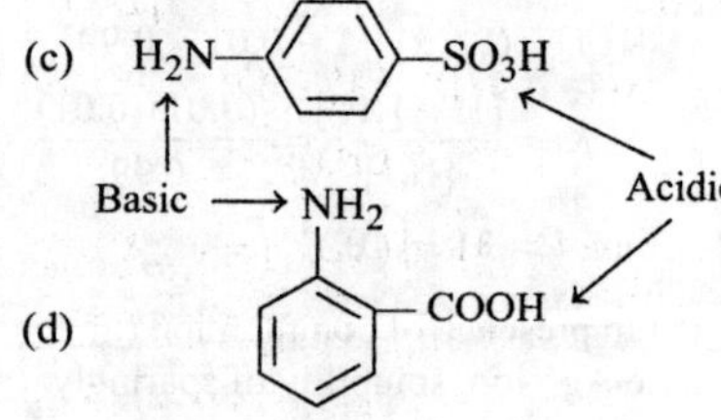

250. (a, c, d)

(a) $[Li^+][OH^-] = 1 \times 10^{-6}$

$\log Li^+ + \log OH^- = -6$

$\therefore \quad p_{Li} + p_{OH} = 6$

$\therefore p_{Li} + (14 - pH) = 6$

$\therefore \quad pH = 8 + p_{Li}$

Thus, (a) is correct.

(b) $[Mg^{2+}][OH^-]^2 = 1 \times 10^{-12}$

$\therefore \quad p_{Mg} + 2p_{OH} = 12$

$p_{Mg} + 2[14 - p_H] = 12$

$\therefore \quad pH = \frac{p_{Mg}}{2} + 8$

Thus, (b) is incorrect.

(c) $[Al^{3+}][OH^-]^3 = 1 \times 10^{-27}$

$\therefore \quad p_{Al} + 3p_{OH} = 27$

$p_{Al} + 3[14 - pH] = 27$

$\therefore \quad pH = \frac{p_{Al}}{3} + 5$

Thus, (c) is correct.

(d) $[Si^{4+}][OH^{-4}] = 1 \times 10^{-28}$

$\therefore \quad p_{Si} + 4p_{OH} = 28$

$p_{Si} + 4[14 - pH] = 28$

$\therefore \quad pH = \left(\frac{p_{Si}}{4} + 7\right)$

Thus, (d) is correct.

251. (a, c, d) $K >> 1$, thus equilibrium is displaced in forward side where weak acid and weak base are formed.

HCN is a weak acid and ONO^- is a weak base and HONO is a stronger acid.

Thus, (a) and (c) are correct.

Also, at equilibrium, $\Delta G = 0$.

252. (a, b, c)

H^+ or OH^-

Benzenoid form (Light colour) ⇌ Quinonoid form (Deep colour)

253. (b, d) $Ag_2CrO_4 \rightleftharpoons 2Ag^+ + CrO_4^{2-}$

$$[Ag^+]^2[CrO_4^{2-}] = K_{sp}$$

$$\log[Ag^+]^2 + \log[CrO_4^{2-}] = \log K_{sp}$$

$$-2\log[Ag^+] - \log[CrO_4^{2-}] = -\log K_{sp}$$

$$\therefore \quad 2p_{Ag} + p_{CrO_4} = pK_{sp}$$

Thus, (a) is incorrect

Also, $[Ag^+] = 2[CrO_4^{2-}]$

$$\therefore \quad (2[CrO_4^{2-}])^2[CrO_4^{2-}] = K_{sp}$$

$$4[CrO_4^{2-}]^3 = K_{sp}$$

$$\therefore \quad \log 4 + 3\log[CrO_4^{2-}] = \log K_{sp}$$

$$-2\log 2 + 3\,p_{CrO_4} = pK_{sp}$$

$$\therefore \quad 3p_{CrO_4} = pK_{sp} + 2\log 2$$

Thus, (b) is correct.

Also, $[CrO_4^{2-}] = \frac{1}{2}[Ag^+]$

$$\therefore [Ag^+]^2\left[\frac{1}{2}Ag^+\right] = K_{sp}$$

$$\frac{1}{2}[Ag^+]^3 = K_{sp}$$

$$-\log 2 + 3\log[Ag^+] = \log K_{sp}$$

$$\therefore \quad \log 2 + 3p_{Ag} = p_{K_{sp}}$$

Thus, (c) is incorrect.

$$[Ag^+] = 2[CrO_4^{2-}]$$

$$\therefore \quad p_{Ag} = -\log 2 + p_{CrO_4}$$

Thus, (d) is correct.

254. (a, c)

I $[Al(OH)_3(H_2O)_3] + OH^- \rightleftharpoons$ (Acid$_1$, Base$_2$)

$[Al(OH)_4(H_2O)_2]^- + H_2O$ (Base$_1$, Acid$_2$)

II. $[Al(OH)_3(H_2O)_3] + H_3O^+ \rightleftharpoons$ (Base$_1$, Acid$_2$)

$[Al(OH)_2(H_2O)_4]^+ + H_2O$ (Acid$_1$, Base$_2$)

Thus, (a) and (c) are correct.

255. (a,d) $BaSO_4$ is precipitated, if

$$[Ba^{2+}][SO_4^{2-}] > K_{sp}$$

	$[Ba^{2+}]_{mix}$	$[SO_4^{2-}]_{mix}$	$[Ba^{2+}][SO_4^{2-}]$	ppt.
(a)	1×10^{-3}M	4.5×10^{-4}M	4.5×10^{-7}	Yes
(b)	1×10^{-4} M	4.5×10^{-8} M	4.5×10^{-12}	No
(c)	3×10^{-4} M	1.5×10^{-8} M	4.5×10^{-12}	No
(d)	2×10^{-4} M	3.0×10^{-4}M	6.0×10^{-8}	Yes

■ On mixing two solutions, volume changes hence, molarity is also affected.

$$M_1V_1 = M(\text{mix})\,V_{\text{mix}}$$

256. (a, d) $\Delta G^\circ < 0$, it means reaction is spontaneous in forward side in which weak acid and weak base are formed.

$$\underset{\text{Weak}}{HA} + \underset{\text{Weak}}{HB} \rightleftharpoons \underset{\text{Acid}}{H_2A^+} + \underset{\text{Base}}{B^-}$$

HA is proton acceptor thus, is a base. HB is proton donor thus, is an acid. Thus, HB is stronger acid than HA.

$$K_a(HB) > K_a(HA)$$

$$\therefore \quad pK_a(HB) < pK_a(HA)$$

Thus, (a) is correct.

Conjugate base B^- is weak base than A^-.

Thus, $K_b(B^-) < K_b(A^-)$

$$pK_b(B^-) > pK_b(A^-)$$

Thus, (d) is correct.

■ If acid is weak, its conjugate base is strong and *vice-versa*.

257. (a, b, c, d)

(a) When first half-equivalence point is reached, mixture contains 50% A and 50% B. Thus, it is a buffer.

Thus,
$$pH = pK_{a_1} + \log\frac{[B]}{[A]} = pK_{a_1} = 2.89$$

Thus, true.

(b) At the first equivalence point, B is formed.

B is proton donor as well as proton acceptor. Thus, it is amphiprotic.

$$pH = \frac{pK_{a_1} + pK_{a_2}}{2}$$

$$= \frac{2.89 + 5.41}{2} = 4.15$$

Thus, true.

(c) When second half-equivalence point is reached, mixture contains 50% B and 50% C.

Thus, it is a buffer.

$$\therefore pH = pK_{a_2} + \log\frac{[C]}{[B]}$$

$$= pK_{a_2} = 5.41$$

Thus, true.

(d) At the second equivalence point, there is complete neutralisation of A changing to

$$A + 2NaOH \longrightarrow C + 2H_2O$$

V mL of 0.01 M A = $2V$ mL of 0.01 M NaOH

C formed = V mL of 0.01 M

But total volume = $3V$

Thus, $[C]_{mix} = \left(\frac{0.01}{3}\right)$ M

C is hydrolysed to B back forming basic solution.

$$C_6H_4(COO^-)_2 + H_2O \rightleftharpoons C_6H_4(COOH)(COO^-) + OH^-$$

$$pH = 7 + \frac{pK_{a_2}}{2} + \frac{\log C}{2}$$

$$= 7 + \frac{5.41}{2} + \frac{\log(0.01/3)}{2}$$

$$= 7 + \frac{5.41}{2} - \frac{2.48}{2} = 8.473$$

Thus, (d) is true.

258. (c, d) $M^{2+} + S^{2-} \longrightarrow MS\downarrow$

MS is precipitated if, $[M^{2+}][S^{2-}] > K_{sp}$

On mixing, total volume = 15 mL.

$$[S^{2-}]_{mix} = 1\times10^{-19}\times\frac{10}{15} = \frac{1\times10^{-18}}{15}\,M$$

$$[M^{2+}]_{mix} = 0.04\times\frac{5}{15} = \frac{0.04}{3}\,M$$

$$[M^{2+}][S^{2-}] = \frac{1\times10^{-18}}{15}\times\frac{0.04}{3}$$

$$= 8.89\times10^{-22}$$

MS	K_{sp} related to $[M^{2+}][S^{2-}]$	ppt.
MnS	$2.5\times10^{-13} > [M^{2+}][S^{2-}]$	No
ZnS	$1.6\times10^{-24} > [M^{2+}][S^{2-}]$	No
CdS	$8.0\times10^{-27} < [M^{2+}][S^{2-}]$	Yes
CuS	$6.3\times10^{-30} < [M^{2+}][S^{2-}]$	Yes

259. (d) Weak acid and salt of weak acid and strong acid together form an acidic buffer.

260. (a, b, c, d)

261. (a, c, d)

$$PO_4^{3-} + H_2O \rightleftharpoons HPO_4^{2-} + OH^-$$

$$K_{h_1} = \frac{K_w}{K_3} = \frac{1\times10^{-14}}{4.5\times10^{-13}} = 2.22\times10^{-2}$$

$$HPO_4^{2-} + H_2O \rightleftharpoons H_2PO_4^- + OH^-$$

$$K_{h_2} = \frac{Kw}{K_2} = \frac{1.0\times10^{-14}}{6.3\times10^{-8}} = 1.60\times10^{-7}$$

$H_2PO_4^- + H_2O \rightleftharpoons H_3PO_4 + OH^-$

$K_{h_3} = \frac{Kw}{K_{h_1}} = \frac{1\times10^{-14}}{7.1\times10^{-3}} = 1.4\times10^{-12}$

Maximum value of K_h is from first step. Thus, this releases maximum $[OH^-]$.

$[OH^-] = Cx = C\sqrt{\frac{K_h}{C}} = \sqrt{CK_h} = \sqrt{C\frac{K_w}{K_3}}$

$= \sqrt{\frac{0.1\times10^{-14}}{4.5\times10^{-13}}} = 4.71\times10^{-2}$ M

$[H_3PO_4]$ is derived from the last step of hydrolysis.

$[H_3PO_4] = Cx = C\sqrt{\frac{K_h}{C}} = \sqrt{K_hC}$

$= \sqrt{1.4\times10^{-12}\times0.1}$

$= 3.74\times10^{-7}$ M

Thus, (a), (c) and (d) are correct.

Type IV. Passage Based MCQs (Comprehension)

Passage 1

K_{sp} of $CaF_2 << K_{sp}$ of SrF_2.

Thus, F^- in saturated solution is contributed by SrF_2.

$SrF_2(s) \rightleftharpoons \underset{(S)}{Sr^{2+}(aq)} + \underset{(2S)}{2F^-(aq)}$

$4S^3 = K_{sp}$

$\therefore S = \left(\frac{K_{sp}}{4}\right)^{1/3} = \left(\frac{2.9\times10^{-9}}{4}\right)^{1/2}$

$= 8.98\times10^{-4}$ M

F^- from $SrF_2 = 8.98\times10^{-4}\times2$ M

$= 1.796\times10^{-3}$ M

$CaF_2(s) \rightleftharpoons Ca^{2+}(aq) + 2F^-(aq)$

$\therefore K_{sp} = [Ca^{2+}][F^-]^2$

$3.4\times10^{-11} = [Ca^{2+}][1.796\times10^{-3}]^2$

$[Ca^{2+}] = 1.05\times10^{-3}$ M

Thus, solubility of CaF_2 in presence of common ion effect of F^- of $SrF_2 = 1.05\times10^{-5}$ M

262.(d)

263.(a)

Passage 2

$HCO_3^- + H_2O \rightleftharpoons H_3O^+ + CO_3^{2-}$

$K_a = \frac{[H_3O^+][CO_3^{2-}]}{[HCO_3^-]} = 4.7\times10^{-11}$

$CO_3^{2-} + H_2O \rightleftharpoons HCO_3^- + OH^-$

Hydrolysis constant

$K_h = \frac{K_w}{K_a} = \frac{[H_3O^+][OH^-]}{\frac{[H_3O^+][CO_3^{2-}]}{[HCO_3^-]}}$

$\frac{[HCO_3^-][OH^-]}{[CO_3^{2-}]} = \frac{K_w}{4.7\times10^{-11}}$ ...(i)

If, pH (buffer) = 8.60

$\therefore [H_3O^+] = 10^{-8.60} = 10^{-9}10^{0.4}$

$= 2.51\times10^{-9}$ M

$\therefore [OH^-] = \frac{K_w}{[H_3O^+]} = \frac{K_w}{2.51\times10^{-9}}$ ...(ii)

From (i) and (ii),

$\therefore \frac{[HCO_3^-]}{[CO_3^{2-}]}\frac{K_w}{(2.51\times10^{-9})} = \frac{K_w}{4.7\times10^{-11}}$

$\frac{[HCO_3^-]}{[CO_3^{2-}]} = \frac{2.51\times10^{-9}}{4.7\times10^{-11}} = 53.4$

$\therefore [HCO_3^-]:[CO_3^{2-}] = 53.4:1$

$\therefore$ Percentage of $[HCO_3^-]$ formed due to hydrolysis of CO_3^{2-} is

$= \frac{53.4}{54.4}\times100$ of CO_3^{2-}

$= 98.16\%$

The carbonate ion which dissolves froms HCO_3^- in 1 : 1 mole ratio or remains unreacted.

Thus,

$[Sr^{2+}] = [HCO_3^-] + [CO_3^{2-}]$

$= 2.2\times10^{-4}$ M (given)

$= 53.4[CO_3^{2-}] + [CO_3^{2-}]$

$\therefore [CO_3^{2-}] = \frac{2.2\times10^{-4}}{54.4}$ M

$\therefore K_{sp} = [Sr^{2+}][CO_3^{2-}]$

$= (2.2\times10^{-4})\left(\frac{2.2\times10^{-4}}{54.4}\right)$

$= 8.9\times10^{-10}$

264.(a)

265.(b)

Passage 3

$CaCO_3(s) \rightleftharpoons Ca^{2+}(aq) + CO_3^{2-}(aq), K_1 = K_{sp}$

$CO_3^{2-}(aq) + H^+(aq) \rightleftharpoons HCO_3^-(aq), K_2 = \frac{1}{K_a}$

$CaCO_3(s) + H^+(aq) \rightleftharpoons \underset{x}{HCO_3^-(aq)} + \underset{x}{CO_3^{2-}(aq)}$

$K_3 = ?$

x = solubility of $CaCO_3$ in a buffer of pH = 8

$\therefore K_3 = K_1K_2 = \frac{K_{sp}}{K_a} = \frac{x^2}{[H^+]}$

$[H^+] = 10^{-pH} = 10^{-8}$ M

$\therefore x^2 = \frac{K_{sp}}{K_a}[H^+] = \frac{(1\times10^{-8})(1\times10^{-8})}{4.7\times10^{-11}}$

$= 2.13\times10^{-6}$

$\because x = 1.45\times10^{-3}$ M

Thus, solubility of $CaCO_3$ in a buffer of pH = 1.45×10^{-3} M.

Also, due to hydrolysis

$CO_3^{2-} + H_2O \rightleftharpoons HCO_3^- + OH^-$

K_h (hydrolysis constant) of CO_3^{2-}

$= \frac{[HCO_3^-][OH^-]}{[CO_3^{2-}]} = \frac{K_w}{K_a}$

$[OH^-] = \frac{K_w}{1\times10^{-8}} = 1\times10^{-6}$ M

$\frac{[HCO_3^-]}{[CO_3^{2-}]} = \frac{1\times10^{-14}\times1}{4.7\times10^{-11}\times10^{-6}} = \frac{212.8}{1}$

Total = $[HCO_3^-] + [CO_3^{2-}]$

$= 212.8 + 1 = 213.8$

$\therefore [CO_3^{2-}] = \frac{1}{213.8}\times100 = 0.471$

266.(d)

267.(c)

Passage 4

$H_2S \rightleftharpoons H^+ + HS^-, \quad K_{a_1}$

$HS^- \rightleftharpoons H^+ + S^{2-}, \quad K_{a_2}$

$H_2S \rightleftharpoons 2H^+ + S^{2-}$

$\therefore K = \frac{[H^+]^2[S^{2-}]}{[H_2S]} = K_{a_1}K_{a_2}$

$[H^+]_{HCl} = 0.022$ M

$\therefore [S^{2-}] = \frac{K_{a_1}K_{a_2}[H_2S]}{[H^+]^2} = \frac{1\times10^{-21}\times0.1}{(0.022)^2}$

$= 2.07\times10^{-19}$ M

CdS is precipitated, if

$[Ca^{2+}][S^{2-}] > K_{sp}$

$(0.001)(2.07\times10^{-19}) = 2.07\times10^{-22} > K_{sp}$

Thus, CdS is precipitated.

$[Cd^{2+}]$ at equilibrium $= \frac{K_{sp}}{[S^{2-}]}$

$= \frac{8\times10^{-27}}{2.07\times10^{-19}} = 3.86\times10^{-8}$ M

$\approx 4.0\times10^{-8}$ M

FeS is precipitated, if $[Fe^{2+}][S^{2-}] > K_{sp}$

$(0.001)(2.07\times10^{-19}) = 2.07\times10^{-22} < K_{sp}$(FeS)

Thus, FeS is not precipitated.

268. (b)

269. (a)

■ Solute *MS* is precipitated, if $[M^{2+}][S^{2-}] > K_{sp}$

Passage 5

$K_{sp} = [Al^{3+}][OH^-]^3$

$1.3\times10^{-33} = (0.0175)[OH^-]^3$

$\therefore [OH^-] = 2.6\times10^{-11}$ M

$\therefore \quad pOH = 10.59$

$\therefore \quad pH = 14 - 10.59 = 3.41$

Mixture of CH_3COOH and CH_3COONa is a buffer. Thus, by Henderson Hasselbalch equation,

$$pH = pK_a + \log\frac{[CH_3COONa]}{[CH_3COOH]}$$

$$3.41 = 4.74 + \log\frac{[CH_3COONa]}{1}$$

$$-1.33 = \log[CH_3COONa]$$

$\therefore [CH_3COONa] = 0.0468\text{ M}$

Thus, $= 0.0468 \times 82\text{ g L}^{-1}$

$$= \frac{0.0468 \times 82 \times 250}{1000}$$

$= 0.96$ g in 250 mL of buffer

270. (b) ***271.*** (a)

Passage 6

$$NH_4OH \rightleftharpoons NH_4^+ + OH^-$$

$$K_b = 1.8 \times 10^{-5} = \frac{[NH_4^+][OH^-]}{[NH_4OH]}$$

$$= \left(\frac{0.25}{0.05}\right)[OH^-]$$

$\therefore \quad [OH^-] = 3.6 \times 10^{-6}\text{ M}$

For $Al(OH)_3$

$$K_{sp} = [Al^{3+}][OH^-]^3$$

$$6.0 \times 10^{-32} = [Al^{3+}](3.6 \times 10^{-6})^3$$

$$[Al^{3+}] = 1.286 \times 10^{-15}\text{ M}$$

For $Mg(OH)_2$,

$$K_{sp} = [Mg^{2+}][OH^-]^2$$

$$8.9 \times 10^{-12} = [Mg^{2+}](36 \times 10^{-6})^2$$

$\therefore \quad [Mg^{2+}] = 0.687\text{ M}$

Thus, solubility of $Mg(OH)_2 > Al(OH)_3$.

In the absence of buffer,

$$K_{sp} = 4S^3$$

$$\therefore \quad S^3 = \frac{K_{sp}}{4}$$

$$S^3 = \frac{8.9 \times 10^{-12}}{4}$$

$$S = \sqrt[3]{\left(\frac{8.9 \times 10^{-12}}{4}\right)}$$

$$S_1 = 1.31 \times 10^{-4}\text{ M}$$

For $Al(OH)_3$, $K_{sp} = 27S^4$

$$\therefore \quad S^4 = \frac{K_{sp}}{27} = \frac{6.0 \times 10^{-32}}{27}$$

$$S_2 = 6.87 \times 10^{-9}\text{ M}$$

$$\frac{S_1}{S_2} = \frac{1.31 \times 10^{-4}}{6.87 \times 10^{-9}} = 19068 \approx 1.9 \times 10^4$$

■ For the solute A_xB_y $K_{sp} = x^x y^y (S)^{x+y}$ where, S is the solubility.

272. (b)

273. (a)

Passage 7

$$Ag_2CrO_4(s) \rightleftharpoons 2Ag^+(aq) + CrO_4^{2-}(aq)$$

$$K_{sp} = [Ag^+]^2[CrO_4^{2-}]$$

$[CrO_4^{2-}]$ required for precipitation of Ag^+ ion

$$= \frac{K_{sp}}{[Ag^+]^2} = \frac{9 \times 10^{-12}}{(0.01)^2}$$

$$= 9 \times 10^{-8}\text{ M}$$

Similarly, $[CrO_4^{2-}]$ required to precipitate Ba^{2+} ion is

$$[CrO_4^{2-}] = \frac{2 \times 10^{-10}}{(0.02)}$$

$$= 1 \times 10^{-8}\text{ M}$$

$[CrO_4^{2-}]$ for $Ba^{2+} < [CrO_4^{2-}]$ for Ag^+

Thus, $[Ba^+]$ is precipitated before $[Ag^+]$ ion

$[CrO_4^{2-}] = 9 \times 10^{-8}$ M when precipitation of Ag^+ ion starts.

At this stage,

$$[Ba^{2+}] = \frac{2 \times 10^{-10}}{9 \times 10^{-8}}$$

$$= 2.2 \times 10^{-3}\text{ M}$$

$[Ba^{2+}]$ at start $= 0.02$ M

Thus, $[Ba^{2+}]$ left $= 0.020 - 0.0022$

$= 0.0178$ M

Thus, % of Ba^{2+} precipitated

$$= \frac{0.0178}{0.020} \times 100 = 89\%$$

274. (a)

275. (d)

Passage 8

We observe that, the volume of NaOH (8.12 mL) used in first stage is half that of the second stage (16.24 mL).

Thus, 50% acid (A) is neutralised.

At this point,

COOH (benzene ring) OH, A $\rightleftharpoons$ COO⁻ (benzene ring) OH, A'

$$[A] = [A']$$

$$\therefore \quad pH = pK_{a_1}\log\frac{[A']}{[A]}$$

$$pH = pK_{a_1} = 4.57$$

After first stage, (A') formed is amphiprotic.

COOH (benzene ring) OH $\underset{H^+}{\rightleftharpoons}$ COO⁻ (benzene ring) OH (A') $\underset{-H^+}{\rightleftharpoons}$ COO⁻ (benzene ring) O⁻

$$\therefore \quad pH = \left(\frac{pK_{a_1} + pK_{a_2}}{2}\right)$$

$$2 \times 7.02 = pK_{a_1} + pK_{a_2}$$

$\therefore \quad pK_{a_2} = 14.04 - 4.57 = 9.47$

276. (c)

277. (a)

Passage 9

$$H_3PO_4 + NaOH \rightleftharpoons NaH_2PO_4 + H_2O$$

$$M_1V_1 = M_2V_2$$

$$20 \times M_1 = 10 \times 0.01$$

M_1(H_3PO_4 taking it monobasic) $= 0.005$ M

$$pH = \frac{1}{2}[pK_{a_1} - \log C]$$

$$= \frac{1}{2}[2.12 - \log 0.005] = 2.21$$

NaH_2PO_4 formed is amphiprotic.

$$H_2PO_4^- \rightleftharpoons H^+ + HPO_4^{2-}$$

$$H_2PO_4^- + H^+ \rightleftharpoons H_3PO_4$$

$$pH = \frac{pK_{a_1} + pK_{a_2}}{2} = \frac{2.12 + 7.22}{2} = 4.67$$

278. (a) ***281.*** (c)

Passage 10

$$pH = 11.30$$

$$pOH = 2.70$$

$$[OH^-] = 10^{-2.70} = 10^{-3}\ 10^{0.30}$$

$$= 2 \times 10^{-3}\text{ M}$$

$[Mg^{2+}]$ remained $= x$

$$(x)[OH^-]^2 = K_{sp}$$

$$x = \frac{1.8 \times 10^{-11}}{(2 \times 10^{-3})^2}$$

$$= 4.5 \times 10^{-6}\text{ M}$$

Percentage Mg^{2+} remained out of 0.059 M

$$= \frac{4.5 \times 10^{-6}}{0.059} \times 100$$

$$= 7.6 \times 10^{-3}\ \%$$

280. (a)

281. (c)

Passage 11

$C_2O_4^{2-}$ is oxidised to CO_2 by MnO_4^- in acidic medium.

$$C_2O_4^{2-} \longrightarrow 2CO_2 + 2e^-$$

$$MnO_4^- + 8H^+ + 5e^- \longrightarrow Mn^{2+} + 4H_2O$$

Thus, 1×10^{-4} M

$$MnO_4^- = 5 \times 10^{-4} \text{ N } MnO_4^-$$

and $x \text{ M } C_2O_4^{2-} = 2x \text{ N } C_2O_4^{2-}$

$$N_1V_1 = N_2V_2$$
$$C_2O_4^{2-} = MnO_4^-$$
$$N_1[C_2O_4^{2-}] \times 1000 = 5 \times 10^{-4} \times 200$$
$$N_1[C_2O_4^{2-}] = 1 \times 10^{-4} \text{ N}$$
$$M_1[C_2O_4^{2-}] = 0.5 \times 10^{-4} \text{ M} = [Ca^{2+}]$$
$$K_{sp} = [Ca^{2+}][C_2O_4^{2-}] = 2.5 \times 10^{-9}$$

In presence of 1×10^{-3} M $CaCl_2$, solubility is decreased due to common ion.

Let solubility be = y mol L^{-1}

$$\underset{y}{CaC_2O_4} \equiv \underset{y}{Ca^{2+}} + C_2O_4^{2-}$$
$$CaCl_2 \equiv Ca^{2+} + 2Cl^- = 1.0 \times 10^{-3} M$$
$$\therefore \quad [Ca^{2+}] = (1 \times 10^{-3} + y) M \approx 1 \times 10^{-3} \text{ M}, \; y << \sqrt{K_{sp}}$$
$$[C_2O_4^{2-}] = y$$
$$[Ca^{2+}][C_2O_4^{2-}] = 2.5 \times 10^{-9}$$
$$\therefore \quad (1 \times 10^{-3})(y) = 2.5 \times 10^{-9}$$
$$\therefore \quad y = 2.5 \times 10^{-6} \text{ M}$$
$$\text{Thus,} \quad \underset{CaC_2O_4}{(2M_1)V_1} = \underset{MnO_4^-}{(5M_2)V_2}$$
$$2 \times 2.5 \times 10^{-6} \times 1000 = 5 \times 1 \times 10^{-4} \times V_2$$
$$\therefore \quad V_2 = 10 \text{ mL}$$

282. (d)

283. (a)

- Normality = Electrons exchanged × molarity

Passage 12

By Henry's law,

$$p_{CO_2} = K_H \, \chi_{CO_2}$$
$$\chi_{CO_2} = \frac{K_H}{p_{CO_2}} = \frac{3.6 \times 10^{-4} \text{ atm}}{(1.25 \times 10^6 / 760) \text{ atm}} = 2.2 \times 10^{-7}$$

Also, $\chi_{CO_2} = \dfrac{n_{(CO_2)}}{n_{(CO_2)} + n_{(H_2O)}} \approx \dfrac{n_{(CO_2)}}{n_{(H_2O)}}$

$n_{(H_2O)}$ in 1 L $H_2O = \dfrac{1000}{18}$ mol $>>> n_{(CO_2)}$

Thus, $n_{(CO_2)} + n_{(H_2O)} \approx n_{(H_2O)}$

$$\therefore n_{(CO_2)} = \chi_{CO_2} \cdot n_{(H_2O)} = 2.2 \times 10^{-7} \times \frac{1000}{18} = 1.2 \times 10^{-5} \text{ mol in 1 L}$$
$$M_{(CO_2)} = 1.2 \times 10^{-5} \text{ M}$$

As H_2CO_3, $H_2CO_3 \rightleftharpoons H^+ + HCO_3^-$

$$[H^+] = \sqrt{K_{a_1} C} = \sqrt{4.3 \times 10^{-7} \times 1.2 \times 10^{-5}} = 2.27 \times 10^{-6} \text{ M}$$
$$pH = -\log[H^+] = 5.64$$

SO_2 (H_2SO_3 in aqueous solution) = 0.12 ppm by volume.

$$= 0.12 \text{ g in } 10^6 \text{ mL } H_2O$$
$$\therefore \quad [H_2SO_3] = \left(\frac{0.12}{64 \times 10^3}\right) \text{mol L}^{-1} = 1.875 \times 10^{-6} \text{ M}$$

H_2SO_3 being strong acid as monobasic,

$$\therefore \quad [H^+] = 1.875 \times 10^{-6} \text{ M}$$
$$\therefore \quad pH = 5.73$$

284. (a)

285. (a)

Passage 13

$$pH = 10.42$$
$$\therefore [H_3O^+] = 10^{-10.42} = 10^{-11} 10^{0.58} = 3.80 \times 10^{-11} M$$
$$\therefore \quad [OH^-] = \frac{K_w}{[H_3O^+]} = \frac{1 \times 10^{-14}}{3.8 \times 10^{-11}} = 2.63 \times 10^{-9} \text{ M}$$
$$Mg(OH)_2 \rightleftharpoons Mg^{2+}(aq) + 2OH^-(aq)$$
$$\text{Thus,} \; [Mg^{2+}] = \frac{1}{2}[OH^-] = \left(\frac{2.63 \times 10^{-4}}{2}\right) M$$
$$K_{sp} = [Mg^{2+}][OH^-]^2 = \left(\frac{2.63 \times 10^{-4}}{2}\right)(2.63 \times 10^{-4})^2 = 9.09 \times 10^{-12}$$

When $[Mg^{2+}] = 0.05$ M

$$[OH^-]^2 = \frac{K_{sp}}{(0.05)} = \frac{9.09 \times 10^{-12}}{0.05}$$
$$[OH^-] = 1.34 \times 10^{-5} \text{ M}$$
$$NH_4OH \rightleftharpoons NH_4^+ + OH^-$$
$$\therefore \quad K_b = \frac{[NH_4^+][OH^-]}{[NH_4OH]}$$
$$\therefore 1.8 \times 10^{-5} = \frac{[NH_4^+](1.34 \times 10^{-5})}{0.05}$$
$$[NH_4^+] = 0.067 \text{ M}$$

286. (d)

287. (c)

Passage 14

$$AgI(s) \rightleftharpoons Ag^+(aq) + I^-(aq)$$
$$K_{sp} = [Ag^+][I^-]$$

$[I^-]$ for precipitating $Ag^+ = \dfrac{K_{sp}}{[Ag^+]}$

$$= \frac{8.5 \times 10^{-17}}{0.1} = 8.5 \times 10^{-16} \text{ M}$$
$$HgI_2(s) \rightleftharpoons Hg^{2+}(aq) + 2I^-(aq)$$
$$K_{sp} = [Hg^{2+}][I^-]^2$$

$[I^-]$ for precipitating of Hg^{2+}

$$= \sqrt{\frac{K_{sp}}{[Hg^{2+}]}} = \sqrt{\frac{2.5 \times 10^{-26}}{0.1}} = 5 \times 10^{-13} \text{ M} > 8.5 \times 10^{-16} \text{ M}$$

Thus, maximum concentration at which AgI gets precipitated

$$= 5 \times 10^{-13} \text{ M}$$

Thus, $[Ag^+]$ unreacted

$$= \frac{8.5 \times 10^{-17}}{5 \times 10^{-13}} = 1.7 \times 10^{-4} \text{ M}$$

Thus, percentage remaining

$$= \frac{1.7 \times 10^{-4}}{0.1} \times 100 = 0.17\,\%$$

Percentage precipitated

$$= 100 - 0.17 = 99.83\,\%$$

288. (a)

289. (d)

- Precipitation always occurs at higher concentration of the added ion,

$$Ag^+ + I^- \longrightarrow AgI$$
$$Hg^{2+} + 2I^- \longrightarrow HgI_2$$

Passage 15

Since, $K_{a_1} >>> K_{a_2} >> K_{a_3}$

Also, $K_h = \dfrac{K_w}{K_a}$

$$K_h \propto \frac{1}{K_a}$$

Thus, smaller the value of K_a, larger the hydrolysis constant, hence $[OH^-]$ from hydrolysis of PO_4^{3-} to HPO_4^{2-} is considered.

$$PO_4^{3-} + H_2O \rightleftharpoons HPO_4^{2-} + OH^-$$
$$K_h = \frac{K_w}{K_{a_3}}$$
$$[OH^-] = Cx = C\sqrt{\frac{K_h}{C}} = \sqrt{\frac{CK_w}{K_{a_3}}} = \sqrt{\frac{0.1 \times 1 \times 10^{-14}}{4.5 \times 10^{-13}}} = 4.71 \times 10^{-2} \text{ M}$$
$$H_3PO_4 \rightleftharpoons 3H^+ + PO_4^{3-}$$
$$\therefore \quad K_1 K_2 K_3 = \frac{[H^+]^3 [PO_4^{3-}]}{[H_3PO_4]}$$

$$[H_3PO_4] = \frac{\left(\frac{K_w}{[OH^-]}\right)^3 [PO_4^{3-}]}{K_1K_2K_3}$$

$$= \frac{\left(\frac{1\times10^{-14}}{0.0471}\right)^3 (0.1)}{7.1\times6.3\times4.5\times10^{-24}}$$

$$= 4.8\times10^{-18}\ M$$

290. (a)

291. (b)

Passage 16

First step ionisation

$$H_2S + H_2O \rightleftharpoons HS^- + H_3O^+$$

$$K_{a_1} = \frac{Cx^2}{(1-x)} \approx Cx^2$$

$$\therefore \quad x = \sqrt{\frac{K_{a_1}}{C}}$$

$$[H_3O^+] = (HS^-) = Cx = \sqrt{K_{a_1}C}$$

$$= \sqrt{1.0\times10^{-7}\times0.05}$$

$$= 7.07\times10^{-5}\ M$$

Second step ionisation

$$HS^- + H_2O \rightleftharpoons H_3O^+ + S^{2-}$$

$$K_{a_2} = 1\times10^{-14} = \frac{[H_3O^+][S^{2-}]}{[HS^-]}$$

As $[H_3O^+] = [HS^-] = 7.07\times10^{-5}$ M

$\therefore \quad [S^{2-}] = K_{a_2} = 1\times10^{-14}$ M

292. (d)

293. (a)

Passage 17

$$Na_2CO_3 + HCl \rightleftharpoons NaHCO_3 + NaCl$$

$NaHCO_3$ is formed.

$[NaHCO_3] = 0.5$ M

(equal volumes cause dilution).

HCO_3^- formed is amphiprotic.

$$pH = \frac{pK_{a_1} + pK_{a_2}}{2}$$

$$pK_{a_1} = -\log K_{a_1}$$
$$= -\log 4.5\times10^{-7} = 6.35$$

$$pK_{a_2} = -\log K_{a_2}$$
$$= -\log 4.7\times10^{-11} = 10.33$$

$$pH = \frac{6.35 + 10.33}{2} = 8.34$$

$$\underset{\text{Acid}}{HCO_3^-} + H_2O \rightleftharpoons CO_3^{2-} + H_3O^+$$

$$K_{a_2} = \frac{[CO_3^{2-}][H_3O^+]}{[HCO_3^-]} \quad \ldots(i)$$

$$\underset{\text{Base}}{HCO_3^-} + H_2O \rightleftharpoons H_2CO_3 + OH^-,$$

Hydrolysis constant of HCO_3^- is

$$K_h = \frac{[H_2CO_3[OH^-]}{[HCO_3^-]} = \frac{K_w}{K_{a_1}} \quad \ldots(ii)$$

(i) × (ii) gives

$$\frac{K_{a_2}\ K_w}{K_{a_1}} = \frac{[CO_3^{2-}][H_3O^+][OH^-][H_2CO_3]}{[HCO_3^-]^2}$$

$$= \frac{[CO_3^{2-}][H_2CO_3][K_w]}{[HCO_3^-]^2}$$

$$\therefore \quad \frac{K_{a_2}}{K_{a_1}} = \frac{[CO_3^{2-}][H_2CO_3]}{[HCO_3^-]^2}$$

$\because \ [H_3O^+][OH^-] = K_w$

Due to hydrolysis,

$$[CO_2] = [H_2CO_3] = [CO_3^{2-}] = x$$

$$\therefore \quad \frac{4.7\times10^{-11}}{4.5\times10^{-7}} = \frac{x^2}{(0.5)^2}$$

$$\therefore \quad \frac{x}{0.5} = 0.01$$

$$\therefore \quad x = 5\times10^{-3}\ M$$

294. (c)

295. (d)

Passage 18

MV (mL) = millimol

HCl = 100 × 1.0 = 100 mmol = 0.1 mol

Enthalpy change in the neutralisation of 0.1 HCl by NaOH in Expt 1

= 0.1 × 57 = 5.7 kJ = 5700 J

Mass of mixture of HCl and NaOH

= 200 mL × 1 gm

Enthalpy change = $ms\Delta T$

= 200 × 4.2 × 5.7

= 4788 J

Thus, total enthalpy change

$(ms\Delta T)_{\text{calorimeter}} + 4788$ J = 5700 J

$ms \times 5.7 = 912$ J

$ms = 160$ J/°C (calorimeter constant)

Enthalpy change in the neutralisation of CH_3COOH

= 200 × 4.2 × 5.6 + 160 × 5.6

= 5600 J = 5.6 kJ

Difference of enthalpy of experiments I and II is used in the dissociation of CH_3COOH. Thus, enthalpy of dissociation of 0.1 mol of CH_3COOH

= 5.7 − 5.6 = 0.1 kJ

∴ Enthalpy of dissociation

$$= \frac{0.1}{0.1} = 1\ \text{kJ mol}^{-1}$$

In experiment II, CH_3COOH is 50% neutralised as CH_3COOH and NaOH are in 2 : 1 molar ratio.

Thus, $[CH_3COOH] = [CH_3COONa]$

$$pH = pK_a = -\log K_a$$
$$= -\log 2\times10^{-5} = 4.7$$

296. (a)

297. (b)

Type V. Numerical Skills

298. **(0.11)**

Oxalic acid solution titrated with NaOH solution using phenolphthalein as an indicator.

$$H_2C_2O_4 + 2NaOH \longrightarrow Na_2C_2O_4 + 2H_2O$$

Equivalent of $H_2C_2O_4$ reacted

= Equivalent of NaOH reacted

$$\frac{5\times2\times0.1}{1000} = \frac{9\times M_{(NaOH)}\times1}{1000}$$

$$M_{(NaOH)} = \frac{1}{9} = 0.11$$

299. **Five (5)** $\underset{\text{Acid}}{BH^+} \rightleftharpoons \underset{\text{Base}}{B + H^+}$

Thus, $\quad pH = pK_a + \log\frac{[B]}{[BH^+]}$

$$(pH - pK_a) = \log\frac{[B]}{[BH^+]}$$

$$0.7 = \log\frac{[B]}{[BH^+]}$$

$$\therefore \quad \frac{[B]}{[BH^+]} = 5.0$$

300. **Six (6)** Isoelectric pH is the pH at which there is no migration of *Zwitter* ion on passing electric current.

$$pH = \frac{pH\ (\text{with NaOH}) + pH(\text{with HCl})}{2}$$

$$= \frac{9.714 + 2.286}{2} = 6$$

301. **Nine (9)** Let initial pH be = y

$\therefore \quad [H^+]_1 = 10^{-y}, V_1 = 10$ mL

Thus final pH = $(y+1)$

$[H^+]_2 = 10^{-(y+1)}, V_2 = (10 + 10x)$

$\because \ N_1V_1 = N_2V_2$

$\therefore \ 10^{-y}\times10 = 10^{-(y+1)}(10 + 10x)$

$10^{-y}\times10 = 10^{-y}\times10^{-1}\times10(1+x)$

$(x+1) = 10$

$x = 9$ mL

302. **(3.00)**

From the given diagram, 6 mL of HA was used till equivalene point. At half of equivalence point, solution will be basic buffer with B and BH^+.

$$\because \quad pOH = pK_b + \log\frac{[BH^+]}{[B]}$$

At half equivalence point : $[BH^+] = [B]$

$\because \quad pH = 11$

Therefore, pOH = pK_b = 14 − 11 = 3

$\because \quad pK_b = 3.00$

303. Six (6)

$$HA \rightleftharpoons H^+ + A^-$$

$$\alpha = \frac{1}{100} = 0.01$$

$$K_a = C\alpha^2 \text{ (by Ostwald's dilution law)}$$

$$= 0.01(0.01)^2 = 1 \times 10^{-6}$$

$$\therefore \ pK_a = 6$$

100 mL of this 0.01 M acid is treated with 25 mL of 0.01 M $Ca(OH)_2$ or 0.02 M (OH^-),

$$Ca(OH)_2 + 2HA \equiv CaA_2 + 2H_2O$$

$$[HA] = \frac{100 \times 0.01}{1000} = 0.0001 \text{ mol}$$

$$[Ca(OH)_2] = \frac{25 \times 0.01}{1000} = 2.5 \times 10^{-4} \text{ mol}$$

HA neutralised by 2.5×10^{-4} mol of $Ca(OH)_2$

$$= 5.0 \times 10^{-4} \text{ mol}$$

Thus, 50% of this acid is neutralised.

At this point $[HA] = [A^-]$

$$\therefore \quad pH = pK_a + \log\frac{[A^-]}{[HA]}$$

$$pH = pK_a = 6$$

304. Nine (9) Let volume of NaOH = x mL

$$N(OH^-) \text{ in mixture} = \frac{1 \times 0.1 + x \times 0.1}{(x+1)}$$

$$= \frac{(x+1)}{10\,(x+1)} = \frac{1}{10}$$

$$0.05 \text{ M } H_2SO_4 = 0.1 \text{ N } H_2SO_4$$

$$N_1V_1(H_2SO_4) = N_2V_2(OH^-)$$

$$10 \times 0.1 = \frac{1}{10}(x+1)$$

$$\therefore \quad (x+1) = 10$$

$$x = 9 \text{ mL}$$

305. Four (4) Equal pH means equal $[H^+]$,

$$[H^+]_{HCOOH} = \sqrt{K_1C_1}$$

$$[H^+]_{CH_3COOH} = \sqrt{K_2C_2}$$

Since, $[H^+]_{HCOOH} = [H^+]_{CH_3COOH}$

$$\therefore \quad \sqrt{K_1C_1} = \sqrt{K_2C_2}$$

$$\frac{K_1}{K_2} = \frac{C_2}{C_1} = \frac{1}{0.25} = 4$$

306. (37) CO_2 gas in 1 kg water at 30 bar = 44 g

Thus, CO_2 gas in 1 kg water at 3.0 bar

$$= 4.4 \text{ g} = \frac{4.4}{44} = 0.1 \text{ mol}$$

As density = 1 g mL^{-1}

Thus, molarity of CO_2 solution

$$= 0.1 \text{ mol L}^{-1}$$

$$H_2CO_3 + H_2O \rightleftharpoons H_3O^+ + HCO_3^-$$

Thus, $[H_3O^+] = \sqrt{K_aC}$

by Ostwald's dilution law

$$= \sqrt{4.0 \times 10^{-7} \times 0.1}$$

$$= 2.0 \times 10^{-4} \text{ M}$$

$$\therefore \quad pH = -\log[H_3O^+]$$

$$= -\log 2.0 \times 10^{-4}$$

$$= 4 - \log 2 = 3.7$$

$$= 37 \times 10^{-1}$$

307. Five (5) $CdS \rightleftharpoons Cd^{2+} + S^{2-}$

$$K_{sp} = [Cd^{2+}][S^{2-}]$$

$[S^{2-}]$ to precipitate 1×10^{-14} M $CdCl_2$

$$= \frac{K_{sp}}{[Cd^{2+}]}$$

$$= \frac{8 \times 10^{-27}}{1 \times 10^{-14}} = 8 \times 10^{-13} \text{ M}$$

$$H_2S \rightleftharpoons 2H^+ + S^{2-}$$

$$\therefore \quad K_{sp} = [H^+]^2[S^{2-}]$$

$$1 \times 10^{-22} = [H^+]^2(8 \times 10^{-13})$$

$$[H^+]^2 = \frac{1 \times 10^{-22}}{8 \times 10^{-13}} = 1.25 \times 10^{-10}$$

$$\therefore \quad [H^+] = 1.11 \times 10^{-5} \text{ M}$$

$$pH = 4.95 \approx 5.0$$

308. Seven (7) It is a case of simultaneous solubility of salts with a common ion.

$$K_{sp\,(CuCl)} >> K_{sp\,(AgCl)}$$

Thus, it can be assumed that Cl^- in a solution comes mainly from CuCl to supress solubility of AgCl.

$$[Cl^-] \text{ in CuCl} = \sqrt{K_{sp}}$$

$$= \sqrt{10^{-6}} = 10^{-3} \text{ M}$$

$$[Ag^+][Cl^-] = K_{sp}$$

$$[Ag^+][10^{-3}] = 1.6 \times 10^{-10}$$

$$\therefore \quad [Ag^+] = 1.6 \times 10^{-7} \text{ M} = 1.6 \times 10^{-x} \text{ M}$$

Thus, $x = 7$

309. Six (6) Acid is said to be diprotic, if it has two ionisable H^+. H attached to electronegative atoms as O, Cl, Br, I, F, is ionised.

(a) H—O—C(=O)—OH

(b) HO—S(=O)(=O)—O—S(=O)(=O)—OH

(c) H—O—Cr(=O)(=O)—O—H

(d) HO—S(=O)—O—H

(e) H—O—B(—O—H)—O—H

(Monobasic Lewis acid)

(f) H—O—P(—H)(=O)—H

(Monobasic)

(g) H—O—P(=O)(—O—H)—OH

(Tribasic)

(h) H—O—S(=O)(=O)—OH

(i) H—O—P(=O)(—H)—OH

(e), (f), (g) are not diprotic acids.

■ $B(OH)_3 + H_2O \rightleftharpoons [B(OH)_4]^- + H^+$

H_3BO_3 or $B(OH)_3$ is a weak monobasic acid. It is Lewis acid

310. Three (3) Aqueous solution of a compound turns red litmus to blue, if it is basic in nature. Salt a weak acid and strong base is basic in nature.

Salt	Made of	Aqueous solution
KCN	(SB + WA)	basic
K_2SO_4	(SA + SB)	neutral
$(NH_4)_2C_2O_4$	(WA + WB)	neutral
NaCl	(SA + SB)	neutral
$Zn(NO_3)_2$	(WB + SA)	acidic
$FeCl_3$	(WB + SA)	acidic
K_2CO_3	(WA + SB)	basic
NH_4NO_3	(WB + SA)	acidic
LiCN	(WA + SB)	basic

311. Six (6) $2NH_3 \rightleftharpoons NH_4^+ + NH_2^-$

K_{NH_3} (ion product)

$$= [NH_4^+][NH_2^-] = 1 \times 10^{-30}$$

Since, $[NH_4^+] = [NH_2^-]$

Hence, $[NH_2^-]^2 = 1 \times 10^{-30}$

$$\therefore \quad [NH_2^-] = 1 \times 10^{-15} \text{ mol dm}^{-3}$$

$$= 1 \times 10^{-15} \text{ mol in 1 dm}^3$$

$$= 1 \times 10^{-15} \text{ mol in } 10^6 \text{ mm}^3$$

$$= 1 \times 10^{-21} \text{ mol in 1 mm}^3$$

$$= 6.00 \times 10^{23} \times 1 \times 10^{-21}$$

NH_2^- ions per $mm^3 = 6 \times 10^2$

Thus, $x = 6$

■ $1\ dm^3 = 10^3\ cm^3 = 10^6 mm^3$

312. **Six (2)** $AB_2(s) \rightleftharpoons A^{2+}(aq) + 2B^-(aq)$

If solubility = S mol L^{-1}

$$\therefore \quad K_{sp} = [A^{2+}][B^-]^2 = 4S^3$$

$$\therefore \quad S = \sqrt[3]{\frac{K_{sp}}{4}}$$

$$\therefore \quad S = \sqrt[3]{\frac{3.2 \times 10^{-11}}{4}}$$

$$= 2 \times 10^{-4} \text{ mol L}^{-1}$$

313. **One (1)** In 1.0×10^{-6} M NaOH,

$$[OH^-] = 1 \times 10^{-6} \text{ M}$$

and $[H_3O^+] = 1 \times 10^{-8}$ M, if ionisation of water is not taken.

If water is ionised,

if $[H_3O^+] = x$ M

then $[OH^-] = x$ M in water

$\therefore$ Total $[OH^-] = (x + 1 \times 10^{-6})$ M

$\therefore$ $[H_3O^+][OH^-] = 1 \times 10^{-14}$

$$\therefore \quad x(x + 10^{-6}) = 1 \times 10^{-14}$$

$$x^2 + 10^{-6}x - 10^{-14} = 0$$

$$\therefore \quad x = \frac{-10^{-6} \pm \sqrt{10^{-12} + 4 \times 10^{-14}}}{2}$$

$$= 9.9 \times 10^{-9}$$

Thus, error = [if ionisation of water is not considered – if ionisation of water is considered]

$$= 1.0 \times 10^{-8} - 9.9 \times 10^{-9}$$

$$= 10 \times 10^{-9} - 9.9 \times 10^{-9}$$

$$= 0.1 \times 10^{-9} \text{ M}$$

Thus, relative percentage error

$$= \frac{0.1 \times 10^{-9}}{9.9 \times 10^{-9}} \times 100 = 1.0\%$$

314. **Five (5)** For a weak base

$$[OH^-] = \sqrt{K_b C}$$

$$\therefore \quad pOH = \frac{1}{2}[pK_b - \log C]$$

If $\quad pH(BOH) = 8.0$

then pOH = 6.0

$$\therefore \quad 6 = \frac{1}{2}[pK_b - \log 10^{-4}]$$

$$12 = [pK_b + 4]$$

$$pK_b = 8 \quad \therefore \quad pK_a = 8$$

For a weak acid,

$$pH = \frac{1}{2}[pK_a - \log C] = \frac{1}{2}[8 - \log 0.01]$$

$$= \frac{1}{2}[8 + 2] = 5.0$$

315. **Three (3)** For a weak acid HA,

$$HA \rightleftharpoons H^+ + A^-$$

	HA	H^+	A^-
Initial	1	0	0
At equil.	$(1 - x)$	x	x

$$K_a = \frac{[H^+][A^-]}{[H]}$$

$$[H^+] = \frac{K_a[HA]}{[A^-]}$$

$$\therefore \quad [H^+] = K_a \frac{(1 - x)}{x}$$

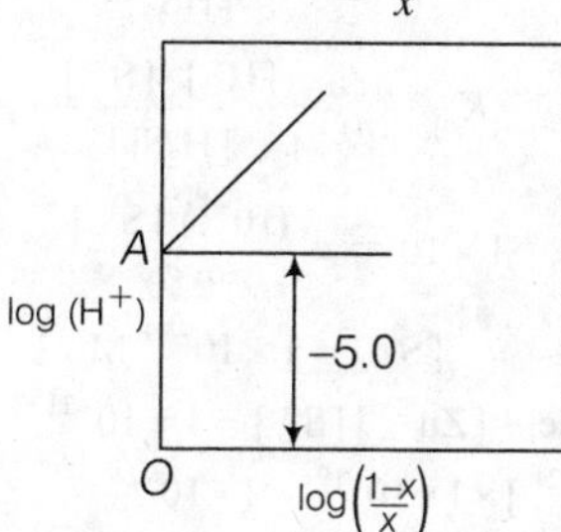

$$\log[H^+] = \log K_a + \log\left(\frac{1 - x}{x}\right)$$

It is linear as

$$y = c + mx$$

On comparison,

$$OA = \log K_a = c = -5$$

Given, $\quad x = 0.01$

$$\therefore \log[H^+] = -5 + \log\frac{0.99}{0.01}$$

$$= -5 + 2 = -3$$

$$pH = -\log[H^+] = 3$$

316. **Two (2)** $K_w = 1.11 \times 10^{-14}$

$\therefore$ $[H_3O^+][OH^-] = 1.11 \times 10^{-14}$

$$\therefore \quad [H_3O^+] = [OH^-] \text{ M}$$

$$= \sqrt{1.11 \times 10^{-14}}$$

$$= 1.053 \times 10^{-7}$$

Also for weak electrolyte, by Ostwald's dilution law

$$[H_3O^+] = \sqrt{K_a C}$$

where, C = molar concentration of water

$$= \frac{1000}{18} \text{ mol L}^{-1}$$

$$\therefore \quad 1.053 \times 10^{-7} = \sqrt{K_a\left(\frac{1000}{18}\right)}$$

$$\therefore \quad K_a = (1.053 \times 10^{-7})^2 \times \frac{18}{1000}$$

$$= 2 \times 10^{-16} = x \times 10^{-16}$$

Thus, $x = 2$

317. **Five (5)** If $HA = x$ mol L^{-1} and $A^- = y$ mol L^{-1}

Then total moles = $(x + y)$ mol L^{-1}

Given $\quad X_{HA} = 0.2 = \left(\dfrac{x}{x + y}\right)$

Thus, $\quad x = 0.2$ mol L^{-1} = [HA]

$$y = 0.8 \text{ mol L}^{-1} = [A^-]$$

$$HA \rightleftharpoons H^+ + A^-$$

$$K_a = \frac{[H^+][A^-]}{[HA]}$$

$$\therefore \quad [H^+] = K_a\frac{[HA]}{[A^-]} = 4 \times 10^{-5} \times \frac{0.2}{0.8}$$

$$\therefore \quad [H^+] = 1 \times 10^{-5} \text{ M}$$

$$\therefore \quad pH = 5$$

318. **One (1)**

$$A_2X_3(s) \rightleftharpoons \underset{2S}{2A^{3+}(aq)} + \underset{3S}{3X^{2-}(aq)}$$

$$K_{sp} = [A^{3+}]^2[X^{2-}]^3 = (2S)^2(3S)^3$$

$$1.1 \times 10^{-23} = 108\ S^5$$

$$S^5 = \frac{1.1 \times 10^{-23}}{108}$$

$$S = 1.0 \times 10^{-5} \text{ M}$$

$$= y \times 10^{-5} \text{ M Thus, } y = 1$$

319. **Eight (8)** CH_3CH_2COONa is a salt of weak acid and strong base. Thus, its aqueous solution is alkaline due to hydrolysis of $CH_3CH_2COO^-$.

$$CH_3CH_2COO^-(aq) + H_2O(l) \rightleftharpoons CH_3CH_2COOH(aq) + OH^-(aq)$$

$$\therefore \quad pH = 7 + \frac{pK_a}{2} + \frac{\log C}{2}$$

$$pH = (\text{constant}) + \frac{1}{2}\log C$$

This represents a straight line

$$y = \text{constant} + mx$$

Constant = intercept

$$= OA = \left(7 + \frac{pK_a}{2}\right) = 9.5$$

and slope $= \dfrac{1}{2} = m$

when, $c = 0.001$ M

$$pH = 9.5 + \frac{1}{2}\log 0.001 = \left(9.5 - \frac{3}{2}\right) = 8.0$$

320. **Six (6)** Any solution i.e. acidic due to hydrolysis turns blue litmus red. Salt of weak base and strong acid is acidic due to hydrolysis.

$$B^+ + H_2O \longrightarrow B(OH) + H^+$$

$KHSO_4$	salt of SA and SB
$FeCl_3$	salt of SA and WB
$AlCl_3$	salt of SA and WB
$CuSO_4$	salt of SA and WB
$NaHCO_3$	salt of WA and SB
CH_3NH_3Cl	salt of WB and SA
$C_5H_5NH.HSO_4$	salt of WB and SA
C_6H_5COONa	salt of WA and SB
Na_2CO_3	salt of WA and SB
$[Zn(H_2O)_4]Cl_2$	salt of WB and SA

Thus, $FeCl_3$, $AlCl_3$, $CuSO_4$, CH_3NH_3Cl $C_5H_5NH.HSO_4$ and $[Zn(H_2O)_4]Cl_2$ turn blue litmus red.

321. Nine (9)

$$Mg(OH)_2(s) \rightleftharpoons Mg^{2+}(aq) + 2OH^-(aq)$$

$$K_{sp} = [Mg^{2+}][OH^-]^2$$

$$1.8 \times 10^{-11} = (0.18)[OH^-]^2$$

$$\therefore \quad [OH^-]^2 = 1 \times 10^{-10}$$

$$[OH^-] = 1 \times 10^{-5} \text{ M}$$

$$\therefore \quad pOH = 5$$

$$\therefore \quad pH = 14 - 5 = 9$$

322. Four (4)

$$PbI_2(s) \rightleftharpoons Pb^{2+}(aq) + 2I^-(aq)$$

$$S \qquad\qquad 2S$$

$$K_{sp} = [Pb^{2+}][I^-]^2 = (S)(2S)^2$$

$$4S^3 = 7.1 \times 10^{-9}$$

$$\therefore \quad S = 1.211 \times 10^{-3} \text{ M}$$

$$\therefore \quad [I^-] = 2S = 2.422 \times 10^{-3} \text{ M}$$

$$Ag^+ + \underset{\text{From } PbI_2}{I^-} \longrightarrow AgI(s)$$

In titration,

$$\underset{AgNO_3}{M_1V_1} = \underset{PbI_2\,(I^-)}{M_2V_2}$$

$$M_1 \times 15.13 = 2.422 \times 10^{-3} \times 25$$

$$M_1 = 4.0 \times 10^{-3} \text{ M} = y \times 10^{-3} \text{ M}$$

$$\therefore \quad y = 4$$

323. Five (5) $[Ag^+][Cl^-] = K_{sp}$

$$\log[Ag^+] + \log[Cl^-] = \log K_{sp}$$

$$\therefore \quad -\log[Ag^+] = -\log K_{sp} + \log[Cl^-]$$

$$p_{Ag^+} = pK_{sp} - p_{Cl^-}$$

$$y = c - mx$$

As p_{Cl^-} increases, p_{Ag^+} decreases

$$\text{Intercept} = pK_{sp} = +9.7448$$

$$pK_{sp} = -\log K_{sp} = 9.7448$$

$$\log K_{sp} = -9.7448$$

$$\therefore \quad K_{sp} = 10^{-9.7448}$$

$$= 10^{-10}\, 10^{0.2552} = 1.8 \times 10^{-10}$$

To precipitate 3.6×10^{-5} M $[AgNO_3]$

$$[Cl^-] = \frac{1.8 \times 10^{-10}}{3.6 \times 10^{-5}} = 5 \times 10^{-6} \text{ M}$$

$$= x \times 10^{-6} \text{ M}$$

Thus, $x = 5$

324. Nine (9) $[Mg^{2+}][OH^-]^2 = 1.0 \times 10^{-12}$

pH = 1,

$$\therefore \quad [H^+] = 10^{-1} \text{M}$$

$$(1 \times 10^{-2})[OH^-]^2 = 1.0 \times 10^{-12}$$

$$\therefore \quad [OH^-]^2 = 1.0 \times 10^{-10}$$

$$\therefore \quad [OH^-] = 1.0 \times 10^{-5} \text{ M}$$

$$\therefore \quad pOH = 5.0$$

$$\therefore \quad pH = 14 - 5 = 9.0$$

325. Two (2) $H_2S \rightleftharpoons H^+ + HS^-$

$$pH = 1, \; [H^+] = 10^{-1} \text{ M}$$

$$K_{a_1} = \frac{[H^+][HS^-]}{[H_2S]}$$

$$HS^- \rightleftharpoons H^+ + S^{2-}$$

$$K_{a_2} = \frac{[H^+][S^{2-}]}{[HS^-]}$$

$$\therefore \quad K_{a_1} \cdot K_{a_2} = \frac{[H^+]^2[S^{2-}]}{[H_2S]}$$

$$1 \times 10^{-20} = \frac{(10^{-1})^2[S^{2-}]}{0.10}$$

$$\therefore \quad [S^{2-}] = 1 \times 10^{-19} \text{ M}$$

Since, $[Zn^{2+}][S^{2-}] = 1 \times 10^{-21}$

$$[Zn^{2+}] \times 1 \times 10^{-19} = 1 \times 10^{-21}$$

$$\therefore \quad [Zn^{2+}] = 0.01 \text{ M}$$

$$\therefore \quad C = [ZnCl_2] = 0.01 \text{ M}$$

$$\therefore \quad p_C = -\log C = -\log 0.01 = 2.0$$

326. Nine (9) For

$$M(OH)_3(s) \rightleftharpoons M^{3+}(aq) + 3OH^-(aq);$$

$$K_{sp} = [M^{3+}][OH^-]^3$$

$$\therefore \quad \log K_{sp} = \log[M^{3+}] + 3\log[OH^-]$$

$$\log[M^{3+}] = \log K_{sp} - 3\log[OH^-]$$

$$\log[M^{3+}] = \log K_{sp} + 3 \text{ pOH}$$

This equation is comparable to

$$y = c + mx$$

$$c = OA = \log K_{sp} \text{ (intercept)} = -16)$$

$$m = 3 = \text{slope}$$

When, $[M^{3+}] = 0.1$ M

$$-1 = -16 + 3 \text{ pOH}$$

$$pOH = 5$$

$$\therefore \quad pH = 14 - 5 = 9$$

327. (12.86)

Initially mixture contains 3 g acetic acid added to 250 mL of 0.1 M HCl, and diluted to 500 mL.

Thus, $[CH_3COOH] = \dfrac{3\text{g}/60 \text{ g mol}^{-1}}{0.5 \text{ L}}$

$$= 0.1 \text{ M}$$

and $\quad [HCl] = \dfrac{0.1}{2} = 0.05$ M

$[H^+]$ in a mixture of weak acid and strong acid is given by

$$[H^+] = \frac{C_2 + \sqrt{C_2^2 + 4K_aC_1}}{2}$$

where, C_1 = molar concentration of weak acid = 0.10 M

C_2 = molar concentration of strong acid = 0.05 M

K_a = ionisation constant of weak acid

$$= 10^{-pK_a} = 10^{-4.75}$$

$$= 10^{0.25} \times 10^{-5.00} = 1.8 \times 10^{-5}$$

$$\therefore \quad [H^+] = \frac{0.05 + \sqrt{(0.05)^2 + 4 \times 1.8 \times 10^{-5} \times 0.10}}{2}$$

$$= \frac{0.05 + 0.05}{2} = 0.05 \text{ M}$$

- We observe that only concentration of HCl is observed in the mixture, and $[H^+]$ due to CH_3COOH has no effect on the total $[H^+]$

To 20 mL of this mixture of CH_3COOH and HCl, 0.5 mL of 5M NaOH is added.

$$M_1V_1(\text{acid}) = 20 \times 0.05 = 1.0$$

$$M_2V_2(\text{base}) = 0.50 \times 5.0 = 2.5$$

$$M_2V_2(\text{base}) > M_1V_1(\text{acid})$$

Thus, mixture is basic.

$$[OH^-]_{mix} = \frac{M_2V_2 - M_1V_1}{V_1 + V_2}$$

$$= \frac{2.5 - 1.0}{20 + 0.5} = \frac{1.5}{20.5} = 0.073 \text{ M}$$

$$\therefore \quad pOH = 1.14$$

$$\therefore \quad pH = 14.00 - 1.14 = 12.86$$

328. Nine (9) $\underset{\substack{\text{Acid}\\ \text{orange}}}{HIn} \rightleftharpoons H^+ + \underset{\substack{\text{Base}\\ \text{yellow}}}{In^-}$

$$K_a = \frac{[H^+][In^-]}{[HIn]}$$

$$[H^+] = K_a \frac{[HIn]}{[In^-]} = K_a \frac{[\text{Orange}]}{[\text{Yellow}]}$$

Case I $[H^+]_1 = 3.0 \times 10^{-4} \times \dfrac{75}{25}$

$$= 9 \times 10^{-4} \text{ M}$$

$$pH = 4 - \log 9$$

Case II $[H^+]_2 = 3 \times 10^{-4} \times \left(\dfrac{25}{75}\right)$

$$= 1 \times 10^{-4} \text{ M}$$

$$pH = 4$$

Thus, change in pH = 4 − (4 − log 9)

$$= \log 9 = \log x$$

Thus, $x = 9$

329. Eight (8) $\underset{\text{Acid}}{HIn} \rightleftharpoons \underset{\text{Base}}{In^-} + H^+$

$$K_a = \frac{[In^-][H^+]}{[HIn]}$$

$$\frac{[In^-]}{[HIn]} = \frac{K_a}{[H^+]} = \frac{9 \times 10^{-5}}{1 \times 10^{-5}} = 4$$

$$\frac{[In^-]}{[HIn] + [In^-]} = \frac{4}{5} = 0.8$$

Thus, percentage = 80%

$$= 10 \times 8 = 10x$$

$$x = 8$$

330. Five (5) $HIn \rightleftharpoons H^+ + In^-$

$$K_a = \frac{[H^+][In^-]}{[HIn]}$$

$\therefore$ $[H^+] = K_a \frac{[HIn]}{[In^-]}$

$\therefore$ $\log[H^+] = \log K_a + \log\frac{[HIn]}{[In^-]}$

$\therefore$ $pH = pK_a + \log\frac{[In^-]}{[HIn]}$

$pH = pK_a + \log y$

It is a straight line equation

Then $OA = pK_a = 4.7$

$\therefore$ $5.4 = 4.7 + \log y$

$\therefore$ $\log y = 0.7$ $\therefore$ $y = 5$

331. Five (5)

$$HgI_2(s) \rightleftharpoons Hg^{2+}(aq) + 2I^-(aq)$$

$$K_{sp} = [Hg^{2+}][I^-]^2$$

$$[I^-] = \sqrt{\frac{K_{sp}}{[Hg^{2+}]}} = \sqrt{\frac{2.5\times10^{-26}}{0.1}}$$

$= 5\times10^{-13}\text{ M} = y\times10^{-13}\text{ M}$

Thus, $y = 5$

332. (10.60)

$$[NaOH] = 4g = \frac{4}{40\text{ g mol}^{-1}}$$

$= 0.1$ mol in 100 L solution

$\therefore$ Molarity of NaOH $= \frac{0.1}{100} = 1\times10^{-3}$ M

Normality of NaOH $= 1\times10^{-3}$ N

(being monoacid base)

$$[H_2SO_4] = 9.8g = \frac{9.8\text{ g}}{98\text{ g mol}^{-1}}$$

$= 0.1$ mol in 100 L solution

$\therefore$ Molarity of $H_2SO_4 = \frac{0.1}{100} = 1\times10^{-3}$ M

Normality of $H_2SO_4 = 2\times10^{-3}$ N

(being dibasic acid)

$N_1V_1(NaOH) = 40\times1\times10^{-3}$ equivalent of A

$N_2V_2(H_2SO_4) = 10\times2\times10^{-3}$ equivlaent of B

$N_1V_1(NaOH) > N_2V_2(H_2SO_4)$

Thus, mixture is basic.

$$N(OH^-) = \frac{N_2V_2 - N_1V_1}{V_1+V_2}$$

$$= \frac{40\times10^{-3} - 20\times10^{-3}}{40+10}$$

$$= \frac{20\times10^{-3}}{50} = 4\times10^{-4}\text{ N}$$

$\therefore$ $pOH = 3.40$

$\therefore$ $pH = 14 - pOH$

$= 14 - 3.40 = 10.60$

333. Nine (9) $HA + NaOH = NaA + H_2O$

NaA is basic due to hydrolysis

$$A^- + H_2O \rightleftharpoons HA + OH^-$$

When equal volumes of HA and NaOH are mixed.

$$[NaA] = \frac{0.1}{2} = 0.05\text{ M}$$

$\therefore$ $pH = 7 + \frac{pK_a}{2} + \frac{\log C}{2}$

$$= 7 + \frac{5.3}{2} + \frac{\log(0.05)}{2} = 9.0$$

334. Eight (8) Solubility of salt of weak acid (AB) in presence of H^+ ions from buffer solution can be calculated with the help of following formula :

$$\text{Solubility} = \sqrt{K_{sp}\left[\frac{[H^+]}{K_a}\right]}$$

Given, pH = 3, so $[H^+] = 10^{-3}$

$K_a = 1\times10^{-8}$ $\Rightarrow$ $K_{sp} = 2\times10^{-10}$

After putting the values in above formula,

$$\text{Solubility} = \sqrt{2\times10^{-10}\left(\frac{10^{-3}}{10^{-8}}\right)}$$

$$= \sqrt{2\times10^{-5}} = 4.47\times10^{-3}\text{ M}$$

Hence, the value of $y = 4.47$

Detailed solution

$AB(s) \rightleftharpoons A^+(aq) + B^-(aq)$, $K_1 = K_{sp}$

$B^-(aq) + H^+(aq) \rightleftharpoons HB(aq)$, $K_2 = \frac{1}{K_a}$

$AB(s) + H^+(aq) \rightleftharpoons A^+(aq) + HB(aq)$, K_3

$$K_3 = K_1K_2 = \frac{K_{sp}}{K_a}$$

Let solubility of $AB(s)$ at pH = 3 be = x then,

$$\frac{K_{sp}}{K_a} = \frac{[A^+](HB)}{[H^+]} = \frac{x^2}{[H^+]}$$

$\therefore$ $x = \sqrt{\frac{K_{sp}}{K_a}[H^+]}$

$$= \sqrt{\frac{2\times10^{-10}}{1\times10^{-8}}\times1\times10^{-3}}$$

$$= \sqrt{2\times10^{-5}}$$

$4.47\times10^{-3}\text{ M} = y\times10^{-3}\text{ M}$

$y = 4.47$

335. Nine (9) Mixture of pyridine and pyridinium chloride makes a basic buffer.

$$pOH = pK_b + \log\frac{[C_5H_5NHCl]}{[C_5H_5N]}$$

$$= 9 - \log1.5 + \log\left(\frac{0.3}{0.2}\right)$$

$$= 9 - \log1.5 + \log1.5 = 9.0$$

336. Six (6) $K_2CO_3 = 50\times0.05$

$= 2.5$ millimol

$HCl = 40\times0.10 = 4.0$ millimol

CO_3^{2-} changes to HCO_3^- and then to H_2CO_3 ($aq.CO_2$) in two stages.

Stage I

	CO_3^{2-} +	H^+ $\longrightarrow$	HCO_3^-
Initial millimol	2.5	4.0	0
After reaction	0	(4.0 – 2.5) = 1.5	2.5 2.5

Stage II (it has 2.5 millimol HCO_3^- and 1.5 millinol H^+).

	HCO_3^- +	H^+ $\longrightarrow$	H_2CO_3
Initial	2.5	1.5	0
At equilibrium	(2.5 – 1.5) = 1.0	0	1.5

Thus, mixture contains 1.0 millimol HCO_3^- and 1.5 millimol H_2CO_3 making a buffer.

$$H_2CO_3 \rightleftharpoons H^+ + HCO_3^-$$

$\therefore$ $pH = pK_{a_1} + \log\frac{[HCO_3^-]}{[H_2CO_3]}$

$$= 6.35 + \log\frac{1.0}{1.5} = 6.35 + \log2 - \log3$$

$= 6.35 + 0.3010 - 0.4771 = 6.173 \approx 6.0$

337. (0.2)

$$ZnS(s) \longrightarrow \underset{(0.05M)}{Zn^{2+}(aq)} + S^{2-}(aq.)$$

$$K_{sp}(ZnS) = [Zn^{2+}][S^{2-}] = 1.25\times10^{-22}$$

$$0.05\times[S^{2-}] = 1.25\times10^{-22}$$

$\Rightarrow$ $[S^{2-}] = \frac{1.25\times10^{-22}}{0.05}$

$\Rightarrow 25\times10^{-22}$

For H_2S: $\underset{(0.1M)}{H_2S} \longrightarrow 2H^+ + \underset{(25\times10^{-22}\text{ M})}{S^{2-}}$

$$K_{Net} = 1\times10^{-21} = \frac{[H^+]^2[S^{2-}]}{[H_2S]}$$

$$1\times10^{-21} = \frac{[H^+]^2\times25\times10^{-22}}{[0.1]}$$

$[H^+]^2 = \frac{1}{25}$ $\Rightarrow [H^+] = \frac{1}{5} = 0.2$ M

338. Eight (8) $A_2B \rightleftharpoons 2A^+ + B^{2-}$

$$K_{sp} = [A^+]^2[B^{2-}]$$

$$\log K_{sp} = 2\log[A^+] + \log[B^{2-}]$$

$$-\log1\times10^{-16} = -2\log[A^+] - \log[B^{2-}]$$

$$16 = 2p_A + p_B$$

$\{\because p_A = -\log[A^+], p_B = -\log[B^{2-}]\}$

$\therefore$ $p_A = 8 - \frac{p_B}{2}$

$y = c - mx$ (straight line)

Thus, $c = OY = 8$

339. **Five (5)** HCl in buffer

$$= \frac{0.006 \text{ mol}}{0.300 \text{ L}} = 0.02 \text{ mol L}^{-1}$$

$$CH_3COONa + HCl \rightleftharpoons CH_3COOH + NaCl$$

Initial	0.56 M	0.02 M	0.25 M
Reacted	– 0.02 M	– 0.02 M	
At equil.	0.54 M	0	0.27 M

Thus, mixture is a buffer.

$$pH = pK_a + \log \frac{[CH_3COO^-]}{[CH_3COOH]}$$

$$= 4.74 + \log \frac{0.54}{0.27} = 5.04 \approx 5.0$$

340. **Two (2)** $NiC_2O_4 \rightleftharpoons Ni^{2+} + C_2O_4^{2-}$

$$x \qquad x$$

$$K_{sp} = [Ni^{2+}][C_2O_4^{2-}] = 4 \times 10^{-10}$$

$$\therefore \quad x^2 = 4 \times 10^{-10}$$

$$x = 2 \times 10^{-5} \text{ M}$$

where, x is the molar solubility of NiC_2O_4.

$$Na_3AlF_6 \rightleftharpoons 3Na^+ + AlF_6^{3-}$$

$$3y \qquad y$$

$$K_{sp} = [Na^+]^3[AlF_6^{3-}] = 4 \times 10^{-10}$$

$$(3y)^3(y) = 4 \times 10^{-10}$$

$$27y^4 = 4 \times 10^{-10}$$

$$y = \sqrt[4]{\frac{4 \times 10^{-10}}{27}} = 2 \times 10^{-3} \text{ M}$$

where, y is the molar solubility of Na_3AlF_6.

$$\therefore \frac{y}{x} = \frac{2 \times 10^{-3}}{2 \times 10^{-5}} = 100 = 10^2 = 10^n$$

Thus, $n = 2$

341. **Nine (9)**

$$H_3BO_3 + H_2O \rightleftharpoons H_2BO_3^- + H_3O^+$$

$$pH = pK_a + \log \frac{[H_2BO_3^-]}{[H_3BO_3]}$$

$$10.10 = 9.14 + \log \frac{[H_2BO_3^-]}{[H_3BO_3]}$$

$$\log \frac{[H_2BO_3^-]}{[H_3BO_3]} = 0.96$$

$$\therefore \frac{[H_2BO_3^-]}{[H_3BO_3]} = 9.12$$

Thus, $[H_2BO_3^-] : [H_3BO_3] = 9.12 : 1.00$

$$[H_2BO_3^-] + [H_3BO_3] = 10.12$$

Thus, percentage of $[H_2BO_3^-]$

$$= \frac{9.12}{10.12} \times 100 = 90.11$$

Thus, NaOH required $= \frac{90.11}{100} \times 0.01$

$$= 9.01 \times 10^{-3} \text{ M}$$

$$\therefore \quad = y \times 10^{-3} \text{ M}$$

Thus, $y = 9$

342. **Three (3)** For weak acid HX is

$$HX(aq) \rightleftharpoons H^+(aq) + X^-(aq)$$

$$K_a(HX) = \frac{[H^+][X^-]}{[HX]}$$

Similarly, for HY $K_a(HY) = \frac{[H^+][Y^-]}{[HY]}$

Given, molar conductivity

$$\lambda_m(HX) = 10\lambda_m(HY)$$

$$\Rightarrow \quad \frac{\lambda_m(HX)}{\lambda_m(HY)} = \frac{1}{10}$$

Also, $\alpha = \frac{\lambda_m}{\lambda_m^\circ}$

$$= \frac{\text{Molar conductivity at given concentration}}{\text{Molar conductivity of very dilute solution}}$$

$$K_a(HX) = C_1\alpha_1^2 = 0.01\left(\frac{\lambda_m(HX)}{\lambda_m^\circ(HX)}\right)^2$$

$$K_a(HY) = C_2\alpha_2^2 = 0.10\left(\frac{\lambda_m(HY)}{\lambda_m^\circ(HY)}\right)^2$$

Also, $\lambda_m^\circ(HX) = \lambda^\circ(HY)$

$$\therefore \quad \frac{K_a(HX)}{K_a(HY)} = \frac{1}{10}\left(\frac{\lambda_m(HX)}{\lambda_m(HY)}\right)^2$$

$$= \frac{1}{10}\left(\frac{1}{10}\right)^2 = 0.001$$

$$\log K_a(HX) - \log K_a(HY)$$

$$= \log \frac{1}{1000} = -3$$

$$\therefore \quad pK_a(HX) - pK_a(HY) = 3$$

Type VI. Matrix Matching

343. (d) $NH_3 + H^+ \longrightarrow NH_4^+$;

$$\Delta H^\circ = -52.2 \text{ kJ mol}^{-1}$$

$$\Delta S^\circ = +1.67 \text{ J mol}^{-1} \text{ K}^{-1}$$

$$H_2O \longrightarrow H^+ + OH^-;$$

$$\Delta H^\circ = +56.6 \text{ kJ mol}^{-10}$$

$$\Delta S^\circ = -78.20 \text{ J mol}^{-1}\text{K}^{-1}$$

$NH_3 + H_2O$ or (NH_4OH)

$$\longrightarrow NH_4^+ + OH^-$$

$$\Delta H^\circ = 4.4 \text{ kJ mol}^{-1},$$

$$\Delta S^\circ = -76.53 \text{ J mol}^{-1} \text{ K}^{-1}$$

Thus, $\Delta H^\circ = 4.4 \text{ kJ mol}^{-1}$

(ii) $\rightarrow$ (r)

$$\Delta S^\circ = -76.53 \text{ J mol}^{-1}\text{K}^{-1}$$

$$= -0.07653 \text{ kJ mol}^{-1} \text{ K}^{-1}$$

(iv) $\rightarrow$ (p)

$$\Delta G^\circ = \Delta H^\circ - T\Delta S^\circ$$

$$= 4.4 - 298(-0.07653)$$

$$= 27.21 \text{ kJ mol}^{-1}$$

Thus, (iii) $\rightarrow$ (s)

$$\Delta G^\circ = -2.303RT \log K_b$$

$$\therefore \quad -\log K_b = \frac{\Delta G^\circ}{2.303RT}$$

$$= \frac{27.21}{2.303 \times 8.314 \times 10^{-3} \times 298}$$

$$pK_b = 4.77$$

Thus, (i) $\rightarrow$ (q)

344. (d) $CH_3COOH + KOH \rightleftharpoons$

$$CH_3COOK + H_2O$$

$$CH_3COOH = 100 \times 0.01 = 1 \text{ millimol}$$

(i) 25 mL of 0.01 M KOH

$$= 0.25 \text{ millimol}$$

(ii) 50 mL of 0.01 M KOH

$$= 0.50 \text{ millimol}$$

(iii) 75 mL of 0.01 M KOH

$$= 0.75 \text{ millimol}$$

(iv) 100 mL of 0.01 M KOH

$$= 1.00 \text{ millimol}$$

After KOH added

Stage	$[CH_3COOH]$ millimol	$[CH_3COOK]$ millimol	$pH = pK_a + \log \frac{[CH_3COOK]}{[CH_3COOH]}$
(i)	0.75	0.25	$4.74 + \log \frac{1}{3} = 4.26$
(ii)	0.50	0.50	4.74
(iii)	0.25	0.75	$4.74 + \log 3 = 5.22$
(iv)	0.00	1.00	8.22

In stages I, II and III, a buffer is formed thus, pH is derived from Henderson-Hasselbalch equation.

After CH_3COOH is completed neutralised, CH_3COOK is hydrolysed back forming a basic solution.

$$CH_3COO^- + H_2O \rightleftharpoons$$

$$CH_3COOH + OH^-$$

$$pH = 7 + \frac{pK_a}{2} + \frac{\log C}{2}$$

Also total volume is = 200 mL containing 1 millimol of CH_3COOK.

$$\therefore \quad [CH_3COOK] = \frac{1 \times 10^{-3} \text{ mol}}{0.2 \text{ L}} = 0.005 \text{ M}$$

$$pH = 7 + \frac{4.74}{2} + \frac{\log 0.005}{2}$$

$$= 7 + 2.37 - 1.15 = 8.22$$

$\therefore$ (i) $\rightarrow$ (q); (ii) $\rightarrow$ (r); (iii) $\rightarrow$ (s), (iv) $\rightarrow$ (p)

345. (b) (i) CH_3COONH_4 it is salt of weak acid and weak base.

$$pH = 7 + \frac{pK_a - pK_b}{2}$$

$$pK_a(CH_3COOH) = 4.74$$

$$pK_a(NH_4^+) = 9.26$$

$$\therefore \quad pK_b(NH_3) = 4.74 \quad \therefore \quad pH = 7$$

Thus, (i) $\rightarrow$ (r)

(ii) C_6H_5COOK, it is salt of weak acid and strong base. Solution is basic.

$$C_6H_5COO^- + H_2O \rightleftharpoons C_6H_5COOH + OH^-$$

$$pH = 7 + \frac{pK_a}{2} + \frac{\log C}{2}$$

$$= 7 + \frac{4.20}{2} + \frac{\log 0.1}{2}$$

$$= 7 + 2.10 - 0.5 = 8.6$$

Thus, (ii) $\rightarrow$ (p)

(iii) $C_6H_5NH_3^+Cl^-$, it is salt of weak base and strong acid. Solution is acidic.

$$C_6H_5NH_3^+ + H_2O \rightleftharpoons C_6H_5NH_3OH + H^+$$

$$pK_a(C_6H_5NH_3^+) = 4.62,$$

$$pK_b(C_6H_5NH_2) = 9.38$$

$$pH = 7 - \frac{pK_b}{2} - \frac{\log C}{2}$$

$$= 7 - \frac{9.38}{2} - \frac{\log 0.1}{2} = 2.81$$

Thus, (iii) $\rightarrow$ (s)

(iv) NaCN is a salt of weak acid and strong base. Solution is basic.

$$CN^- + H_2O \rightleftharpoons HCN + OH^-$$

$$pH = 7 + \frac{pK_a}{2} + \frac{\log C}{2}$$

$$= 7 + \frac{9.21}{2} + \frac{\log 0.1}{2} = 11.1$$

Thus, (iv) $\rightarrow$ (q)

346. (d) $K_{sp}[LiOH] = [Li^+][OH^-] = 1 \times 10^{-6}$

$$\log[Li^+] + \log[OH^-] = -6$$

$$-\log[Li^+] - \log[OH^-] = 6$$

$\therefore \quad p_{Li} + pOH = 6$

But, $\quad pH + pOH = 14$

$\therefore \quad p_{Li} + (14 - pH) = 6$

$\therefore \quad pH = (p_{Li} + 8)$

Thus (i) $\rightarrow$ (r)

$$K_{sp}[Mg(OH)_2] = [Mg^{+2}][OH^-]^2 = 1 \times 10^{-12}$$

$\therefore \quad \log[Mg^{2+}] + 2\log[OH^-] = -12$

$$-\log[Mg^{2+}] - 2\log(OH^-) = 12$$

$\therefore \quad p_{Mg} + 2pOH = 12$

$$p_{Mg} + 2(14 - pH) = 12$$

$$2pH = p_{Mg} + 16$$

$$pH = \frac{(p_{Mg} + 16)}{2}$$

Thus, (ii) $\rightarrow$ (p)

Similarly, (iii) $\rightarrow$ (s) and (iv) $\rightarrow$ (a)

347. (c) Salt of weak acid (HA) and strong base (MOH) is alkaline due to hydrolysis.

$$A^- + H_2O \rightleftharpoons HA + OH^-$$

Thus, $pH = \left(7 + \frac{pK_a}{2}\right) + \frac{\log C}{2}$

$$y = (\text{constant}) + mx$$

Hence, constant = intercept $= \left(7 + \frac{pK_a}{2}\right)$

$$= OA = 9$$

$$m = \text{slope} = \frac{1}{2}$$

thus $\quad 7 + \frac{pK_a}{2} = 9$

$\therefore \quad pK_a = 4$

Thus, (i) $\rightarrow$ (r).

When $C = 0.01$

$$pH = 9 + \frac{\log 0.01}{2} = 9 - \frac{2}{2} = 8$$

Thus, (ii) $\rightarrow$ (p)

pH of weak acid

$$pH = \frac{1}{2}(pK_a - \log C) = \frac{1}{2}[4 - \log 0.01] = 3$$

Thus, (iii) $\rightarrow$ (s)

By Ostwald's dilution law,

$$x = \sqrt{\frac{K_a}{C}} = \sqrt{\frac{10^{-4}}{0.01}} = \sqrt{10^{-2}} = 0.1$$

Thus, percentage ionisation

$$= 0.1 \times 100 = 10\%$$

Thus, (iv) $\rightarrow$ (q)

348. (a) Salt is A_xB_y

$$A_xB_y = xA + yB$$

$\therefore \quad K_{sp} = x^x y^y (s)^{x+y}$

$\therefore \quad \log K_{sp} = [x \log x + y \log y] + (x + y) \log s$

Compare it by equation

$$y = c + mx$$

$$c = \text{intercept}$$

$$= OP = (x \log x + y \log y)$$

$$\text{Slope} = m = (x + y)$$

$$s = \left(\frac{K_{sp}}{x^x y^y}\right)^{\frac{1}{x+y}}$$

	x	y	$C = OP$	s	$(x+y)\log s$
Ag(OH)	1	1	0	1×10^{-5}	−10
$Mg(OH)_2$	1	2	0.6020	1×10^{-4}	−12
$Al(OH)_3$	1	3	1.4314	1×10^{-4}	−16
$Si(OH)_4$	1	4	2.4083	1×10^{-4}	−20

Thus,

(i) - (IV)-(r)

(ii)-(III)-(q)

(iii)-(I)-(p)

(iv)-(II)-(s)

Equation for (Q. 349 to 352)

349. (a)

(A) benzene-1,2-(COOH)(COOH) $\xrightarrow{OH^-}$ (B) benzene-1,2-(COO⁻)(COOH)

$\xrightarrow{OH^-}$ (C) benzene-1,2-(COO⁻)(COO⁻)

(A) is a dibasic acid and 0.01 M

$$= 0.02 \text{ N}$$

$$100 \text{ mL of } 0.02 \text{ N}(A) = \frac{100 \times 0.02}{1000}$$

$$= 2 \times 10^{-3} \text{ equivalent}$$

For first half equivalent point

$$25\% \text{ of } A \text{ reacted} = 2 \times 10^{-3} \times 0.25$$

$$= 0.50 \times 10^{-3}$$

$\therefore \quad V$ mL of 0.02 N KOH $= 0.50 \times 10^{-3}$

$\therefore \quad \frac{V \times 0.02}{1000} = 0.50 \times 10^{-3}$

$\therefore \quad V = 25$ mL

Also, at this stage, $(A) = (B)$

$\therefore \quad pH = pK_{a_1} + \log\frac{[B]}{[A]}$

$$= 2.89 + \log 1 = 2.89$$

$\therefore$ Thus, (1)-IV - (s).

350. (b) At first equivalent point,

50% A reacted $= 2 \times 10^{-3} \times 0.5$ equivalent

$\therefore \quad \frac{V \times 0.2}{1000}$ N KOH $= 2 \times 10^{-3} \times 0.5$

$$V = 50 \text{ mL}$$

The species is amphiprotic, it means A is completely converted into B.

A benzene-1,2-(COOH)(COOH) $\xleftarrow{H^+}$ B benzene-1,2-(COO⁻)(COOH)

$\xrightarrow{H^+}$ C benzene-1,2-(COO⁻)(COO⁻)

$$pH = \frac{pK_{a_1} + pK_{a_2}}{2}$$

$$= \frac{2.89 + 5.41}{2} = 4.15$$

Thus, (ii)-(iii)-(r)

351. (c) At second - half equivalent point,

75% A of reacted $= 2 \times 10^{-3} \times 0.75$

$$= 1.5 \times 10^{-3} \text{ equivalent}$$

Thus, $[OH^-]$ required $= 1.5 \times 10^{-3}$ mol

and $Ca(OH)_2$ required $= \frac{1.5 \times 10^{-3}}{2}$ mol

$\therefore \quad \frac{V \times 0.01}{1000} = \frac{1.5 \times 10^{-3}}{2} = 75$ mL

At this stage, mixture contains 50% of *B* and 50% of *C*.

Thus, $pH = pK_{a_2} + \log\frac{[C]}{[B]} = 5.41$

Thus, (iii) - (II) - q.

352. (a) This is a case of complete conversion of *A* into *C*

Thus, (OH^-) required $= 2\times10^{-3}$ mol

$Ca(OH)_2$ required $= 1\times10^{-3}$ mol

$\therefore \quad \frac{V\times0.01}{1000} = 1\times10^{-3}$

$\therefore \quad V = 100$ mL

Due to dilution volume = 200 mL

$$C_6H_4(COO^-)_2 + H_2O \rightleftharpoons C_6H_4(COOH)(COO^-) + OH^-$$

$$\underset{(A)}{C_6H_4(COOH)_2} + Ca(OH)_2 \longrightarrow \underset{(C)}{C_6H_4(COO)_2Ca} + 2H_2O$$

353. (d) **P :** 10 mL of 0.1 M NaOH = 1 mmol

20 mL of 0.1 M CH_3COOH = 2 mmol

	CH_3COOH	+ NaOH ⇌	CH_3COONa	+ H_2O
Initial	2	1	0	0
At equil.	(2 – 1)	(1 – 1)	1	

Thus, mixture is a buffer containing 1 millimol each of CH_3COOH, and CH_3COONa in 30 mL. On dilution, each part is affected equally thus no change in $[H^+]$.

Thus, (P) - (1)

Q: 20 mL of 0.1 M NaOH = 2 millimol

20 mL of 0.1 M CH_3COOH = 2 millimol

$CH_3COOH \equiv NaOH$

CH_3COOH is neutralised completely and mixture has 2 millimol CH_3COONa in 40 mL.

$\therefore \quad [CH_3COONa]_{Initial} = \frac{2\times10^{-3}\text{ mol}}{0.04\text{ L}} = 0.05$ M

$CH_3COONa(aq)$ is alkaline due to hydrolysis of CH_3COO^-.

$$CH_3COO^- + H_2O \rightleftharpoons CH_3COOH + OH^-$$

$\therefore \quad [H^+]_1 = \sqrt{\frac{K_wK_a}{C}} = \sqrt{\frac{K_wK_a}{0.05}} = \sqrt{20K_wK_a}$

On dilution from 40 mL to 80 mL,

$[CH_3COONa] = \left(\frac{0.05}{2}\right)$

$[H^+]_2 = \sqrt{\frac{K_wK_a}{\frac{0.05}{2}}}$

$\therefore \quad \frac{[H^+]_2}{[H^+]_1} = \sqrt{2}$ times

Thus, Q - 5

R : In this case, NH_4Cl is formed

$NH_4Cl = 2\times10^{-3}$ mol in 40 mL. NH_4Cl solution is acidic due to hydrolysis.

$$NH_4^+ + OH^- \rightleftharpoons NH_4OH + H^+$$

$[NH_4Cl]_{initial} = \frac{2\times10^{-3}\text{mol}}{0.04\text{L}} = 0.05$ M

$\therefore \quad [H^+]_1 = \sqrt{\frac{K_w.C}{K_b}}$

$[H^+]_2$ after dilution to 80 mL, when $[NH_4Cl]$ is $\left(\frac{0.05}{2}\right)$ M

$\therefore \quad [H^+]_2 = \sqrt{\frac{K_w\left(\frac{C}{2}\right)}{K_b}}$

$\frac{[H^+]_2}{[H^+]_1} = \frac{1}{\sqrt{2}}$

Thus, (R) - (4)

S : $Ni(OH)_2(s) \rightleftharpoons Ni^{2+}(aq) + 2OH^-(aq)$

Since, solution is saturated thus even on dilution no change in $[OH^-]$ or $[H^+]$

Thus, (S-1).